W9-ASG-474

UNIVERSITY CASEBOOK SERIES®

BUSINESS ASSOCIATIONS

CASES AND MATERIALS ON AGENCY, PARTNERSHIPS, LLCs, AND CORPORATIONS

NINTH EDITION

by

WILLIAM A. KLEIN
Richard C. Maxwell Distinguished Professor of Law Emeritus
University of California, Los Angeles

J. MARK RAMSEYER
Mitsubishi Professor of Japanese Legal Studies
Harvard Law School

STEPHEN M. BAINBRIDGE
William D. Warren Distinguished Professor of Law
University of California, Los Angeles

444 Cedar Street, Suite 700
St. Paul, MN 55101
1-877-888-1330

Printed in the United States of America

ISBN: 978-1-60930-349-5

Mat #41432634

PREFACE

"You should lay off candy bars for a while," Marlene Dietrich once told Orson Welles. Bloated, he was twice the size of his former self and half the man. Bloated, he resembled nothing so much as the typical corporate law casebook.

We try to be different. And toward that end, in editing this book we follow six basic but apparently widely ignored principles. Each principle is one that we think helps produce a book that teaches students the gist of the law they need to know; that trains them to apply it; and that (perish the thought) almost makes them enjoy the process.

First, we give judges one chance—but only one chance—to explain the law. Most judicial opinions are as bloated as any character Welles ever played, but law schools teach students that point marvelously well in the first year. We see no reason to make the point again in the second. More specifically, we see no reason to force students to plow through fifteen pages of bad prose when a disciplined judge could explain the law in three. We edit the law, and edit it ruthlessly.

Second, working within the "give us the facts, ma'am, just the facts" tradition, we include the facts in all their ambiguity. In corporate law as in most of legal practice, the gist is in the application, and for application the facts matter critically. Although we heavily edit discussions of the law, we include most statements of the facts in full. When helpful, we add extra fact-based problems to explore those applications further.

Third, because lawyers plan at least as often as they litigate, we bring a planner's perspective. In the first half of the book, for example, we explore how the parties to a case could have avoided the disputes at stake. At the end of the book, we use corporate debt to ask both how business executives can structure the relationships among their many investors, and what economic consequences follow from those structural possibilities.

Fourth, we believe in agency and partnership law. We believe they matter not just for their own sake, but for understanding corporate legal practice. Consequently, we include materials on agency and partnership that are complete, that cohere within themselves, and that help explain how the corporate enterprise functions.

Fifth, we offer a *case*book, not a treatise. All of us have already published handbooks on the subject (Klein's *Business Organization and Finance*, with John C. Coffee, Jr., and Frank Partnoy, Foundation Press, Ramseyer's *Business Organizations,* Aspen Publishers, and Bainbridge's *Corporation Law and Economics*, Foundation Press, and *Corporate Law*, Foundation Press). As those handbooks are widely available, we see no need to fill the pages between the cases with long discussions of legal theory and doctrine. Instructors who prefer casebooks without extensive explanatory text will find this the casebook for them; instructors who prefer the explanatory matter should assign one of these other books in conjunction with this casebook.

Last, if a case is no fun, we omit it. There are exceptions, to be sure. Even we could not eliminate some key but dull U.S. and Delaware Supreme Court opinions. In general, however, we include only cases that at least one of us enjoys teaching. Law school drags enough as it is without assigning cases no one wants to read. Corporate law *can* be fascinating. In this book, we do our best to make it so.

The result, we think, is a book that provides simple settings for sophisticated analysis. We offer interesting and challenging cases; we edit them carefully but ruthlessly; we include the necessary statutes; and we add questions and problems where helpful. Through this, we think we offer a book that isolates the basic ideas, eliminates distracting detail, and motivates students to apply those ideas to a world they will soon help shape.

Lean, we think, but not mean. Enjoy the book.

WILLIAM A. KLEIN
J. MARK RAMSEYER
STEPHEN M. BAINBRIDGE

January, 2015

EDITORIAL NOTE AND ACKNOWLEDGMENT

Footnote numbers in cases are as in the original, with no renumbering to take account of omitted footnotes. The numbering of editorial footnotes, which are indicated by asterisk, restarts on each page. Citations in cases are generally omitted, except where the authority cited might be familiar to the student, provides the source of quoted language, or otherwise seemed noteworthy.

We are grateful for permission to reprint copyrighted material from *Knights, Raiders, and Targets: The Impact of the Hostile Takeover,* edited by John C. Coffee, Louis Lowenstein, & Susan Rose-Ackerman. Copyright a 1988 by the Center for Law and Economic Studies. Reprinted by permission of Oxford University Press, Inc.

SUMMARY OF CONTENTS

TABLE OF CONTENTS

TABLE OF CASES

The principal cases are in bold type.

UNIVERSITY CASEBOOK SERIES®

BUSINESS ASSOCIATIONS

CASES AND MATERIALS ON AGENCY, PARTNERSHIPS, LLCs, AND CORPORATIONS

NINTH EDITION

CHAPTER 1

AGENCY

1. WHO IS AN AGENT?

Gorton v. Doty

69 P.2d 136 (Idaho 1937).

In September, 1935, an action was commenced by R. S. Gorton, father of Richard Gorton, to recover expenses incurred by the father for hospitalization, physicians', surgeons', and nurses' fees, and another by the son, by his father as guardian ad litem, to recover damages for injuries sustained as a result of an accident. By stipulation the actions were consolidated for trial. Upon the trial of the cases so consolidated, the jury returned a verdict in favor of the father for $870 and another in favor of the son for $5,000. Separate judgments were then entered upon such verdicts. Thereafter a motion for a new trial was made and denied in each case. The cases come here upon an appeal from each judgment and order denying a new trial.

. . .

It appears that in September, 1934, Richard Gorton, a minor, was a junior in the Soda Springs High School and a member of the football team; that his high school team and the Paris High School team were scheduled to play a game of football at Paris on the 21st. Appellant was teaching at the Soda Springs High School and Russell Garst was coaching the Soda Springs team. On the day the game was played, the Soda Springs High School team was transported to and from Paris in privately owned automobiles. One of the automobiles used for that purpose was owned by appellant. Her car was driven by Mr. Garst, the coach of the Soda Springs High School team.

One of the most difficult questions, if not the most difficult, presented by the record, is, Was the coach, Russell Garst, the agent of appellant while and in driving her car from Soda Springs to Paris, and in returning to the point where the accident occurred?

Briefly stated, the facts bearing upon that question are as follows: That appellant knew the Soda Springs High School football team and the Paris High School football team were to play a game of football at Paris September 21, 1934; that she volunteered her car for use in transporting some of the members of the Soda Springs team to and from the game; that she asked the coach, Russell Garst, the day before the game, if he had all the cars necessary for the trip to Paris the next day; that he said he needed one more; that she told him he might use her car if he drove it; that she was not promised compensation for the use of her car and did not receive any; that the school district paid for the gasoline used on the trip to and from the game; that she testified she loaned the car to Mr. Garst; that she had not employed Mr. Garst at any time and that she had not at any time "directed his work or his services, or what he was doing."

. . .

Broadly speaking, "agency" indicates the relation which exists where one person acts for another. It has these three principal forms: 1. The relation of principal and agent; 2. The relation of master and servant; and, 3. The relation of employer or proprietor and independent contractor. While all have points of similarity, there are, nevertheless, numerous differences. We are concerned here with the first form only.

Specifically, "agency" is the relationship which results from the manifestation of consent by one person to another that the other shall act on his behalf and subject to his control, and consent by the other so to act. [Restatement of Agency § 1.]

[In a subsequent passage, the court indicated that the principal is responsible for the acts of his or her agent: "After having given the jury a correct definition of the term 'agency,' the [trial] court . . . instructed the jury that if they found from the evidence that Russell Garst was, at the time of the accident, the agent of appellant, then that she was chargeable with the acts of her agent as fully and to the same extent as though she had been driving the automobile herself . . ., which is unquestionably the law."]

. . . [This court has not held] that the relationship of principal and agent must necessarily involve some matter of business, but only that where one undertakes to transact some business or manage some affair for another by authority and on account of the latter, the relationship of principal and agent arises.

To enable the Soda Springs football team to play football at Paris, it had to be transported to Paris. Automobiles were to be used and another car was needed. At that juncture, appellant volunteered the use of her car. For what purpose? Necessarily for the purpose of furnishing additional transportation. Appellant, of course, could have driven the car herself, but instead of doing that, she designated the driver (Russell Garst) and, in doing so, made it a condition precedent that the person she designated should drive her car. That appellant thereby at least consented that Russell Garst should act for her and in her behalf, in driving her car to and from the football game, is clear from her act in volunteering the use of her car upon the express condition that he should drive it, and, further, that Mr. Garst consented to so act for appellant is equally clear by his act in driving the car. It is not essential to the existence of authority that there be a contract between principal and agent or that the agent promise to act as such (Restatement Agency, §§ 15, 16, pp. 50–54), nor is it essential to the relationship of principal and agent that they, or either, receive compensation (Restatement Agency, § 16, p. 53).

Furthermore, this court held in Willi v. Schaefer Hitchcock Co., 53 Idaho 367, 25 P.2d 167, in harmony with the clear weight of authority, that the fact of ownership alone (conceded here), regardless of the presence or absence of the owner in the car at the time of the accident, establishes a prima facie case against the owner for the reason that the presumption arises that the driver is the agent of the owner. . . .

It is vigorously contended, however, that the facts and circumstances bearing upon the question under discussion show appellant loaned her car to Mr. Garst. A determination of that question makes it necessary to quote appellant's testimony. She testified as follows:

"Q. On or about the 21st day of September, 1934, state whether or not you permitted Russell Garst to use that car?

"A. I did.

"Q. Under what circumstances?

"A. I loaned it to him.

"Q. When did you loan it to him? Was it that day, or the day before?

"A. On the day before I told him he might have it the next day.

"Q. Did you receive any compensation, or were you promised any compensation, for its use?

"A. No, sir.

"Q. What were the circumstances under which you permitted him to take it?

"A. Well,—"

After having so testified, appellant was then asked:

"Q. You may relate the conversation with him, if there was such conversation.

"A. I asked him if he had all the cars necessary for his trip to Paris the next day. He said he needed one more. I said that he might use mine if he drove it. That was the extent of it."

While it appears that appellant first testified that she permitted Russell Garst to use her car and also that she loaned it to him, it further appears that when she was immediately afterward asked to state the conversation she had with the coach about the matter, she stated that she asked him if he had all the cars necessary for the trip to Paris the next day, that he said he needed one more, that she said he might use her car if he drove it, and, finally, she said that that was the extent of it. It is clear, then, that appellant intended, in relating the conversation she had with the coach, to state the circumstances fully, because, after having testified to the conversation, she concluded by saying, "That was the extent of it." Thus she gave the jury to understand that those were the circumstances, and all of the circumstances, under which Russell Garst drove her car to the football game. If the appellant fully and correctly related the conversation she had with the coach and the circumstances under which he drove her car, as she unquestionably undertook to, and did, do, it follows that, as a matter of fact, she did not say anything whatever to him about loaning her car and he said nothing whatever to her about borrowing it.

We therefore conclude the evidence sufficiently supports the finding of the jury that the relationship of principal and agent existed between appellant and Russell Garst.

. . .

During the course of the closing argument of counsel for respondent, an objection was made by counsel for appellant to certain remarks addressed to the jury. Thereupon the trial court ordered a brief recess and took up such objection in chambers with counsel for the respective parties, whereupon the following proceedings took place outside of the presence of the jury:

"Mr. GLENNON: What I said, your Honor, was in response to counsel's repeated charges that the plaintiff was attempting to mulch [mulct] the defendant in damages, and I stated to the jury in substance, 'That you have a right to draw on your experience as business men in determining the facts in this case, and that you know from your experience as business men that prudent automobile owners usually protect themselves against just such contingencies as are involved in this case.' "

Following that statement by Senator Glennon, counsel for appellant agreed it was substantially correct. Upon returning to the courtroom, the trial judge denied appellant's motion for a mistrial and then instructed the reporter to read the above quoted remarks to the jury, after which the court instructed the jury to disregard the remarks.

Appellant contends that the trial court erred in denying her motion for a mistrial.

Funk & Wagnalls New Standard Dictionary defines the word mulct: "1. To sentence to a pecuniary penalty or forfeiture as a punishment; fine; hence, to fine unjustly, as, to mulct the prisoner in $100. 2. To punish." Appellant had testified during the trial that she volunteered the use of her car. To charge, then, that respondent was attempting to "mulct" her in damages carried the inference that respondent was attempting to punish her in damages for having volunteered the use of her car for the commendable purpose of supplying additional transportation for the home town football team.

And it will be noted that Mr. Glennon stated, and the record shows no denial, that the above-quoted remarks were made by him only in response to repeated charges by appellant's counsel that respondent was attempting to mulct appellant in damages. There is no evidence whatever in the record justifying such charges. They were made during the course of the argument of counsel for appellant, and were as fully and clearly outside the record as the remarks of counsel for respondent. It was a case of meeting improper argument with improper argument. The remarks complained of were provoked by the conduct of counsel for appellant. Hence, we conclude that appellant has no just cause for complaint. Having reached that conclusion, we find it unnecessary to review the cases cited by counsel for the respective parties.

. . .

The judgments and orders are affirmed with costs to respondents.

■ BUDGE, J., Dissenting. I am unable to concur in the majority opinion.

As I read the entire record there is a total lack of evidence to support the allegation in the complaint that Garst was the agent of appellant Doty at or prior to the time of the accident in which respondent Richard Gorton was injured and as such agent was acting within the scope of his authority. An agent is one who acts for another by authority from him, one who undertakes to transact business or manage some affair for another by authority and on account of the latter. (Moreland v. Mason, 45 Idaho 143, 260 P. 1035.) Agency means more than mere passive permission. It involves request, instruction or command. (Klee v. United States, 53 F.2d 58.) . . . As I read the record [Ms. Doty] simply loaned her car to Garst to enable him to furnish means of transportation for the team from Soda Springs to Paris. It was nothing more or less than a kindly gesture on her part to be helpful to Garst, the athletic coach, in arranging transportation for the team. The mere fact that she stated to Garst that he should drive the car was a mere precaution upon her part that the car should not be driven by any one of the young boys, a perfectly natural thing for her to do. It is principally and particularly upon this statement of fact that the majority opinion holds that the relationship of principal and agent was created and that Garst became the agent of Miss Doty, authorized by her to undertake the transportation of the boys from Soda Springs to Paris for her and on her behalf. In other words, Miss Doty is held legally liable for each and every act done or performed by Garst as though she had been personally present and personally performed each and every act that was done or performed by Garst, this in the absence of any contractual relationship between her and Garst or between her and the school district. The rule would seem to be that one who borrows a car for his own use is a gratuitous bailee and not an agent of the owner. (Gochee v. Wagner, 257 N.Y. 344, 178 N.E. 553.). . . .

I am also of the opinion the judgment should be reversed because of the prejudicial remarks of one of counsel for respondent while making his closing argument to the jury as follows:

> "That you have a right to draw on your experience as business men in determining the facts in this case and what you know from your experience as business men that prudent automobile owners usually protect themselves against just such contingencies as are involved in this case."

Upon the making of the above-quoted remarks by respondent's counsel appellant moved for a mistrial basing his motion upon the theory that they suggested that the appellant was carrying insurance and would not have to pay any judgment the jury might render, and, that there was no evidence to support such a theory. The court refused to declare a mistrial but directed counsel for respondent not to argue the point further and directed the jury to disregard that part of counsel's argument. However, the prejudicial effect of the remarks was not cured by the court instructing the jury to disregard that part of counsel's argument. Nothing can be gleaned from the remarks made by learned counsel other than that he, intentionally or otherwise, clearly and unmistakably impressed upon the minds of the jurors that appellant carried insurance on her car and that she personally would not be called upon to pay any verdict that might be rendered against her. Error for injecting the question of insurance in a case of this character is quite clearly stated in [citing numerous authorities]. . . .

The judgment should be reversed and the cause remanded for further proceedings as herein indicated.

ANALYSIS

1. The dissent obviously disagreed with the majority as to the existence of an agency relationship between Doty and the Coach. Did the dissent disagree as to the test to be applied or merely as to the way in which the test should be applied?

2. The majority stated: "It is not essential . . . that there be a contract between principal and agent." What did the court mean by that?

3. Suppose that you were Ms. Doty's attorney and that a few months after the decision was handed down she stopped by your office. She tells you that the new football coach wants to use her car to take some players to another game. She asks for your advice as to how she could avoid liability in the event of an accident. What do you tell her?

4. Was the court using agency concepts to impose liability on the alleged principal in order to achieve some desired outcome? If so, what policy outcome was the court trying to implement?

INTRODUCTORY NOTE

In the next case, A. Gay Jenson Farms Co. v. Cargill, Inc., the context is that of a creditor exercising control over its debtors after the debtor has experienced financial difficulties. The plaintiffs were farmers who sold their grain crops to Warren Grain & Seed Co. (Warren). Warren was a local firm that operated a grain elevator (a storage facility). Cargill is a large, worldwide dealer in grain. On Cargill's view of the facts, Warren bought grain from the farmers and sold it to Cargill. On the farmers' view of the facts, Warren bought grain as an agent for Cargill. Warren became insolvent without having paid the farmers for their grain and they sued Cargill. The case offers a nice illustration of a legal issue of considerable importance to business firms like Cargill that provide trade credit to other firms, as well as to banks and other financial intermediaries.

A. Gay Jenson Farms Co. v. Cargill, Inc.

309 N.W.2d 285 (Minn.1981).

Plaintiffs, 86 individual, partnership or corporate farmers, brought this action against defendant Cargill, Inc. (Cargill) and defendant Warren Grain & Seed Co. (Warren) to recover losses sustained when Warren defaulted on the contracts made with plaintiffs for the sale of grain. After a trial by jury, judgment was entered in favor of plaintiffs, and Cargill brought this appeal. We affirm.

This case arose out of the financial collapse of defendant Warren Seed & Grain Co., and its failure to satisfy its indebtedness to plaintiffs. Warren, which was located in Warren, Minnesota, was operated by Lloyd Hill and his son, Gary Hill. Warren operated a grain elevator and as a result was involved in the purchase of . . . grain from local farmers. The cash grain would be resold through the Minneapolis Grain Exchange or to the terminal grain companies directly. Warren also stored grain for farmers and sold chemicals, fertilizer and steel storage bins. In addition, it operated a seed business which involved buying seed grain from farmers, processing it and reselling it for seed to farmers and local elevators.

Lloyd Hill decided in 1964 to apply for financing from Cargill. Cargill's officials from the Moorhead regional office investigated Warren's operations and recommended that Cargill finance Warren.

Warren and Cargill thereafter entered into a security agreement which provided that Cargill would loan money for working capital to Warren on "open account" financing up to a stated limit, which was originally set as $175,000.[2] Under this contract, Warren would receive funds and pay its expenses by issuing drafts drawn on Cargill through Minneapolis banks. The drafts were imprinted with both Warren's and Cargill's names. Proceeds from Warren's sales would be deposited with Cargill and credited to its account. In return for this financing, Warren appointed Cargill as its grain agent for transaction with the Commodity Credit Corporation. Cargill was also given a right of first refusal to purchase market grain sold by Warren to the terminal market.

A new contract was negotiated in 1967, extending Warren's credit line to $300,000 and incorporating the provisions of the original contract. It was also stated in the contract that Warren would provide Cargill with annual financial statements and that either Cargill would keep the books for Warren or an audit would be conducted by an independent firm. Cargill was given the right of access to Warren's books for inspection.

In addition, the agreement provided that Warren was not to make capital improvements or repairs in excess of $5,000 without Cargill's prior consent. Further, it was not to become liable as guarantor on another's indebtedness, or encumber its assets except with Cargill's permission. Consent by Cargill was required before Warren would be allowed to declare a dividend or sell and purchase stock.

Officials from Cargill's regional office made a brief visit to Warren shortly after the agreement was executed. They examined the annual statement and the accounts receivable, expenses, inventory, seed, machinery and other financial matters. Warren was informed that it would be reminded periodically to make the improvements recommended by Cargill.[3] At approximately this time, a memo was given to the Cargill official in charge of the Warren account, Erhart Becker, which stated in part: "This organization [Warren] needs *very strong* paternal guidance."

In 1970, Cargill contracted with Warren and other elevators to act as its agent to seek growers for a new type of wheat called Bounty 208. Warren, as Cargill's agent for this project, entered into contracts for the growing of the wheat seed, with Cargill named as the contracting party. Farmers were paid directly by Cargill for the seed and all contracts were performed in full. In 1971, pursuant to an agency contract, Warren contracted on Cargill's behalf with various farmers for the growing of sunflower seeds for Cargill. The arrangements were similar to those made in the Bounty 208 contracts, and all those contracts were also completed. Both these agreements were unrelated to the open account financing contract. In addition, Warren, as Cargill's agent in the sunflower seed business, cleaned and packaged the seed in Cargill bags.

During this period, Cargill continued to review Warren's operations and expenses and recommend that certain actions should be taken.[4]

---

[2] Loans were secured by a second mortgage on Warren's real estate and a first chattel mortgage on its inventories of grain and merchandise in the sum of $175,000 with 7% interest. . . .

[3] Cargill headquarters suggested that the regional office check Warren monthly. Also, it was requested that Warren be given an explanation for the relatively large withdrawals from undistributed earnings made by the Hills, since Cargill hoped that Warren's profits would be used to decrease its debt balance. Cargill asked for written requests for withdrawals from undistributed earnings in the future.

[4] Between 1967 and 1973, Cargill suggested that Warren take a number of steps, including: (1) a reduction of seed grain and cash grain inventories; (2) improved collection of accounts receivable; (3) reduction or elimination of its wholesale seed business and its speciality

Warren purchased from Cargill various business forms printed by Cargill and received sample forms from Cargill which Warren used to develop its own business forms.

Cargill wrote to its regional office in 1970 expressing its concern that the pattern of increased use of funds allowed to develop at Warren was similar to that involved in two other cases in which Cargill experienced severe losses. Cargill did not refuse to honor drafts or call the loan, however. A new security agreement which increased the credit line to $750,000 was executed in 1972, and a subsequent agreement which raised the limit to $1,250,000 was entered into in 1976.

Warren was at that time shipping Cargill 90% of its . . . grain. When Cargill's facilities were full, Warren shipped its grain to other companies. Approximately 25% of Warren's total sales was seed grain which was sold directly by Warren to its customers.

As Warren's indebtedness continued to be in excess of its credit line, Cargill began to contact Warren daily regarding its financial affairs. Cargill headquarters informed its regional office in 1973 that, since Cargill money was being used, Warren should realize that Cargill had the right to make some critical decisions regarding the use of the funds. Cargill headquarters also told Warren that a regional manager would be working with Warren on a day-to-day basis as well as in monthly planning meetings. In 1975, Cargill's regional office began to keep a daily debit position on Warren. A bank account was opened in Warren's name on which Warren could draw checks in 1976. The account was to be funded by drafts drawn on Cargill by the local bank.

In early 1977, it became evident that Warren had serious financial problems. Several farmers, who had heard that Warren's checks were not being paid, inquired or had their agents inquire at Cargill regarding Warren's status and were initially told that there would be no problem with payment. In April 1977, an audit of Warren revealed that Warren was $4 million in debt. After Cargill was informed that Warren's financial statements had been deliberately falsified, Warren's request for additional financing was refused. In the final days of Warren's operation, Cargill sent an official to supervise the elevator, including disbursement of funds and income generated by the elevator.

After Warren ceased operations, it was found to be indebted to Cargill in the amount of $3.6 million. Warren was also determined to be indebted to plaintiffs in the amount of $2 million, and plaintiffs brought this action in 1977 to seek recovery of that sum. Plaintiffs alleged that Cargill was jointly liable for Warren's indebtedness as it had acted as principal for the grain elevator.

. . .

The major issue in this case is whether Cargill, by its course of dealing with Warren, became liable as a principal on contracts made by Warren with plaintiffs. Cargill contends that no agency relationship was established with Warren, notwithstanding its financing of Warren's operation and its purchase of the majority of Warren's grain. However,

---

grain operation; (4) marketing fertilizer and steel bins on consignment; (5) a reduction in withdrawals made by officers; (6) a suggestion that Warren's bookkeeper not issue her own salary checks; and (7) cooperation with Cargill in implementing the recommendations. These ideas were apparently never implemented, however.

we conclude that Cargill, by its control and influence over Warren, became a principal with liability for the transactions entered into by its agent Warren.

Agency is the fiduciary relationship that results from the manifestation of consent by one person to another that the other shall act on his behalf and subject to his control, and consent by the other so to act. . . .

In order to create an agency there must be an agreement, but not necessarily a contract between the parties. . . . An agreement may result in the creation of an agency relationship although the parties did not call it an agency and did not intend the legal consequences of the relation to follow. The existence of the agency may be proved by circumstantial evidence which shows a course of dealing between the two parties. . . . When an agency relationship is to be proven by circumstantial evidence, the principal must be shown to have consented to the agency since one cannot be the agent of another except by consent of the latter. . . .

Cargill contends that the prerequisites of an agency relationship did not exist because Cargill never consented to the agency, Warren did not act on behalf of Cargill, and Cargill did not exercise control over Warren. We hold that all three elements of agency could be found in the particular circumstances of this case. By directing Warren to implement its recommendations, Cargill manifested its consent that Warren would be its agent. Warren acted on Cargill's behalf in procuring grain for Cargill as the part of its normal operations which were totally financed by Cargill.[7] Further, an agency relationship was established by Cargill's interference with the internal affairs of Warren, which constituted de facto control of the elevator.

A creditor who assumes control of his debtor's business may become liable as principal for the acts of the debtor in connection with the business. Restatement (Second) of Agency § 14 O (1958). It is noted in comment a to section 14 O that:

> A security holder who merely exercises a veto power over the business acts of his debtor by preventing purchases or sales above specified amounts does not thereby become a principal. However, if he takes over the management of the debtor's business either in person or through an agent, and directs what contracts may or may not be made, he becomes a principal, liable as a principal for the obligations incurred thereafter in the normal course of business by the debtor who has now become his general agent. The point at which the creditor becomes a principal is that at which he assumes de facto control over the conduct of his debtor, whatever the terms of the formal contract with his debtor may be.

A number of factors indicate Cargill's control over Warren, including the following:

(1) Cargill's constant recommendations to Warren by telephone;

(2) Cargill's right of first refusal on grain;

---

[7] Although the contracts with the farmers were executed by Warren, Warren paid for the grain with drafts drawn on Cargill. While this is not in itself significant . . . it is one factor to be taken into account in analyzing the relationship between Warren and Cargill.

(3) Warren's inability to enter into mortgages, to purchase stock or to pay dividends without Cargill's approval;

(4) Cargill's right of entry onto Warren's premises to carry on periodic checks and audits;

(5) Cargill's correspondence and criticism regarding Warren's finances, officers salaries and inventory;

(6) Cargill's determination that Warren needed "strong paternal guidance";

(7) Provision of drafts and forms to Warren upon which Cargill's name was imprinted;

(8) Financing of all Warren's purchases of grain and operating expenses; and

(9) Cargill's power to discontinue the financing of Warren's operations.

We recognize that some of these elements, as Cargill contends, are found in an ordinary debtor-creditor relationship. However, these factors cannot be considered in isolation, but, rather, they must be viewed in light of all the circumstances surrounding Cargill's aggressive financing of Warren.

It is also Cargill's position that the relationship between Cargill and Warren was that of buyer-supplier rather than principal-agent. Restatement (Second) of Agency § 14K (1958) compares an agent with a supplier as follows:

> One who contracts to acquire property from a third person and convey it to another is the agent of the other only if it is agreed that he is to act primarily for the benefit of the other and not for himself.
>
> Factors indicating that one is a supplier, rather than an agent, are:
>
> (1) That he is to receive a fixed price for the property irrespective of price paid by him. This is the most important. (2) That he acts in his own name and receives the title to the property which he thereafter is to transfer. (3) That he has an independent business in buying and selling similar property.

Restatement (Second) of Agency § 14K, comment a (1958).

Under the Restatement approach, it must be shown that the supplier has an independent business before it can be concluded that he is not an agent. The record establishes that all portions of Warren's operation were financed by Cargill and that Warren sold almost all of its market grain to Cargill. Thus, the relationship which existed between the parties was not merely that of buyer and supplier.

. . .

The amici curiae assert that, if the jury verdict is upheld, firms and banks which have provided business loans to county elevators will decline to make further loans. The decision in this case should give no cause for such concern. We deal here with a business enterprise markedly different from an ordinary bank financing, since Cargill was an active participant in Warren's operations rather than simply a financier.

Cargill's course of dealing with Warren was, by its own admission, a paternalistic relationship in which Cargill made the key economic decisions and kept Warren in existence.

Although considerable interest was paid by Warren on the loan, the reason for Cargill's financing of Warren was not to make money as a lender but, rather, to establish a source of market grain for its business. As one Cargill manager noted, "We were staying in there because we wanted the grain." For this reason, Cargill was willing to extend the credit line far beyond the amount originally allocated to Warren. It is noteworthy that Cargill was receiving significant amounts of grain and that, notwithstanding the risk that was recognized by Cargill, the operation was considered profitable.

On the whole, there was a unique fabric in the relationship between Cargill and Warren which varies from that found in normal debtor-creditor situations. We conclude that, on the facts of this case, there was sufficient evidence from which the jury could find that Cargill was the principal of Warren within the definitions of agency set forth in Restatement (Second) of Agency §§ 1 and 14 O.

NOTE

Warren, Minnesota was a town with a population of about 2,000 at the time this case was tried. Warren is located in Marshall County, which is in the northwest corner of Minnesota, on the North Dakota border, with a population of about 15,000. The plaintiffs were local farmers and the defendant was a corporate giant. The case was tried to a jury.

ANALYSIS

1. Why do you suppose Cargill kept extending more and more credit to Warren?

2. What could the farmers have done to protect themselves from the risk of nonpayment?

3. What could Cargill have done to ensure that the grain it bought from Warren was paid for?

4. In light of your answers to questions 2 and 3, does the result in the case place responsibility for avoiding loss on the person with the lower cost of doing so?

5. If Peter says to Amy, "Go out and buy a thousand bushels of corn for me and I'll pay you the usual commission," Amy is Peter's nonservant agent (that is, she acts on behalf of Peter but is not subject to his control over how the objective is achieved). Peter is bound to contracts made by Amy to buy the corn. Control of the manner in which Amy accomplishes the assignment is not an issue. In the *Cargill* case, however, there seems to have been no evidence to support that kind of ordinary nonservant principal/agent relationship. Presumably that is why the court focuses on control and on the Restatement (Second) of Agency § 14 O. Examine the nine factors listed by the court as supporting a conclusion that Cargill exercised control over Warren. How, if at all, does each of these factors tend to establish a principal/agent relationship rather than a relationship of creditor to debtor or buyer to supplier?

6. What is the likely effect of decisions like *Cargill* on the behavior of major creditors? In addressing this question consider the effect on other, minor creditors, like the farmers who sold grain to Warren, as well as major creditors such as Cargill, Inc.

PLANNING

Suppose you are Cargill's lawyer. The chief executive officer (CEO) of the company, after hearing about the decision in the case involving Warren Grain & Seed Co., asks for your recommendations about how Cargill should change the way it does business to avoid liability in the future. She also wants your views on whether, with a supplier like Warren, at the time that its financial condition became desperate, it would have been advisable for Cargill to (a) call in its loans and force the supplier into bankruptcy or (b) notify all other potential creditors that Cargill would not be liable for any purchases by the supplier. What would you say? Bear in mind that you are expected to exercise sound business, as well as legal, judgment, but that your role is to offer alternatives, not to make decisions.

2. LIABILITY OF PRINCIPAL TO THIRD PARTIES IN CONTRACT

A. THE AGENT'S AUTHORITY

Mill Street Church of Christ v. Hogan

785 S.W.2d 263 (Ky.1990).

Mill Street Church of Christ and State Automobile Mutual Insurance Company petition for review of a decision of the New Workers' Compensation Board [hereinafter "New Board"] which had reversed an earlier decision by the Old Workers' Compensation Board [hereinafter "Old Board"]. The Old Board had ruled that Samuel J. Hogan was not an employee of the Mill Street Church of Christ and was not entitled to any workers' compensation benefits. The New Board reversed and ruled that Samuel Hogan was an employee of the church.

. . . In 1986, the Elders of the Mill Street Church of Christ decided to hire church member, Bill Hogan, to paint the church building. The Elders decided that another church member, Gary Petty, would be hired to assist if any assistance was needed. In the past, the church had hired Bill Hogan for similar jobs, and he had been allowed to hire his brother, Sam Hogan, the respondent, as a helper. Sam Hogan had earlier been a member of the church but was no longer a member. . . .

Dr. David Waggoner, an Elder of the church, soon contacted Bill Hogan, and he accepted the job and began work. Apparently Waggoner made no mention to Bill Hogan of hiring a helper at that time. Bill Hogan painted the church by himself until he reached the baptistry portion of the church. This was a very high, difficult portion of the church to paint, and he decided that he needed help. After Bill Hogan had reached this point in his work, he discussed the matter of a helper with Dr. Waggoner at his office. According to both Dr. Waggoner and Hogan, they discussed the possibility of hiring Gary Petty to help Hogan. None of the evidence indicates that Hogan was told that he had to hire Petty. In fact, Dr. Waggoner apparently told Hogan that Petty was difficult to reach. That was basically all the discussion that these two individuals had concerning hiring a helper. None of the other Elders discussed the matter with Bill Hogan.

On December 14, 1986, Bill Hogan approached his brother, Sam, about helping him complete the job. Bill Hogan told Sam the details of the job, including the pay, and Sam accepted the job. On December 15, 1986, Sam began working. A half hour after he began, he climbed the ladder to paint a ceiling corner, and a leg of the ladder broke. Sam fell to the floor and broke his left arm. Sam was taken to the Grayson County Hospital Emergency Room where he was treated. He later was under the care of Dr. James Klinert, a surgeon in Louisville. The church Elders did not know that Bill Hogan had approached Sam Hogan to work as a helper until after the accident occurred.

After the accident, Bill Hogan reported the accident and resulting injury to Charles Payne, a church Elder and treasurer. Payne stated in a deposition that he told Bill Hogan that the church had insurance. At this time, Bill Hogan told Payne the total number of hours worked which included a half hour that Sam Hogan had worked prior to the accident. Payne issued Bill Hogan a check for all of these hours. Further, Bill Hogan did not have to use his own tools and materials in the project. The church supplied the tools, materials, and supplies necessary to complete the project. Bill purchased needed items from Dunn's Hardware Store and charged them to the church's account.

It is undisputed in this case that Mill Street Church of Christ is an insured employer under the Workers' Compensation Act. Sam Hogan filed a claim under the Workers' Compensation Act.* . . .

As part of their argument, petitioners argue the New Board also erred in finding that Bill Hogan possessed implied authority as an agent to hire Sam Hogan. Petitioners contend there was neither implied nor apparent authority in the case at bar.

It is important to distinguish implied and apparent authority before proceeding further. Implied authority is actual authority circumstantially proven which the principal actually intended the agent to possess and includes such powers as are practically necessary to carry out the duties actually delegated. Apparent authority on the other hand is not actual authority but is the authority the agent is held out by the principal as possessing. It is a matter of appearances on which third parties come to rely.

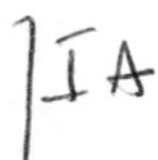

Petitioners attack the New Board's findings concerning implied authority. In examining whether implied authority exists, it is important to focus upon the agent's understanding of his authority. It must be determined whether the agent reasonably believes because of present or past conduct of the principal that the principal wishes him to act in a certain way or to have certain authority. The nature of the task or job may be another factor to consider. Implied authority may be necessary in

* [Eds. If Bill Hogan had authority to hire Sam, then Sam would be deemed the Church's agent (technically, a sub-agent) and its employee for purposes of the Worker's Compensation Act.]

order to implement the express authority. The existence of prior similar practices is one of the most important factors. Specific conduct by the principal in the past permitting the agent to exercise similar powers is crucial.

The person alleging agency and resulting authority has the burden of proving that it exists. Agency cannot be proven by a mere statement, but it can be established by circumstantial evidence including the acts and conduct of the parties such as the continuous course of conduct of the parties covering a number of successive transactions. . . .

In considering the above factors in the case at bar, Bill Hogan had implied authority to hire Sam Hogan as his helper. First, in the past the church had allowed Bill Hogan to hire his brother or other persons whenever he needed assistance on a project. Even though the Board of Elders discussed a different arrangement this time, no mention of this discussion was ever made to Bill or Sam Hogan. In fact, the discussion between Bill Hogan and Church Elder Dr. Waggoner, indicated that Gary Petty would be difficult to reach and Bill Hogan could hire whomever he pleased. Further, Bill Hogan needed to hire an assistant to complete the job for which he had been hired. The interior of the church simply could not be painted by one person. Maintaining a safe and attractive place of worship clearly is part of the church's function, and one for which it would designate an agent to ensure that the building is properly painted and maintained.

Finally, in this case, Sam Hogan believed that Bill Hogan had the authority to hire him as had been the practice in the past. To now claim that Bill Hogan could not hire Sam Hogan as an assistant, especially when Bill Hogan had never been told this fact, would be very unfair to Sam Hogan. Sam Hogan relied on Bill Hogan's representation. The church treasurer in this case even paid Bill Hogan for the half hour of work that Sam Hogan had completed prior to the accident. Considering the above facts, we find that Sam Hogan was within the employment of the Mill Street Church of Christ at the time he was injured.

The decision of the New Workers' Compensation Board is affirmed.

ANALYSIS AND PROBLEMS

1. Is Sam Hogan's belief that his brother Bill had authority to hire Sam relevant to the issue of whether Bill had actual authority to do so?

2. The following problems are based on a simple fact pattern in which Paul owns an apartment building and has hired Ann to manage it.

   a. Paul tells Ann to hire a company to cut the grass. Ann does it. Is Paul bound by the contract?

   b. Without express instructions, Ann hires a janitor to clean the building. Is Paul bound by the employment contract with the janitor? See Restatement (Second) of Agency § 35.

   c. Suppose Paul specifically instructed Ann not to hire a janitor, but that local custom gives apartment managers the power to hire janitors. Would Paul be bound by the contract?

Three-Seventy Leasing Corporation v. Ampex Corporation

528 F.2d 993 (5th Cir.1976).

Three-Seventy Leasing Corporation (370) seeks damages from Ampex Corporation (Ampex) for breach of a contract to sell six computer core memories. The district court, sitting without a jury, found that there was an enforceable contract between 370 and Ampex. . . .

Three-Seventy Leasing Corporation was formed by Joyce, at all times its only active employee, for the purpose of purchasing computer hardware from various manufacturers for lease to end-users. In August of 1972, Kays, a salesman of Ampex and friend of Joyce, initiated discussions with Joyce regarding the possibility of 370 purchasing computer equipment from Ampex. A meeting was arranged between Kays, Joyce, and Mueller, Kays' superior at Ampex. Joyce was informed at this meeting that Ampex could sell to 370 only if 370 could pass Ampex's credit requirements. Joyce informed the two that he did not think this would be a problem.

At approximately the same time, Joyce began negotiations with Electronic Data Systems (EDS), which resulted in EDS's verbal commitment to lease six units of Ampex computer core memory from 370. Desiring to close the two transactions simultaneously, Joyce continued negotiations with Kays. These negotiations resulted in a written document submitted by Kays to Joyce at the direction of Mueller. The document provided for the purchase by Joyce of six core memory units at a price of $100,000 each, with a down payment of $150,000 and the remainder to be paid over a five year period. The document specified that delivery was to be made to EDS. The document also contained a signature block for a representative of 370 and a signature block for a representative of Ampex.

Joyce received this document about November 3, 1972, and executed it on November 6, 1972. The document was never executed by a representative of Ampex. This document forms the core of the present controversy. 370 argues that the document was an offer to sell by Ampex, which was accepted upon Joyce's signature. Ampex contends that the document was nothing more than a solicitation which became an offer to purchase upon execution by Joyce, and that this offer was never accepted by Ampex. 370 counters by arguing in the alternative that even if the document when signed by Joyce was only an offer to purchase, the offer was later accepted by representatives of Ampex.

The district court, in concluding that there existed an enforceable contract, made no determination as to whether the document described above was an offer to sell accepted by Joyce's signature, or an offer to purchase when signed by Joyce which was later accepted by Ampex.

We reject the first alternative as being without evidentiary support. Elemental principles demand that there be a meeting of the minds and a communication that each party has consented to the terms of the agreement in order for a contract to exist. . . . There is no evidence, either written or oral, other than the document itself, which shows that Ampex had the requisite intent necessary to the formation of a contract prior to November 6, 1972, the date the document was executed by Joyce. And the document on its face does not supply that intent. Rather, the fact that the document had a signature block for a representative of Ampex which was unsigned at the time it was submitted to Joyce, in the absence of other evidence, negates any interpretation that Ampex intended this to be an offer to Joyce, without any further acts necessary on the part of Ampex.

Thus, the document, when signed by Joyce, at most constituted an offer by him to purchase. In order for there to be a valid contract, we must therefore find some act of acceptance on the part of Ampex.

On November 9, 1972, Mueller issued an intra-office memorandum which stated in part that "[o]n November 3, 1972, Ampex was awarded an Agreement by Three-Seventy Leasing, Dallas, Texas, for the purchase of six (6) ARM-3360 Memory Units," to be installed at EDS. This memorandum further informed those concerned at Ampex of Joyce's request that all contact with 370 be handled through Kays. On November 17, 1972, Kays sent a letter to Joyce which confirmed the delivery dates for the memory units.[2] We conclude, in light of the circumstances surrounding these negotiations, that the district court was not clearly erroneous when it found that Kays had apparent authority to accept Joyce's offer on behalf of Ampex, and we further conclude that the November 17 letter, in these circumstances, can reasonably be interpreted to be an acceptance.

An agent has apparent authority sufficient to bind the principal when the principal acts in such a manner as would lead a reasonably prudent person to suppose that the agent had the authority he purports to exercise. . . . Further, absent knowledge on the part of third parties to the contrary, an agent has the apparent authority to do those things which are usual and proper to the conduct of the business which he is employed to conduct. . . .

In this case, Kays was employed by Ampex in the capacity of a salesman. It is certainly reasonable for third parties to presume that one employed as salesman has the authority to bind his employer to sell. And Ampex did nothing to dispel this reasonable inference. Rather, its actions and inactions provided a further basis for this belief. First, Kays, at the direction of Mueller, submitted the controversial document to Joyce for signature. The document contained a space for signature by an Ampex representative. Nothing in the document suggests that Kays did not have authority to sign it on behalf of Ampex.[3] Second, Joyce indicated to Kays

---

[2] That letter stated:

Dear John:

With regard to delivery of equipment purchased by Three-Seventy Leasing: Ampex will ship three (3) million bytes of ARM-3360 magnetic core in sufficient time to install 1½ million bytes the weekend of December 16, 1972. The remaining balance of 1½ million bytes will be installed by the weekend of December 30, 1972.

The equipment will be installed in Camphill, Pennsylvania at a predetermined site by Electronic Data Systems.

Regards,

Thomas C. Kays

Sales Representative

[3] It would have been an easy matter to provide in the document that only certain officers of Ampex had authority to sign on its behalf. Any inference to the contrary resulting from Ampex's failure to specify such a limitation must weigh against Ampex.

and Mueller that he wished all communications to be channeled through Kays. Mueller agreed, and acknowledged this in the November 9 intra-company memorandum. Neither Mueller, nor anyone else at Ampex ever informed Joyce that communication regarding acceptance would come through anyone other than Kays. In light of this request and Ampex's agreement, Joyce could reasonably expect that Kays would speak for the company.

Various individuals in the Ampex hierarchy testified at trial that only the contract manager or other supervisor in the company's contract department had authority to sign a contract on behalf of Ampex. However, there is no evidence that this limitation was ever communicated to Joyce in any manner. Absent knowledge of such a limitation by third parties, that limitation will not bar a claim of apparent authority.

Thus, when Joyce received Kays' November 17 letter, he had every reason to believe, based upon Ampex's prior actions, that Kays spoke on behalf of the company. We thus agree with the district court's finding that Kays had apparent authority to act for Ampex.

Having determined that Kays had apparent authority to bind Ampex, we further conclude that his letter of November 17, in light of the pattern of negotiations, could reasonably be interpreted as a promise to ship the six memory units on the dates specified in the letter and on the terms previously set out in the document executed by Joyce and submitted to Ampex. The district court's finding that a contract was formed is therefore not clearly erroneous.

ANALYSIS

1. What was Joyce's function? Was he a sales representative of Ampex? A purchasing agent of EDS? Neither?

2. What was Kays's position and function?

3. Kays did not have authority to enter into the contract. Do you find this surprising as to (a) the agreement to sell the core memory units or (b) the agreement to extend credit, or both?

4. What were the defendant's manifestations that supported a finding of apparent authority?

PLANNING AND ECONOMIC EFFICIENCY

1. What should Ampex have done to protect itself against the problem that arose in this case?

2. What could Joyce have done to protect himself?

3. In light of your answer to questions 1 and 2, does the result in the case place responsibility for avoiding loss on the person with the lower cost of doing so?

QUESTION

As we have seen, contracts entered into on the principal's behalf by an agent lacking actual authority can still be binding on the principal if the agent has apparent authority. Apparent authority only exists, however, "when a third party reasonably believes the actor has authority to act on behalf of the principal and that belief is traceable to the principal's manifestations." Restatement (Third) of Agency § 2.03. What happens if the agent is acting on behalf of a so-called undisclosed principal? ("A principal is undisclosed if, when an agent and a third party interact, the third party has no notice that the agent is acting for a principal." Id. § 1.04(2)(b).) If the third party has no idea that a principal exists, how can there be the manifestation required for apparent authority? The next case considers that problem.

Watteau v. Fenwick

[1893] 1 Queen's Bench 346 (1892).

From the evidence it appeared that one Humble had carried on business at a beerhouse called the Victoria Hotel, at Stockton-on-Tees, which business he had transferred to the defendants, a firm of brewers, some years before the present action. After the transfer of the business, Humble remained as defendants' manager; but the licence was always taken out in Humble's name, and his name was painted over the door. Under the terms of the agreement made between Humble and the defendants, the former had no authority to buy any goods for the business except bottled ales and mineral waters; all other goods required were to be supplied by the defendants themselves. The action was brought to recover the price of goods delivered at the Victoria Hotel over some years, for which it was admitted that the plaintiff gave credit to Humble only: they consisted of cigars, bovril, and other articles. The learned judge allowed the claim for the cigars and bovril only, and gave judgment for the plaintiff for 22*l.* 12*s.* 6*d.* The defendants appealed.

1892. Nov. 19. *Finlay, Q.C.* (*Scott Fox,* with him), for the defendants. The decision of the county court judge was wrong. The liability of a principal for the acts of his agent, done contrary to his secret instructions, depends upon his holding him out as his agent—that is, upon the agent being clothed with an apparent authority to act for his principal. Where, therefore, a man carries on business in his own name through a manager, he holds out his own credit, and would be liable for goods supplied even where the manager exceeded his authority. But where, as in the present case, there is no holding out by the principal, but the business is carried on in the agent's name and the goods are supplied on his credit, a person wishing to go behind the agent and make the principal liable must show an agency in fact.

[Lord Coleridge, C.J. Cannot you, in such a case, sue the undisclosed principal on discovering him?]

Only where the act done by the agent is within the scope of his agency; not where there has been an excess of authority. Where any one has been held out by the principal as his agent, there is a contract with the principal by estoppel, however much the agent may have exceeded his authority; where there has been no holding out, proof must be given of an agency in fact in order to make the principal liable.

Boydell Houghton, for the plaintiff. The defendants are liable in the present action. They are in fact undisclosed principals, who instead of carrying on the business in their own names employed a manager to carry it on for them, and clothed him with authority to do what was necessary to carry on the business. The case depends upon the same principles as *Edmunds v. Bushell,* where the manager of a business which was carried on in his own name with the addition "and Co." accepted a bill of exchange, notwithstanding a stipulation in the agreement with his principal that he should not accept bills; and the Court held that the principal was liable to an indorsee who took the bill without any knowledge of the relations between the principal and agent. In that case there was no holding out of the manager as an agent; it was the simple case of an agent being allowed to act as the ostensible principal without any disclosure to the world of there being any one behind him. Here the defendants have so conducted themselves as to enable their agent to hold himself out to the world as the proprietor of their business, and they are clearly undisclosed principals: *Ramazotti v. Bowring*. All that the plaintiff has to do, therefore, in order to charge the principals, is to show that the goods supplied were such as were ordinarily used in the business—that is to say, that they were within the reasonable scope of the agent's authority. . . .

Dec. 12. Lord Coleridge, C.J. The judgment which I am about to read has been written by my brother Wills, and I entirely concur in it.

■ WILLS, J. The plaintiff sues the defendants for the price of cigars supplied to the Victoria Hotel, Stockton-upon-Tees. The house was kept, not by the defendants, but by a person named Humble, whose name was over the door. The plaintiff gave credit to Humble, and to him alone, and had never heard of the defendants. The business, however, was really the defendants', and they had put Humble into it to manage it for them, and had forbidden him to buy cigars on credit. The cigars, however, were such as would usually be supplied to and dealt in at such an establishment. The learned county court judge held that the defendants were liable. I am of opinion that he was right.

There seems to be less of direct authority on the subject than one would expect. But I think that the Lord Chief Justice during the argument laid down the correct principle, viz., once it is established that the defendant was the real principal, the ordinary doctrine as to principal and agent applies—that the principal is liable for all the acts of the agent which are within the authority usually confided to an agent of that character, notwithstanding limitations, as between the principal and the agent, put upon that authority. It is said that it is only so where there has been a holding out of authority—which cannot be said of a case where the person supplying the goods knew nothing of the existence of a principal. But I do not think so. Otherwise, in every case of undisclosed principal, or at least in every case where the fact of there being a principal was undisclosed, the secret limitation of authority would prevail and defeat the action of the person dealing with the agent and then discovering that he was an agent and had a principal.

But in the case of a dormant partner it is clear law that no limitation of authority as between the dormant and active partner will avail the dormant partner as to things within the ordinary authority of a partner. The law of partnership is, on such a question, nothing but a branch of the general law of principal and agent, and it appears to me to be undisputed and conclusive on the point now under discussion.

The principle laid down by the Lord Chief Justice, and acted upon by the learned county court judge, appears to be identical with that enunciated in the judgments of Cockburn, C.J., and Mellor, J., in Edmunds v. Bushell, the circumstances of which case, though not identical with those of the present, come very near to them. There was no holding out, as the plaintiff knew nothing of the defendant. I appreciate the distinction drawn by Mr. Finlay in his argument, but the principle laid down in the judgments referred to, if correct, abundantly covers the present case. I cannot find that any doubt has ever been expressed that it is correct, and I think it is right, and that very mischievous consequences would often result if that principle were not upheld.

In my opinion this appeal ought to be dismissed with costs.

Appeal dismissed.

NOTE

The Restatement (Second) of Agency included a broad concept called "inherent agency power," which Section 8A of the Restatement defined as follows:

> Inherent agency power is a term used in the restatement of this subject to indicate the power of an agent which is derived not from authority, apparent authority or estoppel, but solely from the agency relation and exists for the protection of persons harmed by or dealing with a servant or other agent.

The Restatement (Second) of Agency § 194 states that an undisclosed principal is liable for acts of an agent "done on his account, if usual or necessary in such transactions, although forbidden by the principal."

Under the Restatement (Second) of Agency § 195, "An undisclosed principal who entrusts an agent with the management of his business is subject to liability to third persons with whom the agent enters into transactions usual in such business and on the principal's account, although contrary to the directions of the principal."

Although some set of rules for dealing with cases like *Watteau* is necessary, the vaguely defined concept of inherent agency power was a poor tool for doing so.

The Restatement (Third) of Agency rejected the concept of inherent agency power in favor of a rule directly targeted at cases like *Watteau*:

> § 2.06 Liability of Undisclosed Principal
>
> (1) An undisclosed principal is subject to liability to a third party who is justifiably induced to make a detrimental change in position by an agent acting on the principal's behalf and without actual authority if the principal, having notice of the agent's conduct and that it might induce others to change their positions, did not take reasonable steps to notify them of the facts.
>
> (2) An undisclosed principal may not rely on instructions given an agent that qualify or reduce the agent's authority to less than the authority a third party would reasonably believe the agent to have under the same circumstances if the principal had been disclosed.

The comments to § 2.06 claim that it reflects the rule of *Watteau* and Restatement (Second) § 195, but the Restatement (Third) rule in fact may be substantially narrower. It concludes with the qualification that the principal is liable "if the principal, having notice of the agent's conduct and that it might induce others to change their position, did not take reasonable steps to notify them of the facts." This makes the rule seem more akin to estoppel than to the old inherent agency power. It seems that the defendants in *Watteau* were not aware that Humble was buying cigars from Watteau and therefore would not be liable under the Restatement (Third) rule—contrary to the actual result in *Watteau*.

ANALYSIS

1. Is there any basis in this case for holding the defendants liable on a theory of apparent authority?

2. Humble had authority to buy "ales and mineral waters" from third parties but not "cigars, bovril, and other articles." (Bovril is a nonalcoholic drink.) The court claims that "mischievous consequences" would result from a decision for the defendants. What are those mischievous consequences? In responding to this question, ask yourself if there is any basis for distinguishing between ales and mineral waters, on the one hand, and cigars and bovril, on the other hand. Bear in mind that the plaintiffs seek recovery from the personal assets of the defendants, not just the assets (if any) invested by the defendants in the Victoria Hotel.

3. The Restatement (Third) offers the following hypothetical:

> P Corporation produces musical recordings and employs A to engage performers. A's counterparts in the recording industry have authority to make unconditional contracts with performers, but B, who is A's superior within P Corporation, directs A to condition all payments to performers on the sales revenues that P Corporation receives from their work. B's direction to A is not known outside P Corporation.

On P's behalf, A enters into a contract with T that is unconditional. T has never met B or anyone else who works for P other than A. Is there a manifestation by P on these facts sufficient to establish apparent authority or do you need some concept like inherent agency power to deal with these sort of cases? See Restatement (Third) § 1.03:

> A person manifests assent or intention through written or spoken words or other conduct.

REVIEW PROBLEMS

1. Suppose Professor Paula Potter has a student research assistant, Allie. Allie is about to graduate and Paula asks her to hire a successor. Paula says that she is willing to pay $9 per hour for 100 hours of work. Allie finds another student, Zelda, who wants the job but points out that the going rate is $10 per hour. Allie says, "Well, if that's the going rate, that's O.K. You have the job." Thereafter Paula tells Zelda that she will pay only $9 and Zelda (who has turned down other job offers) seeks to enforce the contract that she thinks she has for $10 per hour. Who wins? Why? Suppose Paula had said to Allie, "Find the best

available person, tell that person what the job is and how much I am willing to pay, and send her or him to me so I can offer the job if I am satisfied with your choice." Same result?

2. Suppose you are the lawyer for M/M Records, a small record company with good management and exciting prospects. The head of the company, Millie Mogul, has just hired a woman named Sheena Swiftie, who is friendly with a number of leading recording stars and hopes some day to establish herself as an independent agent in the entertainment industry, but wants to start out as an employee (largely because she needs a steady income). Sheena's job is to line up recording stars to make recordings for M/M Records. Sheena will be paid a salary plus bonuses based on what she produces. Millie tells you, "Sheena seems a bit flaky, but I think she can deliver." In recent years, in the recording business, it has become common for record companies to offer substantial guarantees to star performers, but M/M Records does not do so, because it cannot afford to take the risk. Instead, it offers higher royalties than its competitors do. Millie wants Sheena to have authority to pin artists down to contracts when the moment is right, but has emphasized to Sheena the M/M Records policy of no guarantees. Millie asks you if she has anything to worry about and, if she does, what suggestions you might have. You are aware that Millie tends to resent lawyers in general because she thinks they are "deal breakers." What is your response to her?

B. RATIFICATION

Botticello v. Stefanovicz

177 Conn. 22, 411 A.2d 16 (1979).

This case concerns the enforceability of an agreement for the sale of real property when that agreement has been executed by a person owning only an undivided half interest in the property. . . .

The finding of the trial court discloses the following undisputed facts: The defendants, Mary and Walter Stefanovicz (hereinafter "Mary" and "Walter") in 1943 acquired as tenants in common a farm situated in the towns of Colchester and Lebanon. In the fall of 1965, the plaintiff, Anthony Botticello, became interested in the property. When he first visited the farm, Walter advised him that the asking price was $100,000. The following January, the plaintiff again visited the farm and made a counteroffer of $75,000. At that time, Mary stated that there was "no way" she could sell it for that amount. Ultimately the plaintiff and Walter agreed upon a price of $85,000 for a lease with an option to purchase; during these negotiations, Mary stated that she would not sell the property for less than that amount.

The informal agreement was finalized with the assistance of counsel for both Walter and the plaintiff. The agreement was drawn up by Walter's attorney after consultation with Walter and the plaintiff; it was then sent to, and modified by, the plaintiff's attorney. The agreement was signed by Walter and by the plaintiff. Neither the plaintiff nor his attorney, nor Walter's attorney, was then aware of the fact that Walter did not own the property outright. The plaintiff, although a successful businessman with considerable experience in real estate never requested his attorney to do a title search of any kind, and consequently no title search was done. Walter never represented to the plaintiff or the plaintiff's attorney, or to his own attorney, that he was acting for his wife, as her agent. Mary's part ownership came to light in 1968, when a third party sought an easement over the land in question.

Shortly after the execution of the lease and option-to-purchase agreement, the plaintiff took possession of the property. He made substantial improvements on the property and, in 1971, properly exercised his option to purchase. When the defendants refused to honor the option agreement, the plaintiff commenced the present action against both Mary and Walter, seeking specific performance, possession of the premises, and damages.

The trial court found the issues for the plaintiff and ordered specific performance of the option-to-purchase agreement. In their appeal, the defendants [claim] that Mary was never a party to the agreement, and its terms may therefore not be enforced as to her. . . .

The plaintiff alleged, and the trial court agreed, that although Mary was not a party to the lease and option-to-purchase agreement, its terms were nonetheless binding upon her because Walter acted as her authorized agent in the negotiations, discussions, and execution of the written agreement. The defendants have attacked several findings of fact and conclusions of law, claiming that the underlying facts and applicable law do not support the court's conclusion of agency. We agree.

Agency is defined as " 'the fiduciary relationship which results from manifestation of consent by one person to another that the other shall act on his behalf and subject to his control, and consent by the other so to act. . . .' Restatement (Second), 1 Agency § 1." McLaughlin v. Chicken Delight, Inc., 164 Conn. 317, 322, 321 A.2d 456 (1973). Thus, the three elements required to show the existence of an agency relationship include: (1) a manifestation by the principal that the agent will act for him; (2) acceptance by the agent of the undertaking; and (3) an understanding between the parties that the principal will be in control of the undertaking. Restatement (Second), 1 Agency § 1, comment b (1958).

The existence of an agency relationship is a question of fact. The burden of proving agency is on the plaintiff and it must be proven by a fair preponderance of the evidence. Marital status cannot in and of itself prove the agency relationship. Nor does the fact that the defendants owned the land jointly make one the agent for the other.

The facts set forth in the court's finding are wholly insufficient to support the court's conclusion that Walter acted as Mary's authorized agent in the discussions concerning the sale of their farm and in the execution of the written agreement. . . . The finding indicates that when the farm was purchased, and when the couple transferred property to their sons, Walter handled many of the business aspects, including making payments for taxes, insurance, and mortgage. The finding also discloses that Mary and Walter discussed the sale of the farm, and that Mary remarked that she would not sell it for $75,000, and would not sell it for less than $85,000. A statement that one will not sell for less than a certain amount is by no means the equivalent of an agreement to sell for that amount. Moreover, the fact that one spouse tends more to business matters than the other does not, absent other evidence of agreement or authorization, constitute the delegation of power as to an agent. What is most damaging to the plaintiff's case is the court's uncontradicted finding that, although Mary may have acquiesced in Walter's handling of many business matters, Walter never signed any documents as agent for Mary prior to 1966. Mary had consistently signed any deed, mortgage, or mortgage note in connection with their jointly held property.

. . .

The plaintiff argues, alternatively, that even if no agency relationship existed at the time the agreement was signed, Mary was bound by the contract executed by her husband because she ratified its terms by her subsequent conduct. The trial court accepted this alternative argument as well, concluding that Mary had ratified the agreement by receiving and accepting payments from the plaintiff, and by acquiescing in his substantial improvements to the farm. The underlying facts, however, do not support the conclusion of ratification.

Ratification is defined as "the affirmance by a person of a prior act which did not bind him but which was done or professedly done on his account." Restatement (Second), 1 Agency § 82 (1958). Ratification requires "acceptance of the results of the act with an intent to ratify, and with full knowledge of all the material circumstances." Ansonia v. Cooper, 64 Conn. 536, 544, 30 A. 760 (1894). . . .

The finding neither indicates an intent by Mary to ratify the agreement, nor establishes her knowledge of all the material circumstances surrounding the deal. At most, Mary observed the plaintiff occupying and improving the land, received rental payments from the plaintiff from time to time, knew that she had an interest in the property, and knew that the use, occupancy, and rentals were pursuant to a written agreement she had not signed. None of these facts is sufficient to support the conclusion that Mary ratified the agreement and thus bound herself to its terms. It is undisputed that Walter had the power to lease his own undivided one-half interest in the property and the facts found by the trial court could be referable to that fact alone. Moreover, the fact that the rental payments were used for "family" purposes indicates nothing more than one spouse providing for the other.

The plaintiff makes the further argument that Mary ratified the agreement simply by receiving its benefits and by failing to repudiate it. See Restatement (Second), 1 Agency § 98 (1958). The plaintiff fails to recognize that before the receipt of benefits may constitute ratification, the other requisites for ratification must first be present. "Thus if the original transaction was not purported to be done on account of the principal, the fact that the principal receives its proceeds does not make him a party to it." Restatement (Second), 1 Agency § 98, comment f (1958). Since Walter at no time purported to be acting on his wife's behalf, as is essential to effective subsequent ratification, Mary is not bound by the terms of the agreement, and specific performance cannot be ordered as to her.

. . .

We turn now to the question of relief. In view of our holding that Mary never authorized her husband to act as her agent for any purpose connected with the lease and option-to-purchase agreement, recovery against her is precluded. As to Walter, the fact that his ownership was restricted to an undivided one-half interest in no way limited his capacity to contract. He contracted to convey full title and for breach of that contract he may be held liable. The facts of the case are sufficient to furnish a basis for relief to the plaintiff by specific performance or by damages.

There is error as to the judgment against the defendant Mary Stefanovicz; the judgment as to her is set aside and the case remanded with direction to render judgment in her favor. As to the defendant Walter Stefanovicz, there is error only as to the remedy ordered. The judgment as to him is set aside and the case remanded for a new trial limited to the form of relief.

ANALYSIS AND PROBLEMS

Ratification is a means by which the principal can say, "my agent didn't have the right to enter into this contract, but I'm glad she did so. Accordingly, I'll affirm the transaction and agree to be bound by the contract." Any ratification case involves two critical questions: First, what types of acts constitute an affirmation by the principal? Second, what effect should we give to that affirmation?

Obviously, one can expressly affirm a contract. The principal can say something like: "Gosh, what a wonderful deal. I'll go forward with it." Harder questions arise in implied affirmation cases. Consider the following examples:

1. Suppose Pam is a writer. Her husband Alex enters into a contract with ABC Book Publishers under which Pam's next book is to go to ABC. Pam gets a check from ABC, representing the advance on the contract, which she cashes. She then spends the proceeds on a new computer for her office. Some months later Pam tries to sell her new book to another publisher. ABC claims the book. Pam correctly points out that Alex had no authority to act as her agent. ABC responds by saying that she had ratified the contract. Who wins?

2. Suppose Pam argues that she thought the check was for royalties on one of her previous books, which ABC had published. She asserts that she neither knew nor had reason to know that it was an advance on her next book. Who wins?

3. Alan is a slightly deranged fan of Pam's books. Alan goes to a local landscaping company. Pretending to be Pam's butler, he asks the company to cut Pam's grass. Pam arrives home just after the men finished up. Pam thanks them and goes inside. The company sues her for refusing to pay. Pam correctly points out that Alan had no authority to enter into this contract. The company claims she ratified the contract by accepting and retaining its benefits. Who wins?

4. Paula is an investor who has opened an account at a local brokerage. She instructs Al, her broker, only to purchase U.S. treasury bonds for the account. Al disregards those instructions and buys stock in a new very risky high-tech company. Paula does not learn about this until her first monthly statement arrives. She decides to take a wait and see attitude. When her next monthly statement arrives she notices that the stock's price has dropped rather drastically. She calls Al and demands that he close the account and reimburse her for the money she lost. She correctly claims he had no authority to buy the stock. Al closes the

account, but refuses to make Paula's losses good. Al claims Paula ratified the purchase by waiting. Who is right: Paula or Al?

5. Paula owns a mansion called Whiteacre Manor. Alan, having no authority to do so, enters into a sale contract with Ted by which Ted is to purchase Whiteacre Manor. The next day the mansion burns to the ground. Paula then expressly affirms the contract. Ted says she's too late. Who wins?

C. ESTOPPEL

Hoddeson v. Koos Bros.

47 N.J.Super. 224, 135 A.2d 702 (App.Div.1957).

The occurrence which engages our present attention is a little more than conventionally unconventional in the common course of trade. Old questions appear in new styles. A digest of the story told by Mrs. Hoddeson will be informative and perhaps admonitory to the unwary shopper.

The plaintiff Mrs. Hoddeson was acquainted with the spacious furniture store conducted by the defendant, Koos Bros., a corporation, at No. 1859 St. George Avenue in the City of Rahway. On a previous observational visit, her eyes had fallen upon certain articles of bedroom furniture which she ardently desired to acquire for her home. It has been said that "the sea hath bounds but deep desire hath none." Her sympathetic mother liberated her from the grasp of despair and bestowed upon her a gift of $165 with which to consummate the purchase.

It was in the forenoon of August 22, 1956 that Mrs. Hoddeson, accompanied by her aunt and four children, happily journeyed from her home in South River to the defendant's store to attain her objective. Upon entering, she was greeted by a tall man with dark hair frosted at the temples and clad in a light gray suit. He inquired if he could be of assistance, and she informed him specifically of her mission. Whereupon he immediately guided her, her aunt, and the flock to the mirror then on display and priced at $29 which Mrs. Hoddeson identified, and next to the location of the designated bedroom furniture which she had described.

Upon confirming her selections the man withdrew from his pocket a small pad or paper upon which he presumably recorded her order and calculated the total purchase price to be $168.50. Mrs. Hoddeson handed to him the $168.50 in cash. He informed her the articles other than those on display were not in stock, and that reproductions would upon notice be delivered to her in September. Alas, she omitted to request from him a receipt for her cash disbursement. The transaction consumed in time a period from 30 to 40 minutes.

Mrs. Hoddeson impatiently awaited the delivery of the articles of furniture, but a span of time beyond the assured date of delivery elapsed, which motivated her to inquire of the defendant the cause of the unexpected delay. Sorrowful, indeed, was she to learn from the defendant that its records failed to disclose any such sale to her and any such monetary credit in payment.

. . .

Although the amount of money involved is relatively inconsiderable, the defendant has resolved to incur the expense of this appeal. . . .

It eventuated that Mrs. Hoddeson and her aunt were subsequently unable positively to recognize among the defendant's regularly employed salesmen the individual with whom Mrs. Hoddeson had arranged for the purchase, although when she and her aunt were afforded the opportunities to gaze intently at one of the five salesmen assigned to that department of the store, both indicated a resemblance of one of them to the purported salesman, but frankly acknowledged the incertitude of their identification. The defendant's records revealed that the salesman bearing the alleged resemblance was on vacation and hence presumably absent from the store during the week of August 22, 1956.

As you will at this point surmise, the insistence of the defendant at the trial was that the person who served Mrs. Hoddeson was an impostor deceitfully impersonating a salesman of the defendant without the latter's knowledge.

. . .

Where a party seeks to impose liability upon an alleged principal on a contract made by an alleged agent, as here, the party must assume the obligation of proving the agency relationship. It is not the burden of the alleged principal to disprove it.

Concisely stated, the liability of a principal to third parties for the acts of an agent may be shown by proof disclosing (1) express or real authority which has been definitely granted; (2) implied authority, that is, to do all that is proper, customarily incidental and reasonably appropriate to the exercise of the authority granted; and (3) apparent authority, such as where the principal by words, conduct, or other indicative manifestations has "held out" the person to be his agent.

Obviously the plaintiffs' evidence in the present action does not substantiate the existence of any basic express authority or project any question implicating implied authority. The point here debated is whether or not the evidence circumstantiates the presence of apparent authority, and it is at this very point we come face to face with the general rule of law that the apparency and appearance of authority must be shown to have been created by the manifestations of the alleged principal, and not alone and solely by proof of those of the supposed agent. Assuredly the law cannot permit apparent authority to be established by the mere proof that a mountebank in fact exercised it.

. . .

Let us hypothesize for the purposes of our present comments that the acting salesman was not in fact an employee of the defendant, yet he behaved and deported himself during the stated period in the business establishment of the defendant in the manner described by the evidence adduced on behalf of the plaintiffs, would the defendant be immune as a matter of law from liability for the plaintiffs' loss? The tincture of estoppel that gives color to instances of apparent authority might in the law operate likewise to preclude a defendant's denial of liability. It matters little whether for immediate purposes we entitle or characterize the principle of law in such cases as "agency by estoppel" or "a tortious dereliction of duty owed to an invited customer." That which we have in mind are the unique occurrences where solely through the lack of the proprietor's reasonable surveillance and supervision an impostor falsely impersonates in the place of business an agent or servant of his. Certainly the proprietor's duty of care and precaution for the safety and security of the customer encompasses more than the diligent observance and removal of banana peels from the aisles. Broadly stated, the duty of the proprietor also encircles the exercise of reasonable care and vigilance to protect the customer from loss occasioned by the deceptions of an apparent salesman. The rule that those who bargain without inquiry with an apparent agent do so at the risk and peril of an absence of the agent's authority has a patently impracticable application to the customers who patronize our modern department stores.

Our concept of the modern law is that where a proprietor of a place of business by his dereliction of duty enables one who is not his agent conspicuously to act as such and ostensibly to transact the proprietor's business with a patron in the establishment, the appearances being of such a character as to lead a person of ordinary prudence and circumspection to believe that the impostor was in truth the proprietor's agent, in such circumstances the law will not permit the proprietor defensively to avail himself of the impostor's lack of authority and thus escape liability for the consequential loss thereby sustained by the customer.

. . .

In reversing the judgment under review, the interests of justice seem to us to recommend the allowance of a new trial with the privilege accorded the plaintiffs to reconstruct the architecture of their complaint appropriately to project for determination the justiciable issue to which, in view of the inquisitive object of the present appeal, we have alluded. . . .

Reversed and new trial allowed.

ANALYSIS

1. This is one of several cases in this text in which parties vigorously litigated disputes involving seemingly trivial amounts. Why on earth would Koos Bros. have gone to such lengths and expense?

2. What will plaintiff need to prove on remand to justify an estoppel-based verdict in her favor?

3. What result if plaintiff and the alleged imposter had merely entered into a contract for the purchase of the furniture, rather than exchanging money?

D. AGENT'S LIABILITY ON THE CONTRACT

Atlantic Salmon A/S v. Curran

32 Mass.App.Ct. 488, 591 N.E.2d 206 (1992).

These are the plaintiffs' appeals from a Superior Court judgment for the defendant. The issue presented is as to the personal liability of an agent who at the relevant times was acting on behalf of a partially disclosed or unidentified principal. . . .

The facts are not in dispute,. . . . The defendant began doing business with the plaintiffs, Salmonor A/S (Salmonor) and Atlantic Salmon A/S (Atlantic), Norwegian corporations and exporters of salmon, in 1985 and 1987, respectively. At all times, the defendant dealt with the plaintiffs as a representative of "Boston International Seafood Exchange, Inc.," or "Boston Seafood Exchange, Inc." The salmon purchased by the defendant was sold to other wholesalers. Payment checks from the defendant to the plaintiffs were imprinted with the name "Boston International Seafood Exchange, Inc.," and signed by the defendant, using the designation "Treas.," intending thereby to convey the impression that he was treasurer. Wire transfers of payments were also made in the name of Boston International Seafood Exchange, Inc. The defendant gave the plaintiffs' representatives business cards which listed him as "marketing director" of "Boston International Seafood Exchange, Inc." Advertising placed by the defendant appeared in trade journals under both the names "Boston Seafood Exchange, Inc.," and "Boston International Seafood Exchange, Inc." (indicating in one instance as to the latter that it was "Est: 1982"). At the relevant times, no such Massachusetts or foreign corporation had been formed by the defendant or had existed.

On May 31, 1977, a Massachusetts corporation named "Marketing Designs, Inc.," was organized. It was created for the purpose of selling motor vehicles. As of 1983, the defendant was the president, treasurer, clerk, a director and the sole stockholder of that corporation. The extent of activity or solvency of the corporation is not shown on the record. On October 19, 1983, however, Marketing Designs, Inc., was dissolved, apparently for failure to make requisite corporate filings. . . . On December 4, 1987, a certificate was filed with the city clerk of Boston declaring that Marketing Designs, Inc. (then dissolved), was conducting business under the name of Boston Seafood Exchange (not with the designation "Inc." and not also under the name Boston International Seafood Exchange, Inc.). . . .

Salmonor is owed $101,759.65 and Atlantic $153,788.50 for salmon sold to a business known as Boston International Seafood Exchange or Boston Seafood Exchange during 1988. Marketing Designs, Inc., was dissolved at the time the debt was incurred. In that year, advertising in a trade journal appeared in the name of "Boston Seafood Exchange, Inc.," and listed the plaintiffs as suppliers, and the defendant delivered to representatives of the plaintiffs his business card on which he was described as "marketing director" of "Boston International Seafood Exchange, Inc." On July 8, August 19 and 30, and September 9, 1988, the defendant made checks, imprinted with the name "Boston International Seafood Exchange, Inc.," to one or the other of the plaintiffs as payments for shipments of salmon.

The defendant never informed the plaintiffs of the existence of Marketing Designs, Inc., and the plaintiffs did not know of it until after the commencement of the present litigation on November 25, 1988. Marketing Designs, Inc., was revived for all purposes on December 12, 1988. . . .

In the course of his direct testimony, the defendant said: "We do business in seafood, and we're only in seafood. Boston Seafood Exchange is the name we use because it identifies us very closely with the industry and the products that we deal in. 'Marketing Designs, Inc.,' in the seafood business, would have absolutely no bearing or no recall or any factor at all. I picked the name Boston Seafood Exchange, Inc., because it defines where we are, who we deal with, the type of product we're into, and where our specialties are. The reason we have 'Inc.' on there is because also it seemed to me at the time—obviously it seemed to me at the time that it's incumbent upon me to tell people that I'm dealing with and to let them know that they're dealing with a corporation. So, we used 'Inc.' just to notify them; and I signed all my checks 'Treasurer' and so forth."

At trial and on appeal the defendant argues that he was acting as an agent of Marketing Designs, Inc., in 1988 when he incurred the debt which the plaintiffs seek to recover from him individually. It makes no difference that the plaintiffs thought they were dealing with corporate entities which did not exist, the defendant contends, because they were "aware" that they were transacting business with a corporate entity and not with the defendant individually. The judge essentially adopted the defendant's position. . . .[2]

"If the other party [to a transaction] has notice that the agent is or may be acting for a principal but has no notice of the principal's identity, the principal for whom the agent is acting is a partially disclosed principal." Restatement (Second) of Agency § 4(2) (1958). Here, the plaintiffs had notice that the defendant was purporting to act for a corporate principal or principals but had no notice of the identity of the principal as claimed by the defendant in this litigation. "Unless otherwise agreed, a person purporting to make a contract with another for a partially disclosed principal is a party to the contract." Id. at § 321.

It is the duty of the agent, if he would avoid personal liability on a contract entered into by him on behalf of his principal, to disclose not only that he is acting in a representative capacity, but also the identity of his principal. . . .

The judge reasoned that since the defendant had filed a certificate with the city of Boston in December, 1987, that Marketing Designs, Inc., was doing business as Boston Seafood Exchange, the plaintiffs could have discerned "precisely with whom they were dealing by reference to public records before the 1988 credits were extended."[3] But the defendant had dealt with Salmonor, and probably Atlantic, before that date, continued to deal with both under the name Boston International Seafood Exchange, Inc., thereafter, and even proposed to the plaintiffs a corporate restructuring of that nonentity. In any event, it was not the plaintiffs'

---

[2] On the evidence in this case, one might view with considerable skepticism the good faith of the defendant's claim that he was in fact acting as the agent of Marketing Designs, Inc. His use of "Inc." in the description of the two fictitious corporations (a criminal violation, . . .), the methods by which the business was conducted and advertised, the late filing of the business certificate, the purpose of Marketing Designs, Inc., and that in the defendant's own words that name "in the seafood business, would have absolutely no bearing or no recall or any factor at all," the use of only one fictitious name on the doing business certificate, the continuation thereafter of the use of business cards and checks in the other fictitious name of Boston International Seafood Exchange, Inc., and the suggestion to the plaintiffs of the reorganization of that nonentity strongly suggest manipulation and the attempted convenient illusion of personal liability by means of a corporation (then dissolved) never intended to conduct or be responsible for the business of salmon importing. Nevertheless, the judge found that the defendant was not culpable of any relevant "fraud or other reprehensible conduct."

[3] Of course, had the plaintiffs checked the public corporate records, they would have found that Marketing Designs, Inc., had been dissolved.

duty to seek out the identity of the defendant's principal; it was the defendant's obligation fully to reveal it. . . .

It is not sufficient that the plaintiffs may have had the means, through a search of the records of the Boston city clerk, to determine the identity of the defendant's principal. Actual knowledge is the test. . . . "The duty rests upon the agent, if he would avoid personal liability, to disclose his agency, and not upon others to discover it. It is not, therefore, enough that the other party has the means of ascertaining the name of the principal; the agent must either bring to him actual knowledge or, what is the same thing, that which to a reasonable man is equivalent to knowledge or the agent will be bound. There is no hardship to the agent in this rule, as he always has it in his power to relieve himself from personal liability by fully disclosing his principal and contracting only in the latter's name. If he does not do this, it may well be presumed that he intended to make himself personally responsible." 1 Mechem on Agency § 1413 (2d ed. 1914).

Finally, the defendant's use of trade names or fictitious names by which he claimed Marketing Designs, Inc., conducted its business is not in the circumstances a sufficient identification of the alleged principal so as to protect the defendant from personal liability. . . . Indeed, the defendant's own testimony expresses the impossibility of any rational connection. . . .

The judgment is reversed, and new judgments are to be entered against the defendant for Atlantic in the amount of $153,788.50 and for Salmonor in the amount of $101,759.65, both with appropriate interest and costs.

ANALYSIS

1. Suppose that before dealing with the plaintiffs, Curran had reinstated Marketing Designs, Inc. as a lawful corporation and had lawfully and effectively changed its name to Boston International Seafood Exchange, Inc. What result?

2. Does it seem that the plaintiffs got more than they bargained for?

3. What should Curran have done to protect himself from liability.

4. What should the plaintiffs have done to protect against the need for litigation to enforce their claims?

3. LIABILITY OF PRINCIPAL TO THIRD PARTIES IN TORT

A. SERVANT VERSUS INDEPENDENT CONTRACTOR

The first two cases that follow, Humble Oil & Refining Co. v. Martin and Hoover v. Sun Oil Company, again present the issue of organization within the firm versus organization across markets. Here we have large oil companies faced with the business issue of how to sell their principal products, gasoline and oil. One possibility is to sell through independently owned and operated gasoline filling stations. Another possibility is to sell through stations that they own and operate through employees. As the cases illustrate, in practice the arrangements have some characteristics of each of these possibilities.

In the era in which these cases arose, most gasoline stations performed three functions. (1) They sold gasoline, with service. There were no self-serve pumps. (2) They sold tires, batteries, and accessories (TBA). And (3) they performed repair services. The oil companies wanted to supply the gasoline and oil and the tires, batteries, and accessories. The repair services were provided by, or under the direction of, the operator of the station, who generally was himself an automobile mechanic.

The cases involve the liability of the oil companies for personal injuries negligently inflicted by gasoline station personnel. The legal issue turns on whether the operator of the station was an employee—a "servant" in the language of the law—or an independent operator (independent contractor) or, in more modern language, a franchisee. Under the doctrine of respondeat superior, a "master" (employer) is liable for the torts of its servants (employees). A master-servant relationship exists where the servant has agreed (a) to work on behalf of the master and (b) to be subject to the master's control or right to control the "physical conduct" of the servant (that is, the manner in which the job is performed, as opposed to the result alone). See Restatement (Second) of Agency §§ 1 and 2.

Servants are distinguished from independent contractors. The latter are of two types, agents and non-agents. An agent-type independent contractor is one who has agreed to act on behalf of another, the principal, but not subject to the principal's control over how the result is accomplished (that is, over the "physical conduct" of the task). A non-agent independent contractor is one who operates independently and simply enters into arm's length transactions with others. For example, if a carpenter is hired to build a garage for a homeowner, and if it is agreed or understood that the carpenter is simply responsible for getting the job done and is not to take directions from the homeowner, the carpenter is an independent contractor and is not acting as an agent. If the carpenter agrees to buy lumber for the project, on the credit account of the homeowner, the carpenter will still be acting as an independent contractor (assuming again that the homeowner does not have the right to tell the carpenter how to accomplish the task), but, because the carpenter is now acting on behalf of the homeowner in the purchase of the lumber, the carpenter is an (independent-contractor-type) agent of the homeowner. These cases are concerned only with the distinction between servants and independent contractors.

Humble Oil & Refining Co. v. Martin

148 Tex. 175, 222 S.W.2d 995 (1949).

Petitioners Humble Oil & Refining Company and Mrs. A.C. Love and husband complain here of the judgments of the trial court and the Court of Civil Appeals in which they were held [liable] in damages for personal injuries following a special issue verdict at the suit of respondent George F. Martin acting for himself and his two minor daughters. The injuries were inflicted on the three Martins about the noon hour on May 12, 1947, in the City of Austin, by an unoccupied automobile belonging to the petitioners Love, which, just prior to the accident, had been left by Mrs. Love at a filling station owned by petitioner Humble for servicing and thereafter, before any station employee had touched it, rolled by gravity off the premises into and obliquely across the abutting street, striking Mr. Martin and his children from behind as they were walking into the yard of their home, a short distance downhill from the station.

The trial court rendered judgment against petitioners Humble and Mrs. Love jointly and severally and gave the latter judgment over against Humble for whatever she might pay the respondents. The Court of Civil Appeals affirmed the judgment after reforming it to eliminate the judgment over in favor of Mrs. Love, without prejudice to the right of contribution by either defendant under Article 2212, Vernon's Ann.Civ.Stat., 216 S.W.(2d) 251. The petitioners here respectively complain of the judgment in favor of the Martins, and each seeks full indemnity (as distinguished from contribution) from the other.

The apparently principal contention of petitioner, Humble, is that it is liable neither to respondent Martin nor to petitioner Mrs. Love, since the station was in effect operated by an independent contractor, W.T. Schneider, and Humble is accordingly not responsible for his negligence nor that of W.V. Manis, who was the only station employee or representative present when the Love car was left and rolled away. In this connection, the jury convicted petitioner Humble of the following acts of negligence proximately causing the injuries in question: (a) Failure to inspect the Love car to see that the emergency brake was set or the gears engaged; (b) failure to set the emergency brake on the Love car; (c) leaving the Love car unattended on the driveway. The verdict also included findings that Mrs. Love "had delivered her car to the custody of the defendant Humble Oil & Refining Company, before her car started rolling from the position in which she had parked it"; that the accident was not unavoidable; and that no negligent act of either of petitioners was the sole proximate cause of the injuries in question. We think the Court of Civil Appeals properly held Humble responsible for the operation of the station, which admittedly it owned, as it did also the principal products there sold by Schneider under the so-called "Commission Agency Agreement" between him and Humble which was in evidence. The facts that neither Humble, Schneider nor the station employees considered Humble as an employer or master; that the employees were paid and directed by Schneider individually as their "boss," and that a provision of the agreement expressly repudiates any authority of Humble over the employees, are not conclusive against the master-servant relationship, since there is other evidence bearing on the right or power of Humble to control the details of the station work as regards Schneider himself and therefore as to employees which it was expressly contemplated that he would hire. The question is ordinarily one of fact, and where there are items of evidence indicating a master-servant relationship, contrary items such as those above mentioned cannot be given conclusive effect. . . .

Even if the contract between Humble and Schneider were the only evidence on the question, the instrument as a whole indicates a master-servant relationship quite as much as, if not more than, it suggests an arrangement between independent contractors. For example, paragraph 1 includes a provision requiring Schneider "to make reports *and perform other duties in connection with the operation of said station that may be required of him from time to time by Company.*" (Emphasis supplied). And while paragraph 2 purports to require Schneider to pay all operational expenses, the schedule of commissions forming part of the agreement does just the opposite in its paragraph (F), which gives Schneider a 75% "commission" on "the net public utility bills paid" by him and thus requires Humble to pay three-fourths of one of the most important operational expense items. Obviously the main object of the enterprise was the retail marketing of Humble's products with title remaining in Humble until delivery to the consumer. This was done under a strict system of financial control and supervision by Humble, with little or no business discretion reposed in Schneider except as to hiring, discharge, payment and supervision of a few station employees of a more or less laborer status. Humble furnished the all important station location and equipment, the advertising media, the products and a substantial part of the current operating costs. The hours of operation were controlled by Humble. The "Commission Agency Agreement," which evidently was Schneider's only title to occupancy of the premise, was terminable at the will of Humble. The so-called "rentals" were, at least in part, based on the amount of Humble's products sold, being, therefore, involved with the matter of Schneider's remuneration and not rentals in the usual sense. And, as above shown, the agreement required Schneider in effect to do anything Humble might tell him to do. All in all, aside from the stipulation regarding Schneider's assistants, there is essentially little difference between his situation and that of a mere store clerk who happens to be paid a commission instead of a salary. The business was Humble's business, just as the store clerk's business would be that of the store owner. Schneider was Humble's servant, and so accordingly were Schneider's assistants who were contemplated by the contract. Upon facts similar to those at bar but probably less indicative of a master-servant relationship, the latter has been held to exist by respectable authority, which seems to reflect the prevailing view in the nation. . . .

The evidence above discussed serves to distinguish the instant case from The Texas Company v. Wheat, 140 Texas 468, 168 S.W.(2d) 632, upon which petitioner Humble principally relies. In that case the evidence differed greatly from that now before us. It clearly showed a "dealer" type of relationship in which the lessee in charge of the filling station purchased from his landlord, The Texas Company, and sold as his own, and was free to sell at his own price and on his own credit terms, the company products purchased, as well as the products of other oil companies. The contracts contained no provision requiring the lessee to perform any duty The Texas Company might see fit to impose on him, nor did the company pay any part of the lessee's operating expenses, nor control the working hours of the station. . . .

Hoover v. Sun Oil Company

58 Del. 553, 212 A.2d 214 (1965).

This case is concerned with injuries received as the result of a fire on August 16, 1962 at the service station operated by James F. Barone. The fire started at the rear of plaintiff's car where it was being filled with gasoline and was allegedly caused by the negligence of John Smilyk an employee of Barone. Plaintiffs brought suit against Smilyk, Barone and Sun Oil Company (Sun) which owned the service station.

Sun has moved for summary judgment as to it on the basis that Barone was an independent contractor and therefore the alleged negligence of his employee could not result in liability as to Sun. The plaintiffs contend instead that Barone was acting as Sun's agent and that Sun may therefore be responsible for plaintiff's injuries.

Barone began operating this business in October of 1960 pursuant to a lease dated October 17, 1960. The station and all of its equipment, with the exception of a tire-stand and rack, certain advertising displays and miscellaneous hand tools, were owned by Sun. The lease was subject to termination by either party upon thirty days' written notice after the first six months and at the anniversary date thereafter. The rental was partially determined by the volume of gasoline purchased but there was also a minimum and a maximum monthly rental.

At the same time, Sun and Barone also entered into a dealer's agreement under which Barone was to purchase petroleum products from Sun and Sun was to loan necessary equipment and advertising materials. Barone was required to maintain this equipment and to use it solely for Sun products. Barone was permitted under the agreement to sell competitive products but chose to do so only in a few minor areas. As to Sun products, Barone was prohibited from selling them except under the Sunoco label and from blending them with products not supplied by Sun.

Barone's station had the usual large signs indicating that Sunoco products were sold there. His advertising in the classified section of the telephone book was under a Sunoco heading and his employees wore uniforms with the Sun emblem, the uniforms being owned by Barone or rented from an independent company.

Barone, upon the urging of Robert B. Peterson, Sun's area sales representative, attended a Sun school for service station operators in 1961. The school's curriculum was designed to familiarize the station operator with bookkeeping and merchandising, the appearance and proper maintenance of a Sun station, and the Sun Oil products. The course concluded with the operator working at Sun's model station in order to gain work experience in the use of the policy and techniques taught at the school.

Other facts typifying the company-service station relationship were the weekly visits of Sun's sales representative, Peterson, who would take orders for Sun products, inspect the restrooms, communicate customer complaints, make various suggestions to improve sales and discuss any problems that Barone might be having. Besides the weekly visits, Peterson was in contact with Barone on other occasions in order to implement Sun's "competitive allowance system" which enabled Barone to meet local price competition by giving him a rebate on the gasoline in his inventory roughly equivalent to the price decline and a similarly reduced price on his next order of gasoline.

While Peterson did offer advice to Barone on all phases of his operation, it was usually done on request and Barone was under no obligation to follow the advice. Barone's contacts and dealings with Sun were many and their relationship intricate, but he made no written reports to Sun and he alone assumed the overall risk of profit or loss in his business operation. Barone independently determined his own hours of operation and the identity, pay scale and working conditions of his employees, and it was his name that was posted as proprietor.

Plaintiffs contend in effect that the aforegoing facts indicate that Sun controlled the day-to-day operation of the station and consequently Sun is responsible for the negligent acts of Barone's employee. Specifically, plaintiffs contend that there is an issue of fact for the jury to determine as to whether or not there was an agency relationship.

The legal relationships arising from the distribution systems of major oil-producing companies are in certain respects unique. As stated in an annotation collecting many of the cases dealing with this relationship:

"This distribution system has grown up primarily as the result of economic factors and with little relationship to traditional legal concepts in the field of master and servant, so that it is perhaps not surprising that attempts by the court to discuss the relationship in the standard terms have led to some difficulties and confusion." 83 A.L.R.2d 1282, 1284 (1962).

In some situations traditional definitions of principal and agent and of employer and independent contractor may be difficult to apply to service station operations, but the undisputed facts of the case at bar make it clear that Barone was an independent contractor.

Barone's service station, unlike retail outlets for many products, is basically a one-company outlet and represents to the public, through Sunoco's national and local advertising, that it sells not only Sun's quality products but Sun's quality service. Many people undoubtedly come to the service station because of that latter representation.

However, the lease contract and dealer's agreement fail to establish any relationship other than landlord-tenant, and independent contractor. Nor is there anything in the conduct of the individuals which is inconsistent with that relationship so as to indicate that the contracts were mere subterfuge or sham. The areas of close contact between Sun and Barone stem from the fact that both have a mutual interest in the sale of Sun products and in the success of Barone's business.

The cases cited by both plaintiffs and defendant indicate that the result varies according to the contracts involved and the conduct and evidence of control under those contracts. Both lines of cases indicate that the test to be applied is that of whether the oil company has retained the right to control the details of the day-to-day operation of the service station; control or influence over results alone being viewed as insufficient. . . .

The facts of this case differ markedly from those in which the oil company was held liable for the tortious conduct of its service station operator or his employees. Sun had no control over the details of Barone's day-to-day operation. Therefore, no liability can be imputed to Sun from the allegedly negligent acts of Smilyk. Sun's motion for summary judgment is granted.

ANALYSIS

1. Important elements of business relationships include duration, control, risk of loss, and return. Which of these becomes the key issue in the two cases? How can the outcomes in the two cases be reconciled?

2. Pretend you know nothing about the legal rules that distinguish between employees (servants) and people working for themselves (independent contractors).

(a) If you were a person like Schneider (the gas station operator in the *Humble Oil* case), which terms or elements of the relationship with Humble Oil would make you feel like an employee? Which terms would make you feel that you were independent, working for yourself?

(b) If you were a person like Barone (the operator in the *Sun Oil* case), would you feel less like an employee and more like an independent business person than a person like Schneider? Why?

(c) Focus on those terms of each relationship that suggest that the operator is independent. Assume that the oil companies could have changed those terms to make them consistent with an employment relationship. What would the new terms be? Why do you suppose the oil companies chose what may be thought of as a hybrid set of terms?

PLANNING

1. In *Humble Oil* the court states, "The hours of operation were controlled by Humble." In *Sun Oil* the court states, "Barone independently determined his own hours of operation." What do you suppose is the practical difference in the control of each of the oil companies over hours of operation? What do you suppose would happen to Barone if the people at Sun Oil concluded that he was not staying open late enough and that, as a result, Sun Oil was losing sales?

2. If you were advising Humble Oil and wanted to improve the prospects of avoiding liability for personal injuries, what changes would you suggest in the manner in which Humble Oil structured its relationship with its operators? What would be the likely substantive effect of these changes?

POLICY QUESTIONS

In the *Sun Oil* situation, presumably Sun Oil could have insisted that Barone take out a policy of liability insurance, protecting both him and Sun Oil, or that he agree to indemnify Sun Oil for damages and show that he had enough assets to meet his obligation.

1. Do you think that it was irresponsible for Sun Oil to fail to do that?

2. Assume that your answer to part 1 was yes. What if Barone had operated ten gas stations, under his own name (but still bought most of his gasoline and oil and tires, batteries, and accessories from Sun Oil)?

3. Should the law somehow impose an obligation on Sun Oil to ensure that Barone is able to pay his debts?

4. Assume your answer to part 3 was yes. How would you frame the law?

5. What is your general theory of when people who do business with one another should and should not be liable for each other's tort, or contract, damages?

Murphy v. Holiday Inns, Inc.

216 Va. 490, 219 S.E.2d 874 (1975).

On August 21, 1973, Kyran Murphy (plaintiff) filed a motion for judgment against Holiday Inns, Inc. (defendant), a Tennessee Corporation, seeking damages for personal injuries sustained on August 24, 1971, while she was a guest at a motel in Danville. Plaintiff alleged that "Defendant owned and operated" the motel; that "Defendant, its agents and employees, so carelessly, recklessly, and negligently maintained the premises of the motel that Plaintiff did slip and fall on an area of a walk where water draining from an air conditioner had been allowed to accumulate"; and that as a proximate result of such negligence, plaintiff sustained serious and permanent injuries.

Defendant filed grounds of defense and a motion for summary judgment "on the grounds that it has no relationship with regard to the operator of the premises . . . other than a license agreement permitting the operator of a motel on the same premises to use the name 'Holiday Inns' subject to all the terms and conditions of such license agreement." That agreement, filed as an exhibit with defendant's motion for summary judgment, identifies defendant's licensee as Betsy-Len Motor [Hotel] Corporation (Betsy-Len).

Upon a finding that defendant did not own the premises upon which the accident occurred and that "there exists no principal-agent or master-servant relationship between the defendant corporation and Betsy-Len Motor Hotel Corporation," the trial court entered a final order on April 25, 1974, granting summary judgment in favor of defendant.

Plaintiff's sole assignment of error is that the trial court erred "in holding that no principal-agent or master-servant relationship exists."

On brief, plaintiff argues that the license agreement gives defendant "the authority and control over the Betsy-Len Corporation that establishes a true master/servant relationship." . . .

Actual agency is a consensual relationship.

> "Agency is the fiduciary relation which results from the manifestation of consent by one person to another that the other shall act on his behalf and subject to his control, and consent by the other so to act." Restatement (Second) of Agency § 1 (1958).
>
> . . .
>
> "It is the element of continuous subjection to the will of the principal which distinguishes the agent from other fiduciaries and the agency agreement from other agreements." Id., comment (b).

. . .

When an agreement, considered as a whole, establishes an agency relationship, the parties cannot effectively disclaim it by formal "consent." "[T]he relationship of the parties does not depend upon what the parties themselves call it, but rather in law what it actually is." Chandler v. Kelley, 149 Va. 221, 231, 141 S.E. 389, 391–92 (1928). . . . Here, plaintiff and defendant agree that, if the license agreement is sufficient to establish an agency relationship, the disclaimer clause[1] does not defeat it.

Plaintiff and defendant also agree that, in determining whether a contract establishes an agency relationship, the critical test is the nature and extent of the control agreed upon.

The subject matter of the license defendant granted Betsy-Len is a "system." As defined in the agreement, the system is one "providing to the public . . . an inn service . . . of distinctive nature, of high quality, and of other distinguishing characteristics." Those characteristics include trade names using the words "Holiday Inn" and certain variations and combinations of those words, trade marks, architectural designs, insignia, patterns, color schemes, styles, furnishings, equipment, advertising services, and methods of operation.

In consideration of the license to use the "system," the licensee agreed to pay an initial sum of $5000; to construct one or more inns in accordance with plans approved by the licensor; to make monthly payments of 15 cents per room per day (5 cents of which was to be earmarked for national advertising expenditures); and "to conduct the operation of inns . . . in accordance with the terms and provisions of this license and of the Rules of operation of said System".

Plaintiff points to several provisions and rules which he says satisfy the control test and establish the principal-agent relationship. These include requirements:

That licensee construct its motel according to plans, specifications, feasibility studies, and locations approved by licensor;

That licensee employ the trade name, signs, and other symbols of the "system" designated by licensor;

That licensee pay a continuing fee for use of the license and a fee for national advertising of the "system";

That licensee solicit applications for credit cards for the benefit of other licensees;

That licensee protect and promote the trade name and not engage in any competitive motel business or associate itself with any trade association designed to establish standards for motels;

That licensee not raise funds by sale of corporate stock or dispose of a controlling interest in its motel without licensor's approval;

That training for licensee's manager, housekeeper, and restaurant manager be provided by licensor at licensee's expense;

---

[1] That clause provides that "Licensee, in the use of the name 'Holiday Inn' . . . shall identify Licensee as being the owner and operator [and] . . . the parties hereto are completely separate entities, are not partners, joint adventurers, or agents of the other in any sense, and neither has power to obligate or bind the other."

That licensee not employ a person contemporaneously engaged in a competitive motel or hotel business; and

That licensee conduct its business under the "system," observe the rules of operation, make quarterly reports to licensor concerning operations, and submit to periodic inspections of facilities and procedures conducted by licensor's representatives.

The license agreement of which these requirements were made a part is a franchise contract. In the business world, franchising is a crescent phenomenon of billion-dollar proportions.

> "[Franchising is] a system for the selective distribution of goods and/or services under a brand name through outlets owned by independent businessmen, called 'franchisees.' Although the franchisor supplies the franchisee with know-how and brand identification on a continuing basis, the franchisee enjoys the right to profit and runs the risk of loss. The franchisor controls the distribution of his goods and/or services through a contract which regulates the activities of the franchisee, in order to achieve standardization." R. Rosenberg, *Profits From Franchising* 41 (1969). (Italics omitted).

The fact that an agreement is a franchise contract does not insulate the contracting parties from an agency relationship. If a franchise contract so "regulates the activities of the franchisee" as to vest the franchisor with control within the definition of agency, the agency relationship arises even though the parties expressly deny it.

Here, the license agreement contains the principal features of the typical franchise contract, including regulatory provisions. Defendant owned the "brand name," the trade mark, and the other assets associated with the "system." Betsy-Len owned the sales "outlet." Defendant agreed to allow Betsy-Len to use its assets. Betsy-Len agreed to pay a fee for that privilege. Betsy-Len retained the "right to profit" and bore the "risk of loss." With respect to the manner in which defendant's trade mark and other assets were to be used, both parties agreed to certain regulatory rules of operation.

Having carefully considered all of the regulatory provisions in the agreement, we are of opinion that they gave defendant no "control or right to control the methods or details of doing the work," Wells v. Whitaker, 207 Va. 616, 624, 151 S.E.2d 422, 429 (1966), and, therefore, agree with the trial court that no principal-agent or master-servant relationship was created.[2] As appears from the face of the document, the purpose of those provisions was to achieve system-wide standardization of business identity, uniformity of commercial service, and optimum public good will, all for the benefit of both contracting parties. The regulatory provisions did not give defendant control over the day-to-day operation of Betsy-Len's motel. While defendant was empowered to regulate the architectural style of the buildings and the type and style of furnishings and equipment, defendant was given no power to control daily maintenance of the premises. Defendant was given no power to control Betsy-Len's current business expenditures, fix customer rates, or demand a share of the profits. Defendant was given no power to hire or

---

[2] Because defendant had no such control or right to control, the distinction between a principal-agent and a master-servant relationship is not relevant here. . . .

fire Betsy-Len's employees, determine employee wages or working conditions, set standards for employee skills or productivity, supervise employee work routine, or discipline employees for nonfeasance or misfeasance. All such powers and other management controls and responsibilities customarily exercised by an owner and operator of an on-going business were retained by Betsy-Len.

We hold that the regulatory provisions of the franchise contract did not constitute control within the definition of agency, and the judgment is

Affirmed.

ANALYSIS AND PLANNING

1. Restatement (Second) of Agency § 219(1) provides: "A master is subject to liability for the torts of his servants committed while acting in the scope of their employment." The comments to that section make clear that, as a general rule, a principal is not liable for the torts of his non-servant agents—i.e., independent contractors. See also Restatement § 250. Restatement § 1 indicates, as stated by the *Holiday Inns* court, that control is an essential element of the definition of an agency relationship, whether one is dealing with a servant or an independent contractor. A key distinction between the servant and independent contractor types of agents, however, is the differing natures and degrees of control exercised by the principal. See Restatement § 220. Did Holiday Inns have sufficient control over Betsy-Len to make the latter a servant? Are the factors set forth in Restatement § 220 helpful in this regard?

2. According to the court in *Holiday Inns,* "Plaintiff and defendant agree that, in determining whether a contract establishes an agency relationship, the critical test is the nature and extent of the control agreed upon." Is it possible for a franchisor to have a degree of control consistent with the master-servant relationship without that master-servant relationship arising as a matter of law? What other requirement, if any, must be satisfied? See Restatement (Second) of Agency § 1, quoted by the court. To put the issue another way, does it seem to you that the defendant might have prevailed even if it had lost on the control issue? In other words, did the defendant have another, unused, string to its bow?

3. In *Vandemark v. McDonald's Corp.*, 904 A.2d 627 (N.H. 2006), an employee of a McDonald's franchise was injured when the restaurant was robbed. The employee sued McDonald's, claiming that the franchisee was an agent of the franchisor. In support of that claim, the employee pointed to the extensive franchise agreement governing the McDonald's-franchisee relationship and argued that:

> McDonald's has maintained a continuous prescription of what [franchisee] shall and shall not do. McDonald's mandates compliance with the "McDonald's System." McDonald's mandates particular methods for preparing foods, as well as food preparation and service times. McDonald's mandates through the "QSC Play Book" that franchisee restaurants . . . implement "key success factors" in their restaurants. Moreover, McDonald's sends out field consultants . . . to ensure that McDonald's specifications are met. Id. at 634.

The *Vandemark* court rejected the employee's argument, holding that:

> [T]he . . . weight of authority construes franchiser liability narrowly, finding that absent a showing of control over security measures employed by the franchisee, the franchiser cannot be vicariously liable for the security breach. . . .
>
> . . . [T]he trial court relied primarily upon Wendy Hong Wu v. Dunkin' Donuts, Inc., 105 F.Supp.2d 83 (E.D.N.Y.2000), in which the United States District Court for the Eastern District of New York surveyed extensive state and federal case law concerning the vicarious liability of a franchiser for the security breaches of its franchisee. In *Wendy Hong Wu*, an employee of a Dunkin' Donuts' franchisee brought a vicarious liability claim against Dunkin' Donuts after she was raped and assaulted while working the night shift. The court specifically examined whether Dunkin' Donuts had control over the alleged "instrumentality" that caused the harm. The court held that since there was no evidence that Dunkin' Donuts actually mandated specific security equipment or otherwise controlled the steps taken by its franchisees in general to protect employees, it was not vicariously liable for the alleged lapse in security. The court reasoned that the franchise agreement was "primarily designed to maintain uniform appearance among its franchisees and uniform quality among their products and services to protect and enhance the value of the Dunkin' Donuts trademark. [The franchisee] remain[ed] solely responsible for hiring, firing, and training its employees and for making all day-to-day decisions necessary to run the business." In addition to finding a lack of control over security matters within the franchise agreement, the court stated that "the undisputed evidence in the record demonstrates that [Dunkin' Donuts] merely made security equipment available for purchase and suggested that alarm systems and other burglary prevention techniques were important[.]"

. . . [T]he the evidence demonstrates that although the defendant maintained authority to insure the uniformity and standardization of products and services offered by the [franchise] restaurant, such authority did not extend to the control of security operations. Thus, there was no genuine issue of material fact as to whether the defendant exercised control over the relevant security policies at the [franchisee's] restaurant through adopting the QSC Play Book. . . .

Id. at 634–36 (citations omitted).

Does this analysis help explain the outcomes in any or all of *Humble Oil*, *Sun Oil*, or *Holiday Inns*? In particular, if the court's holding that the "issue turns narrowly upon the defendant's level of control over the alleged 'instrumentality' which caused the harm" had been applied in those cases, would the outcome in those cases have changed?

Is such a narrow focus on "control over the alleged 'instrumentality' which caused the harm" consistent with sound social and economic policy?

4. How do firms like Holiday Inns, Inc. make their profit? What are their risks? In their relationships with franchisors, what legal rights are likely to be important to them?

5. How do the franchisees make their profit? What are their risks? In their relationship with the franchisors, what legal rights are likely to be important to them?

6. How much freedom does a franchisee like Betsy-Len have to run its business? Suppose that a field representative of Holiday Inns, Inc. visits the Betsy-Len motor hotel and finds that the desk clerk, who is a son of one of the owners of the franchise, is surly and inefficient, and that the restaurant, managed by the other owner, is badly run, with poor food and slow service. What are the various steps that Holiday Inns, Inc. can take to induce its franchisee to improve its performance? What do your answers to these questions tell you about drafting a franchise contract?

B. TORT LIABILITY AND APPARENT AGENCY

Miller v. McDonald's Corp.

945 P.2d 1107 (Ore. App. 1997).

Plaintiff seeks damages from defendant McDonald's Corporation for injuries that she suffered when she bit into a heart-shaped sapphire stone while eating a Big Mac sandwich that she had purchased at a McDonald's restaurant in Tigard. The trial court granted summary judgment to defendant on the ground that it did not own or operate the restaurant; rather, the owner and operator was a non-party, 3K Restaurants (3K), that held a franchise from defendant. Plaintiff appeals, and we reverse.

. . . 3K owned and operated the restaurant under a License Agreement (the Agreement) with defendant that required it to operate in a manner consistent with the "McDonald's System." The Agreement described that system as including proprietary rights in trade names, service marks and trade marks, as well as "designs and color schemes for restaurant buildings, signs, equipment layouts, formulas and specifications for certain food products, methods of inventory and operation control, bookkeeping and accounting, and manuals covering business practices and policies." . . .

The Agreement described the way in which 3K was to operate the restaurant in considerable detail. It expressly required 3K to operate in compliance with defendant's prescribed standards, policies, practices, and procedures, including serving only food and beverage products that defendant designated. 3K had to follow defendant's specifications and blueprints for the equipment and layout of the restaurant, including adopting subsequent reasonable changes that defendant made, and to maintain the restaurant building in compliance with defendant's standards. 3K could not make any changes in the basic design of the building without defendant's approval.

The Agreement required 3K to keep the restaurant open during the hours that defendant prescribed, including maintaining adequate supplies and employing adequate personnel to operate at maximum capacity and efficiency during those hours. 3K also had to keep the restaurant similar in appearance to all other McDonald's restaurants. 3K's employees had to wear McDonald's uniforms, to have a neat and clean appearance, and to provide competent and courteous service. 3K could use only containers and other packaging that bore McDonald's trademarks. The ingredients for the foods and beverages had to meet defendant's standards, and 3K had to use "only those methods of food handling and preparation that [defendant] may designate from time to time." In order to obtain the franchise, 3K had to represent that the franchisee had worked at a McDonald's restaurant; the Agreement did not distinguish in this respect between a company-run or a franchised restaurant. The manuals gave further details that expanded on many of these requirements.

In order to ensure conformity with the standards described in the Agreement, defendant periodically sent field consultants to the restaurant to inspect its operations. 3K trained its employees in accordance with defendant's materials and recommendations and sent some of them to training programs that defendant administered. Failure to comply with the agreed standards could result in loss of the franchise.

Despite these detailed instructions, the Agreement provided that 3K was not an agent of defendant for any purpose. Rather, it was an independent contractor and was responsible for all obligations and liabilities, including claims based on injury, illness, or death, directly or indirectly resulting from the operation of the restaurant.

Plaintiff went to the restaurant under the assumption that defendant owned, controlled, and managed it. So far as she could tell, the restaurant's appearance was similar to that of other McDonald's restaurants that she had patronized. Nothing disclosed to her that any entity other than defendant was involved in its operation. The only signs that were visible and obvious to the public had the name "McDonald's,"[2] the employees wore uniforms with McDonald's insignia, and the menu was the same that plaintiff had seen in other McDonald's restaurants. The general appearance of the restaurant and the food products that it sold were similar to the restaurants and products that plaintiff had seen in national print and television advertising that defendant had run. To the best of plaintiff's knowledge, only McDonald's sells Big Mac hamburgers.

In short, plaintiff testified, she went to the Tigard McDonald's because she relied on defendant's reputation and because she wanted to obtain the same quality of service, standard of care in food preparation, and general attention to detail that she had previously enjoyed at other McDonald's restaurants. . . .

The kind of actual agency relationship that would make defendant vicariously liable for 3K's negligence requires that defendant have the

[2] This is plaintiff's testimony in her affidavit. Representatives of 3K testified in their depositions that there was a sign near the front counter that identified Bob and Karen Bates and 3K Restaurants as the owners. There is no evidence of the size or prominence of the sign, nor is there evidence of any other non-McDonald's identification in the restaurant.

right to control the method by which 3K performed its obligations under the Agreement. . . .[3]

A number of other courts have applied the right to control test to a franchise relationship. The Delaware Supreme Court, in Billops v. Magness Const. Co., 391 A.2d 196 (Del.1978), stated the test as it applies to that context:

> "If, in practical effect, the franchise agreement goes beyond the stage of setting standards, and allocates to the franchisor the right to exercise control over the daily operations of the franchise, an agency relationship exists." 391 A.2d at 197–98.

This statement expresses the general direction that courts have taken. . . . We therefore adopt it for the purposes of this case.

. . . [We] believe that a jury could find that defendant retained sufficient control over 3K's daily operations that an actual agency relationship existed. The Agreement did not simply set standards that 3K had to meet. Rather, it required 3K to use the precise methods that defendant established. . . . Defendant enforced the use of those methods by regularly sending inspectors and by its retained power to cancel the Agreement. That evidence would support a finding that defendant had the right to control the way in which 3K performed at least food handling and preparation. In her complaint, plaintiff alleges that 3K's deficiencies in those functions resulted in the sapphire being in the Big Mac and thereby caused her injuries. Thus, . . . there is evidence that defendant had the right to control 3K in the precise part of its business that allegedly resulted in plaintiff's injuries. That is sufficient to raise an issue of actual agency.

Plaintiff next asserts that defendant is vicariously liable for 3K's alleged negligence because 3K was defendant's apparent agent.[4] The relevant standard is in Restatement (Second) of Agency, § 267 . . .:

> "One who represents that another is his servant or other agent and thereby causes a third person justifiably to rely upon the care or skill of such apparent agent is subject to liability to the third person for harm caused by the lack of care or skill of the one appearing to be a servant or other agent as if he were such."

. . . We have not applied § 267 to a franchisor/franchisee situation, but courts in a number of other jurisdictions have done so in ways that we find instructive. In most cases the courts have found that there was a jury issue of apparent agency. The crucial issues are whether the putative principal held the third party out as an agent and whether the plaintiff relied on that holding out. . . .

In each of these cases, the franchise agreement required the franchisee to act in ways that identified it with the franchisor. The franchisor imposed those requirements as part of maintaining an image

---

[3] Under the right to control test it does not matter whether the putative principal actually exercises control; what is important is that it has the right to do so. See Peeples v. Kawasaki Heavy Indust., Ltd., 288 Or. 143, 149, 603 P.2d 765 (1979).

[4] Apparent agency is a distinct concept from apparent authority. Apparent agency creates an agency relationship that does not otherwise exist, while apparent authority expands the authority of an actual agent. . . . In this case, the precise issue is whether 3K was defendant's apparent agent, not whether 3K had apparent authority. . . .

of uniformity of operations and appearance for the franchisor's entire system. Its purpose was to attract the patronage of the public to that entire system. The centrally imposed uniformity is the fundamental basis for the courts' conclusion that there was an issue of fact whether the franchisors held the franchisees out as the franchisors' agents.

In this case, for similar reasons, there is an issue of fact about whether defendant held 3K out as its agent. Everything about the appearance and operation of the Tigard McDonald's identified it with defendant and with the common image for all McDonald's restaurants that defendant has worked to create through national advertising, common signs and uniforms, common menus, common appearance, and common standards. The possible existence of a sign identifying 3K as the operator does not alter the conclusion that there is an issue of apparent agency for the jury. There are issues of fact of whether that sign was sufficiently visible to the public, in light of plaintiff's apparent failure to see it, and of whether one sign by itself is sufficient to remove the impression that defendant created through all of the other indicia of its control that it, and 3K under the requirements that defendant imposed, presented to the public.

Defendant does not seriously dispute that a jury could find that it held 3K out as its agent. Rather, it argues that there is insufficient evidence that plaintiff justifiably relied on that holding out. It argues that it is not sufficient for her to prove that she went to the Tigard McDonald's because it was a McDonald's restaurant. Rather, she also had to prove that she went to it because she believed that McDonald's Corporation operated both it and the other McDonald's restaurants that she had previously patronized. It states:

> "All [that] the Plaintiff's affidavit proves is that she went to the Tigard McDonald's based in reliance on her past experiences at other McDonald's. But her affidavit does nothing to link her experiences with ownership of those restaurants by McDonald's Corporation."

Defendant's argument both demands a higher level of sophistication about the nature of franchising than the general public can be expected to have and ignores the effect of its own efforts to lead the public to believe that McDonald's restaurants are part of a uniform national system of restaurants with common products and common standards of quality. A jury could find from plaintiff's affidavit that she believed that all McDonald's restaurants were the same because she believed that one entity owned and operated all of them or, at the least, exercised sufficient control that the standards that she experienced at one would be the same as she experienced at others.

Plaintiff testified in her affidavit that her reliance on defendant for the quality of service and food at the Tigard McDonald's came in part from her experience at other McDonald's restaurants. Defendant's argument that she must show that it, rather than a franchisee, operated those restaurants is, at best, disingenuous. A jury could find that it was defendant's very insistence on uniformity of appearance and standards, designed to cause the public to think of every McDonald's, franchised or unfranchised, as part of the same system, that makes it difficult or impossible for plaintiff to tell whether her previous experiences were at restaurants that defendant owned or franchised. . . .

ANALYSIS

1. What's going on here? Why is the franchisor fighting this case? Isn't it in the franchisor's interest to ensure that plaintiffs like Miller will not have to worry about finding a solvent defendant?

2. If the jury finds that an apparent agency relationship exists between the franchisee and McDonald's, would that suffice for vicarious liability, or would plaintiff also have to show that the franchisee had apparent authority?

3. Should McDonald's reduce the amount of control it exercises over its franchisees, so as to avoid the risk of liability in cases such as this one?

4. Franchising as a way of organizing economic activity arose after the servant/independent contractor dichotomy was well-established. In many ways, the franchisor-franchisee relationship is a hybrid having attributes of both servant and independent contractor status. Accordingly, case outcomes often appear inconsistent and even arbitrary. What might be a better way of handling these cases doctrinally?

5. In its ruling on apparent agency, the court adopts the Restatement's requirement that the plaintiff must have relied on a manifestation by the apparent principal (here, McDonald's) and it must have been that reliance that exposed the plaintiff to harm. In most cases, this requirement makes good sense. Are there cases, however, in which requiring proof of justifiable reliance might seem unfair or inefficient?

PROBLEM

Suppose that the owners of twenty-five motels in a certain state decide that in order to compete they need a trade name and some statewide advertising. They realize that in order to benefit from the trade name they must ensure that each motel maintains high standards and that all the motels set room rates at a figure that is consistent with their intended image. They agree that they will remodel their lobbies to create a common attractive appearance and will require their employees to wear an agreed-upon uniform. They form a corporation called Finest Motels Corp., in which they share ownership. They are required to make periodic payments to Finest Motels Corp. to pay for advertising and for policing compliance with standards. They hire a former executive of Hilton Inns, Inc. and tell her that they want their motels to live up to Hilton standards. Each of the motels is to change its name, with the new name beginning with the location, followed by "Finest Motel"—for example, "Anaheim Finest Motel." If any of the motels become insolvent, is Finest Motel Corp., or any of the other motels, liable for its debts? What suggestions would you offer to protect against that outcome?

C. SCOPE OF EMPLOYMENT

Ira S. Bushey & Sons, Inc. v. United States

398 F.2d 167 (2d Cir.1968).

■ FRIENDLY, CIRCUIT JUDGE:

While the United States Coast Guard vessel Tamaroa was being overhauled in a floating drydock located in Brooklyn's Gowanus Canal, a seaman returning from shore leave late at night, in the condition for which seamen are famed, turned some wheels on the drydock wall. He thus opened valves that controlled the flooding of the tanks on one side of the drydock. Soon the ship listed, slid off the blocks and fell against the wall. Parts of the drydock sank, and the ship partially did—fortunately without loss of life or personal injury. The drydock owner sought and was granted compensation by the District Court for the Eastern District of New York in an amount to be determined, 276 F.Supp. 518; the United States appeals.

. . .

The Tamaroa had gone into drydock on February 28, 1963; her keel rested on blocks permitting her drive shaft to be removed and repairs to be made to her hull. The contract between the Government and Bushey provided in part:

> (o) The work shall, whenever practical, be performed in such manner as not to interfere with the berthing and messing of personnel attached to the vessel undergoing repair, and provision shall be made so that personnel assigned shall have access to the vessel at all times, it being understood that such personnel will not interfere with the work or the contractor's workmen.

Access from shore to ship was provided by a route past the security guard at the gate, through the yard, up a ladder to the top of one drydock wall and along the wall to a gangway leading to the fantail deck, where men returning from leave reported at a quartermaster's shack.

Seaman Lane, whose prior record was unblemished, returned from shore leave a little after midnight on March 14. He had been drinking heavily; the quartermaster made mental note that he was "loose." For reasons not apparent to us or very likely to Lane,[4] he took it into his head, while progressing along the gangway wall, to turn each of three large wheels some twenty times; unhappily, as previously stated, these wheels controlled the water intake valves. After boarding ship at 12:11 A.M., Lane mumbled to an off-duty seaman that he had "turned some valves" and also muttered something about "valves" to another who was standing the engineering watch. Neither did anything; apparently Lane's condition was not such as to encourage proximity. At 12:20 A.M. a crew member discovered water coming into the drydock. By 12:30 A.M. the ship began to list, the alarm was sounded and the crew were ordered ashore. Ten minutes later the vessel and dock were listing over 20

---

[4] Lane disappeared after completing the sentence imposed by a courtmartial and being discharged from the Coast Guard.

degrees; in another ten minutes the ship slid off the blocks and fell against the drydock wall.

The Government attacks imposition of liability on the ground that Lane's acts were not within the scope of his employment. It relies heavily on § 228(1) of the Restatement of Agency 2d which says that "conduct of a servant is within the scope of employment if, but only if: * * * (c) it is actuated, at least in part, by a purpose to serve the master." Courts have gone to considerable lengths to find such a purpose, as witness a well-known opinion in which Judge Learned Hand concluded that a drunken boatswain who routed the plaintiff out of his bunk with a blow, saying "Get up, you big son of a bitch, and turn to," and then continued to fight, might have thought he was acting in the interest of the ship. Nelson v. American-West African Line, 86 F.2d 730 (2 Cir.1936), cert. denied, 300 U.S. 665 (1937). It would be going too far to find such a purpose here; while Lane's return to the Tamaroa was to serve his employer, no one has suggested how he could have thought turning the wheels to be, even if—which is by no means clear—he was unaware of the consequences.

In light of the highly artificial way in which the motive test has been applied, the district judge believed himself obliged to test the doctrine's continuing vitality by referring to the larger purposes respondeat superior is supposed to serve. He concluded that the old formulation failed this test. We do not find his analysis so compelling, however, as to constitute a sufficient basis in itself for discarding the old doctrine. It is not at all clear, as the court below suggested, that expansion of liability in the manner here suggested will lead to a more efficient allocation of resources. As the most astute exponent of this theory has emphasized, a more efficient allocation can only be expected if there is some reason to believe that imposing a particular cost on the enterprise will lead it to consider whether steps should be taken to prevent a recurrence of the accident. Calabresi, The Decision for Accidents: An Approach to Non-fault Allocation of Costs, 78 Harv.L.Rev. 713, 725–34 (1965). And the suggestion that imposition of liability here will lead to more intensive screening of employees rests on highly questionable premises. . . .[5] The unsatisfactory quality of the allocation of resource rationale is especially striking on the facts of this case. It could well be that application of the traditional rule might induce drydock owners, prodded by their insurance companies, to install locks on their valves to avoid similar incidents in the future,[6] while placing the burden on shipowners is much less likely to lead to accident prevention.[7] It is true, of course, that in many cases the plaintiff will not be in a position to insure, and so expansion of liability will, at the very least, serve respondeat superior's loss spreading function. . . . But the fact that the defendant is better able to afford damages is not alone sufficient to justify legal responsibility . . . and this overarching principle must be taken into account in deciding whether to expand the reach of respondeat superior.

---

5 We are not here speaking of cases in which the enterprise has negligently hired an employee whose undesirable propensities are known or should have been. . . .

6 The record reveals that most modern drydocks have automatic locks to guard against unauthorized use of valves.

7 Although it is theoretically possible that shipowners would demand that drydock owners take appropriate action, see Coase, The Problem of Social Cost, 3 J.L. & Economics 1 (1960), this would seem unlikely to occur in real life.

A policy analysis thus is not sufficient to justify this proposed expansion of vicarious liability. This is not surprising since respondeat superior, even within its traditional limits, rests not so much on policy grounds consistent with the governing principles of tort law as in a deeply rooted sentiment that a business enterprise cannot justly disclaim responsibility for accidents which may fairly be said to be characteristic of its activities. It is in this light that the inadequacy of the motive test becomes apparent. Whatever may have been the case in the past, a doctrine that would create such drastically different consequences for the actions of the drunken boatswain in *Nelson* and those of the drunken seaman here reflects a wholly unrealistic attitude toward the risks characteristically attendant upon the operation of a ship. We concur in the statement of Mr. Justice Rutledge in a case involving violence injuring a fellow-worker, in this instance in the context of workmen's compensation:

> Men do not discard their personal qualities when they go to work. Into the job they carry their intelligence, skill, habits of care and rectitude. Just as inevitably they take along also their tendencies to carelessness and camaraderie, as well as emotional make-up. In bringing men together, work brings these qualities together, causes frictions between them, creates occasions for lapses into carelessness, and for fun-making and emotional flare-up. * * * These expressions of human nature are incidents inseparable from working together. They involve risks of injury and these risks are inherent in the working environment.

Hartford Accident & Indemnity Co. v. Cardillo, 72 App.D.C. 52, 112 F.2d 11, 15, cert. denied, 310 U.S. 649 (1940);. . . .

Put another way, Lane's conduct was not so "unforeseeable" as to make it unfair to charge the Government with responsibility. We agree with a leading treatise that "what is reasonably foreseeable in this context (of respondeat superior) * * * is quite a different thing from the foreseeably unreasonable risk of harm that spells negligence * * *. The foresight that should impel the prudent man to take precautions is not the same measure as that by which he should perceive the harm likely to flow from his long-run activity in spite of all reasonable precautions on his own part. The proper test here bears far more resemblance to that which limits liability for workmen's compensation than to the test for negligence. The employer should be held to expect risks, to the public also, which arise 'out of and in the course of' his employment of labor." 2 Harper & James, The Law of Torts 1377–78 (1956). . . . Here it was foreseeable that crew members crossing the drydock might do damage, negligently or even intentionally, such as pushing a Bushey employee or kicking property into the water. Moreover, the proclivity of seamen to find solace for solitude by copious resort to the bottle while ashore has been noted in opinions too numerous to warrant citation. Once all this is granted, it is immaterial that Lane's precise action was not to be foreseen. . . . Consequently, we can no longer accept our past decisions that have refused to move beyond the Nelson rule, . . . since they do not accord with modern understanding as to when it is fair for an enterprise to disclaim the actions of its employees.

One can readily think of cases that fall on the other side of the line. If Lane had set fire to the bar where he had been imbibing or had caused an accident on the street while returning to the drydock, the Government would not be liable; the activities of the "enterprise" do not reach into areas where the servant does not create risks different from those attendant on the activities of the community in general. . . . We agree with the district judge that if the seaman "upon returning to the drydock, recognized the Bushey security guard as his wife's lover and shot him," 276 F.Supp. at 530, vicarious liability would not follow; the incident would have related to the seaman's domestic life, not to his seafaring activity, and it would have been the most unlikely happenstance that the confrontation with the paramour occurred on a drydock rather than at the traditional spot. Here Lane had come within the closed-off area where his ship lay, . . . to occupy a berth to which the Government insisted he have access, . . . and while his act is not readily explicable, at least it was not shown to be due entirely to facets of his personal life. The risk that seamen going and coming from the Tamaroa might cause damage to the drydock is enough to make it fair that the enterprise bear the loss. It is not a fatal objection that the rule we lay down lacks sharp contours; in the end, as Judge Andrews said in a related context, "it is all a question (of expediency,) * * * of fair judgment, always keeping in mind the fact that we endeavor to make a rule in each case that will be practical and in keeping with the general understanding of Mankind." Palsgraf v. Long Island R.R. Co., 248 N.Y. 339, 354–355, 162 N.E. 99, 104, 59 A.L.R. 1253 (1928) (dissenting opinion).

. . .

Affirmed.

NOTE

In Clover v. Snowbird Ski Resort, 808 P.2d 1037 (Utah 1991), Chris Zulliger, an employee of the ski resort, was skiing, at high speed, down an intermediate slope. He had ignored a sign instructing skiers to ski slowly. He reached a crest in the slope and used it to launch himself into a jump. From where he began the jump he was unable to see his landing area, and by the time he was able to see where he would land, he was airborne. He struck and severely injured the plaintiff.

The trial court granted summary judgment in favor of the ski resort, on the theory that the employee was not acting within the scope of his employment. The employee was a chef at one of the resort's restaurants and a supervisor of others. He was expected to ski between restaurant locations. Like many other employees, he had a season ski pass. He was an expert skier. After monitoring the Mid-Gad Restaurant on the mountain, he took about four runs and then started to head for the bottom of the mountain, where he was to begin work as a chef at the resort's Plaza Restaurant. It was on his way down the mountain that he took the reckless and fateful jump.

The Supreme Court concluded that summary judgment should not have been granted in favor of the ski resort and remanded for trial. According to the court, the only doubt about scope of employment arose because Zulliger did not return to the Plaza immediately after monitoring the Mid-Gad. It reasoned, however, that a jury could reasonably find that "Zulliger had resumed his employment and that [his] deviation was not substantial enough to constitute a total abandonment of his employment." The court rejected an alternative argument by the plaintiff, based on *Bushey*, that the employer's liability should depend "not on whether the employee's conduct is motivated by serving the employer's interest, but on whether the employee's conduct is foreseeable." The Utah court noted simply that this is not the test under Utah case law.

ANALYSIS

1. Restatement (Second) of Agency § 228 provides that a servant's conduct "is not within the scope of employment if it is . . . too little actuated by a purpose to serve the master." In *Bushey*, Judge Friendly acknowledged that no purpose to serve the master could be found in this case—no matter how hard one tried. Apparently, the trial court had likewise concluded that no such purpose could be found. Accordingly, the district court opined, the law should be changed. No longer would plaintiffs be required to show that the agent was motivated by a purpose to serve the master. Instead, it would suffice to show that the conduct arose out of and in the course of the employment. The district court's analysis amounted to virtually a rule of strict liability for the torts of an employee as long as any connection in time and space could be made between the conduct and the employment. Judge Friendly affirmed the district court's result but rejected its rationale, noting that it was not at all clear that the proposed rule would lead to a more efficient allocation of resources. On the other hand, does Judge Friendly articulate a standard different from that of the Restatement?

2. Judge Friendly declines to base the decision on considerations of "policy"—that is, economic incentives and deterrence. Instead, he states that respondeat superior derives from "deeply rooted sentiment that a business enterprise cannot justly disclaim responsibility for accidents which may fairly be said to be characteristic of its activities." What is the significance of the court's use of the word "sentiment"? Where does the court find evidence of this sentiment?

3. In what way was Lane's conduct "characteristic of [the] activities" of the Coast Guard?

4. In the last paragraph of the opinion, the court states, "If Lane had set fire to the bar where he had been imbibing or had caused an accident on the street while returning to the drydock, the Government would not be liable. . . ." Why not? What if Lane and other crew members had gone to the bar to relax after a long and arduous voyage and Lane had acted along with several other crew members in setting the fire negligently?

Manning v. Grimsley

643 F.2d 20 (1st Cir.1981).

In this diversity action involving the law of Massachusetts the plaintiff, complaining that he as a spectator at a professional baseball game was injured by a ball thrown by a pitcher, sought in a battery count and in a negligence count to recover damages from the pitcher and his

employer. The district judge directed a verdict for defendants on the battery count and the jury returned a verdict for defendants on the negligence count. The district court having entered judgment for defendants on both counts, the plaintiff appeals from the judgment on the battery count.

(1) In deciding whether the district court correctly directed a verdict for defendants on the battery count, we are to consider the evidence in the light most favorable to the plaintiff. That evidence was to the following effect.

On September 16, 1975 there was a professional baseball game at Fenway Park in Boston between the defendant, the Baltimore Baseball Club, Inc. playing under the name the Baltimore Orioles, and the Boston Red Sox. The defendant Ross Grimsley was a pitcher employed by the defendant Baltimore Club. Some spectators, including the plaintiff, were seated, behind a wire mesh fence, in bleachers located in right field. In order to be ready to pitch in the game, Grimsley, during the first three innings of play, had been warming up by throwing a ball from a pitcher's mound to a plate in the bullpen located near those right field bleachers. The spectators in the bleachers continuously heckled him. On several occasions immediately following heckling Grimsley looked directly at the hecklers, not just into the stands. At the end of the third inning of the game, Grimsley, after his catcher had left his catching position and was walking over to the bench, faced the bleachers and wound up or stretched as though to pitch in the direction of the plate toward which he had been throwing but the ball traveled from Grimsley's hand at more than 80 miles an hour at an angle of 90 degrees to the path from the pitcher's mound to the plate and directly toward the hecklers in the bleachers. The ball passed through the wire mesh fence and hit the plaintiff.

We, unlike the district judge, are of the view that from the evidence that Grimsley was an expert pitcher, that on several occasions immediately following heckling he looked directly at the hecklers, not just into the stands, and that the ball traveled at a right angle to the direction in which he had been pitching and in the direction of the hecklers, the jury could reasonably have inferred that Grimsley intended (1) to throw the ball in the direction of the hecklers, (2) to cause them imminent apprehension of being hit, and (3) to respond to conduct presently affecting his ability to warm up and, if the opportunity came, to play in the game itself.

The foregoing evidence and inferences would have permitted a jury to conclude that the defendant Grimsley committed a battery against the plaintiff. This case falls within the scope of Restatement Torts 2d § 13, which provides, inter alia, that an actor is subject to liability to another for battery if, intending to cause a third person to have an imminent apprehension of a harmful bodily contact, the actor causes the other to suffer a harmful contact. . . . It, therefore, was error for the district court to have directed a verdict for defendant Grimsley on the battery count.

[The court holds that the plaintiff is not collaterally estopped by the jury verdict and non-appealed judgment for the defendants on the negligence count.]

It follows that the plaintiff is entitled to a vacation of the judgment on the battery count in favor of the defendant Grimsley.

The plaintiff is also entitled to a vacation of the judgment on the battery count in favor of the Baltimore Club, Grimsley's employer.

In Massachusetts "where a plaintiff seeks to recover damages from an employer for injuries resulting from an employee's assault . . . [w]hat must be shown is that the employee's assault was in response to the plaintiff's conduct which was presently interfering with the employee's ability to perform his duties successfully. This interference may be in the form of an affirmative attempt to prevent an employee from carrying out his assignments. . . ." Miller v. Federated Department Stores, Inc., 364 Mass. 340, 349–350, 304 N.E.2d 573 (1973).

The defendant Baltimore Club, relying on its reading of the *Miller* case, contends that the heckling from the bleachers constituted words which annoyed or insulted Grimsley and did not constitute "conduct" and that those words did not "presently" interfere with his ability to perform his duties successfully so as to make his employer liable for his assault in response thereto. Our analysis of the *Miller* case leads us to reject the contention. There a porter, whose duties consisted of cleaning the floors and emptying the trash cans in Filene's basement store, slapped a customer who had annoyed or insulted him by a remark that "If you would say 'excuse me,' people could get out of your way." The Massachusetts Supreme Judicial Court held that while the employee "may have been annoyed or insulted by" the customer's remark, "that circumstance alone does not justify imposition of liability on" the employer. 364 Mass. 350–351, 304 N.E.2d 573.

Miller's holding that a critical comment by a customer to an employee did not in the circumstances constitute "conduct" interfering with the employee's performance of his work is obviously distinguishable from the case at bar. Constant heckling by fans at a baseball park would be, within the meaning of *Miller*, conduct. The jury could reasonably have found that such conduct had either the affirmative purpose to rattle or the effect of rattling the employee so that he could not perform his duties successfully. Moreover, the jury could reasonably have found that Grimsley's assault was not a mere retaliation for past annoyance, but a response to continuing conduct which was "presently interfering" with his ability to pitch in the game if called upon to play. Therefore, the battery count against the Baltimore Club should have been submitted to the jury.

Vacated and remanded for a new trial on the battery count.

ANALYSIS

1. Restatement (Second) of Agency § 231 provides that a servant's acts "may be within the scope of employment although consciously criminal or tortious," but the comments to that section indicate that "serious crimes" are outside the scope. Why? Is Manning v. Grimsley inconsistent with the Restatement?

2. Restatement § 228(2) provides that a servant's use of force against another is within the scope of employment if "the use of force is not unexpectable by the master." Consequently, for example, the owner of a nightclub probably would be held liable for injuries inflicted by a bouncer in ejecting someone from the bar. After all, the owner presumably hired the bouncer for the very purpose of using force to eject

drunken or otherwise undesirable patrons. Was Grimley's conduct a use of force that should have been foreseeable by the Club?

3. What could the Club have done to prevent the injury?

4. Once again (see the Analysis following Brill v. Davajon, above), if Manning recovers from the Club, what is the likelihood that it would try to recover from Grimsley?

5. Suppose the jury verdict is that Grimsley is liable, but not the Club, and that Grimsley asks the Club to pay the amount he owes. What would you advise the Club?

D. STATUTORY CLAIMS

Arguello v. Conoco, Inc.

207 F.3d 803 (5th Cir.), cert. denied, 531 U.S. 874 (2000).

The appellants, a group of Hispanic and African-American consumers, filed suit against appellees, Conoco, Inc. ("Conoco" or "Conoco, Inc.") alleging that they were subjected to racial discrimination while purchasing gasoline and other services. Appellants challenge the district court's 12(b)(6) dismissal of their disparate impact claim under 42 U.S.C. § 2000a, and the district court's grant of summary judgment to Conoco on the appellants remaining 42 U.S.C. §§ 1981 and 2000a claims. For the following reasons we affirm in part, and reverse in part.

FACTUAL AND PROCEDURAL BACKGROUND

There are three different incidents which form the background for this appeal. In March 1995, Denise Arguello ("Arguello"), and her father Alberto Govea ("Govea"), along with various other members of their family stopped at a Conoco-owned store[1] in Fort Worth, Texas. After pumping their gasoline Arguello and Govea entered the store to pay for the gasoline and purchase other items. When Arguello approached the counter she presented the store cashier, Cindy Smith ("Smith"), with her items and a credit card. Smith asked to see Arguello's identification. When Arguello gave Smith her Oklahoma driver's license Smith stated that an out-of-state driver's license was not acceptable identification. Arguello disagreed with Smith and Smith began to insult Arguello using profanity and racial epithets. Smith also knocked a six-pack of beer off the counter toward Arguello. After Arguello retreated from the inside of the store, Smith used the store's intercom system to continue yelling racial epithets. Smith also made obscene gestures through the window.

Moments after the incident occurred Arguello and Govea used a pay phone outside the station to call a Conoco customer service phone number and complain about Smith's conduct. Govea also attempted to reenter the store to discover Smith's name. When Govea attempted to reenter the store, Smith and another store employee locked the doors. Linda Corbin ("Corbin"), a district manager, received Arguello and Govea's complaints. Corbin reviewed video tape from the store, which had no audio, and concluded that Smith had acted inappropriately. When she was

[1] We will use the term "Conoco-owned" to denote stores that are owned and operated by Conoco, Inc. "Conoco-branded" stores are stores which are independently owned marketers of Conoco products and are subject to the Petroleum Marketer Agreements.

confronted by Corbin, Smith admitted to using the profanity, racial epithets, and obscene gestures. Corbin counseled Smith about her behavior but did not suspend, or terminate Smith. Several months after the incident Corbin transferred Smith to another store for Smith's protection after receiving phone calls that a group was planning to picket the store at which the incident took place.

In September 1995, Gary Ivory ("Ivory"), Anthony Pickett ("Pickett"), and Michael Ross ("Ross") visited a Conoco-branded store in Fort Worth, Texas. While inside the store they allege that they were followed by a store employee and after complaining about this treatment a store employee told them "we don't have to serve you people" and "you people are always acting like this." The employee refused to serve them and asked them to leave. Eventually the police were summoned and the policeman ordered the store employee to serve the group.

In November 1996, Manuel Escobedo ("Escobedo") and Martha Escobedo ("Mrs. Escobedo") stopped at a Conoco-branded store in San Marcos, Texas. Escobedo claims that while visiting this store the store employee refused to provide toilet paper for the restroom, shouted profanities at his wife, and said "you Mexicans need to go back to Mexico." Escobedo called Conoco to complain about this incident, and was told by a Conoco customer service supervisor, Pamela Harper, that there was nothing Conoco could do because that station was not owned by Conoco. In a separate incident at a Conoco-branded store in Grand Prairie, Texas Escobedo was allegedly told by the store clerk that "you people steal gas." Finally, Escobedo claims that at two Conoco-branded stores in Laredo, Texas he was required to pre-pay for his gasoline while Caucasian customers were allowed to pump their gas first and then pay.

In March 1997, Arguello, Govea, the Escobedos, Ivory, Pickett, and Ross ("plaintiffs" or "appellants") filed suit against Conoco, Inc. . . . In October 1998, the district court granted summary judgment to Conoco on all of the plaintiffs' remaining claims.

DISCUSSION

Appellants raise several issues on appeal. First, appellants contend that the district court erred in finding no agency relationship between Conoco, Inc. and the Conoco-branded stores. Appellants also argue that the district court erred in finding no agency relationship between Conoco, Inc. and Cindy Smith because Smith acted outside the scope of her employment. . . .

B. Agency Relationship between Conoco, Inc. and Conoco-branded Stores

The incidents involving Ivory, Ross, Pickett and the Escobedos occurred at Conoco-branded stores. These Conoco-branded stores are independently owned, and have entered into Petroleum Marketing Agreements ("PMA") that allow them to market and sell Conoco brand gasoline and supplies in their stores. The district court held that no agency relationship existed between Conoco, Inc. and the Conoco branded stores. The district court found that Conoco, Inc. did not control the details of the daily operations of the Conoco branded stores, including personnel decisions.

The Supreme Court has suggested that in order to impose liability on a defendant under § 1981 for the discriminatory actions of a third party, the plaintiff must demonstrate that there is an agency relationship between the defendant and the third party. . . . [T]o establish an agency relationship between Conoco, Inc. and the branded stores the plaintiffs must show that Conoco, Inc. has given consent for the branded stores to act on its behalf and that the branded stores are subject to the control of Conoco, Inc.

Appellants argue that the PMAs establish that Conoco, Inc. has an agency relationship with the branded stores. They argue that the PMAs give Conoco, Inc. control of the branded stores because the PMAs require the branded stores to maintain their businesses according to the standards set forth in the PMAs. Plaintiffs further contend that Conoco, Inc. controls the customer service dimension of the Conoco-branded stores. As evidence the plaintiffs point to a statement in the PMA that instructs the branded stores that "all customers shall be treated fairly, honestly, and courteously." Furthermore, the plaintiffs assert that Conoco, Inc. has the power to debrand the Conoco-branded stations for not complying with the contractual terms of the PMA. Thus, because of this debranding power the plaintiffs reason that Conoco controls the operations of their brand marketers in all areas which are discussed in the PMA, including customer service. The plaintiffs also produced summary judgment evidence that Conoco, Inc. conducts random, bi-yearly inspections of the branded stores to determine if business is being conducted in accordance with the standards of the PMA.[6]

Despite the plaintiffs' interpretation of the PMAs and the evidence of inspections, the plain language of the PMA defines the relationship between Conoco, Inc. and its branded stores. The PMA states:

> Marketer [Conoco branded store] is an independent business and is not, nor are its employees, employees of Conoco. Conoco and Marketer are completely separate entities. They are not partners, general partners . . . nor agents of each other in any sense whatsoever and neither has the power to obligate or bind the other.

In the present case, our review of the record and pleadings do not reveal any allegation by the plaintiffs that the language in the PMA is ambiguous as to its meaning. . . . The language of the PMA, while offering guidelines to the Conoco-branded stores, does not establish that Conoco, Inc. has any participation in the daily operations of the branded stores nor that Conoco, Inc. participates in making personnel decisions.

Therefore, we find that there is no agency relationship between Conoco, Inc. and the branded stores in question, and that Conoco, Inc. as a matter of law cannot be held liable for the unfortunate incidents which happened to Ivory, Pickett, Ross, and the Escobedos at the Conoco-branded stores.

C. Scope of Employment

Arguello and Govea complain of discriminatory treatment at a Conoco-owned store. Appellants argue that the district court erred in

[6] These inspections normally focus on product displays and labeling. Customer service is not considered a main focus of the random inspections.

finding that Conoco could not be held liable . . . for the acts of its store clerk, Smith. The district court found that as a matter of law there was no agency relationship between Smith and Conoco because Smith's acts of discrimination towards Arguello and Govea were outside the scope of Smith's employment. . .

Under general agency principles a master is subject to liability for the torts of his servants while acting in the scope of their employment. See Restatement § 219. Some of the factors used when considering whether an employee's acts are within the scope of employment are: 1) the time, place and purpose of the act; 2) its similarity to acts which the servant is authorized to perform; 3) whether the act is commonly performed by servants; 4) the extent of departure from normal methods; and 5) whether the master would reasonably expect such act would be performed.

First, we must consider the time, place and purpose of Smith's actions. Smith's behavior toward Arguello and Govea occurred while she was on duty inside of the Conoco station where she was employed. The plaintiffs also put forth summary judgment evidence that Smith asked Arguello to present identification for credit card purchases. The purpose of Smith's interaction with Arguello was to complete the sale of gas and other store items. The initial confrontation and subsequent use of racial epithets occurred while Smith was completing Arguello's purchase of her items and processing the credit card transaction.

Second, we must consider whether Smith's actions were similar to those she was authorized by Conoco to perform. The sale of gasoline, other store items, and the completion of credit card purchases are the customary functions of a gasoline store clerk. The plaintiffs presented summary judgment evidence that Smith also used the intercom, which is also a customary action of gasoline store clerks.

Third, we will examine the extent of Smith's departure from normal methods. It is self-evident that Smith did not utilize the normal methods for conducting a sale. There was no summary judgment evidence presented that Conoco expected or anticipated that Smith would perform her functions in this manner. The appellees would have this court adopt the position that because Smith's use of racial epithets is comparable to the commission of an intentional tort, Conoco should not be held liable for Smith's behavior. However, the fact that an employee engages in intentional tortious conduct does not require a finding that the employee was outside the scope of his employment. . . . [A]lthough Conoco could not have expected Smith to shout racial epithets at Arguello and Govea, Smith's actions took place while she was performing her normal duties as a clerk. Conoco, Inc. had authorized Smith to interact with customers as they made purchases. Therefore, although Smith did depart from the normal methods of conducting a purchase this does not lead to the conclusion that as a matter of law she was outside the scope of her employment.

Finally, we must consider whether Conoco could have reasonably expected Smith to act in a racially discriminatory manner. There is no evidence in the record on this prong of the test. However, we note that even if Conoco is able to show that they could not have expected this conduct by Smith, the jury is entitled to find that the other factors outweigh this consideration.

In assessing whether Smith was within the scope of her employment the district court found that the only summary judgment evidence presented by the plaintiffs was that Smith was working in her job as cashier when the offensive behavior occurred. The district court concluded that the summary judgment evidence was insufficient to "overcome the common-sense conclusion" that Smith's offensive actions were not within the scope of her employment. However, we reject the presumption that because Smith behaved in an unacceptable manner that she was obviously outside the scope of her employment. The plaintiffs did present summary judgment evidence that Smith was on duty as a clerk, and that she was performing authorized duties such as conducting sales. This summary judgment evidence is not insignificant. Smith's position as clerk, and her authorization from Conoco to conduct sales allowed her to interact with Arguello and Govea, and put Smith in the position to commit the racially discriminatory acts. The plaintiffs also presented summary judgment evidence that Smith used her authority to conduct credit card transactions and use the gas station intercom system to commit the acts in question.

It is also important to note that Conoco does not challenge whether this incident occurred. Smith admitted to a Conoco district manager that she did subject Arguello and Govea to the use of racial epithets, profanity, and obscene gestures. The only dispute is whether there is a legal remedy for Arguello and Govea by holding Conoco liable for Smith's actions. The plaintiffs contend that the inference that should be drawn from Smith's actions is that Smith was authorized by Conoco to perform the actions of a clerk and that this meant that her actions while on duty as clerk were within the scope of her employment. Conoco, utilizing the same facts asks us to draw the inference that because Smith was acting on personal racial bigotry and animosity that she was outside the scope of her employment.

[The court holds that summary judgment should not have been granted in favor of Conoco on the agency relationship and scope of employment.]

ANALYSIS

1. Do you agree with the court's conclusion that the Conoco-branded stores were not agents of Conoco? Is that decision here consistent with the franchise cases, such as Murphy v. Holiday Inns, Inc., or the gas station cases, i.e., Humble Oil & Refining Co. v. Martin and Hoover v. Sun Oil Company?

2. Do you agree with the court's conclusion that Smith acted within the scope of her employment?

E. LIABILITY FOR TORTS OF INDEPENDENT CONTRACTORS

Majestic Realty Associates, Inc. v. Toti Contracting Co.

30 N.J. 425, 153 A.2d 321 (1959).

Plaintiffs Majestic Realty Associates, Inc., and Bohen's Inc., owner and tenant, sought compensation from defendants Toti Contracting Co.,

Inc. and Parking Authority of the City of Paterson, New Jersey, for damage to Majestic's building and to Bohen's goods. The claim arose out of the activity of Toti in demolishing certain structures owned by the Authority. . . .

Majestic is the owner of the two-story premises at 297 Main Street, Paterson, New Jersey. Bohen's is the tenant of the first floor and basement thereof in which it conducted a dry goods business. The Authority acquired properties along Main Street beginning immediately adjacent to Majestic's building on the south and continuing to Ward Street, the next intersecting street, and then east on the latter street for 150 feet. The motive for the acquisition was to establish a public parking area. Main Street is one of the principal business arteries of the city and the locality was completely built up.

Accomplishment of the Authority's object required demolition of the several buildings on both streets. Some time prior to October 26, 1956, a contract was entered into by the Authority with Toti to do the work. The razing began on the Ward Street side and moved northwardly until the structure next to Majestic's premises was reached. It was at least a story (about 20 feet) higher than Majestic's roof; the northerly wall of the one was 'right up against' the southerly wall of the other and the two walls ran alongside each other for 40 feet.

In the process of leveling this adjacent building, the contractor first removed the roof, then the front and south sidewalls and all of the interior partitions and floors. Thus, the north wall of brick and masonry next to Majestic's structure was left standing free. Expert testimony was adduced to show that the proper method of demolition under the existing circumstances would have been to remove the roof, leaving the interior partition work for support, and to begin to take the north wall down "never leaving any portion (of it) at a higher point than the interior construction of the building would form a brace."

In demolishing the walls, Toti used a large metal ball, said to weigh 3,500 pounds, suspended from a crane which was stationed in the street. There was testimony that during the week prior to the accident, every time the ball would strike a wall, debris and dirt would fly and the Majestic building "rocked." Further expert testimony indicated that in dealing with the free-standing north wall, the ball should have been made to hit the very top on each occasion so as to level it a few bricks at a time. This course was followed at first; the ball was swung from north to south and the dislodged bricks were catapulted away from Majestic's building and onto the adjoining lot. After a time, work ceased for a few minutes. On resumption, the operator of the crane swung the ball in such a manner that it struck at a point some 15 feet below the top of the wall. The impact propelled the uppermost section of the wall back in the direction from which the blow had come with the result that a 15 by 40 foot section fell on Majestic's roof, causing a 25 by 40 foot break therein. One of Bohen's employees, who saw the incident, asked the crane operator in the presence of Toti's president: "What did you do to our building?" He replied, "I goofed."

In characterizing a demolition undertaking of this type in a built up and busy section of a city, and in particular where one building to be razed adjoined another which was to remain untouched, plaintiffs' expert witness said it was "hazardous work"; "one of the most hazardous operations in the building business." And with reference to the leveling of a building so close to another structure which was not to be harmed, he asserted that the recognized procedure is to take it down in small sections so as not to lose control of the operation. This standard conforms with N.J.S.A. 34:5–15 which specifies that "(i)n the demolition of buildings, walls shall be removed part by part."

On the proof outlined, the trial court recognized that the work was hazardous in its very nature, but did not feel that it constituted a nuisance per se. Therefore, he ruled that the Authority, not having had or exercised control over the manner and method or means of performing the demolition operation, could not be held for the negligent act of its independent contractor. [The Appellate Division reversed.]

The problem must be approached with an awareness of the long settled doctrine that ordinarily where a person engages a contractor, who conducts an independent business by means of his own employees, to do work not in itself a nuisance (as our cases put it), he is not liable for the negligent acts of the contractor in the performance of the contract. . . . Certain exceptions have come to be accepted, i.e., (a) where the landowner retains control of the manner and means of the doing of the work which is the subject of the contract; (b) where he engages an incompetent contractor, or (c) where, as noted in the statement of the general rule, the activity contracted for constitutes a nuisance per se. . . .

As to exception (b), noted above, it is not claimed that the proof makes out a jury question on the charge that an incompetent contractor was hired for the task of demolition. Incidental comment thereon, however, may be fruitful.

It has been intimated that the matter of the competency of a contractor should not be restricted to considerations of skill and experience but should encompass financial responsibility to respond to tort claims as well. Research has not disclosed a case where the proposal has been applied. . . .

Inevitably the mind turns to the fact that the injured third party is entirely innocent and that the occasion for his injury arises out of the desire of the contractee to have certain activities performed. The injured has no control over or relation with the contractor. The contractee, true, has no control over the doing of the work and in that sense is also innocent of the wrongdoing; but he does have the power of selection and in the application of concepts of distributive justice perhaps much can be said for the view that a loss arising out of the tortious conduct of a financially irresponsible contractor should fall on the contractee. Professor Morris, in "Torts of Independent Contractors," [29 Ill. L. Rev. 339, 344 (1934)], put it this way:

> If the contractee has to look out for the interests of others by using due care to pick a man with requisite skill to whom to entrust his enterprises, why should he not also have to look out for the interests of others by selecting a man with sufficient financing? And since there is usually a fool proof method of assuring himself that the contractor will meet all tort obligations in requiring an indemnity bond signed by responsible sureties, it would seem that in most cases the contractee would only measure up to the standard of due care so

> as to avoid responsibility when the contractor is able to discharge tort claims arising out of the enterprise.

This passage was written in 1934. At the present time it is a matter of common knowledge that liability insurance to cover such demolition operations is available to contractors and it may be assumed fairly that procurement of that type coverage is regarded as an ordinary business expense. Financial responsibility has nothing to do with legal liability of the contractor. . . .

But this precise facet of the problem of Toti's competency was not raised at the trial or in the briefs. It arose as an emanation of the oral argument. Consequently, no decision is rendered with respect to it and the matter is expressly reserved.

Under exception (c), on which plaintiffs rely principally, liability will be imposed upon the landowner in spite of the engagement of an independent contractor if the work to be done constitutes a nuisance per se. The phrase "nuisance per se," although used with some frequency in the reported cases, is difficult of definition. . . .

Without undertaking an exhaustive review of the cases in our State where the expression appears, it seems proper to say that the legal content of "nuisance per se" and the application thereof in a factual framework such as that now before us, is anything but clear. . . . In Sarno v. Gulf Refining Co., 99 N.J.L. 340, 342 (Sup. Ct. 1924), affirmed 102 N.J.L. 223 (E. & A. 1925), the court equated it with "inherently dangerous" and this appears to have set in motion a trend toward the view now espoused by the Restatement, Torts, §§ 835(e), 416.

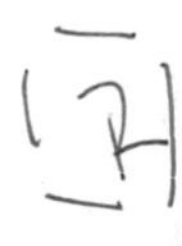

Section 416 of the Restatement propounds a rule which would impose liability upon the landowner who engages an independent contractor to do work which he should recognize as necessarily requiring the creation during its progress of a condition involving a peculiar risk of harm to others unless special precautions are taken, if the contractor is negligent in failing to take those precautions. Such work may be said to be inherently dangerous, i.e., an activity which can be carried on safely only by the exercise of special skill and care, and which involves grave risk of danger to persons or property if negligently done. . . .

It is important to distinguish an operation which may be classed as inherently dangerous from one that is ultra-hazardous. The latter is described as one which "(a) necessarily involves a serious risk of harm to the person, land or chattels of others which cannot be eliminated by the exercise of the utmost care, and (b) is not a matter of common usage." Restatement, supra, § 520. The distinction is important because liability is absolute where the work is ultra-hazardous,. . . .

There is no doubt that the line between work which is ordinary, usual and commonplace, and that which is inherently dangerous because its very nature involves a peculiar and high risk of harm to members of the public or adjoining proprietors of land unless special precautions are taken, is somewhat shadowy. . . . For the present, we need deal only with the case before us. . . . The current New York rule is that the razing of buildings in a busy, built up section of a city is inherently dangerous within the contemplation of section 416 of the Restatement. . . . In our judgment, the doctrine adopted by New York . . . represents the sound and just concept to be applied.

ANALYSIS

1. Under exception (b), for cases in which the principal retained an incompetent contractor, is the principal liable simply upon a showing that the contractor was incompetent? Or should plaintiff be obliged to show that the principal was negligent in selecting an incompetent contractor?

2. Do you agree with the court's dicta implying that hiring a financially irresponsible contractor is tantamount to hiring one who is incompetent? If not, why not? In answering that question, it may be helpful to consider the following: As between Majestic and the Authority, which was best able to monitor Toti's conduct? As between Majestic and the Authority, which was in the best position to insure against these sorts of accidents?

3. Under exception (c), for inherently dangerous activities, is the principal liable simply because the contractor was negligent in failing to take adequate precautions? Or should plaintiff be obliged to show negligence on the principal's part?

4. In light of this decision, what should the Authority do in the future when hiring independent contractors to conduct hazardous activities?

5. Do the exceptions recognized by the *Majestic* opinion swallow the rule that principals are not liable for the tortious acts of their independent contractors?

4. FIDUCIARY OBLIGATION OF AGENTS

We now shift our attention to the fiduciary obligation, or duty of loyalty, owed by agents to their principals. Note that several of the cases to be examined involve agents of corporate principals. They are included in this text because the fact that the principal is a corporation, rather than an individual, is unimportant.

A. DUTIES DURING AGENCY

Reading v. Regem

[1948] 2 KB 268, [1948] 2 All ER 27, [1948] WN 205.

The plaintiff joined the army in 1936, and at the beginning of 1944 he was a sergeant in the Royal Army Medical Corps stationed at the general hospital in Cairo, where he was in charge of the medical stores.*

The plaintiff had not had any opportunities, in his life as a soldier, of making money, but in March, 1944, there were found standing to his credit at banks in Egypt, several thousands of pounds, and he had more thousands of pounds in notes in his flat. He had also acquired a motor car worth £1,500. The Special Investigation Branch of the army looked into the matter, and he was asked how he came by these moneys. He made a statement, from which it appears that they were paid to him by

* [Eds.: Cognizant of Winston Churchill's dictum that the United States and the United Kingdom are "separated by a common language," we have taken the liberty of converting some British legal terms into their American equivalents.]

a man by the name of Manole in these circumstances. A lorry used to arrive loaded with cases, the contents of which were unknown. Then the plaintiff, in full uniform, boarded the lorry, and escorted it through Cairo, so that it was able to pass the civilian police without being inspected. When it arrived at its destination, it was unloaded, or the contents were transferred to another lorry. After the first occasion when this happened, the plaintiff saw Manole in a restaurant in Cairo. Manole handed him an envelope which he put in his pocket. On examining it when he arrived home, he found that it contained £2,000. Two or three weeks later, another load arrived, and another £2,000 was paid. £3,000 was paid after the third load, and so it went on until eventually some £20,000 had gone into the pocket of the suppliant. The services which he rendered for that money were that he accompanied this lorry from one part of Cairo to another, and it is plain that he got it because he was a sergeant in the British army, and, while in uniform, escorted these lorries through Cairo. It is also plain that he was clearly violating his duty in so doing. The military authorities took possession of the money. . . .

In this petition of right, the plaintiff alleges that these moneys are his and should be returned to him by the Crown. In answer, the Crown say: "These were bribes received by you by reason of your military employment, and you hold the money for the Crown. Even if we were wrong in the way in which we seized them, we are entitled to recover the amount of them, and to set off that amount against any claim you may have." In these circumstances, it is not necessary to dwell on the form of the claim. The question is whether or not the Crown is entitled to the money. It is not entitled to it simply because it is the Crown—moneys which are unlawfully obtained are not ipso facto forfeited to the Crown. The claim of the Crown rests on the fact that at the material time it was the plaintiff's employer.

. . . In my judgment, it is a principle of law that, if a servant takes advantage of his service and violates his duty of honesty and good faith to make a profit for himself, in the sense that the assets of which he has control, the facilities which he enjoys, or the position which he occupies, are the real cause of his obtaining the money as distinct from merely affording the opportunity for getting it, that is to say, if they play the predominant part in his obtaining the money, then he is accountable for it to his master. It matters not that the master has not lost any profit nor suffered any damage, nor does it matter that the master could not have done the act himself. If the servant has unjustly enriched himself by virtue of his service without his master's sanction, the law says that he ought not to be allowed to keep the money, but it shall be taken from him and given to his master, because he got it solely by reason of the position which he occupied as a servant of his master. Instances readily occur to mind. Take the case of the master who tells his servant to exercise his horses, and while the master is away, the servant lets them out and makes a profit by so doing. There is no loss to the master, the horses have been exercised, but the servant must account for the profits he makes.

The ATTORNEY-GENERAL put in argument the case of a uniformed policeman who, at the request of thieves and in return for a bribe, directs traffic away from the site of the crime. Is he to be allowed to keep the money? So, also, here, the use of the facilities provided by the Crown in the shape of the uniform and the use of his position in the army were the only reason why the plaintiff was able to get this money. It was solely on that account that he was able to sit in the front of these lorries and give them a safe conduct through Cairo. There was no loss of profit to the Crown. The Crown would have been violating its duty if it had undertaken the task, but the plaintiff was certainly violating his duty, and it is money which must be paid over to his master—in this case, the Crown.

. . . The uniform of the Crown and the position of the plaintiff as a servant of the Crown were the only reasons why he was able to get this money, and that is sufficient to make him liable to hand it over to the Crown. The case is to be distinguished from cases where the service merely gives the opportunity of making money. A servant may, during his master's time, in breach of his contract, do other things to make money for himself, such as gambling, but he is entitled to keep that money himself. The master has a claim for damages for breach of contract, but he has no claim to the money. So, also, the fact that a soldier is stationed in a certain place may give him the opportunity, contrary to the King's Regulations, of engaging in trade and making money in that way. In such a case, the mere fact that his service gave the opportunity for getting the money would not entitle the Crown to it, but if, as here, the wearing of the King's uniform and his position as a soldier is the sole cause of his getting the money and he gets it dishonestly, that is an advantage which he is not allowed to keep. Although the Crown, has suffered no loss, the court orders the money to be handed over to the Crown, because the Crown is the only person to whom it can properly be paid. The plaintiff must not be allowed to enrich himself in this way. He got the money by virtue of his employment, and must hand it over.

DISPOSITION: Petition dismissed with costs.

ANALYSIS

1. The court opines, the sergeant "must not be allowed to enrich himself in this way." Why not?

2. Would a different result obtain under U.S. agency law? Consider Restatement (Third) of Agency § 8.02:

> An agent has a duty not to acquire a material benefit from a third party in connection with transactions conducted or other actions taken on behalf of the principal or otherwise through the agent's use of the agent's position.

Restatement (Third) § 8.05 may also be relevant: "An agent has a duty (1) not to use property of the principal for the agent's own purposes or those of a third party . . . ."

3. Why should the Crown be able to recover even though it "suffered no loss"? Put another way, why is the remedy disgorgement of secret profits rather than actual damages?

PROBLEMS

How, if at all, would you distinguish the following cases from Reading v. Regem?

1. The facts are the same as in the actual case, except that the sergeant had been discharged by the Royal Army before riding along in the smuggler's truck. Would it make a difference if discharged personnel were permitted to wear their uniforms for 30 days, to ease the transition to civilian life?

2. Imagine a U.S. Army Sergeant who, during the Gulf War, single-handedly wiped out an enemy machine gun emplacement; earned the Congressional Medal of Honor; received huge coverage in newspapers and magazines and on television; and became a public hero. One night, while in New York, he went to a popular restaurant, in uniform. The owner of the restaurant called reporters, who arrived and took pictures, which appeared in papers across the country the next day. As the sergeant left the restaurant, the owner gave him an envelope with $1,000 in cash and urged him to return. (And, of course, the owner would not let him pay for his food and drinks.) The sergeant returned many times and received a total of $10,000 in cash.

3. General Norman Schwarzkopf, culminating a long, distinguished career in the U.S. Army, became well known to the public as head of the U.S. military forces in the Gulf War. After that war he published his autobiography, "It Doesn't Take a Hero," for which he presumably received substantial royalties. Assume that, to promote the book, he appeared at various gatherings and on television, always in civilian clothes.

4. Suppose that the long-time Chief Executive Officer of a major corporation authored a book about his experience as CEO and about the principles that he followed in guiding the corporation to its enormous success. The CEO earned substantial royalties, which he gave to charity.

5. Michael Jordan received substantial royalties for the use of his name by a restaurant in Chicago.

6. Suppose an expert witness appeared in court and was identified as a Harvard Law School professor. Her fee for two days of preparation and one day in court was $100,000.

7. A senior executive in an oil company learned that the company's geologists had discovered a huge oil field, but were required to maintain secrecy until the company could buy the drilling rights. The executive bought shares of stock of the company and, after the announcement of the discovery several months later, sold those shares for a large profit.

Rash v. J.V. Intermediate, Ltd

498 F.3d 1201 (10th Cir. 2007).

. . .

I. Factual Background

J.V. Intermediate, Ltd. and J.V. Industrial Companies, Ltd. (collectively, "JVIC") are Texas-based companies which build, refurbish, expand and manage assets for industrial process plants worldwide. JVIC hired W. Clayton Rash to start and manage a Tulsa, Oklahoma division of its industrial plant maintenance business, inspecting, repairing, and maintaining oil refineries and power plants. The parties signed an employment agreement providing Rash a base salary of $125,000, a bonus of 20% of JVIC-Tulsa's net profits, and a termination bonus of 20% of the division's equity. The contract stipulated the use of Texas law and required that Rash "devote [his] full work time and efforts" to JVIC. The agreement was to last for two years, from 1999 to 2001. Rash continued to serve as manager of the Tulsa branch until 2004, without any written contract extension.

Starting in 2001, JVIC claims that Rash actively participated in and owned at least four other businesses, none of which were ever disclosed to JVIC. One of those businesses was Total Industrial Plant Services, Inc. (TIPS), a scaffolding business. TIPS bid on projects for JVIC-Tulsa, and JVIC-Tulsa, with Rash as its manager, often selected TIPS as a subcontractor. At some point during Rash's tenure, JVIC started its own scaffolding business. Between 2001 to 2004, JVIC paid over $1 million to TIPS. The Tulsa division never used JVIC's scaffolding services. . . .

III. Analysis

. . .

A. Fiduciary Duty

1. *Is there a fiduciary relationship?*

. . .

Texas courts . . . recognize that certain relationships constitute formal fiduciary relationships as a matter of law. Examples of these fiduciary relationships are trustee to beneficiary, executor to beneficiary of estates, attorney to client, and partner to partner. Johnson [v. Brewer & Pritchard, P.C., 73 S.W.3d 193], 200 [(Tex. 2003)]. Under Texas common law, the agent to principal relationship also gives rise to a fiduciary duty. . . .

With respect to the agent to principal relationship, the Texas Supreme Court has adopted relevant provisions of the Restatement (Second) of Agency. In particular, § 387 provides: "[U]nless otherwise agreed, an agent is subject to a duty to his principal to act solely for the benefit of the principal in all matters connected with his agency." . . .

[The court concludes that Rash was an agent of JVIC, for several reasons.] First, . . . Rash was hired to build the Tulsa division of JVIC from scratch and had sole management responsibilities for operations at the branch. In Rash's own words, "I did the sales, the operations, and everything out of the Tulsa division." He was charged with finding facilities to operate the business, hiring and training employees, gathering tools and equipment for the branch, and promoting the new venture. Rash solicited and received bids for subcontracts and directly received the invoices for those bids. He set the rates charged to JVIC's customers for work performed by the Tulsa division and kept track of all the costs of the division. In general, Rash conceded that he "ran the shop" and was "responsible for generating business for the Tulsa upstart."

Second, Rash contractually agreed to perform the duties of an agent. . . . In his contract, Rash consented to "devote [his] full work time and efforts to the business and affairs of Joint Venture Piping."

Third, Rash does not deny that he was an agent of JVIC. Instead, he only claims that the scope of his agency did not include scaffolding-related ventures. . . .

2. *Did Rash breach his fiduciary duty?*

Whether Rash breached his fiduciary duty to JVIC turns on the scope of that duty. In *Johnson,* the Texas Supreme Court cautioned courts to "be careful in defining the scope of the fiduciary obligations an employee owes when acting as the employer's agent in the pursuit of business opportunities." 73 S.W.3d at 201. Courts instead inquire whether a fiduciary duty exists with respect to the particular occurrence or transaction at issue. After careful consideration of the question, we are confident that Texas courts would agree on this record that Rash violated his fiduciary duty in failing to disclose his interest in TIPS to JVIC.

Texas law recognizes several basic duties a fiduciary owes the principal:

> Among the agent's fiduciary duties to the principal is the duty to account for profits arising out of the employment, the duty not to act as, or on account of, an adverse party without the principal's consent, the duty not to compete with the principal on his own account or for another in matters relating to the subject matter of the agency, and the duty to deal fairly with the principal in all transactions between them.

Id. at 200 (citing Restatement (Second) of Agency § 13, cmt. a (1958)).3 Additionally and most importantly for this appeal, the "employee has a duty to deal openly with the employer and to fully disclose to the employer information about matters affecting the company's business." Abetter Trucking Co. [v. Arizpe], 113 S.W.3d [503], 510 [(Tex. App. 2003)]. Although "an employee does not owe an absolute duty of loyalty to his or her employer," *Johnson*, 73 S.W.3d at 201 (acknowledging the right of employees to make preparations for a future competing business venture while still employed), at the very least, an employee's independent enterprise cannot compete or contract with the employer without the employer's full knowledge.

. . . Here, Rash presents two defenses: (1) as a manager of JVIC's general industrial plant maintenance work, he owed no specific duty to JVIC's relatively minor scaffolding business, and (2) JVIC's president, Joe Vardell, told him that he had no problem with Rash forming a business which might contract with JVIC. Yet, these defenses, even if true, misapprehend the nature of his fiduciary duty. As discussed above, Rash had a "duty to deal fairly with the principal in *all* transactions between them," id. at 200 (emphasis added), and "to fully disclose to the employer information about matters affecting the company's business," *Abetter Trucking Co.*, 113 S.W.3d at 503 (emphasis added

In other words, Rash had a "general duty of full disclosure respecting matters affecting the principal's interests and a general prohibition against the fiduciary's using the relationship to benefit his personal interest, except with the full knowledge and consent of the principal." United Teachers Ass'n Ins. Co. v. MacKeen & Bailey, Inc., 99 F.3d 645, 650 (5th Cir.1996). Even assuming that Rash had no responsibilities to JVIC regarding the scaffolding division or that Vardell gave him hypothetical permission to engage in other businesses, by failing to inform JVIC specifically of his ownership stake in TIPS, he violated his fiduciary duty . . .

The duty of an agent is to disclose to the principal what the principal should rightly know. The facts are uncontroverted that (1) Rash possessed a significant ownership stake in TIPS, (2) TIPS bid for subcontracts with JVIC-Tulsa, (3) Rash played an instrumental role in selecting JVIC-Tulsa's subcontractors, (4) TIPS was selected as a JVIC-Tulsa subcontractor on several occasions, and (5) Rash never disclosed to JVIC or its president, Vardell, his relationship with TIPS. In fact, Vardell testified that he only learned about Rash's ownership of TIPS through this litigation. In our estimation, this amounts to a breach of his fiduciary duty as a matter of law. . . .

This would be a different case altogether if Rash simply notified Vardell or JVIC about his relationship with TIPS. Since he did not, JVIC was entitled to judgment as a matter of law on its breach of fiduciary claim against Rash.

. . .

ANALYSIS

1. At the time Rash was hired, JVIC did not have a scaffolding business. If JVIC had never formed a scaffolding business, would Rash have violated his fiduciary obligation to JVIC by contracting on its behalf with his company (TIPS)?

2. What should Rash have done to satisfy the court's notion of his duty to disclose?

3. The court notes that "Rash consented to 'devote [his] full work time and efforts to the business and affairs of Joint Venture Piping.' " These so-called best efforts clauses are common in many types of employment agreements. A somewhat more detailed example provides that "employees shall devote their full working time, attention and efforts to the Company's business and shall not, directly or indirectly, engage in any other business or commercial activities which shall conflict or interfere with or distract from in any way the performance of the employee's responsibilities to the Company or which involve any activities similar to the business conducted by the Company." Why are these clauses necessary in light of the fiduciary duties of agents?

B. DUTIES DURING AND AFTER TERMINATION OF AGENCY: HEREIN OF "GRABBING AND LEAVING"

Town & Country House & Home Service, Inc. v. Newbery

3 N.Y.2d 554, 170 N.Y.S.2d 328, 147 N.E.2d 724 (1958).

This action was brought for an injunction and damages against appellants on the theory of unfair competition. The complaint asks to restrain them from engaging in the same business as plaintiff, from soliciting its customers, and for an accounting and damages. The individual appellants were in plaintiff's employ for about three years before they severed their relationships and organized the corporate appellant through which they have been operating. The theory of the complaint is that plaintiff's enterprise "was unique, personal and confidential," and that appellants cannot engage in business at all without breach of the confidential relationship in which they learned its trade secrets, including the names and individual needs and tastes of its customers.

bus. The nature of the enterprise is house and home cleaning by contract with individual householders. Its "unique" quality consists in superseding the drudgery of ordinary house cleaning by mass production methods. The house cleaning is performed by a crew of men who descend upon a home at stated intervals of time, and do the work in a hurry after the manner of an assembly line in a factory. They have been instructed by the housewife but work without her supervision. The householder is supplied with liability insurance, the secrets of the home are kept inviolate, the tastes of the customer are served and each team of workmen is selected as suited to the home to which it is sent. The complaint says that the customer relationship is "impregnated" with a "personal and confidential aspect."

The complaint was dismissed at Special Term on the ground that the individual appellants were not subjected to negative covenants under any contract with plaintiff, and that the methods and techniques used by plaintiff in conducting its business are not confidential or secret as in the case of a scientific formula; that house cleaning and housekeeping "are old and necessary chores which accompany orderly living" and that no violation of duty was involved in soliciting plaintiff's customers by appellants after resigning from plaintiff's employ. The contacts and acquaintances with customers were held not to have been the result of a confidential relationship between plaintiff and defendants or the result of the disclosure of secret or confidential material.

By a divided vote the Appellate Division reversed, but on a somewhat different ground, namely, that while in plaintiff's employ, appellants conspired to terminate their employment, form a business of their own in competition with plaintiff and solicit plaintiff's customers for their business. The overt acts under this conspiracy were found by the Appellate Division to have been that, in pursuance of this plan, they formed the corporate appellant and bought equipment and supplies for their operations—not on plaintiff's time—but during off hours, before they had severed their relations as employees of plaintiff. The Appellate Division concluded that "it is our opinion that their agreement and encouragement to each other to carry out the course of conduct thus planned by them, and their consummation of the plan, particularly their termination of employment virtually en masse, were inimical to, and violative of, the obligations owed by them to appellant as its employees; and that therefore appellant was entitled to relief." . . .

Although the Appellate Division implied more relief than we consider to have been warranted, we think that the trial court erred in dismissing the complaint altogether. The only trade secret which could be involved in this business is plaintiff's list of customers. Concerning that, even where a solicitor of business does not operate fraudulently under the banner of his former employer, he still may not solicit the latter's customers who are not openly engaged in business in advertised locations or whose availability as patrons cannot readily be ascertained but "whose trade and patronage have been secured by years of business effort and advertising, and the expenditure of time and money, constituting a part of the good will of a business which enterprise and foresight have built up" (Witkop & Holmes Co. v. Boyce, 61 Misc. 126, 131, 112 N.Y.S. 874, 878, affirmed 131 App.Div. 922, 115 N.Y.S. 1150, . . .). . . .

The testimony in the instant record shows that the customers of plaintiff were not and could not be obtained merely by looking up their names in the telephone or city directory or by going to any advertised locations, but had to be screened from among many other housewives who did not wish services such as respondent and appellants were equipped to render, but preferred to do their own housework. In most instances housewives do their own house cleaning. The only appeal which plaintiff could have was to those whose cleaning had been done by servants regularly or occasionally employed, except in the still rarer instances where the housewife was on the verge of abandoning doing her own work by hiring some outside agency. In the beginning, prospective customers of plaintiff were discovered by Dorothy Rossmoore, wife of plaintiff's president, by telephoning at random in "sections of Nassau that we thought would be interested in this type of cleaning, and from that we got directories, town directories, and we marked the streets that we had passed down, and I personally called, right down the list." In other words, after selecting a neighborhood which they felt was fertile for their kind of business, they would telephone to all of the residents of a street in the hope of discovering likely prospects. On the first day Mrs. Rossmoore called 52 homes. If she enlisted their interest, an appointment would be made for a personal call in order to sell them the service. At the end of the first year, only 40 to 50 customers had thus been secured. Two hundred to three hundred telephone calls netted 8 to 12 customers. Moreover, during the first year it was not possible to know how much to charge these customers with accuracy, inasmuch as the cleaning requirements of each differed from the others, so that special prices had to be set. In the beginning the customer usually suggested the price which was paid until some kind of cost accounting could demonstrate whether it should be raised or lowered. These costs were entered on cards for every customer, and this represented an accumulated body of experience of considerable value. After three years of operation, and by August, 1952, when the individual appellants resigned their employment by plaintiff, the number of customers amounted to about 240. By that time plaintiff had 7 or 8 crews doing this cleaning work, consisting of 3 men each.

Although appellants did not solicit plaintiff's customers until they were out of plaintiff's employ, nevertheless plaintiff's customers were the only ones they did solicit. Appellants solicited 20 or 25 of plaintiff's customers who refused to do business with appellants and about 13 more of plaintiff's customers who transferred their patronage to appellants. These were all the people that appellants' firm solicited. It would be different if these customers had been equally available to appellants and respondent, but, as has been related, these customers had been screened by respondent at considerable effort and expense, without which their receptivity and willingness to do business with this kind of a service organization could not be known. So there appears to be no question that plaintiff is entitled to enjoin defendants from further solicitation of its customers, or that some profits or damage should be paid to plaintiff by reason of these customers whom they enticed away.

For more than this appellants are not liable. . . .

ANALYSIS

1. Just what could the defendants have done to lure away Town & Country customers, without incurring liability to the plaintiffs?

2. Assume (reasonably) that the law would allow a competitor with no prior relationship with Town & Country to follow Town & Country trucks and thereby discover the addresses, and then the names and telephone numbers, of Town & Country customers, and then to solicit those customers. Is there any good reason why the defendants should not be permitted to hire a detective to do the same sleuthing and then use the list put together by the detective as a basis for telephone solicitation?

CHAPTER 2

PARTNERSHIPS

1. WHAT IS A PARTNERSHIP? AND WHO ARE THE PARTNERS?

A. PARTNERS COMPARED WITH EMPLOYEES

Fenwick v. Unemployment Compensation Commission

133 N.J.L. 295, 44 A.2d 172 (1945).

This is an appeal from a judgment of the Supreme Court reversing a determination of the Unemployment Compensation Commission. The question involved is whether one Arline Chesire was, from January 1, 1939, to January 1, 1942, a partner or an employee of the prosecutor-respondent, John R. Fenwick, trading as United Beauty Shoppe. If she was an employee, then she was the eighth and deciding employee for the purpose of determining the status of the respondent for the year 1939 as an employer subject to the terms of the statute. N.J.S.A. 43:21–1 et seq. [requiring employer payments for unemployment compensation fund]. It is not the contention of the appellant commission that there was a fraudulent intent to avoid the act but the case is submitted as one of legal construction of the relation between Mrs. Chesire and the respondent.

Respondent Fenwick commenced operation of the beauty shop in Newark in November, 1936. In either 1937 or early 1938 he employed Mrs. Chesire as a cashier and reception clerk. Apparently her duties were to receive customers, take their orders for services to be performed by the operators, and collect the charges therefor. The shop did not work on an appointment basis but on a "first come-first served" plan. Mrs. Chesire was employed at a salary of $15 per week and continued at that salary until December, 1938, when she requested an increase. Respondent expressed a willingness to pay higher wages if the income of the shop warranted it. Thereupon an agreement was entered into by the parties. This agreement was drawn by a lawyer who had offices nearby and provided:

> 1. That the parties associate themselves into a partnership to commence January 1, 1939.
>
> 2. That the business shall be the operation of the beauty shop.
>
> 3. That the name shall be United Beauty Shoppe.
>
> 4. That no capital investment shall be made by Mrs. Chesire.
>
> 5. That the control and management of the business shall be vested in Fenwick.

6. That Mrs. Chesire is to act as cashier and reception clerk at a salary of $15 per week and a bonus at the end of the year of 20% of the net profits, if the business warrants it.

7. That as between the partners Fenwick alone is to be liable for debts of the partnership.

8. That both parties shall devote all their time to the shop.

9. That the books are to be open for inspection of each party.

10. That the salary of Fenwick is to be $50 per week and at the end of the year he is to receive 80% of the profits.

11. That the partnership shall continue until either party gives ten days' notice of termination.

The relationship was terminated on January 1, 1942, at the request of Mrs. Chesire who desired to cease work and remain at home with her child.

The Commission held that the agreement was nothing more than an agreement fixing the compensation of an employee. The Supreme Court held that the parties were partners. The court apparently gave great weight to the fact that the parties had entered into the agreement, had called themselves partners, had designated the relationship one of partnership, and held that the surrounding circumstances, the conduct of the parties, etc., were not such as to overcome the force and effect to be given the declaration of the agreement.

Most of the cases wherein the courts have undertaken to determine whether or not a partnership existed, or whether certain persons were members of existing partnerships, have been those in which creditors have sought to impose liability upon alleged partners. In most cases, too, there have been no written partnership agreements to assist in fixing the status. However, the principles of law to be applied are the same. We think there can be no doubt of the right of the Commission, in the circumstances of this case, to raise the question and have a determination of the question of whether a partnership exists in law even though there is this agreement which is called a partnership agreement. We need not consider here what the effect of the agreement on the parties inter sese would be, but only its effect on the application of the unemployment compensation law.

There are several elements that the courts have taken into consideration in determining the existence or non-existence of the partnership relation. The first element is that of the intention of the parties and here, of course, the agreement itself is evidential although not conclusive. Light on the intent of the parties is shed by the testimony of the respondent as follows:

"Q. When was she first hired by you? A. That is what I said, either 1937 or 1938, I can't say definitely what it was without looking it up: I couldn't give you the exact date. And she felt as though she was not getting enough money. Well, we were doing a lot of business, but the prices were very low at the time; it was in the depression and you had to bring your prices down to get business. And I told her I did not want to lose her because she

> was a very very good girl to me in that office, she was what I needed. I told her I couldn't see where I could afford to give her any more. And I did not want to lose her. So it went back and forth, back and forth. Finally I said, 'I will tell you what I will do: If we make any more money I will pay you more, if you want to go along on that agreement.' And that is where the partnership thing came in; that is how we started to be on the partnership concern at that time; that is when that was all discussed and arranged."

That statement is persuasive that the intention of the parties was to enter into an agreement that would provide a possibility of increase of compensation to Mrs. Chesire and at the same time protect Fenwick from being obliged to pay such increase unless business warranted it. The whole thing was prompted and instigated by the demand of the employee for an increase. The employer valued her services and did not wish to lose her. He wished to retain her in the exact same capacity as before but was afraid to promise a straight increase for fear it might mean loss to him. There is no suggestion that anything but the financial relation between the parties, with respect to compensation for services, was the thing they had in mind. After January 1st, 1939, the date the alleged partnership became effective, the operation of the business continued as before. Mrs. Chesire continued to serve in precisely the same capacity as before and Fenwick continued to have complete control of the management of the business. It would seem that, as far as the intention of the parties is concerned, the effect of the statements in the agreement has been met and overcome by the sworn testimony of Fenwick and by the conduct of the parties.

. . .

Another element of partnership is the right to share in profits and clearly that right existed in this case. However, not every agreement that gives the right to share in profits is, for all purposes, a partnership agreement. . . . Therefore, this point is not conclusive.

Another factor is the obligation to share in losses, and this is entirely absent in this case because the agreement provides that Mrs. Chesire is not to share in the losses.

Another is the ownership and control of the partnership property and business. Fenwick contributed all the capital and Mrs. Chesire had no right to share in capital upon dissolution. He likewise reserved to himself control.

The next is community of power in administration, and the reservation in the agreement of the exclusive control of the management of the business in Fenwick excludes this element so far as Mrs. Chesire is concerned. In Wild v. Davenport, Mr. Justice Depue, speaking for this court, said [48 N.J.L. 129, 7 A. 297]:

> "In Voorhees v. Jones [29 N.J.L. 270], the decision that a servant or agent who had a share of profits simply as compensation for services was neither a partner, nor liable for partnership debts, was placed by Chief Justice Whelpley on the ground that such a person had no control over the operation of the firm, and could not direct its investments, nor prevent the contracting of debts; in other words, had none of the

prerogatives of a principal in the management and control of the business."

. . .

Another element is the language in the agreement, and although the parties call themselves partners and the business a partnership, the language used excludes Mrs. Chesire from most of the ordinary rights of a partner.

The conduct of the parties toward third persons is also an element to be considered and the conduct of the parties here does not support a finding that they were partners. They did file partnership income tax returns and held themselves out as partners to the Unemployment Compensation Commission, and Fenwick in his New York state income tax return reported that his income came from the partnership. But to no one else did they hold themselves out as partners. They did not inform the persons they purchased materials from, although Fenwick says this was not necessary since all purchases were for cash and they neither sought nor gave credit. The right to use the trade name had apparently come to Fenwick from one Florence Meola, by lease, and the partnership was given that name by Fenwick. There is no evidence that the trade name was ever registered as that of the partnership.

Another element is the rights of the parties on dissolution and apparently in this case the result of the dissolution, as far as Mrs. Chesire is concerned, was exactly the same as if she had quit an employment. She ceased to work and ceased to receive compensation and everything reverted to the condition it was in prior to 1939, except that Fenwick carried on with a new receptionist.

Under all these circumstances, giving due effect to the written agreement and bearing in mind that the burden of establishing a partnership is upon the one who alleges it to exist, . . ., we think that the partnership has not been established, and that the agreement between these parties, in legal effect, was nothing more than one to provide a method of compensating the girl for the work she had been performing as an employee. She had no authority or control in operating the business, she was not subject to losses, she was not held out as a partner. She got nothing by the agreement but a new scale of wages.

. . .

The Uniform Partnership Act defines a partnership as an association of "two or more persons to carry on as co-owners a business for profit." N.J.S.A. 42:1–6. Essentially the element of co-ownership is lacking in this case. The agreement was one to share the profits resulting from a business owned by Fenwick. He contributed all the capital, managed the business and took over all the assets on dissolution. Ownership was conclusively shown to be in him.

The Act further provides that sharing of profits is prima facie evidence of partnership but "no such inference shall be drawn if such profits were received in payment . . . as wages of an employee," R.S. 42:1–7, N.J.S.A., and it seems that is the legal inference to be drawn from the factual situation here.

The judgment is reversed.

ANALYSIS

1. Near the end of its analysis, the court refers to Mrs. Chesire as "the girl." Fenwick, in his testimony, uses the same description. How might the attitude that may be reflected in this usage affect the decision in a case such as this?

2. What were the "deal points" (that is, the important terms of the economic relationship) between Mr. Fenwick and Mrs. Chesire?

3. Section 18 of the Uniform Partnership Act provides, "The rights and duties of the partners in relation to the partnership shall be determined, *subject to any agreement between them,* by the following rules: . . . (e) All partners have equal rights in the management and conduct of the partnership business." (Emphasis added.) A key finding of the court in the present case seems to have been that "Fenwick continued to have complete control of the management of the business." How might a lawyer draft a "partnership" agreement to make it appear that Chesire had control consistent with the UPA, without in fact depriving Fenwick of the dominant position that he would no doubt insist upon as a matter of business judgment?

4. UPA § 31 provides, in part:

> Dissolution is caused: (1) Without violation of the agreement between the partners, . . . (b) By the express will of any partner when no definite term or particular undertaking is specified.

That leaves the problem of what happens to the partnership property upon dissolution. Presumably Fenwick would want to ensure that upon dissolution he would be entitled to take back all the partnership property needed in the business. How might his lawyer provide for this outcome? UPA § 18 provides, in part, "(a) Each partner shall be repaid his contributions . . . and share equally in the profits and surplus."

5. The court states, "Another factor is the obligation to share losses, and this is entirely absent in this case. . . ." How might the agreement be drafted to weaken this argument?

6. Another possibility that Fenwick might want to consider would be to engage Chesire as an "independent contractor." How would you draft an agreement to achieve this result (without significant change in the substance of the relationship)?

B. PARTNERS COMPARED WITH LENDERS

The next case, Martin v. Peyton, is important for its discussion of legal doctrine and for what it reveals about business relationships. Beyond that, its facts can evoke thoughts about human relationships and feelings—about friendship, trust and distrust, greed, honesty and dishonesty, self-delusion, anger, fear, and so on—that form the background from which the case emerges. Imagine the tale behind this case being turned into a novel or short story by Henry James, John Cheever, or John Updike. Appreciation of the insights of such authors may be as essential to good lawyering as is mastery of legal doctrine.

In this case the question of who is a partner is important because of the rule of partnership law that makes each partner potentially liable for all of the debts of the partnership. As a consequence of this rule, the wealthy defendants in the case were in jeopardy of losing not just the amounts invested in the partnership but all, or a substantial part, of their individual fortunes.

Martin v. Peyton

246 N.Y. 213, 158 N.E. 77 (1927).

. . .

In the case before us the claim that the defendants became partners in the firm of Knauth, Nachod & Kuhne, doing business as bankers and brokers, depends upon the interpretation of certain instruments. [The plaintiff was a creditor of the firm of Knauth, Nachod & Kuhne, and claimed that the defendants (respondents here), who had made investments in the firm (described later in the opinion), were partners and, as such, liable for its debts. The defendants claimed that they were creditors, not partners.] There is nothing in their subsequent acts determinative of or indeed material upon this question. And we are relieved of questions that sometimes arise. "The plaintiff's position is not," we are told, "that the agreements of June 4, 1921, were a false expression or incomplete expression of the intention of the parties. We say that they express defendants' intention and that that intention was to create a relationship which as a matter of law constitutes a partnership." Nor may the claim of the plaintiff be rested on any question of estoppel. "The plaintiff's claim," he stipulates, "is a claim of actual partnership, not of partnership by estoppel. . . ."

Remitted then, as we are, to the documents themselves, we refer to circumstances surrounding their execution only so far as is necessary to make them intelligible. And we are to remember that although the intention of the parties to avoid liability as partners is clear; although in language precise and definite they deny any design to then join the firm of K.N. & K.; although they say their interests in profits should be construed merely as a measure of compensation for loans, not an interest in profits as such; although they provide that they shall not be liable for any losses or treated as partners, the question still remains whether in fact they agree to so associate themselves with the firm as to "carry on as co-owners a business for profit."

In the spring of 1921 the firm of K.N. & K. found itself in financial difficulties. John R. Hall was one of the partners. He was a friend of Mr. Peyton. From him he obtained the loan of almost $500,000 of Liberty bonds, which K.N. & K. might use as collateral to secure bank advances. This, however, was not sufficient. The firm and its members had engaged in unwise speculations, and it was deeply involved. Mr. Hall was also intimately acquainted with George W. Perkins, Jr., and with Edward W. Freeman. He also knew Mrs. Peyton and Mrs. Perkins and Mrs. Freeman. All were anxious to help him. He therefore, representing K.N. & K., entered into negotiations with them. While they were pending a proposition was made that Mr. Peyton, Mr. Perkins, and Mr. Freeman, or some of them, should become partners. It met a decided refusal. Finally an agreement was reached. It is expressed in three documents, executed on the same day, all a part of the one transaction. They were drawn with care and are unambiguous. We shall refer to them as "the agreement," "the indenture," and "the option."

We have no doubt as to their general purpose. The respondents [Peyton, Perkins, and Freeman] were to loan K.N. & K. $2,500,000 worth of liquid securities, which were to be returned to them on or before April 15, 1923. The firm might hypothecate them to secure loans totaling $2,000,000, using the proceeds as its business necessities required. To insure respondents against loss K.N. & K. were to turn over to them a large number of their own securities which may have been valuable, but which were of so speculative a nature that they could not be used as collateral for bank loans. In compensation for the loan the respondents were to receive 40 per cent. of the profits of the firm until the return was made, not exceeding, however, $500,000, and not less than $100,000. Merely because the transaction involved the transfer of securities and not of cash does not prevent its being a loan. . . . The respondents also were given an option to join the firm if they, or any of them, expressed a desire to do so before June 4, 1923.

Many other detailed agreements are contained in the papers. Are they such as may be properly inserted to protect the lenders? Or do they go further? Whatever their purpose, did they in truth associate the respondents with the firm so that they and it together thereafter carried on as co-owners a business for profit? The answer depends upon an analysis of these various provisions.

As representing the lenders, Mr. Peyton and Mr. Freeman are called "trustees." The loaned securities when used as collateral are not to be mingled with other securities of K.N. & K., and the trustees at all times are to be kept informed of all transactions affecting them. To them shall be paid all dividends and income accruing therefrom. They may also substitute for any of the securities loaned securities of equal value. With their consent the firm may sell any of its securities held by the respondents, the proceeds to go, however, to the trustees. In other similar ways the trustees may deal with these same securities, but the securities loaned shall always be sufficient in value to permit of their hypothecation for $2,000,000. If they rise in price, the excess may be withdrawn by the defendants. If they fall, they shall make good the deficiency.

So far, there is no hint that the transaction is not a loan of securities with a provision for compensation. Later a somewhat closer connection with the firm appears. Until the securities are returned, the directing management of the firm is to be in the hands of John R. Hall, and his life is to be insured for $1,000,000, and the policies are to be assigned as further collateral security to the trustees. These requirements are not unnatural. Hall was the one known and trusted by the defendants. Their acquaintance with the other members of the firm was of the slightest. These others had brought an old and established business to the verge of bankruptcy. As the respondents knew, they also had engaged in unsafe speculation. The respondents were about to loan $2,500,000 of good securities. As collateral they were to receive others of problematical value. What they required seems but ordinary caution. Nor does it imply an association in the business.

The trustees are to be kept advised as to the conduct of the business and consulted as to important matters. They may inspect the firm books and are entitled to any information they think important. Finally, they may veto any business they think highly speculative or injurious. Again we hold this but a proper precaution to safeguard the loan. The trustees may not initiate any transaction as a partner may do. They may not bind the firm by any action of their own. Under the circumstances the safety of the loan depended upon the business success of K.N. & K. This success was likely to be compromised by the inclination of its members to engage in speculation. No longer, if the respondents were to be protected, should it be allowed. The trustees therefore might prohibit it, and that their prohibition might be effective, information was to be furnished them. Not dissimilar agreements have been held proper to guard the interests of the lender.

As further security each member of K.N. & K. is to assign to the trustees their interest in the firm. No loan by the firm to any member is permitted and the amount each may draw is fixed. No other distribution of profits is to be made. So that realized profits may be calculated the existing capital is stated to be $700,000, and profits are to be realized as promptly as good business practice will permit. In case the trustees think this is not done, the question is left to them and to Mr. Hall, and if they differ then to an arbitrator. There is no obligation that the firm shall continue the business. It may dissolve at any time. Again we conclude there is nothing here not properly adapted to secure the interest of the respondents as lenders. If their compensation is dependent on a percentage of the profits, still provision must be made to define what these profits shall be.

The "indenture" is substantially a mortgage of the collateral delivered by K.N. & K. to the trustees to secure the performance of the "agreement." It certainly does not strengthen the claim that the respondents were partners.

Finally we have the "option." It permits the respondents, or any of them, or their assignees or nominees to enter the firm at a later date if they desire to do so by buying 50 per cent. or less of the interests therein of all or any of the members at a stated price. Or a corporation may, if the respondents and the members agree, be formed in place of the firm. Meanwhile, apparently with the design of protecting the firm business against improper or ill-judged action which might render the option valueless, each member of the firm is to place his resignation in the hands of Mr. Hall. If at any time he and the trustees agree that such resignation should be accepted, that member shall then retire, receiving the value of his interest calculated as of the date of such retirement.

This last provision is somewhat unusual, yet it is not enough in itself to show that on June 4, 1921, a present partnership was created, nor taking these various papers as a whole do we reach such a result. It is quite true that even if one or two or three like provisions contained in such a contract do not require this conclusion, yet it is also true that when taken together a point may come where stipulations immaterial separately cover so wide a field that we should hold a partnership exists. As in other branches of the law, a question of degree is often the determining factor. Here that point has not been reached. . . .

The judgment appealed from should be affirmed, with costs.

NOTES

1. According to the lower court opinion, K.N. & K. was a large, prominent firm, with substantial foreign banking operations, 300 employees, and total transactions of over $100 million a year. 219 A.D. 297, 220 N.Y.S. 29. Hall had "been indebted to Peyton in [sic] a substantial sum of money since 1913" and Peyton had helped Hall in various business matters. The reason for the loan of securities rather than cash was to avoid the usury laws. (If Peyton, Perkins, and Freeman had not had ready access to cash, presumably they could have used their securities as collateral for a bank loan of cash, which they could then have loaned to K.N. & K.) The losses that gave rise to the litigation resulting in the present decision arose from speculative investments in foreign exchange, which were prohibited by the agreement between K.N. & K. and Perkins and the other investors. Though Hall was not directly involved in making these investments, he knew about them and apparently did not tell his friends Peyton, Perkins, and Freeman.

2. There is an important economic principle relating to risk that may have been at play in the situation described in Martin v. Peyton. Crudely stated, the principle is that you should not allow other people to gamble with your money for their own profit. At the very least, the facts of the case offer a nice opportunity for describing that principle. Suppose that K.N. & K. has suffered losses and has reached a point where its assets have a value of $12 million, including $1 million in a bank account, and its liabilities are $20 million. After about two more weeks of normal operations K.N. & K. will not be able to pay its bills and its creditors will shut it down. K.N. & K. has an opportunity to invest $1 million in a foreign exchange transaction. The expectation is that if the transaction turns out as the K.N. & K. partners hope, the payoff will be $20 million, but the probability of that happening is only one in forty. If the transaction does not turn out as hoped, the entire $1 million will be lost. A one in forty chance of a return of $20 million is worth only $500,000, so the investment appears to be a bad one. But suppose it is K.N. & K.'s last chance. If the investment pays off what is the financial effect for the partners of K.N. & K.? If it does not pay off, what do they lose?

3. The risk of liability for Peyton, Perkins, and Freeman would have been avoided if K.N. & K. had been organized as a corporation. Under that form of organization, the equity investors (the counterparts of partners) enjoy "limited liability"—that is, they are not personally liable for the debts of the firm and therefore stand to lose only the amount they have invested in it. Thus, even if the purported lenders had been treated as shareholders, they would have been shielded from the personal liability that the creditors sought to enforce. (The same would be true if they had formed a limited liability company or limited liability partnership. These forms of business organization, however, were unavailable at the time this transaction occurred.)

ANALYSIS

1. What amount of loss were Peyton, Perkins, and Freeman (PPF) prepared to risk? Why were they willing to take a substantial risk? What is the moral of the story of their investment in K.N. & K.?

2. What were the various elements of return on their investment that PPF bargained for? What does their potential return tell you about the degree of risk that they believed they were accepting?

3. Given the degree of risk to which PPF were exposed, and given the fact that they did not want to be involved in running the business, what kinds of protections would you expect them to want? What protections did they in fact bargain for?

4. As stated above, K.N. & K. violated their agreement with PPF by speculating in foreign exchange and this produced the losses that led to K.N. & K.'s downfall. Why do you suppose PPF did not enforce the agreement and prevent the speculation? What was the value of the prohibition?

5. Apparently PPF relied heavily (and, as it turned out, foolishly) on their friend Hall to protect their interests. Yet the court concludes that Hall was not their agent for the purpose of exercising control over the K.N. & K. operations. Why?

6. Like A. Gay Jenson Farms Co. v. Cargill, Inc. (Chapter 1, § 1, supra), Martin v. Peyton raises the question whether a lender had become so entangled with its borrower as to become responsible for the borrower's debts to others. Although the legal theories differed (agency versus partnership), the same basic principles are at stake. The two cases, of course, reached different results. What distinguishes the relationship between PPF and K. N. & K. from that between Cargill and Warren so as to justify the differing outcomes? Or, was one of the cases incorrectly decided?

PLANNING

The court did not reach its decision in the case without difficulty. It seems fair to say that PPF had a close call with financial disaster. What changes in the agreement might have been made to strengthen their legal position (that is, their claim that they were not partners) without depriving them of important protections?

Southex Exhibitions, Inc. v. Rhode Island Builders Association, Inc.

279 F.3d 94 (1st Cir.2002).

Appellant Southex Exhibitions, Inc. ("Southex") challenges a district court bench ruling that no partnership existed between Southex and the Rhode Island Builder's Association, Inc. ("RIBA"), even though Southex's predecessors in interest had produced home shows for RIBA in Rhode Island ever since 1974. We affirm the district court judgment.

I

BACKGROUND

In 1974, with the construction of the new Providence Civic Center ("Civic Center") and the expansion in RIBA home shows, RIBA's executive director, Ross Dagata, decided to enter into an agreement with Sherman Exposition Management, Inc. ("SEM"), a Massachusetts-based professional show owner and producer, for future productions of the

RIBA home shows at the Civic Center ("the 1974 Agreement"). The preamble in the 1974 Agreement announced that "RIBA wishes to participate in such [s]hows as sponsors and *partners*. . . ." (Emphasis added.) The term of the 1974 Agreement was fixed at five years, renewable by mutual agreement.

RIBA further agreed (i) to sponsor and endorse only shows produced by SEM, (ii) to persuade RIBA members to exhibit at those shows, and (iii) to permit SEM to use RIBA's name for promotional purposes. In turn, SEM undertook, inter alia, to (i) obtain all necessary leases, licenses, permits and insurance, (ii) indemnify RIBA for show-related losses "of whatever sort," (iii) accord RIBA the right to accept or reject any exhibitor, (iv) audit show income, and (v) advance all the capital required to finance the shows. Net show profits were to be shared: 55% to SEM; 45% to RIBA.

The 1974 Agreement further provided that all show dates and admission prices, as well as the Rhode Island banking institution at which show-related business would be transacted, were to be mutually determined by the parties. In the event the Civic Center were to become unavailable for reasons beyond SEM's control, SEM was to be excused from its production duties, provided that SEM promoted no other home show in Rhode Island during the interim; and RIBA retained the right to conduct a home show at another venue, upon appropriate notification to SEM.

In contemporaneous conversations relating to the meaning of the term "partners," Manual Sherman, SEM's president, informed RIBA's Ross Dagata that he "wanted no ownership of the show," because he was uncertain about the financial prospects for home shows in the Rhode Island market. Manual Sherman advised Dagata: "[A]fter the first year, if I'm not happy, we can't produce the show properly or make any money, we'll give you back the show." Although SEM owned other home shows which it produced outside Rhode Island, Manual Sherman consistently described himself simply as the "producer" of the RIBA shows.

In 1994, following a series of assignments and contract renewals agreed to by RIBA, Southex acquired SEM'S interest under the 1974 Agreement. By 1998, Southex determined that in order to maintain its financial stake in the RIBA home shows, the 1974 Agreement either needed to be renegotiated or allowed to expire according to its terms in 1999.* RIBA in turn expressed dissatisfaction with Southex's performance, and eventually entered into a management contract with another producer, Yoffee Exposition Services, Inc.

Southex commenced suit against RIBA in federal district court, to enjoin the RIBA 2000 home show, alleging that the 1974 Agreement established a partnership between RIBA and Southex's predecessor-in-interest (i.e., SEM), and/or that by its silence RIBA had enabled the formation of a partnership-by-estoppel, and that RIBA breached its

* [Eds. [As of March 2002, the show was a five-day event at which the "buying audience [consisted of] consumers from Rhode Island and neighboring communities in Connecticut and Massachusetts . . . looking to build new homes, remodel existing homes, redecorate, landscape, purchase furnishings and appliances, finance or refinance a mortgage, etc." See www.ribahomeshow.com. It is safe to assume that the show generates a substantial profit. Southex presumably concluded that it needed to establish a partnership relationship with RIBA in order to prevent RIBA from being deemed the sole owner of show.]

fiduciary duties to its co-partner, Southex, by its wrongful dissolution of their partnership and its subsequent appointment of another producer. . . .

[T]he district . . . entered judgment for RIBA on the ground that the 1974 Agreement established no partnership under Rhode Island law. . . .

II

DISCUSSION

Under Rhode Island law, a "partnership" is "an association of two (2) or more persons to carry on as *co-owners* a business for profit. . . ." R.I. Gen. Laws. § 7–12–17 [UPA (1914) § 7] (emphasis added). The same statute further provides, inter alia, that—

> [I]n determining whether a partnership exists, these rules apply:
>
> . . .
>
> (2) Joint tenancy, tenancy in common, tenancy by the entireties, joint property, common property, or part ownership does not of itself establish a partnership, whether the co-owners do or do not share any profits made by the use of the property.
>
> . . .
>
> (4) The receipt by a person of a share of the profits of a business is prima facie evidence that he or she is a partner in the business, but no such inference is drawn if profits were received in payment:
>
> (i) As a debt by installments or otherwise;
>
> (ii) As wages of an employee or rent to a landlord;
>
> (iii) As an annuity to a widow or representative of a deceased partner;
>
> (iv) As interest on a loan, though the amount of payment vary with the profits of the business;
>
> (v) As the consideration for the sale of a good will of a business or other property by installments or otherwise. Id. § 7–12–18.

While pure legal issues, such as statutory interpretations, are reviewed de novo . . . the determination as to whether a partnership was formed turned primarily on factual findings, which we review only for clear error.

Southex insists that the 1974 Agreement contains ample indicia that a partnership was formed, including: (1) a 55–45% sharing of profits; (2) mutual control over designated business operations, such as show dates, admission prices, choice of exhibitors, and "partnership" bank accounts; and (3) the respective contributions of valuable property to the partnership by the partners. Given the highly deferential standard of appellate review, however, Southex must do more than point to supportive record evidence. Since it bears the burden of proof, it must demonstrate that the district court ruling, viewed in the light most favorable to RIBA, is not *rationally* supported by the record evidence. . . . In our view, the record evidence indicating a nonpartner relationship cannot be dismissed as insubstantial.

First, the 1974 Agreement is simply entitled "Agreement," rather than "Partnership Agreement." Second, rather than an agreement for an indefinite duration, it prescribed a fixed (albeit renewable) term. Third, rather than undertake to share operating costs with RIBA, SEM not only agreed to advance all monies required to produce the shows, but to indemnify RIBA for all show-related losses as well. State law normally presumes that partners share equally or at least proportionately in partnership losses. . . .

Similarly, although RIBA involved itself in some management decisions, SEM was responsible for the lion's share. . . . Furthermore, Southex not only entered into contracts but conducted business with third parties, in its own name, rather than in the name of the putative partnership. As a matter of fact, their mutual association was never given a name. It is noteworthy as well that Southex stipulated at trial that it never filed either a federal or state partnership tax return. . . .

Similarly, the evidence as to whether either SEM or RIBA contributed any corporate property, with the intent that it become jointly-owned partnership property is highly speculative, particularly since their mutual endeavor simply involved a periodic event, i.e., an annual home show, which neither generated, nor necessitated, ownership interests in significant tangible properties, aside from cash receipts. Unlike tangible real and personal property, whose ownership is more readily established . . ., the intangible intellectual property involved here, such as clientele lists, goodwill, and business expertise, did not so readily lend itself to evidentiary establishment. As a consequence, in the present circumstances the requisite mutual intent to convert intangible intellectual properties into partnership assets may well depend much more importantly upon a clear contractual expression of mutual intention to form a partnership.

Finally, even assuming that the 1974 Agreement, as a whole, is ambiguous, (i) Manuel Sherman testified that he regarded SEM as simply the producer of the annual RIBA shows; and (ii) Dagata testified that SEM specifically disclaimed any ownership interest in the home shows in 1974. . . .

Next, Southex asserts that the district court committed reversible error by not crediting undisputed evidence that RIBA, in 1974, expressly agreed to share business profits with SEM. Southex reasons that since the Rhode Island partnership statute makes such profit sharing prima facie evidence of partnership formation, and RIBA failed to rebut that evidentiary presumption by establishing any of the five exceptions specified in subsection 7–12–18(4), the district court was required to find, as a matter of law, that a partnership was formed. Its reasoning is flawed.

"Partnership" is a notoriously imprecise term, whose definition is especially elusive in practice. . . . Since a partnership can be created absent any written formalities whatsoever, its existence vel non normally must be assessed under a "totality-of-the-circumstances" test. . . .

Similarly, even though the UPA explicitly identifies profit sharing as a particularly probative indicium of partnership formation, and some courts have even held that the absence of profit sharing compels a finding that no partnership existed, . . . it does not necessarily follow that evidence of profit sharing compels a finding of partnership formation. . . .

Furthermore, even though the UPA specifies five instances in which profit sharing does not create a presumption of partnership formation, see R.I. Gen. Laws s 7–12–18(4)(i)–(v), supra, Southex cites (and we have found) no authority for the proposition that the evidentiary presumption created by profit sharing can be overcome only by establishing these five exceptions, rather than by competent evidence of other pertinent factors indicating the absence of an intent to form a partnership (e.g., lack of mutual control over business operations, failure to file partnership tax returns, failure to prescribe loss-sharing). Thus, the undisputed evidence of profit sharing did not compel a determination that Southex and RIBA formed a partnership. Instead, the validity of the ruling below depends upon whether the district court correctly assessed the totality of the circumstances. . . .

Southex next urges that the 1974 Agreement necessitated a finding of partnership formation, in that it unambiguously describes the contracting parties as "partners." Consequently, Southex insists, the district court erred by considering extrinsic evidence regarding the meaning of the term "partners," viz., by crediting testimony that RIBA and Southex's predecessor did not intend, in 1974, to employ the term "partners" in its strict legal sense, but merely in its colloquial sense, as a "cooperative joint effort." Further, Southex asserts that because RIBA concededly reviewed the 1974 Agreement with counsel, we must presume that the term "partners" was employed in its strict legal sense. Once again we must disagree.

First, the term "partner" frequently is defined with a view to its context. . . .

More importantly, the labels the parties assign to their intended legal relationship, while probative of partnership formation, are not necessarily dispositive as a matter of law, particularly in the presence of countervailing evidence. . . .

ANALYSIS

1. Who was entitled to the profits from the show?

2. Who bore the risk of loss?

3. Who had control? Why is it reasonable that control was allocated as it was?

4. What was the duration of the relationship?

5. What is the implication of the answer to each of the above questions as to the existence of a partnership?

6. If the relationship was not that of partnership, what was it?

7. Why does it matter whether or not SEM/Southex and RIBA were partners in the legal sense?

8. What changes in the agreement would have tipped the scales in favor of partnership? Assuming that a partnership was not intended, what could SEM/Southex have done to protect the claim that it sought to enforce in this case?

9. What could RIBA have done to reduce the risk that SEM could successfully claim that a partnership was formed?

C. PARTNERSHIP BY ESTOPPEL

Young v. Jones

816 F. Supp. 1070 (D.S.C. 1992), affirmed sub nom. Young v. Federal Deposit Insurance Corporation, 103 F.3d 1180 (4th Cir.), cert. denied, 522 U.S. 928 (1997).

. . . Plaintiffs are investors from Texas who deposited over a half-million dollars in a South Carolina bank and the funds have disappeared.

PW-Bahamas [Price Waterhouse, Chartered Accountants, a Bahamian partnership] issued an unqualified audit letter regarding the financial statement of Swiss American Fidelity and Insurance Guaranty (SAFIG). Plaintiffs aver that on the basis of that financial statement, they deposited $550,000.00 in a South Carolina bank. Other defendants, not involved in the motions herein, allegedly sent the money from the South Carolina Bank to SAFIG. The financial statement of SAFIG was falsified. The plaintiffs' money and its investment potential has been lost to the plaintiffs and it is for these losses that the plaintiffs seek to recover damages.

. . .

The letterhead [used for the SAFIG audit] identified the Bahamian accounting firm only as "Price Waterhouse." The audit letter also bore a Price Waterhouse trademark and was signed "Price Waterhouse."*

Plaintiffs assert that it was foreseeable to the accounting firm that issued the letter that third-parties would rely upon the financial statement, the subject of the audit letter. According to the plaintiffs, the stamp of approval created by Price Waterhouse's audit letter of SAFIG's financial statement lent credence to the defrauders' claims so that plaintiffs were induced to invest to their detriment.

. . .

Plaintiffs assert that PW-Bahamas and PW-US [the Price Waterhouse partnership in the United States] operate as a partnership, i.e., constitute an association of persons to carry on, as owners, business for profit. In the alternative, plaintiffs contend that if the two associations are not actually operating as partners they are operating as partners by estoppel.

---

* [Eds.—On appeal, the Fourth Circuit further explained: "PW-Bahamas is part of a world-wide organization of separate and independent Price Waterhouse firms that practice accountancy in various countries. The members of each Price Waterhouse firm hold shares in Price Waterhouse World Firm Limited (PW-World Firm), a limited liability company incorporated under the laws of Bermuda. PW-World Firm assists the various Price Waterhouse firms in advancing their respective practices, and it facilitates the maintenance of uniform standards of practice. It does not conduct or supervise client engagements, however. Nor does it play a part in the day-to-day management of the Price Waterhouse firms.

PW-World Firm's bylaws designate twenty-six separate "member firms" in the Price Waterhouse organization. Those member firms include PW-US and Price Waterhouse North Caribbean (PW-North Caribbean), a Cayman Islands partnership authorized to use the Price Waterhouse name pursuant to an agreement with PW-World Firm. PW-North Caribbean sub-licenses PW-Bahamas to use the Price Waterhouse name." Young v. F.D.I.C., 103 F.3d 1180, 1191 n.6 (4th Cir. 1997) (affirming decision in text).]

Defendants PW-US and PW-Bahamas flatly deny that a partnership exists between the two entities and have supplied, under seal, copies of relevant documents executed which establish that the two entities are separately organized. Counsel for plaintiffs admits that he has found nothing which establishes that the two entities are partners in fact. The evidence presented wholly belies plaintiffs' claims that PW-Bahamas and PW-US are operating as a partnership in fact. Thus, the court finds that there is no partnership, in fact, between PW-Bahamas and PW-US.

. . . [T]he argument for estoppel seems to be that if the two partnerships are partners by estoppel then PW-US can be held liable for the negligent acts of its partner PW-Bahamas, so the claim against PW-Bahamas operates as a claim against PW-US. . . .

As a general rule, persons who are not partners as to each other are not partners as to third persons. S.C.Code Ann. § 33–41–220 (Law. Co-op 1976) [U.P.A. § 7(1)]. However, a person who represents himself, or permits another to represent him, to anyone as a partner in an existing partnership or with others not actual partners, is liable to any such person to whom such a representation is made who has, on the faith of the representation, given credit to the actual or apparent partnership. S.C.Code Ann. § 33–41–380(1) [U.P.A. § 16(1)]. . . .

Generally, partners are jointly and severally liable for everything chargeable to the partnership. . . . In South Carolina, a partnership is an entity separate and distinct from the individual partners who compose it. . . . Therefore, plaintiffs' argument is that if the court would find that PW-Bahamas and PW-US are partners by estoppel, PW-US would be jointly and severally liable with PW-Bahamas for everything chargeable to the partnership of the two firms. Moreover, if the two partnerships are partners by estoppel, the individual partners of PW-US would then be jointly and severally liable for the negligent acts of the PW-Bahamas partnership.

Plaintiffs maintain that Price Waterhouse holds itself out to be a partnership with offices around the world. According to the plaintiffs, the U.S. affiliate makes no distinction in its advertising between itself and entities situated in foreign jurisdictions. The foreign affiliates are permitted to use the Price Waterhouse name and trademark. Plaintiffs urge the conclusion of partnership by estoppel from the combination of facts that Price Waterhouse promotes its image as an organization affiliated with other Price Waterhouse offices around the world and that it is common knowledge that the accounting firm of Price Waterhouse operates as a partnership.

Plaintiffs offer for illustration that PW-Bahamas and PW-US hold themselves out to be partners with one another, a Price Waterhouse brochure, picked up by plaintiffs' counsel at a litigation services seminar, that describes Price Waterhouse as one of the "world's largest and most respected professional organizations." The brochure states: "[O]ver 28,000 Price Waterhouse professionals in 400 offices throughout the world can be called upon to provide support for your reorganization and litigation efforts." Plaintiffs assert that assurances like that contained in the brochure cast Price Waterhouse as an established international accounting firm and that the image, promoted by PW-US, is designed to gain public confidence in the firm's stability and expertise.

However, the plaintiffs do not contend that the brochure submitted was seen or relied on by them in making the decision to invest. In addition, plaintiffs point to nothing in the brochure that asserts that the affiliated entities of Price Waterhouse are liable for the acts of another, or that any of the affiliates operate within a single partnership.

PW-US points out that the South Carolina statute, which was cited by plaintiffs in support of their argument for partnership by estoppel, speaks only to the creation of liability to third-persons who, in reliance upon representations as to the existence of a partnership, "[give] credit" to that partnership. . . . There is no evidence, neither has there been an allegation, that credit was extended on the basis of any representation of a partnership existing between PW-Bahamas and the South Carolina members of the PW-US partnership. There is no evidence of any extension of credit to either PW-Bahamas or PW-US, by plaintiffs. Thus, the facts do not support a finding of liability for partners by estoppel under the statutory law of South Carolina.

Further, there is no evidence that plaintiffs relied on any act or statement by any PW-US partner which indicated the existence of a partnership with the Bahamian partnership. Finally, there is no evidence, nor is there a single allegation that any member of the U.S. partnership had anything to do with the audit letter complained of by plaintiffs, or any other act related to the investment transaction.

The court cannot find any evidence to support a finding of partners by estoppel. Therefore, the allegations of negligence against PW-Bahamas cannot serve to hold individual members of the PW-US partnership in the suit. . . .

ANALYSIS

1. Price Waterhouse was, and long had been, a leading accounting firm in the United States. Its name would have been recognized by anyone with any knowledge of business or finance. How did the Bahamian firm become entitled to use the same name? Why would it want to use the name? Should the answers to these questions be relevant to the outcome of the case?

2. What is the difference in proof required for the two separate theories on which the plaintiff relied?

3. Might the plaintiff also have relied on an agency theory?

2. THE FIDUCIARY OBLIGATIONS OF PARTNERS

A. INTRODUCTION

Meinhard v. Salmon

249 N.Y. 458, 164 N.E. 545 (1928).

■ CARDOZO, CH.J. On April 10, 1902, Louisa M. Gerry leased to the defendant Walter J. Salmon the premises known as the Hotel Bristol at the northwest corner of Forty-second street and Fifth avenue in the city of New York. The lease was for a term of twenty years, commencing May 1, 1902, and ending April 30, 1922. The lessee undertook to change the hotel building for use as shops and offices at a cost of $200,000. Alterations and additions were to be accretions to the land.

Salmon, while in course of treaty with the lessor as to the execution of the lease, was in course of treaty with Meinhard, the plaintiff, for the necessary funds. The result was a joint venture with terms embodied in a writing. Meinhard was to pay to Salmon half of the moneys requisite to reconstruct, alter, manage and operate the property. Salmon was to pay to Meinhard 40 per cent of the net profits for the first five years of the lease and 50 per cent for the years thereafter. If there were losses, each party was to bear them equally. Salmon, however, was to have sole power to "manage, lease, underlet and operate" the building. There were to be certain pre-emptive rights for each in the contingency of death.

The two were coadventurers, subject to fiduciary duties akin to those of partners. . . . As to this we are all agreed. The heavier weight of duty rested, however, upon Salmon. He was a coadventurer with Meinhard, but he was manager as well. During the early years of the enterprise, the building, reconstructed, was operated at a loss. If the relation had then ended, Meinhard as well as Salmon would have carried a heavy burden. Later the profits became large with the result that for each of the investors there came a rich return. For each, the venture had its phases of fair weather and of foul. The two were in it jointly, for better or for worse.

When the lease was near its end, Elbridge T. Gerry had become the owner of the reversion. He owned much other property in the neighborhood, one lot adjoining the Bristol Building on Fifth avenue and four lots on Forty-second street. He had a plan to lease the entire tract for a long term to someone who would destroy the buildings then existing, and put up another in their place. In the latter part of 1921, he submitted such a project to several capitalists and dealers. He was unable to carry it through with any of them. Then, in January, 1922, with less than four months of the lease to run, he approached the defendant Salmon. The result was a new lease to the Midpoint Realty Company, which is owned and controlled by Salmon, a lease covering the whole tract, and involving a huge outlay. The term is to be twenty years, but successive covenants for renewal will extend it to a maximum of eighty years at the will of either party. The existing buildings may remain unchanged for seven years. They are then to be torn down, and a new building to cost $3,000,000 is to be placed upon the site. The rental, which under the Bristol lease was only $55,000, is to be from $350,000 to $475,000 for the properties so combined. Salmon personally guaranteed the performance by the lessee of the covenants of the new lease until such time as the new building had been completed and fully paid for.

The lease between Gerry and the Midpoint Realty Company was signed and delivered on January 25, 1922. Salmon had not told Meinhard anything about it. Whatever his motive may have been, he had kept the negotiations to himself. Meinhard was not informed even of the bare existence of a project. The first that he knew of it was in February when the lease was an accomplished fact. He then made demand on the defendants that the lease be held in trust as an asset of the venture, making offer upon the trial to share the personal obligations incidental to the guaranty. The demand was followed by refusal, and later by this suit. A referee gave judgment for the plaintiff, limiting the plaintiff's interest in the lease, however, to 25 per cent. The limitation was on the theory that the plaintiff's equity was to be restricted to one-half of so much of the value of the lease as was contributed or represented by the occupation of the Bristol site. Upon cross-appeals to the Appellate Division, the judgment was modified so as to enlarge the equitable interest to one-half of the whole lease. With this enlargement of plaintiff's interest, there went, of course, a corresponding enlargement of his attendant obligations. The case is now here on an appeal by the defendants.

Joint adventurers, like copartners, owe to one another, while the enterprise continues, the duty of the finest loyalty. Many forms of conduct permissible in a workaday world for those acting at arm's length, are forbidden to those bound by fiduciary ties. A trustee is held to something stricter than the morals of the market place. Not honesty alone, but the punctilio of an honor the most sensitive, is then the standard of behavior. As to this there has developed a tradition that is unbending and inveterate. Uncompromising rigidity has been the attitude of courts of equity when petitioned to undermine the rule of undivided loyalty by the "disintegrating erosion" of particular exceptions (Wendt v. Fischer, 243 N.Y. 439, 444). Only thus has the level of conduct for fiduciaries been kept at a level higher than that trodden by the crowd. It will not consciously be lowered by any judgment of this court.

The owner of the reversion, Mr. Gerry, had vainly striven to find a tenant who would favor his ambitious scheme of demolition and construction. Baffled in the search, he turned to the defendant Salmon in possession of the Bristol, the keystone of the project. He figured to himself beyond a doubt that the man in possession would prove a likely customer. To the eye of an observer, Salmon held the lease as owner in his own right, for himself and no one else. In fact he held it as a fiduciary, for himself and another, sharers in a common venture. If this fact had been proclaimed, if the lease by its terms had run in favor of a partnership, Mr. Gerry, we may fairly assume, would have laid before the partners, and not merely before one of them, his plan of reconstruction. The pre-emptive privilege, or, better, the pre-emptive opportunity, that was thus an incident of the enterprise, Salmon appropriated to himself in secrecy and silence. He might have warned Meinhard that the plan had been submitted, and that either would be free to compete for the award. If he had done this, we do not need to say whether he would have been under a duty, if successful in the competition, to hold the lease so acquired for the benefit of a venture then about to end, and thus prolong by indirection its responsibilities and duties. The trouble about his conduct is that he excluded his coadventurer from any chance to compete, from any chance to enjoy the opportunity for benefit that had come to him alone by virtue of his agency. This chance, if nothing more, he was under a duty to concede. The price of its denial is an extension of the trust at the option and for the benefit of the one whom he excluded.

No answer is it to say that the chance would have been of little value even if seasonably offered. Such a calculus of probabilities is beyond the science of the chancery. Salmon, the real estate operator, might have been preferred to Meinhard, the woolen merchant. On the other hand, Meinhard might have offered better terms, or reinforced his offer by alliance with the wealth of others. Perhaps he might even have persuaded the lessor to renew the Bristol lease alone, postponing for a time, in return for higher rentals, the improvement of adjoining lots. We know that even under the lease as made the time for the enlargement of the building was delayed for seven years. All these opportunities were cut away from him through another's intervention. He knew that Salmon was the manager. As the time drew near for the expiration of the lease, he would naturally assume from silence, if from nothing else, that the lessor was willing to extend it for a term of years, or at least to let it stand as a lease from year to year. Not impossibly the lessor would have done so, whatever his protestations of unwillingness, if Salmon had not given assent to a project more attractive. At all events, notice of termination, even if not necessary, might seem, not unreasonably, to be something to be looked for, if the business was over and another tenant was to enter. In the absence of such notice, the matter of an extension was one that would naturally be attended to by the manager of the enterprise, and not neglected altogether. At least, there was nothing in the situation to give warning to anyone that while the lease was still in being, there had come to the manager an offer of extension which he had locked within his breast to be utilized by himself alone. The very fact that Salmon was in control with exclusive powers of direction charged him the more obviously with the duty of disclosure, since only through disclosure could opportunity be equalized. If he might cut off renewal by a purchase for his own benefit when four months were to pass before the lease would have an end, he might do so with equal right while there remained as many years. . . . He might steal a march on his comrade under cover of the darkness, and then hold the captured ground. Loyalty and comradeship are not so easily abjured.

. . .

We have no thought to hold that Salmon was guilty of a conscious purpose to defraud. Very likely he assumed in all good faith that with the approaching end of the venture he might ignore his coadventurer and take the extension for himself. He had given to the enterprise time and labor as well as money. He had made it a success. Meinhard, who had given money, but neither time nor labor, had already been richly paid. There might seem to be something grasping in his insistence upon more. Such recriminations are not unusual when coadventurers fall out. They are not without their force if conduct is to be judged by the common standards of competitors. That is not to say that they have pertinency here. Salmon had put himself in a position in which thought of self was to be renounced, however hard the abnegation. He was much more than a coadventurer. He was a managing coadventurer. . . . For him and for those like him, the rule of undivided loyalty is relentless and supreme. . . . A different question would be here if there were lacking any nexus of relation between the business conducted by the manager and the opportunity brought to him as an incident of management. . . . For this problem, as for most, there are distinctions of degree. If Salmon had received from Gerry a proposition to lease a building at a location far removed, he might have held for himself the privilege thus acquired, or so we shall assume. Here the subject-matter of the new lease was an extension and enlargement of the subject-matter of the old one. A managing coadventurer appropriating the benefit of such a lease without warning to his partner might fairly expect to be reproached with conduct that was underhand, or lacking, to say the least, in reasonable candor, if the partner were to surprise him in the act of signing the new instrument. Conduct subject to that reproach does not receive from equity a healing benediction.

A question remains as to the form and extent of the equitable interest to be allotted to the plaintiff. The trust as declared has been held to attach to the lease which was in the name of the defendant corporation. We think it ought to attach at the option of the defendant Salmon to the shares of stock which were owned by him or were under his control. The difference may be important if the lessee shall wish to execute an assignment of the lease, as it ought to be free to do with the consent of the lessor. On the other hand, an equal division of the shares might lead to other hardships. It might take away from Salmon the power of control and management which under the plan of the joint venture he was to have from first to last. The number of shares to be allotted to the plaintiff should, therefore, be reduced to such an extent as may be necessary to preserve to the defendant Salmon the expected measure of dominion. To that end an extra share should be added to his half.

Subject to this adjustment, we agree with the Appellate Division that the plaintiff's equitable interest is to be measured by the value of half of the entire lease, and not merely by half of some undivided part. A single building covers the whole area. Physical division is impracticable along the lines of the Bristol site, the keystone of the whole. Division of interests and burdens is equally impracticable. Salmon, as tenant under the new lease, or as guarantor of the performance of the tenant's obligations, might well protest if Meinhard, claiming an equitable interest, had offered to assume a liability not equal to Salmon's, but only half as great. He might justly insist that the lease must be accepted by his coadventurer in such form as it had been given, and not constructively divided into imaginary fragments. What must be yielded to the one may be demanded by the other. The lease as it has been executed is single and entire. If confusion has resulted from the union of adjoining parcels, the trustee who consented to the union must bear the inconvenience. . . .

The judgment should be modified by providing that at the option of the defendant Salmon there may be substituted for a trust attaching to the lease a trust attaching to the shares of stock, with the result that one-half of such shares together with one additional share will in that event be allotted to the defendant Salmon and the other shares to the plaintiff, and as so modified the judgment should be affirmed with costs.

■ ANDREWS, J. (dissenting). . . .

Were this a general partnership between Mr. Salmon and Mr. Meinhard I should have little doubt as to the correctness of this result assuming the new lease to be an offshoot of the old. Such a situation involves questions of trust and confidence to a high degree; it involves questions of good will; many other considerations. As has been said, rarely if ever may one partner without the knowledge of the other acquire for himself the renewal of a lease held by the firm, even if the new lease is to begin after the firm is dissolved. Warning of such an intent, if he is managing partner, may not be sufficient to prevent the application of this rule.

We have here a different situation governed by less drastic principles. I assume that where parties engage in a joint enterprise each owes to the other the duty of the utmost good faith in all that relates to their common venture. Within its scope they stand in a fiduciary relationship. . . .

What then was the scope of the adventure into which the two men entered? . . .

It seems to me that the venture . . . had in view a limited object and was to end at a limited time. There was no intent to expand it into a far greater undertaking lasting for many years. The design was to exploit a particular lease. Doubtless in it Mr. Meinhard had an equitable interest, but in it alone. This interest terminated when the joint adventure terminated. There was no intent that for the benefit of both any advantage should be taken of the chance of renewal—that the adventure should be continued beyond that date. Mr. Salmon has done all he promised to do in return for Mr. Meinhard's undertaking when he distributed profits up to May 1, 1922. Suppose this lease, non-assignable without the consent of the lessor, had contained a renewal option. Could Mr. Meinhard have exercised it? Could he have insisted that Mr. Salmon do so? Had Mr. Salmon done so could he insist that the agreement to share losses still existed or could Mr. Meinhard have claimed that the joint adventure was still to continue for twenty or eighty years? I do not think so. The adventure by its express terms ended on May 1, 1922. The contract by its language and by its whole import excluded the idea that the tenant's expectancy was to subsist for the benefit of the plaintiff. On that date whatever there was left of value in the lease reverted to Mr. Salmon, as it would had the lease been for thirty years instead of twenty. Any equity which Mr. Meinhard possessed was in the particular lease itself, not in any possibility of renewal. There was nothing unfair in Mr. Salmon's conduct.

. . .

The judgment of the courts below should be reversed and a new trial ordered, with costs in all courts to abide the event.

■ POUND, CRANE and LEHMAN, JJ., concur with CARDOZO, CH. J., for modification of the judgment appealed from and affirmance as modified; ANDREWS, J., dissents in opinion in which KELLOGG and O'BRIEN, JJ., concur.

ANALYSIS

1. What was the agreement between Meinhard and Salmon? In particular, what was the agreement as to the duration of the relationship?

2. Did the court conclude that Salmon was obligated to share the new deal with Meinhard or only the opportunity or information? Why?

3. What if Salmon had read in the newspaper about Gerry's interest in developing his property and had approached Gerry with a proposal to participate in the development? Would he have had any obligation to notify Meinhard or let him in on the deal?

PLANNING AND POLICY

1. Suppose you had represented Salmon at the outset of the initial investment transaction in 1902. What kind of provision would you have proposed to include in an agreement with Meinhard to cover the issue that arose in the case?

2. If you had represented Meinhard what kind of provision would you have proposed?

3. If you gave different answers to the preceding two questions, and if Meinhard and Salmon had been called upon to select one, which do you suppose they would have selected?

4. What does your answer to the preceding question tell you about what the legal rule should be in the absence of any discernible agreement?

5. The Revised Uniform Partnership Act (1994) includes the following:

§ 404. General Standards of Partner's Conduct

(a) The only fiduciary duties a partner owes to the partnership and the other partners are the duty of loyalty and the duty of care set forth in subsections (b) and (c).

(b) A partner's duty of loyalty to the partnership and the other partners is limited to the following:

(1) to account to the partnership and hold as trustee for it any property, profit, or benefit derived by the partner in the conduct and winding up of the partnership business or derived from a use by the partner of partnership property, including the appropriation of a partnership opportunity;

(2) to refrain from dealing with the partnership in the conduct or winding up of the partnership business as or on behalf of a party having an interest adverse to the partnership; and

(3) to refrain from competing with the partnership in the conduct of the partnership business before the dissolution of the partnership.

(c) A partner's duty of care to the partnership and the other partners in the conducting and winding up of the partnership business is limited to refraining from engaging in grossly negligent or reckless conduct, intentional misconduct, or a knowing violation of the law.

(d) A partner shall discharge the duties to the partnership and the other partners under this [Act] or under the partnership agreement and exercise any rights consistently with the obligation of good faith and fair dealing.

(e) A partner does not violate a duty or obligation under this [Act] or under the partnership agreement merely because the partner's conduct furthers the partner's own interest.

(f) A partner may lend money to and transact other business with the partnership, and as to each loan or transaction, the rights and obligations of the partners are the same as those of a person who is not a partner, subject to other applicable law.

. . .

a. How, if at all, would the outcome of Meinhard v. Salmon have been affected if the above provision had been the law?

b. What do you suppose Judge Cardozo would have thought about § 404(b)? What do you think?

Sandvick v. LaCrosse

747 N.W.2d 519 (N.D. 2008).

I

In May 1996, Sandvick, Bragg, LaCrosse, and Haughton purchased three oil and gas leases in Golden Valley County, North Dakota. The leases were known as the Horn leases. The Horn leases were standard, paid-up leases with terms of five years and did not contain any provision for extending or renewing them. Empire Oil Company, owned by LaCrosse, held record title to the leases. The leases were purchased from the parties' credits in the Empire Oil Company JV checking account. Sandvick testified the parties' initial intent was to try to sell the leases during the five-year term.

Aside from the Horn leases, the parties had previously owned other oil and gas leases together. Haughton had owned other leases with Sandvick, and LaCrosse was also involved in some of these other leases. Some of the leases were purchased before the Horn leases, and some were purchased after.

In November 2000, Haughton and LaCrosse purchased three oil and gas leases on the Horn property. These leases were referred to as the "Horn Top Leases" and were set to begin at the expiration of the initial Horn Leases. The term "top lease" is defined in Howard R. Williams & Charles J. Meyers, Manual of Oil and Gas Terms 1285 (8th ed.1991), as a "lease granted by a landowner during the existence of a recorded mineral lease which is to become effective if and when the existing lease expires or is terminated." The top leases covered the same acreage as the Horn Leases and had a five-year term, with the title in the name of Empire Oil Company. The top leases were not recorded until December 2001. Prior to purchasing the top leases, LaCrosse and Haughton twice offered to purchase Sandvick's and Bragg's interests in the Horn leases, but Sandvick and Bragg refused. Haughton testified he did not inform either Sandvick or Bragg that he and LaCrosse had purchased the top leases.

In 2004, Sandvick and Bragg sued LaCrosse and Haughton, claiming they breached their fiduciary duties by not offering Sandvick and Bragg an opportunity to purchase the top leases with them. The trial was limited to the issues regarding the existence, life span, and scope of a partnership or joint venture. Following the bench trial, the district court concluded no partnership or joint venture existed.

. . .

II

On appeal, Sandvick and Bragg argue the district court erred in concluding the parties were not partners. In North Dakota, a partnership is "an association of two or more persons to carry on as co-owners a business for profit." [UPA (1997) § 101(6)]. The crucial elements of a partnership are (1) an intention to be partners, (2) co-ownership of the business, and (3) a profit motive. . . .

The district court concluded a partnership did not exist between the parties. In its memorandum opinion following trial, it found the parties were not co-owners of a business. It found the parties' undertaking was very limited and did not coincide with the definition of a business. It found that the parties entered into the leases for a set period of time and that their activity, rather than being a series of acts, was limited to that occurrence.

Under comment 1 to § 202 of the Revised Uniform Partnership Act, a "business" is defined as "a series of acts directed toward an end," and under [UPA (1997) § 101(1)], "includes every trade, occupation, and profession." . . .

In this case, the parties entered into the Horn leases for a specific period. The court found their intention was to try to sell the leases. . . . We conclude the purchase of the Horn leases was a separate act undertaken by the parties, not a series of acts. On the basis of the evidence in the record and the testimony at trial, we conclude the district court did not err in concluding a partnership did not exist.

III

Sandvick and Bragg argue the district court erred in concluding a joint venture did not exist. A joint venture is similar to a partnership but is more limited in scope and duration, and principles of partnership law apply to the joint venture relationship. SPW Associates, LLP v. Anderson, 2006 ND 159, ¶ 8, 718 N.W.2d 580. "For a business enterprise to constitute a joint venture, the following four elements must be present: (1) contribution by the parties of money, property, time, or skill in some common undertaking, but the contributions need not be equal or of the same nature; (2) a proprietary interest and right of mutual control over the engaged property; (3) an express or implied agreement for the sharing of profits, and usually, but not necessarily, of losses; and (4) an express or implied contract showing a joint venture was formed." Id. at ¶ 10 (citations omitted). . . .

The district court concluded the parties were not members of a joint venture when they acquired the Horn leases. It made the following findings of fact, which supported its conclusion:

7. Bragg never talked to Haughton about the investment in the Horn Leases and had no agreement with Haughton concerning the purchase of additional leases, the purchase of Horn minerals, or the purchase of leases on minerals adjacent to the Horn property. Sandvick had no written or oral agreement with either Haughton or Lacrosse concerning the acquisition of a new lease following the expiration of the Horn Leases.

8. At the time of the acquisition of the Horn Leases, Bragg had no agreement with Lacrosse concerning the development of those leases.

Lacrosse never agreed to make Sandvick and Bragg a part of any subsequent lease of the Horn minerals. If Bragg had any expectations concerning the development of the Horn Leases, they were not communicated to Haughton.

. . .

10. No agreement was entered into, express or implied, limiting the parties' abilities to continue activity which did not include the other parties to these proceedings.

11. None of the parties intended to be exclusively involved in this undertaking, and they knew that the other parties would continue to do business which would not include them.

. . .

13. Under the circumstances, the parties had no expectations that the other parties would refrain from investing in the area without offering to the other parties an opportunity to join in the investment.

The court, however, also made findings that reflected a joint venture; specifically, the court found: (1) LaCrosse opened a checking account under the name Empire Oil JV Account; (2) the leases were purchased from the parties' credits in the Empire Oil Company JV account in equal shares; (3) title to the leases was held in Empire Oil Company's name; and (4) the parties' intent in acquiring the leases was to sell them. At trial, Bragg, LaCrosse, and Haughton testified that any profits would have been shared had the Horn leases been sold. This testimony, along with the court's findings above, demonstrates the existence of a joint venture. We conclude a joint venture did exist in regard to the parties' purchase of the Horn leases, because the leases were purchased out of the parties' checking account funds in equal shares, they were titled in Empire Oil's name rather than each of the parties' names, and profits were going to be shared if the leases were sold.

IV

Having concluded a joint venture exists, we look to the scope of the venture and decide whether any fiduciary duties were breached by LaCrosse and Haughton. "The existence and scope of a fiduciary duty depends upon the language of the parties' agreement." Grynberg v. Dome Petroleum Corp., 1999 ND 167, ¶ 21, 599 N.W.2d 261. "[P]rinciples of partnership law apply to the joint venture relationship." Anderson, 2006 ND 159, ¶ 8, 718 N.W.2d 580.

Under [UPA (1997) § 404(a)], a partner owes duties of loyalty and care to the other partners. The duty of loyalty is set forth in [UPA (1997) § 404(b):

> a. To account to the partnership and hold as trustee for it any property, profit, or benefit derived by the partner in the conduct and winding up of the partnership business or derived from a use by the partner of partnership property, including the appropriation of a partnership opportunity;
>
> b. To refrain from dealing with the partnership in the conduct or winding up of the partnership business as or on behalf of a party having an interest adverse to the partnership; and

c. To refrain from competing with the partnership in the conduct of the partnership business before the dissolution of the partnership.

"Joint adventurers, like copartners, owe to one another, while the enterprise continues, the duty of the finest loyalty." Svihl v. Gress, 216 N.W.2d 110, 115 (N.D.1974) (quoting Meinhard v. Salmon, 249 N.Y. 458, 164 N.E. 545, 546 (1928));. . . .

In this case, the scope of the venture was to purchase and then attempt to sell the Horn leases. Approximately six months prior to the expiration of the leases, LaCrosse and Haughton purchased oil and gas leases, known as top leases, that were set to begin upon the expiration of the Horn leases. The top leases were nearly identical in all respects to the original Horn leases. The top leases had the same duration and acreage and were titled in Empire Oil Company's name. An important difference, however, between the original leases and the top leases was that Sandvick and Bragg were not informed of the acquisition of the top leases.

Although the original Horn leases did not contain an extension or renewal provision, the top leases purchased by LaCrosse and Haughton were effectively extensions of the original Horn leases. . . .

LaCrosse and Haughton created a conflict of interest by purchasing the top leases prior to the expiration of the original leases without notifying Sandvick and Bragg. It was in LaCrosse's and Haughton's best interest not to sell the original leases during the remaining six months of the original term. Having excluded Sandvick and Bragg, LaCrosse and Haughton potentially stood to benefit more by waiting to sell the leases until after the original term expired. We conclude LaCrosse and Haughton breached their fiduciary duties of loyalty by taking advantage of a joint venture opportunity when they purchased the top leases without informing Bragg and Sandvick. See Meinhard v. Salmon, 249 N.Y. 458, 164 N.E. 545, 548 (1928) (holding a co-venturer breached his duty of loyalty when he extended the lease on commercial property and excluded his co-venturer from the opportunity). Bragg and Sandvick should have had an opportunity to purchase the top leases with LaCrosse and Haughton. . . .

■ CROTHERS, JUSTICE, concurring in part and dissenting in part.

I concur with Part II of the Majority Opinion affirming the district court's findings and conclusion that the parties were not partners. I respectfully dissent from Parts III and IV where the Majority overlooks the district court's findings of fact and, therefore, overtakes the district court's fact-finding role.

. . .

Even accepting that the present facts require the conclusion that a joint venture was created, the Majority's ultimate decision that liability attaches to the "top leasing" activity is unpersuasive. Rather, North Dakota law allows partners (and therefore joint venturers) to limit the scope of their duty of loyalty to the remaining partners. [UPA (1997) § 103(b)(3)]. This public policy is consistent with other jurisdictions examining the question in the context of mineral development. . . . This also means that, under North Dakota law, the parties could have limited their duty of loyalty. Nevertheless, the Majority presumes without question that the full duty of loyalty existed, and that it formed a basis for liability in this case.

There was no written contract in this case. The parameters of the transaction were unclear. A full trial occurred, with many witnesses testifying about their understanding of the business arrangement. From this, the district court made specific findings regarding the nature of the parties' enterprise, and the scope of their duties to each other [Eds. Here this dissenting opinion quotes the same findings as those in the majority opinion plus the following two findings]:

9. The parties were all involved in other oil and gas related undertakings with various other parties, including, in some instances, the parties that are involved in these proceedings. These undertakings were separate and apart from the Horn Leases.

12. Haughton was interested in the area surrounding the Horn Leases and had various leasehold and mineral interests in the area dating from 1991. Sandvick, Bragg, and LaCrosse were aware of these facts and had reason to believe that he would continue to invest in the area.

Rather than ignoring the district court's findings, our standard of review requires that we respect the trier of fact's ability to see the witnesses, hear the testimony, and determine the scope of the obligations at issue in this case. I therefore would affirm the district court's judgment.

ANALYSIS

1. What is the difference between a partnership and a joint venture?

2. The court asks, first, was there a joint venture, and, then, what was its scope? Are the two questions so clearly separate?

3. According to the majority, what was the "business" of the joint venture?

4. The court invokes Meinhard v. Salmon. Is the argument for the plaintiff that a joint venture existed in that case stronger or weaker than the argument for the plaintiffs in this case?

5. Just what was the obligation of the defendants? What did the Supreme Court think they did wrong?

6. The investors' checking account was entitled "Empire Oil Company JV." According to the appellants' brief, citing the trial transcript, the parties referred to themselves as "partners" in the venture. What is the relevance of these labels?

7. During the term of the leases, Haughton investigated prospects in locations adjacent to the Horn leases and actually acquired leases in those locations. In doing so, did he violate his fiduciary obligations to his co-investors in the Horn leases?

B. GRABBING AND LEAVING

Meehan v. Shaughnessy

404 Mass. 419, 535 N.E.2d 1255 (1989).

The plaintiffs, James F. Meehan (Meehan) and Leo V. Boyle (Boyle), were partners of the law firm, Parker, Coulter, Daley & White (Parker Coulter). After Meehan and Boyle terminated their relationship with Parker Coulter to start their own firm, they commenced this action both to recover amounts they claim the defendants, their former partners, owed them under the partnership agreement, and to obtain a declaration as to amounts they owed the defendants for work done at Parker Coulter on cases they removed to their new firm. The defendants (hereinafter collectively Parker Coulter) counterclaimed that Meehan and Boyle violated their fiduciary duties, breached the partnership agreement, and tortiously interfered with their advantageous business and contractual relationships. As grounds for these claims, Parker Coulter asserted that Meehan and Boyle engaged in improper conduct in withdrawing cases and clients from the firm, and in inducing employees to join the new firm of Meehan, Boyle & Cohen, P.C. (MBC). Parker Coulter also filed a third-party action with similar claims against MBC and against Cynthia J. Cohen (Cohen), a former junior partner, and Steven H. Schafer (Schafer), a former associate, who, among others, left the firm to join MBC.

After a jury-waived trial, a Superior Court judge rejected all of Parker Coulter's claims for relief, and found that Meehan and Boyle were entitled to recover amounts owed to them under the partnership agreement. The judge also found, based on the partnership agreement and a quantum meruit theory, that Parker Coulter was entitled to recover from Meehan and Boyle for time billed and expenses incurred on the cases Meehan and Boyle removed to their own firm. Parker Coulter appealed from the judgment, and we granted direct appellate review.

Although we are in agreement with most of the judge's reasoning and conclusions which he reached after lengthy and painstaking proceedings, we nevertheless reverse the judgment entered below and remand for further findings and a hearing, consistent in all respects with this opinion. This result follows from our conclusion, *infra*, that the judge erred in deciding that Meehan and Boyle acted properly in acquiring consent to remove cases to MBC.[5]

We summarize the facts as found by the judge. . . . Parker, Coulter, Daley & White is a large partnership which specializes in litigation on behalf of both defendants and plaintiffs. Meehan joined the firm in 1959, and became a partner in 1963; his practice focuses primarily on complex tort litigation, such as product liability and aviation defense work. Boyle joined Parker Coulter in 1971, and became a partner in 1980; he has concentrated on plaintiffs' work. Both have developed outstanding

---

[5] We repeatedly, later in this opinion, refer to "preemptive conduct" of Meehan and Boyle, as well as their "breach of duty." Undoubtedly these are accurate descriptions, but we do not wish to leave the impression that the MBC attorneys were unfair in the totality of their conduct in departing from the firm. For instance, we recount early in this opinion that Meehan and Boyle left undisturbed with their partners, and made no attempt to claim, a very large amount of business which Meehan had attracted to Parker Coulter.

reputations as trial lawyers in the Commonwealth. Meehan and Boyle each were active in the management of Parker Coulter. They each served, for example, on the partnership's executive committee and, as members of this committee, were responsible for considering and making policy recommendations to the general partnership. Boyle was also in charge of the "plaintiffs department" within the firm, which managed approximately 350 cases. At the time of their leaving, Meehan's interest in the partnership was 6% and Boyle's interest was 4.8%.

Meehan and Boyle had become dissatisfied at Parker Coulter. On June 27, 1984, after unsuccessfully opposing the adoption of a firm-wide pension plan, the two first discussed the possibility of leaving Parker Coulter. Another partner met with them to discuss leaving but told them their proposed firm would not be suitable for his type of practice. On July 1, Meehan and Boyle decided to leave Parker Coulter and form their own partnership.

Having decided to establish a new firm, Meehan and Boyle then focused on whom they would invite to join them. The two spoke with Cohen, a junior partner and the de facto head of Parker Coulter's appellate department, about joining the new firm as a partner. They arranged to meet with her on July 5, and told her to keep their conversations confidential. The day before the July 5 meeting, Boyle prepared two lists of what he considered to be his cases. The lists contained approximately eighty to 100 cases, and for each case indicated the status, fee arrangement, estimated settlement value, and potential fee to MBC. Boyle gave these lists to Cohen for her to examine in preparation for the July 5 meeting.

At the July 5 meeting, Meehan and Boyle outlined to Cohen their plans for the new firm, including their intent to offer positions to Schafer, Peter Black (Black), and Warren Fitzgerald (Fitzgerald), who were associates at Parker Coulter. Boyle stated that he hoped the clients he had been representing would go with him to the new firm; Meehan said he would take the aviation work he had at Parker Coulter with him. Both stated that they felt others at Parker Coulter were getting paid as much as or more than they were, but were not working as hard. Cohen decided to consider the offer from Meehan and Boyle, and agreed to keep the plans confidential until formal notice of the separation was given to the partnership. Although the partnership agreement required a notice period of three months, the three decided to give only thirty days' notice. They chose to give shorter notice to avoid what they believed would be an uncomfortable situation at the firm, and possible retaliatory measures by the partnership. Meehan and Boyle had agreed that they would leave Parker Coulter on December 31, 1984, the end of Parker Coulter's fiscal year.

During the first week of August, Cohen accepted the offer to join the new firm as a partner. Her primary reason for leaving Parker Coulter to join MBC was that she enjoyed working with Meehan and Boyle.

In July, 1984, Boyle offered a position at MBC to Schafer, who worked closely with Boyle in the plaintiffs department. Boyle told Schafer to organize his cases, and "to keep an eye towards cases to be resolved in 1985 and to handle these cases for resolution in 1985 rather than 1984." He also told Schafer to make a list of cases he could take with him to MBC, and to keep all their conversations confidential.

Late in the summer of 1984, Meehan asked Black and Fitzgerald to become associates at MBC. Fitzgerald had worked with Meehan in the past on general defense work, and Black worked with Meehan, particularly in the aviation area. Meehan was instrumental in attracting Black, who had previously been employed by U.S. Aviation Underwriters (USAU), to Parker Coulter. Although Black had already considered leaving Parker Coulter, he was concerned about whether USAU would follow him to a small firm like MBC, and wanted to discuss his leaving Parker Coulter with the vice president of USAU. In October, 1984, Black and Meehan met with the USAU vice president in New York. They later received assurances from him that he would be interested in sending USAU business to the proposed new firm. Black then accepted the offer to join MBC. Fitzgerald also accepted. Schafer, Black, and Fitzgerald were the only associates Meehan, Boyle, and Cohen approached concerning the new firm.

During July and the following months, Meehan, Boyle, and Cohen made arrangements for their new practice apart from seeking associates. They began to look for office space and retained an architect. In early fall, a lease was executed on behalf of MBC in the name of MBC Realty Trust. They also retained an attorney to advise them on the formation of the new firm.

. . .

Toward the end of November, Boyle prepared form letters to send to clients and referring attorneys as soon as Parker Coulter was notified of the separation. He also drafted a form for the clients to return to him at his home address authorizing him to remove cases to MBC. An outside agency typed these materials on Parker Coulter's letterhead. Schafer prepared similar letters and authorization forms.

While they were planning their departure, from July to approximately December, Meehan, Boyle, Cohen, Schafer, Black, and Fitzgerald all continued to work full schedules. They settled cases appropriately, made reasonable efforts to avoid continuances, tried cases, and worked on discovery. Each generally maintained his or her usual standard of performance.

Meehan and Boyle had originally intended to give notice to Parker Coulter on December 1, 1984. Rumors of their leaving, however, began to circulate before then. During the period from July to early fall, different Parker Coulter partners approached Meehan individually on three separate occasions and asked him if the rumors about his leaving were true. On each occasion, Meehan denied that he was leaving. On November 30, 1984, a partner, Maurice F. Shaughnessy (Shaughnessy), approached Boyle and asked him whether Meehan and Boyle intended to leave the firm. Shaughnessy interpreted Boyle's evasive response as an affirmation of the rumors. Meehan and Boyle then decided to distribute their notice that afternoon, which stated, as their proposed date for leaving, December 31, 1984. A notice was left on the desk of each partner. When Meehan, Boyle, and Cohen gave their notice, the atmosphere at Parker Coulter became "tense, emotional and unpleasant, if not adversarial."

On December 3, the Parker Coulter partners appointed a separation committee and decided to communicate with "important sources of business" to tell them of the separation and of Parker Coulter's desire to continue representing them. . . . Sometime during the week of December 3, the partners sent Boyle a list of cases and requested that he identify the cases he intended to take with him.

Boyle had begun to make telephone calls to referring attorneys on Saturday morning, December 1. He had spoken with three referring attorneys by that date and told them of his departure from Parker Coulter and his wish to continue handling their cases. On December 3, he mailed his previously typed letters and authorization forms, and by the end of the first two weeks of December he had spoken with a majority of referring attorneys, and had obtained authorizations from a majority of clients whose cases he planned to remove to MBC.

Although the partners previously were aware of Boyle's intention to communicate with clients, they did not become aware of the extent of his communications until December 12 or 13. Boyle did not provide his partners with the list they requested of cases he intended to remove until December 17. Throughout December, Meehan, Boyle, and Schafer continued to communicate with referring attorneys on cases they were currently handling to discuss authorizing their transfer to MBC. On December 19, 1984, one of the partners accepted on behalf of Parker Coulter the December 31 departure date and waived the three-month notice period provided for by the partnership agreement. Meehan, Boyle, and Cohen formalized their arrangement as a professional corporation on January 1, 1985.

MBC removed a number of cases from Parker Coulter. Of the roughly 350 contingent fee cases pending at Parker Coulter in 1984, Boyle, Schafer, and Meehan removed approximately 142 to MBC. Meehan advised Parker Coulter that the 4,000 asbestos cases he had attracted to the firm would remain, and he did not seek to take certain other major clients. Black removed thirty-five cases; Fitzgerald removed ten; and Cohen removed three. A provision in the partnership agreement in effect at the separation provided that a voluntarily retiring partner, upon the payment of a "fair charge," could remove "any matter in which the partnership had been representing a client who came to the firm through the personal effort or connection of the retiring partner," subject to the right of the client to stay with the firm. Approximately thirty-nine of the 142 contingent fee cases removed to MBC came to Parker Coulter at least in part through the personal efforts or connections of Parker Coulter attorneys other than Meehan, Boyle, Cohen, Schafer, Black, or Fitzgerald. In all the cases removed to MBC, however, MBC attorneys had direct, existing relationships with the clients. In all the removed cases, MBC attorneys communicated with the referring attorney or with the client directly by telephone or letter. In each case, the client signed an authorization.

Schafer subsequently separated his practice from MBC's. He took with him a number of the cases which had been removed from Parker Coulter to MBC.

Based on these findings, the judge determined that the MBC attorneys did not manipulate cases, or handle them differently as a result of their decision to leave Parker Coulter. He also determined that Parker Coulter failed to prove that the clients whose cases were removed did not freely choose to have MBC represent them. Consequently, he concluded that Meehan and Boyle neither violated the partnership agreement nor breached the fiduciary duty they owed to their partners. In addition, the judge also found that Meehan and Boyle did not tortiously interfere with Parker Coulter's relations with clients or employees. He similarly rejected Parker Coulter's claims against Cohen and Schafer.

. . .

We . . . consider Parker Coulter's claims of wrongdoing. Parker Coulter claims that the judge erred in finding that Meehan, Boyle, Cohen, and Schafer fulfilled their fiduciary duties to the former partnership. In particular, Parker Coulter argues that these attorneys breached their duties (1) by improperly handling cases for their own, and not the partnership's benefit, (2) by secretly competing with the partnership, and (3) by unfairly acquiring from clients and referring attorneys consent to withdraw cases to MBC.[12] We do not agree with Parker Coulter's first two arguments but agree with the third. We first address the claims against Meehan and Boyle, and then turn to those against Cohen and Schafer.

It is well settled that partners owe each other a fiduciary duty of "the utmost good faith and loyalty." Cardullo v. Landau, 329 Mass. 5, 8 (1952). . . . As a fiduciary, a partner must consider his or her partners' welfare, and refrain from acting for purely private gain. . . . Meehan and Boyle owed their copartners at Parker Coulter a duty of the utmost good faith and loyalty, and were obliged to consider their copartners' welfare, and not merely their own.

Parker Coulter first argues that Meehan and Boyle violated their fiduciary duty by handling cases for their own benefit, and challenges the judge's finding that no manipulation occurred.[13] . . . The judge's determination was one of fact, and was based on the assessment of the credibility of individuals with personal knowledge of the facts about which they were testifying. . . .

Parker Coulter also claims that we should disregard the judge's finding of no manipulation because the finding is clearly contradicted by other subsidiary findings, namely that Boyle planned to, and told Schafer to, handle cases for resolution at MBC rather than at Parker Coulter; that Boyle reassigned a number of a departing attorney's cases to himself and Schafer; and that a number of cases which were ready to resolve at Parker Coulter were, in fact, not resolved there. We do not agree that there is a conflict. The judge's finding that Boyle spoke of engaging in improper conduct does not require the conclusion that this conduct actually took place. Similarly, his finding that the reassignment of cases did not establish manipulation is consistent with a determination that the reassignment was based on merit and workload. . . .

Parker Coulter next argues that the judge's findings compel the conclusion that Meehan and Boyle breached their fiduciary duty not to

[12] Parker Coulter does not claim that Meehan and Boyle wrongfully dissolved the partnership by leaving prematurely. . . . .

[13] The judge found, specifically, that: "MBC, Schafer, Black and Fitzgerald worked full schedules from July to November 30, 1984, and some beyond. There was no manipulation of the cases nor were the cases handled differently as a result of the decision by MBC to leave Parker Coulter. They tried cases, worked on discovery, settled cases and made reasonable efforts to avoid continuances, to try their cases when reached, and settle where appropriate and in general maintain the same level of industry and professionalism that they had always demonstrated."

compete with their partners by secretly setting up a new firm during their tenure at Parker Coulter. We disagree. We have stated that fiduciaries may plan to compete with the entity to which they owe allegiance, "provided that in the course of such arrangements they [do] not otherwise act in violation of their fiduciary duties." Chelsea Indus. v. Gaffney, 389 Mass. 1, 10, 11–12 (1983). Here, the judge found that Meehan and Boyle made certain logistical arrangements for the establishment of MBC. These arrangements included executing a lease for MBC's office, preparing lists of clients expected to leave Parker Coulter for MBC, and obtaining financing on the basis of these lists. We believe these logistical arrangements to establish a physical plant for the new firm were permissible. . . .

Lastly, Parker Coulter argues that the judge's findings compel the conclusion that Meehan and Boyle breached their fiduciary duties by unfairly acquiring consent from clients to remove cases from Parker Coulter. We agree that Meehan and Boyle, through their preparation for obtaining clients' consent, their secrecy concerning which clients they intended to take, and the substance and method of their communications with clients, obtained an unfair advantage over their former partners in breach of their fiduciary duties.

A partner has an obligation to "render on demand true and full information of all things affecting the partnership to any partner." G. L. c. 108A, [UPA] § 20. . . . On three separate occasions Meehan affirmatively denied to his partners, on their demand, that he had any plans for leaving the partnership. During this period of secrecy, Meehan and Boyle made preparations for obtaining removal authorizations from clients. Meehan traveled to New York to meet with a representative of USAU and interest him in the new firm. Boyle prepared form letters on Parker Coulter's letterhead for authorizations from prospective MBC clients. Thus, they were "ready to move" the instant they gave notice to their partners. . . .

On giving their notice, Meehan and Boyle continued to use their position of trust and confidence to the disadvantage of Parker Coulter. The two immediately began communicating with clients and referring attorneys. Boyle delayed providing his partners with a list of clients he intended to solicit until mid-December, by which time he had obtained authorization from a majority of the clients.

Finally, the content of the letter sent to the clients was unfairly prejudicial to Parker Coulter. The ABA Committee on Ethics and Professional Responsibility, in Informal Opinion 1457 (April 29, 1980), set forth ethical standards for attorneys announcing a change in professional association.[15] Because this standard is intended primarily

---

[15] These standards provide the following guidelines for notice to clients:

"(a) the notice is mailed; (b) the notice is sent only to persons with whom the lawyer had an active lawyer-client relationship immediately before the change in the lawyer's professional association; (c) the notice is clearly related to open and pending matters for which the lawyer had direct professional responsibility to the client immediately before the change; (d) the notice is sent promptly after the change; (e) the notice does not urge the client to sever a relationship with the lawyer's former firm and does not recommend the lawyer's employment (although it indicates the lawyer's willingness to continue his responsibility for the matters); (f) the notice makes it clear that the client has the right to decide who will complete or continue the matters; and (g) the notice is brief, dignified, and not disparaging of the lawyer's former firm."

to protect clients, proof by Parker Coulter of a technical violation of this standard does not aid them in their claims. See Fishman v. Brooks, 396 Mass. 643, 649 (1986). We will, however, look to this standard for general guidelines as to what partners are entitled to expect from each other concerning their joint clients on the division of their practice. The ethical standard provides that any notice explain to a client that he or she has the right to decide who will continue the representation. Here, the judge found that the notice did not "clearly present to the clients the choice they had between remaining at Parker Coulter or moving to the new firm." By sending a one-sided announcement, on Parker Coulter letterhead, so soon after notice of their departure, Meehan and Boyle excluded their partners from effectively presenting their services as an alternative to those of Meehan and Boyle.

ANALYSIS

1. On December 3, 1984, what options were available to Parker Coulter?

2. Once Meehan and Boyle decided to leave Parker Coulter, what were they free to do to establish their new practice? Did they have an obligation to inform their partners of their decision to leave as soon as that decision was "in concrete"? Even earlier, when it was a strong probability?

3. What about Schafer (the associate who left with Meehan and Boyle)? At some point before his departure, did he have an obligation to advise the Parker Coulter partners of the impending defection?

4. Could, and should, any of the issues of fiduciary obligation have been settled by express prior agreement? If so, what might the agreement have stated?

PROBLEM

Suppose Mark and Norma are lawyers and have practiced as partners for five years. One day Peter comes to the law offices of Mark and Norma, asks to see Mark, and tells Mark that he has a brother who has been seriously injured in an automobile accident and needs a lawyer. Peter says that he has heard that Mark is a good lawyer. Mark quickly concludes that Peter's brother has a strong case and is likely to be able to recover a large judgment. Mark concludes at that moment that it is time to end his partnership with Norma and begin practice on his own. If he does so, what are his obligations to Norma with respect to the representation of Peter's brother?

See also ABA Committee on Ethics and Professional Responsibility Informal Opinion 1466 (Feb. 12, 1981) (extending Informal Opinion 1457 to departing associates as well as partners).

C. EXPULSION

Lawlis v. Kightlinger & Gray

562 N.E.2d 435 (Ind.App.1990).

. . .

The partnership [Kightlinger & Grey] for many years has practiced law in Indianapolis and Evansville under various firm names. [Gerald L.] Lawlis initially became an associate of the partnership in 1966 but resigned after three years to join the staff of Eli Lilly and Company as an attorney. In early 1971, the partnership offered Lawlis a position as a general partner and Lawlis accepted. He signed his first partnership agreement as a general partner in 1972. That agreement remained effective until a new one was executed by the partners, including Lawlis, in 1984. Both these agreements provided for partnership compensation based upon a unit system, i.e., partners participated in the profits according to the number of units assigned to them each year by the partnership. Lawlis became a senior partner in 1975 and continued to practice law with the firm without interruption until 1982.

In that year, Lawlis became an alcohol abuser, and due to that affliction did not practice law for several months in early 1983 and in mid 1984. During each of these periods, he sought treatment for his alcoholism. Lawlis did not reveal his problem with alcohol to the partnership until July of 1983 when he disclosed it to the partnership's Finance Committee. When he did so, it "promptly contacted and met as a group with a physician who had expertise in the area of alcoholism." It then drafted "a document entitled 'Program Outline' which set forth certain conditions for Lawlis's continuing relationship with the Partnership." That document, signed by Lawlis in August, 1983, contained the following understanding: "3. It must be set out and clearly understood that there is no second chance." By March, 1984, Lawlis had resumed the consumption of alcohol. Lawlis again sought treatment, and the firm gave Lawlis a second chance. Its Finance Committee then decided Lawlis would be required to meet specified conditions in order for his relationship with the partnership to continue. These conditions included meetings with specialists selected by the partnership, treatment and consultation regarding his problem, and the obtaining of favorable reports from the specialist as to the likelihood of a favorable treatment outcome. Lawlis was told he would be returned to full partnership status if he complied with the conditions imposed. He has not consumed any alcoholic beverages since his second treatment in an alcoholic clinic in March, 1984.

Two written partnership agreements embodying primarily the same provisions were in effect in 1982 and thereafter, executed in 1972 and 1984, respectively. Lawlis executed both agreements and each annual addendum thereto along with all the other partners of the firm. Under the 1984 agreement, the senior partners by majority vote were to determine (a) the units each partner annually received, (b) the involuntary expulsion of partners, and (c) the involuntary retirement of partners.

As Lawlis battled his problem, his units of participation yearly were reduced by the annual addendum to the partnership agreement. Because he had not consumed alcohol since his second trip to a clinic and had been congratulated by senior partner Wampler, a member of the Finance Committee, and several others as to his "100% turn around," Lawlis felt "a substantial restoration of my previous status was past due." So believing, he met with the Finance Committee on October 1, 1986, and proposed his units of participation be increased from his then 60 to 90 units in 1987.

On October 23, 1986, Wampler told Lawlis the firm's Finance Committee was going to recommend Lawlis's relationship as a senior partner be severed no later than June 30, 1987. Two days later, all the firm's files were removed from Lawlis's office. The severance recommendation was presented at the 1986 year-end senior partners meeting. All except Lawlis voted to accept the Finance Committee's recommendation. At that time, as the Finance Committee also had recommended, Lawlis was assigned one unit of participation for the first six months of 1987 to a maximum total value of $25,000 on a weekly draw. This arrangement permitted Lawlis to retain his status as a senior partner to facilitate transition to other employment and to give him continuing insurance coverage.

Lawlis refused to sign the 1987 addendum containing those provisions and retained counsel to represent his interests. In consequence, he was expelled by a seven to one vote of the senior partners at a meeting held on February 23, 1987. (Lawlis cast the lone dissenting vote.) Article X of the 1984 agreement requires a minimum two-thirds vote of the senior partners to accomplish the involuntary expulsion of a partner. Lawlis filed suit for damages for breach of contract. From the entry of an adverse summary judgment, Lawlis appeals.

. . .

Lawlis first claims his notification by Wampler on October 23, 1986, that the Finance Committee would recommend his severance as a partner coupled with the removal of all partnership files from his office two days later constituted [a] . . . dissolution of the partnership. At that time, he posits he ceased "to be associated in the carrying on as distinguished from the winding up of the business." Deeming such expulsion wrongful because not authorized by a two-thirds vote of the senior partners at that time, Lawlis asserts he has a claim for damages against the partners under IC 23–4–1–18(a)(2) [UPA § 38(a)(2)] for dissolution in contravention of the partnership agreement. We disagree.

It is readily apparent Wampler merely told Lawlis what the Finance Committee proposed to do in the future. No dissolution occurred on that account. That the firm's files were removed from Lawlis's office two days later is immaterial. After their removal, Lawlis still participated in the partnership's profits through a weekly draw even though he evidently had nothing to do. Finally, the undisputed facts clearly demonstrate there was a meeting of the minds he would remain a senior partner after October 23, 1986. The partnership continued to treat Lawlis as a senior partner after that date. The Finance Committee's memorandum of November 25, 1986, regarding Lawlis's partnership status, proposed for 1987 he be given a weekly draw on one unit of participation until June 30, 1987, at which time his relationship with the firm would terminate, unless he withdrew earlier. Further, that committee's minutes for its December 23, 1986 meeting regarding the change in letterhead show Lawlis's name was not to be removed from the letterhead; it was to be placed at the bottom of the list of partners.

Also, Lawlis considered himself to be a senior partner after October 26, 1986. He refused as a senior partner to sign the proposed 1987 addendum "which implemented the decisions made by the Finance Committee concerning Lawlis," Appellant's Brief, p. 8, and cast the lone dissenting vote on his expulsion at the meeting of the senior partners held on February 23, 1987. Article X of the partnership agreement provides:

> *Expulsion of a Partner*
>
> A two-thirds (2/3) majority *of the Senior Partners*, at any time, may expel any partner from the partnership *upon such terms and conditions as set by said Senior Partners*. . . . (Emphasis supplied).

Only a partner could refuse to sign the proposed 1987 addenda after its tender by the firm to Lawlis for signature, and only a senior partner could vote on the Finance Committee's proposal to expel a partner under the partnership agreement. The undisputed facts disclose Lawlis remained a senior partner of the firm until he was expelled as such by vote of the senior partners on February 23, 1987.

Further, the time a dissolution occurs under these circumstances is clearly defined by statute. The Indiana Uniform Partnership Act at IC 23–4–1–31 [UPA § 31] says:

> Sec. 31. Dissolution is caused: (1) Without violation of the agreement between the partners, ...
>
> (d) By the expulsion of any partner from the business bona fide in accordance with such a power conferred by the agreement between the partners.

Lawlis was expelled in accordance with the partnership agreement on February 23, 1987. Thus, dissolution occurred on that date, not when he was notified of the proposal to expel him. Lawlis has no claim for damages under IC 23–4–1–38(a)(2) [UPA § 38(a)(2)].

Lawlis next argues his expulsion contravened the agreement's implied duty of good faith and fair dealing because he was expelled for the "predatory purpose" of "increasing [the firm's] lawyer to partner ratio," as evidenced by the Finance Committee's proposal contained in its November 25, 1986, memo to partners regarding the 1986 year end meeting. The partnership, however, posits Indiana does not recognize a duty of good faith and fair dealing in the context of an at will relationship.

It would be a simple matter to extrapolate the principle that an employer may terminate an at will employee for any cause or no cause without liability and apply it to the roughly comparable at will business relationship we find here, namely, the relationship existing between the partnership as an entity and its individual partners. The Indiana Uniform Partnership Act, however, prevents us from so doing.

As noted above, when a partner is involuntarily expelled from a business, his expulsion must have been "bona fide" or in "good faith" for a dissolution to occur without violation of the partnership agreement. IC

23–4–1–31(1)(d). Said another way, if the power to involuntarily expel partners granted by a partnership agreement is exercised in bad faith or for a "predatory purpose," as Lawlis phrases it, the partnership agreement is violated, giving rise to an action for damages the affected partner has suffered as a result of his expulsion.

Lawlis finds a predatory purpose in the Finance Committee's November 25, 1986, memo to the partners by quoting portions of the memo's section "4. FIVE YEAR PLAN, Firm Growth and Financial Goals." He states:

> The five-year plan stated that, "The goal is to increase the top partners to at least $150,000 within the next two to three years. . . . In order to achieve the goal, we need to continue to improve our lawyer to partner ratio."

Appellant's Brief, at 17. From that quote Lawlis reasons:

> Obviously, the easiest way for the Partnership to improve its lawyer to partner ratio, and thus increase the top partners' salaries, was to eliminate a senior partner. Lawlis' position in the Partnership had been weakened by his absences due to illness. The remaining partners knew this and pounced upon the opportunity to devour Lawlis's partnership interest.

Appellant's Brief, at 18. The undisputed facts demonstrate the total inaccuracy of the final sentence quoted from appellant's brief.

From the time Lawlis's addiction to alcohol became known to the partnership's Finance Committee, it sought to assist and aid him through his medical crisis, even though he was taking substantial amounts of time off from his work to attempt cures in sanatoriums and had concealed the fact of his alcoholism from his partners for many months. The firm permitted him to continue drawing on his partnership account even though he became increasingly unproductive in those years, as reflected by the continuing yearly drop in the number of units assigned him. After signing the Program Outline in August, 1983, which structured his business life by providing among other things for the monitoring of his work product by the firm for a period of one year, recommending he attend Alcoholics Anonymous meetings, setting the specific times he would arrive at and remain in the office, and containing a provision "3. . . . there is no second chance," Lawlis "resumed the consumption of alcohol" in March, 1984. Instead of expelling Lawlis at that time, the partnership acting through its Finance Committee continued to work with Lawlis by drawing up yet another set of conditions he was to meet to remain with the firm. Clearly, these undisputed facts present no "predatory purpose" on the firm's part, nor does the Finance Committee's Five Year Plan when that proposal is read in full.

In essence, the proposal was to change the manner in which the firm valued its performance, and to obtain more production, i.e., billable hours from the attorney associates working for the firm in its various departments to achieve its goal of increased income to the partners. There is no proposal that the number of partners be reduced to accomplish the Five Year Plan's stated goals, nor any reasonable inference arising therefrom to that effect.

Also, in the same memo . . ., the Finance Committee, instead of recommending Lawlis's immediate expulsion as a method of increasing its lawyer to partner ratio, proposed he remain a partner for a maximum total of an additional eight months to give him time to find other employment and retain insurance coverage while so engaged. During that period it proposed he be permitted one participation unit upon which to draw up to $25,000 while he sought other employment. Such proposal again clearly negates a partnership "predatory purpose" for Lawlis's expulsion. Thus, there is no "genuine" issue as to whether the partnership acted in good faith when it expelled Lawlis because it can be foreclosed by reference to the undisputed facts here. . . .

Lawlis next argues the firm's act of expelling him was constructively fraudulent because it constituted a breach of the fiduciary duty owed between partners which requires each to exercise good faith and fair dealing in partnership transactions and toward co-partners. . . . While we agree with Lawlis's bald statement of that concept, it has no application to the facts of this case.

The fiduciary relationship between partners to which the terms "bona fide" and "good faith" relate

> . . . concern the *business aspects or property of the partnership* and prohibit a partner, to wit a fiduciary, from taking any personal advantage touching those subjects. . . . Plaintiffs contend there was substantial evidence indicating the individual partner's breach of fiduciary duties they owed to plaintiffs as members of the bar. In view of our holding that the executive committee *had the right to expel plaintiffs without stating a reason or cause pursuant to the Partnership Agreement, there was no breach of any fiduciary duty.* (Emphasis supplied.)

Holman v. Coie (1974), 11 Wash.App. 195, 522 P.2d 515, 523–524. *Holman* concerned the expulsion of two partners from a law firm for no stated cause, but there was evidence a political speech by one of them had disgruntled the chief executive of one of the firm's major clients, the Boeing Corporation. Substantially the same consideration present in *Holman,* i.e., potential damage to partnership business, is present in this case.

. . .

All the parties involved in this litigation were legally competent and consenting adults well educated in the law who initially dealt at arm's length while negotiating the partnership agreements here involved. At the time the partners negotiated their contract, it is apparent they believed, as in *Holman,* the "guillotine method" of involuntary severance [that is, immediate termination by partnership vote without notice or hearing] would be in the best interests of the partnership. Their intent was to provide a simple, practical, and above all, a speedy method of separating a partner from the firm, if that ever became necessary for any reason. We find no fault with that approach to severance.

Where the remaining partners in a firm deem it necessary to expel a partner under a no cause expulsion clause in a partnership agreement freely negotiated and entered into, the expelling partners act in "good faith" regardless of motivation if that act does not cause a wrongful withholding of money or property legally due the expelled partner at the time he is expelled. . . . Clearly, the senior partners acted in the belief they had the legal right to do so under the partnership agreement, as they did. That they recommended a step-down severance over six months rather than the "guillotine" severance permitted them under the agreement demonstrates a compassionate, not greedy, purpose. If we were to hold otherwise, we would be engrafting a "for cause" requirement upon this agreement when such was not the intent of the parties at the time they entered into their agreement. Mere lapse of time, however long, does not alter that initial intent. Lawlis's constructive fraud argument is without merit.

. . .

Affirmed.

ANALYSIS

1. What would the result have been if Lawlis had been expelled in July 1983 when his partners first discovered that he was suffering from alcoholism?

2. What if he had been expelled in August 1984?

3. Suppose you had been a client of the partnership. What approach would you have wanted it to take?

3. PARTNERSHIP PROPERTY

Putnam v. Shoaf

620 S.W.2d 510 (Ct. App. of Tenn., Western Section, at Jackson, 1981).

This dispute is over the sale of a partnership interest in the Frog Jump Gin Company.

The Frog Jump Gin had operated for a number of years showing losses in some years and profits in others. In the time immediately preceding February, 1976, it appears that the gin operated at a loss. Originally, the gin was operated as an equal partnership between E. C. Charlton, Louise H. Charlton, Lyle Putnam and Carolyn Putnam. In 1974 Mr. Putnam died and Mrs. Putnam, by agreement, succeeded to her husband's interest. The gin operated under that control and management until February 19, 1976, when Mrs. Putnam desired to sever her relationship with the other partners in Frog Jump Gin. At that time the gin was heavily indebted to the Bank of Trenton and Trust Company, and Mrs. Putnam desired to be relieved of this liability. John A. and Maurine H. Shoaf displayed an interest in obtaining Mrs. Putnam's one-half interest in the partnership. An examination by the Shoafs of the financial records of the gin, evidenced by a statement from the gin bookkeeper, indicated a negative financial position of approximately $90,000.00. The Shoafs agreed to take over Mrs. Putnam's position in the partnership if Mrs. Putnam and the Charltons would each pay $21,000.00 into the partnership account. The Shoafs agreed to assume personal liability for all partnership debts. . . . Both the Charltons and Mrs. Putnam paid their respective amounts into the partnership account, and the Shoafs assumed all partnership obligations as aforesaid.

At the time of this agreement the known assets of the Frog Jump Gin consisted primarily of the gin, its equipment, and the land upon which they were located. All gin assets, including the land, were held in the name of the partnership. Mrs. Putnam conveyed her interest in the partnership to the Shoafs by means of a quit claim deed. Upon the Shoafs' assumption of the position of partners, the services of the old bookkeeper were terminated and a new bookkeeper was hired.

In April, 1977, with the assistance of the new bookkeeper, it was learned that the old bookkeeper had engaged in a scheme of systematic embezzlement from the Frog Jump Gin Company from the time of Mr. Putnam's death until the bookkeeper's services were terminated. This disclosure led to suits being filed by the gin against the bookkeeper and the banks that had honored checks forged by the bookkeeper. There is no need to go into the details of all that litigation. Suffice it to say that Mrs. Putnam was allowed to intervene claiming an interest in any fund paid by the banks and the upshot of it all was a judgment paid into Court by the banks in excess of $68,000.00. One-half of that sum, by agreement, has been paid to the Charltons as owners of a one-half interest in the gin, and the other half is the subject of this dispute between the Shoafs and Mrs. Putnam's estate. She has died pending this litigation and the case revived.

. . .

The conveyance between Mrs. Putnam and the Shoafs is evidenced by what is styled a "Quitclaim Deed" executed by Mrs. Putnam on February 19, 1976, which is as follows:

> "FOR AND IN CONSIDERATION of the sum of One Dollar ($1.00), cash in hand paid, the receipt of which is hereby acknowledged, and the assumption by Grantees of all Grantor's obligations arising or by virtue of her partnership interest in the Frog Jump Gin Company, including three notes to Bank of Tenton and Trust Company, I, CAROLYN B. PUTNAM, a widow, have this day bargained and sold and by these presents so hereby sell, transfer, convey and forever quitclaim unto JOHN A. SHOAF and wife, MAURINE H. SHOAF, their heirs and assigns, all the right, title and interest (it being a one-half (1/2) undivided interest) I have in and to the following described real and personal property located in the 25th Civil District of Gibson County, Tennessee, and described as follows; to-wit:"

(The legal description of the real [and personal] property follows.)

> "PERSONAL PROPERTY:
>
> "All of the personal property and machinery in said Frog Jump Gin Company's buildings and on said properties described and used in the operation of its cotton gin plant on the above-described parcel of land, including two Moss Gordin 75 saw gin stands; one Overhead incline cleaner; stick and green leaf machine; two Moss Gordin lint cleaners; two Mitchell Feeders; two Mitchell burners; one Hardwick Etter all steel press; condensers; fans; motors; pulleys; shafting; all piping; belting and machinery and appliances and other personal property, including all cotton trailers, on said parcel of land and used in connection with the operation of said cotton gin, accounts receivable, inventory and all other assets of Frog Jump Gin Company.

"TO HAVE AND TO HOLD the said real and personal property with the appurtenances, estate, title and interest thereto belonging unto the said John A. Shoaf and wife, Maurine H. Shoaf, their heirs and assigns, forever.

"Witness my signature this the 19 day of February, 1976."

On the same day Mrs. Putnam and the Charltons executed the following agreement:

"This Agreement made and entered into on this the 19th day of February, 1976, by and between E. C. Charlton and wife, Louise H. Charlton, party of one part, and Carolyn B. Putnam, party of the other part, all of Trenton, Gibson County, Tennessee;

"WITNESSETH: THAT WHEREAS, the parties have heretofore been conducting a business, as partners, under the firm name and style of Frog Jump Gin Company; and

"WHEREAS, Carolyn B. Putnam has agreed to pay into the partnership the sum of Twenty-one Thousand Dollars ($21,000.00), the receipt of which is hereby acknowledged, and has sold and conveyed her interest in the partnership to John A. Shoaf and wife, Maurine H. Shoaf.

"NOW, THEREFORE, it is mutually agreed that the partnership be and hereby is dissolved. It is further mutually agreed that the parties do hereby release and forever discharge each other from any and all claims and demands on account of, connected with, or growing out of the said partnership, or the division of the assets thereof; and it is expressly understood and agreed that Carolyn B. Putnam is completely released and discharged from any and all liability, debts, or causes of action of the Frog Jump Gin Company, presently existing, contingent, or otherwise, including notes owed to Bank of Trenton and Trust Company, and that E. C. Charlton and wife, Louise H. Charlton assume all liability and indebtedness of the said partnership and covenant to indemnify and save harmless the said Carolyn B. Putnam in the premises.

"In Witness Whereof, the parties have hereunto set their signatures, this day and date first above written."

At approximately the same time, Mrs. Putnam obtained from the Bank of Trenton a complete release from all personal liability for note indebtednesses to the Bank in the face amount of $105,000.00 in consideration of the Shoafs' assumption of all obligations of the Frog Jump Gin.

. . .

First, we must discover the nature of the ownership interest of Mrs. Putnam in that which she conveyed. Under the Uniform Partnership Act, . . . her partnership property rights consisted of her (1) rights in specific partnership property, (2) interest in the partnership and (3) right to participate in management. . . . The right in "specific partnership property" is the partnership tenancy possessory right of equal use or possession by partners for partnership purposes. This possessory right is incident to the partnership and the possessory right does not exist absent the partnership. The possessory right is not the partner's "interest" in the assets of the partnership. . . . The real interest of a partner, as opposed to that incidental possessory right before discussed, is the partner's interest in the partnership which is defined as "his share of the profits and surplus and the same is personal property." . . . Therefore, a co-partner owns no personal specific interest in any specific property or asset of the partnership. The partnership owns the property or the asset. . . . The partner's interest is an undivided interest, as a co-tenant in all partnership property. . . . That interest is the partner's pro rata share of the net value or deficit of the partnership. . . . For this reason a conveyance of partnership property held in the name of the partnership is made in the name of the partnership and not as a conveyance of the individual interests of the partners. . . .

This being true, all Mrs. Putnam had to convey was her interest in the partnership. Accordingly, she had no specific interest in the admittedly unknown choses in action to separately convey or retain. Therefore, the determinative question is: Did Mrs. Putnam intend to convey her interest in the partnership to the Shoafs? There can be no doubt that such was the intent of Mrs. Putnam, as she had no other interest to convey. . . . If we would say otherwise, that is that she intended to convey less, and thereby retain a partnership interest, Mrs. Putnam would have remained a partner unknown to the other parties and, in reality, unknown to herself. It is abundantly evident that the last thing Mrs. Putnam wanted was to remain a partner. She wanted out, and out she got.

. . . This situation is no different from a hypothetical oil discovery on the partnership real property after transfer of a partnership interest with neither party believing oil to be present at the time of the conveyance. The interest in the real property always was and remained in the partnership. Of course, the transferor would not have transferred his partnership interest had he known of the existence of oil on partnership property; but, mutual ignorance of the existence of the oil would not, in our opinion, warrant a "reformation" of the contract for sale of the partnership interest, or warrant a decree in favor of the transferor for a share of the value of the oil.

. . . We wonder what would be the position of Mrs. Putnam, or the estate, had the Frog Jump Gin failed, leaving a sizeable deficit, even after the influx of the bank's refund. Would she accept a partner's share of the Frog Jump Gin's liabilities for a share of the bank's refund? The question answers itself and we pose it only to show that she did not have a specific interest in any specific assets of the Frog Jump Gin, either to retain or convey. All she had was a partner's interest in a "share of the profits" (and losses) which she certainly intended to convey.

ANALYSIS

1. A partnership might be thought of as an entity—like a corporation, which is conceived of as a separate entity, in which individuals may own shares. Alternatively, it might be thought of as an aggregation of assets each of which is owned pro rata by the partners—just as, for example, an individual owning a hardware store might be thought to own directly and personally each and every item in the store's

inventory. Does the court in the present case treat the partnership as an entity or an aggregate? Would it matter?

2. Suppose that after the change of ownership it was discovered, much to everyone's surprise, that an underground stream had undercut the land on which the gin was located and it was necessary to abandon the property. Could the Shoafs have recovered their loss from Ms. Putnam?

4. THE RIGHTS OF PARTNERS IN MANAGEMENT

In many, perhaps most, small partnerships, each of the partners expects to play a role in conducting the business of the partnership. The right of each partner to participate in the operation of the business in some way will be an implicit term of the partnership agreement. At the same time, disagreements may arise over various business decisions. Section 18(e) of the UPA provides that in the absence of an agreement to the contrary, "all partners have equal rights in the management and conduct of the partnership business," and § 18(h) provides that "any difference arising as to ordinary matters connected with the partnership business may be decided by a majority of the partners." (To the same effect is UPA (1997) §§ 103, 401(f) and (j).) Thus, if there are three partners and they disagree as to an "ordinary" matter, the decision of the majority controls. For example, if the partnership operates a grocery store, and two of the partners, for business reasons, want to stop buying bread from a certain supplier, their decision is binding on the third partner. The majority can deprive the minority partner of the authority to buy bread from that supplier. If the supplier is made aware of the limitation, an order for bread from the minority partner would not bind the partnership or the other partners. If, however, there are only two partners, there can be no majority vote that will be effective to deprive either partner of authority to act for the partnership. Similar stalemates can, of course, arise in any partnership with an even number of partners.

National Biscuit Company v. Stroud

249 N.C. 467, 106 S.E.2d 692 (1959).

C.N. Stroud and Earl Freeman entered into a general partnership to sell groceries under the firm name of Stroud's Food Center. There is nothing in the agreed statement of facts to indicate or suggest that Freeman's power and authority as a general partner were in any way restricted or limited by the articles of partnership in respect to the ordinary and legitimate business of the partnership. Certainly, the purchase and sale of bread were ordinary and legitimate business of Stroud's Food Center during its continuance as a going concern.

Several months prior to February 1956 Stroud advised plaintiff that he personally would not be responsible for any additional bread sold by plaintiff to Stroud's Food Center. After such notice to plaintiff, it from 6 February 1956 to 25 February 1956, at the request of Freeman, sold and delivered bread in the amount of $171.04 to Stroud's Food Center.

In Johnson v. Bernheim, 76 N.C. 139, this Court said: "A and B are general partners to do some given business; the partnership is, by operation of law, a power to each to bind the partnership in any manner legitimate to the business. If one partner go to a third person to buy an article on time for the partnership, the other partner cannot prevent it by writing to the third person not to sell to him on time; or, if one party attempt to buy for cash, the other has no right to require that it shall be on time. And what is true in regard to buying is true in regard to selling. What either partner does with a third person is binding on the partnership. It is otherwise where the partnership is not general, but is upon special terms, as that purchases and sales must be with and for cash. There the power to each is special, in regard to all dealings with third persons at least who have notice of the terms." There is contrary authority. 68 C.J.S. Partnership § 143, pp. 578–579. However, this text of C.J.S. does not mention the effect of the provisions of the Uniform Partnership Act.

The General Assembly of North Carolina in 1941 enacted a Uniform Partnership Act, which became effective 15 March 1941. G.S. Ch. 59, Partnership, Art. 2.

G.S. § 59–39 is entitled "Partner Agent of Partnership as to Partnership Business", and subsection (1) reads: "Every partner is an agent of the partnership for the purpose of its business, and the act of every partner, including the execution in the partnership name of any instrument, for apparently carrying on in the usual way the business of the partnership of which he is a member binds the partnership, unless the partner so acting has in fact no authority to act for the partnership in the particular matter, and the person with whom he is dealing has knowledge of the fact that he has no such authority." G.S. § 59–39(4) states: "No act of a partner in contravention of a restriction on authority shall bind the partnership to persons having knowledge of the restriction."

G.S. § 59–45 provides that "all partners are jointly and severally liable for the acts and obligations of the partnership."

G.S. § 59–48 is captioned "Rules Determining Rights and Duties of Partners." Subsection (e) thereof reads: "All partners have equal rights in the management and conduct of the partnership business." Subsection (h) hereof is as follows: "Any difference arising as to ordinary matters connected with the partnership business may be decided by a majority of the partners; but no act in contravention of any agreement between the partners may be done rightfully without the consent of all the partners."

Freeman as a general partner with Stroud, with no restrictions on his authority to act within the scope of the partnership business so far as the agreed statement of facts shows, had under the Uniform Partnership Act "equal rights in the management and conduct of the partnership business." Under G.S. § 59–48(h) Stroud, his co-partner, could not restrict the power and authority of Freeman to buy bread for the partnership as a going concern, for such a purchase was an "ordinary matter connected with the partnership business," for the purpose of its business and within its scope, because in the very nature of things Stroud was not, and could not be, a majority of the partners. Therefore, Freeman's purchases of bread from plaintiff for Stroud's Food Center as a going concern bound the partnership and his co-partner Stroud. The quoted provisions of our Uniform Partnership Act, in respect to the particular facts here, are in accord with the principle of law stated in Johnson v. Bernheim, supra; same case 86 N.C. 339.

In Crane on Partnership, 2d Ed., p. 277, it is said: "In cases of an even division of the partners as to whether or not an act within the scope of the business should be done, of which disagreement a third person has knowledge, it seems that logically no restriction can be placed upon the power to act. The partnership being a going concern, activities within the scope of the business should not be limited, save by the expressed will of the majority deciding a disputed question; half of the members are not a majority."

Slayden, Fakes & Co. v. Lance, 151 N.C. 492, 66 S.E. 449, is distinguishable. That was a case where the terms of the partnership imposed special restrictions on the power of the partner who made the contract.

At the close of business on 25 February 1956 Stroud and Freeman by agreement dissolved the partnership. By their dissolution agreement all of the partnership assets, including cash on hand, bank deposits and all accounts receivable, with a few exceptions, were assigned to Stroud, who bound himself by such written dissolution agreement to liquidate the firm's assets and discharge its liabilities. It would seem a fair inference from the agreed statement of facts that the partnership got the benefit of the bread sold and delivered by plaintiff to Stroud's Food Center, at Freeman's request, from 6 February 1956 to 25 February 1956. . . . But whether it did or not, Freeman's acts, as stated above, bound the partnership and Stroud.

The judgment of the court below is

Affirmed.

ANALYSIS

What could Stroud have done to protect himself from liability for obligations incurred by Freeman?

PLANNING

Suppose Stroud and Freeman come to you before forming their partnership and ask you to draft a partnership agreement for them. What terms might you propose to avert or mitigate the problem that gave rise to the litigation in this case?

Summers v. Dooley

94 Idaho 87, 481 P.2d 318 (1971).

. . . Summers [plaintiff-appellant] entered a partnership agreement with Dooley (defendant-respondent) in 1958 for the purpose of operating a trash collection business. The business was operated by the two men and when either was unable to work, the non-working partner provided a replacement at his own expense. In 1962, Dooley became unable to work and, at his own expense, hired an employee to take his place. In July, 1966, Summers approached his partner Dooley regarding the hiring of an additional employee but Dooley refused. Nevertheless, on his own initiative, Summers hired the man and paid him out of his own pocket. Dooley, upon discovering that Summers had hired an additional man, objected, stating that he did not feel additional labor was necessary and refused to pay for the new employee out of the partnership funds. Summers continued to operate the business using the third man and in October of 1967 instituted suit in the district court for $6,000 against his partner, the gravamen of the complaint being that Summers has been required to pay out more than $11,000 in expenses, incurred in the hiring of the additional man, without any reimbursement from either the partnership funds or his partner. After trial before the court, sitting without a jury, Summers was granted only partial relief and he has appealed. . . .

The principal thrust of appellant's contention is that in spite of the fact that one of the two partners refused to consent to the hiring of additional help, nonetheless, the non-consenting partner retained profits earned by the labors of the third man and therefore the non-consenting partner should be estopped from denying the need and value of the employee, and has by his behavior ratified the act of the other partner who hired the additional man. . . .

An application of the relevant statutory provisions and pertinent case law to the factual situation presented by the instant case indicates that the trial court was correct in its disposal of the issue since a majority of the partners did not consent to the hiring of the third man. I.C. § 53–318(8) [UPA (1914 § 18(h))] provides:

> "Any difference arising as to ordinary matters connected with the partnership business may be decided by a majority of the partners * * *."

. . . A careful reading of the statutory provision[3] indicates that subsection 5 [UPA (1914) § 18(e)] bestows equal rights in the management and conduct of the partnership business upon all of the partners. The concept of equality between partners with respect to management of business affairs is a central theme and recurs throughout the Uniform Partnership law. . . . Thus the only reasonable interpretation of I.C. § 53–318(8) [UPA (1914) § 18(h)] is that business differences must be decided by a majority of the partners provided no other agreement between the partners speaks to the issues.

In the case at bar one of the partners continually voiced objection to the hiring of the third man. He did not sit idly by and acquiesce in the actions of his partner. Under these circumstances it is manifestly unjust to permit recovery of an expense which was incurred individually and not for the benefit of the partnership but rather for the benefit of one partner.

ANALYSIS

1. What should Summers have done?
2. Could the partners have solved this problem by contract?
3. Why could Freeman (in the *National Biscuit* case, supra) bind his partnership but Summers, in this case, could not?

---

[3] Eds.: The court here quotes UPA (1914) § 18(e), which provides: "The rights and duties of the partners in relation to the partnership shall be determined, subject to any agreement between them, by the following rules: . . . (e) All partners have equal rights in the management and conduct of the partnership business."]

PROBLEM

Alison, Bill, and Charles formed a partnership about two years ago to open and operate a grocery store. In accordance with their initial understanding, Alison has served as general manager, Bill has served as assistant general manager and produce manager, and Charles has run the meat department. About six months ago, Charles hired his son Don to work in the meat department. Alison and Bill believe that Don is surly and slow and that he is driving customers away. They have asked Charles to fire him, but Charles has refused to do so. He thinks Don is brash but lovable and that many customers like his style, and he is satisfied that Don works fast enough to get his job done. The relationship of Alison and Bill with Charles and Don is unpleasant.

Alison and Bill come to you for advice. They ask whether they can fire Don and, if so, how they should go about it. What do you say?

Day v. Sidley & Austin

394 F.Supp. 986 (D.D.C.1975), affirmed sub nom. Day v. Avery, 548 F.2d 1018 (D.C.Cir.1976), cert. denied, 431 U.S. 908 (1977).

This case involves a dispute between a former senior partner of Sidley & Austin (S & A), a Chicago law firm, and some of his fellow partners. The controversy centers around the merger between that firm and another Chicago firm, Liebman, Williams, Bennett, Baird and Minow (Liebman firm), and the events subsequent to the merger which ultimately led to plaintiff's resignation. Plaintiff seeks damages claiming a substantial loss of income, damage to his professional reputation and personal embarrassment which resulted from his forced resignation. . . .

The Factual Background

. . . Mr. Day was first associated with Sidley & Austin in 1938. His legal career was interrupted by World War II service in the Navy and by his tenure with both the Illinois state government and as Postmaster General of the United States. Upon leaving the federal government, he was instrumental in establishing a Washington office for the firm in 1963. As a senior underwriting partner, he was entitled to a certain percentage of the firm's profits, and was also privileged to vote on certain matters which were specified in the partnership agreement. He was never a member of the executive committee, however, which managed the firm's day-to-day business. He remained an underwriting partner with Sidley & Austin from 1963 until his resignation in December 1972.

At some time between February 1972 and July 12, 1972, S & A's executive committee explored the idea of a possible merger between that firm and the Liebman firm. S & A partners who were not on the executive committee were unaware of the proposal until it was revealed at a special meeting of its underwriting partners on July 17, 1972. At that meeting, each partner present, including plaintiff, voiced approval of the merger idea and favored pursuing further that possibility in such manner as the executive committee of S & A might think proper or advisable, with the understanding that any proposed agreement would first be submitted to all partners for their consideration before any binding commitments were made. The merger was further discussed at meetings of the underwriting partners held on September 6, September 22, September 26 and

September 28. The plaintiff received timely notice of the meetings but did not attend.

The final Memorandum of Understanding dated September 29, 1972 and the final amended Partnership Agreement, dated October 16, 1972 were executed by all S & A partners, including plaintiff. The Memorandum incorporated a minor change requested by plaintiff.

At a meeting of the executive committee of the combined firm on October 16, 1972, it was decided that the Washington offices and the Washington office committees of the two predecessor firms would be consolidated. The former chairmen of the Washington office committees of the two firms were appointed co-chairmen of the new Washington Office Committee.

In late October of 1972, the new Washington Office Committee recommended to the Management Committee that a combined Washington office be set up at 1730 Pennsylvania Avenue, thus eliminating the old S & A Washington office in the Cafritz Building. A decision was then made to move to the new location despite plaintiff's objections.

Mr. Day resigned from Sidley & Austin effective December 31, 1972 claiming that the changes which occurred after the merger in the Washington office—the appointment of co-chairmen and the relocation of the office—made continued service with the firm intolerable for him. . . .

[Day] alleges that certain active misrepresentations about the results of the proposal also had the effect of voiding the approval of the merger. These other alleged misrepresentations were:

(1) that no Sidley partner would be worse off in any way as a result of the merger, including positions on committees; . . .

Fraud

. . . The key misrepresentation which forms the basis of plaintiff's complaint is that no Sidley partner would be worse off as a result of the merger. Plaintiff interpreted this to mean that he would continue to serve as the sole chairman of the Washington office and that he would wield the commanding authority regarding such matters as expanding office space. It was the change in plaintiff's status at the Washington office which directly precipitated his resignation.

This misrepresentation regarding plaintiff's status cannot support a cause of action for fraud, however, because plaintiff was not deprived of any *legal* right as a result of his reliance on this statement. The 1970 S & A Partnership Agreement, to which plaintiff was a party, sets forth in some detail the relationships among the partners and the structure of the firm. No mention is made of the Washington office or plaintiff's status therein, whereas special arrangements are specified for certain other partners. If chairmanship of the Washington office was of the importance now claimed, the absence of such a provision from the partnership agreement requires a measured explanation which Mr. Day does not supply. Plaintiff's allegations of an unwritten understanding cannot now be heard to contravene the provisions of the Partnership Agreement which seemingly embodied the complete intentions of the parties as to the manner in which the firm was to be operated and managed.

Nor can plaintiff have reasonably believed that no changes would be made in the Washington office since the S & A Agreement gave complete authority to the executive committee to decide questions of firm policy,[8] which would clearly include establishment of committees and the appointment of members and chairpersons. Having read and signed the 1970 and 1972 S & A partnership agreements which implicitly authorized the Executive Committee to create, control or eliminate firm committees, plaintiff could not have reasonably believed that the status of the Washington Office Committee was inviolate and beyond the scope and operation of the Partnership Agreements. Thus, since plaintiff had no right to remain chairman of the Washington office, a misrepresentation regarding his chairmanship does not form the basis for a cause of action in fraud. . . .

Breach of Fiduciary Duty

Plaintiff also alleges that defendants breached their fiduciary duty by beginning negotiations on a merger with the Liebman firm without consulting the other partners who were not on the executive committee and by not revealing information regarding changes that would occur as a result of the merger, such as the co-chairmen arrangement for the Washington office. An examination of the case law on a partner's fiduciary duties, however, reveals that courts have been primarily concerned with partners who make secret profits at the expense of the partnership. Partners have a duty to make a full and fair disclosure to other partners of all information which may be of value to the partnership. . . . The essence of a breach of fiduciary duty between partners is that one partner has advantaged himself at the expense of the firm. . . . The basic fiduciary duties are: 1) a partner must account for any profit acquired in a manner injurious to the interests of the partnership, such as commissions or purchases on the sale of partnership property; 2) a partner cannot without the consent of the other partners, acquire for himself a partnership asset, nor may he divert to his own use a partnership opportunity; and 3) he must not compete with the partnership within the scope of the business. . . .

A typical case of breach of fiduciary duty and fraud between partners cited by plaintiff is Bakalis v. Bressler, 1 Ill.2d 72, 115 N.E.2d 323 (1953). There, a defendant partner had surreptitiously purchased the building which housed the partnership's business and was collecting rents from the partnership for his own profit. What plaintiff is alleging in the instant

[8] Both the 1970 and 1972 S & A Partnership Agreements contained the following language:

> 1. All questions of Firm policy, including determination of salaries, expense, Partners' participation, required balances of Partners, investment of funds, designation of Counsel, and the admission and severance of Partners, shall be decided by an Executive Committee . . . provided, however, that the determination of participation, admission and severance of Partners, shall require the approval of Partners (whether or not members of the Executive Committee) then holding a majority of all voting Percentages. The Committee shall advise and consult with other Partners to such an extent as the Committee may deem advisable and in the best interest of the Firm.
>
> Any amendment of this Agreement or any subsequent agreement, if signed or initialed by Partners then holding a majority of all voting Percentages, shall be as effective as though signed or initialed by all Partners; provided, however, that any agreement providing for the incorporation of the Firm shall be signed by Partners then holding seventy-five percent (75%) of all voting Percentages. . . .

case, however, concerns failure to reveal information regarding changes in the internal structure of the firm. No court has recognized a fiduciary duty to disclose this type of information, the concealment of which does not produce any profit for the offending partners nor any financial loss for the partnership as a whole. Not only was there no financial gain for defendants, but the remaining partners did not acquire any more power within the firm as the result of the alleged withholding of information from plaintiff. They were already members of the executive committee and as such had wide-ranging authority with regard to firm management. Thus plaintiff's claim of breach of fiduciary duty must fail.

What this Court perceives from Mr. Day's pleadings and affidavits is that he may be suffering from a bruised ego but that the facts fail to establish a legal cause of action. As an able and experienced attorney, it should have been clear that the differences and misunderstandings which developed with his former partners were business risks of the sort which cannot be resolved by judicial proceedings. Mr. Day, a knowledgeable, sophisticated and experienced businessman and a responsible member of a large law firm, bound himself to a well-defined contractual arrangement when he executed the 1970 Partnership Agreement. The contract clearly provided for management authority in the executive committee and for majority approval of the merger with the Liebman firm. Even if plaintiff had voted against the merger, he could not have stopped it. Furthermore, the partnership agreement, to which he freely consented denies the existence of a contractual right to any particular status within the firm for plaintiff. If plaintiff's partners did indeed combine against him, it is clear that their alleged activities did not amount to illegality, and that any personal humiliation or injury was a risk that he assumed when he joined with others in the partnership. . . .

NOTE

Suppose a law partnership consists of 200 partners and that one of them retires. Obviously, the remaining 199 partners will continue to practice law without any noticeable change. Technically, however, under UPA (1914) §§ 29 and 31, the old partnership is dissolved by the retirement of any partner and when the remaining partners continue their practice a new partnership is formed. The partners may have a written partnership agreement that specifies what happens when a partner retires—most particularly, how that partner is paid off for her or his interest in the partnership. The agreement may also contain a provision specifying that the remaining partners will continue as partners under the existing agreement. That provision is a "continuation" agreement—that is, an agreement obligating the remaining partners to continue to associate with one another as partners under the existing agreement (or, perhaps, some variation of it). Thus, when Sidley & Austin and the Liebman firm merged, technically, the two firms dissolved (legally, they ceased to exist) and a new firm was formed. But the Sidley & Austin partnership agreement obligated all of its partners to become partners in the new firm. Any partner who objected to the merger could, before the merger, withdraw from the Sidley & Austin partnership, subject to the provisions of the Sidley & Austin agreement relating to withdrawal.

Under UPA (1997), if a partner retires pursuant to an appropriate provision in the partnership agreement (and in various other situations), there is a "dissociation" (§ 601) rather than a "dissolution" (§ 801). Where there has been a dissociation, the partnership continues as to the remaining partners and the dissociated partner is entitled, in the absence of an agreement to the contrary, to be paid an amount determined as if "on the date of dissociation, the assets of the partnership were sold at a price equal to the greater of the liquidation value or the value based on a sale of the entire business as a going concern without the dissociated partner," plus interest from the date of dissociation. § 701(a) and (b).

What is probably most important about Day v. Sidley & Austin is its illustration of the rule of partnership law that partners are free to make any agreement that suits them, without concern about niceties of partnership theory, and its illustration of the principle of contract law, "You made your bed, now you must lie in it."

ANALYSIS

1. Before the merger, to what extent did Mr. Day have a legal right to share in control? Was there any difference in his legal right to share in control after the merger?

2. Does the Sidley & Austin system for control seem to you to be a sensible one? Why?

3. What should Mr. Day have done, at the time he was about to join Sidley & Austin as manager of its Washington office, to protect himself from the mistreatment he claims he suffered?

4. Presumably the Sidley & Austin partnership agreement contained a provision allowing the firm to oust a partner and specifying a formula for determining the amount the ousted partner was to be paid for his or her share in partnership receivables, work in progress, office equipment, etc. Assuming that Mr. Day was correct in his assertion that he was forced out, in what circumstances, if any, should he be entitled to more than the amount so specified?

5. PARTNERSHIP DISSOLUTION

A. THE RIGHT TO DISSOLVE

Owen v. Cohen

19 Cal.2d 147, 119 P.2d 713 (1941).

This is an action in equity brought for the dissolution of a partnership and for the sale of the partnership assets in connection with the settlement of its affairs.

On or about January 2, 1940, plaintiff and defendant entered into an oral agreement whereby they contracted to become partners in the operation of a bowling-alley business in Burbank, California. The parties did not expressly fix any definite period of time for the duration of this undertaking. For the purpose of securing necessary equipment, plaintiff advanced the sum of $6,986.63 to the partnership, with the understanding that the amount so contributed was to be considered a loan to the partnership and was to be repaid to the plaintiff out of the prospective profits of the business as soon as it could reasonably do so. . . .

Plaintiff and defendant opened their partnership bowling-alley on March 15, 1940. From the day of its beginning until the institution of the present action on June 28, 1940—a period of approximately three and one-half months—the business was operated at a profit. During this time the partners paid off a part of the capital indebtedness and each took a salary of $50 per week. However, shortly after the business was begun differences arose between the partners with regard to the management of the partnership affairs and their respective rights and duties under their agreement. This continuing lack of harmonious relationship between the partners had its effect on the monthly gross receipts, which, though still substantial, were steadily declining, and at the date of the filing of this action much of the partnership indebtedness, including the aforementioned loan made by plaintiff, remained unpaid. On July 5, 1940, in response to plaintiff's complaint and upon order to show cause, the court appointed a receiver to take charge of the partnership business, which ever since has been under his control and management.

As the result of the trial of this action the court found . . . that the parties disagreed "on practically all matters essential to the operation of the partnership business and upon matters of policy in connection therewith"; that the defendant had "committed breaches of the partnership agreement" and had "so conducted himself in affairs relating to the business" that it was "not reasonably practicable to carry on the partnership business with him." From this finding it was concluded that the partnership was dissoluble by court decree in accordance with the provisions of section 2426 of the Civil Code.

Pursuant to these findings of fact and conclusions of law, the trial court rendered a decree adjudging the partnership dissolved and ordering the assets sold by the receiver. It was further decreed that the proceeds of such sale and of the receiver's operation of the business on hand upon the consummation of such sale be applied, after allowance for the receiver's fees and expenses, to payment of the partnership debts, including the amount of $6,986.63 loaned by plaintiff to the business; that one-half of the remainder of the proceeds be paid to plaintiff, together with the additional sum of $100.17 for his costs; and that defendant be given what was left. . . .

The principal question presented for consideration is whether or not the evidence warrants a decree of dissolution of the partnership. . . . While the term of the partnership was not expressly fixed, it must be presumed from this agreement that the parties intended the relation should continue until the obligations were liquidated in the manner mutually contemplated. These circumstances negative the existence of a partnership at will, dissoluble at the election of a member thereof . . . .*

* [Eds.: In a subsequent case, the California Supreme Court explained that:

Owen v. Cohen . . . held that when a partner advances a sum of money to a partnership with the understanding that the amount contributed was to be a loan to the partnership and was to be repaid as soon as feasible from the prospective profits of the business, the partnership is for the term reasonably required to repay the loan. It is true that Owen v. Cohen, supra, and other cases hold that partners may impliedly agree to continue in business until a certain sum of money is earned (Mervyn

It is not necessary to enter into a detailed statement of the quarrel between the partners. Whether the disharmony was the result of a difference in disposition or other causes, the effect is the same. Most of the acts of which complaint is made are individually trivial, but from the aggregate the court found, and the record so indicates, that the breach between the partners was due in large measure to defendant's persistent endeavors to become the dominating figure of the enterprise and to humiliate plaintiff before the employees and customers of the bowling-alley. In this connection plaintiff testified that defendant declined to do any substantial amount of the work required for the successful operation of the business; that defendant informed him that he (defendant) "had not worked yet in 47 years and did not intend to start now"; and that he (plaintiff) "should do whatever manual work he could do on the premises, but that he (defendant) would act as manager and wear the dignity." The record also discloses that during the preparation and before the opening of the bowling-alley establishment, defendant told a mutual acquaintance that plaintiff would not be there very long. Corroborative of this evidence is plaintiff's testimony that a few weeks prior to the filing of this action, when he had concluded that he and defendant could not reconcile their differences, he asked defendant to make an offer either to buy out his (plaintiff's) interest in the business or to sell to him (plaintiff); that defendant replied, in effect, that when he was ready to sell to plaintiff, he would set the price himself and it would cost plaintiff plenty to get rid of him. In addition, there is considerable evidence demonstrating that the partners disagreed on matters of policy relating to the operation of the business. One cause of dispute in this connection was defendant's desire to open a gambling room on the second floor of the bowling-alley property and plaintiff's opposition to such move. Another was defendant's dissatisfaction with the agreed salary of $50 per week fixed for each partner to take from the business and his desire to withdraw additional amounts therefrom. This constant dissension over money affairs culminated in defendant's appropriation of small sums from the partnership's funds to his own use without plaintiff's knowledge, approval or consent. In justification of his conduct defendant

Investment Co. v. Biber, 184 Cal. 637, 641–642, 194 P. 1037), or one or more partners recoup their investments (Vangel v. Vangel, 116 Cal.App.2d 615, 625, 254 P.2d 919), or until certain debts are paid (Owen v. Cohen, supra, 19 Cal.2d at page 150, 119 P.2d at page 714), or until certain property could be disposed of on favorable terms (Shannon v. Hudson, 161 Cal.App.2d 44, 48, 325 P.2d 1022). In each of these cases, however, the implied agreement found support in the evidence.

In Owen v. Cohen, supra, the partners borrowed substantial amounts of money to launch the enterprise and there was an understanding that the loans would be repaid from partnership profits. In Vangel v. Vangel, supra, one partner loaned his co-partner money to invest in the partnership with the understanding that the money would be repaid from partnership profits. In Mervyn Investment Co. v. Biber, supra, one partner contributed all the capital, the other contributed his services, and it was understood that upon the repayment of the contributed capital from partnership profits the partner who contributed his services would receive a one-third interest in the partnership assets. In each of these cases the court properly held that the partners impliedly promised to continue the partnership for a term reasonably required to allow the partnership to earn sufficient money to accomplish the understood objective. In Shannon v. Hudson, supra, the parties entered into a joint venture to build and operate a motel until it could be sold upon favorable and mutually satisfactory terms, and the court held that the joint venture was for a reasonable term sufficient to accomplish the purpose of the joint venture.

Page v. Page, 359 P.2d 41, 43 (Cal. 1961).

claimed that on each occasion he set aside a like amount for plaintiff. This extenuating circumstance, however, does not serve to eliminate from the record the fact that monetary matters were a continual source of argument between the partners.

Defendant urges that the evidence shows only petty discord between the partners, and he advances, as applicable here, the general rule that trifling and minor differences and grievances which involve no permanent mischief will not authorize a court to decree a dissolution of a partnership. 20 R.C.L. 958, par. 182. However, as indicated by the same section in Ruling Case Law and previous sections, courts of equity may order the dissolution of a partnership where there are quarrels and disagreements of such a nature and to such extent that all confidence and cooperation between the parties has been destroyed or where one of the parties by his misbehavior materially hinders a proper conduct of the partnership business. It is not only large affairs which produce trouble. The continuance of overbearing and vexatious petty treatment of one partner by another frequently is more serious in its disruptive character than would be larger differences which would be discussed and settled. For the purpose of demonstrating his own preeminence in the business one partner cannot constantly minimize and deprecate the importance of the other without undermining the basic status upon which a successful partnership rests. In our opinion the court in the instant case was warranted in finding from the evidence that there was very bitter, antagonistic feeling between the parties; that under the arrangement made by the parties for the handling of the partnership business, the duties of these parties required cooperation, coordination and harmony; and that under the existent conditions the parties were incapable of carrying on the business to their mutual advantage. As the court concluded, plaintiff has made out a cause for judicial dissolution of the partnership under section 2426 of the Civil Code [U.P.A. § 32]:

"(1) On application by or for a partner the court shall decree a dissolution whenever:. . . .

"(c) A partner has been guilty of such conduct as tends to affect prejudicially the carrying on of the business,

"(d) A partner wilfully or persistently commits a breach of the partnership agreement, or otherwise so conducts himself in matters relating to the partnership business that it is not reasonably practicable to carry on the business in partnership with him,. . . .

"(f) Other circumstances render a dissolution equitable."

Defendant next questions the propriety of that portion of the decree which provides for the payment of plaintiff's loan to the business, to-wit, the sum of $6,986.63, from the proceeds realized upon the sale of the partnership assets. It is his contention that since the partners agreed that the amount so contributed was to be repaid from the profits of the business, which the evidence established to be a profitable enterprise, the court's order directing the discharge of this partnership obligation in a manner violative of the express understanding of the parties is unjustifiable. . . . That a party to a contract may absolutely limit his right to receive a sum of money from a specified source is indisputable. . . . But defendant's argument based upon this settled precept is of no avail here, for his above-described conduct, creative of a condition of disharmony in derogation of the best interests of the partnership, constituted ground for the court's decree of dissolution and its order directing the sale of the assets for the purpose of forwarding the settlement of the partnership affairs. Defendant, whose persistence in the commission of acts provocative of dissension and disagreement between the partners made it impossible for them to carry on the partnership business, is in no position now to insist on its continued operation. These circumstances not only render the assailed provision of the decree invulnerable to defendant's objection, but also establish its complete accord with established principles of equity jurisprudence.

. . .

The judgment is affirmed.

LEGAL ANALYSIS

1. Why do you suppose the plaintiff filed a lawsuit seeking dissolution rather than simply giving notice of dissolution and demanding a winding up?

2. What is the legal effect of the order for dissolution? What is the likely practical effect?

NOTE AND QUESTION

Under Uniform Partnership Act (UPA) (1997) § 801(5) a partnership is dissolved "on application by a partner, [by] a judicial decree that: (i) the economic purpose of the partnership is likely to be reasonably frustrated; (ii) another partner has engaged in conduct relating to the partnership business that makes it not reasonably practicable to carry on the business in partnership with that partner; or (iii) it is not otherwise reasonably practicable to carry on the partnership business in conformity with the partnership agreement." Do you think this is a change in the right direction?

Collins v. Lewis

283 S.W.2d 258 (Texas Court of Civil Appeals, 1955).

This suit was instituted in the District Court of Harris County by the appellants, who, as the owners of a fifty per cent (50%) interest in a partnership known as the L-C Cafeteria, sought a receivership of the partnership business, a judicial dissolution of the partnership, and foreclosure of a mortgage upon appellees' interest in the partnership assets. Appellees denied appellants' right to the relief sought, and filed a cross-action for damages for breach of contract in the event dissolution should be decreed. Appellants' petition for receivership having been denied after a hearing before the court, trial of the issues of dissolution and foreclosure, and of appellees' cross-action, proceeded before the court and a jury. At the conclusion of such trial, the jury, in response to special issues submitted, returned a verdict upon which the trial court entered judgment denying all relief sought by appellants.

The facts are substantially as follows:

In the latter part of 1948 appellee John L. Lewis obtained a commitment conditioned upon adequate financial backing from the Brown-Bellows-Smith Corporation for a lease on the basement space under the then projected San Jacinto Building for the purpose of constructing and operating a large cafeteria therein. Lewis contacted appellant Carr P. Collins, a resident of Dallas, proposing that he (Lewis) would furnish the lease, the experience and management ability for the operation of a cafeteria, and Collins would furnish the money; that all revenue of the business, except for an agreed salary to Lewis, would be applied to the repayment of such money, and that thereafter all profits would be divided equally between Lewis and Collins. These negotiations failed to materialize because of the inability of Lewis to conclude satisfactory terms with the building owners. Thereafter, in 1949, negotiations along substantially the same terms were reopened, and culminated in the execution between the building owners, as lessors, and Lewis and Collins, as lessees, of a lease upon such basement space for a term of 30 years. Thereafter Lewis and Collins entered into a partnership agreement to endure throughout the term of the lease contract. This agreement is in part evidenced by a formal contract between the parties, but both litigants concede that the complete agreement is ascertainable only from the verbal understandings and exchanges of letters between the principals. . . . The substance of the agreement was that Collins was to furnish all of the funds necessary to build, equip, and open the cafeteria for business. Lewis was to plan and supervise such construction, and, after opening for business, to manage the operation of the cafeteria. As a part of his undertaking, he guaranteed that moneys advanced by Collins would be repaid at the rate of at least $30,000, plus interest, in the first year of operation, and $60,000 per year, plus interest, thereafter, upon default of which Lewis would surrender his interest to Collins. In addition Lewis guaranteed Collins against loss to the extent of $100,000. In the partnership agreement fifty per cent interest therein is reflected to be owned by Collins and certain members of his family, in stated proportions, and the other fifty per cent is reflected to be owned by Lewis and members of his family. However, in their conduct of the business of the partnership, it is conceded by all litigants that Lewis and Collins completely controlled the respective equal fifty per cent interests in the business to the same extent as if the actual ownership were so vested. For the purpose of this opinion, they are treated as if that were in fact the case.

Immediately after the lease agreement had been executed Lewis began the preparation of detailed plans and specifications for the cafeteria. Initially Lewis had estimated, and had represented to Collins, that the cost of completing the cafeteria ready for operation would be approximately $300,000. Due to delays on the part of the building owners in completing the building, and delays in procuring the equipment deemed necessary to opening the cafeteria for business, the actual opening did not occur until September 18, 1952, some 2½ years after the lease had been executed. The innumerable problems which arose during that period are in part reflected in the exchange of correspondence between the partners. Such evidence reflects that as to the solution of most of such problems the partners were in entire agreement. It further reflects that such disagreements as did arise were satisfactorily resolved.

It likewise appears that the actual costs incurred during that period greatly exceeded the amount previously estimated by Lewis to be necessary. The cause of such increase is disputed by the litigants. Appellants contend that it was brought about largely by the extravagance and mismanagement of appellee Lewis. Appellees contend that it resulted from inflation, increased labor and material costs, caused by the Korean War, and unanticipated but necessary expenses. Whatever may have been the reason, it clearly appears that Collins, while expressing concern over the increasing cost, and urging the employment of every possible economy, continued to advance funds and pay expenses, which, by the date of opening for business, had exceeded $600,000.

Collins' concern over the mounting costs of the cafeteria appears to have been considerably augmented by the fact that after opening for business the cafeteria showed expenses considerably in excess of receipts. Upon being informed, shortly after the cafeteria had opened for business, that there existed incurred but unpaid items of cost over and above those theretofore paid, Collins made demand upon Lewis that the cafeteria be placed immediately upon a profitable basis, failing which he (Collins) would advance no more funds for any purpose. There followed an exchange of recriminatory correspondence between the parties, Collins on the one hand charging Lewis with extravagant mismanagement, and Lewis on the other hand charging Collins with unauthorized interference with the management of the business. Futile attempts were made by Lewis to obtain financial backing to buy Collins' interest in the business. Numerous threats were made by Collins to cause Lewis to lose his interest in the business entirely. This suit was filed by Collins in January of 1953.

The involved factual background of this litigation was presented to the jury in a trial which extended over five weeks, and is reflected in a record consisting of a transcript of 370 pages, a statement of facts of 1,400 pages, and 163 original exhibits. At the conclusion of the evidence 23 special issues of fact were submitted to the jury. The controlling issues of fact, as to which a dispute existed, were resolved by the jury in their answers to Issues 1 to 5, inclusive, in which they found that Lewis was competent to manage the business of the L-C Cafeteria; that there is not a reasonable expectation of profit under the continued management of Lewis; that but for the conduct of Collins there would be a reasonable expectation of profit under the continued management of Lewis; that such conduct on the part of Collins was not that of a reasonably prudent person acting under the same or similar circumstances; and that such conduct on the part of Collins materially decreased the earnings of the cafeteria during the first year of its operation. . . .

We agree with appellants' premise that there is no such thing as an indissoluble partnership only in the sense that there always exists the power, as opposed to the right, of dissolution. But legal right to dissolution rests in equity, as does the right to relief from the provisions of any legal contract. The jury finding that there is not a reasonable expectation of profit from the L-C Cafeteria under the continued management of Lewis, must be read in connection with their findings that Lewis is competent to manage the business of L-C Cafeteria, and that but for the conduct of Collins there would be a reasonable expectation of profit therefrom. In our view those are the controlling findings upon the issue of dissolution. It was Collins' obligation to furnish the money; Lewis' to furnish the management, guaranteeing a stated minimum repayment of the money. The jury has found that he was competent, and could reasonably have performed his obligation but for the conduct of Collins. We know of no rule which grants Collins, under such circumstances, the right to dissolution of the partnership. . . .

The basic agreement between Lewis and Collins provided that Collins would furnish money in an amount sufficient to defray the cost of building, equipping and opening the L-C Cafeteria for operation. As a part of the agreement between Lewis and Collins, Lewis executed, and delivered to Collins, a mortgage upon Lewis' interest in the partnership "until the indebtedness incurred by the said Carr P. Collins . . . has been paid in full out of income derived from the said L-C Cafeteria, Houston, Texas."

The evidence shows that a substantial portion of the money used to build, equip and open the cafeteria was borrowed by Collins from the First National Bank in Dallas. The bank credit was admittedly extended upon Collins' financial responsibility. In the mechanics of arranging for such credit, however, Collins prepared and requested Lewis and his family to execute notes in the total sum of $175,000 payable to the First National Bank in Dallas on demand. Lewis expressed concern at creating an obligation payable on terms which he felt unable to meet, whereupon Collins addressed a signed letter to Lewis, containing language as follows: ". . . If you are apprehensive because of the fear that there might be a foreclosure of these notes or a failure to renew these notes for a sufficient period of time to liquidate them at a rate of not more than $2,500 per month the first year and $5,000 per month the second year, I can assure you that the notes will be renewed as often as is necessary to protect you on that point. . . ."

. . .

At about the time this suit was instituted, the First National Bank in Dallas made demand upon Lewis for payment of the notes described, thus maturing the liability of Collins upon his endorsement of the notes. The failure of Lewis to pay such notes on demand constitutes the default, by reason of which Collins seeks foreclosure of his mortgage on Lewis' interest in the partnership. We are unable to agree with appellants in this contention, and must overrule their points presenting it. Regardless of the legal relationship between Lewis and the First National Bank in Dallas, created by the notes described, Lewis' obligation to Collins is limited to repaying money advanced by Collins at the minimum rate of $30,000 the first year and $60,000 per year thereafter. Only upon default of that obligation does the right of foreclosure ripen. There is testimony in the record to the effect that Collins, as a director and stockholder in the Dallas Bank had induced the bank to make demand for payment in order to effect foreclosure. That proof appears to us to be entirely immaterial to the determination of the rights of these litigants. The proof is undisputed that the bank, after maturing the notes, took no further steps to effect collection. Aside from that, however, as we construe the partnership agreement, it was Collins' obligation to furnish all money needed to build, equip and open the cafeteria for business. With particular reference to the notes, it was Collins' obligation to protect Lewis against any demand for payment so long as Lewis met his obligation of repaying money advanced by Collins at the rate agreed upon. Failure on Collins' part to protect Lewis on his obligation to the bank would constitute a breach of contract by Collins.

Collins' right to foreclose, therefore, depends upon whether or not Lewis has met his basic obligation of repayment at the rate agreed upon. Appellees contend, we think correctly, that he has, in the following manner: the evidence shows that Collins advanced a total of $636,720 for the purpose of building, equipping and opening the cafeteria for business. The proof also shows that Lewis contended that the actual cost exceeded that amount by over $30,000. The litigants differed in regard to such excess, it being Collins' contention that it represented operating expense rather than cost of building, equipping and opening the cafeteria. The jury heard the conflicting proof relative to these contentions, and resolved the question by their answer to Special Issue 20, whereby they found that the minimum cost of building, equipping and opening the cafeteria for operation amounted to $697,603.36. Under the basic agreement of the partners, therefore, this excess was properly Collins' obligation. Upon the refusal of Collins to pay it, Lewis paid it out of earnings of the business during the first year of its operation. Thus it clearly appears that Lewis met his obligation, and the trial court properly denied foreclosure of the mortgage.

In their brief, appellants repeatedly complain that they should not be forced to endure a continuing partnership wherein there is no reasonable expectation of profit, which they say is the effect of the trial court's judgment. The proper and equitable solution of the differences which arise between partners is never an easy problem, especially where the relationship is as involved as this present one. We do not think it can properly be said, however, that the judgment of the trial court denying appellants the dissolution which they seek forces them to endure a partnership wherein there is no reasonable expectation of profit. We have already pointed out the ever present inherent power, as opposed to the legal right, of any partner to terminate the relationship. Pursuit of that course presents the problem of possible liability for such damages as flow from the breach of contract. The alternative course available to appellants seems clearly legible in the verdict of the jury, whose services in that connection were invoked by appellants.

Judgment affirmed.

NOTE

This case arose before Texas adopted its version of the UPA (1914) or, later, UPA (1997). The rules of these acts are essentially the same as those applied by the court in Collins v. Lewis.

ANALYSIS

1. What did Collins hope to gain by obtaining a decree of dissolution?

2. Where does the court's refusal to order dissolution leave Collins? What is likely to happen next?

PLANNING

What protection should Collins have had in the partnership agreement? If he had sought such protection, is it likely that Lewis would have objected?

Giles v. Giles Land Company

279 P.3d 139 (Kan. App. 2012).

Kelly Giles (Kelly), a general partner in a family farming partnership, filed suit against the partnership and his partners, arguing that he had not been provided access to partnership books and records. The remaining members of the partnership then filed a counterclaim requesting that Kelly be dissociated from the partnership. The trial court held that Kelly was not denied access to the partnership books and records. Kelly does not appeal from this decision. Moreover, the trial court held that Kelly should be dissociated from the partnership. Kelly, however, contends that the trial court's ruling regarding his dissociation from the partnership was improper. We disagree. Accordingly, we affirm.

The dispute in this case centers on a family owned and operated limited partnership, Giles Land Company, L.P. (partnership). On one side is the plaintiff, Kelly, the second youngest of seven children in the Giles family. On the other side are the defendants: the partnership; Norman Lee Giles and Dolores Giles, the mother and father of the seven children involved; and Kelly's six siblings: Norman Roger Giles (Roger), Lorie Giles Horacek, Trudy Giles Giard, Audry Giles Gates, Jody Giles Peintner, and Julie Giles Cox.

Kelly appeals from the trial court's judgment granting the counterclaim filed by the defendants, which included Norman and Dolores Giles along with their six other children, seeking the dissociation of Kelly from the partnership, under K.S.A. 56a–601 [UPA (1997) § 601]. The trial court also denied Kelly's claim that the defendants had failed to provide him full access to the partnership records, but Kelly does not appeal that judgment.

The record reveals the following facts. The partnership was formed in the mid-1990's. One-half of the assets in the partnership came from a trust held for the benefit of the children of Norman and Dolores, and the other half of the assets came from Norman. Over the years, Norman and Dolores transferred interests in the partnership to their children. The ownership in the partnership is as follows:

	General Partnership Interest	Limited Partnership Interest
Norman Lee Giles	4.634500	03.3357145
Dolores N. Giles	4.634500	03.3357145
Trudy Giles Giard		12.857143
Norman Roger Giles	.243667	12.857143
Audry Giles Gates		12.857143
Jody Giles Peintner		12.857143
Lorie Giles Horacek	.243666	12.857143
Kelly K. Giles	.243667	06.185714
Julie Giles Cox		12.857143
Totals:	10.00%	90.00%

The general partnership interests held by Roger, Lorie, and Kelly were gifted to them by their parents.

The partnership owns both ranchland and farmland. This partnership [Giles Land Company] is not the only Giles family business; there is also Giles Ranch Company and H.G. Land and Cattle Company. In 1999, Kelly was a partner in the Giles Ranch Company, but he became so overwhelmed with the debt he had incurred in the operations of the ranch company that he insisted that he be bought out of the ranch company and relieved of all debt. The other partners managed to buy out Kelly's interest in the ranch company. At the time of the lawsuit, Kelly only had an ownership interest in the partnership at issue, *i.e.,* Giles Land Company.

On March 26, 2007, the partnership held a meeting to discuss converting the partnership into a limited liability company. Kelly was unable to attend the meeting, but he later received a letter explaining the family's interest in converting the partnership to a limited liability company. Kelly did not sign the articles of organization for the proposed conversion and instead had his attorney request production of all of the partnership's books and records for his review. Kelly was not satisfied with the records that the partnership had provided, so he filed suit asking the court to force the partnership to turn over all of the documents he was requesting. In response, the defendants filed an answer and a counterclaim seeking to dissociate Kelly from the partnership.

After a 2-day trial, the trial court determined that the partnership had properly complied with the document requests. The trial court also held that Kelly should be dissociated from the partnership under K.S.A. 56a–601(e)(3) [UPA (1997) § 601(5)(iii)] or, in the alternative, K.S.A. 56a–601(e)(1) [UPA (1997) § 601(5)(i)]. The trial court found that due to Kelly's threats and the total distrust between Kelly and his family, it was not practicable to carry on the business of the partnership so long as Kelly was a partner.

Did the Trial Court Err in Finding that Kelly Should Be Dissociated from the Partnership?

On appeal, Kelly argues that the trial court erred in finding that he should be dissociated from the partnership under K.S.A. 56a–601(e)(3) or, alternatively, K.S.A. 56a–601(e)(1). . . .

K.S.A. 56a–601 states the following:

> A partner is dissociated from a partnership upon the occurrence of any of the following events:
>
> . . . .
>
> (e) on application by the partnership or another partner, the partner's expulsion by judicial determination because:
>
> > (1) The partner engaged in wrongful conduct that adversely and materially affected the partnership business;
> >
> > . . . .
> >
> > (3) the partner engaged in conduct relating to the partnership business which makes it not reasonably practicable to carry on the business in partnership with the partner."

The trial court relied primarily on K.S.A. 56a–601(e)(3) to dissociate Kelly; therefore, the record must demonstrate that (1) Kelly engaged in conduct relating to the partnership business and (2) such conduct makes it not reasonably practicable to carry on the business in partnership with Kelly. See K.S.A. 56a–601(e)(3).

Kansas' partnership statutes were . . . changed on the enactment of the Kansas Revised Uniform Partnership Act in 1998. These changes brought about the concept of dissociation, which previously did not formally exist in our law. . . . The statutory dissociation language in K.S.A. 56a–601(e) is very similar to the dissolution provisions set out in K.S.A. 56a–801(e). The comment to § 601 of the UPA, which is the source of K.S.A. 56a–601(e), confirms that the dissociation provisions were based on the preexisting grounds for dissolution under the UPA. . . . Consequently, caselaw addressing the analogous UPA dissolution provisions is probative in analyzing the defendants' dissociation claim.

Kelly first contends that there is no evidence that he engaged in conduct relating to the partnership business. Kelly argues that the trial court erroneously relied on evidence that he had threatened his family members and that the familial relationship was broken. Kelly maintains that this evidence is not related to the partnership business and, therefore, it was not relevant.

Before we address Kelly's argument as to the trial court's use of this evidence in concluding that dissociation was proper, it is helpful to our review to set out some of the trial court's findings. . . .

First, the trial court found that Kelly did not trust the other general partners and that he did not trust some of his sisters who are limited partners in the partnership. The trial court also found that the general partners as well as all of the other partners did not trust Kelly.

The trial court further found that the relationship between Kelly and the other family members was irreparably broken. In reaching that conclusion, the trial court focused on a meeting between the partners in

2006. Kelly turned to each of the general partners and said that they would each die, in turn, and that he would be the last man standing and that he would then get to control the partnership. Although Kelly testified that this was not a threat and that he was simply trying to explain the right of survivorship, the trial court believed the testimony of the rest of the family that it was taken as a threat. The trial court also relied on evidence that Kelly had said that "paybacks are hell" and that he intended to get even with his partners. The trial court also found this to be a threat. Another fact that the trial court relied on in finding that the family relationship was irreparably broken was that it was impossible for any of the family members to communicate with Kelly regarding the partnership. Each family member testified that he or she believed that it was in the best interest of the partnership to not have Kelly remain a partner.

In finding that Kelly should no longer be a partner, the trial court stated:

> This court finds that the testimony of the counterclaimants regarding the plans of Kelly Giles to take over Giles Land Company, L.P., [the partnership], predicting the deaths of the other General Partners, the statement of Kelly Giles that 'paybacks are hell' and that he would get even, is credible. The Court finds that Kelly Giles' version of events as something close to the magnanimous savior of the family lacked credibility. The Court finds that Kelly Giles was not amenable to land acquisitions or working with the family. . . . The Court further finds that given the lack of trust between Kelly Giles and his siblings who are General Partners, the partnership cannot operate in a meaningful fashion, and certainly cannot operate as intended, as a family business where there is cooperation, as long as Kelly Giles is a partner in [the partnership].

. . .

Additionally, to support its argument that the trial court correctly applied K.S.A. 56a–601(e)(3), the defendants direct this court to consider Brennan v. Brennan Associates, 293 Conn. 60, 977 A. 2d 107 (2009). . . . The *Brennan* court held that "an irreparable deterioration of a relationship between partners is a valid basis to order dissolution, and, therefore, is a valid basis for the alternative remedy of dissociation." 293 Conn. at 81, 977 A. 2d 107.

Here, like in *Brennan,* Kelly argues that the evidence that the trial court relied on was not related to the partnership business. Reviewing the record as a whole, it is clear that the trial court found the evidence to be related to the partnership business because this was a family partnership and all of the alleged disputes were between family members in that partnership. It is also telling that both of the parents and all of the other siblings joined in this lawsuit seeking Kelly's dissociation. Clearly, the relationship between Kelly and his family was broken, and although Kelly attempted to argue that their personal issues were not interfering with the partnership, the trial court did not find his testimony to be credible.

In light of the animosity that Kelly harbors toward his partners and his distrust of them (which distrust is mutual), it is clear that Kelly can no longer do business with his partners and vice-versa. Indeed, the partnership has reached an impasse regarding important business because of a lack of communication between Kelly and his partners. The evidence indicated that most communications with Kelly had to be conducted through his attorney. Moreover, Kelly's statement predicting the deaths of his general partners, his statement that "paybacks are hell," and his statement that he would get even showed a naked ambition on his part to control the partnership, contrary to the interests of the other partners.

. . .

Alternative Theory for Dissociation

The trial court also found that there was enough evidence to dissociate Kelly under K.S.A. 56a–601(e)(1). . . .

Under this alternative theory of dissociation, the record must demonstrate (1) that Kelly engaged in wrongful conduct and (2) that the wrongful conduct adversely and materially affected the partnership business. . . .

Kelly first argues that he did not engage in wrongful conduct towards his parents, Norman and Dolores . . . Additionally, Kelly argues that even if his conduct was wrongful, it did not adversely or materially affect the partnership business. Kelly contends the record shows that the partnership continued to operate as it always had and that the partners failed to show how his conduct materially or adversely affected the business of the partnership.

. . .

Kelly had created a situation where the partnership could no longer carry on its business to the mutual advantage of the other partners. For example, Lorie testified that Kelly would berate and belittle Norman in an attempt to make Norman do what Kelly wanted. There was also testimony given by John Horacek, Lorie's husband, that in a phone conversation between Kelly and Norman, Kelly yelled and cursed at his father and his father was in tears by the end of the conversation. Norman further testified that it would be better for everyone if Kelly were no longer in the partnership because it was clear that Kelly did not agree with what the other partners were wanting to do with the future of the partnership. Norman testified: " 'Cause I think the route we're on now, Judge, if we continue on this, and we don't—we're just at a standstill on what we plan to do." There was also evidence that Kelly had frustrated the partnership's opportunities to purchase more land. . . .

Because this is a family partnership, the evidence of Kelly making threats or berating his parents to get them to give him what he wants qualifies as wrongful conduct. None of the partners were able to interact or communicate with Kelly. Additionally, Norman clearly testified that the partnership was at a standstill because of the disputes between Kelly and the rest of the partners. This is evidence that Kelly was materially or adversely affecting the partnership. Moreover, this evidence is clearly enough to support dissolution based on the caselaw listed earlier; therefore, it is also sufficient for dissociation. Based on this evidence, we determine that the trial court properly held that Kelly could also be dissociated under K.S.A. 56a–601(e)(1).

Affirmed.

NOTE AND QUESTION

Under UPA (1997) § 603, when a partner ceases to be associated with the firm, one of two things can happen. In most cases, per Article 7, the nondissociating partners usually may continue the partnership by buying out the dissociating partner's interest. Section 701 explains, in pertinent part, that:

> (a) If a partner is dissociated from a partnership without resulting in a dissolution and winding up of the partnership business under Section 801, the partnership shall cause the dissociated partner's interest in the partnership to be purchased for a buyout price determined pursuant to subsection (b).
>
> (b) The buyout price of a dissociated partner's interest is the amount that would have been distributable to the dissociating partner under Section 807(b) if, on the date of dissociation, the assets of the partnership were sold at a price equal to the greater of the liquidation value or the value based on a sale of the entire business as a going concern without the dissociated partner and the partnership were wound up as of that date. Interest must be paid from the date of dissociation to the date of payment.

In some cases, however, per Article 8, the partners may—and in some cases, must—go forward with a dissolution and winding up of the business. Section 801 explains that:

> A partnership is dissolved, and its business must be wound up, only upon the occurrence of any of the following events:
>
> (1) in a partnership at will, the partnership's having notice from a partner, other than a partner who is dissociated under Section 601(2) through(10), of that partner's express will to withdraw as a partner, or on a later date specified by the partner;
>
> (2) in a partnership for a definite term or particular undertaking:
>
> > (i) within 90 days after a partner's dissociation by death or otherwise under Section 601(6) through (10) or wrongful dissociation under Section 602(b), the express will of at least half of the remaining partners to wind up the partnership business, for which purpose a partner's rightful dissociation pursuant to Section 602(b)(2)(i) constitutes the expression of that partner's will to wind up the partnership business;
> >
> > (ii) the express will of all of the partners to wind up the partnership business; or
> >
> > (iii) the expiration of the term or the completion of the undertaking;
>
> (3) an event agreed to in the partnership agreement resulting in the winding up of the partnership business;

(4) an event that makes it unlawful for all or substantially all of the business of the partnership to be continued, but a cure of illegality within 90 days after notice to the partnership of the event is effective retroactively to the date of the event for purposes of this section;

(5) on application by a partner, a judicial determination that:

(i) the economic purpose of the partnership is likely to be unreasonably frustrated;

(ii) another partner has engaged in conduct relating to the partnership business which makes it not reasonably practicable to carry on the business in partnership with that partner; or

(iii) it is not otherwise reasonably practicable to carry on the partnership business in conformity with the partnership agreement; or

(6) on application by a transferee of a partner's transferable interest, a judicial determination that it is equitable to wind up the partnership business:

(i) after the expiration of the term or completion of the undertaking, if the partnership was for a definite term or particular undertaking at the time of the transfer or entry of the charging order that gave rise to the transfer; or

(ii) at any time, if the partnership was a partnership at will at the time of the transfer or entry of the charging order that gave rise to the transfer.

On the facts of this case, is either the partnership or Kelly entitled to a dissolution under § 801?

ANALYSIS

1. What did UPA (1997) achieve by adding the possibility of dissociation found in § 601?

2. How did Kelly's actions "materially affect[ ] the partnership business" or "make[ ] it not reasonably practicable to carry on the business in partnership with the partner"?

3. What advice might you have offered Kelly about whether to appeal the judgment of the trial court?

4. Was Kelly's conduct more or less reprehensible than that of defendant Cohen in Owen v. Cohen, supra, of defendant John Lewis in Collins v. Lewis, supra? Regardless of what you conclude on that question, would the plaintiff in either of those cases have been entitled to a dissolution under the principles applied in *Giles*?

B. THE CONSEQUENCES OF DISSOLUTION

Prentiss v. Sheffel

20 Ariz.App. 411, 513 P.2d 949 (1973).

OPINION

The question presented by this appeal is whether two majority partners in a three-man partnership-at-will, who have excluded the third partner from partnership management and affairs, should be allowed to purchase the partnership assets at a judicially supervised dissolution sale. We hold that on the facts of this case, such a purchase is proper, and affirm the judgment entered by the trial court.

Suit was originally brought by plaintiffs-appellees seeking dissolution of a partnership they had formed with defendant-appellant. The partnership was created for the purpose of acquiring and operating the West Plaza Shopping Center located at Bethany Home Road and 35th Avenue in Phoenix, Arizona. (Hereinafter referred to as the Center).

As grounds for dissolution the plaintiffs contended that the defendant had in general been derelict in his partnership duties, and in particular that he had failed to contribute the balance of his proportionate share ($6,000) of the operating losses incurred by the Center. The plaintiffs also sought the trial court's permission to continue the partnership business both during the pendency of the suit and thereafter, and requested that a value be fixed on the defendant's interest in the partnership.

Defendant filed a counterclaim seeking a winding up of the partnership and the appointment of a receiver. He contended that his rights as a partner had been violated in that he had been wrongfully excluded from the partnership.

After an extended evidentiary hearing, the trial court made certain pertinent findings of fact which are here summarized:

1. That each of the plaintiffs owned a 42½% interest in the partnership, with an aggregate interest of 85%, while the defendant was the owner of a 15% interest.

2. That no detailed partnership agreement as to how the business would be supervised, how management decisions would be made, or the term of the partnership's existence, was ever made or entered into at any time between the parties, although there were frequent attempts to arrive at such an agreement.

3. That numerous unresolved disputes arose between the parties, most notably as to how title to the partnership property was to be held, and how management decisions should be made.

4. That as a result of these disputes the relationship between the parties deteriorated, culminating with plaintiffs notifying defendant that any further dealings between them should be through their attorney.

5. That defendant had never been denied physical access to the Center; that he visited there from time to time; and that he also engaged in conversations with the resident manager of the Center.

6. That because of his poor financial condition, defendant had not made payments of all of his pro-rata share of the deficits incurred by the Center when called upon to do so.

7. That since its acquisition, the Center's losses from operations had been materially reduced, and certain more advantageous lease provisions had been secured; that there had been no showing of waste nor detriment to the Center as a result of management operations.

8. That there was a freeze-out or exclusion of the defendant from partnership management and affairs.

Based upon these and other findings of fact the trial court concluded that a partnership-at-will existed between the plaintiffs and the defendant which was dissolved as a result of a freeze-out or exclusion of the defendant from the management and affairs of the partnership. A receiver was appointed by the court until the partnership property could be sold and a partition and distribution of assets could be made. The trial court expressly refused the defendant's request that an order be entered forbidding the plaintiffs from bidding at the contemplated judicial sale.

The receiver and the trial court proceeded with the liquidation and sale of the Center. The plaintiffs were the high bidders at the sale which was held in open court. Subsequently, the court entered an order confirming the sale of the Center to them. It is from this order that the defendant appeals.

The principal contention urged by the defendant is that he was *wrongfully* excluded from the management of the partnership, and therefore, because he would in some way be disadvantaged, the plaintiffs should not be allowed to purchase the partnership assets at a judicial sale. The record, however, does not support the defendant's position on two particulars. While the trial court did find that the defendant was excluded from the management of the partnership, there was no indication that such exclusion was done for the wrongful purpose of obtaining the partnership assets in bad faith rather than being merely the result of the inability of the partners to harmoniously function in a partnership relationship.

Moreover, the defendant has failed to demonstrate how he was injured by the participation of the plaintiffs in the judicial sale. To the contrary, from all the evidence it appears that if the plaintiffs had not participated, the sales price would have been considerably lower. Absent the plaintiffs' bid, there would have been only two qualified initial bids, which were $2,076,000 and $2,040,000 respectively. However, with the participation of plaintiffs, whose initial bid was $2,100,000, the final sales price was bid to $2,250,000. Thus it appears that defendant's 15% interest in the partnership was considerably *enhanced* by the plaintiffs' participation.

. . . The defendant characterizes the sale to plaintiffs as a forced sale of his partnership interest. However, defendant was not forced to sell his interest to the plaintiffs. He had the same right to purchase the partnership assets as they did, by submitting the highest bid at the judicial sale. His argument that the plaintiffs were bidding "paper" dollars due to their 85% partnership interest is without force. He too could have bid "paper" dollars to the extent of his 15% interest. Moreover, the fact that the plaintiffs could bid "paper" dollars made it possible, as defendant recognizes in his brief, for them to bid higher than outsiders. As a consequence of this ability to enter a higher bid, the value of the defendant's 15% interest in the sale proceeds increased proportionately.

. . .

The defendant has cited no cases, nor has this court found any, which have prohibited a partner from bidding at a judicial sale of the partnership assets. . . .

It must be emphasized that on this appeal the defendant does not attack the fact that the trial court ordered a sale of the assets. The only area of attack is that plaintiffs have been allowed to participate and bid in that sale. . . .

The judgment of the superior court is affirmed.

ANALYSIS AND PLANNING

1. Prentiss v. Sheffel involves a partnership for the ownership and operation of a shopping center. Among the decisions that must be made for such a venture are the terms of rental agreements (amount of rent, duration of lease, etc.), selection and compensation of a manager, and the budget for advertising, repairs, and maintenance, and amounts to be spent on improvements. Suppose the two plaintiffs have found that the defendant is difficult to work with and generally uninformed and unhelpful. Their inclination is simply to avoid discussing partnership business with him at all, since they invariably outvote him whenever there is disagreement and they do not want to waste any more of their time trying to work with him. They come to you, asking what problems might be created for them if they proceed in accordance with this inclination and what suggestions you might have. What is your response?

2. (a) Property may be worth more to its current owners than to outsiders. One reason for this may be that the outsiders may fear that the owners are aware of some defect that the outsiders cannot observe. It may be that there are no such defects, but the owners may not be able to convince outsiders of that reality. Costs of transfer of ownership and management also may explain why property may be worth more to its current owners than to potential buyers.

(b) Suppose Amy, Bob, and Carol are equal partners in a firm that owns a shopping center. The partnership is terminable at will. Amy and Bob work together well. Their relationship with Carol is unpleasant and unproductive. They would like to buy Carol's one-third interest and would be willing to pay up to $700,000 for it, but they would prefer to pay less. They believe that the most an outsider would be willing to pay for the shopping center would be $1,800,000 ($600,000 for each partner). Consider two possible rules of law. Under Rule A (the rule of Prentiss v. Sheffel), Amy and Bob can dissolve the partnership, can insist on an auction, and can bid for the property themselves, using their interest in the partnership as partial payment. Under Rule B, Amy and Bob can dissolve the partnership, which will result in an auction of the property, but they will not be permitted to bid on the property. Suppose that Amy and Bob offer Carol $610,000 for her interest in the partnership. If Rule A is the law, how is Carol likely to respond? What if Rule B is the law? What do your answers to these questions tell you about which rule you would propose for a partnership agreement if you were advising the parties at the outset, at a time when all the partners anticipate cordial and productive relationships with one another? What are the results under each rule if the parties have different beliefs about what price an outsider would bid at an auction? For example, what if Amy and Bob think an outsider would bid at most $1,800,000, while Carol thinks an outsider would bid $2,400,000? What if these expectations are reversed?

Pav-Saver Corporation v. Vasso Corporation

143 Ill.App.3d 1013, 97 Ill.Dec. 760, 493 N.E.2d 423 (1986).

The matter before us arises out of the dissolution of the parties' partnership, the Pav-Saver Manufacturing Company. The facts are not in dispute, and only those needed to explain our disposition on the issues on appeal will be stated.

Plaintiff, Pav-Saver Corporation ("PSC") is the owner of the Pav-Saver trademark and certain patents for the design and marketing of concrete paving machines. Harry Dale is the inventor of the Pav-Saver "slip-form" paver and the majority shareholder of PSC, located in Moline, Illinois. H. Moss Meersman is an attorney who is also the owner and sole shareholder of Vasso Corporation. In 1974 Dale, individually, together with PSC and Meersman formed Pav-Saver Manufacturing Company for the manufacture and sale of Pav-Saver machines. Dale agreed to contribute his services, PSC contributed the patents and trademark necessary to the proposed operation, and Meersman agreed to obtain financing for it. The partnership agreement was drafted by Meersman and approved by Attorney Charles Peart, president of PSC. The agreement contained two paragraphs which lie at the heart of the appeal and cross-appeal before us:

> "3. The duties, obligations and functions of the respective partners shall be:
>
> A. Meersman shall provide whatever financing is necessary for the joint venture, as required.
>
> B. (1) PAV-SAVER shall grant to the partnership without charge the exclusive right to use on all machines manufactured and sold, its trademark 'PAV-SAVER' during the term of this Agreement. In order to preserve and maintain the good will and other values of the trademark PAV-SAVER, it is agreed between the parties that PAV-SAVER Corporation shall have the right to inspect from time to time the quality of machines upon which the licensed trademark PAV-SAVER is used. . . . Any significant changes in structure, materials or components shall be disclosed in writing or by drawings to PAV-SAVER Corporation.
>
> (2) PAV-SAVER grants to the partnership exclusive license without charge for its patent rights in and to its Patent #3,377,933 for the term of this agreement and exclusive license to use its specifications and drawings for the Slip-form paving machine known as Model MX 6–33, plus any specifications and drawings for any extensions, additions and attachments for said machine for said term. It [is] understood and agreed that same shall remain the property of PAV-SAVER and all copies shall be returned to PAV-SAVER at the expiration of this partnership.

> Further, PAV-SAVER, so long as this agreement is honored and is in force, grants a license under any patents of PAV-SAVER granted in the United States and/or other countries applicable to the Slip-Form paving machine.
>
> . . .
>
> "11. It is contemplated that this joint venture partnership shall be permanent, and same shall not be terminated or dissolved by either party except upon mutual approval of both parties. If, however, either party shall terminate or dissolve said relationship, the terminating party shall pay to the other party, as liquidated damages, a sum equal to four (4) times the gross royalties received by PAV-SAVER Corporation in the fiscal year ending July 31, 1973, as shown by their corporate financial statement. Said liquidated damages to be paid over a ten (10) year period next immediately following the termination, payable in equal installments."

In 1976, upon mutual consent, the PSC/Dale/Meersman partnership was dissolved and replaced with an identical one between PSC and Vasso, so as to eliminate the individual partners.

It appears that the Pav-Saver Manufacturing Company operated and thrived according to the parties' expectations until around 1981, when the economy slumped, sales of the heavy machines dropped off significantly, and the principals could not agree on the direction that the partnership should take to survive. On March 17, 1983, Attorney Charles Peart, on behalf of PSC, wrote a letter to Meersman terminating the partnership and invoking the provisions of paragraph 11 of the parties' agreement.

In response, Meersman moved into an office on the business premises of the Pav-Saver Manufacturing Company, physically ousted Dale, and assumed a position as the day-to-day manager of the business. PSC then sued in the circuit court of Rock Island County for a court-ordered dissolution of the partnership, return of its patents and trademark, and an accounting. Vasso counterclaimed for declaratory judgment that PSC had wrongfully terminated the partnership and that Vasso was entitled to continue the partnership business, and other relief pursuant to the Illinois Uniform Partnership Act. . . . After protracted litigation, the trial court ruled that PSC had wrongfully terminated the partnership; that Vasso was entitled to continue the partnership business and to possess the partnership assets, including PSC's trademark and patents; that PSC's interest in the partnership was $165,000, based on a $330,000 valuation for the business; and that Vasso was entitled to liquidated damages in the amount of $384,612, payable pursuant to paragraph 11 of the partnership agreement. Judgment was entered accordingly.

Both parties appealed. PSC takes issue with the trial court's failure to order the return of its patents and trademark or, in the alternative, to assign a value to them in determining the value of the partnership assets. Further, neither party agrees with the trial court's enforcement of their agreement for liquidated damages. In its cross-appeal, PSC argues that the amount determined by the formula in paragraph 11 is a penalty. Vasso, on the other hand, contends in its appeal that the amount is unobjectionable, but the installment method of pay-out should not be enforced.

In addition to the afore-cited paragraphs of the parties' partnership agreement, the resolution of this case is controlled by the dissolution provision of the Uniform Partnership Act [§ 38] (Ill.Rev.Stat.1983, ch. 106½, pars. 29–43). The Act provides:

> "(2). When dissolution is caused in contravention of the partnership agreement the rights of the partners shall be as follows:
>
> (a) Each partner who has not caused dissolution wrongfully shall have
>
> . . .
>
> II. The right, as against each partner who has caused the dissolution wrongfully, to damage for breach of the agreement.
>
> (b) The partners who have not caused the dissolution wrongfully, if they all desire to continue the business in the same name, either by themselves or jointly with others, may do so, during the agreed term for the partnership and for that purpose may possess the partnership property, provided they secure the payment by bond approved by the court, or pay to any partner who has caused the dissolution wrongfully, the value of his interest in the partnership at the dissolution, less any damages recoverable under clause (2a II) of this section, and in like manner indemnify him against all present or future partnership liabilities.
>
> (c) A partner who has caused the dissolution wrongfully shall have:
>
> . . .
>
> II. If the business is continued under paragraph (2b) of this section the right as against his co-partners and all claiming through them in respect of their interests in the partnership, to have the value of his interest in the partnership, less any damages caused to his co-partners by the dissolution, ascertained and paid to him in cash, or the payment secured by bond approved by the court and to be released from all existing liabilities of the partnership; but in ascertaining the value of the partner's interest the value of the good will of the business shall not be considered."Ill.Rev.Stat.1983, ch. 106½, par. 38(2).

Initially we must reject PSC's argument that the trial court erred in refusing to return Pav-Saver's patents and trademark pursuant to paragraph 3 of the partnership agreement, or in the alternative that the court erred in refusing to assign a value to PSC's property in valuing the partnership assets. The partnership agreement on its face contemplated a "permanent" partnership, terminable only upon mutual approval of the parties (paragraph 11). It is undisputed that PSC's unilateral termination was in contravention of the agreement. The wrongful termination necessarily invokes the provisions of the Uniform

Partnership Act so far as they concern the rights of the partners. Upon PSC's notice terminating the partnership, Vasso elected to continue the business pursuant to section 38(2)(b) of the Uniform Partnership Act. As correctly noted by Vasso, the statute was enacted "to cover comprehensively the problem of dissolution . . . [and] to stabilize business." (Kurtzon v. Kurtzon (1st Dist.1950), 339 Ill.App. 431, 437, 90 N.E.2d 245, 248.) Ergo, despite the parties' contractual direction that PSC's patents would be returned to it upon the mutually approved expiration of the partnership (paragraph 3), the right to possess the partnership property and continue in business upon a wrongful termination must be derived from and is controlled by the statute. Evidence at trial clearly established that the Pav-Saver machines being manufactured by the partnership could not be produced or marketed without PSC's patents and trademark. Thus, to continue in business pursuant to the statutorily-granted right of the party not causing the wrongful dissolution, it is essential that paragraph 3 of the parties' agreement—the return to PSC of its patents—not be honored.

Similarly, we find no merit in PSC's argument that the trial court erred in not assigning a value to the patents and trademark. The only evidence adduced at trial to show the value of this property was testimony relating to good will. It was unrefuted that the name Pav-Saver enjoys a good reputation for a good product and reliable service. However, inasmuch as the Uniform Partnership Act specifically states that "the value of the good will of the business shall not be considered" (Ill.Rev.Stat.1983, ch. 106½, par. 38(2)(c)(II)), we find that the trial court properly rejected PSC's good will evidence of the value of its patents and trademark in valuing its interest in the partnership business.

[In the portion of the opinion omitted here the court rejects PSC's argument that the liquidated damages amount was an unenforceable "penalty." Among other observations, the court notes that the amount, $384,612, was payable in equal installments over a period of 10 years, which means that the present value, or current lump-sum equivalent, was substantially less.]

. . .

Affirmed.

■ JUSTICE STOUDER concurring in part—dissenting in part.

I generally agree with the result of the majority. I cannot, however, accept the majority's conclusion the defendant is entitled to retention of the patents.

. . .

The plaintiff (PSC) brought this action at law seeking dissolution of the partnership before expiration of the agreed term of its existence. Under the Uniform Partnership Act where dissolution is caused by an act in violation of the partnership agreement, the other partner(s) are accorded certain rights. The partnership agreement is a contract, and even though a partner may have the power to dissolve, he does not necessarily have the right to do so. Therefore, if the dissolution he causes is a violation of the agreement, he is liable for any damages sustained by the innocent partner(s) as a result thereof. The innocent partner(s) also have the option to continue the business in the firm name provided they pay the partner causing the dissolution the value of his interest in the partnership. (Ill.Rev.Stat.1983, ch. 106½, par. 38(1), (2).)

The duties and obligations of partners arising from a partnership relation are regulated by the express contract as far as they are covered thereby. A written agreement is not necessary but where it does exist it constitutes the measure of the partners' rights and obligations. While the rights and duties of the partners in relation to the partnership are governed by the Uniform Partnership Act, the uniform act also provides that such rules are subject to any agreement between the parties. . . .

The partnership agreement entered into by PSC and Vasso in pertinent part provides:

> "3.B.(2) [PSC] grants to the partnership exclusive license without charge for its patent rights . . . for the term of this agreement. . . . [I]t being understood and agreed that same shall remain the property of [PSC] . . . and shall be returned to [PSC] at the expiration of this partnership. . . ."

The majority holds this provision in the contract is unenforceable. The only apparent reason for such holding is that its enforcement would affect defendant's option to continue the business. No authority is cited to support such a rule.

The partnership agreement further provides:

> "11. . . . If either party shall terminate or dissolve said [partnership], the terminating party shall pay to the other party as liquidated damages . . . [$384,612]."

This provision becomes operative at the same time as the provision relating to the return of the patents.

. . .

Here, [because] express terms of the partnership agreement deal with the status of the patents and measure of damages, the question is settled thereby. I think it clear the parties agreed the partnership only be allowed the use of the patents during the term of the agreement. The agreement having been terminated, the right to use the patents is terminated. The provisions in the contract do not conflict with the statutory option to continue the business and even if there were a conflict the provisions of the contract should prevail. The option to continue the business does not carry with it any guarantee or assurance of success and it may often well be that liquidation rather than continuation would be the better option for a partner not at fault.

As additional support for my conclusion, it appears the liquidated damages clause was insisted upon by the defendant because of earlier conduct of the plaintiff withdrawing from a former partnership. Thus, the existence of the liquidated damages clause recognizes the right of plaintiff to withdraw the use of his patents in accordance with the specific terms of the partnership agreement. Since liquidated damages depends on return of the patents, I would vacate that part of the judgment providing defendant is entitled to continue use of the patents and provide that use shall remain with plaintiff.

ANALYSIS AND PLANNING

1. Under the decision of the court, what happens next? Is PSC ever entitled to a cash distribution for its interest in the partnership?

2. This case provides a good illustration of a common problem in drafting agreements: the failure to think through and specify how the terms of the agreement are to be carried out. Here the agreement provided for termination, and liquidated damages, but failed to specify, step by step, precisely what would happen following a notice of termination. If you had been called upon to draft the agreement, what questions of implementation, following termination, would you have raised with the parties? What possibilities for resolving those questions would you have been prepared to offer?

NOTE

Under § 701 of the Uniform Partnership Act (1997), if a partner withdraws from a partnership in contravention of the partnership agreement, the partnership does not necessarily dissolve. If it does not, the partnership must buy out the withdrawing ("dissociated") partner for an amount equal to his or her share of the value of the assets of the partnership if "sold at a price equal to the greater of the liquidation value or the value based on a sale of the entire business as a going concern without the dissociated partner." This amount is reduced by any damages for wrongful withdrawal. Contrary to UPA (1914) § 38(2)(c)(II), however, there is no reduction for the value of goodwill.

C. THE SHARING OF LOSSES

Kovacik v. Reed

49 Cal.2d 166, 315 P.2d 314 (Cal. 1957).

[Early in November 1952, Kovacik told Reed that he (Kovacik) had a chance to remodel some kitchens in San Francisco, and asked Reed to become his job superintendent and estimator. Kovacik explained that he had about $10,000.00 to invest and that, if Reed would superintend and estimate the jobs, he would share profits on a 50–50 basis. Kovacik did not ask Reed to share any losses that might result, and Reed did not offer to do so. Indeed, the two did not discuss possible losses at all. Reed accepted Kovacik's proposal and began work on the venture immediately. Through their venture, the two were able to obtain several remodeling jobs. Reed worked on all of the jobs as job superintendent, but contributed no funds. Instead, Kovacik provided the financing. In August, 1953, Kovacik (who kept all of the financial records) told Reed that the venture had lost money. He then demanded that Reed contribute to the amounts that he (Kovacik) had advanced beyond the income he received. Reed claimed that he never agreed to be liable for losses, and refused to pay.*]

Kovacik thereafter instituted this proceeding, seeking an accounting of the affairs of the venture and to recover from Reed one half of the losses. Despite the evidence above set forth from the statement of the oral

* [Eds.—The statement of facts is taken from a stipulated version relied upon by the court.]

proceedings, showing that at no time had defendant agreed to be liable for any of the losses, the trial court "found"—more accurately, we think, concluded as a matter of law—that "plaintiff and defendant were to share equally all their joint venture profits and losses between them," and that defendant "agreed to share equally in the profits and losses of said joint venture." Following an accounting taken by a referee appointed by the court, judgment was rendered awarding plaintiff recovery against defendant of some $4,340, as one half the monetary losses[1] found by the referee to have been sustained by the joint venture.

It is the general rule that in the absence of an agreement to the contrary the law presumes that partners and joint adventurers intended to participate equally in the profits and losses of the common enterprise, irrespective of any inequality in the amounts each contributed to the capital employed in the venture, with the losses being shared by them in the same proportions as they share the profits. . . .

However, it appears that in the cases in which the above stated general rule has been applied, each of the parties had contributed capital consisting of either money or land or other tangible property, or else was to receive compensation for services rendered to the common undertaking which was to be paid before computation of the profits or losses.

Where, however, as in the present case, one partner or joint adventurer contributes the money capital as against the other's skill and labor, all the cases cited, and which our research has discovered, hold that neither party is liable to the other for contribution for any loss sustained. Thus, upon loss of the money the party who contributed it is not entitled to recover any part of it from the party who contributed only services.

The rationale of this rule . . . is that where one party contributes money and the other contributes services, then in the event of a loss each would lose his own capital—the one his money and the other his labor. Another view would be that in such a situation the parties have, by their agreement to share equally in profits, agreed that the values of their contributions—the money on the one hand and the labor on the other—were likewise equal; it would follow that upon the loss, as here, of both money and labor, the parties have shared equally in the losses. Actually, of course, plaintiff here lost only some $8,680—or somewhat less than the $10,000 which he originally proposed and agreed to invest. . . .

The judgment is reversed.

---

[1] The record is silent as to the factors taken into account by the referee in determining the "loss" suffered by the venture. However, there is no contention that defendant's services were ascribed any value whatsoever. It may also be noted that the trial court "found" that "neither plaintiff nor defendant was to receive compensation for their services rendered to said joint venture, but plaintiff and defendant were to share equally all their joint venture profits and losses between them." Neither party suggests that plaintiff actually rendered services to the venture in the same sense that defendant did. And, as is clear from the settled statement, plaintiff's proposition to defendant was that plaintiff would provide the money as against defendant's contribution of services as estimator and superintendent.

NOTES AND QUESTIONS

1. The relevant statutory provisions are UPA (1914) §§ 18(a) and 40. The former provides, in pertinent part:

> The rights and duties of the partners in relation to the partnership shall be determined, subject to any agreement between them, by the following rules:
>
> (a) Each partner shall be repaid his contributions, whether by way of capital or advances to the partnership property and share equally in the profits and surplus remaining after all liabilities, including those to partners, are satisfied; and must contribute towards the losses, whether of capital or otherwise sustained by the partnership according to his share in the profits.

Section 40(b) provides that, subject to any contrary agreement, upon dissolution, liabilities of the partnership shall be paid in the following order:

> I. Those owing to creditors other than partners,
>
> II. Those owing to partners other than for capital and profits,
>
> III. Those owing to partners in respect of capital,
>
> IV. Those owing to partners in respect of profits.

Subsection 40(d) further provides, in pertinent part: "The partners shall contribute, as provided by section 18(a) the amount necessary to satisfy the liabilities [set forth in § 40(b)]."

Is the holding in *Kovacik* consistent with the plain meaning, if any, of these provisions? The drafters of the revised Uniform Partnership Act (1997) apparently did not believe so. Section 401(b) readopts the loss sharing rule of UPA section 18(a): "Each partner is entitled to an equal share of the partnership profits and is chargeable with a share of partnership losses in proportion to the partner's share of the profits." Even more to the point, the official comment thereto expressly rejects *Kovacik*.

> Subsection (b) establishes the default rules for the sharing of partnership profits and losses. The UPA § 18(a) rules that profits are shared equally and that losses, whether capital or operating, are shared in proportion to each partner's share of the profits are continued. . . . The default rules apply, as does UPA § 18(a), where one or more of the partners contribute no capital, although there is case law to the contrary [citing, inter alia, *Kovacik*].

2. What result if Reed had made even a nominal monetary contribution to the partnership's capital or had received some compensation for his services? What result if Kovacik had done as much work on the partnership's jobs as had Reed? What if Kovacik had done about half—or one quarter—as much work as Reed?

3. Were Kovacik and Reed free to adopt any rule they wanted for sharing of losses? If so, why do you suppose they failed to do so?

4. Is it likely in this case that Kovacik was more wealthy than Reed? Is it more likely in most cases that the contributor of capital will be more wealthy than the contributor of services? If so, how should that affect the outcome of the case?

5. Should the outcome in a case like *Kovacik* turn on which of the partners originated the project or business? If so, should the legal rule turn on the how this issue is resolved in each case or on how it is likely to turn out in most cases?

6. Under the *Kovacik* rule, the services-only partner does not share in loss of the amount initially invested by the capital-only partner. What concern might the capital-only partner have about the effect of this rule on the job performance or the decisionmaking by the services-only partner? How might that concern affect the bargain over loss sharing?

7. It appears that Kovacik and Reed had not bargained over, or even discussed, the question of allocating losses in the event the partnership failed. If they had bargained, what rule do you suppose they would have adopted? Would they likely have agreed that Reed had no obligation to contribute to partnership losses? Does your answer to that question inform your analysis of the merits of the rule announced in *Kovacik*?

D. BUYOUT AGREEMENTS

A buy-out, or buy-sell, agreement is an agreement that allows a partner to end her or his relationship with the other partners and receive a cash payment, or series of payments, or some assets of the firm, in return for her or his interest in the firm. There are many possible approaches. A good buy-out agreement must be tailored to the needs and circumstances of each firm. Here is a brief outline of some of the issues and alternatives:

I. "Trigger" events
   A. Death
   B. Disability
   C. Will of any partner
II. Obligation to buy versus option
   A. Firm
   B. Other investors
   C. Consequences of refusal to buy
      i. If there is an obligation
      ii. If there is no obligation
III. Price
   A. Book value
   B. Appraisal
   C. Formula (e.g., five times earnings)
   D. Set price each year
   E. Relation to duration (e.g., lower price in first five years)

IV. Method of payment
   A. Cash
   B. Installments (with interest?)
V. Protection against debts of partnership
VI. Procedure for offering either to buy or sell
   A. First mover sets price to buy or sell
   B. First mover forces others to set price

What terms would you propose for a buy-out agreement in the situations described in each of the cases presented in the preceding section?

G & S Investments v. Belman

145 Ariz. 258, 700 P.2d 1358 (Ct. App., Div. 2, 1984).

This case involves a partnership dispute arising out of the misconduct and subsequent death of Thomas N. Nordale. There are two principal issues in this case: whether the surviving general partner, G & S Investments, is entitled to continue the partnership after the death of Nordale, and how the value of Nordale's interest in partnership property is to be computed. The trial court, after making findings of fact and conclusions of law, entered judgment in favor of G & S Investments, finding that it had the right to continue the partnership and that the estate was owed $4,867.57. . . .

Century Park, Ltd., is a limited partnership which was formed to receive ownership of a 62-unit apartment complex in Tucson. In 1982 the general partners were G & S Investments (51 per cent) and Nordale (25.5 per cent). The remaining partnership interest was owned by the limited partners, Jones and Chapin.

In 1979 Nordale began using cocaine, which caused a personality change. He became suspicious of his partners and other people, and he could not communicate with other people. He stopped going to work and stopped keeping normal business hours. He stopped returning phone calls and became hyperactive, agitated and angry toward people for no reason. Commencing in 1980 he made threats to some of the other partners, stating that he was going to get them and fix them.

Nordale lived in the apartment complex. This led to several problems. He sexually solicited an underage female tenant of the complex. Despite repeated demands, he refused to give up possession or pay rent on an apartment that the partnership had allowed him to use temporarily during his divorce. His lifestyle in the apartment complex created a great deal of tension and disturbance and frightened the tenants. At least one tenant was lost because of the disturbances.

Fundamental business and management disputes also arose. Nordale irrationally insisted upon converting the apartment complex into condominiums despite adverse tax consequences and mortgage interest rates that were at an all-time high. He also insisted on raising the rents despite the fact that recent attempts to do so had resulted in mass vacancies which had a devastating economic effect on the partnership enterprise.

By 1981 Gary Gibson and Steven Smith (G & S Investments) had come to the conclusion that Nordale was incapable of making rational business decisions and that they should seek a dissolution of the partnership which would allow them to carry on the business and buy out Nordale's interest.

The original complaint, filed on September 11, 1981, sought a judicial dissolution and the right to carry on the business and buy out Nordale's interest as permitted by [UPA (1914) § 38].

. . .

After the filing of the complaint, on February 16, 1982, Nordale died. On June 28, 1982, appellees filed a supplemental complaint invoking their right to continue the partnership and acquire Nordale's interest under article 19 of the partnership's Articles of Limited Partnership. The key provisions of article 19 are as follows:

> "(a) In the interest of a continuity of the partnership it is agreed that upon the death, retirement, insanity or resignation of one of the general partners . . . *the surviving or remaining general partners may continue the partnership business. . . .*
>
> . . .
>
> (e) Rules as to resignation or retirement [which under Article 19(d) includes death].
>
> . . .
>
> (2) In the event the surviving or remaining general partner shall desire to continue the partnership business, *he shall purchase the interest of the retiring or resigning general partner. . . .* "(Emphasis added)

. . .

THE FILING OF THE ORIGINAL COMPLAINT

Appellant contends that the mere filing of the complaint acted as a dissolution of the partnership, requiring the liquidation of the assets and distribution of the net proceeds to the partners. He takes this position because he believes the estate will receive more money under this theory than if the other partners are allowed to carry on the business upon payment of the amount which was due to Nordale under the partnership agreement. Appellees contend that the filing of the complaint did not cause a dissolution but that the wrongful conduct of Nordale, in contravention of the partnership agreement, gave the court the power to dissolve the partnership and allow them to carry on the business by themselves. See [UPA (1914) § 38.] We agree with appellees.

Contrary to appellant's contention, Nordale's conduct was in contravention of the partnership agreement. Nordale's conduct affected the carrying on of the business and made it impracticable to continue in partnership with him. His conduct was wrongful and was in contravention of the partnership agreement, thus allowing the court to permit appellees to carry on the business. . . . [UPA (1914) § 32] authorizes the court to dissolve a partnership when:

> "(2) A partner becomes in any other way incapable of performing his part of the partnership contract.

(3) A partner has been guilty of such conduct as tends to affect prejudicially the carrying on of the business.

(4) A partner willfully or persistently commits a breach of the partnership agreement, or otherwise so conducts himself in matters relating to the partnership business that it is not reasonably practicable to carry on the business in partnership with him. . . ."

In the case of Cooper v. Isaacs, 448 F.2d 1202 (D.C.Cir.1971) the court was met with the same contention made here, to-wit, that the mere filing of the complaint acted as a dissolution. The court rejected this contention. To paraphrase the reasoning of the court in Cooper v. Isaacs, supra, because the Uniform Partnership Act provides for dissolution for cause by decree of court and appellees have alleged facts which would entitle them to a dissolution on this ground if proven, their filing of the complaint cannot be said to effect a dissolution, wrongful or otherwise, under the act; dissolution would occur only when decreed by the court or when brought about by other acts.

ARTICLE 19 OF THE ARTICLES OF PARTNERSHIP

Article 19 of the Articles of Partnership provides that upon the death, retirement, insanity or resignation of one of the general partners the surviving or remaining general partners may continue the partnership business. It further provides that should the surviving or remaining general partners desire to continue the partnership business, they must purchase the interest of the retiring or resigning general partner. . . .

THE BUY-OUT FORMULA

Article 19(e)(2)(i) contains the following buy-out provision:

"The amount shall be calculated as follows:

By the addition of the sums of the amount of the resigning or retiring general partner's *capital account* plus an amount equal to the average of the prior three years' profits and gains actually paid to the general partner, or as agreed upon by the general partners, provided said agreed sum does not exceed the calculated sum in dollars." (Emphasis added)

Appellant claims that the term "capital account" in article 19(e)(2)(i) is ambiguous. The estate relies on the testimony of an accountant, Jon Young, that the term "capital account" is ambiguous merely because there is no definition of the term in the articles. He claimed that it was not clear whether the cost basis or the fair market value of the partnership's assets should be used in determining the capital account. Even on direct examination, however, Young admitted that read literally the buy-out formula takes the capital account of the deceased partner and adds to that amount the average of the prior three years' earnings. On cross-examination he admitted that generally accepted accounting principles require the partnership capital accounts be maintained on a cost basis and that he has never seen a partnership in which the capital accounts in the books and records were based on the fair market value. . . .

In contrast, Gibson and Smith testified that the parties actually intended and understood "capital account" to mean exactly what it literally says, the account which shows a partner's capital contribution to the partnership plus profits minus losses.* Smith, an accountant, further testified that while there is a relationship between the capital accounts and valuation of the partnership assets, the valuation of the assets does not affect the actual entries made on the capital account.

There was no dispute that Nordale's capital account showed a negative balance of $44,510.09, . . . [while] the fair market value of his interest in the partnership . . . would have amounted to the sum of $76,714.24.

. . .

The words "capital account" are not ambiguous and clearly mean the partner's capital account as it appears on the books of the partnership. Our conclusion is further buttressed by the entire language of article 19(e)(2)(i) which requires, for a buy-out, the payment of the amount of the partner's capital account plus other sums. This is "capital account" language and not "fair market value" language.

. . .

Because partnerships result from contract, the rights and liabilities of the partners among themselves are subject to such agreements as they may make. . . .

Partnership buy-out agreements are valid and binding although the purchase price agreed upon is less or more than the actual value of the interest at the time of death. . . .

We do not have the power to rewrite article 19 based upon subjective notions of fairness arising long after the agreement was made or because the agreement did not turn out to be an advantageous one. Modern business practice mandates that the parties be bound by the contract they enter into, absent fraud or duress. . . . It is not the province of this court to act as a post-transaction guardian for either party.

PLANNING

1. What, if any, are the virtues of the buyout agreement in this case?

---

* [Eds.—The capital account is also reduced by the amount of any distributions. To illustrate, suppose the total cash amount initially contributed by the partners was $400,000; that Nordale contributed $100,000 (25 percent), which is his initial capital account; that there were no further contributions; that the partnership had net profits of $40,000 in each of its first three years (a total of $120,000). Nordale's share of the profit would be $30,000, which would increase his capital account to $130,000. If there had been a total distribution of $40,000 to the partners, Nordale would have received $10,000 and that would have reduced his capital account to $120,000. If there had been total losses of $500,000 in the first three years, and no distributions, Nordale's share of the losses would have been $125,000 and his capital account would have been a negative $25,000. Any change in the value of the partnership's real estate investment is ignored. Suppose, for example, that there had been total losses of $500,000, financed by borrowing against the security of the real estate, which had increased in fair market value by $1.3 million. The fair market value of Nordale's interest would have increased by $200,000 (25 percent of the $1.3 million increase in fair market value less 25 percent of the $500,000 loan). But his capital account would still be a negative $25,000. The court in the present case observes that "capital account" and "book value," though not "synonymous," are "functional equivalents."]

2. What alternative valuation formula would you suggest? What other terms would you want to discuss if you were representing the parties?

3. Might your advice vary depending on whether you represented Nordale or G & S Investments?

6. LIMITED PARTNERSHIPS

Holzman v. De Escamilla

86 Cal.App.2d 858, 195 P.2d 833 (1948).

This is an appeal by James L. Russell and H.W. Andrews from a judgment decreeing they were general partners in Hacienda Farms, Limited, a limited partnership, from February 27, to December 1, 1943, and as such were liable as general partners to the creditors of the partnership.

Early in 1943, Hacienda Farms, Limited, was organized as a limited partnership (Secs. 2477 et seq., Civil Code) with Ricardo de Escamilla as the general partner and James L. Russell and H.W. Andrews as limited partners.

The partnership went into bankruptcy in December, 1943, and Lawrence Holzman was appointed and qualified as trustee of the estate of the bankrupt. On November 13, 1944, he brought this action for the purpose of determining that Russell and Andrews, by taking part in the control of the partnership business, had become liable as general partners to the creditors of the partnership. The trial court found in favor of the plaintiff on this issue and rendered judgment to the effect that the three defendants were liable as general partners.

The findings supporting the judgment are so fully supported by the testimony of certain witnesses, although contradicted by Russell and Andrews, that we need mention but a small part of it. We will not mention conflicting evidence as conflicts in the evidence are settled in the trial court and not here.

De Escamilla was raising beans on farm lands near Escondido at the time the partnership was formed. The partnership continued raising vegetable and truck crops which were marketed principally through a produce concern controlled by Andrews.

The record shows the following testimony of de Escamilla:

> "A. We put in some tomatoes.
>
> "Q. Did you have a conversation or conversations with Mr. Andrews or Mr. Russell before planting the tomatoes? A. We always conferred and agreed as to what crops we would put in. . . .
>
> "Q. Who determined that it was advisable to plant watermelons? A. Mr. Andrews. . . .
>
> "Q. Who determined that string beans should be planted? A. All of us. There was never any planting done—except the first crop that was put into the partnership as an asset by myself, there was never any crop that was planted or contemplated in

planting that wasn't thoroughly discussed and agreed upon by the three of us; particularly Andrews and myself."

De Escamilla further testified that Russell and Andrews came to the farms about twice a week and consulted about the crops to be planted. He did not want to plant peppers or egg plant because, as he said, "I don't like that country for peppers or egg plant; no, sir," but he was overruled and those crops were planted. The same is true of the watermelons.

Shortly before October 15, 1943, Andrews and Russell requested de Escamilla to resign as manager, which he did, and Harry Miller was appointed in his place.

Hacienda Farms, Limited, maintained two bank accounts, one in a San Diego bank and another in an Escondido bank. It was provided that checks could be drawn on the signatures of any two of the three partners. It is stated in plaintiff's brief, without any contradiction (the checks are not before us) that money was withdrawn on twenty checks signed by Russell and Andrews and that all other checks except three bore the signatures of de Escamilla, the general partner, and one of the other defendants. The general partner had no power to withdraw money without the signature of one of the limited partners.

Section 2483 of the Civil Code provides as follows:

> "A limited partner shall not become liable as a general partner, unless, in addition to the exercise of his rights and powers as a limited partner, he takes part in the control of the business."

The foregoing illustrations sufficiently show that Russell and Andrews both took "part in the control of the business." The manner of withdrawing money from the bank accounts is particularly illuminating. The two men had absolute power to withdraw all the partnership funds in the banks without the knowledge or consent of the general partner. Either Russell or Andrews could take control of the business from de Escamilla by refusing to sign checks for bills contracted by him and thus limit his activities in the management of the business. They required him to resign as manager and selected his successor. They were active in dictating the crops to be planted, some of them against the wish of Escamilla. This clearly shows they took part in the control of the business of the partnership and thus became liable as general partners. . . .

Judgment affirmed.

QUESTION

The Revised Uniform Limited Partnership Act (RULPA) § 303(a) now provides that: "a limited partner is not liable for the obligations of a limited partnership unless the limited partner is also a general partner or, in addition to the exercise of his rights and powers as a limited partner, he takes part in the control of the business. However, if the limited partner takes part in the control of the business and is not also a general partner, the limited partner is liable only to persons who transact business with the limited partnership and who reasonably believe, based upon the limited partner's conduct, that the limited partner is a general partner." RULPA § 303(b) also provides that "a limited partner does not participate in control . . . solely by . . . (2) consulting with and advising a general partner with respect to the business of the limited partnership." In Mt. Vernon Sav. and Loan v. Partridge Associates, 679 F.Supp. 522 (D.Md.1987), the court stated:

> [A] limited partner who disregards the limited partnership form to such an extent that he becomes substantially the same as a general partner has unlimited liability regardless of a plaintiff's knowledge of his role. At the same time, a limited partner may have unlimited liability for exercising less than a general partner's power if the fact that he acted as more than a limited partner was actually known to the plaintiff.

Is the court's statement consistent with the statutory text?

Under these rules, suppose that a creditor of Hacienda Farms, who had delivered fertilizer to the farm on de Escamilla's order, saw and heard Andrews and Russell engaging in the conversations about which de Escamilla testified. Would Andrews and Russell be liable to the creditor? What if, in addition, the creditor had in the past received payment by checks that bore the signatures of Andrews and of Russell?

In re: El Paso Pipeline Partners, L.P. Derivative Litigation

2014 WL 2768782 (Del. Ch.).

. . .

I. FACTUAL BACKGROUND

. . .

A. The Partnership Structure

El Paso MLP is a Delaware limited partnership headquartered in Houston, Texas. El Paso MLP operates as a master limited partnership ("MLP"), a term that refers to a publicly traded limited partnership that is treated as a pass-through entity for federal income tax purposes.[1] El Paso MLP owns interests in companies that operate natural gas pipelines, liquid natural gas ("LNG") terminals, and storage facilities throughout the United States. Its common units trade on the New York Stock Exchange under the symbol "EPB."

MLPs that focus on transporting and storing oil and natural gas, like El Paso MLP, are commonly referred to as midstream MLPs. Midstream MLPs are typically "sponsored" by a corporation with MLP-qualifying assets that generate stable cash flows. The sponsor seeks to maximize the market value of those assets by selling them to an MLP that can issue publicly traded securities on the strength of the cash flows and distribute the cash periodically to investors in a tax-efficient manner. In the typical

[1] [Eds.—Under federal income tax law most publicly traded entities, including partnerships, are taxed as corporations, with a corporate-rate tax paid by the partnership. See Int. Rev. Code § 7704(a). There is an exception, however, for certain partnerships, such as the one in this case, that, broadly speaking, do not actively engage in business but instead passively hold assets for investment. See Int. Rev. Code § 7704(c), (d)(E). These partnerships, like partnerships that are not publicly traded, are taxed on a "pass through" basis, meaning that no tax is paid at the entity level. Instead the income is allocated annually to the investors and reported by them (but some investors may be nontaxable entities such as pension plans and private universities).]

structure, the sponsor owns 100% of the general partner of the MLP, giving the sponsor control over the MLP. The sponsor initially contributes a block of assets to the MLP and, over time, sells additional assets to the MLP. Because the assets move from the sponsor level down to the MLP level, the sales are referred to colloquially as "drop-downs."

In August 2007, El Paso Corporation ("El Paso Parent") formed El Paso MLP and contributed to El Paso MLP an initial set of MLP-qualifying assets. On November 15, El Paso MLP announced an initial public offering of 25,000,000 common units. The IPO prospectus cautioned that El Paso Parent would have no obligation to drop down additional assets into El Paso MLP. Despite this disclosure, El Paso Parent was plainly creating a sponsored MLP, implying that El Paso MLP over time would acquire assets from El Paso Parent.

Consistent with the typical MLP structure, El Paso Parent indirectly owns 100% of defendant El Paso Pipeline GP Company, L.L.C., . . . the general partner of El Paso MLP (the "General Partner"). The General Partner in turn owns a 2% general partner interest in El Paso MLP. By virtue of the general partner interest, El Paso Parent has a 2% economic interest in El Paso MLP and, more importantly, exercises control over El Paso MLP. . . . As is customary with sponsored MLPs, El Paso MLP has no employees of its own. Employees of El Paso Parent manage and operate El Paso MLP's business.

At the time of the March 2010 transaction, defendants Douglas L. Foshee, James C. Yardley, John R. Suit, D. Mark Leland, Ronald L. Kuehn, William A. Smith, and Arthur C. Reichstetter (together, the "Individual Defendants") constituted the board of directors of the General Partner (the "GP Board"). Four of the Individual Defendants [Foshee, Yardley, Suit, and Leland] held [all the top] management positions with El Paso Parent or the General Partner. . . . Each of the management directors beneficially owned equity stakes in El Paso Parent that dwarfed their equity stakes in El Paso MLP.

The other three members of the GP Board [Kuehn, Smith, and Reichstetter] were outside directors, although two had past ties to El Paso Parent. Kuehn was Interim CEO of El Paso Parent in 2003 and served as Chairman of the Board of El Paso Parent from 2003 until 2009, one year before the challenged transaction occurred. Smith was an Executive Vice President of El Paso Parent and Chairman of El Paso Merchant Energy's Global Gas Group until 2002. Reichstetter was the only director without past ties to El Paso Parent.

. . .

B. The Drop-Down Proposal

On February 9, 2010, El Paso Parent offered to sell to El Paso MLP . . . interests in Southern LNG and Elba Express . . . for . . . $1,053 billion. This decision refers to El Paso MLP's eventual purchase of . . . Southern LNG and Elba Express as the "Drop-Down."

Southern LNG owned an LNG terminal on Elba Island, a private 840-acre island off the coast of Georgia. Elba Express owned a 190-mile natural gas pipeline that connected the Elba Island terminal to four major interstate natural gas pipelines. . . .

By 2010, when El Paso Parent proposed the Drop-Down, domestic discoveries of shale gas and improved techniques for its extraction had led to higher levels of domestic production and lower gas prices. As a result, the market for imported LNG had weakened. Demand at the Elba Island facility fell to less than 10% of capacity. . . . At the time, the principal sources of revenue for Southern LNG and Elba Express were existing contracts with subsidiaries of Shell and British Gas (the "Service Agreements"). Under the Service Agreements, the subsidiaries had reserved 100% of the firm capacity of the Elba Island terminal and the Elba Express pipeline, guaranteeing that Shell and British Gas would have the capacity to transport or store gas at any time for a set charge. Because the Service Agreements were firm contracts, Southern LNG and Elba Express would charge fees to Shell and British Gas regardless of whether they actually stored or transported gas. The Service Agreements had terms of 25 to 30 years.

Despite their lengthy terms and firm pricing, the Service Agreements were not sure things. The Shell and British Gas counterparties were special purpose entities with no assets of their own. If the Service Agreements became sufficiently unprofitable, then Shell and British Gas could walk away from their subsidiaries, leaving Southern LNG and Elba Express to collect from judgment-proof shells. . . .

The plaintiffs believe that because of the weakened domestic market for imported LNG, El Paso Parent faced a significant risk that Shell and British Gas would choose to breach the Service Agreements, leaving Southern LNG and Elba Express with less than 20% of their anticipated revenue. The plaintiffs argue that through the Drop-Down, El Paso Parent sought to off-load these now-risky assets onto El Paso MLP at an inflated price.

C. The Conflicts Committee

Because El Paso Parent controlled El Paso MLP through the General Partner, and because El Paso Parent owned the assets that El Paso MLP would be acquiring, the Drop-Down created a conflict of interest for the General Partner. El Paso MLP's limited partnership agreement (the "LP Agreement" or "LPA") contemplated that El Paso MLP could proceed with a transaction that presented a conflict of interest for the General Partner . . . if the conflict-of-interest transaction received "Special Approval." The LP Agreement defined this form of approval as "approval by a majority of the members of the Conflicts Committee acting in good faith." LPA § 1.1. The LP Agreement in turn defined the Conflicts Committee as

> a committee of the Board of Directors of the General Partner composed of two or more directors, each of whom (a) is not a security holder, officer or employee of the General Partner, (b) is not an officer, director or employee of any Affiliate of the General Partner, (c) is not a holder of any ownership interest in the Partnership Group other than Common Units and awards that may be granted to such director under the Long Term Incentive Plan and (d) meets the independence standards required of directors who serve on an audit committee of a board of directors established by the Securities Exchange Act and the rules and regulations of the Commission thereunder and by the

> National Securities Exchange on which the Common Units are listed or admitted to trading.

Id.

At El Paso MLP, the Conflicts Committee was not a standing committee of the GP Board, but rather a committee constituted on an ad hoc basis to consider specific conflict-of-interest transactions. On February 12, 2010, the GP Board resolved to seek Special Approval for the Drop-Down. . . .

The resolution granted the Conflicts Committee, for the period of existence, the power and authority

> to evaluate and assess whether the [Drop-Down] is fair and reasonable to the Partnership and, if the Conflicts Committee so determines, (a) to approve the [Drop-Down] as provided by Section 7.9(a) of the Limited Partnership Agreement and (b) to make a recommendation to the [GP] Board whether or not to approve such terms and conditions of the [Drop-Down].

. . .

The resolution named [the outside directors] Reichstetter, Kuehn, and Smith as the members of the committee. . . . At some point, the committee retained Akin Gump Strauss Hauer & Feld LLP ("Akin Gump") as its legal advisor and Tudor, Pickering, Holt & Co. ("Tudor") as its financial advisor. The engagements appear to have happened as a matter of course before the Conflicts Committee ever formally met.

As suggested by the ready hiring of Akin Gump and Tudor, the record reflects that El Paso Parent, the GP Board, and the individuals who served on the Conflicts Committee have developed a level of comfort with the Special Approval process:

- Between 2008 and 2012, El Paso Parent and El Paso MLP engaged in eight drop-down transactions. . . .
- El Paso Parent initiated each transaction. El Paso MLP never initiated a transaction.
- On each occasion, the General Partner opted to proceed by Special Approval and formed a Conflicts Committee.
- On each occasion, the members of the Conflicts Committee were Kuehn, Smith, and Reichstetter.

. . .

- On each occasion, the committee hired Tudor as its financial advisor.
- On each occasion, the Conflicts Committee obtained some marginal improvement in the terms of El Paso Parent's original proposal.
- On each occasion, Tudor opined that the resulting deal was fair and collected a $500,000 fee plus expenses.

The Special Approval process for the Drop-Down fit this pattern.

D. Special Approval Is Granted

Over the course of the next month and a half, the Conflicts Committee met five times to review El Paso Parent's proposal. . . . El

Paso Parent management gave Tudor a fifty-four page presentation that provided an overview of the proposed transaction and Southern LNG's and Elba Express's assets, including a summary of the Service Agreements. . . .

. . .

After the meeting on March 2, 2010, Reichstetter met with representatives of El Paso Parent to negotiate the transaction price. After some limited back and forth, they agreed upon consideration of $963 million,. . . .

On March 24, 2010, the Conflicts Committee met for the fifth and final time. . . . Tudor opined that the proposed transaction was "fair, from a financial point of view, to the holders of the Common Units of [El Paso MLP], other than [the General Partner] and its affiliates." The Conflicts Committee then unanimously approved resolutions recommending that El Paso MLP enter into the Drop-Down. . . .

E. El Paso Parent Declines To Exercise [An Option To Buy Other LNG Assets]

Unbeknownst to the Conflicts Committee, at the same time that El Paso Parent was proposing to sell LNG assets to El Paso MLP and touting their value, El Paso Parent was [declining to exercise its option] to buy LNG assets for itself [at a price that reflected] an EBITDA multiple of 9.1x* . . .

During the negotiation of the Drop-Down, the Conflicts Committee did not know about [this] transaction . . . .

According to the plaintiffs, the fact that El Paso Parent decided not to acquire an LNG asset at a lower implied EBITDA multiple while at the same time selling its own LNG assets to El Paso MLP for a higher implied EBITDA multiple was highly material information that should have been provided to the Conflicts Committee. The plaintiffs contend that the Gulf LNG deal illustrated arm's-length pricing for a comparable LNG asset, such that the Conflicts Committee's decision to buy a similar LNG asset at a significantly higher implied EBITDA multiple gives rise to an inference of bad faith. . . .

---

* [Eds.—EBITDA stands for annual Earnings Before Interest Taxes Depreciation and Amortization. In essence it is a measure of the annual net cash flow from an asset, independent of taxes and financing cost. EBITDA can be used in a number of ways to arrive at the value of the asset. One common, though crude, method is to multiply EBITDA by some widely accepted multiplier, which may vary, among other considerations, with the riskiness of the asset. For example, it the EBITDA (cash flow) of an asset is $10,000 and the appropriate multiplier for similar assets is 9, the value is $90,000. An asset with the same EBITDA but with greater risk would have a lower multiplier—say, 7, which would generate a value of $70,000. There is, of course, considerable uncertainty—one might say guesswork—in estimates of future EBITDA and in the choice of the appropriate multiplier.]

II. LEGAL ANALYSIS

. . .

A. Breach Of The Express Terms Of The LP Agreement

. . .

2. The Operative Contractual Framework

. . . Section 7.9(e) of the LP Agreement eliminates all common law duties that the General Partner and the Individual Defendants might otherwise owe to El Paso MLP and its limited partners, including fiduciary duties. The LP Agreement replaces those duties with contractual commitments. . . .

Under Section 7.9(a), if the General Partner takes action in its capacity as the General Partner, and the action involves a conflict of interest, then the action will be "permitted and deemed approved by all Partners" and "not constitute a breach" of the LP Agreement or "any duty stated or implied by law or equity" as long as the [action is (among other possibilities)] "approved by Special Approval." . . .

The LP Agreement defines Special Approval as "approval by a majority of the members of the Conflicts Committee acting in good faith." LPA § 1.1. The LP Agreement [further provides]:

> Whenever the Conflicts Committee makes a determination or takes or declines to take any other action, it shall make such determinations or take or decline to take such other action in good faith and shall not be subject to any other or different standards (including fiduciary standards). . . . In order for a determination or other action to be in "good faith" for purposes of this Agreement, the Person or Persons making such determination or taking or declining to take such other action must believe that the determination or other action is in the best interests of the Partnership.

Id. § 7.9(b).

Under Delaware law, the standard for good faith that applies to the Conflicts Committee requires a subjective belief that the determination or other action is in the best interests of El Paso MLP. . . .

3. The Application Of The Subjective Good Faith Standard

Under the subjective good faith standard, "the ultimate inquiry must focus on the subjective belief of the specific directors accused of wrongful conduct." [Allen v.] Encore Energy [P'rs, P.P.], 72 A.3d [93], 107 [(Del. 2013)]. The Delaware Supreme Court has admonished that when applying the subjective belief standard, "[t]rial judges should avoid replacing the actual directors with hypothetical reasonable people." Id. Nevertheless, because science has not yet developed a reliable method of reading minds, objective facts are logically and legally relevant to the extent they permit an inference that the defendants lacked the necessary subjective belief. Id. The high court has provided illustrations of this concept:

> Some actions may objectively be so egregiously unreasonable . . . that they "seem[ ] essentially inexplicable on any ground other than [subjective] bad faith." It may also be reasonable to infer subjective bad faith in less egregious transactions when a

> plaintiff alleges objective facts indicating that a transaction was not in the best interests of the partnership and that the directors knew of those facts. Therefore, objective factors may inform an analysis of a defendant's subjective belief to the extent they bear on the defendant's credibility when asserting that belief. . . .

Id.

. . .

In this case, the plaintiffs contend that the members of the Conflicts Committee failed to appreciate how easy it would be for Shell and British Gas to walk away from the Service Agreements, that Shell and British Gas would have a significant economic incentive to do so given the weakness in the domestic gas market, and that the value of the projected revenue under the Service Agreements had to be discounted significantly in light of that risk. The plaintiffs also fault the Special Committee for failing to take into account the fact that on February 9, 2010, the same day El Paso Parent made its initial proposal to sell LNG assets to El Paso MLP at a multiple of 12.2x EBITDA, El Paso Parent was analyzing and later decided not to exercise a right to purchase a 30% interest in Gulf LNG at 9.1x EBITDA. As additional evidence of the Conflicts Committee's bad faith, the plaintiffs cite an email Kuehn sent early in the process in which he suggested an EBITDA multiple well below where the Conflicts Committee began negotiating and ultimately ended up. The plaintiffs also rely on two expert reports.

a. The Service Agreements

The plaintiffs focus primarily on the risk that Shell and British Gas would walk away from the Service Agreements. . . . The plaintiffs . . . have introduced evidence establishing that the contractual counterparties to the Service Agreements were corporate shells and that only 17% of the projected revenue from the Service Agreements was guaranteed by entities with meaningful assets. Despite these limitations, the Conflicts Committee and Tudor valued the Service Agreements based on 100% of their projected revenue, without any discounting for the risk of breach.

The record establishes that there is no genuine dispute about whether the Conflicts Committee understood the state of the natural gas market. The members of the Conflicts Committee had extensive experience in the energy industry, and they received presentations about the condition of the natural gas market.

. . .

. . . Contrary to the plaintiffs' position, the record evidence establishes that the Conflicts Committee considered the revenue risk. Unlike the plaintiffs, the members of the Conflicts Committee believed that the guarantees were meaningful and that even if the guarantees covered only a portion of the Service Agreements' revenue, neither Shell nor British Gas would default. The Conflicts Committee saw little to no risk in the agreements because of El Paso MLP's ongoing relationships with Shell and British Gas, the interests that Shell and British Gas have in maintaining the availability of shipping and storage capacity, and the importance to Shell and British Gas of having a reputation for fulfilling their contracts.

What the plaintiffs really dispute is the weight the Conflicts Committee should have given to risks that both the Conflicts Committee and the plaintiffs identified. Reasonable minds could disagree about the judgment made by the Conflicts Committee, but the Conflicts Committee's judgment was not so extreme that it could support a potential finding of bad faith, nor was the committee's process sufficiently egregious to support such an inference. . . .

b. El Paso Parent's Decision Not To Invest In Gulf LNG

. . .

The plaintiffs contend that El Paso Parent's decision not to acquire an LNG asset at a 9.lx EBITDA multiple while at the same time proposing to sell its own LNG assets to El Paso MLP at a 12.2x EBITDA multiple supports an inference that the Drop-Down was approved in bad faith. The plaintiffs first argue that because El Paso Parent concealed information from the Conflicts Committee, Special Approval for the Drop-Down was not properly obtained. But the subjective good faith of the members of the Conflicts Committee cannot be challenged based on information that the plaintiffs admit the members did not have. The contractual language of the Special Approval provision turns only on the subjective good faith of the Conflicts Committee. It does not address whether Special Approval is valid if the General Partner withholds information from the Conflicts Committee. That gap in the LP Agreement must be filled, if necessary, by the implied covenant of good faith and fair dealing.

. . .

If the Conflicts Committee or its advisors knew about the Gulf LNG data point contemporaneously with the Drop-Down, then the pricing disparity might be sufficient to support an inference of bad faith when evaluated under the current procedural standard. Such a ruling would not mean that the defendants would lose and be held liable, only that a trial would be necessary to resolve a disputed question of fact as to their intent. In this case, however, the plaintiffs admit that the Conflicts Committee did not know about the Gulf LNG data point for purposes of the Drop-Down. That concession is dispositive.

. . .

e. Summary Judgment On Count I For The Drop-Down

. . . Summary judgment is therefore granted in favor of the General Partner, as well as the other defendants, . . . as to the claim that the Drop-Down violated the express requirements of the LP Agreement.

B. Breach Of The Implied Terms Of The LP Agreement

In addition to contending that the defendants breached their express contractual obligations under the LP Agreement, Count I of the First Complaint asserts that the defendants violated unwritten obligations supplied by the implied covenant of good faith and fair dealing. Because a claim for breach of the implied covenant of good faith and fair dealing is a claim for breach of contract, the General Partner is the only defendant potentially liable on this claim. [The court observes that the Limited Partnership Agreement does not expressly eliminate a good faith obligation of El Paso Parent to offer information, and that, consequently, the role of the court is to determine what the parties would have agreed to if they had addressed the issue. In this case, the court concludes, various terms of the actual Agreement suggest that had the parties addressed the issue, no such obligation would have been imposed. Thus, the court grants summary judgment to the defendants.]

ANALYSIS

1. Given the inherent conflict in the sale of assets from El Paso Parent to El Paso MLP, why would anyone invest in El Paso MLP?

2. The court recognizes that the failure of El Paso Parent to purchase LNG assets at 9.1x EBITDA while selling similar assets to El Paso MLP at 12.2x EBITDA may have been relevant to the conflicts committee but that Parent had no obligation to offer that information to the committee. What does this tell you about the legal relationship between Parent and MLP?

3. Among the key "deal points" in any transaction are control (who's in charge and with what constraints?), returns (who gets what?), and duration (how long does it last and how can it be ended?). In this El Paso transaction, what are the terms as to each of these elements? How might the limited partners want to change these terms?

CHAPTER 3

The Nature of the Corporation

1. The Corporate Entity and Its Formation and Structure

We begin with a set of hypothetical cases designed to introduce the key concept of the corporation as a separate entity and how that concept affects the relationships among individuals involved in the corporate enterprise. We then turn to how a corporation is formed and some of the basic elements of corporate structure: shareholders, the board of directors, articles of incorporation and bylaws.

HYPOTHETICAL CASES: FIDUCIARY OBLIGATIONS

The following set of hypotheticals is derived from a famous pair of cases involving the Old Dominion Copper Company. Old Dominion Copper Mining & Smelting Co. v. Lewisohn, 210 U.S. 206, 28 S.Ct. 634, 52 L.Ed. 1025 (1908); Old Dominion Copper Mining & Smelting Co. v. Bigelow, 203 Mass. 159, 89 N.E. 193 (1909), affirmed, 225 U.S. 111, 32 S.Ct. 641, 56 L.Ed. 1009 (1912).

Case 1. Ann buys land for $125,000 and shortly thereafter sells it to a total stranger, Sean, for $200,000. Ann makes no misrepresentations. Sean does not ask what Ann paid for the property, or when she bought it, and Ann does not say. Thus, there is no basis for a common-law action for fraud or deceit. There is no fiduciary obligation of Ann to Sean and no duty to disclose the purchase price. Ann is entitled to keep her $75,000 profit. Of course, if Ann lies to Sean, she may be liable to him for damages. What if he asks her what she paid for the land? If she is reluctant to reveal her purchase price but wants to avoid liability, how might she respond? Suppose Sean says, "I heard that you bought the land for $125,000 only a month ago. Is that true?" Assuming that Ann in fact bought the land two months ago, for $125,000, how might she respond?

Case 2. Art has recently bought land for $125,000. Shortly thereafter he meets Paula, an individual for whom he has in the past served as agent in the acquisition of land. Paula expresses an interest in the land that Art has just bought but does not know that Art is the owner and Art does nothing to inform her. Paula asks Art to represent her in seeking to acquire the land. Art agrees to do so. Art then sells the land to Paula for $200,000, without revealing his interest in the transaction. Assume that the land is in fact worth $200,000 (and that Art had in fact been offered $195,000 for it). Can Paula recover the $75,000 profit that Art has made? The relevant legal doctrine is stated as follows in Section 388 of the Restatement of Agency (Second): "Unless otherwise agreed, an agent who makes a profit in connection with transactions conducted by him on behalf of the principal is under a duty to give such profit to the principal." Does that seem to you to be a good rule? Why?

Breach of duty of loyalty?

Case 3. With the basic principles reflected in the first two cases in mind, we can turn to the question of how the results are affected by the interposition of a corporation. Suppose the facts are the same as in Case 2, except that the buyer is a corporation, P Corp., instead of an individual, and that the corporation is owned by Paula (that is, she owns all the shares of its stock). Suppose further that Paula is the president of the corporation and she conducts the negotiations with Art by virtue of which he agrees to act for the corporation. Art would become an agent of the corporation and its legal position would be the same as that of Paula in Case 2. Paula herself would not be allowed to proceed as an individual against Art, either in her role as shareholder or in her role as president of the corporation.

Case 4. Suppose that Art has just bought land for $125,000 and contemplates selling it to Paula for use in a residential development. Art has developed a plan that contemplates that the development will be conducted by a corporation called Art Corp., in which he will have no interest. He considers three approaches to selling his land to Paula. Under the first approach he causes a corporation to be formed. The corporation then sells all the shares of its stock in the corporation to Paula for $200,000 cash. Paula, her husband Peter, and her daughter Peggy become the directors of the corporation and Paula becomes its president. Art then sells the land to the corporation for $200,000; the transaction is approved by the corporation's board of directors. In this scenario, the relevant general rule of corporate law is that Art, as a promoter, owes a fiduciary obligation to the corporation. His obligation is like that of an agent to a principal (as in Case 2). If he does not reveal his interest in the land, and his profit, and adequately secure the approval of directors of the corporation (or, possibly, the approval of Paula as sole shareholder), can the corporation recover the $75,000 profit? In other words, can Art deal with the corporation at arm's length? Is there any good reason why he should not be allowed to do so? That is, is there any good reason why the result here should be different from the result in Case 1?

Under a second approach, Art sells the land to Paula for $200,000. Paula then forms the corporation and contributes the land to it in exchange for all of its shares of common stock. If this approach is followed, under what legal theories, if any, might Paula or the corporation recover Art's $75,000 profit? Can you think of any good reason why the result should be different under this approach than it would be under the first approach?

Under the third approach, Art forms a corporation and contributes $200,000 cash to it in return for all of its shares of common stock. He elects himself, his wife Alice, and his son Abe as directors and the directors appoint him president. He sells the land to the corporation for $200,000; the transaction is approved by the board of directors. Five days later, according to a preconceived plan, Art sells all his shares to Paula for $200,000. Art, Alice, and Abe are immediately replaced as directors of the corporation by Paula, Peter, and Peggy, and Paula replaces Art as president. Assume that Paula has no cause of action on a theory of common law fraud (which requires misrepresentation and reliance) or under any state or federal laws affecting the sale of securities. Should the corporation be allowed to recover the $75,000 secret profit, without proof of unfairness? (Don't leap to conclusions. The U.S. Supreme Court and the Massachusetts Supreme Judicial Court reached opposite conclusions on a question much like this one in the *Old Dominion* cases referred to above.) If you conclude that the corporation should be allowed to recover the $75,000, suppose Paula had held the shares for six months, during which time she had done nothing to develop or use the land, and then had sold the shares for $250,000 to a shrewd real estate investor who had thoroughly inspected the land, and that thereafter it is discovered for the first time that Art made the $75,000 profit. Should the corporation still be allowed to recover the profit? What if the amount contributed to the corporation by Art and used by the corporation to buy the property was $125,000 instead of $200,000, but Art nonetheless sold the shares to Paula for $200,000?

Corporate Formation

In most states, incorporating a business is an astonishingly simple process. Articles of incorporation meeting certain minimal statutory requirements are drafted. One or more incorporators sign the articles and deliver them to the state of incorporation's secretary of state's office, along with a check for any applicable fees or taxes. The secretary of state retains the original articles and returns a copy to the incorporator with a receipt for the fee. Unless the articles provide to the contrary, the corporation comes into existence at the moment the secretary of state's office accepts the articles for filing.

Modern articles of incorporation usually are bare-bones documents, containing little more than the statutorily mandated terms. Model Business Corporation Act (MBCA) § 2.02(a), for example, requires the articles to contain only four items:

- *Name.* A corporation's name may not be the same or confusingly similar to that of another corporation incorporated or qualified to do business in the state of incorporation. The name must also include some word or abbreviation indicating that the business is incorporated, such as corporation, company, "Inc." or the like.
- *Authorized shares.* The articles must state the maximum number of shares the corporation is authorized to issue.
- *Registered agent.* The articles must state the name of the corporation's registered agent and the address of its registered office. The registered office must be located within the state of incorporation. The registered agent receives service of process when the corporation is sued.
- *Incorporators.* The articles must state the name and address of each incorporator.

Under MBCA § 2.02(b), the articles of incorporation also may contain a host of optional provisions. Some of these options alternatively may be included in the bylaws, but many must be included in the articles of incorporation in order to be effective. Some of the more common and important optional provisions include:

- *Statement of purpose.* The articles may state the nature of the corporation's business or the purposes for which it was formed.[1]
- *Classes and series of shares.* Corporate stock may be separated into multiple classes and series. If the corporation wishes to do so, the articles must identify the different classes and state the number of shares of each class the corporation is authorized to issue. Where one or more classes of shares have certain preferential rights over other classes, those rights must be spelled out in this part of the articles.
- *Director and officer indemnification and liability limitation.* We will see many situations throughout this text in which directors or officers of a corporation may be held liable for misconduct. Most corporate statutes now permit the articles to include provisions limiting the scope of a director's liability and/or permitting indemnification of directors.

The articles of incorporation may be amended at any time. A three-step process is normally involved. First, the board of directors must recommend the amendment to the shareholders. Second, the shareholders must approve the amendment. Finally, the amendment must be filed with the secretary of state's office.

Bylaws are the rules a corporation adopts to govern its internal affairs. Bylaws tend to be far more detailed than the articles of incorporation, for three reasons: (1) bylaws need not be filed with the state government, which means they are not part of any public record; (2) bylaws are more easily amended than articles of incorporation (see below); and (3) officers and directors tend to be more familiar with bylaws than with the articles, which makes them a ready repository of organizational rules. In the event of a conflict between a bylaw and the articles, the latter controls.

The bylaws typically deal with such matters as number and qualifications of directors, board vacancies, board committees, quorum and notice requirement for shareholder and board meetings, procedures for calling special shareholder and board meetings, any special voting procedures, any limits on the transferability of shares, and titles and duties of the corporation's officers.

Boilermakers Local 154 Retirement Fund v. Chevron Corporation

73 A.3d 934 (Del.Ch.2013).

I. *Introduction*

The board of Chevron, the oil and gas major, has adopted a bylaw providing that litigation relating to Chevron's internal affairs should be conducted in Delaware, the state where Chevron is incorporated and

---

[1] A number of states, prominently including Delaware, still require that the articles contain a statement of corporate purpose. It is sufficient, however, to state that "the purpose of the corporation is to engage in any lawful act or activity. . . ." DGCL § 102(a)(3).

whose substantive law Chevron's stockholders know governs the corporation's internal affairs. The board of the logistics company FedEx, which is also incorporated in Delaware and whose internal affairs are also therefore governed by Delaware law, has adopted a similar bylaw providing that the forum for litigation related to FedEx's internal affairs should be the Delaware Court of Chancery. . . .

The plaintiffs, stockholders in Chevron and FedEx, have sued the boards for adopting these "forum selection bylaws." The plaintiffs' complaints are nearly identical and were filed only a few days apart by clients of the same law firm. In Count I, the plaintiffs claim that the bylaws are statutorily invalid because they are beyond the board's authority under the Delaware General Corporation Law ("DGCL"). In Count IV, the plaintiffs allege that the bylaws are contractually invalid, . . . because they were unilaterally adopted by the Chevron and FedEx boards using their power to make bylaws. . . . The plaintiffs have also claimed that the boards of Chevron and FedEx breached their fiduciary duties in adopting the bylaws.

II. *Background And Procedural Posture*

A. *The Chevron And FedEx Forum Selection Bylaws*

Critical to the resolution of this motion is an understanding of who has the power to adopt, amend, and repeal the bylaws, and what subjects the bylaws may address under the DGCL. 8 Del. C. § 109(a) identifies who has the power to adopt, amend, and repeal the bylaws:

> [T]he power to adopt, amend or repeal bylaws shall be in the stockholders entitled to vote. . . . Notwithstanding the foregoing, any corporation may, in its certificate of incorporation, confer the power to adopt, amend or repeal bylaws upon the directors. . . . The fact that such power has been so conferred upon the directors . . . shall not divest the stockholders . . . of the power, nor limit their power to adopt, amend or repeal bylaws.

8 Del. C. § 109(b) states the subject matter the bylaws may address:

> The bylaws may contain any provision, not inconsistent with law or with the certificate of incorporation, relating to the business of the corporation, the conduct of its affairs, and its rights or powers or the rights or powers of its stockholders, directors, officers or employees.

Both Chevron's and FedEx's certificates of incorporation conferred on the boards the power to adopt bylaws under 8 Del. C. § 109(a). Thus, all investors who bought stock in the corporations whose forum selection bylaws are at stake knew that (i) the DGCL allows for bylaws to address the subjects identified in 8 Del. C. § 109(b), (ii) the DGCL permits the certificate of incorporation to contain a provision allowing directors to adopt bylaws unilaterally, and (iii) the certificates of incorporation of Chevron and FedEx contained a provision conferring this power on the boards.

Acting consistent with the power conferred to the board in Chevron's certificate of incorporation, the board amended the bylaws and adopted a forum selection bylaw . . . that provided:

> Unless the Corporation consents in writing to the selection of an alternative forum, the Court of Chancery of the State of

> Delaware shall be the sole and exclusive forum for (i) any derivative action or proceeding brought on behalf of the Corporation, (ii) any action asserting a claim of breach of a fiduciary duty owed by any director, officer or other employee of the Corporation to the Corporation or the Corporation's stockholders, (iii) any action asserting a claim arising pursuant to any provision of the Delaware General Corporation Law, or (iv) any action asserting a claim governed by the internal affairs doctrine. Any person or entity purchasing or otherwise acquiring any interest in shares of capital stock of the Corporation shall be deemed to have notice of and consented to the provisions of this [bylaw].

Several months later, on March 14, 2011, the board of FedEx, a Delaware corporation headquartered in Tennessee, adopted a forum selection bylaw identical to Chevron's. Like Chevron, FedEx's board had been authorized by the certificate of incorporation to adopt bylaws without a stockholder vote, and the FedEx board adopted the bylaw unilaterally.

Chevron's board amended its bylaw on March 28, 2012 to provide that suits could be filed in any state or federal court in Delaware with jurisdiction over the subject matter and the parties. The amended bylaw also provides that the bylaw would not apply unless the court in Delaware had personal jurisdiction over all the parties that were "indispensable" to the action.

In their briefing, the boards of Chevron and FedEx state that . . . these bylaws are not intended to regulate *what* suits may be brought against the corporations, only *where* internal governance suits may be brought.

B. *The Defendant Boards Have Identified Multiforum Litigation Over Single Corporate Transactions Or Decisions As The Reason Why They Adopted The Bylaws*

The Chevron and FedEx boards say that they have adopted forum selection bylaws in response to corporations being subject to litigation over a single transaction or a board decision in more than one forum simultaneously, so-called "multiforum litigation." The defendants' opening brief . . . describes how, for jurisdictional purposes, a corporation is a citizen both of the state where it is incorporated and of the state where it has its principal place of business. Because a corporation need not be, and frequently is not, headquartered in the state where it is incorporated, a corporation may be subject to personal jurisdiction as a defendant in a suit involving corporate governance matters in two states. . . . Furthermore, both state and federal courts may have jurisdiction over the claims against the corporation. The result is that any act that the corporation or its directors undertake may be challenged in various forums within those states simultaneously. The boards of Chevron and FedEx argue that multiforum litigation, when it is brought by dispersed stockholders in different forums, directly or derivatively, to challenge a single corporate action, imposes high costs on the corporations and hurts investors by causing needless costs that are ultimately born by stockholders, and that these costs are not justified by rational benefits for stockholders from multiforum filings.

. . .

C. *The Plaintiffs Challenge The Forum Selection Bylaws*

. . . [B]ecause Chevron and FedEx had made persuasive arguments that addressing the facial challenges to the bylaws would avoid unnecessary costs or delay, . . . the court consolidated their cases to resolve those common and narrow questions of law: (i) whether the forum selection bylaws are facially invalid under the DGCL (Count I); and (ii) whether the board-adopted forum selection bylaws are facially invalid as a matter of contract law (Count IV). . . .

III. *The Standard Of Review*

The standard of review on this motion is important in framing this consolidated motion. . . . [T]his motion is only concerned with the facial statutory and contractual validity of the bylaws, and the motion is expressly not concerned with how the bylaws might be applied in any future, real-world situation. The plaintiffs' proposed standard, by contrast, is based on a case in which this court resolved an actual, live controversy over whether a bylaw could be applied to the real human events underlying that case.

. . . [T]he plaintiffs' burden on this motion challenging the facial statutory and contractual validity of the bylaws is a difficult one: they must show that the bylaws cannot operate lawfully or equitably *under any circumstances.* So, the plaintiffs must show that the bylaws do not address proper subject matters of bylaws as defined by the DGCL in 8 Del. C. § 109(b), and can never operate consistently with law. . . .

IV. *Legal Analysis*

A. *The Board-Adopted Forum Selection Bylaws Are Statutorily Valid*

. . . First, . . . the court must determine whether the adoption of the forum selection bylaws was beyond the board's authority in the sense that they do not address a proper subject matter under 8 Del. C. § 109(b), which provides that:

> The bylaws may contain any provision, not inconsistent with law or with the certificate of incorporation, relating to the business of the corporation, the conduct of its affairs, and its rights or powers or the rights or powers of its stockholders, directors, officers or employees.

. . .

1. *The Forum Selection Bylaws Regulate A Proper Subject Matter Under 8 Del. C. § 109(b)*

. . . As a matter of easy linguistics, the forum selection bylaws address the "rights" of the stockholders, because they regulate where stockholders can exercise their right to bring certain internal affairs claims against the corporation and its directors and officers. They also plainly relate to the conduct of the corporation by channeling internal affairs cases into the courts of the state of incorporation, providing for the opportunity to have internal affairs cases resolved authoritatively by our Supreme Court if any party wishes to take an appeal. . . .

Perhaps recognizing the weakness of any argument that the forum selection bylaws fall outside the plain language of 8 Del. C. § 109(b), the plaintiffs try to argue that judicial gloss put on the language of the statute renders the bylaws facially invalid. The plaintiffs contend that the bylaws . . . attempt to regulate an "external" matter, as opposed to, an "internal" matter of corporate governance. The plaintiffs attempt to support this argument with a claim that traditionally there have only been three appropriate subject matters of bylaws: stockholder meetings, the board of directors and its committees, and officerships.

But even if one assumes that judicial statements could limit the plain statutory words in the way the plaintiffs claim (which is dubious), the judicial decisions do not aid the plaintiffs. The plaintiffs take a cramped view of the proper subject matter of bylaws. The bylaws of Delaware corporations have a "procedural, process-oriented nature."[74] It is doubtless true that our courts have said that bylaws typically do not contain substantive mandates, but direct how the corporation, the board, and its stockholders may take certain actions. 8 Del. C. § 109(b) has long been understood to allow the corporation to set "self-imposed rules and regulations [that are] deemed expedient for its convenient functioning."[76] The forum selection bylaws here fit this description. They are process-oriented, because they regulate *where* stockholders may file suit, not *whether* the stockholder may file suit or the kind of remedy that the stockholder may obtain on behalf of herself or the corporation. The bylaws also clearly address cases of the kind that address "the business of the corporation, the conduct of its affairs, and . . . the rights or powers of its stockholders, directors, officers or employees," because they govern where internal affairs cases governed by state corporate law may be heard. These are the kind of claims most central to the relationship between those who manage the corporation and the corporation's stockholders.

By contrast, the bylaws would be regulating external matters if the board adopted a bylaw that purported to bind a plaintiff, even a stockholder plaintiff, who sought to bring a tort claim against the company based on a personal injury she suffered that occurred on the company's premises or a contract claim based on a commercial contract with the corporation. The reason why those kinds of bylaws would be beyond the statutory language of 8 Del. C. § 109(b) is obvious: the bylaws would not deal with the rights and powers of the plaintiff-stockholder *as a stockholder*. . . .

Nor is it novel for bylaws to regulate how stockholders may exercise their rights as stockholders. For example, an advance notice bylaw "requires stockholders wishing to make nominations or proposals at a corporation's annual meeting to give notice of their intention in advance of so doing."[79] Like such bylaws, which help organize what could otherwise be a chaotic stockholder meeting, the forum selection bylaws are designed to bring order to what the boards of Chevron and FedEx say they perceive to be a chaotic filing of duplicative and inefficient derivative and corporate suits against the directors and the corporations.

The plaintiffs' argument, then, reduces to the claim that the bylaws do not speak to a "traditional" subject matter, and should be ruled invalid

---

[74] CA, Inc. v. AFSCME Emps. Pension Plan, 953 A.2d 227, 236–37 (Del.2008).

[76] Gow v. Consol. Coppermines Corp., 165 A. 136, 140 (Del.Ch.1933).

[79] JANA Master Fund, Ltd. v. CNET Networks, Inc., 954 A.2d 335, 344 (Del.Ch.2008) (citation omitted), aff'd, 947 A.2d 1120 (Del.2008) (Table).

for that reason alone. For starters, the factual premise of this argument is not convincing. . . . But in any case, the Supreme Court long ago rejected the position that board action should be invalidated or enjoined simply because it involves a novel use of statutory authority. In *Moran v. Household International* in 1985, . . . the court reiterated that "our corporate law is not static. It must grow and develop in response to, indeed in anticipation of, evolving concepts and needs. Merely because the General Corporation Law is silent as to a specific matter does not mean that it is prohibited."[84]

. . .

2. *The Board-Adopted Bylaws Are Not Contractually Invalid As Forum Selection Clauses Because They Were Adopted Unilaterally By The Board*

Despite the contractual nature of the stockholders' relationship with the corporation under our law, the plaintiffs argue, in Count IV of their complaints, that the forum selection bylaws by their nature are different and cannot be adopted by the board unilaterally. The plaintiffs' argument is grounded in the contention that a board-adopted forum selection bylaw cannot be a *contractual* forum selection clause because the stockholders do not vote in advance of its adoption to approve it. The plaintiffs acknowledge that contractual forum selection clauses are "prima facie valid" under *The Bremen v. Zapata Off-Shore Co.* and *Ingres Corp. v. CA, Inc.*, and that they are presumptively enforceable.[92] But, the plaintiffs say, the forum selection bylaws are contractually invalid in this case, because they were adopted by a board, rather than by Chevron's and FedEx's dispersed stockholders. The plaintiffs argue that this method of adopting a forum selection clause is invalid as a matter of contract law, because it does not require the assent of the stockholders who will be affected by it. Thus, in the plaintiffs' view, there are two types of bylaws: (i) contractually binding bylaws that are adopted by stockholders; (ii) non-contractually binding bylaws that are adopted by boards using their statutory authority conferred by the certificate of incorporation.

. . .

In an unbroken line of decisions dating back several generations, our Supreme Court has made clear that the bylaws constitute a binding part of the contract between a Delaware corporation and its stockholders. Stockholders are on notice that, as to those subjects that are subject of regulation by bylaw under 8 Del. C. § 109(b), the board itself may act unilaterally to adopt bylaws addressing those subjects. Such a change by the board is not extra-contractual simply because the board acts unilaterally; rather it is the kind of change that the overarching statutory and contractual regime the stockholders buy into explicitly allows the board to make on its own. In other words, the Chevron and FedEx stockholders have assented to a contractual framework established by the DGCL and the certificates of incorporation that explicitly recognizes that stockholders will be bound by bylaws adopted unilaterally by their boards. Under that clear contractual framework, the stockholders assent

---

[84] [Eds.: Moran v. Household Int'l, Inc., 500 A.2d 1346, 1351 (Del.1985) (quoting Unocal Corp. v. Mesa Petroleum Co., 493 A.2d 946, 957 (Del.1985)).]

[92] [Eds.: The Bremen v. Zapata Off-Shore Co., 407 U.S. 1, 92 S.Ct. 1907, 32 L.Ed.2d 513 (1972); Ingres Corp. v. CA, Inc., 8 A.3d 1143 (Del.2010).]

to not having to assent to board-adopted bylaws. The plaintiffs' argument that stockholders must approve a forum selection bylaw for it to be contractually binding is an interpretation that contradicts the plain terms of the contractual framework chosen by stockholders who buy stock in Chevron and FedEx. . . .

Even so, the statutory regime provides protections for the stockholders, through the indefeasible right of the stockholders to adopt and amend bylaws themselves. "[B]y its terms Section 109(a) vests in the shareholders a power to adopt, amend or repeal bylaws that is legally sacrosanct, *i.e.,* the power cannot be non-consensually eliminated or limited by anyone other than the legislature itself."[104] Thus, even though a board may, as is the case here, be granted authority to adopt bylaws, stockholders can check that authority by repealing board-adopted bylaws. And, of course, because the DGCL gives stockholders an annual opportunity to elect directors, stockholders have a potent tool to discipline boards who refuse to accede to a stockholder vote repealing a forum selection clause. Thus, a corporation's bylaws are part of an inherently flexible contract between the stockholders and the corporation under which the stockholders have powerful rights they can use to protect themselves if they do not want board-adopted forum selection bylaws to be part of the contract between themselves and the corporation.

. . .

V. *Conclusion*

For these reasons, the court finds that the challenged bylaws are statutorily valid under 8 Del. C. § 109(b), and are contractually valid and enforceable as forum selection clauses. Judgment is entered for the defendants dismissing Counts I and IV of the plaintiffs' complaints against Chevron and FedEx, with prejudice. IT IS SO ORDERED.

ANALYSIS

1. In a portion of the opinion we have omitted, the court explains that "neither the wisdom of the Chevron and FedEx boards in adopting the forum selection bylaws to address the prevalence of multiforum litigation, [n]or in proceeding by way of a bylaw, rather than proposing an amendment to the certificate of incorporation, are proper matters for this court to address." Are forum selection provisions wise? And, if so, is it wise to adopt them in the bylaws rather than the articles of incorporation?

2. The court emphasized that the plaintiffs had made a facial challenge to the bylaws and, accordingly, the possibility that the bylaws might operate inequitably under some circumstances was not before the court. In what circumstances, if any, might a forum selection bylaw operate inequitably?

3. The court noted that "contractual nature of the stockholders' relationship with the corporation under our law." What does it mean to say that that relationship is contractual in nature?

---

[104] *CA, Inc.*, 953 A.2d at 232.

2. THE CORPORATE ENTITY AND LIMITED LIABILITY

Walkovszky v. Carlton

18 N.Y.2d 414, 276 N.Y.S.2d 585, 223 N.E.2d 6 (1966).

■ FULD, JUDGE.

This case involves what appears to be a rather common practice in the taxicab industry of vesting the ownership of a taxi fleet in many corporations, each owning only one or two cabs.

The complaint alleges that the plaintiff was severely injured four years ago in New York City when he was run down by a taxicab owned by the defendant Seon Cab Corporation and negligently operated at the time by the defendant Marchese. The individual defendant, Carlton, is claimed to be a stockholder of 10 corporations, including Seon, each of which has but two cabs registered in its name, and it is implied that only the minimum automobile liability insurance required by law (in the amount of $10,000) is carried on any one cab. Although seemingly independent of one another, these corporations are alleged to be "operated . . . as a single entity, unit and enterprise" with regard to financing, supplies, repairs, employees and garaging, and all are named as defendants.[1] The plaintiff asserts that he is also entitled to hold their stockholders personally liable for the damages sought because the multiple corporate structure constitutes an unlawful attempt "to defraud members of the general public" who might be injured by the cabs.

The defendant Carlton has moved, pursuant to CPLR 3211(a)7, to dismiss the complaint on the ground that as to him it "fails to state a cause of action." The court at Special Term granted the motion but the Appellate Division, by a divided vote, reversed, holding that a valid cause of action was sufficiently stated. The defendant Carlton appeals to us, from the nonfinal order, by leave of the Appellate Division on a certified question.

The law permits the incorporation of a business for the very purpose of enabling its proprietors to escape personal liability . . . but, manifestly, the privilege is not without its limits. Broadly speaking, the courts will disregard the corporate form, or, to use accepted terminology, "pierce the corporate veil", whenever necessary "to prevent fraud or to achieve equity." International Aircraft Trading Co. v. Manufacturers Trust Co., 297 N.Y. 285, 292, 79 N.E.2d 249, 252. In determining whether liability should be extended to reach assets beyond those belonging to the corporation, we are guided, as Judge Cardozo noted, by "general rules of agency." Berkey v. Third Ave. Ry. Co., 144 N.Y. 84, 95, 155 N.E. 58, 61, 50 A.L.R. 599. In other words, whenever anyone uses control of the corporation to further his own rather than the corporation's business, he will be liable for the corporation's acts "upon the principle of *respondeat superior* applicable even where the agent is a natural person." Rapid Tr. Subway Constr. Co. v. City of New York, 259 N.Y. 472, 488, 182 N.E. 145, 150. Such liability, moreover, extends not only to the corporation's commercial dealings . . . but to its negligent acts as well.

. . .

---

[1] The corporate owner of a garage is also included as a defendant.

In the case before us, the plaintiff has explicitly alleged that none of the corporations "had a separate existence of their own" and, as indicated above, all are named as defendants. However, it is one thing to assert that a corporation is a fragment of a larger corporate combine which actually conducts the business. . . . It is quite another to claim that the corporation is a "dummy" for its individual stockholders who are in reality carrying on the business in their personal capacities for purely personal rather than corporate ends. . . . Either circumstance would justify treating the corporation as an agent and piercing the corporate veil to reach the principal but a different result would follow in each case. In the first, only a larger *corporate* entity would be held financially responsible . . . while, in the other the stockholder would be personally liable. . . . Either the stockholder is conducting the business in his individual capacity or he is not. If he is, he will be liable; if he is not, then, it does not matter—insofar as his personal liability is concerned—that the enterprise is actually being carried on by a larger "enterprise entity."

At this stage in the present litigation, we are concerned only with the pleadings and, since CPLR 3014 permits causes of action to be stated "alternatively or hypothetically," it is possible for the plaintiff to allege both theories as the basis for his demand for judgment. . . . Reading the complaint in this case most favorably and liberally, we do not believe that there can be gathered from its averments the allegations required to spell out a valid cause of action against the defendant Carlton.

The individual defendant is charged with having "organized, managed, dominated and controlled" a fragmented corporate entity but there are no allegations that he was conducting business in his individual capacity. Had the taxicab fleet been owned by a single corporation, it would be readily apparent that the plaintiff would face formidable barriers in attempting to establish personal liability on the part of the corporation's stockholders. The fact that the fleet ownership has been deliberately split up among many corporations does not ease the plaintiff's burden in that respect. The corporate form may not be disregarded merely because the assets of the corporation, together with the mandatory insurance coverage of the vehicle which struck the plaintiff, are insufficient to assure him the recovery sought. If Carlton were to be held individually liable on those facts alone, the decision would apply equally to the thousands of cabs which are owned by their individual drivers who conduct their businesses through corporations organized pursuant to section 401 of the Business Corporation Law, Consol.Laws, c. 4 and carry the minimum insurance required by subdivision 1 (par. [a]) of section 370 of the Vehicle and Traffic Law, Consol.Laws, c. 71. These taxi owner-operators are entitled to form such corporations . . . and we agree with the court at Special Term that, if the insurance coverage required by statute "is inadequate for the protection of the public, the remedy lies not with the courts but with the Legislature." It may very well be sound policy to require that certain corporations must take out liability insurance which will afford adequate compensation to their potential tort victims. However, the responsibility for imposing conditions on the privilege of incorporation has been committed by the Constitution to the Legislature (N.Y. Const. art. X, § 1) and it may not be fairly implied, from any statute, that the Legislature intended, without the slightest discussion or debate, to require of taxi corporations that they carry automobile liability insurance over and above that mandated by the Vehicle and Traffic Law.

This is not to say that it is impossible for the plaintiff to state a valid cause of action against the defendant Carlton. However, the simple fact is that the plaintiff has just not done so here. While the complaint alleges that the separate corporations were undercapitalized and that their assets have been intermingled, it is barren of any "sufficiently particular[ized] statements" (CPLR 3013) . . . that the defendant Carlton and his associates are actually doing business in their individual capacities, shuttling their personal funds in and out of the corporations "without regard to formality and to suit their immediate convenience." Weisser v. Mursam Shoe Corp., 2d Cir., 127 F.2d 344, 345, 145 A.L.R. 467, supra. Nothing of the sort has in fact been charged, and it cannot reasonably or logically be inferred from the happenstance that the business of Seon Cab Corporation may actually be carried on by a larger corporate entity composed of many corporations which, under general principles of agency, would be liable to each other's creditors in contract and in tort.

In point of fact, the principle relied upon in the complaint to sustain the imposition of personal liability is not agency but fraud. Such a cause of action cannot withstand analysis. If it is not fraudulent for the owner-operator of a single cab corporation to take out only the minimum required liability insurance, the enterprise does not become either illicit or fraudulent merely because it consists of many such corporations. The plaintiff's injuries are the same regardless of whether the cab which strikes him is owned by a single corporation or part of a fleet with ownership fragmented among many corporations. Whatever rights he may be able to assert against parties other than the registered owner of the vehicle come into being not because he has been defrauded but because, under the principle of *respondeat superior,* he is entitled to hold the whole enterprise responsible for the acts of its agents.

In sum, then, the complaint falls short of adequately stating a cause of action against the defendant Carlton in his individual capacity. . . .

■ KEATING, JUDGE (dissenting).

The defendant Carlton, the shareholder here sought to be held for the negligence of the driver of a taxicab, was a principal shareholder and organizer of the defendant corporation which owned the taxicab. The corporation was one of 10 organized by the defendant, each containing two cabs and each cab having the "minimum liability" insurance coverage mandated by section 370 of the Vehicle and Traffic Law. The sole assets of these operating corporations are the vehicles themselves and they are apparently subject to mortgages.*

From their inception these corporations were intentionally undercapitalized for the purpose of avoiding responsibility for acts which were bound to arise as a result of the operation of a large taxi fleet having cars out on the street 24 hours a day and engaged in public transportation. And during the course of the corporations' existence all

* It appears that the medallions, which are of considerable value, are judgment proof. (Administrative Code of City of New York, § 436–2.0.)

income was continually drained out of the corporations for the same purpose.

The issue presented by this action is whether the policy of this State, which affords those desiring to engage in a business enterprise the privilege of limited liability through the use of the corporate device, is so strong that it will permit that privilege to continue no matter how much it is abused, no matter how irresponsibly the corporation is operated, no matter what the cost to the public. I do not believe that it is.

Under the circumstances of this case the shareholders should all be held individually liable to this plaintiff for the injuries he suffered. . . .

The policy of this State has always been to provide and facilitate recovery for those injured through the negligence of others. The automobile, by its very nature, is capable of causing severe and costly injuries when not operated in a proper manner. The great increase in the number of automobile accidents combined with the frequent financial irresponsibility of the individual driving the car led to the adoption of section 388 of the Vehicle and Traffic Law which had the effect of imposing upon the owner of the vehicle the responsibility for its negligent operation. It is upon this very statute that the cause of action against both the corporation and the individual defendant is predicated.

In addition the Legislature, still concerned with the financial irresponsibility of those who owned and operated motor vehicles, enacted a statute requiring minimum liability coverage for all owners of automobiles. The important public policy represented by both these statutes is outlined in section 310 of the Vehicle and Traffic Law. That section provides that: "The legislature is concerned over the rising toll of motor vehicle accidents and the suffering and loss thereby inflicted. The legislature determines that it is a matter of grave concern that motorists shall be financially able to respond in damages for their negligent acts, so that innocent victims of motor vehicle accidents may be recompensed for the injury and financial loss inflicted upon them."

The defendant Carlton claims that, because the minimum amount of insurance required by the statute was obtained, the corporate veil cannot and should not be pierced despite the fact that the assets of the corporation which owned the cab were "trifling compared with the business to be done and the risks of loss" which were certain to be encountered. I do not agree.

The Legislature in requiring minimum liability insurance of $10,000, no doubt, intended to provide at least some small fund for recovery against those individuals and corporations who just did not have and were not able to raise or accumulate assets sufficient to satisfy the claims of those who were injured as a result of their negligence. It certainly could not have intended to shield those individuals who organized corporations, with the specific intent of avoiding responsibility to the public, where the operation of the corporate enterprise yielded profits sufficient to purchase additional insurance. Moreover, it is reasonable to assume that the Legislature believed that those individuals and corporations having substantial assets would take out insurance far in excess of the minimum in order to protect those assets from depletion. Given the costs of hospital care and treatment and the nature of injuries sustained in auto collisions, it would be unreasonable to assume that the

Legislature believed that the minimum provided in the statute would in and of itself be sufficient to recompense "innocent victims of motor vehicle accidents . . . for the injury and financial loss inflicted upon them".

The defendant, however, argues that the failure of the Legislature to increase the minimum insurance requirements indicates legislative acquiescence in this scheme to avoid liability and responsibility to the public. In the absence of a clear legislative statement, approval of a scheme having such serious consequences is not to be so lightly inferred.

. . .

The defendant contends that a decision holding him personally liable would discourage people from engaging in corporate enterprise.

What I would merely hold is that a participating shareholder of a corporation vested with a public interest, organized with capital insufficient to meet liabilities which are certain to arise in the ordinary course of the corporation's business, may be held personally responsible for such liabilities. Where corporate income is not sufficient to cover the cost of insurance premiums above the statutory minimum or where initially adequate finances dwindle under the pressure of competition, bad times or extraordinary and unexpected liability, obviously the shareholder will not be held liable. . . .

The only types of corporate enterprises that will be discouraged as a result of a decision allowing the individual shareholder to be sued will be those such as the one in question, designed solely to abuse the corporate privilege at the expense of the public interest.

For these reasons I would vote to affirm the order of the Appellate Division.

■ DESMOND, C.J., and VAN VOORHIS, BURKE and SCILEPPI, JJ., concur with FULD, J.

■ KEATING, J., dissents and votes to affirm in an opinion in which BERGAN, J., concurs.

Order reversed, etc.

ANALYSIS

There are three separate legal doctrines that the plaintiff might invoke in a case like Walkovszky v. Carlton: (a) enterprise liability; (b) respondeat superior (agency); and (c) disregard of the corporate entity ("piercing the corporate veil"). Assume that the shares of each of the ten corporations in *Walkovszky* were owned 75 percent by Carlton, who ran the business and served as president of each corporation, as well as being a director; 10 percent each by two investors who were also directors but were otherwise inactive; and 5 percent by an investor who had inherited his shares, and had no role in the management of the business and only a vague idea of how it operated.

1. Articulate more fully each of the three legal doctrines and distinguish it from the others.

2. What facts would the plaintiff hope to find and seek to prove in support of each theory?

3. What persons are liable under each theory?

PLANNING AND POLICY

1. Assume that the law is correctly stated and applied by Judge Fuld in the majority opinion in *Walkovszky*. If you had acted as lawyer for Carlton and the other investors at the inception of the business, what advice would you have given them about what they must do to achieve their goals of insulating themselves from personal liability and insulating each corporation from the obligations of the others? How would your answer change if you had advised an individual who owned only two cabs and drove one of them himself?

2. Assume that the law is correctly stated and applied by Judge Keating in the dissenting opinion. How would your advice to Carlton and the other investors have changed? What about your advice to the individual with only two cabs?

3. What, if anything, do your answers to the preceding questions add to the policy debate between Judge Fuld and Judge Keating?

Sea-Land Services, Inc. v. Pepper Source

941 F.2d 519 (7th Cir.1991).

■ BAUER, CHIEF JUDGE.

This spicy case finds its origin in several shipments of Jamaican sweet peppers. Appellee Sea-Land Services, Inc. ("Sea-Land"), an ocean carrier, shipped the peppers on behalf of The Pepper Source ("PS"), one of the appellants here. PS then stiffed Sea-Land on the freight bill, which was rather substantial. Sea-Land filed a federal diversity action for the money it was owed. On December 2, 1987, the district court entered a default judgment in favor of Sea-Land and against PS in the amount of $86,767.70. But PS was nowhere to be found; it had been "dissolved" in mid-1987 for failure to pay the annual state franchise tax. Worse yet for Sea-Land, even had it not been dissolved, PS apparently had no assets. With the well empty, Sea-Land could not recover its judgment against PS. Hence the instant lawsuit.

In June 1988, Sea-Land brought this action against Gerald J. Marchese and five business entities he owns: PS, Caribe Crown, Inc., Jamar Corp., [and] Salescaster Distributors, Inc., ... Sea-Land sought by this suit to pierce PS's corporate veil and render Marchese personally liable for the judgment owed to Sea-Land, and then "reverse pierce" Marchese's other corporations so that they, too, would be on the hook for the $87,000. Thus, Sea-Land alleged in its complaint that all of these corporations "are alter egos of each other and hide behind the veils of alleged separate corporate existence for the purpose of defrauding plaintiff and other creditors." Not only are the corporations alter egos of each other, alleged Sea-Land, but also they are alter egos of Marchese, who should be held individually liable for the judgment because he created and manipulated these corporations and their assets for his own personal uses. Count III, paras. 9–10. (Hot on the heels of the filing of Sea-Land's complaint, PS took the necessary steps to be reinstated as a corporation in Illinois.)

In early 1989, Sea-Land filed an amended complaint adding Tie-Net International, Inc., as a defendant. Unlike the other corporate defendants, Tie-Net is not owned solely by Marchese; he holds half of the stock, and an individual named George Andre owns the other half. Sea-Land alleged that, despite this shared ownership, Tie-Net is but another alter ego of Marchese and the other corporate defendants, and thus it also should be held liable for the judgment against PS.

Through 1989, Sea-Land pursued discovery in this case, including taking a two-day deposition from Marchese. In December 1989, Sea-Land moved for summary judgment. In that motion—which, with the brief in support and the appendices, was about three inches thick—Sea-Land argued that it was "entitled to judgment as a matter of law, since the evidence including deposition testimony and exhibits in the appendix will show that piercing the corporate veil and finding the status of an alter ego is merited in this case." Marchese and the other defendants filed brief responses.

In an order dated June 22, 1990, the court granted Sea-Land's motion. The court discussed and applied the test for corporate veil-piercing explicated in Van Dorn Co. v. Future Chemical and Oil Corp., 753 F.2d 565 (7th Cir.1985). Analyzing Illinois law, we held in *Van Dorn*:

> [A] corporate entity will be disregarded and the veil of limited liability pierced when two requirements are met: First, there must be such unity of interest and ownership that the separate personalities of the corporation and the individual [or other corporation] no longer exist; and second, circumstances must be such that adherence to the fiction of separate corporate existence would sanction a fraud or promote injustice.

753 F.2d at 569–70 (quoting Macaluso v. Jenkins, 95 Ill.App.3d 461, 420 N.E.2d 251, 255 (1981)) (other citations omitted). . . . As for determining whether a corporation is so controlled by another to justify disregarding their separate identities, the Illinois cases . . . focus on four factors: "(1) the failure to maintain adequate corporate records or to comply with corporate formalities, (2) the commingling of funds or assets, (3) undercapitalization, and (4) one corporation treating the assets of another corporation as its own." 753 F.2d at 570 (citations omitted). . . .

Following the lead of the parties, the district court in the instant case laid the template of *Van Dorn* over the facts of this case. The court concluded that both halves and all features of the test had been satisfied, and, therefore, entered judgment in favor of Sea-Land and against PS, Caribe Crown, Jamar, Sales-caster, Tie-Net, and Marchese individually. These defendants were held jointly liable for Sea-Land's $87,000 judgment, as well as for post-judgment interest under Illinois law. From that judgment Marchese and the other defendants brought a timely appeal. . . .

The first and most striking feature that emerges from our examination of the record is that these corporate defendants are, indeed, little but Marchese's playthings. Marchese is the sole shareholder of PS, Caribe Crown, Jamar, and Salescaster. He is one of the two shareholders of Tie-Net. Except for Tie-Net, none of the corporations ever held a single corporate meeting. (At the handful of Tie-Net meetings held by Marchese and Andre, no minutes were taken.) During his deposition, Marchese did not remember any of these corporations ever passing articles of incorporation, bylaws, or other agreements. As for physical facilities,

Marchese runs all of these corporations (including Tie-Net) out of the same, single office, with the same phone line, the same expense accounts, and the like. And how he does "run" the expense accounts. When he fancies to, Marchese "borrows" substantial sums of money from these corporations—interest free, of course. The corporations also "borrow" money from each other when need be, which left at least PS completely out of capital when the Sea-Land bills came due. What's more, Marchese has used the bank accounts of these corporations to pay all kinds of personal expenses, including alimony and child support payments to his ex-wife, education expenses for his children, maintenance of his personal automobiles, health care for his pet—the list goes on and on. Marchese did not even have a personal bank account. (With "corporate" accounts like these, who needs one?) And Tie-Net is just as much a part of this as the other corporations. On appeal, Marchese makes much of the fact that he shares ownership of Tie-Net, and that Sea-Land has not been able to find an example of funds flowing from PS to Tie-Net to the detriment of Sea-Land and PS's other creditors. So what? The record reveals that, in all material senses, Marchese treated Tie-Net like his other corporations: he "borrowed" over $30,000 from Tie-Net; money and "loans" flowed freely between Tie-Net and the other corporations; and Marchese charged up various personal expenses (including $460 for a picture of himself with President Bush) on Tie-Net's credit card. Marchese was not deterred by the fact that he did not hold all of the stock of Tie-Net; why should his creditors be?

In sum, we agree with the district court that there can be no doubt that the "shared control/unity of interest and ownership" part of the *Van Dorn* test is met in this case: corporate records and formalities have not been maintained; funds and assets have been commingled with abandon; PS, the offending corporation, and perhaps others have been undercapitalized; and corporate assets have been moved and tapped and "borrowed" without regard to their source. Indeed, Marchese basically punted this part of the inquiry before the district court by coming forward with little or no evidence in response to Sea-Land's extensively supported argument on these points. That fact alone was enough to do him in; opponents to summary judgment motions cannot simply rest on their laurels, but must come forward with specific facts showing that there is a genuine issue for trial. . . . Regarding the elements that make up the first half of the *Van Dorn* test, Marchese and the other defendants have not done so. Thus, Sea-Land is entitled to judgment on these points.

The second part of the *Van Dorn* test is more problematic, however. "Unity of interest and ownership" is not enough; Sea-Land also must show that honoring the separate corporate existences of the defendants "would sanction a fraud or promote injustice." *Van Dorn*, 753 F.2d at 570. This last phrase truly is disjunctive:

> Although an intent to defraud creditors would surely play a part if established, the Illinois test does not require proof of such intent. Once the first element of the test is established, *either* the sanctioning of a fraud (intentional wrongdoing) or the promotion of injustice, will satisfy the second element.

Id. (emphasis in original). Seizing on this, Sea-Land has abandoned the language in its two complaints that make repeated references to "fraud" by Marchese, and has chosen not to attempt to prove that PS and

Marchese intended to defraud it—which would be quite difficult on summary judgment. Instead, Sea-Land has argued that honoring the defendants' separate identities would "promote injustice."

But what, exactly, does "promote injustice" mean, and how does one establish it on summary judgment? These are the critical, troublesome questions in this case. To start with, as the above passage from *Van Dorn* makes clear, "promote injustice" means something less than an affirmative showing of fraud—but how much less? In its one-sentence treatment of this point, the district court held that it was enough that "Sea-Land would be denied a judicially-imposed recovery." Sea-Land defends this reasoning on appeal, arguing that "permitting the appellants to hide behind the shield of limited liability would clearly serve as an injustice against appellee" because it would "impermissibly deny appellee satisfaction." Appellee's Brief at 14–15. But that cannot be what is meant by "promote injustice." The prospect of an unsatisfied judgment looms in every veil-piercing action; why else would a plaintiff bring such an action? Thus, if an unsatisfied judgment is enough for the "promote injustice" feature of the test, then every plaintiff will pass on that score, and *Van Dorn* collapses into a one-step "unity of interest and ownership" test.

Because we cannot abide such a result, we will undertake our own review of Illinois cases to determine how the "promote injustice" feature of the veil-piercing inquiry has been interpreted. In Pederson [v. Paragon Enterprises, 214 Ill.App.3d 815, 158 Ill.Dec. 371, 373, 574 N.E.2d 165, 167 (1st Dist.1991)], . . . the court offered the following summary: "Some element of unfairness, something akin to fraud or deception or the existence of a compelling public interest must be present in order to disregard the corporate fiction." 214 Ill.App.3d at 821, 158 Ill.Dec. at 375, 574 N.E.2d at 169. . . .

The light shed on this point by other Illinois cases can be seen only if we examine the cases on their facts. Perivoliotis v. Pierson, 167 Ill.App.3d 259, 521 N.E.2d 254 (1988), was a complicated adverse possession case that addresses briefly the meaning of the "injustice" requirement. The issue in the case was whether an individual (Woulfe) could possess a strip of land adversely to a corporation (TomDon) that held title to the land, when Woulfe was the president and one of only two shareholders (the other, his wife) of TomDon. The court held that, because TomDon was merely Woulfe's alter ego, Woulfe could not possess the land "adversely." In so holding, the court stated that "the running of the prescriptive period against a corporation's property during a period when the corporation's principal owner and president mistakenly possessed the encroachment area in his individual capacity defies common sense and is the type of 'injustice' that would justify piercing the corporate veil." Id. at 256.

Gromer, Wittenstrom & Meyer, P.C. v. Strom, 140 Ill.App.3d 349, 489 N.E.2d 370 (1986), was another unfortunately complicated case in which our issue was addressed. Basically, three individuals, W, M, and S, were partners. All three signed a note agreeing to be jointly and severally liable for a debt owed to a bank. S left the partnership and it dissolved. W & M then formed a new corporation, W & M Co., of which they were the sole shareholders. W & M Co. paid off the bank and became the assignee of the note, and then promptly sued S for collection on the note. Putting to one side the rather abstruse procedural posture of the case, suffice it to say that W & M Co. won at the trial level and appealed [sic]. On appeal, S claimed that the court should pierce the corporate veil and recognize W & M Co. for what it really was—his former partners and cosigners on the note; the reason being that cosigners cannot payoff [sic] a note and then take judgment on the note against another cosigner. The appellate court agreed and vacated the judgment:

> We believe that these facts and arguments sufficiently indicate that to recognize [W & M Co.] as an entity separate from its shareholders would be to sanction an injustice. Where such an injustice would result and there is such unity of interest between the corporation and the individual shareholders that the separate personalities no longer exist, the corporate veil must be pierced.

Id. at 374 (citations omitted).

In B. Kreisman & Co. v. First Arlington Nat'l Bank of Arlington Heights, 91 Ill.App.3d 847, 415 N.E.2d 1070 (1980), the appellate court reversed the trial court's refusal to pierce the veil. Defendant corporation stiffed plaintiff for the bill on some restaurant equipment, so plaintiff sued for a mechanics lien. Plaintiff won at trial, but the trial court would not pierce the defendant corporation's veil and also hold liable the individual who was the "dominant force" controlling the defendant corporation. Noting that the equipment, though never paid for, was used by the defendant corporation for several years, the appellate court stated, "Under these circumstances we believe the corporate veil should be pierced to require [the 'dominant individual'] to be personally liable; to say otherwise would promote an injustice and permit her to be unjustly enriched at plaintiff's expense." Id. at 1073 (citations omitted).

. . .

Generalizing from these cases, we see that the courts that properly have pierced corporate veils to avoid "promoting injustice" have found that, unless it did so, some "wrong" beyond a creditor's inability to collect would result: the common sense rules of adverse possession would be undermined; former partners would be permitted to skirt the legal rules concerning monetary obligations; a party would be unjustly enriched; a parent corporation that caused a sub's liabilities and its inability to pay for them would escape those liabilities; or an intentional scheme to squirrel assets into a liability-free corporations while heaping liabilities upon an asset-free corporation would be successful. Sea-Land, although it alleged in its complaint the kind of intentional asset- and liability-shifting found in *Van Dorn*, has yet to come forward with evidence akin to the "wrongs" found in these cases. Apparently, it believed, as did the district court, that its unsatisfied judgment was enough. That belief was in error, and the entry of summary judgment premature. We, therefore, reverse the judgment and remand the case to the district court.

On remand, the court should require that Sea-Land produce, if it desires summary judgment, evidence and argument that would establish the kind of additional "wrong" present in the above cases. For example, perhaps Sea-Land could establish that Marchese, like Roth in *Van Dorn*, used these corporate facades to avoid its responsibilities to creditors; or that PS, Marchese, or one of the other corporations will be "unjustly enriched" unless liability is shared by all. Of course, Sea-Land is not required fully to prove intent to defraud, which it probably could not do on summary judgment anyway. But it is required to show the kind of injustice to merit the evocation of the court's essentially equitable power to prevent "injustice." . . .

REVERSED and REMANDED with instructions.

NOTE

On remand of *Sea-Land*, the district court found in favor of Sea-Land and entered a judgment against Marchese for $86,768 plus post-judgment interest of $31,365. In concluding that protecting Marchese would "sanction a fraud or promote injustice," the court relied on the fact that Marchese had engaged in blatant tax fraud by treating his personal expenses as deductible corporate business expenses, and had used corporate funds for his own benefit while avoiding corporate debts. The court also found that Marchese had assured a Sea-Land representative in a telephone conversation that the freight bill would be paid, even though he knew at the time that he would "manipulate" the corporate funds "to insure there would not be funds to pay" the Sea-Land bills. This, said the court, constituted "fraud." Sea-Land Services, Inc. v. Pepper Source, 1992 WL 168537 (N.D.Ill.1992). The district court judgment was affirmed on appeal, Sea-Land Services, Inc. v. Pepper Source, 993 F.2d 1309 (7th Cir.1993), with the observation that there was more than the mere fact that Marchese's corporations did not pay their debts: he had received "countless benefits at the expense of" Sea-Land and other creditors, including loans and salaries paid in such a way as to "insur[e] that his corporations had insufficient funds with which to pay their debts."

QUESTIONS

1. Once the plaintiff had pierced PS's corporate veil to impose personal liability on Marchese, it could have levied on the stock he owned in the other affiliated firms. What would it gain by having the court "reverse pierce" the other corporate veils?

2. Why is not the owner of a corporation that has escaped personal liability for its debts necessarily unjustly enriched?

INTRODUCTORY NOTE

In the following case a corporation owns all the shares of common stock of another corporation. The first corporation is generally referred to as a "parent" corporation and the second as a "subsidiary." Why would the parent choose this form of organization rather than simply run all its activities out of a single corporation (with "divisions" for separate activities)? There are a number of reasons, but one important one is that generally the parent, like any other shareholder, is not liable for the debts of the subsidiary, so the parent can undertake an activity without putting at risk its own assets, beyond those it decides to commit to the subsidiary. Like an individual shareholder, however, a corporate shareholder must be aware of the danger that if it is not careful, the creditors of the subsidiary may be able to pierce the corporate veil of the subsidiary. The parent must also be careful not to become directly liable by virtue of its participation in the activities of the subsidiary.

In re Silicone Gel Breast Implants Products Liability Litigation

887 F.Supp. 1447 (N.D.Ala.1995).

■ POINTER, CHIEF JUDGE.

Under submission after appropriate discovery, extensive briefing, and oral argument is the motion for summary judgment filed by defendant Bristol-Myers Squibb Co. Bristol is the sole shareholder of Medical Engineering Corporation, a major supplier of breast implants, but has never itself manufactured or distributed breast implants. Bristol asserts that the evidence is insufficient for the plaintiffs' claims to proceed against it, whether through piercing the corporate veil or under a theory of direct liability. The parties agree that, with discovery substantially complete, this motion is ripe for decision. For the reasons stated below, the court concludes that Bristol is not entitled to summary judgment.

. . .

II. CHOICE OF LAW

In federal multidistrict proceedings, the transferee court applies the substantive law of the transferor courts. . . . The transferor courts in diversity cases would be bound to apply the law of the forum state, including its choice of law rules. . . .

This MDL proceeding involves diversity-jurisdiction cases filed in, or removed to, federal courts in 90 of the 94 districts, located in virtually every state, the District of Columbia, Puerto Rico, and the Virgin Islands. This court must therefore look to the laws of the several states to determine whether Bristol's motion should be granted. Many states would call for this court, when addressing "alter ego" and other "veil piercing" issues, to apply the law of Delaware, where Bristol and MEC are incorporated. But, under choice-of-law rules in other jurisdictions, this court may be obliged to apply the laws of many different states. Because of variations in applicable state law, summary judgment could be proper in some cases while not warranted in others.

III. FACTS

For purposes of Bristol's summary judgment motion, the court treats the following facts as established, either because they are not in genuine dispute or because they are supported by evidence viewed in the light most favorable to the plaintiffs.

MEC was incorporated in Wisconsin in 1969, with its principal place of business in Racine. It was an independent, privately-held corporation manufacturing a variety of medical and plastic surgery devices, including breast implants. In 1982, after an extensive due diligence review that included information regarding capsular contracture, rupture, and gel bleed, Bristol, a Delaware corporation, purchased MEC's stock for $28 million through a series of mergers and corporate reorganizations. [After a series of formalistic transactions, MEC became, in 1982, a Delaware corporation, wholly owned by Bristol.]

In 1988 Bristol expanded its breast implant business by purchasing from the Cooper Companies two other breast-implant manufacturers, Natural Y Surgical Specialties, Inc. and Aesthetech Corporation. Though executed in the name of MEC and the Cooper Companies, the purchase was negotiated between Bristol and the Cooper Companies, and the purchase price of $8.7 million was paid from a Bristol account (though charged to MEC). The due diligence review, which indicated potential hazards and possible liability relating to polyurethane-coated breast implants, was conducted jointly by MEC and Bristol.

Documents reflect that MEC has had, at least in form, a board of three directors, generally consisting of the Bristol Vice President then serving as President of Bristol's Health Care Group, another Bristol executive, and MEC's president. Bristol's Health Care Group President, who reported to Bristol's president or chairman, could not be outvoted by the other two MEC board members. Several of the former MEC presidents did not recall that MEC had a board, let alone that they were members; and one of these stated that he did not attend, call, or receive notice of board meetings in his five years of service because he had a designated Bristol officer to contact. The few resolutions that were adopted by MEC's board were apparently prepared by Bristol officials.

MEC prepared "significant event" reports for Bristol's Corporate Policy Committee. These reports included information on breast implant production, such as publicity, testing, expenses, lawsuit settlements, and backorders caused by sterilization difficulties. Neither Bristol managers nor MEC Presidents recall any orders or recommendations being issued by Bristol as a result of these reviews. Bristol also required MEC to prepare and submit a five-year plan for its review.

MEC submitted budgets for approval by Bristol's senior management. For this submission, MEC filled out a series of standard Bristol forms that included information on projected sales, profits and losses, cash flow, balance sheets, and capital requirements. Bristol had the authority to modify this budget, though it rarely, if ever, actually did so. Cash received by MEC was transferred to an account maintained by Bristol. This money was credited to MEC, but the interest earned was credited to Bristol. Bristol was MEC's banker, providing such loans as it determined MEC needed. Bristol required MEC to obtain its approval for capital appropriations,[1] though most, if not all, of these requests were approved.

Bristol set the employment policies and wage scales that applied to MEC's employees. Before hiring a top executive or negotiating the salary, MEC was required to seek Bristol's approval. Before hiring a vice president of MEC, MEC's president and his superior at Bristol interviewed the candidate. Key executive employees were rated on the Bristol schedule. Bristol set a target for salary increases below the key executive level and approved those for employees above that level. Key executives of MEC received stock options for Bristol stock. MEC employees could participate in Bristol's pension and savings plans.

Bristol provided various services to MEC. Zimmer International, another Bristol subsidiary, distributed MEC breast implants but did not

[1] The evidence reflects, for example, that MEC sought this approval before purchasing a laboratory sink costing $4,600.

receive any benefit for doing so. Bristol's corporate development group assisted MEC in seeking out new product lines. Bristol's scientific experts researched the hazards of breast implants and polyurethane foam. Bristol provided funds for MEC to conduct sales contests. Bristol funded tests on breast implants. Another Bristol subsidiary, ConvaTec, assisted MEC in developing its premarket approval application (PMAA) regarding breast implants for the FDA. In addition to this assistance, Bristol hired an outside laboratory to verify ConvaTec's analysis. Bristol also conducted post-market surveillance at the request of the FDA. Some of Bristol's in-house counsel acted as MEC attorneys. These attorneys advised MEC on virtually every aspect of its business including budgets, price increases, new product development, package inserts, liability, compliance with FDA regulations, and negotiated settlements with individuals claiming damages from breast implants. They also developed the system for handling complaints about MEC products. They reviewed all breast implant promotional materials and responses to allegations of harm and liability.

Bristol's Technical Evaluation and Service Department ("TESD") performed auditing and review functions for MEC once or twice a year. They performed all Good Manufacturing Practices (GMP) audits at MEC. These audits were designed to ensure consistent quality of MEC's products. Bristol expected MEC to comply with any manufacturing deficiencies TESD found. A number of the conditions listed as needing corrective action regarded breast implants. TESD also audited MEC's sterilization and lab companies.

Bristol's public relations department issued statements regarding the allegations of TDA production and cancer in rats implanted with polyurethane implants. Bristol's corporate communication department prepared question and answer scripts for MEC employees for use in responding to questions about breast implant safety. Bristol's public affairs department developed a strategic plan to address concerns about the MEME implant and to respond to questions and concerns about the safety of breast implants in general. Bristol's press releases consistently represented that Bristol was researching breast implant safety. For example, in a release dated July 9, 1991, Bristol stated that tests underway would "confirm the well-established safety profile of polyurethane coated breast implants" and that Bristol completed testing which showed that earlier findings concerning the production of TDA from the breakdown of polyurethane were the result of inappropriate testing conditions. In a statement dated July 24, 1991, Bristol represented that numerous other studies were being undertaken to assure the public and the FDA of the safety of polyurethane coated breast implants.

Bristol's name and logo were contained in the package inserts and promotional products regarding breast implants, apparently as a marketing tool to increase confidence in the product. Bristol's name was used in all sales and promotional communications with physicians.

MEC posted a profit every year between 1983 and 1990. Total sales increased from approximately $14 million in 1983 to $65 million in 1990. Bristol never received dividends from MEC. Bristol prepared consolidated federal income tax returns but MEC prepared its own

Wisconsin tax forms. Bristol also purchased insurance for MEC under its policy. This insurance has a face value of over $2 billion.

Bristol's executive vice president suspended MEC's sales of polyurethane coated breast implants on April 17, 1991, and determined not to submit a PMAA for the implants to the FDA. MEC ceased its breast implant business in 1991 and later that year MEC ceased all operations by selling its urology division. This sale could not have occurred without Bristol's approval, and proceeds from the sale were turned over to Bristol, which then executed a low-interest demand note for $57,518,888 payable to MEC. MEC's only assets at this time are this demand note and its indemnity insurance.

IV. ANALYSIS

The various theories of recovery made by plaintiffs against Bristol can be generally divided between those involving "corporate control" and those asserting direct liability. The corporate control claims deal with piercing the corporate veil to abrogate limited liability and hold Bristol responsible for actions of MEC. The direct liability theories include strict products liability, negligence, negligent failure to warn, negligence per se for not complying with FDA regulations, misrepresentation, fraud, and participation.

A. "Corporate Control" Claims

The potential for abuse of the corporate form is greatest when, as here, the corporation is owned by a single shareholder. The evaluation of corporate control claims cannot, however, disregard the fact that, no different from other stockholders, a parent corporation is expected—indeed, required—to exert some control over its subsidiary. Limited liability is the rule, not the exception. . . . However, when a corporation is so controlled as to be the alter ego or mere instrumentality of its stockholder, the corporate form may be disregarded in the interests of justice. So far as this court has been able to determine, some variation of this theory of liability is recognized in all jurisdictions.

An initial question is whether veil-piercing may ever be resolved by summary judgment. Ordinarily the fact-intensive nature of the issue will require that it be resolved only through a trial. Summary judgment, however, can be proper if, as occurred earlier in this litigation with respect to claims against Dow Chemical and Corning, the evidence presented could lead to but one result. Because the court concludes that a jury (or in some jurisdictions, the judge acting in equity) could—and, under the laws of many states, probably should—find that MEC was but the alter ego of Bristol, summary judgment must be denied.

The totality of circumstances must be evaluated in determining whether a subsidiary may be found to be the alter ego or mere instrumentality of the parent corporation. Although the standards are not identical in each state, all jurisdictions require a showing of substantial domination. Among the factors to be considered are whether:

- the parent and the subsidiary have common directors or officers
- the parent and the subsidiary have common business departments

- the parent and the subsidiary file consolidated financial statements and tax returns
- the parent finances the subsidiary
- the parent caused the incorporation of the subsidiary
- the subsidiary operates with grossly inadequate capital
- the parent pays the salaries and other expenses of the subsidiary
- the subsidiary receives no business except that given to it by the parent
- the parent uses the subsidiary's property as its own
- the daily operations of the two corporations are not kept separate
- the subsidiary does not observe the basic corporate formalities, such as keeping separate books and records and holding shareholder and board meetings.

. . .

The fact-finder at a trial could find that the evidence supports the conclusion that many of these factors have been proven: two of MEC's three directors were Bristol directors; MEC was part of Bristol's Health Care group and used Bristol's legal, auditing, and communications departments; MEC and Bristol filed consolidated federal tax returns and Bristol prepared consolidated financial reports; Bristol operated as MEC's finance company, providing loans for the purchase of Aesthetech and Natural Y, receiving interest on MEC's funds, and requiring MEC to make requests for capital appropriations; Bristol effectively used MEC's resources as its own by obtaining interest on MEC's money and requiring MEC to make requests for capital appropriations to obtain its own funds; some members of MEC's board were not aware that MEC had a board of directors, let alone that they were members; and the senior Bristol member of MEC's board could not be out-voted by the other two directors. These facts, even apart from evidence that might establish some of the other factors listed above, would provide significant support for a finding at trial that MEC is Bristol's alter ego.

Bristol contends that a finding of fraud or like misconduct is necessary to pierce the corporate veil. Despite Bristol's contentions to the contrary, Delaware courts—to which Bristol would have this court look—do not necessarily require a showing of fraud if a subsidiary is found to be the mere instrumentality or alter ego of its sole stockholder. . . . In addition, many jurisdictions that require a showing of fraud, injustice, or inequity in a contract case do not in a tort situation. . . . A rational distinction can be drawn between tort and contract cases. In actions based on contract, "the creditor has willingly transacted business with the subsidiary" although it could have insisted on assurances that would make the parent also responsible. [United States v. Jon-T Chemicals, Inc., 768 F.2d 686, 693 (5th Cir.1985), cert. denied, 475 U.S. 1014, 106 S.Ct. 1194, 89 L.Ed.2d 309 (1986).] In a tort situation, however, the injured party had no such choice; the limitations on corporate liability were, from its standpoint, fortuitous and non-consensual.

There is, however, evidence precluding summary judgment even in jurisdictions that require a finding of fraud, inequity, or injustice. This conclusion is not based merely on the evidence that, even accepting Bristol's contentions regarding the amount of insurance available to MEC, MEC may have insufficient funds to satisfy the potential risks of responding to, and defending against, the numerous existing and potential claims of the plaintiffs. Equally significant is the fact that Bristol permitted its name to appear on breast implant advertisements, packages, and product inserts to improve sales by giving the product additional credibility. Combined with the evidence of potentially insufficient assets, this fact would support a finding that it would be inequitable and unjust to allow Bristol now to avoid liability to those induced to believe Bristol was vouching for this product.

Because the evidence available at a trial could support—if not, under some state laws, perhaps mandate—a finding that the corporate veil should be pierced, Bristol is not entitled through summary judgment to dismissal of the claims against it.

B. Direct Liability Claims

There is an additional reason why Bristol is not entitled to summary judgment. Under the law in most jurisdictions, it may also be subject to liability under at least one of the direct liability claims made by plaintiffs; namely, the theory of negligent undertaking pursuant to Restatement (Second) of Torts § 324A. That section provides:

> One who undertakes, gratuitously or for consideration, to render services to another which he should recognize as necessary for the protection of a third person or his things, is subject to liability to the third person for physical harm resulting from his failure to exercise reasonable care to [perform] his undertakings, if
>
> (a) his failure to exercise reasonable care increases the risk of harm, or
>
> (b) he has undertaken to perform a duty owed by the other to the third person, or
>
> (c) the harm is suffered because of a reliance of the other or the third person upon the undertaking.

Under this theory, frequently applied in connection with safety inspections by insurers or with third-party repairs to equipment or premises, a duty that would not otherwise have existed can arise when an individual or company nevertheless undertakes to perform some action. . . . The potential liability for failure to use reasonable care in such circumstances extends to persons who may reasonably be expected to suffer harm from that negligence. Doctrinally, a cause of action under § 324A does not involve an assertion of derivative liability but one of direct liability, since it is based on the actions of defendant itself. The existence of a parent-subsidiary relationship, while not required, is obviously no defense to such a claim.

. . .

By allowing its name to be placed on breast implant packages and product inserts, Bristol held itself out as supporting the product, apparently to increase confidence in the product and to increase sales.

Bristol also issued press releases stating that polyurethane-coated breast implants were safe. Having engaged in this type of marketing, it cannot now deny its potential responsibility under § 324A. . . .

V. CONCLUSION

By separate order, Bristol's motion for summary judgment will be denied. As with other orders denying summary judgment, this decision is interlocutory and does not constitute a holding that Bristol is liable to the plaintiffs. . . .

QUESTIONS

1. Which of the various "factors to be considered" are most important and which, if any, seem irrelevant, and why?

2. What is the relevance of the use of Bristol's name on "advertisements, packages, and product inserts" under a theory of (a) piercing the corporate veil or (b) direct liability under Restatement (Second) of Torts § 324A?

3. Is there any other theory under which the use of Bristol's name would be relevant?

4. If you had been Bristol's lawyer, what advice would you have given (if asked) about how to avoid liability for the debts of MEC? Bear in mind the importance of the need of Bristol to exercise control over MEC in a practical manner and the distaste of people in business for pettifogging lawyers.

INTRODUCTORY NOTE

Beginning in the 1960s, limited partnerships came into widespread use for "tax shelter" investments. Tax shelter investments are ones that show losses for tax purposes even though they may be successful economically. Such investments were of considerable economic importance (particularly in certain sectors, such as real estate and oil and gas) until the tax benefits were substantially curtailed in the 1980s, particularly in 1986. The tax advantage of the use of the limited partnership form of organization was that the investors were able to claim their pro rata share of the (economically artificial) losses of the partnership on their individual tax returns, which is not possible for tax-shelter-type investments if the corporate form is used. While the basic partnership form bestowed this tax benefit—the so called "pass-through" of losses—the use of the *limited* partnership form gave the limited partners the corporate advantage of limited liability. Beginning in the late 1960s, lawyers for the promoters of tax shelter investments developed a variation on the basic limited partnership: a limited partnership with a corporation as the sole general partner. With the use of this form, no individual was liable for the debts of the partnership. Initially some observers thought that that was too good to be true, but eventually it became accepted as a standard form of tax shelter organization. As the preceding material in this section suggests, however, it is often easier for a lawyer to form a corporation (or a limited partnership with a corporate general partner) than for the clients to respect the form and thereby make it effective.

Frigidaire Sales Corporation v. Union Properties, Inc.

88 Wash. 2d 400, 562 P.2d 244 (1977).

Petitioner, Frigidaire Sales Corporation, sought review of a Court of Appeals decision which held that limited partners do not incur general liability for the limited partnership's obligations simply because they are officers, directors, or shareholders of the corporate general partner. . . . We granted review, and now affirm the decision of the Court of Appeals.

. . . Petitioner entered into a contract with Commercial Investors (Commercial), a limited partnership. Respondents, Leonard Mannon and Raleigh Baxter, were limited partners of Commercial. Respondents were also officers, directors, and shareholders of Union Properties, Inc., the only general partner of Commercial. Respondents controlled Union Properties, and through their control of Union Properties they exercised the day-to-day control and management of Commercial. Commercial breached the contract, and petitioner brought suit against Union Properties and respondents. The trial court concluded that respondents did not incur general liability for Commercial's obligations by reason of their control of Commercial, and the Court of Appeals affirmed.

We first note that petitioner does not contend that respondents acted improperly by setting up the limited partnership with a corporation as the sole general partner. Limited partnerships are a statutory form of business organization, and parties creating a limited partnership must follow the statutory requirements. In Washington, parties may form a limited partnership with a corporation as the sole general partner. . . .

Petitioner's sole contention is that respondents should incur general liability for the limited partnership's obligations [under the Uniform Limited Partnership Act provision that removes the limitation of liability of a limited partner who "takes part in the control of the business"], because they exercised the day-to-day control and management of Commercial. Respondents, on the other hand, argue that Commercial was controlled by Union Properties, a separate legal entity, and not by respondents in their individual capacities.

[The court distinguishes Delaney v. Fidelity Lease Ltd., 526 S.W.2d 543 (Tex.1975), in which, among other things, the Texas Supreme Court expressed concern about the use of corporate general partners with "minimum capitalization and therefore minimum liability."]

However, we agree with our Court of Appeals analysis that this concern with minimum capitalization is not peculiar to limited partnerships with corporate general partners, but may arise anytime a creditor deals with a corporation. . . . Because our limited partnership statutes permit parties to form a limited partnership with a corporation as the sole general partner, this concern about minimal capitalization, standing by itself, does not justify a finding that the limited partners incur general liability for their control of the corporate general partner. . . . If a corporate general partner is inadequately capitalized, the rights of a creditor are adequately protected under the "piercing-the-corporate-veil" doctrine of corporation law. . . .

Furthermore, petitioner was never led to believe that respondents were acting in any capacity other than in their corporate capacities. The parties stipulated at the trial that respondents never acted in any direct, personal capacity. When the shareholders of a corporation, who are also the corporation's officers and directors, conscientiously keep the affairs of the corporation separate from their personal affairs, and no fraud or manifest injustice is perpetrated upon third persons who deal with the corporation, the corporation's separate entity should be respected. . . .

For us to find that respondents incurred general liability for the limited partnership's obligations . . . would require us to . . . totally ignore the corporate entity of Union Properties, when petitioner knew it was dealing with that corporate entity. There can be no doubt that respondents, in fact, controlled the [limited partnership]. However, they did so only in their capacities as agents for their principal, the corporate general partner. Although the corporation was a separate entity, it could act only through its board of directors, officers, and agents. . . . Petitioner entered into the contract with Commercial. Respondents signed the contract in their capacities as president and secretary-treasurer of Union Properties, the general partner of Commercial. In the eyes of the law it was Union Properties, as a separate corporate entity, which entered into the contract with petitioner and controlled the limited partnership.

Further, because respondents scrupulously separated their actions on behalf of the corporation from their personal actions, petitioner never mistakenly assumed that respondents were general partners with general liability. . . . Petitioner knew Union Properties was the sole general partner and did not rely on respondents' control by assuming that they were also general partners. If petitioner had not wished to rely on the solvency of Union Properties as the only general partner, it could have insisted that respondents personally guarantee contractual performance. Because petitioner entered into the contract knowing that Union Properties was the only party with general liability, and because in the eyes of the law it was Union Properties, a separate entity, which controlled the limited partnership, there is no reason for us to find that respondents incurred general liability for their acts done as officers of the corporate general partner.

The decision of the Court of Appeals is affirmed.

ANALYSIS

In *Frigidaire* the individual defendants were limited partners of Commercial Investors as well as officers, directors and shareholders of Union Properties, Inc., the general partner. If they had not been limited partners might they still have been personally liable (if they had not been so scrupulous about respecting the corporate form)? On what theory or theories? How would the proof differ, depending on whether they were or were not limited partners?

3. SHAREHOLDER DERIVATIVE ACTIONS

A. INTRODUCTION

Cohen v. Beneficial Industrial Loan Corp.

337 U.S. 541, 69 S.Ct. 1221, 93 L.Ed. 1528 (1949).

■ MR. JUSTICE JACKSON delivered the opinion of the Court.

The ultimate question here is whether a federal court, having jurisdiction of a stockholder's derivative action only because the parties are of diverse citizenship, must apply a statute of the forum state which makes the plaintiff, if unsuccessful, liable for the reasonable expenses, including attorney's fees, of the defense and entitles the corporation to require security for their payment.

Petitioners' decedent, as plaintiff, brought in the United States District Court for New Jersey an action in the right of the Beneficial Industrial Loan Corporation, a Delaware corporation doing business in New Jersey. The defendants were the corporation and certain of its managers and directors. The complaint alleged generally that since 1929 the individual defendants engaged in a continuing and successful conspiracy to enrich themselves at the expense of the corporation. Specific charges of mismanagement and fraud extended over a period of eighteen years and the assets allegedly wasted or diverted thereby were said to exceed $100,000,000. The stockholder had demanded that the corporation institute proceedings for its recovery but, by their control of the corporation, the individual defendants prevented it from doing so. This stockholder, therefore, sought to assert the right of the corporation. One of 16,000 stockholders, he owned 100 of its more than two million shares, so that his holdings, together with 150 shares held by the intervenor, approximated 0.0125% of the outstanding stock and had a market value that had never exceeded $9,000.

The action was brought in 1943, and various proceedings had been taken therein when, in 1945, New Jersey enacted the statute which is here involved.[1] Its general effect is to make a plaintiff having so small an

---

1 Chapter 131, New Jersey Laws of 1945, provides in pertinent part as follows:

"1. In any action instituted or maintained in the right of any domestic or foreign corporation by the holder or holders of shares, or of voting trust certificates representing shares, of such corporation having a total par value or stated capital value of less than five per centum (5%) of the aggregate par value or stated capital value of all the outstanding shares of such corporation's stock of every class . . . unless the shares or voting trust certificates held by such holder or holders have a market value in excess of fifty thousand dollars ($50,000.00), the corporation in whose right such action is brought shall be entitled, at any stage of the proceeding before final judgment, to require the complainant or complainants to give security for the reasonable expenses, including counsel fees, which may be incurred by it in connection with such action and by the other parties defendant in connection therewith for which it may become subject pursuant to law, its certificate of incorporation, its by-laws or under equitable principles, to which the corporation shall have recourse in such amount as the court having jurisdiction shall determine upon the termination of such action. . . .

"2. In any action, suit or proceeding brought or maintained in the right of a domestic or foreign corporation by the holder or holders of shares, or of voting trust certificates representing shares, of such corporation, it must be made to appear that the complainant was a shareholder or the holder of a voting trust certificate at the time

interest liable for the reasonable expenses and attorney's fees of the defense if he fails to make good his complaint and to entitle the corporation to indemnity before the case can be prosecuted. These conditions are made applicable to pending actions. The corporate defendant therefore moved to require security, pointed to its by-laws by which it might be required to indemnify the individual defendants, and averred that a bond of $125,000 would be appropriate.

Constitutionality.

Petitioners deny the validity of the statute under the Federal Constitution. . . .

The background of stockholder litigation with which this statute deals requires no more than general notice. As business enterprise increasingly sought the advantages of incorporation, management became vested with almost uncontrolled discretion in handling other people's money. The vast aggregate of funds committed to corporate control came to be drawn to a considerable extent from numerous and scattered holders of small interests. The director was not subject to an effective accountability. That created strong temptation for managers to profit personally at expense of their trust. The business code became all too tolerant of such practices. Corporate laws were lax and were not self-enforcing, and stockholders, in face of gravest abuses, were singularly impotent in obtaining redress of abuses of trust.

Equity came to the relief of the stockholder, who had no standing to bring civil action at law against faithless directors and managers. Equity, however, allowed him to step into the corporation's shoes and to seek in its right the restitution he could not demand in his own. It required him first to demand that the corporation vindicate its own rights, but when, as was usual, those who perpetrated the wrongs also were able to obstruct any remedy, equity would hear and adjudge the corporation's cause through its stockholder with the corporation as a defendant, albeit a rather nominal one. This remedy, born of stockholder helplessness, was long the chief regulator of corporate management and has afforded no small incentive to avoid at least grosser forms of betrayal of stockholders' interests. It is argued, and not without reason, that without it there would be little practical check on such abuses.

Unfortunately, the remedy itself provided opportunity for abuse, which was not neglected. Suits sometimes were brought not to redress real wrongs, but to realize upon their nuisance value. They were bought off by secret settlements in which any wrongs to the general body of share owners were compounded by the suing stockholder, who was mollified by payments from corporate assets.* These litigations were aptly characterized in professional slang as "strike suits." And it was said that these suits were more commonly brought by small and irresponsible than

---

of the transaction of which he complains or that his share or voting trust certificate thereafter devolved upon him by operation of law.

"3. This act shall take effect immediately and shall apply to all such actions, suits or proceedings now pending in which no final judgment has been entered, and to all future actions, suits and proceedings."

* [Eds.—Generally it was not the shareholder who was "mollified by payments from corporate assets," but the shareholder's lawyer, who received a generous legal fee. To this day, the principal effective incentive that generates derivative actions is legal fees, not shareholder dissatisfaction.]

by large stockholders, because the former put less to risk and a small interest was more often within the capacity and readiness of management to compromise than a large one.

We need not determine the measure of these abuses or the evils they produced on the one hand or prevented and redressed on the other. The Legislature of New Jersey, like that of other states, considered them sufficient to warrant some remedial measures.

. . . [A] stockholder who brings suit on a cause of action derived from the corporation assumes a position, not technically as a trustee perhaps, but one of a fiduciary character. He sues, not for himself alone, but as representative of a class comprising all who are similarly situated. The interests of all in the redress of the wrongs are taken into his hands, dependent upon his diligence, wisdom and integrity. And while the stockholders have chosen the corporate director or manager, they have no such election as to a plaintiff who steps forward to represent them. He is a self-chosen representative and a volunteer champion. The Federal Constitution does not oblige the state to place its litigating and adjudicating processes at the disposal of such a representative, at least without imposing standards of responsibility, liability and accountability which it considers will protect the interests he elects himself to represent. . . . We conclude that the state has plenary power over this type of litigation.

. . .

In considering whether the statute offends the Due Process Clause we can judge it only by its own terms, for it has had no interpretation or application as yet. It imposes liability and requires security for "the *reasonable* expenses, including counsel fees, which may be incurred" (emphasis supplied) by the corporation and by other parties defendant. The amount of security is subject to increase if the progress of the litigation reveals that it is inadequate, or to decrease if it is proved to be excessive. A state may set the terms on which it will permit litigations in its courts. No type of litigation is more susceptible of regulation than that of a fiduciary nature. And it cannot seriously be said that a state makes such *unreasonable* use of its power as to violate the Constitution when it provides liability and security for payment of *reasonable* expenses if a litigation of this character is adjudged to be unsustainable. . . .

The contention that the statute denies equal protection of the laws is based upon the fact that it enables a stockholder who owns 5% of a corporation's outstanding shares, or $50,000 in market value, to proceed without either security or liability and imposes both upon those who elect to proceed with a smaller interest. We do not think the state is forbidden to use the amount of one's financial interest, which measures his individual injury from the misconduct to be redressed, as some measure of the good faith and responsibility of one who seeks at his own election to act as custodian of the interests of all stockholders, and as an indication that he volunteers for the large burdens of the litigation from a real sense of grievance and is not putting forward a claim to capitalize personally on its harassment value. These may not be the best ways of precluding "strike lawsuits," but we are unable to say that a classification for these purposes, based upon the percentage or market value of the stock alleged to be injured by the wrongs, is an unconstitutional one.

Applicability in Federal Court.

The Rules of Decision Act, in effect since the First Congress of the United States and now found at 28 U.S.C. § 1652, provides: "The laws of the several states, except where the Constitution or treaties of the United States or Acts of Congress otherwise require or provide, shall be regarded as rules of decision in civil actions in the courts of the United States, in cases where they apply." This Court in Erie R. Co. v. Tompkins, 304 U.S. 64, held that judicial decisions are laws of the states within its meaning. But *Erie R. Co. v. Tompkins* and its progeny have wrought a more far-reaching change in the relation of state and federal courts and the application of state law in the latter whereby in diversity cases the federal court administers the state system of law in all except details related to its own conduct of business. . . . The only substantial argument that this New Jersey statute is not applicable here is that its provisions are mere rules of procedure rather than rules of substantive law.

Even if we were to agree that the New Jersey statute is procedural, it would not determine that it is not applicable. Rules which lawyers call procedural do not always exhaust their effect by regulating procedure. But this statute is not merely a regulation of procedure. With it or without it the main action takes the same course. However, it creates a new liability where none existed before, for it makes a stockholder who institutes a derivative action liable for the expense to which he puts the corporation and other defendants, if he does not make good his claims. Such liability is not usual and it goes beyond payment of what we know as "costs." If all the Act did was to create this liability, it would clearly be substantive. But this new liability would be without meaning and value in many cases if it resulted in nothing but a judgment for expenses at or after the end of the case. Therefore, a procedure is prescribed by which the liability is insured by entitling the corporate defendant to a bond of indemnity before the outlay is incurred. We do not think a statute which so conditions the stockholder's action can be disregarded by the federal court as a mere procedural device.

We hold that the New Jersey statute applies in federal courts and that the District Court erred in declining to fix the amount of indemnity reasonably to be exacted as a condition of further prosecution of the suit.

The judgment of the Court of Appeals is

Affirmed.

■ [Eds.—The dissenting opinions of JUSTICE DOUGLAS (joined by JUSTICE FRANKFURTER) and JUSTICE RUTLEDGE are omitted.]

ANALYSIS

1. Think about the role of the shareholder in the legal structure of the corporation. Why is the derivative action one in equity rather than at law?

2. Is there anything unique about derivative actions that has led New Jersey and other states to reject the normal rule of American law that each party bears her or his own legal expenses, regardless of who prevails?

Eisenberg v. Flying Tiger Line, Inc.

451 F.2d 267 (2d Cir.1971).

■ IRVING R. KAUFMAN, CIRCUIT JUDGE:

Max Eisenberg, a resident of New York, "as stockholder of The Flying Tiger Line, Inc. [Flying Tiger], on behalf of himself and all other stockholders of said corporation similarly situated" commenced this action in the Supreme Court of the State of New York to enjoin the effectuation of a plan of reorganization and merger.* Flying Tiger, a Delaware corporation with its principal place of business in California, removed the action to the District Court for the Eastern District of New York.

Flying Tiger pleaded several affirmative defenses and moved for an order to require Eisenberg to comply with New York Business Corporation Law § 627 (McKinney's Consol.Laws, c. 4 1963), which requires a plaintiff suing derivatively on behalf of a corporation to post security for the corporation's costs. Judge Travia granted the motion without opinion and afforded Eisenberg thirty days to post security in the sum of $35,000. Eisenberg did not comply, his action was dismissed and he appeals. We find Eisenberg's cause of action to be personal and not derivative within the meaning of § 627. We therefore reverse the dismissal.

In this action, Eisenberg is seeking to overturn a reorganization and merger which Flying Tiger effected in 1969. He charges that a series of corporate maneuvers were intended to dilute his voting rights. In order to achieve this end, he alleges, Flying Tiger in July 1969 organized a wholly owned Delaware subsidiary, the Flying Tiger Corporation ("FTC"). In August, FTC in turn organized a wholly owned subsidiary, FTL Air Freight Corporation ("FTL"). The three Delaware corporations then entered into a plan of reorganization, subject to stockholder approval, by which Flying Tiger merged into FTL and only FTL survived. A proxy statement dated August 11 was sent to stockholders, who approved the plan by the necessary two-thirds vote at the stockholders' meeting held on September 15.

Upon consummation of this merger Flying Tiger ceased as the operating company, FTL took over operations and Flying Tiger shares were converted into an identical number of FTC shares. Thereafter, FTL changed its name to "Flying Tiger Line, Inc.," for the obvious purpose of continuing without disruption the business previously conducted by Flying Tiger. The approximately 4,500,000 shares of the company traded on the New York and Pacific Coast stock exchanges are now those of the holding company, FTC, rather than those of the operating company, Flying Tiger. The effect of the merger is that business operations are now confined to a wholly owned subsidiary of a holding company whose stockholders are the former stockholders of Flying Tiger.

It is of passing interest that Eisenberg contends that the end result of this complex plan was to deprive minority stockholders of any vote or any influence over the affairs of the newly spawned company. Flying Tiger insists the plan was devised to bring about diversification without interference from the Civil Aeronautics Board, which closely regulates

* [Eds.—Eisenberg represented himself.]

air carriers, and to better use available tax benefits. Even if any of these motives prove to be relevant, the alleged illegality is not relevant to the questions before this court. We are called on to decide, assuming Eisenberg's complaint is sufficient on its face, only whether he should have been required to post security for costs as a condition to prosecuting his action.

To resolve this question we look first to Cohen v. Beneficial Industrial Loan Corp., 337 U.S. 541 (1949), which instructs that a federal court with diversity jurisdiction must apply a state statute providing security for costs if the state court would require the security in similar circumstances. . . . [T]his Court still must determine whether to apply the New York costs security statute, Business Corporation Law § 627, or, as Eisenberg contends, Delaware law, which has no such requirement. New York clearly has indicated that § 627 will be applied in its courts whether or not New York substantive law controls the merits of the case. . . . Since New York courts would invoke its own law on security for costs rather than Delaware's, we are required to do the same. . . .

Eisenberg argues, however, that New York courts would refuse to invoke § 627 in the instant case because the section applies exclusively to derivative actions. . . . He urges that his class action is representative and not derivative.

We are told that if the gravamen of the complaint is injury to the corporation the suit is derivative, but "if the injury is one to the plaintiff as a stockholder and to him individually and not to the corporation," the suit is individual in nature and may take the form of a representative class action. 13 Fletcher, Private Corporation § 5911 (1970 Rev.Vol.). This generalization is of little use in our case which is one of those "borderline cases which are more or less troublesome to classify." Id. The essence of Eisenberg's claimed injury is that the reorganization has deprived him and fellow stockholders of their right to vote on the operating company affairs and that this right in no sense ever belonged to Flying Tiger itself. This right, he says, belonged to the stockholders *per se.* Flying Tiger notes, however, that the stockholders were harmed, if at all, only because their company was dissolved, and their vote can be restored only if that company is revived. It insists, therefore, that stockholders are affected only secondarily or derivatively because we must first breathe life back into their dissolved corporation before the stockholders can be helped.

Despite a leading New York case which would seem at first glance to support Flying Tiger's position, we find that its contention misses the mark by a wide margin in its failure to distinguish between derivative and non-derivative class actions. In Gordon v. Elliman, 306 N.Y. 456, 119 N.E.2d 331 (1954), by a vote of 4 to 3, the Court of Appeals took an expansive view of the coverage of § 627's predecessor, General Corporation Law § 61–b. The majority held that an action to compel the payment of a dividend was derivative in nature and security for costs could be required. The test formulated by the majority was "whether the object of the lawsuit is to recover upon a chose in action belonging directly to the stockholders, or whether it is to compel the performance of corporate acts which good faith requires the directors to take in order to perform a duty which they owe to the corporation, and through it, to its stockholders." 306 N.Y. at 459, 119 N.E.2d at 334. Pursuant to this test it is argued that, if Flying Tiger's directors had a duty not to merge the corporation, that duty was owed to the corporation and only derivatively to its stockholders. Both the 4–1 Appellate Division and the 4–3 Court of Appeals opinions evoked the quick and unanimous condemnation of commentators. Moreover, this test, "which appears to sweep away the distinction between a representative and a derivative action," in effect classifying all stockholder class actions as derivative, has been limited strictly to its facts by lower New York courts. Lazar v. Knolls Cooperative Section No. 2, Inc., 205 Misc. 748, 130 N.Y.S.2d 407, 410 (Sup.Ct.1954). . . . In *Lazar,* a stockholder sought to force directors to call a stockholders' meeting. The court stated security for costs could not be required where a plaintiff:

> "does not challenge acts of the management on behalf of the corporation. He challenges the right of the present management to exclude him and other stockholders from proper participation in the affairs of the corporation. He claims that the defendants are interfering with the plaintiff's rights and privileges as stockholders."

130 N.Y.S. at 410, 205 Misc. at 752. In substance, this is similar to what Eisenberg challenges here.

The legislature also was concerned with the sweeping breadth of *Gordon.* In the recodification of corporate statutes completed in 1963, it added three words to the definition of derivative suits contained in § 626. Suits are now derivative only if brought in the right of a corporation to procure a judgment "in its favor." This was to "forestall any such pronouncement in the future as that made by the Court of Appeals in Gordon v. Elliman." Hornstein, "Analysis of Business Corporation Law," 6 McKinney's Consolidated Laws of New York Ann. 483 (1963).

. . .

Eisenberg's position is even stronger than it would be in the ordinary merger case. In routine merger circumstances the stockholders retain a voice in the operation of the company, albeit a corporation other than their original choice. Here, however, the reorganization deprived him and other minority stockholders of any voice in the affairs of their previously existing operating company.

It is thus clear to us that *Gordon* is factually distinguishable from the instant case. Moreover, a close analysis of other New York cases, the amendment to § 626 and the major treatises, lead us to conclude that *Gordon* has lost its viability as stating a broad principle of law.

Perhaps the strongest string in Eisenberg's bow is one he helped to fashion when he made an investment some forty years ago in Central Zone Property Corp. In 1952 that New York corporation obtained stockholder approval to transfer its assets to a new Delaware corporation in return for the new company's stock. The stock was to be held by trustees in a voting trust, and the former stockholders received voting trust certificates. Eisenberg complained that this effectively deprived him of a voice in the operation of his company which would be run in the future by the trustees of the voting trust. The Court of Appeals agreed that New York law did not permit such a reorganization. Eisenberg v. Central Zone Property Corp., 203 Misc. 59, 116 N.Y.S.2d 154, aff'd, 306 N.Y. 58, 115 N.E.2d 652 (1953). Although we have emphasized that we do not reach the merits of Eisenberg's present complaint, it is of some interest that security for costs was neither sought nor was it discussed in the *Central Zone* opinions, even though Eisenberg did not own five percent of the shares of the corporation. It was clear to all that the allegations of the complaint, quite similar in character to the instant one, stated a representative cause of action. . . . We believe Eisenberg's actions should not have been dismissed for failure to post security pursuant to § 627.

Reversed.

ANALYSIS

1. How, if at all, was Eisenberg deprived of voting rights by the Flying Tiger reorganization?

2. Would the result in the case have been different if Eisenberg had alleged that the directors of Flying Tiger Line, Inc., had violated their duty of loyalty to the corporation and had sought damages in the amount of the legal and other costs of effecting the reorganization?

3. In *Eisenberg*, the Second Circuit is applying New York law. In Delaware, many courts long used the so-called "special injury" test to determine whether a suit was direct or derivative. A special injury was defined as a wrong that "is separate and distinct from that suffered by other shareholders, . . . or a wrong involving a contractual right of a shareholder, such as the right to vote, or to assert majority control, which exists independently of any right of the corporation." Moran v. Household Int'l, Inc., 490 A.2d 1059, 1070 (Del.Ch.1985), aff'd 500 A.2d 1346 (Del.1986 1985). Is the test used in *Eisenberg* the same as the special injury test?

In Tooley v. Donaldson, Lufkin, & Jenrette, Inc., 2004 WL 728354 (Del.Supr.), the Delaware supreme court rejected the special injury test, in favor of a two-pronged standard to be used in determining whether a stockholder's claim is derivative or direct: (1) who suffered the alleged harm, the corporation or the suing stockholders, individually; and (2) who would receive the benefit of any recovery or other remedy, the corporation or the stockholders, individually. Would the result in *Eisenberg* change if this standard were applied to that facts of that case?

NOTE ON SETTLEMENTS AND ATTORNEY FEES

If a derivative action is settled before judgment, the corporation can pay the legal fees of the plaintiff and of the defendants. If, on the other hand, a judgment for money damages is imposed on the defendants, except to the extent that they are covered by insurance, they will be required to pay those damages and may be required to bear the cost of their defense as well. See Del.Gen.Corp.Law § 145(b) (The corporation may pay the defendants' expenses only if the court determines that "despite the adjudication of liability but in view of all the circumstances of the case, [the defendant] is fairly entitled to indemnity."); Cal.Corp.Code § 317(c) (to the same effect). On the plaintiff's side the real party in interest in a derivative action often is the attorney. Putting these rules and observations together, corporate managers who have harmed the corporation generally will be relieved of risk of personal losses if the corporation pays large fees to the plaintiff's attorneys in return for their willingness to accept a settlement, especially one with a form of relief other than money damages. The plaintiff's attorneys may be willing to accept such a settlement in order to avoid the risks of litigation or simply because they are well paid to do so. The court in which the derivative suit is filed must approve any settlement, but a busy judge is not likely to challenge a settlement that is supported by both the parties.

In re General Tire and Rubber Company Securities Litigation, 726 F.2d 1075 (6th Cir.), cert. denied, 469 U.S. 858 (1984), provides a nice illustration of a non-monetary settlement with seemingly generous attorney fees. In that case, General Tire, and its subsidiary, RKO General, had engaged in "ubiquitous corporate improprieties and apparent illegalities." The Securities and Exchange Commission (SEC) brought an action that resulted in recommendations for administrative changes such as expanded review by independent accountants. Derivative actions were also filed, complaining, in part, about dishonest reports by RKO General that led to the loss of a TV license worth over $100 million. The derivative actions were settled, with judicial approval, with the payment of $500,000 as fees to the plaintiffs' attorney. The settlement agreement "acknowledge[d] the plaintiffs' role in implementing remedial action to prevent future improprieties," but in light of the SEC role in the matter, this language seems to be a smokescreen. The only substantive relief was an agreement by General Tire that it would for three years appoint to the RKO board two members who were neither officers nor employees of General Tire or RKO. As the dissenting judge pointed out this relief provided "no real benefit in view of the absolute control of RKO by General Tire."

NOTE AND QUESTION ON INDIVIDUAL RECOVERY IN A DERIVATIVE ACTION

Sometimes a court awards an individual recovery in a derivative action. For example, in Lynch v. Patterson, 701 P.2d 1126 (Wyo.1985), Pat Patterson, Birl Lynch, and R.C. Lynch had carried on an oil-field consulting business in corporate form. Patterson owned 30 percent of the common stock and Birl Lynch and R.C. Lynch each owned 35 percent. Patterson quit working for the corporation and set up his own consulting business. Thereafter, Birl Lynch and R.C. Lynch increased their own pay and ultimately, it was found, paid themselves $266,000 in excess compensation. Patterson filed a derivative action to recover the excess salaries of $266,000 from the Lynches. The trial court awarded him damages as an individual in the amount of 30 percent of the $266,000, or $79,800. The Wyoming Supreme Court upheld this judgment, noting that "corporate recovery would simply return the funds to the control of the wrongdoers." Suppose Patterson's legal fees were $21,000. Should he have been entitled to recover part or all of this outlay? If so, how much? (There is no mention of this issue in the opinion.)

B. THE REQUIREMENT OF DEMAND ON THE DIRECTORS

Grimes v. Donald

673 A.2d 1207 (Del.Sup.Ct.1996).

In this appeal we address the following issues: (1) the distinction between a direct claim of a stockholder and a derivative claim; (2) a direct claim of alleged abdication by a board of directors of its statutory duty; (3) when a pre-suit demand in a derivative suit is required or excused; and (4) the consequences of demand by a stockholder and the refusal by the board to act on such a demand.

. . .

We hold as follows: First, an abdication claim can be stated by a stockholder as a direct claim, as distinct from a derivative claim, but here the complaint fails to state a claim upon which relief can be granted. Second, when a stockholder demands that the board of directors take action on a claim allegedly belonging to the corporation and demand is refused, the stockholder may not thereafter assert that demand is excused with respect to other legal theories in support of the same claim, although the stockholder may have a remedy for wrongful refusal or may submit further demands which are not repetitious.

Accordingly, on the state of this record, we AFFIRM the dismissal of this action by the Court of Chancery.

I. The Facts

C.L. Grimes ("Grimes"), plaintiff below-appellant, appeals from the dismissal, for failure to state a claim, of his complaint against James L. Donald ("Donald") (the CEO) and the Board of Directors (the "Board") of DSC Communications Corporation ("DSC" or the "Company"). Grimes seeks a declaration of the invalidity of the Agreements between Donald and the Company. He also seeks an award of damages against Donald and other members of the Board. He alleges that the Board has breached its fiduciary duties by abdicating its authority, failing to exercise due care and committing waste.

The following facts have been drawn from the face of the complaint. The Company is a Delaware corporation headquartered in Plano, Texas, a suburb of Dallas. The Company, whose shares are traded on the Nasdaq National Market System, designs, manufactures, markets and services telecommunication systems.

The Agreements, executed during 1990, are the focus of the complaint. The Employment Agreement provides that Donald "shall be responsible for the general management of the affairs of the company . . .," and that Donald "shall report to the Board." The Employment Agreement runs until the earlier of Donald's 75th birthday or his termination (1) by reason of death or disability; (2) for cause; or (3) without cause. Under the Employment Agreement, Donald can declare a "Constructive Termination Without Cause" by the Company of his employment as a result of, inter alia, "unreasonable interference, in the good-faith judgment of . . . [Donald], by the Board or a substantial stockholder of the Company, in [Donald's] carrying out his duties and responsibilities under the [Employment] Agreement." A Constructive

Termination Without Cause takes effect after delivery of notice by Donald and the failure by the Board to remedy such interference.

In the event of a Termination Without Cause, constructive or otherwise, Donald is entitled to the following:

severance package

> 1. Continued payment of his "Base Salary" at the level in effect immediately prior to termination for the remainder of his "Term of Employment," which, as stated, will be 6 1/2 years unless Donald dies or turns 75 first. In 1992, Donald's Base Salary exceeded $650,000.
>
> 2. Annual incentive awards for the remainder of the Term of Employment equal to the average of the three highest annual bonuses awarded to Donald during his last ten years as CEO. In 1992, such award allegedly equaled $300,000.
>
> 3. Medical benefits for Donald and his wife for life, as well as his children until the age of 23.
>
> 4. Continued participation in all employee benefit plans in which Donald is participating on the date of termination until the earlier of the expiration of the Term of Employment or the date on which he receives equivalent benefits from a subsequent employer.
>
> 5. Other (unidentified) benefits in accordance with DSC's plans and programs.

Grimes v. Donald, Del. Ch., 20 Del.J.Corp.L. 757, 765, 1995 WL 54441 (1995).

The Income Continuation Plan provides, inter alia, that after Base Salary payments cease under the Employment Agreement, Donald is entitled to receive, for the remainder of his life, annual payments equal to the average of the sum of his Base Salary plus bonuses in the three highest years, multiplied by 3%, multiplied by his years of service. Donald has also been awarded 200,000 "units" under the Long Term Incentive Plan. In the event of a Change of Control, as defined in the Incentive Plan, Donald will have the right to cash payments for his units, which Grimes alleges could total $60,000,000 at the stock price in effect at the time the complaint was filed.

As required by Court of Chancery Rule 23.1, Grimes alleges in his complaint that he wrote to the Board on September 23, 1993 and demanded that the Board abrogate the Agreements. . . .

The Board refused the demand in a letter dated November 8, 1993, which states in part:

> The Compensation Committee of our Board of Directors, as well as the entire Board, have seriously considered the issues set forth in your letter of September 29. To assist in the review, the Board obtained reports analyzing the relevant issues from the Company's outside benefits consultant, Hirschfeld, Stern, Moyer & Ross, Inc. and from the Company's outside legal counsel, Jones, Day, Reavis & Pogue. The Compensation Committee and the full Board of Directors believe that a thorough analysis of the applicable provisions of Delaware law necessarily leads to a conclusion that Mr. Donald's duties as described in the Employment Agreement do not constitute an

impermissible delegation of the duties of the Board of Directors. . . .

II. Grimes Has Not Stated a Claim for Abdication of Directorial Duty

. . . The due care, waste and excessive compensation claims asserted here are derivative and will be considered as such. Kramer v. Western Pacific Indus., Inc., Del.Supr., 546 A.2d 348, 353 (1988). The abdication claim, however, is a direct claim. In order to reach this conclusion, we believe a further exploration of the distinction between direct and derivative claims is appropriate.

A. Distinction Between Direct and Derivative Claims, Generally

As the Court of Chancery has noted: "Although the tests have been articulated many times, it is often difficult to distinguish between a derivative and an individual action." In re Rexene Corp. Shareholders Litig., Del.Ch., 17 Del.J.Corp.L. 342, 348, 1991 WL 77529 (1991); . . . The distinction depends upon " 'the nature of the wrong alleged' and the relief, if any, which could result if plaintiff were to prevail." Kramer v. Western Pacific, 546 A.2d at 352 (quoting Elster v. American Airlines, Inc., Del.Ch., 100 A.2d 219, 221–223 (1953)). . . .*

With respect to the abdication claim, Grimes seeks only a declaration of the invalidity of the Agreements. Monetary recovery will not accrue to the corporation as a result. Chancellor Seitz illustrated this distinction in Bennett [v. Breuil Petroleum Corp., Del.Ch., 99 A.2d 236 (1953)]. The Court of Chancery there allowed the plaintiff-stockholder to proceed individually on his claim that stock was issued for an improper purpose and entrenchment; he proceeded derivatively on his claim that the stock was issued for an insufficient price. 99 A.2d at 241.

. . .

C. Analysis of Grimes' Abdication Claim

In the case before us, the abdication claim fails as a matter of law. Grimes claims that the potentially severe financial penalties which the Company would incur in the event that the Board attempts to interfere in Donald's management of the Company will inhibit and deter the Board from exercising its duties under Section 141(a). The Court of Chancery assumed that, if a contract could have the practical effect of preventing a board from exercising its duties, it would amount to a de facto abdication of directorial authority. The Chancellor concluded, however, that Grimes has not set forth well-pleaded allegations which would establish such a situation. We agree.

. . .

Directors may not delegate duties which lie "at the heart of the management of the corporation." Chapin v. Benwood, Del.Ch., 402 A.2d 1205, 1210 (1979), aff'd sub nom. Harrison v. Chapin, Del.Supr., 415 A.2d 1068 (1980). A court "cannot give legal sanction to agreements which

* [Eds.: In Tooley v. Donaldson, Lufkin, & Jenrette, Inc., 2004 WL 728354 (Del.Supr.), the Delaware supreme court clarified the standard, holding that in determining whether a stockholder's claim is derivative or direct, the issue must turn solely on the following questions: (1) who suffered the alleged harm, the corporation or the suing stockholders, individually; and (2) who would receive the benefit of any recovery or other remedy, the corporation or the stockholders, individually.]

have the effect of removing from directors in a very substantial way their duty to use their own best judgment on management matters." Abercrombie v. Davies, Del.Ch., 123 A.2d 893, 899 (1956), rev'd on other grounds, Del.Supr., 130 A.2d 338 (1957). Distinguishing these cases, however, the Court of Chancery stated: "[U]nlike the agreements considered in *Abercrombie* and *Chapin*, the Donald Agreements do not formally preclude the DSC board from exercising its statutory powers and fulfilling its fiduciary duty." *Grimes*, 20 Del.J.Corp.L. at 774–775. Compare Rosenblatt v. Getty Oil Co., Del.Supr., 493 A.2d 929, 943–44 (1985) (delegation to independent appraiser of responsibility to value oil and gas reserves as part of a merger agreement was proper exercise of business judgment).

With certain exceptions, "an informed decision to delegate a task is as much an exercise of business judgment as any other." *Rosenblatt*, 493 A.2d at 943. Likewise, business decisions are not an abdication of directorial authority merely because they limit a board's freedom of future action. A board which has decided to manufacture bricks has less freedom to decide to make bottles. In a world of scarcity, a decision to do one thing will commit a board to a certain course of action and make it costly and difficult (indeed, sometimes impossible) to change course and do another. This is an inevitable fact of life and is not an abdication of directorial duty.

If the market for senior management, in the business judgment of a board, demands significant severance packages, boards will inevitably limit their future range of action by entering into employment agreements. Large severance payments will deter boards, to some extent, from dismissing senior officers. If an independent and informed board, acting in good faith, determines that the services of a particular individual warrant large amounts of money, whether in the form of current salary or severance provisions, the board has made a business judgment. That judgment normally will receive the protection of the business judgment rule unless the facts show that such amounts, compared with the services to be received in exchange, constitute waste or could not otherwise be the product of a valid exercise of business judgment. . . .

The Board of DSC retains the ultimate freedom to direct the strategy and affairs of the Company. If Donald disagrees with the Board, the Company may or may not (depending on the circumstances) be required to pay him a substantial sum of money in order to pursue its chosen course of action. So far, we have only a rather unusual contract, but not a case of abdication.[4] The Chancellor correctly dismissed the abdication claim.

[4] The unfortunate choice of language in the Employment Agreement should not obscure the fact that, in many cases, large severance payments do not necessarily preclude a formerly passive board from asserting its power over a CEO. The Court of Chancery, in dismissing the claim, nonetheless disparaged as "foolish" and "ill-conceived" the language of the agreement introducing the concept of the Board committing "unreasonable interference" in the discharge of Donald's duties, "in the good faith judgment of the Executive . . ." 20 Del.J.Corp.L. at 777. We agree that, on the surface, this unfortunate choice of words is "badly flawed" in terms of traditional concepts of corporate governance. Id. When the Employment Agreement is read as a whole, however, the initial perception of unlawful delegation gives way to the reality that the Agreement is not—on its face—a wrongful delegation. . . .

III. Grimes' Demand on The Board With Respect to The Derivative Claim Conceded That Demand Was Required

. . .

A. The Demand Requirement in Perspective

. . .

If a claim belongs to the corporation, it is the corporation, acting through its board of directors, which must make the decision whether or not to assert the claim. . . . "[T]he derivative action impinges on the managerial freedom of directors." Pogostin v. Rice, Del. Supr., 480 A.2d 619, 624 (1984). "[T]he demand requirement is a recognition of the fundamental precept that directors manage the business and affairs of the corporation." Aronson v. Lewis, Del.Supr., 473 A.2d 805, 812 (1984).

A stockholder filing a derivative suit must allege either that the board rejected his pre-suit demand that the board assert the corporation's claim or allege with particularity why the stockholder was justified in not having made the effort to obtain board action. One ground for alleging with particularity that demand would be futile is that a "reasonable doubt" exists that the board is capable of making an independent decision to assert the claim if demand were made. The basis for claiming excusal would normally be that: (1) a majority of the board has a material financial or familial interest; (2) a majority of the board is incapable of acting independently for some other reason such as domination or control;[8] or (3) the underlying transaction is not the product of a valid exercise of business judgment. If the stockholder cannot plead such assertions consistent with Chancery Rule 11, after using the "tools at hand"[11] to obtain the necessary information before filing a derivative action, then the stockholder must make a pre-suit demand on the board.

---

[8] Rales v. Blasband, Del.Supr., 634 A.2d 927, 936 (1993). Demand is not excused simply because plaintiff has chosen to sue all directors. Id. Likewise, a plaintiff cannot necessarily disqualify all directors simply by attacking a transaction in which all participated. Pogostin v. Rice, 480 A.2d at 627.

[11] In *Rales* we undertook to describe some of those "tools at hand":

> Although derivative plaintiffs may believe it is difficult to meet the particularization requirement of Aronson because they are not entitled to discovery to assist their compliance with Rule 23.1, see Levine, 591 A.2d [194], 208–10 [(Del.1991)], they have many avenues available to obtain information bearing on the subject of their claims. For example, there is a variety of public sources from which the details of a corporate act may be discovered, including the media and governmental agencies such as the Securities and Exchange Commission. In addition, a stockholder who has met the procedural requirements and has shown a specific proper purpose may use the summary procedure embodied in 8 Del.C. § 220 [shareholder right to inspect books and records] to investigate the possibility of corporate wrongdoing. Compaq Computer Corp. v. Horton, Del.Supr., 631 A.2d 1 (1993). . . . Surprisingly, little use has been made of section 220 as an information-gathering tool in the derivative context. Perhaps the problem arises in some cases out of an unseemly race to the court house, chiefly generated by the "first to file" custom seemingly permitting the winner of the race to be named lead counsel. The result has been a plethora of superficial complaints that could not be sustained. Nothing requires the Court of Chancery, or any other court having appropriate jurisdiction, to countenance this process by penalizing diligent counsel who has employed these methods, including section 220, in a deliberate and thorough manner in preparing a complaint that meets the demand excused test of Aronson.

634 A.2d at 934–935 n. 10.

The demand requirement serves a salutary purpose. First, by requiring exhaustion of intracorporate remedies, the demand requirement invokes a species of alternative dispute resolution procedure which might avoid litigation altogether. Second, if litigation is beneficial, the corporation can control the proceedings. Third, if demand is excused or wrongfully refused, the stockholder will normally control the proceedings.[13]

policy

The jurisprudence of *Aronson* and its progeny is designed to create a balanced environment which will: (1) on the one hand, deter costly, baseless suits by creating a screening mechanism to eliminate claims where there is only a suspicion expressed solely in conclusory terms; and (2) on the other hand, permit suit by a stockholder who is able to articulate particularized facts showing that there is a reasonable doubt either that (a) a majority of the board is independent for purposes of responding to the demand, or (b) the underlying transaction is protected by the business judgment rule.

Aronson introduced the term "reasonable doubt" into corporate derivative jurisprudence. Some courts and commentators have questioned why a concept normally present in criminal prosecution would find its way into derivative litigation. Yet the term is apt and achieves the proper balance. Reasonable doubt can be said to mean that there is a reason to doubt.[17] This concept is sufficiently flexible and workable to provide the stockholder with "the keys to the courthouse" in an appropriate case where the claim is not based on mere suspicions or stated solely in conclusory terms.

B. Wrongful Refusal Distinguished from Excusal

Demand has been excused in many cases in Delaware under the *Aronson* test. The law regarding wrongful refusal is not as well developed, however. Although Delaware law does not require demand in every case[21] because Delaware does have the mechanism of demand excusal, it is important that the demand process be meaningful. Therefore, a stockholder who makes a demand is entitled to know promptly what action the board has taken in response to the demand. A

---

[13] This Court has held that in demand-excused cases the board of directors may sometimes reassert its authority over a derivative claim in certain instances through the device of the Special Litigation Committee ("SLC"). Zapata Corp. v. Maldonado, Del.Supr., 430 A.2d 779 (1981). The use of a committee of the board formed to respond to a demand or to advise the board on its duty in responding to a demand is not the same as the SLC process contemplated by Zapata, however. It is important that these discrete and quite different processes not be confused.

[17] Stated obversely, the concept of reasonable doubt is akin to the concept that the stockholder has a "reasonable belief" that the board lacks independence or that the transaction was not protected by the business judgment rule. . . .

[21] The ALI [American Law Institute] Principles [of Corporate Governance: Analysis and Recommendations (1992)] and the American Bar Association's Model Business Corporation Act § 7.42(1), both are premised upon the concept of universal demand—that is, a requirement that demand must be made in every case. The Principles and the Model Act then go in directions which are different from Delaware law and different from each other in determining the manner in which derivative litigation is to be conducted or terminated after demand has been made. In reversing the decision of the United States Court of Appeals for the Seventh Circuit, which had adopted the universal demand rule in a derivative suit under the Investment Company Act of 1940, the Supreme Court of the United States held that state law applied and analyzed the implications of the universal demand rule compared with the traditional rule exemplified by Delaware law. Kamen v. Kemper Fin. Svcs., Inc., 500 U.S. 90, 101–08 (1991).

stockholder who makes a serious demand and receives only a peremptory refusal has the right to use the "tools at hand" to obtain the relevant corporate records, such as reports or minutes, reflecting the corporate action and related information in order to determine whether or not there is a basis to assert that demand was wrongfully refused. . . .

If a demand is made, the stockholder has spent one—but only one—"arrow" in the "quiver." The spent "arrow" is the right to claim that demand is excused. The stockholder does not, by making demand, waive the right to claim that demand has been wrongfully refused.

Simply because the composition of the board provides no basis ex ante for the stockholder to claim with particularity and consistently with Rule 11 that it is reasonable to doubt that a majority of the board is either interested or not independent, it does not necessarily follow ex post that the board in fact acted independently, disinterestedly or with due care in response to the demand. . . . If a demand is made and rejected, the board rejecting the demand is entitled to the presumption of the business judgment rule unless the stockholder can allege facts with particularity creating a reasonable doubt that the board is entitled to the benefit of the presumption. If there is reason to doubt that the board acted independently or with due care in responding to the demand, the stockholder may have the basis ex post to claim wrongful refusal. The stockholder then has the right to bring the underlying action with the same standing which the stockholder would have had, ex ante, if demand had been excused as futile. . . .

C. Application to This Case

In the case before the Court, plaintiff made a pre-suit demand. Later, however, plaintiff contended that demand was excused. Under the doctrine articulated by this Court in Spiegel v. Buntrock, [571 A.2d 767 (Del.1990)] plaintiff, by making a demand, waived his right to contest the independence of the board. As the Court of Chancery properly held, plaintiff may not bifurcate his theories relating to the same claim. Thus, demand having been made as to the propriety of the Agreements, it cannot be excused as to the claim that the Agreements constituted waste, excessive compensation or was the product of a lack of due care.

. . .

In *Spiegel*, this Court held that "[a] shareholder who makes a demand can no longer argue that demand is excused." 571 A.2d at 775. Permitting a stockholder to demand action involving only one theory or remedy and to argue later that demand is excused as to other legal theories or remedies arising out of the same set of circumstances as set forth in the demand letter would create an undue risk of harassment.

In this case, the Board of DSC considered and rejected the demand. After investing the time and resources to consider and decide whether or not to take action in response to the demand, the Board is entitled to have its decision analyzed under the business judgment rule unless the presumption of that rule can be rebutted. . . . Grimes cannot avoid this result by holding back or bifurcating legal theories based on precisely the same set of facts alleged in the demand.

Since Grimes made a pre-suit demand with respect to all claims arising out of the Agreements, he was required by Chancery Rule 23.1 to plead with particularity why the Board's refusal to act on the derivative claims was wrongful. . . . The complaint recites the Board's rejection of Grimes' demand and proceeds to assert why Grimes disagrees with the Board's conclusion. The complaint generally asserts that the refusal could not have been the result of an adequate, good faith investigation since the Board decided not to act on the demand. Such conclusory, ipse dixit, assertions are inconsistent with the requirements of Chancery Rule 23.1. . . . The complaint fails to include particularized allegations which would raise a reasonable doubt that the Board's decision to reject the demand was the product of a valid business judgment.

ANALYSIS

1. Under Delaware law, what is the legal effect and likely consequence of a shareholder demand that the board pursue a corporate cause of action?

2. Under Delaware law, when is demand excused? What must a shareholder allege in her or his complaint to establish that demand is excused? How does the plaintiff find the necessary facts?

3. In a derivative suit in which the plaintiff seeks money damages from corporate officers, and in which the plaintiff is required to post a bond to pay the defendant's legal expenses if the defendant prevails, what justification is there for allowing the board to dismiss the suit? What does the corporation have to lose?

4. Is it not true that a derivative suit is always a challenge to the wisdom, judgment, or competence of the board? Suppose you have been a member of the board of a corporation for ten years and a suit is filed naming other long-time members of the board as defendants. Do you think you could be fair and unbiased in deciding whether the suit should be dismissed? If not, what would you do?

5. Suppose a plaintiff in a derivative suit seeks recovery of funds embezzled by one of the corporation's officers and alleges with particularity the facts of the embezzlement and the failure of the board to seek recovery. Under the Delaware rule, is demand required? Should it be?

Marx v. Akers

644 N.Y.S.2d 121, 666 N.E.2d 1034 (1996).

Plaintiff commenced this shareholder derivative action against International Business Machines Corporation (IBM) and IBM's board of directors without first demanding that the board initiate a lawsuit. The amended complaint (complaint) alleges that the board wasted corporate assets by awarding excessive compensation to IBM's executives and outside directors. The issues raised on this appeal are whether the Appellate Division abused its discretion by dismissing plaintiff's complaint for failure to make a demand and whether plaintiff's complaint fails to state a cause of action. . . .

Facts and Procedural History

The complaint alleges that during a period of declining profitability at IBM the director defendants engaged in self-dealing by awarding excessive compensation to the 15 outside directors on the 18-member board. Although the complaint identifies only one of the three inside directors as an IBM executive (defendant Akers is identified as a former chief executive officer of IBM), plaintiff also appears to allege that the director defendants violated their fiduciary duties to IBM by voting for unreasonably high compensation for IBM executives.

. . .

Background

. . .

[New York] Business Corporation Law § 626(c) provides that in any shareholders' derivative action, "the complaint shall set forth with particularity the efforts of the plaintiff to secure the initiation of such action by the board or the reasons for not making such effort." Enacted in 1961 (L.1961, ch. 855), § 626(c) codified a rule of equity developed in early shareholder derivative actions requiring plaintiffs to demand that the corporation initiate an action, unless such demand was futile, before commencing an action on the corporation's behalf (Barr v. Wackman, 36 N.Y.2d 371, 377, 368 N.Y.S.2d 497, 329 N.E.2d 180). The purposes of the demand requirement are to (1) relieve courts from deciding matters of internal corporate governance by providing corporate directors with opportunities to correct alleged abuses, (2) provide corporate boards with reasonable protection from harassment by litigation on matters clearly within the discretion of directors, and (3) discourage "strike suits" commenced by shareholders for personal gain rather than for the benefit of the corporation. . . . By their very nature, shareholder derivative actions infringe upon the managerial discretion of corporate boards. . . . Consequently, we have historically been reluctant to permit shareholder derivative suits, noting that the power of courts to direct the management of a corporation's affairs should be "exercised with restraint" (Gordon v. Elliman, 306 N.Y. 456, 462, 119 N.E.2d 331).

In permitting a shareholder derivative action to proceed because a demand on the corporation's directors would be futile,

> "the object is for the court to chart the course for the corporation which the directors should have selected, and which it is presumed that they would have chosen if they had not been actuated by fraud or bad faith. Due to their misconduct, the court substitutes its judgment ad hoc for that of the directors in the conduct of its business" (id., at 462, 119 N.E.2d 331).

Achieving a balance between preserving the discretion of directors to manage a corporation without undue interference, through the demand requirement, and permitting shareholders to bring claims on behalf of the corporation when it is evident that directors will wrongfully refuse to bring such claims, through the demand futility exception, has been accomplished by various jurisdictions in different ways. One widely cited approach to demand futility which attempts to balance these competing concerns has been developed by Delaware courts and applies a two-pronged test to each case to determine whether a failure to serve a demand is justified. At the other end of the spectrum is a universal demand requirement which would abandon particularized determinations in favor of requiring a demand in every case before a shareholder derivative suit may be filed.

The Delaware Approach

[The court summarizes Delaware law, which is described in *Grimes*, supra.]

The two branches of the [Delaware] test are disjunctive. . . . Once director interest has been established, the business judgment rule becomes inapplicable and the demand excused without further inquiry. . . . Whether a board has validly exercised its business judgment must be evaluated by determining whether the directors exercised procedural (informed decision) and substantive (terms of the transaction) due care. . . .

Universal Demand

A universal demand requirement would dispense with the necessity of making case-specific determinations and impose an easily applied bright line rule. The Business Law Section of the American Bar Association has proposed requiring a demand in all cases, without exception, and [prohibits] the commencement of a derivative proceeding within 90 days of the demand unless the demand is rejected earlier. . . . However, plaintiffs may file suit before the expiration of 90 days, even if their demand has not been rejected, if the corporation would suffer irreparable injury as a result. . . .

. . . At least 11 States have adopted, by statute, the universal demand requirement proposed in the Model Business Corporation Act. [The states identified by the court are Arizona, Connecticut, Georgia, Michigan, Mississippi, Montana, Nebraska, New Hampshire, North Carolina, Virginia, and Wisconsin.]

New York State has also considered and continues to consider implementing a universal demand requirement. However, even though bills to adopt a universal demand have been presented over three legislative sessions, the Legislature has yet to enact a universal demand requirement. . . .

New York's Approach to Demand Futility

Although instructive, neither the universal demand requirement nor the Delaware approach to demand futility is adopted here. Since New York's demand requirement is codified in Business Corporation Law § 626(c), a universal demand may only be adopted by the Legislature. Delaware's approach, which resembles New York law in some respects, incorporates a "reasonable doubt" standard which, as we have already pointed out, has provoked criticism as confusing and overly subjective. An analysis of the *Barr* decision compels the conclusion that in New York, a demand would be futile if a complaint alleges with particularity that (1) a majority of the directors are interested in the transaction, or (2) the directors failed to inform themselves to a degree reasonably necessary about the transaction, or (3) the directors failed to exercise their business judgment in approving the transaction.

In Barr v. Wackman, 36 N.Y.2d 371, 368 N.Y.S.2d 497, 329 N.E.2d 180, supra, we considered whether the plaintiff was excused from making a demand where the board of Talcott National Corporation (Talcott), consisting of 13 outside directors, a director affiliated with a related company and four interested inside directors, rejected a merger proposal involving Gulf & Western Industries (Gulf & Western) in favor of another proposal on allegedly less favorable terms for Talcott and its shareholders. The merger proposal, memorialized in a board-approved "agreement in principle," proposed exchanging one share of Talcott common stock for approximately $24 consisting of $17 in cash and 0.6 of a warrant to purchase Gulf & Western stock, worth approximately $7. This proposal was abandoned in favor of a cash tender offer for Talcott shares by Associates First Capital Corporation (a Gulf & Western subsidiary) at $20 per share—$4 less than proposed for the merger.

The plaintiff in *Barr* alleged that Talcott's board discarded the merger proposal after the four "controlling" inside directors received pecuniary and personal benefits from Gulf & Western in exchange for ceding control of Talcott on terms less favorable to Talcott's shareholders. As alleged in the complaint, these benefits included new and favorable employment contracts for nine Talcott officers, including five-year employment contracts for three of the controlling directors. In addition to his annual salary of $125,000 with Talcott, defendant Silverman (a controlling director) would allegedly receive $60,000 a year under a five-year employment contract with Associates First Capital, and an aggregate of $275,000 for the next five years in an arrangement with Associates First Capital to serve as a consultant. This additional compensation would be awarded to Silverman after control of Talcott passed to Associates First Capital and Gulf & Western. Plaintiff also alleged that Gulf & Western and Associates First Capital paid an excessive "finder's fee" of $340,000 to a company where Silverman's son was an executive vice-president. In addition to alleging that the controlling defendants obtained personal benefits, the complaint also alleged that Talcott's board agreed to sell a Talcott subsidiary at a net loss of $6,100,000 solely to accommodate Gulf & Western.

In *Barr*, we held that insofar as the complaint attacked the controlling directors' acts in causing the corporation to enter into a transaction for their own financial benefit, demand was excused because of the self-dealing, or self-interest of those directors in the challenged transaction. . . .

We also held in *Barr*, however, that as to the disinterested outside directors, demand could be excused even in the absence of their receiving any financial benefit from the transaction. That was because the complaint alleged that, by approving the terms of the less advantageous offer, those directors were guilty of a "breach of their duties of due care and diligence to the corporation" (id., at 380, 368 N.Y.S.2d 497, 329 N.E.2d 180). Their performance of the duty of care would have "put them on notice of the claimed self-dealing of the affiliated directors" (id.). The complaint charged that the outside directors failed "to do more than passively rubber-stamp the decisions of the active managers" (id., at 381, 368 N.Y.S.2d 497, 329 N.E.2d 180) resulting in corporate detriment. These allegations, the *Barr* Court concluded, also excused demand as to the charges against the disinterested directors.

Barr also makes clear that "[i]t is not sufficient * * * merely to name a majority of the directors as parties defendant with conclusory allegations of wrongdoing or control by wrongdoers" (id., at 379, 368 N.Y.S.2d 497, 329 N.E.2d 180) to justify failure to make a demand. Thus, *Barr* reflects the statutory requirement that the complaint "shall set forth with particularity the * * * reasons for not making such effort" (Bus. Corp. Law § 626[c]).

Unfortunately, various courts have overlooked the explicit warning that conclusory allegations of wrongdoing against each member of the board are not sufficient to excuse demand and have misinterpreted *Barr* as excusing demand whenever a majority of the board members who approved the transaction are named as defendants. . . .

We thus deem it necessary to offer the following elaboration of *Barr*'s demand/futility standard. (1) Demand is excused because of futility when a complaint alleges with particularity that a majority of the board of directors is interested in the challenged transaction. Director interest may either be self-interest in the transaction at issue . . ., or a loss of independence because a director with no direct interest in a transaction is "controlled" by a self-interested director. (2) Demand is excused because of futility when a complaint alleges with particularity that the board of directors did not fully inform themselves about the challenged transaction to the extent reasonably appropriate under the circumstances. . . . (3) Demand is excused because of futility when a complaint alleges with particularity that the challenged transaction was so egregious on its face that it could not have been the product of sound business judgment of the directors.

The Current Appeal

. . .

As in *Barr*, we look to the complaint here to determine whether the allegations are sufficient and establish with particularity that demand would have been futile.* Here, the plaintiff alleges that the compensation awarded to IBM's outside directors . . . was excessive.

Defendants' motion to dismiss for failure to make a demand as to the allegations concerning the compensation paid to IBM's executive officers was properly granted. A board is not interested "in voting compensation for one of its members as an executive or in some other nondirectorial capacity, such as a consultant to the corporation," although "so-called 'back-scratching' arrangements, pursuant to which all directors vote to approve each other's compensation as officers or employees, do not constitute disinterested directors' action" (1 ALI, [Principles of Corporate Governance], § 5.03, Comment g, at 250 [1992]). Since only three directors are alleged to have received the benefit of the executive compensation scheme, plaintiff has failed to allege that a majority of the board was interested in setting executive compensation. . . . The complaint does not allege particular facts in contending that the board failed to deliberate or exercise its business judgment in setting those levels. Consequently, the failure to make a demand regarding the fixing

* [Eds.—The court reproduced and focused on the following language from the complaint: Plaintiff has made no demand upon the directors of IBM to institute this lawsuit because such demand would be futile. As set forth above, each of the directors authorized, approved, participated and/or acquiesced in the acts and transactions complained of herein and are liable therefor. Further, each of the Non-Employee [outside] Directors has received and retained the benefit of his excessive compensation and each of the other directors has received and retained the benefit of the incentive compensation described above. The defendants cannot be expected to vote to prosecute an action against themselves. Demand upon the company to bring action [sic] to redress the wrongs herein is therefore unnecessary.]

of executive compensation was fatal to that portion of the complaint challenging that transaction.

However, a review of the complaint indicates that plaintiff also alleged that a majority of the board was self-interested in setting the compensation of outside directors because the outside directors comprised a majority of the board.

Directors are self-interested in a challenged transaction where they will receive a direct financial benefit from the transaction which is different from the benefit to shareholders generally. . . . A director who votes for a raise in directors' compensation is always "interested" because that person will receive a personal financial benefit from the transaction not shared in by stockholders. . . . Consequently, a demand was excused as to plaintiff's allegations that the compensation set for outside directors was excessive.

Corporate Waste

Our conclusion that demand should have been excused as to the part of the complaint challenging the fixing of directors' compensation does not end our inquiry. We must also determine whether plaintiff has stated a cause of action regarding director compensation, i.e., some wrong to the corporation. We conclude that plaintiff has not, and thus dismiss the complaint in its entirety.

. . . [A] complaint challenging the excessiveness of director compensation must—to survive a dismissal motion—allege compensation rates excessive on their face or other facts which call into question whether the compensation was fair to the corporation when approved, the good faith of the directors setting those rates, or that the decision to set the compensation could not have been a product of valid business judgment.

Applying the foregoing principles to plaintiff's complaint, it is clear that it must be dismissed. The complaint alleges that the directors increased their compensation rates from a base of $20,000 plus $500 for each meeting attended to a retainer of $55,000 plus 100 shares of IBM stock over a five-year period. . . .

These conclusory allegations do not state a cause of action. There are no factually based allegations of wrongdoing or waste which would, if true, sustain a verdict in plaintiff's favor.

ANALYSIS

1. How do you suppose this case would have been decided under Delaware law as described by the court in this case and by the *Grimes* court?

2. The court lists three "purposes" for the demand requirement. How well does the requirement serve each of these purposes?

3. What is the function of demand under a requirement of universal demand? Is the court correct in stating that a requirement of universal demand "would dispense with the necessity of making case-specific determinations"?

4. In *Marx*, the court determined that demand should be excused but that plaintiff had failed to state a cause of action. Accordingly,

plaintiff's complaint was dismissed on the merits. What would have happened if the court had made the opposite determination; i.e., that demand was required, but that the complaint stated a cause of action?

PROBLEMS

Agricorp Corp. is an agribusiness: it owns and operates many large farms. It has five directors, including Alice Adams, who is the Chairman of the Board and Chief Executive Officer. Adams learns of an opportunity to purchase a large farm in Indiana.

1. Adams and two of the other directors decide to buy the Indiana farm for themselves. Assume that this constitutes self-dealing in violation of the duty of loyalty. A shareholder wants to sue. Is this a direct or derivative lawsuit?

2. Assuming the lawsuit is derivative in nature, is demand required or excused under New York and/or Delaware law?

3. Suppose only Adams is going to buy the land. She discloses the opportunity to the other directors. The other directors vote to have the corporation reject the opportunity and to approve Adams's personal purchase of the land. A derivative suit is to be brought. Is demand required or excused under New York and/or Delaware law?

4. Suppose that the other directors had not voted on Adams's purchase, but had merely acquiesced in it. Is demand required or excused under New York and/or Delaware law?

C. THE ROLE OF SPECIAL COMMITTEES

Auerbach v. Bennett

47 N.Y.2d 619, 419 N.Y.S.2d 920, 393 N.E.2d 994 (1979).

■ JONES, JUDGE.

. . .

In the summer of 1975 the management of General Telephone & Electronics Corporation, in response to reports that numerous other multinational companies had made questionable payments to public officials or political parties in foreign countries, directed that an internal preliminary investigation be made to ascertain whether that corporation had engaged in similar transactions. On the basis of the report of this survey, received in October, 1975, management brought the issue to the attention of the corporation's board of directors. At a meeting held on November 6 of that year the board referred the matter to the board's audit committee. The audit committee retained as its special counsel the Washington, D.C., law firm of Wilmer, Cutler & Pickering, which had not previously acted as counsel to the corporation. With the assistance of such special counsel and Arthur Andersen & Co., the corporation's outside auditors, the audit committee engaged in an investigation into the corporation's world-wide operations, focusing on whether, in the period January 1, 1971 to December 31, 1975, corporate funds had been (1) paid directly or indirectly to any political party or person or to any officer, employee, shareholder or director of any governmental or private customer, or (2) used to reimburse any officer of the corporation or other person for such payments.

On March 4, 1976 the audit committee released its report which was filed with the Securities and Exchange Commission and disclosed to the corporation's shareholders in a proxy statement prior to the annual meeting of shareholders held in April, 1976. The audit committee reported that it had found evidence that in the period from 1971 to 1975 the corporation or its subsidiaries had made payments abroad and in the United States constituting bribes and kickbacks in amounts perhaps totaling more than 11 million dollars and that some of the individual defendant directors had been personally involved in certain of the transactions.

Almost immediately Auerbach, a shareholder in the corporation, instituted the present shareholders' derivative action on behalf of the corporation against the corporation's directors, Arthur Andersen & Co. and the corporation. The complaint alleged that in connection with the transactions reported by the audit committee defendants, present and former members of the corporation's board of directors, and Arthur Andersen & Co., are liable to the corporation for breach of their duties to the corporation and should be made to account for payments made in those transactions.

On April 21, 1976 the board of directors of the corporation adopted a resolution creating a special litigation committee "for the purpose of establishing a point of contract [sic] between the Board of Directors and the Corporation's General Counsel concerning the position to be taken by the Corporation in certain litigation involving shareholder derivative claims on behalf of the Corporation against certain of its directors and officers" and authorizing that committee "to take such steps from time to time as it deems necessary to pursue its objectives including the retention of special outside counsel." The special committee comprised three disinterested directors who had joined the board after the challenged transactions had occurred. The board subsequently additionally vested in the committee "all of the authority of the Board of Directors to determine, on behalf of the Board, the position that the Corporation shall take with respect to the derivative claims alleged on its behalf" in the present and similar shareholder derivative actions.

The special litigation committee reported under date of November 22, 1976. It found that defendant Arthur Andersen & Co. had conducted its examination of the corporation's affairs in accordance with generally accepted auditing standards and in good faith and concluded that no proper interest of the corporation or its shareholders would be served by the continued assertion of a claim against it. The committee also concluded that none of the individual defendants had violated the New York State statutory standard of care, that none had profited personally or gained in any way, that the claims asserted in the present action are without merit, that if the action were allowed to proceed the time and talents of the corporation's senior management would be wasted on lengthy pretrial and trial proceedings, that litigation costs would be inordinately high in view of the unlikelihood of success, and that the continuing publicity could be damaging to the corporation's business. The committee determined that it would not be in the best interests of the corporation for the present derivative action to proceed, and, exercising the authority delegated to it, directed the corporation's general counsel to take that position in the present litigation as well as in pending comparable shareholders' derivative actions.

[The original plaintiff, Auerbach, decided not to appeal, and Stanley Wallenstein was substituted as plaintiff.]

As all parties and both courts below recognize, the disposition of this case on the merits turns on the proper application of the business judgment doctrine, in particular to the decision of a specially appointed committee of disinterested directors acting on behalf of the board to terminate a shareholders' derivative action. . . .

In this instance our inquiry, to the limited extent to which it may be pursued, has a two-tiered aspect. The complaint initially asserted liability on the part of defendants based on the payments made to foreign governmental customers and privately owned customers, some unspecified portions of which were allegedly passed on to officials of the customers, i.e., the focus was on first-tier bribes and kickbacks. Then subsequent to the service of the complaint there came the report of a special litigation committee, particularly appointed by the corporation's board of directors to consider the merits of the present and similar shareholders' derivative actions, and its determination that it would not be in the best interests of the corporation to press claims against defendants based on their possible first-tier liability. The motions for summary judgment were predicated principally on the report and determination of the special litigation committee and on the contention that this second-tier corporate action insulated the first-tier transactions from judicial inquiry and was itself subject to the shelter of the business judgment doctrine.

. . .

We [conclude] that the determination of the special litigation committee forecloses further judicial inquiry in this case.

It appears to us that the business judgment doctrine, at least in part, is grounded in the prudent recognition that courts are ill equipped and infrequently called on to evaluate what are and must be essentially business judgments. . . .

In the present case we confront a special instance of the application of the business judgment rule and inquire whether it applies in its full vigor to shield from judicial scrutiny the decision of a three-person minority committee of the board acting on behalf of the full board not to prosecute a shareholder's derivative action. The record in this case reveals that the board is a 15-member board, and that the derivative suit was brought against four of the directors. Nothing suggests that any of the other directors participated in any of the challenged first-tier transactions. Indeed the report of the audit committee on which the complaint is based specifically found that no other directors had any prior knowledge of or were in any way involved in any of these transactions. Other directors had, however, been members of the board in the period during which the transactions occurred. Each of the three director members of the special litigation committee joined the board thereafter.

The business judgment rule does not foreclose inquiry by the courts into the disinterested independence of those members of the board chosen by it to make the corporate decision on its behalf—here the members of the special litigation committee. Indeed the rule shields the deliberations and conclusions of the chosen representatives of the board only if they possess a disinterested independence and do not stand in a dual relation which prevents an unprejudicial exercise of judgment. . . .

We examine then the proof submitted by defendants. It is not disputed that the members of the special litigation committee were not members of the corporation's board of directors at the time of the first-tier transactions in question. . . . Notwithstanding the vigorous and imaginative hypothesizing and innuendo of counsel there is nothing in this record to raise a triable issue of fact as to the independence and disinterested status of these three directors.

The contention of Wallenstein that any committee authorized by the board of which defendant directors were members must be held to be legally infirm and may not be delegated power to terminate a derivative action must be rejected. In the very nature of the corporate organization it was only the existing board of directors which had authority on behalf of the corporation to direct the investigation and to assure the cooperation of corporate employees, and it is only that same board by its own action—or as here pursuant to authority duly delegated by it—which had authority to decide whether to prosecute the claims against defendant directors. The board in this instance, with slight adaptation, followed prudent practice in observing the general policy that when individual members of a board of directors prove to have personal interests which may conflict with the interests of the corporation, such interested directors must be excluded while the remaining members of the board proceed to consideration and action. . . .

Courts have consistently held that the business judgment rule applies where some directors are charged with wrongdoing, so long as the remaining directors making the decision are disinterested and independent. . . .

To accept the assertions of the intervenor and to disqualify the entire board would be to render the corporation powerless to make an effective business judgment with respect to prosecution of the derivative action. The possible risk of hesitancy on the part of the members of any committee, even if composed of outside, independent, disinterested directors, to investigate the activities of fellow members of the board where personal liability is at stake is an inherent, inescapable, given aspect of the corporation's predicament. . . .

We turn then to the action of the special litigation committee itself, which comprised two components. First, there was the selection of procedures appropriate to the pursuit of its charge, and second, there was the ultimate substantive decision, predicated on the procedures chosen and the data produced thereby, not to pursue the claims advanced in the shareholders' derivative actions. The latter, substantive decision falls squarely within the embrace of the business judgment doctrine, involving as it did the weighing and balancing of legal, ethical, commercial, promotional, public relations, fiscal and other factors familiar to the resolution of many if not most corporate problems. To this extent the conclusion reached by the special litigation committee is outside the scope of our review. . . .

As to the other component of the committee's activities, however, the situation is different. . . . As to the methodologies and procedures best suited to the conduct of an investigation of facts and the determination of legal liability, the courts are well equipped by long and continuing experience and practice to make determinations. . . .

While the court may properly inquire as to the adequacy and appropriateness of the committee's investigative procedures and methodologies, it may not under the guise of consideration of such factors trespass in the domain of business judgment. At the same time those responsible for the procedures by which the business judgment is reached may reasonably be required to show that they have pursued their chosen investigative methods in good faith. What evidentiary proof may be required to this end will, of course, depend on the nature of the particular investigation, and the proper reach of disclosure at the instance of the shareholders will in turn relate inversely to the showing made by the corporate representatives themselves. The latter may be expected to show that the areas and subjects to be examined are reasonably complete and that there has been a good-faith pursuit of inquiry into such areas and subjects. What has been uncovered and the relative weight accorded in evaluating and balancing the several factors and considerations are beyond the scope of judicial concern. Proof, however, that the investigation has been so restricted in scope, so shallow in execution, or otherwise so *pro forma* or halfhearted as to constitute a pretext or sham, consistent with the principles underlying the application of the business judgment doctrine, would raise questions of good faith or conceivably fraud which would never be shielded by that doctrine.

In addition to the issue of the disinterested independence of the special litigation committee, addressed above, the disposition of the present appeal turns, then, on whether on defendants' motions for summary judgment predicated on the investigation and determination of the special litigation committee, Wallenstein by tender of evidentiary proof in admissible form has shown facts sufficient to require a trial of any material issue of fact as to the adequacy or appropriateness of the *modus operandi* of that committee or has demonstrated acceptable excuse for failure to make such tender. . . . We conclude that the requisite showing has not been made on this record.

On the submissions made by defendants in support of their motions, we do not find either insufficiency or infirmity as to the procedures and methodologies chosen and pursued by the special litigation committee. That committee promptly engaged eminent special counsel to guide its deliberations and to advise it. The committee reviewed the prior work of the audit committee, testing its completeness, accuracy and thoroughness by interviewing representatives of Wilmer, Cutler & Pickering, reviewing transcripts of the testimony of 10 corporate officers and employees before the Securities and Exchange Commission, and studying documents collected by and work papers of the Washington law firm. Individual interviews were conducted with the directors found to have participated in any way in the questioned payments, and with representatives of Arthur Andersen & Co. Questionnaires were sent to and answered by each of the corporation's nonmanagement directors. At the conclusion of its investigation the special litigation committee sought and obtained pertinent legal advice from its special counsel. The selection of appropriate investigative methods must always turn on the nature and characteristics of the particular subject being investigated, but we find nothing in this record that requires a trial of any material issue of fact concerning the sufficiency or appropriateness of the procedures chosen by this special litigation committee. Nor is there anything in this record to raise a triable issue of fact as to the good-faith pursuit of its examination by that committee.

■ COOKE, CHIEF JUDGE (dissenting).

. . .

Since the continuation of the suit is dependent, in large measure, upon the motives and actions of the defendants and the special litigation committee, and since knowledge of these matters "is peculiarly in the possession of the defendants themselves", summary judgment should not be granted prior to disclosure proceedings. . . .

ANALYSIS

1. By way of review, note that in Auerbach v. Bennett there is no mention of the demand issue. Presumably the parties assumed that demand was excused. Were they right about that?

2. In the Auerbach v. Bennett situation, how do you suppose the three new, independent members of the board were selected? Who do you suppose identified them as likely prospects? What other methods of selection might be sensible?

Zapata Corp. v. Maldonado

430 A.2d 779 (Del.1981).

■ QUILLEN, JUSTICE: . . .

In June, 1975, William Maldonado, a stockholder of Zapata, instituted a derivative action in the Court of Chancery on behalf of Zapata against ten officers and/or directors of Zapata, alleging, essentially, breaches of fiduciary duty. Maldonado did not first demand that the board bring this action, stating instead such demand's futility because all directors were named as defendants and allegedly participated in the acts specified. . . .

By June, 1979, four of the defendant-directors were no longer on the board, and the remaining directors appointed two new outside directors to the board. The board then created an "Independent Investigation Committee" (Committee), composed solely of the two new directors, to investigate Maldonado's actions, as well as a similar derivative action then pending in Texas, and to determine whether the corporation should continue any or all of the litigation. The Committee's determination was stated to be "final, . . . not . . . subject to review by the Board of Directors and . . . in all respects . . . binding upon the Corporation."

Following an investigation, the Committee concluded, in September, 1979, that each action should "be dismissed forthwith as their continued maintenance is inimical to the Company's best interests. . . ." Consequently, Zapata moved for dismissal or summary judgment. . . .

We limit our review in this interlocutory appeal to whether the Committee has the power to cause the present action to be dismissed.

We begin with an examination of the carefully considered opinion of the Vice Chancellor which states, in part, that the "business judgment" rule does not confer power "to a corporate board of directors to terminate a derivative suit," [Maldonado v. Flynn, 413 A.2d 1251, 1257 (Del.Ch.1980)]. His conclusion is particularly pertinent because several federal courts, applying Delaware law, have held that the business judgment rule enables boards (or their committees) to terminate derivative suits, decisions now in conflict with the holding below.

As the term is most commonly used, and given the disposition below, we can understand the Vice Chancellor's comment that "the business judgment rule is irrelevant to the question of whether the Committee has the authority to compel the dismissal of this suit." 413 A.2d at 1257. Corporations, existing because of legislative grace, possess authority as granted by the legislature. Directors of Delaware corporations derive their managerial decision making power, which encompasses decisions whether to initiate, or refrain from entering, litigation, from 8 Del.C. § 141(a).[6] This statute is the fount of directorial powers. The "business judgment" rule is a judicial creation that presumes propriety, under certain circumstances, in a board's decision. Viewed defensively, it does not create authority. In this sense the "business judgment" rule is not relevant in corporate decision making until after a decision is made. It is generally used as a defense to an attack on the decision's soundness. The board's managerial decision making power, however, comes from § 141(a). The judicial creation and legislative grant are related because the "business judgment" rule evolved to give recognition and deference to directors' business expertise when exercising their managerial power under § 141(a).

In the case before us, although the corporation's decision to move to dismiss or for summary judgment was, literally, a decision resulting from an exercise of the directors' (as delegated to the Committee) business judgment, the question of "business judgment," in a defensive sense, would not become relevant until and unless the decision to seek termination of the derivative lawsuit was attacked as improper. . . . This question was not reached by the Vice Chancellor because he determined that the stockholder had an individual right to maintain this derivative action. . . .

Thus, the focus in this case is on the power to speak for the corporation as to whether the lawsuit should be continued or terminated. As we see it, this issue in the current appellate posture of this case has three aspects: the conclusions of the Court below concerning the continuing right of a stockholder to maintain a derivative action; the corporate power under Delaware law of an authorized board committee

[6] 8 Del.C. § 141(a) states:

"The business and affairs of every corporation organized under this chapter shall be managed by or under the direction of a board of directors, except as may be otherwise provided in this chapter or in its certificate of incorporation. If any such provision is made in the certificate of incorporation, the powers and duties conferred or imposed upon the board of directors by this chapter shall be exercised or performed to such extent and by such person or persons as shall be provided in the certificate of incorporation."

to cause dismissal of litigation instituted for the benefit of the corporation; and the role of the Court of Chancery in resolving conflicts between the stockholder and the committee.

Accordingly, we turn first to the Court of Chancery's conclusions concerning the right of a plaintiff stockholder in a derivative action. We find that its determination that a stockholder, once demand is made and refused, possesses an independent, individual right to continue a derivative suit for breaches of fiduciary duty over objection by the corporation, . . . as an absolute rule, is erroneous. The Court of Chancery relied principally upon Sohland v. Baker, Del.Supr., 141 A. 277 (1927), for this statement of the Delaware rule. . . . *Sohland* is sound law. But *Sohland* cannot be fairly read as supporting the broad proposition which evolved in the opinion below.

In *Sohland,* the complaining stockholder was allowed to file the derivative action in equity after making demand and after the board refused to bring the lawsuit. But the question before us relates to the power of the corporation by motion to terminate a lawsuit properly commenced by a stockholder without prior demand. No Delaware statute or case cited to us directly determines this new question and we do not think that *Sohland* addresses it by implication.

The language in *Sohland* relied on by the Vice Chancellor negates the contention that the case stands for the broad rule of stockholder right which evolved below. This Court therein stated that "a stockholder *may sue* in his own name for the purpose of enforcing corporate rights . . . in a proper case if the corporation on the demand of the stockholder refuses to bring suit." 141 A. at 281 (emphasis added). The Court also stated that "whether ['[t]he right of a stockholder *to file a bill* to litigate corporate rights'] exists necessarily depends on the facts of each particular case." 141 A. at 282 (emphasis added). Thus, the precise language only supports the stockholder's right to initiate the lawsuit. It does not support an absolute right to continue to control it.

Additionally, the issue and context in *Sohland* are simply different from this case. Baker, a stockholder, suing on behalf of Bankers' Mortgage Co., sought cancellation of stock issued to Sohland, a director of Bankers', in a transaction participated in by a "great majority" of Bankers' board. Before instituting his suit, Baker requested the board to assert the cause of action. The board refused. Interestingly, though, on the same day the board refused, it authorized payment of Baker's attorneys fees so that he could pursue the claim; one director actually escorted Baker to the attorneys suggested by the board. At this chronological point, Sohland had resigned from the board, and it was he, not the board, who was protesting Baker's ability to bring suit. In sum, despite the board's refusal to bring suit, it is clear that the board supported Baker in his efforts. It is not surprising then that he was allowed to proceed as the corporation's representative "for the prevention of injustice," because "the corporation itself refused to litigate an apparent corporate right." 141 A. at 282.

Moreover, McKee v. Rogers, Del.Ch., 156 A. 191 (1931), stated "as a general rule" that "a stockholder cannot be permitted . . . to invade the discretionary field committed to the judgment of the directors and sue in the corporation's behalf when the managing body refuses. This rule is a well settled one." 156 A. at 193.

The *McKee* rule, of course, should not be read so broadly that the board's refusal will be determinative in every instance. Board members, owing a well-established fiduciary duty to the corporation, will not be allowed to cause a derivative suit to be dismissed when it would be a breach of their fiduciary duty. Generally disputes pertaining to control of the suit arise in two contexts.

Consistent with the purpose of requiring a demand, a board decision to cause a derivative suit to be dismissed as detrimental to the company, after demand has been made and refused, will be respected unless it was wrongful.[10] . . . A claim of a wrongful decision not to sue is thus the first exception and the first context of dispute. Absent a wrongful refusal, the stockholder in such a situation simply lacks legal managerial power. . . .

But it cannot be implied that, absent a wrongful board refusal, a stockholder can never have an individual right to initiate an action. For, as is stated in *McKee,* a "well settled" exception exists to the general rule.

> "[A] stockholder may sue in equity in his derivative right to assert a cause of action in behalf of the corporation, *without prior demand* upon the directors to sue, when it is apparent that a demand would be futile, that the officers are under an influence that sterilizes discretion and could not be proper persons to conduct the litigation."

156 A. at 193 (emphasis added). This exception, the second context for dispute, is consistent with the Court of Chancery's statement below, that "[t]he stockholders' individual right to bring the action does not ripen, however, . . . unless he can show a demand to be futile." *Maldonado,* 413 A.2d at 1262.

These comments in *McKee* and in the opinion below make obvious sense. A demand, when required and refused (if not wrongful), terminates a stockholder's legal ability to initiate a derivative action. But where demand is properly excused, the stockholder does possess the ability to initiate the action on his corporation's behalf.

These conclusions, however, do not determine the question before us. Rather, they merely bring us to the question to be decided. It is here that we part company with the Court below. Derivative suits enforce corporate rights and any recovery obtained goes to the corporation. . . . "The right of a stockholder to file a bill to litigate corporate rights is, therefore, solely for the purpose of preventing injustice where it is apparent that material corporate rights would not otherwise be protected." *Sohland,* 141 A. at 282. We see no inherent reason why the "two phases" of a derivative suit, the stockholder's suit to compel the corporation to sue and the corporation's suit (see 413 A.2d at 1261–62), should automatically result in the placement in the hands of the litigating stockholder sole control of the corporate right throughout the litigation. To the contrary, it seems to us that such an inflexible rule would recognize the interest of one person or group to the exclusion of all

---

[10] In other words, when stockholders, after making demand and having their suit rejected, attack the board's decision as improper, the board's decision falls under the "business judgment" rule and will be respected if the requirements of the rule are met. . . . That situation should be distinguished from the instant case, where demand was not made, and the *power* of the board to seek a dismissal, due to disqualification, presents a threshold issue. . . .

others within the corporate entity. Thus, we reject the view of the Vice Chancellor as to the first aspect of the issue on appeal.

The question to be decided becomes: When, if at all, should an authorized board committee be permitted to cause litigation, properly initiated by a derivative stockholder in his own right, to be dismissed? As noted above, a board has the power to choose not to pursue litigation when demand is made upon it, so long as the decision is not wrongful. If the board determines that a suit would be detrimental to the company, the board's determination prevails. Even when demand is excusable, circumstances may arise when continuation of the litigation would not be in the corporation's best interests. Our inquiry is whether, under such circumstances, there is a permissible procedure under § 141(a) by which a corporation can rid itself of detrimental litigation. If there is not, a single stockholder in an extreme case might control the destiny of the entire corporation. This concern was bluntly expressed by the Ninth Circuit in Lewis v. Anderson, 9th Cir., 615 F.2d 778, 783 (1979), cert. denied, ___ U.S. ___, 101 S.Ct. 206, 66 L.Ed.2d 89 (1980): "To allow one shareholder to incapacitate an entire board of directors merely by leveling charges against them gives too much leverage to dissident shareholders." But, when examining the means, including the committee mechanism examined in this case, potentials for abuse must be recognized. This takes us to the second and third aspects of the issue on appeal.

Before we pass to equitable considerations as to the mechanism at issue here, it must be clear that an independent committee possesses the corporate power to seek the termination of a derivative suit. Section 141(c) allows a board to delegate all of its authority to a committee. Accordingly, a committee with properly delegated authority would have the power to move for dismissal or summary judgment if the entire board did.

Even though demand was not made in this case and the initial decision of whether to litigate was not placed before the board, Zapata's board, it seems to us, retained all of its corporate power concerning litigation decisions. If Maldonado had made demand on the board in this case, it could have refused to bring suit. Maldonado could then have asserted that the decision not to sue was wrongful and, if correct, would have been allowed to maintain the suit. The board, however, never would have lost its statutory managerial authority. The demand requirement itself evidences that the managerial power is retained by the board. When a derivative plaintiff is allowed to bring suit after a wrongful refusal, the board's authority to choose whether to pursue the litigation is not challenged although its conclusion—reached through the exercise of that authority—is not respected since it is wrongful. . . .

The corporate power inquiry then focuses on whether the board, tainted by the self-interest of a majority of its members, can legally delegate its authority to a committee of two disinterested directors. We find our statute clearly requires an affirmative answer to this question. As has been noted, under an express provision of the statute, § 141(c), a committee can exercise all of the authority of the board to the extent provided in the resolution of the board. Moreover, at least by analogy to our statutory section on interested directors, 8 Del.C. § 144, it seems clear that the Delaware statute is designed to permit disinterested directors to act for the board.* . . .

We do not think that the interest taint of the board majority is per se a legal bar to the delegation of the board's power to an independent committee composed of disinterested board members. The committee can properly act for the corporation to move to dismiss derivative litigation that is believed to be detrimental to the corporation's best interest.

Our focus now switches to the Court of Chancery which is faced with a stockholder assertion that a derivative suit, properly instituted, should continue for the benefit of the corporation and a corporate assertion, properly made by a board committee acting with board authority, that the same derivative suit should be dismissed as inimical to the best interests of the corporation.

At the risk of stating the obvious, the problem is relatively simple. If, on the one hand, corporations can consistently wrest bona fide derivative actions away from well-meaning derivative plaintiffs through the use of the committee mechanism, the derivative suit will lose much, if not all, of its generally-recognized effectiveness as an intra-corporate means of policing boards of directors. . . . If, on the other hand, corporations are unable to rid themselves of meritless or harmful litigation and strike suits, the derivative action, created to benefit the corporation, will produce the opposite, unintended result. . . . It thus appears desirable to us to find a balancing point where bona fide stockholder power to bring corporate causes of action cannot be unfairly trampled on by the board of directors, but the corporation can rid itself of detrimental litigation.

As we noted, the question has been treated by other courts as one of the "business judgment" of the board committee. If a "committee, composed of independent and disinterested directors, conducted a proper review of the matters before it, considered a variety of factors and reached, in good faith, a business judgment that [the] action was not in the best interest of [the corporation]," the action must be dismissed. See, e.g., Maldonado v. Flynn, [485 F.Supp. 274, 282, 286 (S.D.N.Y.1980)]. The issues become solely independence, good faith, and reasonable investigation. The ultimate conclusion of the committee, under that view, is not subject to judicial review.

We are not satisfied, however, that acceptance of the "business judgment" rationale at this stage of derivative litigation is a proper balancing point. While we admit an analogy with a normal case respecting board judgment, it seems to us that there is sufficient risk in the realities of a situation like the one presented in this case to justify caution beyond adherence to the theory of business judgment.

The context here is a suit against directors where demand on the board is excused. We think some tribute must be paid to the fact that the lawsuit was properly initiated. It is not a board refusal case. Moreover, this complaint was filed in June of 1975 and, while the parties undoubtedly would take differing views on the degree of litigation activity, we have to be concerned about the creation of an "Independent Investigation Committee" four years later, after the election of two new outside directors. Situations could develop where such motions could be

* [Eds.—See Chapter 5, Sec. 2.]

filed after years of vigorous litigation for reasons unconnected with the merits of the lawsuit.

Moreover, notwithstanding our conviction that Delaware law entrusts the corporate power to a properly authorized committee, we must be mindful that directors are passing judgment on fellow directors in the same corporation and fellow directors, in this instance, who designated them to serve both as directors and committee members. The question naturally arises whether a "there but for the grace of God go I" empathy might not play a role. And the further question arises whether inquiry as to independence, good faith and reasonable investigation is sufficient safeguard against abuse, perhaps subconscious abuse. . . .

Whether the Court of Chancery will be persuaded by the exercise of a committee power resulting in a summary motion for dismissal of a derivative action, where a demand has not been initially made, should rest, in our judgment, in the independent discretion of the Court of Chancery. We thus steer a middle course between those cases which yield to the independent business judgment of a board committee and this case as determined below which would yield to unbridled plaintiff stockholder control. In pursuit of the course, we recognize that "[t]he final substantive judgment whether a particular lawsuit should be maintained requires a balance of many factors—ethical, commercial, promotional, public relations, employee relations, fiscal as well as legal." Maldonado v. Flynn, supra, 485 F.Supp. at 285. But we are content that such factors are not "beyond the judicial reach" of the Court of Chancery which regularly and competently deals with fiduciary relationships, disposition of trust property, approval of settlements and scores of similar problems. We recognize the danger of judicial overreaching but the alternatives seem to us to be outweighed by the fresh view of a judicial outsider. Moreover, if we failed to balance all the interests involved, we would in the name of practicality and judicial economy foreclose a judicial decision on the merits. At this point, we are not convinced that is necessary or desirable.

After an objective and thorough investigation of a derivative suit, an independent committee may cause its corporation to file a pretrial motion to dismiss in the Court of Chancery. The basis of the motion is the best interests of the corporation, as determined by the committee. The motion should include a thorough written record of the investigation and its findings and recommendations. Under appropriate Court supervision, akin to proceedings on summary judgment, each side should have an opportunity to make a record on the motion. As to the limited issues presented by the motion noted below, the moving party should be prepared to meet the normal burden under Rule 56 that there is no genuine issue as to any material fact and that the moving party is entitled to dismiss as a matter of law. The Court should apply a two-step test to the motion.

First, the Court should inquire into the independence and good faith of the committee and the bases supporting its conclusions. Limited discovery may be ordered to facilitate such inquiries. The corporation should have the burden of proving independence, good faith and a reasonable investigation, rather than presuming independence, good faith and reasonableness. If the Court determines either that the committee is not independent or has not shown reasonable bases for its conclusions, or, if the Court is not satisfied for other reasons relating to the process, including but not limited to the good faith of the committee, the Court shall deny the corporation's motion. If, however, the Court is satisfied under Rule 56 standards that the committee was independent and showed reasonable bases for good faith findings and recommendations, the Court may proceed, in its discretion, to the next step.

The second step provides, we believe, the essential key in striking the balance between legitimate corporate claims as expressed in a derivative stockholder suit and a corporation's best interests as expressed by an independent investigating committee. The Court should determine, applying its own independent business judgment, whether the motion should be granted. This means, of course, that instances could arise where a committee can establish its independence and sound bases for its good faith decisions and still have the corporation's motion denied. The second step is intended to thwart instances where corporate actions meet the criteria of step one, but the result does not appear to satisfy its spirit, or where corporate actions would simply prematurely terminate a stockholder grievance deserving of further consideration in the corporation's interest. The Court of Chancery of course must carefully consider and weigh how compelling the corporate interest in dismissal is when faced with a non-frivolous lawsuit. The Court of Chancery should, when appropriate, give special consideration to matters of law and public policy in addition to the corporation's best interests.

If the Court's independent business judgment is satisfied, the Court may proceed to grant the motion, subject, of course, to any equitable terms or conditions the Court finds necessary or desirable.

The interlocutory order of the Court of Chancery is reversed and the cause is remanded for further proceedings consistent with this opinion.

ANALYSIS

1. Why does the *Zapata* court distinguish between cases where the independent litigation committee investigates whether to sue after a derivative plaintiff has made demand on the firm, and cases where the plaintiff's demand on the firm has been excused? Should the *Zapata* court's two-step review of the litigation committee's decision also apply to cases where a plaintiff demands of the board that it litigate the alleged corporate claim and the board refuses to do so?

2. What is the likely difference in practical effect of the various rules relating to special committees? Suppose you are counsel to a special litigation committee of a Delaware corporation, appointed to decide whether to seek dismissal of a derivative suit. What advice would you give as to how the committee should proceed? How, if at all, would your advice be different in the case of a New York corporation?

In re Oracle Corp. Derivative Litigation

824 A.2d 917 (Del. Ch. 2003).

■ STRINE, VICE CHANCELLOR.

In this opinion, I address the motion of the special litigation committee ("SLC") of Oracle Corporation to terminate this action, "the Delaware Derivative Action," and other such actions pending in the name of Oracle against certain Oracle directors and officers. . . . The SLC bears the burden of persuasion on this motion and must convince me that there is no material issue of fact calling into doubt its independence. . . .

I. Factual Background

. . . The Delaware Derivative Complaint centers on alleged insider trading by four members of Oracle's board of directors—Lawrence Ellison, Jeffrey Henley, Donald Lucas, and Michael Boskin (collectively, the "Trading Defendants"). . . .

Ellison is Oracle's Chairman, Chief Executive Officer, and its largest stockholder, owning nearly twenty-five percent of Oracle's voting shares. . . . By virtue of his managerial position, Ellison has regular access to a great deal of information about how Oracle is performing on a week-to-week basis. . . . Henley is Oracle's Chief Financial Officer, Executive Vice President, and a director of the corporation. . . . Lucas is a director who chairs Oracle's Executive Committee and its Finance and Audit Committee. . . . Boskin is a director, Chairman of the Compensation Committee, and a member of the Finance and Audit Committee. . . .

Into early to mid-February, Oracle allegedly continued to assure the market that it would meet its December guidance. Then, on March 1, 2001, the company announced that rather than posting 12 cents per share in quarterly earnings and 25% license revenue growth as projected, the company's earnings for the quarter would be 10 cents per share and license revenue growth only 6%. The stock market reacted swiftly and negatively to this news, with Oracle's share price dropping as low as $15.75 before closing at $16.88—a 21% decline in one day. These prices were well below the above $30 per share prices at which the Trading Defendants sold in January 2001. . . .

The plaintiffs make two central claims in their amended complaint in the Delaware Derivative Action. First, the plaintiffs allege that the Trading Defendants breached their duty of loyalty by misappropriating inside information and using it as the basis for trading decisions. . . . Second, as to the other defendants—who are the members of the Oracle board who did not trade—the plaintiffs allege a *Caremark*[6] violation, in the sense that the board's indifference to the deviation between the company's December guidance and reality was so extreme as to constitute subjective bad faith. . . .

On February 1, 2002, Oracle formed the SLC in order to investigate the Delaware Derivative Action and to determine whether Oracle should press the claims raised by the plaintiffs, settle the case, or terminate it. . . . Two Oracle board members were named to the SLC. Both of them joined the Oracle board on October 15, 2001, more than a half a year after

[6] In re Caremark Int'l Derivative Litig., 698 A.2d 959 (Del.Ch.1996).

Oracle's 3Q FY 2001 closed. The SLC members also share something else: both are tenured professors at Stanford University. . . . Professor Hector Garcia-Molina is Chairman of the Computer Science Department at Stanford. . . . The other SLC member, Professor Joseph Grundfest, is the W.A. Franke Professor of Law and Business at Stanford University. . . .

. . . Before deciding to join the Oracle board, Grundfest, in particular, did a good deal of due diligence. His review included reading publicly available information. . . . Grundfest then met with defendants Ellison and Henley, among others. . . . Grundfest testified that . . . he had [not] concluded that the claims . . . had no merit, only that Ellison's and Henley's explanations of their conduct were plausible. Grundfest did, however, conclude that these were reputable businessmen with whom he felt comfortable serving as a fellow director. . . .

The most important advisors retained by the SLC were its counsel from Simpson Thacher & Bartlett LLP. Simpson Thacher had not performed material amounts of legal work for Oracle or any of the individual defendants before its engagement, and the plaintiffs have not challenged its independence. . . . National Economic Research Advisors ("NERA") was retained by the SLC to perform some analytical work. The plaintiffs have not challenged NERA's independence. . . .

The SLC's investigation was, by any objective measure, extensive. The SLC reviewed an enormous amount of paper and electronic records. SLC counsel interviewed seventy witnesses, some of them twice. SLC members participated in several key interviews, including the interviews of the Trading Defendants. . . .

During the course of the investigation, the SLC met with its counsel thirty-five times for a total of eighty hours. In addition to that, the SLC members, particularly Professor Grundfest, devoted many more hours to the investigation.

In the end, the SLC produced an extremely lengthy Report totaling 1,110 pages (excluding appendices and exhibits) that concluded that Oracle should not pursue the plaintiffs' claims against the Trading Defendants or any of the other Oracle directors serving during the 3Q FY 2001. . . .

. . . [T]he SLC concluded that even a hypothetical Oracle executive who possessed all information regarding the company's performance in December and January of 3Q FY 2001 would not have possessed material, non-public information that the company would fail to meet the earnings and revenue guidance it provided the market in December. . . .

[T]aking into account all the relevant information sources, the SLC concluded that even Ellison and Henley—who were obviously the two Trading Defendants with the most access to inside information—did not possess material, non-public information. As to Lucas and Boskin, the SLC noted that they did not receive the weekly updates (of various kinds) that allegedly showed a weakening in Oracle's performance during 3Q FY 2001. As a result, there was even less of a basis to infer wrongdoing on their part. . . .

IV. Is the SLC Independent?

A. The Facts Disclosed in the Report

In its Report, the SLC took the position that its members were independent. In support of that position, the Report noted several factors including:

- the fact that neither Grundfest nor Garcia-Molina received compensation from Oracle other than as directors;
- the fact that neither Grundfest nor Garcia-Molina were on the Oracle board at the time of the alleged wrongdoing;
- the fact that both Grundfest and Garcia-Molina were willing to return their compensation as SLC members if necessary to preserve their status as independent;
- the absence of any other material ties between Oracle, the Trading Defendants, and any of the other defendants, on the one hand, and Grundfest and Garcia-Molina, on the other; and
- the absence of any material ties between Oracle, the Trading Defendants, and any of the other defendants, on the one hand, and the SLC's advisors, on the other.

Noticeably absent from the SLC Report was any disclosure of several significant ties between Oracle or the Trading Defendants and Stanford University, the university that employs both members of the SLC. In the Report, it was only disclosed that:

- defendant Boskin was a Stanford professor;
- the SLC members were aware that Lucas had made certain donations to Stanford; and
- among the contributions was a donation of $50,000 worth of stock that Lucas donated to Stanford Law School after Grundfest delivered a speech to a venture capital fund meeting in response to Lucas's request. It happens that Lucas's son is a partner in the fund and that approximately half the donation was allocated for use by Grundfest in his personal research.

B. The "Stanford" Facts that Emerged During Discovery

In view of the modesty of these disclosed ties, it was with some shock that a series of other ties among Stanford, Oracle, and the Trading Defendants emerged during discovery. Although the plaintiffs have embellished these ties considerably beyond what is reasonable, the plain facts are a striking departure from the picture presented in the Report. . . .

1. Boskin

Defendant Michael J. Boskin is the T.M. Friedman Professor of Economics at Stanford University. . . . During the 1970s, Boskin taught Grundfest when Grundfest was a Ph.D. candidate. Although Boskin was not Grundfest's advisor and although they do not socialize, the two have remained in contact over the years, speaking occasionally about matters of public policy.

Furthermore, both Boskin and Grundfest are senior fellows and steering committee members at the Stanford Institute for Economic Policy Research, which was previously defined as "SIEPR." . . . [B]oth Boskin and Grundfest publish working papers under the SIEPR rubric and . . . SIEPR helps to publicize their respective works. . . .

2. Lucas

. . . Lucas's ties with Stanford are far, far richer than the SLC Report lets on. To begin, Lucas is a Stanford alumnus, having obtained both his undergraduate and graduate degrees there. By any measure, he has been a very loyal alumnus. [The court then detailed numerous financial contributions to Stanford by Lucas and a family foundation with which he was affiliated.] From these undisputed facts, it is inarguable that Lucas is a very important alumnus of Stanford and a generous contributor to not one, but two, parts of Stanford important to Grundfest: the Law School and SIEPR. . . .

3. Ellison

There can be little doubt that Ellison is a major figure in the community in which Stanford is located. The so-called Silicon Valley has generated many success stories, among the greatest of which is that of Oracle and its leader, Ellison. One of the wealthiest men in America, Ellison is a major figure in the nation's increasingly important information technology industry. Given his wealth, Ellison is also in a position to make—and, in fact, he has made—major charitable contributions to Stanford. . . .

In order to buttress the argument that Stanford did not feel beholden to him, Ellison shared with the court the (otherwise private) fact that one of his children had applied to Stanford in October 2000 and was not admitted. If Stanford felt comfortable rejecting Ellison's child, the SLC contends, why should the SLC members hesitate before recommending that Oracle press insider trading-based fiduciary duty claims against Ellison?

But the fact remains that Ellison was still talking very publicly and seriously about the possibility of endowing a graduate interdisciplinary studies program at Stanford during the summer after his child was rejected from Stanford's undergraduate program.

C. The SLC's Argument

The SLC contends that even together, these facts regarding the ties among Oracle, the Trading Defendants, Stanford, and the SLC members do not impair the SLC's independence. In so arguing, the SLC places great weight on the fact that none of the Trading Defendants have the practical ability to deprive either Grundfest or Garcia-Molina of their current positions at Stanford. Nor, given their tenure, does Stanford itself have any practical ability to punish them for taking action adverse to Boskin, Lucas, or Ellison—each of whom, as we have seen, has contributed (in one way or another) great value to Stanford as an institution. . . .

In so arguing, the SLC focuses on the language of previous opinions of this court and the Delaware Supreme Court that indicates that a director is not independent only if he is dominated and controlled by an interested party, such as a Trading Defendant. . . . Put another way, much of our law focuses the bias inquiry on whether there are economically material ties between the interested party and the director whose impartiality is questioned, treating the possible effect on one's personal wealth as the key to the independence inquiry. Putting a point on this, the SLC cites certain decisions of Delaware courts concluding that directors who are personal friends of an interested party were not, by virtue of those personal ties, to be labeled non-independent. . . .

E. The Court's Analysis of the SLC's Independence

. . . [I]n my view, an emphasis on "domination and control" would serve only to fetishize much-parroted language, at the cost of denuding the independence inquiry of its intellectual integrity. Take an easy example. Imagine if two brothers were on a corporate board, each successful in different businesses and not dependent in any way on the other's beneficence in order to be wealthy. The brothers are brothers, they stay in touch and consider each other family, but each is opinionated and strong-willed. A derivative action is filed targeting a transaction involving one of the brothers. The other brother is put on a special litigation committee to investigate the case. If the test is domination and control, then one brother could investigate the other. Does any sensible person think that is our law? I do not think it is.

And it should not be our law. Delaware law should not be based on a reductionist view of human nature that simplifies human motivations on the lines of the least sophisticated notions of the law and economics movement. Homo sapiens is not merely homo economicus. We may be thankful that an array of other motivations exist that influence human behavior; not all are any better than greed or avarice, think of envy, to name just one. But also think of motives like love, friendship, and collegiality, think of those among us who direct their behavior as best they can on a guiding creed or set of moral values.

Nor should our law ignore the social nature of humans. To be direct, corporate directors are generally the sort of people deeply enmeshed in social institutions. Such institutions have norms, expectations that, explicitly and implicitly, influence and channel the behavior of those who participate in their operation. Some things are "just not done," or only at a cost, which might not be so severe as a loss of position, but may involve a loss of standing in the institution. In being appropriately sensitive to this factor, our law also cannot assume—absent some proof of the point—that corporate directors are, as a general matter, persons of unusual social bravery, who operate heedless to the inhibitions that social norms generate for ordinary folk.

For all these reasons, this court has previously held that the Delaware Supreme Court's teachings on independence can be summarized thusly:

> At bottom, the question of independence turns on whether a director is, for any substantial reason, incapable of making a decision with only the best interests of the corporation in mind. That is, the Supreme Court cases ultimately focus on impartiality and objectivity.[49] . . .

[49] Parfi Holding AB v. Mirror Image Internet, Inc., 794 A.2d 1211, 1232 (Del.Ch.2001) (footnotes omitted) (emphasis in original), rev'd in part on other grounds, 817 A.2d 149 (Del.2002), cert. denied, ___ U.S. ___, 123 S.Ct. 2076, 155 L.Ed.2d 1061 (2003).

1. The Contextual Nature of the Independence Inquiry Under Delaware Law

. . . Thus, in assessing the independence of the Oracle SLC, I necessarily examine the question of whether the SLC can independently make the difficult decision entrusted to it: to determine whether the Trading Defendants should face suit for insider trading-based allegations of breach of fiduciary duty. An affirmative answer by the SLC to that question would have potentially huge negative consequences for the Trading Defendants, not only by exposing them to the possibility of a large damage award but also by subjecting them to great reputational harm. To have Professors Grundfest and Garcia-Molina declare that Oracle should press insider trading claims against the Trading Defendants would have been, to put it mildly, "news." Relatedly, it is reasonable to think that an SLC determination that the Trading Defendants had likely engaged in insider trading would have been accompanied by a recommendation that they step down as fiduciaries until their ultimate culpability was decided. . . .

2. The SLC Has Not Met Its Burden to Demonstrate the Absence of a Material Dispute of Fact About Its Independence

Using the contextual approach I have described, I conclude that the SLC has not met its burden to show the absence of a material factual question about its independence. I find this to be the case because the ties among the SLC, the Trading Defendants, and Stanford are so substantial that they cause reasonable doubt about the SLC's ability to impartially consider whether the Trading Defendants should face suit. The concern that arises from these ties can be stated fairly simply, focusing on defendants Boskin, Lucas, and Ellison in that order, and then collectively.

As SLC members, Grundfest and Garcia-Molina were already being asked to consider whether the company should level extremely serious accusations of wrongdoing against fellow board members. As to Boskin, both SLC members faced another layer of complexity: the determination of whether to have Oracle press insider trading claims against a fellow professor at their university. Even though Boskin was in a different academic department from either SLC member, it is reasonable to assume that the fact that Boskin was also on faculty would—to persons possessing typical sensibilities and institutional loyalty—be a matter of more than trivial concern. . . . To accuse a fellow professor—whom one might see at the faculty club or at inter-disciplinary presentations of academic papers—of insider trading cannot be a small thing—even for the most callous of academics.

As to Boskin, Grundfest faced an even more complex challenge than Garcia-Molina. . . . Grundfest (I infer) would have more difficulty objectively determining whether Boskin engaged in improper insider trading than would a person who was not a fellow professor, had not been a student of Boskin, had not kept in touch with Boskin over the years, and who was not a senior fellow and steering committee member at SIEPR.

In so concluding, I necessarily draw on a general sense of human nature. It may be that Grundfest is a very special person who is capable of putting these kinds of things totally aside. But the SLC has not provided evidence that that is the case. In this respect, it is critical to note that I do not infer that Grundfest would be less likely to recommend suit against Boskin than someone without these ties. Human nature being what it is, it is entirely possible that Grundfest would in fact be tougher on Boskin than he would on someone with whom he did not have such connections. The inference I draw is subtly, but importantly, different. What I infer is that a person in Grundfest's position would find it difficult to assess Boskin's conduct without pondering his own association with Boskin and their mutual affiliations. Although these connections might produce bias in either a tougher or laxer direction, the key inference is that these connections would be on the mind of a person in Grundfest's position, putting him in the position of either causing serious legal action to be brought against a person with whom he shares several connections (an awkward thing) or not doing so (and risking being seen as having engaged in favoritism toward his old professor and SIEPR colleague).

The same concerns also exist as to Lucas. For Grundfest to vote to accuse Lucas of insider trading would require him to accuse SIEPR's Advisory Board Chair and major benefactor of serious wrongdoing—of conduct that violates federal securities laws. . . .

And, for both Grundfest and Garcia-Molina, service on the SLC demanded that they consider whether an extremely generous and influential Stanford alumnus should be sued by Oracle for insider trading. Although they were not responsible for fundraising, as sophisticated professors they undoubtedly are aware of how important large contributors are to Stanford, and they share in the benefits that come from serving at a university with a rich endowment. A reasonable professor giving any thought to the matter would obviously consider the effect his decision might have on the University's relationship with Lucas, it being (one hopes) sensible to infer that a professor of reasonable collegiality and loyalty cares about the well-being of the institution he serves. . . .

The SLC's motion to terminate is DENIED. . . .

ANALYSIS

1. If you had been in Grundfest's shoes, would you have felt uncomfortable taking on the role of determining whether Boskin, Ellison, and Lucas had engaged in illegal insider trading? Would you have accepted the assignment to the SLC?

2. Why did the Board of Oracle appoint Grundfest and Garcia-Molina to the SLC? What were the alternatives? What would you have advised?

SUBSEQUENT DEVELOPMENTS

In Beam ex rel. Martha Stewart Living Omnimedia, Inc. v. Stewart, 845 A.2d 1040 (Del. 2004), the Delaware supreme court addressed the question of when a director is deemed independent of alleged wrongdoers:

> A variety of motivations, including friendship, may influence the demand futility inquiry. But, to render a director

> unable to consider demand, a relationship must be of a bias-producing nature. Allegations of mere personal friendship or a mere outside business relationship, standing alone, are insufficient to raise a reasonable doubt about a director's independence.

Id. at 1050. The opinion, however, also included a section entitled "A Word About the Oracle Case," in which the Court cautioned that:

> *Oracle* involved the issue of the independence of the Special Litigation Committee (SLC) appointed by the Oracle board to determine whether or not the corporation should cause the dismissal of a corporate claim by stockholder-plaintiffs against directors. The Court of Chancery undertook a searching inquiry of the relationships between the members of the SLC and Stanford University in the context of the financial support of Stanford by the corporation and its management. The Vice Chancellor concluded, after considering the SLC Report and the discovery record, that those relationships were too close for purposes of the SLC analysis of independence.[41]
>
> An SLC is a unique creature that was introduced into Delaware law by Zapata v. Maldonado in 1981.[42] The SLC procedure is a method sometimes employed where presuit demand has already been excused and the SLC is vested with the full power of the board to conduct an extensive investigation into the merits of the corporate claim with a view toward determining whether—in the SLC's business judgment—the corporate claim should be pursued. Unlike the demand-excusal context, where the board is presumed to be independent, the SLC has the burden of establishing its own independence by a yardstick that must be "like Caesar's wife"—"above reproach."[43] Moreover, unlike the presuit demand context, the SLC analysis contemplates not only a shift in the burden of persuasion but also the availability of discovery into various issues, including independence.
>
> We need not decide whether the substantive standard of independence in an SLC case differs from that in a presuit demand case. As a practical matter, the procedural distinction relating to the diametrically-opposed burdens and the availability of discovery into independence may be outcome-determinative on the issue of independence. Moreover, because the members of an SLC are vested with enormous power to seek dismissal of a derivative suit brought against their director-colleagues in a setting where presuit demand is already excused, the Court of Chancery must exercise careful oversight of the bona fides of the SLC and its process. Aside from the

---

[41] *Oracle*, 824 A.2d at 921. It is noteworthy that the Vice Chancellor was concerned and expressed "some shock" that the extent of the Stanford ties was not revealed in the Report of the SLC and was unearthed only in discovery. He noted that "the plain facts are a striking departure from the picture presented in the Report." Id. at 929–30.

[42] 430 A.2d 779 (Del.Supr.1981).

[43] Lewis v. Fuqua, 502 A.2d 962, 967 (Del.Ch.1985).

procedural distinctions, the Stanford connections in *Oracle* are factually distinct from the relationships present here.

Id. at 1054–55.

4. THE ROLE AND PURPOSES OF CORPORATIONS

A.P. Smith Mfg. Co. v. Barlow

13 N.J. 145, 98 A.2d 581, appeal dismissed, 346 U.S. 861 (1953).

The Chancery Division, in a well-reasoned opinion by Judge Stein, determined that a donation by the plaintiff The A.P. Smith Manufacturing Company to Princeton University was *intra vires*. . . .

The company was incorporated in 1896 and is engaged in the manufacture and sale of valves, fire hydrants and special equipment, mainly for water and gas industries. Its plant is located in East Orange and Bloomfield and it has approximately 300 employees. Over the years the company has contributed regularly to the local community chest and on occasions to Upsala College in East Orange and Newark University, now part of Rutgers, the State University. On July 24, 1951 the board of directors adopted a resolution which set forth that it was in the corporation's best interests to join with others in the 1951 Annual Giving to Princeton University, and appropriated the sum of $1,500 to be transferred by the corporation's treasurer to the university as a contribution towards its maintenance. When this action was questioned by stockholders the corporation instituted a declaratory judgment action in the Chancery Division and trial was had in due course.

Mr. Hubert F. O'Brien, the president of the company, testified that he considered the contribution to be a sound investment, that the public expects corporations to aid philanthropic and benevolent institutions, that they obtain good will in the community by so doing, and that their charitable donations create favorable environment for their business operations. In addition, he expressed the thought that in contributing to liberal arts institutions, corporations were furthering their self-interest in assuring the free flow of properly trained personnel for administrative and other corporate employment. . . . Mr. Irving S. Olds, former chairman of the board of the United States Steel Corporation, pointed out that corporations have a self-interest in the maintenance of liberal education as the bulwark of good government. He stated that "Capitalism and free enterprise owe their survival in no small degree to the existence of our private, independent universities" and that if American business does not aid in their maintenance it is not "properly protecting the long-range interest of its stockholders, its employees and its customers." Similarly, Dr. Harold W. Dodds, President of Princeton University, suggested that if private institutions of higher learning were replaced by governmental institutions our society would be vastly different and private enterprise in other fields would fade out rather promptly. Further on he stated that "democratic society will not long endure if it does not nourish within itself strong centers of non-governmental fountains of knowledge, opinions of all sorts not governmentally or politically originated. If the time comes when all these centers are absorbed into government, then freedom as we know it, I submit, is at an end."

The objecting stockholders have not disputed any of the foregoing testimony nor the showing of great need by Princeton and other private institutions of higher learning and the important public service being rendered by them for democratic government and industry alike. Similarly, they have acknowledged that for over two decades there has been state legislation on our books which expresses a strong public policy in favor of corporate contributions such as that being questioned by them. Nevertheless, they have taken the position that (1) the plaintiff's certificate of incorporation does not expressly authorize the contribution and under common-law principles the company does not possess any implied or incidental power to make it, and (2) the New Jersey statutes which expressly authorize the contribution may not constitutionally be applied to the plaintiff, a corporation created long before their enactment. . . .

In his discussion of the early history of business corporations Professor Williston refers to a 1702 publication where the author stated flatly that "The general intent and end of all civil incorporations is for better government." And he points out that the early corporate charters, particularly their recitals, furnish additional support for the notion that the corporate object was the public one of managing and ordering the trade as well as the private one of profit for the members. . . . However, with later economic and social developments and the free availability of the corporate device for all trades, the end of private profit became generally accepted as the controlling one in all businesses other than those classed broadly as public utilities. . . . As a concomitant the common-law rule developed that those who managed the corporation could not disburse any corporate funds for philanthropic or other worthy public cause unless the expenditure would benefit the corporation. . . . During the 19th Century when corporations were relatively few and small and did not dominate the country's wealth, the common-law rule did not significantly interfere with the public interest. But the 20th Century has presented a different climate. . . . Control of economic wealth has passed largely from individual entrepreneurs to dominating corporations, and calls upon the corporations for reasonable philanthropic donations have come to be made with increased public support. In many instances such contributions have been sustained by the courts within the common-law doctrine upon liberal findings that the donations tended reasonably to promote the corporate objectives. . . .

When the wealth of the nation was primarily in the hands of individuals they discharged their responsibilities as citizens by donating freely for charitable purposes. With the transfer of most of the wealth to corporate hands and the imposition of heavy burdens of individual taxation, they have been unable to keep pace with increased philanthropic needs. They have therefore, with justification, turned to corporations to assume the modern obligations of good citizenship in the same manner as humans do. . . . In actual practice corporate giving has correspondingly increased. Thus, it is estimated that annual corporate contributions throughout the nation aggregate over 300 million dollars, with over 60 million dollars thereof going to universities and other educational institutions. . . .

During the first world war corporations loaned their personnel and contributed substantial corporate funds in order to insure survival;

during the depression of the '30s they made contributions to alleviate the desperate hardships of the millions of unemployed; and during the second world war they again contributed to insure survival. They now recognize that we are faced with other, though nonetheless vicious, threats from abroad which must be withstood without impairing the vigor of our democratic institutions at home and that otherwise victory will be pyrrhic indeed. More and more they have come to recognize that their salvation rests upon sound economic and social environment which in turn rests in no insignificant part upon free and vigorous nongovernmental institutions of learning. It seems to us that just as the conditions prevailing when corporations were originally created required that they serve public as well as private interests, modern conditions require that corporations acknowledge and discharge social as well as private responsibilities as members of the communities within which they operate. . . .

In 1930 a statute was enacted in our State which expressly provided that any corporation could cooperate with other corporations and natural persons in the creation and maintenance of community funds and charitable, philanthropic or benevolent instrumentalities conducive to public welfare, and could for such purposes expend such corporate sums as the directors "deem expedient and as in their judgment will contribute to the protection of the corporate interests." L.1930, c. 105; L.1931, c. 290; R.S. 14:3–13, N.J.S.A. See 53 N.J.L.J. 335 (1930). Under the terms of the statute donations in excess of 1% of the capital stock required 10 days' notice to stockholders and approval at a stockholders' meeting if written objections were made by the holders of more than 25% of the stock; in 1949 the statute was amended to increase the limitation to 1% of capital and surplus. See L.1949, c. 171. In 1950 a more comprehensive statute was enacted. L.1950, c. 220; N.J.S.A. 14:3–13.1 et seq. . . .

The appellants contend that the foregoing New Jersey statutes may not be applied to corporations created before their passage. Fifty years before the incorporation of The A.P. Smith Manufacturing Company our Legislature provided that every corporate charter thereafter granted "shall be subject to alteration, suspension and repeal, in the discretion of the legislature." L.1846, p. 16; R.S. 14:2–9, N.J.S.A. A similar reserved power was placed into our State Constitution in 1875 (Art. IV, Sec. VII, par. 11), and is found in our present Constitution. Art. IV, Sec. VII, par. 9. In the early case of Zabriskie v. Hackensack & New York Railroad Company, 18 N.J.Eq. 178 (Ch.1867), the court was called upon to determine whether a railroad could extend its line, above objection by a stockholder, under a legislative enactment passed under the reserve power after the incorporation of the railroad. Notwithstanding the breadth of the statutory language and persuasive authority elsewhere . . . it was held that the proposed extension of the company's line constituted a vital change of its corporate object which could not be accomplished without unanimous consent. . . . The court announced the now familiar New Jersey doctrine that although the reserved power permits alterations in the public interest of the contract between the state and the corporation, it has no effect on the contractual rights between the corporation and its stockholders and between stockholders *inter se*. Unfortunately, the court did not consider whether it was not contrary to the public interest to permit the single minority stockholder before it to restrain the railroad's normal corporate growth and development as authorized by the Legislature and approved, reasonably and in good faith, by the corporation's managing directors and majority stockholders. Although the later cases in New Jersey have not disavowed the doctrine of the *Zabriskie* case, it is noteworthy that they have repeatedly recognized that where justified by the advancement of the public interest the reserved power may be invoked to sustain later charter alterations even though they affect contractual rights between the corporation and its stockholders and between stockholders *inter se*. . . .

State legislation adopted in the public interest and applied to pre-existing corporations under the reserved power has repeatedly been sustained by the United States Supreme Court above the contention that it impairs the rights of stockholders and violates constitutional guarantees under the Federal Constitution. . . .

It seems clear to us that the public policy supporting the statutory enactments under consideration is far greater and the alteration of pre-existing rights of stockholders much lesser than in the cited cases sustaining various exercises of the reserve power. In encouraging and expressly authorizing reasonable charitable contributions by corporations, our State has not only joined with other states in advancing the national interest but has also specially furthered the interests of its own people who must bear the burdens of taxation resulting from increased state and federal aid upon default in voluntary giving. . . .

In the light of all of the foregoing we have no hesitancy in sustaining the validity of the donation by the plaintiff. There is no suggestion that it was made indiscriminately or to a pet charity of the corporate directors in furtherance of personal rather than corporate ends. On the contrary, it was made to a preeminent institution of higher learning, was modest in amount and well within the limitations imposed by the statutory enactments, and was voluntarily made in the reasonable belief that it would aid the public welfare and advance the interests of the plaintiff as a private corporation and as part of the community in which it operates. We find that it was a lawful exercise of the corporation's implied and incidental powers under common-law principles and that it came within the express authority of the pertinent state legislation. . . .

The judgment entered in the Chancery Division is in all respects

Affirmed.

ANALYSIS

1. What is the holding of this case?

2. What is its likely effect on shareholders and on contributions to charities? What charities are likely to benefit the most? In this connection consider the following comment (made as part of a panel discussion) by Warren Buffet, who is one of the most successful and respected investors in recent decades:

> I have a friend who is the chief fundraiser for a philanthropy. Been that for about five years. And he calls on corporate officers and he has a very simple technique when he calls. All he wants is to take some other big shot with him who will sort of nod affirmatively while he meets with the CEO [chief executive officer]. He has found that what many big shots love

> is what I call elephant bumping. I mean they like to go to the places where other elephants are, because it reaffirms the fact that when they look around the room and they see all these other elephants that they must be an elephant too, or why would they be there? . . . So my friend always takes an elephant with him when he goes to call on another elephant. And the soliciting elephant, as my friend goes through his little pitch, nods and the receiving elephant listens attentively, and as long as the visiting elephant is appropriately large, my friend gets his money. And it's rather interesting, in the last five years he's raised 8 million dollars. He's raised it from 60 corporations. It almost never fails if he has the right elephant. And in the process of raising this 8 million dollars from 60 corporations from people who nod and say it's a marvelous idea, its prosocial, etc., not one CEO has reached in his pocket and pulled out 10 bucks of his own to give to this marvelous charity. They've given 8 million dollars collectively of other people's money. And so far he's yet to get his first 10-dollar bill. So far, the Salvation Army has done better at Christmas than essentially he's done with all these well-reasoned arguments that lead people to spend other people's money.

From J. Coffee, L. Lowenstein, and S. Rose-Ackerman, Knights, Raiders, and Targets: The Impact of the Hostile Takeover 14 (1988).

NOTE

The Delaware General Corporation Law, § 122, provides, "Every corporation created under this chapter shall have the power to . . . (9) Make donation for the public welfare or for charitable, scientific or educational purposes, and in time of war or other national emergency in aid thereof. . . ." Note, however, that this is one of the powers that a corporation has. Other listed powers include the power to "sue and be sued" and the power to "make contracts, including contracts of guaranty and suretyship." Thus, § 122(9) can be read merely as an authorization to make charitable contributions that serve the basic purpose of business corporations, which is to maximize profit. The courts have been extremely tolerant, however, in accepting the business judgment of the officers and directors of corporations, including their business judgment about whether a charitable donation will be good for the corporation in the long run. One of the rare exceptions to the judicial deference to the business judgment of a board of directors is found in the next case to be considered, Dodge v. Ford Motor Company.

The California Corporations Code, § 207(e), gives corporations the power to "make donations, regardless of *specific* corporate benefit, for the public welfare or for community fund, hospital, charitable, educational, scientific, civic or similar purposes." (Emphasis supplied.)

The New York Business Corporations Law, § 202(a)(12) (McKinney, 1986), includes in the general powers of corporations, the power "to make donations, irrespective of corporate benefit, for the public welfare or for community fund, hospital, charitable, educational, scientific, civic or similar purposes, and in time of war or other national emergency in aid thereof."

A Pennsylvania provision, enacted in 1990, provides, as part of its rules on duties of directors, that directors "may, in considering the best interests of the corporation," consider the effects of their actions on "any or all groups affected by such actions, including shareholders, employees, suppliers, customers and creditors of the corporation, and upon communities in which offices or other establishments of the corporation are located." Penn.Consol. Statutes, Title 15, § 102(d). This provision then goes further by providing that the directors "shall not be required, in considering the best interests of the corporation or the effects of any action, to regard any corporate interest or the interests of any particular group affected by such action as a dominant or controlling interest or factor." This language was part of a package of provisions intended primarily to allow Pennsylvania corporations to fend off hostile takeovers (see Chapter 7), but is not limited to such situations. The basic rule of corporate choice of law in all states is that the law of the state of incorporation controls on issues relating to a corporation's "internal affairs," which includes responsibilities of directors to shareholders. Thus, under the Pennsylvania statute, if a corporation is incorporated in Pennsylvania, its directors can take account of the effects of their actions on people in other states. But the actions of directors of a corporation that has its headquarters in Pennsylvania and does most of its business in that state, but is incorporated in, say, Delaware, are controlled by Delaware law.

Under the federal income tax law (Int.Rev.Code of 1986, § 170(b)(2)), the deduction for charitable contributions by corporations is limited to 10 percent of taxable income. The deduction is not dependent on the existence of a business purpose for the contribution.

PROBLEM

Suppose you are outside counsel to a public corporation engaged in the manufacture and sale of automobile replacement parts. The CEO calls you for advice about having the corporation make a gift of $100,000 to a charitable organization in which a good friend of his is involved. The organization operates a private school for poor minority children and has had considerable success over a number of years in motivating and educating children who might otherwise not have had much of a chance to succeed academically. The before-tax earnings of the corporation for the current year will be about $20 million. The CEO says that he is beseiged by requests for charitable donations and, to avoid creating ill will with people seeking funds for other causes (some of whom are important customers), wants the corporation's gift to the school to be anonymous. He asks if there is any problem with doing so. Assume the corporation is incorporated in Delaware. What is your advice? What if the state of incorporation is California? New York? Pennsylvania?

PLANNING

It is possible for corporations to adopt charter provisions expressly limiting or prohibiting charitable contributions. Such provisions are unheard of. Suppose you are about to invest, as a 20 percent shareholder, in a new corporation; that two other individuals will each own 40 percent of the shares; and that, while you admire the business acumen of the other two, you are deeply at odds with them on political and social issues. Would you want to include in the charter a provision limiting the power of the corporation to make charitable or political contributions? If so, what language would you propose?

Dodge v. Ford Motor Co.

204 Mich. 459, 170 N.W. 668 (1919).

[Ford Motor Co. was incorporated in 1903 with an investment of $150,000. Henry Ford was the majority shareholder and the brothers Horace E. Dodge and John F. Dodge were among the other shareholders. In 1908 the amount invested was increased to $2 million. The company grew rapidly. The car it made sold initially for $900, but by 1916, despite improvements, the price had been lowered to $440, and in August of that year was lowered to $360. Profits soared. For the three fiscal years ending July 31, 1916, the total number of cars sold was 472,350 and the total profit was almost $60 million. Beginning in 1911, regular yearly dividends were $1.2 million, or 60 percent of the amount initially invested. In addition, the following special dividends were paid:

1911	$ 1,000,000
1912	4,000,000
1913	10,000,000
1914	11,000,000
1915	10,000,000

The company's profits were far in excess of the amount of these dividends—a cumulative total at the end of the 1916 fiscal year of almost $174 million. At that time the company had more than $50 million cash on hand.*

In 1916 Henry Ford, who owned 58 percent of the common shares, announced that in the future no special dividends would be paid. Profits would be reinvested in the business—for example, to expand the existing plant and to build an iron ore smelting plant so as to permit the company to make its own metal parts. In addition, the price of the company's cars would be reduced.

The Dodge brothers owned 10 percent of the common shares; they were not members of the board of directors and were not employed by the company. In 1915 their share of the regular dividend was $120,000 and their share of the special dividend was $1 million, with a prospect of even greater dividends in the future. Under Henry Ford's announced policy they could expect to receive only $120,000 per year for the indefinite future. In 1913 they had formed an auto company of their own, which competed with Ford. In 1916, after the announcement of the new

* The facts are taken from the opinion and from P. Collier and D. Horowitz, The Fords: An American Epic 80–81 (1987). In 1913, upon the urging of one of his top employees, Ford raised the wages of the company's workers overnight from $2.50 per day to $5.00 per day. Other automakers accused him of being a "traitor to his class," but Ford apparently believed that the new wage would be good for the image of the company, would help sell cars, and, presumably, would enable him to hire more productive workers. Ford also hired social workers to improve the workers' "sobriety and industry." Id. at 66–67.

dividend policy, John Dodge met with Henry Ford, complained of the new dividend policy, and offered to sell his and his brother's shares to Ford for $35 million. Ford expressed no interest in buying at any price. The Dodge brothers then sued, attacking both the dividend policy and Ford's proposed plans to expand the company's manufacturing facilities. They prevailed in the lower court, which enjoined the building of the new smelting plant and ordered the payment of a dividend of $19.3 million out of what amounted to spare cash.]

[T]he case for plaintiffs must rest upon the claim, and the proof in support of it, that the proposed expansion of the business of the corporation, involving the further use of profits as capital, ought to be enjoined because inimical to the best interests of the company and its shareholders, and upon the further claim that in any event the withholding of the special dividend asked for by plaintiffs is arbitrary action of the directors requiring judicial interference.

The rule which will govern courts in deciding these questions is not in dispute. . . . This court, in Hunter v. Roberts, Throp & Co., 83 Mich. 63, 71, 47 N.W. 131, 134, recognized the rule in the following language:

> "It is a well-recognized principle of law that the directors of a corporation, and they alone, have the power to declare a dividend of the earnings of the corporation, and to determine its amount. 5 Amer. & Eng.Enc.Law, 725. Courts of equity will not interfere in the management of the directors unless it is clearly made to appear that they are guilty of fraud or misappropriation of the corporate funds, or refuse to declare a dividend when the corporation has a surplus of net profits which it can, without detriment to its business, divide among its stockholders, and when a refusal to do so would amount to such an abuse of discretion as would constitute a fraud, or breach of that good faith which they are bound to exercise towards the stockholders."

. . .

When plaintiffs made their complaint and demand for further dividends, the Ford Motor Company had concluded its most prosperous year of business. The demand for its cars at the price of the preceding year continued. It could make and could market in the year beginning August 1, 1916, more than 500,000 cars. Sales of parts and repairs would necessarily increase. The cost of materials was likely to advance, and perhaps the price of labor; but it reasonably might have expected a profit for the year of upwards of $60,000,000. It had assets of more than $132,000,000, a surplus of almost $112,000,000, and its cash on hand and municipal bonds were nearly $54,000,000. Its total liabilities, including capital stock, was a little over $20,000,000. It had declared no special dividend during the business year except the October, 1915, dividend. It had been the practice, under similar circumstances, to declare larger dividends. Considering only these facts, a refusal to declare and pay further dividends appears to be not an exercise of discretion on the part of the directors, but an arbitrary refusal to do what the circumstances required to be done. These facts and others call upon the directors to justify their action, or failure or refusal to act. In justification, the defendants have offered testimony tending to prove, and which does prove, the following facts: It had been the policy of the corporation for a considerable time to annually reduce the selling price of cars, while keeping up, or improving, their quality. As early as in June, 1915, a general plan for the expansion of the productive capacity of the concern by a practical duplication of its plant had been talked over by the executive officers and directors and agreed upon; not all of the details having been settled, and no formal action of directors having been taken. The erection of a smelter was considered, and engineering and other data in connection therewith secured. In consequence, it was determined not to reduce the selling price of cars for the year beginning August 1, 1915, but to maintain the price and to accumulate a large surplus to pay for the proposed expansion of plant and equipment, and perhaps to build a plant for smelting ore. It is hoped, by Mr. Ford, that eventually 1,000,000 cars will be annually produced. The contemplated changes will permit the increased output.

The plan, as affecting the profits of the business for the year beginning August 1, 1916, and thereafter, calls for a reduction in the selling price of the cars. It is true that this price might be at any time increased, but the plan called for the reduction in price of $80 a car. The capacity of the plant, without the additions thereto voted to be made (without a part of them at least), would produce more than 600,000 cars annually. This number, and more, could have been sold for $440 instead of $360, a difference in the return for capital, labor, and materials employed of at least $48,000,000. In short, the plan does not call for and is not intended to produce immediately a more profitable business, but a less profitable one; not only less profitable than formerly, but less profitable than it is admitted it might be made. The apparent immediate effect will be to diminish the value of shares and the returns to shareholders.

It is the contention of plaintiffs that the apparent effect of the plan is intended to be the continued and continuing effect of it, and that it is deliberately proposed, not of record and not by official corporate declaration, but nevertheless proposed, to continue the corporation henceforth as a semi-eleemosynary institution and not as a business institution. In support of this contention, they point to the attitude and to the expressions of Mr. Henry Ford.

Mr. Henry Ford is the dominant force in the business of the Ford Motor Company. No plan of operations could be adopted unless he consented, and no board of directors can be elected whom he does not favor. One of the directors of the company has no stock. One share was assigned to him to qualify him for the position, but it is not claimed that he owns it. A business, one of the largest in the world, and one of the most profitable, has been built up. It employs many men, at good pay.

"My ambition," said Mr. Ford, "is to employ still more men, to spread the benefits of this industrial system to the greatest possible number, to help them build up their lives and their homes. To do this we are putting the greatest share of our profits back in the business."

With regard to dividends, the company paid sixty per cent. on its capitalization of two million dollars, or $1,200,000, leaving $58,000,000 to reinvest for the growth of the company. This is Mr. Ford's policy at present, and it is understood that the other stockholders cheerfully accede to this plan.

He had made up his mind in the summer of 1916 that no dividends other than the regular dividends should be paid, "for the present."

"Q. For how long? Had you fixed in your mind any time in the future, when you were going to pay—A. No.

"Q. That was indefinite in the future? A. That was indefinite; yes, sir."

The record, and especially the testimony of Mr. Ford, convinces that he has to some extent the attitude towards shareholders of one who has dispensed and distributed to them large gains and that they should be content to take what he chooses to give. His testimony creates the impression, also, that he thinks the Ford Motor Company has made too much money, has had too large profits, and that, although large profits might be still earned, a sharing of them with the public, by reducing the price of the output of the company, ought to be undertaken. We have no doubt that certain sentiments, philanthropic and altruistic, creditable to Mr. Ford, had large influence in determining the policy to be pursued by the Ford Motor Company—the policy which has been herein referred to.

It is said by his counsel that:

> "Although a manufacturing corporation cannot engage in humanitarian works as its principal business, the fact that it is organized for profit does not prevent the existence of implied powers to carry on with humanitarian motives such charitable works as are incidental to the main business of the corporation."

. . .

In discussing this proposition, counsel have referred to decisions such as Hawes v. Oakland, 104 U.S. 450, 26 L.Ed. 827. . . . These cases, after all, like all others in which the subject is treated, turn finally upon the point, the question, whether it appears that the directors were not acting for the best interests of the corporation. We do not draw in question, nor do counsel for the plaintiffs do so, the validity of the general proposition stated by counsel nor the soundness of the opinions delivered in the cases cited. The case presented here is not like any of them. The difference between an incidental humanitarian expenditure of corporate funds for the benefit of the employés, like the building of a hospital for their use and the employment of agencies for the betterment of their condition, and a general purpose and plan to benefit mankind at the expense of others, is obvious. There should be no confusion (of which there is evidence) of the duties which Mr. Ford conceives that he and the stockholders owe to the general public and the duties which in law he and his codirectors owe to protesting, minority stockholders. A business corporation is organized and carried on primarily for the profit of the stockholders. The powers of the directors are to be employed for that end. The discretion of directors is to be exercised in the choice of means to attain that end, and does not extend to a change in the end itself, to the reduction of profits, or to the nondistribution of profits among stockholders in order to devote them to other purposes.

. . .

It is said by appellants that the motives of the board members are not material and will not be inquired into by the court so long as their acts are within their lawful powers. As we have pointed out, and the proposition does not require argument to sustain it, it is not within the lawful powers of a board of directors to shape and conduct the affairs of a corporation for the merely incidental benefit of shareholders and for the primary purpose of benefiting others, and no one will contend that, if the avowed purpose of the defendant directors was to sacrifice the interests of shareholders, it would not be the duty of the courts to interfere.

We are not, however, persuaded that we should interfere with the proposed expansion of the business of the Ford Motor Company. In view of the fact that the selling price of products may be increased at any time, the ultimate results of the larger business cannot be certainly estimated. The judges are not business experts. It is recognized that plans must often be made for a long future, for expected competition, for a continuing as well as an immediately profitable venture. The experience of the Ford Motor Company is evidence of capable management of its affairs. . . .

Defendants say, and it is true, that a considerable cash balance must be at all times carried by such a concern. But, as has been stated, there was a large daily, weekly, monthly, receipt of cash. The output was practically continuous and was continuously, and within a few days, turned into cash. Moreover, the contemplated expenditures were not to be immediately made. The large sum appropriated for the smelter plant was payable over a considerable period of time. So that, without going further, it would appear that, accepting and approving the plan of the directors, it was their duty to distribute on or near the 1st of August, 1916, a very large sum of money to stockholders.

. . .

[The Court reversed the portion of the decree of the lower court enjoining the building of the smelting plant, but upheld the portion of that decree ordering the payment of a dividend of $19.3 million.]

Shlensky v. Wrigley

95 Ill.App.2d 173, 237 N.E.2d 776 (1968).

This is an appeal from a dismissal of plaintiff's amended complaint on motion of the defendants. The action was a stockholders' derivative suit against the directors for negligence and mismanagement. The corporation was also made a defendant. Plaintiff sought damages and an order that defendants cause the installation of lights in Wrigley Field and the scheduling of night baseball games.

Plaintiff is a minority stockholder of defendant corporation, Chicago National League Ball Club (Inc.), a Delaware corporation with its principal place of business in Chicago, Illinois. Defendant corporation owns and operates the major league professional baseball team known as the Chicago Cubs. The corporation also engages in the operation of Wrigley Field, the Cubs' home park, the concessionaire sales during Cubs' home games, television and radio broadcasts of Cubs' home games, the leasing of the field for football games and other events and receives its share, as visiting team, of admission moneys from games played in other National League stadia. The individual defendants are directors of the Cubs and have served for varying periods of years. Defendant Philip K. Wrigley is also president of the corporation and owner of approximately 80% of the stock therein.

Plaintiff alleges that since night baseball was first played in 1935 nineteen of the twenty major league teams have scheduled night games. In 1966, out of a total of 1620 games in the major leagues, 932 were played at night. Plaintiff alleges that every member of the major leagues, other than the Cubs, scheduled substantially all of its home games in 1966 at night, exclusive of opening days, Saturdays, Sundays, holidays and days prohibited by league rules. Allegedly this has been done for the specific purpose of maximizing attendance and thereby maximizing revenue and income.

The Cubs, in the years 1961–65, sustained operating losses from its direct baseball operations. Plaintiff attributes those losses to inadequate attendance at Cubs' home games. He concludes that if the directors continue to refuse to install lights at Wrigley Field and schedule night baseball games, the Cubs will continue to sustain comparable losses and its financial condition will continue to deteriorate.

Plaintiff alleges that, except for the year 1963, attendance at Cubs' home games has been substantially below that at their road games, many of which were played at night.

Plaintiff compares attendance at Cubs' games with that of the Chicago White Sox, an American League club, whose weekday games were generally played at night. The weekend attendance figures for the two teams were similar; however, the White Sox week-night games drew many more patrons than did the Cubs' weekday games.

Plaintiff alleges that the funds for the installation of lights can be readily obtained through financing and the cost of installation would be far more than offset and recaptured by increased revenues and incomes resulting from the increased attendance.

Plaintiff further alleges that defendant Wrigley has refused to install lights, not because of interest in the welfare of the corporation but because of his personal opinions "that baseball is a 'daytime sport' and that the installation of lights and night baseball games will have a deteriorating effect upon the surrounding neighborhood." It is alleged that he has admitted that he is not interested in whether the Cubs would benefit financially from such action because of his concern for the neighborhood, and that he would be willing for the team to play night games if a new stadium were built in Chicago.

Plaintiff alleges that the other defendant directors, with full knowledge of the foregoing matters, have acquiesced in the policy laid down by Wrigley and have permitted him to dominate the board of directors in matters involving the installation of lights and scheduling of night games, even though they knew he was not motivated by a good faith concern as to the best interests of defendant corporation, but solely by his personal views set forth above. It is charged that the directors are acting for a reason or reasons contrary and wholly unrelated to the business interests of the corporation; that such arbitrary and capricious acts constitute mismanagement and waste of corporate assets, and that the directors have been negligent in failing to exercise reasonable care and prudence in the management of the corporate affairs.

The question on appeal is whether plaintiff's amended complaint states a cause of action. It is plaintiff's position that fraud, illegality and conflict of interest are not the only bases for a stockholder's derivative

action against the directors. Contrariwise, defendants argue that the courts will not step in and interfere with honest business judgment of the directors unless there is a showing of fraud, illegality or conflict of interest.

The cases in this area are numerous and each differs from the others on a factual basis. However, the courts have pronounced certain ground rules which appear in all cases and which are then applied to the given factual situation. . . .

. . . In Davis v. Louisville Gas & Electric Co., 16 Del.Ch. 157, 142 A. 654, a minority shareholder sought to have the directors enjoined from amending the certificate of incorporation. The court said on page 659:

> "We have then a conflict in view between the responsible managers of a corporation and an overwhelming majority of its stockholders on the one hand and a dissenting minority on the other—a conflict touching matters of business policy, such as has occasioned innumerable applications to courts to intervene and determine which of the two conflicting views should prevail. The response which courts make to such applications is that it is not their function to resolve for corporations questions of policy and business management. The directors are chosen to pass upon such questions and their judgment *unless shown to be tainted with fraud* is accepted as final. The judgment of the directors of corporations enjoys the benefit of a presumption that it was formed in good faith and was designed to promote the best interests of the corporation they serve." (Emphasis supplied)

Similarly, the court in Toebelman v. Missouri-Kansas Pipe Line Co., D.C., 41 F.Supp. 334, said at page 339:

> "The general legal principle involved is familiar. Citation of authorities is of limited value because the facts of each case differ so widely. Reference may be made to the statement of the rule in Helfman v. American Light & Traction Company, 121 N.J.Eq. 1, 187 A. 540, 550, in which the Court stated the law as follows: 'In a purely business corporation . . . the authority of the directors in the conduct of the business of the corporation must be regarded as absolute when they act within the law, and the court is without authority to substitute its judgment for that of the directors.'"

Plaintiff argues that the allegations of his amended complaint are sufficient to set forth a cause of action under the principles set out in Dodge v. Ford Motor Co., 204 Mich. 459, 170 N.W. 668. In that case plaintiff, owner of about 10% of the outstanding stock, brought suit against the directors seeking payment of additional dividends and the enjoining of further business expansion. In ruling on the request for dividends the court indicated that the motives of Ford in keeping so much money in the corporation for expansion and security were to benefit the public generally and spread the profits out by means of more jobs, etc. The court felt that these were not only far from related to the good of the stockholders, but amounted to a change in the ends of the corporation and that this was not a purpose contemplated or allowed by the corporate charter. . . . [Nonetheless] it is clear that the [*Dodge*] court felt that there must be fraud or a breach of that good faith which directors are bound to exercise toward the stockholders in order to justify the courts entering into the internal affairs of corporations. This is made clear when the court refused to interfere with the directors' decision to expand the business. . . .

Plaintiff in the instant case argues that the directors are acting for reasons unrelated to the financial interest and welfare of the Cubs. However, we are not satisfied that the motives assigned to Philip K. Wrigley, and through him to the other directors, are contrary to the best interests of the corporation and the stockholders. For example, it appears to us that the effect on the surrounding neighborhood might well be considered by a director who was considering the patrons who would or would not attend the games if the park were in a poor neighborhood. Furthermore, the long run interest of the corporation in its property value at Wrigley Field might demand all efforts to keep the neighborhood from deteriorating. By these thoughts we do not mean to say that we have decided that the decision of the directors was a correct one. That is beyond our jurisdiction and ability. We are merely saying that the decision is one properly before directors and the motives alleged in the amended complaint showed no fraud, illegality or conflict of interest in their making of that decision.

While all the courts do not insist that one or more of the three elements must be present for a stockholder's derivative action to lie, nevertheless we feel that unless the conduct of the defendants at least borders on one of the elements, the courts should not interfere. The trial court in the instant case acted properly in dismissing plaintiff's amended complaint.

We feel that plaintiff's amended complaint was also defective in failing to allege damage to the corporation. . . .

There is no allegation that the night games played by the other nineteen teams enhanced their financial position or that the profits, if any, of those teams were directly related to the number of night games scheduled. There is an allegation that the installation of lights and scheduling of night games in Wrigley Field would have resulted in large amounts of additional revenues and incomes from increased attendance and related sources of income. Further, the cost of installation of lights, funds for which are allegedly readily available by financing, would be more than offset and recaptured by increased revenues. However, no allegation is made that there will be a net benefit to the corporation from such action, considering all increased costs.

Plaintiff claims that the losses of defendant corporation are due to poor attendance at home games. However, it appears from the amended complaint, taken as a whole, that factors other than attendance affect the net earnings or losses. For example, in 1962, attendance at home and road games decreased appreciably as compared with 1961, and yet the loss from direct baseball operation and of the whole corporation was considerably less.

The record shows that plaintiff did not feel he could allege that the increased revenues would be sufficient to cure the corporate deficit. The only cost plaintiff was at all concerned with was that of installation of lights. No mention was made of operation and maintenance of the lights or other possible increases in operating costs of night games and we cannot speculate as to what other factors might influence the increase or decrease of profits if the Cubs were to play night home games.

. . . [P]laintiff's allegation that the minority stockholders and the corporation have been seriously and irreparably damaged by the wrongful conduct of the defendant directors is a mere conclusion and not based on well pleaded facts in the amended complaint.

Finally, we do not agree with plaintiff's contention that failure to follow the example of the other major league clubs in scheduling night games constituted negligence. Plaintiff made no allegation that these teams' night schedules were profitable or that the purpose for which night baseball had been undertaken was fulfilled. Furthermore, it cannot be said that directors, even those of corporations that are losing money, must follow the lead of the other corporations in the field. Directors are elected for their business capabilities and judgment and the courts cannot require them to forego their judgment because of the decisions of directors of other companies. Courts may not decide these questions in the absence of a clear showing of dereliction of duty on the part of the specific directors and mere failure to "follow the crowd" is not such a dereliction.

For the foregoing reasons the order of dismissal entered by the trial court is affirmed.

Affirmed.

ANALYSIS

1. If Shlensky was unhappy with the way Wrigley wanted to operate, why did he not just sell his shares?

2. Does the decision in the case leave open the possibility that Shlensky might have prevailed?

3. Suppose you represent Shlensky, that the case is being tried, and that you have called Wrigley as a hostile witness. What strategy would you adopt in your questioning of him?

NOTE: THE AMERICAN LAW INSTITUTE APPROACH

The American Law Institute took the following approach in § 2.01 of its Principles of Corporate Governance: Analysis and Recommendations (1994):

> (a) Subject to the provisions of Subsection (b) and § 6.02 (Action of Directors That Has the Foreseeable Effect of Blocking Unsolicited Tender Offers), a corporation should have as its objective the conduct of business activities with a view to enhancing corporate profit and shareholder gain.
>
> (b) Even if corporate profit and shareholder gain are not thereby enhanced, the corporation, in the conduct of its business:
>
> > (1) Is obliged, to the same extent as a natural person, to act within the boundaries set by law;

(2) May take into account ethical considerations that are reasonably regarded as appropriate to the responsible conduct of business; and

(3) May devote a reasonable amount of resources to public welfare, humanitarian, educational, and philanthropic purposes.*

PROBLEMS

1. Ann and Bill long ago established a salami making business, with a factory, machinery, etc. For many years they made high-quality salami. Ann died several years ago and left her share of the business to her daughter Carol. Carol is an expert in marketing and thinks the salami can be made at lower cost by using cheaper meat and more nitrate and that this will have no adverse effect on sales. She has strong evidence to support her position. Bill does not disagree with her facts but says that he and Ann always believed in making a high-quality product because that way they slept better. Moreover, if the method of making salami were changed, there would no longer be jobs for some of the long-time employees, and Bill feels an obligation to them. If the business is in corporate form and Bill owns 60 percent, is President, and controls the board of directors, what chance does Carol have in succeeding by litigation in forcing Bill to abandon his old-style methods of making salami and adopting her proposals?

2. The basic facts about Bill and Carol and the salami factory are the same as in the preceding problem. Bill has a heart attack, following which he becomes well informed about the role of animal fat in coronary artery disease. Carol's income consists entirely of her dividends from the corporation. Bill has substantial income from other sources. Bill decides that salami is bad for one's health; it substantially increases the risk of heart attacks. He wants to produce low-fat salami. He says that he must do this as a matter of social responsibility. He admits that this will reduce, and possibly even eliminate, profits. Since he is wealthy he doesn't care about profits. If Bill proceeds with his plan for producing low-fat salami, does Carol have a good cause of action? Should she have? If she does, what is the proper remedy? What if Bill had claimed that it would be possible to make big profits from low-fat salami?

NOTE: THE PUBLIC BENEFIT CORPORATION

In 2013 Delaware enacted new provisions to its General Corporation Law allowing the formation of a new hybrid type of entity called a "public benefit corporation" (PBC). A PBC is defined in § 362 as a "for-profit corporation . . . that is intended to produce a public benefit or benefits and to operate in a responsible and sustainable manner." The "public benefit" must be specified in the firm's certificate of incorporation and consist of "a positive effect . . . on one or more categories of persons, entities, communities or interests (other than stockholders in their capacities as stockholders) including, but not limited to, effects of an artistic, charitable, cultural, economic, educational, environmental, literary, medical, religious, scientific or technological nature." Existing for-profit corporations may convert to PBCs only with the approval of 90 percent of outstanding shares, with the dissenting shareholders entitled to appraisal (that is, the right to be cashed out at fair market value). The PBC must, at least biennially, provide its shareholders with a statement that includes "objective factual information . . . regarding [its] success in meeting [its] objectives for promoting [its specified] public benefits and interests."

Other states have adopted similar provisions, with variations, particularly as to public disclosure, and third-party assessment, of the public benefit.

If a case like Dodge v. Ford Motor Company were to arise today, would the availability of this type of organization add force to the plaintiffs' argument? What might be the relevance to this question of a provision such as § 368 of the Delaware PBC law, which provides that enactment of the new set of provisions "shall not affect a statute or rule of law that is applicable to a corporation that is not a public benefit corporation"?

CHAPTER 4

THE LIMITED LIABILITY COMPANY

The Limited Liability Company (LLC) is an alternative form of business organization that combines certain features of the corporate form with others more closely resembling general partnerships. In an LLC the investors are called "members." Like the traditional corporation, the LLC provides a liability shield for its members. It allows somewhat more flexibility than the corporation in developing rules for management and control. The LLC may be managed by all its members (as in a partnership) or by managers, who may or may not be members (as in a corporation). The LLC also offers advantageous tax treatment as compared with a corporation. A corporation pays tax on its profits as earned and the shareholders (the equity investors) pay a second tax when those profits are distributed to them. Investors in an LLC are taxed, like partners, only once on its profits, as those profits are earned. Moreover, the investors in an LLC can take account, on their individual tax returns, of any losses of the LLC as those losses are incurred; the losses are said to "pass through." A corporation's losses can be carried forward to offset any future profits but cannot be used by its shareholders. In addition, the LLC allows greater freedom than a corporation in allocating profit and loss for tax purposes.

The formation of an LLC, like the formation of a corporation, requires some paperwork and filings with a state agency. Some states impose fees and taxes (generally modest) on LLCs that are not imposed on partnerships.

Another recent development is the Limited Liability Partnership (LLP). Limited liability is achieved by filing a document with a state official. Most LLP statutes provide limited liability only for partnership debts arising from negligence and similar misconduct (other than misconduct for which the partner is directly responsible), not for contractual obligations, although a few provide protection for both contract and tort liabilities. The principal impetus for the enactment of the first LLP legislation, in Texas in 1991, was the concern of lawyers for malpractice liability, following the collapse of the savings and loan industry and the potentially devastating effect of the collapse of one such institution on a leading Dallas law firm. See Robert W. Hamilton, Registered Limited Liability Partnerships: Present at the Birth (Nearly), 66 U. Colo. L. Rev. 1065, 1069 (1995). Professor Hamilton noted that "more than 1,200 law firms, including virtually all of the state's largest firms, elected to become LLPs within one year after . . . enactment" of the Texas LLP legislation. Id. at 1065. All 50 states now have LLP legislation.

1. FORMATION

Duray Development, LLC v. Perrin

288 Mich.App. 143, 792 N.W.2d 749 (2010).

. . .

I. BASIC FACTS AND PROCEDURAL HISTORY

Duray Development is a residential development company whose sole member is Robert Munger. . . . In 2004, Duray Development purchased 40 acres of undeveloped property . . . in Caledonia Township, Michigan.

On September 30, 2004, Duray Development entered into a contract with Perrin [and] Perrin Excavating, . . .for excavating [the property]. In that contract, . . . Perrin signed on behalf of himself and Perrin Excavating,. . . .

On October 27, 2004, Duray Development and Perrin entered into a new contract, intended to supersede the September 30, 2004 contract. The new contract contained the same language and provisions as the earlier contract. However, the new contract was between Duray Development and Outlaw [Excavating, LLC], and Perrin and Perrin Excavating . . . were not parties. Outlaw was an excavation company that Perrin . . . had recently formed. Perrin . . . signed the new contract on behalf of Outlaw, and held [himself] out to Duray Development as the owner . . . of the company. . . . Once [the contract was] signed, all parties proceeded under the contract as if Outlaw were the contractor for the Copper Corners development.

Two contracts were drafted because Perrin had not yet formed Outlaw at the time of the first contract. However, Duray Development did not want to wait for Perrin to finish forming the company before starting the excavation. . . . Therefore, the parties entered into the first contract on September 30, 2004, and then entered into the second contract once the parties thought Outlaw was a valid limited liability company.

Defendants began excavation and grading work pursuant to the contracts, but did not perform satisfactorily or on time. Duray Development then sued defendants for breach of contract. . . . Duray Development later learned through discovery that Outlaw did not obtain a "filed" status as a limited liability company until November 29, 2004, and therefore Outlaw was not a valid limited liability company at the time the parties executed the second contract.[1]

. . . After trial, the trial court ruled in favor of Duray Development, finding that Perrin was in breach of contract and owed $96,367.68 in damages to Duray Development.

In a posttrial memorandum, Perrin argued that he was not personally liable for Duray Development's damages. He asserted that, although Outlaw was not a valid limited liability company at the time of

---

1 According to the Limited Liability Company Act, MCL 450.4101 et seq., a limited liability company does not exist until the state administrator endorses the articles of organization with the word "filed." MCL 450.4104(2) and (6).

the execution of the second contract, Outlaw was nevertheless liable to Duray Development under the doctrine of de facto corporation. The trial court opined that if Outlaw were a corporation, then the de facto corporation doctrine most likely would have applied. However, the trial court concluded that the Limited Liability Company Act "clearly and specifically provides for the time that a limited liability company comes into existence and has powers to contract" and therefore superseded the de facto corporation doctrine and made it inapplicable to limited liability companies altogether. Perrin now appeals.

Perrin argument

II. PERRIN'S PERSONAL LIABILITY

A. STANDARD OF REVIEW

. . . According to Perrin, even though Outlaw was not yet a properly formed limited liability company, the parties all treated the contract as though Outlaw was a properly formed limited liability company and, therefore, the doctrine of de facto corporation shielded Perrin from personal liability. He further argues that the doctrine of corporation by estoppel precluded Duray Development from arguing that he is personally liable.

. . .

THE LIMITED LIABILITY COMPANY ACT

The Limited Liability Company Act provides precisely when a limited liability company comes into existence. MCL 450.4202(2) provides that "[t]he existence of the limited liability company begins on the effective date of the articles of organization as provided in [MCL 450.4104]." MCL 450.4104(1) requires that the articles of organization be delivered to the administrator of the Michigan Department of Energy, Labor and Economic Growth (DELEG). Under MCL 450.4104(2), after delivery of the articles of organization, "the administrator shall endorse upon it the word 'filed' with his or her official title and the date of receipt and of filing[.]" And under MCL 450.4104(6), "[a] document filed under [MCL 450.4104(2)] is effective at the time it is endorsed[.]"

. . .

In this case, Perrin signed the articles of organization for Outlaw on the same day as the second contract, October 27, 2004. Perrin then signed the October 27, 2004 contract on behalf of Outlaw. However, the DELEG administrator did not endorse the articles of organization until November 29, 2004. Therefore, pursuant to the Limited Liability Company Act, Outlaw was not in existence on October 27, 2004. And Outlaw did not adopt or ratify the second contract. Therefore, Perrin became personally liable for Outlaw's obligations unless a de facto limited liability company existed or limited liability company by estoppel applied.

C. DE FACTO CORPORATION AND CORPORATION BY ESTOPPEL

De facto corporation and corporation by estoppel are separate and distinct doctrines that warrant individual treatment. The de facto corporation doctrine provides that a defectively formed corporation—that is, one that fails to meet the technical requirements for forming a de jure corporation—may attain the legal status of a de facto corporation if certain requirements are met, as discussed later in this opinion. The most important aspect of a de facto corporation is that courts perceive and treat it in all respects as if it were a properly formed de jure corporation. . . .

Corporation by estoppel, on the other hand, is an equitable remedy and does not concern legal status. The general rule is: "Where a body assumes to be a corporation and acts under a particular name, a third party dealing with it under such assumed name is estopped to deny its corporate existence."[20] . . . [T]he de facto corporation doctrine establishes the legal existence of the corporation. By contrast, the corporation by estoppel doctrine merely prevents one from arguing against it, and does nothing to establish its actual existence in the eyes of the rest of the world.

. . .

D. THE DE FACTO CORPORATION DOCTRINE

The Michigan Supreme Court established the four elements for a de facto corporation long ago:

> "When incorporators have [1] proceeded in good faith, [2] under a valid statute, [3] for an authorized purpose, and [4] have executed and acknowledged articles of association pursuant to that purpose, a corporation de facto instantly comes into being. A de facto corporation is an actual corporation. As to all the world, except the State, it enjoys the status and powers of a de jure corporation."[25]

Here, there is no question that elements (2), (3), and (4) were satisfied. . . .

It is less obvious whether the first element of the doctrine—good faith—was satisfied. There is little guidance in Michigan caselaw for a definition, or application, of this specific element. But in Newcomb-Endicott Co. v. Fee,[26] the Michigan Supreme Court, although applying a different set of elements, did state that in the absence of a claim or evidence of fraud or false representation on the part of the incorporators, and in light of a bona fide attempt to incorporate, there was no reason to deny a company the status of a de facto corporation.

Here, Duray Development does not allege that Perrin set up the corporation through fraud or false representations; that is, Duray Development does not allege that Perrin set up the corporation as a sham, for fraudulent purposes, or as a mere instrumentality under a theory of piercing the corporate veil. Rather, as the record indicates, Duray Development did not learn until after filing the complaint in this case that Outlaw was not a valid limited liability company on October 27, 2004. Duray Development at all times dealt with Outlaw as a valid corporation [sic] with which it contracted. Duray Development's sole member, Munger, testified that once the second contract took effect, Duray Development no longer considered Perrin or Perrin Excavating as parties to the contract, but instead considered Outlaw to be the new "contractor." There is no evidence whatsoever to suggest that Perrin formed Outlaw in anything other than good faith. Accordingly, the trial court was correct to conclude that, had Outlaw been formed as a

---

20 [Estey Mfg. Co. v. Runnells, 55 Mich. 130, 133, 20 N.W. 823 (1884).]

25 Tisch Auto Supply [Co. v. Nelson], 222 Mich. [196,] 200, 192 N.W. 600 [(1923)]. . . .

26 167 Mich. [574,] 582, 133 N.W. 540 [(1911)].

corporation instead of a limited liability company, it would have been a de facto corporation for purposes of liability on the October 27, 2004 contract. Thus, all elements of a de facto corporation were present in this case.

The trial court, however, concluded that the de facto *corporation* doctrine does not apply to *limited liability companies* and therefore did not apply to Outlaw. It reasoned that the plain reading of the Limited Liability Company Act "clearly and specifically provides for the time that a limited liability company comes into existence and has powers to contract." . . .

Neither this Court nor the Supreme Court has addressed whether the de facto corporation doctrine can be extended or applied to a limited liability company. That is not to say, however, that the doctrine cannot be applied to a limited liability company. . . .

. . . [T]he similarities between the Business Corporation Act and the Limited Liability Company Act support the conclusion that the de facto corporation doctrine applies to both. The purposes for forming a limited liability company and a corporation are similar. Notably, the Limited Liability Company Act states, "A limited liability company may be formed under this act for any lawful purpose for which a domestic corporation or a domestic partnership could be formed, except as otherwise provided by law."[36] Further, both the Limited Liability Company Act and the Business Corporation Act contemplate the moment in time when a limited liability company or corporation comes into existence. Because the Business Corporation Act and the Limited Liability Company Act relate to the common purpose of forming a business and because both statutes contemplate the moment of existence for each, they should be interpreted in a consistent manner.

Accordingly, we conclude that the de facto corporation doctrine applies to Outlaw, a limited liability company. As a result, Outlaw, and not Perrin, individually, is liable for the breach of the October 27, 2004 contract.

E. CORPORATION BY ESTOPPEL

. . . The Supreme Court in Estey Mfg. Co. v. Runnells,[41] summarized the principle of corporation by estoppel as follows: "Where a body assumes to be a corporation and acts under a particular name, a third party dealing with it under such assumed name is estopped to deny its corporate existence."

As with the doctrine of de facto corporation, this Court has not addressed whether corporation by estoppel can be applied to limited liability companies. However, corporation by estoppel is an equitable remedy, and its purpose is to prevent one who contracts with a corporation from later denying its existence in order to hold the individual officers or partners liable. . . .

With this in mind, and in light of the purpose of corporation by estoppel, the corporate structure has little impact on the equitable principles at stake. In other words, there is no reason or purpose to draw a distinction on the basis of corporate form. Furthermore, like de facto

---

[36] MCL 450.4201; see also MCL 450.1251(1).

[41] [55 Mich. 130, 133, 20 N.W. 823 (1884).]

corporation, because corporation by estoppel coexists with the Business Corporation Act, so too can it coexist with the Limited Liability Company Act.

. . .

. . . [H]ere, the record clearly supports a finding of "limited liability company by estoppel" through the extension of the corporation by estoppel doctrine. Perrin was an individual party to the first contract, as was his limited liability company, Perrin Excavating. However, only Outlaw became a party to the second contract, which superseded the first. And all parties dealt with the second contract as though Outlaw were a party. After the second contract, Duray Development received billings from Outlaw, and not from Perrin. Duray Development also received a certificate of liability insurance for Outlaw. Munger testified that he dealt with Perrin, Perrin Excavating, and KDM Excavating before the second contract and only dealt with Outlaw after. Duray Development continued to assume Outlaw was a valid limited liability company after filing the lawsuit and only learned of the filing and contract discrepancies once litigation began in July 2006.

. . .

ANALYSIS

1. Suppose that Perrin, chronically short of funds, finds it hard both to hire a lawyer to form a new firm and to keep his excavating equipment properly maintained. Perrin discusses this problem with Munger (Duray's owner), and Munger encourages him to defer hiring a lawyer. "Keep your equipment maintained," he tells Perrin. "You can always form your LLC later." Perrin takes his advice, and does not hire a lawyer. Does either the de facto or the estoppel doctrine apply? Does the analysis depend on whether Munger is suing Perrin, or the mechanic who worked on Perrin's excavating equipment is suing Perrin?

2. Suppose that Perrin had failed to pay his legal bills and that, as a result his lawyer, after preparing initial drafts of the required documents for forming an LLC, refused to do any more work until Perrin finally paid, months later as the work on the Duray project was coming to an end. Would, and should, Perrin still be entitled to the benefit of the de facto LLC or estoppel doctrine?

3. Obviously, both the de facto corporation doctrine and the corporation by estoppel doctrine originated in corporate law. The drafters of the Model Business Corporation Act (MBCA) have repeatedly tried to abolish these doctrines by statute. Section 50 the 1969 MBCA required that a certificate of incorporation be issued in order for a de jure corporation to exist and § 139 imposed full personal liability on the promoters unless a de jure corporation existed. In the comments to § 50, the drafters stated that these provisions intended to abolish the de facto corporation doctrine.

The 1984 MBCA's drafters recognized that courts were resisting their predecessors' attempt to abolish the de facto corporation and corporation by estoppel doctrines. Accordingly, the drafters chose to relax the statutory standard slightly. MBCA § 2.04 now provides: "All persons purporting to act as or on behalf of a corporation, knowing there was no incorporation under [the MBCA], are jointly and severally liable for all liabilities created while so acting." By negative inference, neither inactive investors nor active investors who are unaware of the defective incorporation may be held personally liable.

What policy arguments, if any, support the MBCA drafters' efforts to eliminate the common law doctrines?

2. THE OPERATING AGREEMENT

Elf Atochem North America, Inc. v. Jaffari

727 A.2d 286 (Del. Sup. Ct. 1999).

■ VEASEY, CHIEF JUSTICE:

. . .

This is a purported derivative suit brought on behalf of a Delaware LLC calling into question whether: (1) the LLC, which did not itself execute the LLC agreement in this case ("the Agreement") defining its governance and operation, is nevertheless bound by the Agreement; and (2) contractual provisions directing that all disputes be resolved exclusively by arbitration or court proceedings in California are valid under the Act. Resolution of these issues requires us to examine the applicability and scope of certain provisions of the Act in light of the Agreement.

We hold that: (1) the Agreement is binding on the LLC as well as the members; and (2) since the Act does not prohibit the members of an LLC from vesting exclusive subject matter jurisdiction in arbitration proceedings (or court enforcement of arbitration) in California to resolve disputes, the contractual forum selection provisions must govern.

Accordingly, we affirm the judgment of the Court of Chancery dismissing the action brought in that court on the ground that the Agreement validly predetermined the fora in which disputes would be resolved, thus stripping the Court of Chancery of subject matter jurisdiction.

Facts

Plaintiff below-appellant Elf Atochem North America, Inc., a Pennsylvania Corporation ("Elf"), manufactures and distributes solvent-based maskants to the aerospace and aviation industries throughout the world. Defendant below-appellee Cyrus A. Jaffari is the president of Malek, Inc., a California Corporation. Jaffari had developed an innovative, environmentally-friendly alternative to the solvent-based maskants that presently dominate the market.

For decades, the aerospace and aviation industries have used solvent-based maskants in the chemical milling process.[3] Recently, however, the Environmental Protection Agency ("EPA") classified solvent-based maskants as hazardous chemicals and air contaminants.

---

[3] Manufacturers of airplanes and missiles use maskants in the process of chemical milling in order to reduce the weight of their products. Chemical milling is a process where a caustic substance is placed on metal parts in order to dissolve the metal with which it comes into contact. Maskants are used to protect those areas of metal intended to be preserved.

To avoid conflict with EPA regulations, Elf considered developing or distributing a maskant less harmful to the environment.

In the mid-nineties, Elf approached Jaffari and proposed investing in his product and assisting in its marketing. Jaffari found the proposal attractive since his company, Malek, Inc., possessed limited resources and little international sales expertise. Elf and Jaffari agreed to undertake a joint venture that was to be carried out using a limited liability company as the vehicle.

On October 29, 1996, Malek, Inc. caused to be filed a Certificate of Formation with the Delaware Secretary of State, thus forming Malek LLC, a Delaware limited liability company under the Act. The certificate of formation is a relatively brief and formal document that is the first statutory step in creating the LLC as a separate legal entity. The certificate does not contain a comprehensive agreement among the parties, and the statute contemplates that the certificate of formation is to be complemented by the terms of the Agreement.

Next, Elf, Jaffari and Malek, Inc. entered into a series of agreements providing for the governance and operation of the joint venture. Of particular importance to this litigation, Elf, Malek, Inc., and Jaffari entered into the Agreement, a comprehensive and integrated document of 38 single-spaced pages setting forth detailed provisions for the governance of Malek LLC, which is not itself a signatory to the Agreement. Elf and Malek LLC entered into an Exclusive Distributorship Agreement in which Elf would be the exclusive, worldwide distributor for Malek LLC. The Agreement provides that Jaffari will be the manager of Malek LLC. Jaffari and Malek LLC entered into an employment agreement providing for Jaffari's employment as chief executive officer of Malek LLC.

The Agreement is the operative document for purposes of this Opinion, however. Under the Agreement, Elf contributed $1 million in exchange for a 30 percent interest in Malek LLC. Malek, Inc. contributed its rights to the water-based maskant in exchange for a 70 percent interest in Malek LLC. The Agreement contains an arbitration clause covering all disputes. The clause, Section 13.8, provides that "any controversy or dispute arising out of this Agreement, the interpretation of any of the provisions hereof, or the action or inaction of any Member or Manager hereunder shall be submitted to arbitration in San Francisco, California. . . ." Section 13.8 further provides: "No action . . . based upon any claim arising out of or related to this Agreement shall be instituted in any court by any Member except (a) an action to compel arbitration . . . or (b) an action to enforce an award obtained in an arbitration proceeding. . . ." The Agreement also contains a forum selection clause, Section 13.7, providing that all members consent to: "exclusive jurisdiction of the state and federal courts sitting in California in any action on a claim arising out of, under or in connection with this Agreement or the transactions contemplated by this Agreement, provided such claim is not required to be arbitrated pursuant to Section 13.8"; and personal jurisdiction in California. The Distribution Agreement contains no forum selection or arbitration clause.

Elf's Suit in the Court of Chancery

On April 27, 1998, Elf sued Jaffari and Malek LLC, individually and derivatively on behalf of Malek LLC, in the Delaware Court of Chancery, seeking equitable remedies. Among other claims, Elf alleged that Jaffari breached his fiduciary duty to Malek LLC, pushed Malek LLC to the brink of insolvency by withdrawing funds for personal use, interfered with business opportunities, failed to make disclosures to Elf, and threatened to make poor quality maskant and to violate environmental regulations. Elf also alleged breach of contract, tortious interference with prospective business relations, and (solely as to Jaffari) fraud.

The Court of Chancery granted defendants' motion to dismiss based on lack of subject matter jurisdiction. The court held that Elf's claims arose under the Agreement, or the transactions contemplated by the agreement, and were directly related to Jaffari's actions as manager of Malek LLC. Therefore, the court found that the Agreement governed the question of jurisdiction and that only a court of law or arbitrator in California is empowered to decide these claims. Elf now appeals the order of the Court of Chancery dismissing the complaint.

. . .

General Summary of Background of the Act

The phenomenon of business arrangements using "alternative entities" has been developing rapidly over the past several years. Long gone are the days when business planners were confined to corporate or partnership structures.

[The court describes the history of the adoption and amendment of the Delaware Limited Partnership (LP) Act, the present version of which is based on the Revised Uniform Limited Partnership Act (RULPA).]

The Delaware [LLC] Act was adopted in October 1992. . . . The LLC is an attractive form of business entity because it combines corporate-type limited liability with partnership-type flexibility and tax advantages. The Act can be characterized as a "flexible statute" because it generally permits members to engage in private ordering with substantial freedom of contract to govern their relationship, provided they do not contravene any mandatory provisions of the Act. . . .

The Delaware Act has been modeled on the popular Delaware LP Act. In fact, its architecture and much of its wording is almost identical to that of the Delaware LP Act. Under the Act, a member of an LLC is treated much like a limited partner under the LP Act. The policy of freedom of contract underlies both the Act and the LP Act.

. . .

Policy of the Delaware Act

The basic approach of the Delaware Act is to provide members with broad discretion in drafting the Agreement and to furnish default provisions when the members' agreement is silent. The Act is replete with fundamental provisions made subject to modification in the Agreement (e.g. "unless otherwise provided in a limited liability company agreement. . . .").[26]

---

[26] . . . For example, members are free to contract among themselves concerning management of the LLC, including who is to manage the LLC, the establishment of classes of

Although business planners may find comfort in working with the Act in structuring transactions and relationships, it is a somewhat awkward document for this Court to construe and apply in this case. To understand the overall structure and thrust of the Act, one must wade through provisions that are prolix, sometimes oddly organized, and do not always flow evenly. Be that as it may as a problem in mastering the Act as a whole, one returns to the narrow and discrete issues presented in this case.

Freedom of Contract

Section 18–1101(b) of the Act, like the essentially identical Section 17–1101(c) of the LP Act, provides that "[i]t is the policy of [the Act] to give the maximum effect to the principle of freedom of contract and to the enforceability of limited liability company agreements." Accordingly, the following observation relating to limited partnerships applies as well to limited liability companies:

> The Act's basic approach is to permit partners to have the broadest possible discretion in drafting their partnership agreements and to furnish answers only in situations where the partners have not expressly made provisions in their partnership agreement. Truly, the partnership agreement is the cornerstone of a Delaware limited partnership, and effectively constitutes the entire agreement among the partners with respect to the admission of partners to, and the creation, operation and termination of, the limited partnership. Once partners exercise their contractual freedom in their partnership agreement, the partners have a great deal of certainty that their partnership agreement will be enforced in accordance with its terms.[27]

In general, the commentators observe that only where the agreement is inconsistent with mandatory statutory provisions will the members' agreement be invalidated. Such statutory provisions are likely to be those intended to protect third parties, not necessarily the contracting members. As a framework for decision, we apply that principle to the issues before us, without expressing any views more broadly.

The Arbitration and Forum Selection Clauses in the Agreement are a Bar to Jurisdiction in the Court of Chancery

In vesting the Court of Chancery with jurisdiction, the Act accomplished at least three purposes: (1) it assured that the Court of Chancery has jurisdiction it might not otherwise have because it is a court of limited jurisdiction that requires traditional equitable relief or specific legislation to act; (2) it established the Court of Chancery as the default forum in the event the members did not provide another choice of forum or dispute resolution mechanism; and (3) it tends to center interpretive litigation in Delaware courts with the expectation of uniformity. Nevertheless, the arbitration provision of the Agreement in this case fosters the Delaware policy favoring alternate dispute

---

members, voting, procedures for holding meetings of members, or considering matters without a meeting.

[27] Martin I. Lubaroff & Paul Altman, Delaware Limited Partnerships § 1.2 (1999) (footnote omitted). . . .

resolution mechanisms, including arbitration. Such mechanisms are an important goal of Delaware legislation, court rules, and jurisprudence.

Malek LLC's Failure to Sign the Agreement Does Not Affect the Members' Agreement Governing Dispute Resolution

Elf argues that because Malek LLC, on whose behalf Elf allegedly brings these claims, is not a party to the Agreement, the derivative claims it brought on behalf of Malek LLC are not governed by the arbitration and forum selection clauses of the Agreement.

. . .

We are not persuaded by this argument. Section 18–101(7) defines the limited liability company agreement as "any agreement, written or oral, of the member or members as to the affairs of a limited liability company and the conduct of its business." Here, Malek, Inc. and Elf, the members of Malek LLC, executed the Agreement to carry out the affairs and business of Malek LLC and to provide for arbitration and forum selection.

Notwithstanding Malek LLC's failure to sign the Agreement, Elf's claims are subject to the arbitration and forum selection clauses of the Agreement. The Act is a statute designed to permit members maximum flexibility in entering into an agreement to govern their relationship. It is the members who are the real parties in interest. The LLC is simply their joint business vehicle. This is the contemplation of the statute in prescribing the outlines of a limited liability company agreement.

Classification by Elf of its Claims as Derivative is Irrelevant

Elf argues that the Court of Chancery erred in failing to classify its claims against Malek LLC as derivative. Elf contends that, had the court properly characterized its claims as derivative instead of direct, the arbitration and forum selection clauses would not have applied to bar adjudication in Delaware.

. . .

Although Elf correctly points out that Delaware law allows for derivative suits against management of an LLC, Elf contracted away its right to bring such an action in Delaware and agreed instead to dispute resolution in California. That is, Section 13.8 of the Agreement specifically provides that the parties (i.e., Elf) agree to institute "[n]o action at law or in equity based upon any claim arising out of or related to this Agreement" except an action to compel arbitration or to enforce an arbitration award. Furthermore, under Section 13.7 of the Agreement, each member (i.e., Elf) "consent[ed] to the exclusive jurisdiction of the state and federal courts sitting in California in any action on a claim arising out of, under or in connection with this Agreement or the transactions contemplated by this Agreement."

Sections 13.7 and 13.8 of the Agreement do not distinguish between direct and derivative claims. They simply state that the members may not initiate any claims outside of California. Elf initiated this action in the Court of Chancery in contravention of its own contractual agreement. As a result, the Court of Chancery correctly held that all claims, whether derivative or direct, arose under, out of or in connection with the Agreement, and thus are covered by the arbitration and forum selection clauses.

This prohibition is so broad that it is dispositive of Elf's claims . . . that purport to be under the Distributorship Agreement that has no choice of forum provision. Notwithstanding the fact that the Distributorship Agreement is a separate document, in reality these counts are all subsumed under the rubric of the Agreement's forum selection clause for any claim "arising out of" and those that are "in connection with" the Agreement or transactions "contemplated by" or "related to" that Agreement under Sections 13.7 and 13.8. . . .

The Court of Chancery was correct in holding that Elf's claims bear directly on Jaffari's duties and obligations under the Agreement. Thus, we decline to disturb its holding.

The Argument that Chancery Has "Special" Jurisdiction for Derivative Claims Must Fail

Elf claims that 6 Del.C. §§ 18–110(a), 18–111 and 18–1001 vest the Court of Chancery with subject matter jurisdiction over this dispute. According to Elf, the Act grants the Court of Chancery subject matter jurisdiction over its claims for breach of fiduciary duty and removal of Jaffari, even though the parties contracted to arbitrate all such claims in California. In effect, Elf argues that the Act affords the Court of Chancery "special" jurisdiction to adjudicate its claims, notwithstanding a clear contractual agreement to the contrary.

Again, we are not persuaded by Elf's argument. Elf is correct that 6 Del.C. §§ 18–110(a) and 18–111 vest jurisdiction with the Court of Chancery in actions involving removal of managers and interpreting, applying or enforcing LLC agreements respectively. As noted above, Section 18–1001 provides that a party may bring derivative actions in the Court of Chancery. Such a grant of jurisdiction may have been constitutionally necessary if the claims do not fall within the traditional equity jurisdiction. Nevertheless, for the purpose of designating a more convenient forum, we find no reason why the members cannot alter the default jurisdictional provisions of the statute and contract away their right to file suit in Delaware.

. . . [B]ecause the policy of the Act is to give the maximum effect to the principle of freedom of contract and to the enforceability of LLC agreements, the parties may contract to avoid the applicability of Sections 18–110(a), 18–111, and 18–1001. . . .

Our conclusion is bolstered by the fact that Delaware recognizes a strong public policy in favor of arbitration. Normally, doubts on the issue of whether a particular issue is arbitrable will be resolved in favor of arbitration. . . . If we were to hold otherwise, arbitration clauses in existing LLC agreements could be rendered meaningless. By resorting to the alleged "special" jurisdiction 296 of the Court of Chancery, future plaintiffs could avoid their own arbitration agreements simply by couching their claims as derivative. Such a result could adversely affect many arbitration agreements already in existence in Delaware.

. . .

ANALYSIS

1. Elf obviously objected to arbitration in California (or perhaps anywhere). So why did it agree to the arbitration clause?

2. Suppose that the parties had included in their LLC operating agreement a provision of the following sort:

> Each member agrees that the other shall be relieved of and immune to liability for any act against the other or against the LLC, whether in tort or contract or in law or equity, regardless of any allegation of willfulness, intention, or gross negligence.

What result?

3. What result if the vehicle for the joint venture had been a corporation rather than an LLC?

4. Is there any good reason why the parties should not be allowed to contract as to jurisdiction and arbitration?

Fisk Ventures, LLC v. Segal

2008 WL 1961156 (Del. Ch.), aff'd sub nom., Segal v. Fisk Ventures, LLC, 984 A.2d 124 (Del. 2009).

. . .

I. BACKGROUND

. . .

A. The Company, its Structure, and the LLC Agreement

Genitrix, LLC, is a Delaware limited liability company formed to develop and market biomedical technology. Dr. Segal founded the Company in 1996 following his postdoctoral fellowship at the Whitehead Institute for Biomedical Research [at MIT]. Originally formed as a Maryland limited liability company, Genitrix was moved in 1997 to Delaware at the behest of Dr. H. Fisk Johnson, who invested heavily.

Equity in Genitrix is divided into three classes of membership. In exchange for the patent rights he obtained from the Whitehead Institute, Segal's capital account was credited with $500,000. This allowed him to retain approximately 55% of the Class A membership interest. The remainder of the Class A interest was apparently granted to other individuals not involved in this suit. In the initial round of investment, Johnson contributed $843,000 in return for a sizeable portion of the Class B membership interest. The remainder of the Class B interest is held by Fisk Ventures, LLC, and Stephen Rose. Finally, various other investors contributed over $1 million for membership interests in Class C. These Class C investors are apparently mostly passive; the power in the LLC is essentially divided by the LLC Agreement (the "Agreement") between the Class A and Class B members.

Under the Agreement, the Board of Member Representatives (the "Board") manages the business and affairs of the Company. As originally contemplated by the Agreement, the Board consisted of four members: two of whom were appointed by Johnson and two of whom were appointed by Segal. In early 2007, however, the balance of power seemingly shifted. Because the Company failed to meet certain benchmarks, the Board expanded to five seats and the Class B members were able to appoint a representative to the newly created seat. Nevertheless, because the Agreement requires the approval of 75% of the Board for most actions, the combined 60% stake of Fisk Ventures and Johnson is insufficient to control the Company. In other words, the LLC Agreement was drafted in such a way as to require the cooperation of the Class A and B members.

B. The Parties . . .

Dr. Andrew Segal, fresh out of residency training, worked for the Whitehead Institute for Biomedical Research in Cambridge, Massachusetts from 1994 to early 1996. While there, Segal researched and worked on projects relating to how the human immune system could be manipulated effectively to attack cancer and infectious diseases. In early 1996, Dr. Segal left the Whitehead Institute and obtained a license to certain patent rights related to his research.

With these patent rights in hand, Dr. Segal formed Genitrix. Intellectual property rights alone, however, could not fund the research, testing, and trials necessary to bring Dr. Segal's ideas to some sort of profitable fruition. Consequently, Segal sought and obtained capital for the Company. Originally, Segal served as both President and Chief Executive Officer, and the terms of his employment were governed by contract (the "Segal Employment Agreement"). Under the Segal Employment Agreement, any intellectual property rights developed by Dr. Segal during his tenure with Genitrix would be assigned to the Company. . . .

Fisk Ventures is a Delaware limited liability company controlled by Dr. H. Fisk Johnson, who owns 99% of it. Fisk is a Class B member and is entitled to appoint one person to the Board. Fisk filed the initial petition in this action seeking dissolution of the Company. . . .

Dr. Johnson is the controlling member of Fisk and is himself a Class B shareholder in the Company who is personally now entitled to appoint two members to the Board. . . .

Stephen Rose and William Freund are Class B Members of the Company and are Class B Representatives on the Board who were appointed by Johnson. Johnson also employs both Rose and Freund in a number of capacities outside of Genitrix, and Segal alleges that they are therefore dependant on Johnson or his affiliates for their livelihood.

C. The Company's Woes . . .

1. *Early Difficulties, the Fisk Ventures Note, and the Class B Put Right*

From its inception, Genitrix found itself strapped for cash. Segal's allegations contain numerous references to the tight budget and reminders that he worked for the Company for little or no pay in order to ease Genitrix's financial pain. In the earliest part of this decade, the Company hobbled along on grants from the National Institutes of Health and a series of relatively small financing transactions. Between November 2000 and August 2002, Johnson contributed another $550,000 in convertible debt,* much of which was subsequently converted to Class

* [Eds.—Convertible debt is debt that is convertible into equity, generally at the option of the holder of the debt (that is, the lender). It gives an investor some downside advantage—that is, a priority over other investors in the event of insolvency. It also offers upside potential in that it can be converted to equity if the firm prospers. In addition, it offers an "exit" possibility in that there will usually be some date when the debt must be repaid.]

B equity, and other investors provided $100,000 in convertible debt that was subsequently converted to Class C equity.

This influx of financing was insufficient, however. In the summer of 2003, Segal communicated to the Board that the Company would require $2.6 million to allow for human trials of the technology. Johnson, who by that point had contributed about $1.4 million, stated that he was unwilling to be the sole financier of the Company. Nevertheless, Johnson and Fisk Ventures agreed to contribute another $2 million in convertible debt if the Company agreed to try to raise an additional $5 million from other investors over the following two years.

Over the course of negotiating the terms of the Fisk Ventures note, Segal proposed that the "Put Right" of the Class B investors be suspended to allow him to more easily woo other investors. [The Put Right provided that] the Class B Members may, at any time, force the Company to purchase any or all of their Class B membership interests at a price determined by an independent appraisal. If the purchase price exceeds 50% of the Company's tangible assets, the Members who exercised the Put Right would receive notes secured by all of the assets of the Company. In other words, the Put—if exercised—would subrogate what would otherwise be senior claims of new investors. Though Segal believed this right would scare off potential investors, the Class B Members refused to suspend or relinquish their contractual rights, though they did communicate that they had no immediate or foreseeable intention of exercising the right. Segal alleges that, based on his conversations with Rose, he believed the Class B Members would be "more flexible with respect to the Put" once there was a prospective investment "on the table."

2. *Failed Efforts to Raise Money from New Investors*

To meet the $5 million challenge put forth in the Fisk Ventures Note, the Company retained an investment banking consultant to help it raise money from venture capital funds. This effort failed to generate any investment. By the summer of 2005—almost two years after the creation of the Fisk Ventures Note—the Company had failed to raise the needed $5 million,. . . .

. . . Dr. Segal turned his attention to individual, high-net-worth investors. Early indications were positive, but, Segal alleges, several potential investors complained about the Class B Put Right, one of whom called it a "deal killer." Thus, Segal again asked the Class B members to relinquish or suspend the Put Right. The Class B members again refused.

3. *The Private Placement Memorandum, . . .*

Meanwhile, in August 2005, Segal took it upon himself to [draft a document, a "private placement memorandum," that he could use to seek funds from] high-net-worth individuals. . . . When he attempted to get the approval of the Board in December, the Class B representatives refused to consent, citing the haste with which Segal was then acting. Once again, moreover, Segal wanted the Class B members to suspend or relinquish their Put Right. . . .

Segal stressed the Company's need to quickly secure additional funding and encouraged the Class B members to [approve], but the Class B Members instead offered a counterproposal of $500,000 in convertible debt from Fisk Ventures. The terms of that note would have required the

Company to meet certain benchmarks. If the Company failed to meet them, the Class B members would obtain control of the Board. . . .

[Segal next sought funds from Scott Tilson, a Class C investor, who was prepared to provide the funds only if the Class B members suspended their Put Right for three years, which they refused to do.]

4. *Segal's Removal as CEO*

The LLC Agreement contains a provision that allows the Class B members to replace Segal's Board representatives if the Company fails to adhere to certain covenants while Segal serves as CEO. Concerned that the Company was dangerously close to breaching those covenants and worried that he would lose his Board representation, Segal circulated to the Board in March 2006 a proposal to remove himself as CEO. Instead of discussing and approving this resolution, however, the Class B representatives, who represented over 50% of the Board, executed and circulated their own resolution, which replaced Segal with Chris Pugh, another employee of Genitrix, as "interim" CEO. . . .

5. *The Company's Current State*

In March 2006, the Company ran out of operating cash. Fisk Ventures provided another $125,000 capital contribution to pay the remaining employees and to cover some expenses, but larger problems loomed. The Board met in the third week of April to discuss its options.

Keeping with the common theme in this case, Dr. Segal and the Class B members had different ideas of what the Company should do. Dr. Segal proposed splitting Genitrix in two; the Class B members flatly rejected this proposal. The Class B members advocated a "buy down" proposal in which the Company would raise $3.5 million, in exchange for which the Class B members would find their interest in the Company reduced to 25% and would become largely passive investors. Although Dr. Segal initially expressed some interest in this proposal, he rejected it when he saw the actual terms set forth in writing by the Class B members about a month later.

In August 2006, Pugh left Genitrix to work for another firm, leaving the Company with just two employees (including Dr. Segal). That other employee left in May 2007. The Company has no office, no capital funds, no grant funds, and generates no revenue. The Board has not met since the fall of 2006 because the Class A representatives have refused to participate in any meetings. In May 2007 and at the invitation of the Class B members, Dr. Segal proposed terms under which the Class B members might purchase his interest in the Company. The Class B members rejected those terms in June 2007 and subsequently Fisk Ventures initiated this suit, seeking dissolution of Genitrix.

D. The Counterclaims/Third-Party Claims and the Parties' Contentions

. . . Segal contends that the counterclaim/third-party defendants breached the LLC Agreement, breached the implied covenant of good faith and fair dealing implicit in the LLC Agreement, breached their fiduciary duties to the Company, and tortiously interfered with the Segal Employment Agreement. Segal passionately contends that the Class B defendants failed to comply with their duties to Segal and to the Company by standing in the way of proposed financing. . . .

III. FAILURE TO STATE A CLAIM

. . . Because Segal has not stated facts that either show he is entitled or from which I can infer he is entitled to relief, I dismiss his claims.

A. *Breach of Contract*

. . . Dr. Segal's counterclaims and third-party claims contend—perhaps reasonably—that Genitrix suffered because the Class B members refused to accede to Segal's proposals with respect to research, financing, and other matters. It may very well be that Genitrix would be a thriving company today if only the Class B members had seen things Segal's way. However, it may very well be that Genitrix would also be a thriving company today if only Dr. Segal had gone along with what the Class B members wanted. Indeed, the LLC Agreement endows both the Class A and Class B members with certain rights and protections. In no way does it obligate one class to acquiesce to the wishes of the other simply because the other believes its approach is superior or in the best interests of the Company. To find otherwise—that is, to find that the Court must decide whose business judgment was more in keeping with the LLC's best interests—would cripple the policy underlying the LLC Act promoting freedom of contract. . . .

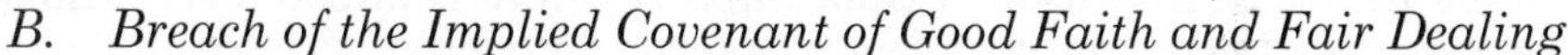

B. *Breach of the Implied Covenant of Good Faith and Fair Dealing*

Every contract contains an implied covenant of good faith and fair dealing that "requires a 'party in a contractual relationship to refrain from arbitrary or unreasonable conduct which has the effect of preventing the other party to the contract from receiving the fruits' of the bargain."[45] Although occasionally described in broad terms, the implied covenant is not a panacea for the disgruntled litigant. In fact, it is clear that "a court cannot and should not use the implied covenant of good faith and fair dealing to fill a gap in a contract with an implied term unless it is clear from the contract that the parties would have agreed to that term had they thought to negotiate the matter."[47] Only rarely invoked successfully, the implied covenant of good faith and fair dealing protects the spirit of what was *actually bargained and negotiated for* in the contract. Moreover, because the implied covenant is, by definition, *implied,* and because it protects the *spirit* of the agreement rather than the form, it cannot be invoked where the contract itself expressly covers the subject at issue.

Here, Segal argues that Fisk, Rose, and Freund breached the implied covenant of good faith and fair dealing by frustrating or blocking the financing opportunities proposed by Segal. However, neither the LLC Agreement nor any other contract endowed him with the right to unilaterally decide what fundraising or financing opportunities the Company should pursue, and his argument is "another in a long line of cases in which a plaintiff has tried, unsuccessfully, to argue that the implied covenant grants [him] a substantive right that [he] did not extract during negotiation."[51] Moreover, the LLC Agreement *does* address the subject of financing, and it specifically requires the approval

---

[45] Dunlap v. State Farm Fire & Cas. Co., 878 A.2d 434, 442 (Del.2005) (quoting Wilgus v. Salt Pond Inv. Co., 498 A.2d 151, 159 (Del.Ch.1985)).

[47] Corp. Prop. Assocs. 14 Inc. v. CHR Holding Corp., C.A. No. 3231–VCS, 2008 WL 963048 at *5 Del. Ch. Apr. 10, 2008). . . .

[51] Allied Capital [Corp. v. GC-Sun Holding, LP], 910 A.2d [1020], 1024 [(Del. Ch. 2006)].

of 75% of the Board. Implicit in such a requirement is the right of the Class B Board representatives to disapprove of and therefore block Segal's proposals. As this Court has previously noted, "[t]he mere exercise of one's contractual rights, without more, cannot constitute . . . a breach [of the implied covenant of good faith and fair dealing]."[52] Negotiating forcefully and within the bounds of rights granted by the LLC agreement does not translate to a breach of the implied covenant on the part of the Class B members. . . .

NOTE

In a subsequent stage of the litigation, the Chancery Court granted Fisk Ventures' motion for a judicial order of dissolution, on the statutory ground that it was no longer "reasonably practicable to carry on the business." Fisk Ventures, LLC v. Segal, 2009 WL 73957 (Del. Ch. 2009) The court observed that the Delaware LLC statute "does not specify what a court must consider in evaluating the 'reasonably practicable' standard, but several convincing factual circumstances have pervaded the case law: (1) the members' vote is deadlocked at the Board level; (2) the operating agreement gives no means of navigating around the deadlock; and (3) due to the financial condition of the company, there is effectively no business to operate." The Genetrix situation satisfied each of these criteria. Segal had sought to require that Fisk exercise its Put Right, which, according to Segal, would have allowed him to raise funds from other investors. The court rejected Segal's request, pointing out that the Put Right gave Fisk an *option* to seek a buyout; it did not give Genetrix or Segal a right to force Fisk to sell.

ANALYSIS

1. What does this case teach us about the wisdom of a provision that, in effect, gave each of the principal parties a veto power over all decisions? Why do well-advised entrepreneurs and investors agree to such a provision? In this case, did either party benefit from the veto power? Should the parties have anticipated some sort of stalemate and included a tie-breaker in the LLC agreement? If so, what sort of tie breaker?

2. What was the function of the "Put Right"? Why would a new investor insist on waiver of that right and why was Dr. Johnson unwilling to provide the waiver?

3. Suppose there was clear and convincing evidence that Genitrix's financial problems could be solved by an additional investment of $1 million. Further suppose that the holders of the Class B membership interests could easily afford to make such an investment. Should the court have ordered them to do so? If so, on what terms?

4. Can the result in this case be reconciled with that of Collins v. Lewis (Chapter 2, Sec. 6(A))?

---

[52] Shenandoah Life Ins. Co. v. Valero Energy Corp., C.A. No. 9032, 1988 WL 63491, at *8 (Del. Ch. June 21, 1988).

3. PIERCING THE LLC VEIL

NetJets Aviation, Inc. v. LHC Communications, LLC

537 F.3d 168 (2d Cir. 2008).

. . .

I. BACKGROUND

NetJets is engaged in the business of leasing fractional interests in airplanes and providing related air-travel services.* LHC is a Delaware limited liability company whose sole member-owner is Zimmerman. . . .

A. The Contracts Between NetJets and LHC

On August 1, 1999, LHC entered into two contracts with NetJets. In the first (the "Lease Agreement"), NetJets leased to LHC a 12.5 percent interest in an airplane, for which LHC was to pay NetJets a fixed monthly rental fee. The lease term was five years, with LHC having a qualified right of early termination. The second contract (the "Management Agreement") required NetJets to manage LHC's interest in the leased airplane and to provide services such as maintenance and piloting with respect to that airplane, or substitute aircraft, at specified hourly rates. It required LHC to pay a monthly management fee, as well as fuel charges, taxes, and other fees associated with LHC's air travel. The Management Agreement allotted to LHC use of the airplane for an average of 100 hours per year for the five-year term of the lease ("LHC air hours"), and it provided that if the leased airplane were unavailable at a time when LHC wished to use it, NetJets would provide substitute aircraft. NetJets regularly sent LHC invoices for the services provided under the Lease and Management Agreements.

. . .

In July 2000, LHC terminated its agreements with NetJets. LHC's chief financial officer ("CFO") James P. Whittier sent a letter, addressed to a NetJets vice president, stating, in pertinent part, that "[t]he present outstanding is $440,840.39 and we are requesting that you apply the deposit of $100,000 against the outstanding and contact this office to resolve the balance.". . .

As requested, NetJets contacted LHC and applied the $100,000 deposit against LHC's debt; however, it did not receive payment of the remaining balance of $340,840.39. In 2001, LHC ceased operations.

B. The Present Action and the Decision of the District Court

NetJets commenced the present diversity action in 2002, asserting claims against LHC and Zimmerman for breach of contract, account stated, and unjust enrichment. . . .

Following a period of discovery, NetJets moved for summary judgment against both defendants on the breach-of-contract and account-

* [Eds.: NetJets is a leading provider of private-jet services. In 1998 it was acquired by Berkshire Hathaway Inc., which was founded and is headed by greatly admired Warren Buffett, and which holds investments in a wide variety of businesses. Buffett, through his investment in the company, became one of the world's wealthiest people.]

stated claims. NetJets contended that Zimmerman should be held liable for the debts of LHC as its alter ego based on evidence, described in greater detail in Part II.B. below, of, inter alia, (a) the frequent use of LHC air hours for personal travel by Zimmerman and his friends and family, (b) the frequent transfers of funds between LHC and Zimmerman's other companies, (c) Zimmerman's frequent withdrawal of funds from LHC for his own personal use, and (d) the fact that LHC is no longer in business and has no assets with which to pay its debt to NetJets, a condition that NetJets contends was caused by Zimmerman's withdrawals.

In a Memorandum and Order dated June 12, 2006, the district court granted NetJets's summary judgment motion in part, awarding it $340,840.39 against LHC on the account-stated claims. . . .

Although Zimmerman had not moved for summary judgment in his favor, the court *sua sponte* granted summary judgment dismissing all of NetJets's claims against him.

II. DISCUSSION

. . .

For the reasons that follow, we conclude . . . that NetJets is entitled to trial on its contract and account-stated claims against Zimmerman as LHC's alter ego.

. . .

B. NetJets's Claims Against Zimmerman

1. Limitations on Limited Liability

. . . The shareholders of a corporation and the members of an LLC generally are not liable for the debts of the entity, and a plaintiff seeking to persuade a Delaware court to disregard the corporate structure faces "a difficult task," Harco National Insurance Co. v. Green Farms, Inc., No. CIV. A. 1331, 1989 WL 110537, at *4 (Del. Ch. Sept. 19, 1989) ("Harco").

Nonetheless, in appropriate circumstances, the distinction between the entity and its owner "may be disregarded" to require an owner to answer for the entity's debts. Pauley Petroleum Inc. v. Continental Oil Co., 239 A.2d 629, 633 (Del. 968). In general, with respect to the limited liability of owners of a corporation, Delaware law permits a court to pierce the corporate veil "where there is fraud or where [the corporation] is in fact a mere instrumentality or alter ego of its owner." Geyer v. Ingersoll Publications Co., 621 A.2d 784, 793 (Del.Ch.1992); . . .

To prevail under the alter-ego theory of piercing the veil, a plaintiff need not prove that there was actual fraud but must show a mingling of the operations of the entity and its owner plus an "overall element of injustice or unfairness." Harco, 1989 WL 110537, at *4.

> "[A]n alter ego analysis must start with an examination of factors which reveal how the corporation operates and the particular defendant's relationship to that operation. These factors include whether the corporation was adequately capitalized for the corporate undertaking; whether the corporation was solvent; whether dividends were paid, corporate records kept, officers and directors functioned properly, and other corporate formalities were observed;

whether the dominant shareholder siphoned corporate funds; and whether, in general, the corporation simply functioned as a facade for the dominant shareholder."

Id. at *4. . . .

"[N]o single factor c[an] justify a decision to disregard the corporate entity, but . . . some combination of them [i]s required, and . . . *an overall element of injustice or unfairness must always be present, as well.*" Harco, [1989 WL 110537, at *5] (quoting Golden Acres, 702 F.Supp. at 1104).

Harper v. Delaware Valley Broadcasters, Inc., 743 F.Supp. 1076, 1085 (D.Del.1990) ("Harper") (emphasis added), aff'd, 932 F.2d 959 (3d Cir.1991).

. . . Our Court has stated this as a two-pronged test focusing on (1) whether the entities in question operated as a single economic entity, and (2) whether there was an overall element of injustice or unfairness. . . .

These principles are generally applicable as well where one of the entities in question is an LLC rather than a corporation. In the alter-ego analysis of an LLC, somewhat less emphasis is placed on whether the LLC observed internal formalities because fewer such formalities are legally required. . . .

3. The Evidence that LHC and Zimmerman Operated as One

With respect to the question of whether LHC and Zimmerman operated as a single entity, the record contains, inter alia, financial records of LHC and deposition testimony from Zimmerman and LHC's CFO, Whittier. The evidence discussed below, taken in the light most favorable to NetJets, shows, inter alia, that LHC, of which Zimmerman is the sole member-owner, was started with a capitalization of no more than $20,100; that LHC proceeded to invest millions of dollars supplied by Zimmerman, including some $22 million in an internet technology company eventually called Bazillion, Inc. ("Bazillion"); and that Zimmerman put money into LHC as LHC needed it, and took money out of LHC as Zimmerman needed it.

Whittier, who had known Zimmerman since 1980 and worked with him full time from 1996 until April 2002, was LHC's only officer other than Zimmerman. In addition to LHC, Zimmerman directly or indirectly owned or controlled a number of companies, including Landover Telecom Corporation ("Landover Telecom"), LandTel N.V. ("LandTel"), IP II Partners, LP ("IP II"),. . . . Whittier acted as CFO for each of those companies. During most of the period 1996 to April 2002, Whittier "got paid from either Mr. Zimmerman or one of his corporations."

Zimmerman formed LHC in 1998; for most of its operating life, it shared office space with some of Zimmerman's other companies; LHC employed no more than five-to-seven people at any given time; and some of its employees worked for both LHC and Zimmerman's other companies or for LHC and Zimmerman personally. Whittier ran much of LHC's day-to-day operations based on instructions, general or specific, received from Zimmerman.

Zimmerman formed LHC "to be used as an investment vehicle for Mr. Zimmerman for him to make investments." "With regards to investments, Mr. Zimmerman reviewed investments. If he decided to go forward after his review, he would make an investment through [LHC] to an investment corporation he wanted to invest in." Although Zimmerman sought Whittier's advice as to the best way of accomplishing something he had decided he wanted to do, the ultimate decisions were always made by Zimmerman. "There were no decisions, financial decisions, made with regard to LHC without Mr. Zimmerman's approval."

Whittier testified that LHC also "was an operating company which maintained a consulting agreement with another entity called Landtel NV." But LandTel, which was wholly owned by Zimmerman's Landover Telecom—and was apparently LHC's only paying client—did not come into existence until January 2000, and LHC records do not show receipt of any consulting fees from LandTel until July 2000. Until LandTel was formed, therefore, the day-to-day LHC operations run by Whittier apparently consisted only of making Zimmerman's investments and carrying on Zimmerman's personal business. . . .

Whittier's compensation was paid sometimes by LHC and sometimes by Zimmerman personally.

In connection with Zimmerman's personal business, LHC's records show numerous transfers of money by Zimmerman to LHC, as well as numerous transfers of money from LHC to Zimmerman. Some of the transfers by Zimmerman to LHC were for the purpose of having LHC make investments,. . . . Other transfers by Zimmerman to LHC were made for the purpose of meeting LHC's operating expenses. . . .

Whittier testified that Zimmerman would transfer funds to LHC "as needed." ("Monies would go in . . . LHC based on the need."). Often those funds would come from Zimmerman's personal bank accounts. However, because Zimmerman generally waited until the eleventh hour to provide money to meet LHC's operating needs, sometimes "shortcuts" were taken by having the money come to LHC directly from one of Zimmerman's other companies . . ., none of which had any business relationship with LHC.

Whittier testified also that "[m]onies would go . . . out of LHC based on the need." For example, Zimmerman would take money out of LHC to "mak[e] an investment in another entity." In addition, at several brokerage firms, Zimmerman had personal accounts that were unrelated to LHC's operations; he had many margin calls in those accounts because he "utilized margin debt very aggressively," especially with respect to two stocks whose market prices dropped sharply in 2000 (one "from a high of above 90 down to the 60s" and the other "from a high of 93 down to 3"). Zimmerman had LHC make payments to meet some of these margin calls in his personal accounts. On May 15 and 16, 2000, for example, LHC wired a total of $2 million to Salomon Smith Barney to meet margin calls or reduce the margin debt on Zimmerman's personal brokerage accounts. On August 22 and October 6, 2000, LHC sent Paine Webber, another firm at which Zimmerman personally had "big brokerage accounts," checks totaling $2 million. . . .

LHC also transferred money to Zimmerman, or to third persons on his behalf, in connection with his living expenses. For example, LHC made payments to Fox Lair (consistently called "Fox Liar" in LHC's general ledger), a Zimmerman corporation that owned a $15 million New

York apartment on Park Avenue, which was characterized by Zimmerman as "a corporate residence" but was used by no one other than Zimmerman and his family. Fox Lair needed money "to pay phone bills and cleaning people and things of that nature"; according to LHC's ledgers, from December 5, 2000, through July 2, 2001, Fox Lair received some $70,000 from LHC. In addition, LHC made periodic payments to the Screen Actors Guild (of which Zimmerman's wife was a member) for health insurance for Zimmerman and his family; LHC purchased a Bentley automobile at a cost of approximately $350,000 for Zimmerman's personal use, placing title in his name; and LHC made a payment of $110,000, characterized in its general ledger as "Loan receivable" and in its check register as "Interest Expense," to a person who had no connection with LHC but who held a mortgage on a property owned by Zimmerman personally.

In addition, many of the air hours to which LHC was entitled under its agreements with NetJets were used by Zimmerman personally. Of the 40-odd LHC flights invoiced by NetJets, Zimmerman acknowledges that "approximately 6" were for vacations for himself and/or his wife. But in addition to those six, there were at least an equal number of flights that apparently had no relation to LHC's business. These flights included several that transported Zimmerman's family to and from Europe or to and from one of Zimmerman's five homes. Zimmerman contends that use of LHC air hours for these purposes was "part of [his compensation] package" and "[o]ne of the perks of being the chairman." That may be; but for purposes of determining whether Zimmerman and LHC were alter egos, it is pertinent that Zimmerman made all of LHC's financial decisions; Zimmerman alone decided what his perks and package would be.

In LHC's general ledger, each of the transfers of money between LHC and Zimmerman—in either direction—is labeled "Loan receivable." They were also so labeled regardless of whether Zimmerman's payment to LHC was to be used to make an investment or was to be used for operating expenses. . . . The decision that those transactions would be labeled loans or loan repayments was made by Zimmerman.

"There were no written agreements" with regard to any of Zimmerman's loans; nor were there any "set repayment program" or agreements as to repayment terms: "Money was put in as needed and when money was not needed and Mr. Zimmerman needed money elsewhere, he might transfer it out. That was his decision to make." "There was no procedure. Money was put in and taken out as needed."

In all, LHC's financial records for the period January 1, 2000, through June 18, 2002, show—in addition to some two dozen transactions between LHC and Zimmerman's other companies—approximately 60 transfers of money directly from Zimmerman to LHC and approximately 60 transfers of money out of LHC directly to Zimmerman. In sum, there is evidence that, inter alia, Zimmerman created LHC to be one of his personal investment vehicles; that he was the sole decisionmaker with respect to LHC's financial actions; that Zimmerman frequently put money into LHC as LHC needed it to meet operating expenses; that LHC used some of that money, as well as some moneys it received from selling shares of one of its assets, to pay more than $4.5 million to third persons for Zimmerman's personal expenses including margin calls, mortgage payments, apartment expenses, and automobiles; and that with no written agreements or documentation or procedures in place, Zimmerman directly, on the average of twice a month for 2 1/2 years, took money out of LHC at will in order to make other investments or to meet his other personal expenses. This evidence is ample to permit a reasonable factfinder to find that Zimmerman completely dominated LHC and that he essentially treated LHC's bank account as one of his pockets, into which he reached when he needed or desired funds for his personal use. Accordingly, we reject Zimmerman's contention that the district court should have granted summary judgment in his favor on the ground that he and LHC did not operate as a single economic entity.

4. The Evidence of Fraud, Illegality, or Injustice

. . . NetJets adduced sufficient evidence of fraud, illegality, or unfairness to warrant a trial on its contract and account-stated claims against Zimmerman as LHC's alter ego. For example, in an effort to parry NetJets's contention that LHC was undercapitalized, Zimmerman submitted an affidavit from LHC's accountant [Balaban] stating that "it was not intended by Zimmerman to treat the monies paid into LHC as loans" and that all of Zimmerman's payments into LHC were in fact capital contributions. Yet, as discussed above, Whittier testified that Zimmerman instructed him that those payments were to be characterized as loans, in order to allow Zimmerman to take money out of LHC at will and to do so without tax consequences.

Further, although the Balaban affidavit stops short of giving an opinion as to how to characterize Zimmerman's withdrawals of money from LHC, it would appear that, if his payments to LHC were capital contributions as the Balaban affidavit opines, LHC's payments to Zimmerman would be properly characterized as distributions. Yet the DLLCA provides generally, with some qualifications, that an LLC "shall not make a distribution to a member to the extent that at the time of the distribution, after giving effect to the distribution, all liabilities of the limited liability company . . . exceed the fair value of the assets of the limited liability company." Del.Code tit. 6, § 18–607(a). Given that LHC ceased operating and was unable to pay its debt to NetJets, if Zimmerman's withdrawals left LHC in that condition those withdrawals may well have been prohibited by § 18–607(a). A factfinder could infer that Zimmerman's payments to LHC were deliberately mischaracterized as loans in order to mask the fact that Zimmerman was making withdrawals from LHC that were forbidden by law, and could thereby properly find fraud or an unfair siphoning of LHC's assets.

The record also includes other evidence from which a reasonable factfinder could find that Zimmerman operated LHC in his own self-interest in a manner that unfairly disregarded the rights of LHC's creditors. For example, it could find

— that although LHC was apparently unable in 2000 to pay its $340,840.39 (net of LHC's deposit) debt to NetJets, in that year LHC bought, and gave Zimmerman title to, a Bentley automobile for $350,210.95;

— that LHC's only paying client for its consulting services began paying LHC for those services in July 2000 (the month in which LHC terminated its agreements with

NetJets), sending LHC a first payment of approximately $675,000 on July 9, and that on that day Zimmerman withdrew that amount and more from LHC;

— that from the point at which LHC terminated its relationship with NetJets in July 2000 until the end of 2001—the year in which NetJets ceased operations—LHC's records of its transactions directly with Zimmerman indicate that Zimmerman withdrew from LHC approximately $750,000 more than he put in;

— and that, excluding moneys put into LHC solely for its investments in Bazillion, the total amount of money taken out of LHC by Zimmerman and his other companies appears to exceed the amount that he and those companies put into LHC by some $3 million.

From this record, a reasonable factfinder could properly find that there was an overall element of injustice in Zimmerman's operation of LHC. . . .

CONCLUSION

. . . For the reasons stated above, the judgment of the district court is vacated . . . [and] the case is remanded for further proceedings not inconsistent with this opinion.

ANALYSIS

1. What should NetJets have done before the LHC default to protect its interests? Is it fair to say that NetJets got a windfall—that is, more than it bargained for?

2. What should Zimmerman have done to protect himself from personal liability?

3. What is the relevance of the fact that Zimmerman made all the decisions, including the amount of his own compensation, and that LHC was purely an investment company?

4. Uniform Limited Liability Company Act § 303(b) provides that: "The failure of a limited liability company to observe the usual company formalities or requirements relating to the exercise of its company powers or management of its business is not a ground for imposing personal liability on the members or managers for liabilities of the company." In the absence of such a statute, what weight, if any, should a court give to evidence tending to show that the LLC's members failed to observe the sorts of organizational formalities referred to above? Put another way, what are the important differences between an LLC and a corporation that are relevant to piercing?

4. FIDUCIARY OBLIGATION

McConnell v. Hunt Sports Enterprises

132 Ohio App.3d 657, 725 N.E.2d 1193 (1999).

[On October 31, 1996, several wealthy individuals and their controlled entities formed Columbus Hockey Limited, L.L.C. (CHL) for the purpose of seeking a National Hockey League franchise for Columbus Ohio. The two leading figures in the story that unfolded were John H. McConnell and Lamar Hunt, who were investors in CHL and wound up on opposite sides of the present law suit. To secure the NHL franchise, CHL needed an arena and sought public financing through an increase in the countywide sales tax. Unfortunately for CHL, the voters rejected the sales tax increase. Shortly thereafter, Nationwide Insurance Enterprise developed an interest in building the arena and leasing it to the holder of the franchise. With this in mind, Dimon McPherson, Nationwide's chairman and chief executive officer, met with Hunt, who purported to act for CHL, but without consulting with the other CHL investors. Nationwide made a proposal for the lease, which Hunt rejected. Meanwhile, an NHL deadline was fast approaching. Having received several rebuffs from Hunt, McPherson approached McConnell, who said that if Hunt would not agree to lease the arena, he would. McPherson conveyed this information to the Nationwide board of directors. Thereafter, Hunt again stated to Nationwide's representatives that he found the lease unacceptable, but was still interested in pursuing the matter.

On June 4, 1997, the NHL franchise expansion committee was advised of McConnell's unconditional backup offer and recommended to the NHL board of governors that a franchise be awarded for the city of Columbus.

On June 9, the CHL investors met. Hunt and his allies stated that they found Nationwide's lease offer unacceptable. McConnell and his allies, on the other hand, accepted the lease offer and signed an agreement in their own names (after the elimination of "Columbus Hockey Limited" from the signature line). On June 17, 1997, the NHL expansion committee recommended that the Columbus franchise be awarded to McConnell's group. On the same date the McConnell group filed the present law suit seeking a declaratory judgment to establish its legal right to the franchise without inclusion of Hunt or CHL. The suit relied on the express language of the CHL operating agreement that is discussed by the court below. The Hunt group filed an answer and counterclaim on behalf of itself and CHL and also filed a suit on behalf of CHL against McConnell and some of his group in a New York state court.

On June 25, 1997, the NHL board of governors awarded a franchise to Columbus with McConnell's group as owner.

In the present Ohio declaratory judgment action there was a flurry of motions and countermotions, a jury trial, and finally, on May 18, 1998, a directed verdict in favor of McConnell on the main counts. On appeal, the court issued a lengthy opinion, parts of which follow, beginning with a response to the Hunt group's argument that the lower court erred in refusing to allow introduction of extrinsic evidence of the meaning of the crucial language in the CHL operating agreement.]

The construction of written contracts is a matter of law. . . . If a contract is clear and unambiguous, there is no issue of fact to be determined,. . . . Only where the language of a contract is unclear or ambiguous or when the circumstances surrounding the agreement invest the language of the contract with a special meaning, will extrinsic evidence be considered in an effort to give effect to the parties' intentions. . . .

The test for determining whether a term is ambiguous is that common words in a written contract will be given their ordinary meaning unless manifest absurdity results or unless some other meaning is clearly evidenced from the face or overall content of the contract. . . . For the reasons that follow, we conclude that section 3.3 is plain and unambiguous and allowed members of CHL to compete against CHL for an NHL franchise.

Section 3.3 of the operating agreement states:

> "Members May Compete. Members shall not in any way be prohibited from or restricted in engaging or owning an interest in any other business venture of any nature, including any venture which might be competitive with the business of the Company."

Appellant emphasizes the word "other" in the above language and states, in essence, that it means any business venture that is different from the business of the company. . . .

Appellant's interpretation of section 3.3 goes beyond the plain language of the agreement and adds words or meanings not stated in the provision. Section 3.3, for example, does not state "[m]embers shall not be prohibited from or restricted in engaging or owning an interest in any other business venture that is different from the business of the company." Rather, section 3.3 states: "any other business venture of any nature." It then adds to this statement: "including any venture which might be competitive with the business of the Company." The words "any nature" could not be broader, and the inclusion of the words "any venture which might be competitive with the business of the Company" makes it clear that members were not prohibited from engaging in a venture that was competitive with CHL's investing in and operating an NHL franchise. . . .

[The court next turns to the trial court's direction to the jury that the McConnell group] did not violate any [fiduciary] duty by forming and joining COLHOC [Limited Partnership], by allegedly excluding appellant from participating in an NHL franchise, by preparing to compete against CHL and in not providing additional capital for CHL.

Such instruction was proper because, as discussed [above], appellees [the McConnell group] were permitted to compete against CHL for a hockey franchise, and there was no requirement that CHL members contribute additional capital. As will be addressed in more detail infra, these acts in and of themselves would not constitute breach of fiduciary duty because the operating agreement allowed such acts. . . .

Before we can review the propriety of the directed verdict in this case, the law on fiduciary duty and interference with a prospective business relationship must be addressed. The term "fiduciary relationship" has been defined as a relationship in which special confidence and trust is reposed in the integrity and fidelity of another, and there is a resulting position of superiority or influence acquired by virtue of this special trust. . . . In the case at bar, a limited liability company is involved which, like a partnership, involves a fiduciary relationship. Normally, the presence of such a relationship would preclude direct competition between members of the company. However, here we have an operating agreement that by its very terms allows members to compete with the business of the company. Hence, the question we are presented with is whether an operating agreement of a limited liability company may, in essence, limit or define the scope of the fiduciary duties imposed upon its members. We answer this question in the affirmative.

. . .

. . . In becoming members of CHL, appellant and appellees agreed to abide by the terms of the operating agreement, and such agreement specifically allowed competition with the company by its members. As such, the duties created pursuant to such undertaking did not include a duty not to compete. Therefore, there was no duty on the part of appellees to refrain from subjecting appellant to the injury complained of herein.

We find further support for our conclusion in case law concerning close corporations and partnerships. . . .

Given the above, we conclude as a matter of law that it was not a breach of fiduciary duty for appellees to form COLHOC and obtain an NHL franchise to the exclusion of CHL. In so concluding, we are not stating that no act related to such obtainment could be considered a breach of fiduciary duty. In general terms, members of limited liability companies owe one another the duty of utmost trust and loyalty. However, such general duty in this case must be considered in the context of members' ability, pursuant to operating agreement, to compete with the company.

We now turn to the elements of tortious interference with a prospective business relationship. The tort of interference with a business relationship occurs when a person, without a privilege to do so, induces or otherwise purposely causes a third person not to enter into or continue a business relationship with another. . . .

. . . [A]ppellees were permitted under the operating agreement to compete with CHL and, as discussed above, this in and of itself cannot constitute a breach of fiduciary duty. Further, in so competing, appellees did not engage in any acts that would otherwise constitute wrongful behavior. Nationwide contacted McConnell only after appellant indicated the lease terms were unacceptable. Even then, McConnell stated he would accept the lease terms and obtain the franchise on his own only if appellant did not. There is no evidence that McConnell acted in any secretive manner in his actions leading up to the franchise award or that he used CHL assets for personal gain. In short, the evidence shows that appellees obtained the NHL franchise to the exclusion of CHL. Appellees did nothing beyond this that could constitute a breach of fiduciary duty.

Likewise, the evidence does not show that appellees tortiously interfered with appellant's prospective business relationships with Nationwide and the NHL. The evidence does not show that appellees induced or otherwise purposely caused Nationwide and the NHL not to enter into or continue a business relationship with appellant. Indeed, and as indicated above, the evidence shows that McConnell stated he would lease the arena and obtain the franchise only if appellant did not. It was only after appellant rejected the lease proposal on several occasions that McConnell stepped in. Appellant had yet another opportunity on June 9, 1997 to participate in the Nationwide arena lease and the NHL franchise. Appellant again found the lease proposal unacceptable, and without a signed lease term sheet, there would have been no franchise from the NHL. McPherson testified that Nationwide would accept a lease agreement with whomever the successful franchise applicant was. In addition, it is clear . . . that the NHL was still considering appellant as a potential franchise owner up until the last moment. Again, the evidence does not show that appellees' actions constituted an intentional interference with appellant's business relationships. It must be noted that appellees had the right to compete against CHL. However, even given such right, McConnell did not approach Nationwide or the NHL. Nationwide approached McConnell only after appellant indicated the lease terms were unacceptable. In short, it was appellant's actions that caused the termination of any relationship or potential relationship it had with Nationwide and the NHL. In conclusion, there was not sufficient material evidence presented at trial so as to create a factual question for the jury on the issues of breach of fiduciary duty and tortious interference with business relationships. Therefore, a directed verdict in favor of appellees . . . was appropriate.

[The court next addresses the trial court's directed verdict in favor of the McConnell group on its claim of the Hunt group's] breach of contract in unilaterally rejecting the Nationwide lease proposal, in failing to negotiate with Nationwide in good faith, in allowing Nationwide's deadline to expire without response, and in wrongfully and unlawfully usurping control of CHL. In granting appellees' motion for a directed verdict, the trial court found appellant violated the CHL operating agreement in failing to ask for and obtain the authorization of CHL members, other than appellees, prior to filing the answer and counterclaim in this action and the suit in New York. . . . The trial court awarded appellees $1.00 in damages.

. . . Appellant [Hunt's firm] contends that under the operating agreement, it could only be liable for willful misconduct. In addition, appellant contends it was the "operating member" of CHL and, therefore, had full authority to act on CHL's behalf. For the reasons that follow, we conclude that a directed verdict in favor of appellees . . . was appropriate.

First, there was no evidence at trial that appellant was the operating member of CHL. The operating agreement, which sets forth the entire agreement between the members of CHL, does not name any person or entity the operating or managing member of CHL. Instead, all members of CHL had an equal number of units in CHL, as reflected by the amount of their capital contributions shown on Schedule A of the operating agreement. Pursuant to section 4.1 of the operating agreement, no member was permitted to take any action on behalf of the company unless such action was approved by the specified number of members, which was, at the very least, a majority of the units allocated.

This brings us to the question of whether appellant breached the operating agreement by failing to obtain the approval of the other CHL members prior to filing, in CHL's name, the answer and counterclaim in this suit [and] the suit in New York. . . . Again, section 4.1(b) of the operating agreement requires at least majority approval prior to taking any action on behalf of CHL. Further, the approval of the members as to any action on behalf of CHL must have been evidenced by minutes of a meeting properly noticed and held or by an action in writing signed by the requisite number of members. . . .

There is no evidence that appellant obtained the approval of CHL members prior to filing the actions listed above. Indeed, there is no evidence that appellant even asked permission of any member to file the actions, let alone held a meeting or requested approval in writing. The evidence does show that appellant, in the name of CHL, filed the answer and counterclaim in the present suit [and] the action in New York. . . . This was contrary to sections 4.1 and 4.2 of the operating agreement and constituted breach of such agreement.

Appellant points to section 4.4 of the operating agreement and contends appellees had to show willful misconduct on its part in filing such actions. Section 4.4 states:

> "Exculpation of Members; Indemnity. In carrying out their duties hereunder, the Members shall not be liable to the Company or to any other Member for their good faith actions, or failure to act, or for any errors of judgment, or for any act or omission believed in good faith to be within the scope of authority conferred by this Agreement, but only for their own willful misconduct in the performance of their obligations under this Agreement. Actions or omissions taken in reliance upon the advice of legal counsel as being within the scope of authority conferred by this Agreement shall be conclusive evidence of such good faith; however, good faith may be determined without obtaining such advice."

Section 4.4's provisions are in the context of members carrying out their duties under the operating agreement. There was no duty on appellant's part to unilaterally file the actions at issue. Indeed, we have determined that appellant did not act properly under the operating agreement in filing such actions. Hence, the provision in section 4.4 indicating members were only liable to other members for their own willful misconduct in the performance of their obligations under the operating agreement does not even apply to the actions taken by appellant.

However, even if we applied this provision, the evidence shows appellant engaged in willful misconduct in filing the actions at issue. As indicated above, appellant was a member of CHL at the time of its formation. As a member of CHL, appellant agreed to be bound by the terms of the operating agreement. Hunt read the operating agreement prior to signing it. The agreement required a majority vote prior to taking any action on behalf of CHL, such as the filing of the actions at issue.

ANALYSIS

1. Suppose that Hunt, with the approval of all the other members of CHL, had been negotiating with Nationwide and was near an agreement and that McConnell had then made a good offer to Nationwide and secured the right to lease the arena and, with that in hand, had secured the franchise. What result?

2. Do you agree that the language of Section 3.3 of the operating agreement was clear and unambiguous? How might it have been drafted to remove all possible doubt in its application to this case?

5. ADDITIONAL CAPITAL

Racing Investment Fund 2000, LLC v. Clay Ward Agency, Inc.

320 S.W.3d 654 (Ky. 2010).

Racing Investment Fund 2000, LLC is a limited liability company created in August 2000, to purchase, train and race thoroughbred horses. [Pursuant to the Operating Agreement, investors would buy 50 units at $100,000 per unit.] In May, 2004, Racing Investment entered into an agreed judgment with its former equine insurance firm, Clay Ward Agency, Inc., for past-due insurance premiums. Shortly thereafter, Racing Investment partially paid the judgment by tendering all of the remaining assets of the then-defunct limited liability company. When Racing Investment failed to pay the remainder of the amount owed, Clay Ward succeeded in having Racing Investment held in contempt of court for its failure to pay the entire judgment amount. Specifically, the trial court ruled that a provision in Racing Investment's Operating Agreement which allowed the limited liability company's Manager to call for additional capital contributions, as needed, from all members on a pro rata basis for "operating, administrative or other business expenses" provided a means of satisfying the Clay Ward judgment [for $57,139.68]. The trial court ordered that Racing Investment "act accordingly to satisfy the Judgment within a reasonable period of time" or face other sanctions. After the Court of Appeals affirmed, this Court granted discretionary review to consider whether the capital call provision can be invoked by a court to obtain funds from the limited liability company's members in order to satisfy a judgment against the limited liability company. Having concluded that KRS 275.150 provides for immunity from personal liability for a limited liability company's debts unless a member agrees otherwise and, further, that members of Racing Investment did not, by signing an operating agreement allowing for periodic capital calls from the Manager, subject themselves to personal liability, we reverse. . . .

Analysis

In 1994, Kentucky joined a growing national trend by recognizing limited liability companies (LLCs) through the adoption of the "Kentucky Limited Liability Company Act" codified at KRS Chapter 275. As early commentators noted, the hallmark of this new form of business entity is its combination of the income tax advantages of a partnership with the business advantages of a corporation. Thomas Rutledge and Lady Booth, The Limited Liability Company Act: Understanding Kentucky's New Organizational Option, 83 Ky. L.J. 1 (1994–95). The "centerpiece" of a limited liability company is its "provision for limited liability of its members and managers in regard to the debts and obligations of the LLC. . . ." Id. at 6. . . . One indicia of the strength of that limited liability protection is the Internal Revenue Service's recognition that federal employment tax liabilities incurred by an LLC cannot be collected from the LLC's members. Id. citing Rev. Rul.2004–41, 2004–1 C.B. 845.1

Kentucky codified the limited liability feature of a limited liability company at KRS 275.150—"Immunity from personal liability":

> (1) Except as provided in subsection (2) of this section or as otherwise specifically set forth in other sections in this chapter, no member, manager, employee, or agent of a limited liability company, including a professional limited liability company, shall be personally liable by reason of being a member, manager, employee, or agent of the limited liability company, under a judgment, decree, or order of a court, agency, or tribunal of any type, or in any other manner, in this or any other state, or on any other basis, for a debt, obligation, or liability of the limited liability company, whether arising in contract, tort, or otherwise. The status of a person as a member, manager, employee, or agent of a limited liability company, including a professional limited liability company, shall not subject the person to personal liability for the acts or omissions, including any negligence, wrongful act, or actionable misconduct, of any other member, manager, agent, or employee of the limited liability company.
>
> (2) Notwithstanding the provisions of subsection (1) of this section, under a written operating agreement or under another written agreement, a member or manager may agree to be obligated personally for any of the debts, obligations, and liabilities of the limited liability company.

Notably, the statute contains a strong, detailed declaration of personal immunity followed by recognition in subsection (2) that a member or members may agree in writing to be personally liable for the LLC's debts, obligations and liabilities. As one national commentator has noted, "[s]ince most LLCs are created for the purpose of obtaining limited liability, few LLCs take advantage of the opportunity to allow their members to waive limited liability under the act." Steven C. Alberty, Limited Liability Companies: A Planning and Drafting Guide § 3.06(b)(2) (2003).

. . .

Section 4.3(a) of the Racing Investment Operating Agreement, entitled "Additional Capital Contributions" provides:

> The Investor Members . . . shall be obligated to contribute to the capital of the Company, on a prorata basis in accordance with their respective Percentage Interests, such amounts as may be reasonably deemed advisable by the Manager from time to time in order to pay operating, administrative, or other business expenses of the Company which have been incurred, or which the Manager reasonably anticipates will be incurred, by the Company. Except under unusual circumstances, such additional capital contributions ("Additional Capital Contributions") shall not be required more often than quarterly and shall be due and payable by each Investor Member . . . within fifteen (15) days after such Investor Member receives written notice from the Company of the amount due (a "Quarterly Bill"), The Manager shall not be required to make any additional capital contributions.

This is the provision relied upon by Clay Ward in contending that Racing Investment was in contempt of court for not having paid the agreed judgment in full. Under Clay Ward's interpretation, Racing Investment incurred a legitimate business expense for the equine insurance premiums prior to its dissolution and the members of the LLC, by agreeing to the periodic capital contribution provision, are subject to a "last call" to satisfy the outstanding balance on the judgment. In accepting this construction, the trial court and Court of Appeals essentially concluded that, by agreeing to make periodic capital contributions pursuant to Section 4.3(a), individual members of Racing Investment are legally responsible for their pro rata share of the entity's business debt. Indeed, under this theory, any outstanding debt that remains unpaid by the LLC can be satisfied through application for a court-ordered capital call. We reject this construction as contrary to the plain terms of the Operating Agreement and the letter and spirit of the Kentucky Limited Liability Company Act.

As discussed above, an operating agreement providing for future capital contributions by the LLC's members is neither "unique" as suggested by Clay Ward nor "atypical" as described by the Court of Appeals. Many businesses choosing the limited liability company form have circumstances that require periodic capital infusion. . . . Section 4.3(a) is a provision designed to assure members will contribute additional capital, as deemed necessary by the Manager, to advance Racing Investment's thoroughbred racing venture. While Clay Ward's insurance premiums were indeed a legitimate business expense for which the Manager could have made a capital call, that premise alone does not lead . . . to the relief ordered by the trial court. Simply put, Section 4.3(a) is a not-uncommon, on-going capital infusion provision, not a debt-collection mechanism by which a court can order a capital call and, by doing so, impose personal liability on the LLC's members for the entity's outstanding debt. Clay Ward insists that its quest to be paid is not about individual member liability, but there is no other way to construe what occurs when a court orders a capital call be made to pay for a particular LLC debt. From any viewpoint, the shield of limited liability has been lifted and the LLC's members have been held individually liable for its debt.

KRS 275.150 emphatically rejects personal liability for an LLC's debt unless the member or members, as the case may be, have agreed through the operating agreement or another written agreement to assume personal liability. Any such assumption of personal liability, which is contrary to the very business advantage reflected in the name "limited liability company," must be stated clearly in unequivocal language which leaves no room for doubt about the parties' intent. Section 4.3(a) of Racing Investment's Operating Agreement does not begin to meet this standard. A provision designed to provide on-going capital infusion as necessary, at the Manager's discretion, for the conduct of the entity's business affairs is simply not an agreement "to be obligated personally for any of the debts, obligations and liabilities of the limited liability company." KRS 275.150(2). To reiterate, assumption of personal liability by a member of an LLC is so antithetical to the purpose of a limited liability company that any such assumption must be stated in unequivocal terms leaving no doubt that the member or members intended to forego a principal advantage of this form of business entity. On this score, Section 4.3(a) simply does not qualify.

. . .

ANALYSIS

1. Litigation Strategy. The defendant in the case is Racing Investment. The members are not joined as defendants. Why not? Why does the court focus on the limited liability of the members?

2. Failure to Contribute. What is the function of the following provision in the Operating Agreement (quoted in the Racing Investment brief but not referred to in the court's opinion) concerning the possibility of a member failing to respond to a call for a contribution, and how does it work?

> The Managing Member: . . . may notify all Investor Members . . . of such default and disclose any information with respect thereto as the Manager deems advisable, and/or (ii) may, but shall not be obligated to, borrow the amount of the Additional Capital Contribution which the Defaulting Investor Member failed or neglected to pay from the Manager, any member, any officer, any Affiliate of the Manager, or any member or officer, any bank, or any other source on such terms and conditions . . . as the Manager, in the Manager's sole discretion, may deem advisable.

If the Managing Member calls for additional contributions and some or all the members fail to contribute, what are the next steps?

3. Negotiating the Operating Agreement. If you had represented a potential investor in Racing Investment and had been asked for your opinion on the Operating Agreement, what would you have said about the provision on calls for additional contributions (Section 4.3(a))?

PLANNING: ADDITIONAL CAPITAL

Suppose that in the Racing Investment Fund situation there were 10 members, each of whom had initially invested $500,000 for 10 units and had been making periodic additional contributions for several years. Now suppose that the manager sends to each of the investors a letter stating:

> I regret to report that our horses have not done well, but I have high hopes for the future. We are out of money and need an additional contribution from each of you of $20,000, a total of $200,000. This sum is needed to continue operations for another season and sell the horses in an orderly manner. My best estimate is that if we have a successful racing season the orderly sale will result in net proceeds (after payment of debts) of as much as $5,000,000; if we have a bad season, the net will be zero. Our consultants, who are the best in the business, say that the probability of netting the $5,000,000 is about 50%, with an equal probability of netting nothing. Without the additional contribution I will be obliged to take the best offer I can get right now for all the horses, which I firmly believe will be barely enough to pay off our debts. Thus, if each of you contributes $20,000 you can expect, within the next year or so, liquidating distribution of $500,000, if all goes well. Without the additional

> contributions you will probably receive nothing. As you all know, it is presently impossible for us to borrow the needed funds from a bank or other third party without personal guarantees from each of you, and my understanding is that few if any of you would be willing to provide such a guarantee.

A week after this letter is received by the members, eight of the ten members have agreed to contribute the additional $20,000, but the other two have refused. The manager goes back to the eight members who have agreed to contribute and asks them to commit to an additional $5,000. These additional amounts would be recoverable from the liquidating distribution (if any) of the members who have refused to contribute.

1. The Dilemma. If you are a member who has agreed to contribute $20,000 and you are now asked for the additional $5,000, what is your reaction?

2. Solution? How might the operating agreement have been drafted to mitigate the problem suggested by the immediately preceding question?

6. DISSOLUTION

New Horizons Supply Cooperative v. Haack

1999 WL 33499 (Wis.App.).

Allison Haack appeals a small claims judgment in the amount of $1,009.99 plus costs entered against her in favor of New Horizons Supply Cooperative. Haack contends the trial court erred in denying her defense that because the debt was incurred by Kickapoo Valley Freight LLC, a limited liability company under ch. 183, Stats., she was not personally liable for the cooperative's claim. We conclude, however, that Haack did not establish at trial that the amount of New Horizons' claim exceeded the value of any liquidation distribution she may have received from the dissolved company. See § 183.0909(2), Stats. (quoted below in text). Accordingly, we affirm the appealed judgment.

BACKGROUND

On May 30, 1995, Haack signed a "CARDTROL AGREEMENT" whereby the "Patron" agreed "to be responsible for payment of all fuel purchased with" the "Cardtrol Card" issued under the agreement by a predecessor to New Horizons. "Kickapoo Valley Freight, LLC" is shown as the "Patron" in the first paragraph of the form agreement, and it is signed by "Allison Haack," with no designation indicating whether her signature was given individually or in a representative capacity on behalf of Kickapoo Valley.

An employee of New Horizons testified at trial that in September 1997, when the Kickapoo Valley account was in arrears, she contacted Robert Koch about the bill. Koch referred her to his sister, Haack, who apparently took care of paying the bills for the company. When contacted, Haack told the New Horizons employee that she would start paying $100 per month on the account. When no payment was received in October, Haack was contacted again, and she then informed New Horizons that Kickapoo Valley had dissolved, "that she was . . . a partner, that Robert had moved out of state, and that she planned to assume responsibility and would again start to make a hundred dollars per month beginning in October." The employee also testified that during the October telephone conversation, Haack told her she had the assets of the business: a truck, which was secured by the bank; and some accounts receivable "that they were trying to collect."

When contacted in November, Haack again promised a payment, but in December, Haack told the New Horizons employee "not to call her at work anymore." When attempts to contact Haack at her home phone number proved unsuccessful, New Horizons commenced this action to collect the account balance, $1,009.99, from Haack "DBA KICKAPOO VALLEY FREIGHT." Haack testified that Kickapoo Valley had been organized as a limited liability company, but she did not introduce articles of organization or an operating agreement into evidence.

Haack did offer as exhibits a Wisconsin Department of Revenue registration certificate, as well as some correspondence from the department, showing the enterprise identified as "Kickapoo Valley Freight LLC." Haack stated her defense to New Horizons' claim was that the account was in the business name, that she was not personally liable for debts of the limited liability company, and that she had not personally guaranteed the obligation.

According to Haack, her brother, Robert Koch, had suffered a nervous breakdown and left the state; the truck was sold, with all proceeds going to the bank who held the lien on it; and there were "no additional assets," but that she was "left with quite a lot of debt that I had signed for." She acknowledged that she told New Horizons that she "would try to take care" of the account "several times" after the business ceased operations. Finally, Haack testified that she had not filed articles of dissolution or notified creditors of the termination of the business when it ceased operations in the fall of 1997.

In response to questions from the court regarding her investment in the company, and the limits of her liability and that of Mr. Koch, Haack answered that both of them had "lost" their investments in the company. She also testified that the company was taxed as a partnership, and that she had with her copies of a sale agreement whereby "the assets" of the company were sold and the proceeds were given to the bank in order to release the lien on the truck. None of those documents were introduced as exhibits, however, and they are not a part of the record. Haack later testified that the assets that were sold consisted of a "truck, a pallet jack and the customer list." She did not testify as to the disposition of any cash or accounts receivable remaining at the time the business was dissolved.

The trial court began its oral decision by noting that "the problem the court has, nobody's filed with this court any documents to show what the limited liability agreement stated. I don't know . . . who bore what responsibilities." The court went on to conclude that "the rules of dissolution apparently were not followed" because articles of dissolution had not been filed nor creditors notified. It awarded judgment to New Horizons in the amount claimed, on the following basis:

> Haack signed . . . an agreement for Kickapoo Valley Freight LLC, but it would appear to me that the corporation was just a shell around which there were no real intentions to operate like

> a corporation because there was no intent even to dissolve the corporation, and the court's going to find that the corporate veil is pierced by the fact that the people were acting like a partnership, being taxed like a partnership. . . .
>
> . . .
>
> I'm treating this as a partnership and assessing liability to the remaining partner. . . . That's the evidence that's before me, and unless I would have some other evidence that was not presented, I have to treat this matter as a partnership and assume that the limited liability agreement did not alter the normal partnership liability situation.

Haack appeals the judgment entered against her for $1,009.99 plus costs.

ANALYSIS

[T]he gravamen of Haack's appeal is that the court erred in applying the law to the largely undisputed facts of record. Thus, we are called upon to decide a legal question: Were Haack's testimony and exhibits sufficient to establish a defense under § 183.0304, STATS., which provides that "a member or manager of a limited liability company is not personally liable for any debt, obligation or liability of the limited liability company"? . . . [W]e will not overturn a judgment where the record reveals that the trial court's decision was right, although for the wrong reason.

New Horizons seeks to defend the trial court's judgment, and its rationale of "piercing the corporate veil," by noting that ch. 183, Stats., expressly permits the importation of concepts such as "piercing the veil" from business corporation law:

> Notwithstanding sub. (1) [which sets forth the limitation on member liability], nothing in this chapter shall preclude a court from ignoring the limited liability company entity under principles of common law of this state that are similar to those applicable to business corporations and shareholders in this state and under circumstances that are not inconsistent with the purposes of this chapter.

Section 183.0304(2), Stats. The cooperative argues that the court properly applied the concept of "piercing the veil" to the facts adduced at the trial of this matter. We disagree, and conclude, as Haack contends, that the court's comments imply that it erroneously deemed Kickapoo Valley's treatment as a partnership for tax purposes to be conclusive. There is little in the record, moreover, to support a conclusion that Haack "organized, controlled and conducted" company affairs to the extent that it had "no separate existence of its own and [was Haack's] mere instrumentality," which she "used to evade an obligation, to gain an unjust advantage or to commit an injustice." See Wiebke v. Richardson & Sons, Inc., 83 Wis.2d 359, 363, 265 N.W.2d 571, 573 (1978).

Rather, we conclude that entry of judgment against Haack on the New Horizons' claim was proper because she failed to establish that she took appropriate steps to shield herself from liability for the company's debts following its dissolution and the distribution of its assets. Section 183.0201, Stats. provides that "[o]ne or more persons may organize a limited liability company by signing and delivering articles of organization to the [Department of Financial Institutions] for filing." The filing of articles by the department constitutes "conclusive proof that the limited liability company is organized and formed under this chapter." Section 183.0204, Stats. As we have noted, Haack testified that an attorney had drafted and filed the necessary paperwork to establish Kickapoo Valley Freight LLC, but no direct evidence of the filing of articles with the department was presented to the court. Be that as it may, a fact-finder could have inferred from Haack's testimony and from her exhibits showing that the Department of Revenue apparently recognized Kickapoo Valley as an "LLC," that Haack and her brother had properly formed a limited liability company.

The record is devoid, however, of any evidence showing that appropriate steps were taken upon the dissolution of the company to shield its members from liability for the entity's obligations. Although it appears that filing articles of dissolution is optional, see § 183.0906, STATS., the order for distributing the company's assets following dissolution is fixed by statute, and the company's creditors enjoy first priority, see § 183.0905, STATS. A dissolved limited liability company may "dispose of known claims against it" by filing articles of dissolution, and then providing written notice to its known creditors containing information regarding the filing of claims. See § 183.0907, STATS. The testimony at trial indicates that Haack knew of New Horizons' claim at the time Kickapoo Valley was dissolved. It is also clear from the record that articles of dissolution for Kickapoo Valley Freight LLC were not filed, nor was the cooperative formally notified of a claim filing procedure or deadline.

Section 183.0909, Stats., provides in relevant part as follows:

> A claim not barred under § 183.0907 or 183.0908 may be enforced under this section against any of the following:
>
> . . .
>
> (2) If the dissolved limited liability company's assets have been distributed in liquidation, a member of the limited liability company to the extent of the member's proportionate share of the claim or to the extent of the assets of the limited liability company distributed to the member in liquidation, whichever is less, but a member's total liability for all claims under this section may not exceed the total value of assets distributed to the member in liquidation.

It appears from the record that certain of Kickapoo Valley's assets were sold, and that the proceeds from that sale were remitted to the bank which held a lien on the company's truck. There is nothing in the record, however, showing the disposition of other company assets, such as cash and accounts receivable. New Horizons' witness testified that, in October 1997, Haack had claimed to be attempting to collect the accounts of the dissolved company and hoped to pay the instant debt from those proceeds. We do not know the value of the accounts receivable in question, however, or the amounts of any other company debts to which the proceeds of the accounts may have been applied, because Haack presented no testimony on the issue.

In this regard, we agree with the trial court's comments regarding the lack of evidence in the record to show that Kickapoo Valley's affairs were properly wound up following its dissolution occasioned by Robert Koch's dissociation from the enterprise. . . .

Thus, although Haack correctly contends that the judgment cannot be sustained on the ground relied upon by the trial court, we "nevertheless . . . look to facts in the record 'in favor of respondent which [seem] to be insurmountable.' " See State v. Alles, 106 Wis.2d 368, 391–92, 316 N.W.2d 378, 388–89 (1982) (citation omitted).

ANALYSIS

1. The opinion states that the lower court "erroneously deemed Kickapoo Valley's treatment as a partnership for tax purposes to be conclusive." Does Kickapoo Valley's treatment as a partnership for tax purposes have any relevance at all?

2. Was there any theory of liability on which the plaintiff might have relied, other than those considered by the court?

3. Suppose that Haack had proved that she had invested $2,000 in the LLC and that upon dissolution she had pocketed (after paying off the LLC's other debts) $500. For what amount would she be liable to New Horizons?

CHAPTER 5

THE DUTIES OF OFFICERS, DIRECTORS, AND OTHER INSIDERS

1. THE OBLIGATIONS OF CONTROL: DUTY OF CARE

Kamin v. American Express Company

86 Misc.2d 809, 383 N.Y.S.2d 807, affirmed, 54 A.D.2d 654, 387 N.Y.S.2d 993 (1st Dept.1976).

In this stockholders' derivative action, the individual defendants, who are the directors of the American Express Company, move for an order dismissing the complaint for failure to state a cause of action pursuant to CPLR 3211(a)(7), and alternatively, for summary judgment pursuant to CPLR 3211(c).

The complaint is brought derivatively by two minority stockholders of the American Express Company, asking for a declaration that a certain dividend in kind is a waste of corporate assets, directing the defendants not to proceed with the distribution, or, in the alternative, for monetary damages. The motion to dismiss the complaint requires the Court to presuppose the truth of the allegations. It is the defendants' contention that, conceding everything in the complaint, no viable cause of action is made out.

After establishing the identity of the parties, the complaint alleges that in 1972 American Express acquired for investment 1,954,418 shares of common stock of Donaldson, Lufkin and Jenrette, Inc. (hereafter DLJ), a publicly traded corporation, at a cost of \$29.9 million. It is further alleged that the current market value of those shares is approximately \$4.0 million. On July 28, 1975, it is alleged, the Board of Directors of American Express declared a special dividend to all stockholders of record pursuant to which the shares of DLJ would be distributed in kind. Plaintiffs contend further that if American Express were to sell the DLJ shares on the market, it would sustain a capital loss of \$25 million, which could be offset against taxable capital gains on other investments. Such a sale, they allege, would result in tax savings to the company of approximately \$8 million, which would not be available in the case of the distribution of DLJ shares to stockholders. It is alleged that on October 8, 1975 and October 16, 1975, plaintiffs demanded that the directors rescind the previously declared dividend in DLJ shares and take steps to preserve the capital loss which would result from selling the shares. This demand was rejected by the Board of Directors on October 17, 1975.

It is apparent that all the previously-mentioned allegations of the complaint go to the question of the exercise by the Board of Directors of business judgment in deciding how to deal with the DLJ shares. The crucial allegation which must be scrutinized to determine the legal sufficiency of the complaint is paragraph 19, which alleges:

> "19. All of the defendant Directors engaged in or acquiesced in or negligently permitted the declaration and payment of the Dividend in violation of the fiduciary duty owed by them to Amex to care for and preserve Amex's assets in the same manner as a man of average prudence would care for his own property."

Plaintiffs never moved for temporary injunctive relief, and did nothing to bar the actual distribution of the DLJ shares. The dividend was in fact paid on October 31, 1975. Accordingly, that portion of the complaint seeking a direction not to distribute the shares is deemed to be moot, and the Court will deal only with the request for declaratory judgment or for damages.

Examination of the complaint reveals that there is no claim of fraud or self-dealing, and no contention that there was any bad faith or oppressive conduct. The law is quite clear as to what is necessary to ground a claim for actionable wrongdoing.

> "In actions by stockholders, which assail the acts of their directors or trustees, courts will not interfere unless the powers have been illegally or unconscientiously executed; or unless it be made to appear that the acts were fraudulent or collusive, and destructive of the rights of the stockholders. Mere errors of judgment are not sufficient as grounds for equity interference, for the powers of those entrusted with corporate management are largely discretionary." Leslie v. Lorillard, 110 N.Y. 519, 532, 18 N.E. 363, 365. . . .

More specifically, the question of whether or not a dividend is to be declared or a distribution of some kind should be made is exclusively a matter of business judgment for the Board of Directors.

> ". . . Courts will not interfere with such discretion unless it be first made to appear that the directors have acted or are about to act in bad faith and for a dishonest purpose. It is for the directors to say, acting in good faith of course, when and to what extent dividends shall be declared. . . . The statute confers upon the directors this power, and the minority stockholders are not in a position to question this right, so long as the directors are acting in good faith. . . ." Liebman v. Auto Strop Co., 241 N.Y. 427, 433–4, 150 N.E. 505, 506.
>
> . . .

Thus, a complaint must be dismissed if all that is presented is a decision to pay dividends rather than pursuing some other course of conduct. . . . A complaint which alleges merely that some course of action other than that pursued by the Board of Directors would have been more advantageous gives rise to no cognizable cause of action. Courts have more than enough to do in adjudicating legal rights and devising remedies for wrongs. The directors' room rather than the courtroom is the appropriate forum for thrashing out purely business questions which will have an impact on profits, market prices, competitive situations, or tax advantages. . . .

It is not enough to allege, as plaintiffs do here, that the directors made an imprudent decision, which did not capitalize on the possibility of using a potential capital loss to offset capital gains. More than imprudence or mistaken judgment must be shown.

> . . . Section 720(a)(1)(A) of the Business Corporation Law permits an action against directors for "the neglect of, or failure to perform, or other violation of his duties in the management and disposition of corporate assets committed to his charge." This does not mean that a director is chargeable with ordinary negligence for having made an improper decision, or having acted imprudently. The "neglect" referred to in the statute is neglect of duties (i.e., malfeasance or nonfeasance) and not misjudgment. To allege that a director "negligently permitted the declaration and payment" of a dividend without alleging fraud, dishonesty or nonfeasance, is to state merely that a decision was taken with which one disagrees.

Nor does this appear to be a case in which a potentially valid cause of action is inartfully stated. The defendants have moved alternatively for summary judgment and have submitted affidavits under CPLR 3211(c), and plaintiffs likewise have submitted papers enlarging upon the allegations of the complaint. The affidavits of the defendants and the exhibits annexed thereto demonstrate that the objections raised by the plaintiffs to the proposed dividend action were carefully considered and unanimously rejected by the Board at a special meeting called precisely for that purpose at the plaintiffs' request. The minutes of the special meeting indicate that the defendants were fully aware that a sale rather than a distribution of the DLJ shares might result in the realization of a substantial income tax saving. Nevertheless, they concluded that there were countervailing considerations primarily with respect to the adverse effect such a sale, realizing a loss of $25 million, would have on the net income figures in the American Express financial statement. Such a reduction of net income would have a serious effect on the market value of the publicly traded American Express stock. This was not a situation in which the defendant directors totally overlooked facts called to their attention. They gave them consideration, and attempted to view the total picture in arriving at their decision. While plaintiffs contend that according to their accounting consultants the loss on the DLJ stock would still have to be charged against current earnings even if the stock were distributed, the defendants' accounting experts assert that the loss would be a charge against earnings only in the event of a sale, whereas in the event of distribution of the stock as a dividend, the proper accounting treatment would be to charge the loss only against surplus. While the chief accountant for the SEC raised some question as to the appropriate accounting treatment of this transaction, there was no basis for any action to be taken by the SEC with respect to the American Express financial statement.

The only hint of self-interest which is raised, not in the complaint but in the papers on the motion, is that four of the twenty directors were officers and employees of American Express and members of its Executive Incentive Compensation Plan. Hence, it is suggested, by virtue of the action taken earnings may have been overstated and their compensation affected thereby. Such a claim is highly speculative and standing alone can hardly be regarded as sufficient to support an inference of self-dealing. There is no claim or showing that the four company directors dominated and controlled the sixteen outside members of the Board. Certainly, every action taken by the Board has some impact on earnings and may therefore affect the compensation of those whose earnings are keyed to profits. That does not disqualify the inside directors, nor does it put every policy adopted by the Board in question. All directors have an obligation, using sound business judgment, to maximize income for the benefit of all persons having a stake in the welfare of the corporate entity. . . . What we have here as revealed both by the complaint and by the affidavits and exhibits, is that a disagreement exists between two minority stockholders and a unanimous Board of Directors as to the best way to handle a loss already incurred on an investment. The directors are entitled to exercise their honest business judgment on the information before them, and to act within their corporate powers. That they may be mistaken, that other courses of action might have differing consequences, or that their action might benefit some shareholders more than others presents no basis for the superimposition of judicial judgment, so long as it appears that the directors have been acting in good faith. The question of to what extent a dividend shall be declared and the manner in which it shall be paid is ordinarily subject only to the qualification that the dividend be paid out of surplus (Business Corporation Law Section 510, subd. b). The Court will not interfere unless a clear case is made out of fraud, oppression, arbitrary action, or breach of trust.

. . .

In this case it clearly appears that the plaintiffs have failed as a matter of law to make out an actionable claim. Accordingly, the motion by the defendants for summary judgment and dismissal of the complaint is granted.

ANALYSIS

1. What standard does the court adopt for the duty of care of directors? What must a plaintiff prove?

2. The directors of American Express had two possible courses of action. They could have sold the shares of DLJ and distributed the proceeds to the shareholders of American Express. The alternative, which they adopted, was to distribute the DLJ shares in kind to the American Express shareholders. According to the facts pleaded by the plaintiff, the cost to American Express of the second course of action was $8 million in lost tax benefits. What was the offsetting benefit? What was the likelihood that the value to the shareholders of that benefit would be greater than the cost?

3. The court says that the decision not to sell the DLJ shares might have benefited four of the defendants who were employees of American Express, because of the operation of the corporation's incentive compensation plan (under which, presumably, bonuses or other benefits were based on reported profits). What does this suggest to you about how incentive compensation provisions of employment contracts should be drafted?

Smith v. Van Gorkom

488 A.2d 858 (Del.Sup.Ct.1985).

■ HORSEY, JUSTICE (for the majority):

This appeal from the Court of Chancery involves a class action brought by shareholders of the defendant Trans Union Corporation . . . against the defendant members of the Board of Directors. . . .

Following trial, the former Chancellor granted judgment for the defendant directors . . .

Speaking for the majority of the Court, we . . . reverse and direct that judgment be entered in favor of the plaintiffs and against the defendant directors for the fair value of the plaintiffs' stockholdings in Trans Union, in accordance with Weinberger v. UOP, Inc., Del.Supr., 457 A.2d 701 (1983).

I.

. . . Trans Union was a publicly-traded, diversified holding company, the principal earnings of which were generated by its railcar leasing business. During the period here involved, the Company had a cash flow of hundreds of millions of dollars annually. However, the Company had difficulty in generating sufficient taxable income [to be able to make use of certain federal income tax benefits called] investment tax credits (ITCs). . . .

On August 27, 1980, [Trans Union CEO Jerome] Van Gorkom met with Senior Management of Trans Union. . . . Various alternatives were suggested and discussed preliminarily, including the sale of Trans Union to a company with a large amount of taxable income.

Donald Romans, Chief Financial Officer of Trans Union, stated that his department had done a "very brief bit of work on the possibility of a leveraged buy-out."* . . . The work consisted of a "preliminary study" of the cash which could be generated by the Company if it participated in a leveraged buy-out. . . .

On September 5, at another Senior Management meeting which Van Gorkom attended, Romans again brought up the idea of a leveraged buy-out . . . Romans and Bruce S. Chelberg, President and Chief Operating Officer of Trans Union, had been working on the matter in preparation for the meeting. According to Romans: They did not "come up" with a price for the Company. They merely "ran the numbers" at $50 a share and at $60 a share with the "rough form" of their cash figures at the time. Their "figures indicated that $50 would be very easy to do but $60 would be very difficult to do under those figures." . . .

At this meeting, Van Gorkom stated that he would be willing to take $55 per share for his own 75,000 shares. He vetoed the suggestion of a leveraged buy-out by Management, however, as involving a potential conflict of interest for Management. Van Gorkom, a certified public accountant and lawyer, had been an officer of Trans Union for 24 years, its Chief Executive Officer for more than 17 years, and Chairman of its

* [Eds.—A leveraged buyout (LBO) is simply a purchase of a company financed by a relatively small amount of equity (common stock) and a large amount of debt (which provides the leverage). Often assets of the company are sold to pay off part of the debt.]

Board for 2 years. It is noteworthy in this connection that he was then approaching 65 years of age and mandatory retirement.

. . .

Van Gorkom decided to meet with Jay A. Pritzker, a well-known corporate takeover specialist and a social acquaintance. However, rather than approaching Pritzker simply to determine his interest in acquiring Trans Union, Van Gorkom assembled a proposed per share price for sale of the Company and a financing structure by which to accomplish the sale. Van Gorkom did so without consulting either his Board or any members of Senior Management except one: Carl Peterson, Trans Union's Controller. Telling Peterson that he wanted no other person on his staff to know what he was doing, but without telling him why, Van Gorkom directed Peterson to calculate the feasibility of a leveraged buy-out at an assumed price per share of $55. Apart from the Company's historic stock market price [in the $30 to $40 price range] and Van Gorkom's long association with Trans Union, the record is devoid of any competent evidence that $55 represented the per share intrinsic value of the Company.

Having thus chosen the $55 figure, based solely on the availability of a leveraged buy-out, Van Gorkom multiplied the price per share by the number of shares outstanding to reach a total value of the Company of $690 million. Van Gorkom told Peterson to use this $690 million figure and to assume a $200 million equity contribution by the buyer. Based on these assumptions, Van Gorkom directed Peterson to determine whether the debt portion of the purchase price could be paid off in five years or less if financed by Trans Union's cash flow as projected in the Five Year Forecast, and by the sale of certain weaker divisions identified in a study done for Trans Union by the Boston Consulting Group ("BCG study"). Peterson reported that, of the purchase price, approximately $50–80 million would remain outstanding after five years. Van Gorkom was disappointed, but decided to meet with Pritzker nevertheless.

Van Gorkom arranged a meeting with Pritzker at the latter's home on Saturday, September 13, 1980. Van Gorkom prefaced his presentation by stating to Pritzker: "Now as far as you are concerned, I can, I think, show how you can pay a substantial premium over the present stock price and pay off most of the loan in the first five years. . . ."

Van Gorkom then reviewed with Pritzker his calculations based upon his proposed price of $55 per share. Although Pritzker mentioned $50 as a more attractive figure, no other price was mentioned. However, Van Gorkom stated that to be sure that $55 was the best price obtainable, Trans Union should be free to accept any better offer. Pritzker demurred, stating that his organization would serve as a "stalking horse" for an "auction contest" only if Trans Union would permit Pritzker to buy 1,750,000 shares of Trans Union stock at market price which Pritzker could then sell to any higher bidder. . . .

On Monday, September 15, Pritzker advised Van Gorkom that he was interested in the $55 cash-out merger proposal and requested more information on Trans Union. . . . Van Gorkom was "astounded that events were moving with such amazing rapidity."

On Thursday, September 18, Van Gorkom met again with Pritzker. At that time, Van Gorkom knew that Pritzker intended to make a cash-out merger offer at Van Gorkom's proposed $55 per share. Pritzker instructed his attorney, a merger and acquisition specialist, to begin drafting merger documents. There was no further discussion of the $55 price. However, the number of shares to be offered [by the company] to Pritzker was negotiated down to one million shares; the price was set at $38–75 cents above the per share price at the close of the market on September 19. At this point, Pritzker insisted that the Trans Union Board act on his merger proposal within the next three days, stating to Van Gorkom: "We have to have a decision by no later than Sunday [evening, September 21] before the opening of the English stock exchange on Monday morning." . . .

On Friday, September 19, Van Gorkom, Chelberg, and Pritzker consulted with Trans Union's lead bank regarding the financing of Pritzker's purchase of Trans Union. The bank indicated that it could form a syndicate of banks that would finance the transaction. . . .

On Friday, September 19, Van Gorkom called a special meeting of the Trans Union Board for noon the following day. He also called a meeting of the Company's Senior Management to convene at 11:00 a.m., prior to the meeting of the Board. . . .

Senior Management's reaction to the Pritzker proposal was completely negative. No member of Management, except Chelberg and Peterson, supported the proposal. . . . Nevertheless, Van Gorkom proceeded to the Board meeting as scheduled without further delay. . . .

Van Gorkom began the Special Meeting of the Board with a twenty-minute oral presentation. Copies of the proposed Merger Agreement were delivered too late for study before or during the meeting. He reviewed the Company's ITC and depreciation problems and the efforts theretofore made to solve them. He discussed his initial meeting with Pritzker and his motivation in arranging that meeting. Van Gorkom did not disclose to the Board, however, the methodology by which he alone had arrived at the $55 figure, or the fact that he first proposed the $55 price in his negotiations with Pritzker.

Van Gorkom outlined the terms of the Pritzker offer as follows: Pritzker would pay $55 in cash for all outstanding shares of Trans Union stock upon completion of which Trans Union would be merged into New T Company, a subsidiary wholly-owned by Pritzker and formed to implement the merger; for a period of 90 days, Trans Union could receive, but could not actively solicit, competing offers; the offer had to be acted on by the next evening, Sunday, September 21; Trans Union could only furnish to competing bidders published information, and not proprietary information; the offer was subject to Pritzker obtaining the necessary financing by October 10, 1980; if the financing contingency were met or waived by Pritzker, Trans Union was required to sell to Pritzker one million newly-issued shares of Trans Union at $38 per share.

Van Gorkom took the position that putting Trans Union "up for auction" through a 90-day market test would validate a decision by the Board that $55 was a fair price. He told the Board that the "free market will have an opportunity to judge whether $55 is a fair price." Van Gorkom framed the decision before the Board not as whether $55 per share was the highest price that could be obtained, but as whether the

$55 price was a fair price that the stockholders should be given the opportunity to accept or reject. . . .

Chelberg, Trans Union's President, supported Van Gorkom's presentation and representations. . . .

The Board meeting of September 20 lasted about two hours. Based solely upon Van Gorkom's oral presentation, Chelberg's supporting representations, Romans' oral statement [describing the feasibility study], Brennan's legal advice, and their knowledge of the market history of the Company's stock, the directors approved the proposed Merger Agreement. However, the Board later claimed to have attached two conditions to its acceptance: (1) that Trans Union reserved the right to accept any better offer that was made during the market test period; and (2) that Trans Union could share its proprietary information with any other potential bidders. While the Board now claims to have reserved the right to accept any better offer received after the announcement of the Pritzker agreement (even though the minutes of the meeting do not reflect this), it is undisputed that the Board did not reserve the right to actively solicit alternate offers.

The Merger Agreement was executed by Van Gorkom during the evening of September 20 at a formal social event that he hosted for the opening of the Chicago Lyric Opera. Neither he nor any other director read the agreement prior to its signing and delivery to Pritzker.

. . . Within 10 days of the public announcement, dissent among Senior Management over the merger had become widespread. Faced with threatened resignations of key officers, Van Gorkom met with Pritzker who agreed to several modifications of the Agreement. Pritzker was willing to do so provided that Van Gorkom could persuade the dissidents to remain on the Company payroll for at least six months after consummation of the merger.

Van Gorkom reconvened the Board on October 8 and secured the directors' approval of the proposed amendments [to the merger agreement]—sight unseen. The Board also authorized the employment of Salomon Brothers, its investment banker, to solicit other offers for Trans Union during the proposed "market test" period. . . . Salomon Brothers' efforts over a three-month period from October 21 to January 21 produced only one serious suitor for Trans Union-General Electric Credit Corporation ("GE Credit"), a subsidiary of the General Electric Company. However, GE Credit was unwilling to make an offer for Trans Union unless Trans Union first rescinded its Merger Agreement with Pritzker. When Pritzker refused, GE Credit terminated further discussions with Trans Union in early January.

In the meantime, in early December, the investment firm of Kohlberg, Kravis, Roberts & Co. ("KKR"), the only other concern to make a firm offer for Trans Union, withdrew its offer under circumstances hereinafter detailed. . . .

On February 10, the stockholders of Trans Union approved the Pritzker merger proposal. Of the outstanding shares, 69.9% were voted in favor of the merger; 7.25% were voted against the merger; and 22.85% were not voted.

II.

We turn to the issue of the application of the business judgment rule to the September 20 meeting of the Board. . . .

Under Delaware law, the business judgment rule is the offspring of the fundamental principle, codified in 8 Del.C. § 141(a), that the business and affairs of a Delaware corporation are managed by or under its board of directors. . . . The rule itself "is a presumption that in making a business decision, the directors of a corporation acted on an informed basis, in good faith and in the honest belief that the action taken was in the best interests of the company." [Aronson v. Lewis, 473 A.2d 805, 812 (Del.1984).] . . . Thus, the party attacking a board decision as uninformed must rebut the presumption that its business judgment was an informed one.

The determination of whether a business judgment is an informed one turns on whether the directors have informed themselves "prior to making a business decision, of all material information reasonably available to them." Id.

Under the business judgment rule there is no protection for directors who have made "an unintelligent or unadvised judgment." Mitchell v. Highland-Western Glass, Del.Ch., 167 A. 831, 833 (1933). . . . [As we have held in other contexts, however,] we think the concept of gross negligence is the proper standard for determining whether a business judgment reached by a board of directors was an informed one.

In the specific context of a proposed merger of domestic corporations, a director has a duty under 8 Del.C. 251(b), along with his fellow directors, to act in an informed and deliberate manner in determining whether to approve an agreement of merger before submitting the proposal to the stockholders. Certainly in the merger context, a director may not abdicate that duty by leaving to the shareholders alone the decision to approve or disapprove the agreement. . . .

III.

. . . [T]he question of whether the directors reached an informed business judgment in agreeing to sell the Company, pursuant to the terms of the September 20 Agreement presents, in reality, two questions: (A) whether the directors reached an informed business judgment on September 20, 1980; and (B) if they did not, whether the directors' actions taken subsequent to September 20 were adequate to cure any infirmity in their action taken on September 20. . . .

-A-

On the record before us, we must conclude that the Board of Directors did not reach an informed business judgment on September 20, 1980 in voting to "sell" the Company for $55 per share pursuant to the Pritzker cash-out merger proposal. . . .

The directors (1) did not adequately inform themselves as to Van Gorkom's role in forcing the "sale" of the Company and in establishing the per share purchase price; (2) were uninformed as to the intrinsic value of the Company; and (3) given these circumstances, at a minimum, were grossly negligent in approving the "sale" of the Company upon two hours' consideration, without prior notice, and without the exigency of a crisis or emergency.

As has been noted, the Board based its September 20 decision to approve the cash-out merger primarily on Van Gorkom's representations. None of the directors, other than Van Gorkom and Chelberg, had any prior knowledge that the purpose of the meeting was to propose a cash-out merger of Trans Union. No members of Senior Management were present, other than Chelberg, Romans and Peterson; and the latter two had only learned of the proposed sale an hour earlier. . . .

Without any documents before them concerning the proposed transaction, the members of the Board were required to rely entirely upon Van Gorkom's 20-minute oral presentation of the proposal. No written summary of the terms of the merger was presented; the directors were given no documentation to support the adequacy of the $55 price per share for sale of the Company; and the Board had before it nothing more than Van Gorkom's statement of his understanding of the substance of an agreement which he admittedly had never read, nor which any member of the Board had ever seen.

Under 8 Del.C. § 141(e), "directors are fully protected in relying in good faith on reports made by officers." Michelson v. Duncan, Del.Ch., 386 A.2d 1144, 1156 (1978); aff'd in part and rev'd in part on other grounds, Del.Supr., 407 A.2d 211 (1979). . . . The term "report" has been liberally construed to include reports of informal personal investigations by corporate officers. . . . However, there is no evidence that any "report," as defined under § 141(e), concerning the Pritzker proposal, was presented to the Board on September 20. Van Gorkom's oral presentation of his understanding of the terms of the proposed Merger Agreement, which he had not seen, and Romans' brief oral statement of his preliminary study regarding the feasibility of a leveraged buy-out of Trans Union do not qualify as § 141(e) "reports" for these reasons: The former lacked substance because Van Gorkom was basically uninformed as to the essential provisions of the very document about which he was talking. Romans' statement was irrelevant to the issues before the Board since it did not purport to be a valuation study. At a minimum for a report to enjoy the status conferred by § 141(e), it must be pertinent to the subject matter upon which a board is called to act, and otherwise be entitled to good faith, not blind, reliance. . . .

The defendants rely on the following factors to sustain the Trial Court's finding that the Board's decision was an informed one: (1) the magnitude of the premium or spread between the $55 Pritzker offering price and Trans Union's current market price of $38 per share; (2) the amendment of the Agreement as submitted on September 20 to permit the Board to accept any better offer during the "market test" period; (3) the collective experience and expertise of the Board's "inside" and "outside" directors; and (4) their reliance on Brennan's legal advice that the directors might be sued if they rejected the Pritzker proposal. . . .

(1)

A substantial premium may provide one reason to recommend a merger, but in the absence of other sound valuation information, the fact of a premium alone does not provide an adequate basis upon which to assess the fairness of an offering price. . . .

The record is clear that before September 20, Van Gorkom and other members of Trans Union's Board knew that the market had consistently undervalued the worth of Trans Union's stock, despite steady increases in the Company's operating income in the seven years preceding the merger. The Board related this occurrence in large part to Trans Union's inability to use its ITCs as previously noted. . . .

The parties do not dispute that a publicly-traded stock price is solely a measure of the value of a minority position and, thus, market price represents only the value of a single share. Nevertheless, on September 20, the Board assessed the adequacy of the premium over market, offered by Pritzker, solely by comparing it with Trans Union's current and historical stock price.

Indeed, as of September 20, the Board had no other information on which to base a determination of the intrinsic value of Trans Union as a going concern. As of September 20, the Board had made no evaluation of the Company designed to value the entire enterprise, nor had the Board ever previously considered selling the Company or consenting to a buy-out merger. . . .

The record also establishes that the Board accepted without scrutiny Van Gorkom's representation as to the fairness of the $55 price per share for sale of the Company—a subject that the Board had never previously considered. The Board thereby failed to discover that Van Gorkom had suggested the $55 price to Pritzker and, most crucially, that Van Gorkom had arrived at the $55 figure based on calculations designed solely to determine the feasibility of a leveraged buy-out. No questions were raised either as to the tax implications of a cash-out merger or how the price for the one million share option granted Pritzker was calculated. . . .

(2)

This brings us to the post-September 20 "market test" upon which the defendants ultimately rely to confirm the reasonableness of their September 20 decision to accept the Pritzker proposal. In this connection, the directors present a two-part argument: (a) that by making a "market test" of Pritzker's $55 per share offer a condition of their September 20 decision to accept his offer, they cannot be found to have acted impulsively or in an uninformed manner on September 20; and (b) that the adequacy of the $17 premium for sale of the Company was conclusively established over the following 90 to 120 days by the most reliable evidence available—the marketplace. . . .

Again, the facts of record do not support the defendants' argument. There is no evidence: (a) that the Merger Agreement was effectively amended to give the Board freedom to put Trans Union up for auction sale to the highest bidder; or (b) that a public auction was in fact permitted to occur. . . .

Van Gorkom states that the Agreement as submitted incorporated the ingredients for a market test by authorizing Trans Union to receive competing offers over the next 90-day period. However, he concedes that the Agreement barred Trans Union from actively soliciting such offers and from furnishing to interested parties any information about the Company other than that already in the public domain. . . .

(3)

The directors' unfounded reliance on both the premium and the market test as the basis for accepting the Pritzker proposal undermines the defendants' remaining contention that the Board's collective experience and sophistication was a sufficient basis for finding that it reached its September 20 decision with informed, reasonable deliberation. . . .

-B-

We now examine the Board's post-September 20 conduct for the purpose of determining first, whether it was informed and not grossly negligent; and second, if informed, whether it was sufficient to legally rectify and cure the Board's derelictions of September 20.[23]

(1)

. . .

Van Gorkom . . . called a special meeting of Trans Union's Board for October 8. . . . [T]he primary purpose of the October 8 Board meeting was to amend the Merger Agreement, in a manner agreeable to Pritzker, to permit Trans Union to conduct a "market test." Van Gorkom understood that the proposed amendments were intended to give the Company an unfettered "right to openly solicit offers down through January 31." Van Gorkom presumably so represented the amendments to Trans Union's Board members on October 8. In a brief session, the directors approved Van Gorkom's oral presentation of the substance of the proposed amendments, the terms of which were not reduced to writing until October 10. But rather than waiting to review the amendments, the Board again approved them sight unseen and adjourned, giving Van Gorkom authority to execute the papers when he received them. . . .

The next day, October 9, and before the Agreement was amended, Pritzker moved swiftly to off-set the proposed market test amendment. First, Pritzker informed Trans Union that he had completed arrangements for financing its acquisition and that the parties were thereby mutually bound to a firm purchase and sale arrangement. Second, Pritzker announced the exercise of his option to purchase one million shares of Trans Union's treasury stock at $38 per share—75 cents above the current market price. . . .

The next day, October 10, Pritzker delivered to Trans Union the proposed amendments to the September 20 Merger Agreement. Van Gorkom promptly proceeded to countersign all the instruments on behalf of Trans Union without reviewing the instruments to determine if they were consistent with the authority previously granted him by the Board. . . .

The October 10 amendments to the Merger Agreement did authorize Trans Union to solicit competing offers, but the amendments had more far-reaching effects. The most significant change was in the definition of the third-party "offer" available to Trans Union as a possible basis for withdrawal from its Merger Agreement with Pritzker. Under the October 10 amendments, a better *offer* was no longer sufficient to permit Trans Union's withdrawal. Trans Union was now permitted to terminate the Pritzker Agreement and abandon the merger only if, prior to February 10, 1981, Trans Union had either consummated a merger (or sale of assets) with a third party or had entered into a "definitive" merger agreement more favorable than Pritzker's and for a greater

[23] As will be seen, we do not reach the second question.

consideration—subject only to stockholder approval. Further, the "extension" of the market test period to February 10, 1981 was circumscribed by other amendments which required Trans Union to file its preliminary proxy statement on the Pritzker merger proposal by December 5, 1980 and use its best efforts to mail the statement to its shareholders by January 5, 1981. Thus, the market test period was effectively reduced, not extended....

In our view, the record compels the conclusion that the directors' conduct on October 8 exhibited the same deficiencies as did their conduct on September 20. The Board permitted its Merger Agreement with Pritzker to be amended in a manner it had neither authorized nor intended....

... Our review of the record compels a finding that confirmation of the appropriateness of the Pritzker offer by an unfettered or free market test was virtually meaningless in the face of the terms and time limitations of Trans Union's Merger Agreement with Pritzker as amended October 10, 1980....

VI.

To summarize: we hold that the directors of Trans Union breached their fiduciary duty to their stockholders (1) by their failure to inform themselves of all information reasonably available to them and relevant to their decision to recommend the Pritzker merger; and (2) by their failure to disclose all material information such as a reasonable stockholder would consider important in deciding whether to approve the Pritzker offer....

On remand, the Court of Chancery shall conduct an evidentiary hearing to determine the fair value of the shares represented by the plaintiffs' class, based on the intrinsic value of Trans Union on September 20, 1980.... Thereafter, an award of damages may be entered to the extent that the fair value of Trans Union exceeds $55 per share.

■ MCNEILLY, JUSTICE, dissenting:

The majority opinion reads like an advocate's closing address to a hostile jury. And I say that not lightly. Throughout the opinion great emphasis is directed only to the negative, with nothing more than lip service granted the positive aspects of this case. . . . The first and most important error made is the majority's assessment of the directors' knowledge of the affairs of Trans Union and their combined ability to act in this situation under the protection of the business judgment rule.

Trans Union's Board of Directors consisted of ten men, five of whom were "inside" directors and five of whom were "outside" directors. The "inside" directors were Van Gorkom, Chelberg, Bonser, William B. Browder, Senior Vice-President-Law, and Thomas P. O'Boyle, Senior Vice-President-Administration. At the time the merger was proposed the inside five directors had collectively been employed by the Company for 116 years and had 68 years of combined experience as directors. The "outside" directors were A.W. Wallis, William B. Johnson, Joseph B. Lanterman, Graham J. Morgan and Robert W. Reneker. With the exception of Wallis, these were all chief executive officers of Chicago based corporations that were at least as large as Trans Union. The five "outside" directors had 78 years of combined experience as chief executive officers, and 53 years cumulative service as Trans Union directors....

Directors of this caliber are not ordinarily taken in by a "fast shuffle." I submit they were not taken into this multi-million dollar corporate transaction without being fully informed and aware of the state of the art as it pertained to the entire corporate panorama of Trans Union. . . . I do not believe that to be the case here. These men knew Trans Union like the back of their hands and were more than well qualified to make on the spot informed business judgments concerning the affairs of Trans Union including a 100% sale of the corporation. Lest we forget, the corporate world of then and now operates on what is so aptly referred to as "the fast track." These men were at the time an integral part of that world, all professional business men, not intellectual figureheads. . . .

AFTERMATH

Following remand, the case was settled, with the approval of the trial court, for $23 million. Of this, $10 million came from insurance covering the directors and almost $11 million came from the Pritzkers. The rest was paid by the directors, but Van Gorkom paid "substantially more" than the five outside directors. See Chicago Tribune, Feb. 8, 1987, § 7, p. 9, col. 4, and Feb. 15, 1987, § C, p. 2.

Van Gorkom claimed after the decision that the board had not intended to take the position that $55 per share was a "fair" price. Instead, he said, "We decided that $55 was too good a price to take away from shareholders without giving them the opportunity to vote and decide for themselves whether or not they wanted to take the offer." Not too long after sale to the Pritzkers, there developed a glut of rail cars. Rates plummeted and two of Trans Union's competitors filed for bankruptcy. Id.

NOTE ON CINERAMA, INC. V. TECHNICOLOR, INC.

Smith v. Van Gorkom was decided in 1985. In 1983, Ronald Perelman, operating through MacAndrews and Forbes Group, Inc., of which he was the chairman and controlling shareholder, acquired Technicolor, Inc. at a price of $23 per share. The pre-offer price was $11 per share. The acquisition proved to be highly profitable for Perelman, who later acquired Revlon, Inc. (see Chapter 7, Section 2(B)) and became one of the richest men in America.

Cinerama, Inc. was a Technicolor shareholder. It opposed the acquisition; it voted against the merger of Technicolor into a MacAndrews & Forbes subsidiary and perfected its appraisal rights. While pursuing its appraisal remedy, Cinerama discovered facts that led it to file an action in the Delaware Chancery Court opposing the merger and claiming the nonappraisal remedy of rescission (which would have resulted in a substantial recovery because of a post-merger increase in the value of Technicolor). Cinerama was allowed to proceed with both actions (see Cede & Co. v. Technicolor, Inc., 542 A.2d 1182 (1988) (Cede I).

In the action for rescission (or other remedies) the Chancery Court found that the Technicolor board had violated its duty of care. The story was similar to that in Smith v. Van Gorkom in that the CEO had in effect made the deal with Perelman and then presented it to the board, which approved it quickly, without adequate information and adequate deliberation and without conducting a "market check." The case was more favorable to the defendants in that the CEO had done a thorough job of investigation, had bargained hard (raising the price from an initial offer of $15 per share and from a later, more serious, offer of $20 per share), and had hired experts who had done a thorough job in support of the fairness of the deal for Technicolor. This, however, did not relieve the board of its own obligations.

Despite the defect in the process of approval, the Chancery Court rejected Cinerama's action on the theory that the price was fair, so there was no harm and, therefore, no cause of action. In short, "no harm, no foul." This ruling was reversed on appeal and the case was remanded. Cede & Co. v. Technicolor, Inc., 634 A.2d 345 (1993), modified upon motion for reargument 636 A.2d 956 (1994) (Cede II).

On remand, the Chancery Court found that the defendant had met its burden of proving entire fairness and dismissed the action. On appeal the Delaware Supreme Court affirmed. Cinerama, Inc. v. Technicolor, Inc., 663 A.2d 1156 (1995). The Supreme Court opinion opened with the following statement of basic legal principles:

> . . . A combination of the fiduciary duties of care and loyalty gives rise to the requirement that "a director disclose to shareholders all material facts bearing upon a merger vote. . . ." Zirn v. VLI Corp., Del.Supr., 621 A.2d 773, 778 (1993). Moreover, in Delaware, "existing law and policy have evolved into a virtual per se rule of [awarding] damages for breach of the fiduciary duty of disclosure." In re Tri-Star Pictures, Inc. Litig., 634 A.2d at 333.

The court then distinguished *Van Gorkom*:

> In *Van Gorkom,* this Court concluded that the board of directors' failure to inform itself before recommending a merger to the stockholders constituted a breach of the fiduciary duty of care and rebutted the presumptive protection of the business judgment rule. Smith v. Van Gorkom, 488 A.2d at 893. In *Van Gorkom,* this Court also concluded that the directors had violated the duty of disclosure. This Court then held that the directors were liable for damages, since the record after trial reflected that the compound breaches of the duties of care and disclosure could not withstand an entire fairness analysis. Consequently, . . . the only issue to remand was the amount of damages the Court of Chancery should assess. . . .

The court then proceeded to discuss various factors that must be considered in an analysis of the entire fairness of a transaction: the timing, initiation, negotiation, and structure of the transaction, the disclosure to and approval by the directors, and the disclosure to and approval by the shareholders. The court upheld the Chancery Court decision for the defendants after quoting the following portion of that court's summary description of the important facts:

> (1) CEO Kamerman consistently sought the highest price that Perelman would pay; (2) Kamerman was better informed about the strengths and weaknesses of Technicolor as a business than anyone else; . . . (3) Kamerman and later the board were advised by firms who were among the best in the country; (4) the

> negotiations led to a price that was very high when compared to the prior market price of the stock (about a 100% premium over unaffected market price) or when compared to premiums paid in more or less comparable transactions during the period; (5) while the company was not shopped, there is no indication in the record that more money was possible from Mr. Perelman or likely from anyone else; management declined to do an MBO transaction at a higher price and while I did conclude that the deal was "probably locked up," if the value of the company at that time was or appeared to be remotely close to the value Cinerama claimed at trial, any "lock-up" arrangement present would not have created an insuperable financial or legal obstacle to an alternative buyer. Indeed the conclusion that the transaction was probably locked up was logically and actually premised upon the belief that the $23 price was high.

The Supreme Court decision left Cinerama with its appraisal action. In 2003 (twenty years after the transaction at issue), the Chancery court issued a lengthy opinion, with the conclusion that Cinerama was entitled to $21.98 per share, $1.02 less than the price it rejected it 1983, plus post-judgment interest. Cede & Co. v. Technicolor, Inc., 2003 WL 23700218 (Del. Ch. 2003, as revised July 9, 2004). In turn, the Supreme Court affirmed the judgment in 2005, although it reversed Chancery's finding on the amount of debt and the discount rate. See Cede & Co. v. Technicolor, Inc., 884 A.2d 26 (2005).

ANALYSIS

1. The *Van Gorkom* court refers to the board's views about the "intrinsic" value of the shares of stock of Trans Union. In the case of a publicly held corporation what is the difference, if any, between the "intrinsic" value and the market price?

2. If $55 per share was good enough for Van Gorkom, who held 75,000 shares, why was it not good enough for the rest of the shareholders? Did Van Gorkom's interests or goals differ from those of a typical shareholder?

3. Is it the assumption of the court in *Van Gorkom* that the duty of the directors was to obtain the highest possible price for the company or was the assumption that the duty was simply to obtain a "fair" price, whatever that may mean? What duty should directors be charged with? Note that in a situation like that facing the directors of Trans Union, a decision to seek a higher price creates a risk that the favorable deal at hand may fall through, with the shareholders left with shares trading at their old price. How serious, in fact, do you suppose that risk was? Do you suppose that when Pritzker put a short time limit on his offer he was bluffing?

4. One way in which directors faced with the opportunity to sell the company can protect themselves is to hire an investment banking firm to issue an opinion as to the fairness of the price that has been offered. Should directors be encouraged to ask for such "second opinions"? What might an investment banker have known that the outside directors of Trans Union did not know? Is it likely that there was any information about Trans Union known by its employees that would not be known by

investors in general and that would be important to them? Who should pay for the investment banker's fairness opinion? What is the relevance, if any, of time constraints imposed on an existing offer?

5. After the decision in Smith v. Van Gorkom, is a board of directors permitted to accept an offer for the company without shopping for a better offer? Should it be? Was it wrong for the directors to approve the sale of the one million shares to Pritzker for $38 per share?

6. What is the likely effect of this decision on the behavior of directors? On the welfare of shareholders? On the welfare of lawyers and investment bankers?

7. In the *Cede* case discussed above, the Delaware Supreme Court described the business judgment rule as "a powerful presumption" against judicial interference with board decision making. It then stated:

> Thus, a shareholder plaintiff challenging a board decision has the burden at the outset to rebut the rule's presumption. To rebut the rule, a shareholder plaintiff assumes the burden of providing evidence that directors, in reaching their challenged decision, breached any one of the triads of their fiduciary duty—good faith, loyalty or due care. If a shareholder plaintiff fails to meet this evidentiary burden, the business judgment rule attaches to protect corporate officers and directors and the decisions they make, and our courts will not second-guess these business judgments. If the rule is rebutted, the burden shifts to the defendant directors, the proponents of the challenged transaction, to prove to the trier of fact the "entire fairness" of the transaction to the shareholder plaintiff.

Id. at 361. Is this statement of the business judgment rule consistent with *Kamin* and *Van Gorkom*? Does this statement treat the business judgment rule as a doctrine of abstention or as a standard of liability?

NOTE ON LEGISLATIVE RESPONSE

The decision in Smith v. Van Gorkom caused considerable consternation and anxiety among corporate directors. To relieve the anxiety, many states adopted provisions designed to afford directors protection from liability. The Delaware legislation is found in Del.Gen.Corp.Law § 102(b)(7), which allows any corporation to include in its certificate of incorporation:

> A provision eliminating or limiting the personal liability of a director to the corporation or its stockholders for monetary damages for breach of fiduciary duty as a director, provided that such provision shall not eliminate or limit the liability of a director: (i) For any breach of the director's duty of loyalty to the corporation or its stockholders; (ii) for acts or omissions not in good faith or which involve intentional misconduct or a knowing violation of law; (iii) under § 174 of this title [relating to payment of dividends]; or (iv) for any transaction from which the director derived an improper personal benefit. . . .

There has been widespread adoption, with shareholder approval, of amendments to corporate certificates of incorporation to provide the protection contemplated by this provision (and provisions in other states with similar objectives).

Francis v. United Jersey Bank

432 A.2d 814 (N.J. 1981).

[Pritchard & Baird Intermediaries Corp. (Pritchard & Baird) was in the business of acting as a reinsurance broker. Reinsurance is the process by which an insurance company that has agreed to insure a risk (the ceding company) assigns all or a portion of that risk to another company (the reinsurer), along with a share of the premium. The broker acts as intermediary. In doing so, it receives funds from ceding companies and is obligated to pay these funds over to the reinsurers. Lillian Pritchard had inherited a 48 percent interest in Pritchard & Baird from her husband, Charles Pritchard, Sr. She was the largest single shareholder and a director. The remaining shares of the corporation were owned by her sons, Charles, Jr. and William, who also served as directors. Charles, Jr. dominated the management of the corporation after the death of his father. Charles, Jr. and William over a period of several years withdrew large sums of money from the corporation in the form of "loans." By the time the corporation finally became bankrupt, the total of the loans was over $12 million. The loans were taken from funds that the corporation was supposed to hold in trust for its clients. In effect, the purported loans were simply misappropriations by the two sons. After the discovery of the misappropriations and the consequent insolvency of the corporation, Mrs. Pritchard died. The present suit is by the trustee in bankruptcy (representing the interests of the various creditors) against Mrs. Pritchard's estate to recover the misappropriated amounts.]

Mrs. Pritchard was not active in the business of Pritchard & Baird and knew virtually nothing of its corporate affairs. She briefly visited the corporate offices in Morristown on only one occasion, and she never read or obtained the annual financial statements. She was unfamiliar with the rudiments of reinsurance and made no effort to assure that the policies and practices of the corporation, particularly pertaining to the withdrawal of funds, complied with industry custom or relevant law. Although her husband had warned her that Charles, Jr. would "take the shirt off my back," Mrs. Pritchard did not pay any attention to her duties as a director or to the affairs of the corporation.

After her husband died in December 1973, Mrs. Pritchard became incapacitated and was bedridden for a six-month period. She became listless at this time and started to drink rather heavily. Her physical condition deteriorated, and in 1978 she died. The trial court rejected testimony seeking to exonerate her because she "was old, was grief-stricken at the loss of her husband, sometimes consumed too much alcohol and was psychologically overborne by her sons." 162 N.J.Super. at 371, 392 A.2d 1233. That court found that she was competent to act and that the reason Mrs. Pritchard never knew what her sons "were doing was because she never made the slightest effort to discharge any of her responsibilities as a director of Pritchard & Baird." 162 N.J.Super. at 372, 392 A.2d 1233.

. . . Individual liability of a corporate director for acts of the corporation is a prickly problem. Generally directors are accorded broad immunity and are not insurers of corporate activities. The problem is particularly nettlesome when a third party asserts that a director, because of nonfeasance, is liable for losses caused by acts of insiders, who in this case were officers, directors and shareholders. Determination of the liability of Mrs. Pritchard requires findings that she had a duty to the clients of Pritchard & Baird, that she breached that duty and that her breach was a proximate cause of their losses.

The New Jersey Business Corporation Act, which took effect on January 1, 1969, was a comprehensive revision of the statutes relating to business corporations. One section, N.J.S.A. 14A:6–14, concerning a director's general obligation had no counterpart in the old Act. That section makes it incumbent upon directors to

> discharge their duties in good faith and with that degree of diligence, care and skill which ordinarily prudent men would exercise under similar circumstances in like positions. [N.J.S.A. 14A:6–14]

. . .

Because N.J.S.A. 14A:6–14 is modeled in part upon section 717 of the New York statute, N.Y.Bus.Corp. Law § 717 (McKinney), we consider also the law of New York in interpreting the New Jersey statute. . . .

Prior to the enactment of section 717, the New York courts, like those of New Jersey, had espoused the principle that directors owed that degree of care that a businessman of ordinary prudence would exercise in the management of his own affairs. . . . In addition to requiring that directors act honestly and in good faith, the New York courts recognized that the nature and extent of reasonable care depended upon the type of corporation, its size and financial resources. Thus, a bank director was held to stricter accountability than the director of an ordinary business.[1]

. . .

As a general rule, a director should acquire at least a rudimentary understanding of the business of the corporation. Accordingly, a director should become familiar with the fundamentals of the business in which the corporation is engaged. . . . Because directors are bound to exercise ordinary care, they cannot set up as a defense lack of the knowledge needed to exercise the requisite degree of care. If one "feels that he has not had sufficient business experience to qualify him to perform the duties of a director, he should either acquire the knowledge by inquiry, or refuse to act." Ibid.

Directors are under a continuing obligation to keep informed about the activities of the corporation. . . .

Directors may not shut their eyes to corporate misconduct and then claim that because they did not see the misconduct, they did not have a duty to look. The sentinel asleep at his post contributes nothing to the enterprise he is charged to protect. . . .

---

[1] The obligations of directors of banks involve some additional consideration because of their relationship to the public generally and depositors in particular. Statutes impose certain requirements on bank directors. For example, directors of national banks must take an oath that they will diligently and honestly administer the affairs of the bank and will not permit violation of the banking laws. . . .

Directorial management does not require a detailed inspection of day-to-day activities, but rather a general monitoring of corporate affairs and policies. . . .

While directors are not required to audit corporate books, they should maintain familiarity with the financial status of the corporation by a regular review of financial statements. . . .

Of some relevance in this case is the circumstance that the financial records disclose the "shareholders' loans." Generally directors are immune from liability if, in good faith,

> they rely upon the opinion of counsel for the corporation or upon written reports setting forth financial data concerning the corporation and prepared by an independent public accountant or certified public accountant or firm of such accountants or upon financial statements, books of account or reports of the corporation represented to them to be correct by the president, the officer of the corporation having charge of its books of account, or the person presiding at a meeting of the board. [N.J.S.A. 14A:6–14]

The review of financial statements, however, may give rise to a duty to inquire further into matters revealed by those statements. . . . Upon discovery of an illegal course of action, a director has a duty to object and, if the corporation does not correct the conduct, to resign. . . .

In certain circumstances, the fulfillment of the duty of a director may call for more than mere objection and resignation. Sometimes a director may be required to seek the advice of counsel. . . . A director may have a duty to take reasonable means to prevent illegal conduct by co-directors; in any appropriate case, this may include threat of suit. . . .

A director's duty of care does not exist in the abstract, but must be considered in relation to specific obligees. In general, the relationship of a corporate director to the corporation and its stockholders is that of a fiduciary. . . . Shareholders have a right to expect that directors will exercise reasonable supervision and control over the policies and practices of a corporation. The institutional integrity of a corporation depends upon the proper discharge by directors of those duties.

While directors may owe a fiduciary duty to creditors also, that obligation generally has not been recognized in the absence of insolvency. . . . With certain corporations, however, directors are deemed to owe a duty to creditors and other third parties even when the corporation is solvent. Although depositors of a bank are considered in some respects to be creditors, courts have recognized that directors may owe them a fiduciary duty. . . . Directors of nonbanking corporations may owe a similar duty when the corporation holds funds of others in trust. . . .

The most striking circumstances affecting Mrs. Pritchard's duty as a director are the character of the reinsurance industry, the nature of the misappropriated funds and the financial condition of Pritchard & Baird. The hallmark of the reinsurance industry has been the unqualified trust and confidence reposed by ceding companies and reinsurers in reinsurance brokers. Those companies entrust money to reinsurance intermediaries with the justifiable expectation that the funds will be transmitted to the appropriate parties. Consequently, the companies could have assumed rightfully that Mrs. Pritchard, as a director of a reinsurance brokerage corporation, would not sanction the comingling and the conversion of loss and premium funds for the personal use of the principals of Pritchard & Baird.

As a reinsurance broker, Pritchard & Baird received annually as a fiduciary millions of dollars of clients' money which it was under a duty to segregate. To this extent, it resembled a bank rather than a small family business. Accordingly, Mrs. Pritchard's relationship to the clientele of Pritchard & Baird was akin to that of a director of a bank to its depositors. All parties agree that Pritchard & Baird held the misappropriated funds in an implied trust. That trust relationship gave rise to a fiduciary duty to guard the funds with fidelity and good faith. . . .

As a director of a substantial reinsurance brokerage corporation, she should have known that it received annually millions of dollars of loss and premium funds which it held in trust for ceding and reinsurance companies. Mrs. Pritchard should have obtained and read the annual statements of financial condition of Pritchard & Baird. Although she had a right to rely upon financial statements prepared in accordance with N.J.S.A. 14A:6–14, such reliance would not excuse her conduct. The reason is that those statements disclosed on their face the misappropriation of trust funds.

From those statements, she should have realized that, as of January 31, 1970, her sons were withdrawing substantial trust funds under the guise of "Shareholders' Loans." The financial statements for each fiscal year commencing with that of January 31, 1970, disclosed that the working capital deficits and the "loans" were escalating in tandem. Detecting a misappropriation of funds would not have required special expertise or extraordinary diligence; a cursory reading of the financial statements would have revealed the pillage. Thus, if Mrs. Pritchard had read the financial statements, she would have known that her sons were converting trust funds. When financial statements demonstrate that insiders are bleeding a corporation to death, a director should notice and try to stanch the flow of blood.

In summary, Mrs. Pritchard was charged with the obligation of basic knowledge and supervision of the business of Pritchard & Baird. Under the circumstances, this obligation included reading and understanding financial statements, and making reasonable attempts at detection and prevention of the illegal conduct of other officers and directors. She had a duty to protect the clients of Pritchard & Baird against policies and practices that would result in the misappropriation of money they had entrusted to the corporation. She breached that duty.

IV

Nonetheless, the negligence of Mrs. Pritchard does not result in liability unless it is a proximate cause of the loss. . . .

Usually a director can absolve himself from liability by informing the other directors of the impropriety and voting for a proper course of action. . . . Conversely, a director who votes for or concurs in certain actions may be "liable to the corporation for the benefit of its creditors or shareholders, to the extent of any injuries suffered by such persons, respectively, as a result of any such action." N.J.S.A. 14A:6–12 (Supp.1981–1982). A director who is present at a board meeting is presumed to concur in corporate action taken at the meeting unless his dissent is entered in the minutes of the meeting or filed promptly after adjournment. N.J.S.A. 14A:6–13. In many, if not most, instances an objecting director whose dissent is noted in accordance with N.J.S.A. 14A:6–13 would be absolved after attempting to persuade fellow directors to follow a different course of action. Cf. *McGlynn* [*v. Schultz,* 90 N.J. Super. 505, 520–521, 218 A.2d 408 (Ch.Div.1966), aff'd 95 N.J.Super. 412, 231 A.2d 386 (App.Div.), cert. den. 50 N.J. 409, 235 A.2d 901 (1967)] (receiver had no case against director who advised president that certain funds should be escrowed, wrote to executive committee to that effect, and objected at special meeting of board of directors); *Selheimer v. Manganese Corp.,* 423 Pa. 563, 572, 584, 224 A.2d 634, 640, 646 (Sup.Ct.1966) (dissenting minority director in publicly held corporation absolved because he did all he could to divert majority directors from their course of conduct by complaining to management, threatening to institute suit and organizing a stockholders' committee).

Even accepting the hypothesis that Mrs. Pritchard might not be liable if she had objected and resigned, there are two significant reasons for holding her liable. First, she did not resign until just before the bankruptcy. Consequently, there is no factual basis for the speculation that the losses would have occurred even if she had objected and resigned. Indeed, the trial court reached the opposite conclusion: "The actions of the sons were so blatantly wrongful that it is hard to see how they could have resisted any moderately firm objection to what they were doing." 162 N.J.Super. at 372, 392 A.2d 1233. Second, the nature of the reinsurance business distinguishes it from most other commercial activities in that reinsurance brokers are encumbered by fiduciary duties owed to third parties. In other corporations, a director's duty normally does not extend beyond the shareholders to third parties.

In this case, the scope of Mrs. Pritchard's duties was determined by the precarious financial condition of Pritchard & Baird, its fiduciary relationship to its clients and the implied trust in which it held their funds. Thus viewed, the scope of her duties encompassed all reasonable action to stop the continuing conversion. Her duties extended beyond mere objection and resignation to reasonable attempts to prevent the misappropriation of the trust funds. . . .

Within Pritchard & Baird, several factors contributed to the loss of the funds: comingling of corporate and client monies, conversion of funds by Charles, Jr. and William and dereliction of her duties by Mrs. Pritchard. The wrongdoing of her sons, although the immediate cause of the loss, should not excuse Mrs. Pritchard from her negligence which also was a substantial factor contributing to the loss. . . . Her sons knew that she, the only other director, was not reviewing their conduct; they spawned their fraud in the backwater of her neglect. Her neglect of duty contributed to the climate of corruption; her failure to act contributed to the continuation of that corruption. Consequently, her conduct was a substantial factor contributing to the loss.

. . .

The judgment of the Appellate Division is affirmed.

PROBLEM

Assume you are a member of the board of directors of a corporation that operates a chain of "health spas." Business has not been good and rents and salaries are high. The corporation is deeply in debt to landlords, suppliers, utilities, and employees. The corporation's method of operation is to require customers to pay a membership fee of $500 for one year, in advance. All the money collected this way within the past year has been spent, except for $5,000 collected within the past week or so. At a regular meeting of the board, the CEO reviews the financial status of the corporation and says that he intends to spend the $5,000 on an advertising campaign that he hopes will turn the business around. If that does not work, there will be no alternative but to close the doors and go out of business, in which case there will be no assets available for creditors or to pay wages owed to employees. A member of the board whose business judgment you respect says that in her opinion the chance of success of the advertising campaign is about 5 percent. In the meantime, you know that the corporation is continuing to sign up new customers (at $500 each) and to hire new employees. Some of the shareholders of the corporation are people of modest means who are your friends and who invested on the basis of your recommendation. Consider both the ethical and legal implications of your actions. As a director, what would you do? Assume, initially, that you have ruled out resignation.

On the possibility of resignation, assume that the corporation is incorporated in Delaware. Del.Gen.Corp.L. § 141(b) provides: "Each director shall hold office until his successor is elected or until his earlier resignation or removal." What would you think about the possibility of resigning?

PROBLEMS

1. Suppose you are a member of the board of directors of a trucking company that operates tank trucks carrying bulk liquids between Florida and New York. In all the states along the route between Florida and New York except Pennsylvania, trucks are permitted a maximum weight of up to 60,000 pounds (including the equipment), but in Pennsylvania the maximum weight is 45,000 pounds. The penalty for violation of the maximum weight law is a fine of $200. Under Pennsylvania law it is plain that the fine is "penal"; it is not regarded as a type of toll or use tax. The risk of being caught and fined on any one trip is about 20 percent. The practice of your corporation and, as far as you are aware, of all your competitors, is to ignore the 45,000 maximum weight law and treat the fines as a cost of doing business. The alternative is either to comply with the 45,000 pound limit along the entire route or to reduce the load at the border of Pennsylvania, carry the excess to the other border in another truck, and then load the excess back onto the through-route truck. The cost of either alternative would make it impossible to compete with other trucking firms and with individual truckers and with other forms of transportation without losing money. Moreover, compliance with the 45,000 limit would require carrying less than a full load and would increase safety hazards. You have just learned of these facts. What do you do?

2. Suppose the facts are the same as in the preceding paragraph, but you also learn that it is often possible to avoid the $200 fine by paying a bribe of $50 to the state official at the weight station whenever a violation is discovered and that your drivers have been instructed to do that whenever possible. Bribery of a public official is a felony punishable by a fine and a jail sentence, but there has been virtually no enforcement. What do you do? (Assume that the corporation is privately held and thus is not subject to the accounting rules imposed by the securities laws.)

3. Suppose the facts are the same as in the preceding paragraph except that time has passed and you and the other directors have ordered the CEO to do what is required to prevent the payment of bribes by the company's drivers. The CEO has complied and the result has been an increase in costs such that the company no longer can operate at a profit. The CEO proposes that the company sell all its tractors (the part of the rig that contains the engine and cab) and hire independent tractor owners to haul the company's trailers. What is your reaction?

2. DUTY OF LOYALTY

A. DIRECTORS AND MANAGERS

Bayer v. Beran

49 N.Y.S.2d 2 (Sup.Ct.1944).

. . .

To encourage freedom of action on the part of directors, or to put it another way, to discourage interference with the exercise of their free and independent judgment, there has grown up what is known as the "business judgment rule." . . . "Questions of policy of management, expediency of contracts or action, adequacy of consideration, lawful appropriation of corporate funds to advance corporate interests, are left solely to their honest and unselfish decision, for their powers therein are without limitation and free from restraint, and the exercise of them for the common and general interests of the corporation may not be questioned, although the results show that what they did was unwise or inexpedient." Pollitz v. Wabash R. Co., 207 N.Y. 113, 124, 100 N.E. 721, 724. Indeed, although the concept of "responsibility" is firmly fixed in the law, it is only in a most unusual and extraordinary case that directors are held liable for negligence in the absence of fraud, or improper motive, or personal interest.

The "business judgment rule," however, yields to the rule of undivided loyalty. This great rule of law is designed "to avoid the possibility of fraud and to avoid the temptation of self-interest." Conway, J., in Matter of Ryan's Will, 291 N.Y. 376, 406, 52 N.E.2d 909, 923. It is "designed to obliterate all divided loyalties which may creep into a fiduciary relation. . . ." Thatcher, J., in City Bank Farmers Trust Co. v. Cannon, 291 N.Y. 125, 132, 51 N.E.2d 674, 676. "Included within its scope is every situation in which a trustee chooses to deal with another in such close relation with the trustee that possible advantage to such other person might influence, consciously or unconsciously, the judgment of the trustee. . . ." Lehman, Ch. J., in Albright v. Jefferson County National

Bank, 292 N.Y. 31, 39, 53 N.E.2d 753, 756. The dealings of a director with the corporation for which he is the fiduciary are therefore viewed "with jealousy by the courts." Globe Woolen Co. v. Utica Gas & Electric Co., 224 N.Y. 483, 121 N.E. 378, 380. Such personal transactions of directors with their corporations, such transactions as may tend to produce a conflict between self-interest and fiduciary obligation, are, when challenged, examined with the most scrupulous care, and if there is any evidence of improvidence or oppression, any indication of unfairness or undue advantage, the transactions will be voided. . . . "Their dealings with the corporation are subjected to rigorous scrutiny and where any of their contracts or engagements with the corporation are challenged the burden is on the director not only to prove the good faith of the transaction but also to show its inherent fairness from the viewpoint of the corporation and those interested therein." Pepper v. Litton, 308 U.S. 295, 306, 60 S.Ct. 238, 245, 84 L.Ed. 281.

The . . . "advertising" cause of action charges the directors with negligence, waste and improvidence in embarking the corporation [Celanese Corporation of America] upon a radio advertising program beginning in 1942 and costing about $1,000,000 a year. It is further charged that they were negligent in selecting the type of program and in renewing the radio contract for 1943. More serious than these allegations is the charge that the directors were motivated by a noncorporate purpose in causing the radio program to be undertaken and in expending large sums of money therefor. It is claimed that this radio advertising was for the benefit of Miss Jean Tennyson, one of the singers on the program, who in private life is Mrs. Camille Dreyfus, the wife of the president of the company and one of its directors; that it was undertaken to "further, foster and subsidize her career"; to "furnish a vehicle" for her talents.

Eliminating for the moment the part played by Miss Tennyson in the radio advertising campaign, it is clear that the character of the advertising, the amount to be expended therefor, and the manner in which it should be used, are all matters of business judgment and rest peculiarly within the discretion of the board of directors. Under the authorities previously cited, it is not, generally speaking, the function of a court of equity to review these matters or even to consider them. Had the wife of the president of the company not been involved, the advertising cause of action could have been disposed of summarily. Her connection with the program, however, makes it necessary to go into the facts in some detail.

Before 1942 the company had not resorted to radio advertising. While it had never maintained a fixed advertising budget, the company had, through its advertising department, spent substantial sums of money for advertising purposes. In 1941, for example, the advertising expense was $683,000, as against net sales for that year of $62,277,000 and net profits (before taxes) of $13,972,000. The advertising was at all times directed towards the creation of a consumer preference which would compel or induce the various trade elements linking the corporation to the consumer to label the corporation's products so that the consumer would know he was buying the material he wanted. The company had always claimed that its products, which it had called or labeled "Celanese," were different from rayon, chemically and physically;

that its products had qualities, special and unique, which made them superior to rayon. The company had never called or designated its products as rayon.

As far back as ten years ago, a radio program was considered, but it did not seem attractive. In 1937, the Federal Trade Commission promulgated a rule, the effect of which was to require all celanese products to be designated and labeled rayon. The name "Celanese" could no longer be used alone. The products had to be called or labeled "rayon" or "celanese rayon." This gave the directors much concern. As one of them expressed it, "When we were compelled to put our product under the same umbrella with rayon rather than being left outside as a separate product, a thermo-plastic such as nylon is, we believed we were being treated in an unfair manner and that it was up to us, however, to do the best we could to circumvent the situation in which we found ourselves.... All manner of things were considered but there seemed only one thing we could do. We could either multiply our current advertising and our method of advertising in the same mediums we had been using, or we could go into radio."

The directors, in considering the matter informally, but not collectively as a board, decided towards the end of 1941 to resort to the radio and to have the company go on the air with a dignified program of fine music, the kind of program which they felt would be in keeping with what they believed to be the beauty and superior quality of their products. The radio program was not adopted on the spur of the moment or at the whim of the directors. They acted after studies reported to them, made by the advertising department, beginning in 1939. A radio consultant was employed to advise as to time and station. An advertising agency of national repute was engaged to take charge of the formulation and production of the program. It was decided to expend about $1,000,000 a year, but the commitments were to be subject to cancellation every thirteen weeks, so that the maximum obligation of the company would be not more than $250,000.

So far, there is nothing on which to base any claim of breach of fiduciary duty. Some care, diligence and prudence were exercised by these directors before they committed the company to the radio program. It was for the directors to determine whether they would resort to radio advertising; it was for them to conclude how much to spend; it was for them to decide the kind of program they would use. It would be an unwarranted act of interference for any court to attempt to substitute its judgment on these points for that of the directors, honestly arrived at. The expenditure was not reckless or unconscionable. Indeed, it bore a fair relationship to the total amount of net sales and to the earnings of the company. . . . That a program of classical and semiclassical music was selected, rather than a variety program, or a news commentator program, furnishes no ground for legal complaint. True, variety programs have a wider popular appeal than do musicals, but it would be a very sad thing if the former were the only kind of radio programs to be used. Some of the largest industrial concerns in the country have recognized this and have maintained fine musical programs on the radio for many years.

Now we have to take up an unfortunate incident, one which cannot be viewed with the complacency displayed by some of the directors of the company. This is not a closely held family corporation. The Doctors

Dreyfus and their families own about 135,000 shares of common stock, the other directors about 10,000 shares out of a total outstanding issue of 1,376,500 shares. Some of these other directors were originally employed by Dr. Camille Dreyfus, the president of the company. His wife, to whom he has been married for about twelve years, is known professionally as Miss Jean Tennyson and is a singer of wide experience.

Dr. Dreyfus, as was natural, consulted his wife about the proposed radio program; he also asked the advertising agency, that had been retained, to confer with her about it. She suggested the names of the artists, all stars of the Metropolitan Opera Company, and the name of the conductor, prominent in his field. She also offered her own services as a paid artist. All of her suggestions as to personnel were adopted by the advertising agency. While the record shows Miss Tennyson to be a competent singer, there is nothing to indicate that she was indispensable or essential to the success of the program. She received $500 an evening. It would be far-fetched to suggest that the directors caused the company to incur large expenditures for radio advertising to enable the president's wife to make $24,000 in 1942 and $20,500 in 1943.

Of course it is not improper to appoint relatives of officers or directors to responsible positions in a company. But where a close relative of the chief executive officer of a corporation, and one of its dominant directors, takes a position closely associated with a new and expensive field of activity, the motives of the directors are likely to be questioned. The board would be placed in a position where selfish, personal interests might be in conflict with the duty it owed to the corporation. That being so, the entire transaction, if challenged in the courts, must be subjected to the most rigorous scrutiny to determine whether the action of the directors was intended or calculated "to subserve some outside purpose, regardless of the consequences to the company, and in a manner inconsistent with its interests."

After such careful scrutiny I have concluded that, up to the present, there has been no breach of fiduciary duty on the part of the directors. The president undoubtedly knew that his wife might be one of the paid artists on the program. The other directors did not know this until they had approved the campaign of radio advertising and the general type of radio program. The evidence fails to show that the program was designed to foster or subsidize "the career of Miss Tennyson as an artist" or to "furnish a vehicle for her talents." That her participation in the program may have enhanced her prestige as a singer is no ground for subjecting the directors to liability, as long as the advertising served a legitimate and a useful corporate purpose and the company received the full benefit thereof.

The musical quality of "Celanese Hour" has not been challenged, nor does the record contain anything reflecting on Miss Tennyson's competence as an artist. There is nothing in the testimony to show that some other soprano would have enhanced the artistic quality of the program or its advertising appeal. There is no suggestion that the present program is inefficient or that its cost is disproportionate to what a program of that character reasonably entails. Miss Tennyson's contract with the advertising agency retained by the directors was on a standard form, negotiated through her professional agent. Her compensation, as well as that of the other artists, was in conformity with that paid for comparable work. She received less than any of the other artists on the program. Although she appeared with greater regularity than any other singer, she received no undue prominence, no special build-up. Indeed, all of the artists were subordinated to the advertisement of the company and of its products. The company was featured. It appears also that the popularity of the program has increased since it was inaugurated.

It is clear, therefore, that the directors have not been guilty of any breach of fiduciary duty, in embarking upon the program of radio advertising and in renewing it. . . .

It is urged that the expenditures were illegal because the radio advertising program was not taken up at any formal meeting of the board of directors, and no resolution approving it was adopted by the board or by the executive committee. The general rule is that directors acting separately and not collectively as a board cannot bind the corporation. There are two reasons for this: first, that collective procedure is necessary in order that action may be deliberately taken after an opportunity for discussion and an interchange of views; and second, that directors are the agents of the stockholders and are given by law no power to act except as a board. . . . Liability may not, however, be imposed on directors because they failed to approve the radio program by resolution at a board meeting.

It is desirable to follow the regular procedure, prescribed by law, which is something more than what has, at times, thoughtlessly been termed red tape. Long experience has demonstrated the necessity for doing this in order to safeguard the interests of all concerned, particularly where, as here, the company has over 1,375,000 shares outstanding in the hands of the public, of which about 10% are held by the officers and directors.

But the failure to observe the formal requirements is by no means fatal. . . . The directorate of this company is composed largely of its executive officers. It is a close, working directorate. Its members are in daily association with one another and their full time is devoted to the business of the company with which they have been connected for many years. In this respect it differs from the boards of many corporations of comparable size, where the directorate is made up of men of varied interests who meet only at stated, and somewhat infrequent, intervals.

The same informal practice followed in this transaction had been the customary procedure of the directors in acting on corporate projects of equal and greater magnitude. All of the members of the executive committee were available for daily consultation and they discussed and approved the plan for radio advertising. While a greater degree of formality should undoubtedly be exercised in the future, it is only just and proper to point out that these directors, with all their loose procedure, have done very well for the corporation. Under their administration the company has thrived and prospered. . . .

The expenditures for radio advertising, although made without resolution at a formal meeting of the board, were approved and authorized by the members individually, and may in no sense be considered to have been ultra vires. The resolution adopted by the board on July 6, 1943, with all of the directors present, except two who were resident in England, while expressly ratifying only the renewal of the broadcasting contract, may be deemed a ratification of all prior action taken in connection with the radio advertising. When this resolution was adopted, the Celanese Hour had been on the air to the knowledge of all the directors for eighteen months. Moreover, acceptance and retention of the benefits of the radio advertising, with full knowledge thereof, was as complete a ratification as would have resulted from any formal all-inclusive resolution. . . .

On the entire case, the directors acted in the free exercise of their honest business judgment and their conduct in the transactions challenged did not constitute negligence, waste or improvidence. The complaint is accordingly dismissed on the merits.

NOTE

Late-nineteenth-century courts generally held that a corporation could freely void any contract between it and one of its directors or officers. By the early twentieth century, courts hesitated to let firms void their contracts so easily. As a result, if a disinterested majority of directors had ratified a contract and if the complaining party could not prove it unfair, the courts generally held the contract valid. *Bayer* takes the rule one step further: because the contract is fair, it is valid even though disinterested directors have not formally ratified it.

Benihana of Tokyo, Inc. v. Benihana, Inc.

906 A.2d 114 (Del. 2006).

. . .

Factual and Procedural Background

Rocky Aoki founded Benihana of Tokyo, Inc. (BOT), and its subsidiary, Benihana, which own and operate Benihana restaurants in the United States and other countries. Aoki owned 100% of BOT until 1998, when he pled guilty to insider trading charges. In order to avoid licensing problems created by his status as a convicted felon, Aoki transferred his stock to the Benihana Protective Trust. The trustees of the Trust were [three of Aoki's six children] (Kana Aoki Nootenboom, Kyle Aoki and Kevin Aoki) and Darwin Dornbush (who was then the family's attorney, a Benihana director, and, effectively, the company's general counsel).

Benihana, a Delaware corporation, has two classes of common stock. There are approximately 6 million shares of Class A common stock outstanding. Each share has 1/10 vote and the holders of Class A common are entitled to elect 25% of the directors. There are approximately 3 million shares of Common stock outstanding. Each share of Common has one vote and the holders of Common stock are entitled to elect the remaining 75% of Benihana's directors. Before the transaction at issue, BOT owned 50.9% of the Common stock and 2% of the Class A stock. The nine-member board of directors is classified and the directors serve three-year terms.[1]

---

[1] The directors at the time of the challenged transaction were: Dornbush, John E. Abdo, Norman Becker, Max Pine, Yoshihiro Sano, Joel Schwartz, Robert B. Sturges, Takanori Yoshimoto, and Kevin Aoki.

In 2003, shortly after Aoki married Keiko Aoki, conflicts arose between Aoki and his children. In August, the children were upset to learn that Aoki had changed his will to give Keiko control over BOT [upon his death]. Joel Schwartz, Benihana's president and chief executive officer, also was concerned about this change in control. He discussed the situation with Dornbush, and they briefly considered various options, including the issuance of sufficient Class A stock to trigger a provision in the certificate of incorporation that would allow the Common and Class A to vote together for 75% of the directors.

The Aoki family's turmoil came at a time when Benihana also was facing challenges. Many of its restaurants were old and outmoded. Benihana hired WD Partners to evaluate its facilities and to plan and design appropriate renovations. The resulting Construction and Renovation Plan anticipated that the project would take at least five years and cost $56 million or more. . . . [Benihana hired Morgan Joseph & Co. to develop financing options.]

On January 9, 2004, after evaluating Benihana's financial situation and needs, Fred Joseph, of Morgan Joseph, met with Schwartz, Dornbush and John E. Abdo, the board's executive committee. Joseph expressed concern that Benihana would not have sufficient available capital to complete the Construction and Renovation Plan and pursue appropriate acquisitions. Benihana was conservatively leveraged, and Joseph discussed various financing alternatives, including bank debt, high yield debt, convertible debt or preferred stock, equity and sale/leaseback options.

The full board met with Joseph on January 29, 2004. He reviewed all the financing alternatives that he had discussed with the executive committee, and recommended that Benihana issue convertible preferred stock. Joseph explained that the preferred stock would provide the funds needed for the Construction and Renovation Plan and also put the company in a better negotiating position if it sought additional financing from Wachovia [a major banking and financial services institution].

Joseph gave the directors a board book, marked "Confidential," containing an analysis of the proposed stock issuance (the Transaction). The book included, among others, the following anticipated terms: (i) issuance of $20,000,000 of preferred stock, convertible into Common stock; (ii) dividend of 6% +/- 0.5%; (iii) conversion premium of 20% +/- 2.5%; (iv) buyer's approval required for material corporate transactions; and (v) one to two board seats to the buyer. At trial, Joseph testified that the terms had been chosen by looking at comparable stock issuances and analyzing the Morgan Joseph proposal under a theoretical model.

The board met again on February 17, 2004, to review the terms of the Transaction. The directors discussed Benihana's preferences and Joseph predicted what a buyer likely would expect or require. . . .

Shortly after the February meeting, Abdo contacted Joseph and told him that BFC Financial Corporation was interested in buying the new convertible stock.[5] In April 2005, Joseph sent BFC a private placement memorandum. Abdo [representing BFC] negotiated with Joseph for several weeks. They agreed to the Transaction on the following basic

[5] BFC, a publicly traded Florida corporation, is a holding company for several investments. Abdo is a director and vice chairman. He owns 30% of BFC's stock.

terms: (i) $20 million issuance in two tranches of $10 million each, with the second tranche to be issued one to three years after the first; (ii) BFC obtained one seat on the board, and one additional seat if Benihana failed to pay dividends for two consecutive quarters; (iii) BFC obtained preemptive rights on any new voting securities; (iv) 5% dividend; . . . (vi) BFC had the right to force Benihana to redeem the preferred stock in full after ten years; and (vii) the stock would have immediate "as if converted" voting rights.* Joseph testified that he was satisfied with the negotiations, as he had obtained what he wanted with respect to the most important points.

On April 22, 2004, Abdo sent a memorandum to Dornbush, Schwartz and Joseph, listing the agreed terms of the Transaction. He did not send the memorandum to any other members of the Benihana board. Schwartz did tell Becker, Sturges, Sano, and possibly Pine that BFC was the potential buyer. At its next meeting, held on May 6, 2004, the entire board was officially informed of BFC's involvement in the Transaction. Abdo made a presentation on behalf of BFC and then left the meeting. Joseph distributed an updated board book, which explained that Abdo had approached Morgan Joseph on behalf of BFC, and included the negotiated terms. The trial court found that the board was not informed that Abdo had negotiated the deal on behalf of BFC. But the board did know that Abdo was a principal of BFC. After discussion, the board reviewed and approved the Transaction, subject to the receipt of a fairness opinion.

On May 18, 2004, after he learned that Morgan Joseph was providing a fairness opinion, Schwartz publicly announced the stock issuance. Two days later, Aoki's counsel sent a letter asking the board to abandon the Transaction and pursue other, more favorable, financing alternatives. The letter expressed concern about the directors' conflicts, the dilutive effect of the stock issuance, and its "questionable legality." Schwartz gave copies of the letter to the directors at the May 20 board meeting, and Dornbush advised that he did not believe that Aoki's concerns had merit. Joseph and another Morgan Joseph representative then joined the meeting by telephone and opined that the Transaction was fair from a financial point of view. The board then approved the Transaction.

During the following two weeks, Benihana received three alternative financing proposals. Schwartz asked Becker, Pine and Sturges to act as an independent committee and review the first offer. The committee decided that the offer was inferior and not worth pursuing. Morgan Joseph agreed with that assessment. Schwartz referred the next two proposals to Morgan Joseph, with the same result.

On June 8, 2004, Benihana and BFC executed the Stock Purchase Agreement. On June 11, 2004, the board met and approved resolutions ratifying the execution of the Stock Purchase Agreement and authorizing the stock issuance. Schwartz then reported on the three alternative proposals that had been rejected by the ad hoc committee and Morgan Joseph. On July 2, 2004, BOT filed this action against all of Benihana's directors, except Kevin Aoki, alleging breaches of fiduciary duties; and

* [Editors.—According to the lower court opinion, "[t]he Transaction caused a decrease in BOT's voting power in two steps: first to 42.5% and then to 36.5%." Benihana of Tokyo, Inc. v. Benihana, Inc., 891 A.2d 150, 155 (Del. Ch. 2005).]

against BFC, alleging that it aided and abetted the fiduciary violations. Three months later, as the parties were filing their pre-trial briefs, the board again reviewed the Transaction. After considering the allegations in the amended complaint, the board voted once more to approve it. . . .

Discussion

. . .

A. *Section 144(a)(1) approval*

Section 144 of the Delaware General Corporation Law provides a safe harbor for interested transactions, like this one, if "[t]he material facts as to the director's . . . relationship or interest and as to the contract or transaction are disclosed or are known to the board of directors . . . and the board . . . in good faith authorizes the contract or transaction by the affirmative votes of a majority of the disinterested directors. . . ." After approval by disinterested directors, courts review the interested transaction under the business judgment rule.

BOT argues that § 144(a)(1) is inapplicable because, when they approved the Transaction, the disinterested directors did not know that Abdo had negotiated the terms for BFC. Abdo's role as negotiator is material, according to BOT, because Abdo had been given the confidential term sheet prepared by Joseph and knew which of those terms Benihana was prepared to give up during negotiations. We agree that the board needed to know about Abdo's involvement in order to make an informed decision. The record clearly establishes, however, that the board possessed that material information when it approved the Transaction on May 6, 2004 and May 20, 2004.

Shortly before the May 6 meeting, Schwartz told Becker, Sturges and Sano that BFC was the proposed buyer. Then, at the meeting, Abdo made the presentation on behalf of BFC. Joseph's board book also explained that Abdo had made the initial contact that precipitated the negotiations. The board members knew that Abdo is a director, vice-chairman, and one of two people who control BFC. Thus, although no one ever said, "Abdo negotiated this deal for BFC," the directors understood that he was BFC's representative in the Transaction. . . .

B. *Abdo's alleged fiduciary violation*

BOT next argues that the Court of Chancery should have reviewed the Transaction under an entire fairness standard because Abdo breached his duty of loyalty when he used Benihana's confidential information to negotiate on behalf of BFC. This argument starts with a flawed premise. The record does not support BOT's contention that Abdo used any confidential information against Benihana. Even without Joseph's comments at the February 17 board meeting, Abdo knew the terms a buyer could expect to obtain in a deal like this. Moreover, as the trial court found, "the negotiations involved give and take on a number of points" and Benihana "ended up where [it] wanted to be" for the most important terms. Abdo did not set the terms of the deal; he did not deceive the board; and he did not dominate or control the other directors' approval of the Transaction. In short, the record does not support the claim that Abdo breached his duty of loyalty.

C. *Dilution of BOT's voting power*

Finally, BOT argues that the board's primary purpose in approving the Transaction was to dilute BOT's voting control. BOT points out that Schwartz was concerned about BOT's control in 2003 and even discussed with Dornbush the possibility of issuing a huge number of Class A shares. Then, despite the availability of other financing options, the board decided on a stock issuance, and agreed to give BFC "as if converted" voting rights. . . .

It is settled law that, "corporate action . . . may not be taken for the sole or primary purpose of entrenchment."[19] Here, however, the trial court found that "the primary purpose of the . . . Transaction was to provide what the directors subjectively believed to be the best financing vehicle available for securing the necessary funds to pursue the agreed upon Construction and Renovation Plan for the Benihana restaurants." That factual determination has ample record support, especially in light of the trial court's credibility determinations. . . .

ANALYSIS

1. (a) What alternatives might there have been that would have met Benihana's needs without depriving BOT (and Rocky and Keiko) of control? (b) Assuming that a voting security of some sort would be issued, with BOT losing majority voting control, why do you suppose Benihana did not seek to sell plain common stock? (c) Should the shift in control have affected the board's obligations and the standard of review applied by the court?

2. The preferred stock in this case can be thought of as a hybrid of debt and equity. What are its important elements? Why would BFC want each element and why might Benihana be reluctant to include each element? What are the tradeoffs? What arguments would you make, from either side of the negotiating table, for each element?

PROBLEMS

1. Susan Alexander is a "singer" who is trying to break into the big-time opera circuit. A few years ago, she took up with wealthy Charlie Kane, and has now married him. He would like to promote her career. Kane is CEO and majority shareholder in the Chicago *Inquirer*. The shares of the *Inquirer* are worth a total of $100 million.

A. Suppose that the *Inquirer*'s board of directors votes to make a $20 million donation to start a Chicago City Opera Co. (CCO). The Chicago community is eager to have this opera company, and the company thus stands to receive much goodwill in the area. If Alexander does not sing with the company, is there a problem?

B. Suppose that, out of appreciation for Kane, the music director of the CCO offers to star Alexander as the lead soprano in a new production of the opera "Rosebud." Is there a problem? Suppose that, when offered the lead, Alexander responds: "Thanks, you're so sweet. But Charlie is so rich, you know, and

[19] Williams v. Geier, 671 A.2d 1368, 1381 n. 28 (Del.1996).

we really don't need more money. I'd love to sing the lead, but how would it be if I did it for free?"

C. Suppose that Kane owns 100% of the stock of the *Inquirer*. Do your answers to the questions above change?

D. Suppose that Alexander is a genuine star, and the CCO offers her the "Rosebud" lead after holding an audition at which the judges unanimously voted her the best lyric soprano.

2. X Corp. is a public corporation that has been through troubled times but recently installed an effective team of managers, who have solved many operations problems. Cash flow has turned positive. The managers and the board members consider that the price of the company's shares does not reflect the firm's improved prospects, despite optimistic statements in the most recent annual report.

The CEO owns 7 percent of the common stock and other members of the management team own, collectively, 6 percent. The board members own, collectively, 8 percent. The CEO, who is also chair of the board, proposes to the board that the company purchase shares on the open market.

A. Would such purchases violate the board's fiduciary obligation to the selling shareholders? What about the board's duty to nonselling shareholders?

B. How would the selling shareholders be harmed, if at all?

C. Suppose the managers and the board members also have substantial numbers of stock options giving them the right to buy the stock at fixed prices. Suppose further that a majority of the shares are held by nontaxable institutions that have urged that all spare cash be used to pay dividends rather than to purchase shares. Is there a legally cognizable conflict of interest between the managers and board members and the institutions?

B. CORPORATE OPPORTUNITIES

Broz v. Cellular Information Systems, Inc.

673 A.2d 148 (Del.1996).

. . .

I. THE CONTENTIONS OF THE PARTIES AND THE DECISION BELOW

Robert F. Broz ("Broz") is the President and sole stockholder of RFB Cellular, Inc. ("RFBC"), a Delaware corporation engaged in the business of providing cellular telephone service in the Midwestern United States. At the time of the conduct at issue in this appeal, Broz was also a member of the board of directors of plaintiff below . . ., Cellular Information Systems, Inc. ("CIS"). CIS is a publicly held Delaware corporation and a competitor of RFBC.

The conduct before the Court involves the purchase by Broz of a cellular telephone service license for the benefit of RFBC. The license in question, known as the Michigan–2 Rural Service Area Cellular License ("Michigan–2"), is issued by the Federal Communications Commission ("FCC") and entitles its holder to provide cellular telephone service to a portion of northern Michigan. . . .

II. FACTS

. . . RFBC owns and operates an FCC license area, known as the Michigan–4 Rural Service Area Cellular License ("Michigan–4"). The license entitles RFBC to provide cellular telephone service to a portion of rural Michigan. Although Broz' efforts have been devoted primarily to the business operations of RFBC, he also served as an outside director of CIS at the time of the events at issue in this case. . . .

In April of 1994, Mackinac Cellular Corp. ("Mackinac") sought to divest itself of Michigan–2, the license area immediately adjacent to Michigan–4. To this end, Mackinac contacted Daniels & Associates ("Daniels") and arranged for the brokerage firm to seek potential purchasers for Michigan–2. In compiling a list of prospects, Daniels included RFBC as a likely candidate. In May of 1994, David Rhodes, a representative of Daniels, contacted Broz and broached the subject of RFBC's possible acquisition of Michigan–2. . . .

Michigan–2 was not, however, offered to CIS. Apparently, Daniels did not consider CIS to be a viable purchaser for Michigan–2 in light of CIS' recent financial difficulties. The record shows that, at the time Michigan–2 was offered to Broz, CIS had recently emerged from lengthy and contentious [insolvency reorganization]. . . .

During the period from early 1992 until the time of CIS' emergence from bankruptcy in 1994, CIS divested itself of some fifteen separate cellular license systems. CIS contracted to sell four additional license areas on May 27, 1994, leaving CIS with only five remaining license areas, all of which were outside of the Midwest.

On June 13, 1994, following a meeting of the CIS board, Broz spoke with CIS' Chief Executive Officer, Richard Treibick ("Treibick"), concerning his interest in acquiring Michigan–2. Treibick communicated to Broz that CIS was not interested in Michigan–2.[16] Treibick further stated that he had been made aware of the Michigan–2 opportunity prior to the conversation with Broz, and that any offer to acquire Michigan–2 was rejected. . . . [I]n August of 1994, Broz contacted another CIS director, Peter Schiff ("Schiff"), to discuss the possible acquisition of Michigan–2 by RFBC. Schiff, like Treibick, indicated that CIS had neither the wherewithal nor the inclination to purchase Michigan–2. In late September of 1994, Broz also contacted Stanley Bloch ("Bloch"), a director and counsel for CIS, to request that Bloch represent RFBC in its dealings with Mackinac. Bloch agreed to represent RFBC, and, like Schiff and Treibick, expressed his belief that CIS was not at all interested in the transaction. Ultimately, all the CIS directors testified at trial that, had Broz inquired at that time, they each would have expressed the opinion that CIS was not interested in Michigan–2.[17]

[16] In fact, during a deposition given in March of 1995, Treibick testified that he didn't "know who frankly was hawking [the Michigan–2 license] . . . at the time. . . . [W]e said forget it. It was not something we would have bought if they offered it to us for nothing."

[17] We assume arguendo that informal contacts and individual opinions of board members are not a substitute for a formal process of presenting an opportunity to a board of directors.

On June 28, 1994, following various overtures from PriCellular concerning an acquisition of CIS, six CIS directors entered into agreements with PriCellular to sell their shares in CIS at a price of $2.00 per share. These agreements were contingent upon, inter alia, the consummation of a PriCellular tender offer* for all CIS shares at the same price. . . .

. . . Financing difficulties ultimately caused PriCellular to delay the closing date of the tender offer from September 16, 1994 until October 14, 1994 and then again until November 9, 1994.

On August 6, September 6 and September 21, 1994, Broz submitted written offers to Mackinac for the purchase of Michigan–2. During this time period, PriCellular also began negotiations with Mackinac to arrange an option for the purchase of Michigan–2. PriCellular's interest in Michigan–2 was fully disclosed to CIS' chief executive, Treibick, who did not express any interest in Michigan–2, and was actually incredulous that PriCellular would want to acquire the license. . . .

In late September of 1994, PriCellular reached agreement with Mackinac on an option to purchase Michigan–2. The exercise price of the option agreement was set at $6.7 million, with the option remaining in force until December 15, 1994. . . . The agreement further provided that Mackinac was free to sell Michigan–2 to any party who was willing to exceed the exercise price of the Mackinac-PriCellular option contract by at least $500,000. On November 14, 1994, Broz agreed to pay Mackinac $7.2 million for the Michigan–2 license, thereby meeting the terms of the option agreement. An asset purchase agreement was thereafter executed by Mackinac and RFBC.

Nine days later, on November 23, 1994, PriCellular completed its financing and closed its tender offer for CIS. Prior to that point, PriCellular owned no equity interest in CIS. . . .

IV. APPLICATION OF THE CORPORATE OPPORTUNITY DOCTRINE

The doctrine of corporate opportunity represents but one species of the broad fiduciary duties assumed by a corporate director or officer. A corporate fiduciary agrees to place the interests of the corporation before his or her own in appropriate circumstances. . . . The classic statement of the doctrine is derived from the venerable case of Guth v. Loft, Inc., [5 A.2d 503 (Del.1939)]. In *Guth*, this Court held that:

> if there is presented to a corporate officer or director a business opportunity which the corporation is financially able to undertake, is, from its nature, in the line of the corporation's business and is of practical advantage to it, is one in which the corporation has an interest or a reasonable expectancy, and, by embracing the opportunity, the self-interest of the officer or

Nevertheless, in our view such a formal process was not necessary under the circumstances of this case in order for Broz to avoid liability. These contacts with individual board members do, however, tend to show that Broz was not acting surreptitiously or in bad faith.

* [Eds.—A "tender offer" is an offer to buy shares of stock from shareholders, who are invited to tender their shares to the offeror for purchase at a specified price within some specified period of time. Often the completion of the transaction is made contingent on the offeror receiving some specified number of shares, sufficient, for example, to give it control of the target corporation.]

> director will be brought into conflict with that of the corporation, the law will not permit him to seize the opportunity for himself.

Guth, 5 A.2d at 510–11.

. . .

We note at the outset that Broz became aware of the Michigan–2 opportunity in his individual and not his corporate capacity. . . . In fact, it is clear from the record that Mackinac did not consider CIS a viable candidate for the acquisition of Michigan–2. Accordingly, Mackinac did not offer the property to CIS. In this factual posture, many of the fundamental concerns undergirding the law of corporate opportunity are not present (e.g., misappropriation of the corporation's proprietary information). The burden imposed upon Broz to show adherence to his fiduciary duties to CIS is thus lessened to some extent. . . . Nevertheless, this fact is not dispositive. . . .

We turn now to an analysis of the factors relied on by the trial court. First, we find that CIS was not financially capable of exploiting the Michigan–2 opportunity. Although the Court of Chancery concluded otherwise, we hold that this finding was not supported by the evidence. The record shows that CIS was in a precarious financial position at the time Mackinac presented the Michigan–2 opportunity to Broz. . . .

. . .

[Moreover], while it may be said with some certainty that the Michigan–2 opportunity was within CIS' line of business, it is not equally clear that CIS had a cognizable interest or expectancy in the license. . . . Despite the fact that the nature of the Michigan–2 opportunity was historically close to the core operations of CIS, changes were in process. At the time the opportunity was presented, CIS was actively engaged in the process of divesting its cellular license holdings. CIS' articulated business plan did not involve any new acquisitions. Further, as indicated by the testimony of the entire CIS board, the Michigan–2 license would not have been of interest to CIS even absent CIS' financial difficulties and CIS' then current desire to liquidate its cellular license holdings. Thus, CIS had no interest or expectancy in the Michigan–2 opportunity. . . .

Finally, the corporate opportunity doctrine is implicated only in cases where the fiduciary's seizure of an opportunity results in a conflict between the fiduciary's duties to the corporation and the self-interest of the director as actualized by the exploitation of the opportunity. In the instant case, Broz' interest in acquiring and profiting from Michigan–2 created no duties that were inimical to his obligations to CIS. . . . Broz . . . comported himself in a manner that was wholly in accord with his obligations to CIS. Broz took care not to usurp any opportunity which CIS was willing and able to pursue. Broz sought only to compete with an outside entity, PriCellular, for acquisition of an opportunity which both sought to possess. Broz was not obligated to refrain from competition with PriCellular. . . .

In concluding that Broz had usurped a corporate opportunity, the Court of Chancery placed great emphasis on the fact that Broz had not formally presented the matter to the CIS board. . . . In so holding, the trial court erroneously grafted a new requirement onto the law of corporate opportunity, viz., the requirement of formal presentation under circumstances where the corporation does not have an interest, expectancy or financial ability.

The teaching of *Guth* and its progeny is that the director or officer must analyze the situation ex ante to determine whether the opportunity is one rightfully belonging to the corporation. If the director or officer believes, based on one of the factors articulated above, that the corporation is not entitled to the opportunity, then he may take it for himself. Of course, presenting the opportunity to the board creates a kind of "safe harbor" for the director, which removes the specter of a post hoc judicial determination that the director or officer has improperly usurped a corporate opportunity. . . . It is not the law of Delaware that presentation to the board is a necessary prerequisite to a finding that a corporate opportunity has not been usurped.

. . .

In concluding that Broz usurped an opportunity properly belonging to CIS, the Court of Chancery held that "[f]or practical business reasons CIS' interests with respect to the Mackinac transaction came to merge with those of PriCellular, even before the closing of its tender offer for CIS stock." Based on this fact, the trial court concluded that Broz was required to consider PriCellular's prospective, post-acquisition plans for CIS in determining whether to forgo the opportunity or seize it for himself. Had Broz done this, the Court of Chancery determined that he would have concluded that CIS was entitled to the opportunity by virtue of the alignment of its interests with those of PriCellular.

We disagree. Broz was under no duty to consider . . . the contingent and uncertain plans of PriCellular in reaching his determination of how to proceed.

. . .

Broz, as an active participant in the cellular telephone industry, was entitled to proceed in his own economic interest in the absence of any countervailing duty. The right of a director or officer to engage in business affairs outside of his or her fiduciary capacity would be illusory if these individuals were required to consider every potential, future occurrence in determining whether a particular business strategy would implicate fiduciary duty concerns. . . .

V. CONCLUSION

. . . [W]e hold that Broz did not breach his fiduciary duties to CIS. . . .

ANALYSIS

1. Suppose that PriCellular had had no financial problems and could easily have invested enough money in CIS to buy Michigan–2. What would the result have been?

2. Suppose that RFBC had had shareholders other than Broz and that CIS had a potential interest in Michigan–2, unknown to Rhodes (the broker for the seller), and the ability to finance a purchase. What should Broz have done? Was he obligated only to inform CIS or, rather, to allow CIS to proceed without competition from RFBC?

3. Suppose Broz had been an officer (e.g., vice president for development) of CIS, in addition to his board membership at CIS and his

RFBC positions. Assuming all the other facts remain the same, what result? Suppose we change one other fact as well: Rhodes, in bringing the opportunity to Broz, did not distinguish between Broz's role in CIS and his role in RFBC? What result?

4. Why did PriCellular not simply outbid Broz and buy Michigan–2 for itself?

5. Was the court fair in treating CIS's interest in Michigan–2 as separate from that of PriCellular?

6. The court suggests that a rule that would have required Broz to formally present the opportunity to the CIS board would generate uncertainty and economic inefficiency. How does the court know this to be true? Do you agree?

In re eBay, Inc. Shareholders Litigation

2004 WL 253521 (Del.Ch.) (Memorandum Opinion).

Shareholders of eBay, Inc. filed these consolidated derivative actions against certain eBay directors and officers for usurping corporate opportunities. Plaintiffs allege that eBay's investment banking advisor, Goldman Sachs Group, engaged in "spinning," a practice that involves allocating shares of lucrative initial public offerings of stock to favored clients. In effect, the plaintiff shareholders allege that Goldman Sachs bribed certain eBay insiders, using the currency of highly profitable investment opportunities—opportunities that should have been offered to, or provided for the benefit of, eBay rather than the favored insiders. . . .

I. BACKGROUND FACTS

The facts, as alleged in the complaint, are straightforward. In 1995, defendants Pierre M. Omidyar and Jeffrey Skoll founded nominal defendant eBay, a Delaware corporation, as a sole proprietorship. eBay is a pioneer in online trading platforms, providing a virtual auction community for buyers and sellers to list items for sale and to bid on items of interest. In 1998, eBay retained Goldman Sachs and other investment banks to underwrite an initial public offering [IPO] of common stock. Goldman Sachs was the lead underwriter. The stock was priced at $18 per share. Goldman Sachs purchased about 1.2 million shares. Shares of eBay stock became immensely valuable during 1998 and 1999, rising to $175 per share in early April 1999. Around that time, eBay made a secondary offering, issuing 6.5 million shares of common stock at $170 per share for a total of $1.1 billion. Goldman Sachs again served as lead underwriter. Goldman Sachs was asked in 2001 to serve as eBay's financial advisor in connection with an acquisition by eBay of PayPal, Inc. For these services, eBay has paid Goldman Sachs over $8 million. During this same time period, Goldman Sachs "rewarded" the individual defendants by allocating to them thousands of IPO shares, managed by Goldman Sachs, at the initial offering price. Because the IPO market during this particular period of time was extremely active, prices of initial stock offerings often doubled or tripled in a single day. Investors who were well connected, either to Goldman Sachs or to similarly situated investment banks serving as IPO underwriters, were able to flip these investments into instant profit by selling the equities in a few days or even in a few hours after they were initially purchased. The essential allegation of the complaint is that Goldman Sachs provided these IPO share allocations to the individual defendants to show appreciation for eBay's business and to enhance Goldman Sachs' chances of obtaining future eBay business. In addition to co-founding eBay, defendant Omidyar has been eBay's CEO, CFO [Chief Financial Officer] and President. He is eBay's largest stockholder, owning more than 23% of the company's equity. Goldman Sachs allocated Omidyar shares in at least forty IPOs at the initial offering price. Omidyar resold these securities in the public market for millions of dollars in profit. [Four other defendants, each of whom was an eBay officer or director, or both, profited to the tune of "millions of dollars" each on numerous issues of IPO stock allocated to them by Goldman Sachs.]

II. ANALYSIS

. . . [In a section of the opinion omitted here the court rejects the defendants' motion to dismiss for failure to make a demand of the eBay board of Directors. The court concludes that demand was excused because it would have been "futile."]

B. *Corporate Opportunity*

Plaintiffs have stated a claim that defendants usurped a corporate opportunity of eBay. Defendants insist that Goldman Sachs' IPO allocations to eBay's insider directors were "collateral investments opportunities" that arose by virtue of the inside directors status as wealthy individuals. They argue that this is not a corporate opportunity within the corporation's line of business or an opportunity in which the corporation had an interest or expectancy.[3] These arguments are unavailing.

First, no one disputes that eBay financially was able to exploit the opportunities in question. Second, eBay was in the business of investing in securities. The complaint alleges that eBay "consistently invested a portion of its cash on hand in marketable securities." According to eBay's 1999 10-K, for example, eBay had more than $550 million invested in equity and debt securities. eBay invested more than $181 million in "short-term investments" and $373 million in "long-term investments." Thus, investing was "a line of business" of eBay. Third, the facts alleged in the complaint suggest that investing was integral to eBay's cash management strategies and a significant part of its business. Finally, it is no answer to say, as do defendants, that IPOs are risky investments. It is undisputed that eBay was never given an opportunity to turn down the IPO allocations as too risky.

Defendants also argue that to view the IPO allocations in question as corporate opportunities will mean that every advantageous investment opportunity that comes to an officer or director will be considered a corporate opportunity. On the contrary, the allegations in the complaint in this case indicate that unique, below-market-price investment opportunities were offered by Goldman Sachs to the insider defendants as financial inducements to maintain and secure corporate business. This was not an instance where a broker offered advice to a director about an investment in a marketable security. The conduct

---

[3] See Broz v. Cellular Info. Sys. Inc., 673 A.2d 148, 155 (Del.1996) (listing factors to find corporate opportunity).

challenged here involved a large investment bank that regularly did business with a company steering highly lucrative IPO allocations to select insider directors and officers at that company, allegedly both to reward them for past business and to induce them to direct future business to that investment bank. This is a far cry from the defendants' characterization of the conduct in question as merely "a broker's investment recommendations" to a wealthy client.

Nor can one seriously argue that this conduct did not place the insider defendants in a position of conflict with their duties to the corporation. One can realistically characterize these IPO allocations as a form of commercial discount or rebate for past or future investment banking services. Viewed pragmatically, it is easy to understand how steering such commercial rebates to certain insider directors places those directors in an obvious conflict between their self-interest and the corporation's interest. . . .

Finally, even if one assumes that IPO allocations like those in question here do not constitute a corporate opportunity, a cognizable claim is nevertheless stated on the common law ground that an agent is under a duty to account for profits obtained personally in connection with transactions related to his or her company. The complaint gives rise to a reasonable inference that the insider directors accepted a commission or gratuity that rightfully belonged to eBay but that was improperly diverted to them. Even if this conduct does not run afoul of the corporate opportunity doctrine, it may still constitute a breach of the fiduciary duty of loyalty.[7] Thus, even if one does not consider Goldman Sachs' IPO allocations to these corporate insiders-allocations that generated millions of dollars in profit-to be a corporate opportunity, the defendant directors were nevertheless not free to accept this consideration from a company, Goldman Sachs, that was doing significant business with eBay and that arguably intended the consideration as an inducement to maintaining the business relationship in the future.[8]

III. CONCLUSION

For all of the above reasons, I deny the defendants' motions to dismiss the complaint in this consolidated action.

ANALYSIS

1. In Beam ex rel. Martha Stewart Living Omnimedia, Inc. v. Stewart, 833 A.2d 961 (Del.Ch. 2003), aff'd, 845 A.2d 1040 (Del. 2004), plaintiff Beam raised a corporate opportunity claim described by Vice Chancellor Chandler as follows:

> In January 2002, Stewart and the Martha Stewart Family Partnership sold 3,000,000 shares of [Martha Stewart Omnimedia] Class A stock to [a consortium of investors and investment funds] designated in the amended complaint as "ValueAct." In March 2002, Kleiner, Perkins, acting through its general partner, Doerr [a member of MSO's board of directors], sold 1,999,403 shares of MSO to ValueAct.

---

[7] Gibralt Capital Corp. v. Smith, 2001 WL 647837, at *9 (Del. Ch. May 8, 2001); Thorpe v. CERBCO, Inc., 676 2d 436, 444 (Del.1996).

[8] Restatement (Second) of Agency § 388 (1957).

> . . .
>
> Count III of the amended complaint alleges that Stewart and Doerr breached their fiduciary duty of loyalty, usurping a corporate opportunity by selling large blocks of MSO stock to ValueAct.

In other words, plaintiff alleged that Stewart and Doerr took a corporate opportunity by selling some of their MSO stock to a group of investors. The opportunity allegedly usurped from MSO was one of raising capital by selling stock, which was preempted by Stewart's and Doerr's sales.

Chandler held that in the 4 factor-test set out in Broz v. Cellular Information Systems, Inc., *supra*, "no single factor is dispositive. Instead the Court must balance all factors as they apply to a particular case." After doing so, Chandler held that Stewart and Doerr had not usurped a corporate opportunity from MSO. On the basis of which of the *Broz* factors do you suppose Chancellor Chandler so concluded? Do you think his analysis might have changed if Stewart and Doerr had possessed material nonpublic information suggesting that the shares were worth less than their market value? How does the eBay defendant's conduct differ from that of Stewart and Doerr?

2. In the *Beam* case, Chancellor Chandler held that an opportunity is within the corporation's line of business when it is "an activity as to which [the corporation] has fundamental knowledge, practical experience and ability to pursue." Is spinning IPO shares with a corporation's line of business under that standard? Most publicly held corporations invest at least some of their available cash in marketable securities. Does the *eBay* decision suggest that spinning IPO shares therefore is within the lines of business of essentially all companies? Is it relevant to your analysis that, according to eBay's 1999 Form 10-K, eBay had a total of just under $949 million in assets of which approximately $550 million consisted of the investments referred to by the court?

3. Suppose the independent members of eBay's board of directors had authorized the defendants to accept the allocated shares. What result on those facts?

4. As an alternative theory of liability, the court invokes the common law restated by Restatement (Second) of Agency § 388, which provides:

> Unless otherwise agreed, an agent who makes a profit in connection with transactions conducted by him on behalf of the principal is under a duty to give such profit to the principal.

Comment a following this statement of the rule reads:

> [T]hus, an agent who, without the knowledge of the principal, receives something in connection with, or because of, a transaction conducted for the principal, has a duty to pay this to the principal even though otherwise he has acted with perfect fairness to the principal and violates no duty of loyalty in receiving the amount.

What were the "transactions conducted" by the defendants "on behalf of the principal" in this case?

Should the court instead have relied upon Restatement § 387, which provides:

> Unless otherwise agreed, an agent is subject to a duty to his principal to act solely for the benefit of the principal in all matters connected with his agency.

Clearly, agency law does not preclude an agent from making personal investments. Why then is spinning IPO shares sufficiently "connected with his agency" relationship to justify imposing a constructive trust for the benefit of the principal on the profits from such transactions?

5. Spinning of IPO shares in circumstances such as those alleged in the *eBay* case is widely regarded as unethical. Should that factor into the analysis? Where there is a quid pro quo between the investment bank and the recipient of the share allocation, whereby the recipient directs business to the bank in return for the allocation, the transaction may be an illegal bribe. Even where there is a quid pro quo, however, proving that the transaction was illegal is regarded as a difficult task. How should that factor into the analysis, if at all?

PROBLEMS

George is Vice-President for Marketing of Zapco Enterprises, Inc., a manufacturer of video game software used in arcades and home systems (such as the Nintendo system). One of George's duties is to test competitor models. One day George leaves work and travels to a near-by video arcade to test a new game put out by Zapco's principal competitor. While visiting the arcade, George meets two young computer software engineers who have developed a new voice recognition program for personal computers. After further meetings with the engineers, George decides the program has promise and offers to help market it. The two engineers set up a new corporation called "Wordco, Inc.," and hire George as a marketing consultant. George receives 10 percent of Wordco's common stock and also becomes entitled to a commission of $10 for every copy of the program sold by Wordco. Zapco sues George for violating the corporate opportunity doctrine.

1. Assuming Zapco is incorporated in Delaware, has George violated the corporate opportunity doctrine?

2. What if the engineers had approached George at Zapco's booth at a computer trade fair?

3. Would it be relevant to the outcome that the two engineers refused to work with Zapco, because they refused to work with a mere game company?

4. Assume that after meeting with the engineers, but before signing the contract with Wordco, George approached Zapco's Chief Executive Officer and told him about this project. The CEO said Zapco had no interest in the project and no objection to George working for Wordco as long as it did not interfere with his Zapco duties. Result?

5. Suppose the transaction was a corporate opportunity. In perfect good faith, George takes it for himself. He then mentions to the firm's lawyer that he (George) is working on this word-processing project on the side. The lawyer sees that this is a corporate opportunity, which should have been offered to the company. Based on the lawyer's advice, George tells the board of directors about the opportunity, offers it to the

corporation, and asks the board to ratify his taking the opportunity. The board does so. Is George insulated from liability?

C. DOMINANT SHAREHOLDERS

Sinclair Oil Corp. v. Levien

280 A.2d 717 (Del.1971).

This is an appeal by the defendant, Sinclair Oil Corporation (hereafter Sinclair), from an order of the Court of Chancery, 261 A.2d 911, in a derivative action requiring Sinclair to account for damages sustained by its subsidiary, Sinclair Venezuelan Oil Company (hereafter Sinven), organized by Sinclair for the purpose of operating in Venezuela, as a result of dividends paid by Sinven, the denial to Sinven of industrial development, and a breach of contract between Sinclair's wholly owned subsidiary, Sinclair International Oil Company, and Sinven.

Sinclair, operating primarily as a holding company, is in the business of exploring for oil and of producing and marketing crude oil and oil products. At all times relevant to this litigation, it owned about 97% of Sinven's stock. The plaintiff owns about 3000 of 120,000 publicly held shares of Sinven. Sinven, incorporated in 1922, has been engaged in petroleum operations primarily in Venezuela and since 1959 has operated exclusively in Venezuela.

Sinclair nominates all members of Sinven's board of directors. The Chancellor found as a fact that the directors were not independent of Sinclair. Almost without exception, they were officers, directors, or employees of corporations in the Sinclair complex. By reason of Sinclair's domination, it is clear that Sinclair owed Sinven a fiduciary duty. . . .

The Chancellor held that because of Sinclair's fiduciary duty and its control over Sinven, its relationship with Sinven must meet the test of intrinsic fairness. The standard of intrinsic fairness involves both a high degree of fairness and a shift in the burden of proof. Under this standard the burden is on Sinclair to prove, subject to careful judicial scrutiny, that its transactions with Sinven were objectively fair. . . .

Sinclair argues that the transactions between it and Sinven should be tested, not by the test of intrinsic fairness with the accompanying shift of the burden of proof, but by the business judgment rule under which a court will not interfere with the judgment of a board of directors unless there is a showing of gross and palpable overreaching. . . .

A board of directors enjoys a presumption of sound business judgment, and its decisions will not be disturbed if they can be attributed to any rational business purpose. A court under such circumstances will not substitute its own notions of what is or is not sound business judgment.

We think, however, that Sinclair's argument in this respect is misconceived. When the situation involves a parent and a subsidiary, with the parent controlling the transaction and fixing the terms, the test of intrinsic fairness, with its resulting shifting of the burden of proof, is applied. . . . The basic situation for the application of the rule is the one in which the parent has received a benefit to the exclusion and at the expense of the subsidiary. . . .

A parent does indeed owe a fiduciary duty to its subsidiary when there are parent-subsidiary dealings. However, this alone will not evoke the intrinsic fairness standard. This standard will be applied only when the fiduciary duty is accompanied by self-dealing—the situation when a parent is on both sides of a transaction with its subsidiary. Self-dealing occurs when the parent, by virtue of its domination of the subsidiary, causes the subsidiary to act in such a way that the parent receives something from the subsidiary to the exclusion of, and detriment to, the minority stockholders of the subsidiary.

We turn now to the facts. The plaintiff argues that, from 1960 through 1966, Sinclair caused Sinven to pay out such excessive dividends that the industrial development of Sinven was effectively prevented, and it became in reality a corporation in dissolution.

From 1960 through 1966, Sinven paid out $108,000,000 in dividends ($38,000,000 in excess of Sinven's earnings during the same period). The Chancellor held that Sinclair caused these dividends to be paid during a period when it had a need for large amounts of cash. Although the dividends paid exceeded earnings, the plaintiff concedes that the payments were made in compliance with 8 Del.C. § 170, authorizing payment of dividends out of surplus or net profits. However, the plaintiff attacks these dividends on the ground that they resulted from an improper motive—Sinclair's need for cash. The Chancellor, applying the intrinsic fairness standard, held that Sinclair did not sustain its burden of proving that these dividends were intrinsically fair to the minority stockholders of Sinven. . . .

We do not accept the argument that the intrinsic fairness test can never be applied to a dividend declaration by a dominated board, although a dividend declaration by a dominated board will not inevitably demand the application of the intrinsic fairness standard. . . .

If such a dividend is in essence self-dealing by the parent, then the intrinsic fairness standard is the proper standard. For example, suppose a parent dominates a subsidiary and its board of directors. The subsidiary has outstanding two classes of stock, X and Y. Class X is owned by the parent and Class Y is owned by minority stockholders of the subsidiary. If the subsidiary, at the direction of the parent, declares a dividend on its Class X stock only, this might well be self-dealing by the parent. It would be receiving something from the subsidiary to the exclusion of and detrimental to its minority stockholders. This self-dealing, coupled with the parent's fiduciary duty, would make intrinsic fairness the proper standard by which to evaluate the dividend payments.

Consequently it must be determined whether the dividend payments by Sinven were, in essence, self-dealing by Sinclair. The dividends resulted in great sums of money being transferred from Sinven to Sinclair. However, a proportionate share of this money was received by the minority shareholders of Sinven. Sinclair received nothing from Sinven to the exclusion of its minority stockholders. As such, these dividends were not self-dealing. We hold therefore that the Chancellor erred in applying the intrinsic fairness test as to these dividend payments. The business judgment standard should have been applied.

We conclude that the facts demonstrate that the dividend payments complied with the business judgment standard and with 8 Del.C. § 170. The motives for causing the declaration of dividends are immaterial unless the plaintiff can show that the dividend payments resulted from improper motives and amounted to waste. The plaintiff contends only that the dividend payments drained Sinven of cash to such an extent that it was prevented from expanding.

The plaintiff proved no business opportunities which came to Sinven independently and which Sinclair either took to itself or denied to Sinven. As a matter of fact, with two minor exceptions which resulted in losses, all of Sinven's operations have been conducted in Venezuela, and Sinclair had a policy of exploiting its oil properties located in different countries by subsidiaries located in the particular countries.

From 1960 to 1966 Sinclair purchased or developed oil fields in Alaska, Canada, Paraguay, and other places around the world. The plaintiff contends that these were all opportunities which could have been taken by Sinven. . . .

However, the plaintiff could point to no opportunities which came to Sinven. Therefore, Sinclair usurped no business opportunity belonging to Sinven. Since Sinclair received nothing from Sinven to the exclusion of and detrimental to Sinven's minority stockholders, there was no self-dealing. Therefore, business judgment is the proper standard by which to evaluate Sinclair's expansion policies.

Since there is no proof of self-dealing on the part of Sinclair, it follows that the expansion policy of Sinclair and the methods used to achieve the desired result must, as far as Sinclair's treatment of Sinven is concerned, be tested by the standards of the business judgment rule. Accordingly, Sinclair's decision, absent fraud or gross overreaching, to achieve expansion through the medium of its subsidiaries, other than Sinven, must be upheld.

Even if Sinclair was wrong in developing these opportunities as it did, the question arises, with which subsidiaries should these opportunities have been shared? No evidence indicates a unique need or ability of Sinven to develop these opportunities. The decision of which subsidiaries would be used to implement Sinclair's expansion policy was one of business judgment with which a court will not interfere absent a showing of gross and palpable overreaching. . . . No such showing has been made here.

Next, Sinclair argues that the Chancellor committed error when he held it liable to Sinven for breach of contract.

In 1961 Sinclair created Sinclair International Oil Company (hereafter International), a wholly owned subsidiary used for the purpose of coordinating all of Sinclair's foreign operations. All crude purchases by Sinclair were made thereafter through International.

On September 28, 1961, Sinclair caused Sinven to contract with International whereby Sinven agreed to sell all of its crude oil and refined products to International at specified prices. The contract provided for minimum and maximum quantities and prices. The plaintiff contends that Sinclair caused this contract to be breached in two respects. Although the contract called for payment on receipt, International's payments lagged as much as 30 days after receipt. Also, the contract required International to purchase at least a fixed minimum amount of crude and refined products from Sinven. International did not comply with this requirement.

Clearly, Sinclair's act of contracting with its dominated subsidiary was self-dealing. Under the contract Sinclair received the products produced by Sinven, and of course the minority shareholders of Sinven were not able to share in the receipt of these products. If the contract was breached, then Sinclair received these products to the detriment of Sinven's minority shareholders. We agree with the Chancellor's finding that the contract was breached by Sinclair, both as to the time of payments and the amounts purchased.

Although a parent need not bind itself by a contract with its dominated subsidiary, Sinclair chose to operate in this manner. As Sinclair has received the benefits of this contract, so must it comply with the contractual duties.

Under the intrinsic fairness standard, Sinclair must prove that its causing Sinven not to enforce the contract was intrinsically fair to the minority shareholders of Sinven. Sinclair has failed to meet this burden. Late payments were clearly breaches for which Sinven should have sought and received adequate damages. As to the quantities purchased, Sinclair argues that it purchased all the products produced by Sinven. This, however, does not satisfy the standard of intrinsic fairness. Sinclair has failed to prove that Sinven could not possibly have produced or in some way have obtained the contract minimums. As such, Sinclair must account on this claim. . . .

We will therefore reverse that part of the Chancellor's order that requires Sinclair to account to Sinven for damages sustained as a result of dividends paid between 1960 and 1966, and by reason of the denial to Sinven of expansion during that period. We will affirm the remaining portion of that order and remand the cause for further proceedings.

ANALYSIS

1. Perhaps the best-known statement of corporate fiduciary duties appears in the Supreme Court bankruptcy case of Pepper v. Litton, 308 U.S. 295, 306 (1939):

> A director is a fiduciary. . . . So is a dominant or controlling stockholder or group of stockholders. . . . Their powers are in trust. . . . Their dealings with the corporation are subjected to rigorous scrutiny and where any of their contracts or engagements with the corporation is challenged the burden is on the director or shareholder not only to prove the good faith of the transaction but also to show its inherent fairness from the viewpoint of the corporation and those interested therein.

2. Was the shareholder duty-of-loyalty analysis necessary to decide *Sinclair*? How might one have resolved the case using only the law regarding the duty of loyalty of directors?

3. When corporation P owns a large percentage of the stock of corporation S, P almost inevitably dominates S. However hard P tries to insulate S from P's influence, S managers will know that P can decide whether to fire them or promote them. Given that fact, how might P try

to deal with the risk that the minority shareholders in S may file fiduciary duty suits against it? We shall revisit this issue in our discussion of mergers and acquisitions in Chapter 7, Section 1.

Zahn v. Transamerica Corporation

162 F.2d 36 (3d Cir.1947).

Zahn, a holder of Class A common stock of Axton-Fisher Tobacco Company, a corporation of Kentucky, sued Transamerica Corporation, a Delaware company, on his own behalf and on behalf of all stockholders similarly situated, in the District Court of the United States for the District of Delaware. His complaint as amended asserts that Transamerica caused Axton-Fisher to redeem its Class A stock at $80.80 per share on July 1, 1943, instead of permitting the Class A stockholders to participate in the assets on the liquidation of their company in June, 1944. He alleges in brief that if the Class A stockholders had been allowed to participate in the assets on liquidation of Axton-Fisher and had received their respective shares of the assets, he and the other Class A stockholders would have received $240 per share instead of $80.80. . . .

Prior to April 30, 1943, Axton-Fisher had authorized and outstanding three classes of stock, designated respectively as preferred stock, Class A stock and Class B stock. Each share of preferred stock had a par value of $100 and was entitled to cumulative dividends at the rate of $6 per annum and possessed a liquidation value of $105 plus accrued dividends. The Class A stock, specifically described in the charter as a "common" stock, was entitled to an annual cumulative dividend of $3.20 per share. The Class B stock was next entitled to receive an annual dividend of $1.60 per share. If further funds were made available by action of the board of directors by way of dividends, the Class A stock and the Class B stock were entitled to share equally therein. Upon liquidation of the company and the payment of the sums required by the preferred stock, the Class A stock was entitled to share with the Class B stock in the distribution of the remaining assets, but the Class A stock was entitled to receive twice as much per share as the Class B stock.[2]

Each share of Class A stock was convertible at the option of the shareholder into one share of Class B stock. All or any of the shares of Class A stock were callable by the corporation at any quarterly dividend date upon sixty days' notice to the shareholders, at $60 per share with

---

[2] The charter provides as follows:

"In the event of the dissolution, liquidation, merger or consolidation of the corporation, or sale of substantially all its assets, whether voluntary or involuntary, there shall be paid to the holders of the preferred stock then outstanding $105 per share, together with all unpaid accrued dividends thereon, before any sum shall be paid to or any assets distributed among the holders of the Class A common stock and/or the holders of the Class B common stock. After such payment to the holders of the preferred stock, and all unpaid accrued dividends on the Class A common stock shall have been paid, then all remaining assets and funds of the corporation shall be divided among and paid to the holders of the Class A common stock and to the holders of the Class B common stock in the ratio of 2 to 1; that is to say, there shall be paid upon each share of Class A common stock twice the amount paid upon each share of Class B common stock, in any such event."

accrued dividends.[3] The voting rights were vested in the Class B stock but if there were four successive defaults in the payment of quarterly dividends, the class or classes of stock as to which such defaults occurred gained voting rights equal share for share with the Class B stock. By reason of this provision the Class A stock had possessed equal voting rights with the Class B stock since on or about January 1, 1937.

On or about May 16, 1941, Transamerica purchased 80,160 shares of Axton-Fisher's Class B common stock. This was about 71.5% of the outstanding Class B stock and about 46.7% of the total voting stocks of Axton-Fisher. By August 15, 1942, Transamerica owned 5,332 shares of Class A stock and 82,610 shares of Class B stock. By March 31, 1943, the amount of Class A stock of Axton-Fisher owned by Transamerica had grown to 30,168 shares or about 66⅔% of the total amount of this stock outstanding, and the amount of Class B stock owned by Transamerica had increased to 90,768 shares or about 80% of the total outstanding. . . . Since May 16, 1941, Transamerica had control of and had dominated the management, directorate, financial policies, business and affairs of Axton-Fisher. Since the date last stated Transamerica had elected a majority of the board of directors of Axton-Fisher. These individuals are in large part officers or agents of Transamerica.

In the fall of 1942 and in the spring of 1943 Axton-Fisher possessed as its principal asset leaf tobacco which had cost it about $6,361,981. This asset was carried on Axton-Fisher's books in that amount. The value of leaf tobacco had risen sharply and, to quote the words of the complaint, "unbeknown to the public holders of . . . Class A common stock of Axton-Fisher, but known to Transamerica, the market value of . . . [the] tobacco had, in March and April of 1943, attained the huge sum of about $20,000,000."

The complaint then alleges the gist of the plaintiff's grievance, viz., that Transamerica, knowing of the great value of the tobacco which Axton-Fisher possessed, conceived a plan to appropriate the value of the tobacco to itself by redeeming the Class A stock at the price of $60 a share plus accrued dividends, the redemption being made to appear as if "incident to the continuance of the business of Axton-Fisher as a going concern," and thereafter, the redemption of the Class A stock being completed, to liquidate Axton-Fisher; that this would result, after the disbursal of the sum required to be paid to the preferred stock, in Transamerica gaining for itself most of the value of the warehouse tobacco. The complaint further alleges that in pursuit of this plan Transamerica, by a resolution of the Board of Directors of Axton-Fisher on April 30, 1943, called the Class A stock at $60 and, selling a large part of the tobacco to Phillip-Morris Company, Ltd., Inc., together with

---

3 The charter provides as follows:

"The whole or any part of the Class A common stock of the corporation, at the option of the Board of Directors, may be redeemed on any quarterly dividend payment date by paying therefor in cash Sixty dollars ($60.00) per share and all unpaid and accrued dividends thereon at the date fixed for such redemption, upon sending by mail to the registered holders of the Class A common stock at least sixty (60) days' notice of the exercise of such option. If at any time the Board of Directors shall determine to redeem less than the whole amount of Class A common stock then outstanding, the particular stock to be so redeemed shall be determined in such manner as the Board of Directors shall prescribe; provided, however, that no holder of Class A common stock shall be preferred over any other holder of such stock."

substantially all of the other assets of Axton-Fisher, thereafter liquidated Axton-Fisher, paid off the preferred stock and pocketed the balance of the proceeds of the sale. Warehouse receipts representing the remainder of the tobacco were distributed to the Class B stockholders.

Assuming as we must that the allegations of the complaint are true, it will be observed that agents or representatives of Transamerica constituted Axton-Fisher's board of directors at the times of the happening of the events complained of, and that Transamerica was Axton-Fisher's principal and controlling stockholder at such times. . . .

. . .

The circumstances of the case at bar are *sui generis* and we can find no Kentucky decision squarely in point. In our opinion, however, the law of Kentucky imposes upon the directors of a corporation or upon those who are in charge of its affairs by virtue of majority stock ownership or otherwise the same fiduciary relationship in respect to the corporation and to its stockholders as is imposed generally by the laws of Kentucky's sister States or which was imposed by federal law prior to Erie R. Co. v. Tompkins, 304 U.S. 64.

The tenor of the federal decisions in respect to the general fiduciary duty of those in control of a corporation is unmistakable. The Supreme Court in Southern Pacific Co. v. Bogert, 250 U.S. 483, 487, 488, said: "The rule of corporation law and of equity invoked is well settled and has been often applied. The majority has the right to control; but when it does so, it occupies a fiduciary relation toward the minority, as much so as the corporation itself or its officers and directors." . . .

It is appropriate to emphasize at this point that the right to call the Class A stock for redemption was confided by the charter of Axton-Fisher to the directors and not to the stockholders of that corporation. We must also emphasize . . . that there is a radical difference when a stockholder is voting strictly as a stockholder and when voting as a director; that when voting as a stockholder he may have the legal right to vote with a view of his own benefits and to represent himself only; but that when he votes as a director he represents all the stockholders in the capacity of a trustee for them and cannot use his office as a director for his personal benefit at the expense of the stockholders.

Two theories are presented on one of which the case at bar must be decided: One, vigorously asserted by Transamerica and based on its interpretation of the decision in the Taylor case, is that the board of directors of Axton-Fisher, whether or not dominated by Transamerica, the principal Class B stockholder, at any time and for any purpose, might call the Class A stock for redemption; the other, asserted with equal vigor by Zahn, is that the board of directors of Axton-Fisher as fiduciaries were not entitled to favor Transamerica, the Class B stockholder, by employing the redemption provisions of the charter for its benefit.

We must of course treat the decision of the Court of Appeals of Kentucky [in another case arising from the same transactions] as evidence of what is the law of Kentucky. The Court took the position on that record that the directors at any time might call the Class A stock for redemption and that the redemption provision of the charter was written as much for the benefit of the Class B stock as for the Class A stock. It is argued by Transamerica very persuasively that what the Court of

Appeals of Kentucky held was that when the Class A stock received its allocation of $60 a share plus accrued dividends it received its full due and that the directors had the right at any time to eliminate Class A stock from the corporate setup for the benefit of the Class B stock. It does not appear from the opinion of the Court of Appeals of Kentucky whether or not the subsequent liquidation of Axton-Fisher was brought to the attention of the Court. But it is clear from the pleading that the subsequent liquidation was not an issue in the case. . . . We think that it is the settled law of Kentucky that directors may not declare or withhold the declaration of dividends for the purpose of personal profit or, by analogy, take any corporate action for such a purpose.

The difficulty in accepting Transamerica's contentions in the case at bar is that the directors of Axton-Fisher, if the allegations of the complaint be accepted as true, were the instruments of Transamerica, were directors voting in favor of their special interest, that of Transamerica, could not and did not exercise an independent judgment in calling the Class A stock, but made the call for the purpose of profiting their true principal, Transamerica. In short a puppet-puppeteer relationship existed between the directors of Axton-Fisher and Transamerica.

The act of the board of directors in calling the Class A stock, an act which could have been legally consummated by a disinterested board of directors, was here effected at the direction of the principal Class B stockholder in order to profit it. Such a call is voidable in equity at the instance of a stockholder injured thereby. It must be pointed out that under the allegations of the complaint there was no reason for the redemption of the Class A stock to be followed by the liquidation of Axton-Fisher except to enable the Class B stock to profit at the expense of the Class A stock. As has been hereinbefore stated the function of the call was confided to the board of directors by the charter and was not vested by the charter in the stockholders of any class. It was the intention of the the framers of Axton-Fisher's charter to require the board of directors to act disinterestedly if that body called the Class A stock, and to make the call with a due regard for its fiduciary obligations. If the allegations of the complaint be proved, it follows that the directors of Axton-Fisher, the instruments of Transamerica, have been derelict in that duty. Liability which flows from the dereliction must be imposed upon Transamerica which, under the allegations of the complaint, constituted the board of Axton-Fisher and controlled it.

. . .

. . . In our opinion, if the allegations of the complaint be proved, Zahn may maintain his cause of action to recover from Transamerica the value of the stock retained by him as that shall be represented by its aliquot share of the proceeds of Axton-Fisher on dissolution. . . .

The judgment will be reversed.

AFTERMATH

The case was returned to the district court for a determination of the amount of damages. The district court ruling, on *Zahn* and related cases, was reviewed by the court of appeals in Speed v. Transamerica Corporation, 235 F.2d 369 (3d Cir.1956), with the following result:

In the Zahn and Friedman actions the district court found that Transamerica had exercised its position as controlling stockholder to cause the board of directors of Axton-Fisher to call the Class A stock for redemption and that although Transamerica at that time knew that the board was doing so on the assumption that it was for the purpose of improving the capital structure of the company as a going concern, the real purpose of Transamerica in causing the call to be made was by liquidation, merger, consolidation or sale of Axton-Fisher's assets to gain for itself the appreciation in the value of those assets. Accordingly the district court held Transamerica accountable to the Class A stockholders, both those who had redeemed their stock pursuant to the call and those who had not done so. . . . The court found that a disinterested board of directors of Axton-Fisher would undoubtedly have exercised its powers to call the Class A stock before liquidation, disclosing the intention to liquidate together with full information as to the appreciated value of Axton-Fisher's tobacco inventory, and that the Class A stockholders would thereupon have exercised their privilege to convert their stock, share for share, into Class B stock and would thus have participated equally with the Class B stockholders in the proceeds of the liquidation. Applying this rule in the Friedman and Zahn cases, after deducting the sum of $80.80 per share received by the Class A stockholders or set aside for them on the redemption call of April 30, 1943, the court found those stockholders entitled to $21.02 per share. . . .

As we have indicated, the district court concluded that Transamerica was liable both in tort for fraud and deceit and because of its violation of Rule X–10B–5 of the Securities and Exchange Commission. These conclusions were based upon its finding of Transamerica's deceptive concealment of the great appreciation in value of Axton-Fisher's tobacco inventory and of its secret intention to capture that appreciation for itself to the exclusion of the public stockholders. . . .

The Court of Appeals of Kentucky has held that the Axton-Fisher Class A stock, although designated as a common stock was in the nature of a junior preferred stock, and that the provision of the charter for the redemption of the Class A stock was a continuing option allowed to the holders of the Class B common stock which the board of directors could exercise in their favor.* This construction of the Axton-Fisher charter by the highest court of the state of its incorporation was, of course, binding on the district court. We agree with the district court that the provisions of the Axton-Fisher charter with respect to liquidation must be read realistically with the provisions for redemption of the Class A stock and its conversion into Class B stock. When so read it becomes apparent that a disinterested board of directors discharging its responsibility to the Class B stockholders in case of liquidation would call the Class A stock for redemption at $60 per share if it appeared that the

* [Eds.—Taylor v. Axton-Fisher Tobacco Co., 1943, 295 Ky. 226, 229–231, 173 S.W.2d 377, 379–380, 148 A.L.R. 834, 837–838.]

distribution in liquidation to that stock would exceed that figure on a two-to-one basis. Since the board would have the right to do this and the Class B stockholders would be entitled to such action, the failure to do so would be an arbitrary act which would confer a windfall to which they were not entitled under the charter upon the Class A stockholders at the direct expense of the holders of the Class B stock. The district court was therefore quite right in determining that the damages to be awarded to the Class A stockholders should be measured by what they would have received if they had converted their shares into Class B stock prior to the liquidation. . . .

ANALYSIS

1. What purpose was served by having the two classes of stock that were the focus of attention in this case? In the situation that gave rise to the case, the Class A shareholders should have converted their A shares to B shares, and would have done so if they had had full information. What, then, is the function of the provision in the corporate charter for redemption of the Class A shares at $60 per share? What about the provision for a 2:1 division of assets, in favor of the Class A shares, in the event of liquidation?

2. What is the relevance, if any, of the *Zahn* court's discussion of the duty of controlling shareholders to minority shareholders?

D. RATIFICATION

Fliegler v. Lawrence

361 A.2d 218 (Del. 1976).

In this shareholder derivative action brought on behalf of Agau Mines, Inc., a Delaware corporation, (Agau) against its officers and directors and United States Antimony Corporation, a Montana corporation (USAC), we are asked to decide whether the individual defendants, in their capacity as directors and officers of both corporations, wrongfully usurped a corporate opportunity belonging to Agau, and whether all defendants wrongfully profited by causing Agau to exercise an option to purchase that opportunity. . . .

I

In November, 1969, defendant, John C. Lawrence (then president of Agau, a publicly held corporation engaged in a dual-phased gold and silver exploratory venture) in his individual capacity, acquired certain antimony properties under a lease-option for $60,000. Lawrence offered to transfer the properties, which were then 'a raw prospect', to Agau, but after consulting with other members of Agau's board of directors, he and they agreed that the corporation's legal and financial position would not permit acquisition and development of the properties at that time. Thus, it was decided to transfer the properties to USAC, (a closely held corporation formed just for this purpose and a majority of whose stock was owned by the individual defendants) where capital necessary for development of the properties could be raised without risk to Agau through the sale of USAC stock; it was also decided to grant Agau a long-term option to acquire USAC if the properties proved to be of commercial value.

In January, 1970, the option agreement was executed by Agau and USAC. Upon its exercise and approval by Agau shareholders, Agau was to deliver 800,000 shares of its restricted investment stock for all authorized and issued shares of USAC. The exchange was calculated on the basis of reimbursement to USAC and its shareholders for their costs in developing the properties to a point where it could be ascertained if they had commercial value.

. . .

In July, 1970, the Agau board resolved to exercise the option, an action which was approved by majority vote of the shareholders in October, 1970. Subsequently, plaintiff instituted this suit on behalf of Agau to recover the 800,000 shares and for an accounting. . . .

III

A.

Preliminarily, defendants argue that they have been relieved of the burden of proving fairness by reason of shareholder ratification of the Board's decision to exercise the option. They rely on 8 Del.C. § 144(a)(2) and Gottlieb v. Heyden Chemical Corp., Del.Supr., 33 Del.Ch. 177, 91 A.2d 57 (1952).

In *Gottlieb*, this Court stated that shareholder ratification of an "interested transaction," although less than unanimous, shifts the burden of proof to an objecting shareholder to demonstrate that the terms are so unequal as to amount to a gift or waste of corporate assets. . . . The Court explained:

> "[T]he entire atmosphere is freshened and a new set of rules invoked where formal approval has been given by a majority of independent, fully informed [share]holders." 91 A.2d at 59.

The purported ratification by the Agau shareholders would not affect the burden of proof in this case because the majority of shares voted in favor of exercising the option were cast by defendants in their capacity as Agau shareholders. Only about one-third of the "disinterested" shareholders voted, and we cannot assume that such non-voting shareholders either approved or disapproved. Under these circumstances, we cannot say that "the entire atmosphere has been freshened" and that departure from the objective fairness test is permissible. . . . In short, defendants have not established factually a basis for applying *Gottlieb*.

Nor do we believe the Legislature intended a contrary policy and rule to prevail by enacting 8 Del.C. § 144, which provides, in part:

> (a) No contract or transaction between a corporation and 1 or more of its directors or officers, or between a corporation and any other corporation, partnership, association, or other organization in which 1 or more of its directors or officers, are directors or officers, or have a financial interest, shall be void or voidable solely for this reason, or solely because the director or officer is present at or participates in the meeting of the board or committee which authorizes the contract or transaction, or solely because his or their votes are counted for such purpose, if:

(1) The material facts as to his relationship or interest and as to the contract or transaction are disclosed or are known to the board of directors or the committee, and the board or committee in good faith authorizes the contract or transaction by the affirmative votes of a majority of the disinterested directors, even though the disinterested directors be less than a quorum; or

(2) The material facts as his relationship or interest and as to the contract or transaction are disclosed or are known to the shareholders entitled to vote thereon, and the contract or transaction is specifically approved in good faith by vote of the shareholders; or

(3) The contract or transaction is fair as to the corporation as of the time it is authorized, approved or ratified, by the board of directors, a committee, or the shareholders.

Defendants argue that the transaction here in question is protected by § 144(a)(2) which, they contend, does not require that ratifying shareholders be "disinterested" or "independent"; nor, they argue, is there warrant for reading such a requirement into the statute. . . .

We do not read the statute as providing the broad immunity for which defendants contend. It merely removes an "interested director" cloud when its terms are met and provides against invalidation of an agreement "solely" because such a director or officer is involved. Nothing in the statute sanctions unfairness to Agau or removes the transaction from judicial scrutiny.

[After an elaborate inquiry into the economics of the transaction, the court held:]

Considering all of the above factors, we conclude that defendants have proven the intrinsic fairness of the transaction. Agau received properties which by themselves were clearly of substantial value. But more importantly, it received a promising, potentially self-financing and profit generating enterprise with proven markets and commercial capability which could well be expected to provide Agau at the very least with the cash it sorely needed to undertake further exploration and development of its own properties if not to stay in existence. For those reasons, we believe that the interest given to the USAC shareholders was a fair price to pay. Accordingly, we have no doubt but that this transaction was one which at that time would have commended itself to an independent corporation in Agau's position.

Affirmed.

ANALYSIS

1. Section 144 of the Delaware statute provides that a properly ratified contract between a corporation and one of its directors is not necessarily "void or voidable" because of the conflict of interest. What does this mean? Is a *non*ratified contract between a corporation and one of its directors necessarily void or voidable? If not, then what difference could ratification make?

2. Section 144 provides that a ratified contract is not void or voidable "solely" because of the conflict. What purpose does the "solely" serve? Does it mean the fact that a ratified contract involves an interested director will continue to be a factor that contributes to the contract's voidability? What other reasons might there be?

3. Suppose you had represented the corporation in the negotiations with Jean Tennyson over the Celanese Hour. What procedures would you have followed if the statute quoted in *Fliegler* had governed?

In re Wheelabrator Technologies, Inc. Shareholders Litigation

663 A.2d 1194 (Del.Ch.1995).

Opinion

■ JACOBS, VICE CHANCELLOR.

[Waste Management, Inc. (Waste) and Wheelabrator Technologies, Inc. (WTI) were both in the "waste management" industry. In 1988, Waste bought 22 percent of WTI stock and elected four of its own directors to serve on WTI's eleven-member board. In 1990, for reasons never made clear by the court, Waste and WTI negotiated a "merger" agreement in which (i) Waste would acquire another 33 percent of WTI stock, and (ii) WTI shareholders would receive .574 WTI shares and .469 Waste shares for each WTI share they held.

To consider this agreement, WTI's board held a special meeting. All members other than the Waste designees attended. They reviewed copies of the agreement and materials furnished by the investment bankers involved (Lazard Freres and Salomon Brothers). They also listened to presentations from both these investment bankers and WTI's attorneys. All of the speakers declared that the transaction was fair.

The seven non-Waste directors of WTI then unanimously approved the merger agreement. Upon the completion of that vote, the four Waste directors joined the meeting and the full board unanimously approved it as well. The two firms then distributed a proxy statement explaining the transaction to WTI shareholders. At a special shareholders meeting, a majority of WTI shareholders (not counting Waste) approved the agreement.]

. . .

IV. THE DISCLOSURE CLAIM

Delaware law imposes upon a board of directors the fiduciary duty to disclose fully and fairly all material facts within its control that would have a significant effect upon a stockholder vote. . . . The plaintiffs argue that the defendants breached their duty of disclosure because the proxy statement issued in connection with the merger was materially misleading in several respects. . . .

[T]he plaintiffs contend that the proxy disclosure that the WTI Board had "carefully considered the financial, business and tax aspects" of the merger was materially misleading. In fact, plaintiffs argue, the WTI board had deliberated for only three hours before voting to approve and recommend the merger to WTI shareholders.

This argument also lacks evidentiary support. The assertion that the WTI board could not have considered the merger proposal carefully rests upon an unsupported inference from one fact: the three hour length of the March 30, 1990 board meeting. Given the other undisputed facts of record, that inference is unreasonable and does not create a triable fact issue. First, the board meeting was attended by WTI's investment bankers and outside counsel who made presentations and thereafter answered the board members' questions. Second, the proxy statement describes in detail the various factors that the board considered in deciding whether to approve and recommend the merger. . . . The plaintiffs offer no evidence that that description was in any way inaccurate. Third, Waste and WTI had had a close business relationship for over two years before the merger, during which time many discussions concerning the future of that relationship had taken place. It is reasonable to (and I do) infer that WTI's directors already had, and were able to draw upon, a substantial working knowledge of Waste during the March 30, 1990 meeting.

. . .

For the foregoing reasons, summary judgment will be granted dismissing the remaining duty of disclosure claim.

V. THE FIDUCIARY DUTY CLAIMS

In rejecting the disclosure claim, the Court necessarily has determined that the merger was approved by a fully informed vote of a majority of WTI's disinterested stockholders. . . .

A. The Duty of Care Claim.

As noted, the plaintiffs concede that if the WTI shareholder vote was fully informed, the effect of that informed vote would be to extinguish the claim that the WTI board failed to exercise due care in negotiating and approving the merger. Given the ratification holding of Smith v. Van Gorkom, Del.Supr., 488 A.2d 858, 889–90 (1985), that concession is not surprising. In *Van Gorkom,* the defendant directors argued that the shareholder vote approving a challenged merger agreement "had the legal effect of curing any failure of the board to reach an informed business judgment in its approval of the merger." Id. at 889. Accepting that legal principle (but not its application to the facts before it), the Supreme Court stated:

> The parties tacitly agree that a discovered failure of the Board to reach an informed business judgment constitutes a voidable, rather than a void, act. Hence, the merger can be sustained, notwithstanding the infirmity of the Board's actions, if its approval by majority vote of the shareholders is found to have been based on an informed electorate.

Id. at 889.

Accordingly, summary judgment dismissing the plaintiffs' due care claim will be granted. . . .

B. The Duty of Loyalty Claim.

. . .

The [Delaware] ratification decisions that involve duty of loyalty claims are of two kinds: (a) "interested" transaction cases between a corporation and its directors (or between the corporation and an entity in which the corporation's directors are also directors or have a financial interest), and (b) cases involving a transaction between the corporation and its controlling shareholder.

Regarding the first category, 8 Del.C. § 144(a)(2) pertinently provides that an "interested" transaction of this kind will not be voidable if it is approved in good faith by a majority of disinterested stockholders. Approval by fully informed, disinterested shareholders pursuant to § 144(a)(2) invokes "the business judgment rule and limits judicial review to issues of gift or waste with the burden of proof upon the party attacking the transaction." Marciano v. Nakash, 535 A.2d 400, 405 n. 3 (Del.Supr.1987). The result is the same in "interested" transaction cases not decided under § 144:

> Where there has been independent shareholder ratification of interested director actions, the objecting stockholder has the burden of showing that no person of ordinary sound business judgment would say that the consideration received for the options was a fair exchange for the options granted.

Michelson, 407 A.2d at 224 (quoting Kaufman v. Shoenberg, Del.Ch., 91 A.2d 786, 791 (1952), at 791);. . . .

The second category concerns duty of loyalty cases arising out of transactions between the corporation and its controlling stockholder. Those cases involve primarily parent-subsidiary mergers that were conditioned upon receiving "majority of the minority" stockholder approval. In a parent-subsidiary merger, the standard of review is ordinarily entire fairness, with the directors having the burden of proving that the merger was entirely fair. Weinberger v. UOP, Inc., 457 A.2d 701, 703. But where the merger is conditioned upon approval by a "majority of the minority" stockholder vote, and such approval is granted, the standard of review remains entire fairness, but the burden of demonstrating that the merger was unfair shifts to the plaintiff. . . . That burden-shifting effect of ratification has also been held applicable in cases involving mergers with a de facto controlling stockholder, and in a case involving a transaction other than a merger.

. . .

C. The Appropriate Review Standard and Burden of Proof.

Having determined what effect shareholder ratification does not have, the Court must now determine what effect it does have. The plaintiffs argue that their duty of loyalty claim is governed by the entire fairness standard, with ratification operating only to shift the burden on the fairness issue to the plaintiffs. That is incorrect, because this merger did not involve an interested and controlling stockholder.

[T]he [Delaware] Supreme Court determined that the effect of a fully informed shareholder vote was to shift the burden of proof within the *entire fairness* standard of review. [Emphasis added.] . . . Critical to the result in those cases was that the transaction involved a de facto . . . or de jure . . . controlling stockholder. That circumstance brought those cases within the purview of the ratification doctrine articulated in [cases] involving mergers between a corporation and its majority stockholder-parent. The participation of the controlling interested stockholder is critical to the application of the entire fairness standard because . . . the potential for process manipulation by the controlling stockholder, and the concern that the controlling stockholder's continued presence might influence even a fully informed shareholder vote, justify the need for the exacting judicial scrutiny and procedural protection afforded by the entire fairness form of review.

In this case, there is no contention or evidence that Waste, a 22% stockholder of WTI, exercised de jure or de facto control over WTI. . . . Accordingly, the review standard applicable to this merger is business judgment, with the plaintiffs having the burden of proof.

The final question concerns the proper application of that review standard to the facts at bar. Because no party has yet been heard on that subject, that issue cannot be determined on this motion. Its resolution must await further proceedings, which counsel may present (if they so choose) on a supplemental motion for summary judgment.

. . .

ANALYSIS

1. Why should the effect of a fully informed shareholder vote on the standard of review be different for duty of care cases than for duty of loyalty cases not involving de jure or de facto control?

2. What must the plaintiff in *Wheelabrator* be prepared to prove at trial or to resist a renewed motion for summary judgment? What do you suppose is the likelihood of success?

3. In Smith v. Van Gorkom, why was the shareholder action in approving the merger, by an overwhelming majority, not a complete defense to the action against the directors?

PROBLEMS

DreamTeam, Inc. (DTI), which is incorporated in Delaware, is a Hollywood studio owned in equal parts by Mouse, Duck, and Flintstone. The three also constitute the board. DTI has recently signed a contract with director Olivia Stone for a new movie, *Fillmore.* Stone has based the film on (what she considers) the scandalous presidency of Millard Fillmore. In the movie, Stone will star Flintstone as the diabolical mastermind behind (what Stone claims is) the newly discovered CIA plot to assassinate Fillmore. For directing this movie, Stone will receive $25 million; for playing the villain, Flintstone will receive $5 million.

1. The Stone contract was approved by a 2–1 vote among the board of directors, with Mouse objecting. Mouse now brings a derivative suit to enjoin the contract. What result?

2. The Flintstone contract was approved by a 2–1 vote among the board of directors, with Mouse objecting. Mouse similarly sues to enjoin the contract. What result?

3. Stone will use the movie to push her distinctive fringe-left political philosophy. Mouse shares this philosophy; Duck does not share it, but does not care as long as the movie makes money; Flintstone objects

to the philosophy. Can Flintstone block the use of a DTI movie for political ends?

4. Suppose Mouse had been absent when the Flintstone contract was considered by the board. The contract was approved by a vote of 2–0, both Duck and Flintstone voting in the affirmative. Mouse objects (a) that the action was invalid for lack of a quorum and (b) that the contract should be enjoined as unfair and unauthorized. What result?

3. THE OBLIGATION OF GOOD FAITH

INTRODUCTION

The notion that directors ought to act in good faith pervades Delaware's corporate governance jurisprudence. Only directors who, inter alia, act in good faith are entitled to indemnification of legal expenses. DGCL § 145. Only directors who, inter alia, rely in good faith on corporate books and records or reports from corporate officers or certain advisors are "fully protected" against shareholder claims. DGCL § 141(e). Related party transactions are partially insulated from judicial review, inter alia, only if they are approved by the disinterested directors or shareholders in good faith. DGCL § 144(a)(1)–(2). The business judgment rule presumes that directors acted, inter alia, in good faith.* And so on.

Despite these longstanding references to good faith, however, it is fair to say that the concept remained essentially undefined until quite recently. Instead, a director's obligation to act in good faith traditionally was "subsumed in a court's inquiry into the director's satisfaction of her duties of care and loyalty."** If there was no breach of either of those duties, courts did not perform a separate inquiry on the issue of good faith.

The process of giving content to good faith began with the Delaware Supreme Court's decision in Cede & Co. v. Technicolor, Inc., 634 A.2d 345 (Del. 1993):

> [A] shareholder plaintiff challenging a board decision has the burden at the outset to rebut the rule's presumption. To rebut the rule, a shareholder plaintiff assumes the burden of providing evidence that directors, in reaching their challenged decision, breached any one of *the triads of their fiduciary duty-good faith, loyalty or due care*. If a shareholder plaintiff fails to meet this evidentiary burden, the business judgment rule attaches to protect corporate officers and directors and the decisions they make, and our courts will not second-guess these business judgments. If the rule is rebutted, the burden shifts to the defendant directors, the proponents of the challenged

* See, e.g., Aronson v. Lewis, 473 A.2d 805, 812 (Del. 1984) (defining the business judgment rule as "a presumption that in making a business decision the directors of a corporation acted on an informed basis, in good faith and in the honest belief that the action taken was in the best interests of the company").

** Arthur Fleischer, Jr. & Alexander Sussman, Directors' Fiduciary Duties in Takeovers and Mergers, 1388 PLI/CORP 911, 918 (2003).

transaction, to prove to the trier of fact the "entire fairness" of the transaction to the shareholder plaintiff.

Id. at 361 (emphasis supplied; citations omitted). The court's use of the term "triad" signaled the then-novel proposition that good faith was a freestanding fiduciary obligation having equal dignity with the traditional concepts of care and loyalty.

The cases that follow trace the development of the so-called triad and the obligation of good faith in two key areas: executive compensation and oversight.

A. COMPENSATION

In re The Walt Disney Co. Derivative Litigation

906 A.2d 27 (Del. June 8, 2006).*

In August 1995, Michael Ovitz ("Ovitz") and The Walt Disney Company ("Disney" or the "Company") entered into an employment agreement under which Ovitz would serve as President of Disney for five years. In December 1996, only fourteen months after he commenced employment, Ovitz was terminated without cause, resulting in a severance payout to Ovitz valued at approximately $130 million.

In January 1997, several Disney shareholders brought derivative actions in the Court of Chancery, on behalf of Disney, against Ovitz and the directors of Disney who served at the time of the events complained of (the "Disney defendants"). The plaintiffs claimed that the $130 million severance payout was the product of fiduciary duty and contractual breaches by Ovitz, and breaches of fiduciary duty by the Disney defendants, and a waste of assets. . . . In August 2005, the Chancellor handed down a well-crafted 174 page Opinion and Order, determining that "the director defendants did not breach their fiduciary duties or commit waste." . . . We conclude, for the reasons that follow, that the Chancellor's factual findings and legal rulings were correct. . . .

I. THE FACTS

. . . In 1994 Disney lost in a tragic helicopter crash its President and Chief Operating Officer, Frank Wells, who together with Michael Eisner, Disney's Chairman and Chief Executive Officer, had enjoyed remarkable success at the Company's helm. Eisner temporarily assumed Disney's presidency, but only three months later, heart disease required Eisner to undergo quadruple bypass surgery. Those two events persuaded Eisner and Disney's board of directors that the time had come to identify a successor to Eisner.

Eisner's prime candidate for the position was Michael Ovitz, who was the leading partner and one of the founders of Creative Artists Agency ("CAA"), the premier talent agency whose business model had reshaped the entire industry. By 1995, CAA had 550 employees and a roster of about 1400 of Hollywood's top actors, directors, writers, and musicians. That roster generated about $150 million in annual revenues

* [Some paragraphs in the original have been consolidated.—Eds.]

and an annual income of over $20 million for Ovitz, who was regarded as one of the most powerful figures in Hollywood.

Eisner and Ovitz had enjoyed a social and professional relationship that spanned nearly 25 years. . . . Although in the past the two men had casually discussed possibly working together, in 1995, when Ovitz began negotiations to leave CAA and join Music Corporation of America ("MCA"), Eisner became seriously interested in recruiting Ovitz to join Disney. Eisner shared that desire with Disney's board members on an individual basis.

A. Negotiation of the Ovitz Employment Agreement

Eisner and Irwin Russell, who was a Disney director and chairman of the compensation committee, first approached Ovitz about joining Disney. Their initial negotiations were unproductive, however, because at that time MCA had made Ovitz an offer that Disney could not match. The MCA-Ovitz negotiations eventually fell apart, and Ovitz returned to CAA in mid-1995. . . . [Soon, negotiations with Disney were again] in full swing.

. . . [A]t some point during the negotiations Ovitz came to believe that he and Eisner would run Disney, and would work together in a relation akin to that of junior and senior partner. Unfortunately, Ovitz's belief was mistaken, as Eisner had a radically different view of what their respective roles at Disney should be.

. . . Ovitz owned 55% of CAA and earned approximately $20 to $25 million a year from that company. From the beginning Ovitz made it clear that he would not give up his 55% interest in CAA without "downside protection." Considerable negotiation then ensued over downside protection issues.

. . . During the summer of 1995, the parties agreed to a draft version of Ovitz's employment agreement (the "OEA") modeled after Eisner's and the late Mr. Wells' employment contracts. As described by the Chancellor, the draft agreement included the following terms:

Under the proposed OEA, Ovitz would receive a five-year contract with two tranches of options. The first tranche consisted of three million options vesting in equal parts in the third, fourth, and fifth years, and if the value of those options at the end of the five years had not appreciated to $50 million, Disney would make up the difference. The second tranche consisted of two million options that would vest immediately if Disney and Ovitz opted to renew the contract.

The proposed OEA sought to protect both parties in the event that Ovitz's employment ended prematurely, and provided that absent defined causes, neither party could terminate the agreement without penalty. If Ovitz, for example, walked away, for any reason other than those permitted under the OEA, he would forfeit any benefits remaining under the OEA and could be enjoined from working for a competitor. Likewise, if Disney fired Ovitz for any reason other than gross negligence or malfeasance, Ovitz would be entitled to a non-fault payment (Non-Fault Termination or "NFT"), which consisted of his remaining salary, $7.5 million a year for unaccrued bonuses, the immediate vesting of his first tranche of options and a $10 million cash out payment for the second tranche of options.

As the basic terms of the OEA were crystallizing, Russell prepared and gave Ovitz and Eisner a "case study" to explain those terms. . . . Russell acknowledged . . . that Ovitz was an "exceptional corporate executive" . . . who merited "downside protection and upside opportunity." Both would be required to enable Ovitz to adjust to the reduced cash compensation he would receive from a public company, in contrast to the greater cash distributions and other perquisites more typically available from a privately held business. But, Russell did caution that Ovitz's salary would be at the top level for any corporate officer and significantly above that of the Disney CEO. Moreover, the stock options granted under the OEA would exceed the standards applied within Disney and corporate America and would "raise very strong criticism." . . .

To assist in evaluating the financial terms of the OEA, Russell recruited Graef Crystal, an executive compensation consultant, and Raymond Watson, a member of Disney's compensation committee and a past Disney board chairman who had helped structure Wells' and Eisner's compensation packages. . . . On August 10, Russell, Watson, and Crystal met. They discussed and generated a set of values using different and various inputs and assumptions, accounting for different numbers of options, vesting periods, and potential proceeds of option exercises at various times and prices. . . . Two days later, Crystal faxed to Russell a memorandum concluding that the OEA would provide Ovitz with approximately $23.6 million per year for the first five years, or $23.9 million a year over seven years if Ovitz exercised a two-year renewal option. . . . Those sums, Crystal opined, would approximate Ovitz's current annual compensation at CAA.

Addressing Crystal's concerns, Russell made clear that the guarantee would not function as Crystal believed it might. Crystal then revised his original letter, adjusting the value of the OEA (assuming a two year renewal) to $24.1 million per year. Up to that point, only three Disney directors—Eisner, Russell and Watson—knew the status of the negotiations with Ovitz and the terms of the draft OEA.

While Russell, Watson, and Crystal were finalizing their analysis of the OEA, Eisner and Ovitz reached a separate agreement. Eisner told Ovitz that: (1) the number of options would be reduced from a single grant of five million to two separate grants, the first being three million options for the first five years and the second consisting of two million more options if the contract was renewed; and (2) Ovitz would join Disney only as President, not as a co-CEO with Eisner. After deliberating, Ovitz accepted those terms, and that evening Ovitz, Eisner, Sid Bass and their families celebrated Ovitz's decision to join Disney. . . .

On August 14, Eisner and Ovitz signed a letter agreement (the "OLA"), which outlined the basic terms of Ovitz's employment, and stated that the agreement (which would ultimately be embodied in a formal contract) was subject to approval by Disney's compensation committee and board of directors. . . . Eisner [, Russell, and Watson] . . . contacted each of the . . . board members . . . to inform them of the impending new hire. . . .

Once the OLA was signed, Joseph Santaniello, a Vice President and counsel in Disney's legal department, began to embody in a draft OEA the terms that Russell and Goldman had agreed upon and had been memorialized in the OLA. [Several amendments were then made.] . . . On September 26, 1995, the Disney compensation committee (which consisted of Messrs. Russell, Watson, Poitier, and Lozano) met for one hour to consider, among other agenda items, the proposed terms of the OEA. . . . The committee voted unanimously to approve the OEA terms, subject to "reasonable further negotiations within the framework of the terms and conditions" described in the OEA.

Immediately after the compensation committee meeting, the Disney board met in executive session. . . . Eisner led the discussion relating to Ovitz, and Watson then explained his analysis, and both Watson and Russell responded to questions from the board. After further deliberation, the board voted unanimously to elect Ovitz as President. . . .

B. Ovitz's Performance as President of Disney

Ovitz's tenure as President of the Walt Disney Company officially began on October 1, 1995, the date that the OEA was executed. When Ovitz took office, the initial reaction was optimistic, and Ovitz did make some positive contributions while serving as President of the Company. By the fall of 1996, however, it had become clear that Ovitz was "a poor fit with his fellow executives." . . .

Although the plaintiffs attempted to show that Ovitz acted improperly (*i.e.*, with gross negligence or malfeasance) while in office, the Chancellor found that the trial record did not support those accusations. . . . The Chancellor also rejected the appellants' second claim—that Ovitz was a habitual liar. . . . Lastly, the Chancellor found that the record did not support, and often contradicted, the appellants' third claim—that Ovitz had violated the Company's policies relating to expenses and to reporting gifts he received while President of Disney. . . .

On September 30, 1996, the Disney board met. During an executive session of that meeting, and in small group discussions where Ovitz was not present, Eisner told the other board members of the continuing problems with Ovitz's performance. . . . Those interchanges set the stage for Ovitz's eventual termination as Disney's President.

C. Ovitz's Termination at Disney

After the discussions between Litvack and Ovitz, Eisner and Ovitz met several times. During those meetings they discussed Ovitz's future, including Ovitz's employment prospects at Sony. Eisner believed that because Ovitz had a good, longstanding relationship with many Sony senior executives, Sony would be willing to take Ovitz in "trade" from Disney. Eisner favored such a trade, which would not only remove Ovitz from Disney, but also would relieve Disney of any obligation to pay Ovitz under the OEA. Thereafter, in October 1996, Ovitz, with Eisner's permission, entered into negotiations with Sony. Those negotiations did not prove fruitful, however. . . .

In response to this unwelcome news, Eisner wrote (but never sent) a letter to Ovitz on November 11, in which Eisner attempted to make it clear that Ovitz was no longer welcome at Disney. Instead of sending that letter, Eisner met with Ovitz personally on November 13, and discussed much of what the letter contained. . . .

During this period Eisner was also working with Litvack to explore whether they could terminate Ovitz under the OEA for cause. If so,

Disney would not owe Ovitz the NFT payment. From the very beginning, Litvack advised Eisner that he did not believe there was cause to terminate Ovitz under the OEA. Litvack's advice never changed.

At the end of November 1996, Eisner again asked Litvack if Disney had cause to fire Ovitz and thereby avoid the costly NFT payment. Litvack proceeded to examine that issue more carefully. He studied the OEA, refreshed himself on the meaning of "gross negligence" and "malfeasance," and reviewed all the facts concerning Ovitz's performance of which he was aware. Litvack also consulted Val Cohen, co-head of Disney's litigation department and Joseph Santaniello, in Disney's legal department. Cohen and Santaniello both concurred in Litvack's conclusion that no basis existed to terminate Ovitz for cause. . . .

. . . Ovitz met with Eisner on December 3, to discuss his termination. Ovitz asked for several concessions, all of which Eisner ultimately rejected. Eisner told Ovitz that all he would receive was what he had contracted for in the OEA. . . .

II. *SUMMARY OF APPELLANTS' CLAIMS OF ERROR*

. . . The appellants' claims of error are most easily analyzed in two separate groupings: (1) the claims against the Disney defendants and (2) the claims against Ovitz. The first category encompasses the claims that the Disney defendants breached their fiduciary duties to act with due care and in good faith by (1) approving the OEA, and specifically, its NFT provisions; and (2) approving the NFT severance payment to Ovitz upon his termination—a payment that is also claimed to constitute corporate waste. . . . Falling into the second category are the claims being advanced against Ovitz. Appellants claim that Ovitz breached his fiduciary duties of care and loyalty to Disney by (i) negotiating for and accepting the NFT severance provisions of the OEA, and (ii) negotiating a full NFT payout in connection with his termination. . . . In Part III, we analyze the claims relating to Ovitz. In Part IV, we address the claims asserted against the Disney defendants.

III. *THE CLAIMS AGAINST OVITZ*

. . . [A]ppellants contend that the Court of Chancery erred by dismissing their claim, as a summary judgment matter, that Ovitz had breached his fiduciary duties to Disney by negotiating and entering into the OEA. On summary judgment the Chancellor determined that Ovitz had breached no fiduciary duty to Disney, because Ovitz did not become a fiduciary until he formally assumed office on October 1, 1995, by which time the essential terms of the NFT provision had been negotiated. . . .

That ruling was erroneous, appellants argue, because even though Ovitz did not formally assume the title of President until October 1, 1995, he became a *de facto* fiduciary before then. . . . That conclusion is compelled, appellants urge, because Ovitz's substantial contacts with third parties, and his receipt of confidential Disney information and request for reimbursement of expenses before October 1, prove that Eisner and Disney had already vested Ovitz with at least apparent authority before his formal investiture in office.

. . . [T]he *de facto* officer argument lacks merit, both legally and factually. A *de facto* officer is one who actually assumes possession of an office under the claim and color of an election or appointment and who is actually discharging the duties of that office, but for some legal reason lacks *de jure* legal title to that office. Here, Ovitz did not assume, or purport to assume, the duties of the Disney presidency before October 1, 1995. In his post-trial Opinion, the Chancellor found as fact that all of Ovitz's pre-October 1 conduct upon which appellants rely to establish *de facto* officer status, represented Ovitz's preparations to assume the duties of President after he was formally in office. The record amply supports those findings. . . .

IV. *THE CLAIMS AGAINST THE DISNEY DEFENDANTS*

. . . [T]he claims of error that relate to the Disney defendants . . . are subdivisible into two groups: (A) claims arising out of the approval of the OEA and of Ovitz's election as President; and (B) claims arising out of the NFT severance payment to Ovitz upon his termination.

A. Claims Arising From the Approval of The OEA and Ovitz's Election as President

. . . [T]he appellants' core argument in the trial court was that the Disney defendants' approval of the OEA and election of Ovitz as President were not entitled to business judgment rule protection, because those actions were either grossly negligent or not performed in good faith. . . .

1. The Due Care Determinations

. . . The appellants claim that the Chancellor erred by: (1) treating as distinct questions whether the plaintiffs had established by a preponderance of the evidence either gross negligence or a lack of good faith; (2) ruling that the old board was not required to approve the OEA; . . . (4) concluding that the compensation committee members did not breach their duty of care in approving the NFT provisions of the OEA; and (5) holding that the remaining members of the old board (*i.e.*, the directors who were not members of the compensation committee) had not breached their duty of care in electing Ovitz as Disney's President. . . .

(a) Treating Due Care and Bad Faith as Separate Grounds for Denying Business Judgment Rule Review

This argument is best understood against the backdrop of the presumptions that cloak director action being reviewed under the business judgment standard. Our law presumes that "in making a business decision the directors of a corporation acted on an informed basis, in good faith, and in the honest belief that the action taken was in the best interests of the company." Those presumptions can be rebutted if the plaintiff shows that the directors breached their fiduciary duty of care or of loyalty or acted in bad faith. If that is shown, the burden then shifts to the director defendants to demonstrate that the challenged act or transaction was entirely fair to the corporation and its shareholders.

Because no duty of loyalty claim was asserted against the Disney defendants, the only way to rebut the business judgment rule presumptions would be to show that the Disney defendants had either breached their duty of care or had not acted in good faith. At trial, the plaintiff-appellants attempted to establish both grounds, but the Chancellor determined that the plaintiffs had failed to prove either.

. . .

(b) Ruling That the Full Disney Board Was Not Required To Consider and Approve the OEA

The appellants . . . challenge the Court of Chancery's determination that the full Disney board was not required to consider and approve the OEA, because the Company's governing instruments allocated that decision to the compensation committee. . . .

The Delaware General Corporation Law (DGCL) expressly empowers a board of directors to appoint committees and to delegate to them a broad range of responsibilities, which may include setting executive compensation. Nothing in the DGCL mandates that the entire board must make those decisions. . . .

(d) Holding That the Compensation Committee Members Did Not Fail To Exercise Due Care in Approving the OEA

The appellants next challenge the Chancellor's determination that although the compensation committee's decision-making process fell far short of corporate governance "best practices," the committee members breached no duty of care in considering and approving the NFT terms of the OEA. That conclusion is reversible error, the appellants claim, because the record establishes that the compensation committee members did not properly inform themselves of the material facts and, hence, were grossly negligent in approving the NFT provisions of the OEA. . . .

In our view, a helpful approach is to compare what actually happened here to what would have occurred had the committee followed a "best practices" (or "best case") scenario, from a process standpoint. In a "best case" scenario, all committee members would have received, before or at the committee's first meeting on September 26, 1995, a spreadsheet or similar document prepared by (or with the assistance of) a compensation expert (in this case, Graef Crystal). Making different, alternative assumptions, the spreadsheet would disclose the amounts that Ovitz could receive under the OEA in each circumstance that might foreseeably arise. One variable in that matrix of possibilities would be the cost to Disney of a non-fault termination for each of the five years of the initial term of the OEA. The contents of the spreadsheet would be explained to the committee members, either by the expert who prepared it or by a fellow committee member similarly knowledgeable about the subject. That spreadsheet, which ultimately would become an exhibit to the minutes of the compensation committee meeting, would form the basis of the committee's deliberations and decision.

Had that scenario been followed, there would be no dispute (and no basis for litigation) over what information was furnished to the committee members or when it was furnished. Regrettably, the committee's informational and decisionmaking process used here was not so tidy. That is one reason why the Chancellor found that although the committee's process did not fall below the level required for a proper exercise of due care, it did fall short of what best practices would have counseled.

The Disney compensation committee met twice: on September 26 and October 16, 1995. The minutes of the September 26 meeting reflect that the committee approved the terms of the OEA (at that time embodied in the form of a letter agreement), except for the option grants, which were not approved until October 16—after the Disney stock incentive plan had been amended to provide for those options. At the September 26 meeting, the compensation committee considered a "term sheet" which, in summarizing the material terms of the OEA, relevantly disclosed that in the event of a non-fault termination, Ovitz would receive: (i) the present value of his salary ($1 million per year) for the balance of the contract term, (ii) the present value of his annual bonus payments (computed at $7.5 million) for the balance of the contract term, (iii) a $10 million termination fee, and (iv) the acceleration of his options for 3 million shares, which would become immediately exercisable at market price.

Thus, the compensation committee knew that in the event of an NFT, Ovitz's severance payment alone could be in the range of $40 million cash, plus the value of the accelerated options. Because the actual payout to Ovitz was approximately $130 million, of which roughly $38.5 million was cash, the value of the options at the time of the NFT payout would have been about $91.5 million. Thus, the issue may be framed as whether the compensation committee members knew, at the time they approved the OEA, that the value of the option component of the severance package could reach the $92 million order of magnitude if they terminated Ovitz without cause after one year. The evidentiary record shows that the committee members were so informed.

On this question the documentation is far less than what best practices would have dictated. There is no exhibit to the minutes that discloses, in a single document, the estimated value of the accelerated options in the event of an NFT termination after one year. The information imparted to the committee members on that subject is, however, supported by other evidence, most notably the trial testimony of various witnesses about spreadsheets that were prepared for the compensation committee meetings.

The compensation committee members derived their information about the potential magnitude of an NFT payout from two sources. The first was the value of the "benchmark" options previously granted to Eisner and Wells and the valuations by Watson of the proposed Ovitz options. Ovitz's options were set at 75% of parity with the options previously granted to Eisner and to Frank Wells. Because the compensation committee had established those earlier benchmark option grants to Eisner and Wells and were aware of their value, a simple mathematical calculation would have informed them of the potential value range of Ovitz's options. Also, in August and September 1995, Watson and Russell met with Graef Crystal to determine (among other things) the value of the potential Ovitz options, assuming different scenarios. Crystal valued the options under the Black-Scholes method, while Watson used a different valuation metric. Watson recorded his calculations and the resulting values on a set of spreadsheets that reflected what option profits Ovitz might receive, based upon a range of different assumptions about stock market price increases. Those spreadsheets were shared with, and explained to, the committee members at the September meeting.

The committee's second source of information was the amount of "downside protection" that Ovitz was demanding. Ovitz required financial protection from the risk of leaving a very lucrative and secure position at CAA, of which he was a controlling partner, to join a publicly held corporation to which Ovitz was a stranger, and that had a very different culture and an environment which prevented him from completely controlling his destiny. The committee members knew that by leaving CAA and coming to Disney, Ovitz would be sacrificing "booked" CAA commissions of $150 to $200 million—an amount that Ovitz demanded as protection against the risk that his employment relationship with Disney might not work out. Ovitz wanted at least $50 million of that compensation to take the form of an "up-front" signing bonus. Had the $50 million bonus been paid, the size of the option grant would have been lower. Because it was contrary to Disney policy, the compensation committee rejected the up-front signing bonus demand, and elected instead to compensate Ovitz at the "back end," by awarding him options that would be phased in over the five-year term of the OEA.

It is on this record that the Chancellor found that the compensation committee was informed of the material facts relating to an NFT payout. If measured in terms of the documentation that would have been generated if "best practices" had been followed, that record leaves much to be desired. The Chancellor acknowledged that, and so do we. But, the Chancellor also found that despite its imperfections, the evidentiary record was sufficient to support the conclusion that the compensation committee had adequately informed itself of the potential magnitude of the entire severance package, including the options, that Ovitz would receive in the event of an early NFT.

The OEA was specifically structured to compensate Ovitz for walking away from $150 million to $200 million of anticipated commissions from CAA over the five-year OEA contract term. This meant that if Ovitz was terminated without cause, the earlier in the contract term the termination occurred the larger the severance amount would be to replace the lost commissions. Indeed, because Ovitz was terminated after only one year, the total amount of his severance payment (about $130 million) closely approximated the lower end of the range of Ovitz's forfeited commissions ($150 million), less the compensation Ovitz received during his first and only year as Disney's President. Accordingly, the Court of Chancery had a sufficient evidentiary basis in the record from which to find that, at the time they approved the OEA, the compensation committee members were adequately informed of the potential magnitude of an early NFT severance payout. . . .

(e) Holding That the Remaining Disney Directors Did Not Fail To Exercise Due Care in Approving the Hiring Of Ovitz as the President of Disney

The appellants' final claim in this category is that the Court of Chancery erroneously held that the remaining members of the old Disney board had not breached their duty of care in electing Ovitz as President of Disney. . . . The Chancellor determined that in electing Ovitz, the directors were informed of all information reasonably available and, thus, were not grossly negligent. We agree.

The Chancellor found and the record shows the following: well in advance of the September 26, 1995 board meeting the directors were fully aware that the Company needed—especially in light of Wells' death and Eisner's medical problems—to hire a "number two" executive and potential successor to Eisner. There had been many discussions about that need and about potential candidates who could fill that role even before Eisner decided to try to recruit Ovitz. Before the September 26 board meeting Eisner had individually discussed with each director the possibility of hiring Ovitz, and Ovitz's background and qualifications. The directors thus knew of Ovitz's skills, reputation and experience, all of which they believed would be highly valuable to the Company. The directors also knew that to accept a position at Disney, Ovitz would have to walk away from a very successful business—a reality that would lead a reasonable person to believe that Ovitz would likely succeed in similar pursuits elsewhere in the industry. The directors also knew of the public's highly positive reaction to the Ovitz announcement, and that Eisner and senior management had supported the Ovitz hiring. Indeed, Eisner, who had long desired to bring Ovitz within the Disney fold, consistently vouched for Ovitz's qualifications and told the directors that he could work well with Ovitz.

The board was also informed of the key terms of the OEA (including Ovitz's salary, bonus and options). Russell reported this information to them at the September 26, 1995 executive session, which was attended by Eisner and all non-executive directors. Russell also reported on the compensation committee meeting that had immediately preceded the executive session. And, both Russell and Watson responded to questions from the board. Relying upon the compensation committee's approval of the OEA and the other information furnished to them, the Disney directors, after further deliberating, unanimously elected Ovitz as President.

Based upon this record, we uphold the Chancellor's conclusion that, when electing Ovitz to the Disney presidency the remaining Disney directors were fully informed of all material facts, and that the appellants failed to establish any lack of due care on the directors' part.

2. *The Good Faith Determinations*

The Court of Chancery held that the business judgment rule presumptions protected the decisions of the compensation committee and the remaining Disney directors, not only because they had acted with due care but also because they had not acted in bad faith. . . .

In its Opinion the Court of Chancery defined bad faith as follows:

> Upon long and careful consideration, I am of the opinion that the concept of *intentional dereliction of duty,* a *conscious disregard for one's responsibilities,* is an appropriate (although not the only) standard for determining whether fiduciaries have acted in good faith. Deliberate indifference and inaction *in the face of a duty to act* is, in my mind, conduct that is clearly disloyal to the corporation. It is the epitome of faithless conduct.

. . . Because of the increased recognition of the importance of good faith, some conceptual guidance to the corporate community may be helpful. . . .

The precise question is whether the Chancellor's articulated standard for bad faith corporate fiduciary conduct—intentional dereliction of duty, a conscious disregard for one's responsibilities—is legally correct. In approaching that question, we note that the Chancellor characterized that definition as "*an* appropriate *(although not the only)* standard for determining whether fiduciaries have acted in good faith."

That observation is accurate and helpful, because as a matter of simple logic, at least three different categories of fiduciary behavior are candidates for the "bad faith" pejorative label.

The first category involves so-called "subjective bad faith," that is, fiduciary conduct motivated by an actual intent to do harm. That such conduct constitutes classic, quintessential bad faith is a proposition so well accepted in the liturgy of fiduciary law that it borders on axiomatic. We need not dwell further on this category, because no such conduct is claimed to have occurred, or did occur, in this case.

The second category of conduct, which is at the opposite end of the spectrum, involves lack of due care—that is, fiduciary action taken solely by reason of gross negligence and without any malevolent intent. In this case, appellants assert claims of gross negligence to establish breaches not only of director due care but also of the directors' duty to act in good faith. Although the Chancellor found, and we agree, that the appellants failed to establish gross negligence, to afford guidance we address the issue of whether gross negligence (including a failure to inform one's self of available material facts), without more, can also constitute bad faith. The answer is clearly no.

. . . Both our legislative history and our common law jurisprudence distinguish sharply between the duties to exercise due care and to act in good faith. . . .

That leaves the third category of fiduciary conduct, which falls in between the first two categories of (1) conduct motivated by subjective bad intent and (2) conduct resulting from gross negligence. This third category is what the Chancellor's definition of bad faith—intentional dereliction of duty, a conscious disregard for one's responsibilities—is intended to capture. The question is whether such misconduct is properly treated as a non-exculpable, nonindemnifiable violation of the fiduciary duty to act in good faith. In our view it must be, for at least two reasons.

First, the universe of fiduciary misconduct is not limited to either disloyalty in the classic sense (*i.e.*, preferring the adverse self-interest of the fiduciary or of a related person to the interest of the corporation) or gross negligence. Cases have arisen where corporate directors have no conflicting self-interest in a decision, yet engage in misconduct that is more culpable than simple inattention or failure to be informed of all facts material to the decision. To protect the interests of the corporation and its shareholders, fiduciary conduct of this kind, which does not involve disloyalty (as traditionally defined) but is qualitatively more culpable than gross negligence, should be proscribed. A vehicle is needed to address such violations doctrinally, and that doctrinal vehicle is the duty to act in good faith. The Chancellor implicitly so recognized in his Opinion, where he identified different examples of bad faith as follows:

> The good faith required of a corporate fiduciary includes not simply the duties of care and loyalty, in the narrow sense that I have discussed them above, but all actions required by a true faithfulness and devotion to the interests of the corporation and its shareholders. A failure to act in good faith may be shown, for instance, where the fiduciary intentionally acts with a purpose other than that of advancing the best interests of the corporation, where the fiduciary acts with the intent to violate

> applicable positive law, or where the fiduciary intentionally fails to act in the face of a known duty to act, demonstrating a conscious disregard for his duties. There may be other examples of bad faith yet to be proven or alleged, but these three are the most salient.

Those articulated examples of bad faith are not new to our jurisprudence. Indeed, they echo pronouncements our courts have made throughout the decades. Second, the legislature has also recognized this intermediate category of fiduciary misconduct, which ranks between conduct involving subjective bad faith and gross negligence. Section 102(b)(7)(ii) of the DGCL expressly denies money damage exculpation for "acts or omissions not in good faith or which involve intentional misconduct or a knowing violation of law." By its very terms that provision distinguishes between "intentional misconduct" and a "knowing violation of law" (both examples of subjective bad faith) on the one hand, and "acts . . . not in good faith," on the other. Because the statute exculpates directors only for conduct amounting to gross negligence, the statutory denial of exculpation for "acts . . . not in good faith" must encompass the intermediate category of misconduct captured by the Chancellor's definition of bad faith.

For these reasons, we uphold the Court of Chancery's definition as a legally appropriate, although not the exclusive, definition of fiduciary bad faith. We need go no further. To engage in an effort to craft (in the Court's words) "a definitive and categorical definition of the universe of acts that would constitute bad faith" would be unwise and is unnecessary to dispose of the issues presented on this appeal.

. . .

B. Claims Arising From the Payment of the NFT Severance Payout to Ovitz

The appellants advance three alternative claims . . . whose overall thrust is that even if the OEA approval was legally valid, the NFT severance payout to Ovitz pursuant to the OEA was not. Specifically, the appellants contend that: (1) only the full Disney board with the concurrence of the compensation committee—but not Eisner alone—was authorized to terminate Ovitz; (2) because Ovitz could have been terminated for cause, Litvack and Eisner acted without due care and in bad faith in reaching the contrary conclusion; and (3) the business judgment rule presumptions did not protect the new Disney board's acquiescence in the NFT payout, because the new board was not entitled to rely upon Eisner's and Litvack's contrary advice. . . . We disagree.

1. Was Action By The New Board Required To Terminate Ovitz As The President of Disney?

The Chancellor determined that although the board as constituted upon Ovitz's termination (the "new board") had the authority to terminate Ovitz, neither that board nor the compensation committee was required to act, because Eisner also had, and properly exercised, that authority. The new board, the Chancellor found, was not required to terminate Ovitz under the company's internal documents. Without such a duty to act, the new board's failure to vote on the termination could not give rise to a breach of the duty of care or the duty to act in good faith. . . .

Article Tenth of the Company's certificate of incorporation in effect at the termination plainly states that:

> The officers of the Corporation shall be chosen in such a manner, shall hold their offices for such terms and shall carry out such duties as are determined solely by the Board of Directors, subject to the right of the Board of Directors to remove any officer or officers at any time with or without cause.

Article IV of Disney's bylaws provided that the Board Chairman/CEO "shall, subject to the provisions of the Bylaws and the control of the Board of Directors, have general and active management, direction, and supervision over the business of the Corporation and over its officers. . . ." . . . The issue is whether the Chancellor's interpretation of these instruments, as giving the board and the Chairman/CEO concurrent power to terminate a lesser officer, is legally permissible. . . . Read together, the governing instruments do not yield a single, indisputably clear answer, and could reasonably be interpreted either way. . . .

Where corporate governing instruments are ambiguous, our case law permits a court to determine their meaning by resorting to well-established legal rules of construction, which include the rules governing the interpretation of contracts. One such rule is that where a contract is ambiguous, the court must look to extrinsic evidence to determine which of the reasonable readings the parties intended.

Here, the extrinsic evidence clearly supports the conclusion that the board and Eisner understood that Eisner, as Board Chairman/CEO had concurrent power with the board to terminate Ovitz as President. In that regard, the Chancellor credited the testimony of new board members that Eisner, as Chairman and CEO, was empowered to terminate Ovitz without board approval or intervention; and also Litvack's testimony that during his tenure as general counsel, many Company officers were terminated and the board never once took action in connection with their terminations. . . .

2. In Concluding That Ovitz Could Not Be Terminated For Cause, Did Litvack or Eisner Breach Any Fiduciary Duty?

It is undisputed that Litvack and Eisner (based on Litvack's advice) both concluded that if Ovitz was to be terminated, it could only be without cause, because no basis existed to terminate Ovitz for cause. . . . [T]he Chancellor determined independently, as a matter of fact and law, that (1) Ovitz had not engaged in any conduct as President that constituted gross negligence or malfeasance—the standard for an NFT under the OEA; and (2) in arriving at that same conclusion in 1996, Litvack and Eisner did not breach their fiduciary duty of care or their duty to act in good faith. . . .

At the trial level, the appellants attempted to show, as a factual matter, that Ovitz's conduct as President met the standard for a termination for cause, because (i) Ovitz intentionally failed to follow Eisner's directives and was insubordinate, (ii) Ovitz was a habitual liar, and (iii) Ovitz violated Company policies relating to expenses and to reporting gifts he gave while President of Disney. The Court found the facts contrary to appellants' position. . . .

With respect to Eisner, the Chancellor found that faced with a situation where he was unable to work well with Ovitz, who required close and constant supervision, Eisner had three options: 1) keep Ovitz as President and continue trying to make things work; 2) keep Ovitz at Disney, but in a role other than as President; or 3) terminate Ovitz. The first option was unacceptable, and the second would have entitled Ovitz to the NFT, or at the very least would have resulted in a costly lawsuit to determine whether Ovitz was so entitled. After an unsuccessful effort to "trade" Ovitz to Sony, that left only the third option, which was to terminate Ovitz and pay the NFT. The Chancellor found that in choosing this alternative, Eisner had breached no duty and had exercised his business judgment . . . :

Even though the Chancellor found much to criticize in Eisner's "imperial CEO" style of governance, nothing has been shown to overturn the factual basis for the Court's conclusion that, in the end, Eisner's conduct satisfied the standards required of him as a fiduciary.

3. Were the Remaining Directors Entitled to Rely upon Eisner's And Litvack's Advice That Ovitz Could Not Be Fired for Cause

The appellants' third claim of error challenges the Chancellor's conclusion that the remaining new board members could rely upon Litvack's and Eisner's advice that Ovitz could be terminated only without cause. The short answer to that challenge is that, for the reasons previously discussed, the advice the remaining directors received and relied upon was accurate. Moreover, the directors' reliance on that advice was found to be in good faith. . . .

V. *THE WASTE CLAIM*

The appellants' final claim is that even if the approval of the OEA was protected by the business judgment rule presumptions, the payment of the severance amount to Ovitz constituted waste. This claim is rooted in the doctrine that a plaintiff who fails to rebut the business judgment rule presumptions is not entitled to any remedy unless the transaction constitutes waste. The Court of Chancery rejected the appellants' waste claim, and the appellants claim that in so doing the Court committed error.

To recover on a claim of corporate waste, the plaintiffs must shoulder the burden of proving that the exchange was "so one sided that no business person of ordinary, sound judgment could conclude that the corporation has received adequate consideration." A claim of waste will arise only in the rare, "unconscionable case where directors irrationally squander or give away corporate assets." This onerous standard for waste is a corollary of the proposition that where business judgment presumptions are applicable, the board's decision will be upheld unless it cannot be "attributed to any rational business purpose."

. . . The claim that the payment of the NFT amount to Ovitz, without more, constituted waste is meritless on its face, because at the time the NFT amounts were paid, Disney was contractually obligated to pay them. The payment of a contractually obligated amount cannot constitute waste, unless the contractual obligation is itself wasteful. Accordingly, the proper focus of a waste analysis must be whether the amounts required to be paid in the event of an NFT were wasteful *ex ante*. . . . Specifically, the OEA gave Ovitz every incentive to leave the Company before serving out the full term of his contract. The appellants urge that although the OEA may have induced Ovitz to join Disney as President, no contractual safeguards were in place to retain him in that position. In essence, appellants claim that the NFT provisions of the OEA created an irrational incentive for Ovitz to get himself fired.

That claim does not come close to satisfying the high hurdle required to establish waste. The approval of the NFT provisions in the OEA had a rational business purpose: to induce Ovitz to leave CAA, at what would otherwise be a considerable cost to him, in order to join Disney. . . .

ANALYSIS

1. In *Brehm v. Eisner,* 746 A.2d 244 (Del. 2000), in which the Delaware Supreme Court reversed Chancellor Chandler's original grant of a motion to dismiss and sent the Ovitz case back down to Chancery for the trial that resulted in the appeal denied in this opinion, then Chief Justice Norman Veasey wrote for the Court:

> As for the plaintiffs' contention that the directors failed to exercise "substantive due care," we should note that such a concept is foreign to the business judgment rule. Courts do not measure, weigh or quantify directors' judgments. We do not even decide if they are reasonable in this context. Due care in the decisionmaking context is process due care only. Irrationality is the outer limit of the business judgment rule. Irrationality may be the functional equivalent of the waste test or it may tend to show that the decision is not made in good faith, which is a key ingredient of the business judgment rule.

Is the Court's decision in the present case consistent with Veasey's analysis or has the court introduced an element of substantive due care analysis into the business judgment rule? In other words, after the present case, will the business judgment rule still preclude Delaware judges from attempting to measure the reasonableness of a board's decision?

2. Under this decision, is proof of bad faith (a) a basis for rebutting the business judgment rule's presumption against judicial review of director decision making, (b) a separate basis for imposing liability on directors even in the absence of a showing that the directors violated their duty of care or loyalty, or (c) both?

3. Does an intentional decision by the board to break the law constitute bad faith? If so, should it?

4. By this point in your law school career, you should be quite familiar with devising hypotheticals to test the application of some doctrine. Try your hand at devising a hypothetical set of facts in which the directors have acted in bad faith without also violating either their duty of care or of loyalty.

5. The Court's decision leaves two issues unresolved: (a) Should courts assess director compliance with the preconditions of the business judgment rule and their fiduciary duties on an individual director-by-director basis or on the basis of an analysis of the actions of the collective board? (b) Does the business judgment rule preclude judicial review of

the merits of decisions made by officers, as well as those of directors? How should a future court rule on those issues?

6. What is the single most important thing the Disney directors could have done when making decisions about Ovitz's compensation to avoid the risk and great expense associated with this trial?

NOTE ON SAY ON PAY

In response to the financial crisis of 2007–2008, Congress passed The Wall Street Reform and Consumer Protection Act of 2010 ("Dodd-Frank").[1] Most of the Act deals with financial regulation. Several provisions of the Act, however, impose new corporate governance regulations not just on Wall Street banks but also on all Main Street public corporations. In particular, two address executive compensation.

Section 951 of Dodd-Frank creates a so-called "say on pay" mandate, requiring periodic shareholder advisory votes on executive compensation, about which more in a moment. Section 952 mandates that the compensation committees of the board of directors of public companies must be fully independent and that those committees be given responsibility for setting CEO pay, among other things.

Dodd-Frank § 951 creates a new § 14A of the Securities Exchange Act, pursuant to which reporting companies must conduct a shareholder advisory vote on specified executive compensation not less frequently than every three years. At least once every six years, shareholders also must vote on how frequently to hold such an advisory vote (i.e., annually, biannually, or triennially).

The vote must be tabulated and disclosed. Larger public corporations are further required to disclose whether and how their compensation policies and decisions take into account the results of the say on pay vote.

The results of the vote are not binding on the board of directors. Indeed, the Act makes clear that the vote shall not be deemed either to effect or affect the fiduciary duties of directors.

B. OVERSIGHT

INTRODUCTION

Directors are not expected to know, in minute detail, everything that happens on a day-to-day basis. At the very least, however, a director must have a rudimentary understanding of the firm's business and how it works, keep informed about the firm's activities, engage in a general monitoring of corporate affairs, attend board meetings regularly, and routinely review financial statements. Beyond these obligations, however, the question remained as to whether boards must adopt rules and procedures to ensure that corporate officers and other employees do not engage in illegal or unlawful conduct, and must make reasonable efforts to monitor compliance with those rules and procedures.

---

[1] The Wall Street Reform and Consumer Protection Act of 2010, Pub. L. No. 111–203, 124 Stat. 1376 (2010) (hereinafter cited as "Dodd Frank").

In *In re Caremark Int'l Inc. Deriv. Litig.*, 698 A.2d 959 (Del. Ch. 1996), Delaware Chancellor Allen described the obligations of members of the board as follows:

> [I]t would, in my opinion, be a mistake to conclude that . . . corporate boards may satisfy their obligation to be reasonably informed concerning the corporation, without assuring themselves that information and reporting systems exist in the organization that are reasonably designed to provide to senior management and to the board itself timely, accurate information sufficient to allow management and the board, each within its scope, to reach informed judgments concerning both the corporation's compliance with law and its business performance. . . .
>
> Thus, I am of the view that a director's obligation includes a duty to attempt in good faith to assure that a corporate information and reporting system, which the board concludes is adequate, exists, and that failure to do so under some circumstances may, in theory at least, render a director liable for losses caused by non-compliance with applicable legal standards.

Id. at 970. Does that obligation arise under the duty of care, loyalty, or good faith? Does it matter?

Stone v. Ritter

911 A.2d 362 (Del. 2006).

This is an appeal from a final judgment of the Court of Chancery dismissing a derivative complaint against fifteen present and former directors of AmSouth Bancorporation ("AmSouth"), a Delaware corporation. . . .

The Court of Chancery characterized the allegations in the derivative complaint as a "classic *Caremark* claim," a claim that derives its name from *In re Caremark Int'l Deriv. Litig.* In *Caremark*, the Court of Chancery recognized that: "[g]enerally where a claim of directorial liability for corporate loss is predicated upon ignorance of liability creating activities within the corporation . . . only a sustained or systematic failure of the board to exercise oversight—such as an utter failure to attempt to assure a reasonable information and reporting system exists-will establish the lack of good faith that is a necessary condition to liability."[2]

. . .

Facts

. . . During the relevant period, AmSouth's wholly-owned subsidiary, AmSouth Bank, operated about 600 commercial banking branches in six states throughout the southeastern United States and employed more than 11,600 people.

In 2004, AmSouth and AmSouth Bank paid $40 million in fines and $10 million in civil penalties to resolve government and regulatory

[2] In re Caremark Int'l Inc. Deriv. Litig., 698 A.2d at 971. . . .

investigations pertaining principally to the failure by bank employees to file "Suspicious Activity Reports" ("SARs"), as required by the federal Bank Secrecy Act ("BSA") and various anti-money-laundering ("AML") regulations. . . . No fines or penalties were imposed on AmSouth's directors, and no other regulatory action was taken against them.

[The government contended that although "at least one" AmSouth Bank employee suspected that a banking client was engaged in illegal activities, the Bank failed to file SARs.]

On October 12, 2004, the Federal Reserve and the Alabama Banking Department concurrently issued a Cease and Desist Order against AmSouth, requiring it, for the first time, to improve its BSA/AML program. That Cease and Desist Order required AmSouth to (among other things) engage an independent consultant "to conduct a comprehensive review of the Bank's AML Compliance program and make recommendations, as appropriate, for new policies and procedures to be implemented by the Bank." KPMG Forensic Services ("KPMG") performed the role of independent consultant and issued its report on December 10, 2004 (the "KPMG Report").

Also on October 12, 2004, [the Treasury's Financial Crimes Enforcement Network (FinCEN)] and the Federal Reserve jointly assessed a $10 million civil penalty against AmSouth for operating an inadequate anti-money-laundering program and for failing to file SARs. . . . Among FinCEN's specific determinations were its conclusions that "AmSouth's [AML compliance] program lacked adequate board and management oversight," and that "reporting to management for the purposes of monitoring and oversight of compliance activities was materially deficient." AmSouth neither admitted nor denied FinCEN's determinations in this or any other forum.

Demand Futility and Director Independence

. . .

In this appeal, the plaintiffs concede that "[t]he standards for determining demand futility in the absence of a business decision" are set forth in *Rales v. Blasband*.[10] To excuse demand under *Rales*, "a court must determine whether or not the particularized factual allegations of a derivative stockholder complaint create a reasonable doubt that, as of the time the complaint is filed, the board of directors could have properly exercised its independent and disinterested business judgment in responding to a demand."

Critical to this demand excused argument is the fact that the directors' potential personal liability depends upon whether or not their conduct can be exculpated by the section 102(b)(7) provision contained in the AmSouth certificate of incorporation. Such a provision can exculpate directors from monetary liability for a breach of the duty of care, but not for conduct that is not in good faith or a breach of the duty of loyalty. The standard for assessing a director's potential personal liability for failing to act in good faith in discharging his or her oversight responsibilities has evolved beginning with our decision in *Graham v. Allis-Chalmers Manufacturing Company*,[15] through the Court of Chancery's *Caremark*

---

[10] Rales v. Blasband, 634 A.2d 927 (Del.1993).

[15] Graham v. Allis-Chalmers Mfg. Co., 188 A.2d 125 (Del.1963).

decision to our most recent decision in *Disney*. A brief discussion of that evolution will help illuminate the standard that we adopt in this case.

Graham and *Caremark*

Graham was a derivative action brought against the directors of Allis-Chalmers for failure to prevent violations of federal anti-trust laws by Allis-Chalmers employees. There was no claim that the Allis-Chalmers directors knew of the employees' conduct that resulted in the corporation's liability. Rather, the plaintiffs claimed that the Allis-Chalmers directors should have known of the illegal conduct by the corporation's employees. In *Graham*, this Court held that "*absent cause for suspicion* there is no duty upon the directors to install and operate a corporate system of espionage to ferret out wrongdoing which they have no reason to suspect exists."[17]

In *Caremark*, . . . [we] narrowly construed our holding in *Graham* "as standing for the proposition that, absent grounds to suspect deception, neither corporate boards nor senior officers can be charged with wrongdoing simply for assuming the integrity of employees and the honesty of their dealings on the company's behalf."[19] The *Caremark* Court opined it would be a "mistake" to interpret this Court's decision in *Graham* to mean that:

> corporate boards may satisfy their obligation to be reasonably informed concerning the corporation, without assuring themselves that information and reporting systems exist in the organization that are reasonably designed to provide to senior management and to the board itself timely, accurate information sufficient to allow management and the board, each within its scope, to reach informed judgments concerning both the corporation's compliance with law and its business performance.[20]

. . . The Court of Chancery then formulated the following standard for assessing the liability of directors where the directors are unaware of employee misconduct that results in the corporation being held liable:

> Generally where a claim of directorial liability for corporate loss is predicated upon ignorance of liability creating activities within the corporation, as in *Graham* or in this case, . . . only a sustained or systematic failure of the board to exercise oversight-such as an utter failure to attempt to assure a reasonable information and reporting system exists—will establish the lack of good faith that is a necessary condition to liability.[23]

Caremark Standard Approved

As evidenced by the language quoted above, the *Caremark* standard for so-called "oversight" liability draws heavily upon the concept of director failure to act in good faith. That is consistent with the definition(s) of bad faith recently approved by this Court in its recent *Disney* decision, where we held that a failure to act in good faith requires

---

[17] Graham v. Allis-Chalmers Mfg. Co., 188 A.2d at 130 (emphasis added).

[19] [In re Caremark Int'l Inc. Deriv. Litig., 698 A.2d 959, 969 (Del.Ch.1996).]

[20] Id. at 970.

[23] In re Caremark Int'l Inc. Deriv. Litig., 698 A.2d at 971.

conduct that is qualitatively different from, and more culpable than, the conduct giving rise to a violation of the fiduciary duty of care (i.e., gross negligence). In *Disney*, we identified the following examples of conduct that would establish a failure to act in good faith:

> A failure to act in good faith may be shown, for instance, where the fiduciary intentionally acts with a purpose other than that of advancing the best interests of the corporation, where the fiduciary acts with the intent to violate applicable positive law, or where the fiduciary intentionally fails to act in the face of a known duty to act, demonstrating a conscious disregard for his duties. There may be other examples of bad faith yet to be proven or alleged, but these three are the most salient.[26]

The third of these examples describes, and is fully consistent with, the lack of good faith conduct that the *Caremark* court held was a "necessary condition" for director oversight liability, i.e., "a sustained or systematic failure of the board to exercise oversight—such as an utter failure to attempt to assure a reasonable information and reporting system exists. . . ." . . .

It is important, in this context, to clarify a doctrinal issue that is critical to understanding fiduciary liability under *Caremark* as we construe that case. The phraseology used in *Caremark* and that we employ here—describing the lack of good faith as a "necessary condition to liability"—is deliberate. The purpose of that formulation is to communicate that a failure to act in good faith is not conduct that results, ipso facto, in the direct imposition of fiduciary liability. The failure to act in good faith may result in liability because the requirement to act in good faith "is a subsidiary element[,]" i.e., a condition, "of the fundamental duty of loyalty."[30] It follows that because a showing of bad faith conduct, in the sense described in *Disney* and *Caremark*, is essential to establish director oversight liability, the fiduciary duty violated by that conduct is the duty of loyalty.

This view of a failure to act in good faith results in two additional doctrinal consequences. First, although good faith may be described colloquially as part of a "triad" of fiduciary duties that includes the duties of care and loyalty, the obligation to act in good faith does not establish an independent fiduciary duty that stands on the same footing as the duties of care and loyalty. Only the latter two duties, where violated, may directly result in liability, whereas a failure to act in good faith may do so, but indirectly. The second doctrinal consequence is that the fiduciary duty of loyalty is not limited to cases involving a financial or other cognizable fiduciary conflict of interest. It also encompasses cases where the fiduciary fails to act in good faith. As the Court of Chancery aptly put it in *Guttman*, "[a] director cannot act loyally towards the corporation unless she acts in the good faith belief that her actions are in the corporation's best interest."[32]

We hold that *Caremark* articulates the necessary conditions predicate for director oversight liability: (a) the directors utterly failed to implement any reporting or information system or controls; or (b) having

---

[26] [In re Walt Disney Co. Deriv. Litig., 906 A.2d 27, 67 (Del.2006).]

[30] Guttman v. Huang, 823 A.2d 492, 506 n. 34 (Del.Ch.2003).

[32] Guttman v. Huang, 823 A.2d 492, 506 n. 34 (Del.Ch.2003).

implemented such a system or controls, consciously failed to monitor or oversee its operations thus disabling themselves from being informed of risks or problems requiring their attention. In either case, imposition of liability requires a showing that the directors knew that they were not discharging their fiduciary obligations. Where directors fail to act in the face of a known duty to act, thereby demonstrating a conscious disregard for their responsibilities, they breach their duty of loyalty by failing to discharge that fiduciary obligation in good faith.

. . .

Reasonable Reporting System Existed

[The plaintiffs contend that demand is excused under Rule 23.1 because AmSouth's directors breached their oversight duty and, as a result, face a "substantial likelihood of liability" as a result of their "utter failure" to act in good faith to put into place policies and procedures to ensure compliance with BSA and AML obligations.] The KPMG Report evaluated the various components of AmSouth's longstanding BSA/AML compliance program. The KPMG Report reflects that AmSouth's Board dedicated considerable resources to the BSA/AML compliance program and put into place numerous procedures and systems to attempt to ensure compliance. . . .

The KPMG Report describes the numerous AmSouth employees, departments and committees established by the Board to oversee AmSouth's compliance with the BSA and to report violations to management and the Board:

> BSA Officer. Since 1998, AmSouth has had a "BSA Officer" "responsible for all BSA/AML-related matters including employee training, general communications, CTR reporting and SAR reporting," and "presenting AML policy and program changes to the Board of Directors, the managers at the various lines of business, and participants in the annual training of security and audit personnel[;]"
>
> BSA/AML Compliance Department. AmSouth has had for years a BSA/AML Compliance Department, headed by the BSA Officer and comprised of nineteen professionals, including a BSA/AML Compliance Manager and a Compliance Reporting Manager;
>
> Corporate Security Department. AmSouth's Corporate Security Department has been at all relevant times responsible for the detection and reporting of suspicious activity as it relates to fraudulent activity, and William Burch, the head of Corporate Security, has been with AmSouth since 1998 and served in the U.S. Secret Service from 1969 to 1998; and
>
> Suspicious Activity Oversight Committee. Since 2001, the "Suspicious Activity Oversight Committee" and its predecessor, the "AML Committee," have actively overseen AmSouth's BSA/AML compliance program. The Suspicious Activity Oversight Committee's mission has for years been to "oversee the policy, procedure, and process issues affecting the Corporate Security and BSA/AML Compliance Programs, to ensure that an effective program exists at AmSouth to deter, detect, and

report money laundering, suspicious activity and other fraudulent activity."

The KPMG Report reflects that the directors not only discharged their oversight responsibility to establish an information and reporting system, but also proved that the system was designed to permit the directors to periodically monitor AmSouth's compliance with BSA and AML regulations. For example, as KPMG noted in 2004, AmSouth's designated BSA Officer "has made annual high-level presentations to the Board of Directors in each of the last five years." Further, the Board's Audit and Community Responsibility Committee (the "Audit Committee") oversaw AmSouth's BSA/AML compliance program on a quarterly basis. The KPMG Report states that "the BSA Officer presents BSA/AML training to the Board of Directors annually," and the "Corporate Security training is also presented to the Board of Directors."

The KPMG Report shows that AmSouth's Board at various times enacted written policies and procedures designed to ensure compliance with the BSA and AML regulations. For example, the Board adopted an amended bank-wide "BSA/AML Policy" on July 17, 2003—four months before AmSouth became aware that it was the target of a government investigation. . . . Among other things, the July 17, 2003, BSA/AML Policy directs all AmSouth employees to immediately report suspicious transactions or activity to the BSA/AML Compliance Department or Corporate Security.

Complaint Properly Dismissed

. . .

[The standard] of liability—lack of good faith as evidenced by sustained or systematic failure of a director to exercise reasonable oversight—is quite high. But, a demanding test of liability in the oversight context is probably beneficial to corporate shareholders as a class, as it is in the board decision context, since it makes board service by qualified persons more likely, while continuing to act as a stimulus to *good faith performance of duty* by such directors.[42]

The KPMG Report . . . [shows] that the Board received and approved relevant policies and procedures, delegated to certain employees and departments the responsibility for filing SARs and monitoring compliance, and exercised oversight by relying on periodic reports from them. . . .

With the benefit of hindsight, the plaintiffs' complaint seeks to equate a bad outcome with bad faith. The lacuna in the plaintiffs' argument is a failure to recognize that the directors' good faith exercise of oversight responsibility may not invariably prevent employees from violating criminal laws, or from causing the corporation to incur significant financial liability, or both. . . . In the absence of red flags, good faith in the context of oversight must be measured by the directors' actions "to assure a reasonable information and reporting system exists" and not by second-guessing after the occurrence of employee conduct that results in an unintended adverse outcome. Accordingly, we hold that the Court of Chancery properly . . . dismissed the plaintiffs' derivative complaint for failure to excuse demand. . . .

---

[42] [In re Caremark Int'l Inc. Deriv. Litig., 698 A.2d at 971 (emphasis in original).]

ANALYSIS

1. If *Caremark* claims are to be recharacterized as loyalty claims, what other duty of care claims also logically should be recharacterized as violations of the duty of loyalty?

2. Review the Problems following *Francis* (Chapter 5, Section 1, supra), in which the board of directors of a trucking company authorizes corporate employees to break a traffic regulation. After *Stone*, how would your analysis of those problems change, if at all?

3. At common law, the owner of a dog was liable to someone whom the dog had bitten only if the owner was on notice that the dog had a propensity to bite. The requisite propensity could be shown by either a prior bite (hence, the colloquialism "every dog gets one bite") or where the dog was of a vicious breed. Does that rule make policy sense, especially compared to the modern trend of holding dog owners strictly liable even for first bites? If so, is that policy appropriate for modern corporate governance?

4. Suppose that the board of directors of AmSouth had considered the issue and then affirmatively decided not to adopt any law compliance program. Would it be liable if that decision resulted in corporate losses?

5. After *Stone*, on what grounds, if any, could a plaintiff bring a *Caremark* claim in cases in which the board of directors had implemented a reasonable compliance program and reporting system?

6. In footnote 112 of the *Disney* decision, reprinted above, the Delaware Supreme Court stated ". . . we do not reach or otherwise address the issue of whether the fiduciary duty to act in good faith is a duty that, like the duties of care and loyalty, can serve as an independent basis for imposing liability upon corporate officers and directors. That issue is not before us on this appeal." What is the status of the "fiduciary duty to act in good faith" after *Stone*?

7. What are the practical consequences of this decision in the following areas: (a) Whether an exculpation provision adopted pursuant to DGCL § 102(b)(7) precludes monetary liability in *Caremark* claims? (b) To what extent is a plaintiff likely entitled to discovery in *Caremark* claims, as compared to standard duty of care claims such as those at issue in cases like *Brehm v. Eisner* (Chapter 5, Section 1, supra)? (c) What remedy is available to a plaintiff who successfully brings a *Caremark* claim? (d) The doctrinal distinctions between the duty of loyalty and the duty of care?

8. Taken together, do *Disney* and *Stone* appear to make directors of Delaware corporations more or less vulnerable to claims of breach of fiduciary duty?

C. DERIVATIVE ASPECTS

INTRODUCTORY NOTE

Cases involving alleged oversight failures almost never reach the merits of the claims. Instead, in the vast majority of cases the plaintiff files a derivative suit without making demand on the board of directors, in response to which the defendants move to dismiss the suit for failure to comply with Delaware Rule of Civil Procedure 23.1's demand requirement. The case is thus joined on the issue of whether demand was excused as futile. The following case illustrates how the *Caremark* standards fit into the demand excused context, explains the special rules on demand futility applicable to oversight cases, and provides an opportunity to review both oversight and demand futility.

In re China Agritech, Inc. Shareholder Derivative Litigation

2013 WL 2181514 (Del.Ch. 2013).

China Agritech, Inc. . . . purportedly operates a fertilizer manufacturing business in China. According to lead plaintiff Albert Rish, China Agritech is a fraud that serves only to enrich its co-founders, defendants Yu Chang and Xiao Rong Teng. Rish has sued derivatively to recover damages resulting from (i) the Company's purchase of stock from a corporation owned by Chang and Teng, (ii) the suspected misuse of $23 million raised by the Company in a secondary offering, (iii) the mismanagement that occurred during a remarkable twenty-four month period that witnessed the terminations of two outside auditing firms and the resignations of six outside directors and two senior officers, and (iv) the Company's failure to make any federal securities filings since November 2010 and concomitant delisting by NASDAQ. . . .

The defendants have moved to dismiss pursuant to Rule 23.1, contending that the complaint fails to plead that demand was made on the board or would have been futile. . . .

I. FACTUAL BACKGROUND

. . .

A. China Agritech

According to its public filings, China Agritech is a Delaware corporation that develops, manufactures, and markets environmentally friendly fertilizer products in the People's Republic of China. The Company accessed the domestic securities markets in February 2005 through a reverse merger with an inactive corporation that had retained its NASDAQ listing.* "[U]sing a defunct Delaware corporation that happens to retain a public listing to evade the regulatory regime established by the federal securities laws is contrary to Delaware public policy." Williams v. Calypso Wireless, Inc., 2012 WL 424880, at *1 n. 1 (Del. Ch. Feb. 8, 2012). . . .

Defendant Chang founded China Agritech. Chang has served as the Company's President, Chief Executive Officer, Secretary, and Chairman of the board since February 2005. He owns approximately 55% of China Agritech's outstanding common stock, holding 34.1% directly and another 20.8% beneficially through China Tailong Group Limited. By

---

* [Eds.: When two or more corporations merge, only one of the constituent corporations survives. In a forward merger, which is by far the more common type, the acquiring corporation survives. In a reverse merger, by contrast, the acquired corporation is the one that survives. In such a merger, the newly formed entity retains all the rights of the surviving corporation, including its listing on a US stock exchange. By using this technique, a corporation thus can go public on US capital markets without the delay and expense of an initial public offering (IPO).]

virtue of his stock ownership and positions with the Company, Chang controls China Agritech.

Defendant Teng co-founded China Agritech. Teng has served as a director of the Company since June 2005. From February 3, 2005 until March 13, 2009, she served as the Company's Chief Operating Officer. She owns 1.68% of the Company's common stock directly.

. . .

B. Problems With Internal Controls

In its [annual] Form 10-K for the year ending December 31, 2007, filed with the SEC on March 28, 2008, the Company disclosed that it "did not have in place the financial controls and procedures required to comply with U.S. financial reporting standards." . . .

In an effort to correct its control problems, the Company hired new executives and expanded its board. On October 22, 2008, defendant Yau-Sing Tang ("Y.Tang") joined China Agritech as its CFO and controller. On that same date, defendants Gene Michael Bennett, Lun Zhang Dai, and Hai Ling Zhang ("H.Zhang") became directors. The board then established an Audit Committee, a Compensation Committee, and a Nominating and Governance Committee (the "Governance Committee"), each populated with the new outside directors. Beginning with its Form 10-K for the year ending December 31, 2008, filed with the SEC on March 28, 2009, China Agritech disclosed that its internal controls and procedures were effective as of December 31, 2008.

C. The Yinlong Transaction

On February 12, 2009, Yinlong Industrial Co., Ltd. ("Yinlong") sold China Agritech the remaining 10% equity interest in China Agritech's otherwise 90% owned subsidiary, Pacific Dragon Fertilizers Co. Ltd. ("Pacific Dragon"). Chang and Teng owned 85% and 15%, respectively, of Yinlong's shares, making the deal an interested transaction. . . .

China Agritech acquired the Pacific Dragon shares through a wholly owned subsidiary, China Tailong Holdings Company Ltd. ("Tailong"). China Agritech agreed to pay Yinlong $7,980,000 for the shares, with all but $1 million coming in the form of an interest-free promissory note from Tailong to Yinlong. The transaction closed on May 15, 2009. On the day of the closing, the parties entered into a supplemental purchase agreement. The supplemental purchase agreement amended the "settlement of the purchase consideration" to a cash payment of $1 million and the issuance of 1,745,000 restricted shares of China Agritech common stock. . . .

Chang, Teng, Dai, Bennett, and H. Zhang comprised the board at the time of the Yinlong Transaction. Dai, Bennett, and H. Zhang comprised both the Audit Committee and the Governance Committee.

In March 2009, defendant Ming Gang Zhu became China Agritech's Chief Operating Officer, taking over from Teng. In December 2009, defendant Zheng Wang joined the board as a designee of a fund that invested in the Company. Because of her affiliation, the board did not consider her to be an independent director. . . .

In early January 2010, Charles Law became an outside director. He joined the Governance Committee and the Compensation Committee.

D. The $23 Million Offering

In April 2010, China Agritech announced a public offering of 1,243,000 shares of common stock, plus an underwriter's option on an additional 186,450 shares, which the underwriter exercised (the "Offering"). The stated purpose of the Offering was to finance the construction of distribution centers for China Agritech's fertilizer products. The Offering raised total gross proceeds of $23 million. According to the Complaint, the funds have not been used to construct distribution centers or for any other discernible business purpose, suggesting either that the funds have been misused or that the stated purpose was false. At the time of the Offering, Chang, Teng, Dai, Bennett, H. Zhang, Law, and Wang comprised the board.

E. The Material Weaknesses Return

In its [quarterly] Form 10-Q dated August 16, 2010, China Agritech disclosed that material weaknesses had again undermined its disclosure controls and procedures. . . . The material weaknesses necessitated making adjustments to the Company's reported results for first quarter 2010.

In its Form 10-Q dated November 10, 2010, the Company claimed to have fixed its internal controls problem: "[M]anagement enhanced the supervision and review of the financial reporting process" and deemed that the "remediation steps correct[ed] the material weaknesses" previously identified. The November 2010 Form 10-Q was the last time that China Agritech made a federally mandated securities filing. . . .

On November 13, 2010, three days after claiming that the material weaknesses were solved, the Company fired its outside auditor, Crowe Horwath LLP. The Audit Committee approved the termination. Dai, Bennett, and H. Zhang comprised the Audit Committee.

F. The Company Hires Ernst & Young.

Effective as of November 13, 2010, the Company hired Ernst & Young Hua Ming ("Ernst & Young") as its new outside auditor. . .

On December 15, 2010, Ernst & Young provided a letter to the Audit Committee describing matters which, if not appropriately addressed, could result in audit adjustments, significant deficiencies or material weaknesses, and delays in the filing of the Company's Form 10-K for 2010. Company management claimed to have addressed the issues, but Ernst & Young did not agree.

G. The McGee Report

While Ernst & Young was raising issues with Company management, Lucas McGee was investigating China Agritech. McGee is a self-described "consultant and private investor with more than ten years of business and finance experience throughout Asia, including China, Hong Kong and Vietnam." On February 3, 2011, McGee posted a report titled "China Agritech: A Scam" (the "McGee Report") on the investor website www.seekingalpha.com. McGee disclosed that he held a short position in the Company's stock and stood to profit from a decline in the Company's common stock price.

The McGee Report identified a series of alleged problems with the Company's business, including:

- Factories are idle: After visiting [China Agritech's] reported manufacturing facilities . . . we found virtually no manufacturing underway. The single exception was the facility in Pinggu County on the outskirts of Beijing, where the plant was not in operation on the Friday when we visited but local people told us that it has sporadically produced some liquid fertilizer over the last year. Plants in Bengbu, Anhui (supposedly the largest), Harbin, and Xinjiang were completely shuttered.
- Harbin plant for sale: The Harbin facility—supposedly a major manufacturing facility for the $100 million revenue business—whose name has never been officially changed in government documentation from "Pacific Dragon," had a sign hanging on the gates last summer reading "this factory is for sale."
- No contract with Sinochem: A January [China Agritech] announcement states: "In May 2010, the Company signed a renewed contract supplying organic liquid compound fertilizers to Sinochem, China's largest fertilizer distributor." . . . But a manager with Sinochem told us that Sinochem has no contract with [China Agritech] and in fact has never bought or sold organic liquid fertilizers. . . .
- [China Agritech] not permitted to make granular fertilizer: [China Agritech] claims that most of its sales volume now derives from granular compound fertilizers. But government officials familiar with the [China Agritech] operation say that [China Agritech] has not received a license to manufacture granular compound fertilizer and does not sell any.
- Unable to buy the product: Although the [C]ompany has announced 21 regional distribution centers, we have not been able to locate any. . . .
- Fictional Revenue: [W]e have received an analysis of audited [China Agritech] revenues reported to the Chinese government for the year 2009 In its [third quarter 2010 10-Q], [China Agritech] claims that it has 100,000 metric tons of production capacity in Anhui, 50,000 metric tons in Harbin, and 50,000 tons in Xinjiang. But a total value of . . . $3,000 in plant and equipment in Xinjiang would be insufficient to support 50,000 tons of production capacity. Indeed, when we visited the site of the Xinjiang plant, we found little more than a warehouse, shared with two other companies and demonstrating no activity.
- Our early attempts to find the Xinjiang factory were unsuccessful. . . . [A]fter searching the area and asking county officials, we were able to discover a factory bearing [China Agritech's] name along with the names of two other companies [at a different location than the registered address]. . . . The facility, however, is idle and we were told by local people that there is no production activity there.

- In Anhui, which [China Agritech] calls its principal production facility . . . [w]e visited and found a small plant on a rutted road outside Bengbu, completely deserted.
- The Beijing plant is larger, but plant staff said in our presence that the facility was idle. The [C]ompany would not allow us in, but we drove around the plant and saw a few people on site washing clothes but no evidence of production. Local government officials said that [China Agritech] had not been able to obtain a production license for granular fertilizer and that it produced a very small volume of liquid fertilizer.
- No distribution centers: In May 2010, [China Agritech] issued over 1.4 million new shares, raising just under $19 million for the construction of distribution centers. But we have not been able to find evidence that any distribution centers were actually built.
- Mysterious suppliers: The companies that [China Agritech] lists in its corporate materials as suppliers of raw materials . . . cannot be found in any directory under possible Chinese names that would correspond to the transliterated names or under the alphabetic names.
- Financial anomalies:

. . .

3. The Xinjiang company reports zero fixed assets, meaning that it owns no equipment for production. . . .

4. The Beijing facility has licensed registered capital of $20 million, but by the end of 2009 had received 88 million RMB, so only more than half of the legally required amount. But despite the missing capital, half of the registered capital was still sitting in the account in cash in 2009, indicating that the company had not purchased much, if any, equipment. . . .

McGee concluded that China Agritech "is not a currently functioning business that is manufacturing products. Instead it is, in our view, simply a vehicle for transferring shareholder wealth from outside investors into the pockets of the founders and inside management." . . .

On February 4, 2011, the day after the McGee Report issued, the Company posted a press release on its website denying the allegations. On February 10, the Company issued a second press release in the form of an open letter from Chang to "Fellow Shareholders and Potential Investors" in which he contested key elements of the McGee Report. . . .

On February 10, 2011, Law resigned from the board. The remaining directors appointed X. Zhang to fill his seat.

H. The Company Fires Ernst & Young.

On March 8, 2011, Ernst & Young met with the Audit Committee to discuss potential violations of law, including the United States securities laws. The issues identified by Ernst & Young included goods delivery notes that appeared to be modified after the fact; time sheets and related data for the Harbin facility that appeared to be destroyed; material purchases apparently made without supporting official tax invoice or with duplicative official tax invoice; a tax notice from the Harbin City tax bureau that appeared to be falsified; and what appeared to be material undisclosed related party transactions. Ernst & Young expressed concern about whether the firm could continue to rely on management's representations. . . . Ernst & Young asked the Audit Committee to take "timely and appropriate action."

On March 10, 2011, the board formed a Special Investigation Committee (the "Special Committee") to investigate Ernst & Young's allegations. The original members of the Special Committee were Wang, Dai, Bennett, and H. Zhang. Because Dai, Bennett, and H. Zhang were members of the Audit Committee, they faced the awkward task of investigating, evaluating, and passing on the propriety of their own actions as members of the Audit Committee. Wang was the only member of the Special Committee who did not face the prospect of investigating her own actions, but she was also a director whom the board did not regard as independent.

On March 12, 2011, Company management drafted a press release stating that the Special Committee had been formed and explaining that the action was taken due to allegations "made by third parties" with respect to the Company and certain issues "identified in connection with the performance of the Company's year end audit." When the actual press release was issued, it omitted the phrase "identified in connection with the performance of the Company's year end audit." Ernst & Young immediately advised Company counsel that the deletion of the reference to audit issues was a material omission. Ernst & Young stated that it would resign if a corrective press release was not issued. No correction was made.

On March 14, 2011, Chang informed Ernst & Young that the Audit Committee had terminated its engagement. Ernst & Young had no prior notice regarding its potential termination and had no reason to believe its termination was under consideration before the dispute over the press release. . . .

On March 15, 2011, Ernst & Young sent the Company a letter detailing its concerns about its termination and the accuracy of the Company's purported reasons. The letter noted that it was being sent to fulfill Ernst & Young's obligations "under Section 10A(b)(2) of the Securities Exchange Act of 1934," which requires an independent auditor to report directly to a company's board of directors if it believes an (i) "illegal act" has occurred that materially affects the issuer's financial statements and (ii) that management had not, either independently or as required by the board, yet taken "timely and appropriate remedial action."

Wang, the chair of the Special Committee, resigned from the board on March 15, 2011. She "was a Special Committee member only for one day." Def. Op. Br. at 38 n. 14. The other members of the Special Committee continued to serve. Bennett, the Chair of the Audit Committee, took over as Chair of the Special Committee.

On April 25, 2011, the remaining directors appointed defendant Kai Wai Sim to fill Wang's seat. On the same day, Bennett resigned from both the Audit Committee and Special Committee, although for the time being he remained a member of the board. . . .

In April 2011, NASDAQ notified the Company that it would be delisted "based on public interest concerns and the Company's failure to file its 2010 form 10-K on time." . . .

On May 27, 2011, the Company announced that Zhu, the Company's COO, had resigned. . . .

J. The Special Committee's "Findings"

On December 1, 2011, the Company issued a press release announcing that the Special Committee had completed its investigation. The Company noted that "[t]he investigation was subject to certain limitations," including that "[Ernst & Young] did not cooperate with the investigation. . . ." It is not clear what other limitations, if any, existed.

Without providing any details or explanation, the Company reported that according to the Special Committee, all was well:

[T]he [Special] Committee concluded that the investigation appropriately addressed all material issues raised by [Ernst & Young], the circumstances of [Ernst & Young]'s termination, and the allegations in [the McGee Report]. With specific regard to [the McGee Report], the [Special] Committee concluded that the allegations were either factually incorrect or that there were reasonable explanations as to their non-materiality. . . .

K. The Parade Of Resignations

On January 6, 2012, Rish filed this lawsuit. At the time, defendants Chang, Teng, Dai, Sim, Bennett, H. Zhang, and X. Zhang comprised the board (the "Demand Board"). Sim, Dai, H. Zhang, and X. Zhang served on the Special Committee, and Sim, H. Zhang, and X. Zhang served on the Audit Committee. [Shortly thereafter, Sim, Y.Tang, H. Zhang, X. Zhang, and Bennett resigned from the board.] . . .

The resignations left Chang, Teng, and Dai as the only members of the board. To recapitulate, Chang and Teng are the Company's co-founders. Chang controls a mathematical majority of China Agritech's outstanding voting power, and he is the Company's President, CEO, Secretary, and Chairman of the Board. . . .

II. LEGAL ANALYSIS

. . .

A. Rule 23.1

When a corporation suffers harm, the board of directors is the institutional actor legally empowered under Delaware law to determine what, if any, remedial action the corporation should take, including pursuing litigation against the individuals involved. "A cardinal precept of the General Corporation Law of the State of Delaware is that directors, rather than shareholders, manage the business and affairs of the corporation." Aronson v. Lewis, 473 A.2d 805, 811 (Del.1984). . . .

In a derivative suit, a stockholder seeks to displace the board's authority over a litigation asset and assert the corporation's claim. *Aronson*, 473 A.2d at 811. . . .

Because directors are empowered to manage, or direct the management of, the business and affairs of the corporation, the right of a stockholder to prosecute a derivative suit is limited to situations where the stockholder has demanded that the directors pursue the corporate claim and they have wrongfully refused to do so or where demand is excused because the directors are incapable of making an impartial decision regarding such litigation.

Rish concedes that he did not make a litigation demand on the Demand Board, and the Company opposes his efforts to pursue litigation. Consequently, for Rish to obtain authority to move forward on behalf of China Agritech, his Complaint must "allege with particularity . . . the reasons . . . for not making the effort [to make a litigation demand]," and this Court must determine based on those allegations that "demand is excused because the directors are incapable of making an impartial decision regarding whether to institute such litigation." Stone v. Ritter, 911 A.2d 362, 367 (Del.2006). . . .

The Delaware Supreme Court has established two tests for determining whether the allegations of a complaint sufficiently plead demand futility. In *Aronson*, the seminal demand-futility decision, the Delaware Supreme Court crafted a specific two-part test that applies when a derivative plaintiff challenges an earlier board decision made by the same directors who remain in office at the time suit is filed. The Court of Chancery "must decide whether, under the particularized facts alleged, a reasonable doubt is created that: (1) the directors are disinterested and independent and (2) the challenged transaction was otherwise the product of a valid exercise of business judgment." [*Aronson*, 473 A.2d at 814.] The first of the two inquiries examines "the independence and disinterestedness of the directors" with respect to the decision that the derivative action would challenge. Id.* . . . If the underlying transaction was approved by a disinterested and independent board majority, then the court moves to the second inquiry: whether the plaintiff "has alleged facts with particularity which, if taken as true, support a reasonable doubt that the challenged transaction was the product of a valid exercise of business judgment." Id. at 815. A plaintiff might allege sufficiently, for example, that the directors were grossly negligent in approving the transaction.

. . .

In [Rales v. Blasband, 634 A.2d 927 (Del.1993)], the Delaware Supreme Court confronted a board whose members had not participated in the underlying decision that the derivative action would challenge, and therefore "the test enunciated in [*Aronson*] . . . [was] not implicated." [Id.] at 930. In response, the Delaware Supreme Court framed a second and more comprehensive demand futility standard that asks "whether or not the particularized factual allegations of a derivative stockholder complaint create a reasonable doubt that, as of the time the complaint is filed, the board of directors could have properly exercised its independent and disinterested business judgment in responding to a demand." Id. at 934. The Delaware Supreme Court envisioned that the *Rales* test would

* [Eds.: Later in the opinion, the Vice Chancellor stated: "A director is deemed 'interested' if he 'has received, or is entitled to receive, a personal financial benefit from the challenged transaction which is not equally shared by the stockholders.' Pogostin v. Rice, 480 A.2d 619, 624 (Del.1984)."]

be used in three principal scenarios: (1) where a business decision was made by the board of a company, but a majority of the directors making the decision have been replaced; (2) where the subject of the derivative suit is not a business decision of the board; and (3) where . . . the decision being challenged was made by the board of a different corporation.

A director cannot consider a litigation demand under *Rales* if the director is interested in the alleged wrongdoing, not independent, or would face a "substantial likelihood" of liability if suit were filed. *Rales*, 634 A.2d at 936 (internal quotation marks omitted). To show that a director faces a "substantial risk of liability," a plaintiff does not have to demonstrate a reasonable probability of success on the claim. In *Rales*, the Delaware Supreme Court rejected such a requirement as "unduly onerous." Id. at 935. The plaintiff need only "make a threshold showing, through the allegation of particularized facts, that their claims have some merit." Id. at 934. . . .

The *Aronson* and *Rales* have been described as complementary versions of the same inquiry. This case illustrates that reality. The fundamental question presented by the defendant's Rule 23.1 motion is whether the Demand Board could have validly considered a litigation demand. The Complaint challenges at least three events that involved actual decisions: the Yinlong Transaction, the terminations of the outside auditors, and the Special Committee's determination to take no action. Five of the seven members of the Demand Board were directors at the time those decisions were made. Because less than "a majority of the directors making the decision have been replaced," Rales, 634 A.2d at 935, *Aronson* provides the demand futility standard for the five participating directors. *Rales* would provide the standard for the two remaining directors, but because the *Aronson* analysis establishes demand futility, I do not reach the *Rales* aspect. . . .

The litigation also alleges a systematic lack of oversight at China Agritech. That challenge does not involve an actual board decision, so *Rales* governs.* . . .

The board of a Delaware corporation has a fiduciary obligation to adopt internal information and reporting systems that are "reasonably designed to provide to senior management and to the board itself timely, accurate information sufficient to allow management and the board, each within its scope, to reach informed judgments concerning both the corporation's compliance with law and its business performance." In re Caremark Int'l Inc. Deriv. Litig., 698 A.2d 959, 970 (Del. Ch.1996). If a corporation suffers losses proximately caused by fraud or illegal conduct, and if the directors failed "to attempt in good faith to assure that a corporate information and reporting system, which the board concludes is adequate, exists," then there is a sufficient connection between the occurrence of the illegal conduct and board level action or conscious inaction to support liability. Id. "[I]mposition of liability requires a showing that the directors knew that they were not discharging their fiduciary obligations." *Stone*, 911 A.2d at 370.

---

* [Eds.: Recall that earlier in the decision the court had explained that *Rales* applies "where the subject of the derivative suit is not a business decision of the board." When plaintiff alleges a Caremark violation by the board for failing its oversight duties, by definition there has been no business decision and the second *Rales* prong is applicable.]

The burden on a plaintiff who seeks to establish liability under a failure-to-monitor theory "is quite high." *Caremark*, 698 A.2d at 971.

> Generally where a claim of directorial liability for corporate loss is predicated upon ignorance of liability creating activities within the corporation, as in Graham [v. Allis-Chalmers Manufacturing Co., 188 A.2d 125 (Del.1963)] or in [the *Caremark* case itself], . . . only a sustained or systematic failure of the board to exercise oversight—such as an utter failure to attempt to assure a reasonable information and reporting system exists—will establish the lack of good faith that is a necessary condition to liability.

Id. "Concretely, this latter allegation might take the form of facts that show the company entirely lacked an audit committee or other important supervisory structures, or that a formally constituted audit committee failed to meet." [David B.] Shaev [Profit Sharing Account v. Armstrong], 2006 WL 391931, at *5 [(Del. Ch. Feb. 13, 2006)]. (footnote omitted). . . .

The allegations of the Complaint support a reasonable inference that China Agritech had a "formally constituted audit committee [that] failed to meet." *Shaev*, 2006 WL 391931, at *5. In response to the Section 220 Demand, China Agritech did not produce any Audit Committee meeting minutes for 2009 or 2010. The Company's proxy statement filed on July 22, 2010 similarly implies that the Audit Committee did not meet during 2009, although it did take action by written consent on three occasions.

During 2009 and 2010, the Company engaged in the Yinlong Transaction, conducted the Offering, disclosed a material weakness in its disclosure controls and procedures, claimed to have fixed the problem, terminated Crowe Horwath as its outside auditor, hired Ernst & Young as its new outside auditor, and named Dai's daughter as head of China Agritech's internal audit department. Yet there is no documentary evidence that the Audit Committee ever held a single meeting during this two year period. . . .

Discrepancies in the Company's public filings with governmental agencies reinforce the inference of an Audit Committee that existed in name only. During its time as a publicly listed entity in the United States, the federal securities laws mandated that the Company make periodic filings with the SEC. Regulatory requirements in China mandated that the Company make periodic filings with the State Administration for Industry and Commerce ("SAIC"). The Complaint alleges that in four of five years that the Company reported large profits in its filings with the SEC, the Company reported net losses to the SAIC. In the fifth year, the Company reported a large profit in its filings with the SEC, and one-fifth of that profit to the SAIC.

. . .

Taken together, the factual allegations of the Complaint support a reasonable inference that the members of the Audit Committee acted in bad faith in the sense that they consciously disregarded their duties. Unlike the parade of hastily filed *Caremark* complaints that Delaware courts have dismissed, and like those rare *Caremark* complaints that prior decisions have found adequate, the Complaint supports these allegations with references to books and records . . ., and with inferences that this Court can reasonably draw from the absence of books and records that the Company could be expected to produce.

Because of their service on the Audit Committee, Dai, Bennett, and H. Zhang face a substantial risk of liability for knowingly disregarding their duty of oversight. These directors could not validly consider a litigation demand concerning the problems that occurred on their watch. Dai also could not validly consider a litigation demand for the additional reason that his daughter, Lingxiao Dai, served as Vice President of Finance from May 1, 2009 until November 19, 2010, and as head of the internal audit department thereafter. A director lacks independence when "the director is unable to base his or her decisions on the corporate merits of the issue before the board." Litt v. Wycoff, 2003 WL 1794724, at *3 (Del. Ch. Mar. 28, 2003). A meaningful investigation into or litigation regarding China Agritech's lack of internal controls, financial reporting deficiencies, and potential violations of law would necessitate an investigation into Dai's daughter and could lead to a finding of wrongdoing against her. Close family relationships, like the parent-child relationship, create a reasonable doubt as to the independence of a director. . . . Dai also cannot consider a demand that would place Chang or Teng at risk because his daughter's primary employment depends on the good wishes of the Company's controlling stockholders. . . .

Lastly, Chang could not validly consider a demand because he would face a substantial risk of liability in connection with the events of the 2009 through 2010 period. Chang was the Company's Chairman, CEO, and controlling stockholder. The disputes between the Company and Crowe Horwath and Ernst & Young pitted Chang and his management team against the outside auditors. Ernst & Young pointed the finger directly at Chang and his management team by advising the Audit Committee that it did not believe it could rely on management's statements. Ernst & Young also contended that it was senior management that made a materially misleading disclosure regarding Ernst & Young's termination.

Chang, Dai, Bennett, and H. Zhang comprise a majority of the Demand Board. Demand is therefore futile under *Rales* for purposes of the *Caremark* claim, rendering it unnecessary to consider the other three directors.

. . .

C. Section 102(b)(7)*

The defendants argue that the Complaint should be dismissed because it does not assert a claim for which the defendants could be held liable in light of the exculpatory provision in China Agritech's certificate of incorporation. Because the Complaint pleads claims that implicate the duty of loyalty, including its embedded requirement of good faith, the defendants cannot invoke the exculpatory provision as a defense at this stage.

The Complaint challenges the Yinlong Transaction, an interested transaction with a controlling stockholder where entire fairness provides the presumptive standard of review. When the entire fairness standard of review applies, "the inherently interested nature of those transactions"

* [Eds.: See supra Chapter 5, § 1.]

renders the claims "inextricably intertwined with issues of loyalty." Emerald P'rs v. Berlin, 787 A.2d 85, 93 (Del.2001). Chang and Teng benefitted directly from the Yinlong Transaction, and Dai, Bennett, and H. Zhang approved it. Given the standard of review, I cannot dismiss these defendants.

The balance of the Complaint states claims that raise questions about whether the directors acted in good faith. A Section 102(b)(7) provision "can exculpate directors from monetary liability for a breach of the duty of care, but not for conduct that is not in good faith or a breach of the duty of loyalty." *Stone*, 911 A.2d at 367. The standard for *Caremark* liability parallels the standard for imposing liability when directors failed to act in good faith. See Stephen M. Bainbridge et al., The Convergence of Good Faith and Oversight, 55 UCLA L.Rev. 559 (2008) (discussing the re-interpretation of Caremark as a good faith case and the potential liability risks to directors that result).

> A failure to act in good faith may be shown, for instance, [1] where the fiduciary intentionally acts with a purpose other than that of advancing the best interests of the corporation, [2] where the fiduciary acts with the intent to violate applicable positive law, or [3] where the fiduciary intentionally fails to act in the face of a known duty to act, demonstrating a conscious disregard for his duties. There may be other examples of bad faith yet to be proven or alleged, but these three are the most salient.

In re Walt Disney Co. Deriv. Litig., 906 A.2d 27, 67 (Del.2006) (quoting In re Walt Disney Co. Deriv. Litig., 907 A.2d 693, 755–56 (Del. Ch.2005), aff'd, 906 A.2d 27 (Del.2006). . . . The ruling that the Complaint states an oversight claim against the defendants prevents them from invoking the Company's exculpatory provision at the pleading stage.

. . .

ANALYSIS

1. In this opinion, the court was resolving the defendant's motion to dismiss for failure to make demand. As the court noted in a portion we omitted, at that stage of the case, "plaintiffs receive the benefit of all reasonable inferences." If the case goes to trial, however, the court will be obliged to make credibility determinations. Is there any reason to be skeptical of elements of the plaintiff's evidence such as the McGee Report?

2. Although the Vice Chancellor stated that the *Aronson* and *Rales* tests are "complementary versions of the same inquiry," the opinion also quotes Delaware Supreme Court precedents indicating that *Aronson* is not "implicated" where *Rales* applies and vice-versa. What are the differences between the *Aronson* and *Rales* standards and why did the Delaware Supreme Court create the latter standard to govern the specified cases?

3. In Rich v. Chong, 66 A.3d 963 (Del. Ch. 2013), the Delaware Chancery Court faced a case, similar to *China Agritech*, involving a Chinese corporation—Fuqi International, Inc.—that had accessed the US capital markets via a reverse merger into a US shell company listed on NASDAQ. In 2009, Fuqi announced that it would be unable to file its quarterly and annual SEC disclosure statements due to "certain errors

related to the accounting of the Company's inventory and cost of sales." In 2010, Fuqi disclosed that the SEC had begun an investigation of Fuqi's failures to file SEC reports on a timely basis and other potential violations. Thereafter, Fuqi disclosed accounting errors, internal control failures, and other management problems.

Plaintiff Rich brought a derivative suit alleging that Fuqi's board of directors had violated its *Caremark* duties. The court explained that:

> One way a plaintiff may successfully plead a Caremark claim is to plead facts showing that a corporation had no internal controls in place. Fuqi had some sort of compliance system in place. For example, it had an Audit Committee and submitted financial statements to the SEC in 2009. However, accepting the Plaintiff's allegations as true, the mechanisms Fuqi had in place appear to have been woefully inadequate. In its press releases, Fuqi has detailed its extensive problems with internal controls. . . . These disclosures lead me to believe that Fuqi had no *meaningful* controls in place. The board of directors may have had regular meetings, and an Audit Committee may have existed, but there does not seem to have been any regulation of the company's operations *in China*.

Id. at 982–83 (footnotes omitted) (emphasis in original). Did China Agritech likewise have no meaningful controls in place, such that a *Caremark* case could be successfully pled?

The *Rich* court further explained that:

> As the Supreme Court held in Stone v. Ritter, if the directors have implemented a system of controls, a finding of liability is predicated on the directors' having "consciously failed to monitor or oversee [the system's] operations thus disabling themselves from being informed of risks or problems requiring their attention." One way that the plaintiff may plead such a conscious failure to monitor is to identify "red flags," obvious and problematic occurrences, that support an inference that the Fuqi directors knew that there were material weaknesses in Fuqi's internal controls and failed to correct such weaknesses. . . .
>
> First, Fuqi was a preexisting Chinese company that gained access to the U.S. capital markets through the Reverse Merger. Thus, Fuqi's directors were aware that there may be challenges in bringing Fuqi's internal controls into harmony with the U.S. securities reporting systems. Notwithstanding that fact, according to the Complaint, the directors did nothing to ensure that its reporting mechanisms were accurate. Second, the board knew that it had problems with its accounting and inventory processes by March 2010 at the latest, because it announced that the 2009 financial statements would need restatement at that time. In the same press release, Fuqi also acknowledged the likelihood of material weaknesses in its internal controls. Third, Fuqi received a letter from NASDAQ in April 2010 warning Fuqi that it would face delisting if Fuqi did not bring its reporting requirements up to date with the SEC.

> It seems reasonable to infer that, because of these "red flags," the directors knew that there were deficiencies in Fuqi's internal controls.

Id. at 983–84 (footnotes omitted). Are there comparable red flags in *China Agritech* that would permit one to draw the same inference in that case?

4. If the directors in either *China Agritech* or *Rich* were aware that their company's internal controls were inadequate, have they failed to act in the face of a known duty such that they can be deemed to have acted in bad faith?

5. As to at least one of the transactions, namely the related party transaction between China Agritech and directors Chang and Teng, it appears that not all the directors were personally interested in the transaction. Can such directors nevertheless be held liable under *Caremark* even if they were not complicit in the underlying transaction?

6. As the *China Agritech* court indicates, *Caremark* claims are not exculpable under § 102(b)(7) clauses. Why not? Should they be exculpable?

7. In cases like these, in which a corporation with the vast bulk of its operations in a foreign country becomes a US corporation via a reverse merger with a US shell corporation, and appoints US residents to the board of directors, what should those directors do to ensure that they comply with their duties as set forth in Stone v. Ritter, supra, and Francis v. United Jersey Bank, supra? Would you have been willing to serve as a director of China Agritech? What do you suppose motivates people to serve on the boards of such corporations?

4. DISCLOSURE AND FAIRNESS

Trading in corporate securities, such as stocks or bonds, takes place on two basic types of markets: (1) the primary market, in which the issuer of the securities—i.e., the company that created the securities—sells them to investors; and (2) the secondary market, in which investors trade securities among themselves without any significant participation by the original issuer. An initial public offering by a corporation, for example, takes place in the primary market. In contrast, trading between investors on the floor of the New York Stock Exchange is a highly organized and regulated example of a secondary market.

Regulation of the primary market in this country began with the passage of the first state "blue sky law" by Kansas in 1911.* These statutes had a limited jurisdictional reach, they contained many special interest exemptions, and the states had limited enforcement resources.

* All states still have so-called "blue-sky" laws. The name comes from the claim that such statutes protect investors from "speculative schemes which have no more basis than so many feet of 'blue sky.'" Hall v. Geiger-Jones Co., 242 U.S. 539, 550 (1917). Some of these statutes are much more restrictive than the Securities Act. They may, for example, allow the state administrator to deny registration if he or she considers the securities too speculative or otherwise unsatisfactory. When Apple Computer Inc. "went public" in 1980, Massachusetts banned the sale of its stock for just that reason. From time to time, the SEC and various scholars and regulators have tried to reduce the costs that overlapping and inconsistent state and federal securities laws impose. They have had modest (if incomplete) success. The Uniform Securities Act, adopted (in modified form) by a majority of the states, does reduce some of those costs.

In the aftermath of the Great Crash of 1929 and subsequent Great Depression, there was general agreement that the time had come for federal regulation of the securities markets. Between 1933 and 1940 Congress passed 7 statutes regulating various aspects of the industry. Of these, the most important for our purposes are the Securities Act of 1933 and the Securities Exchange Act of 1934.

The Securities Act is principally concerned with the primary market. In drafting it, Congress rejected proposals for federal merit review of securities. Instead, Congress concentrated on two goals: mandating disclosure of material information to investors and prevention of fraud. As to disclosure, the Securities Act follows a transactional disclosure model—i.e. mandating disclosures by issuers in connection with primary market transactions.

The Securities Exchange Act ("Exchange Act") is principally concerned with secondary market transactions. A whole host of issues fall within its purview, including a number that figure prominently in this course: insider trading and other forms of securities fraud, short-swing profits by corporate insiders, regulation of shareholder voting via proxy solicitations, and regulation of tender offers. Another important element of the Exchange Act is its requirement of periodic disclosures by publicly held corporations.

The Exchange Act is also important because it created the Securities and Exchange Commission as the primary federal agency charged with administering the various securities laws. There are five Commissioners, who must be confirmed by the Senate and no more than three of whom can belong to the same political party. Most of the work, of course, is done not by the Commissioners but by the professional staff. The staff is mainly comprised of lawyers, although there are a fair number of accountants and other specialists, and is organized into Divisions and Offices having various responsibilities. The staff has three primary functions: it provides interpretative guidance to private parties raising questions about the application of the securities laws to a particular transaction; it advises the Commission as to new rules or revisions of existing rules; and it investigates and prosecutes violations of the securities laws. Those of you who ultimately decide to practice in this area will spend most of your careers dealing with the staff; only very rarely will you actually have occasion to deal with the Commissioners.

A. DEFINITION OF A SECURITY

It is perhaps a cheap way of getting your attention, but it is nevertheless worth pointing out that securities regulation issues reportedly are the single most common source of legal malpractice claims against business lawyers. Why? Put bluntly, because there are so many ways the lawyer can go awry. One of the easiest mistakes a lawyer can make is to fail to recognize that he or she is dealing with a security. This typically has adverse consequences for the client, which often turns out to have adverse consequences for the lawyer.

Knowing whether or not a particular type of instrument or investment will be deemed to be a security is important for at least two reasons. First, it tells you whether the registration requirements of the Securities Act apply to the transaction. One need only go through the registration process if the thing your client is selling is a security. If the SEC or a private plaintiff sues your client for failing to register securities, your first response thus might be that what you sold is not a security. If that doesn't work, you will next argue that one of the exemptions from registration is available. And if that doesn't work, you'll try to settle the case on the best terms you can get.

The other reason the definition of a security is important relates to the antifraud provisions of the Acts. In general, plaintiffs have a much easier time when they bring suit under the securities laws than they would if they had to bring suit under state common law fraud rules. For one thing, the elements of federal securities fraud are less demanding and thus easier to prove. For another thing, there are certain procedural advantages, such as liberal venue and service of process provisions. As a result, plaintiffs defrauded in what looks like a garden variety fraud often allege that a security is present in the scheme so as to bring their claims under the federal securities laws. Such attempts not infrequently succeed, because the securities laws apply to lots of things that don't look very much like securities at first glance. For example, investments in worm farms. Smith v. Gross, 604 F.2d 639 (9th Cir.1979).

The statutory definition of a security in § 2(1) of the Securities Act is divided into two broad categories. (The Exchange Act definitional section is substantially identical and the two are usually interpreted as in pari materia.) First, a list of rather specific instruments, including "stock," "notes," and "bonds." Second, a list of general, catch-all phrases, such as "evidence of indebtedness," "investment contracts" and, in perhaps the most general description of them all, "any instrument commonly known as a 'security.' " The situation is further complicated by the first sentence of § 2, which provides that the terms used in the Act shall be defined in accordance with the various provisions of § 2, "unless the context otherwise requires." This "context" clause is an escape hatch. Courts have sometimes used it to hold that although an instrument appears to fall within one of the listed types of securities, the instrument shall not be held to constitute a security for purposes of the securities laws if "the context otherwise requires." In other words, the "context" clause can be used to say: yes, this thing looks like a security, but given the nature of the transaction we're going to hold that it does not come within the Securities Act. And vice-versa.

Most of the litigation involving atypical instruments claimed to be securities turns on whether the instrument in question falls within one of the catch-all phrases in § 2, especially the term "investment contract." The following case provides a good example of the issues business lawyers often face in this context.

Robinson v. Glynn

349 F.3d 166 (4th Cir. 2003).

Plaintiff James Robinson filed suit against Thomas Glynn, Glynn Scientific, Inc., and GeoPhone Company, LLC, alleging that Glynn committed federal securities fraud when he sold Robinson a partial interest in Geophone Company. The district court found that Robinson's membership interest in GeoPhone was not a security within the meaning of the federal securities laws, and it dismissed Robinson's securities fraud claim. Because Robinson was an active and knowledgeable executive at GeoPhone, rather than a mere passive investor in the company, we affirm. To do otherwise would unjustifiably expand the scope of the federal securities laws by treating an ordinary commercial venture as an investment contract.

I.

. . . In 1995, Glynn organized GeoPhone Corporation to develop and commercially market the GeoPhone telecommunications system. The GeoPhone system was designed around a signal processing technology, Convolutional Ambiguity Multiple Access (CAMA), that Glynn purportedly designed. Glynn was GeoPhone Corporation's majority shareholder and chairman. In September 1995, GeoPhone Corporation became a limited liability company, GeoPhone Company, LLC. . . .

In March 1995, Glynn and his associates contacted James Robinson, a businessman with no prior telecommunications experience, in an effort to raise capital for GeoPhone. Over the next several months, Glynn met and corresponded with Robinson, attempting to convince Robinson to invest in GeoPhone. Glynn described to Robinson the CAMA technology, its centrality to the GeoPhone system, and Geo-Phone's business plan. In July 1995, Robinson agreed to loan Glynn $1 million so that Glynn could perform a field test of the GeoPhone system and the CAMA technology.

In addition to Robinson's loan, in August 1995 Robinson and Glynn executed a "Letter of Intent," in which Robinson pledged to invest up to $25 million in GeoPhone, LLC if the field test indicated that CAMA worked in the GeoPhone system. Robinson's $25 million investment was to be comprised of his initial $1 million loan, an immediate $14 million investment upon successful completion of the field test, and a later $10 million investment. In October 1995, engineers hired by Glynn performed the field test, but, apparently with Glynn's knowledge, they did not use CAMA in the test. Nevertheless, Glynn allegedly told Robinson that the field test had been a success.

Consistent with the Letter of Intent, in December 1995 Robinson and Glynn executed an "Agreement to Purchase Membership Interests in GeoPhone" (APMIG). Under the APMIG, Robinson agreed to convert his $1 million loan and his $14 million investment into equity and subsequently to invest the additional $10 million. Robinson and Glynn also entered into an "Amended and Restated GeoPhone Operating Agreement" (ARGOA), which detailed the capital contribution, share ownership, and management structure of GeoPhone.

Pursuant to the ARGOA, Robinson received 33,333 of GeoPhone's 133,333 shares. On the back of the share certificates that Robinson received, the restrictive legend referred to the certificates as "shares" and "securities." It also specified that the certificates were exempt from registration under the Securities Act of 1933, and stated that the certificates could not be transferred without proper registration under the federal and state securities laws.

In addition, the ARGOA established a seven-person board of managers that was authorized to manage GeoPhone's affairs. Two of the managers were to be appointed by Robinson with the remaining five appointed by Glynn and his brother. Finally, the ARGOA vested management of GeoPhone in Robinson and Glynn based on each member's ownership share. Robinson was named GeoPhone's treasurer, and he was appointed to the board of managers and the company's executive committee. Glynn served as GeoPhone's chairman and was intimately involved in the company's operations and technical development. . . .

Yet in 1998 Robinson allegedly learned for the first time that the CAMA technology had never been implemented in the GeoPhone system—not even in the field test that had provided the basis for Robinson's investment. Robinson then filed suit in federal court, claiming violation of the federal securities laws, specifically § 10(b) of the Securities Exchange Act of 1934 and Rule 10b–5. The district court, however, granted summary judgment to Glynn, because it found that Robinson's membership interest in GeoPhone, LLC did not constitute a security under the federal securities laws. Robinson now challenges the district court's dismissal of his federal securities law claim.

II.

In order to establish a claim under Rule 10b–5, Robinson must prove fraud in connection with the purchase of securities. The Securities Act of 1933 and the Securities Exchange Act of 1934 define a "security" broadly as "any note, stock, treasury stock, security future, bond, debenture, . . ., investment contract, . . ., or, in general, any interest or instrument commonly known as a 'security.' "[2] In this case, Robinson claims that his membership interest in GeoPhone, a limited liability company (LLC), qualifies as either an "investment contract" or "stock" under the Securities Acts.

. . . The Supreme Court has defined an investment contract as "a contract, transaction or scheme whereby a person invests his money in a common enterprise and is led to expect profits solely from the efforts of the promoter or a third party." S.E.C. v. W.J. Howey, Co., 328 U.S. 293, 298–99, 66 S.Ct. 1100, 90 L.Ed. 1244 (1946). The parties agree that Robinson invested his money in a common enterprise with an expectation of profits. Their disagreement concerns whether Robinson expected profits "solely from the efforts" of others, most notably Glynn.

Since *Howey*, however, the Supreme Court has endorsed relaxation of the requirement that an investor rely only on others' efforts, by omitting the word "solely" from its restatements of the *Howey* test. And neither our court nor our sister circuits have required that an investor like Robinson expect profits "solely" from the efforts of others. Requiring investors to rely wholly on the efforts of others would exclude from the protection of the securities laws any agreement that involved even slight efforts from investors themselves. It would also exclude any agreement that offered investors control in theory, but denied it to them in fact. Agreements do not annul the securities laws by retaining nominal powers for investors unable to exercise them. . . .

What matters more than the form of an investment scheme is the "economic reality" that it represents. The question is whether an investor, as a result of the investment agreement itself or the factual

[2] The Securities Acts' definitions of "security" differ in wording only slightly and are generally treated as identical in meaning.

circumstances that surround it, is left unable to exercise meaningful control over his investment. . . .

In looking at the powers accorded Robinson under GeoPhone's operating agreement, as well as Robinson's activity as an executive at GeoPhone, it is clear that Robinson was no passive investor heavily dependent on the efforts of others like Glynn. Under the ARGOA, management authority for GeoPhone resided in a board of managers. Robinson not only had the power to appoint two of the board members, but he himself assumed one of the board seats and was named as the board's vice-chairman. The board, in turn, delegated extensive responsibility to a four-person executive committee of which Robinson was also a member.

In addition, Robinson served as GeoPhone's Treasurer. Among his powers were the ability to select external financial and legal consultants; to consult with GeoPhone's Chief Financial Officer on all financial matters relating to the company; to review status reports from the President and other officers; and to assemble the executive committee in order to discuss variations from GeoPhone's operating plan. Beyond even these fairly extensive powers, the ARGOA forbade GeoPhone from either incurring any indebtedness outside the normal course of business without Robinson's approval or diluting his interest in GeoPhone without first consulting him. In short, Robinson carefully negotiated for a level of control "antithetical to the notion of member passivity" required to find an investment contract under the federal securities laws. Keith v. Black Diamond Advisors, Inc., 48 F.Supp.2d 326, 333 (S.D.N.Y.1999). . . .

Robinson argues, however, that his lack of technological expertise relative to Glynn prevented him from meaningfully exercising his rights. . . . To the extent that Robinson needed assistance in understanding any particular aspect of the CAMA technology, nothing prevented him from seeking it from outside parties or others at GeoPhone. . . .

Indeed, the record amply supports the district court's conclusion that Robinson exercised his management rights despite his lack of technical expertise. For instance, Robinson reviewed GeoPhone's technology and financial records, as well as weekly status reports from GeoPhone's President, Chief Operating Officer, and Chief Financial Officer covering numerous aspects of GeoPhone's operation. He disapproved disbursements and proposed licenses of the GeoPhone technology. Robinson even expressed to the board of managers problems he perceived with GeoPhone, including the company's technological development, its management, and marketability. In the end, Robinson generally asserts that he lacked technical sophistication, without explaining in any detail what was beyond his ken or why it left him powerless to exercise his management rights. . . .

Finally, Robinson argues that he and Glynn considered his interest in GeoPhone a security, based on language in the APMIG, in the ARGOA, and on the back of Robinson's GeoPhone certificates. For instance, the restrictive legend on the back of Robinson's certificates refers to the certificates as "shares" and "securities." While this may be persuasive evidence that Robinson and Glynn believed the securities laws to apply, it does not indicate that their understanding was well-founded. Just as agreements cannot evade the securities laws by reserving powers to members unable to exercise them, neither can agreements invoke those same laws simply by labeling commercial ventures as securities. It is the "economic reality" of a particular instrument, rather than the label attached to it, that ultimately determines whether it falls within the reach of the securities laws. See Great Rivers Coop. v. Farmland Indus., Inc., 198 F.3d 685, 701 (8th Cir.1999). The "economic reality" here is that Robinson was not a passive investor relying on the efforts of others, but a knowledgeable executive actively protecting his interest and position in the company.

III.

Robinson further claims that his membership interest in GeoPhone was not only an "investment contract" within the meaning of the federal securities laws, but "stock" as well. Congress intended catch-all terms like "investment contract" to encompass the range of novel and unusual instruments whose economic realities invite application of the securities laws; but the term "stock" refers to a narrower set of instruments with a common name and characteristics. See Landreth Timber Co. v. Landreth, 471 U.S. 681, 686, 105 S.Ct. 2297, 85 L.Ed.2d 692 (1985). Thus the securities laws apply "when an instrument is both called 'stock' and bears stock's usual characteristics." *Id.* Yet Robinson's membership interest was neither denominated stock by the parties, nor did it possess all the usual characteristics of stock.

The characteristics typically associated with common stock are (i) the right to receive dividends contingent upon an apportionment of profits; (ii) negotiability; (iii) the ability to be pledged or hypothecated; (iv) the conferring of voting rights in proportion to the number of shares owned; and (v) the capacity to appreciate in value. Robinson's membership interest in GeoPhone lacked several of these characteristics.

First, as is common with interests in LLCs, GeoPhone's members did not share in the profits in proportion to the number of their shares. Pursuant to the ARGOA, Robinson was to receive 100 percent of GeoPhone's net profits up to a certain amount, only after which were funds to be distributed pro rata to the members in proportion to their relative shares.

Second, like interests in LLCs more generally, Robinson's membership interests were not freely negotiable. According to the ARGOA, Robinson could only transfer his interests if he first offered other members the opportunity to purchase his interests on similar terms. Moreover, unlike with stock (except some stock in close corporations), anyone to whom Robinson or other members transferred their interests would not have thereby acquired any of the control or management rights that normally attend a stock transfer. . . .

Similarly, Robinson could pledge his interest, but the pledgee would acquire only distribution rights and not control rights. . . . As for the apportionment of voting rights, the parties dispute whether voting rights were conferred in proportion to members' interests in GeoPhone. Even resolving this dispute in Robinson's favor, it remains clear that Robinson's membership interest lacked the ordinary attributes of stock.

Finally, from the very beginning Robinson and Glynn consistently viewed Robinson's investment as a "membership interest," and never as "stock." The purchase and operating agreements that Robinson and

Glynn executed, as well as the agreement in which Robinson bought out Glynn's interest in GeoPhone, all termed Robinson's investment as a "membership interest" rather than "stock." Even the shares that Robinson received as a result of his investments declared Robinson the holder of "membership interests in GeoPhone Company, L.L.C., within the meaning of the Delaware Limited Liability Company Act." . . .

IV.

The parties have vigorously urged us to rule broadly in this case, asking that we generally classify interests in limited liability companies, or LLCs, as investment contracts (Robinson's view) or non-securities (Glynn's view). LLCs are particularly difficult to categorize under the securities laws, however, because they are hybrid business entities that combine features of corporations, general partnerships, and limited partnerships. As their name indicates, LLCs can limit the liability of their members, which may mean that LLC members are more likely to be passive investors who need the protection of the securities laws. However, LLC members are also able to actively participate in management without piercing the veil of their liability, which would suggest that LLC members are more likely than limited partners or corporate shareholders to be active investors not in need of the securities statutes.

Precisely because LLCs lack standardized membership rights or organizational structures, they can assume an almost unlimited variety of forms. It becomes, then, exceedingly difficult to declare that LLCs, whatever their form, either possess or lack the economic characteristics associated with investment contracts. Even drawing firm lines between member-managed and manager-managed LLCs threatens impermissibly to elevate form over substance. . . .

We decline, therefore, the parties' invitation for a broader holding. . . .

ANALYSIS

1. The Court says that Geophone was originally formed as a corporation and later "became a limited liability company, GeoPhone Company, LLC." How does a corporation "become" an LLC? Compare Uniform Limited Liability Company Act § 902 and $904.

2. An LLC was not the parties' only option, as indicated by the conversion of Geophone from a corporation to an LLC. (A) Suppose that Geophone still had been organized as a close corporation at the time Robinson bought an interest in it through the purchase of shares of Geophone stock. Would the transaction have been subject to Rule 10b–5? (B) Suppose Geophone had been organized as a general partnership. What result?

B. THE REGISTRATION PROCESS

The Securities Act prohibits the sale of securities unless the company issuing the securities (the issuer) has "registered" them with the SEC. More specifically, § 5 of the Act imposes three basic rules: (1) a security may not be offered for sale through the mails or by use of other means of interstate commerce unless a registration statement has been filed with the SEC; (2) securities may not be sold until the registration statement has become effective; and (3) the prospectus (a disclosure document) must be delivered to the purchaser before a sale.

To register securities, the issuer must give the Commission extensive information about its finances and business. A large company about to sell stock to the public for the first time will need to file a registration statement that can easily exceed a hundred pages. In the process, it will involve its general counsel and outside accountants. The lawyers' fees alone can exceed $100,000, and the investment banking firm that underwrites the issue (i.e., attempts to find buyers for the stock) will charge a fee several times that amount.

When the SEC reviews a registration statement, it does not ask whether the security would be a good investment. Instead, it asks whether the registration statement contains the disclosures required by the statute and the SEC rules thereunder and whether that information appears to be accurate. The core of the registration statement thus is the "prospectus," the principal disclosure document issuers are required by the Securities Act to give prospective buyers. Until the SEC has approved the disclosures made in the prospectus, companies cannot sell the new securities.*

Because of the cost and delay associated with the registration process, many issuers work hard to find ways to sell securities without registering them. The Securities Act includes two types of exemptions to the registration requirement: it exempts some securities entirely and exempts some transactions in securities not otherwise exempt. In general, an exempt security need never be registered, either when initially sold by the issuer or in any subsequent transaction. Exempt transactions, in contrast, are one-time exemptions. If A sells a non-exempt security to B in an exempt transaction, B is not automatically free to resell that security. B must either register it or utilize another exempt transaction. Because exempt securities tend to be highly specialized, business lawyers are far more likely to encounter transactional exemptions, such as the statutory private placement exemption discussed in the following case.

Doran v. Petroleum Management Corp.

545 F.2d 893 (5th Cir.1977).

In this case a sophisticated investor who purchased a limited partnership interest in an oil drilling venture seeks to rescind. The question raised is whether the sale was part of a private offering

---

* To be sure, the Securities Act technically allows the issuer to sell securities twenty days after it files a registration statement with the SEC (unless the SEC issues an order halting the process). Hence, issuers could simply file the statement, wait twenty days, and then sell. In practice, however, the scheme would not work: the proposed price of a security is part of the registration statement, and issuers seldom know the price they should charge twenty days in advance. Accordingly, issuers wait until the SEC finds the registration statement satisfactory. They then price the security, amend the registration statement to incorporate that price, and ask the SEC to make the amendment effective immediately. As the SEC is satisfied with the issuer's disclosure, it agrees.

exempted by § 4(2) of the Securities Act of 1933, from the registration requirements of that Act.[1]. . .

We hold that in the absence of findings of fact that each offeree had been furnished information about the issuer that a registration statement would have disclosed or that each offeree had effective access to such information, the district court erred in concluding that the offering was a private placement. Accordingly, we reverse and remand.

I. Facts

Prior to July 1970, Petroleum Management Corporation (PMC) organized a California limited partnership for the purpose of drilling and operating four wells in Wyoming. . . . As found by the district court, PMC contacted only four other persons with respect to possible participation in the partnership. All but the plaintiff declined.

During the late summer of 1970, plaintiff William H. Doran, Jr., received a telephone call from a California securities broker previously known to him. The broker, Phillip Kendrick, advised Doran of the opportunity to become a "special participant" in the partnership. PMC then sent Doran the drilling logs and technical maps of the proposed drilling area. PMC informed Doran that two of the proposed four wells had already been completed. Doran agreed to become a "special participant" in the Wyoming drilling program. In consideration for his partnership share, Doran agreed to contribute $125,000 toward the partnership. . . .

During 1970 and 1971, PMC periodically sent Doran production information on the completed wells of the limited partnership. Throughout this period, however, the wells were deliberately overproduced in violation of the production allowances established by the Wyoming Oil and Gas Conservation Commission. As a consequence, on November 16, 1971, the Commission ordered the partnership's wells sealed for a period of 338 days. On May 1, 1972, the Commission notified PMC that production from the wells could resume on August 9, 1972. After August 9, the wells yielded a production income level below that obtained prior to the Commission's order.

Following the cessation of production payments between November 1971 and August 1972 and the decreased yields thereafter, the Mid-Continent note upon which Doran was primarily liable went into default. Mid-Continent subsequently obtained a state court judgment against Doran, PMC, and the two signatory officers of PMC for $50,815.50 plus interest and attorney's fees.

On October 16, 1972, Doran filed this suit in federal district court seeking damages for breach of contract, rescission of the contract based on violations of the Securities Acts of 1933 and 1934, and a judgment declaring the defendants liable for payment of the state judgment obtained by Mid-Continent.

The court below found that the offer and sale of the "special participant" interest was a private offering because Doran was a

---

[1] Section 4. The provisions of section 5 shall not apply to:

(1) transactions by any person other than an issuer, underwriter, or dealer.

(2) transactions by an issuer not involving any public offering.

sophisticated investor who did not need the protection of the Securities Acts. . . .

II. The Private Offering Exemption

No registration statement was filed with any federal or state regulatory body in connection with the defendants' offering of securities.[4] Along with two other factors that we may take as established—that the defendants sold or offered to sell these securities, and that the defendants used interstate transportation or communication in connection with the sale or offer of sale—the plaintiff thus states a prima facie case for a violation of the federal securities laws. . . .[5]

The defendants do not contest the existence of the elements of plaintiff's prima facie case but raise an affirmative defense that the relevant transactions came within the exemption from registration found in § 4(2), 15 U.S.C. § 77d(2). Specifically, they contend that the offering of securities was not a public offering. The defendants, who of course bear the burden of proving this affirmative defense, must therefore show that the offering was private. . . .

This court has in the past identified four factors relevant to whether an offering qualifies for the exemption. The consideration of these factors, along with the policies embodied in the 1933 Act, structure the inquiry. . . . The relevant factors include the number of offerees and their relationship to each other and the issuer, the number of units offered, the size of the offering, and the manner of the offering. . . .

The term, "private offering," is not defined in the Securities Act of 1933. The scope of the § 4(2) private offering exemption must therefore be determined by reference to the legislative purposes of the Act. In SEC v. Ralston Purina Co., [346 U.S. 119 (1953)], the SEC had sought to enjoin a corporation's offer of unregistered stock to its employees, and the Court grappled with the corporation's defense that the offering came within the private placement exemption. The Court began by looking to the statutory purpose:

> Since exempt transactions are those as to which "there is no practical need for . . . [the bill's] application," the applicability of [§ 4(2)] should turn on whether the particular class of persons

---

[4] The district court correctly concluded that the limited partnership interest was a "security" as that term is defined by the Securities Act of 1933 and the Securities and Exchange Act of 1934. . . .

[5] Section 5. (a) Unless a registration statement is in effect as to a security, it shall be unlawful for any person, directly or indirectly:

> (1) to make use of any means or instruments of transportation or communication in interstate commerce or of the mails to sell such security through the use or medium of any prospectus or otherwise . . .

(b) It shall be unlawful for any person, directly or indirectly—

> (1) to make use of any means or instruments of transportation or communication in interstate commerce or of the mails to carry or transmit any prospectus relating to any security with respect to which a registration statement has been filed under this title, unless such prospectus meets the requirements of section 10 [specifying the required contents of a prospectus] . . .

(c) It shall be unlawful for any person, directly or indirectly, to make use of any means or instruments of transportation or communication in interstate commerce or of the mails to offer to sell or offer to buy through the use or medium of any prospectus or otherwise any security, unless a registration statement has been filed as to such security, . . .

> affected need the protection of the Act. An offering to those who are shown to be able to fend for themselves is a transaction "not involving any public offering."

346 U.S. at 124, 73 S.Ct. at 984. According to the Court, the purpose of the Act was "to protect investors by promoting full disclosure of information thought necessary to informed investment decisions." Id. at 124, 73 S.Ct. at 984. It therefore followed that "the exemption question turns on the knowledge of the offerees." Id. at 126–27, 73 S.Ct. at 985. That formulation remains the touchstone of the inquiry into the scope of the private offering exemption. It is most nearly reflected in the first of the four factors: the number of offerees and their relationship to each other and to the issuer.

In the case at bar, the defendants may have demonstrated the presence of the latter three factors. A small number of units offered, relatively modest financial stakes, and an offering characterized by personal contact between the issuer and offerees free of public advertising or intermediaries such as investment bankers or securities exchanges—these aspects of the instant transaction aid the defendants' search for a § 4(2) exemption.

Nevertheless, with respect to the first, most critical, and conceptually most problematic factor, the record does not permit us to agree that the defendants have proved that they are entitled to the limited sanctuary afforded by § 4(2). We must examine more closely the importance of demonstrating both the number of offerees and their relationship to the issuer in order to see why the defendants have not yet gained the § 4(2) exemption.

A. *The Number of Offerees*

Establishing the number of persons involved in an offering is important both in order to ascertain the magnitude of the offering and in order to determine the characteristics and knowledge of the persons thus identified.

The number of offerees, not the number of purchasers, is the relevant figure in considering the number of persons involved in an offering. . . . A private placement claimant's failure to adduce any evidence regarding the number of offerees will be fatal to the claim. . . . The number of offerees is not itself a decisive factor in determining the availability of the private offering exemption. Just as an offering to few may be public, so an offering to many may be private. . . . Nevertheless, "the more offerees, the more likelihood that the offering is public." . . . In the case at bar, the record indicates that eight investors were offered limited partnership shares in the drilling program—a total that would be entirely consistent with a finding that the offering was private. . . .

In considering the number of offerees solely as indicative of the magnitude or scope of an offering, the difference between one and eight offerees is relatively unimportant. Rejecting the argument that Doran was the sole offeree is significant, however, because it means that in considering the need of the offerees for the protection that registration would have afforded we must look beyond Doran's interests to those of all his fellow offerees. Even the offeree-plaintiff's 20–20 vision with respect to the facts underlying the security would not save the exemption if any one of his fellow offerees was blind.

B. *The Offerees' Relationship to the Issuer*

Since SEC v. Ralston, supra, courts have sought to determine the need of offerees for the protections afforded by registration by focusing on the relationship between offerees and issuer and more particularly on the information available to the offerees by virtue of that relationship. . . .

1. *The role of investment sophistication*

The lower court's finding that Doran was a sophisticated investor is amply supported by the record, as is the sophistication of the other offerees. Doran holds a petroleum engineering degree from Texas A & M University. His net worth is in excess of $1,000,000. His holdings of approximately twenty-six oil and gas properties are valued at $850,000.

Nevertheless, evidence of a high degree of business or legal sophistication on the part of all offerees does not suffice to bring the offering within the private placement exemption. We clearly established that proposition in Hill York Corp. v. American International Franchises, Inc., [448 F.2d 680, 690 (5th Cir.1971)]. We reasoned that "if the plaintiffs did not possess the information requisite for a registration statement, they could not bring their sophisticated knowledge of business affairs to bear in deciding whether or not to invest. . . ." Sophistication is not a substitute for access to the information that registration would disclose. As we said in *Hill York,* although the evidence of the offerees' expertise "is certainly favorable to the defendants, the level of sophistication will not carry the point. In this context, the relationship between the promoters and the purchasers and the 'access to the kind of information which registration would disclose' become highly relevant factors." . . .

In short, there must be sufficient basis of accurate information upon which the sophisticated investor may exercise his skills. Just as a scientist cannot be without his specimens, so the shrewdest investor's acuity will be blunted without specifications about the issuer. For an investor to be invested with exemptive status he must have the required data for judgment.

2. *The requirement of available information*

More specifically, we shall require on remand that the defendants demonstrate that all offerees, whatever their expertise, had available the information a registration statement would have afforded a prospective investor in a public offering. Such a showing is not independently sufficient to establish that the offering qualified for the private placement exemption, but it is necessary to gain the exemption and is to be weighed along with the sophistication and number of the offerees, the number of units offered, and the size and manner of the offering. . . .

Because in this case these latter factors weigh heavily in favor of the private offering exemption, satisfaction of the necessary condition regarding the availability of relevant information to the offerees would compel the conclusion that this offering fell within the exemption. . . .

C. *On Remand: The Issuer-Offeree Relationship*

In determining on remand the extent of the information available to the offerees, the district court must keep in mind that the "availability" of information means either disclosure of or effective access to the relevant information. The relationship between issuer and offeree is most critical when the issuer relies on the latter route.

To begin with, if the defendants could prove that all offerees were actually furnished the information a registration statement would have provided, whether the offerees occupied a position of access pre-existing such disclosure would not be dispositive of the status of the offering. . . .

Alternatively it might be shown that the offeree had access to the files and record of the company that contained the relevant information. Such access might be afforded merely by the position of the offeree or by the issuer's promise to open appropriate files and records to the offeree as well as to answer inquiries regarding material information. . . .

IV. Conclusion

An examination of the record and the district court's opinion in this case leaves unanswered the central question in all cases that turn on the availability of the § 4(2) exemption. Did the offerees know or have a realistic opportunity to learn facts essential to an investment judgment? We remand so that the trial court can answer that question.

. . . In adjusting the generalities of § 4(2) to the realities of the contemporary market, we have seized on the availability to all offerees of pertinent facts. We have conditioned the private offering exemption on either actual disclosure of the information registration would provide or the offerees' effective access to such information. If the issuer has not disclosed but instead relies on the offerees' access, the privileged status of the offerees relative to the issuer must be shown. . . .

NOTE ON OTHER EXEMPTIONS

Most of the transactions exempted from the Securities Act appear in § 4. These include the "private placements" under § 4(2) discussed in *Doran,* and "transactions by any person other than an issuer, underwriter, or dealer" (§ 4(1)). Private placements are common—and becoming ever more so. As the § 4(2) exemption is notably imprecise, however, most issuers who hope to rely on it will turn to the SEC's Regulation D (rules 501–506).*

Regulation D provides a series of safe-harbors that issuers can use to come within the private-placement exemption and avoid (or reduce) their required disclosure. For example, if an issuer raises no more than $1 million through the securities, it generally may sell them to an unlimited number of buyers without registering the securities. (Rule 504.) If it raises no more than $5 million, it may sell the securities to 35 buyers but no more. (Rule 505.) And if it raises more than $5 million, it may sell to no more than 35 buyers, and each buyer must pass various tests of financial sophistication. (Rule 506.) In most cases, the issuer cannot widely advertise the security, and in all cases must file with the SEC a notice of the sale shortly after it issues the securities. The limits on the number of buyers do not apply to "accredited investors," such as banks, brokers, and other financial institutions and wealthy buyers. In most cases, the issuer must give buyers some information about the

* Issuers could also make offerings of under $5 million under another set of safe harbor rules—"Regulation A"—and take advantage of Regulation A's reduced disclosure requirements. The attractiveness of Regulation D, however, has reduced the number of firms using Regulation A.

company, but the extent of the information required varies with the amount of money at stake in the issue.

Regulation D (and § 4(2)) generally exempts only the initial sale. As a result, most buyers can resell the securities only if they find another exemption. If the buyer is not "an issuer, underwriter, or dealer," he or she will be able to rely on § 4(1). But this exclusion may be misleading. Suppose Mary buys stock because she sees it as a good deal, and plans to resell it quickly at a higher price. Because § 2(11) defines an underwriter as someone who buys the security "with a view to" reselling it, Mary may be an underwriter. If so, § 4(1) will not exempt her sale. Worse, should she resell her shares to a large number of people, a court could integrate her resale into the initial offering and invalidate the issuer's exemption for the entire issue.

To deal with these resale problems, Regulation D provides that issuers can protect the exemption by using "reasonable care" to make sure the buyers are planning to hold the stock themselves. To show that care, they should exercise "reasonable inquiry" into the buyer's plans, disclose to the buyers that the stock is unregistered and subject to various resale restrictions, and print those restrictions directly on the stock. In addition, many lawyers will rely on yet another safe-harbor rule—Rule 144. Subject to various qualifications, the rule allows buyers to resell stock they acquire in a Regulation D offering if they first hold it for one year and then resell it in limited volumes.

NOTE ON SECURITIES ACT CIVIL LIABILITIES

Before the adoption of Securities Act of 1933, securities fraud was solely a matter for state law. At common law, plaintiff had to prove that the defendant had misrepresented a material fact. Plaintiff also had to prove all of the other elements of common law fraud: reliance, causation, scienter and injury. Plaintiff's recovery was limited to the amount of loss: the difference between what he or she paid and what the security was worth. The common law of misrepresentation thus was almost incapable of dealing with securities fraud. Consider the reliance element. Many securities cases involve omissions: failures to speak. But how do you rely on silence? Even if the fraud involved a misrepresentation, what happens if only some investors received the misrepresentations? The causation element also caused problems. It is always hard to prove what portion of one's loss was caused by the fraud and what portion of the loss was caused by other factors, such as general market conditions.

If the Securities Act had left it to the common law, civil liability to private party plaintiffs would not have played an important enforcement role.* However, Congress considered civil liability to private parties to be

---

* Section 20(a) of the Securities Act gives the SEC broad power to investigate violations of the Act or the SEC rules adopted under the Act. Section 20(b) gives the SEC the power to bring a civil action in US District Court seeking an injunction against on-going or future violations. A number of other sanctions are potentially available under other statutes. For example, the SEC can suspend or bar a professional underwriter, broker or dealer from working in the securities industry. The SEC may also impose a variety of administrative penalties on violators.

Section 20(b) also authorizes the SEC to refer violations to the Attorney General who may then institute criminal proceedings against the violator. Section 24 provides the criminal penalties associated with securities violations: each violation subjects the perpetrator to a potential penalty of a fine of up to $10,000 and/or a prison term of up to five years. The penalties

an important deterrent and therefore enacted various express private rights of action for private parties injured by securities law violations. In addition, the courts have implied private rights of action under several other provisions of the Acts. The most important of these is under Exchange Act § 10(b), which is discussed in the following section.

Securities Act § 11 is the principal express cause of action directed at fraud committed in connection with the sale of securities through the use of a registration statement. Because the material misrepresentation or omission must be in the registration statement, § 11 may not be used in connection with an exempt offering. Neither reliance nor causation generally are an element of the plaintiff's prima facie case. To the contrary, in a curious twist, it is the defendant who has the burden of proving that its misconduct did not cause plaintiff's damages. Pursuant to § 11(e), a defendant may reduce the amount of damages if it is able to prove that the reduction in value was caused by some other factor.

Because § 11 does not contain any privity requirement, the list of potential defendants is quite expansive. It includes: everyone who signed the registration statement, which by statute must at a minimum include the issuer, its principal executive officers, and a majority of its board of directors; every director of the issuer at the time the registration statement became effective, including directors who did not sign the registration statement; every person named in the registration statement as someone about to become a director; every "expert" named as having prepared or certified any part of the statement, or as having prepared any report or valuation used in connection with the statement; and every underwriter involved in the distribution.

Securities Act § 12(a)(1) imposes strict liability on sellers of securities for offers or sales made in violation of § 5. Section 12(a)(1) liability thus arises, for example, where the seller improperly fails to register the securities. Section 12(a)(1) is also available if the seller registers but fails to deliver a statutory prospectus, violates the gun-jumping rules, or commits any other violation of § 5. Under § 12(a)(1) the main remedy is rescission: the buyer can recover the consideration paid, plus interest, less income received on the security. If the buyer is no longer the owner of the securities he or she can recover damages comparable to those which would be provided by rescission.

Section 12(a)(2) imposes private civil liability on any person who offers or sells a security in interstate commerce, who makes a material misrepresentation or omission in connection with the offer or sale, and cannot prove he did not know of the misrepresentation or omission and could not have known even with the exercise of reasonable care. Plaintiff's prima facie case has six elements: (1) the sale of a security; (2) through instruments of interstate commerce or the mails; (3) by means of a prospectus or oral communication; (4) containing an untrue statement or omission of a material fact; (5) by a defendant who offered or sold the security; and (6) which defendant knew or should have known of the untrue statement (if plaintiff pleads defendant's knowledge, the burden of proving otherwise shifts to the defendant). Notice that plaintiff need not prove reliance. Until the Supreme Court's decision in Gustafson

for violating the 1934 Act are even more severe, because they were recently raised to create greater deterrents against illegal insider trading. Section 32 of that Act no provides for fines of up to $2.5 million and a jail term of up to 10 years.

v. Alloyd Co., 513 U.S. 561 (1995), most lawyers assumed that § 12(a)(2)'s scope was considerably broader than that of § 11. It was assumed to apply not only to fraudulent registration statements, but also to fraudulent selling materials and oral communications. It was assumed to apply to exempt offerings, whereas § 11 is limited to registered offerings. Finally, most lawyers assumed that § 12(a)(2) reached secondary market transactions. In Gustafson, however, the Supreme Court held that liability arises under § 12(a)(2) only with respect to material misrepresentations or omissions made in written documents or oral communications used in connection with public offerings. Although the concept of public offering seems to include some unregistered offerings, the Court's opinion makes clear that liability under § 12(a)(2) at a minimum does not arise in secondary market transactions or private placements.

For a plaintiff's lawyer, these provisions are like an artist's palette: you have an array of options, each having unique advantages and disadvantages. Exchange Act § 10(b) requires the plaintiff to prove that the defendant acted with scienter, for example, while § 11 does not require plaintiff to prove anything about defendant's state of mind. Similar disparities could be cited about each of the sections. The lawyer's task thus is to identify the remedy best suited to the facts at bar.

For a transactional lawyer representing an issuer or other participant in the offering process, due diligence is the principal fallout of these provisions. At common law, plaintiff had to prove scienter—i.e., that defendant acted with the intent to commit fraud. In a § 11 case, by contrast, as to the issuer, plaintiff need not prove anything with respect to the defendant's state of mind. Once plaintiff makes out his prima facie case, the issuer is strictly liable. The issuer can be held liable even if the misrepresentation or omission was an inadvertent mistake. As to defendants other than the issuer, the degree of fault required is essentially a negligence standard. The burden of proof, however, is on the defendants to prove that they were not negligent in connection with the preparation of the registration statement. Similarly, under § 12(a)(2), defendants who conduct a reasonable investigation cannot be held liable. Taken together, these defenses gave rise to the due diligence process.

Due diligence is not an affirmative obligation; if the client does not want to perform it, the client is not required to do so. All rational participants in a registered offering perform due diligence, however, because it is usually the only viable defense to a § 11 claim. In practice, due diligence review is delegated to lawyers. The issuer's officers and directors delegate their due diligence obligations to the firm's lawyers. The underwriters will delegate their due diligence the lead underwriter's counsel. If the lawyers fail to carry out an adequate due diligence review, any defendants who delegated their due diligence tasks to that counsel will lose the defense. On the other hand, such defendants have a claim for legal malpractice against the lawyers who failed to do a proper due diligence review, which is why the following case is at least as scary for lawyers as it is for clients.

Escott v. BarChris Construction Corp.

283 F.Supp. 643 (S.D.N.Y.1968).

This is an action by purchasers of 5½ per cent convertible subordinated fifteen year debentures of BarChris Construction Corporation (BarChris). Plaintiffs purport to sue on their own behalf and "on behalf of all other . . . present and former holders" of the debentures. . . .

The action is brought under § 11 of the Securities Act of 1933 (15 U.S.C. § 77k). Plaintiffs allege that the registration statement with respect to these debentures filed with the Securities and Exchange Commission, which became effective on May 16, 1961, contained material false statements and material omissions.

Defendants fall into three categories: (1) the persons who signed the registration statement; (2) the underwriters, consisting of eight investment banking firms, led by Drexel & Co. (Drexel); and (3) BarChris's auditors, Peat, Marwick, Mitchell & Co. (Peat, Marwick).

The signers, in addition to BarChris itself, were the nine directors of BarChris, plus its controller, defendant Trilling, who was not a director. Of the nine directors, five were officers of BarChris, i.e., defendants Vitolo, president; Russo, executive vice president; Pugliese, vice president; Kircher, treasurer; and Birnbaum, secretary. Of the remaining four, defendant Grant was a member of the firm of Perkins, Daniels, McCormack & Collins, BarChris's attorneys. He became a director in October 1960. Defendant Coleman, a partner in Drexel, became a director on April 17, 1961, as did the other two, Auslander and Rose, who were not otherwise connected with BarChris. . . .

. . . On the main issue of liability, the questions to be decided are (1) did the registration statement contain false statements of fact, or did it omit to state facts which should have been stated in order to prevent it from being misleading; (2) if so, were the facts which were falsely stated or omitted "material" within the meaning of the Act; (3) if so, have defendants established their affirmative defenses?

Before discussing these questions, some background facts should be mentioned. At the time relevant here, BarChris was engaged primarily in the construction of bowling alleys, somewhat euphemistically referred to as "bowling centers." These were rather elaborate affairs. They contained not only a number of alleys or "lanes," but also, in most cases, bar and restaurant facilities. . . .

The introduction of automatic pin setting machines in 1952 gave a marked stimulus to bowling. It rapidly became a popular sport, with the result that "bowling centers" began to appear throughout the country in rapidly increasing numbers. BarChris benefited from this increased interest in bowling. Its construction operations expanded rapidly. It is estimated that in 1960 BarChris installed approximately three per cent of all lanes built in the United States. . . .

BarChris's sales increased dramatically from 1956 to 1960. According to the prospectus, net sales, in round figures, in 1956 were some $800,000, in 1957 $1,300,000, in 1958 $1,700,000. In 1959 they increased to over $3,300,000, and by 1960 they had leaped to over $9,165,000. . . .

BarChris was compelled to expend considerable sums in defraying the cost of construction before it received reimbursement. As a consequence, BarChris was in constant need of cash to finance its operations, a need which grew more pressing as operations expanded.

In December 1959, BarChris sold 560,000 shares of common stock to the public at $3.00 per share. This issue was underwritten by Peter Morgan & Company, one of the present defendants.

By early 1961, BarChris needed additional working capital. The proceeds of the sale of the debentures involved in this action were to be devoted, in part at least, to fill that need.

The registration statement of the debentures, in preliminary form, was filed with the Securities and Exchange Commission on March 30, 1961. A first amendment was filed on May 11 and a second on May 16. The registration statement became effective on May 16. The closing of the financing took place on May 24. On that day BarChris received the net proceeds of the financing.

By that time BarChris was experiencing difficulties in collecting amounts due from some of its customers. Some of them were in arrears in payments due to factors on their discounted notes. As time went on those difficulties increased. Although BarChris continued to build alleys in 1961 and 1962, it became increasingly apparent that the industry was overbuilt. Operators of alleys, often inadequately financed, began to fail. Precisely when the tide turned is a matter of dispute, but at any rate, it was painfully apparent in 1962.

In May of that year BarChris made an abortive attempt to raise more money by the sale of common stock. It filed with the Securities and Exchange Commission a registration statement for the stock issue which it later withdrew. In October 1962 BarChris came to the end of the road. On October 29, 1962, it filed in this court a petition for an arrangement under Chapter XI of the Bankruptcy Act. BarChris defaulted in the payment of the interest due on November 1, 1962 on the debentures.

[The court then undertook a lengthy analysis of the accuracy of BarChris's documents.]

Summary

For convenience, the various falsities and omissions which I have discussed in the preceding pages are recapitulated here. They were as follows:

1.	1960 Earnings		
	(a)	Sales	
		As per prospectus	$9,165,320
		Correct figure	$8,511,420
		Overstatement	$ 653,900
	(b)	Net Operating Income	
		As per prospectus	$1,742,801
		Correct figure	$1,496,196
		Overstatement	$ 246,605
	(c)	Earnings per Share	
		As per prospectus	$ .75

Correct figure	$ .65
Overstatement	$ .10
2. 1960 Balance Sheet	
Current Assets	
As per prospectus	$4,524,021
Correct figure	$3,914,332
Overstatement	$ 609,689
3. Contingent Liabilities as of December 31, 1960 on Alternative Method of Financing	
As per prospectus	$ 750,000
Correct figure	$1,125,795
Understatement	$ 375,795
Capitol Lanes should have been shown as a direct liability	$ 325,000
4. Contingent Liabilities as of April 30, 1961	
As per prospectus	$ 825,000
Correct figure	$1,443,853
Understatement	$ 618,853
Capitol Lanes should have been shown as a direct liability	$ 314,166
5. Earnings Figures for Quarter ending March 31, 1961	
(a) Sales	
As per prospectus	$2,138,455
Correct figure	$1,618,645
Overstatement	$ 519,810
(b) Gross Profit	
As per prospectus	$ 483,121
Correct figure	$ 252,366
Overstatement	$ 230,755
6. Backlog as of March 31, 1961	
As per prospectus	$6,905,000
Correct figure	$2,415,000
Overstatement	$4,490,000
7. Failure to Disclose Officers' Loans Outstanding and Unpaid on May 16, 1961	$ 386,615
8. Failure to Disclose Use of Proceeds in Manner not Revealed in Prospectus	
Approximately	$1,160,000
9. Failure to Disclose Customers' Delinquencies in May 1961 and BarChris's Potential Liability with Respect Thereto	
	Over $1,350,000

Materiality

It is a prerequisite to liability under § 11 of the Act that the fact which is falsely stated in a registration statement, or the fact that is omitted when it should have been stated to avoid misleading, be "material." The regulations of the Securities and Exchange Commission pertaining to the registration of securities define the word as follows. . . .

> "The term 'material', when used to qualify a requirement for the furnishing of information as to any subject, limits the information required to those matters as to which an average prudent investor ought reasonably to be informed before purchasing the security registered."

What are "matters as to which an average prudent investor ought reasonably to be informed"? It seems obvious that they are matters which such an investor needs to know before he can make an intelligent, informed decision whether or not to buy the security. . . .

The average prudent investor is not concerned with minor inaccuracies or with errors as to matters which are of no interest to him. The facts which tend to deter him from purchasing a security are facts which have an important bearing upon the nature or condition of the issuing corporation or its business.

Judged by this test, there is no doubt that many of the misstatements and omissions in this prospectus were material. This is true of all of them which relate to the state of affairs in 1961, i.e., the overstatement of sales and gross profit for the first quarter, the understatement of contingent liabilities as of April 30, the overstatement of orders on hand and the failure to disclose the true facts with respect to officers' loans, customers' delinquencies, application of proceeds and the prospective operation of several alleys.

The misstatements and omissions pertaining to BarChris's status as of December 31, 1960, however, present a much closer question. The 1960 earnings figures, the 1960 balance sheet and the contingent liabilities as of December 31, 1960 were not nearly as erroneous as plaintiffs have claimed. But they were wrong to some extent, as we have seen. Would it have deterred the average prudent investor from purchasing these debentures if he had been informed that the 1960 sales were $8,511,420 rather than $9,165,320, that the net operating income was $1,496,196 rather than $1,742,801 and that the earnings per share in 1960 were approximately 65rather than 75? According to the unchallenged figures, sales in 1959 were $3,320,121, net operating income was $441,103, and earnings per share were 33. Would it have made a difference to an average prudent investor if he had known that in 1960 sales were only 256 per cent of 1959 sales, not 276 per cent; that net operating income was up by only $1,055,093, not by $1,301,698, and that earnings per share, while still approximately twice those of 1959, were not something more than twice?

These debentures were rated "B" by the investment rating services. They were thus characterized as speculative, as any prudent investor must have realized. It would seem that anyone interested in buying these convertible debentures would have been attracted primarily by the conversion feature, by the growth potential of the stock. The growth which the company enjoyed in 1960 over prior years was striking, even on the correct figures. It is hard to see how a prospective purchaser of this type of investment would have been deterred from buying if he had been advised of these comparatively minor errors in reporting 1960 sales and earnings.

This leaves for consideration the errors in the 1960 balance sheet figures which have previously been discussed in detail. Current assets were overstated by approximately $600,000. Liabilities were understated by approximately $325,000 by the failure to treat the liability on Capitol Lanes as a direct liability of BarChris on a consolidated basis. Of this $325,000 approximately $65,000, the amount payable on Capitol within one year, should have been treated as a current liability.

As per balance sheet, cash was $285,482. In fact, $145,000 of this had been borrowed temporarily from Talcott [with whom BarChris had a financing arrangement] and was to be returned by January 16, 1961 so that realistically, cash was only $140,482. Trade accounts receivable were overstated by $150,000 by including Howard Lanes Annex, an alley which was not sold to an outside buyer.

As per balance sheet, total current assets were $4,524,021, and total current liabilities were $2,413,867, a ratio of approximately 1.9 to 1. This was bad enough, but on the true facts, the ratio was worse. As corrected, current assets, as near as one can tell, were approximately $3,924,000, and current liabilities approximately $2,478,000, a ratio of approximately 1.6 to 1.

Would it have made any difference if a prospective purchaser of these debentures had been advised of these facts? There must be some point at which errors in disclosing a company's balance sheet position become material, even to a growth-oriented investor. On all the evidence I find that these balance sheet errors were material within the meaning of § 11.

Since there was an abundance of material misstatements pertaining to 1961 affairs, whether or not the errors in the 1960 figures were material does not affect the outcome of this case except to the extent that it bears upon the liability of Peat, Marwick. That subject will be discussed hereinafter.

The "Due Diligence" Defenses

Section 11 . . . of the Act provides that:

> [§ 11. (a) In case any part of the registration statement, when such part became effective, contained an untrue statement of a material fact or omitted to state a material fact required to be stated therein or necessary to make the statements therein not misleading, any person acquiring such security (unless it is proved that at the time of such acquisition he knew of such untruth or omission) may, . . . sue:
>
> (1) every person who signed the registration statement;
>
> (2) every person who was a director of . . . the issuer . . .; . . .
>
> (4) every accountant, engineer, or appraiser, or any person whose profession gives authority to a statement made by him, who has with his consent been named as having prepared or certified any part of the registration statement, with respect to the statement in such registration

statement, . . . which purports to have been prepared or certified by him;

(5) every underwriter with respect to such security. . . .

(b) Notwithstanding the provisions of subsection (a) no person, other than the issuer, shall be liable as provided therein who shall sustain the burden of proof . . .

(3) that (A) as regards any part of the registration statement not purporting to be made on the authority of an expert, . . . he had, after reasonable investigation, reasonable ground to believe and did believe, at the time such part of the registration statement became effective, that the statements therein were true and that there was no omission to state a material fact required to be stated therein or necessary to make the statements therein not misleading; and (B) as regards any part of the registration statement purporting to be made upon his authority as an expert . . . (i) he had, after reasonable investigation, reasonable ground to believe and did believe, at the time such part of the registration statement became effective, that the statements therein were true and that there was no omission to state a material fact required to be stated therein or necessary to make the statements therein not misleading, or (ii) such part of the registration statement did not fairly represent his statement as an expert or was not a fair copy of or extract from his report or valuation as an expert; and (C) as regards any part of the registration statement purporting to be made on the authority of an expert (other than himself) . . . he had no reasonable ground to believe and did not believe, at the time such part of the registration statement became effective, that the statements therein were untrue or that there was an omission to state a material fact required to be stated therein or necessary to make the statements therein not misleading, or that such part of the registration statement did not fairly represent the statement of the expert or was not a fair copy of or extract from the report or valuation of the expert;. . . .]

Section 11(c) defines "reasonable investigation" as follows:

"In determining, for the purpose of paragraph (3) of subsection (b) of this section, what constitutes reasonable investigation and reasonable ground for belief, the standard of reasonableness shall be that required of a prudent man in the management of his own property."

Every defendant, except BarChris itself, to whom, as the issuer, these defenses are not available, . . . has pleaded these affirmative defenses. . . .

Before considering the evidence, a preliminary matter should be disposed of. The defendants do not agree among themselves as to who the "experts" were or as to the parts of the registration statement which were expertised. Some defendants say that Peat, Marwick was the expert, others say that BarChris's attorneys, Perkins, Daniels, McCormack &

Collins, and the underwriters' attorneys, Drinker, Biddle & Reath, were also the experts. On the first view, only those portions of the registration statement purporting to be made on Peat, Marwick's authority were expertised portions. On the other view, everything in the registration statement was within this category, because the two law firms were responsible for the entire document.

The first view is the correct one. To say that the entire registration statement is expertised because some lawyer prepared it would be an unreasonable construction of the statute. Neither the lawyer for the company nor the lawyer for the underwriters is an expert within the meaning of § 11. The only expert, in the statutory sense, was Peat, Marwick, and the only parts of the registration statement which purported to be made upon the authority of an expert were the portions which purported to be made on Peat, Marwick's authority.

Here again, the more narrow view is the correct one. The registration statement contains a report of Peat, Marwick as independent public accountants dated February 23, 1961. This relates only to the consolidated balance sheet of BarChris and consolidated subsidiaries as of December 31, 1960, and the related statement of earnings and retained earnings for the five years then ended. This is all that Peat, Marwick purported to certify. It is perfectly clear that it did not purport to certify the 1961 figures, some of which are expressly stated in the prospectus to have been unaudited. . . .

Vitolo and Pugliese

They were the founders of the business who stuck with it to the end. Vitolo was president and Pugliese was vice president. Despite their titles, their field of responsibility in the administration of BarChris's affairs during the period in question seems to have been less all-embracing than Russo's. Pugliese in particular appears to have limited his activities to supervising the actual construction work.

Vitolo and Pugliese are each men of limited education. It is not hard to believe that for them the prospectus was difficult reading, if indeed they read it at all.

But whether it was or not is irrelevant. The liability of a director who signs a registration statement does not depend upon whether or not he read it or, if he did, whether or not he understood what he was reading.

And in any case, Vitolo and Pugliese were not as naive as they claim to be. They were members of BarChris's executive committee. At meetings of that committee BarChris's affairs were discussed at length. They must have known what was going on. Certainly they knew of the inadequacy of cash in 1961. They knew of their own large advances to the company which remained unpaid. They knew that they had agreed not to deposit their checks until the financing proceeds were received. They knew and intended that part of the proceeds were to be used to pay their own loans.

All in all, . . . Vitolo and Pugliese . . . could not have believed that the registration statement was wholly true and that no material facts had been omitted. And in any case, there is nothing to show that they made any investigation of anything which they may not have known about or understood. They have not proved their due diligence defenses.

Kircher

Kircher was treasurer of BarChris and its chief financial officer. He is a certified public accountant and an intelligent man. He was thoroughly familiar with BarChris's financial affairs. . . . He knew of the customers' delinquency problem. . . .

Kircher worked on the preparation of the registration statement. He conferred with Grant and on occasion with Ballard [the underwriters' counsel]. He supplied information to them about the company's business. He read the prospectus and understood it. He knew what it said and what it did not say.

Kircher's contention is that he had never before dealt with a registration statement, that he did not know what it should contain, and that he relied wholly on Grant, Ballard and Peat, Marwick to guide him. He claims that it was their fault, not his, if there was anything wrong with it. He says that all the facts were recorded in BarChris's books where these "experts" could have seen them if they had looked. He says that he truthfully answered all their questions. In effect, he says that if they did not know enough to ask the right questions and to give him the proper instructions, that is not his responsibility.

There is an issue of credibility here. In fact, Kircher was not frank in dealing with Grant and Ballard. He withheld information from them. But even if he had told them all the facts, this would not have constituted the due diligence contemplated by the statute. Knowing the facts, Kircher had reason to believe that the expertised portion of the prospectus, i.e., the 1960 figures, was in part incorrect. He could not shut his eyes to the facts and rely on Peat, Marwick for that portion. . . .

Birnbaum

Birnbaum was a young lawyer, admitted to the bar in 1957, who, after brief periods of employment by two different law firms and an equally brief period of practicing in his own firm, was employed by BarChris as house counsel and assistant secretary in October 1960. Unfortunately for him, he became secretary and a director of BarChris on April 17, 1961, after the first version of the registration statement had been filed with the Securities and Exchange Commission. He signed the later amendments, thereby becoming responsible for the accuracy of the prospectus in its final form.

Although the prospectus, in its description of "management," lists Birnbaum among the "executive officers" and devotes several sentences to a recital of his career, the fact seems to be that he was not an executive officer in any real sense. He did not participate in the management of the company. As house counsel, he attended to legal matters of a routine nature. Among other things, he incorporated subsidiaries, with which BarChris was plentifully supplied. . . .

Birnbaum examined contracts. In that connection he advised BarChris that the T-Bowl contracts were not legally enforceable. He was thus aware of that fact. . . .

It seems probable that Birnbaum did not know of many of the inaccuracies in the prospectus. He must, however, have appreciated some of them. In any case, he made no investigation and relied on the others to get it right. . . . As a lawyer, he should have known his obligations under the statute. He should have known that he was required to make a reasonable investigation of the truth of all the statements in the unexpertised portion of the document which he signed. Having failed to make such an investigation, he did not have reasonable ground to believe that all these statements were true. Birnbaum has not established his due diligence defenses except as to the audited 1960 figures.

Auslander

Auslander was an "outside" director, i.e., one who was not an officer of BarChris. He was chairman of the board of Valley Stream National Bank in Valley Stream, Long Island. In February 1961 Vitolo asked him to become a director of BarChris. Vitolo gave him an enthusiastic account of BarChris's progress and prospects. As an inducement, Vitolo said that when BarChris received the proceeds of a forthcoming issue of securities, it would deposit $1,000,000 in Auslander's bank.

In February and early March 1961, before accepting Vitolo's invitation, Auslander made some investigation of BarChris. He obtained Dun & Bradstreet reports which contained sales and earnings figures for periods earlier than December 31, 1960. He caused inquiry to be made of certain of BarChris's banks and was advised that they regarded BarChris favorably. . . .

On March 3, 1961, Auslander indicated his willingness to accept a place on the board. Shortly thereafter, on March 14, Kircher sent him a copy of BarChris's annual report for 1960. Auslander observed that BarChris's auditors were Peat, Marwick. They were also the auditors for the Valley Stream National Bank. He thought well of them.

Auslander was elected a director on April 17, 1961. The registration statement in its original form had already been filed, of course without his signature. On May 10, 1961, he signed a signature page for the first amendment to the registration statement which was filed on May 11, 1961. This was a separate sheet without any document attached. Auslander did not know that it was a signature page for a registration statement. He vaguely understood that it was something "for the SEC." . . .

In considering Auslander's due diligence defenses, a distinction is to be drawn between the expertised and non-expertised portions of the prospectus. As to the former, Auslander knew that Peat, Marwick had audited the 1960 figures. He believed them to be correct because he had confidence in Peat, Marwick. He had no reasonable ground to believe otherwise.

As to the non-expertised portions, however, Auslander is in a different position. He seems to have been under the impression that Peat, Marwick was responsible for all the figures. This impression was not correct, as he would have realized if he had read the prospectus carefully. Auslander made no investigation of the accuracy of the prospectus. He relied on the assurance of Vitolo and Russo, and upon the information he had received in answer to his inquiries back in February and early March. These inquiries were general ones, in the nature of a credit check. . . .

It is true that Auslander became a director on the eve of the financing. He had little opportunity to familiarize himself with the company's affairs. The question is whether, under such circumstances,

Auslander did enough to establish his due diligence defense with respect to the non-expertised portions of the prospectus. . . .

Section 11 imposes liability in the first instance upon a director, no matter how new he is. He is presumed to know his responsibility when he becomes a director. He can escape liability only by using that reasonable care to investigate the facts which a prudent man would employ in the management of his own property. In my opinion, a prudent man would not act in an important matter without any knowledge of the relevant facts, in sole reliance upon representations of persons who are comparative strangers and upon general information which does not purport to cover the particular case. To say that such minimal conduct measures up to the statutory standard would, to all intents and purposes, absolve new directors from responsibility merely because they are new. . . .

I find and conclude that Auslander has not established his due diligence defense with respect to the misstatements and omissions in those portions of the prospectus other than the audited 1960 figures. . . .

Grant

Grant became a director of BarChris in October 1960. His law firm was counsel to BarChris in matters pertaining to the registration of securities. Grant drafted the registration statement for the stock issue in 1959 and for the warrants in January 1961. He also drafted the registration statement for the debentures. In the preliminary division of work between him and Ballard, the underwriters' counsel, Grant took initial responsibility for preparing the registration statement, while Ballard devoted his efforts in the first instance to preparing the indenture.

Grant is sued as a director and as a signer of the registration statement. This is not an action against him for malpractice in his capacity as a lawyer. Nevertheless, in considering Grant's due diligence defenses, the unique position which he occupied cannot be disregarded. As the director most directly concerned with writing the registration statement and assuring its accuracy, more was required of him in the way of reasonable investigation than could fairly be expected of a director who had no connection with this work.

There is no valid basis for plaintiffs' accusation that Grant knew that the prospectus was false in some respects and incomplete and misleading in others. Having seen him testify at length, I am satisfied as to his integrity. I find that Grant honestly believed that the registration statement was true and that no material facts had been omitted from it.

In this belief he was mistaken, and the fact is that for all his work, he never discovered any of the errors or omissions which have been recounted at length in this opinion, with the single exception of Capitol Lanes. He knew that BarChris had not sold this alley and intended to operate it, but he appears to have been under the erroneous impression that Peat, Marwick had knowingly sanctioned its inclusion in sales because of the allegedly temporary nature of the operation.

Grant contends that a finding that he did not make a reasonable investigation would be equivalent to a holding that a lawyer for an issuing company, in order to show due diligence, must make an independent audit of the figures supplied to him by his client. I do not consider this to be a realistic statement of the issue. There were errors and omissions here which could have been detected without an audit. The question is whether, despite his failure to detect them, Grant made a reasonable effort to that end.

Much of this registration statement is a scissors and paste-pot job. Grant lifted large portions from the earlier prospectuses, modifying them in some instances to the extent that he considered necessary. But BarChris's affairs had changed for the worse by May 1961. Statements that were accurate in January were no longer accurate in May. Grant never discovered this. He accepted the assurances of Kircher and Russo that any change which might have occurred had been for the better, rather than the contrary.

It is claimed that a lawyer is entitled to rely on the statements of his client and that to require him to verify their accuracy would set an unreasonably high standard. This is too broad a generalization. It is all a matter of degree. To require an audit would obviously be unreasonable. On the other hand, to require a check of matters easily verifiable is not unreasonable. Even honest clients can make mistakes. The statute imposes liability for untrue statements regardless of whether they are intentionally untrue. The way to prevent mistakes is to test oral information by examining the original written record.

There were things which Grant could readily have checked which he did not check. For example, he was unaware of the provisions of the agreements between BarChris and Talcott. He never read them. Thus, he did not know, although he readily could have ascertained, that BarChris's contingent liability on Type B leaseback arrangements was 100 per cent, not 25 per cent. . . .

Grant was entitled to rely on Peat, Marwick for the 1960 figures. He had no reasonable ground to believe them to be inaccurate. But the matters which I have mentioned were not within the expertised portion of the prospectus. As to this, Grant, was obliged to make a reasonable investigation. I am forced to find that he did not make one. After making all due allowances for the fact that Bar Chris's officers misled him, there are too many instances in which Grant failed to make an inquiry which he could easily have made which, if pursued, would have put him on his guard. In my opinion, this finding on the evidence in this case does not establish an unreasonably high standard in other cases for company counsel who are also directors. Each case must rest on its own facts. I conclude that Grant has not established his due diligence defenses except as to the audited 1960 figures. . . .

Peat, Marwick

The part of the registration statement purporting to be made upon the authority of Peat, Marwick as an expert was, as we have seen, the 1960 figures. But because the statute requires the court to determine Peat, Marwick's belief, and the grounds thereof, "at the time such part of the registration statement became effective," for the purposes of this affirmative defense, the matter must be viewed as of May 16, 1961, and the question is whether at that time Peat, Marwick, after reasonable investigation, had reasonable ground to believe and did believe that the 1960 figures were true and that no material fact had been omitted from the registration statement which should have been included in order to make the 1960 figures not misleading. . . .

Peat, Marwick's work was in general charge of a member of the firm, Cummings, and more immediately in charge of Peat, Marwick's manager, Logan. Most of the actual work was performed by a senior accountant, Berardi. . . .

Berardi was then about thirty years old. He was not yet a C.P.A. He had had no previous experience with the bowling industry. This was his first job as a senior accountant. He could hardly have been given a more difficult assignment.

After obtaining a little background information on BarChris by talking to Logan and reviewing Peat, Marwick's work papers on its 1959 audit, Berardi examined the results of test checks of BarChris's accounting procedures which one of the junior accountants had made, and he prepared an "internal control questionnaire" and an "audit program." Thereafter, for a few days subsequent to December 30, 1960, he inspected BarChris's inventories and examined certain alley construction. Finally, on January 13, 1961, he began his auditing work which he carried on substantially continuously until it was completed on February 24, 1961. Toward the close of the work, Logan reviewed it and made various comments and suggestions to Berardi.

It is unnecessary to recount everything that Berardi did in the course of the audit. We are concerned only with the evidence relating to what Berardi did or did not do with respect to those items which I have found to have been incorrectly reported in the 1960 figures in the prospectus. More narrowly, we are directly concerned only with such of those items as I have found to be material. . . .

First and foremost is Berardi's failure to discover that Capitol Lanes had not been sold. This error affected both the sales figure and the liability side of the balance sheet. . . .

Berardi knew from various BarChris records that Capitol Lanes, Inc. was paying rentals to Talcott. Also, a Peat, Marwick work paper bearing Kennedy's initials recorded that Capitol Lanes, Inc. held certain insurance policies, including a fire insurance policy on "contents," a workmen's compensation and a public liability policy. . . .

Berardi testified that he inquired of Russo about Capitol Lanes and that Russo told him that Capitol Lanes, Inc. was going to operate an alley some day but as yet it had no alley. Berardi testified that he understood that the alley had not been built and that he believed that the rental payments were on vacant land.

I am not satisfied with this testimony. If Berardi did hold this belief, he should not have held it. The entries as to insurance and as to "operation of alley" should have alerted him to the fact that an alley existed. He should have made further inquiry on the subject. It is apparent that Berardi did not understand this transaction.

[The court continued with a discussion of other mistakes by Berardi.]

In substance, what Berardi did is similar to what Grant and Ballard did. He asked questions, he got answers which he considered satisfactory, and he did nothing to verify them. . . .

Accountants should not be held to a standard higher than that recognized in their profession. I do not do so here. Berardi's review did not come up to that standard. He did not take some of the steps which Peat, Marwick's written program prescribed. He did not spend an adequate amount of time on a task of this magnitude. Most important of all, he was too easily satisfied with glib answers to his inquiries.

. . .

Defendants' motions to dismiss this action, upon which decision was reserved at the trial, are denied. . . .

QUESTIONS

1. How does Peat Marwick's potential liability differ from that of the directors? Why should it differ?

2. Is BarChris itself liable under the statute? Why?

3. Should a director who also serves as general counsel to the issuer be held to a different standard than the other directors?

4. How should a law firm respond to a request from a client that a partner serve on its board of directors?

5. Who was harmed by the defendants' misconduct? Did anyone benefit from it?

PROBLEM

US Way is a marketing firm. Sales agents for the firm sell microwave ovens door-to-door, keep a 6 percent commission on any sales they make, and forward the remainder to their supervising manager. Those managers (who recruit the sales agents) keep a 6 percent commission for themselves and forward the rest to USW. USW then pays the wholesalers and the firm's salaried officers. Neither the sales staff nor the managers earn any other compensation.

Sales staff may become managers if they recruit other sales agents to work under them. If, however, total commissions would otherwise exceed 15 percent of the sales price (as would happen if a manager recruited a sales agent who in turn recruited another sales agent and all three collected 6 percent) the managers and sales staff in the chain divide the 15 percent equally.

1. Suppose the USW president owns all the stock of USW. Would USW need to register with the SEC?

2. Suppose the stock of USW is traded on the New York Stock Exchange. Suppose further that in March scientists discover that microwave ovens present a non-negligible risk of causing brain cancer, particularly among small children. In April, USW issues additional stock to the public for $50 per share.

(a) Suppose that the market for microwave ovens collapses in May and USW becomes insolvent. A buyer of one of the April USW shares sues the directors personally, on the ground that the registration statement inadequately disclosed the cancer-risk problem. If a court finds the registration statement materially misleading, can the buyer recover?

Must the buyer have seen the registration statement before buying the stock? What would be the buyer's damages?

(b) Suppose again the facts as stated in 2(a). Is the buyer likely to be successful in a suit against the accounting firm that audited the registration statement?

NOTE ON INTEGRATED DISCLOSURE AND EXCHANGE ACT DISCLOSURES

The Securities Act and the Exchange Act originally established two separate disclosure systems. The former requires disclosures with respect to particular transactions, such as new issues of stocks or bonds to the public, while the latter imposes a system of periodic disclosures on certain companies—most importantly, the obligation to file annual and quarterly reports.

For publicly traded companies that must file periodic disclosure reports under the Exchange Act, there was a substantial amount of overlap and duplication between those reports and the Securities Act registration statement disclosures it was obliged to make when selling securities to the public. In response to the substantial regulatory burden this overlap created, the SEC adopted the modern integrated disclosure system.

Integrated disclosure starts with the reports that must be filed under the Exchange Act. We therefore begin with the question—who must file? A full answer to that question is complicated, involving a convoluted review of multiple sections of the Exchange Act. For our purposes, it suffices to say that effectively all publicly traded companies, as well as some large close corporations, are required to file Exchange Act reports.

Covered corporations must register with the SEC by filing an initial Form 10. This form only needs to be filed once with respect to a particular class of securities—the first time the issuer registers that class of securities under the Act. It contains exhaustive disclosures similar to those required in a Securities Act registration statement.* The corporation thereafter must annually file a Form 10-K, which contains audited financial statements and management's report of the previous year's activities and usually also incorporates the annual report sent to shareholders. The company also must file a Form 10-Q for each of first three quarters of the year. It will contain unaudited financial statements and management's report on material recent developments. Finally, the corporation must file a Form 8-K within 4 days after certain important events affecting the company's operations or financial condition. In other words, if a major event happens, the company must report it immediately

* Be careful to distinguish registration of a class of securities under the Exchange Act from registration of an offering of securities under the Securities Act—a company that has registered a class of securities under the Exchange Act will still have to register a particular offering of securities of that class under the Securities Act. For example, suppose ABC Corporation has registered its common stock under the Exchange Act. ABC now wants to sell an additional 1 million shares of common stock in a new public offering. Unless an exemption is available, the shares to be sold in the offering must still be registered under the Securities Act, even though the class itself is registered under the Exchange Act. Although it is slightly inaccurate, it might be helpful if you think about the difference as follows: the Exchange Act registers companies; the Securities Act registers offerings.

instead of waiting for the next quarterly or annual report. The Form specifies events that are considered sufficiently important to require filing, such as sales or purchases of significant assets or a change in control of the company.

In addition to the periodic disclosure obligations, registering a class of securities under the Exchange Act triggers a variety of other requirements. For example, the issuer becomes subject to the proxy rules under § 14, the tender offer rules under sections 13 and 14, and certain of the anti-fraud provisions of the Act.

Before the integrated disclosure system came into being, a reporting company that wished to sell securities in a registered public offering was obliged to prepare a registration statement containing most of the information that had already been disclosed in its Exchange Act periodic disclosure reports. Worse yet, the Securities Act and Exchange Act forms differed somewhat both as to style and content. As a result, the disclosure process was enormously expensive for reporting firms.

To economists all of this duplication of effort required by the two Acts was not only expensive, but was also unnecessary. The efficient capital markets hypothesis posits that all publicly available information is more or less instantaneously incorporated into the market price of its securities. Because the theory is reasonably well-accepted for this purpose, we may assume that all of the information released in the firm's regular Exchange Act disclosure statements will be digested by securities analysts and reflected in the firm's market price. Because virtually all securities offerings by established companies are made either at the current market price of its securities or at a slight discount from market price, there is no need to reiterate all of the Exchange Act information in a Securities Act filing. The market has already gotten the information and accounted for it.

The SEC eventually saw the efficient capital markets hypothesis as providing a way out of the box—a way of eliminating the complex and expensive dual disclosure system. It therefore adopted the so-called "Integrated Disclosure System," one of the truly major changes in its history. Under the integrated disclosure system, an issuer planning a registered offering first looks to the various registration statement forms to determine which form it is eligible to use. The forms then direct the drafter to Regulation S-K for the substantive disclosure requirements. Regulation S-K adopted uniform disclosure standards for both Acts, so that virtually all filings are now prepared under identical instructions. As a result, the style and content of disclosure documents under both Acts are now essentially identical. Thus, for example, the annual 10-K report contains information that can be directly transferred into a registration statement.

Each of the main registration statement forms requires disclosure of two basic types of information: information about the transaction and information about the issuer (a/k/a registrant). Form S-1, the basic registration statement form, requires detailed disclosure about both categories. But Form S-3 only requires disclosure of information about the transaction. Information about the issuer is incorporated by reference from the last 10-K and other Exchange Act disclosure documents. In order to use Form S-3, an issuer must meet two basic requirements—it must be large and seasoned. It must have a substantial number of shares outstanding and must have been a reporting company for several years. The basic idea is that an issuer eligible to use Form S-3 will be one that is regularly providing disclosure to the market about itself and whose securities are traded in an efficient market that impounds the disclosed information into price quickly. Given these criteria, the SEC posited that registrant-related information would be unnecessarily duplicative.

C. RULE 10b–5

Where Congress is silent as to whether or not a private right of action exists under a particular statute, courts have sometimes implied a private right of action. In securities law, the most important of these undoubtedly is the private right of action under Exchange Act § 10(b) and Rule 10b–5 thereunder. Section 10(b) provides:

> It shall be unlawful for any person, directly or indirectly, by the use of any means or instrumentality of interstate commerce or of the mails, or of any facility of any national securities exchange. . . .
>
> > (b) To use or employ, in connection with the purchase or sale of any security registered on a national securities exchange or any security not so registered . . ., any manipulative or deceptive device or contrivance in contravention of such rules and regulations as the Commission may prescribe as necessary or appropriate in the public interest or for the protection of investors. . . .

Notice that § 10(b) applies to any security, including securities of closely held corporations that generally are not subject to the Exchange Act and to transactions in government securities. Notice also that § 10(b) is not self-executing—it did not prohibit anything until the SEC adopted rules implementing it.

Our attention therefore turns to Rule 10b–5—easily the most famous, and arguably the most important, of all the SEC's many rules:

> It shall be unlawful for any person, directly or indirectly, by the use of any means or instrumentality of interstate commerce, or of the mails or of any facility of any national securities exchange,
>
> > (a) To employ any device, scheme, or artifice to defraud,
> >
> > (b) To make any untrue statement of a material fact or to omit to state a material fact necessary in order to make the statements made, in the light of the circumstances under which they were made, not misleading, or
> >
> > (c) To engage in any act, practice, or course of business which operates or would operate as a fraud or deceit upon any person,
>
> in connection with the purchase or sale of any security.

The central theme of the rule's history is one of repeated judicial glosses on this relatively innocuous—and vague—text. As Justice Rehnquist has observed, Rule 10b–5 is now "a judicial oak which has grown from little more than a legislative acorn." Blue Chip Stamps v. Manor Drug Stores, 421 U.S. 723 (1975). In a very real sense, Rule 10b–5 jurisprudence is a species of federal common law only loosely tied to the statutory text.

Halliburton Co. v. Erica P. John Fund, Inc.

134 S.Ct. 2398 (2014).

■ CHIEF JUSTICE ROBERTS delivered the opinion of the Court.

Investors can recover damages in a private securities fraud action only if they prove that they relied on the defendant's misrepresentation in deciding to buy or sell a company's stock. In Basic Inc. v. Levinson, 485 U.S. 224 (1988), we held that investors could satisfy this reliance requirement by invoking a presumption that the price of stock traded in an efficient market reflects all public, material information—including material misstatements. In such a case, we concluded, anyone who buys or sells the stock at the market price may be considered to have relied on those misstatements.

We also held, however, that a defendant could rebut this presumption in a number of ways, including by showing that the alleged misrepresentation did not actually affect the stock's price—that is, that the misrepresentation had no "price impact." The questions presented are whether we should overrule or modify *Basic*'s presumption of reliance and, if not, whether defendants should nonetheless be afforded an opportunity in securities class action cases to rebut the presumption at the class certification stage, by showing a lack of price impact.

I

Respondent Erica P. John Fund, Inc. (EPJ Fund), is the lead plaintiff in a putative class action against Halliburton and one of its executives . . . alleging violations of section 10(b) of the Securities Exchange Act of 1934, and Securities and Exchange Commission Rule 10b–5. According to EPJ Fund, between June 3, 1999, and December 7, 2001, Halliburton made a series of misrepresentations regarding its potential liability in asbestos litigation, its expected revenue from certain construction contracts, and the anticipated benefits of its merger with another company—all in an attempt to inflate the price of its stock. Halliburton subsequently made a number of corrective disclosures, which, EPJ Fund contends, caused the company's stock price to drop and investors to lose money.

EPJ Fund moved to certify a class comprising all investors who purchased Halliburton common stock during the class period. . . . Halliburton argued that class certification was inappropriate because the evidence . . . showed that none of its alleged misrepresentations had actually affected its stock price. By demonstrating the absence of any "price impact," Halliburton contended, it had rebutted *Basic*'s presumption that the members of the proposed class had relied on its alleged misrepresentations simply by buying or selling its stock at the market price. And without the benefit of the *Basic* presumption, investors would have to prove reliance on an individual basis, meaning that individual issues would predominate over common ones. . . .

We . . . granted certiorari . . . to resolve a conflict among the Circuits over whether securities fraud defendants may attempt to rebut the *Basic* presumption at the class certification stage with evidence of a lack of price impact. We also accepted Halliburton's invitation to reconsider the presumption of reliance for securities fraud claims that we adopted in *Basic*.

II

. . .

A

Section 10(b) of the Securities Exchange Act of 1934 and the Securities and Exchange Commission's Rule 10b–5 prohibit making any material misstatement or omission in connection with the purchase or sale of any security. Although section 10(b) does not create an express private cause of action, we have long recognized an implied private cause of action to enforce the provision and its implementing regulation. See Blue Chip Stamps v. Manor Drug Stores, 421 U.S. 723 (1975). To recover damages for violations of section 10(b) and Rule 10b–5, a plaintiff must prove " '(1) a material misrepresentation or omission by the defendant; (2) scienter; (3) a connection between the misrepresentation or omission and the purchase or sale of a security; (4) reliance upon the misrepresentation or omission; (5) economic loss; and (6) loss causation.' " Amgen Inc. v. Connecticut Retirement Plans and Trust Funds, 568 U.S. ___, ___ (2013). . . .

The reliance element " 'ensures that there is a proper connection between a defendant's misrepresentation and a plaintiff's injury.' " 568 U.S., at ___. . . . "The traditional (and most direct) way a plaintiff can demonstrate reliance is by showing that he was aware of a company's statement and engaged in a relevant transaction—*e.g.,* purchasing common stock—based on that specific misrepresentation." Id., at ___. . . .

In *Basic,* however, we recognized that requiring such direct proof of reliance "would place an unnecessarily unrealistic evidentiary burden on the Rule 10b–5 plaintiff who has traded on an impersonal market." 485 U.S., at 245. . . . We also noted that "[r]equiring proof of individualized reliance" from every securities fraud plaintiff "effectively would . . . prevent[ ] [plaintiffs] from proceeding with a class action" in Rule 10b–5 suits. Id., at 242. . . .

To address these concerns, *Basic* held that securities fraud plaintiffs can in certain circumstances satisfy the reliance element of a Rule 10b–5 action by invoking a rebuttable presumption of reliance, rather than proving direct reliance on a misrepresentation. The Court based that presumption on what is known as the "fraud-on-the-market" theory, which holds that "the market price of shares traded on well-developed markets reflects all publicly available information, and, hence, any material misrepresentations." Id., at 246. The Court also noted that, rather than scrutinize every piece of public information about a company for himself, the typical "investor who buys or sells stock at the price set by the market does so in reliance on the integrity of that price"—the belief that it reflects all public, material information. Id., at 247. . . .

Based on this theory, a plaintiff must make the following showings to demonstrate that the presumption of reliance applies in a given case: (1) that the alleged misrepresentations were publicly known, (2) that they were material, (3) that the stock traded in an efficient market, and (4) that the plaintiff traded the stock between the time the misrepresentations were made and when the truth was revealed. See id., at 248, n. 27. . . .

At the same time, *Basic* emphasized that the presumption of reliance was rebuttable rather than conclusive. Specifically, "[a]ny showing that severs the link between the alleged misrepresentation and either the price received (or paid) by the plaintiff, or his decision to trade at a fair market price, will be sufficient to rebut the presumption of reliance." 485 U.S., at 248. So for example, if a defendant could show that the alleged misrepresentation did not, for whatever reason, actually affect the market price, or that a plaintiff would have bought or sold the stock even had he been aware that the stock's price was tainted by fraud, then the presumption of reliance would not apply. Id., at 248–249. . . .

B

. . .

2

Halliburton's primary argument for overruling *Basic* is that the decision rested on two premises that can no longer withstand scrutiny. The first premise concerns what is known as the "efficient capital markets hypothesis." *Basic* stated that "the market price of shares traded on well-developed markets reflects all publicly available information, and, hence, any material misrepresentations." Id., at 246. From that statement, Halliburton concludes that the *Basic* Court espoused "a robust view of market efficiency" that is no longer tenable, for " 'overwhelming empirical evidence' now 'suggests that capital markets are not fundamentally efficient.' " Brief for Petitioners 14–16. . . . To support this contention, Halliburton cites studies purporting to show that "public information is often not incorporated immediately (much less rationally) into market prices." Brief for Petitioners 17. . . .

Halliburton does not, of course, maintain that capital markets are *always* inefficient. Rather, in its view, *Basic's* fundamental error was to ignore the fact that " 'efficiency is not a binary, yes or no question.' " Brief for Petitioners 20. . . . The markets for some securities are more efficient than the markets for others, and even a single market can process different kinds of information more or less efficiently, depending on how widely the information is disseminated and how easily it is understood. . . .

Halliburton's criticisms fail to take *Basic* on its own terms. Halliburton focuses on the debate among economists about the degree to which the market price of a company's stock reflects public information about the company. . . . That debate is not new. Indeed, the *Basic* Court acknowledged it and declined to enter the fray, declaring that "[w]e need not determine by adjudication what economists and social scientists have debated through the use of sophisticated statistical analysis and the application of economic theory." 485 U.S., at 246–247, n. 24. . . . The Court instead based the presumption on the fairly modest premise that "market professionals generally consider most publicly announced material statements about companies, thereby affecting stock market prices." Id., at 247, n. 24. . . . Indeed, in making the presumption rebuttable, *Basic* recognized that market efficiency is a matter of degree and accordingly made it a matter of proof.

The academic debates discussed by Halliburton have not refuted the modest premise underlying the presumption of reliance. Even the foremost critics of the efficient-capital-markets hypothesis acknowledge that public information generally affects stock prices. . . . Debates about the precise degree to which stock prices accurately reflect public information are thus largely beside the point. "That the . . . price [of a stock] may be inaccurate does not detract from the fact that false statements affect it, and cause loss," which is "all that Basic requires." Schleicher v. Wendt, 618 F.3d 679, 685 (C.A.7 2010) (Easterbrook, C. J.).

Halliburton also contests a second premise underlying the *Basic* presumption: the notion that investors "invest 'in reliance on the integrity of [the market] price.'" Reply Brief 14. . . . Halliburton identifies a number of classes of investors for whom "price integrity" is supposedly "marginal or irrelevant." Reply Brief 14. The primary example is the value investor, who believes that certain stocks are undervalued or overvalued and attempts to "beat the market" by buying the undervalued stocks and selling the overvalued ones. . . .

But *Basic* never denied the existence of such investors. As we recently explained, *Basic* concluded only that "it is reasonable to presume that *most* investors—knowing that they have little hope of outperforming the market in the long run based solely on their analysis of publicly available information—will rely on the security's market price as an unbiased assessment of the security's value in light of all public information." *Amgen,* 568 U.S., at ___. . . .

C

. . . . Halliburton and its amici contend that, by facilitating securities class actions, the *Basic* presumption produces a number of serious and harmful consequences. Such class actions, they say, allow plaintiffs to extort large settlements from defendants for meritless claims; punish innocent shareholders, who end up having to pay settlements and judgments; impose excessive costs on businesses; and consume a disproportionately large share of judicial resources. . . .

These concerns are more appropriately addressed to Congress, which has in fact responded, to some extent, to many of the issues raised by Halliburton and its amici. Congress has, for example, enacted the Private Securities Litigation Reform Act of 1995 (PSLRA), 109 Stat. 737, which sought to combat perceived abuses in securities litigation with heightened pleading requirements, limits on damages and attorney's fees, a "safe harbor" for certain kinds of statements, restrictions on the selection of lead plaintiffs in securities class actions, sanctions for frivolous litigation, and stays of discovery pending motions to dismiss. . . . Such legislation demonstrates Congress's willingness to consider policy concerns of the sort that Halliburton says should lead us to overrule *Basic.*

III

Halliburton proposes two alternatives to overruling *Basic* that would alleviate what it regards as the decision's most serious flaws. The first alternative would require plaintiffs to prove that a defendant's misrepresentation actually affected the stock price—so-called "price impact"—in order to invoke the *Basic* presumption. . . . Halliburton's second proposed alternative would allow defendants to rebut the presumption of reliance with evidence of a *lack* of price impact, not only at the merits stage—which all agree defendants may already do—but also before class certification.

A

As noted, to invoke the *Basic* presumption, a plaintiff must prove that: (1) the alleged misrepresentations were publicly known, (2) they were material, (3) the stock traded in an efficient market, and (4) the plaintiff traded the stock between when the misrepresentations were made and when the truth was revealed. . . . Each of these requirements follows from the fraud-on-the-market theory underlying the presumption. If the misrepresentation was not publicly known, then it could not have distorted the stock's market price. So too if the misrepresentation was immaterial—that is, if it would not have " 'been viewed by the reasonable investor as having significantly altered the "total mix" of information made available,' " Basic, supra, at 231–232. . .—or if the market in which the stock traded was inefficient. And if the plaintiff did not buy or sell the stock after the misrepresentation was made but before the truth was revealed, then he could not be said to have acted in reliance on a fraud-tainted price.

The first three prerequisites are directed at price impact—"whether the alleged misrepresentations affected the market price in the first place." *Halliburton I,* 563 U.S., at ___. . . . In the absence of price impact, *Basic*'s fraud-on-the-market theory and presumption of reliance collapse. . . .

Halliburton argues that since the *Basic* presumption hinges on price impact, plaintiffs should be required to prove it directly in order to invoke the presumption. . . .

Far from a modest refinement of the *Basic* presumption, this proposal would radically alter the required showing for the reliance element of the Rule 10b–5 cause of action. What is called the *Basic* presumption actually incorporates two constituent presumptions: First, if a plaintiff shows that the defendant's misrepresentation was public and material and that the stock traded in a generally efficient market, he is entitled to a presumption that the misrepresentation affected the stock price. Second, if the plaintiff also shows that he purchased the stock at the market price during the relevant period, he is entitled to a further presumption that he purchased the stock in reliance on the defendant's misrepresentation.

By requiring plaintiffs to prove price impact directly, Halliburton's proposal would take away the first constituent presumption. Halliburton's argument for doing so is the same as its primary argument for overruling the *Basic* presumption altogether: Because market efficiency is not a yes-or-no proposition, a public, material misrepresentation might not affect a stock's price even in a generally efficient market. But as explained, *Basic* never suggested otherwise; that is why it affords defendants an opportunity to rebut the presumption by showing, among other things, that the particular misrepresentation at issue did not affect the stock's market price. . . .

B

Even if plaintiffs need not directly prove price impact to invoke the *Basic* presumption, Halliburton contends that defendants should at least be allowed to defeat the presumption at the class certification stage through evidence that the misrepresentation did not in fact affect the stock price. We agree.

1

There is no dispute that defendants may introduce such evidence at the merits stage to rebut the *Basic* presumption. . . .

Nor is there any dispute that defendants may introduce price impact evidence at the class certification stage, so long as it is for the purpose of countering a plaintiff's showing of market efficiency, rather than directly rebutting the presumption. . . .

After all, plaintiffs themselves can and do introduce evidence of the *existence* of price impact in connection with "event studies"—regression analyses that seek to show that the market price of the defendant's stock tends to respond to pertinent publicly reported events. . . . In this case, for example, EPJ Fund submitted an event study of various episodes that might have been expected to affect the price of Halliburton's stock, in order to demonstrate that the market for that stock takes account of material, public information about the company. . . .

Defendants—like plaintiffs—may accordingly submit price impact evidence prior to class certification. What defendants may not do, EPJ Fund insists and the Court of Appeals held, is rely on that same evidence prior to class certification for the particular purpose of rebutting the presumption altogether.

This restriction makes no sense, and can readily lead to bizarre results. Suppose a defendant at the certification stage submits an event study looking at the impact on the price of its stock from six discrete events, in an effort to refute the plaintiffs' claim of general market efficiency. All agree the defendant may do this. Suppose one of the six events is the specific misrepresentation asserted by the plaintiffs. All agree that this too is perfectly acceptable. Now suppose the district court determines that, despite the defendant's study, the plaintiff has carried its burden to prove market efficiency, but that the evidence shows no price impact with respect to the specific misrepresentation challenged in the suit. The evidence at the certification stage thus shows an efficient market, on which the alleged misrepresentation had no price impact. And yet under EPJ Fund's view, the plaintiffs' action should be certified and proceed as a class action (with all that entails), even though the fraud-on-the-market theory does not apply and common reliance thus cannot be presumed.

Such a result is inconsistent with *Basic*'s own logic. Under *Basic*'s fraud-on-the-market theory, market efficiency and the other prerequisites for invoking the presumption constitute an indirect way of showing price impact. As explained, it is appropriate to allow plaintiffs to rely on this indirect proxy for price impact, rather than requiring them to prove price impact directly, given *Basic*'s rationales for recognizing a presumption of reliance in the first place.

But an indirect proxy should not preclude direct evidence when such evidence is available. As we explained in *Basic,* "[a]ny showing that severs the link between the alleged misrepresentation and . . . the price received (or paid) by the plaintiff . . . will be sufficient to rebut the presumption of reliance" because "the basis for finding that the fraud had been transmitted through market price would be gone." 485 U.S., at 248. And without the presumption of reliance, a Rule 10b–5 suit cannot proceed as a class action: Each plaintiff would have to prove reliance individually, so common issues would not "predominate" over individual ones, as required by Rule 23(b)(3). Id., at 242. Price impact is thus an essential precondition for any Rule 10b–5 class action. . . .

It is so ordered.

■ JUSTICE THOMAS, with whom JUSTICE SCALIA and JUSTICE ALITO join, concurring in the judgment.

The implied Rule 10b–5 private cause of action is "a relic of the heady days in which this Court assumed common-law powers to create causes of action," Correctional Services Corp. v. Malesko, 534 U.S. 61, 75 . . . (2001). . . . We have since ended that practice because the authority to fashion private remedies to enforce federal law belongs to Congress alone. . . .

Basic Inc. v. Levinson, 485 U.S. 224 . . . (1988), demonstrates the wisdom of this rule. *Basic* presented the question how investors must prove the reliance element of the implied Rule 10b–5 cause of action—the requirement that the plaintiff buy or sell stock in reliance on the defendant's misstatement—when they transact on modern, impersonal securities exchanges. Were the Rule 10b–5 action statutory, the Court could have resolved this question by interpreting the statutory language. Without a statute to interpret for guidance, however, the Court began instead with a particular policy "problem": for investors in impersonal markets, the traditional reliance requirement was hard to prove and impossible to prove as common among plaintiffs bringing 10b–5 class-action suits. Id., at 242, 245. With the task thus framed as "resol[ving]" that " 'problem' " rather than interpreting statutory text, *id.*, at 242, the Court turned to nascent economic theory and naked intuitions about investment behavior in its efforts to fashion a new, easier way to meet the reliance requirement. The result was an evidentiary presumption, based on a "fraud on the market" theory, that paved the way for class actions under Rule 10b–5.

Today we are asked to determine whether *Basic* was correctly decided. The Court suggests that it was, and that stare decisis demands that we preserve it. I disagree. . . .

II

Basic's reimagined reliance requirement was a mistake, and the passage of time has compounded its failings. First, the Court based both parts of the presumption of reliance on a questionable understanding of disputed economic theory and flawed intuitions about investor behavior. Second, *Basic*'s rebuttable presumption is at odds with our subsequent Rule 23 cases, which require plaintiffs seeking class certification to " 'affirmatively demonstrate' " certification requirements like the predominance of common questions. Comcast Corp. v. Behrend, 569 U.S. ___, ___ (2013). . . . Finally, *Basic*'s presumption that investors rely on the integrity of the market price is virtually irrebuttable in practice, which means that the "essential" reliance element effectively exists in name only.

A

Basic based the presumption of reliance on two factual assumptions. The first assumption was that, in a "well-developed market," public statements are generally "reflected" in the market price of securities. 485

U.S., at 247. The second was that investors in such markets transact "in reliance on the integrity of that price." Ibid. In other words, the Court created a presumption that a plaintiff had met the two-part, fraud-on-the-market version of the reliance requirement because, in the Court's view, "common sense and probability" suggested that each of those parts would be met. Id., at 246.

In reality, both of the Court's key assumptions are highly contestable and do not provide the necessary support for *Basic*'s presumption of reliance. The first assumption—that public statements are "reflected" in the market price—was grounded in an economic theory that has garnered substantial criticism since *Basic*. The second assumption—that investors categorically rely on the integrity of the market price—is simply wrong.

1

The Court's first assumption was that "most publicly available information"—including public misstatements—"is reflected in [the] market price" of a security. *Id.,* at 247. The Court grounded that assumption in "empirical studies" testing a then-nascent economic theory known as the efficient capital markets hypothesis. Id., at 246–247. Specifically, the Court relied upon the "semi-strong" version of that theory, which posits that the average investor cannot earn above-market returns (*i.e.,* "beat the market") in an efficient market by trading on the basis of publicly available information. . . .

This view of market efficiency has since lost its luster. . . . Further, and more importantly, "overwhelming empirical evidence" now suggests that even when markets do incorporate public information, they often fail to do so accurately. Lev and de Villiers, Stock Price Crashes and 10b–5 Damages: A Legal, Economic and Policy Analysis, 47 Stan. L.Rev. 7, 20–21 (1994). . . . In sum, economists now understand that the price impact *Basic* assumed would happen reflexively is actually far from certain even in "well-developed" markets. . . .

2

The *Basic* Court also grounded the presumption of reliance in a second assumption: that "[a]n investor who buys or sells stock at the price set by the market does so in reliance on the integrity of that price." 485 U.S., at 247. . . .

The Court's rather superficial analysis does not withstand scrutiny. It cannot be seriously disputed that a great many investors do *not* buy or sell stock based on a belief that the stock's price accurately reflects its value. Many investors in fact trade for the opposite reason—that is, because they think the market has under- or overvalued the stock, and they believe they can profit from that mispricing. . . .

Other investors trade for reasons entirely unrelated to price—for instance, to address changing liquidity needs, tax concerns, or portfolio balancing requirements. . . .

B

Basic's presumption of reliance also conflicts with our more recent cases clarifying Rule 23's class-certification requirements. Those cases instruct that "a party seeking to maintain a class action 'must affirmatively demonstrate his compliance' with Rule 23." *Comcast,* 569

U.S., at ___. . . . To prevail on a motion for class certification, a party must demonstrate through "evidentiary proof" that " 'questions of law or fact common to class members predominate over any questions affecting only individual members.' " 569 U.S., at ___. . . .

Basic permits plaintiffs to bypass that requirement of evidentiary proof. Under *Basic,* plaintiffs who invoke the presumption of reliance (by proving its predicates) are deemed to have met the predominance requirement of Rule 23(b)(3). . . .

Basic thus exempts Rule 10b–5 plaintiffs from Rule 23's proof requirement. Plaintiffs who invoke the presumption of reliance are deemed to have shown predominance as a matter of law, even though the resulting rebuttable presumption leaves individualized questions of reliance in the case and predominance still unproved. . . .

For these reasons, *Basic* should be overruled in favor of the straightforward rule that "[r]eliance by the plaintiff upon the defendant's deceptive acts"—actual reliance, not the fictional "fraud-on-the-market" version—"is an essential element of the § 10(b) private cause of action." *Stoneridge,* 552 U.S., at 159.

ANALYSIS

1. Will the *Halliburton* decision reduce the incentive for plaintiffs to bring so-called strike suits—i.e., nuisance suits brought in hopes of extracting a small settlement from defendants for whom it is cheaper to settle than to litigate the case?

2. Most securities fraud cases that survive a motion to dismiss or for summary judgment settle before going to trial. How does the *Halliburton* decision affect the relative bargaining position of plaintiffs and defendants, if at all?

3. Although the majority opinion explains "that market efficiency is a matter of degree," it did not eliminate the requirement that plaintiff show, among other things, that "the stock traded in an efficient market" in order to invoke the fraud on the market presumption of reliance. How does one prove that the market for the stock is efficient?

4. Do you need a fancy economic theory to justify the fraud on the market presumption of reliance?

5. If you rely on the "integrity" of the market price, does it follow that you think that that price is the "true value" of your shares?

6. What is the class of individuals who will recover damages in *Halliburton*, if a violation of § 10(b) and Rule 10b–5 is established? What individuals will bear the burden of those damages?

PROBLEM

Suppose that 30 percent of the shares of Tanaka Corp. are owned by the Tanaka family. The head of the family, and founder of the corporation, is Ken Tanaka, who has effective control and serves on the board (but is not an officer or otherwise employed), and has decided to sell out to Big Blue Corp. Negotiations have taken place between representatives of Big Blue and Ken Tanaka, as a result of which a tentative agreement has been reached that Big Blue will buy all of the

Tanaka family shares for $30 per share and will offer to buy all the remaining, publicly held shares for the same price. A number of nonprice terms of the agreement, including Ken Tanaka's role in the merged firm, have not yet been resolved.

The Big Blue representatives have told Ken Tanaka that they are not willing to get into a bidding war and that if news of their interest in buying is disclosed prematurely they may withdraw their offer. There have been rumors, some published in the Wall Street Journal, of the possibility of a sale, and the price of the Tanaka Corp. shares trading on the NYSE has risen over the past two weeks from $20 per share to $23 per share.

A financial reporter calls the public relations officer of Tanaka Corp., Abe Ahnust, and asks if there is any truth to the rumors and whether there is any other explanation for the rise in the price of the shares. Abe, who is fully informed about the negotiations between Ken Tanaka and representatives of Big Blue, makes the following statement: "I am aware of no corporate development that would explain the recent rise in the price of the shares." Following the issuance of this statement, the price of the Tanaka Corp. shares falls to $22 per share. (a) Has Abe, or Tanaka Corp., violated § 10(b) and rule 10b–5? (b) If your answer to the preceding question is yes, would it change if Abe had not been informed of the negotiations between Ken Tanaka and Big Blue's representatives? (c) Suppose Abe's statement was not authorized by Ken but that Ken reads it the following day in the Wall Street Journal. Does Ken have any duty to make a further announcement or tell Abe to do so?

West v. Prudential Securities, Inc.

282 F.3d 935 (7th Cir. 2002).

■ EASTERBROOK, CIRCUIT JUDGE. According to the complaint in this securities-fraud action, James Hofman, a stockbroker working for Prudential Securities, told 11 of his customers that Jefferson Savings Bancorp was "certain" to be acquired, at a big premium, in the near future. Hofman continued making this statement for seven months (repeating it to some clients); it was a lie, for no acquisition was impending. And if the statement had been the truth, then Hofman was inviting unlawful trading on the basis of material non-public information. He is a securities offender coming or going, . . . as are any customers who traded on what they thought to be confidential information if Hofman said what the plaintiffs allege, a subject still to be determined. What we must decide is whether the action may proceed, not on behalf of those who received Hofman's "news" in person but on behalf of *everyone* who bought Jefferson stock during the months when Hofman was misbehaving. The district judge certified such a class, invoking the fraud-on-the-market doctrine of Basic, Inc. v. Levinson, 485 U.S. 224, 241–49, (1988). Prudential asks us to entertain an interlocutory appeal under Fed. R. Civ. P. 23(f). For two reasons, this is an appropriate case for such an appeal, which we now accept. . . .

First, the district court's order marks a substantial extension of the fraud-on-the-market approach. *Basic* held that "because most publicly available information is reflected in market price, an investor's reliance on any public material misrepresentations, therefore, may be presumed for purposes of a Rule 10b–5 action." 485 U.S. at 247. The theme of *Basic* and other fraud-on-the-market decisions is that *public* information reaches professional investors, whose evaluations of that information and trades quickly influence securities prices. But Hofman did not release information to the public, and his clients thought that they were receiving and acting on non-public information; its value (if any) lay precisely in the fact that other traders did not know the news. No newspaper or other organ of general circulation reported that Jefferson was soon to be acquired. As plaintiffs summarize their position, their "argument in a nutshell is that it is unimportant for purposes of the fraud-on-the-market doctrine whether the information was 'publicly available' in the . . . sense that . . . the information was disseminated through a press release, or prospectus or other written format." Yet extending the fraud-on-the-market doctrine in this way requires not only a departure from *Basic* but also a novelty in fraud cases as a class. . . . [O]ral frauds have not been allowed to proceed as class actions, for the details of the deceit differ from victim to victim, and the nature of the loss also may be statement-specific. . . .

Second, very few securities class actions are litigated to conclusion, so review of this novel and important legal issue may be possible only through the Rule 23(f) device. What is more, some scholars believe that the settlements in securities cases reflect high risk of catastrophic loss, which together with imperfect alignment of managers' and investors' interests leads defendants to pay substantial sums even when the plaintiffs have weak positions. . . . The strength of this effect has been debated, . . . but its existence is established. The effect of a class certification in inducing settlement to curtail the risk of large awards provides a powerful reason to take an interlocutory appeal. . . .

Causation is the shortcoming in this class certification. . . . Professional investors monitor news about many firms; good news implies higher dividends and other benefits, which induces these investors to value the stock more highly, and they continue buying until the gains are exhausted. With many professional investors alert to news, markets are efficient in the sense that they rapidly adjust to all public information; if some of this information is false, the price will reach an incorrect level, staying there until the truth emerges. . . . [F]ew propositions in economics are better established than the quick adjustment of securities prices to public information. . . .

No similar mechanism explains how prices would respond to non-public information, such as statements made by Hofman to a handful of his clients. These do not come to the attention of professional investors or money managers, so the price-adjustment mechanism just described does not operate. Sometimes full-time market watchers can infer important news from the identity of a trader (when the corporation's CEO goes on a buying spree, this implies good news) or from the sheer volume of trades (an unprecedented buying volume may suggest that a bidder is accumulating stock in anticipation of a tender offer), but neither the identity of Hofman's customers nor the volume of their trades would have conveyed information to the market in this fashion. No one these days accepts the strongest version of the efficient capital market hypothesis, under which non-public information automatically affects prices. That version is empirically false: the public announcement of news (good and bad) has big effects on stock prices, which could not happen if prices already incorporated the effect of non-public information. Thus it is hard to see how Hofman's non-public statements could have caused changes in the price of Jefferson Savings stock. *Basic* founded the fraud-on-the-market doctrine on a causal mechanism with both theoretical and empirical power; for non-public information there is nothing comparable.

The district court did not identify any causal link between non-public information and securities prices, let alone show that the link is as strong as the one deemed sufficient . . . in *Basic*. . . . Instead the judge observed that each side has the support of a reputable financial economist (Michael J. Barclay for the plaintiffs, Charles C. Cox for the defendant) and thought the clash enough by itself to support class certification and a trial on the merits. That amounts to a delegation of judicial power to the plaintiffs, who can obtain class certification just by hiring a competent expert. A district judge may not duck hard questions by observing that each side has some support, or that considerations relevant to class certification also may affect the decision on the merits. Tough questions must be faced and squarely decided, if necessary by holding evidentiary hearings and choosing between competing perspectives. . . .

Because the record here does not demonstrate that non-public information affected the price of Jefferson Savings' stock, a remand is unnecessary. What the plaintiffs have going for them is that Jefferson's stock *did* rise in price (by about $5, or 20% of its trading price) during the months when Hofman was touting an impending acquisition, plus a model of demand-pull price increases offered by their expert. Barclay started with a model devised by another economist, in which trades themselves convey information to the market and thus affect price. . . . [This] model assumes that some trades are by informed traders and some by uninformed traders, and that the market may be able to draw inferences about which is which. The model has not been verified empirically. Barclay approached the issue differently, assuming that *all* trades affect prices by raising demand even if no trader is well informed—as if there were an economic market in "Jefferson Savings stock" as there is in dill pickles or fluffy towels. Hofman's tips raised the demand for Jefferson Savings stock and curtailed the supply (for the tippees were less likely to sell their own shares); that combination of effects raised the stock's price. Yet investors do not want Jefferson Savings *stock* (as if they sought to paper their walls with beautiful certificates); they want monetary returns (at given risk levels), returns that are available from many financial instruments. One fundamental attribute of efficient markets is that *information*, not demand in the abstract, determines stock prices. . . . There are so many substitutes for any one firm's stock that the effective demand curve is horizontal. It may shift up or down with new information but is not sloped like the demand curve for physical products. That is why institutional purchases (which can be large in relation to normal trading volume) do not elevate prices, while relatively small trades by insiders can have substantial effects; the latter trades convey information, and the former do not. . . .

Data may upset theory, and if Barclay had demonstrated that demand by itself elevates securities prices, then the courts would be required to attend closely. What Barclay did is inquire whether the price of Jefferson Savings stock rose during the period of additional demand by Hofman's customers. He gave an affirmative answer and stopped. Yet it is not possible to prove a relation between demand and price without considering *other* potential reasons. Was there perhaps some truthful Jefferson-specific information released to the market at the time? . . . By failing to test for and exclude other potential sources of price movement, Barclay undercut the power of the inference that he advanced.

Indeed, Barclay's report calls into question his belief that the market for Jefferson Savings stock is efficient, the foundation of the fraud-on-the-market doctrine. In an efficient market, how could *one* ignorant outsider's lie cause a long-term rise in price? Professional investors would notice the inexplicable rise and either investigate for themselves (discovering the truth) or sell short immediately, driving the price back down. In an efficient market, a lie told by someone with nothing to back up the statement (no professional would have thought Hofman a person "in the know") will self-destruct long before eight months have passed. Hofman asserted that an acquisition was imminent. That statement might gull people for a month, but after two or three months have passed the lack of a merger or tender offer puts the lie to the assertion; professional investors then draw more astute inferences and the price effect disappears. That this did not occur implies either that Jefferson Savings was not closely followed by professional investors (and that the market therefore does not satisfy Basic's efficiency requirement) or that something other than Hofman's statements explains these price changes.

. . . The order certifying a class is REVERSED.

ANALYSIS

The plaintiffs' expert witness claimed that the additional demand for Jefferson Savings shares created by people who believed and relied on Hofman's lies was sufficient by itself to drive up the price of those shares. Superficially, this claim would seem to represent a simple application of standard supply and demand principles. Rejecting the claim, Judge Easterbrook writes:

> Yet investors do not want Jefferson Savings *stock* (as if they sought to paper their walls with beautiful certificates); they want monetary returns (at given risk levels), returns that are available from many financial instruments. One fundamental attribute of efficient markets is that *information*, not demand in the abstract, determines stock prices. . . . There are so many substitutes for any one firm's stock that the effective demand curve is horizontal.

The demand curve at issue is the market demand for Jefferson Savings stock. When Judge Easterbrook says that the demand for Jefferson Savings stock is "horizontal" (or, perfectly elastic), he means that an increase in the price of the stock (absent public information justifying the increase) will cause investors to substitute other shares for it. With ordinary household products, an increase in price will cause demand to fall, but not to 0. Even at a higher price, some buyers will still want that particular product. According to standard finance theory, however, stock is different. Investors (more specifically, the large investors who move sufficient quantities of money to influence stock prices) do not pick a given stock because they like it. They pick it because they want to assemble a diversified portfolio of shares, and for that portfolio need stock that provides a given package of attributes (risk, expected return, and so forth). Given that any number of different shares can offer such a package of attributes, an increase in the price of stock A will simply cause those investors to switch to stock B or C.

So when will the price of a given stock change? According to standard finance principles, it will change whenever investors (again, the large investors who control enough funds to affect prices) acquire new information about the stock. For example, if those investors change their estimate of the returns they can expect to earn from the stock (estimates based on the expected cash flows at the firm), they will change the price they are willing to pay for it. Recall, in this regard, that these large investors also have access to the very best securities analysts. These investors will not learn new information from the purchases or sales of a few misled investors. As a result, reasons Judge Easterbrook, if the people who believed Hofman's lies were to bid up the price of Jefferson Savings shares, the more sophisticated investors would simply sell. In the process, they would drive the price back down to where it was without the effect of the gullible, misinformed buyers.

Within the finance community, there is an on-going debate as to whether the demand curve for corporate securities is indeed horizontal, with respectable recent studies indicating that it is not. Resolving the debate is outside the scope of any law school class in corporate law, but Judge Easterbrook's opinion raises some important questions. When should a judge rely on finance principles? Should he or she avoid such reliance whenever a debate exists within the academic community? Should Judge Easterbrook have let the case go to trial, and let the jury decide the question? On issues of corporate finance, when should judges throw the question to the jury? What in this case induced Judge Easterbrook to dismiss it without a trial?

NOTE ON JUDICIAL LIMITATIONS ON ACTIONS UNDER RULE 10b–5

Standing: In Blue Chip Stamps v. Manor Drug Stores, 421 U.S. 723 (1975), the Court put some bite in the rule that the protections of Rule 10b–5 extend only to purchasers and sellers of a corporation's securities. In that case the defendant corporation had been required by an antitrust action to offer its common stock to some of its customers, including the plaintiff. The plaintiff claimed that it had been misled by the defendant's prospectus, which the plaintiff argued was unduly pessimistic. Because it relied on that prospectus, explained the plaintiff, it had not exercised its right to buy shares on which it would have made a profit. The Court held that the plaintiff had no cause of action under Rule 10b–5 because it had neither bought nor sold shares.

Scienter: In Ernst & Ernst v. Hochfelder, 425 U.S. 185 (1976), the Court held that liability for issuance of a false or misleading statement required proof of a state of mind referred to as "scienter"; that is, the person making the false statement must have made it with an "intent to deceive, manipulate, or defraud." The Court reserved judgment on the question whether recklessness would be sufficient, but later decisions have answered that question affirmatively.

Secondary Liability and Scope of Interpretation: Until quite recently, Rule 10b–5 was regarded as an example of interstitial lawmaking in which the courts used common-law adjudicatory methods to flesh out the text's bare bones. In Central Bank of Denver v. First Interstate Bank, 511 U.S. 164 (1994), however, the Supreme Court held that there was no implied private right of action against those who aid and abet violations of Rule 10b–5. *Central Bank* thus substantially limited the scope of secondary liability under the rule, at least insofar as private party causes of action are concerned. For our purposes, however, the case is more significant for its methodology than its holding. The court held that the scope of conduct prohibited by § 10(b) (and thus Rule 10b–5) is controlled by the text of the statute. Where the plain text does not resolve some aspect of the Rule 10b–5 cause of action, courts must "infer 'how the 1934 Congress would have addressed the issue had the 10b–5 action been included as an express provision of the 1934 Act.' " Id. at 178 (quoting Musick, Peeler & Garrett v. Employers Ins., 508 U.S. 286, 294 (1993)). The court admits this is an "awkward task." Lampf, Pleva, Lipkind, Prupis & Petigrow v. Gilbertson, 501 U.S. 350, 357 (1991). Justice Scalia put it more colorfully: "We are imagining here." Id. at 360. *Central Bank* constrained this imaginative process by requiring courts to "use the express causes of action in the securities acts as the primary model for the § 10(b) action." *Central Bank*, 511 U.S. at 178.

Santa Fe Industries, Inc. v. Green

430 U.S. 462, 97 S.Ct. 1292, 51 L.Ed.2d 480 (1977).

. . .

I

In 1936, petitioner Santa Fe Industries, Inc. (Santa Fe), acquired control of 60% of the stock of Kirby Lumber Corp. (Kirby), a Delaware corporation. Through a series of purchases over the succeeding years, Santa Fe increased its control of Kirby's stock to 95%; the purchase prices during the period 1968–1973 ranged from $65 to $92.50 per share. In 1974, wishing to acquire 100% ownership of Kirby, Santa Fe availed itself of § 253 of the Delaware Corporation Law, known as the "short-form merger" statute. Section 253 permits a parent corporation owning at least 90% of the stock of a subsidiary to merge with that subsidiary, upon approval by the parent's board of directors, and to make payment in cash for the shares of the minority stockholders. The statute does not require the consent of, or advance notice to, the minority stockholders. However, notice of the merger must be given within 10 days after its effective date, and any stockholder who is dissatisfied with the terms of the merger may petition the Delaware Court of Chancery for a decree ordering the surviving corporation to pay him the fair value of his shares, as determined by a court-appointed appraiser subject to review by the court. . . .

Santa Fe obtained independent appraisals of the physical assets of Kirby—land, timber, buildings, and machinery—and of Kirby's oil, gas, and mineral interests. These appraisals, together with other financial information, were submitted to Morgan Stanley & Co. (Morgan Stanley), an investment banking firm retained to appraise the fair market value of Kirby stock. Kirby's physical assets were appraised at $320 million (amounting to $640 for each of the 500,000 shares); Kirby's stock was valued by Morgan Stanley at $125 per share. Under the terms of the merger, minority stockholders were offered $150 per share.

The provisions of the short-form merger statute were fully complied with. The minority stockholders of Kirby were notified the day after the merger became effective and were advised of their right to obtain an appraisal in Delaware court if dissatisfied with the offer of $150 per share. They also received an information statement containing, in addition to the relevant financial data about Kirby, the appraisals of the value of Kirby's assets and the Morgan Stanley appraisal concluding that the fair market value of the stock was $125 per share.

Respondents, minority stockholders of Kirby, objected to the terms of the merger, but did not pursue their appraisal remedy in the Delaware Court of Chancery. Instead, they brought this action in federal court on behalf of the corporation and other minority stockholders, seeking to set aside the merger or to recover what they claimed to be the fair value of their shares. The amended complaint asserted that, based on the fair market value of Kirby's physical assets as revealed by the appraisal included in the information statement sent to minority shareholders, Kirby's stock was worth at least $772 per share. The complaint alleged further that the merger took place without prior notice to minority stockholders; that the purpose of the merger was to appropriate the difference between the "conceded pro rata value of the physical assets," App. 103a, and the offer of $150 per share—to "freez[e] out the minority stockholders at a wholly inadequate price," id., at 100a; and that Santa Fe, knowing the appraised value of the physical assets, obtained a "fraudulent appraisal" of the stock from Morgan Stanley and offered $25 above that appraisal "in order to lull the minority stockholders into erroneously believing that [Santa Fe was] generous." Id., at 103a. This course of conduct was alleged to be "a violation of Rule 10b–5 because defendants employed a 'device, scheme, or artifice to defraud' and engaged in an 'act, practice or course of business which operates or would operate as a fraud or deceit upon any person, in connection with the purchase or sale of any security.' " Ibid. . . .

The District Court dismissed the complaint for failure to state a claim upon which relief could be granted. As the District Court understood the complaint, respondents' case rested on two distinct grounds. First, federal law was assertedly violated because the merger was for the sole purpose of eliminating the minority from the company, therefore lacking any justifiable business purpose, and because the merger was undertaken without prior notice to the minority shareholders. Second, the low valuation placed on the shares in the cash-exchange offer was itself said to be a fraud actionable under Rule 10b–5. In rejecting the first ground for recovery, the District Court reasoned that Delaware law required neither a business purpose for a short-form merger nor prior notice to the minority shareholders who the statute contemplated would be removed from the company, and that Rule 10b–5 did not override these provisions of state corporate law by independently placing a duty on the majority not to merge without prior notice and without a justifiable business purpose.

As for the claim that actionable fraud inhered in the allegedly gross undervaluation of the minority shares, the District Court . . . thought that if "full and fair disclosure is made, transactions eliminating minority interests are beyond the purview of Rule 10b–5," and concluded that the "complaint fail[ed] to allege an omission, misstatement or fraudulent course of conduct that would have impeded a shareholder's judgment of the value of the offer." [391 F. Supp. 849, 854 (S.D.N.Y.1975).] The complaint therefore failed to state a claim and was dismissed.

A divided Court of Appeals for the Second Circuit reversed. . . . As to the first aspect of the case, the Court of Appeals did not disturb the District Court's conclusion that the complaint did not allege a material misrepresentation or nondisclosure with respect to the value of the stock; and the court declined to rule that a claim of gross undervaluation itself would suffice to make out a rule 10b–5 case. With respect to the second aspect of the case, however, the court fundamentally disagreed with the District Court as to the reach and coverage of rule 10b–5. The Court of Appeals' view was that, although the rule plainly reached material misrepresentations and nondisclosures in connection with the purchase or sale of securities, neither misrepresentation nor nondisclosure was a necessary element of a rule 10b–5 action; the rule reached "breaches of fiduciary duty by a majority against minority shareholders without any charge of misrepresentation or lack of disclosure." [533 F.2d 1283, 1287 (2d Cir.1976).] . . .

II

Section 10(b) of the 1934 Act makes it "unlawful for any person . . . to use or employ . . . any manipulative or deceptive device or contrivance in contravention of [SEC rules]"; rule 10b–5, promulgated by the SEC under § 10(b), prohibits, in addition to nondisclosure and misrepresentation, any "artifice to defraud" or any act "which operates or would operate as a fraud or deceit." . . .

[Ernst & Ernst v. Hochfelder, 425 U.S. 185 (1976)] makes clear that in deciding whether a complaint states a cause of action for "fraud" under rule 10b–5, "we turn first to the language of § 10(b), for '[t]he starting point in every case involving construction of a statute is the language itself.'" Id., at 197, quoting Blue Chip Stamps v. Manor Drug Stores, 421 U.S. 723, 756 (1975) (Powell, J., concurring). . . .

The language of § 10(b) gives no indication that Congress meant to prohibit any conduct not involving manipulation or deception. Nor have we been cited to any evidence in the legislative history that would support a departure from the language of the statute. "When a statute speaks so specifically in terms of manipulation and deception, . . . and when its history reflects no more expansive intent, we are quite unwilling to extend the scope of the statute. . . ." Id., at 214. Thus the claim of fraud and fiduciary breach in this complaint states a cause of action under any part of rule 10b–5 only if the conduct alleged can be fairly viewed as "manipulative or deceptive" within the meaning of the statute.

III

It is our judgment that the transaction, if carried out as alleged in the complaint, was neither deceptive nor manipulative and therefore did not violate either § 10(b) of the Act or rule 10b–5.

As we have indicated, the case comes to us on the premise that the complaint failed to allege a material misrepresentation or material failure to disclose. The finding of the District Court, undisturbed by the

Court of Appeals, was that there was no "omission" or "misstatement" in the information statement accompanying the notice of merger. On the basis of the information provided, minority shareholders could either accept the price offered or reject it and seek an appraisal in the Delaware Court of Chancery. Their choice was fairly presented, and they were furnished with all relevant information on which to base their decision.

We therefore find inapposite the cases relied upon by respondents and the court below, in which the breaches of fiduciary duty held violative of rule 10b–5 included some element of deception. Those cases forcefully reflect the principle that "[§] 10(b) must be read flexibly, not technically and restrictively" and that the statute provides a cause of action for any plaintiff who "suffer[s] an injury as a result of deceptive practices touching its sale [or purchase] of securities. . . ." Superintendent of Insurance v. Bankers Life & Cas. Co., 404 U.S. 6, 12–13 (1971). But the cases do not support the proposition, adopted by the Court of Appeals below and urged by respondents here, that a breach of fiduciary duty by majority stockholders, without any deception, misrepresentation, or nondisclosure, violates the statute and the rule.

It is also readily apparent that the conduct alleged in the complaint was not "manipulative" within the meaning of the statute. "Manipulation" is "virtually a term of art when used in connection with securities markets." *Ernst & Ernst,* 425 U.S., at 199. The term refers generally to practices, such as wash sales, matched orders, or rigged prices, that are intended to mislead investors by artificially affecting market activity. . . . Section 10(b)'s general prohibition of practices deemed by the SEC to be "manipulative"—in this technical sense of artificially affecting market activity in order to mislead investors—is fully consistent with the fundamental purpose of the 1934 Act " 'to substitute a philosophy of full disclosure for the philosophy of *caveat emptor*. . . .' " Affiliated Ute Citizens v. United States, 406 U.S. 128, 151 (1972), quoting SEC v. Capital Gains Research Bureau, 375 U.S. 180, 186 (1963). Indeed, nondisclosure is usually essential to the success of a manipulative scheme. No doubt Congress meant to prohibit the full range of ingenious devices that might be used to manipulate securities prices. But we do not think it would have chosen this "term of art" if it had meant to bring within the scope of § 10(b) instances of corporate mismanagement such as this, in which the essence of the complaint is that shareholders were treated unfairly by a fiduciary.

IV

The language of the statute is, we think, "sufficiently clear in its context" to be dispositive here, *Ernst & Ernst,* supra, at 201; but even if it were not, there are additional considerations that weigh heavily against permitting a cause of action under rule 10b–5 for the breach of corporate fiduciary duty alleged in this complaint. Congress did not expressly provide a private cause of action for violations of § 10(b). Although we have recognized an implied cause of action under that section in some circumstances, . . . we have also recognized that a private cause of action under the antifraud provisions of the Securities Exchange Act should not be implied where it is "unnecessary to ensure the fulfillment of Congress' purposes" in adopting the Act. Piper v. Chris-Craft Industries, [430 U.S. 1, 41 (1977)]. . . . As we noted earlier, the Court repeatedly has described the "fundamental purpose" of the Act as implementing a "philosophy of full disclosure"; once full and fair disclosure has occurred, the fairness of the terms of the transaction is at most a tangential concern of the statute. . . . As in Cort v. Ash, 422 U.S. 66, 80 (1975), we are reluctant to recognize a cause of action here to serve what is "at best a subsidiary purpose" of the federal legislation.

A second factor in determining whether Congress intended to create a federal cause of action in these circumstances is "whether 'the cause of action [is] one traditionally relegated to state law. . . .' " Piper v. Chris-Craft Industries, Inc., ante, at 40, quoting Cort v. Ash, supra, at 78. The Delaware Legislature has supplied minority shareholders with a cause of action in the Delaware Court of Chancery to recover the fair value of shares allegedly undervalued in a short-form merger. . . . Of course, the existence of a particular state-law remedy is not dispositive of the question whether Congress meant to provide a similar federal remedy, but as in *Cort* and *Piper,* we conclude that "it is entirely appropriate in this instance to relegate respondent and others in his situation to whatever remedy is created by state law." 422 U.S., at 84; ante, at 41.

The reasoning behind a holding that the complaint in this case alleged fraud under rule 10b–5 could not be easily contained. It is difficult to imagine how a court could distinguish, for purposes of rule 10b–5 fraud, between a majority stockholder's use of a short-form merger to eliminate the minority at an unfair price and the use of some other device, such as a long-form merger, tender offer, or liquidation, to achieve the same result; or indeed how a court could distinguish the alleged abuses in these going private transactions from other types of fiduciary self-dealing involving transactions in securities. The result would be to bring within the rule a wide variety of corporate conduct traditionally left to state regulation. In addition to posing a "danger of vexatious litigation which could result from a widely expanded class of plaintiffs under rule 10b–5," Blue Chip Stamps v. Manor Drug Stores, [421 U.S. 723, 740 (1975)], this extension of the federal securities laws would overlap and quite possibly interfere with state corporate law. Federal courts applying a "federal fiduciary principle" under rule 10b–5 could be expected to depart from state fiduciary standards at least to the extent necessary to ensure uniformity within the federal system. Absent a clear indication of congressional intent, we are reluctant to federalize the substantial portion of the law of corporations that deals with transactions in securities, particularly where established state policies of corporate regulation would be overridden. As the Court stated in *Cort v. Ash,* supra: "Corporations are creatures of state law, and investors commit their funds to corporate directors on the understanding that, except where federal law *expressly* requires certain responsibilities of directors with respect to stockholders, state law will govern the internal affairs of the corporation." 422 U.S., at 84 (emphasis added).

We thus adhere to the position that "Congress by § 10(b) did not seek to regulate transactions which constitute no more than internal corporate mismanagement." Superintendent of Insurance v. Bankers Life & Cas. Co., 404 U.S., at 12. There may well be a need for uniform federal fiduciary standards to govern mergers such as that challenged in this complaint. But those standards should not be supplied by judicial extension of § 10(b) and rule 10b–5 to "cover the corporate universe."

The judgment of the Court of Appeals is reversed, and the case is remanded for further proceedings consistent with this opinion.

NOTE

The holders of about 5,000 shares of Kirby Lumber dissented from the merger and demanded appraisal. After litigation, it was determined that they were entitled to $254.40 per share, representing the value of the corporation as a going concern. See Bell v. Kirby Lumber Corp., 413 A.2d 137 (Del.1980). In upholding this appraisal amount, the Delaware Supreme Court observed that, based on one appraisal, Santa Fe "could have liquidated Kirby and realized $670 per share for each stockholder." The court concluded, however, that since Santa Fe, as 95 percent owner, "had the power [right?] to do with Kirby what it chose," the liquidation value was essentially irrelevant.

ANALYSIS

1. Many states have short-form merger statutes similar to the one used in *Santa Fe.* Suppose that the Supreme Court had affirmed the Court of Appeals. What would have been the practical effect on these statutes?

2. Suppose that the defendants in *Santa Fe* had used the short-form merger, but had issued a misleading notice to the minority shareholders in connection with the merger. What would the Court have likely held?

Deutschman v. Beneficial Corp.

841 F.2d 502 (3d Cir. 1988), cert. den'd, 490 U.S. 1114 (1989).

Robert M. Deutschman appeals from a Fed.R.Civ.P. 12(b)(6) dismissal of his amended class action complaint against Beneficial Corporation (Beneficial), Finn M.W. Caspersen, Beneficial's Chairman and Chief Executive Officer, and Andrew C. Halvorsen, its Chief Financial Officer. The . . . complaint alleges that the defendants violated § 10(b) . . . of the Securities Exchange Act of 1934. . . .

. . . Deutschman alleges that in 1986 and part of 1987 Beneficial's insurance division suffered severe losses which had an adverse impact on Beneficial's financial condition; that Caspersen and Halvorsen held stock and stock options in Beneficial which would be adversely affected by a decline in the market price of that stock; that disclosures were made about the losses in Beneficial's insurance division which caused declines in that market price; that in order to prevent further declines Caspersen and Halvorsen, on Beneficial's behalf, issued statements about the problems in the insurance division, which they knew to be false and misleading, to the effect that those problems were behind it and were covered by sufficient reserves; that these misleading statements placed an artificial floor under the market price of Beneficial stock; that purchasers of Beneficial stock and purchasers of call options in Beneficial stock made purchases at prices which were artificially inflated by the market's reliance on defendants' misstatements, and that both purchasers of Beneficial stock and purchasers of Beneficial call options suffered losses as a consequence. Beneficial stock is traded on the New

York Stock Exchange and on other national stock exchanges. Options on Beneficial stock are traded on the Pacific Stock Exchange. The complaint does not allege that Beneficial, Caspersen, or Halvorsen, during the time period complained of, traded in Beneficial stock or in put or call options on Beneficial stock. It alleges that Deutschman suffered losses when, upon disclosure of the facts, call options on Beneficial's stock that he had purchased in reliance on the market price created by defendants' misstatements, became worthless. It does not allege that Deutschman purchased Beneficial stock.

The district court held that option traders who suffered losses as a result of intentional misstatements by the management of a corporation, the stock of which is the subject of those options, lack standing to assert a cause of action for damages under § 10(b) of the 1934 Act and rule 10b–5 of the Securities and Exchange Commission. The court reasoned that in the absence of an allegation that Deutschman bought or sold Beneficial stock, or of an allegation that the defendants bought or sold options, there was no duty owed to him to refrain even from affirmative misstatements which would affect the market price of Beneficial stock.

Put and call options have been a feature of the national financial markets since 1790. Under these contracts a seller agrees to sell or a purchaser agrees to buy a security at a fixed price on or before a fixed date in the future. Such contracts permit investors to hedge against future movements in the market price of securities. Prior to the early 1970s the utility of put and call options was limited because of high transaction costs, and because of the absence of a secondary market for the option contracts. In 1973, the Chicago Board Options Exchange became the first registered exchange for trading in option contracts. Within a short time that exchange had been joined by the American, Philadelphia, Pacific, and Midwest exchanges. By 1985, those exchanges were trading options on over 400 stocks, and the volume of contracts traded exceeded 118.6 million. . . .

The option contract gives its owner the right to buy (call) or sell (put) a fixed number of shares of a specified underlying stock at a given price (the striking price) on or before the expiration date of the contract. For this option a premium is paid, and the contract is worth more or less than the premium depending upon the direction of the market price of the underlying stock relative to the striking price. The market price for options is directly responsive, therefore, to changes in the market price of the underlying stock, and to information affecting that price. . . .

Because the market value of an option contract is responsive to changes in the market price of the underlying stock, holders of option contracts are susceptible to two separate types of deceptive practices: insider trading and affirmative misrepresentation. Insiders trading on undisclosed material information can injure option holders either by market activity which causes the price of the underlying stock to move, or by market activity directly in the options market. Insiders or others who do not trade in either market can injure option holders by misstating material facts to the public, thereby causing a distortion in the market price of the underlying security, and in the necessarily related market price of the option contract. Only the second type of harm is pleaded by Deutschman: affirmative misrepresentation by corporate managers having the effect of artificially supporting the market price of the underlying stock, and concomitantly the market price of the option contract for that stock.

Section 10(b) prohibits the use "in connection with the purchase or sale of any security . . . [of] any manipulative or deceptive device or contrivance in contravention of such rules and regulations as the [SEC] may prescribe." . . . The defendants do not deny that the affirmative misrepresentations pleaded by Deutschman would, if proved, amount to untrue statements of material fact which would operate to deceive a purchaser of Beneficial stock. The complaint alleges that the misrepresentations were made intentionally or with reckless disregard of the truth. It, therefore, satisfies the § 10(b) scienter requirement. . . . Thus defendants do not dispute that even though they did not trade in Beneficial stock they could, if Deutschman's allegations are proved, be held liable in a suit by a purchaser of such stock. . . . Finally, defendants do not dispute that Deutschman is a purchaser of a security. Congress placed that question beyond debate when . . . it amended the Securities and Exchange Act of 1934 and other federal statutes so as explicitly to include option contracts. . . .

The only standing limitation recognized by the Supreme Court with respect to § 10(b) damage actions is the requirement that the plaintiff be a purchaser or seller of a security. See Blue Chip Stamps v. Manor Drug Stores, 421 U.S. 723, 95 S.Ct. 1917, 44 L.Ed.2d 539 (1975); Birnbaum v. Newport Steel Corp., 193 F.2d 461 (2d Cir.), cert. denied, 343 U.S. 956, 72 S.Ct. 1051, 96 L.Ed. 1356 (1952). When in *Manor Drug Stores* the Supreme Court adopted the *Birnbaum* requirement that a § 10(b) plaintiff be a purchaser or seller of a security, however, it expressly recognized that such plaintiffs need not be in any relationship of privity with the defendant charged with misrepresentation. The underlying purpose of the 1934 Act was the protection of actual participants in the securities markets, and the *Birnbaum* rule was consistent with that purpose because it limited "the class of plaintiffs to those who have at least dealt in the security to which the prospectus, representation, or omission relates."

Deutschman's complaint appears, therefore, to satisfy every requirement for a § 10(b) damage action imposed by the Supreme Court when dealing with affirmative misrepresentations which may affect the market price of a security. . . .

Another policy argument advanced by the defendants is that although purchasers of option contracts do purchase securities they are entitled to less protection under the 1934 Act because option trading, like blackjack or craps, is "gambling." By characterizing option traders as "gamblers" the defendants hope that we will draw the conclusion that they are fair game for affirmative misrepresentation, while stock traders are not. We are not persuaded that the difference between trading in the two types of securities should lead to different treatment. Since the price of option contracts is closely dependent upon the price of the underlying stocks, the degree of risk involved in trading in one over the other is not self-evidently greater. The time element of a put or call option does increase exposure to price movements, but the ability to buy or sell such options in the interim does not. Moreover, the availability of option contracts permits traders in common stocks to engage in hedging transactions, which are often used as a means of reducing exposure to market fluctuations and are thus risk reducing. This method of risk reduction, formerly available only through put and call options in an over-the-counter market, has since 1973 been available at lower cost. Finally, it is not our role as a court to pass judgment on the soundness of the legislative policy judgments which led to the creation of exchanges for option contracts, and their treatment as securities. Congress, the Securities and Exchange Commission, the Board of Governors of the Federal Reserve System, and the Commodity Futures Trading Commission all have had a role in the evolution of the market for these securities, and the policy judgment was their responsibility, not ours.

We hold that Deutschman has standing as a purchaser of an option contract to seek damages under § 10(b) for the affirmative misrepresentations he alleges were made by the defendants, Beneficial, Caspersen, and Halvorsen. The judgment dismissing Deutschman's § 10(b) claim must therefore be reversed. . . .

PROBLEMS

1. Monarch Mining Corporation is a publicly held corporation in the business of exploring for, developing, and mining various ores. At a quarterly meeting of its board of directors, the CEO announces that she has received good reports about a major exploration project. The reports are preliminary, however. It may turn out that the project will turn into a major discovery, but it is still possible that it will turn out to be worthless. The present price of a share of Monarch's common stock is $69. The board members are aware that certain publicly traded call options on some of its shares have an exercise price of $72 per share and will expire in three days. It is reasonable to suppose that if the good news is released, the price of the shares will rise to $75. The CEO proposes that the news not be released, because her experience leads her to believe that shareholders and analysts become disgruntled when favorable prospects are reported and it later turns out that the prospects come to nothing. If the board decides to hold off on the release of the news, is there any liability under § 10(b) and rule 10b–5 or under common-law rules of fiduciary obligation? What if there is no basis for concern about adverse reaction to favorable announcements that do not pan out?

2. Cashrich Corporation is a publicly held corporation that recently sold one of its divisions and is holding the cash from the sale. Cashrich has no debts. Its common shares are currently selling for $69 per share. Certain options on some of the shares have an exercise price of $70 and will expire in two months. At the quarterly board meeting the CEO presents two alternatives for use of the cash on hand. Alternative A is to use it to pay a dividend of $20 per share one month hence. It is reasonable to suppose that after payment of the dividend, the price of the shares will fall by $20 per share. Alternative B is to invest the cash in a project that the staff has studied. This is a risky project and it is unclear how investors might react to it. The best guess of the more sophisticated members of the board is that there is a 50 percent chance that the Cashrich shares will rise to $73 and a 50 percent chance that they will fall to $65. If the directors decide to adopt Alternative A (payment of a dividend), might they be liable to the option holders?

5. INSIDE INFORMATION

Goodwin v. Agassiz

283 Mass. 358, 186 N.E. 659 (1933).

A stockholder in a corporation seeks in this suit relief for losses suffered by him in selling shares of stock in Cliff Mining Company by way of accounting, rescission of sales, or redelivery of shares. The named defendants are MacNaughton, a resident of Michigan not served or appearing, and Agassiz, a resident of this commonwealth, the active party defendant. . . .

. . . The defendants, in May, 1926, purchased through brokers on the Boston stock exchange seven hundred shares of stock of the Cliff Mining Company which up to that time the plaintiff had owned. Agassiz was president and director and MacNaughton a director and general manager of the company. They had certain knowledge, material as to the value of the stock, which the plaintiff did not have. The plaintiff contends that such purchase in all the circumstances without disclosure to him of that knowledge was a wrong against him. That knowledge was that an experienced geologist had formulated in writing in March, 1926, a theory as to the possible existence of copper deposits under conditions prevailing in the region where the property of the company was located. That region was known as the mineral belt in Northern Michigan, where are located mines of several copper mining companies. Another such company, of which the defendants were officers, had made extensive geological surveys of its lands. In consequence of recommendations resulting from that survey, exploration was started on property of the Cliff Mining Company in 1925. That exploration was ended in May, 1926, because completed unsuccessfully, and the equipment was removed. The defendants discussed the geologist's theory shortly after it was formulated. Both felt that the theory had value and should be tested, but they agreed that, before starting to test it, options should be obtained by another copper company of which they were officers on land adjacent to or nearby in the copper belt, that if the geologist's theory were known to the owners of such other land there might be difficulty in securing options, and that that theory should not be communicated to any one unless it became absolutely necessary. Thereafter, options were secured which, if taken up, would involve a large expenditure by the other company. The defendants both thought, also that, if there was any merit in the geologist's theory, the price of Cliff Mining Company stock in the market would go up. Its stock was quoted and bought and sold on the Boston Stock Exchange. Pursuant to agreement, they bought many shares of that stock through agents on joint account. The plaintiff first learned of the closing of exploratory operations on property of the Cliff Mining Company from an article in a paper on May 15, 1926, and immediately sold his shares of stock through brokers. It does not appear that the defendants were in any way responsible for the publication of that article. The plaintiff did not know that the purchase was made for the defendants and they did not know that his stock was being bought for them. There was no communication between them touching the subject. The plaintiff would not have sold his stock if he had known of the geologist's theory. The finding is express that the defendants were not guilty of fraud, that they committed no breach of duty owed by them to the Cliff Mining Company, and that that company was not harmed by the nondisclosure of the geologist's theory, or by their purchases of its stock, or by shutting down the exploratory operations.

The contention of the plaintiff is that the purchase of his stock in the company by the defendants without disclosing to him as a stockholder their knowledge of the geologist's theory, their belief that the theory was true, . . ., the keeping secret the existence of the theory, discontinuance by the defendants of exploratory operations begun in 1925 on property of the Cliff Mining Company and their plan ultimately to test the value of the theory, constitute actionable wrong for which he as stockholder can recover. . . .

The directors of a commercial corporation stand in a relation of trust to the corporation and are bound to exercise the strictest good faith in respect to its property and business. . . . The contention that directors also occupy the position of trustee toward individual stockholders in the corporation is plainly contrary to repeated decisions of this court and cannot be supported. . . .

The principle thus established is supported by an imposing weight of authority in other jurisdictions. . . .

While the general principle is as stated, circumstances may exist requiring that transactions between a director and a stockholder as to stock in the corporation be set aside. The knowledge naturally in the possession of a director as to the condition of a corporation places upon him a peculiar obligation to observe every requirement of fair dealing when directly buying or selling its stock. Mere silence does not usually amount to a breach of duty, but parties may stand in such relation to each other that an equitable responsibility arises to communicate facts. . . . Purchases and sales of stock dealt in on the stock exchange are commonly impersonal affairs. An honest director would be in a difficult situation if he could neither buy nor sell on the stock exchange shares of stock in his corporation without first seeking out the other actual ultimate party to the transaction and disclosing to him everything which a court or jury might later find that he then knew affecting the real or speculative value of such shares. Business of that nature is a matter to be governed by practical rules. Fiduciary obligations of directors ought not to be made so onerous that men of experience and ability will be deterred from accepting such office. Law in its sanctions is not coextensive with morality. It cannot undertake to put all parties to every contract on an equality as to knowledge, experience, skill and shrewdness. It cannot undertake to relieve against hard bargains made between competent parties without fraud. On the other hand, directors cannot rightly be allowed to indulge with impunity in practices which do violence to prevailing standards of upright business men. Therefore, where a director personally seeks a stockholder for the purpose of buying his shares without making disclosure of material facts within his peculiar knowledge and not within reach of the stockholder, the transaction will be closely scrutinized and relief may be granted in appropriate instances. . . .

The precise question to be decided in the case at bar is whether on the facts found the defendants as directors had a right to buy stock of the plaintiff, a stockholder. Every element of actual fraud or misdoing by the defendants is negatived by the findings. Fraud cannot be presumed; it must be proved. . . . The facts found afford no ground for inferring fraud or conspiracy. The only knowledge possessed by the defendants not open to the plaintiff was the existence of a theory formulated in a thesis by a geologist as to the possible existence of copper deposits where certain geological conditions existed common to the property of the Cliff Mining Company and that of other mining companies in its neighborhood. This thesis did not express an opinion that copper deposits would be found at any particular spot or on property of any specified owner. Whether that theory was sound or fallacious, no one knew, and so far as appears has never been demonstrated. The defendants made no representations to anybody about the theory. No facts found placed upon them any obligation to disclose the theory. A few days after the thesis expounding the theory was brought to the attention of the defendants, the annual report by the directors of the Cliff Mining Company for the calendar year 1925, signed by Agassiz for the directors, was issued. It did not cover the time when the theory was formulated. The report described the status of the operations under the exploration which had been begun in 1925. At the annual meeting of the stockholders of the company held early in April, 1926, no reference was made to the theory. It was then at most a hope, possibly an expectation. It had not passed the nebulous stage. No disclosure was made of it. The Cliff Mining Company was not harmed by the nondisclosure. There would have been no advantage to it, so far as appears, from a disclosure. The disclosure would have been detrimental to the interests of another mining corporation in which the defendants were directors. In the circumstances there was no duty on the part of the defendants to set forth to the stockholders at the annual meeting their faith, aspirations and plans for the future. Events as they developed might render advisable radical changes in such views. Disclosure of the theory, if it ultimately was proved to be erroneous or without foundation in fact, might involve the defendants in litigation with those who might act on the hypothesis that it was correct. The stock of the Cliff Mining Company was bought and sold on the stock exchange. The identity of buyers and seller of the stock in question in fact was not known to the parties and perhaps could not readily have been ascertained. The defendants caused the shares to be bought through brokers on the stock exchange. They said nothing to anybody as to the reasons actuating them. The plaintiff was no novice. He was a member of the Boston Stock Exchange and had kept a record of sales of Cliff Mining Company stock. He acted upon his own judgment in selling his stock. He made no inquiries of the defendants or of other officers of the company. The result is that the plaintiff cannot prevail.

PROBLEMS

1. Martha, a successful lawyer in Boston, inherited a tract of ranch land in Oklahoma several years ago. She leased out the land through a local Oklahoma real estate agent, Rose, who found the lessee, took care of all the details, and sent checks to Martha for the net amount after deducting her commission and expenses. A month ago Martha was in Oklahoma on business and drove to the town nearest to the ranch. She made some inquiries that caused her to think there might be oil on the land, whereupon she hired a geologist to advise her. The geologist was optimistic about finding oil. Martha also spoke briefly with Rose and Rose

mentioned in passing that Martha's distant cousin, George, whom Martha had not seen for twenty years, had inherited the adjacent ranch and had been leasing it through Rose. Rose also told Martha that George was a stock broker in San Francisco.

Martha then returned to Boston and called George. After some friendly conversation about their family ties, Martha steered the conversation to their ranches and offered to buy George's ranch for a price reflecting its value as ranch land with little prospect of producing oil. George accepted the offer. Before doing so, he called Rose and was told that the price offered by Martha was a fair price for ranch land. Rose was unaware that Martha had inspected the land and was unaware of any of the information that led Martha to hire the geologist. Shortly after she bought George's land, Martha sold the land to a Texas oil speculator for a price that gave her a substantial profit on the land that she had just bought. (a) Is George legally entitled to recover this profit from Martha? (b) Should he be? (c) Suppose that when Martha called him, George had asked, "Do you know anything about the land, such as evidence that there might be oil under it, that might give it value beyond its value simply as ranch land?" Martha had responded, "How would I know anything more than what you know?"—which George, not knowing of Martha's trip to Oklahoma, took to mean "No."

Suppose that Rose had hired the geologist and, after receiving the report suggesting that there was oil under George's ranch, bought George's ranch from him without revealing to him this information. Would George be legally entitled to recover from Rose any profit she made on the sale of the ranch?

2. Juan and Betty were partners in a cattle ranch in Oklahoma. The land on which the ranch was operated was owned as partnership property. It is located in an area in which there has never been any significant discovery of oil. One night in a bar Juan met a young geologist who had some new theories about how oil is deposited and had convincing evidence of a high probability of finding oil under the Juan/Betty ranch. Juan, knowing that Betty wanted to retire from cattle ranching and go to law school, offered to buy her out. He did not tell her what he knew about the possibility of finding oil under the land. Betty accepted Juan's offer. Shortly thereafter Juan sold the ranch to a Texas oil speculator for a handsome profit. Is Betty legally entitled to recover this profit from Juan?

3. Eve is a shareholder in Maximine Corp., a mining company with claims in Wyoming. Maximine Corp. shares are traded on the New York Stock Exchange. While traveling in Wyoming on vacation, Eve overheard a conversation in a bar between two of Maximine Corp.'s geologists and concluded that the corporation's crews had discovered a valuable ore deposit. She spent more time hanging around, listening, and asking questions, and confirmed her conclusion. She then approached Bob, an acquaintance back home in Chicago who, she knew, owned shares of Maximine Corp. stock. She bought Bob's shares without telling him what she knew about the ore discovery. Shortly thereafter the information about the ore discovery was disclosed in a press release by Maximine Corp. and Eve sold the shares she bought from Bob at a substantial profit. (a) Is Bob legally entitled to recover the profit from Eve? (b) Should he be?

4. The facts about Maximine Corp. are the same as in the preceding paragraph. Carlos is the CEO of Maximine Corp. and learned of the ore discovery because of his position in the firm.

(a) Carlos called his broker and told the broker to buy 1,000 shares of Maximine Corp. stock for him at the market price of $10 per share. A week later the news of the ore discovery was released and the price of the shares started to rise. Two weeks later Carlos sold the 1,000 shares at $18 per share. At common law, has Carlos incurred any legal liability?

(b) Suppose the shares of Maximine Corp. are not publicly traded. There are 50 shareholders and only two or three purchases and sales each year. Carlos knew that Wilma, the widow of a former executive of the company, owned 1,000 shares of stock of Maximine Corp. and that she needed money. He went to her home, asked how she was doing, and offered to buy her shares for $10 per share. Based on her knowledge of a few previous sales and of the earnings and dividends of Maximine Corp., Wilma decided that this was a fair price and accepted the offer. A week later the news of the ore discovery was published. Does Wilma have a common-law cause of action against Carlos?

Securities and Exchange Commission v. Texas Gulf Sulphur Co.

401 F.2d 833 (2d Cir.), cert. denied sub nom. Coates v. S.E.C., 394 U.S. 976 (1969).

[In the late 1950s, the mining firm Texas Gulf Sulphur (TGS) began exploratory drilling in eastern Canada. Defendant TGS Vice President Richard D. Mollison, a mining engineer, supervised the project. Defendant Richard H. Clayton, an electrical engineer, was also on the site. On October 29 and 30, 1963, TGS located a segment of land that looked especially promising. It drilled an exploratory hole (K–55–1) on it in early November and found extraordinarily high mineral content. By November 12 it decided that it should buy the land in the area.

To preserve the opportunity for the company to buy the land without driving up prices, defendant TGS President Claude O. Stephens ordered company employees to keep drilling results secret. By March 27, 1964, the company had bought enough of the land that it could safely resume drilling. The on-site officials began to send daily reports to Stephens and defendant Vice President Charles F. Fogarty.

From November 12, 1963 to March 31, 1964, several TGS employees and their "tippees" bought TGS stock and calls (options) on stock. Where in November they had owned 1135 shares of TGS and no calls, by the end of March they owned 8,235 shares and 12,300 calls. Other defendants discussed below include TGS director Frances G. Coates and TGS Secretary David M. Crawford.]

Meanwhile, rumors that a major ore strike was in the making had been circulating throughout Canada. On the morning of Saturday, April 11, Stephens at his home in Greenwich, Conn., read in the New York Herald Tribune and in the New York Times unauthorized reports of the TGS drilling which seemed to infer a rich strike from the fact that the drill cores had been flown to the United States for chemical assay.

Stephens immediately contacted Fogarty at his home in Rye, N.Y., who in turn telephoned and later that day visited Mollison at Mollison's home in Greenwich to obtain a current report and evaluation of the drilling progress. The following morning, Sunday, Fogarty again telephoned Mollison, inquiring whether Mollison had any further information and told him to return to Timmins with Holyk, the TGS Chief Geologist, as soon as possible "to move things along." With the aid of one Carroll, a public relations consultant, Fogarty drafted a press release designed to quell the rumors, which release, after having been channeled through Stephens and Huntington, a TGS attorney, was issued at 3:00 P.M. on Sunday, April 12, and which appeared in the morning newspapers of general circulation on Monday, April 13. It read in pertinent part as follows:

> NEW YORK, April 12—The following statement was made today by Dr. Charles F. Fogarty, executive vice president of Texas Gulf Sulphur Company, in regard to the company's drilling operations near Timmins, Ontario, Canada. Dr. Fogarty said:
>
> "During the past few days, the exploration activities of Texas Gulf Sulphur in the area of Timmins, Ontario, have been widely reported in the press, coupled with rumors of a substantial copper discovery there. These reports exaggerate the scale of operations, and mention plans and statistics of size and grade of ore that are without factual basis and have evidently originated by speculation of people not connected with TGS.
>
> "The facts are as follows. TGS has been exploring in the Timmins area for six years as part of its overall search in Canada and elsewhere for various minerals—lead, copper, zinc, etc. During the course of this work, in Timmins as well as in Eastern Canada, TGS has conducted exploration entirely on its own, without the participation by others. Numerous prospects have been investigated by geophysical means and a large number of selected ones have been core-drilled. These cores are sent to the United States for assay and detailed examination as a matter of routine and on advice of expert Canadian legal counsel. No inferences as to grade can be drawn from this procedure.
>
> "Most of the areas drilled in Eastern Canada have revealed either barren pyrite or graphite without value; a few have resulted in discoveries of small or marginal sulphide ore bodies.
>
> "Recent drilling on one property near Timmins has led to preliminary indications that more drilling would be required for proper evaluation of this prospect. The drilling done to date has not been conclusive, but the statements made by many outside quarters are unreliable and include information and figures that are not available to TGS.
>
> "The work done to date has not been sufficient to reach definite conclusions and any statement as to size and grade of ore would be premature and possibly misleading. When we have progressed to the point where reasonable and logical conclusions can be made, TGS will issue a definite statement to its

stockholders and to the public in order to clarify the Timmins project."

* * * * * *

The release purported to give the Timmins drilling results as of the release date, April 12. From Mollison, Fogarty had been told of the developments through 7:00 P.M. on April 10, and of the remarkable discoveries made up to that time, detailed supra, which discoveries, according to the calculations of the experts who testified for the SEC at the hearing, demonstrated that TGS had already discovered 6.2 to 8.3 million tons of proven ore having gross assay values from $26 to $29 per ton. TGS experts, on the other hand, denied at the hearing that proven or probable ore could have been calculated on April 11 or 12 because there was then no assurance of continuity in the mineralized zone.

The evidence as to the effect of this release on the investing public was equivocal and less than abundant. On April 13 the New York Herald Tribune in an article head-noted "Copper Rumor Deflated" quoted from the TGS release of April 12 and backtracked from its original April 11 report of a major strike but nevertheless inferred from the TGS release that "recent mineral exploratory activity near Timmins, Ontario, has provided preliminary favorable results, sufficient at least to require a step-up in drilling operations." Some witnesses who testified at the hearing stated that they found the release encouraging. On the other hand, a Canadian mining security specialist, Roche, stated that "earlier in the week [before April 16] we had a Dow Jones saying that they [TGS] didn't have anything basically" and a TGS stock specialist for the Midwest Stock Exchange became concerned about his long position in the stock after reading the release. The trial court stated only that "While, in retrospect, the press release may appear gloomy or incomplete, this does not make it misleading or deceptive on the basis of the facts then known." . . .

While drilling activity ensued to completion, TGS officials were taking steps toward ultimate disclosure of the discovery. On April 13, a previously-invited reporter for The Northern Miner, a Canadian mining industry journal, visited the drillsite, interviewed Mollison, Holyk and Darke, and prepared an article which confirmed a 10 million ton ore strike. This report, after having been submitted to Mollison and returned to the reporter unamended on April 15, was published in the April 16 issue. A statement relative to the extent of the discovery, in substantial part drafted by Mollison, was given to the Ontario Minister of Mines for release to the Canadian media. Mollison and Holyk expected it to be released over the airways at 11 P.M. on April 15th, but, for undisclosed reasons, it was not released until 9:40 A.M. on the 16th. An official detailed statement, announcing a strike of at least 25 million tons of ore, based on the drilling data set forth above, was read to representatives of American financial media from 10:00 A.M. to 10:10 or 10:15 A.M. on April 16, and appeared over Merrill Lynch's private wire at 10:29 A.M. and, somewhat later than expected, over the Dow Jones ticker tape at 10:54 A.M.

Between the time the first press release was issued on April 12 and the dissemination of the TGS official announcement on the morning of April 16, the only defendants before us on appeal who engaged in market activity were Clayton and Crawford and TGS director Coates. Clayton ordered 200 shares of TGS stock through his Canadian broker on April 15 and the order was executed that day over the Midwest Stock Exchange. Crawford ordered 300 shares at midnight on the 15th and another 300 shares at 8:30 A.M. the next day, and these orders were executed over the Midwest Exchange in Chicago at its opening on April 16. Coates left the TGS press conference and called his broker son-in-law Haemisegger shortly before 10:20 A.M. on the 16th and ordered 2,000 shares of TGS for family trust accounts of which Coates was a trustee but not a beneficiary; Haemisegger executed this order over the New York and Midwest Exchanges, and he and his customers purchased 1500 additional shares.

During the period of drilling in Timmins, the market price of TGS stock fluctuated but steadily gained overall. On Friday, November 8, when the drilling began, the stock closed at 17⅜; on Friday, November 15, after K–55–1 had been completed, it closed at 18. After a slight decline to 16⅜ by Friday, November 22, the price rose to 20⅞ by December 13, when the chemical assay results of K–55–1 were received, and closed at a high of 24⅛ on February 21, the day after the stock options had been issued. It had reached a price of 26 by March 31, after the land acquisition program had been completed and drilling had been resumed, and continued to ascend to 30⅛ by the close of trading on April 10, at which time the drilling progress up to then was evaluated for the April 12th press release. On April 13, the day on which the April 12 release was disseminated, TGS opened at 30⅛, rose immediately to a high of 32 and gradually tapered off to close at 30⅞. It closed at 30¼ the next day, and at 29⅜ on April 15. On April 16, the day of the official announcement of the Timmins discovery, the price climbed to a high of 37 and closed at 36⅜. By May 15, TGS stock was selling at 58¼.*

I. The Individual Defendants

A. *Introductory*

Rule 10b–5, 17 CFR 240.10b–5, on which this action is predicated, provides:

> It shall be unlawful for any person, directly or indirectly, by the use of any means or instrumentality of interstate commerce, or of the mails, or of any facility of any national securities exchange,
>
> (1) to employ any device, scheme, or artifice to defraud,
>
> (2) to make any untrue statement of a material fact or to omit to state a material fact necessary in order to make the statements made, in the light of the circumstances under which they were made, not misleading, or
>
> (3) to engage in any act, practice, or course of business which operates or would operate as a fraud or deceit upon any person,
>
> in connection with the purchase or sale of any security.

* [Eds.—The Dow-Jones Industrial Average, a widely used index of general stock market performance, was 755 on October 30, 815 on March 30, and 820 on May 28.]

Rule 10b–5 . . . is based in policy on the justifiable expectation of the securities marketplace that all investors trading on impersonal exchanges have relatively equal access to material information. . . .

The essence of the Rule is that anyone who, trading for his own account in the securities of a corporation, has "access, directly or indirectly, to information intended to be available only for a corporate purpose and not for the personal benefit of anyone" may not take "advantage of such information knowing it is unavailable to those with whom he is dealing," i.e., the investing public. Matter of Cady, Roberts & Co., 40 SEC 907, 912 (1961). Insiders, as directors or management officers are, of course, by this Rule, precluded from so unfairly dealing, but the Rule is also applicable to one possessing the information who may not be strictly termed an "insider" within the meaning of Sec. 16(b) of the Act. Cady, Roberts, supra. Thus, anyone in possession of material inside information must either disclose it to the investing public, or, if he is disabled from disclosing it in order to protect a corporate confidence, or he chooses not to do so, must abstain from trading in or recommending the securities concerned while such inside information remains undisclosed. So, it is here no justification for insider activity that disclosure was forbidden by the legitimate corporate objective of acquiring options to purchase the land surrounding the exploration site; if the information was, as the SEC contends, material,[9] its possessors should have kept out of the market until disclosure was accomplished. Cady, Roberts, supra at 911.

B. *Material Inside Information*

An insider is not, of course, always foreclosed from investing in his own company merely because he may be more familiar with company operations than are outside investors. An insider's duty to disclose information or his duty to abstain from dealing in his company's securities arises only in "those situations which are essentially extraordinary in nature and which are reasonably certain to have a substantial effect on the market price of the security if [the extraordinary situation is] disclosed." Fleischer, Securities Trading and Corporate Information Practices: The Implications of the Texas Gulf Sulphur Proceeding, 51 Va.L.Rev. 1271, 1289.

Nor is an insider obligated to confer upon outside investors the benefit of his superior financial or other expert analysis by disclosing his educated guesses or predictions.

This is not to suggest, however, as did the trial court, that "the test of materiality must necessarily be a conservative one, particularly since many actions under Section 10(b) are brought on the basis of hindsight," 258 F.Supp. 262 at 280, in the sense that the materiality of facts is to be assessed solely by measuring the effect the knowledge of the facts would have upon prudent or conservative investors. As we stated in List v. Fashion Park, Inc., 340 F.2d 457, 462, "The basic test of materiality . . . is whether a *reasonable* man would attach importance . . . in determining his choice of action in the transaction in question. Restatement, Torts § 538(2)(a); accord Prosser, Torts 554–55; I Harper & James, Torts 565–66." (Emphasis supplied.) This, of course, encompasses any fact ". . .

[9] Congress intended by the Exchange Act to eliminate the idea that the use of inside information for personal advantage was a normal emolument of corporate office. . . .

which in reasonable and objective contemplation *might* affect the value of the corporation's stock or securities. . . ." List v. Fashion Park, Inc., supra at 462, quoting from Kohler v. Kohler Co., 319 F.2d 634, 642 (7 Cir.1963). (Emphasis supplied.) Such a fact is a material fact and must be effectively disclosed to the investing public prior to the commencement of insider trading in the corporation's securities. The speculators and chartists of Wall and Bay Streets are also "reasonable" investors entitled to the same legal protection afforded conservative traders. Thus, material facts include not only information disclosing the earnings and distributions of a company but also those facts which affect the probable future of the company and those which may affect the desire of investors to buy, sell, or hold the company's securities.

In each case, then, whether facts are material within Rule 10b–5 when the facts relate to a particular event and are undisclosed by those persons who are knowledgeable thereof will depend at any given time upon a balancing of both the indicated probability that the event will occur and the anticipated magnitude of the event in light of the totality of the company activity. Here, notwithstanding the trial court's conclusion that the results of the first drill core, K–55–1, were "too 'remote' . . . to have had any significant impact on the market, i.e., to be deemed material," 258 F.Supp. at 283, knowledge of the possibility, which surely was more than marginal, of the existence of a mine of the vast magnitude indicated by the remarkably rich drill core located rather close to the surface (suggesting mineability by the less expensive open-pit method) within the confines of a large anomaly (suggesting an extensive region of mineralization) might well have affected the price of TGS stock and would certainly have been an important fact to a reasonable, if speculative, investor in deciding whether he should buy, sell, or hold. After all, this first drill core was "unusually good and . . . excited the interest and speculation of those who knew about it." 258 F.Supp. at 282.

. . . Our survey of the facts found below conclusively establishes that knowledge of the results of the discovery hole, K–55–1, would have been important to a reasonable investor and might have affected the price of the stock.[12] On April 16, The Northern Miner, a trade publication in wide circulation among mining stock specialists, called K–55–1, the discovery hole, "one of the most impressive drill holes completed in modern times."

Finally, a major factor in determining whether the K–55–1 discovery was a material fact is the importance attached to the drilling results by those who knew about it. In view of other unrelated recent developments favorably affecting TGS, participation by an informed person in a regular stock-purchase program, or even sporadic trading by an informed person, might lend only nominal support to the inference of the materiality of the K–55–1 discovery; nevertheless, the timing by those who knew of it of

[12] We do not suggest that material facts must be disclosed immediately; the timing of disclosure is a matter for the business judgment of the corporate officers entrusted with the management of the corporation within the affirmative disclosure requirements promulgated by the exchanges and by the SEC. Here, a valuable corporate purpose was served by delaying the publication of the K–55–1 discovery. We do intend to convey, however, that where a corporate purpose is thus served by withholding the news of a material fact, those persons who are thus quite properly true to their corporate trust must not during the period of non-disclosure deal personally in the corporation's securities or give to outsiders confidential information not generally available to all the corporations' stockholders and to the public at large.

their stock purchases and their purchases of *short-term* calls—purchases in some cases by individuals who had never before purchased calls or even TGS stock—virtually compels the inference that the insiders were influenced by the drilling results. . . .

Our decision to expand the limited protection afforded outside investors by the trial court's narrow definition of materiality is not at all shaken by fears that the elimination of insider trading benefits will deplete the ranks of capable corporate managers by taking away an incentive to accept such employment. Such benefits, in essence, are forms of secret corporate compensation, . . . derived at the expense of the uninformed investing public and not at the expense of the corporation which receives the sole benefit from insider incentives. Moreover, adequate incentives for corporate officers may be provided by properly administered stock options and employee purchase plans of which there are many in existence. In any event, the normal motivation induced by stock ownership, i.e., the identification of an individual with corporate progress, is ill-promoted by condoning the sort of speculative insider activity which occurred here; for example, some of the corporation's stock was sold at market in order to purchase short-term calls upon that stock, calls which would never be exercised to increase a stockholder equity in TGS unless the market price of that stock rose sharply.

The core of Rule 10b–5 is the implementation of the Congressional purpose that all investors should have equal access to the rewards of participation in securities transactions. It was the intent of Congress that all members of the investing public should be subject to identical market risks—which market risks include, of course the risk that one's evaluative capacity or one's capital available to put at risk may exceed another's capacity or capital. The insiders here were not trading on an equal footing with the outside investors. . . .

We hold, therefore, that all transactions in TGS stock or calls by individuals apprised of the drilling results of K–55–1 were made in violation of Rule 10b–5. Inasmuch as the visual evaluation of that drill core (a generally reliable estimate though less accurate than a chemical assay) constituted material information, those advised of the results of the visual evaluation as well as those informed of the chemical assay traded in violation of law. The geologist Darke possessed undisclosed material information and traded in TGS securities. Therefore we reverse the dismissal of the action as to him and his personal transaction. . . .

Coates was absolved by the court below because his telephone order was placed shortly before 10:20 A.M. on April 16, which was after the announcement had been made even though the news could not be considered already a matter of public information. . . . This result seems to have been predicated upon a misinterpretation of dicta in *Cady, Roberts,* where the SEC instructed insiders to "keep out of the market until the established procedures for public release of the information are *carried out* instead of hastening to execute transactions in advance of, and in frustration of, the objectives of the release," 40 SEC at 915 (emphasis supplied). The reading of a news release, which prompted Coates into action, is merely the first step in the process of dissemination required for compliance with the regulatory objective of providing all investors with an equal opportunity to make informed investment judgments. Assuming that the contents of the official release could instantaneously be acted upon,[18] at the minimum Coates should have waited until the news could reasonably have been expected to appear over the media of widest circulation, the Dow Jones broad tape, rather than hastening to insure an advantage to himself and his broker son-in-law.

. . .

II. The Corporate Defendant

A. *Introductory*

At 3:00 P.M. on April 12, 1964, evidently believing it desirable to comment upon the rumors concerning the Timmins project, TGS issued the press release quoted in pertinent part in the text at [above]. The SEC argued below and maintains on this appeal that this release painted a misleading and deceptive picture of the drilling progress at the time of its issuance, and hence violated Rule 10b–5(2). TGS relies on the holding of the court below that "The issuance of the release produced no unusual market action" and "In the absence of a showing that the purpose of the April 12 press release was to affect the market price of TGS stock to the advantage of TGS or its insiders, the issuance of the press release did not constitute a violation of Section 10(b) or Rule 10b–5 since it was not issued 'in connection with the purchase or sale of any security' " and, alternatively, "even if it had been established that the April 12 release was issued in connection with the purchase or sale of any security, the Commission has failed to demonstrate that it was false, misleading or deceptive." 258 F.Supp. at 294.

. . .

B. *The "In Connection With . . ." Requirement*

. . .

[I]t seems clear from the legislative purpose Congress expressed in the Act, and the legislative history of Section 10(b) that Congress when it used the phrase "in connection with the purchase or sale of any security" intended only that the device employed, whatever it might be, be of a sort that would cause reasonable investors to rely thereon, and, in connection therewith, so relying, cause them to purchase or sell a corporation's securities. There is no indication that Congress intended that the corporations or persons responsible for the issuance of a misleading statement would not violate the section unless they engaged in related securities transactions or otherwise acted with wrongful motives; indeed, the obvious purposes of the Act to protect the investing public and to secure fair dealing in the securities markets would be seriously undermined by applying such a gloss onto the legislative language. . . .

---

[18] Although the only insider who acted after the news appeared over the Dow Jones broad tape is not an appellant and therefore we need not discuss the necessity of considering the advisability of a "reasonable waiting period" during which outsiders may absorb and evaluate disclosures, we note in passing that, where the news is of a sort which is not readily translatable into investment action, insiders may not take advantage of their advance opportunity to evaluate the information by acting immediately upon dissemination. In any event, the permissible timing of insider transactions after disclosures of various sorts is one of the many areas of expertise for appropriate exercise of the SEC's rule-making power, which we hope will be utilized in the future to provide some predictability and certainty for the business community.

C. *Did the Issuance of the April 12 Release Violate Rule 10b–5?*

Turning first to the question of whether the release was misleading, i.e., whether it conveyed to the public a false impression of the drilling situation at the time of its issuance, we note initially that the trial court did not actually decide this question. Its conclusion that "the Commission has failed to demonstrate that it was false, misleading or deceptive," 258 F.Supp. at 294, seems to have derived from its views that "The defendants are to be judged *on the facts known to them* when the April 12 release was issued," 258 F.Supp. at 295 (emphasis supplied), that the draftsmen "exercised reasonable business judgment under the circumstances," 258 F.Supp. at 296, and that the release was not "misleading or deceptive *on the basis of the facts then known,*" 258 F.Supp. at 296 (emphasis supplied) rather than from an appropriate primary inquiry into the meaning of the statement to the reasonable investor and its relationship to truth. While we certainly agree with the trial court that "in retrospect, the press release may appear gloomy or incomplete," 258 F.Supp. at 296, we cannot, from the present record, by applying the standard Congress intended, definitively conclude that it was deceptive or misleading to the reasonable investor, or that he would have been misled by it. Certain newspaper accounts of the release viewed the release as confirming the existence of preliminary favorable developments, and this optimistic view was held by some brokers, so it could be that the reasonable investor would have read between the lines of what appears to us to be an inconclusive and negative statement and would have envisioned the actual situation at the Kidd segment on April 12. On the other hand, in view of the decline of the market price of TGS stock from a high of 32 on the morning of April 13 when the release was disseminated to 29⅜ by the close of trading on April 15, and the reaction to the release by other brokers, it is far from certain that the release was generally interpreted as a highly encouraging report or even encouraging at all. Accordingly, we remand this issue to the district court that took testimony and heard and saw the witnesses for a determination of the character of the release in the light of the facts existing at the time of the release, by applying the standard of whether the reasonable investor, in the exercise of due care, would have been misled by it.

. . .

NOTES AND QUESTIONS

1. There has been considerable academic debate over the years about whether insider trading should be prohibited. Part of the argument for elimination of the prohibition rests on the fact that most insider trading escapes detection. If the existence of the legal prohibition conveys to the public the impression that stock market trading is an unrigged game that anyone can play, that impression may be misleading. Another line of analysis questions whether there are any victims deserving of protection. Here there are two issues, (a) whether a person suffers a loss and (b) whether that person should be owed any duty by the insider. In the TGS context, consider four possible market participants, all of whom bought or sold 100 shares of TGS common stock on January 30, 1964, at the market price of $23 per share.

i. Grace bought 100 shares on the basis of her broker's advice and her own study of financial data.

ii. Isabel sold 100 shares that she had held for five years. She sold because she needed the money for the downpayment on a house.

iii. Christine sold 100 shares that she had bought six months earlier for $17 per share. She sold because she concluded, based on the information available to her, that the shares were worth no more than $20 per share.

iv. Alison never owned any TGS shares. On January 30, 1964, she considered buying 100 shares but concluded that the price at that time ($23 per share) was too high. If the price had been $22 or less she would have bought.

2. Part of the debate over whether insider trading should be prohibited is based on judgments about whether allowing insider trading would be a good way of compensating employees. Suppose that federal law allowed insider trading by officers, directors, or other employees, or by the corporation, if such trading is permitted in the corporation's articles of incorporation; that you are a member of the board of directors of a corporation whose articles authorize the board to permit individuals whom it identifies to trade on inside information; and that the corporation's business is similar to that of TGS.

(a) Whom would you authorize to take advantage of the opportunity to engage in trading on nonpublic information, when would you do so, and what limits, if any, would you impose?

(b) How would you react to a proposal that the corporation itself buy or sell shares based on nonpublic information?

(c) Suppose you are an investor with a large portfolio of stocks and you are considering the purchase of shares of stock of two different corporations that seem to you to be equally attractive in all other respects, except that the articles of one authorize insider trading and the articles of the other do not. Which would you buy?

3. *Texas Gulf Sulphur* was an SEC enforcement action. It had previously been established that § 10(b) gave rise to a private cause of action for damages, though the question of who can sue whom for what amounts has given rise to considerable litigation and is still largely unsettled. In a private action for damages the plaintiff must prove (1) defendant made a material misrepresentation or omission in connection with the purchase or sale of a security, (2) reliance, (3) scienter, and (4) causation.

In 1984, Congress amended § 21(d) of the '34 Act to allow the SEC to seek a civil penalty up to three times the insider's profits. In the Insider Trading and Securities Fraud Enforcement Act of 1988, Congress added § 20A to the '34 Act. This provision gives an express cause of action for damages to contemporaneous traders against inside traders and tippers. "Contemporaneous" is not defined. The amount that can be recovered is limited to the amount of the insider's profit reduced by any amount disgorged in an SEC enforcement action. Section 20A(d) preserves but does not clarify existing law relating to implied causes of action under § 10(b) and Rule 10b–5. The Act provides expressly for derivative liability of employers for the actions of their employees (for example, the actions of employees of brokerage firms), but (contrary to the general rule for vicarious tort liability) not if the employer is able to prove good faith and noninducement.

INTRODUCTORY NOTE ON CURRENT LAW

Chiarella v. United States, 445 U.S. 222 (1980), involved a criminal prosecution. The defendant had been a "markup man" in the composing room of a financial printing company. The printing company had been retained by the acquiring corporation in connection with a tender offer for the shares of another corporation. The acquiring corporation made every reasonable effort to keep the identity of the tender offer target a secret, even from the employees of the printer. Chiarella, by virtue of his job and ingenuity, correctly identified the target and bought shares of its stock through a broker. When the tender offer was announced, the target shares rose in value and Chiarella sold his shares at a profit. When his conduct was brought to light he was fired and he agreed to give up ("disgorge," in the current parlance) his profit. In addition, he was indicted for violating § 10(b) and Rule 10b–5.

The Supreme Court, reversing the court of appeals, held that Chiarella's conduct was not a violation because he was not an "insider" of the corporation whose shares he had traded (that is, the target corporation). Starting with the observation that the "case concerns the legal effect of [Chiarella's] silence," and the basic proposition that, under § 10(b) and Rule 10b–5, "a corporate insider must abstain from trading in the shares of his corporation unless he has first disclosed all material inside information known to him," the Court concluded that the duty to abstain arises from the relationship of trust between a corporation's shareholders and its employees. Since there was no relationship of trust between Chiarella and the shareholders of the corporations whose shares he traded, he had no duty to "disclose or abstain." Citing *Santa Fe Industries, Inc.*, supra, Chapter 4, Sec. 3, the Court stated, "not every instance of financial unfairness constitutes fraudulent activity under § 10(b)." As an alternative theory to support Chiarella's conviction, the government argued that he had violated a duty to the acquiring corporation; the theory is that Chiarella "misappropriated" information. The Court declined to consider this alternative theory because it was not submitted to the jury.

Chief Justice Burger dissented on the basis of the "misappropriation" theory. This theory was presented to the Court later in United States v. O'Hagan, immediately following *Dirks*.

Dirks v. Securities & Exchange Commission

463 U.S. 646, 103 S.Ct. 3255, 77 L.Ed.2d 911 (1983).

■ JUSTICE POWELL delivered the opinion of the Court.

Petitioner Raymond Dirks received material nonpublic information from "insiders" of a corporation with which he had no connection. He disclosed this information to investors who relied on it in trading in the shares of the corporation. The question is whether Dirks violated the antifraud provisions of the federal securities laws by this disclosure.

I

In 1973, Dirks was an officer of a New York broker-dealer firm who specialized in providing investment analysis of insurance company securities to institutional investors. On March 6, Dirks received information from Ronald Secrist, a former officer of Equity Funding of America. Secrist alleged that the assets of Equity Funding, a diversified corporation primarily engaged in selling life insurance and mutual funds, were vastly overstated as the result of fraudulent corporate practices. Secrist also stated that various regulatory agencies had failed to act on similar charges made by Equity Funding employees. He urged Dirks to verify the fraud and disclose it publicly.

Dirks decided to investigate the allegations. He visited Equity Funding's headquarters in Los Angeles and interviewed several officers and employees of the corporation. The senior management denied any wrongdoing, but certain corporation employees corroborated the charges of fraud. Neither Dirks nor his firm owned or traded any Equity Funding stock, but throughout his investigation he openly discussed the information he had obtained with a number of clients and investors. Some of these persons sold their holdings of Equity Funding securities, including five investment advisers who liquidated holdings of more than $16 million.[2]

While Dirks was in Los Angeles, he was in touch regularly with William Blundell, the Wall Street Journal's Los Angeles bureau chief. Dirks urged Blundell to write a story on the fraud allegations. Blundell did not believe, however, that such a massive fraud could go undetected and declined to write the story. He feared that publishing such damaging hearsay might be libelous.

During the 2-week period in which Dirks pursued his investigation and spread word of Secrist's charges, the price of Equity Funding stock fell from $26 per share to less than $15 per share. This led the New York Stock Exchange to halt trading on March 27. Shortly thereafter California insurance authorities impounded Equity Funding's records and uncovered evidence of the fraud. Only then did the Securities and Exchange Commission (SEC) file a complaint against Equity Funding and only then, on April 2, did the Wall Street Journal publish a front-page story based largely on information assembled by Dirks. Equity Funding immediately went into receivership.

The SEC began an investigation into Dirks' role in the exposure of the fraud. After a hearing by an Administrative Law Judge, the SEC found that Dirks had aided and abetted violations of [Securities Exchange Act § 10(b) and Rule 10b–5 thereunder, among other provisions] by repeating the allegations of fraud to members of the investment community who later sold their Equity Funding stock. The SEC concluded: "Where 'tippees'—regardless of their motivation or occupation—come into possession of material 'corporate information that

---

[2] Dirks received from his firm a salary plus a commission for securities transactions above a certain amount that his clients directed through his firm. . . . But "[i]t is not clear how many of those with whom Dirks spoke promised to direct some brokerage business through [Dirks' firm] to compensate Dirks, or how many actually did so." 220 U.S.App.D.C., at 316, 681 F.2d, at 831. The Boston Company Institutional Investors, Inc., promised Dirks about $25,000 in commissions, but it is unclear whether Boston actually generated any brokerage business for his firm . . .

they know is confidential and know or should know came from a corporate insider,' they must either publicly disclose that information or refrain from trading." 21 S.E.C. Docket 1401, 1407 (1981) (footnote omitted) (quoting Chiarella v. United States, 445 U.S. 222, 230, n. 12 (1980)). Recognizing, however, that Dirks "played an important role in bringing [Equity Funding's] massive fraud to light," 21 S.E.C. Docket, at 1412, the SEC only censured him.

II

In the seminal case of In re Cady, Roberts & Co., 40 S.E.C. 907 (1961), the SEC recognized that the common law in some jurisdictions imposes on "corporate 'insiders,' particularly officers, directors, or controlling stockholders" an "affirmative duty of disclosure . . . when dealing in securities." Id., at 911, and n. 13. The SEC found that not only did breach of this common-law duty also establish the elements of a Rule 10b–5 violation, but that individuals other than corporate insiders could be obligated either to disclose material nonpublic information before trading or to abstain from trading altogether. Id., at 912. In *Chiarella,* we accepted the two elements set out in *Cady, Roberts* for establishing a Rule 10b–5 violation: "(i) the existence of a relationship affording access to inside information intended to be available only for a corporate purpose, and (ii) the unfairness of allowing a corporate insider to take advantage of that information by trading without disclosure." 445 U.S., at 227. In examining whether Chiarella had an obligation to disclose or abstain, the Court found that there is no general duty to disclose before trading on material nonpublic information, and held that "a duty to disclose under § 10(b) does not arise from the mere possession of nonpublic market information." Such a duty arises rather from the existence of a fiduciary relationship.

Not "all breaches of fiduciary duty in connection with a securities transaction," however, come within the ambit of Rule 10b–5. Santa Fe Industries, Inc. v. Green, 430 U.S. 462, 472 (1977). There must also be "manipulation or deception." Id., at 473. In an inside-trading case this fraud derives from the "inherent unfairness involved where one takes advantage" of "information intended to be available only for a corporate purpose and not for the personal benefit of anyone." In re Merrill Lynch, Pierce, Fenner & Smith, Inc., 43 S.E.C. 933, 936 (1968). Thus, an insider will be liable under Rule 10b–5 for inside trading only where he fails to disclose material nonpublic information before trading on it and thus makes "secret profits." *Cady, Roberts,* supra, at 916, n. 31.

III

We were explicit in *Chiarella* in saying that there can be no duty to disclose where the person who has traded on inside information "was not [the corporation's] agent, . . . was not a fiduciary, [or] was not a person in whom the sellers [of the securities] had placed their trust and confidence." 445 U.S., at 232. Not to require such a fiduciary relationship, we recognized, would "depar[t] radically from the established doctrine that duty arises from a specific relationship between two parties" and would amount to "recognizing a general duty between all participants in market transactions to forgo actions based on material, nonpublic information." Id., at 232, 233. This requirement of a specific relationship between the shareholders and the individual trading on inside information has created analytical difficulties for the SEC and courts in policing tippees who trade on inside information. Unlike insiders who have independent fiduciary duties to both the corporation and its shareholders, the typical tippee has no such relationships.[14] In view of this absence, it has been unclear how a tippee acquires the *Cady, Roberts* duty to refrain from trading on inside information.

A

The SEC's position, as stated in its opinion in this case, is that a tippee "inherits" the *Cady, Roberts* obligation to shareholders whenever he receives inside information from an insider:

> "In tipping potential traders, Dirks breached a duty which he had assumed as a result of knowingly receiving confidential information from [Equity Funding] insiders. Tippees such as Dirks who receive non-public, material information from insiders become 'subject to the same duty as [the] insiders.' *Shapiro v. Merrill Lynch, Pierce, Fenner & Smith, Inc.* [495 F.2d 228, 237 (C.A.2 1974) (quoting *Ross v. Licht,* 263 F.Supp. 395, 410 (S.D.N.Y.1967))]. Such a tippee breaches the fiduciary duty which he assumes from the insider when the tippee knowingly transmits the information to someone who will probably trade on the basis thereof. . . . Presumably, Dirks' informants were entitled to disclose the [Equity Funding] fraud in order to bring it to light and its perpetrators to justice. However, Dirks—standing in their shoes—committed a breach of the fiduciary duty which he had assumed in dealing with them, when he passed the information on to traders." 21 S.E.C. Docket, at 1410, n. 42.

This view differs little from the view that we rejected as inconsistent with congressional intent in *Chiarella.* In that case, the Court of Appeals agreed with the SEC and affirmed Chiarella's conviction, holding that "*[a]nyone*—corporate insider or not—who regularly receives material nonpublic information may not use that information to trade in securities without incurring an affirmative duty to disclose." United States v. Chiarella, 588 F.2d 1358, 1365 (C.A.2 1978) (emphasis in original). Here, the SEC maintains that anyone who knowingly receives nonpublic material information from an insider has a fiduciary duty to disclose before trading.

In effect, the SEC's theory of tippee liability in both cases appears rooted in the idea that the antifraud provisions require equal information among all traders. This conflicts with the principle set forth in *Chiarella* that only some persons, under some circumstances, will be barred from trading while in possession of material nonpublic information.

Imposing a duty to disclose or abstain solely because a person knowingly receives material nonpublic information from an insider and

---

[14] Under certain circumstances, such as where corporate information is revealed legitimately to an underwriter, accountant, lawyer, or consultant working for the corporation, these outsiders may become fiduciaries of the shareholders. The basis for recognizing this fiduciary duty is not simply that such persons acquired nonpublic corporate information, but rather that they have entered into a special confidential relationship in the conduct of the business of the enterprise and are given access to information solely for corporate purposes. . . .

For such a duty to be imposed, however, the corporation must expect the outsider to keep the disclosed nonpublic information confidential, and the relationship at least must imply such a duty.

trades on it could have an inhibiting influence on the role of market analysts, which the SEC itself recognizes is necessary to the preservation of a healthy market.[17] It is commonplace for analysts to "ferret out and analyze information," 21 S.E.C. Docket, at 1406,[18] and this often is done by meeting with and questioning corporate officers and others who are insiders. And information that the analysts obtain normally may be the basis for judgments as to the market worth of a corporation's securities. The analyst's judgment in this respect is made available in market letters or otherwise to clients of the firm. It is the nature of this type of information, and indeed of the markets themselves, that such information cannot be made simultaneously available to all of the corporation's stockholders or the public generally.

B

The conclusion that recipients of inside information do not invariably acquire a duty to disclose or abstain does not mean that such tippees always are free to trade on the information. The need for a ban on some tippee trading is clear. Not only are insiders forbidden by their fiduciary relationship from personally using undisclosed corporate information to their advantage, but they also may not give such information to an outsider for the same improper purpose of exploiting the information for their personal gain. . . .

Similarly, the transactions of those who knowingly participate with the fiduciary in such a breach are "as forbidden" as transactions "on behalf of the trustee himself." Mosser v. Darrow, 341 U.S. 267, 272 (1951). . . . Thus, the tippee's duty to disclose or abstain is derivative from that of the insider's duty. . . . As we noted in *Chiarella,* "[t]he tippee's obligation has been viewed as arising from his role as a participant after the fact in the insider's breach of a fiduciary duty."

Thus, some tippees must assume an insider's duty to the shareholders not because they receive inside information, but rather because it has been made available to them *improperly*. And for Rule 10b–5 purposes, the insider's disclosure is improper only where it would violate his *Cady, Roberts* duty. Thus, a tippee assumes a fiduciary duty to the shareholders of a corporation not to trade on material nonpublic

[17] The SEC expressly recognized that "[t]he value to the entire market of [analysts'] efforts cannot be gainsaid; market efficiency in pricing is significantly enhanced by [their] initiatives to ferret out and analyze information, and thus the analyst's work redounds to the benefit of all investors." 21 S.E.C. Docket, at 1406. The SEC asserts that analysts remain free to obtain from management corporate information for purposes of "filling in the 'interstices in analysis' . . . ." Brief for Respondent 42 (quoting *Investors Management Co.,* 44 S.E.C., at 646). But this rule is inherently imprecise, and imprecision prevents parties from ordering their actions in accord with legal requirements.

[18] On its facts, this case is the unusual one. Dirks is an analyst in a broker-dealer firm, and he did interview management in the course of his investigation. He uncovered, however, startling information that required no analysis or exercise of judgment as to its market relevance. Nonetheless, the principle at issue here extends beyond these facts. The SEC's rule—applicable without regard to any breach by an insider—could have serious ramifications on reporting by analysts of investment views.

Despite the unusualness of Dirks' "find," the central role that he played in uncovering the fraud at Equity Funding, and that analysts in general can play in revealing information that corporations may have reason to withhold from the public, is an important one. Dirks' careful investigation brought to light a massive fraud at the corporation. And until the Equity Funding fraud was exposed, the information in the trading market was grossly inaccurate. But for Dirks' efforts, the fraud might well have gone undetected longer.

information only when the insider has breached his fiduciary duty to the shareholders by disclosing the information to the tippee and the tippee knows or should know that there has been a breach.

C

In determining whether a tippee is under an obligation to disclose or abstain, it thus is necessary to determine whether the insider's "tip" constituted a breach of the insider's fiduciary duty. All disclosures of confidential corporate information are not inconsistent with the duty insiders owe to shareholders. In contrast to the extraordinary facts of this case, the more typical situation in which there will be a question whether disclosure violates the insider's *Cady, Roberts* duty is when insiders disclose information to analysts. In some situations, the insider will act consistently with his fiduciary duty to shareholders, and yet release of the information may affect the market. For example, it may not be clear—either to the corporate insider or to the recipient analyst—whether the information will be viewed as material nonpublic information. Corporate officials may mistakenly think the information already has been disclosed or that it is not material enough to affect the market. Whether disclosure is a breach of duty therefore depends in large part on the purpose of the disclosure. This standard was identified by the SEC itself in *Cady, Roberts:* a purpose of the securities laws was to eliminate "use of inside information for personal advantage." 40 S.E.C., at 912, n. 15. . . . Thus, the test is whether the insider personally will benefit, directly or indirectly, from his disclosure. Absent some personal gain, there has been no breach of duty to stockholders. And absent a breach by the insider, there is no derivative breach.[22] . . .

IV

Under the inside-trading and tipping rules set forth above, we find that there was no actionable violation by Dirks. It is undisputed that Dirks himself was a stranger to Equity Funding, with no pre-existing fiduciary duty to its shareholders. He took no action, directly or indirectly, that induced the shareholders or officers of Equity Funding to repose trust or confidence in him. There was no expectation by Dirks' sources that he would keep their information in confidence. Nor did Dirks misappropriate or illegally obtain the information about Equity Funding. Unless the insiders breached their *Cady, Roberts* duty to shareholders in disclosing the nonpublic information to Dirks, he breached no duty when he passed it on to investors as well as to the Wall Street Journal.

It is clear that neither Secrist nor the other Equity Funding employees violated their *Cady, Roberts* duty to the corporation's shareholders by providing information to Dirks. The tippers received no

[22] An example of a case turning on the court's determination that the disclosure did not impose any fiduciary duties on the recipient of the inside information is Walton v. Morgan Stanley & Co., 623 F.2d 796 (C.A.2 1980). There, the defendant investment banking firm, representing one of its own corporate clients, investigated another corporation that was a possible target of a takeover bid by its client. In the course of negotiations the investment banking firm was given, on a confidential basis, unpublished material information. Subsequently, after the proposed takeover was abandoned, the firm was charged with relying on the information when it traded in the target corporation's stock. For purposes of the decision, it was assumed that the firm knew the information was confidential, but that it had been received in arm's-length negotiations. See id., at 798. In the absence of any fiduciary relationship, the Court of Appeals found no basis for imposing tippee liability on the investment firm. See id., at 799.

monetary or personal benefit for revealing Equity Funding's secrets, nor was their purpose to make a gift of valuable information to Dirks. As the facts of this case clearly indicate, the tippers were motivated by a desire to expose the fraud. . . . In the absence of a breach of duty to shareholders by the insiders, there was no derivative breach by Dirks. . . . Dirks therefore could not have been "a participant after the fact in [an] insider's breach of a fiduciary duty." *Chiarella,* 445 U.S., at 230, n. 12.

V

We conclude that Dirks, in the circumstances of this case, had no duty to abstain from use of the inside information that he obtained. The judgment of the Court of Appeals therefore is

Reversed.

ANALYSIS

1. Why did the Court absolve Secrist of wrongdoing?

2. What is the scope of the Court's doctrine on breaches of fiduciary duties? What if Dirks and Secrist had routinely exchanged stock tips? What if Secrist had disclosed the Equity Funding fraud in part because he had been fired over an unrelated matter? What if Dirks merely overheard Secrist describing the fraud in a public elevator?

3. Suppose Secrist had disclosed inside information (not involving fraud) to Dirks because of a bribe from Dirks. Dirks then advised his clients to sell their Equity Funding stock. Dirks, of course, would have violated Rule 10b–5. Would his clients also have violated the rule?

4. Stock analysts such as Dirks earn their livelihoods in part by supplying investors with analysis of public information. To this extent the activities of stock analysts seem unobjectionable. But analysts also spend time trying to obtain information that is not clearly public. They spend time talking with executives of the corporations in which they have an interest. It seems clear that the executives, the analysts, and the investors who pay for the services of the analysts all think that the analysts are able to obtain valuable information from their communications with the executives. The objective of the corporate executives is generally to paint a favorable picture of their corporations. The analysts seek an informational advantage for their investors over other investors. They do not receive discrete, material items of information of the sort described in the cases we have examined in this section. Rather, what they tend to get are details and analysis. They get answers to perceptive, sophisticated questions. The activities of stock analysts are widespread and their propriety seems generally to be regarded as beyond question. Is that as it should be? Should corporate insiders be prohibited from providing private briefings to analysts (or anyone else)? Suppose you are a major shareholder of a public corporation. Is there anything wrong with the CEO spending a couple of hours once or twice a year with you, answering your questions about the corporation's business?

The SEC recently concluded that selective disclosure to analysts undermined public confidence in the integrity of the stock markets. The SEC further concluded that Dirks' tipping regime was an inadequate constraint on the selective disclosure practice because, inter alia, it can be difficult to prove that the tipper received a personal benefit in connection with a disclosure. In 2000, the SEC adopted Regulation FD to create a non-insider trading-based mechanism for restricting selective disclosure. If someone acting on behalf of a public corporation discloses material nonpublic information to securities market professionals or "holders of the issuer's securities who may well trade on the basis of the information," the issuer must also disclose that information to the public. Exchange Act Rel. No. 43,154 (Aug. 15, 2000). Where the disclosure is intentional, the issuer must simultaneously disclose the information in a manner designed to convey it to the general public. Hence, for example, if the issuer holds a briefing for selected analysts, it must simultaneously announce the same information through, say, a press release to "a widely disseminated news or wire service." The SEC encouraged issuers to make use of the Internet and other new information technologies, such as by webcasting conference calls with analysts. Where the disclosure was not intentional, as where a corporate officer "let something slip," the issuer must make public disclosure "promptly" after a senior officer learns of the disclosure.

United States v. O'Hagan

521 U.S. 642, 117 S.Ct. 2199, 138 L.Ed.2d 724 (1997).

This case concerns the interpretation and enforcement of § 10(b) and § 14(e) of the Securities Exchange Act of 1934, and rules made by the Securities and Exchange Commission pursuant to these provisions, Rule 10b–5 and Rule 14e–3(a). Two prime questions are presented. . . . (1) Is a person who trades in securities for personal profit, using confidential information misappropriated in breach of a fiduciary duty to the source of the information, guilty of violating § 10(b) and Rule 10b–5? (2) Did the Commission exceed its rulemaking authority by adopting Rule 14e–3(a), which proscribes trading on undisclosed information in the tender offer setting, even in the absence of a duty to disclose? Our answer to the first question is yes, and to the second question, viewed in the context of this case, no.

I

Respondent James Herman O'Hagan was a partner in the law firm of Dorsey & Whitney in Minneapolis, Minnesota. In July 1988, Grand Metropolitan PLC (Grand Met), a company based in London, England, retained Dorsey & Whitney as local counsel to represent Grand Met regarding a potential tender offer for the common stock of the Pillsbury Company, headquartered in Minneapolis. Both Grand Met and Dorsey & Whitney took precautions to protect the confidentiality of Grand Met's tender offer plans. . . . [O]n October 4, 1988, Grand Met publicly announced its tender offer for Pillsbury stock.

On August 18, 1988, while Dorsey & Whitney was still representing Grand Met, O'Hagan began purchasing call options for Pillsbury stock. Each option gave him the right to purchase 100 shares of Pillsbury stock by a specified date in September 1988. . . . By the end of September, he owned 2,500 unexpired Pillsbury options, apparently more than any other individual investor. O'Hagan also purchased, in September 1988, some 5,000 shares of Pillsbury common stock, at a price just under $39 per share. When Grand Met announced its tender offer in October, the price of Pillsbury stock rose to nearly $60 per share. O'Hagan then sold his Pillsbury call options and common stock, making a profit of more than $4.3 million.

The Securities and Exchange Commission (SEC or Commission) initiated an investigation into O'Hagan's transactions, culminating in a 57-count indictment. The indictment alleged that O'Hagan defrauded his law firm and its client, Grand Met, by using for his own trading purposes material, nonpublic information regarding Grand Met's planned tender offer. According to the indictment, O'Hagan used the profits he gained through this trading to conceal his previous embezzlement and conversion of unrelated client trust funds.[2] . . . O'Hagan was charged with 20 counts of mail fraud; 17 counts of securities fraud, in violation of § 10(b) of the Securities Exchange Act of 1934 (Exchange Act), and SEC Rule 10b–5; 17 counts of fraudulent trading in connection with a tender offer, in violation of § 14(e) of the Exchange Act, and SEC Rule 14e–3(a); and 3 counts of violating federal money laundering statutes. A jury convicted O'Hagan on all 57 counts, and he was sentenced to a 41-month term of imprisonment.

A divided panel of the Court of Appeals for the Eighth Circuit reversed all of O'Hagan's convictions. Liability under § 10(b) and Rule 10b–5, the Eighth Circuit held, may not be grounded on the "misappropriation theory" of securities fraud on which the prosecution relied. The Court of Appeals also held that Rule 14e–3(a)—which prohibits trading while in possession of material, nonpublic information relating to a tender offer—exceeds the SEC's § 14(e) rulemaking authority because the rule contains no breach of fiduciary duty requirement. The Eighth Circuit further concluded that O'Hagan's mail fraud and money laundering convictions rested on violations of the securities laws, and therefore could not stand once the securities fraud convictions were reversed. . . .

Decisions of the Courts of Appeals are in conflict on the propriety of the misappropriation theory under § 10(b) and Rule 10b–5, and on the legitimacy of Rule 14e–3(a) under § 14(e). We granted certiorari, and now reverse the Eighth Circuit's judgment.

II

. . .

A

. . .

Under the "traditional" or "classical theory" of insider trading liability, § 10(b) and Rule 10b–5 are violated when a corporate insider trades in the securities of his corporation on the basis of material, nonpublic information. Trading on such information qualifies as a "deceptive device" under § 10(b), we have affirmed, because "a relationship of trust and confidence [exists] between the shareholders of a corporation and those insiders who have obtained confidential information by reason of their position with that corporation." Chiarella v. United States, 445 U.S. 222, 228 (1980). That relationship, we recognized, "gives rise to a duty to disclose [or to abstain from trading]

[2] O'Hagan was convicted of theft in state court, sentenced to 30 months' imprisonment, and fined. . . . The Supreme Court of Minnesota disbarred O'Hagan from the practice of law. . . .

because of the 'necessity of preventing a corporate insider from . . . taking unfair advantage of . . . uninformed . . . stockholders.'" Id., at 228–229 (citation omitted). The classical theory applies not only to officers, directors, and other permanent insiders of a corporation, but also to attorneys, accountants, consultants, and others who temporarily become fiduciaries of a corporation. See Dirks v. SEC, 463 U.S. 646, 655, n. 14 (1983).

The "misappropriation theory" holds that a person commits fraud "in connection with" a securities transaction, and thereby violates § 10(b) and Rule 10b–5, when he misappropriates confidential information for securities trading purposes, in breach of a duty owed to the source of the information. Under this theory, a fiduciary's undisclosed, self-serving use of a principal's information to purchase or sell securities, in breach of a duty of loyalty and confidentiality, defrauds the principal of the exclusive use of that information. In lieu of premising liability on a fiduciary relationship between company insider and purchaser or seller of the company's stock, the misappropriation theory premises liability on a fiduciary-turned-trader's deception of those who entrusted him with access to confidential information.

The two theories are complementary, each addressing efforts to capitalize on nonpublic information through the purchase or sale of securities. The classical theory targets a corporate insider's breach of duty to shareholders with whom the insider transacts; the misappropriation theory outlaws trading on the basis of nonpublic information by a corporate "outsider" in breach of a duty owed not to a trading party, but to the source of the information. The misappropriation theory is thus designed to "protect the integrity of the securities markets against abuses by 'outsiders' to a corporation who have access to confidential information that will affect the corporation's security price when revealed, but who owe no fiduciary or other duty to that corporation's shareholders." [Brief for United States 14.]

In this case, the indictment alleged that O'Hagan, in breach of a duty of trust and confidence he owed to his law firm, Dorsey & Whitney, and to its client, Grand Met, traded on the basis of nonpublic information regarding Grand Met's planned tender offer for Pillsbury common stock. This conduct, the Government charged, constituted a fraudulent device in connection with the purchase and sale of securities.[5]

B

We agree with the Government that misappropriation, as just defined, satisfies § 10(b)'s requirement that chargeable conduct involve a "deceptive device or contrivance" used "in connection with" the purchase or sale of securities. We observe, first, that misappropriators, as the Government describes them, deal in deception. A fiduciary who "[pretends] loyalty to the principal while secretly converting the principal's information for personal gain," Brief for United States 17, "dupes" or defrauds the principal.

. . .

[5] The Government could not have prosecuted O'Hagan under the classical theory, for O'Hagan was not an "insider" of Pillsbury, the corporation in whose stock he traded.

. . . Deception through nondisclosure is central to the theory of liability for which the Government seeks recognition. As counsel for the Government stated in explanation of the theory at oral argument: "To satisfy the common law rule that a trustee may not use the property that [has] been entrusted [to] him, there would have to be consent. To satisfy the requirement of the Securities Act that there be no deception, there would only have to be disclosure."[6]

The misappropriation theory advanced by the Government is consistent with Santa Fe Industries, Inc. v. Green, 430 U.S. 462 (1977), a decision underscoring that § 10(b) is not an all-purpose breach of fiduciary duty ban; rather, it trains on conduct involving manipulation or deception. . . . In contrast to the Government's allegations in this case, in *Santa Fe Industries*, all pertinent facts were disclosed by the persons charged with violating § 10(b) and Rule 10b–5 . . .; therefore, there was no deception through nondisclosure to which liability under those provisions could attach. . . . Similarly, full disclosure forecloses liability under the misappropriation theory: Because the deception essential to the misappropriation theory involves feigning fidelity to the source of information, if the fiduciary discloses to the source that he plans to trade on the nonpublic information, there is no "deceptive device" and thus no § 10(b) violation—although the fiduciary-turned-trader may remain liable under state law for breach of a duty of loyalty.[7]

We turn next to the § 10(b) requirement that the misappropriator's deceptive use of information be "in connection with the purchase or sale of [a] security." This element is satisfied because the fiduciary's fraud is consummated, not when the fiduciary gains the confidential information, but when, without disclosure to his principal, he uses the information to purchase or sell securities. The securities transaction and the breach of duty thus coincide. This is so even though the person or entity defrauded is not the other party to the trade, but is, instead, the source of the nonpublic information. . . . A misappropriator who trades on the basis of material, nonpublic information, in short, gains his advantageous market position through deception; he deceives the source of the information and simultaneously harms members of the investing public. . . .

The misappropriation theory comports with § 10(b)'s language, which requires deception "in connection with the purchase or sale of any security," not deception of an identifiable purchaser or seller. The theory is also well-tuned to an animating purpose of the Exchange Act: to insure honest securities markets and thereby promote investor confidence. . . . Although informational disparity is inevitable in the securities markets, investors likely would hesitate to venture their capital in a market where trading based on misappropriated nonpublic information is unchecked by law. An investor's informational disadvantage vis-a-vis a

---

[6] Under the misappropriation theory urged in this case, the disclosure obligation runs to the source of the information, here, Dorsey & Whitney and Grand Met. Chief Justice Burger, dissenting in *Chiarella*, advanced a broader reading of § 10(b) and Rule 10b–5; the disclosure obligation, as he envisioned it, ran to those with whom the misappropriator trades. . . . The Government does not propose that we adopt a misappropriation theory of that breadth.

[7] Where, however, a person trading on the basis of material, nonpublic information owes a duty of loyalty and confidentiality to two entities or persons—for example, a law firm and its client—but makes disclosure to only one, the trader may still be liable under the misappropriation theory.

misappropriator with material, nonpublic information stems from contrivance, not luck; it is a disadvantage that cannot be overcome with research or skill. . . .

In sum, considering the inhibiting impact on market participation of trading on misappropriated information, and the congressional purposes underlying § 10(b), it makes scant sense to hold a lawyer like O'Hagan a § 10(b) violator if he works for a law firm representing the target of a tender offer, but not if he works for a law firm representing the bidder. The text of the statute requires no such result.[9] The misappropriation at issue here was properly made the subject of a § 10(b) charge because it meets the statutory requirement that there be "deceptive" conduct "in connection with" securities transactions. . . .

III

We consider next the ground on which the Court of Appeals reversed O'Hagan's convictions for fraudulent trading in connection with a tender offer, in violation of § 14(e) of the Exchange Act and SEC Rule 14e–3(a). A sole question is before us as to these convictions: Did the Commission, as the Court of Appeals held, exceed its rulemaking authority under § 14(e) when it adopted Rule 14e–3(a) without requiring a showing that the trading at issue entailed a breach of fiduciary duty? We hold that the Commission, in this regard and to the extent relevant to this case, did not exceed its authority.

The governing statutory provision, § 14(e) of the Exchange Act, reads in relevant part:

> "It shall be unlawful for any person . . . to engage in any fraudulent, deceptive, or manipulative acts or practices, in connection with any tender offer. . . . The [SEC] shall, for the purposes of this subsection, by rules and regulations define, and prescribe means reasonably designed to prevent, such acts and practices as are fraudulent, deceptive, or manipulative."

. . .

Relying on § 14(e)'s rulemaking authorization, the Commission, in 1980, promulgated Rule 14e–3(a). That measure provides:

> "(a) If any person has taken a substantial step or steps to commence, or has commenced, a tender offer (the 'offering person'), it shall constitute a fraudulent, deceptive or manipulative act or practice within the meaning of section 14(e) of the [Exchange] Act for any other person who is in possession of material information relating to such tender offer which information he knows or has reason to know is nonpublic and which he knows or has reason to know has been acquired directly or indirectly from:

[9] As noted earlier, however, the textual requirement of deception precludes § 10(b) liability when a person trading on the basis of nonpublic information has disclosed his trading plans to, or obtained authorization from, the principal—even though such conduct may affect the securities markets in the same manner as the conduct reached by the misappropriation theory. . . . [O]nce a disloyal agent discloses his imminent breach of duty, his principal may seek appropriate equitable relief under state law. Furthermore, in the context of a tender offer, the principal who authorizes an agent's trading on confidential information may, in the Commission's view, incur liability for an Exchange Act violation under Rule 14e–3(a).

"(1) The offering person,

"(2) The issuer of the securities sought or to be sought by such tender offer, or

"(3) Any officer, director, partner or employee or any other person acting on behalf of the offering person or such issuer,

"to purchase or sell or cause to be purchased or sold any of such securities or any securities convertible into or exchangeable for any such securities or any option or right to obtain or to dispose of any of the foregoing securities, unless within a reasonable time prior to any purchase or sale such information and its source are publicly disclosed by press release or otherwise."

. . .

In the Eighth Circuit's view, because Rule 14e–3(a) applies whether or not the trading in question breaches a fiduciary duty, the regulation exceeds the SEC's § 14(e) rulemaking authority. . . .

We need not resolve in this case whether the Commission's authority under § 14(e) to "define . . . such acts and practices as are fraudulent" is broader than the Commission's fraud-defining authority under § 10(b), [as the Government contended,] for we agree with the United States that Rule 14e–3(a), as applied to cases of this genre, qualifies under § 14(e) as a "means reasonably designed to prevent" fraudulent trading on material, nonpublic information in the tender offer context.[17] A prophylactic measure, because its mission is to prevent, typically encompasses more than the core activity prohibited. . . .

. . . [I]t is a fair assumption that trading on the basis of material, nonpublic information will often involve a breach of a duty of confidentiality to the bidder or target company or their representatives. The SEC, cognizant of the proof problem that could enable sophisticated traders to escape responsibility, placed in Rule 14e–3(a) a "disclose or abstain from trading" command that does not require specific proof of a breach of fiduciary duty. That prescription, we are satisfied, applied to this case, is a "means reasonably designed to prevent" fraudulent trading on material, nonpublic information in the tender offer context. . . .

NOTES AND QUESTIONS

1. The Supreme Court previously considered the misappropriation theory in Carpenter v. United States, 484 U.S. 19 (1987). R. Foster Winans wrote the widely read "Heard on the Street" column for the Wall Street Journal, which provides investing information and advice. Because that column apparently had a short-lived effect on the price of the stocks it covered, someone who knew the column's contents in advance could profit by trading in the affected stocks. Although Wall Street Journal policy stated that prior to their publication the contents of columns were the Journal's confidential property, Winans, before publication, disclosed the contents of his columns to several friends who

---

[17] We leave for another day, when the issue requires decision, the legitimacy of Rule 14e–3(a) as applied to "warehousing," which the Government describes as "the practice by which bidders leak advance information of a tender offer to allies and encourage them to purchase the target company's stock before the bid is announced." . . .

then traded in the affected stocks. Winans and his friends were convicted of securities fraud and mail and wire fraud.* The Supreme Court affirmed on all counts, but affirmed the securities fraud convictions (as opposed to the mail and wire fraud counts) only by an evenly divided Court (4–4) with respect to the misappropriation theory. By long-standing tradition, a decision by an evenly-divided court affirms the lower court result but has no precedential or stare decisis effect, leaving the validity of the misappropriation theory uncertain until *O'Hagan*. Would Winans' conviction stand under *O'Hagan*? Suppose the Wall Street Journal had a policy permitting employees to trade on the basis of information about forthcoming articles. What result after *O'Hagan*? Could the Wall Street Journal itself trade on the basis of information about forthcoming articles?

2. In United States v. Chestman, 947 F.2d 551 (2d Cir.1991), cert. denied 503 U.S. 1004 (1992), Ira Waldbaum was the president and controlling shareholder of Waldbaum, Inc., a publicly-traded supermarket chain. Ira decided to sell Waldbaum to A & P at $50 per share, a 100% premium over the prevailing market price. Ira informed his sister Shirley of the forthcoming transaction. Shirley told her daughter Susan Loeb, who in turn told her husband Keith Loeb. Each person in the chain told the next to keep the information confidential. Keith passed an edited version of the information to his stock broker, one Robert Chestman, who then bought Waldbaum stock for his own account and the accounts of other clients. Chestman was accused of violating Rule 10b–5. According to the Government's theory of the case, Keith Loeb misappropriated information from his wife Susan, which he then tipped to Chestman. The Second Circuit held that "a person violates Rule 10b–5 when he misappropriates material nonpublic information in breach of a fiduciary duty or similar relationship of trust and confidence and uses that information in a securities transaction." Id. at 566. The Court further held that in the absence of any evidence that Keith regularly participated in confidential business discussions, the familial relationship standing alone did not create a fiduciary relationship between Keith and Susan or any members of her family. Accordingly, Loeb's actions did not give rise to the requisite breach of fiduciary duty. Would *O'Hagan* change the Second Circuit's analysis in any material respect?

In 2000, the SEC addressed the *Chestman* problem by adopting Rule 10b5–2, which provides "a non-exclusive list of three situations in which a person has a duty of trust or confidence for purposes of the 'misappropriation' theory. . . ." Exchange Act Rel. No. 43,154 (Aug. 15, 2000). First, such a duty exists whenever someone agrees to maintain information in confidence. Second, such a duty exists between two people who have a pattern or practice of sharing confidences such that the

* The federal mail and wire fraud statutes, 18 U.S.C. §§ 1341 and 1343, respectively prohibit the use of the mails and "wire, radio, or television communication" for the purpose of executing any "scheme or artifice to defraud." The mail and wire fraud statutes protect only property rights, McNally v. U.S., 483, U.S. 350 (1987), but confidential business information is deemed to be property for purposes of those statutes. Carpenter v. U.S., 484 U.S. 19, 25 (1987). Hence, the Supreme Court held, the Wall Street Journal owned the information used by Winans and his co-conspirators and, moreover, that their use of the mails and wire communications to trade on the basis of that information constituted the requisite scheme to defraud. Arguably, after *Carpenter* and *O'Hagan*, if there is a Rule 10b–5 violation there will also be a mail and wire fraud violation and vice-versa.

recipient of the information knows or reasonably should know that the speaker expects the recipient to maintain the information's confidentiality. Third, such a duty exists when someone receives or obtains material nonpublic information from a spouse, parent, child, or sibling. Query whether Rule 10b5–2 is consistent with the Supreme Court's insider trading jurisprudence as set forth in *Dirks* and *O'Hagan*? If not, should the SEC have adopted it?

3. Does a duty to disclose to the source of the information arise before trading in all fiduciary relationships? Consider ABA Model Rule of Professional Conduct 1.8(b), which states: "A lawyer shall not use information relating to representation of a client to the disadvantage of the client unless the client consents after consultation. . . ." Does a lawyer's use of confidential client information for insider trading purposes always operate to the client's disadvantage? If not, and assuming the Model Rule accurately states the lawyer's fiduciary obligation, does trading by a lawyer on the basis of confidential client information nevertheless always violate § 10(b) in the absence of disclosure by the lawyer to the client?

4. According to the Court, liability under § 10(b) could not have been imposed if O'Hagan had disclosed "to the source of the information" that he planned to trade on the nonpublic information. Recall that O'Hagan was a partner in the Dorsey & Whitney law partnership. To whom should O'Hagan have made the requisite disclosure?

5. Suppose O'Hagan had informed Dorsey & Whitney of his intentions to buy Pillsbury stock and the firm had approved. What result?

6. Suppose O'Hagan had informed both Dorsey & Whitney and Grand Met of his intentions to buy Pillsbury stock for his own benefit, at least one of them had objected, but O'Hagan bought anyway. What result?

7. The Court states that "investors likely would hesitate to venture their capital in a market where trading based on misappropriated nonpublic information is unchecked." On what facts, if any, is the court's intuition premised? Do you agree with the Court?

8. Is *O'Hagan* premised mainly on an economic analysis of how capital markets function or on a moral intuition that insider trading is wrong? Is there an economic justification for prohibiting insider trading? Is there a moral justification for prohibiting insider trading? Is either economics or morality relevant to a case like *O'Hagan*, which after all purports to involve interpreting a statute?

9. Assuming arguendo that insider trading ought to be regulated, is it necessary to make a federal case out of it? As the fiduciary duty-based rationale for regulating insider trading suggests, the real concern in this area goes to the duty of loyalty rather than disclosure. It is the theft of information by an agent from his principal that is being punished here, not his failure to disclose information to those with whom he trades. Given that all other fiduciary duty issues have been left to state law, why is insider trading governed by federal law?

10. One of the long open questions of insider trading jurisprudence was whether liability could be imposed solely on those who traded *on the basis of* material nonpublic information or could be imposed more

generally on all who traded *while in possession of* such information. Suppose Jane Doe sold Acme Corporation stock knowing Acme was about to suffer severe financial reverses, but can demonstrate that she would have sold under any circumstances in order to pay catastrophic medical bills. In SEC v. Adler, 137 F.3d 1325 (11th Cir. 1998), the Eleventh Circuit opined that mere knowing possession of material nonpublic information by an inside trader was not a per se violation of 10b–5, as the SEC asserted. Instead, the court relied on causation concepts: Trading while in possession of such information merely raises a strong inference that the insider traded on the basis of that information. The insider can rebut that presumption by showing that he or she did not use such information in making trading decisions. In United States v. Smith, 155 F.3d 1051 (9th Cir. 1998), the Ninth Circuit largely agreed with *Adler*'s analysis. Because *Smith* was a criminal case, however, the Ninth Circuit did not believe it could even permit the inference of use allowed by *Adler*—instead, the government must prove the insider used inside information as the basis for his or her trading activity.

In 2000, the SEC addressed this issue by adopting Rule 10b5–1, which states that Rule 10b–5's prohibition of insider trading is violated whenever someone trades "on the basis of" material nonpublic information. However, because one is deemed, subject to certain narrow exceptions, to have traded "on the basis of" material nonpublic information if one was aware of such information at the time of the trade, Rule 10b5–1 effectively rejects the *Adler* and *Smith* position.

6. SHORT-SWING PROFITS

In addition to banning insider trading through the judicial interpretation of § 10(b) (discussed in Section 4, supra), the 1934 Securities Exchange Act contains a prophylactic rule against it in § 16(b): officers, directors, and 10 percent shareholders must pay to the corporation any profits they make, within a six-month period, from buying and selling the firm's stock.* As with most prophylactic rules, the

* Section 16(b) provides:

For the purpose of preventing the unfair use of information which may have been obtained by such beneficial owner, director, or officer by reason of his relationship to the issuer, any profit realized by him from any purchase and sale, or any sale and purchase, of any equity security of such issuer (other than an exempted security) or a security-based swap agreement (as defined in section 206B of the Gramm-Leach-Bliley Act) involving any such equity security within any period of less than six months, unless such security or security-based swap agreement was acquired in good faith in connection with a debt previously contracted, shall inure to and be recoverable by the issuer, irrespective of any intention on the part of such beneficial owner, director, or officer in entering into such transaction of holding the security or security-based swap agreement purchased or of not repurchasing the security or security-based swap agreement sold for a period exceeding six months. Suit to recover such profit may be instituted at law or in equity in any court of competent jurisdiction by the issuer, or by the owner of any security of the issuer in the name and in behalf of the issuer if the issuer shall fail or refuse to bring such suit within sixty days after request or shall fail diligently to prosecute the same thereafter; but no such suit shall be brought more than two years after the date such profit was realized. This subsection shall not be construed to cover any transaction where such beneficial owner was not such both at the time of the purchase and sale, or the sale and purchase, of the security or security based swap agreement (as defined in section 206B of the Gramm-Leach-Bliley Act) involved, or any transaction or transactions which the Commission by rules and regulations may exempt as not comprehended within the purpose of this subsection.

section is both over- and under-inclusive. It both penalizes insiders for trades unrelated to non-public information and misses many trades based squarely on such information. But as with other prophylactic rules, it does draw sharp distinctions. The *Reliance Electric and Foremost-McKesson cases,* and the accompanying notes, trace the more prominent of those distinctions; the problems at the end of this section illustrate how they apply.

Reliance Electric Co. v. Emerson Electric Co.

404 U.S. 418, 92 S.Ct. 596, 30 L.Ed.2d 575, rehearing denied, 405 U.S. 969 (1972).

Section 16(b) of the Securities Exchange Act of 1934, 48 Stat. 896, 15 U.S.C. § 78p(b), provides, among other things, that a corporation may recover for itself the profits realized by an owner of more than 10% of its shares from a purchase and sale of its stock within any six-month period, provided that the owner held more than 10% "both at the time of the purchase and sale." In this case, the respondent, the owner of 13.2% of a corporation's shares, disposed of its entire holdings in two sales, both of them within six months of purchase. The first sale reduced the respondent's holdings to 9.96%, and the second disposed of the remainder. The question presented is whether the profits derived from the second sale are recoverable by the Corporation under § 16(b). We hold that they are not.

I

On June 16, 1967, the respondent, Emerson Electric Co., acquired 13.2% of the outstanding common stock of Dodge Manufacturing Co., pursuant to a tender offer made in an unsuccessful attempt to take over Dodge. The purchase price for this stock was $63 per share. Shortly thereafter, the shareholders of Dodge approved a merger with the petitioner, Reliance Electric Co. Faced with the certain failure of any further attempt to take over Dodge, and with the prospect of being forced to exchange its Dodge shares for stock in the merged corporation in the near future, Emerson, following a plan outlined by its general counsel, decided to dispose of enough shares to bring its holdings below 10%, in order to immunize the disposal of the remainder of its shares from liability under § 16(b). Pursuant to counsel's recommendation, Emerson on August 28 sold 37,000 shares of Dodge common stock to a brokerage house at $68 per share. This sale reduced Emerson's holdings in Dodge to 9.96% of the outstanding common stock. The remaining shares were then sold to Dodge at $69 per share on September 11.

After a demand on it by Reliance for the profits realized on both sales, Emerson filed this action seeking a declaratory judgment as to its liability under § 16(b). Emerson first claimed that it was not liable at all, because it was not a 10% owner at the time of the *purchase* of the Dodge shares. The District Court disagreed, holding that a purchase of stock falls within § 16(b) where the purchaser becomes a 10% owner by virtue of the purchase. The Court of Appeals affirmed this holding, and

The term "such beneficial owner" refers to one who owns "more than 10 per centum of any class of any equity security (other than an exempted security) which is registered pursuant to section 12 of this title." Securities Exchange Act of 1934, § 16(a), 15 U.S.C. § 78p(a).

Emerson did not cross-petition for certiorari. Thus that question is not before us.

Emerson alternatively argued to the District Court that, assuming it was a 10% stockholder at the time of the purchase, it was liable only for the profits on the August 28 sale of 37,000 shares, because after that time it was no longer a 10% owner within the meaning of § 16(b). After trial on the issue of liability alone, the District Court held Emerson liable for the entire amount of its profits. The court found that Emerson's sales of Dodge stock were "effected pursuant to a single predetermined plan of disposition with the overall intent and purpose of avoiding Section 16(b) liability," and construed the term "time of . . . sale" to include "the entire period during which a series of related transactions take place pursuant to a plan by which a 10% beneficial owner disposes of his stock holdings" 306 F.Supp. 588, 592.

On an interlocutory appeal under 28 U.S.C. § 1292(b), the Court of Appeals upheld the finding that Emerson "split" its sale of Dodge stock simply in order to avoid most of its potential liability under § 16(b), but it held this fact irrelevant under the statute so long as the two sales are "not legally tied to each other and [are] made at different times to different buyers. . . ." 434 F.2d 918, 926. Accordingly, the Court of Appeals reversed the District Court's judgment as to Emerson's liability for its profits on the September 11 sale, and remanded for a determination of the amount of Emerson's liability on the August 28 sale. Reliance filed a petition for certiorari, which we granted in order to consider an unresolved question under an important federal statute. 401 U.S. 1008.

II

The history and purpose of § 16(b) have been exhaustively reviewed by federal courts on several occasions since its enactment in 1934. . . .

Those courts have recognized that the only method Congress deemed effective to curb the evils of insider trading was a flat rule taking the profits out of a class of transactions in which the possibility of abuse was believed to be intolerably great. As one court observed:

> "In order to achieve its goals, Congress chose a relatively arbitrary rule capable of easy administration. The objective standard of Section 16(b) imposes strict liability upon substantially all transactions occurring within the statutory time period, regardless of the intent of the insider or the existence of actual speculation. This approach maximized the ability of the rule to eradicate speculative abuses by reducing difficulties in proof. Such arbitrary and sweeping coverage was deemed necessary to insure the optimum prophylactic effect." Bershad v. McDonough, 428 F.2d 693, 696.

Thus Congress did not reach every transaction in which an investor actually relies on inside information. A person avoids liability if he does not meet the statutory definition of an "insider," or if he sells more than six months after purchase. . . .

Among the "objective standards" contained in § 16(b) is the requirement that a 10% owner be such "both at the time of the purchase and sale . . . of the security involved." Read literally, this language clearly contemplates that a statutory insider might sell enough shares to bring his holdings below 10%, and later—but still within six months—sell additional shares free from liability under the statute. Indeed, commentators on the securities laws have recommended this exact procedure for a 10% owner who, like Emerson, wishes to dispose of his holdings within six months of their purchase.

Under the approach urged by Reliance, and adopted by the District Court, the apparent immunity of profits derived from Emerson's second sale is lost where the two sales, though independent in every other respect, are "interrelated parts of a single plan." 306 F.Supp., at 592. But a "plan" to sell that is conceived within six months of purchase clearly would not fall within § 16(b) if the sale were made after the six months had expired, and we see no basis in the statute for a different result where the 10% requirement is involved rather than the six-month limitation. . . .

The judgment is

Affirmed.

Foremost-McKesson, Inc. v. Provident Securities Company

423 U.S. 232, 96 S.Ct. 508, 46 L.Ed.2d 464 (1976).

This case presents an unresolved issue under § 16(b) of the Securities Exchange Act of 1934 (Act). That section of the Act was designed to prevent a corporate director or officer or "the beneficial owner of more than 10 per centum" of a corporation from profiteering through short-swing securities transactions on the basis of inside information. It provides that a corporation may capture for itself the profits realized on a purchase and sale, or sale and purchase, of its securities within six months by a director, officer, or beneficial owner. Section 16(b)'s last sentence, however, provides that it "shall not be construed to cover any transaction where such beneficial owner was not such both at the time of the purchase and sale, or the sale and purchase, of the security involved. . . ." The question presented here is whether a person purchasing securities that put his holdings above the 10% Level is a beneficial owner "at the time of the purchase" so that he must account for profits realized on a sale of those securities within six months. The United States Court of Appeals for the Ninth Circuit answered this question in the negative. 506 F.2d 601 (1974). We affirm. . . . Respondent, Provident Securities Co., was a personal holding company.* In 1968 Provident decided tentatively to liquidate and dissolve, and it engaged an agent to find a purchaser for its assets. Petitioner, Foremost-McKesson, Inc., emerged as a potential purchaser, but extensive negotiations were required to resolve a disagreement over the nature of the consideration Foremost would pay. Provident wanted cash in order to facilitate its dissolution, while Foremost wanted to pay with its own securities.

Eventually a compromise was reached, and Provident and Foremost executed a purchase agreement embodying their deal on September 25, 1969. The agreement provided that Foremost would buy two-thirds of

* [Eds.—This is an investment vehicle largely earning passive income, such as interest, dividends, royalties, or rents.]

Provident's assets for $4.25 million in cash and $49.75 million in Foremost convertible subordinated debentures. The agreement further provided that Foremost would register under the Securities Act of 1933 $25 million in principal amount of the debentures and would participate in an underwriting agreement by which those debentures would be sold to the public. At the closing on October 15, 1969, Foremost delivered to Provident the cash and a $40 million debenture which was subsequently exchanged for two debentures in the principal amounts of $25 million and $15 million. Foremost also delivered a $2.5 million debenture to an escrow agent on the closing date. On October 20 Foremost delivered to Provident a $7.25 million debenture representing the balance of the purchase price. These debentures were immediately convertible into more than 10% of Foremost's outstanding common stock.

On October 21 Provident, Foremost, and a group of underwriters executed an underwriting agreement to be closed on October 28. The agreement provided for sale to the underwriters of the $25 million debenture. On October 24 Provident distributed the $15 million and $7.25 million debentures to its stockholders, reducing the amount of Foremost common into which the company's holdings were convertible to less than 10%. On October 28 the closing under the underwriting agreement was accomplished. Provident thereafter distributed the cash proceeds of the debenture sale to its stockholders and dissolved.

Provident's holdings in Foremost debentures as of October 20 were large enough to make it a beneficial owner of Foremost within the meaning of § 16. Having acquired and disposed of these securities within six months, Provident faced the prospect of a suit by Foremost to recover any profits realized on the sale of the debenture to the underwriters. Provident therefore sued for a declaration that it was not liable to Foremost under s 16(b). The District Court granted summary judgment for Provident, and the Court of Appeals affirmed.

. . .

The meaning of the exemptive provision has been disputed since § 16(b) was first enacted. The discussion has focused on the application of the provision to a purchase-sale sequence, the principal disagreement being whether "at the time of the purchase" means "before the purchase" or "immediately after the purchase." The difference in construction is determinative of a beneficial owner's liability in cases such as Provident's where such owner sells within six months of purchase the securities the acquisition of which made him a beneficial owner. The commentators divided immediately over which construction Congress intended, and they remain divided. The Courts of Appeals also are in disagreement over the issue. . . .

The exemptive provision, which applies only to beneficial owners and not to other statutory insiders, must have been included in § 16(b) for a purpose. Although the extensive legislative history of the Act is bereft of any explicit explanation of Congress' intent, the evolution of § 16(b) from its initial proposal through passage does shed significant light on the purpose of the exemptive provision. . . .

The legislative record . . . reveals that the drafters focused directly on the fact that [the original draft of the bill that became § 16(b)] covered a short-term purchase-sale sequence by a beneficial owner only if his status existed before the purchase, and no concern was expressed about the wisdom of this requirement. But the explicit requirement was omitted from the operative language of the section when it was restructured to cover sale-repurchase sequences. In the same draft, however, the exemptive provision was added to the section. On this record we are persuaded that the exemptive provision was intended to preserve the requirement of beneficial ownership before the purchase.... We hold that, in a purchase-sale sequence, a beneficial owner must account for profits only if he was a beneficial owner "before the purchase." . . .

Our construction of § 16(b) also is supported by the distinction Congress recognized between short-term trading by mere stockholders and such trading by directors and officers. The legislative discourse revealed that Congress thought that all short-swing trading by directors and officers was vulnerable to abuse because of their intimate involvement in corporate affairs. But trading by mere stockholders was viewed as being subject to abuse only when the size of their holdings afforded the potential for access to corporate information. These different perceptions simply reflect the realities of corporate life.

It would not be consistent with this perceived distinction to impose liability on the basis of a purchase made when the percentage of stock ownership requisite to insider status had not been acquired. . . . While this reasoning might not compel our construction of the exemptive provision, it explains why Congress may have seen fit to draw the line it did.

NOTES ON § 16(b)

1. *Issuers:* Section 16(b) applies only to companies that register their stock under the 1934 Act. These include companies with stock traded on a national exchange, and companies with assets of at least $10 million and 500 or more shareholders. See Securities Exchange Act § 12(g); Rule 12g–1.

2. *Officers:* In addition to trades by 10 percent owners, § 16(b) applies to trades by directors and officers. Rule 16a–1(f) provides, "The term 'officer' shall mean an issuer's president, principal financial officer, principal accounting officer (or, if there is no such accounting officer, the controller), any vice-president of the issuer in charge of a principal business unit, division or function (such as sales, administration or finance), and other officer who performs a policy-making function, or any other person who performs similar policy-making functions for the issuer." If an officer or director trades stock, that trade generally cannot be paired with a transaction that occurred prior to his or her appointment. It can, however, be paired with one that occurs after he or she ceases to be an officer or director. See Rule 16a–2.

3. *Deputization:* If a firm's employee serves as a director of another firm, § 16(b) may apply to the first firm's trades in the stock of the second. Suppose X Corp. asks one of its officers to serve on the board of directors of Y Corp. If X profits on Y stock within a six-month period, X may be liable under § 16(b) on the theory that it "deputized" the officer. See Blau v. Lehman, 368 U.S. 403, 408–10, 82 S.Ct. 451, 454–55, 7 L.Ed.2d 403

(1962); Feder v. Martin Marietta Corp., 406 F.2d 260, 263 (2d Cir.1969), cert. denied, 396 U.S. 1036 (1970).

4. *Stock classes and convertible debentures:* To determine stock percentages under § 16(b), courts consider classes of stock separately. Thus, a shareholder who owns 10 percent of one class of stock is subject to § 16(b), even if he or she does not own 10 percent of another class, or 10 percent of the company's total stock. That shareholder will be liable for the short-swing profits that he or she makes on *any* class of stock.

Section 16(b) applies only to "equity securities." The term covers convertible debt, but not other bonds or debentures. Suppose Alice holds a convertible bond. To decide what percentage of the equity security she holds, courts calculate the percentage of stock that she would own if she converted the bond into stock. See Chemical Fund, Inc. v. Xerox Corp., 377 F.2d 107 (2d Cir.1967).

5. *§ 16(b) Litigation:* Although recovery under § 16(b) accrues to the corporation, shareholders may enforce it derivatively. As a result, the American bar includes a cadre of lawyers who make their living finding § 16(b) claims, filing derivative suits, and then claiming attorneys' fees. See Gilson v. Chock Full O'Nuts Corp., 326 F.2d 246 (2d Cir.1964); Smolowe v. Delendo Corp., 136 F.2d 231, 241 (2d Cir.1943), cert. denied, 320 U.S. 751 (1943). They generally obtain the information about the inside trades by scrutinizing the stock transaction reports that the insiders must file with the SEC. In most cases, they settle the suits out of court.

6. *Matching stock:* To calculate a company's recovery under § 16(b), a court must match a defendant's purchases with her or his sales. Because shareholders may buy and sell a company's stock at a wide variety of prices within any given six-month period, this is no easy task. The solution that the courts have adopted, however, is for many observers the harshest principle of all in § 16(b) jurisprudence. Simply put, the courts match stock sales and purchases in whatever way (within the confines of the rules above) maximizes the amount the company can recover. They do not use any of the standard accounting tools (e.g., FIFO: first-in, first-out). Much less do they let shareholders identify specific shares of stock (e.g., "In November I sold the share I bought in January, not the share I bought in October.") Instead, they match the lowest priced purchases and the highest priced sales. (See Smolowe v. Delendo Corp., 136 F.2d 231 (2d Cir.), cert. denied, 320 U.S. 751 (1943).)

Consider an example. Brown is president of Techniflex, Inc., a successful software company. On January 1, he bought 800 shares of Techniflex at $30 per share. In February, during a temporary slowdown in production, he bought 200 shares at $10. In March, he sold 300 shares for $50. Brown owes Techniflex $10,000. Whichever shares Brown actually sold in March, he is treated as though he sold the 200 shares he bought at the lower price ($10), plus another 100 shares he bought at the higher price ($30). Thus, he owes (200)($50 – $10) + (100)($50 – $30) = $10,000. He owes this amount even if he sold the remaining shares in June for $1 per share, and thus generated a net loss on all transactions over the six-month period.

7. *Options.* Form almost always triumphs over substance in § 16(b) cases. There are some exceptions, however, the most notable of which is

the unconventional transaction doctrine. The Exchange Act defines "sale" very broadly: it includes every disposition of a security for value. For purposes of § 16(b), however, certain transactions are not deemed sales; namely, so-called unconventional transactions.

The leading case in this area is *Kern County Land Co. v. Occidental Petroleum Corp.,* 411 U.S. 582 (1973). In 1967, Occidental launched a tender offer for 500,000 shares of Kern County Land Co. (Old Kern). The offer later was extended and the number of shares being sought was increased. When the offer closed in June, Occidental owned more than 10% of Old Kern's stock. To avoid being taken over by Occidental, Old Kern negotiated a defensive merger with Tenneco. Under the merger agreement, Old Kern stock would be exchanged for Tenneco stock. In order to avoid becoming a minority shareholder in Tenneco, Occidental sold to a Tenneco subsidiary an option to purchase the Tenneco shares Occidental would acquire in the merger, which could not be exercised until the § 16(b) six month period had elapsed. Tenneco and Old Kern merged during the six month period following Occidental's tender offer. Somewhat later, more than 6 months after the tender offer, Occidental sold Tenneco stock pursuant to the option.

The successor corporation to Old Kern (New Kern) sued under § 16(b). It offered two theories. First, the merger and resulting exchange of Old Kern for Tenneco stock constituted a sale, which had occurred less than six months after the purchase effected by the tender offer. Second, the tender offer constituted a purchase and the grant of the option (rather than the exercise of the option) constituted a sale. Because the option was granted less than six months after the tender offer, New Kern argued that Occidental was liable for any profit earned on the shares covered by the option. The Supreme Court rejected both of New Kern's arguments, holding that Occidental had no § 16(b) liability. Both the merger and the grant of the option were unconventional transactions and, as such, were not deemed a sale for § 16(b) purposes.

Courts have identified three factors to be considered in deciding whether a transaction is conventional or unconventional: (1) whether the transaction is volitional; (2) whether the transaction is one over which the beneficial owner has any influence; and (3) whether the beneficial owner had access to confidential information about the transaction or the issuer. In the case at bar, Occidental as a hostile bidder had no access to confidential information about Old Kern or Tenneco. In addition, as to the merger, the exchange was involuntary—as the merger had been approved by the other shareholders, Occidental had no option but to exchange its shares.

Although *Kern* still stands for the proposition that substance sometimes triumphs over form even in § 16(b), it no longer states the rule for options. Instead, in 1991 the SEC announced that it would treat the acquisition of an option as the purchase (or sale) of the underlying stock. Thus, the purchase of an option to buy stock (a call) could be matched either with a sale of the underlying stock or with the purchase of an option to sell the stock (a put). For example, suppose an investor bought call options on 10 shares for \$1 each, exercisable at \$50 per share. If he exercised the options and sold the stock for \$60 a share, he would have § 16(b) liability of $\$60 \times 10 - (10 \times \$1 + 10 \times \$50) = \$90$. A purchase of stock could similarly be matched with the purchase of a put. See SEC Release No. 34–28869 (Feb. 21, 1991).

PROBLEMS

1. Bill is chief executive officer of SCLaw, Inc. (SCLI), a chain of proprietary law schools in southern California. SCLI stock is registered under the 1934 Act, and 1,000,000 shares are outstanding. On January 1, Bill purchased 200,000 shares of SCLI common stock for $10 per share. Determine his liability, if any, under § 16(b):

(a) If he sells all 200,000 shares on May 1 for $50 per share.

(b) If he sells 110,000 shares on May 1 for $50 per share, and the remainder on May 2 at the same price.

(c) If he sells 110,000 shares on May 1 for $50 per share, resigns from SCLI, and sells the remainder on May 2 at the same price.

2. Renée is a shrewd investor with 200,000 shares of SCLI stock that she has held for several years. She is not an officer or director of the company. Determine her liability, if any, under § 16(b):

(a) If she sells her entire holding of SCLI shares (200,000 shares) on January 1 at $50 per share, buys 50,000 shares on May 1 for $10 per share, and buys 110,000 more shares on May 2 at the same price.

(b) If she sells her entire portfolio of SCLI shares (200,000 shares) on January 1 at $50 per share, buys 110,000 shares on May 1 for $10 per share, and 50,000 more shares on May 2 at the same price.

(c) If she sells 110,000 shares on January 1 at $50 per share, sells the remainder of her shares (90,000 shares) on January 2 at the same price, and buys 300,000 shares on May 1 for $10 per share.

3. Bill, still the SCLI CEO, buys 100,000 shares on March 1 at $10 per share, 700,000 shares on April 1 at $90 per share, and sells all his shares on May 1 at $30 per share. Did he make any money? For what amount, if any, is he liable under § 16(b)?

4. Suppose Renée owns none of the 1,000,000 shares of SCLI stock, but has owned, for several years, 5,000 convertible debentures, with a face amount of $1,000 each, for which she paid $1,000 each or $5,000,000 total. Each of the debentures is convertible into 100 shares of common stock. Suppose that Renée buys 100 additional debentures on March 1 at $800 each. Without converting any debentures, she then sells 100 debentures on April 1 at $900 each. Is she liable under § 16(b)? If so, for how much?

5. Suppose there are 1,000,000 shares of class A SCLI stock, and 1,000,000 shares of class B SCLI stock. On March 1, Mary (not an officer or director) buys 110,000 shares of Class A at $10 per share. On March 2, she buys 50,000 shares of Class B at $10 per share. On April 1, she sells all her stock for $50 per share. What is the amount, if any, of her liability?

7. INDEMNIFICATION AND INSURANCE

Most states have detailed statutory provisions covering the authority or obligation of a corporation to indemnify officers and directors for any damages they might incur in connection with their corporate activities, and for the expenses of defending themselves. In considering these statutes, several points should be kept in mind. First, there are several different situations that might give rise to liability. One situation involves claims by third persons—for example, where an officer or director is driving a company car on company business and negligently injures someone. Another situation involves injury to the corporation or its shareholders, as in the cases we have examined in this Chapter. Many of the suits in which officers and directors become defendants, along with the corporation, are brought by employees (for wrongful discharge or for violation of anti-discrimination laws), customers (for example, for harmful drugs sold by a pharmaceutical company), competitors (for violation of the anti-trust or unfair-competition laws), or government agencies. One may think of the corporation as being the principal defendant in these cases, but officers and directors cannot ignore their potential personal liability. Note that Delaware's protective provision, § 102(b)(7), applies only to "liability of a director to the corporation or its stockholders for monetary damages for breach of fiduciary duty as a director."

Second, the risk of liability may be remote, but the amount of the damages can be large in relation to the individual wealth of the officers and directors and there may be forms of relief other than money damages (for example, an injunction in the context of a takeover attempt). Even if no money damages are awarded, the expenses of defense can be substantial. Individual defendants will want to be assured not only of reimbursement of expenses, but also of advancement of expenses or assumption by the corporation of the obligation to provide a defense. (Bear in mind, it may be necessary for the corporation and the individual defendants to have separate counsel and for various individuals to have separate counsel.)

Third, corporations may be able to buy insurance to cover damages and expenses of defense (see discussion in the next note), but if they are allowed to do that, the question arises, why not allow them to become self-insurers? That is, is there any good reason for prohibiting a corporation from indemnifying an officer or director from liability when it would be permitted to provide insurance to cover that liability?

Fourth, officers and directors need to be concerned about the possibility that the corporation will be taken over by people hostile to them. That possibility affects the value of a right to reimbursement that is within the discretion of the board. Officers and directors also must be concerned in many cases about the risk that the corporation will become insolvent and that no funds will be available to reimburse them for judgments against them or (probably more important to conscientious directors) for their legal fees in defending themselves.

Statutory rules for indemnification are found in the corporate laws of the various states. The law of Delaware, reflected in the two cases in this section, is typical. You will note that it begins, in § 145(a), with a provision relating to suits by third parties allowing indemnification in certain circumstances for "expenses . . ., judgments, fines, and amounts paid in settlement." The next paragraph, § 145(b), covers indemnification for suits "by or in the right of the corporation"—that is, derivative suits; it allows indemnification only for expenses and, if the person seeking indemnification has been found liable to the corporation, only with judicial approval. Under § 145(c) expenses must be reimbursed if the defendant was successful. Advancement of expenses, which may be of the utmost importance, is specifically addressed by § 145(e). Insurance is authorized by § 145(g).

Perhaps of most interest to officers, directors, and other employees is § 145(f), which expressly contemplates agreements that provide greater protection than does the statute by itself. The scope of this paragraph is not as clear as one might hope: Does "other rights" contemplate only those rights not of the same type as those covered by the statute? Can a corporation agree to indemnify against judgments payable to the corporation? Would such an agreement be nullified as a violation of "public policy"? These are interesting and important questions, but of greater importance for our purposes is the attention this provision draws to written indemnification agreements.

Waltuch v. Conticommodity Services, Inc.

88 F.3d 87 (2d Cir.1996).

Famed silver trader Norton Waltuch spent $2.2 million in unreimbursed legal fees to defend himself against numerous civil lawsuits and an enforcement proceeding brought by the Commodity Futures Trading Commission (CFTC). In this action under Delaware law, Waltuch seeks indemnification of his legal expenses from his former employer. The district court denied any indemnity, and Waltuch appeals.

As vice-president and chief metals trader for Conticommodity Services, Inc., Waltuch traded silver for the firm's clients, as well as for his own account. In late 1979 and early 1980, the silver price spiked upward as the then-billionaire Hunt brothers and several of Waltuch's foreign clients bought huge quantities of silver futures contracts. Just as rapidly, the price fell until (on a day remembered in trading circles as "Silver Thursday") the silver market crashed. Between 1981 and 1985, angry silver speculators filed numerous lawsuits against Waltuch and Conticommodity, alleging fraud, market manipulation, and antitrust violations. All of the suits eventually settled and were dismissed with prejudice, pursuant to settlements in which Conticommodity paid over $35 million to the various suitors. Waltuch himself was dismissed from the suits with no settlement contribution. His unreimbursed legal expenses in these actions total approximately $1.2 million. Waltuch was also the subject of an enforcement proceeding brought by the CFTC, charging him with fraud and market manipulation. The proceeding was settled, with Waltuch agreeing to a penalty that included a $100,000 fine and a six-month ban on buying or selling futures contracts from any exchange floor. Waltuch spent $1 million in unreimbursed legal fees in the CFTC proceeding.

Waltuch brought suit in the United States District Court for the Southern District of New York (Lasker, J.) against Conticommodity and its parent company, Continental Grain Co. (together "Conti"), for indemnification of his unreimbursed expenses. Only two of Waltuch's claims reach us on appeal.

Waltuch first claims that Article Ninth of Conticommodity's articles of incorporation requires Conti to indemnify him for his expenses in both the private and CFTC actions. Conti responds that this claim is barred by subsection (a) of § 145 of Delaware's General Corporation Law, which permits indemnification only if the corporate officer acted "in good faith," something that Waltuch has not established. Waltuch counters that subsection (f) of the same statute permits a corporation to grant indemnification rights outside the limits of subsection (a), and that Conticommodity did so with Article Ninth (which has no stated good-faith limitation). The district court held that, notwithstanding § 145(f), Waltuch could recover under Article Ninth only if Waltuch met the "good faith" requirement of § 145(a). On the factual issue of whether Waltuch had acted "in good faith," the court denied Conti's summary judgment motion and cleared the way for trial. The parties then stipulated that they would forgo trial on the issue of Waltuch's "good faith," agree to an entry of final judgment against Waltuch on his claim under Article Ninth and § 145(f), and allow Waltuch to take an immediate appeal of the judgment to this Court. Thus, as to Waltuch's first claim, the only question left is how to interpret §§ 145(a) and 145(f), assuming Waltuch acted with less than "good faith." As we explain in part I below, we affirm the district court's judgment as to this claim and hold that § 145(f) does not permit a corporation to bypass the "good faith" requirement of § 145(a).

Waltuch's second claim is that subsection (c) of § 145 requires Conti to indemnify him because he was "successful on the merits or otherwise" in the private lawsuits. The district court ruled for Conti on this claim as well. The court explained that, even though all the suits against Waltuch were dismissed without his making any payment, he was not "successful on the merits or otherwise," because Conti's settlement payments to the plaintiffs were partially on Waltuch's behalf. For the reasons stated in part II below, we reverse this portion of the district court's ruling, and hold that Conti must indemnify Waltuch under § 145(c) for the $1.2 million in unreimbursed legal fees he spent in defending the private lawsuits.

I

Article Ninth, on which Waltuch bases his first claim, is categorical and contains no requirement of "good faith":

> The Corporation shall indemnify and hold harmless each of its incumbent or former directors, officers, employees and agents . . . against expenses actually and necessarily incurred by him in connection with the defense of any action, suit or proceeding threatened, pending or completed, in which he is made a party, by reason of his serving in or having held such position or capacity, except in relation to matters as to which he shall be adjudged in such action, suit or proceeding to be liable for negligence or misconduct in the performance of duty.

Conti argues that § 145(a) of Delaware's General Corporation Law, which does contain a "good faith" requirement, fixes the outer limits of a corporation's power to indemnify; Article Ninth is thus invalid under

Delaware law, says Conti, to the extent that it requires indemnification of officers who have acted in bad faith. The affirmative grant of power in § 145(a) is as follows:

> *A corporation shall have power to indemnify* any person who was or is a party . . . to any threatened, pending or completed action . . ., whether civil, criminal, administrative or investigative (other than an action by or in the right of the corporation) by reason of the fact that he is or was a director, officer, employee or agent of the corporation, . . . against expenses (including attorneys' fees), judgments, fines and amounts paid in settlement actually and reasonably incurred by him in connection with such action, . . . *if he acted in good faith and in a manner he reasonably believed to be in or not opposed to the best interests of the corporation*, and, with respect to any criminal action or proceeding, had no reasonable cause to believe his conduct was unlawful.

(Emphasis added.)

In order to escape the "good faith" clause of § 145(a), Waltuch argues that § 145(a) is not an exclusive grant of indemnification power, because § 145(f) expressly allows corporations to indemnify officers in a manner broader than that set out in § 145(a). The "nonexclusivity" language of § 145(f) provides:

> The indemnification and advancement of expenses provided by, or granted pursuant to, the other subsections of this section *shall not be deemed exclusive of any other rights* to which those seeking indemnification or advancement of expenses may be entitled under any bylaw, agreement, vote of stockholders or disinterested directors or otherwise, both as to action in his official capacity and as to action in another capacity while holding such office.

(Emphasis added.) . . .

A. *Delaware Cases*

No Delaware court has decided the very issue presented here; but the applicable cases tend to support the proposition that a corporation's grant of indemnification rights cannot be *inconsistent* with the substantive statutory provisions of § 145, notwithstanding § 145(f). We draw this rule of "consistency" primarily from our reading of the Delaware Supreme Court's opinion in Hibbert v. Hollywood Park, Inc., 457 A.2d 339 (Del.1983). In that case, Hibbert and certain other directors sued the corporation and the remaining directors, and then demanded indemnification for their expenses and fees related to the litigation. The company refused indemnification on the ground that directors were entitled to indemnification only as defendants in legal proceedings. The court reversed the trial court and held that Hibbert was entitled to indemnification under the plain terms of a company bylaw that did not draw an express distinction between plaintiff directors and defendant directors. Id. at 343. The court then proceeded to test the bylaw for consistency with § 145(a):

> Furthermore, *indemnification here is consistent with current Delaware law*. Under 8 Del.C. § 145(a) . . ., "a corporation may indemnify any person who was or is a party or is threatened to

> be made a party to any threatened, pending or completed" derivative or third-party action. By this language, indemnity is *not limited* to only those who stand as a defendant in the main action. The corporation can also grant indemnification rights beyond those provided by statute.

Id. at 344 (emphasis added and citations omitted). . . . This passage contains two complementary propositions. Under § 145(f), a corporation may provide indemnification rights that go "beyond" the rights provided by § 145(a) and the other substantive subsections of § 145. At the same time, any such indemnification rights provided by a corporation must be "consistent with" the substantive provisions of § 145, including § 145(a). In *Hibbert*, the corporate bylaw was "consistent with" § 145(a), because this subsection was "not limited to" suits in which directors were defendants. *Hibbert*'s holding may support an inverse corollary that illuminates our case: if § 145(a) had been expressly limited to directors who were named as defendants, the bylaw could not have stood, regardless of § 145(f), because the bylaw would not have been "consistent with" the substantive statutory provision.

A more recent opinion of the Delaware Supreme Court, analyzing a different provision of § 145, also supports the view that the express limits in § 145's substantive provisions are not subordinated to § 145(f). In Citadel Holding Corp. v. Roven, 603 A.2d 818, 823 (Del.1992), a corporation's bylaws provided indemnification "to the full extent permitted by the General Corporation Law of Delaware." The corporation entered into an indemnification agreement with one of its directors, reciting the parties' intent to afford enhanced protection in some unspecified way. The director contended that the agreement was intended to afford mandatory advancement of expenses, and that this feature (when compared with the merely permissive advancement provision of § 145(e)) was the enhancement intended by the parties.* The corporation, seeking to avoid advancement of expenses, argued instead that the agreement enhanced the director's protection only in the sense that the pre-contract indemnification rights were subject to statute, whereas his rights under the contract could not be diminished without his consent. Id.

In rejecting that argument, the court explained that indemnification rights provided by contract could not exceed the "scope" of a corporation's indemnification powers as set out by the statute:

> If the General Assembly were to amend Delaware's director indemnification statute with the effect of curtailing the scope of indemnification a corporation may grant a director, the fact that [the director's] rights were also secured by contract would be of little use to him. Private parties may not circumvent the legislative will simply by agreeing to do so.

---

* [Eds. § 145(e) provides:

(e) Expenses (including attorneys' fees) incurred by an officer or director in defending any civil, criminal, administrative or investigative action, suit or proceeding may be paid by the corporation in advance of the final disposition of such action, suit or proceeding upon receipt of an undertaking by or on behalf of such director or officer to repay such amount if it shall ultimately be determined that such person is not entitled to be indemnified by the corporation as authorized in this section. . . .]

Id. *Citadel* thus confirms the dual propositions stated in *Hibbert*: indemnification rights may be broader than those set out in the statute, but they cannot be inconsistent with the "scope" of the corporation's power to indemnify, as delineated in the statute's substantive provisions. . . .

B. *Statutory Reading.*

The "consistency" rule suggested by these Delaware cases is reinforced by our reading of § 145 as a whole. Subsections (a) (indemnification for third-party actions) and (b) (similar indemnification for derivative suits) expressly grant a corporation the power to indemnify directors, officers, and others, if they "acted in good faith and in a manner reasonably believed to be in or not opposed to the best interest of the corporation."* These provisions thus limit the scope of the power that they confer. They are permissive in the sense that a corporation may exercise less than its full power to grant the indemnification rights set out in these provisions. . . . By the same token, subsection (f) permits the corporation to grant additional rights: the rights provided in the rest of § 145 "shall not be deemed exclusive of any other rights to which those seeking indemnification may be entitled." But crucially, subsection (f) merely acknowledges that one seeking indemnification may be entitled to "other rights" (of indemnification or otherwise); it does not speak in terms of corporate power, and therefore cannot be read to free a corporation from the "good faith" limit explicitly imposed in subsections (a) and (b). . . .

When the Legislature intended a subsection of § 145 to augment the powers limited in subsection (a), it set out the additional powers expressly. Thus subsection (g) explicitly allows a corporation to circumvent the "good faith" clause of subsection (a) by purchasing a directors and officers liability insurance policy. Significantly, that subsection is framed as a grant of corporate power:

> A corporation shall have power to purchase and maintain insurance on behalf of any person who is or was a director, officer, employee or agent of the corporation . . . against any liability asserted against him and incurred by him in any such capacity, or arising out of his status as such, *whether or not the corporation would have the power to indemnify him against such liability under this section.*

---

* Eds. Section 145(b) provides:

(b) A corporation shall have power to indemnify any person who was or is a party . . . to any threatened, pending or completed action . . . by or in the right of the corporation to procure a judgment in its favor by reason of the fact that the person is or was a director, officer, employee or agent of the corporation, . . . against expenses (including attorneys' fees) actually and reasonably incurred by the person in connection with the defense or settlement of such action or suit if the person acted in good faith and in a manner the person reasonably believed to be in or not opposed to the best interests of the corporation and except that no indemnification shall be made in respect of any claim, issue or matter as to which such person shall have been adjudged to be liable to the corporation unless and only to the extent that the Court of Chancery or the court in which such action or suit was brought shall determine upon application that, despite the adjudication of liability but in view of all the circumstances of the case, such person is fairly and reasonably entitled to indemnity for such expenses which the Court of Chancery or such other court shall deem proper.]

(Emphasis added.) The italicized passage reflects the principle that corporations have the power under § 145 to indemnify in some situations and not in others. Since § 145(f) is neither a grant of corporate power nor a limitation on such power, subsection (g) must be referring to the limitations set out in § 145(a) and the other provisions of § 145 that describe corporate power. If § 145 (through subsection (f) or another part of the statute) gave corporations unlimited power to indemnify directors and officers, then the final clause of subsection (g) would be unnecessary: that is, its grant of "power to purchase and maintain insurance" (exercisable regardless of whether the corporation itself would have the power to indemnify the loss directly) is meaningful only because, in some insurable situations, the corporation simply lacks the power to indemnify its directors and officers directly.

. . . [W]e hold that Conti's Article Ninth, which would require indemnification of Waltuch even if he acted in bad faith, is inconsistent with § 145(a) and thus exceeds the scope of a Delaware corporation's power to indemnify. Since Waltuch has agreed to forgo his opportunity to prove at trial that he acted in good faith, he is not entitled to indemnification under Article Ninth for the $2.2 million he spent in connection with the private lawsuits and the CFTC proceeding. We therefore affirm the district court on this issue.

II

Unlike § 145(a), which grants a discretionary indemnification power, § 145(c) affirmatively requires corporations to indemnify its officers and directors for the "successful" defense of certain claims:

> To the extent that a director, officer, employee or agent of a corporation has been successful on the merits or otherwise in defense of any action, suit or proceeding referred to in subsections (a) and (b) of this section, or in defense of any claim, issue or matter therein, he shall be indemnified against expenses (including attorneys' fees) actually and reasonably incurred by him in connection therewith.

Waltuch argues that he was "successful on the merits or otherwise" in the private lawsuits, because they were dismissed with prejudice without any payment or assumption of liability by him. Conti argues that the claims against Waltuch were dismissed only because of Conti's $35 million settlement payments, and that this payment was contributed, in part, "on behalf of Waltuch."

The district court agreed with Conti that "the successful settlements cannot be credited to Waltuch but are attributable solely to Conti's settlement payments. It was not Waltuch who was successful, but Conti who was successful for him." 833 F.Supp. at 311. The district court held that § 145(c) mandates indemnification when the director or officer "is vindicated," but that there was no vindication here:

> Vindication is also ordinarily associated with a dismissal with prejudice without any payment. However, a director or officer is not vindicated when the reason he did not have to make a settlement payment is because someone else assumed that liability. Being bailed out is not the same thing as being vindicated.

Id. We believe that this understanding and application of the "vindication" concept is overly broad and is inconsistent with a proper interpretation of § 145(c).

No Delaware court has applied § 145(c) in the context of indemnification stemming from the settlement of civil litigation. One lower court, however, has applied that subsection to an analogous case in the criminal context, and has illuminated the link between "vindication" and the statutory phrase, "successful on the merits or otherwise." In Merritt-Chapman & Scott Corp. v. Wolfson, 321 A.2d 138 (Del.Super.Ct.1974), the corporation's agents were charged with several counts of criminal conduct. A jury found them guilty on some counts, but deadlocked on the others. The agents entered into a "settlement" with the prosecutor's office by pleading nolo contendere to one of the counts in exchange for the dropping of the rest. Id. at 140. The agents claimed entitlement to mandatory indemnification under § 145(c) as to the counts that were dismissed. In opposition, the corporation raised an argument similar to the argument raised by Conti:

> [The corporation] argues that the statute and sound public policy require indemnification only where there has been vindication by a finding or concession of innocence. *It contends that the charges against [the agents] were dropped for practical reasons*, not because of their innocence. . . .
>
> The statute requires indemnification to the extent that the claimant "has been successful on the merits or otherwise." *Success is vindication*. In a criminal action, any result other than conviction must be considered success. *Going behind the result*, as [the corporation] attempts, is neither authorized by subsection (c) nor consistent with the presumption of innocence.

Id. at 141 (emphasis added).

Although the underlying proceeding in *Merritt* was criminal, the court's analysis is instructive here. The agents in *Merritt* rendered consideration—their guilty plea on one count—to achieve the dismissal of the other counts. The court considered these dismissals both "success" and (therefore) "vindication," and refused to "go[ ] behind the result" or to appraise the reason for the success. In equating "success" with "vindication," the court thus rejected the more expansive view of vindication urged by the corporation. Under *Merritt*'s holding, then, vindication, when used as a synonym for "success" under § 145(c), does not mean moral exoneration. Escape from an adverse judgment or other detriment, for whatever reason, is determinative. According to *Merritt*, the only question a court may ask is what the result was, not why it was.

Conti's contention that, because of its $35 million settlement payments, Waltuch's settlement without payment should not really count as settlement without payment, is inconsistent with the rule in *Merritt*. Here, Waltuch was sued, and the suit was dismissed without his having paid a settlement. Under the approach taken in *Merritt*, it is not our business to ask why this result was reached. Once Waltuch achieved his settlement gratis, he achieved success "on the merits or otherwise." And, as we know from *Merritt*, success is sufficient to constitute vindication (at least for the purposes of § 145(c)). Waltuch's settlement thus vindicated him.

ANALYSIS

1. First consider only the $1.2 million of expenses Waltuch incurred in the private actions. Generally, private indemnification provisions such as Article Ninth of Conticommodity's articles of incorporation are intended to expand the right to reimbursement allowed or required by statute. Why did Waltuch lose his argument for reimbursement under Article Ninth and win under § 145(c)? Why is there a good faith requirement in § 145(a) but not in § 145(c)?

2. Turning to the expenses in the CFTC action, disregarding § 145(a), does the language of Article Ninth require reimbursement?

3. Suppose that Conticommodity, pursuant to a unanimous vote of its board of directors, had in fact reimbursed all of Waltuch's expenses and a shareholder files a derivative action to recover the amount of the reimbursement from the directors. What result?

4. Why would a state legislature want to limit the power of a corporation to indemnify to those situations in which the officer or director acted in good faith? What if the directors and a majority (or all) of the shareholders were informed of the conduct in question (such as Waltuch's manipulation of silver prices) and approved because it was likely to enhance profits?

5. In light of the court's analysis, is section 145(f) mere surplusage? Describe an indemnification provision that is "consistent" with section 145(a) but which requires section 145(f) in order to be valid.

Citadel Holding Corporation v. Roven

603 A.2d 818 (Del.1992).

This is an appeal from a decision of the Superior Court awarding damages in an action brought by a former director against Citadel Holding Corporation ("Citadel") under an indemnification agreement. The court ruled that the director, Alfred Roven ("Roven"), was entitled to reimbursement for sums paid or incurred by him to defray litigation expenses in a federal court action brought against him by Citadel. . . . We affirm the Superior Court's ruling on the merits of the contractual dispute. . . .

I

Citadel, a savings and loan holding company, is a Delaware corporation having its principal place of business in Glendale, California. Roven was a director of Citadel from July, 1985 to July, 1988. During most of that time, he beneficially owned 9.8 percent of Citadel's common stock.

In May of 1987, Citadel and Roven entered into an Indemnity Agreement ("the Agreement"). The stated purpose of the Agreement was to provide Roven with protection greater than already provided him by Citadel's Certificate of Incorporation, Bylaws and insurance.

. . .

The body of the Agreement consists of twelve numbered paragraphs, only a few of which are relevant here. Paragraph 1 contains Citadel's general obligation to indemnify Roven. That section provides, in part:

> 1. The Corporation shall indemnify the Agent against any expense or liability incurred in connection with any threatened, pending or completed action, suit or proceeding, whether civil or criminal, administrative or investigative, to which he is a party or is threatened to be made a party by reason of his service as a director. . . .

This general undertaking to indemnify for "any expense or liability" is limited later in the Agreement, however, by specific exceptions to the obligation. The exception which has pertinence to the present dispute is contained in paragraph 5(e):

> 5. The Corporation shall not be obligated under this Agreement to make payment in regard to any liability or expense of the Agent:
>
> (e) for an accounting of profits made from the purchase or sale by the Agent of securities of the Corporation within the meaning of Section 16(b) of the Securities Exchange Act of 1934 and amendments thereto or similar provisions of any state statutory law or common law; . . .

Under Paragraph 7 of the agreement Roven is entitled to require Citadel to advance the costs of defending certain lawsuits. This paragraph was invoked by Roven as the basis for his Superior Court breach of contract action. It states:

> 7. Costs and expenses (including attorneys' fees) incurred by the Agent in defending or investigating any action, suit, proceeding or investigation shall be paid by the Corporation in advance of the final disposition of such matter, if the Agent shall undertake in writing to repay any such advances in the event that it is ultimately determined that the Agent is not entitled to indemnification under the terms of this Agreement.

Roven's claim for indemnification and reimbursement was prompted by a suit brought by Citadel against him in the United States District Court for the Central District of California ("the federal action"). In that proceeding, which is ongoing, Citadel alleged that Roven violated Section 16(b) of the Securities and Exchange Act of 1934 by purchasing certain options to buy Citadel stock while he was a director. Roven is contesting the claim that his option purchases violated Section 16(b) and contends that the federal action is but one chapter in a continuing fight for control of Citadel between Roven and another director of Citadel, James J. Cotter. . . .

II

. . .

Initially, Citadel argues that paragraph 7, the advancement provision of the Agreement, was never intended to cover the federal action in any event. To support this proposition, it points to language of the advancement provision which requires Roven to secure any advance by a written promise to repay the advances "in the event that it is ultimately determined that [Roven] is not entitled to indemnification under the terms of this Agreement." It further argues that the expense of defending the federal action is not subject to indemnification because the Section 16(b) claim does not arise "by reason of his service as a director" as required by the indemnification provision found in Paragraph 1. Rather, it arises by reason of the fact that he is a director. Furthermore, Citadel argues, a suit under Section 16(b) is specifically excluded from indemnification by Paragraph 5(e) which limits the scope of Paragraph 1. Because Roven has no right to indemnification, the argument goes, he has no right to advances. . . . This was a suit to enforce the advancement provision of the Agreement, not the indemnity provision. The language of Paragraph 7 is therefore critical to any analysis of the obligations of the parties.

The language found in that paragraph in no way renders the right to advances dependent upon the right to indemnity. The phrase "under the terms of this Agreement," relied upon by Citadel, refers only to the ultimate determination that the Agent is not entitled to indemnification. It describes, and thus conditions, the breadth of the written promise Roven is required to make to secure Citadel's advances. It does not limit Roven's right to those advances initially. Citadel's arguments regarding the exception in Paragraph 5(e) and the phrase "by reason of his service as a director" in Paragraph 1 are therefore irrelevant to the scope of Roven's rights under Paragraph 7. Those provisions speak to Roven's right to indemnification, not advances. It is clear, therefore, that nothing in Paragraph 1 or Paragraph 5(e) compels the conclusion that Roven is not entitled to advances for the costs of defending the federal action.

. . .

The General Corporation Law of Delaware expressly allows a corporation to advance the costs of defending a suit to a director. 8 Del. C. § 145(e).* The authority conferred is permissive. The corporation "may" pay an officer or director's expenses in advance. The Agreement, on the other hand, renders the corporation's duty mandatory in providing that expenses shall be paid in advance. Under the Agreement, Citadel is required to advance to Roven the costs of defending suits, rather than merely permitting it to make such advances as provided in the statute. The use of the word "shall" therefore simply reflects the parties' intention to provide Roven expanded protection.

Under both the statute and the Agreement, the corporation's obligation to pay expenses is subject to a reasonableness requirement. We can assume that under the statute alone Citadel would never choose to advance unreasonable expenses, although it has the option to make reasonable advances. As the Superior Court correctly determined, under the Agreement, Citadel is not required to advance unreasonable expenses but is required to advance reasonable ones. Thus, although Citadel need not write Roven a blank check, Roven still achieves far greater protection by reason of his agreement as long as his expenses are deemed reasonable. This interpretation of the disputed provision advances the intent of the parties without producing an absurd result. . . .

This interpretation also clears up the ambiguity of the phrase "any action." For example, a demand for advances of costs incurred during a legal proceeding the subject of which was totally unrelated to the business of Citadel would clearly be unreasonable. We think it clear that the advancement provision of the agreement was never intended to cover unrelated legal proceedings.

---

* [Eds.—§ 145(e) is quoted at page TBA supra.]

. . .

V

In conclusion, we hold that the Agreement requires Citadel to advance to Roven all reasonable costs incurred in defending the federal action. . . . Finally, we note again that our decision here concerns Roven's right to advances under the Agreement, not his right to indemnification. At the appropriate time in the future, if necessary, the parties may litigate their rights under the indemnification provision of the Agreement.

AFTERMATH

As to the substance of Citadel's claim against Roven under § 16(b), the trial court's grant of Roven's motion for summary judgment was affirmed in Citadel Holding Corp. v. Roven, 26 F.3d 960 (9th Cir.1994). The options at issue had been bought by Roven in privately negotiated transactions with two brokerage firms and were subject to substantial restrictions. In upholding the judgment in favor of Roven, the appellate court relied on the fact that the options had not been immediately exercisable. This being a sufficient basis for the result, it did not reach the alternative grounds on which the lower court had relied—namely, that there had been no purchase and sale within six months and no profits had been "realized" within six months. The appellate court decided the case under § 16(b) rules relating to the treatment of options that were in force at the time the case arose rather than the new rules that were adopted in 1991 and are now in force.

ANALYSIS

Would, and should, the result have been different if Roven had not claimed that "the federal action is but one chapter in a continuing fight for control of Citadel between Roven and another director of Citadel, James J. Cotter"?

PLANNING

1. How would you rewrite paragraph 7 of the agreement between Citadel and Roven to achieve a reasonable result and minimize the risk of litigation?

2. How would you define the types of expenses that would be reimbursed? Is it reasonable to cover expenses associated with actions arising under § 16(b)?

NOTE ON INSURANCE

Most publicly held, and many privately held, corporations carry director and officer (D & O) liability insurance. There have been reports of individuals refusing to serve as directors without such insurance. In recent years such insurance has become expensive and, in some instances, impossible to obtain. The policies often have high deductibles and worrisome maximum coverages, and some of them have important exclusions (e.g., for violation of anti-pollution laws, for conduct in connection with resistance to a takeover, for actions by regulatory agencies, and for certain violations of the securities laws). Some corporations have combined to form their own “captive” insurance companies for writing D & O coverage. Others have established trust funds to pay damages or expenses, or both.

CHAPTER 6

PROBLEMS OF CONTROL

1. PROXY FIGHTS

INTRODUCTION

Corporations hold annual meetings of shareholders for election of directors and, where necessary, for voting on other matters. Corporations may also call special meetings—for example, for shareholder approval or disapproval of a merger. Despite the potential importance of actions taken at shareholder meetings, few shareholders of public corporations actually attend them. Few shareholders own enough shares to make any difference at the meeting, even institutional shareholders such as pension funds and mutual funds (though the role of such shareholders, despite various legal and other obstacles, seems to be moving toward greater involvement in corporate governance). Even if individuals own shares worth tens of thousands of dollars, their stake will generally be too small to affect the outcome. As a result, such shareholders seldom find it cost-effective to become well informed about corporate disputes, much less to attend any meeting in person.

Thus, most annual shareholder meetings are uneventful, quiet affairs, where directors are reelected without opposition and certain other routine matters are attended to. The events preceding such meetings can become contentious, however, if insurgents seek to take control of the firm by electing themselves and their allies to the board. Contention can also arise when issues that require shareholder approval are scheduled for determination at the annual meeting, or at a special meeting called to decide certain issues basic to the corporation. Such issues include whether to amend the articles of incorporation (for example, to limit director liability), to liquidate the firm, to sell all or substantially all of the assets, or to engage in a merger.

With small firms, by contrast, shareholders may appear at the meeting and help decide the firm's business strategy. Shareholders of such firms may find it worthwhile to attend shareholder meetings because they own enough shares to affect the outcome of any vote.

Because few shareholders of public corporations attend the annual meeting, the outcome will generally depend on which group has collected the most "proxies." (Proxy voting is also available, but less common, for small corporations.) Under corporate law, shareholders may appoint an agent to attend the meeting and vote on their behalf. That agent is the shareholder's "proxyholder," sometimes simply called the shareholder's "proxy"; the document by which the shareholder appoints the agent is also called the "proxy" (or "proxy card"). Because the outcome of the meeting depends on the number of votes cast, the person with the most proxies usually wins.

Generally, the incumbent managers of a large firm will solicit proxies from shareholders directly. Shortly before the annual meeting, they will write to the "shareholders of record" and ask them to sign and return the enclosed proxy card. By doing so, the shareholders authorize the management representative to vote on their behalf. If the stock is held in "street name," the broker or bank will forward the material to the "beneficial owner."*

"Proxy fights" result when an insurgent group tries to oust incumbent managers by soliciting proxy cards and electing its own representatives to the board. Such fights were relatively common in the 1950s, but fell out of favor when insurgent investors turned to tender offers as a more efficient way to gain corporate control. In the 1980s and 1990s, however, many corporations adopted defenses against tender offers and many states passed statutes that increased the difficulty and reduced the cost-effectiveness of tender offers. (On all of these developments, see Chapter 7, Sec. 2). Accordingly, insurgent shareholders again be turned to proxy fights, but now typically as part of a larger tender offer effort. An insurgent group could initiate a tender offer, for example, but combine it with a proxy fight to put added pressure on the incumbents. It might try to replace the existing board through the proxy fight, or use the proxies to fight any defensive measures that the management hopes to implement. Like tender offers, proxy fights are subject both to the 1934 Securities Exchange Act and to state corporate statutes.

A. STRATEGIC USE OF PROXIES

Levin v. Metro-Goldwyn-Mayer, Inc.

264 F.Supp. 797 (S.D.N.Y.1967).

This action was filed by six stockholders of Metro-Goldwyn-Mayer, Inc. (MGM), a Delaware corporation with its principal place of business in New York.** The defendants named are MGM and five of the thirteen members of its Board of Directors. They are part of present MGM corporate management; all of them serve as officers or as members of the Executive Committee.

Plaintiff, Philip Levin, is and has been a director of MGM since February, 1965 and all of the plaintiffs hold substantial blocks of MGM common stock.[3]

The present action flows from a conflict for corporate control between present management—called "the O'Brien group" and "the Levin group."

* Traditionally, an investor who bought stock notified the company and recorded the stock in his or her own name. Before the annual meeting, the board of directors would announce a given date as the "record date" for the meeting (or the by-laws would specify a date). People listed on the corporation's stock ledger as owning the stock on that date were called the "shareholders of record" and, even if they thereafter sold the stock before the meeting, were the people entitled to vote at the meeting. In part to facilitate trades, however, many shareholders no longer bother to notify the company when they purchase. Instead, they simply leave the stock in the name of their broker (or depository trust company). Such stock is said to be held "in street name," and the investor is known as the "beneficial owner."

** [Eds.—Jurisdiction was based both on diversity and on a federal cause of action arising out of alleged SEC proxy rule violations.]

3 Plaintiffs own 552,705 shares of MGM common stock, approximately 11% of the total outstanding shares, with a market value of nearly $20,000,000. Levin, one of the plaintiffs, also states by affidavit that he has other stockholders associated with him in the proxy contest who hold 127,150 shares of MGM common, with a market value of approximately $4,323,100.

Each group intends to nominate a slate of directors at the MGM stockholder annual meeting which is to be held on February 23, 1967; each has been actively soliciting proxies for this meeting. . . .

Plaintiffs complain of the manner, method and means employed by defendants in the solicitation of proxies for the coming annual meeting of MGM stockholders. Specifically, plaintiffs charged that the defendants, in connection with the proxy solicitation contest, have wrongfully committed MGM to pay for the services of specially retained attorneys, a public relations firm and proxy soliciting organizations, and, in addition, have improperly used the offices and employees of MGM in proxy solicitation and the good-will and business contacts of MGM to secure support for the present management. Plaintiffs, in their complaint, pray for temporary and permanent injunctive relief against defendants' continuing this method of solicitation of proxies and against defendants' voting the proxies so obtained at the annual meeting. They also seek money damages of $2,500,000 on behalf of MGM from the individual defendants. . . .

Plaintiffs maintain the injunctive relief sought is required to prevent (1) the unlawful use of the corporate organization—its employees, good-will and offices and of corporate funds in the solicitation of proxies, (2) the retention of "the four top proxy-soliciting concerns and the passing of their bill for their services to the corporation rather than to the individuals" and (3) the employment at corporate expense of special counsel "for the sole and exclusive and no other purpose than the waging of a proxy contest on behalf of the individual defendants who have every right to pay for his valuable services" with their own private funds, particularly in view of the fact that regularly employed attorneys are available to represent the corporate interests of MGM.

Because of the nature of plaintiffs' allegations, we weigh the merits of this application for injunctive relief against the financial and business background of MGM. As of August 31, 1966, MGM had total assets of $251,132,000 and a gross income for its 1966 fiscal year of approximately $185,000,000. It is one of the major producers and distributors of motion pictures in the world and markets to exhibitors films produced by others as well as its own films. . . . MGM is one of the "giants" in the entertainment industry.

. . . Defendants point with unabashed pride to the results they have achieved in their direction of the affairs of MGM. We do not question that the successful operation of MGM has been accomplished in no small measure by diligent and intelligent application to corporate affairs and by the exercise of sound and informed business judgment. The decision as to the continuance of the present management, however, rests entirely with the stockholders. A court may not override or dictate on a matter of this nature to stockholders.

. . . It is the concern of the law and of the Court that they be fully and truthfully informed as to the merits of the contentions of those soliciting their proxy. It is equally important that the Court should not unnecessarily exercise its injunctive power in such matters lest such judicial action operate to unduly influence a stockholder's decision as to which faction should receive his proxy.

It is quite plain that the differences between "the O'Brien group" and "the Levin group" are much more than mere personality conflicts. These might readily be resolved by reasoning and hard-headed, profit-minded business men. There are definite business policies advocated by each group, so divergent that reconciliation does not seem possible. They appear so evident from the papers before us that detailed analysis would be a waste of time.[7] However, in such a situation the right of an independent stockholder to be fully informed is of supreme importance. The controlling question presented on this application is whether illegal or unfair means of communication, such as demand judicial intervention, are being employed by the present management. We find that they are not and conclude that the injunctive relief now sought should be denied.

The proxy statement filed by MGM under date of January 6, 1967, opens with the statement that "MGM will bear all cost in connection with the management solicitation of proxies." . . . It discloses the employment of Georgeson & Co. at $15,000 and Kissel-Blake Organization, Inc. at $5,000 for services and estimated out-of-pocket expenses. . . .

It advises that "Proxies may also be solicited in newspapers or other publications" and that the total amount which it is estimated will be spent in the management solicitation is $125,000 "exclusive of amounts normally expended for a solicitation for an election of directors and costs represented by salaries and wages of regular employees and officers."

We do not find the amounts recited to be paid excessive, or the method of operation disclosed by MGM management to be unfair or illegal. It contravenes no federal statute or S.E.C. rule or regulation. . . .

Motion denied.

PROBLEM

Suppose you own 25 percent of the stock of True Love, Inc., a publisher of gothic romance novels. On the supposition that the novel market is shrinking, True Love has decided to start a new division, Amore Comics, to produce gothic romance comic books. You believe that the Amore Comics venture is doomed, and launch a proxy fight to install yourself and your literati friends on the board. Incumbent managers fight back by using corporate funds to hire a public relations firm that will mastermind their tactics.

You file a derivative suit challenging that use of the corporate treasury. What result? How would your answer change if you establish that 80 percent of the stock of the public relations firm is held by the older brother of the True Love CEO? What if you could also establish that

---

[7] The fundamental policy differences between the contesting groups concern, among other matters:

a. The annual number of feature pictures MGM should produce; management policy would limit them to approximately 25 top productions (with cost per picture from $5,000,000 to $8,000,000) and the balance costing down to approximately $500,000; "the Levin group" policy advocates up to 50 top productions a year.

b. "The Levin" policy would provide for a slow release of pictures to TV showing; management would license to TV pictures of more recent release date. . . .

d. Levin policy would build up cash funds available for productions by reducing dividends, and thus reduce necessity for financing; present management policy is different.

three of the eleven True Love directors are personal friends of Lady Lucy Duff Gordon, the illustrator retained to draw the Amore Comics?

B. REIMBURSEMENT OF COSTS

Rosenfeld v. Fairchild Engine & Airplane Corp.

309 N.Y. 168, 128 N.E.2d 291 (1955).

■ FROESSEL, JUDGE.

In a stockholder's derivative action brought by plaintiff, an attorney, who owns 25 out of the company's over 2,300,000 shares, seeks to compel the return of $261,522, paid out of the corporate treasury to reimburse both sides in a proxy contest for their expenses. The Appellate Division, . . . has unanimously affirmed a judgment of an Official Referee, . . . dismissing plaintiff's complaint on the merits, and we agree. . . .

Of the amount in controversy $106,000 was spent out of corporate funds by the old board of directors while still in office in defense of their position in said contest; $28,000 was paid to the old board by the new board after the change of management following the proxy contest, to compensate the former directors for such of the remaining expenses of their unsuccessful defense as the new board found was fair and reasonable; payment of $127,000, representing reimbursement of expenses to members of the prevailing group, was expressly ratified by a 16 to 1 majority vote of the stockholders.

. . . The Appellate Division found that the difference between plaintiff's group and the old board "went deep into the policies of the company", and that among these Ward's contract was one of the "main points of contention."

By way of contrast with the findings here, in Lawyers' Advertising Co. v. Consolidated Ry., Lighting & Refrigerating Co., 187 N.Y. 395, . . . which was an action to recover for the cost of publishing newspaper notices not authorized by the board of directors, it was expressly found that the proxy contest there involved was "by one faction in its contest with another for the control of the corporation . . . a contest for the perpetuation of their offices and control." We there said by way of *dicta* that under *such* circumstances the publication of certain notices on behalf of the management faction was not a corporate expenditure which the directors had the power to authorize.

Other jurisdictions and our own lower courts have held that management may look to the corporate treasury for the reasonable expenses of soliciting proxies to defend its position in a bona fide policy contest. . . .

It should be noted that plaintiff does not argue that the aforementioned sums were fraudulently extracted from the corporation; indeed, his counsel conceded that "the charges were fair and reasonable," but denied "they were legal charges which may be reimbursed for." . . .

If directors of a corporation may not in good faith incur reasonable and proper expenses in soliciting proxies in these days of giant corporations with vast numbers of stockholders, the corporate business might be seriously interfered with because of stockholder indifference and the difficulty of procuring a quorum, where there is no contest. In the event of a proxy contest, if the directors may not freely answer the challenges of outside groups and in good faith defend their actions with respect to corporate policy for the information of the stockholders, they and the corporation may be at the mercy of persons seeking to wrest control for their own purposes, so long as such persons have ample funds to conduct a proxy contest. The test is clear. When the directors act in good faith in a contest over policy, they have the right to incur reasonable and proper expenses for solicitation of proxies and in defense of their corporate policies, and are not obliged to sit idly by. . . .

It is also our view that the members of the so-called new group could be reimbursed by the corporation for their expenditures in this contest by affirmative vote of the stockholders. . . .

The rule then which we adopt is simply this: In a contest over policy, as compared to a purely personal power contest, corporate directors have the right to make reasonable and proper expenditures, subject to the scrutiny of the courts when duly challenged, from the corporate treasury for the purpose of persuading the stockholders of the correctness of their position and soliciting their support for policies which the directors believe, in all good faith, are in the best interests of the corporation. The stockholders, moreover, have the right to reimburse successful contestants for the reasonable and bona fide expenses incurred by them in any such policy contest, subject to like court scrutiny. That is not to say, however, that corporate directors can, under any circumstances, disport themselves in a proxy contest with the corporation's moneys to an unlimited extent. Where it is established that such moneys have been spent for personal power, individual gain or private advantage, and not in the belief that such expenditures are in the best interests of the stockholders and the corporation, or where the fairness and reasonableness of the amounts allegedly expended are duly and successfully challenged, the courts will not hesitate to disallow them.

The judgment of the Appellate Division should be affirmed, without costs.

■ VAN VOORHIS, JUDGE (dissenting).

. . .

No resolution was passed by the stockholders approving payment to the management group. It has been recognized that not all of the $133,966 in obligations paid or incurred by the management group was designed merely for information of stockholders. This outlay included payment for all of the activities of a strenuous campaign to persuade and cajole in a hard-fought contest for control of this corporation. It included, for example, expenses for entertainment, chartered airplanes and limousines, public relations counsel and proxy solicitors. However legitimate such measures may be on behalf of stockholders themselves in such a controversy, most of them do not pertain to a corporate function but are part of the familiar apparatus of aggressive factions in corporate contests. . . .

The Appellate Division acknowledged in the instant case that "It is obvious that the management group here incurred a substantial amount of needless expense which was charged to the corporation," but this conclusion should have led to a direction that those defendants who were incumbent directors should be required to come forward with an explanation of their expenditures under the familiar rule that where it has been established that directors have expended corporate money for their own purposes, the burden of going forward with evidence of the propriety and reasonableness of specific items rests upon the directors. . . .

The second ground assigned by the Appellate Division for dismissing the complaint against incumbent directors is stockholder ratification of reimbursement to the insurgent group. Whatever effect or lack of it this resolution had upon expenditures by the insurgent group, clearly the stockholders who voted to pay the insurgents entertained no intention of reimbursing the management group for their expenditures. . . . Upon the contrary, they were removing the incumbents from control mainly for the reason that they were charged with having mulcted the corporation by a long-term salary and pension contract to one of their number, J. Carlton Ward, Jr. . . .

What expenses of the incumbent group should be allowed and what should be disallowed should be remitted to the trial court to ascertain, after taking evidence, in accordance with the rule that the incumbent directors were required to assume the burden of going forward in the first instance with evidence explaining and justifying their expenditures. Only such as were reasonably related to informing the stockholders fully and fairly concerning the corporate affairs should be allowed. The concession by plaintiff that such expenditures as were made were reasonable in amount does not decide this question. By way of illustration, the costs of entertainment for stockholders may have been, and it is stipulated that they were, at the going rates for providing similar entertainment. That does not signify that entertaining stockholders is reasonably related to the purposes of the corporation. . . .

Regarding the $127,556 paid by the new management to the insurgent group for their campaign expenditures, the question immediately arises whether that was for a corporate purpose. The Appellate Division has recognized that upon no theory could such expenditures be reimbursed except by approval of the stockholders and, as has been said, it is the insurgents' expenditures alone to which the stockholders' resolution of ratification was addressed. If *unanimous* stockholder approval had been obtained and no rights of creditors or of the public intervened, it would make no practical difference whether the purpose were *ultra vires*—i.e., not a corporate purpose. . . . Upon the other hand, an act which is *ultra vires* cannot be ratified merely by a majority of the stockholders of a corporation.

The . . . cases which are cited consist of Hall v. Trans-Lux Daylight Picture Screen Corp., 20 Del.Ch. 78, 171 A. 226, . . . and the Federal cases applying Delaware law, Hand v. Missouri-Kansas Pipe Line Co., D.C., 54 F.Supp. 649, and Steinberg v. Adams, [90 F.Supp. 604]. . . .

The case most frequently cited and principally relied upon from among these Delaware decisions is Hall v. Trans-Lux Daylight Picture Screen Corp., supra. There the English case was followed of Peel v. London & North Western Ry. Co., [1 Ch. 5 (1907)], which distinguished between expenses merely for the purpose of maintaining control, and contests over policy questions of the corporation. In the *Hall* case the issues concerned a proposed merger, and a proposed sale of stock of a subsidiary corporation. These were held to be policy questions, and payment of the management campaign expenses was upheld.

In our view, the impracticability of such a distinction is illustrated by the statement in the *Hall* case, . . . that "It is impossible in many cases of intracorporate contests over directors, to sever questions of policy from those of persons." This circumstance is stressed in Judge Rifkind's opinion in the *Steinberg* case . . .:

"The simple fact, of course, is that generally policy and personnel do not exist in separate compartments. A change in personnel is sometimes indispensable to a change of policy. A new board may be the symbol of the shift in policy as well as the means of obtaining it."

That may be all very well, but the upshot of this reasoning is that inasmuch as it is generally impossible to distinguish whether "policy" or "personnel" is the dominant factor, any averments must be accepted at their face value that questions of policy are dominant. Nowhere do these opinions mention that the converse is equally true and more pervasive, that neither the "ins" nor the "outs" ever say that they have no program to offer to the shareholders, but just want to acquire or to retain control, as the case may be. In common experience, this distinction is unreal. . . .

The main question of "policy" in the instant corporate election, as is stated in the opinions below and frankly admitted, concerns the long-term contract with pension rights of a former officer and director, Mr. J. Carlton Ward, Jr. The insurgents' chief claim of benefit to the corporation from their victory consists in the termination of that agreement, resulting in an alleged actuarial saving of $350,000 to $825,000 to the corporation, and the reduction of other salaries and rent by more than $300,000 per year. The insurgents had contended in the proxy contest that these payments should be substantially reduced so that members of the incumbent group would not continue to profit personally at the expense of the corporation. If these charges were true, which appear to have been believed by a majority of the shareholders, then the disbursements by the management group in the proxy contest fall under the condemnation of the English and the Delaware rule.

These circumstances are mentioned primarily to illustrate how impossible it is to distinguish between "policy" and "personnel," as Judge Rifkind expressed it, but they also indicate that personal factors are deeply rooted in this contest. That is certainly true insofar as the former management group is concerned. It would be hard to find a case to which the careful reservation made by the English Judge in the *Peel* case, supra, was more directly applicable.

NOTES ON THE REGULATION OF PROXY FIGHTS

1. *The Regulatory Scheme.* Section 14(a) of the 1934 Act prohibits people from soliciting proxies in violation of SEC rules. Consider the scope of this statement. First, courts construe the concept of "solicitation" broadly. In Studebaker Corp. v. Gittlin, 360 F.2d 692 (2d Cir.1966), for example, an insurgent shareholder planned to solicit proxies from the other shareholders, and for that purpose wanted access to the list of the firm's shareholders. Because he held insufficient shares to demand the list under state law, he asked some other shareholders to join him in his effort. The court held that these preliminary requests constituted a proxy

solicitation—he solicited proxies when he asked selected shareholders to join him in demanding the shareholder list, even though his purpose in getting the list was *then* to ask the shareholders for their proxies for the annual meeting. In 1992, however, the SEC amended Rule 14a–2 to specify that a shareholder does not (subject to several qualifications) fall under the general SEC filing requirements if it does not solicit proxies for itself. A pension fund that submits a shareholder proposal, for example, may not be subject to the requirements since, even if it campaigns on behalf of its proposal, it is not asking shareholders to give it proxies.

Second, the rules require people who solicit proxies to furnish each shareholder with a "proxy statement." In it, they must disclose information that may be relevant to the decision the shareholder must make. Generally, for example, the management must include an annual report, and anyone soliciting the proxies must disclose conflicts of interest and any major issues he or she expects to raise at the shareholder meeting. In the case of proxies for contested meetings, the rules require particularly extensive disclosure. Under Rule 14a–6, the parties soliciting the proxies must file copies of this material with the SEC.

Third, when an insurgent group wants to contest management and solicit proxies, Rule 14a–7 gives management a choice: it can either mail the insurgent group's material to the shareholders directly and charge the group for the cost, or it can give the group a copy of the shareholder list and let it distribute its own material. Because the management often prefers to keep the list confidential, it generally opts for the former. Naturally, if the insurgent has a right to the shareholders list under state law (as discussed in several cases below), Rule 14a–7 does not circumscribe that right.

2. *The economics of proxy fights.* Proxy fights fell out of favor in corporate control contests for simple economic reasons: if an insurgent group organized a proxy fight and lost, it bore the entire cost of soliciting the proxies; if it won and made the firm more profitable, it gained only a fraction of that increased profitability. To see the point, suppose you own 10 percent of a firm worth \$8 million (\$800,000), but believe it to be badly managed. You conclude that by firing the managers, you could raise the value of the firm by 20 percent (or \$1.6 million). Your lawyer tells you that you could replace the managers in two ways: (a) you could organize a tender offer, buy up all the stock, and then replace the directors, or (b) you could solicit proxies from the existing shareholders and elect new directors. Of these two, the tender offer will almost always require a larger outlay. Because you will buy the stock itself, you will need at least \$7.2 million (for 90 percent of the stock of an \$8 million company). If you do so, however, you will capture all of the gains from any improvement you make to the company. (You could, of course, simply buy another 41 percent of the stock and gain majority control. You would then, however, capture only half of any increased profitability you generate.)

By contrast, suppose you organize a proxy fight. If you succeed, your stock will rise by only \$160,000 (20% of your \$800,000 investment). True, if you succeed, the firm may reimburse you for your proxy expenses. If you fail, though, you bear the entire cost of the proxy fight. As a result, you bear large risks, but stand to earn only a small portion of any gains you create. More generally, the point is this: investors who expect to incur large financial risks in rehabilitating a badly managed firm will prefer to keep for themselves any increased value they create. With a tender offer, they can buy all the corporate stock and do so. With a proxy fight, they must share that value with the other shareholders.

3. *Statutory reform in Delaware re expenses*: In 2009, the Delaware legislature adopted new Delaware General Corporation Law § 113, which states that:

> (a) The bylaws may provide for the reimbursement by the corporation of expenses incurred by a stockholder in soliciting proxies in connection with an election of directors, subject to such procedures or conditions as the bylaws may prescribe, including:
>
> (1) Conditioning eligibility for reimbursement upon the number or proportion of persons nominated by the stockholder seeking reimbursement or whether such stockholder previously sought reimbursement for similar expenses;
>
> (2) Limitations on the amount of reimbursement based upon the proportion of votes cast in favor of 1 or more of the persons nominated by the stockholder seeking reimbursement, or upon the amount spent by the corporation in soliciting proxies in connection with the election;
>
> (3) Limitations concerning elections of directors by cumulative voting pursuant to § 214 of this title; or
>
> (4) Any other lawful condition.
>
> (b) No bylaw so adopted shall apply to elections for which any record date precedes its adoption.

Section 113 was adopted following the Delaware Supreme Court's decision in CA, Inc. v. AFSCME Employees Pension Plan, 953 A.2d 227 (Del. 2008). As of yet, however, § 113-based bylaws have not significantly changed the economic analysis of proxy contests. In October 2011, for example, Society of Corporate Secretaries and Governance Professionals CEO Kenneth Bertsch stated that only two public companies had adopted § 113-based bylaws. Kenneth A. Bertsch, Dealing With Proxy Access, BoardMember.com (Oct 3, 2011).

QUESTIONS

1. In order to find an inefficiently managed firm, a potential insurgent group will need to investigate many firms. Under *Rosenfeld,* it may be compensated for the cost of a proxy fight if it wins. Yet it will not be compensated either for the cost of investigating firms that it discovers are properly managed, or for the cost of proxy fights it loses. How does this affect the incentive to renovate inefficiently managed firms?

2. As a matter of policy, should a successful insurgent group receive a multiple of its expenses to compensate it for the proxy fights it loses? For the cost of investigating firms that it discovers are properly managed? Should it be compensated directly for proxy fights it loses?

3. If insurgent groups are reimbursed only when they win, should incumbents be reimbursed when they lose?

PROBLEM

Kane is a rich man who likes to run newspapers. He is the editor-in-chief of the New York *Inquirer* and CEO and 33 percent owner of the Inquirer Corp., the parent firm. Geddes owns 10 percent of the Inquirer Corp. and thinks he himself would make a better CEO and editor. He decides to launch a proxy fight.

Kane throws a lavish party at Xanadu, his country estate, for the lead shareholders (assorted managers of pension funds and mutual funds). He gives a short lecture about why the status quo should continue, and then invites everyone to party until dawn. Can Kane charge his expenses to the company?

Geddes throws a lean-and-mean party aboard his yacht, the *Geddes Princess,* at which he harangues the same lead shareholders about Kane's mismanagement and about his own ability to run a newspaper. Can Geddes obtain reimbursement from the Inquirer Corp. if he wins? If he loses?

C. PRIVATE ACTIONS FOR PROXY RULE VIOLATIONS

J.I. Case Co. v. Borak

377 U.S. 426, 84 S.Ct. 1555, 12 L.Ed.2d 423 (1964).

This is a civil action brought by respondent, a stockholder of petitioner J. I. Case Company, charging [that] a merger between Case and the American Tractor Corporation . . . was effected through the circulation of a false and misleading proxy statement by those proposing the merger. The complaint . . . alleged a violation of § 14(a)[1] of the Securities Exchange Act of 1934 with reference to the proxy solicitation material. The trial court held that as to this count it had no power to redress the alleged violations of the Act but was limited solely to the granting of declaratory relief thereon under § 27 of the Act.[2] On

[1] Section 14(a) of the Securities Exchange Act of 1934, 48 Stat. 895, 15 U.S.C. § 78n(a), provides: 'It shall be unlawful for any person, by the use of the mails or by any means or instrumentality of interstate commerce or of any facility of any national securities exchange or otherwise to solicit or to permit the use of his name to solicit any proxy or consent or authorization in respect of any security (other than an exempted security) registered on any national securities exchange in contravention of such rules and regulations as the (Securities and Exchange) Commission may prescribe as necessary or appropriate in the public interest or for the protection of investors.'

[2] Section 27 of the Act, 48 Stat. 902–903, 15 U.S.C. § 78aa, provides in part: 'The district courts of the United States, the Supreme Court of the District of Columbia, and the United States courts of any Territory or other place subject to the jurisdiction of the United States shall have exclusive jurisdiction of violations of this title or the rules and regulations thereunder, and of all suits in equity and actions at law brought to enforce any liability or duty created by this title or the rules and regulations thereunder. Any criminal proceeding may be brought in the district wherein any act or transaction constituting the violation occurred. Any suit or action to enforce any liability or duty created by this title or rules and regulations thereunder, or to enjoin any violation of such title or rules and regulations, may be brought in any such district or in the district wherein the defendant is found or is an inhabitant or transacts business, and process in

interlocutory appeal the Court of Appeals reversed. . . . We consider only the question of whether § 27 of the Act authorizes a federal cause of action for rescission or damages to a corporate stockholder with respect to a consummated merger which was authorized pursuant to the use of a proxy statement alleged to contain false and misleading statements violative of § 14(a) of the Act. . . .

I.

Respondent, the owner of 2,000 shares of common stock of Case acquired prior to the merger, brought this suit based on diversity jurisdiction seeking the enjoin a proposed merger between Case and the American Tractor Corporation (ATC) on various grounds, including breach of the fiduciary duties of the Case directors, self-dealing among the management of Case and ATC and misrepresentations contained in the material circulated to obtain proxies. The injunction was denied and the merger was thereafter consummated. Subsequently successive amended complaints were filed. . . . They alleged: that petitioners, or their predecessors, solicited or permitted their names to be used in the solicitation of proxies of Case stockholders for use at a special stockholders' meeting at which the proposed merger with ATC was to be voted upon; that the proxy solicitation material so circulated was false and misleading in violation of § 14(a) of the Act and Rule 14a–9 which the Commission had promulgated thereunder;[4] that the merger was approved at the meeting by a small margin of votes and was thereafter consummated; that the merger would not have been approved but for the false and misleading statements in the proxy solicitation material; and that Case stockholders were damaged thereby. The respondent sought judgment holding the merger void and damages for himself and all other stockholders similarly situated, as well as such further relief 'as equity shall require.'. . . .

II.

It appears clear that private parties have a right under § 27 to bring suit for violation of § 14(a) of the Act. Indeed, this section specifically grants the appropriate District Courts jurisdiction over "all suits in equity and actions at law brought to enforce any liability or duty created" under the Act. The petitioners make no concessions, however, emphasizing that Congress made no specific reference to a private right of action in § 14(a); that, in any event, the right would not extend to derivative suits and should be limited to prospective relief only. In addition, some of the petitioners argue that the merger can be dissolved only if it was fraudulent or non-beneficial, issues upon which the proxy material would not bear. But the causal relationship of the proxy

---

such cases may be served in any other district of which the defendant is an inhabitant or wherever the defendant may be found.'

[4] 17 CFR s 240.14a–9 provides: 'False or misleading statements. No solicitation subject to §§ 240.14a–1 to 240.14a–10 shall be made by means of any proxy statement, form of proxy, notice of meeting, or other communication written or oral containing any statement which at the time and in the light of the circumstances under which it is made, is false or misleading with respect to any material fact, or which omits to state any material fact necessary in order to make the statements therein not false or misleading or necessary to correct an statement in any earlier communication with respect to the solicitation of a proxy for the same meeting or subject matter which has become false or misleading.'

material and the merger are questions of fact to be resolved at trial, not here. We therefore do not discuss this point further.

III.

While the respondent contends that his Count 2 claim is not a derivative one, we need not embrace that view, for we believe that a right of action exists as to both derivative and direct causes.

The purpose of § 14(a) is to prevent management or others from obtaining authorization for corporate action by means of deceptive or inadequate disclosure in proxy solicitation. The section stemmed from the congressional belief that "(f)air corporate suffrage is an important right that should attach to every equity security bought on a public exchange." H.R. Rep. No. 1383, 73d Cong., 2d Sess., 13. It was intended to "control the conditions under which proxies may be solicited with a view to preventing the recurrence of abuses which * * * (had) frustrated the free exercise of the voting rights of stockholders." Id., at 14. "Too often proxies are solicited without explanation to the stockholder of the real nature of the questions for which authority to cast his vote is sought." S. Rep.No.792, 73d Cong., 2d Sess., 12. These broad remedial purposes are evidenced in the language of the section which makes it "unlawful for any person * * * to solicit or to permit the use of his name to solicit any proxy or consent or authorization in respect of any security * * * registered on any national securities exchange in contravention of such rules and regulations as the Commission may prescribe as necessary or appropriate in the public interest or for the protection of investors." While this language makes no specific reference to a private right of action, among its chief purposes is "the protection of investors," which certainly implies the availability of judicial relief where necessary to achieve that result.

The injury which a stockholder suffers from corporate action pursuant to a deceptive proxy solicitation ordinarily flows from the damage done the corporation, rather than from the damage inflicted directly upon the stockholder. The damage suffered results not from the deceit practiced on him alone but rather from the deceit practiced on the stockholders as a group. To hold that derivative actions are not within the sweep of the section would therefore be tantamount to a denial of private relief. Private enforcement of the proxy rules provides a necessary supplement to Commission action. As in anti-trust treble damage litigation, the possibility of civil damages or injunctive relief serves as a most effective weapon in the enforcement of the proxy requirements. The Commission advises that it examines over 2,000 proxy statements annually and each of them must necessarily be expedited. Time does not permit an independent examination of the facts set out in the proxy material and this results in the Commission's acceptance of the representations contained therein at their face value, unless contrary to other material on file with it. Indeed, on the allegations of respondent's complaint, the proxy material failed to disclose alleged unlawful market manipulation of the stock of ATC, and this unlawful manipulation would not have been apparent to the Commission until after the merger.

We, therefore, believe that under the circumstances here it is the duty of the courts to be alert to provide such remedies as are necessary to make effective the congressional purpose. . . . It is for the federal courts "to adjust their remedies so as to grant the necessary relief" where federally secured rights are invaded. "And it is also well settled that where legal rights have been invaded, and a federal statute provides for a general right to sue for such invasion, federal courts may use any available remedy to make good the wrong done." Bell v. Hood, 327 U.S. 678, 684, 66 S.Ct. 773, 777, 90 L.Ed. 939 (1946). Section 27 grants the District Courts jurisdiction "of all suits in equity and actions at law brought to enforce any liability or duty created by this title * * *."

> "The power to enforce implies the power to make effective the right of recovery afforded by the Act. And the power to make the right of recovery effective implies the power to utilize any of the procedures or actions normally available to the litigant according to the exigencies of the particular case." [Deckert v. Independence Shares Corp., 311 U.S. 282, 288 (1940).]
>
> . . .

Nor do we find merit in the contention that such remedies are limited to prospective relief. . . . [I]f federal jurisdiction were limited to the granting of declaratory relief, victims of deceptive proxy statements would be obliged to go into state courts for remedial relief. And if the law of the State happened to attach no responsibility to the use of misleading proxy statements, the whole purpose of the section might be frustrated. Furthermore, the hurdles that the victim might face (such as . . . security for expenses statutes . . ., etc.) might well prove insuperable to effective relief.

IV.

Our finding that federal courts have the power to grant all necessary remedial relief is not to be construed as any indication of what we believe to be the necessary and appropriate relief in this case. We are concerned here only with a determination that federal jurisdiction for this purpose does exist. Whatever remedy is necessary must await the trial on the merits.

The other contentions of the petitioners are denied.

Affirmed.

ANALYSIS

Nothing in the Securities Exchange Act or the SEC rules thereunder creates an express cause of action for shareholders suing over proxy violations. What then was the statutory basis for finding a federal cause of action?

Mills v. Electric Auto-Lite Co.

396 U.S. 375, 90 S.Ct. 616, 24 L.Ed.2d 593 (1970).

This case requires us to consider a basic aspect of the implied private right of action for violation of § 14(a) of the Securities Exchange Act of 1934, recognized by this Court in J. I. Case Co. v. Borak, 377 U.S. 426 (1964). As in *Borak* the asserted wrong is that a corporate merger was accomplished through the use of a proxy statement that was materially false or misleading. The question with which we deal is what causal relationship must be shown between such a statement and the merger to establish a cause of action based on the violation of the Act.

I

Petitioners were shareholders of the Electric Auto-Lite Company until 1963, when it was merged into Mergenthaler Linotype Company. They brought suit on the day before the shareholders' meeting at which the vote was to take place on the merger against Auto-Lite, Mergenthaler, and a third company, American Manufacturing Company, Inc. The complaint sought an injunction against the voting by Auto-Lite's management of all proxies obtained by means of an allegedly misleading proxy solicitation; however, it did not seek a temporary restraining order, and the voting went ahead as scheduled the following day. Several months later petitioners filed an amended complaint, seeking to have the merger set aside and to obtain such other relief as might be proper.

In Count II of the amended complaint, which is the only count before us,[2] petitioners predicated jurisdiction on § 27 of the 1934 Act. They alleged that the proxy statement sent out by the Auto-Lite management to solicit shareholders' votes in favor of the merger was misleading, in violation of § 14(a) of the Act and SEC Rule 14a–9 thereunder. Petitioners recited that before the merger Mergenthaler owned over 50% of the outstanding shares of Auto-Lite common stock, and had been in control of Auto-Lite for two years. American Manufacturing in turn owned about one-third of the outstanding shares of Mergenthaler, and for two years had been in voting control of Mergenthaler and, through it, of Auto-Lite. Petitioners charged that in light of these circumstances the proxy statement was misleading in that it told Auto-Lite shareholders that their board of directors recommended approval of the merger without also informing them that all 11 of Auto-Lite's directors were nominees of Mergenthaler and were under the 'control and domination of Mergenthaler.' Petitioners asserted the right to complain of this alleged violation both derivatively on behalf of Auto-Lite and as representatives of the class of all its minority shareholders.

On petitioners' motion for summary judgment with respect to Count II, the District Court for the Northern District of Illinois ruled as a matter of law that the claimed defect in the proxy statement was, in light of the circumstances in which the statement was made, a material omission. The District Court concluded, from its reading of the *Borak* opinion, that it had to hold a hearing on the issue whether there was "a causal connection between the finding that there has been a violation of the disclosure requirements of § 14(a) and the alleged injury to the plaintiffs" before it could consider what remedies would be appropriate.

After holding such a hearing, the court found that under the terms of the merger agreement, an affirmative vote of two-thirds of the Auto-Lite shares was required for approval of the merger, and that the respondent companies owned and controlled about 54% of the outstanding shares. Therefore, to obtain authorization of the merger, respondents had to secure the approval of a substantial number of the minority shareholders. At the stockholders' meeting, approximately 950,000 shares, out of 1,160,000 shares outstanding, were voted in favor of the merger. This included 317,000 votes obtained by proxy from the minority shareholders, votes that were 'necessary and indispensable to

[2] In the other two counts, petitioners alleged common-law fraud and that the merger was ultra vires under Ohio law.

the approval of the merger.' The District Court concluded that a causal relationship had thus been shown. . . .

[R]espondents took an interlocutory appeal to the Court of Appeals for the Seventh Circuit. That court affirmed the District Court's conclusion that the proxy statement was materially deficient, but reversed on the question of causation. The court acknowledged that, if an injunction had been sought a sufficient time before the stockholders' meeting, "corrective measures would have been appropriate." However, since this suit was brought too late for preventive action, the courts had to determine "whether the misleading statement and omission caused the submission of sufficient proxies," as a prerequisite to a determination of liability under the Act. If the respondents could show, "by a preponderance of probabilities, that the merger would have received a sufficient vote even if the proxy statement had not been misleading in the respect found," petitioners would be entitled to no relief of any kind.

The Court of Appeals acknowledged that this test corresponds to the common-law fraud test of whether the injured party relied on the misrepresentation. However, rightly concluding that "[r]eliance by thousands of individuals, as here, can scarcely be inquired into," the court ruled that the issue was to be determined by proof of the fairness of the terms of the merger. If respondents could show that the merger had merit and was fair to the minority shareholders, the trial court would be justified in concluding that a sufficient number of shareholders would have approved the merger had there been no deficiency in the proxy statement. In that case respondents would be entitled to a judgment in their favor.

Claiming that the Court of Appeals has construed this Court's decision in *Borak* in a manner that frustrates the statute's policy of enforcement through private litigation, the petitioners then sought review in this Court.

II

As we stressed in *Borak*, § 14(a) stemmed from a congressional belief that "[f]air corporate suffrage is an important right that should attach to every equity security bought on a public exchange." H.R. Rep. No.1383, 73d Cong., 2d Sess., 13. The provision was intended to promote "the free exercise of the voting rights of stockholders" by ensuring that proxies would be solicited with "explanation to the stockholder of the real nature of the questions for which authority to cast his vote is sought." Id. at 14. The decision below, by permitting all liability to be foreclosed on the basis of a finding that the merger was fair, would allow the stockholders to be by-passed, at least where the only legal challenge to the merger is a suit for retrospective relief after the meeting has been held. A judicial appraisal of the merger's merits could be substituted for the actual and informed vote of the stockholders.

The result would be to insulate from private redress an entire category of proxy violations—those relating to matters other than the terms of the merger. Even outrageous misrepresentations in a proxy solicitation, if they did not relate to the terms of the transaction, would give rise to no cause of action under § 14(a). Particularly if carried over to enforcement actions by the Securities and Exchange Commission itself, such a result would subvert the congressional purpose of ensuring full and fair disclosure to shareholders.

Further, recognition of the fairness of the merger as a complete defense would confront small shareholders with an additional obstacle to making a successful challenge to a proposal recommended through a defective proxy statement. The risk that they would be unable to rebut the corporation's evidence of the fairness of the proposal, and thus to establish their cause of action, would be bound to discourage such shareholders from the private enforcement of the proxy rules that "provides a necessary supplement to Commission action." J. I. Case Co. v. Borak, 377 U.S., at 432, 84 S.Ct. at 1560.

. . . In *Borak*, which came to this Court on a dismissal of the complaint, the Court limited its inquiry to whether a violation of § 14(a) gives rise to "a federal cause of action for rescission or damages," 377 U.S., at 428, 84 S.Ct. at 1558. Referring to the argument made by petitioners there "that the merger can be dissolved only if it was fraudulent or non-beneficial, issues upon which the proxy material would not bear," the Court stated: "But the causal relationship of the proxy material and the merger are questions of fact to be resolved at trial, not here. We therefore do not discuss this point further." Id., at 431, 84 S.Ct. at 1559. In the present case there has been a hearing specifically directed to the causation problem. The question before the Court is whether the facts found on the basis of that hearing are sufficient in law to establish petitioners' cause of action, and we conclude that they are.

Where the misstatement or omission in a proxy statement has been shown to be "material," as it was found to be here, that determination itself indubitably embodies a conclusion that the defect was of such a character that it might have been considered important by a reasonable shareholder who was in the process of deciding how to vote.[6] This requirement that the defect have a significant propensity to affect the voting process is found in the express terms of Rule 14a–9, and it adequately serves the purpose of ensuring that a cause of action cannot be established by proof of a defect so trivial, or so unrelated to the transaction for which approval is sought, that correction of the defect or imposition of liability would not further the interests protected by § 14(a).

There is no need to supplement this requirement, as did the Court of Appeals, with a requirement of proof of whether the defect actually had a decisive effect on the voting. Where there has been a finding of materiality, a shareholder has made a sufficient showing of causal relationship between the violation and the injury for which he seeks redress if, as here, he proves that the proxy solicitation itself, rather than the particular defect in the solicitation materials, was an essential link in the accomplishment of the transaction. This objective test will avoid

---

[6] . . . In this case, where the misleading aspect of the solicitation involved failure to reveal a serious conflict of interest on the part of the directors, the Court of Appeals concluded that the crucial question in determining materiality was "whether the minority shareholders were sufficiently alerted to the board's relationship to their adversary to be on their guard." An adequate disclosure of this relationship would have warned the stockholders to give more careful scrutiny to the terms of the merger than they might to one recommended by an entirely disinterested board. Thus, the failure to make such a disclosure was found to be a material defect "as a matter of law," thwarting the informed decision at which the statute aims, regardless of whether the terms of the merger were such that a reasonable stockholder would have approved the transaction after more careful analysis.

the impracticalities of determining how many votes were affected, and, by resolving doubts in favor of those the statute is designed to protect, will effectuate the congressional policy of ensuring that the shareholders are able to make an informed choice when they are consulted on corporate transactions.[7]

III

Our conclusion that petitioners have established their case by showing that proxies necessary to approval of the merger were obtained by means of a materially misleading solicitation implies nothing about the form of relief to which they may be entitled. We held in *Borak* that upon finding a violation the courts were "to be alert to provide such remedies as are necessary to make effective the congressional purpose," noting specifically that such remedies are not to be limited to prospective relief. 377 U.S., at 433, 434, 84 S.Ct. at 1560. In devising retrospective relief for violation of the proxy rules, the federal courts should consider the same factors that would govern the relief granted for any similar illegality or fraud. One important factor may be the fairness of the terms of the merger. Possible forms of relief will include setting aside the merger or granting other equitable relief, but, as the Court of Appeals below noted, nothing in the statutory policy "requires the court to unscramble a corporate transaction merely because a violation occurred." In selecting a remedy the lower courts should exercise "the sound discretion which guides the determinations of courts of equity," keeping in mind the role of equity as "the instrument for nice adjustment and reconciliation between the public interest and private needs as well as between competing private claims." Hecht Co. v. Bowles, 321 U.S. 321, 329–330, 64 S.Ct. 587, 591–592, 88 L.Ed. 754 (1944), quoting from Meredith v. Winter Haven, 320 U.S. 228, 235, 64 S.Ct. 7, 11, 88 L.Ed. 9 (1943).

. . .

[A] determination of what relief should be granted in Auto-Lite's name must hinge on whether setting aside the merger would be in the best interests of the shareholders as a whole. In short, in the context of a suit such as this one, . . . the merger should be set aside only if a court of equity concludes, from all the circumstances, that it would be equitable to do so.

Monetary relief will, of course, also be a possibility. Where the defect in the proxy solicitation relates to the specific terms of the merger, the district court might appropriately order an accounting to ensure that the shareholders receive the value that was represented as coming to them. On the other hand, where, as here, the misleading aspect of the solicitation did not relate to terms of the merger, monetary relief might be afforded to the shareholders only if the merger resulted in a reduction of the earnings or earnings potential of their holdings. In short, damages

[7] We need not decide in this case whether causation could be shown where the management controls a sufficient number of shares to approve the transaction without any votes from the minority. Even in that situation, if the management finds it necessary for legal or practical reasons to solicit proxies from minority shareholders, at least one court has held that the proxy solicitation might be sufficiently related to the merger to satisfy the causation requirement, see Laurenzano v. Einbender, 264 F.Supp. 356 (D.C.E.D.N.Y.1966) . . . . [Eds.: In Virginia Bankshares, Inc. v. Sandberg, 501 U.S. 1083 (1991), however, the Supreme Court held that causation could not be established in such situations.]

should be recoverable only to the extent that they can be shown. If commingling of the assets and operations of the merged companies makes it impossible to establish direct injury from the merger, relief might be predicated on a determination of the fairness of the terms of the merger at the time it was approved. These questions, of course, are for decision in the first instance by the District Court on remand, and our singling out of some of the possibilities is not intended to exclude others.

IV

Although the question of relief must await further proceedings in the District Court, our conclusion that petitioners have established their cause of action indicates that the Court of Appeals should have affirmed the partial summary judgment on the issue of liability. The result would have been not only that respondents, rather than petitioners, would have borne the costs of the appeal, but also, we think, that petitioners would have been entitled to an interim award of litigation expenses and reasonable attorneys' fees. We agree with the position taken by petitioners, and by the United States as amicus, that petitioners, who have established a violation of the securities laws by their corporation and its officials, should be reimbursed by the corporation or its survivor for the costs of establishing the violation.

The absence of express statutory authorization for an award of attorneys' fees in a suit under § 14(a) does not preclude such an award in cases of this type. . . .

While the general American rule is that attorneys' fees are not ordinarily recoverable as costs, both the courts and Congress have developed exceptions to this rule for situations in which overriding considerations indicate the need for such a recovery. A primary judge-created exception has been to award expenses where a plaintiff has successfully maintained a suit, usually on behalf of a class, that benefits a group of others in the same manner as himself. To allow the others to obtain full benefit from the plaintiff's efforts without contributing equally to the litigation expenses would be to enrich the others unjustly at the plaintiff's expense. This suit presents such a situation. The dissemination of misleading proxy solicitations was a "deceit practiced on the stockholders as a group," J. I. Case Co. v. Borak, 377 U.S., at 432, 84 S.Ct. at 1560, and the expenses of petitioners' lawsuit have been incurred for the benefit of the corporation and the other shareholders.

The fact that this suit has not yet produced, and may never produce, a monetary recovery from which the fees could be paid does not preclude an award based on this rationale. Although the earliest cases recognizing a right to reimbursement involved litigation that had produced or preserved a "common fund" for the benefit of a group, nothing in these cases indicates that the suit must actually bring money into the court as a prerequisite to the court's power to order reimbursement of expenses. "[T]he foundation for the historic practice of granting reimbursement for the costs of litigation other than the conventional taxable costs is part of the original authority of the chancellor to do equity in a particular situation." Sprague v. Ticonic Nat. Bank, 307 U.S. 161, 166, 59 S.Ct. 777, 780, 83 L.Ed. 1184 (1939).

Other cases have departed further from the traditional metes and bounds of the doctrine, to permit reimbursement in cases where the litigation has conferred a substantial benefit on the members of an ascertainable class, and where the court's jurisdiction over the subject matter of the suit makes possible an award that will operate to spread the costs proportionately among them. This development has been most pronounced, in shareholders' derivative actions, where the courts increasingly have recognized that the expenses incurred by one shareholder in the vindication of a corporate right of action can be spread among all shareholders through an award against the corporation, regardless of whether an actual money recovery has been obtained in the corporation's favor. For example, awards have been sustained in suits by stockholders complaining that shares of their corporation had been issued wrongfully for an inadequate consideration. A successful suit of this type, resulting in cancellation of the shares, does not bring a fund into court or add to the assets of the corporation, but it does benefit the holders of the remaining shares by enhancing their value. . . .

In many of these instances the benefit conferred is capable of expression in monetary terms, if only by estimating the increase in market value of the shares attributable to the successful litigation. However, an increasing number of lower courts have acknowledged that a corporation may receive a "substantial benefit" from a derivative suit, justifying an award of counsel fees, regardless of whether the benefit is pecuniary in nature.

> "Where an action by a stockholder results in a substantial benefit to a corporation he should recover his costs and expenses. * * * [A] substantial benefit must be something more than technical in its consequence and be one that accomplishes a result which corrects or prevents an abuse which would be prejudicial to the rights and interests of the corporation or affect the enjoyment or protection of an essential right to the stockholder's interest." [Bosch v. Meeker Cooperative Light & Power Assn., 101 N.W.2d 423, 425–27 (Minn. 1960).]

In many suits under § 14(a), particularly where the violation does not relate to the terms of the transaction for which proxies are solicited, it may be impossible to assign monetary value to the benefit. Nevertheless, the stress placed by Congress on the importance of fair and informed corporate suffrage leads to the conclusion that, in vindicating the statutory policy, petitioners have rendered a substantial service to the corporation and its shareholders. Whether petitioners are successful in showing a need for significant relief may be a factor in determining whether a further award should later be made. But regardless of the relief granted, private stockholders' actions of this sort "involve corporate therapeutics,"[23] and furnish a benefit to all shareholders by providing an important means of enforcement of the proxy statute. To award attorneys' fees in such a suit to a plaintiff who has succeeded in establishing a cause of action is not to saddle the unsuccessful party with the expenses but to impose them on the class that has benefited from them and that would have had to pay them had it brought the suit.

For the foregoing reasons we conclude that the judgment of the Court of Appeals should be vacated and the case remanded to that court for further proceedings consistent with this opinion.

---

[23] Murphy v. North American Light & Power Co., 33 F.Supp. 567, 570 (D.C.S.D.N.Y.1940).

ANALYSIS

1. What policy goal was the Supreme Court pursuing in creating the implied private right of action under § 14(a)? Put another way, whose incentives was the Supreme Court seeking to affect?

2. In TSC Industries, Inc. v. Northway, Inc., 426 U.S. 438 (1976), the Supreme Court held that a fact is material "if there is a substantial likelihood that a reasonable shareholder would consider it important in deciding how to vote." Id. at 449. Is the omitted fact at issue in *Mills* material under this standard?

PROBLEM

Cypress Club, Inc. (CC) owns an upscale and overpriced restaurant in the foothills of Topanga Canyon, northwest of Los Angeles. Because of the glut of upscale overpriced restaurants in the area, CC is losing money. Its stock is publicly traded on the over-the-counter market. Issued for $50 per share just five years ago, it now trades at $3.00. An elderly financier named General Guy Sternwood owns 65 percent of the stock.

1. Suppose that CC directors propose a merger with Sternwood Investments, Inc. (SII). Through the merger, CC shareholders will receive for each CC share SII shares worth $3.30. For the merger to take place, it must be approved by a majority of the CC shares. Suppose further, however, that the proxy materials explaining the terms of the merger do not disclose (i) that Sternwood and one Eddie Mars each own 30 percent of SII and (ii) that Mars and Sternwood are about to be indicted in Tokyo for their role in a stock-manipulation scheme on the Tokyo Stock Exchange.

You, as a CC shareholder, discover the TSE connection and sue to block the vote. Will you win? Suppose you discover the TSE connection when the indictments are issued after the vote has taken place. Can you recover damages? What would they be? Does it matter whether SII stock is publicly traded?

2. Suppose that CC directors propose a merger with West Publishing Company. Through the merger, CC shareholders will receive for each CC share West shares worth $2.70. Suppose further that the management disclosed all the details of the merger, but few CC shareholders bothered to read the proxy material. Accordingly, 95 percent of the shareholders approved the merger. You sue for damages. What result?

Seinfeld v. Bartz

2002 WL 243597 (N.D.Cal. 2002).

. . .

FACTUAL BACKGROUND

Plaintiff is a shareholder of Defendant Cisco Systems, Inc. ("Cisco") and brings this suit as a derivative action against the company and its ten directors. At issue in this case is a 1999 amendment to Cisco's Automatic Option Grant Program for outside directors. The amendment, which was approved by shareholder vote at the November 1999 annual meeting, raised the number of stock options granted to outside directors upon joining the board from 20,000 shares to 30,000 shares.* Additionally, the amendment raised the number of options granted annually to each continuing outside director from 10,000 shares to 15,000 shares.

Plaintiff alleges that Defendants acted negligently in preparing their statement to solicit proxies to vote in favor of the amendment. The disputed proxy statement states that Cisco paid each outside director, except for Defendant Sarin, a $32,000 annual retainer fee for fiscal year 1999, and that it paid Defendant Sarin a $40,000 retainer fee to include board service commencing in September 1998. In addition, the statement represents that each director would receive periodic option grants under the Automatic Option Grant Program and was eligible to participate in the Discretionary Option Grant Program. The statement goes on to explain the number of options granted to each director, as well as the options' exercise prices and vesting requirements.

Plaintiff alleges that Defendants violated SEC proxy rules by failing to include the value of the option grants based on the theoretical Black-Scholes option pricing model.** According to Plaintiff's Black-Scholes calculations, the value of the options granted to each of the continuing outside directors in 1998 was $369,500 on November 12, 1998 (the date of the grant) and $1,020,600 on September 27, 1999 (the date of the proxy statement). Plaintiff asserts that Cisco uses Black-Scholes to prepare its annual financial statements,*** and that it therefore would have been

* [Eds.—Options come in two basic forms: (1) call options, which give their holder the right to buy from the issuer of the option an underlying asset, such as the common stock of a company, at a set price (called the strike price or the exercise price), usually with an expiration date; and (2) put options, which give their holder the right to sell to the issuer of the option an underlying asset, such as the common stock of a company, at a set price, usually with an expiration date. Options on corporate stock may be issued and traded by individuals (so-called market options) or, as in this case, call options may be issued by corporations to their employees as compensation (so-called compensatory stock options). Options issued to employees have become an important part of executive compensation and, at many firms, are also used to compensate nonexecutive employees.]

** [Eds.—The value of an option depends, among other things, on the value of the underlying asset at the time the option is exercised. Suppose, for example, that you hold a call option giving you the right to buy one share of Acme Corporation stock at a strike price of $1. If the value of Acme's stock exceeds $1, at which point it is said to be "in the money," the option has value because you can buy the share for $1 and then immediately sell it at the higher price. At the time the option was issued, however, the issuer has no way of knowing what the stock price will be when the option is exercised. Options therefore are notoriously difficult to value when issued. The so-called Black-Scholes formula was developed by economists Fischer Black and Myron Scholes to value options. Although the formula is complex, and its derivation bewilderingly mathematical, it has become the most widely accepted method for valuing options. In brief, the Black-Scholes formula considers five factors in valuing an option: (1) the current value of the underlying asset; (2) the exercise price; (3) the current discount rate (i.e., the rate at which sums to be received in the future are discounted to present value); (4) the price volatility of the underlying asset; and (5) the amount of time remaining until expiration of the option.]

*** [Eds.—Employee compensation is an expense, which under generally accepted accounting principles must be deducted from revenue to determine a firm's income. Before the corporate accounting scandals of 2002, however, corporations commonly refused to recognize the value of stock options granted as compensation to employees as an expense. In footnotes to their financial statements, public corporations are obliged to disclose the number and estimated value of stock options issued as compensation. Presumably Cisco used the Black-Scholes formula to estimate the value of the options for this purpose. Under prevailing accounting standards, however, corporations had an option as to the income statement treatment of stock options. The

easy for Defendants to include the Black-Scholes valuations in the proxy statement. More significantly, Plaintiff alleges that Defendants' statement of a $32,000 annual retainer fee plus stock options materially misrepresents the compensation of each outside director. Plaintiff contends that, using Black-Scholes, each director received compensation valued at well over $32,000.

In addition, Plaintiff alleges that the following sentence contained in the proxy statement is materially false and misleading: "Unless the market price of the Common Stock appreciates over the option term, no value will be realized from the option grants made to the executive officers." Plaintiff asserts that this statement is false because the grant of stock options results in the immediate realization of value, which is best determined using Black-Scholes. . . .

DISCUSSION

Plaintiff alleges that Defendants negligently violated Section 14(a) of the Securities Exchange Act of 1934 and Rule 14a–9 of the Securities and Exchange Commission ("SEC"). Section 14(a) makes it unlawful to solicit proxies in violation of SEC rules. 15 U.S.C. § 78n(a) (2002). SEC Rule 14a–9 prohibits solicitation of a proxy by a statement containing either (1) a false or misleading declaration of material fact or (2) an omission of material fact that makes any portion of the statement false or misleading. . . . An omitted fact is "material" if "there is a substantial likelihood that a reasonable shareholder would consider it important in deciding how to vote." TSC Industries, Inc. v. Northway, Inc., 426 U.S. 438, 449 (1976). A plaintiff does not have to demonstrate that disclosure of the fact in question would have caused a reasonable shareholder to change his or her vote. Id. Instead, it is sufficient to establish a substantial likelihood that, "under all of the circumstances, the omitted fact would have assumed actual significance in the deliberations of the reasonable shareholder." Id. In other words, "there must be a substantial likelihood that the disclosure of the omitted fact would have been viewed by the reasonable investor as having significantly altered the 'total mix' of information made available." Id.

Failure to Include Black-Scholes Valuations in the Proxy Statement

Here, Plaintiff asserts that the Black-Scholes valuations of the option grants to the outside directors are omitted material facts. As Defendants point out, however, four courts that have considered Plaintiff's argument have rejected it at the pleading stage. See Resnik v. Swartz, No. 00 Civ. 5355(LMM), 2001 WL 15671 (S.D.N.Y. Jan. 8, 2001); In re 3Com Corp. Shareholders Litig., No. C.A. 16721, 1999 WL 1009210 (Del. Ch. Oct. 25, 1999); Cohen v. Calloway, 667 N.Y.S.2d 249 (N.Y.App.Div.1998); Lewis v. Vogelstein, 699 A.2d 327 (Del. Ch.1997). The courts in all four of these cases held that Black-Scholes valuations are not material as a matter of law. To the parties' and the Court's knowledge, no court has ever held to the contrary. . . .

---

corporation could treat stock options as an expense, again using the Black-Scholes formula (or some other plausible method) to estimate the size of that expense, but was not obliged to do so. Most chose not to do so. Since 2006, an SEC rule has required that options be treated as expenses in the financial reports of registered companies.]

While not controlling precedent, the above cases are highly persuasive because of the factual similarities they share with the instant case.

Plaintiff attempts to distinguish the three state-court cases—but, notably, does not even mention *Resnik* in his written opposition—on grounds that they were applying state, rather than federal, law. Plaintiff correctly points out that the plaintiffs in the Delaware cases alleged breach of the state-law-based duty of candor, and not the federally defined Rule 14a–9. However, the New York and Delaware courts applied the same "materiality" standard that this Court is bound to apply under the U.S. Supreme Court's decision in *TSC Industries*. Thus, the fact that the state cases addressed state-law causes of action does not require this Court to reject the analysis in those cases.

Plaintiff next argues that a Ninth Circuit case, Custom Chrome, Inc. v. Commissioner of Internal Revenue, 217 F.3d 1117 (9th Cir.2000), requires this Court to break new ground and reject the decisions made by the four courts discussed above. In *Custom Chrome*, the Ninth Circuit noted in a footnote that Black-Scholes was a reliable method of determining the value of the options at issue in that case. Id. at 1124 n. 10. However, as Defendants correctly point out, the court explicitly distinguished the options at issue—which were issued as part of a loan transaction—from options granted for services rendered.* Id. at 1122. In this case, Defendants received options for the services they rendered as Cisco's directors, and *Custom Chrome* is therefore distinguishable.

Custom Chrome is further distinguishable because tax regulations require that the options in that case be valued at the time of grant. Id. at 1122. Here, by contrast, nothing requires Defendants to calculate the value of the options at time of grant. Plaintiff argues that SEC regulations require Black-Scholes calculations, but he points to no specific regulation that requires them. . . .

Based on the persuasive case law presented by Defendants, and the lack of convincing rebuttal by Plaintiff, this Court rules that, as a matter of law, Black-Scholes valuations are not material for purposes of Rule 14a–9 analysis. . . .

ANALYSIS

1. In the fifth paragraph of the opinion, the court quotes this sentence from Cisco's proxy statement:

> Unless the market price of the Common Stock appreciates over the option term, no value will be realized from the option grants made to the executive officers.

Is this statement accurate?

---

* [Eds.—Custom Chrome, Inc. v. Commissioner of Internal Revenue, 217 F.3d 1117 (9th Cir.2000), was a tax case. The taxpayer had borrowed money from a bank and, as part of the transaction, had issued warrants (options issued by a corporation on its own stock) to the bank. The court determined that the value of the options was, in effect, a reduction in the amount received by the borrower as loan proceeds. This resulted in "original issue discount" (discount from the face amount of the loan), which had important tax consequences. In order to determine that amount of the original issue discount (OID), it was necessary to value the warrants, and the court identified the Black-Scholes formula as the proper method for doing so.]

2. Suppose Helen owns the house she lives in free and clear and that its market value is $200,000. Now suppose Helen grants to Owen the option to buy the house any time within the next five years for $200,000. Do you suppose Helen could still sell the house for $200,000 to someone else? Do you suppose that on the date of receipt of the option Owen would feel any richer, even though the market value of the house had not risen? Suppose that Helen is a lawyer and that she granted the option to Owen in return for Owen's services to her as her secretary for the past year. If Helen wants to be realistic about her income for the year, should she ignore the option grant?

3. Do you agree with the court that the omission of the Black-Scholes valuation was not material as a matter of law?

4. Suppose the options had been treated as compensation at the time of grant, so the recipients would have income and Cisco would have a deduction in computing its income. Now suppose that the duration of the options when issued was five years and that a year later the market price of the stock had fallen and, consequently, the value of the options had fallen by an even greater percentage. How should this reality be reflected in Cisco's annual report of its income?

D. SHAREHOLDER PROPOSALS

Lovenheim v. Iroquois Brands, Ltd.

618 F.Supp. 554 (D.D.C.1985).

I. BACKGROUND

Plaintiff Peter C. Lovenheim, owner of two hundred shares of common stock in Iroquois Brands, Ltd. (hereinafter "Iroquois/Delaware"), seeks to bar Iroquois/Delaware from excluding from the proxy materials being sent to all shareholders in preparation for an upcoming shareholder meeting information concerning a proposed resolution he intends to offer at the meeting. Mr. Lovenheim's proposed resolution relates to the procedure used to force-feed geese for production of pâté de foie gras in France,[2] a type of pâté imported by Iroquois/Delaware. Specifically, his resolution calls upon the Directors of Iroquois/Delaware to:

---

[2] Pâté de foie gras is made from the liver of geese. According to Mr. Lovenheim's affidavit, force-feeding is frequently used in order to expand the liver and thereby produce a larger quantity of pâté. Mr. Lovenheim's affidavit also contains a description of the force-feeding process:

> Force-feeding usually begins when the geese are four months old. On some farms where feeding is mechanized, the bird's body and wings are placed in a metal brace and its neck is stretched. Through a funnel inserted 10–12 inches down the throat of the goose, a machine pumps up to 400 grams of corn-based mash into its stomach. An elastic band around the goose's throat prevents regurgitation. When feeding is manual, a handler uses a funnel and stick to force the mash down.

Affidavit of Peter C. Lovenheim at para. 7. Plaintiff contends that such force-feeding is a form of cruelty to animals. Id.

Plaintiff has offered no evidence that force-feeding is used by Iroquois/Delaware's supplier in producing the pâté imported by Iroquois/Delaware. However his proposal calls upon the committee he seeks to create to investigate this question.

> form a committee to study the methods by which its French supplier produces pâté de foie gras, and report to the shareholders its findings and opinions, based on expert consultation, on whether this production method causes undue distress, pain or suffering to the animals involved and, if so, whether further distribution of this product should be discontinued until a more humane production method is developed.

Attachment to Affidavit of Peter C. Lovenheim.

Mr. Lovenheim's right to compel Iroquois/Delaware to insert information concerning his proposal in the proxy materials turns on the applicability of § 14(a) of the Securities Exchange Act of 1934 . . . ("the Exchange Act"), and the shareholder proposal rule promulgated by the Securities and Exchange Commission ("SEC"), Rule 14a–8. That rule states in pertinent part:

> If any security holder of an issuer notifies the issuer of his intention to present a proposal for action at a forthcoming meeting of the issuer's security holders, the issuer shall set forth the proposal in its proxy statement and identify it in its form of proxy and provide means by which security holders [presenting a proposal may present in the proxy statement a statement of not more than [500] words in support of the proposal].

Iroquois/Delaware has refused to allow information concerning Mr. Lovenheim's proposal to be included in proxy materials being sent in connection with the next annual shareholders meeting. In doing so, Iroquois/Delaware relies on an exception to the general requirement of Rule 14a–8, Rule 14a–8([i])(5). That exception provides that an issuer of securities "may omit a proposal and any statement in support thereof" from its proxy statement and form of proxy:

> if the proposal relates to operations which account for less than 5 percent of the issuer's total assets at the end of its most recent fiscal year, and for less than 5 percent of its net earnings and gross sales for its most recent fiscal year, and is not otherwise significantly related to the issuer's business. . . .

II. LIKELIHOOD OF PLAINTIFF PREVAILING ON MERITS

. . .

C. Applicability of Rule 14a–8([i])(5) Exception

. . . [T]he likelihood of plaintiff's prevailing in this litigation turns primarily on the applicability to plaintiff's proposal of the exception to the shareholder proposal rule contained in Rule 14a–8([i])(5).

Iroquois/Delaware's reliance on the argument that this exception applies is based on the following information contained in the affidavit of its president: Iroquois/Delaware has annual revenues of $141 million with $6 million in annual profits and $78 million in assets. In contrast, its pâté de foie gras sales were just $79,000 last year, representing a net loss on pâté sales of $3,121. Iroquois/Delaware has only $34,000 in assets related to pâté. Thus none of the company's net earnings and less than .05 percent of its assets are implicated by plaintiff's proposal. These levels are obviously far below the five percent threshold set forth in the first portion of the exception claimed by Iroquois/Delaware.

Plaintiff does not contest that his proposed resolution relates to a matter of little economic significance to Iroquois/Delaware. Nevertheless he contends that the Rule 14a–8([i])(5) exception is not applicable as it cannot be said that his proposal "is not otherwise significantly related to the issuer's business" as is required by the final portion of that exception. In other words, plaintiff's argument that Rule 14a–8 does not permit omission of his proposal rests on the assertion that the rule and statute on which it is based do not permit omission merely because a proposal is not economically significant where a proposal has "ethical or social significance."[3] . . .

The Court would note that the applicability of the Rule 14a–8([i])(5) exception to Mr. Lovenheim's proposal represents a close question given the lack of clarity in the exception itself. In effect, plaintiff relies on the word "otherwise," suggesting that it indicates the drafters of the rule intended that other noneconomic tests of significance be used. Iroquois/Delaware relies on the fact that the rule examines other significance in relation to the issuer's business. Because of the apparent ambiguity of the rule, the Court considers the history of the shareholder proposal rule in determining the proper interpretation of the most recent version of that rule.

Prior to 1983, paragraph 14a–8([i])(5) excluded proposals "not significantly related to the issuer's business" but did not contain an objective economic significance test such as the five percent of sales, assets, and earnings specified in the first part of the current version. Although a series of SEC decisions through 1976 allowing issuers to exclude proposals challenging compliance with the Arab economic boycott of Israel allowed exclusion if the issuer did less than one percent of their business with Arab countries or Israel, the Commission stated later in 1976 that it did "not believe that subparagraph ([i])(5) should be hinged solely on the economic relativity of a proposal." Securities Exchange Act Release No. 12,999, 41 Fed. Reg. 52,994, 52,997 (1976). Thus the Commission required inclusion "in many situations in which the related business comprised less than one percent" of the company's revenues, profits or assets "where the proposal has raised policy questions important enough to be considered 'significantly related' to the issuer's business."

As indicated above, the 1983 revision adopted the five percent test of economic significance in an effort to create a more objective standard. Nevertheless, in adopting this standard, the Commission stated that proposals will be includable notwithstanding their "failure to reach the

---

[3] The assertion that the proposal is significant in an ethical and social sense relies on plaintiff's argument that "the very availability of a market for products that may be obtained through the inhumane force-feeding of geese cannot help but contribute to the continuation of such treatment." Plaintiff's brief characterizes the humane treatment of animals as among the foundations of western culture and cites in support of this view the Seven Laws of Noah, an animal protection statute enacted by the Massachusetts Bay Colony in 1641, numerous federal statutes enacted since 1877, and animal protection laws existing in all fifty states and the District of Columbia. An additional indication of the significance of plaintiff's proposal is the support of such leading organizations in the field of animal care as the American Society for the Prevention of Cruelty to Animals and The Humane Society of the United States for measures aimed at discontinuing use of force-feeding.

specified economic thresholds if a significant relationship to the issuer's business is demonstrated on the face of the resolution or supporting statement." Securities Exchange Act Release No. 19,135, 47 Fed. Reg. 47,420, 47,428 (1982). Thus it seems clear based on the history of the rule that "the meaning of 'significantly related' is not limited to economic significance." . . .

. . . The Court therefore holds that in light of the ethical and social significance of plaintiff's proposal and the fact that it implicates significant levels of sales, plaintiff has shown a likelihood of prevailing on the merits with regard to the issue of whether his proposal is "otherwise significantly related" to Iroquois/Delaware's business.[3]

NOTE

The SEC reluctantly referees the shareholder proposal process. If the subject corporation's management believes the proposal can be excluded from the proxy statement, it files a notice with the SEC that the firm intends to exclude the proposal. If the SEC staff agrees that the proposal can be excluded, it will issue a so-called no-action letter, which simply states that the staff will not recommend that the Commission bring an enforcement proceeding against the issuer if the proposal is excluded. On the other hand, if the staff determines that the proposal should be included in management's proxy statement, the staff will notify the issuer that the SEC may bring an enforcement action if the proposal is excluded. The SEC staff can also take an intermediate position; in effect, it says to the proponent: "As your proposal or your supporting statement are presently drafted, they can be excluded under Rule 14a–8. However, if you revise them as follows, we believe that management must include the proposal." Whichever side loses at the staff level in theory can ask the actual Commissioners to review the staff's decision. After review by the Commissioners, the losing party can in theory seek judicial review by the United States Circuit Court of Appeals for the District of Columbia. These reviews are very rare; more typically, if management is the losing party it will simply acquiesce in the staff's decision. If the shareholder proponent loses, he or she may seek an injunction in federal district court, as did the plaintiff in the *Lovenheim* case.

ANALYSIS

1. Why did Lovenheim merely ask Iroquois Brands' board to form a study committee? Put another way, why didn't Lovenheim offer a proposal prohibiting the company from selling pâté?

2. Think about your favorite social or political cause. Suppose you wanted to get a shareholder proposal relating on that cause on a corporate proxy statement. Assume that the proposal would not meet the 5 percent economic significance test of Rule 14a–8(i)(5). On what basis would you show that the proposal has sufficient ethical or social

---

[3] The result would, of course, be different if plaintiff's proposal was ethically significant in the abstract but had no meaningful relationship to the business of Iroquois/Delaware as Iroquois/Delaware was not engaged in the business of importing pâté de foie gras.

significance to justify its inclusion in the proxy statement under Lovenheim?

3. Although Iroquois Brands contended that Lovenheim's proposal might cause investors to conclude that the company was involved in cruelty to animals, the court dismissed that concern as "largely speculative." Was the court correct in giving such short shrift to this possibility?

AFSCME v. AIG, Inc.

462 F.3d 121 (2d Cir. 2006).

This case raises the question of whether a shareholder proposal requiring a company to include certain shareholder-nominated candidates for the board of directors on the corporate ballot can be excluded from the corporate proxy materials on the basis that the proposal "relates to an election" under Securities Exchange Act Rule 14a–8(i)(8) . . . ("election exclusion" or "Rule 14a–8(i)(8)"). Complicating this question is not only the ambiguity of Rule 14a–8(i)8) itself but also the fact that the [SEC] has ascribed two different interpretations to the Rule's language. The SEC's first interpretation was published in 1976, the same year that it last revised the election exclusion. The Division of Corporation Finance (the "Division"), the group within the SEC that handles investor disclosure matters and issues no-action letters, continued to apply this interpretation consistently for fifteen years until 1990, when it began applying a different interpretation, although at first in an ad hoc and inconsistent manner. The result of this gradual interpretive shift is the SEC's second interpretation, as set forth in its amicus brief to this Court. We believe that an agency's interpretation of an ambiguous regulation made at the time the regulation was implemented or revised should control unless that agency has offered sufficient reasons for its changed interpretation. Accordingly, we hold that a shareholder proposal that seeks to amend the corporate bylaws to establish a procedure by which shareholder-nominated candidates may be included on the corporate ballot does not relate to an election within the meaning of the Rule and therefore cannot be excluded from corporate proxy materials under that regulation.

Background

The American Federation of State, County & Municipal Employees ("AFSCME") is one of the country's largest public service employee unions. Through its pension plan, AFSCME holds 26,965 shares of voting common stock of American International Group ("AIG" or "Company"), a multi-national corporation operating in the insurance and financial services sectors. On December 1, 2004, AFSCME submitted to AIG for inclusion in the Company's 2005 proxy statement a shareholder proposal that, if adopted by a majority of AIG shareholders at the Company's 2005 annual meeting, would amend the AIG bylaws to require the Company, under certain circumstances, to publish the names of shareholder-nominated candidates for director positions together with any candidates nominated by AIG's board of directors ("Proposal"). AIG sought the input of the Division regarding whether AIG could exclude the Proposal from its proxy statement under the election exclusion on the basis that it "relates to an election." The Division issued a no-action letter in which it indicated that it would not recommend an enforcement action against AIG should the Company exclude the Proposal from its proxy statement. . . .

Armed with the no-action letter, AIG then proceeded to exclude the Proposal from the Company's proxy statement. In response, AFSCME brought suit in the United States District Court for the Southern District of New York (Stanton, J.) seeking a court order compelling AIG to include the Proposal in its next proxy statement. . . . [T]he district court entered final judgment denying plaintiff's claims for declaratory and injunctive relief and dismissing plaintiff's complaint.

Discussion

Rule 14a–8(i)(8), also known as "the town meeting rule," regulates what are referred to as "shareholders proposals," that is, "recommendation[s] or requirement[s] that the company and/or its board of directors take [some] action, which [the submitting shareholder(s)] intend to present at a meeting of the company's shareholders," [Rule] 14a–8(a). If a shareholder seeking to submit a proposal meets certain eligibility and procedural requirements, the corporation is required to include the proposal in its proxy statement and identify the proposal in its form of proxy, unless the corporation can prove to the SEC that a given proposal may be excluded based on one of thirteen grounds enumerated in the regulations. . . . One of these grounds, Rule 14a–8(i)(8), provides that a corporation may exclude a shareholder proposal "[i]f the proposal relates to an election for membership on the company's board of directors or analogous governing body."

We must determine whether, under Rule 14a–8(i)(8), a shareholder proposal "relates to an election" if it seeks to amend the corporate bylaws to establish a procedure by which certain shareholders are entitled to include in the corporate proxy materials their nominees for the board of directors ("proxy access bylaw proposal"). . . . The relevant language here—"relates to an election"—is not particularly helpful. AFSCME reads the election exclusion as creating an obvious distinction between proposals addressing a particular seat in a particular election (which AFSCME concedes are excludable) and those, like AFSCME's proposal, that simply set the background rules governing elections generally (which AFSCME claims are not excludable). AFSCME's distinction rests on Rule 14a–8(i)(8)'s use of the article "an," which AFSCME claims "necessarily implies that the phrase 'relates to an election' is intended to relate to proposals that address particular elections, instead of simply 'elections' generally." It is at least plausible that the words "an election" were intended to narrow the scope of the election exclusion, confining its application to proposals relating to "a particular election and not elections generally." It is, however, also plausible that the phrase was intended to create a comparatively broader exclusion, one covering "a particular election or elections generally" since any proposal that relates to elections in general will necessarily relate to an election in particular. The language of Rule 14a8(i)(8) provides no reason to adopt one interpretation over the other.

When the language of a regulation is ambiguous, we typically look for guidance in any interpretation made by the agency that promulgated the regulation in question. . . . We are aware of two statements published by the SEC that offer informal interpretations of Rule 14a–8(i)(8). The first is a statement appearing in the amicus brief that the SEC filed in this case at our request. The second interpretation is contained in a statement the SEC published in 1976, the last time the SEC revised the election exclusion. Neither of these interpretations has the force of law. But, while agency interpretations that lack the force of law do not warrant deference when they interpret ambiguous statutes, they do normally warrant deference when they interpret ambiguous regulations. . . .

The 1976 Statement clearly reflects the view that the election exclusion is limited to shareholder proposals used to oppose solicitations dealing with an identified board seat in an upcoming election and rejects the somewhat broader interpretation that the election exclusion applies to shareholder proposals that would institute procedures making such election contests more likely. The SEC suggested as much when, four months after its 1976 Statement, it explained that the scope of the election exclusion does not cover shareholder proposals dealing with matters such as cumulative voting and general director requirements, both of which have the potential to increase the likelihood of election contests. . . . That the 1976 statement adopted this narrower view of the election exclusion finds further support in the fact that it was also the view that the Division adopted for roughly sixteen years following publication of the SEC's 1976 Statement. . . . It was not until 1990 that the Division first signaled a change of course by deeming excludable proposals that might result in contested elections, even if the proposal only purports to alter general procedures for nominating and electing directors. . . .

Because the interpretation of Rule 14a–8(i)(8) that the SEC advances in its amicus brief-that the election exclusion applies to proxy access bylaw proposals-conflicts with the 1976 Statement, it does not merit the usual deference we would reserve for an agency's interpretation of its own regulations. . . . The SEC has not provided, nor to our knowledge has it or the Division ever provided, reasons for its changed position regarding the excludability of proxy access bylaw proposals. Although the SEC has substantial discretion to adopt new interpretations of its own regulations in light of, for example, changes in the capital markets or even simply because of a shift in the Commission's regulatory approach, it nevertheless has a "duty to explain its departure from prior norms." Atchison, T. & S.F. Ry. Co. v. Wichita Bd. of Trade, 412 U.S. 800, 808, 93 S.Ct. 2367, 37 L.Ed.2d 350 (1973) (citing Sec. of Agric. v. United States, 347 U.S. 645, 652–53, 74 S.Ct. 826, 98 L.Ed. 1015 (1954)). . . .

Accordingly, we deem it appropriate to defer to the 1976 Statement, which represents the SEC's interpretation of the election exclusion the last time the Rule was substantively revised. . . .

In deeming proxy access bylaw proposals non-excludable under Rule 14a–8(i)(8), we take no side in the policy debate regarding shareholder access to the corporate ballot. There might be perfectly good reasons for permitting companies to exclude proposals like AFSCME's, just as there may well be valid policy reasons for rendering them non-excludable. However, Congress has determined that such issues are appropriately the province of the SEC, not the judiciary.

BACKGROUND AND AFTERMATH

In 2003, the SEC proposed a new Rule 14a–11 that would permit shareholders, upon the occurrence of certain specified events and subject to various restrictions, to have their nominees placed on the company's proxy statement and ballot. If the rule had been adopted, a shareholder-nominated director thus could be elected to the board in a fashion quite similar to the way shareholder-sponsored proposals are now put to a shareholder vote under SEC Rule 14a–8. The proposal received considerable opposition from the business community, while also being criticized by shareholder activists as not going far enough. The SEC never acted on the proposal, allowing it to die a quiet death.

Shareholder activists such as AFSCME then tried using Rule 14a–8 to bypass the SEC's failure to act by putting forward shareholder proposals adopting bylaws allowing shareholders to nominate directors. In addition, shareholder activists also began putting forward similar proposals to adopt bylaws under which directors would be elected by majority vote rather than the traditional plurality.

In the wake of the *AIG* decision, the SEC began a rulemaking process to determine whether Rule 14a–8(i)(8) should be amended to permit or deny shareholder access to the corporate ballot. On November 28, 2007, the SEC announced an amendment to Rule 14a–8(i)(8), pursuant to which the Rule would read:

> (i) Question 9: If I have complied with the procedural requirements, on what other bases may a company rely to exclude my proposal? . . .
>
> > (8) Relates to election: If the proposal relates to a nomination or an election for membership on the company's board of directors or analogous governing body or a procedure for such nomination or election.

The amendment thus reversed the 1976 statement and effectively overturned the substantive result of the *AIG* case. At the same time, however, the SEC announced its intention to continue studying the issue.

Proponents of proxy access persuaded Congress to include a provision in the Dodd-Frank financial reform legislation of 2010 affirming that the SEC has authority to adopt a rule along the lines of the 2003 proposal. Section 971 of the Act did not require that the SEC do so. On the other hand, if the SEC chose to do so, § 971 expressed Congress' intent that the SEC "should have wide latitude in setting the terms of such proxy access." In particular, § 971 expressly authorizes the SEC to exempt "an issuer or class of issuers" from any proxy access rule and specifically requires the SEC to "take into account, among other considerations, whether" proxy access "disproportionately burdens small issuers."

Section 971 probably was unnecessary. An SEC rulemaking proceeding on proxy access was well advanced long before Dodd-Frank was adopted, so a shove from Congress was superfluous. As to the question of SEC authority, proxy access almost certainly fell within the disclosure and process sphere over which the SEC has unquestioned authority. By adopting § 971, however, Congress did preempt an expected challenge to any forthcoming SEC regulation.

In any case, the ink was hardly dry on Dodd-Frank when the SEC announced final adoption of new Rule 14a–11. The rule required companies to include in their proxy materials, alongside the nominees of the incumbent board, the nominees of shareholders who own at least 3 percent of the company's shares and have done so continuously for at least the prior three years. A shareholder could only put forward a short slate, consisting of at least 1 nominee or up to 25% of the company's board of directors whichever was greater. Oddly, this entitlement applied even to minority shareholders of a corporation that had a controlling shareholder with sufficient voting power to elect the entire board. Application of the rule to small companies was to be deferred for three years, while the SEC studied its impact.

As was the case with the 2003 proposal, in order for an individual to be eligible to be nominated under Rule 14a–11, that individual would have to satisfy the applicable stock exchange listing standard definition of independence from the company. The 2003 proposal also contemplated that the nominee must satisfy a number of independence criteria (e.g., no family or employment relationships) vis-à-vis the nominating shareholder or group. The SEC at that time clearly was concerned that the proposal would be used to put forward special interest directors who would not broadly represent the shareholders as a whole but rather only the narrow interests of those who nominated them. As adopted, Rule 14a–11 contained no such requirement. Accordingly, there was a very real risk shareholder nominated directors would perceive themselves as representatives of their electoral constituency rather than all shareholders.

Insurgents could not, however, use the rule to bypass a proxy contest for control. Shareholders whose disclosed intent was to seek control of the company could not use the rule to nominate directors. Likewise, shareholders whose disclosed intent was to elect more directors than the number authorized by the rule could not use the rule to nominate directors. In either case, such shareholders would have had to run a traditional proxy contest.

Concurrently, the SEC amended Rule 14a–8(i)(8). As amended, the new rule stated that a proposal may be excluded if it:

> (i) Would disqualify a nominee who is standing for election; (ii) Would remove a director from office before his or her term expired; (iii) Questions the competence, business judgment, or character of one or more nominees or directors; (iv) Seeks to include a specific individual in the company's proxy materials for election to the board of directors; or (v) Otherwise could affect the outcome of the upcoming election of directors.

In adopting these amendments, the SEC explained that proxy access bylaws no longer were automatically excludable. To the contrary, bylaws that expand proxy access rights to a broader group of shareholders or create alternative proxy access rights were expressly authorized. A shareholder proposal to eliminate or restrict proxy access rights, however, was impermissible.

In Business Roundtable v. S.E.C., 647 F.3d 1144 (D.C. Cir. 2011), however, the U.S. Court of Appeals for the District of Columbia struck down Rule 14a–11 in a lawsuit brought by the Business Roundtable and the U.S. Chamber of Commerce. Even though the SEC clearly had authority to adopt the rule, the court found that the SEC had:

> [A]cted arbitrarily and capriciously for having failed . . . adequately to assess the economic effects of [the] new rule. Here the Commission inconsistently and opportunistically framed the costs and benefits of the rule; failed adequately to quantify the certain costs or to explain why those costs could not be quantified; neglected to support its predictive judgments; contradicted itself; and failed to respond to substantial problems raised by commenters.

The court agreed with those who argue that, if the proxy access rule had been validly adopted, a board often would have not just the right—but the duty—to oppose shareholder nominees:

> [T]he American Bar Association Committee on Federal Regulation of Securities commented: "If the [shareholder] nominee is determined [by the board] not to be as appropriate a candidate as those to be nominated by the board's independent nominating committee . . ., then the board will be compelled by its fiduciary duty to make an appropriate effort to oppose the nominee, as boards now do in traditional proxy contests."

The court also decisively rejected the SEC's claim that shareholder activism is beneficial for corporate performance:

> The petitioners also maintain, and we agree, the Commission relied upon insufficient empirical data when it concluded that Rule 14a–11 will improve board performance and increase shareholder value by facilitating the election of dissident shareholder nominees. . . . The Commission acknowledged the numerous studies submitted by commenters that reached the opposite result. . . .One commenter, for example, submitted an empirical study showing that "when dissident directors win board seats, those firms underperform peers by 19 to 40% over the two years following the proxy contest." . . .. The Commission completely discounted those studies "because of questions raised by subsequent studies, limitations acknowledged by the studies' authors, or [its] own concerns about the studies' methodology or scope."
>
> The Commission instead relied exclusively and heavily upon two relatively unpersuasive studies, one concerning the effect of "hybrid boards" (which include some dissident directors) and the other concerning the effect of proxy contests in general, upon shareholder value. . . . Indeed, the Commission "recognize[d] the limitations of the Cernich (2009) study," and noted "its long-term findings on shareholder value creation are difficult to interpret." . . . In view of the admittedly (and at best) "mixed" empirical evidence, . . . we think the Commission has not sufficiently supported its conclusion that increasing the potential for election of directors nominated by shareholders will result in improved board and company performance and shareholder value. . . .

Likewise, the Court agreed with those who argue that certain institutional investors—most notably union pension funds and state and local government pension funds—would use proxy access as leverage to extract private gains at the expense of other investors:

> Notwithstanding the ownership and holding requirements, there is good reason to believe institutional investors with special interests will be able to use the rule and, as more than one commenter noted, "public and union pension funds" are the institutional investors "most likely to make use of proxy access." . . . Nonetheless, the Commission failed to respond to comments arguing that investors with a special interest, such as unions and state and local governments whose interests in jobs may well be greater than their interest in share value, can be expected to pursue self-interested objectives rather than the goal of maximizing shareholder value, and will likely cause companies to incur costs even when their nominee is unlikely to be elected.

The D.C. Circuit opinion is not the end of the story. After the D.C. Circuit decision, the SEC put its planned amendments to Rule 14a–8 into effect. Accordingly, shareholders who want proxy access now can put forward proposals under that rule to amend the issuer's bylaws so as to permit shareholder nominees to be included on the proxy card.

ANALYSIS

1. In the final paragraph of its opinion the court writes that "[t]here might be perfectly good reasons for permitting companies to exclude proposals like AFSCME's, just as there may well be valid policy reasons for rendering them non-excludable." What might some "perfectly good reasons" for excluding the proposal be?

2. If you were a shareholder in AIG, would you favor the proposed change? If you were a director?

3. Suppose a neo-Nazi group tried to use a corporate election as a forum for its positions. Should different rules apply? Labor unions (and their pension plans) often support changes of the sort proposed in AIG—why?

CA, Inc. v. AFSCME Employees Pension Plan

953 A.2d 227 (Del. 2008).

This proceeding arises from a certification by the United States Securities and Exchange Commission (the "SEC"), to this Court, of two questions of law pursuant to Article IV, Section 11(8) of the Delaware Constitution[1] and Supreme Court Rule 41. . . .

I. *FACTS*

CA is a Delaware corporation whose board of directors consists of twelve persons, all of whom sit for reelection each year. . . .

---

[1] Article IV, Section 11(8) was amended in 2007 to authorize this Court to hear and determine questions of law certified to it by (in addition to the tribunals already specified therein) the United States Securities and Exchange Commission. 76 Del. Laws 2007, ch. 37 § 1, effective May 3, 2007. This certification request is the first submitted by the SEC to this Court.

AFSCME, a CA stockholder, is associated with the American Federation of State, County and Municipal Employees. On March 13, 2008, AFSCME submitted a proposed stockholder bylaw (the "Bylaw" or "proposed Bylaw") for inclusion in the Company's proxy materials for its 2008 annual meeting of stockholders. The Bylaw, if adopted by CA stockholders, would amend the Company's bylaws to provide as follows:

> RESOLVED, that pursuant to section 109 of the Delaware General Corporation Law and Article IX of the bylaws of CA, Inc., stockholders of CA hereby amend the bylaws to add the following Section 14 to Article II:
>
> The board of directors shall cause the corporation to reimburse a stockholder or group of stockholders (together, the "Nominator") for reasonable expenses ("Expenses") incurred in connection with nominating one or more candidates in a contested election of directors to the corporation's board of directors, including, without limitation, printing, mailing, legal, solicitation, travel, advertising and public relations expenses, so long as (a) the election of fewer than 50% of the directors to be elected is contested in the election, (b) one or more candidates nominated by the Nominator are elected to the corporation's board of directors, (c) stockholders are not permitted to cumulate their votes for directors, and (d) the election occurred, and the Expenses were incurred, after this bylaw's adoption. The amount paid to a Nominator under this bylaw in respect of a contested election shall not exceed the amount expended by the corporation in connection with such election.

CA's current bylaws and Certificate of Incorporation have no provision that specifically addresses the reimbursement of proxy expenses. . . .

It is undisputed that the decision whether to reimburse election expenses is presently vested in the discretion of CA's board of directors, subject to their fiduciary duties and applicable Delaware law.

On April 18, 2008, CA notified the SEC's Division of Corporation Finance (the "Division") of its intention to exclude the proposed Bylaw from its 2008 proxy materials. The Company requested from the Division a "no-action letter" stating that the Division would not recommend any enforcement action to the SEC if CA excluded the AFSCME proposal.[2]
. . .

III. *THE FIRST QUESTION*

A. *Preliminary Comments*

The first question [certified to us by the SEC] is whether the Bylaw is a proper subject for shareholder action, more precisely, whether the Bylaw may be proposed and enacted by shareholders without the concurrence of the Company's board of directors. Before proceeding

---

[2] Under Sections (i)(1) and (i)(2) of SEC Rule 14a–8, a company may exclude a stockholder proposal from its proxy statement if the proposal "is not a proper subject for action by the shareholders under the laws of the jurisdiction of the company's organization," or where the proposal, if implemented, "would cause the company to violate any state law to which it is subject." See17 C.F.R. § 240.14a–8.

further, we make some preliminary comments in an effort to delineate a framework within which to begin our analysis.

First, the DGCL empowers both the board of directors and the shareholders of a Delaware corporation to adopt, amend or repeal the corporation's bylaws. 8 Del. C. § 109(a) relevantly provides that:

> After a corporation has received any payment for any of its stock, the power to adopt, amend or repeal bylaws shall be in the stockholders entitled to vote . . . ; provided, however, any corporation may, in its certificate of incorporation, confer the power to adopt, amend or repeal bylaws upon the directors. . . . The fact that such power has been so conferred upon the directors . . . shall not divest the stockholders . . . of the power, nor limit their power to adopt, amend or repeal bylaws.

Pursuant to Section 109(a), CA's Certificate of Incorporation confers the power to adopt, amend or repeal the bylaws upon the Company's board of directors. . . .

Second, the vesting of that concurrent power in both the board and the shareholders raises the issue of whether the stockholders' power is coextensive with that of the board, and vice versa. As a purely theoretical matter that is possible, and were that the case, then the first certified question would be easily answered. That is, under such a regime any proposal to adopt, amend or repeal a bylaw would be a proper subject for either shareholder or board action, without distinction. But the DGCL has not allocated to the board and the shareholders the identical, coextensive power to adopt, amend and repeal the bylaws. Therefore, how that power is allocated between those two decision-making bodies requires an analysis that is more complex.

Moving from the theoretical to this case, by its terms Section 109(a) vests in the shareholders a power to adopt, amend or repeal bylaws that is legally sacrosanct, i.e., the power cannot be non-consensually eliminated or limited by anyone other than the legislature itself. If viewed in isolation, Section 109(a) could be read to make the board's and the shareholders' power to adopt, amend or repeal bylaws identical and coextensive, but Section 109(a) does not exist in a vacuum. It must be read together with 8 Del. C. § 141(a), which pertinently provides that:

> The business and affairs of every corporation organized under this chapter shall be managed by or under the direction of a board of directors, except as may be otherwise provided in this chapter or in its certificate of incorporation.

No such broad management power is statutorily allocated to the shareholders. Indeed, it is well established that stockholders of a corporation subject to the DGCL may not directly manage the business and affairs of the corporation, at least without specific authorization in either the statute or the certificate of incorporation. Therefore, the shareholders' statutory power to adopt, amend or repeal bylaws is not coextensive with the board's concurrent power and is limited by the board's management prerogatives under Section 141(a). . . .

B. *Analysis*

1.

. . .

Implicit in CA's argument is the premise that *any* bylaw that in *any* respect might be viewed as limiting or restricting the power of the board of directors automatically falls outside the scope of permissible bylaws. That simply cannot be. That reasoning, taken to its logical extreme, would result in eliminating altogether the shareholders' statutory right to adopt, amend or repeal bylaws. Bylaws, by their very nature, set down rules and procedures that bind a corporation's board and its shareholders. In that sense, most, if not all, bylaws could be said to limit the otherwise unlimited discretionary power of the board. Yet Section 109(a) carves out an area of shareholder power to adopt, amend or repeal bylaws that is expressly inviolate. Therefore, to argue that the Bylaw at issue here limits the board's power to manage the business and affairs of the Company only begins, but cannot end, the analysis needed to decide whether the Bylaw is a proper subject for shareholder action. The question left unanswered is what is the scope of shareholder action that Section 109(b) permits yet does not improperly intrude upon the directors' power to manage corporation's business and affairs under Section 141(a). . . .

2.

It is well-established Delaware law that a proper function of bylaws is not to mandate how the board should decide specific substantive business decisions, but rather, to define the process and procedures by which those decisions are made. As the Court of Chancery has noted:

> Traditionally, the bylaws have been the corporate instrument used to set forth the rules by which the corporate board conducts its business. To this end, the DGCL is replete with specific provisions authorizing the bylaws to establish the procedures through which board and committee action is taken. . . . [T]here is a general consensus that bylaws that regulate the process by which the board acts are statutorily authorized.
>
> . . .
>
> . . . Sections 109 and 141, taken in totality,. . . . make clear that bylaws may pervasively and strictly regulate the process by which boards act, subject to the constraints of equity.

Examples of the procedural, process-oriented nature of bylaws are found in both the DGCL and the case law. For example, 8 Del. C. § 141(b) authorizes bylaws that fix the number of directors on the board, the number of directors required for a quorum (with certain limitations), and the vote requirements for board action. 8 Del. C. § 141(f) authorizes bylaws that preclude board action without a meeting. And, almost three decades ago this Court upheld a shareholder-enacted bylaw requiring unanimous board attendance and board approval for any board action, and unanimous ratification of any committee action.[18] Such purely

[18] Frantz Mfg. Co. v. EAC Indus., 501 A.2d 401 (Del.1985). See also Hollinger, 844 A.2d at 1079–80 (shareholder-enacted bylaw abolishing a board committee created by board resolution does not impermissibly interfere with the board's authority under Section 141(a)).

procedural bylaws do not improperly encroach upon the board's managerial authority under Section 141(a). . . .

Although CA concedes that "restrictive procedural bylaws (such as those requiring the presence of all directors and unanimous board consent to take action) are acceptable," it points out that even facially procedural bylaws can unduly intrude upon board authority. The Bylaw being proposed here is unduly intrusive, CA claims, because, by mandating reimbursement of a stockholder's proxy expenses, it limits the board's broad discretionary authority to decide whether to grant reimbursement at all. CA further claims that because (in defined circumstances) the Bylaw mandates the expenditure of corporate funds, its subject matter is necessarily substantive, not process-oriented, and, therefore falls outside the scope of what Section 109(b) permits.[19]

Because the Bylaw is couched as a command to reimburse ("The board of directors shall cause the corporation to reimburse a stockholder"), it lends itself to CA's criticism. But the Bylaw's wording, although relevant, is not dispositive of whether or not it is process-related. The Bylaw could easily have been worded differently, to emphasize its process, as distinguished from its mandatory payment, component. By saying this we do not mean to suggest that this Bylaw's reimbursement component can be ignored. What we do suggest is that a bylaw that requires the expenditure of corporate funds does not, for that reason alone, become automatically deprived of its process-related character. A hypothetical example illustrates the point. Suppose that the directors of a corporation live in different states and at a considerable distance from the corporation's headquarters. Suppose also that the shareholders enact a bylaw that requires all meetings of directors to take place in person at the corporation's headquarters. Such a bylaw would be clearly process-related, yet it cannot be supposed that the shareholders would lack the power to adopt the bylaw because it would require the corporation to expend its funds to reimburse the directors' travel expenses. Whether or not a bylaw is process-related must necessarily be determined in light of its context and purpose.

The context of the Bylaw at issue here is the process for electing directors—a subject in which shareholders of Delaware corporations have a legitimate and protected interest. The purpose of the Bylaw is to promote the integrity of that electoral process by facilitating the nomination of director candidates by stockholders or groups of stockholders. Generally, and under the current framework for electing directors in contested elections, only board-sponsored nominees for election are reimbursed for their election expenses. Dissident candidates are not, unless they succeed in replacing at least a majority of the entire board. The Bylaw would encourage the nomination of non-management board candidates by promising reimbursement of the nominating

---

[19] CA actually conflates two separate arguments that, although facially similar, are analytically distinct. The first argument is that the Bylaw impermissibly intrudes upon board authority because it mandates the expenditure of corporate funds. The second is that the Bylaw impermissibly leaves no role for board discretion and would require reimbursement of the costs of a subset of CA's stockholders, even in circumstances where the board's fiduciary duties would counsel otherwise. Analytically, the first argument is relevant to the issue of whether the Bylaw is a proper subject for unilateral stockholder action, whereas the second argument more properly goes to the separate question of whether the Bylaw, if enacted, would violate Delaware law.

stockholders' proxy expenses if one or more of its candidates are elected. In that the shareholders also have a legitimate interest, because the Bylaw would facilitate the exercise of their right to participate in selecting the contestants. . . .

The shareholders of a Delaware corporation have the right "to participate in selecting the contestants" for election to the board. The shareholders are entitled to facilitate the exercise of that right by proposing a bylaw that would encourage candidates other than board-sponsored nominees to stand for election. The Bylaw would accomplish that by committing the corporation to reimburse the election expenses of shareholders whose candidates are successfully elected. That the implementation of that proposal would require the expenditure of corporate funds will not, in and of itself, make such a bylaw an improper subject matter for shareholder action. Accordingly, we answer the first question certified to us in the affirmative.

That, however, concludes only part of the analysis. The DGCL also requires that the Bylaw be "not inconsistent with law."[23] Accordingly, we turn to the second certified question, which is whether the proposed Bylaw, if adopted, would cause CA to violate any Delaware law to which it is subject.

IV. *THE SECOND QUESTION*

In answering the first question, we have already determined that the Bylaw does not facially violate any provision of the DGCL or of CA's Certificate of Incorporation. The question thus becomes whether the Bylaw would violate any common law rule or precept. . . .

This Court has previously invalidated contracts that would require a board to act or not act in such a fashion that would limit the exercise of their fiduciary duties. In *Paramount Communications, Inc. v. QVC Network, Inc.*,[27] we invalidated a "no shop" provision of a merger agreement with a favored bidder (Viacom) that prevented the directors of the target company (Paramount) from communicating with a competing bidder (QVC) the terms of its competing bid in an effort to obtain the highest available value for shareholders. We held that:

> The No-Shop Provision could not validly define or limit the fiduciary duties of the Paramount directors. To the extent that a contract, or a provision thereof, purports to require a board to act or not act in such a fashion as to limit the exercise of fiduciary duties, it is invalid and unenforceable. [. . .] [T]he Paramount directors could not contract away their fiduciary obligations. Since the No-Shop Provision was invalid, Viacom never had any vested contract rights in the provision.

. . . [*QVC* involved a binding contractual arrangement] that the board of directors had voluntarily imposed upon themselves. This case involves a binding bylaw that the shareholders seek to impose involuntarily on the directors in the specific area of election expense reimbursement. Although this case is distinguishable in that respect, the distinction is one without a difference. The reason is that the internal governance contract—which here takes the form of a bylaw—is one that would also

[23] 8 Del. C. § 109(b).

[27] 637 A.2d 34 (Del.1994).

prevent the directors from exercising their full managerial power in circumstances where their fiduciary duties would otherwise require them to deny reimbursement to a dissident slate. That this limitation would be imposed by a majority vote of the shareholders rather than by the directors themselves, does not, in our view, legally matter.[32]

. . . AFSCME argues that it is unfair to claim that the Bylaw prevents the CA board from discharging its fiduciary duty where the effect of the Bylaw is to relieve the board entirely of those duties in this specific area.

That response, in our view, is more semantical than substantive. No matter how artfully it may be phrased, the argument concedes the very proposition that renders the Bylaw, as written, invalid: the Bylaw mandates reimbursement of election expenses in circumstances that a proper application of fiduciary principles could preclude. That such circumstances could arise is not far fetched. . . .[34]

It is in this respect that the proposed Bylaw, as written, would violate Delaware law if enacted by CA's shareholders. As presently drafted, the Bylaw would afford CA's directors full discretion to determine what *amount* of reimbursement is appropriate, because the directors would be obligated to grant only the "reasonable" expenses of a successful short slate.* Unfortunately, that does not go far enough, because the Bylaw contains no language or provision that would reserve to CA's directors their full power to exercise their fiduciary duty to decide whether or not it would be appropriate, in a specific case, to award reimbursement at all.

In arriving at this conclusion, we express no view on whether the Bylaw as currently drafted, would create a better governance scheme from a policy standpoint. We decide only what is, and is not, legally permitted under the DGCL. That statute, as currently drafted, is the expression of policy as decreed by the Delaware legislature. Those who believe that CA's shareholders should be permitted to make the proposed Bylaw as drafted part of CA's governance scheme, have two alternatives. They may seek to amend the Certificate of Incorporation to include the substance of the Bylaw; *or* they may seek recourse from the Delaware General Assembly.

Accordingly, we answer the second question certified to us in the affirmative.

ANALYSIS

1. At the end of its opinion, the court suggests that the shareholders might "seek to amend the Certificate of Incorporation to include the substance of the Bylaw." Under DGCL § 242(b) (1), however, the Board must propose amendments to the Certificate before a

---

[32] Only if the Bylaw provision were enacted as an amendment to CA's Certificate of Incorporation would that distinction be dispositive. See8 Del. C. § 102(b)(1) and § 242.

[34] Such a circumstance could arise, for example, if a shareholder group affiliated with a competitor of the company were to cause the election of a minority slate of candidates committed to using their director positions to obtain, and then communicate, valuable proprietary strategic or product information to the competitor.

* [Eds.—In a short slate proxy contest, the shareholder conducting the contests nominates fewer individuals than the number of vacancies to be filled.]

shareholder vote may be taken. What do you suppose is the likelihood that the Board of CA, Inc., would agree to propose the amendment, so that the shareholders could vote on it?

Is the proposal a good idea? One way to think about the issue is to imagine a successful information-technology firm owned and controlled by its three founders. Suppose they have decided to "go public"—that is, sell shares to individuals willing to buy in a "public offering." Suppose further that the founders will sell a substantial portion of their own shares in the public offering, in order to cash in on their success (the great American dream fulfilled). They ask you for the pros and cons of including in the Certificate the language of the bylaw at issue in the *CA* opinion (an unlikely request, to be sure, but let's pretend). What do you have to say?

2. Suppose the shareholders of Acme, Inc., adopted a reimbursement bylaw with the requisite fiduciary out.* Sometime later a shareholder successfully conducted a short slate proxy contest. The shareholder sought reimbursement under the bylaw. The board concluded that reimbursement would be inconsistent with its fiduciary duties. The shareholder sues. Should the court apply the business judgment rule or some more exacting standard of review to the issue?

3. In AFSCME v. AIG, 462 F.3d 121 (2nd Cir. 2006) (excerpted immediately preceding the present case), AFSCME proposed the following amendment to AIG's bylaws:

> "The Corporation shall include in its proxy materials for a meeting of stockholders the name, together with the Disclosure and Statement (both defined below), of any person nominated for election to the Board of Directors by a stockholder or group thereof that satisfies the requirements of this section 6.10 (the "Nominator"), and allow stockholders to vote with respect to such nominee on the Corporation's proxy card. Each Nominator may nominate one candidate for election at a meeting.
>
> To be eligible to make a nomination, a Nominator must:
>
> (a) have beneficially owned 3% or more of the Corporation's outstanding common stock (the "Required Shares") for at least one year;
>
> (b) provide written notice received by the Corporation's Secretary within the time period specified in section 1.11 of the Bylaws containing (i) with respect to the nominee, (A) the information required by Items 7(a), (b) and (c) of SEC Schedule 14A (such information is referred to herein as the "Disclosure") and (B) such nominee's consent to being named in the proxy statement and to serving as a director if elected; and (ii) with respect to the Nominator, proof of ownership of the Required Shares; and

* [Eds.—A fiduciary out is a provision contained in the articles of incorporation, the bylaws, or a contract that allows the board of directors to decline to carry out the specified task if the board concludes that doing so would violate its fiduciary duties. In the present cases, the term refers to a provision in the bylaw that, as the Supreme Court mandated, "would reserve to CA's directors their full power to exercise their fiduciary duty to decide whether or not it would be appropriate, in a specific case, to award reimbursement at all."]

> (c) execute an undertaking that it agrees (i) to assume all liability of any violation of law or regulation arising out of the Nominator's communications with stockholders, including the Disclosure (ii) to the extent it uses soliciting material other than the Corporation's proxy materials, comply with all laws and regulations relating thereto.
>
> The Nominator shall have the option to furnish a statement, not to exceed 500 words, in support of the nominee's candidacy (the "Statement"), at the time the Disclosure is submitted to the Corporation's Secretary. The Board of Directors shall adopt a procedure for timely resolving disputes over whether notice of a nomination was timely given and whether the Disclosure and Statement comply with this section 6.10 and SEC Rules."

Would this bylaw be a proper subject of shareholder action under Delaware law? Should the bylaw include a fiduciary out in order to pass muster?

4. In *CA,* the Court declined "to articulate with doctrinal exactitude a bright line that divides those bylaws that shareholders may unilaterally adopt under Section 109(b) from those which they may not under Section 141(a)," explaining in a footnote that they were deciding only the validity of the specific bylaw in question:

> We do not attempt to delineate the location of that bright line in this Opinion. What we do hold is case specific; that is, wherever may be the location of the bright line that separates the shareholders' bylaw-making power under Section 109 from the directors' exclusive managerial authority under Section 141(a), the proposed Bylaw at issue here does not invade the territory demarcated by Section 141(a).

In light of this decision, consider the Problems immediately following the present case and materials. On which side of the "bright line" do the various bylaws discussed in those problems fall?

5. Is the process/substance "bright line" consistent with the language of Section 109(b), which provides in pertinent part that "bylaws may contain any provision, not inconsistent with law or with the certificate of incorporation, relating to the business of the corporation, the conduct of its affairs, and its rights or powers or the rights or powers of its stockholders, directors, officers or employees"?

PROBLEMS

1. PeopleAuto (PA) has long specialized in the production of small economy cars. Recently, it moved into the low-end of the luxury car market with several fancy sports sedan models.

To increase consumer interest in its sporty models, PA acquired the long-abandoned Duesenberg marque, and launched the Duesenberg Phaeton. The Phaeton produces 1001 horsepower, will (when driven by a professional) hit 200 mph, and sells for $1,200,000. PA anticipates an initial production run of 48 cars. It does not anticipate ever making money on the Phaeton. Instead, its managers believe that the Phaeton increases the sales of its other models by consolidating its image as the producer of exciting cars.

PA (incorporated in Delaware) has received several shareholder proposals for this year's annual meeting. You are the firm's in-house lawyer. Your boss asks you whether she can exclude them:

> Proposal A: Resolved, that the Company shall discontinue the Phaeton.
>
> Proposal B: Resolved, that the shareholders recommend that the company discontinue the Phaeton.
>
> Proposal C: Resolved, that the by-laws of the Company are hereby amended to include the following Section 12.2:
>
> 12.2 The Company shall produce no automobiles with a top speed of more than 100 m.p.h.

The proponents of A, B, and C argue simply that the company loses so much money on the Phaeton that it should stop producing it.

Section 109(a) of the Delaware General Corporation Law provides that by-laws may be adopted, amended, or repealed by the stockholders and, in addition by the directors if the certificate of incorporation so provides. Section 109(b) provides:

> The by-laws may contain any provision, not inconsistent with law or with the certificate of incorporation, relating to the business of the corporation, the conduct of its affairs, and its rights or power or the rights or powers of its stockholders, directors, officers or employees.

2. Your law firm is approached by a group of high-tech entrepreneurs about to form a corporation. They anticipate difficulties raising equity capital, and believe that investors will be more willing to buy stock if they (the investors) can readily remove incumbent managers. Toward that end, they propose including in the firm's articles of incorporation a provision much like that proposed in AIG. Would the provision be a good idea?

3. Your law firm is approached by another group of entrepreneurs who think investors are tired of the shareholder proposal system, and would like to contract out of it. Accordingly, they would like to include in their firm's articles of incorporation a provision that would allow management to refuse to include in its proxy solicitation material any proposal submitted by any shareholder. Suppose the provision were legal. Who would lose if the firm adopted such a provision?

E. SHAREHOLDER INSPECTION RIGHTS

INTRODUCTION

Suppose you own shares of a firm you believe is badly managed. Suppose further that you want to communicate with the firm's other shareholders about that mismanagement. Under the federal proxy rules, you may, as we have seen, be able to force the incumbent board to include a proposal you draft in its proxy solicitation materials. But suppose you want to elect your own slate of directors and thereby gain control of the corporation. You cannot require the corporation to include your slate in its solicitation materials, so you will need to do your own proxy solicitation. If you pay the costs you may be able to require the corporation to mail your solicitation materials. More precisely, under Rule 14a–7, the firm can choose either to mail your material and bill you for the costs or to give you the shareholder list instead. Most incumbent managements choose to mail the material themselves and keep the list confidential.

The well-counseled insurgent will be unwilling to rely on management's good offices. In a battle for control, information about shareholder identity may be crucial, for in such a battle you will not consider all shareholders alike. Instead, you will want to identify the holders of large blocks of stock and to spend most of your efforts trying to convince those major shareholders to support you. You will want the "shareholder list." Precisely because information about shareholder identity is valuable to you, incumbent managers are likely to resist your efforts to obtain it. There is nothing in the federal proxy rules requiring the corporation to give you the shareholder list, but the federal rules do not impair any rights you may have under state law. Thus, battles for the shareholder list are fought under state laws, as the cases in this section illustrate.

Crane Co. v. Anaconda Co.

39 N.Y.2d 14, 382 N.Y.S.2d 707, 346 N.E.2d 507 (1976).

In August, 1975, respondent Crane Company, an Illinois corporation, publicly announced a proposed offer to exchange up to 100 million dollars in subordinated debentures for as many as 5 million shares of common stock of the appellant Anaconda Company, a Montana corporation. This offer was vigorously opposed by Anaconda's management which sent four letters to shareholders asserting, *inter alia,* that the exchange offer was not in the best interests of Anaconda. Before the exchange offer could proceed Crane was obligated to file with the Securities and Exchange Commission a registration statement detailing the material facts of the offer in a prospectus. . . .

On November 19, 1975, Crane's registration statement became effective and Crane proceeded to distribute its prospectus to numerous brokers, dealers, commercial banks and trust companies for use in soliciting Anaconda stockholders. The next day Crane requested a copy of Anaconda's list of shareholders claiming that Anaconda had a fiduciary duty to its shareholders to present them with all the information pertinent to the pending tender offer.* Crane owned no Anaconda stock at this time and Anaconda refused contending that there was no basis for Crane's request. However, as of December 11, 1975, approximately 2,350,000 Anaconda shares had been tendered to Crane, making Crane Anaconda's largest stockholder. The following day, a formal written demand to produce its stock book for inspection was made by Crane on Anaconda. This demand, accompanied by an affidavit stating that the inspection was "not desired for a purpose which is in the interest of a business or object other than the business of Anaconda," was made pursuant to section 1315 of the Business Corporation Law** and the

* [Tender offers are discussed at Chapter 7, Section 2.—Eds.]

** [Eds.—The New York statute provided:

(a) Any resident of this state who shall have been a shareholder of record, for at least six months immediately preceding his demand, of a foreign corporation doing

common-law right to inspect corporate records. Anaconda rejected the demand but offered to mail Crane's prospectus to its shareholders at Crane's expense. . . .

In its petition Crane stated that it held in excess of 11% of Anaconda's common stock and that its request conformed to the requirements of the Business Corporation Law in that the inspection was not required for a purpose other than the business of Anaconda and that Crane had not participated in the sale of any stockholder list within the last five years. . . . Crane also stated in substance that it desired to communicate directly with its fellow stockholders to inform them of the terms of . . . its tender offer . . ., to reply to misleading statements issued and distributed by Anaconda to its stockholders, and thereby to dispel any misconceptions and facilitate the further tender of Crane debentures. Anaconda answered by asserting that Crane's alleged reasons for inspection were not purposes relating to the business of Anaconda within the meaning of section 1315 of the Business Corporation Law.

Special Term found that neither Crane's overriding purpose to further its tender offer nor its ancillary purposes were proper in this context and dismissed the petition. The Appellate Division reversed, with two Justices dissenting. The majority concluded that the matter was proper being one of general interest to Anaconda's shareholders by virtue of their common interest in the corporation as shareholders. We agree with this determination.

Succinctly put, the issue here is whether a qualified stockholder may inspect the corporation's stock register to ascertain the identity of fellow stockholders for the avowed purpose of informing them directly of its exchange offer and soliciting tenders of stock. In our view this question should be answered in the affirmative. A shareholder desiring to discuss relevant aspects of a tender offer should be granted access to the shareholder list unless it is sought for a purpose inimical to the corporation or its stockholders—and the manner of communication selected should be within the judgment of the shareholder.

The significance of this appeal is evident in view of the fact that this right is the one most frequently litigated by stockholders . . . and the fact that the tender offer is the primary method of corporate acquisition. . . . The conceptual basis for this right is derived from the shareholder's

---

business in this state, or any resident of this state holding, or thereunto authorized in writing by the holders of, at least five percent of any class of the outstanding shares, upon at least five days' written demand may require such foreign corporation to produce a record of its shareholders setting forth the names and addresses of all shareholders, the number and class of shares held by each and the dates when they respectively became the owners of record thereof and shall have the right to examine . . . the record of shareholders or an exact copy thereof certified as correct by the corporate officer or agent responsible for keeping or producing such record and to make extracts therefrom. . . .

(b) An examination authorized by paragraph (a) may be denied to such shareholder or other person upon his refusal to furnish to the foreign corporation . . . an affidavit that such inspection is not desired for a purpose which is in the interest of a business or object other than the business of the foreign corporation and that such shareholder or other person has not within five years sold or offered for sale any list of shareholders of any corporation of any type or kind, whether or not formed under the laws of this state, or aided or abetted any person in procuring any such record of shareholders for any such purpose.

beneficial ownership of corporate assets and the concomitant right to protect his investment. . . .

The present statute (Business Corporation Law, §§ 1315, 624) was enacted in 1961 and provid[es] that access [must] be permitted to qualified shareholders on written demand, subject to denial if the petitioner refused to furnish an affidavit that the "inspection is not desired for a purpose . . . other than the business" of the corporation and that the petitioner has not been involved in the sale of stock lists within the last five years (Business Corporation Law, § 1315, subd. [b]; § 624, subd. [c]). . . .

In attempting to sustain its burden of proof, appellant contends that inspection should not be compelled where the stockholder desires to obtain the identity of other stockholders to convince them to sell their stock, since this does not involve the business of the corporation. . . . We read this authority to compel the opposite conclusion.

Although everything affecting the shareholders will not affect the corporation, the converse is not true. Whenever the corporation faces a situation having potential substantial effect on its wellbeing or value, the shareholders qua shareholders are necessarily affected and the business of the corporation is involved within the purview of section 1315 of the Business Corporation Law. This statute should be liberally construed in favor of the stockholder whose welfare as a stockholder or the corporation's welfare may be affected. To say, as Anaconda would, that a pending tender offer involving over one fifth of the corporation's common stock is a purpose other than the business of the corporation is myopic. Since the pendency of such an exchange offer may well affect not only the future direction of the corporation but the continued vitality of the shareholders' investment, inspection of the stock book should be allowed so that qualified shareholders may have the means to independently evaluate the situation. Nor do we consider it significant that the petitioning shareholder precipitated that which may affect the corporation or shareholders; the right adheres as one of property in the shareholder and one for the protection of that interest. . . .

Early in the proceedings Anaconda offered to have the corporation's transfer agent transmit the tender offer prospectus to all the stockholders. This was declined by Crane as much too expensive and not a productive way of soliciting tenders. . . . Obviously then, Crane was and is interested in pursuing a selective and direct approach by other means to stockholders. This is not by itself improper and is due to the pragmatics of soliciting tenders from likely prospects who hold sufficient shares. . . . Accordingly, since it appears that Anaconda has failed to sustain its burden of proving an improper purpose and it cannot be said that the court below abused its discretion, we conclude that inspection should be compelled.

State ex rel. Pillsbury v. Honeywell, Inc.

291 Minn. 322, 191 N.W.2d 406 (1971).

Petitioner appeals from an order and judgment of the district court denying all relief prayed for in a petition for writs of mandamus to compel respondent, Honeywell, Inc., (Honeywell) to produce its original shareholder ledger, current shareholder ledger, and all corporate records dealing with weapons and munitions manufacture. We must affirm. . . .

Petitioner attended a meeting on July 3, 1969, of a group involved in what was known as the "Honeywell Project." Participants in the project believed that American involvement in Vietnam was wrong, that a substantial portion of Honeywell's production consisted of munitions used in that war, and that Honeywell should stop this production of munitions. Petitioner had long opposed the Vietnam war, but it was at the July 3rd meeting that he first learned of Honeywell's involvement. He was shocked at the knowledge that Honeywell had a large government contract to produce anti-personnel fragmentation bombs. Upset because of knowledge that such bombs were produced in his own community by a company which he had known and respected, petitioner determined to stop Honeywell's munitions production.

On July 14, 1969, petitioner ordered his fiscal agent to purchase 100 shares of Honeywell. He admits that the sole purpose of the purchase was to give himself a voice in Honeywell's affairs so he could persuade Honeywell to cease producing munitions. . . . In his deposition testimony petitioner made clear the reason for his purchase of Honeywell's shares:

> "Q . . . [D]o I understand that you requested Mr. Lacey to buy these 100 shares of Honeywell in order to follow up on the desire you had to bring to Honeywell management and to stockholders these theses that you have told us about here today?
>
> "A Yes. That was my motivation."

The "theses" referred to are petitioner's beliefs concerning the propriety of producing munitions for the Vietnam war. . . .

Prior to the instigation of this suit, petitioner submitted two formal demands to Honeywell requesting that it produce its original shareholder ledger, current shareholder ledger, and all corporate records dealing with weapons and munitions manufacture. Honeywell refused. . . .

In the deposition petitioner outlined his beliefs concerning the Vietnam war and his purpose for his involvement with Honeywell. He expressed his desire to communicate with other shareholders in the hope of altering Honeywell's board of directors and thereby changing its policy. To this end, he testified, business records are necessary to insure accuracy.

A hearing was held on January 8, 1970, during which Honeywell introduced the deposition, conceded all material facts stated therein, and argued that petitioner was not entitled to any relief as a matter of law. Petitioner asked that alternative writs of mandamus issue for all the relief requested in his petition. On April 8, 1970, the trial court dismissed the petition, holding that the relief requested was for an improper and indefinite purpose. Petitioner contends in this appeal that the dismissal was in error.

1. Honeywell is a Delaware corporation doing business in Minnesota.

. . .

Under the Delaware statute the shareholder must prove a proper purpose to inspect corporate records other than shareholder lists. Del.Code Ann. tit. 8, § 220. . . .*

2. The trial court ordered judgment for Honeywell, ruling that petitioner had not demonstrated a proper purpose germane to his interest as a stockholder. Petitioner contends that a stockholder who disagrees with management has an absolute right to inspect corporate records for purposes of soliciting proxies. He would have this court rule that such solicitation is per se a "proper purpose." Honeywell argues that a "proper purpose" contemplates concern with investment return. We agree with Honeywell. . . .

The act of inspecting a corporation's shareholder ledger and business records must be viewed in its proper perspective. In terms of the corporate norm, inspection is merely the act of the concerned owner checking on what is in part his property. In the context of the large firm, inspection can be more akin to a weapon in corporate warfare. The effectiveness of the weapon is considerable:

> "Considering the huge size of many modern corporations and the necessarily complicated nature of their bookkeeping, it is plain that to permit their thousands of stockholders to roam at will through their records would render impossible not only any attempt to keep their records efficiently, but the proper carrying on of their businesses."

. . . Because the power to inspect may be the power to destroy, it is important that only those with a bona fide interest in the corporation enjoy that power. . . .

Petitioner had utterly no interest in the affairs of Honeywell before he learned of Honeywell's production of fragmentation bombs. Immediately after obtaining this knowledge, he purchased stock in Honeywell for the sole purpose of asserting ownership privileges in an effort to force Honeywell to cease such production. We agree with the

---

* [Eds.—The statute provided:

(b) Any stockholder . . . shall, upon written demand under oath stating the purpose thereof, have the right during the usual hours for business to inspect for any proper purpose the corporation's stock ledger, a list of its stockholders, and its other books and records, and to make copies or extracts therefrom. A proper purpose shall mean a purpose reasonably related to such person's interest as a stockholder. . . .

(c) If the corporation . . . refuses to permit an inspection sought by a stockholder . . . pursuant to sub-section (b) or does not reply to the demand within five business days after the demand has been made, the stockholder may apply to the Court of Chancery for an order to compel such inspection. . . . The Court may summarily order the corporation to permit the stockholder to inspect the corporation's stock ledger, an existing list of stockholders, and its other books and records, and to make copies or extracts therefrom; or the Court may order the corporation to furnish to the stockholder a list of its stockholders as of a specific date on condition that the stockholder first pay to the corporation the reasonable cost of obtaining and furnishing such list and on such other conditions as the Court deems appropriate. Where the stockholder seeks to inspect the corporation's books and records, other than its stock ledger or list of stockholders, he shall first establish (1) that he has complied with the provisions of this section respecting the form and manner of making demand for inspection of such document; and (2) that the inspection he seeks is for a proper purpose. Where the stockholder seeks to inspect the corporation's stock ledger or list of stockholders and he has complied with the provisions of this section respecting the form and manner of making demand for inspection of such documents, the burden of proof shall be upon the corporation to establish that the inspection he seeks is for an improper purpose.]

court in Chas. A. Day & Co. v. Booth, 123 Maine 443, 447, 123 A. 557, 558 (1924) that "where it is shown that such stockholding is only colorable, or solely for the purpose of maintaining proceedings of this kind, [we] fail to see how the petitioner can be said to be a 'person interested,' entitled as of right to inspect. . . ." But for his opposition to Honeywell's policy, petitioner probably would not have bought Honeywell stock, would not be interested in Honeywell's profits and would not desire to communicate with Honeywell's shareholders. His avowed purpose in buying Honeywell stock was to place himself in a position to try to impress his opinions favoring a reordering of priorities upon Honeywell management and its other shareholders. Such a motivation can hardly be deemed a proper purpose germane to his economic interest as a shareholder. . . .

We do not mean to imply that a shareholder with a bona fide investment interest could not bring this suit if motivated by concern with the long-or short-term economic effects on Honeywell resulting from the production of war munitions. Similarly, this suit might be appropriate when a shareholder has a bona fide concern about the adverse effects of abstention from profitable war contracts on his investment in Honeywell.

In the instant case, however, the trial court, in effect, has found from all the facts that petitioner was not interested in even the long-term well-being of Honeywell or the enhancement of the value of his shares. His sole purpose was to persuade the company to adopt his social and political concerns, irrespective of any economic benefit to himself or Honeywell. This purpose on the part of one buying into the corporation does not entitle the petitioner to inspect Honeywell's books and records. . . .

The order of the trial court denying the writ of mandamus is affirmed.

QUESTIONS

1. Should companies be able to limit access to shareholder lists? Should shareholder lists be treated differently from the firm's financial records? From its other business documents? What costs might firms incur if forced to give unrestricted access to the shareholder lists?

2. Should a firm be able to expand or contract the shareholder inspection right?

3. If a shareholder has a "proper purpose" in demanding the shareholder list, should it matter that he or she may have other purposes? Suppose, for example, that the shareholder making the demand is a broker trying to open a mail-order investment consulting service.

4. In light of *Pillsbury,* how might you coach a client who wants access to corporate records for a political cause?

Sadler v. NCR Corporation

928 F.2d 48 (2d Cir.1991).

This appeal concerns a limited but potentially important tactic in proxy contests—a stockholder's demand for a list of record shareholders and a list of beneficial owners of shares who do not object to disclosure of their names ("NOBO list"). The appeal raises issues under New York state law and the United States Constitution as to the power of New York to require an out-of-state corporation, doing business within New York, to provide resident shareholders with the list of record stockholders and to compile and produce the NOBO list, under circumstances where the requesting shareholders could not obtain such lists under the law of the state of incorporation. The lists are sought in connection with a tender offer and the solicitation of proxy votes in an effort to replace directors. . . .

We conclude that New York law authorizes production of the shareholder and NOBO lists in the circumstances of this case and that application of New York law does not violate the Commerce Clause of the Constitution. . . .

Background

NCR, a large computer company, is incorporated in Maryland and has its principal place of business in Dayton, Ohio. It is undisputed that NCR maintains at least eight offices in New York and conducts substantial business there. NCR has 75,000 shareholders. AT & T, the well-known telecommunications company, is a New York corporation with its principal executive offices in New York City. AT & T became a beneficial owner of 100 shares of NCR stock on November 21, 1990. The Sadlers are New York residents who own more than 6,000 shares of NCR stock and have been record holders of NCR stock for more than six months prior to this lawsuit.

On December 6, 1990, AT & T began a tender offer for the shares of NCR, offering to purchase all of the common stock of NCR for $90 a share. In compliance with Rule 14d–5 of the Securities and Exchange Commission, 17 C.F.R. § 240.14d–5 (1990), NCR mailed the offer to purchase to all NCR stockholders. The NCR board rejected the tender offer and declined to redeem a "poison pill" shareholders' rights plan, which presented and continues to present an obstacle to a hostile tender offer.* AT & T responded to this opposition by soliciting NCR shareholders to convene a special meeting of stockholders to replace a majority of the NCR directors so that the barriers to the tender offer could be removed. Maryland law permits a special meeting of stockholders to be called upon the request of stockholders entitled to cast 25 percent of the votes at the meeting. Md. Corps. & Ass'ns Code Ann. § 2–502 (1985 & Supp. 1990). NCR's corporate charter permits directors to be replaced at a special meeting of stockholders upon the affirmative vote of 80 percent of all outstanding shares. Soon after soliciting calls for a special meeting, AT & T submitted to NCR requests for a special meeting from holders of more than half of NCR stock. NCR subsequently scheduled a special meeting for March 28, 1991, the date selected for its annual meeting.

Beginning in early January 1991, AT & T and the Sadlers, acting at AT & T's request, sought from NCR its stockholder list and related materials to facilitate communication with owners of NCR shares. In addition to the list of record owners, AT & T sought a magnetic computer tape of the list and daily transfer sheets showing changes in shareholders from the date of demand to the date of the annual meeting. AT & T also

* [Poison pills are discussed at Chapter 7, Section 2(B).—Eds.]

sought two other lists, a "CEDE list" and a "NOBO list." A "CEDE list" identifies the brokerage firms and other record owners who bought shares in a street name for their customers and who have placed those shares in the custody of depository firms such as Depository Trust Co.; these shares are reflected in the corporation's records only under the names of nominees used by such depository firms. Depository Trust Co. uses "Cede & Co." as the name of the nominee for shares it holds for brokerage firms, and such lists, regardless of the nominee names adopted by other depository firms, are known as "CEDE lists." . . . A "NOBO list" (non-objecting beneficial owners) contains the names of those owning beneficial interests in shares of a corporation who have given consent to the disclosure of their identities. The Securities and Exchange Commission requires brokers and other record holders of stock in street name to compile a NOBO list at a corporation's request. . . .

Upon NCR's refusal to produce the requested materials, the Sadlers and AT & T brought this suit in the Southern District, relying on section 1315 of the New York Business Corporation Law, N.Y. Bus. Corp. Law § 1315 (McKinney 1986). Section 1315, which we consider in detail below, enables New York residents owning shares of a foreign corporation to obtain a list of the corporation's shareholders. On January 28, 1991, the District Court ruled that the Sadlers qualified under section 1315 to obtain NCR's stockholder list and that the statute could constitutionally be applied to require NCR to comply with their request, notwithstanding NCR's Commerce Clause objections. Later that day, [the district court judge] issued a supplemental ruling rejecting NCR's contention that the NOBO list was not producible under section 1315 because it was not then in existence but required compilation. He entered an order requiring NCR to produce all the materials sought by the Sadlers and AT & T.

Discussion

I. Application of section 1315

Section 1315(a) permits any New York resident who for six months has been a stockholder of record of a foreign corporation doing business in New York, or who holds or acts for those who hold five percent of any class of outstanding shares to require the corporation, on five days' written notice, to produce "a record of its shareholders setting forth the names and addresses of all shareholders, the number and class of shares held by each and the dates when they respectively became the owners of record." N.Y. Bus. Corp. Law (McKinney 1986). Such a resident is also entitled "to examine in person or by agent . . . the record of shareholders" at specified locations. Id. The corporation may require the requesting shareholder to furnish an affidavit assuring that "inspection is not desired for a purpose . . . other than the business of" the corporation and that the shareholder has not engaged in the sale of stockholder lists within the past five years. Id. § 1315(b). A substantially similar provision of New York law applies to stockholder lists of New York corporations. N.Y. Bus. Corp. Law § 624 (McKinney 1986). See Crane Co. v. Anaconda Co., 39 N.Y.2d 14, 18–20, 346 N.E.2d 507, 510–11, 382 N.Y.S.2d 707, 710–11 (1976) (outlining origin of the New York statutory right to inspect stockholder lists).

A. Eligibility of the Sadlers.

The Sadlers qualify under section 1315 as persons entitled to obtain a "record" of NCR's shareholders. The Sadlers are residents of New York and have owned NCR stock for six months prior to their demand. The corporation whose stockholder list they seek does business in New York.

Nevertheless, NCR challenges the Sadlers' right to invoke section 1315 because of the arrangement between the Sadlers and AT & T under which the Sadlers initiated their request. Since AT & T had not held its NCR stock for more than six months, it sought out a New York resident who qualified under section 1315. AT & T's agreement with the Sadlers provides that the Sadlers will demand the NCR stockholder list, that AT & T will reimburse the Sadlers for any expenses and indemnify them for any losses arising out of the demand, and that the Sadlers will not settle any claim or lawsuit concerning the demand without the consent of AT & T, which will not be unreasonably withheld. Pursuant to this agreement, the Sadlers requested that NCR produce the stockholder records to AT & T, which it characterized as "our agent," and informed NCR that AT & T would reimburse NCR for any expenses incurred in complying with the demand. NCR contends that AT & T is not the agent of the Sadlers, but in reality is the principal, using the Sadlers as its agent for a demand that AT & T itself is not entitled to make.

We agree with [the district court judge] that the agreement between the Sadlers and AT & T does not disqualify the Sadlers from invoking section 1315. Though section 1315 permits an "agent" to act for the qualifying New York resident in inspecting the shareholder record, it does not inevitably apply all the technical aspects of the law of agency to the permissible relationship between the requesting shareholder and another entity with whom the shareholder chooses to act. Section 1315 "should be liberally construed in favor of the stockholder," *Crane Co.*, 39 N.Y.2d at 20–21, 346 N.E.2d at 512, 382 N.Y.S.2d at 712. Once the resident shareholder alleges compliance with the statute, "the bona fides of the shareholder will be assumed . . . and it becomes incumbent on the corporation to justify its refusal by showing an improper purpose or bad faith." Id. at 20, 346 N.E.2d at 511, 382 N.Y.S.2d at 711 (citations omitted).

We see no reason to believe that New York would deny the Sadlers the right to invoke section 1315 because of the arrangement they have made with AT & T. . . .

B. The demand for the NOBO list.

Whether New York law entitles the Sadlers to require NCR to assemble a NOBO list presents a more substantial question. The parties agree that section 1315 applies to NOBO lists in a corporation's possession, but it is undisputed that at the time of the demand, NCR did not have a NOBO list in its possession. It is also undisputed that a corporation can obtain a NOBO list, normally within ten days, by requesting compilation of the list by firms that offer data processing services for this task. NCR reads section 1315 as limited to production of lists in existence, as distinguished from those readily capable of being compiled. . . .

The text of section 1315 does not resolve the dispute, although a narrow reading of its terms might favor NCR. The statute could be read to be limited to production or examination of lists already in existence and could also be limited to lists reflecting the names and addresses of owners of record. But New York courts have made clear that the statute is to be "liberally construed," Crane Co., 39 N.Y.2d at 20–21, 346 N.E.2d at 512, 382 N.Y.S.2d at 712, to "facilitate communication among shareholders on issues respecting corporate affairs," Bohrer [v. International Banknote Co.], 150 A.D.2d 196, 540 N.Y.S.2d 445, 446 [(1st Dep't 1989)]. . . . A narrow reading of section 1315 would therefore not accord with New York law. . . .

Other courts, however, construing statutes similar to section 1315, have expressly declined to order compilation of NOBO lists. RB Associates [v. The Gillette Co., C.A. No. 9711, 1988 WL 27731 (Del.Ch., Mar.22, 1988)]; Cenergy Corp. v. Bryson Oil & Gas P.L.C., 662 F.Supp. 1144, 1148 (D.Nev.1987). The matter was given extended consideration by Chancellor Allen in *RB Associates*. In declining to order compilation of a NOBO list, he distinguished it in two respect from CEDE lists, which Delaware and New York require a corporation to compile upon request of a qualified shareholder. . . . CEDE lists, he pointed out, can be generated rapidly by a computer, whereas a NOBO list takes up to ten days to compile. Second, he expressed the view that it would be extremely inefficient without a CEDE list to attempt to distribute proxy materials to persons for whom a depository company holds shares, whereas a NOBO list "plays no central role in a proxy contest." *RB Associates*, supra.

We do not find either distinction compelling. Since compilation of a NOBO list is a relatively simple mechanical task, the fact that compilation takes longer than for a CEDE list is an insubstantial basis for distinction. As to both sets of information, the underlying data exist in discrete records readily available to be compiled into an aggregate list. Nor are the functions of the lists significantly dissimilar. Both facilitate direct communication with stockholders, in the case of a NOBO list, at least with those beneficial owners who have indicated no objection to disclosure of their names and addresses.

Though Delaware chooses to construe the reach of its requirements on stockholder list disclosure narrowly in this respect, we think New York would construe section 1315 more generously. Once the Securities and Exchange Commission has acted to enable a corporation to obtain from brokers and other record owners a list of beneficial owners of its shares who do not object to such disclosure, we think New York would apply section 1315 to permit a qualifying shareholder to require the compilation and production of such a list.

Even if the statute might not require compilation of NOBO lists routinely, . . . compilation was properly ordered in this case. The effect of NCR's 80 percent rule is to count as a "no" vote on the replacement of directors every share that is not voted at the special meeting. Thus, the shares of non-voting beneficial owners who might oppose management if solicited by management opponents armed with a NOBO list are counted in favor of management. Denying such opponents an opportunity to contact the NOBOs is inconsistent with the statute's objective of seeking "to the extent possible, to place shareholders on an equal footing with management in obtaining access to shareholders." *Bohrer*, 150 A.D.2d at 196–97, 540 N.Y.S.2d at 446. In effect, NCR already has the votes of those

NOBOs who, for lack of solicitation, decline to vote. As to them, NCR has all the access it needs.

. . .

[NCR claimed] that section 1315 subjects it to inconsistent regulation of a sort that the dormant Commerce Clause power prohibits. . . . [S]tates have traditionally exercised authority to require disclosure of stockholder lists of foreign corporations doing business within their borders. Moreover, such authority will not normally create, and does not create in this case, the sort of irreconcilable conflict that would arise if a state purported to regulate voting rights or other aspects of the internal affairs of a foreign corporation that "admit only of one uniform system, or plan of regulation," Cooley v. Board of Wardens, 53 U.S. (12 How.) 299, 319 (1851). Access to stockholder lists is a recognized exception to the internal affairs doctrine as a matter of corporate law and conflicts of law, and it should take a substantial threat of conflict adversely affecting interstate commerce before a court invalidates a state's assertion of this traditional authority. Though Maryland may well have balanced limited shareholder access to stockholder lists with generous authority for calling special meetings, it did so against the background of traditional foreign state regulation of such access, and it cannot expect courts to provide constitutional insulation for the particular arrangements it adopted. If the traditional role of states concerning access to stockholder lists of foreign corporations is to be circumscribed, that alteration will have to be undertaken by Congress.

NCR's remaining Commerce Clause contentions require little discussion. Section 1315 creates no discrimination against interstate commerce. . . . [I]t applies (for all practical purposes) equally to foreign and domestic corporations. . . .

Equally unavailing is the claim that section 1315 imposes unjustified burdens on interstate commerce. . . .

AFTERMATH

Subsequent to the decision in *Sadler*, New York law was amended to provide that, in response to shareholder requests for information, "[t]he corporation shall not be required to obtain information about beneficial owners not in its possession." McKinney's Business Corporation Law § 1315(a).

PROBLEMS

McWindsor, Inc., which is incorporated in New York, is a maker of upscale British-style fashions. To date, it has specialized in $1,000 all-cotton pea-green trench coats and $100 all-cotton umbrellas. Both sport the distinctive McWindsor plaid fabric, said to have been designed for the kilts of an obscure Scottish regiment in 1656. McWindsor stock trades at about $1,000 per share. Some shareholders have asked the company to perform a 10–for–1 stock split (each shareholder would tender his or her stock to the company, and receive 10 new shares of stock for each old share of stock). By doing so, the company would reduce the price of a share of McWindsor stock to about $100. The shareholders explain that these lower share prices would let them more easily fit McWindsor shares into diversified stock portfolios. The company has refused. Far better, CEO Prince George McWindsor announces, for stock to trade at the price of a rain coat than for it to trade at the price of an umbrella.

1. Suppose X (a manufacturer of expensive sports cars) buys several shares of McWindsor stock and requests a shareholders list. Must McWindsor give X the list? What kind of list? Suppose X announces a sale/tender offer: it will exchange one sports car (generally selling at $180,000) for every 150 shares of McWindsor stock tendered to X by McWindsor shareholders. If it again asks for the shareholder list, must McWindsor give it the list?

2. Suppose an investor holding three McWindsor shares asks for the shareholder list. He explains that he wants to contact other shareholders and ask them to join him in demanding that the company effect a stock split. Must McWindsor provide the list?

3. Suppose an investment bank holding 300 McWindsor shares asks for the list. It explains that its stock analysts have developed a new formula for fitting McWindsor shares into diversified stock portfolios. It thus wants to offer their services to McWindsor shareholders. Must McWindsor provide the list? Suppose instead that the investment bank forms a mutual fund called Diversified McWindsor, Inc. [DWI]. In exchange for several thousand shares of DWI stock, it has contributed several thousand shares of 20 companies that, together with McWindsor, form a well-diversified stock portfolio. DWI now announces a tender offer for McWindsor stock: in exchange for every McWindsor share tendered, it will provide 10 shares (each worth $100) of DWI. In order to publicize the tender offer, DWI asks for the shareholders list. Must McWindsor provide the list?

4. Suppose a group of shareholders ask for all records relating to the employment practices of McWindsor's supplier in Northern Ireland. The shareholders explain that they have heard rumors that McWindsor's supplier discriminates against Catholic workers, and want to ascertain whether the rumors are true. Must McWindsor provide the records?

2. SHAREHOLDER VOTING CONTROL

Stroh v. Blackhawk Holding Corp.

48 Ill.2d 471, 272 N.E.2d 1 (1971).

The only issue before this court is the validity of the 500,000 shares of Class B stock, which by the articles of incorporation of Blackhawk were limited in their rights by the provision "none of the shares of Class B stock shall be entitled to dividends either upon voluntary or involuntary liquidation or otherwise." It is the plaintiffs' contention that because of the foregoing limitation—depriving the Class B shares of the "economic" incidents of shares of stock, or of the proportionate interest in the corporate assets—the Class B shares do not in fact constitute shares of stock.

Blackhawk Holding Corporation was organized under the Illinois Business Corporation Act in November of 1963. Its articles of incorporation authorized the issuance of 3,000,000 shares of Class A stock with a par value of $1, and 500,000 shares of Class B stock without par value. . . . Pursuant to the preorganization subscription agreements, 21 promoters purchased 87,868 shares of the Class A stock at the price of $3.40 per share ($298,751.20), and the 500,000 shares of Class B stock at ¼ per share ($1,250). Thereafter, the corporation registered the Class A shares with the securities division of the office of the Secretary of State of Illinois for the sale of 500,000 shares thereof to the general public at a price of $4 per share. The prospectus for the registration described the Class A and Class B stock, and quoted from the articles of incorporation relative to their respective rights and preferences. The prospectus explained that every share of each class of stock would be entitled to one vote on all general matters submitted to a vote of the shareholders. . . .

The prospectus also explained that no Class B stock was being offered for sale in that all of such stock has been previously issued. Under the heading "Organization and Development," the prospectus also stated: "Subscriptions for a total of $300,001.20 were sold to twenty-one persons, representing 87,868 class A shares, the class now being offered, at the price of $3.40 per share ($298,751.20) and 500,000 class B shares, at a price of one-fourth of a cent per share ($1,250.00); thus said subscribers by virtue of a $300,001.20 investment, have control of the corporation having an initial capitalization of $2,000,000.00 after this offering."

In August of 1964, there was a 2 for 1 split of the Class A stock, increasing the shares outstanding from 587,863 to 1,175,736 shares. The corporation sold additional Class A stock to the public in 1965 for $4 a share. As of June 1968, there were 1,237,681 Class A shares and 500,000 Class B shares outstanding, the latter representing 28.78% of the total voting shares of the company.

. . .

Under the Illinois constitution of 1870, a stockholder in an Illinois corporation is guaranteed the right to vote based upon the number of shares owned by him. (Ill.Const. art. XI, sec. 3, S.H.A.) Section 14 of the Business Corporation Act (Ill.Rev.Stat.1969, ch. 32, par. 157.14) provides that shares of stock in an Illinois corporation may be divided into classes,

> "with such designations, preferences, qualifications, limitations, restrictions and such special or relative rights as shall be stated in the articles of incorporation. The articles of incorporation shall not limit or deny the voting power of the shares of any class.
>
> Without limiting the authority herein contained, a corporation when so provided in its articles of incorporation, may issue shares of preferred or special classes:
>
> . . .
>
> (c) Having preference over any other class or classes of shares as to the payment of dividends.
>
> (d) Having preference as to the assets of the corporation over any other class or classes of shares upon the voluntary or involuntary liquidation of the corporation."

. . .

Section 2.6 of the Act, in defining "shares" states, " 'Shares' means the units into which the proprietary interests in a corporation are divided." (Ill.Rev.Stat.1969, ch. 32, par. 157.2–6.) This was formerly section 2(f) of the Act (Ill.Rev.Stat.1955, ch. 32, par. 157.2(f)) which defined shares as "units into which shareholders' rights to participate in the control of a corporation, in its surplus or profits, or in the distribution of its assets, are divided." . . .

To the plaintiffs, "proprietary," as used in the definition of shares, means a property right, and shares must then represent some economic interest, or interest in the property or assets of the corporation. However, the word "proprietary" does not necessarily denote economic or asset rights, although it has been defined as synonymous with ownership or to denote legal title . . . and "proprietary rights" have been defined as those conferred by virtue of ownership of a thing. . . .

We agree with the defendants' construction. We interpret this statutory definition to mean that the proprietary rights conferred by the ownership of stock may consist of one or more of the rights to participate "in the control of the corporation, in its surplus or profits, *or* in the distribution of its assets." The use of the disjunctive conjunction "*or*" indicates that one or more of the three named rights may inure to a stockholder by virtue of his stock ownership. . . .

We must here decide the extent to which economic attributes of shares of stock may be eliminated. . . .

Section 14 of the Act clearly expresses the intent of the legislature to be that parties to a corporate entity may create whatever restrictions and limitations they may want with regard to their corporate stock by expressing such restrictions and limitations in the articles of incorporation. These rights and powers granted by the legislature to the corporation to make the terms of its contract with its shareholders are limited only by the proviso that the articles may not limit or deny the voting power of any share. This section of the Act expressly confers the right to prefer a class of shares over another with regard to dividends and assets. Section 2.6 defines shares as "The units into which the proprietary interests in a corporation are divided."

In seeking the intent of the legislature, a statute should be construed as a whole and its separate parts considered together. Our present constitution requires only that a shareholder not be deprived of his voice in management. It does not require that a shareholder, in addition to the management aspect of ownership, must also have an economic interest.

Thus, section 14, like the constitution, limits the power of a corporation only as to the voting aspect of ownership. . . .

When the relevant sections of the Act are read together with the constitution, it seems apparent that it was the intent of the legislature that the proprietary interests represented by the shares of stock consist of management or control rights, rights to earnings, and rights to assets. There are other rights which are incidental to these. Under our laws, the rights to earnings and the rights to assets—the "economic" rights—may be removed and eliminated from the other attributes of a share of stock. Only the management incident of ownership may not be removed.

. . .

The constitution requires only that the right to vote be proportionate to the number of shares owned, not to the investment made in a corporation. It has long been the common practice in Illinois to classify shares of stock such that one may invest less than another in a corporation, and yet have control. One . . . shareholder may purchase ten shares of a class of stock issued at its par value of $1,000 per share, and his business partner may purchase 100 shares of another class of the corporate stock issued at its par value of $10 per share. The parties, for varying reasons, may be very willing that the party investing the $1,000 have control of the management of the corporation, as opposed to the party having the investment of $10,000. . . .

If there is overreaching or fraud in establishing the different relative voting rights of shares, that is another matter and there is a remedy available. We are aware that the classification of shares, so as to enable one class to obtain greater voting rights with the same or lesser investment in a corporation than another class, may carry with it the possibility for wrongdoing. However, it also often serves a valid purpose and there is nothing inherently wrong in such a scheme. The fact that a corporation makes a public offering of stock does not render the procedure outlined above less valid. The securities division of the Secretary of State's office has its particular guidelines to protect the public in such an offering.

In this case the parties went one step further than is customary. The stock which could be bought cheaper, and yet carry the same voting power per share, was not permitted to share at all in the dividends or assets of the corporation. This additional step did not invalidate the stock.

We find nothing in the declared public policy of this State to condemn stock of this nature. . . .

Affirmed and remanded, with directions.

■ SCHAEFER, JUSTICE (dissenting).

. . .

"Under our laws," say the majority, "the rights to earnings and the rights to assets—the 'economic' rights—may be removed and eliminated from the other attributes of a share of stock. Only the management incident of ownership may not be removed." This seems to me to be saying that the ownership incidents of ownership may be eliminated. What remains, then, is a disembodied right to manage the assets of a corporation, divorced from any financial interest in those assets except such as may accrue from the power to manage them. In my opinion, what is left after the economic rights are "removed and eliminated" is not a share of corporate stock under the law of Illinois.

. . .

ANALYSIS

1. What might be the public policy underlying a prohibition of nonvoting shares? Would that policy also be offended by shares with unequal voting power?

2. The opinion of the lower appellate court in *Stroh* reveals that in 1967 the Class A shares were selling for substantially less than the $4 per share initial offering price. At the same time, the Class B shares were selling for "about 20 times the original price." 253 N.E.2d 692, at 694. Does this tend to show that the initial investors in Class A shares were

treated unfairly? Why would the Class B shares have any value at all? How would you determine what the value is?

3. At the time this case arose, the Illinois constitution contained provisions that in effect required all common shares to have equal voting rights. In a 1970 constitutional revision, these requirements were dropped. The Illinois Business Corporation Act of 1983, § 7.40(b), now provides that corporations, in their articles, "may limit or deny voting rights or may provide special voting rights as to any class or classes or series of shares." Under this law, how might the original 21 investors in Blackhawk Holding Corp. have accomplished their apparent purpose (voting control disproportionate to profit claim) without using the peculiar Class B shares?

4. The original 21 investors in Blackhawk Holding Corp. obviously wanted to protect their control. One reason why people want control is that they (or their relations or friends) are, or expect to be, employed by the corporation and they want to protect their salaries and perquisites. To that extent, their interests may diverge from the interests of other shareholders. Are there reasons for wanting control that do not involve such blatant conflict of interest?

5. Suppose you have money to invest and are offered shares in a corporation with a control structure like that of Blackhawk Holding Corp. Suppose you believe that the people who will hold disproportionately large voting control will use their control to provide themselves and their children with jobs at salaries above the market rate and that there is no reasonable prospect that there will be anything you can do about it. Might you still be willing to buy shares in the corporation?

NOTE AND QUESTIONS

In Providence and Worcester Co. v. Baker, 378 A.2d 121 (Del.1977), the plaintiff owned 28 percent of the single class of voting shares of the Providence and Worcester Company (P & W). The corporation's articles of incorporation provided that "each shareholder shall be entitled to one vote for every share of the common stock of said company owned by him not exceeding fifty shares, and one vote for every twenty shares more than fifty owned by him; provided, that no stockholder shall be entitled to vote upon more than one fourth part of the whole number of shares issued and outstanding. . . ." The result of this provision was that the plaintiff, with 28 percent of the shares, had only 3 percent of the votes. The plaintiff argued that the corporation's voting rule violated § 151(a) of the Delaware corporation law, which provides that corporations may issue various classes or series of stock, "which classes or series may have such voting powers, full or limited, or no voting powers . . . as shall be stated and expressed in the certificate of incorporation." The plaintiff argued that this section of the Delaware law allows differences in voting power between classes of stock but not within a single class of stock and that, consequently, the P & W voting rule was impermissible. The Delaware Supreme Court rejected this argument and upheld the P & W rule.

Assume that at the time of its formation, P & W issued 35,000 shares and no shareholder held more than 200 shares. What legitimate purpose might be served by a voting rule like that of P & W? As a potential original investor in 100 of the P & W shares, what potential harm to your interests might you be concerned about as a result of the rule?

PROBLEM

Suppose a corporation is formed with 1 million Class A common shares, which are sold at $4 per share. No other shares are outstanding. Two years later the shares are selling on the market for $6 per share. The managers of the corporation own 300,000 shares and control the board of directors. The board adopts the following plan: For each share of Class A stock that a shareholder owns, he or she will be entitled to buy either (i) one additional share of Class A Stock at $5.00 per share or (ii) five shares of a new Class B stock at 1 cent per share. The Class B shares will carry one vote per share but will be entitled to no dividends (current or liquidating). All the members of the management group will buy Class B shares. They will therefore wind up with their original Class A shares (300,000 votes) plus 1,500,000 Class B shares (1,500,000 votes). Suppose you own 1,000 of the original shares (now called Class A). You believe that there is a group of outside investors that would be willing to buy the entire corporation for $9 million ($9 per share for the existing shares). In fact, you believe that the reason for the board's plan to offer the new shares is its concern about the outside group taking over. The time has come when you must decide whether to buy new A shares or B shares, or neither. (a) What do you do? (b) Do you think the board should be allowed to put you to this choice? (c) Suppose you had been entitled to vote on whether the new Class B shares should have been authorized. How would you have voted?

3. CONTROL IN CLOSELY HELD CORPORATIONS

Ringling Bros.-Barnum & Bailey Combined Shows v. Ringling

29 Del.Ch. 610, 53 A.2d 441 (Del.Sup.Ct.1947).

The Court of Chancery was called upon to review an attempted election of directors at the 1946 annual stockholders meeting of the corporate defendant. The pivotal questions concern an agreement between two of the three present stockholders, and particularly the effect of this agreement with relation to the exercise of voting rights by these two stockholders. At the time of the meeting, the corporation had outstanding 1000 shares of capital stock held as follows: 315 by petitioner Edith Conway Ringling; 315 by defendant Aubrey B. Ringling Haley (individually or as executrix and legatee of a deceased husband); and 370 by defendant John Ringling North. The purpose of the meeting was to elect the entire board of seven directors. The shares could be voted cumulatively. Mrs. Ringling asserts that by virtue of the operation of an agreement between her and Mrs. Haley, the latter was bound to vote her shares for an adjournment of the meeting, or in the alternative, for a certain slate of directors. Mrs. Haley contends that she was not so bound for reason that the agreement was invalid, or at least revocable.

The two ladies entered into the agreement in 1941. It makes like provisions concerning stock of the corporate defendant and of another corporation, but in this case, we are concerned solely with the agreement as it affects the voting of stock of the corporate defendant. The agreement recites that each party was the owner "subject only to possible claims of creditors of the estates of Charles Ringling and Richard Ringling, respectively" (deceased husbands of the parties), of 300 shares of the capital stock of the defendant corporation; that in 1938 these shares had been deposited under a voting trust agreement which would terminate in 1947, or earlier, upon the elimination of certain liability of the corporation; that each party also owned 15 shares individually; that the parties had "entered into an agreement in April 1934 providing for joint action by them in matters affecting their ownership of stock and interest in" the corporate defendant; that the parties desired "to continue to act jointly in all matters relating to their stock ownership or interest in" the corporate defendant (and the other corporation). The agreement then provides as follows:

"Now, Therefore, in consideration of the mutual covenants and agreements hereinafter contained the parties hereto agree as follows:

. . .

"2. In exercising any voting rights to which either party may be entitled by virtue of ownership of stock or voting trust certificates held by them in either of said corporations, each party will consult and confer with the other and the parties will act jointly in exercising such voting rights in accordance with such agreement as they may reach with respect to any matter calling for the exercise of such voting rights.

"3. In the event the parties fail to agree with respect to any matter covered by paragraph 2 above, the question in disagreement shall be submitted for arbitration to Karl D. Loos, of Washington, D.C. as arbitrator and his decision thereon shall be binding upon the parties hereto. Such arbitration shall be exercised to the end of assuring for the respective corporations good management and such participation therein by the members of the Ringling family as the experience, capacity and ability of each may warrant. The parties may at any time by written agreement designate any other individual to act as arbitrator in lieu of said Loos. . . .

"5. This agreement shall be in effect from the date hereof and shall continue in effect for a period of ten years unless sooner terminated by mutual agreement in writing by the parties hereto.

". . ."

The Mr. Loos mentioned in the agreement is an attorney and has represented both parties since 1937, and, before and after the voting trust was terminated in late 1942, advised them with respect to the exercise of their voting rights. At the annual meetings in 1943 and the two following years, the parties voted their shares in accordance with mutual understandings arrived at as a result of discussions. In each of these years, they elected five of the seven directors. Mrs. Ringling and Mrs. Haley each had sufficient votes, independently of the other, to elect two of the seven directors. By both voting for an additional candidate, they could be sure of his election regardless of how Mr. North, the remaining stockholder, might vote.[1]

Some weeks before the 1946 meeting, they discussed with Mr. Loos the matter of voting for directors. They were in accord that Mrs. Ringling should cast sufficient votes to elect herself and her son; and that Mrs. Haley should elect herself and her husband; but they did not agree upon a fifth director. The day before the meeting, the discussions were continued, Mrs. Haley being represented by her husband since she could not be present because of illness. In a conversation with Mr. Loos, Mr. Haley indicated that he would make a motion for an adjournment of the meeting for sixty days, in order to give the ladies additional time to come to an agreement about their voting. On the morning of the meeting, however, he stated that because of something Mrs. Ringling had done, he would not consent to a postponement. Mrs. Ringling then made a demand upon Mr. Loos to act under the third paragraph of the agreement "to arbitrate the disagreement" between her and Mrs. Haley in connection with the manner in which the stock of the two ladies should be voted. At the opening of the meeting, Mr. Loos read the written demand and stated that he determined and directed that the stock of both ladies be voted for an adjournment of sixty days. Mrs. Ringling then made a motion for adjournment and voted for it. Mr. Haley, as proxy for his wife, and Mr. North voted against the motion. Mrs. Ringling (herself or through her attorney, it is immaterial which) objected to the voting of Mrs. Haley's stock in any manner other than in accordance with Mr. Loos' direction. The chairman ruled that the stock could not be voted contrary to such direction, and declared the motion for adjournment had carried. Nevertheless, the meeting proceeded to the election of directors. Mrs. Ringling stated that she would continue in the meeting "but without prejudice to her position with respect to the voting of the stock and the fact that adjournment had not been taken." Mr. Loos directed Mrs. Ringling to cast her votes

882 for Mrs. Ringling,

882 for her son, Robert, and

441 for a Mr. Dunn,

who had been a member of the board for several years. She complied. Mr. Loos directed that Mrs. Haley's votes be cast

882 for Mrs. Haley,

882 for Mr. Haley, and

441 for Mr. Dunn.

Instead of complying, Mr. Haley attempted to vote his wife's shares

1103 for Mrs. Haley, and

1102 for Mr. Haley.

---

[1] Each lady was entitled to cast 2205 votes (since each had the cumulative voting rights of 315 shares, and there were 7 vacancies in the directorate). The sum of the votes of both is 4410, which is sufficient to allow 882 votes for each of 5 persons. Mr. North, holding 370 shares, was entitled to cast 2590 votes, which obviously cannot be divided so as to give to more than two candidates as many as 882 votes each. It will be observed that in order for Mrs. Ringling and Mrs. Haley to be sure to elect five directors (regardless of how Mr. North might vote) they must act together in the sense that their combined votes must be divided among five different candidates and at least one of the five must be voted for by both Mrs. Ringling and Mrs. Haley.

Mr. North voted his shares

864 for a Mr. Woods,

863 for a Mr. Griffin, and

863 for Mr. North.

The chairman ruled that the five candidates proposed by Mr. Loos, together with Messrs. Woods and North, were elected. The Haley-North group disputed this ruling insofar as it declared the election of Mr. Dunn; and insisted that Mr. Griffin, instead, had been elected. A directors' meeting followed in which Mrs. Ringling participated after stating that she would do so "without prejudice to her position that the stockholders' meeting had been adjourned and that the directors' meeting was not properly held." Mr. Dunn and Mr. Griffin, although each was challenged by an opposing faction, attempted to join in voting as directors for different slates of officers. Soon after the meeting, Mrs. Ringling instituted this proceeding.

The Vice Chancellor determined that the agreement to vote in accordance with the direction of Mr. Loos was valid as a "stock pooling agreement" with lawful objects and purposes, and that it was not in violation of any public policy of this state. He held that where the arbitrator acts under the agreement and one party refuses to comply with his direction, "the Agreement constitutes the willing party . . . an implied agent possessing the irrevocable proxy of the recalcitrant party for the purpose of casting the particular vote." It was ordered that a new election be held before a master, with the direction that the master should recognize and give effect to the agreement if its terms were properly invoked.

Before taking up defendants' objections to the agreement, let us analyze particularly what it attempts to provide with respect to voting, including what functions and powers it attempts to repose in Mr. Loos, the "arbitrator." The agreement recites that the parties desired "to continue to act jointly in all matters relating to their stock ownership or interest in" the corporation. The parties agreed to consult and confer with each other in exercising their voting rights and to act jointly—that is, concertedly; unitedly; towards unified courses of action—in accordance with such agreement as they might reach. Thus, so long as the parties agree for whom or for what their shares shall be voted, the agreement provides no function for the arbitrator. His role is limited to situations where the parties fail to agree upon a course of action. In such cases, the agreement directs that "the question in disagreement shall be submitted for arbitration" to Mr. Loos "as arbitrator and his decision thereon shall be binding upon the parties." These provisions are designed to operate in aid of what appears to be a primary purpose of the parties, "to act jointly" in exercising their voting rights, by providing a means for fixing a course of action whenever they themselves might reach a stalemate.

Should the agreement be interpreted as attempting to empower the arbitrator to carry his directions into effect? Certainly there is no express delegation or grant of power to do so, either by authorizing him to vote the shares or to compel either party to vote them in accordance with his directions. The agreement expresses no other function of the arbitrator than that of deciding questions in disagreement which prevent the effectuation of the purpose "to act jointly." The power to enforce a decision does not seem a necessary or usual incident of such a function. Mr. Loos is not a party to the agreement. It does not contemplate the transfer of any shares or interest in shares to him, or that he should undertake any duties which the parties might compel him to perform. They provided that they might designate any other individual to act instead of Mr. Loos. The agreement does not attempt to make the arbitrator a trustee of an express trust. What the arbitrator is to do is for the benefit of the parties, not for his own benefit. Whether the parties accept or reject his decision is no concern of his, so far as the agreement or the surrounding circumstances reveal. We think the parties sought to bind each other, but to be bound only to each other, and not to empower the arbitrator to enforce decisions he might make.

From this conclusion, it follows necessarily that no decision of the arbitrator could ever be enforced if both parties to the agreement were unwilling that it be enforced, for the obvious reason that there would be no one to enforce it. Under the agreement, something more is required after the arbitrator has given his decision in order that it should become compulsory: at least one of the parties must determine that such decision shall be carried into effect. Thus, any "control" of the voting of the shares, which is reposed in the arbitrator, is substantially limited in action under the agreement in that it is subject to the overriding power of the parties themselves.

The agreement does not describe the undertaking of each party with respect to a decision of the arbitrator other than to provide that it "shall be binding upon the parties." It seems to us that this language, considered with relation to its context and the situations to which it is applicable, means that each party promised the other to exercise her own voting rights in accordance with the arbitrator's decision. The agreement is silent about any exercise of the voting rights of one party by the other. The language with reference to situations where the parties arrive at an understanding as to voting plainly suggests "action" by each, and "exercising" voting rights by each, rather than by one for the other. There is no intimation that this method should be different where the arbitrator's decision is to be carried into effect. Assuming that a power in each party to exercise the voting rights of the other might be a relatively more effective or convenient means of enforcing a decision of the arbitrator than would be available without the power, this would not justify implying a delegation of the power in the absence of some indication that the parties bargained for that means. The method of voting actually employed by the parties tends to show that they did not construe the agreement as creating powers to vote each other's shares; for at meetings prior to 1946 each party apparently exercised her own voting rights, and at the 1946 meeting, Mrs. Ringling, who wished to enforce the agreement, did not attempt to cast a ballot in exercise of any voting rights of Mrs. Haley. We do not find enough in the agreement or in the circumstances to justify a construction that either party was empowered to exercise voting rights of the other.

Having examined what the parties sought to provide by the agreement, we come now to defendants' contention that the voting provisions are illegal and revocable. They say that the courts of this state have definitely established the doctrine "that there can be no agreement, or any device whatsoever, by which the voting power of stock of a

Delaware corporation may be irrevocably separated from the ownership of the stock, except by an agreement which complies with Section 18" of the Corporation Law, Rev.Code 1935, § 2050, and except by a proxy coupled with an interest. . . . The statute reads, in part, as follows:

"Sec. 18. Fiduciary Stockholders; Voting Power of; Voting Trusts:—Persons holding stock in a fiduciary capacity shall be entitled to vote the shares so held, and persons whose stock is pledged shall be entitled to vote, unless in the transfer by the pledgor on the books of the corporation he shall have expressly empowered the pledgee to vote thereon, in which case only the pledgee, or his proxy may represent said stock and vote thereon.

"One or more stockholders may by agreement in writing deposit capital stock of an original issue with or transfer capital stock to any person or persons, or corporation or corporations authorized to act as trustee, for the purpose of vesting in said person or persons, corporation or corporations, who may be designated Voting Trustee or Voting Trustees, the right to vote thereon for any period of time determined by such agreement, not exceeding ten years, upon the terms and conditions stated in such agreement. Such agreement may contain any other lawful provisions not inconsistent with said purpose. . . . Said Voting Trustees may vote upon the stock so issued or transferred during the period in such agreement specified; stock standing in the names of such Voting Trustees may be voted either in person or by proxy, and in voting said stock, such Voting Trustees shall incur no responsibility as stockholder, trustee or otherwise, except for their own individual malfeasance."[2]

In our view, neither the cases nor the statute sustain the rule for which the defendants contend. Their sweeping formulation would impugn well-recognized means by which a shareholder may effectively confer his voting rights upon others while retaining various other rights. For example, defendants' rule would apparently not permit holders of voting stock to confer upon stockholders of another class, by the device of an amendment of the certificate of incorporation, the exclusive right to vote during periods when dividends are not paid on stock of the latter class. The broad prohibitory meaning which defendants find in Section 18 seems inconsistent with their concession that proxies coupled with an interest may be irrevocable, for the statute contains nothing about such proxies. The statute authorizes, among other things, the deposit or transfer of stock in trust for a specified purpose, namely, "vesting" in the transferee "the right to vote thereon" for a limited period; and prescribes numerous requirements in this connection. Accordingly, it seems reasonable to infer that to establish the relationship and accomplish the purpose which the statute authorizes, its requirements must be complied with. But the statute does not purport to deal with agreements whereby shareholders attempt to bind each other as to how they shall vote their shares. Various forms of such pooling agreements, as they are sometimes called, have been held valid and have been distinguished from voting trusts. . . . We think the particular agreement before us does not violate Section 18 or constitute an attempted evasion of its requirements, and is

[2] Omitted portions of the section provide requirements for the filing of a copy of the agreement in the principal Delaware office of the corporation for the issuance of certificates of stock to the voting trustees, for the voting of stock where there are more than one voting trustee, and for the extension of the agreement for additional periods, not exceeding ten years each.

not illegal for any other reason. Generally speaking, a shareholder may exercise wide liberality of judgment in the matter of voting, and it is not objectionable that his motives may be for personal profit, or determined by whims or caprice, so long as he violates no duty owed his fellow shareholders. . . . The ownership of voting stock imposes no legal duty to vote at all. A group of shareholders may, without impropriety, vote their respective shares so as to obtain advantages of concerted action. They may lawfully contract with each other to vote in the future in such way as they, or a majority of their group, from time to time determine. . . . Reasonable provisions for cases of failure of the group to reach a determination because of an even division in their ranks seem unobjectionable. The provision here for submission to the arbitrator is plainly designed as a deadlock-breaking measure, and the arbitrator's decision cannot be enforced unless at least one of the parties (entitled to cast one-half of their combined votes) is willing that it be enforced. We find the provision reasonable. It does not appear that the agreement enables the parties to take any unlawful advantage of the outside shareholder, or of any other person. It offends no rule of law or public policy of this state of which we are aware.

Legal consideration for the promises of each party is supplied by the mutual promises of the other party. The undertaking to vote in accordance with the arbitrator's decision is a valid contract. The good faith of the arbitrator's action has not been challenged and, indeed, the record indicates that no such challenge could be supported. Accordingly, the failure of Mrs. Haley to exercise her voting rights in accordance with his decision was a breach of her contract. It is no extenuation of the breach that her votes were cast for two of the three candidates directed by the arbitrator. His directions to her were part of a single plan or course of action for the voting of the shares of both parties to the agreement, calculated to utilize an advantage of joint action by them which would bring about the election of an additional director. The actual voting of Mrs. Haley's shares frustrates that plan to such an extent that it should not be treated as a partial performance of her contract.

Throughout their argument, defendants make much of the fact that all votes cast at the meeting were by the registered shareholders. The Court of Chancery may, in a review of an election, reject votes of a registered shareholder where his voting of them is found to be in violation of rights of another person. . . . It seems to us that upon the application of Mrs. Ringling, the injured party, the votes representing Mrs. Haley's shares should not be counted. Since no infirmity in Mr. North's voting has been demonstrated, his right to recognition of what he did at the meeting should be considered in granting any relief to Mrs. Ringling; for her rights arose under a contract to which Mr. North was not a party. With this in mind, we have concluded that the election should not be declared invalid, but that effect should be given to a rejection of the votes representing Mrs. Haley's shares. No other relief seems appropriate in this proceeding. Mr. North's vote against the motion for adjournment was sufficient to defeat it. With respect to the election of directors, the return of the inspectors should be corrected to show a rejection of Mrs. Haley's votes, and to declare the election of the six persons for whom Mr. North and Mrs. Ringling voted.

This leaves one vacancy in the directorate. The question of what to do about such a vacancy was not considered by the court below and has not been argued here. For this reason, and because an election of directors at the 1947 annual meeting (which presumably will be held in the near future) may make a determination of the question unimportant, we shall not decide it on this appeal. If a decision of the point appears important to the parties, any of them may apply to raise it in the Court of Chancery, after the mandate of this court is received there.

An order should be entered directing a modification of the order of the Court of Chancery in accordance with this opinion.

ANALYSIS

1. If you had been in the position of Loos, attorney for several years for Mrs. Ringling and Mrs. Haley, what would you have said when they asked you to act as arbitrator under their agreement?

2. Did Mrs. Haley win or lose?

3. Note that Mrs. Ringling did not seek specific performance. The suit she filed was to review an election. What would the result have been if she had sought specific performance?

4. How should the agreement have been drafted to make a lawsuit unnecessary?

McQuade v. Stoneham

263 N.Y. 323, 189 N.E. 234 (1934).

■ POUND, CHIEF JUDGE. The action is brought to compel specific performance of an agreement between the parties, entered into to secure the control of National Exhibition Company, also called the Baseball Club (New York Nationals or "Giants"). This was one of Stoneham's enterprises which used the New York polo grounds for its home games. McGraw was manager of the Giants. McQuade was at the time the contract was entered into a city magistrate. He resigned December 8, 1930.

Defendant Stoneham became the owner of 1,306 shares, or a majority of the stock of National Exhibition Company. Plaintiff and defendant McGraw each purchased 70 shares of his stock. Plaintiff paid Stoneham $50,338.10 for the stock he purchased. As a part of the transaction, the agreement in question was entered into. It was dated May 21, 1919. Some of its pertinent provisions are

"VIII. The parties hereto will use their best endeavors for the purpose of continuing as directors of said Company and as officers thereof the following:

"Directors:

"Charles A. Stoneham,

"John J. McGraw,

"Francis X. McQuade

"—with the right to the party of the first part [Stoneham] to name all additional directors as he sees fit:

"Officers:

"Charles A. Stoneham, President,

"John J. McGraw, Vice-President,

"Francis X. McQuade, Treasurer.

"IX. No salaries are to be paid to any of the above officers or directors, except as follows:

"President	$45,000
"Vice-President	7,500
"Treasurer	7,500

"X. There shall be no change in said salaries, no change in the amount of capital, or the number of shares, no change or amendment of the by-laws of the corporation or any matters regarding the policy of the business of the corporation or any matters which may in anywise affect, endanger or interfere with the rights of minority stockholders, excepting upon the mutual and unanimous consent of all of the parties hereto. . . .

"XIV. This agreement shall continue and remain in force so long as the parties or any of them or the representative of any, own the stock referred to in this agreement, to wit, the party of the first part, 1,166 shares, the party of the second part 70 shares and the party of the third part 70 shares, except as may otherwise appear by this agreement. . . ."

In pursuance of this contract Stoneham became president and McGraw vice president of the corporation. McQuade became treasurer. In June, 1925, his salary was increased to $10,000 a year. He continued to act until May 2, 1928, when Leo J. Bondy was elected to succeed him. The board of directors consisted of seven men. The four outside of the parties hereto were selected by Stoneham and he had complete control over them. At the meeting of May 2, 1928, Stoneham and McGraw refrained from voting, McQuade voted for himself, and the other four voted for Bondy. Defendants did not keep their agreement with McQuade to use their best efforts to continue him as treasurer. On the contrary, he was dropped with their entire acquiescence. At the next stockholders' meeting he was dropped as a director although they might have elected him.

The courts below have refused to order the reinstatement of McQuade, but have given him damages for wrongful discharge, with a right to sue for future damages.

The cause for dropping McQuade was due to the falling out of friends. McQuade and Stoneham had disagreed. The trial court has found in substance that their numerous quarrels and disputes did not affect the orderly and efficient administration of the business of the corporation; that plaintiff was removed because he had antagonized the dominant Stoneham by persisting in challenging his power over the corporate treasury and for no misconduct on his part. The court also finds that plaintiff was removed by Stoneham for protecting the corporation and its minority stockholders. We will assume that Stoneham put him out when he might have retained him, merely in order to get rid of him.

Defendants say that the contract in suit was void because the directors held their office charged with the duty to act for the corporation according to their best judgment and that any contract which compels a director to vote to keep any particular person in office and at a stated salary is illegal. Directors are the exclusive executive representatives of the corporation, charged with administration of its internal affairs and the management and use of its assets. They manage the business of the corporation. (General Corporation Law, Consol. Laws, c. 23, § 27.) "An agreement to continue a man as president is dependent upon his continued loyalty to the interests of the corporation." Fells v. Katz, 256 N.Y. 67, 72, 175 N.E. 516, 517. So much is undisputed.

Plaintiff contends that the converse of this proposition is true and that an agreement among directors to continue a man as an officer of a corporation is not to be broken so long as such officer is loyal to the interests of the corporation and that, as plaintiff has been found loyal to the corporation, the agreement of defendants is enforceable.

Although it has been held that an agreement among stockholders whereby it is attempted to divest the directors of their power to discharge an unfaithful employee of the corporation is illegal as against public policy (Fells v. Katz, supra), it must be equally true that the stockholders may not, by agreement among themselves, control the directors in the exercise of the judgment vested in them by virtue of their office to elect officers and fix salaries. Their motives may not be questioned so long as their acts are legal. The bad faith or the improper motives of the parties does not change the rule. . . . Directors may not by agreements entered into as stockholders abrogate their independent judgment. . . .

Stockholders may, of course, combine to elect directors. That rule is well settled. As Holmes, C.J., pointedly said (Brightman v. Bates, 175 Mass. 105, 111, 55 N.E. 809, 811): "If stockholders want to make their power felt, they must unite. There is no reason why a majority should not agree to keep together." The power to unite is, however, limited to the election of directors and is not extended to contracts whereby limitations are placed on the power of directors to manage the business of the corporation by the selection of agents at defined salaries.

The minority shareholders whose interests McQuade says he has been punished for protecting, are not, aside from himself, complaining about his discharge. He is not acting for the corporation or for them in this action. It is impossible to see how the corporation has been injured by the substitution of Bondy as treasurer in place of McQuade. As McQuade represents himself in this action and seeks redress for his own wrongs, "we prefer to listen to [the corporation and the minority stockholders] before any decision as to their wrongs." Faulds v. Yates, 57 Ill. 416, 417, 11 Am.Rep. 24.

It is urged that we should pay heed to the morals and manners of the market place to sustain this agreement and that we should hold that its violation gives rise to a cause of action for damages rather than base our decision on any outworn notions of public policy. Public policy is a dangerous guide in determining the validity of a contract and courts should not interfere lightly with the freedom of competent parties to make their own contracts. We do not close our eyes to the fact that such agreements, tacitly or openly arrived at, are not uncommon, especially in close corporations where the stockholders are doing business for convenience under a corporate organization. We know that majority stockholders, united in voting trusts, effectively manage the business of a corporation by choosing trustworthy directors to reflect their policies in the corporate management. Nor are we unmindful that McQuade has, so the court has found, been shabbily treated as a purchaser of stock from Stoneham. We have said: "A trustee is held to something stricter than the morals of the market place" (Meinhard v. Salmon, 249 N.Y. 458, 464, 164 N.E. 545, 546), but Stoneham and McGraw were not trustees for McQuade as an individual. Their duty was to the corporation and its stockholders, to be exercised according to their unrestricted lawful judgment. They were under no legal obligation to deal righteously with McQuade if it was against public policy to do so.

The courts do not enforce mere moral obligations, nor legal ones either, unless someone seeks to establish rights which may be waived by custom and for convenience. We are constrained by authority to hold that a contract is illegal and void so far as it precludes the board of directors, at the risk of incurring legal liability, from changing officers, salaries, or policies or retaining individuals in office, except by consent of the contracting parties. On the whole, such a holding is probably preferable to one which would open the courts to pass on the motives of directors in the lawful exercise of their trust.

A further reason for reversal exists. At the time the contract was made the plaintiff was a city magistrate. . . .

The Inferior Criminal Courts Act (Laws of 1910, c. 659, as amended) provides that no "city magistrate shall engage in any other business, profession or hold any other public office or shall serve as the representative of any political party for any assembly, aldermanic, senatorial or congressional district in the executive committee or other governing body of any political party organization or political party association. No city magistrate shall engage in any other business or profession or act as referee, or receiver, but each of said justices and magistrates shall devote his whole time and capacity, so far as the public interest demands, to the duties of his office. . . ." (Section 161, Laws 1933, c. 746, formerly section 102, as amended, Laws 1915, c. 531.) The contract contemplated that the plaintiff should hold an executive office at a stipulated and substantial salary. . . .

Until the date when the defendant repudiated the agreement, its performance constituted a violation of the statute. . . .

■ LEHMAN, JUDGE.

I concur in the decision of the court on the second ground stated in the opinion. I desire to state the reasons why I do not accept the first ground.

. . .

We have said: "An ordinary agreement, among a minority in number, but a majority in shares, for the purpose of obtaining control of the corporation by the election of particular persons as directors is not illegal." Manson v. Curtis, 223 N.Y. 313, 319, 119 N.E. 559, 561, Ann.Cas. 1918E, 247. We are agreed that, if the contract had provided only for the election of directors, it would not have been illegal. Its vice, if any, is inherent in the provisions intended to give assurance that the directors so elected would act according to the prearranged design of the stockholders in apportioning the corporate offices and emoluments of such offices among the majority stockholders.

. . .

There can, I think, be no doubt that shareholders owning a majority of the corporate stock may combine to obtain and exercise any control which a single owner of such stock could exercise. What may lawfully be done by an individual may ordinarily be lawfully done by a combination, but no combination is legal if formed to accomplish an illegal object. No such combination or agreement may "contravene any express charter or statutory provision or contemplate any fraud, oppression or wrong against other stockholders or other illegal object." Manson v. Curtis, supra.

In that case we held invalid, on that ground, an agreement for the selection "of directors who should remain passive or mechanical to the will and word" of one of the parties to the agreement. Now it is said that, for the same reason, this agreement must be held unenforceable, though here the agreement contemplated no restriction upon the powers of the board of directors, and no dictation or interference by stockholders except in so far as concerns the election and remuneration of officers and the adhesion by the corporation to established policies.

It seems difficult to reconcile such a decision with the statements in the opinion in Manson v. Curtis that "it is not illegal or against public policy for two or more stockholders owning the majority of the shares of stock to unite upon a course of corporate policy or action, or upon the officers whom they will elect," and that "shareholders have the right to combine their interests and voting powers to secure such control of the corporation and the adoption of and adhesion by it to a specific policy and course of business." Obviously, a combination intended to effect the election of certain officers and to obtain control of the corporation and adhesion by it to a specific policy and course of business can accomplish its ends only to the extent that directors will bow to the will of those who united to elect them. The directors have the power and the duty to act in accordance with their own best judgment so long as they remain directors. The majority stockholders can compel no action by the directors, but at the expiration of the term of office of the directors the stockholders have the power to replace them with others whose actions coincide with the judgment or desires of the holders of a majority of the stock. The theory that directors exercise in all matters an independent judgment in practice often yields to the fact that the choice of directors lies with the majority stockholders and thus gives the stockholders a very effective control of the action by the board of directors. In truth the board of directors may check the arbitrary will of those who would otherwise completely control the corporation, but cannot indefinitely thwart their will.

A contract which destroys this check contravenes "express charter or statutory provisions" and is, therefore, illegal. A contract which merely provides that stockholders shall in combination use their power to achieve a legitimate purpose is not illegal. They may join in the election of directors who, in their opinion, will be in sympathy with the policies of the majority stockholders and who, in the choice of executive officers, will be influenced by the wishes of the majority stockholders. The directors so chosen may not act in disregard of the best interests of the corporation and its minority stockholders, but with that limitation they may and, in practice, usually are swayed by the wishes of the majority. Otherwise there would be no continuity of corporate policy and no continuity in management of corporate affairs.

The contract now under consideration provides, in a narrow field, for corporate action within these limitations. . . . A contract which merely provides for the election of fit officers and adhesion to particular policy determined in advance constitutes an agreement by which men in combination exercise a power which could be lawfully exercised if lodged in a single man. It is legal, if designed to protect legitimate interests without wrong to others. Public policy should be governed by facts, not abstractions. The contract is, in my opinion, valid. It is unenforceable only because it resulted in an employment which was itself illegal.

■ CRANE, KELLOGG, O'BRIEN, and HUBBS, JJ., concur with POUND, C.J.

■ LEHMAN, J., concurs in result in opinion in which CROUCH, J., concurs.

Clark v. Dodge

269 N.Y. 410, 199 N.E. 641 (1936).

. . .

The two corporate defendants are New Jersey corporations manufacturing medicinal preparations by secret formulae. The main office, factory, and assets of both corporations are located in the state of New York. In 1921, and at all times since, Clark owned 25 per cent. and Dodge 75 per cent. of the stock of each corporation. Dodge took no active part in the business, although he was a director, and through ownership of their qualifying shares, controlled the other directors of both corporations. He was the president of Bell & Co., Inc., and nominally general manager of Hollings-Smith Company, Inc. The plaintiff, Clark, was a director and held the offices of treasurer and general manager of Bell & Co., Inc., and also had charge of the major portion of the business of Hollings-Smith Company, Inc. The formulae and methods of manufacture of the medicinal preparations were known to him alone. Under date of February 15, 1921, Dodge and Clark, the sole owners of the stock of both corporations, entered into a written agreement under seal, which after reciting the stock ownership of both parties, the desire of Dodge that Clark should continue in the efficient management and control of the business of Bell & Co., Inc., so long as he should "remain faithful, efficient and competent to so manage and control the said business"; and his further desire that Clark should not be the sole custodian of a specified formula, but should share his knowledge thereof and of the method of manufacture with a son of Dodge, provided, in substance, as follows: That Dodge during his lifetime and, after his death, a trustee to be appointed by his will, would so vote his stock and so vote as a director that the plaintiff (a) should continue to be a director of Bell & Co., Inc.; and (b) should continue as its general manager so long as he should be "faithful, efficient and competent"; (c) should during his life receive one-fourth of the net income of the corporations either by way of salary or dividends; and (d) that no unreasonable or incommensurate salaries should be paid to other officers or agents which would so reduce the net income as materially to affect Clark's profits. Clark on his part agreed to disclose the specified formula to the son and to instruct him in the details and methods of manufacture; and, further, at the end of his life to bequeath his stock—if no issue survived him—to the wife and children of Dodge.

It was further provided that the provisions in regard to the division of net profits and the regulation of salaries should also apply to the Hollings-Smith Company.

The complaint alleges due performance of the contract by Clark and breach thereof by Dodge in that he has failed to use his stock control to continue Clark as a director and as general manager, and has prevented Clark from receiving his proportion of the income, while taking his own, by causing the employment of incompetent persons at excessive salaries, and otherwise.

The relief sought is reinstatement as director and general manager and an accounting by Dodge and by the corporations for waste and for the proportion of net income due plaintiff, with an injunction against further violations.

The only question which need be discussed is whether the contract is illegal as against public policy within the decision in McQuade v. Stoneham, 263 N.Y. 323, 189 N.E. 234, upon the authority of which the complaint was dismissed by the Appellate Division.

"The business of a corporation shall be managed by its board of directors." General Corporation Law (Consol.Laws, c. 23) § 27. That is the statutory norm. Are we committed by the McQuade Case to the doctrine that there may be no variation, however slight or innocuous, from that norm, where salaries or policies or the retention of individuals in office are concerned? There is ample authority supporting that doctrine, . . . and something may be said for it, since it furnishes a simple, if arbitrary, test. Apart from its practical administrative convenience, the reasons upon which it is said to rest are more or less nebulous. Public policy, the intention of the Legislature, detriment to the corporation, are phrases which in this connection mean little. Possible harm to bona fide purchasers of stock or to creditors or to stockholding minorities have more substance; but such harms are absent in many instances. If the enforcement of a particular contract damages nobody—not even, in any perceptible degree, the public—one sees no reason for holding it illegal, even though it impinges slightly upon the broad provision of section 27. Damage suffered or threatened is a logical and practical test, and has come to be the one generally adopted by the courts. . . . Where the directors are the sole stockholders, there seems to be no objection to enforcing an agreement among them to vote for certain people as officers. There is no direct decision to that effect in this court, yet there are strong indications that such a rule has long been recognized. The opinion in Manson v. Curtis, 223 N.Y. 313, 325, 119 N.E. 559, 562, Ann.Cas. 1918E, 247, closed its discussion by saying: "The rule that all the stockholders by their universal consent may do as they choose with the corporate concerns and assets, provided the interests of creditors are not affected, because they are the complete owners of the corporation, cannot be invoked here." That was because all the stockholders were not parties to the agreement there in question. So, where the public was not affected, "the parties in interest, might, by their original agreement of incorporation, limit their respective rights and powers," even where there was a conflicting statutory standard. Ripin v. United States Woven Label Co., 205 N.Y. 442, 448, 98 N.E. 855, 857. . . .

Except for the broad dicta in the McQuade opinion, we think there can be no doubt that the agreement here in question was legal and that the complaint states a cause of action. There was no attempt to sterilize the board of directors, as in the Manson and McQuade Cases. The only restrictions on Dodge were (a) that as a stockholder he should vote for Clark as a director—a perfectly legal contract; (b) that as director he should continue Clark as general manager, so long as he proved faithful, efficient, and competent—an agreement which could harm nobody; (c) that Clark should always receive as salary or dividends one-fourth of the "net income." For the purposes of this motion, it is only just to construe that phrase as meaning whatever was left for distribution after the directors had in good faith set aside whatever they deemed wise; (d) that no salaries to other officers should be paid, unreasonable in amount or incommensurate with services rendered—a beneficial and not a harmful agreement.

If there was any invasion of the powers of the directorate under that agreement, it is so slight as to be negligible; and certainly there is no damage suffered by or threatened to anybody. The broad statements in the McQuade opinion, applicable to the facts there, should be confined to those facts.

ANALYSIS AND PLANNING

1. In McQuade v. Stoneham, the court says that it is a matter of "public policy" that "stockholders may not, by agreement among themselves, control the directors in the exercise of the judgment vested in them by virtue of their office to elect officers and fix salaries." What, if any, are the goals or criteria of good government that underlie that public policy?

2. Was McQuade assured of representation on the board of directors? What legal devices are available to provide assurance of a seat on the board?

3. If McQuade had been assured of representation on the board of directors, how might he have been assured of continuation in his role as treasurer of the corporation?

4. Subsequent to the decisions in these cases, the New York Business Corporation Law was changed. It now provides, in § 620:

> (a) An agreement between two or more shareholders, if in writing and signed by the parties thereto, may provide that in exercising any voting rights, the shares held by them shall be voted as therein provided, or as they may agree, or as determined in accordance with a procedure agreed upon by them.
>
> (b) A provision in the certificate of incorporation otherwise prohibited by law because it improperly restricts the board in its management of the business of the corporation, or improperly transfers to one or more shareholders or to one of more persons or corporations to be selected by him or them, all or any part of such management otherwise within the authority

> of the board under this chapter, shall nevertheless be valid: (1) If all the incorporators or holders of record of all outstanding shares, whether or not having voting power, have authorized such provision in the certificate of incorporation or an amendment thereof; and (2) If, subsequent to the adoption of such provision, shares are transferred or issued only to persons who had knowledge or notice thereof or consented in writing to such provision.

Under this provision, how might you have protected McQuade's interests?

5. Section 141(a) of the Delaware General Corporation Law provides:

> (a) The business and affairs of every corporation organized under this chapter shall be managed by or under the direction of a board of directors, except as may be otherwise provided in this chapter or in its certificate of incorporation. If any such provision is made in the certificate of incorporation, the powers and duties conferred or imposed upon the board of directors by this chapter shall be exercised or performed to such extent and by such person or persons as shall be provided in the certificate of incorporation.

Section 142(b) provides, in part:

> (b) Officers shall be chosen in such manner and shall hold their offices for such terms as are prescribed by the by-laws or determined by the board of directors or other governing body.

With these provisions to rely upon, how might you have protected McQuade's interests?*

6. In Clark v. Dodge the court in effect granted specific performance of the agreement. Do you agree that this is the appropriate remedy?

7. Dodge and Clark agreed, according to the court, that Clark "should continue as [the corporation's] general manager so long as he should be 'faithful, efficient and competent.' " What do you think about the wisdom and efficacy of this agreement?

CORPORATE PLANNING BY USE OF EMPLOYMENT CONTRACTS

One way to give McQuade, in McQuade v. Stoneham, or Clark, in Clark v. Dodge, what he seemed to have wanted might have been to have the corporation enter into an employment contract with him. Here, in outline form, is a list of some issues that are presented by employment contracts.

I. Duration

   A. Number of years. Then what?

---

* Compare New York Business Corporation Law, § 715(b) ("The certificate of incorporation may provide that all officers or that specified officers shall be elected by the shareholders instead of by the board."); California Corporations Code, § 312(b) ("Except as otherwise provided by the articles or bylaws, officers shall be chosen by the board and serve at the pleasure of the board, . . .").

- B. Termination for cause
  - 1. By whom?
  - 2. What is "cause"?
- C. Effect of illness, incapacity, etc.

II. Compensation
- A. Salary
- B. Adjustments (e.g., for inflation)
- C. Bonuses, stock options, etc.
- D. Benefits
- E. Travel and other expenses
- F. Perquisites

III. Duties and status
- A. Job description
- B. Other duties
- C. Amount of time; vacation
- D. Outside activities

IV. Competition and Trade Secrets

V. Consequences of termination
- A. Liquidated damages
- B. Duty to mitigate

VI. Parties
- A. Mergers, etc.
- B. Guarantee by majority shareholder

Assume that you represent McQuade, except that the time is now, and that he is about to invest a substantial amount of money in a major league baseball team and become its treasurer and chief financial officer. He wants to sit down with you and have you explain to him what the issues are and what he might reasonably seek in an employment contract and in any related agreements that you think important. What would you be prepared to ask him and tell him?

What if it were Clark, rather than McQuade, whom you were about to advise?

Do you think that the interests of the parties in the two cases would have been better served by the use of employment contracts than by the use of voting agreements? What other legal device should have been recommended?

NOTE ON SHAREHOLDER AGREEMENTS, VOTING TRUSTS, STATUTORY CLOSE CORPORATIONS, AND INVOLUNTARY DISSOLUTION

Shareholder agreements (sometimes called "pooling" agreements), designed to achieve objectives such as those reflected in McQuade v. Stoneham and in Clark v. Dodge, have often been used. Agreements by which the shareholders simply commit to electing themselves, or their representatives, as directors, are generally considered unobjectionable, and are now expressly validated in many jurisdictions (see, e.g., New York Bus. Corp. Law, § 620(a), validating shareholder voting agreements with other objectives as well). They do not interfere with the obligations of the directors to exercise their sound judgment in managing the affairs of the corporation.

The courts have had more difficulty with shareholder agreements requiring the appointment of particular individuals as officers or employees of the corporation, since such agreements do deprive the directors of one of their most important functions. The modern view, reflected in the next case (Galler v. Galler) and in the Note following it (summarizing Zion v. Kurtz), is that such agreements are enforceable, at least for closely held corporations, as long as they are signed by all shareholders (and, perhaps, in situations in which any nonsigning minority shareholders cannot or do not object).

Another device that can be used for control is the voting trust, a device specifically authorized by the corporation laws of most states. With a voting trust, shareholders who wish to act in concert turn their shares over to a trustee. The trustee then votes all the shares, in accordance with instructions in the document establishing the trust. Voting trusts are often used to maintain control of a corporation by a family or group, when there is a fear that some members of the family or group might form a coalition with minority shareholders to shift control. For example, suppose that five members of a family own 60 percent of the voting shares of the corporation. They can create a voting trust and instruct the trustee to vote all the shares for directors, and on other matters submitted to shareholder vote, in accordance with decisions reached by the five members by majority vote. Voting trusts generally must be made public. See Del.Gen.Corp. Law § 218.

Many states now have special statutory provisions for closely held corporations. These provisions vary widely from state to state. Generally they allow certain corporations to elect (it's voluntary) close corporation status (whereupon the corporation is said to be a statutory close corporation). For example, under the Delaware General Corporation Law close corporation status may be elected by corporations with not more than 30 shareholders. § 342(1). Under § 351, "The certificate of incorporation of a close corporation may provide that the business of the corporation shall be managed by the stockholders of the corporation rather than by a board of directors." Thus, one advantage of close corporation status is avoidance of any need to provide for certain corporate formalities (where otherwise the failure to do so might give rise to personal liability of shareholders for corporate debts). In many situations, however, electing close corporation status may be more trouble than it is worth. Most of what investors should have to protect their interests and ensure the effective control of their venture can be accomplished by adaptations of the articles of incorporation and bylaws, together with ancillary agreements such as voting agreements, employment agreements, and buy-sell agreements.

Of more current relevance is the recent innovation in small-business organization, the Limited Liability Company (LLC). With an LLC, issues of control are left largely to individual choice, reflected in a document, drafted by (or for) the investors (the "members") and called "regulations" or "operating agreement" or something of the sort. Broadly speaking, an

LLC may be "member managed" (like a partnership) or "manager managed" (like a corporation), with virtually infinite variety available. Additional flexibility in organization and control is provided by the availability in most states of a Limited Liability Partnership (LLP) or Limited Liability Limited Partnership (LLLP).

A final aspect of corporate law affecting closely held corporations is the development of provisions in corporations codes allowing for involuntary dissolution by court order. These provisions can operate, in certain circumstances, as a bail-out remedy for shareholders who have failed to enter into effective control or buy-sell agreements. These agreements are examined in Section 5 of this Chapter.

Galler v. Galler

32 Ill.2d 16, 203 N.E.2d 577 (1964).

There is no substantial dispute as to the facts in this case. From 1919 to 1924, Benjamin and Isadore Galler, brothers, were equal partners in the Galler Drug Company, a wholesale drug concern. In 1924 the business was incorporated under the Illinois Business Corporation Act, each owning one half of the outstanding 220 shares of stock. In 1945 each contracted to sell 6 shares to an employee, Rosenberg, at a price of $10,500 for each block of 6 shares, payable within 10 years. . . . Rosenberg was not involved in this litigation either as a party or as a witness, and in July of 1961, prior to the time that the master in chancery hearings were concluded, defendants Isadore and Rose Galler purchased the 12 shares from Rosenberg. A supplemental complaint was filed by the plaintiff, Emma Galler, asserting an equitable right to have 6 of the 12 shares transferred to her and offering to pay the defendants one half of the amount that the defendants paid Rosenberg. The parties have stipulated that pending disposition of the instant case, these shares will not be voted or transferred. For approximately one year prior to the entry of the decree by the chancellor in July of 1962, there were no outstanding minority shareholder interests.

In March, 1954, Benjamin and Isadore, on the advice of their accountant, decided to enter into an agreement for the financial protection of their immediate families and to assure their families, after the death of either brother, equal control of the corporation. In June, 1954, while the agreement was in the process of preparation by an attorney-associate of the accountant, Benjamin suffered a heart attack. Although he resumed his business duties some months later, he was again stricken in February, 1955, and thereafter was unable to return to work. During his brother's illness, Isadore asked the accountant to have the shareholders' agreement put in final form in order to protect Benjamin's wife, and this was done by another attorney employed in the accountant's office. On a Saturday night in July, 1955, the accountant brought the agreement to Benjamin's home, and 6 copies of it were executed there by the two brothers and their wives. . . . Between the execution of the agreement in July, 1955, and Benjamin's death in December, 1957, the agreement was not modified. Benjamin suffered a stroke late in July, 1955. . . . Because of the state of Benjamin's health, nothing further was said to him by any of the parties concerning the agreement. It appears from the evidence that some months after the agreement was signed, the defendants Isadore and Rose Galler and their son, the defendant, Aaron Galler sought to have the agreements destroyed. The evidence is undisputed that defendants had decided prior to Benjamin's death they would not honor the agreement, but never disclosed their intention to plaintiff [Emma] or her husband [Benjamin].

On July 21, 1956, Benjamin executed an instrument creating a trust naming his wife as trustee. The trust covered, among other things, the 104 shares of Galler Drug Company stock and the stock certificates were endorsed by Benjamin and delivered to Emma. When Emma presented the certificates to defendants for transfer into her name as trustee, they sought to have Emma abandon the 1955 agreement or enter into some kind of a noninterference agreement as a price for the transfer of the shares. Finally, in September, 1956, after Emma had refused to abandon the shareholders' agreement, she did agree to permit defendant Aaron to become president for one year and agreed that she would not interfere with the business during that year. The stock was then reissued in her name as trustee. During the year 1957 while Benjamin was still alive, Emma tried many times to arrange a meeting with Isadore to discuss business matters but he refused to see her.

Shortly after Benjamin's death, Emma went to the office and demanded the terms of the 1955 agreement be carried out. Isadore told her that anything she had to say could be said to Aaron, who then told her that his father would not abide by the agreement. He offered a modification of the agreement by proposing the salary continuation payment but without her becoming a director. When Emma refused to modify the agreement and sought enforcement of its terms, defendants refused and this suit followed.

During the last few years of Benjamin's life both brothers drew an annual salary of $42,000. Aaron, whose salary was $15,000 as manager of the warehouse prior to September, 1956, has since the time that Emma agreed to his acting as president drawn an annual salary of $20,000. In 1957, 1958, and 1959 a $40,000 annual dividend was paid. Plaintiff has received her proportionate share of the dividend.

The July, 1955, agreement in question here, entered into between Benjamin, Emma, Isadore and Rose, recites that Benjamin and Isadore each own 47½% of the issued and outstanding shares of the Galler Drug Company, an Illinois corporation, and that Benjamin and Isadore desired to provide income for the support and maintenance of their immediate families. No reference is made to the shares then being purchased by Rosenberg. The essential features of the contested portions of the agreement are substantially as set forth in the opinion of the Appellate Court: (2) that the bylaws of the corporation will be amended to provide for a board of four directors; that the necessary quorum shall be three directors; and that no directors' meeting shall be held without giving ten days notice to all directors. (3) The shareholders will cast their votes for the above named persons (Isadore, Rose, Benjamin and Emma) as directors at said special meeting and at any other meeting held for the purpose of electing directors. (4, 5) In the event of the death of either brother his wife shall have the right to nominate a director in place of the decedent. (6) Certain annual dividends will be declared by the corporation. The dividend shall be $50,000 payable out of the accumulated earned surplus in excess of $500,000. If 50% of the annual net profits after taxes exceeds the minimum $50,000, then the directors shall have discretion to declare a dividend up to 50% of the annual net profits. If the net profits are less than $50,000, nevertheless the minimum $50,000 annual dividend shall be declared, providing the $500,000 surplus is maintained. Earned surplus is defined. (9) The certificates evidencing the said shares of Benjamin Galler and Isadore Galler shall bear a legend that the shares are subject to the terms of this agreement. (10) A salary continuation agreement shall be entered into by the corporation which shall authorize the corporation upon the death of Benjamin Galler or Isadore Galler, or both, to pay a sum equal to twice the salary of such officer, payable monthly over a five-year period. Said sum shall be paid to the widow during her widowhood, but should be paid to such widow's children if the widow remarries within the five-year period. . . .

The Appellate Court found the 1955 agreement void because "the undue duration, stated purpose and substantial disregard of the provisions of the Corporation Act outweigh any considerations which might call for divisibility" and held that "the public policy of this state demands voiding this entire agreement."

While the conduct of defendants towards plaintiff was clearly inequitable, the basically controlling factor is the absence of an objecting minority interest, together with the absence of public detriment. . . .

At this juncture it should be emphasized that we deal here with a so-called close corporation. . . . For our purposes, a close corporation is one in which the stock is held in a few hands, or in a few families, and wherein it is not at all, or only rarely, dealt in by buying or selling. . . . Moreover, it should be recognized that shareholder agreements similar to that in question here are often, as a practical consideration, quite necessary for the protection of those financially interested in the close corporation. While the shareholder of a public-issue corporation may readily sell his shares on the open market should management fail to use, in his opinion, sound business judgment, his counterpart of the close corporation often has a large total of his entire capital invested in the business and has no ready market for his shares should he desire to sell. He feels, understandably, that he is more than a mere investor and that his voice should be heard concerning all corporate activity. Without a shareholder agreement, specifically enforceable by the courts, insuring him a modicum of control, a large minority shareholder might find himself at the mercy of an oppressive or unknowledgeable majority. Moreover, as in the case at bar, the shareholders of a close corporation are often also the directors and officers thereof. With substantial shareholding interests abiding in each member of the board of directors, it is often quite impossible to secure, as in the large public-issue corporation, independent board judgment free from personal motivations concerning corporate policy. For these and other reasons too voluminous to enumerate here, often the only sound basis for protection is afforded by a lengthy, detailed shareholder agreement securing the rights and obligations of all concerned.

As the preceding review of the applicable decisions of this court points out, there has been a definite, albeit inarticulate, trend toward eventual judicial treatment of the close corporation as *sui generis.* Several shareholder-director agreements that have technically "violated" the letter of the Business Corporation Act have nevertheless been upheld in the light of the existing practical circumstances, i.e., no apparent public injury, the absence of a complaining minority interest, and no apparent prejudice to creditors. However, we have thus far not attempted to limit these decisions as applicable only to close corporations and have seemingly implied that general considerations regarding judicial supervision of all corporate behavior apply. . . .

. . . "New needs compel fresh formulation of corporate 'norms.' There is no reason why mature men should not be able to adapt the statutory form to the structure they want, so long as they do not endanger other stockholders, creditors, or the public, or violate a clearly mandatory provision of the corporation laws. In a typical close corporation the stockholders' agreement is usually the result of careful deliberation among all initial investors. In the large public-issue corporation, on the other hand, the 'agreement' represented by the corporate charter is not consciously agreed to by the investors; they have no voice in its formulation, and very few ever read the certificate of incorporation. Preservation of the corporate norms may there be necessary for the protection of the public investors." Hornstein, Stockholders' Agreements in the Closely Held Corporation, 59 Yale L. Journal, 1040, 1056.

This court has recognized, albeit *sub silentio,* the significant conceptual differences between the close corporation and its public-issue counterpart in, among other cases, Kantzler v. Benzinger, 214 Ill. 589, where an agreement quite similar to the one under attack here was upheld. Where, as in *Kantzler* and here, no complaining minority interest appears, no fraud or apparent injury to the public or creditors is present, and no clearly prohibitory statutory language is violated, we can see no valid reason for precluding the parties from reaching any arrangements concerning the management of the corporation which are agreeable to all. . . .

We now, in the light of the foregoing, turn to specific provisions of the 1955 agreement.

The Appellate Court correctly found many of the contractual provisions free from serious objection, and we need not prolong this opinion with a discussion of them here. That court did, however, find difficulties in the stated purpose of the agreement as it relates to its duration, the election of certain persons to specific offices for a number of years, the requirement for the mandatory declaration of stated dividends (which the Appellate Court held invalid), and the salary continuation agreement.

Since the question as to the duration of the agreement is a principal source of controversy, we shall consider it first. The parties provided no specific termination date, and while the agreement concludes with a paragraph that its terms "shall be binding upon and shall inure to the benefits of" the legal representatives, heirs and assigns of the parties, this clause is, we believe, intended to be operative only as long as one of the parties is living. It further provides that it shall be so construed as to carry out its purposes, and we believe these must be determined from a consideration of the agreement as a whole. Thus viewed, a fair construction is that its purposes were accomplished at the death of the survivor of the parties. While these life spans are not precisely ascertainable, and the Appellate Court noted Emma Galler's life expectancy at her husband's death was 26.9 years, we are aware of no statutory or public policy provision against stockholder's agreements which would invalidate this agreement on that ground. . . .

The clause that provides for the election of certain persons to specified offices for a period of years likewise does not require invalidation. In Kantzler v. Benzinger, 214 Ill. 589, this court upheld an agreement entered into by all the stockholders providing that certain parties would be elected to the offices of the corporation for a fixed period. In Faulds v. Yates, 57 Ill. 416, we upheld a similar agreement among the majority stockholders of a corporation, notwithstanding the existence of a minority which was not before the court complaining thereof. See also Hornstein, "Judicial Tolerance of the Incorporated Partnership," 18 Law and Contemporary Problems 435 at page 444.

We turn next to a consideration of the effect of the stated purpose of the agreement upon its validity. The pertinent provision is: "The said Benjamin A. Galler and Isadore A. Galler desire to provide income for the support and maintenance of their immediate families." Obviously, there is no evil inherent in a contract entered into for the reason that the persons originating the terms desired to so arrange their property as to provide post-death support for those dependent upon them. Nor does the fact that the subject property is corporate stock alter the situation so long as there exists no detriment to minority stock interests, creditors or other public injury. It is, however, contended by defendants that the methods provided by the agreement for implementation of the stated purpose are, as a whole, violative of the Business Corporation Act . . . to such an extent as to render it void *in toto.*

The terms of the dividend agreement require a minimum annual dividend of $50,000, but this duty is limited by the subsequent provision that it shall be operative only so long as an earned surplus of $500,000 is maintained. It may be noted that in 1958, the year prior to commencement of this litigation, the corporation's net earnings after taxes amounted to $202,759 while its earned surplus was $1,543,270, and this was increased in 1958 to $1,680,079 while earnings were $172,964. The minimum earned surplus requirement is designed for the protection of the corporation and its creditors, and we take no exception to the contractual dividend requirements as thus restricted. . . .

The salary continuation agreement is a common feature, in one form or another, of corporate executive employment. It requires that the widow should receive a total benefit, payable monthly over a five-year period, aggregating twice the amount paid her deceased husband in one year. This requirement was likewise limited for the protection of the corporation by being contingent upon the payments being income tax-deductible by the corporation. The charge made in those cases which have considered the validity of payments to the widow of an officer and shareholder in a corporation is that a gift of its property by a noncharitable corporation is in violation of the rights of its shareholders and *ultra vires.* Since there are no shareholders here other than the parties to the contract, this objection is not here applicable, and its effect, as limited, upon the corporation is not so prejudicial as to require its invalidation. . . .

We hold defendants must account for all monies received by them from the corporation since September 25, 1956, in excess of that theretofore authorized.

ANALYSIS

1. In Galler v. Galler, as in Clark v. Dodge, the court in effect ordered specific performance. Is there a better remedy? If you think there is, what does that suggest about whether there was a better form of agreement available to the parties at the outset?

2. Under the court's order, what is the likelihood of a change in the salaries paid to Isadore and to Aaron as long as Emma lives?

3. Was there anything in the agreement about which Rosenberg might reasonably have complained? If he had complained, and had sided with the defendants in the litigation that resulted in the decision of the Illinois Supreme Court, what would the outcome have been?

4. The court in Galler v. Galler says, "Without a shareholder agreement, specifically enforceable by the courts, insuring him a modicum of control, a large minority shareholder might find himself at the mercy of an oppressive or unknowledgeable majority." Later the court says, "often the only sound basis for protection is afforded by a lengthy, detailed shareholder agreement securing the rights and obligations of all concerned." Does it follow that a lawyer who is asked to form a corporation for people about to embark on a business venture and who fails to urge the adoption of various protective agreements is guilty of malpractice?

5. At the time this case arose the use of the corporate form could produce some federal income tax advantages. Under the current tax regime those tax advantages have largely disappeared. Most closely held corporations are eligible to be treated for tax purposes as so-called S corporations, which are taxed much the same as partnerships. Moreover, closely held businesses can achieve desired tax outcomes by organizing as Limited Liability Companies, Limited Liability Partnerships, Limited Partnerships, or Limited Liability Limited Partnerships. Thus, tax considerations do not play an important role in crafting the substantive elements of a business organization. Do you think that in the Gallers' family business the partnership form would have been better than the corporate form? In answering this question think of the basic rules of partnership and corporate law relating to control, duration and termination, and share of profit and loss, and about how those rules need to be modified.

Ramos v. Estrada

8 Cal.App.4th 1070 10 Cal.Rptr.2d 833 (1992).

[Two groups of people separately sought from the Federal Communications Commission a permit to form a Spanish language television station in Ventura County. One group was called the Broadcast Group and included Leopoldo Ramos and his wife and Tila Estrada and her husband. The Ramoses owned 50 percent of the Broadcast Group and the Estradas and four other couples each owned 10 percent. The other group seeking the permit was called Ventura 41. Ultimately the two groups combined in a corporation called Television, Inc. and at some time in 1986 the shares of this corporation were issued to the individual members of each group. Initially, 5,000 shares of Television, Inc. were issued to the members of the Broadcast Group and 5,000 to the members of Ventura 41. The board of directors was to have eight members, four from each group. After the station was operated at full power for six months, however, two additional shares were to go to the Broadcast Group and the membership of the board of directors was to be increased to nine, of whom five would be elected by the Broadcast Group.

In June 1987, the members of Broadcast Group entered into an agreement to vote all their shares of Television, Inc. in a manner determined by a majority of them. The agreement also restricted transfer of the shares and provided that if any member of the group failed to abide by the voting provision, that member's shares would be sold to the other members at cost plus 8 percent per year.

The initial eight-member board of Television, Inc. elected Leopoldo Ramos as president. Tila Estrada was a member of the board. Thereafter, however, Estrada defected from the Broadcast Group, as described by the court below.]

At a special directors' meeting held on October 8, 1988, Tila Estrada voted with the Ventura 41 group block to remove Ramos as president and to replace him with Walter Ulloa, a member of Ventura 41. She also joined Ventura 41 in voting to remove Romualdo Ochoa, a Broadcast Group member, as secretary and to replace him with herself.

Under the June Broadcast Agreement and the Merger Agreement, each of the groups were required to vote for the directors upon whom a majority of each respective group had agreed. The terms of that agreement expressly state that failure to adhere to the agreement constitutes an election by the shareholder to sell his or her shares pursuant to buy/sell provisions of the agreement. The agreement also calls for specific enforcement of such buy/sell provisions.

On October 15, 1988, the Broadcast Group noticed another meeting to decide how its members would vote their shares for directors at the annual meeting. All members attended except the Estradas. The group agreed to nominate *another* slate of directors which did not include either of the Estradas. The Estradas were notified of the results of this meeting.

The Estradas unilaterally declared the June Broadcast Agreement null and void as of October 15, 1988, in a letter dictated for them by Paul Zevnik, the attorney for Ventura 41. Tila Estrada refused to recognize the October 15 vote of the majority of the Broadcast Group to replace her as a director of Television Inc. Ramos et al. sued the Estradas for breach of the June Broadcast Agreement, among other things.

The court ruled that the Estradas materially breached the valid June Broadcast Agreement, and it ordered their shares sold in accordance with the specific enforcement provisions of the June Broadcast Agreement. The court restrained the Estradas from voting their shares other than as provided in the June Broadcast Agreement.

Discussion

The Estradas contend that the June Broadcast Agreement is void because it constitutes an expired proxy which the Estradas validly revoked. . . .

Corporations Code [California] section 178 defines a proxy to be "a written authorization signed . . . by a shareholder . . . giving another person or persons power to vote with respect to the shares of such shareholder."

Section 7.1 of the June Broadcast Agreement details the voting arrangement among the shareholders. It states, in pertinent part: "The Stockholders agree that they shall consult with each other prior to voting their shares in the Company. They shall attempt in good faith to reach a consensus as to the outcome of any such vote. In the case of a vote for directors, they agree that no director shall be selected who is not acceptable to at least one member (i.e., spousal unit) of each of Group A and Group B. (See P 1.2(b)(1) above [which states that 'The Stockholders shall be divided into two groups, Group "A" being composed of Leopoldo Ramos and Cecilia Morris, and Group "B" being composed of all the other Stockholders'].) In the case of all *votes of Stockholders* they agree that, following consultation and compliance with the other provisions of this paragraph, *they will all vote their stock in the manner voted by a majority of the Stockholders*." (Second emphasis in original.)

No proxies are created by this agreement. The agreement has the characteristics of a shareholders' voting agreement expressly authorized by section 706, subdivision (a) for close corporations. . . . Although the articles of incorporation do not contain the talismanic statement that "This corporation is a close corporation," the arrangements of this corporation, and in particular this voting agreement, are strikingly similar to ones authorized by the Code for close corporations.

Section 706, subdivision (a) states, in pertinent part: "an agreement between two or more shareholders of a close corporation, if in writing and signed by the parties thereto, may provide that in exercising any voting rights the shares held by them shall be voted as provided by the agreement, or as the parties may agree or as determined in accordance with a procedure agreed upon by them. . . ."

Here, the members of this corporation executed a written agreement providing that they shall try to reach a consensus on all votes and that they shall consult with one another and vote their own stock in accordance with the majority of the stockholders. They entered into this agreement because they "mutually desired" to limit the transferability of their stock to ensure "the Company does not pass into the control of persons whose interests might be incompatible with the interests of the Company and of the Stockholders, establishing their mutual rights and obligations in the event of death, and establishing a mechanism for determining how the Stockholders' voting rights in the Company shall be exercised. . . ."

Even though this corporation does not qualify as a close corporation, this agreement is valid and binding on the Estradas. Section 706, subdivision (d) states: "This section shall not invalidate any voting or other agreement among shareholders . . . which agreement . . . is not otherwise illegal."

The Legislative Committee comment regarding section 706, subdivision (d) states that "this subdivision is intended to preserve any agreements which would be upheld under court decisions *even though they do not comply with one or more of the requirements of this section, including voting agreements of corporations other than close corporations.*" (West's Ann. Corp. Code, § 706 (1990) p. 330, emphasis added.)

The California Practice Guide indicates that such "pooling" agreements are valid not only for close corporations, but also "among any number of shareholders of other corporations as well." (Friedman, Cal. Practice Guide Corporations (1992) § 3:159.2, p. 3–31.)

The instant agreement is valid, enforceable and supported by consideration. It states, in pertinent part, that the stockholders entered into the agreement for the purposes of "limiting the transferability of . . . stock in the Company, ensuring that the Company does not pass into the control of persons whose interests might be incompatible with the interests of the Company and of the Stockholders, establishing their mutual rights and obligations in the event of death, and establishing a mechanism for determining how the Stockholders' voting rights . . . shall be exercised. . . ."

Section 7.2 of the agreement states that "the Stockholders understand and acknowledge that the purpose of the foregoing arrangement is to preserve their relative voting power in the Company. . . . Accordingly, in the event that a Stockholder fails to abide by this arrangement for whatever reason, that failure shall constitute on [sic] irrevocable election by the Stockholder to sell his stock in the Company, triggering the same rights of purchase provided in Article IV above."

The agreement calls for enforcement by specific performance of its terms because the stock is not readily marketable. [Corporations Code] Section 709, subdivision (c) expressly permits enforcement of shareholder voting agreements by such equitable remedies. It states, in pertinent part: "The court may determine the person entitled to the office of director or may order a new election to be held or appointment to be made, may determine the validity, effectiveness and construction of voting agreements . . . and the right of persons to vote and may direct such other relief as may be just and proper."

The Estradas contend that the forced sale provision is unconscionable and oppressive. They portray themselves as naive, small-town business people who were forced to sign an adhesion agreement without reviewing its contents.

Substantial evidence supports the findings that Tila Estrada has been a licensed real estate broker. She is an astute businesswoman experienced with contracts concerning real property. The consent and signatures of the Estradas to the agreement were not procured by fraud, duress or other wrongful conduct of Ramos. The Estradas read and discussed with other members of Broadcast Group, and with their own counsel, the voting, buy/sell and other provisions of the agreement and the January Broadcast Agreement, as well as various drafts of these documents, and they freely signed these agreements.

On direct examination, under Evidence Code section 776, Tila Estrada admitted she owns and operates a real estate brokerage business; she regularly reviews a broad variety of real estate documents; she and her husband own and manage investment property; and she has considered herself "to be an astute business woman" since 1985. Tila Estrada also has been a participant and owner in another application before the FCC, for an FM radio station, before the instant suit was filed.

Ms. Estrada stated she got copies "of all the drafts and all the Shareholders Agreements." She discussed these agreements with other members of Broadcast Group and with its counsel, Mr. Howard Weiss.

The June Broadcast Agreement, including its voting and buy/sell provisions, was unanimously executed after the Estradas had a full and fair opportunity to consider it in its entirety. As the trial court found, the buy-out provisions at issue here are valid, favored by courts and enforceable by specific performance. . . .

The Estradas breached the agreement by their written repudiation of it. Their breach constituted an election to sell their Television Inc. shares in accordance with the terms of the buy/sell provisions in the agreement. This election does not constitute a forfeiture—they violated the agreement voluntarily, aware of the consequences of their acts and they are provided full compensation, per their agreement.

The judgment is affirmed. Costs to Ramos.

ANALYSIS

1. If you had been consulted by Tila Estrada before she signed the June Broadcast Agreement, what advice would you have given her?

2. If Tila Estrada had consulted you after she formed the intent to defect from the Broadcast Group and vote with the Ventura 41 Group, what advice would you have given her (assuming you did not have the decision in the case as an authority on which to rely)?

NOTE ON THE LAW IN OTHER STATES

In Zion v. Kurtz, 50 N.Y.2d 92, 428 N.Y.S.2d 199, 405 N.E.2d 681 (1980), the Court of Appeals of New York, applying a basic choice-of-law rule, decided a shareholder-agreement case under Delaware law, but stated that the result would be the same under New York law. The facts in the case were complex and unusual. There were essentially two shareholders, with Kurtz holding the majority interest and Zion the minority. An agreement between them narrowly defined the intended activities of the corporation and provided that no other activities could be engaged in without the minority shareholder's consent.* In supporting

* Note that the shareholders' objective could have been achieved by use of a narrow statement of purposes in the articles of incorporation. Such a limitation might not have been enforceable as against a third party (see, e.g., Del.Gen.Corp.Law § 124), but the same would be true of the limitation in the contract in Zion v. Kurtz. A limitation in the articles might have created problems in selling shares to others, but again the problem also seems to arise with the use of a contract. Some shares were in fact sold to others, but subject to the terms of the agreement of the two original shareholders. Presumably the two could have abandoned their agreement without the consent of the new shareholders. Amendment of the articles of incorporation requires a vote of the shareholders, which might or might not have been a problem.

its view that the agreement did not violate the public policy of Delaware, the court cited the Delaware provisions relating to statutory close corporations, although the corporation involved in the case was not a statutory close corporation and the restriction in the agreement was not made part of the articles of incorporation, as might be required in the case of a statutory close corporation (under Del.Gen.Corp.Law § 351). See also N.Y.Bus.Corp.Law § 620(b), set forth following Clark v. Dodge.

PROBLEM

Curlie, Moe, and Larry incorporate a restaurant. They each receive one-third of the stock.

1. If they agree to exercise their best efforts to ensure that each is elected to the board of directors, is the agreement enforceable? If they agree that they will, as directors, elect each other officers of the corporation, is the agreement enforceable?

2. Suppose Curlie and Moe (but not Larry) agree to exercise their best efforts to ensure that each is elected to the board and agree that they will, as directors, elect each other as officers. Is either agreement enforceable? Does the result change if they agree to elect each other as officers, "so long as each shall remain faithful, efficient and competent to manage and control the restaurant"?

NOTE AND QUESTIONS ON LIMITED LIABILITY COMPANIES

Under the Delaware Limited Liability Company Act, § 18–704(a),

> An assignee of a limited liability company interest may become a member . . . upon:
>
> (1) The approval of all of the members of the limited liability company . . . ; or
>
> (2) Compliance with any procedure provided for in the limited liability company agreement.

Notwithstanding the permissive language of (a)(2), do you think that most LLCs would be well advised to provide in their organizational documents for freely transferrable membership interests? What are the sensible alternatives?

4. ABUSE OF CONTROL

Wilkes v. Springside Nursing Home, Inc.

370 Mass. 842, 353 N.E.2d 657 (1976).

In 1951 Wilkes acquired an option to purchase a building and lot located on the corner of Springside Avenue and North Street in Pittsfield, Massachusetts, the building having previously housed the Hillcrest Hospital. Though Wilkes was principally engaged in the roofing and siding business, he had gained a reputation locally for profitable dealings in real estate. Riche, an acquaintance of Wilkes, learned of the option, and interested Quinn (who was known to Wilkes through membership on the draft board in Pittsfield) and Pipkin (an acquaintance of both Wilkes and Riche) in joining Wilkes in his investment. The four men met and decided to participate jointly in the purchase of the building and lot as a real estate investment which, they believed, had good profit potential on resale or rental.

The parties later determined that the property would have its greatest potential for profit if it were operated by them as a nursing home. Wilkes consulted his attorney, who advised him that if the four men were to operate the contemplated nursing home as planned, they would be partners and would be liable for any debts incurred by the partnership and by each other. On the attorney's suggestion, and after consultation among themselves, ownership of the property was vested in Springside, a corporation organized under Massachusetts law.

Each of the four men invested $1,000 and subscribed to ten shares of $100 par value stock in Springside. At the time of incorporation it was understood by all of the parties that each would be a director of Springside and each would participate actively in the management and decision making involved in operating the corporation.[7] It was, further, the understanding and intention of all the parties that, corporate resources permitting, each would receive money from the corporation in equal amounts as long as each assumed an active and ongoing responsibility for carrying a portion of the burdens necessary to operate the business.

The work involved in establishing and operating a nursing home was roughly apportioned, and each of the four men undertook his respective tasks.[8] Initially, Riche was elected president of Springside, Wilkes was elected treasurer, and Quinn was elected clerk.[9] Each of the four was listed in the articles of organization as a director of the corporation.

At some time in 1952, it became apparent that the operational income and cash flow from the business were sufficient to permit the four stockholders to draw money from the corporation on a regular basis. Each of the four original parties initially received $35 a week from the corporation. As time went on the weekly return to each was increased until, in 1955, it totalled $100.

In 1959, after a long illness, Pipkin sold his shares in the corporation to Connor, who was known to Wilkes, Riche and Quinn through past transactions with Springside in his capacity as president of the First Agricultural National Bank of Berkshire County. Connor received a weekly stipend from the corporation equal to that received by Wilkes, Riche and Quinn. He was elected a director of the corporation but never

---

[7] Wilkes testified before the master that, when the corporate officers were elected, all four men "were . . . guaranteed directorships." Riche's understanding of the parties' intentions was that they all wanted to play a part in the management of the corporation and wanted to have some "say" in the risks involved; that, to this end, they all would be directors; and that "unless you [were] a director and officer you could not participate in the decisions of [the] enterprise."

[8] Wilkes took charge of the repair, upkeep and maintenance of the physical plant and grounds; Riche assumed supervision over the kitchen facilities and dietary and food aspects of the home; Pipkin was to make himself available if and when medical problems arose; and Quinn dealt with the personnel and administrative aspects of the nursing home, serving informally as a managing director. Quinn further coordinated the activities of the other parties and served as a communication link among them when matters had to be discussed and decisions had to be made without a formal meeting.

[9] Riche held the office of president from 1951 to 1963; Quinn served as president from 1963 on, as clerk from 1951 to 1967, and as treasurer from 1967 on; Wilkes was treasurer from 1951 to 1967.

held any other office. He was assigned no specific area of responsibility in the operation of the nursing home but did participate in business discussions and decisions as a director and served additionally as financial adviser to the corporation.

In 1965 the stockholders decided to sell a portion of the corporate property to Quinn who, in addition to being a stockholder in Springside, possessed an interest in another corporation which desired to operate a rest home on the property. Wilkes was successful in prevailing on the other stockholders of Springside to procure a higher sale price for the property than Quinn apparently anticipated paying or desired to pay. After the sale was consummated, the relationship between Quinn and Wilkes began to deteriorate.

The bad blood between Quinn and Wilkes affected the attitudes of both Riche and Connor. As a consequence of the strained relations among the parties, Wilkes, in January of 1967, gave notice of his intention to sell his shares for an amount based on an appraisal of their value. In February of 1967 a directors' meeting was held and the board exercised its right to establish the salaries of its officers and employees.[10] A schedule of payments was established whereby Quinn was to receive a substantial weekly increase and Riche and Connor were to continue receiving $100 a week. Wilkes, however, was left off the list of those to whom a salary was to be paid. The directors also set the annual meeting of the stockholders for March, 1967.

At the annual meeting in March, Wilkes was not reelected as a director, nor was he reelected as an officer of the corporation. He was further informed that neither his services nor his presence at the nursing home was wanted by his associates.

The meetings of the directors and stockholders in early 1967, the master found, were used as a vehicle to force Wilkes out of active participation in the management and operation of the corporation and to cut off all corporate payments to him. Though the board of directors had the power to dismiss any officers or employees for misconduct or neglect of duties, there was no indication in the minutes of the board of directors' meeting of February, 1967, that the failure to establish a salary for Wilkes was based on either ground. The severance of Wilkes from the payroll resulted not from misconduct or neglect of duties, but because of the personal desire of Quinn, Riche and Connor to prevent him from continuing to receive money from the corporation. Despite a continuing deterioration in his personal relationship with his associates, Wilkes had consistently endeavored to carry on his responsibilities to the corporation in the same satisfactory manner and with the same degree of competence he had previously shown. Wilkes was at all times willing to carry on his responsibilities and participation if permitted so to do and provided that he receive his weekly stipend.

1. We turn to Wilkes's claim for damages based on a breach of the fiduciary duty owed to him by the other participants in this venture. In light of the theory underlying this claim, we do not consider it vital to our

[10] The by-laws of the corporation provided that the directors, subject to the approval of the stockholders, had the power to fix the salaries of all officers and employees. This power, however, up until February, 1967, had not been exercised formally; all payments made to the four participants in the venture had resulted from the informal but unanimous approval of all the parties concerned.

approach to this case whether the claim is governed by partnership law or the law applicable to business corporations. This is so because, as all the parties agree, Springside was at all times relevant to this action, a close corporation as we have recently defined such an entity in Donahue v. Rodd Electrotype Co. of New England, Inc., 367 Mass. 578, 585–586 (1975).

In *Donahue,* we held that "stockholders in the close corporation owe one another substantially the same fiduciary duty in the operation of the enterprise that partners owe to one another." Id. at 593 (footnotes omitted), 328 N.E.2d at 515. As determined in previous decisions of this court, the standard of duty owed by partners to one another is one of "utmost good faith and loyalty." Cardullo v. Landau, 329 Mass. 5, 8, 105 N.E.2d 843 (1952), and cases cited. . . .

Thus, we concluded in *Donahue,* with regard to "their actions relative to the operations of the enterprise and the effects of that operation on the rights and investments of other stockholders," "[s]tockholders in close corporations must discharge their management and stockholder responsibilities in conformity with this strict good faith standard. They may not act out of avarice, expediency or self-interest in derogation of their duty of loyalty to the other stockholders and to the corporation." 367 Mass. at 593, n. 18.

In the *Donahue* case we recognized that one peculiar aspect of close corporations was the opportunity afforded to majority stockholders to oppress, disadvantage or "freeze out" minority stockholders. In *Donahue* itself, for example, the majority refused the minority an equal opportunity to sell a ratable number of shares to the corporation at the same price available to the majority. The net result of this refusal, we said, was that the minority could be forced to "sell out at less than fair value," 367 Mass. at 593, since there is by definition no ready market for minority stock in a close corporation.

"Freeze outs," however, may be accomplished by the use of other devices. One such device which has proved to be particularly effective in accomplishing the purpose of the majority is to deprive minority stockholders of corporate offices and of employment with the corporation. . . . This "freeze-out" technique has been successful because courts fairly consistently have been disinclined to interfere in those facets of internal corporate operations, such as the selection and retention or dismissal of officers, directors and employees, which essentially involve management decisions subject to the principle of majority control. . . . As one authoritative source has said, "[M]any courts apparently feel that there is a legitimate sphere in which the controlling [directors or] shareholders can act in their own interest even if the minority suffers." F.H. O'Neal, ["Squeeze-Outs" of Minority Shareholders 59 (1975)] (footnote omitted). . . .

The denial of employment to the minority at the hands of the majority is especially pernicious in some instances. A guaranty of employment with the corporation may have been one of the "basic reason[s] why a minority owner has invested capital in the firm." Symposium—The Close Corporation, 52 Nw.U.L.Rev. 345, 392 (1957).

. . .

The minority stockholder typically depends on his salary as the principal return on his investment, since the "earnings of a close corporation . . . are distributed in major part in salaries, bonuses and retirement benefits." 1 F.H. O'Neal, Close Corporations § 1.07 (1971). Other noneconomic interests of the minority stockholder are likewise injuriously affected by barring him from corporate office. . . . Such action severely restricts his participation in the management of the enterprise, and he is relegated to enjoying those benefits incident to his status as a stockholder. . . . In sum, by terminating a minority stockholder's employment or by severing him from a position as an officer or director, the majority effectively frustrate the minority stockholder's purposes in entering on the corporate venture and also deny him an equal return on his investment.

The *Donahue* decision acknowledged, as a "natural outgrowth" of the case law of this Commonwealth, a strict obligation on the part of majority stockholders in a close corporation to deal with the minority with the utmost good faith and loyalty. On its face, this strict standard is applicable in the instant case. The distinction between the majority action in *Donahue* and the majority action in this case is more one of form than of substance. Nevertheless, we are concerned that untempered application of the strict good faith standard enunciated in *Donahue* to cases such as the one before us will result in the imposition of limitations on legitimate action by the controlling group in a close corporation which will unduly hamper its effectiveness in managing the corporation in the best interests of all concerned. The majority, concededly, have certain rights to what has been termed "selfish ownership" in the corporation which should be balanced against the concept of their fiduciary obligation to the minority. . . .

Therefore, when minority stockholders in a close corporation bring suit against the majority alleging a breach of the strict good faith duty owed to them by the majority, we must carefully analyze the action taken by the controlling stockholders in the individual case. It must be asked whether the controlling group can demonstrate a legitimate business purpose for its action. . . . In asking this question, we acknowledge the fact that the controlling group in a close corporation must have some room to maneuver in establishing the business policy of the corporation. It must have a large measure of discretion, for example, in declaring or withholding dividends, deciding whether to merge or consolidate, establishing the salaries of corporate officers, dismissing directors with or without cause, and hiring and firing corporate employees.

When an asserted business purpose for their action is advanced by the majority, however, we think it is open to minority stockholders to demonstrate that the same legitimate objective could have been achieved through an alternative course of action less harmful to the minority's interest. . . . If called on to settle a dispute, our courts must weigh the legitimate business purpose, if any, against the practicability of a less harmful alternative.

Applying this approach to the instant case it is apparent that the majority stockholders in Springside have not shown a legitimate business purpose for severing Wilkes from the payroll of the corporation or for refusing to reelect him as a salaried officer and director. The master's subsidiary findings relating to the purpose of the meetings of the directors and stockholders in February and March, 1967, are supported by the evidence. There was no showing of misconduct on Wilkes's part as a director, officer or employee of the corporation which would lead us to approve the majority action as a legitimate response to the disruptive nature of an undesirable individual bent on injuring or destroying the corporation. On the contrary, it appears that Wilkes had always accomplished his assigned share of the duties competently, and that he had never indicated an unwillingness to continue to do so.

It is an inescapable conclusion from all the evidence that the action of the majority stockholders here was a designed "freeze out" for which no legitimate business purpose has been suggested. Furthermore, we may infer that a design to pressure Wilkes into selling his shares to the corporation at a price below their value well may have been at the heart of the majority's plan.[14]

In the context of this case, several factors bear directly on the duty owed to Wilkes by his associates. At a minimum, the duty of utmost good faith and loyalty would demand that the majority consider that their action was in disregard of a long-standing policy of the stockholders that each would be a director of the corporation and that employment with the corporation would go hand in hand with stock ownership; that Wilkes was one of the four originators of the nursing home venture; and that Wilkes, like the others, had invested his capital and time for more than fifteen years with the expectation that he would continue to participate in corporate decisions. Most important is the plain fact that the cutting off of Wilkes's salary, together with the fact that the corporation never declared a dividend . . . assured that Wilkes would receive no return at all from the corporation.

2. The question of Wilkes's damages at the hands of the majority has not been thoroughly explored on the record before us. Wilkes, in his original complaint, sought damages in the amount of the $100 a week he believed he was entitled to from the time his salary was terminated up until the time this action was commenced. However, the record shows that, after Wilkes was severed from the corporate payroll, the schedule of salaries and payments made to the other stockholders varied from time to time. In addition, the duties assumed by the other stockholders after Wilkes was deprived of his share of the corporate earnings appear to have changed in significant respects.[15] Any resolution of this question must take into account whether the corporation was dissolved during the pendency of this litigation.

Therefore our order is as follows: So much of the judgment as dismisses Wilkes's complaint and awards costs to the defendants is reversed. The case is remanded to the Probate Court for Berkshire County for further proceedings concerning the issue of damages. Thereafter a judgment shall be entered declaring that Quinn, Riche and Connor breached their fiduciary duty to Wilkes as a minority stockholder

[14] This inference arises from the fact that Connor, acting on behalf of the three controlling stockholders, offered to purchase Wilkes's shares for a price Connor admittedly would not have accepted for his own shares.

[15] In fairness to Wilkes, who, as the master found, was at all times ready and willing to work for the corporation, it should be noted that neither the other stockholders nor their representatives may be heard to say that Wilkes's duties were performed by them and that Wilkes's damages should, for that reason, be diminished.

in Springside, and awarding money damages therefor. Wilkes shall be allowed to recover from Riche, the estate of T. Edward Quinn and the estate of Lawrence R. Connor, ratably, according to the inequitable enrichment of each, the salary he would have received had he remained an officer and director of Springside. In considering the issue of damages the judge on remand shall take into account the extent to which any remaining corporate funds of Springside may be diverted to satisfy Wilkes's claim.

So ordered.

ANALYSIS

1. According to normal, fundamental rules of corporate law, the board of directors appoints officers and sets their salaries. The earlier cases in this section reveal the difficulties that courts generally have with deviations from the corporate norm of management by the board of directors. In the present case, the parties did not, by written shareholder agreement, attempt to "sterilize" the board. Why is it, then, that the plaintiff in this case, Wilkes, was not required to cast his argument in terms of abuse of discretion by the board?

2. Suppose that the Springside Nursing Home board in 1967 had declared a dividend of $1,000 payable to each of Connor, Riche, and Quinn, with no dividend payable to Wilkes. Would Wilkes have had a legal entitlement to object? How would you frame the objection? Does this line of inquiry suggest another approach to the actual case?

3. Suppose there had been evidence in the case that the board had found another person to perform the duties that were being performed by Wilkes, but at a lower salary, and, after due deliberation, had fired Wilkes and hired the other person. Would Wilkes still have prevailed?

4. If the venture had been operated as a partnership, relying on the basic rules of the Uniform Partnership Act, what would Wilkes's position have been? Could the other partners have fired him? If they refused to pay him a salary, could they continue to pay themselves salaries?

5. The court refers to a right of "selfish ownership" in a close corporation. Suppose that Connor, Quinn, and Riche had decided on a substantial expansion of the nursing home; that this expansion would require suspension of the payment of salaries or dividends and would require considerable borrowing; and that there would, as a result, be a substantial risk of failure and loss of the entire investment. Suppose that Connor, Quinn, and Riche were all wealthy and could afford the loss, but that Wilkes was a man of modest means and could not afford the loss. Would Wilkes have been legally entitled to block the action of the majority? Should he have been? Would your answer be different if the majority had offered to buy out Wilkes's interest at a price about 40 percent below its existing market value? How would your answers to these questions change, if at all, if the venture had been organized as a partnership?

6. What is the appropriate remedy in this case? If Wilkes is entitled to damages, what about the duty to mitigate? Assuming that the corporation is to continue in existence, and that Connor, Quinn, and Riche are willing to forgo salary payments, must they pay dividends?

7. What planning techniques were available to the investors that would have allowed them to avoid litigation? If the lawyer who assisted in the formation of the corporation failed to discuss those planning techniques, is she or he guilty of malpractice? How does the decision in this case affect the obligations of lawyers in similar situations in the future?

8. Could the outcome in this case have been reached by applying ordinary principles of contract, rather than principles of fiduciary obligation? If so, would that have been a better approach? If you had been Wilkes's lawyer, which approach would you have emphasized?

Ingle v. Glamore Motor Sales, Inc.

73 N.Y.2d 183, 538 N.Y.S.2d 771, 535 N.E.2d 1311 (1989).

■ BELLACOSA, JUDGE.

. . .

In 1964, plaintiff-appellant Ingle sought to purchase an equity interest in respondent Glamore Motor Sales, Inc. from its then sole shareholder, respondent James Glamore. Ingle was not sold an interest in the corporation initially, but he was hired as sales manager. There was no express agreement between the parties establishing either the duration or conditions of employment.

In 1966, Glamore and Ingle entered into a written shareholders' agreement which provided that Ingle would purchase 22 of Glamore's 100 shares in the corporation, that Ingle would have a five-year option to purchase an additional 18 shares, and that Glamore would nominate and vote Ingle as a director and secretary of the corporation. The agreement also gave Glamore the right to repurchase all of Ingle's stock if "Ingle shall cease to be an employee of the Corporation *for any reason*" (emphasis added). Ingle later purchased the 18 additional shares and the parties executed a new shareholders' agreement, which updated some facets and eliminated outdated ones. The repurchase provision of the 1973 agreement tracked identically the 1966 version.

On January 1, 1982, the corporation issued 60 additional shares of stock. Glamore purchased 22 shares of the new issue and his two sons (respondents William and Robert Glamore) each purchased 19 shares. The three Glamores and Ingle, the only four shareholders, entered into a third agreement reflecting the corporate relationship. The repurchase provision pertinent to this litigation is: "(b) *Termination of employment.* In the event that any Stockholder shall *cease to be an employee of the Corporation for any reason,* Glamore shall have the option, for a period of 30 days after such termination of employment, to purchase all of the shares of stock then owned by such Stockholder" (emphasis supplied).

At a special meeting of the board of directors held on May 9, 1983, Ingle was voted out of his corporate posts and fired from his employment as operating manager of the business. The termination was effective May 31, 1983. On June 1, Glamore notified Ingle that he was exercising the repurchase-upon-termination-of-employment option and in due course paid Ingle $96,000 for his 40 shares in the corporation.

Plaintiff argues that as a minority shareholder of a closely held corporation, employed without the benefit of a contract containing a durational employment protection and without any limitation on the employer's right to discharge, he is nevertheless entitled by reason of his minority shareholder status to a fiduciary-rooted protection against being fired. His theory is that his employment status should not be governed by the employment at-will doctrine but, rather, that as a minority shareholder in a close corporation he should be treated as a co-owner, equivalent to a partner, whose employment rights flow from a special duty of loyalty and good faith. He next urges that an implicit covenant of good faith and fair dealing under the shareholders' agreement precluded his termination without cause, despite the express language and nature of the agreement in that regard. He concludes that even if he is an at-will employee, an action properly lies for the respondents' breach of fiduciary duties and for wrongful interference with his employment. Ingle started two separate actions seeking damages via seven causes of action alleging breach of fiduciary duty and of contract. Eventually all causes of action were dismissed—we believe correctly.

A minority shareholder in a close corporation, by that status alone, who contractually agrees to the repurchase of his shares upon termination of his employment for any reason, acquires no right from the corporation or majority shareholders against at-will discharge. There is nothing in law, in the agreement, or in the relationship of the parties to warrant such a contradictory and judicial alteration of the employment relationship or the express agreement. It is necessary in this case to appreciate and keep distinct the duty a corporation owes to a minority shareholder *as a shareholder* from any duty it might owe him as an employee.

Both lower courts agree, as do we, that Ingle did not sufficiently present facts raising a triable issue regarding the existence of either an oral or written employment contract fixing employment of a definite duration. . . . Under the established common-law rule—and without any reference to the shareholders' agreement—the corporation had the right to discharge plaintiff at will. . . .

The twist in this fact pattern is an asserted liability based on allegations that the corporate officers breached fiduciary duties of good faith and fair dealing arising from the shareholders' agreement and on tortious interference with Ingle's employment. The twist does not support a deviation from the governing principle in this case.

In Murphy v. American Home Prods. Corp., 58 N.Y.2d 293, 461 N.Y.S.2d 232, 448 N.E.2d 86, we concluded that there is no implied obligation of good faith and fair dealing in an employment at will, as that would be incongruous to the legally recognized jural relationship in that kind of employment relationship. . . .

Plaintiff confuses and tries to avoid the sequential relationship of his employment status to his shareholders' agreement by extracting an obligation from the agreement to manufacture a legally unrecognized employment security. Divestiture of his status as a shareholder, by operation of the repurchase provision, is a contractually agreed to consequence flowing directly from the firing, not vice versa. The dissent similarly confuses and inverts the Appellate Division's and our holding. . . .

As noted, Ingle argued that the corporation discharged him because James Glamore would then have a right to repurchase his shares under the terms of the shareholders' agreement. Notably, however, Ingle never asserted that the $2,400 per share paid to him upon termination was not fairly representative of his equity interest in the corporation. He does not contend that the corporation undervalued his shares, and he accepted payment from Glamore without reservation. Indeed, that, too, was fixed by the parties' buy-out agreement. . . .

Ingle's and the dissent's reliance on Fender v. Prescott, 101 A.D.2d 418, 422, 476 N.Y.S.2d 128, *expressly affirmed on grounds other than the corporate relationship discussion,* 64 N.Y.2d 1077, 1078–1079, 489 N.Y.S.2d 880, 479 N.E.2d 225, for an exception based on the close corporate form in which this employer and employee find themselves is unavailing. No duty of loyalty and good faith akin to that between partners, precluding termination except for cause, arises among those operating a business in the corporate form who "have only the rights, duties and obligations of stockholders" and not those of partners. . . .

Finally, the dissent essentially invokes an equity appeal. While we have no quarrel whatsoever with that magnificent juridical jewel applied in its proper setting, this lawsuit does not qualify. Here, fair principles of well-settled law, affecting employment and contractual relationships between private parties, govern and are entitled to respect and efficacy from this court. We cannot merely substitute our preferred notions for those of the parties themselves in such matters.

. . .

If there was no protection against discharge of an at-will employee in *Murphy* (supra) . . ., where there was no contractual arrangement at all, there surely can be none here where the related contract expressly confirms the unavailability of that protection. Moreover, to hold otherwise on the facts and pleadings of this case would confuse our recent holdings in an area of the law where certainty, predictability and reliability are highly prized common-law goals.

. . .

Accordingly, the order of the Appellate Division, 140 A.D.2d 493, 528 N.Y.S.2d 602, should be affirmed, with costs.

■ HANCOCK, JUDGE (dissenting).

This appeal presents a clear-cut legal question: whether plaintiff's status as an officer, director, substantial part owner and active participant in the affairs and management of Glamore Motor Sales, a close corporation, gives him equitable rights and remedies which are not subject to the ordinary legal rules of master and servant? The majority answers "no" and writes off the case as a routine application of New York's employment at-will rule. Because this produces a result which is egregiously unfair and one which, I am convinced, is not warranted under existing case law, I respectfully dissent.

By treating the essence of plaintiff's complaints as a claimed breach of a hiring contract by the employer rather than an unfair squeeze-out of a minority shareholder in a close corporation by the majority, the court simply concludes that plaintiff has no rights at all. . . .

The majority's decision summarily rejects, without discussion, plaintiff's underlying theory which is rooted in his equitable rights as a minority shareholder and principal in a close corporation and the fiduciary duty of fair dealing owed him by the majority shareholders—rights and duties which have been widely recognized in statutory and decisional law in this and other jurisdictions (*see, e.g.,* . . . Wilkes v. Springside Nursing Home, 370 Mass. 842, 353 N.E.2d 657 [1976], . . .).

. . .

What is remarkable about the majority opinion is that it appears to treat the employment at-will rule as a sort of categorical imperative which necessarily dictates the result in this case. There can be no question about the harshness of the outcome—assuming plaintiff's allegations to be true: the controlling shareholders are permitted to have the corporation fire plaintiff arbitrarily and in bad faith solely for the purpose of getting rid of him as a 25% stock owner.[1] . . .

The Appellate Division, in dismissing plaintiff's complaints, and the majority of the court, in its affirmance, have adopted defendants' literal interpretation of the phrase in paragraph 7(b) of the stockholders' agreement—"cease to be an employee of the Corporation for any reason"—as giving defendants the unfettered right to repurchase plaintiff's shares by firing him, even if arbitrarily or in bad faith.

The plain wording of the buy-back provision and its sense, when read in the context of the entire agreement and the circumstances surrounding its execution, by no means unequivocally support this interpretation. Plaintiff states that the purpose and intent of paragraph 7(b) was to protect James Glamore in case *plaintiff chose* to leave the business, not to give Glamore the right—at any time, for any reason or for no reason—to deprive plaintiff of all expectancies as coprincipal in the agency. He points to the other two contingencies giving Glamore the right to repurchase his shares: plaintiff's decision to sell his stock (para. 7[a]) and plaintiff's death (para. 7[c]); he argues that the purpose of paragraph 7(b) like that of the other provisions was solely to protect Glamore by

[1] The notion that plaintiff's loss must somehow be viewed as less onerous because he is not contesting the $2,400 per share cash-out price misses the point of the lawsuit. Plaintiff wants to *keep his stock*—not to sell it. The injury to plaintiff is that he is being involuntarily cashed out as a stockholder through the buy-back agreement and forced out of his investment and participation in Glamore Motor Sales, Inc. Obviously, if the buy-back agreement is held to be enforceable against plaintiff, he is precluded from complaining about the amount. He has agreed to it.

Moreover, it cannot seriously be suggested that plaintiff should be pleased with being repaid a total of $96,000 in 1983 for his $75,000 cash outlay made 17 to 15 years earlier, particularly in light of the high risk he assumed in guaranteeing the corporation's loans up to $1,000,000. That he agreed to such buy-back figure, of course, supports his contention that he thought the buy-back agreement was intended to protect Glamore's control over plaintiff's stock by giving Glamore the right to repurchase the stock in the event that plaintiff died, wished to sell or transfer his shares, or voluntarily decided to quit; and that it was never in plaintiff's contemplation that the clause was to apply as the price for his shares in the event that he was involuntarily terminated. . . .

William Glamore and Robert Glamore, sons of James H. Glamore, were elected vice-president and secretary-treasurer, respectively; and . . ., thereafter, upon exercise of the purchase option in the shareholders' agreement, plaintiff was compelled to deliver his shares for the sum of $2,400 per share. About these facts there is no dispute.

giving him the right to repurchase upon the happening of a contingency beyond Glamore's control—i.e., in paragraph 7(b), plaintiff's voluntary decision to leave. The very choice of the wording to describe the contingency of plaintiff's leaving—i.e., "ceases to be an employee" rather than "is terminated"—tends to support plaintiff's argument. The word "ceases" suggests that it was action by plaintiff not by the employer in ending the relationship which was contemplated. Thus, in my opinion the repurchase option of 7(b) is not free from ambiguity. . . .

There is no employment agreement between plaintiff and the corporation. Nothing in the original stockholders' agreement between plaintiff and James Glamore or in the subsequent agreement between plaintiff and the additional members of the Glamore family as stockholders purports to set the terms of plaintiff's relationship with the corporation or to state when or under what circumstances it may be terminated. . . . Upholding the corporation's right to discharge plaintiff here, therefore, must rest squarely on the application of the employment at-will doctrine, "that where an employment is for an indefinite term it is presumed to be a hiring at will which may be freely terminated by either party at any time for any reason or even for no reason" (Murphy v. American Home Prods. Corp., 58 N.Y.2d [293,] 300, 461 N.Y.S.2d 232, 448 N.E.2d 86). Whether this rule may be properly and fairly applied in this case is the central issue on which we disagree.

II

New York, like many other States, unquestionably recognizes that the status of a minority shareholder in a close corporation requires special protection from the courts. . . .

Thus, for purposes of asserting rights as a minority shareholder under Business Corporation Law § 1104–a, we have held that a shareholder "who reasonably expected that ownership in the corporation would entitle him or her to a job, a share of corporate earnings, a place in corporate management, or some other form of security, would be oppressed in a very real sense when others in the corporation seek to defeat those expectations and there exists no effective means of salvaging the investment" (Matter of Kemp & Beatley [Gardstein], 64 N.Y.2d supra, at 72–73, 484 N.Y.S.2d 799, 473 N.E.2d 1173).

A person who, like plaintiff, buys a minority interest in a close corporation does so not only in the hope of enjoying an increase in value of his stake in the business but for the assurance of employment in the business in a managerial position. . . .

Thus, the relationship of a minority shareholder to a close corporation, if fairly viewed, cannot possibly be equated with an ordinary hiring and, in the absence of a contract, regarded as nothing more than an employment at will. But this is exactly how the majority of the court has treated plaintiff's association with Glamore Motor Sales. And it has done so by not addressing the multiple relationships and the expectancies and vulnerabilities peculiar to the status of a minority shareholder in plaintiff's position—those very considerations which call for the relief that only a court of equity can give. . . .

ANALYSIS

1. Is it possible to reconcile the result in *Ingle* with the result in *Wilkes?*

2. What should Ingle have done to protect the rights he claimed he had? What should Glamore have done to make clear that Ingle had no such rights?

3. On what basis did the dissent conclude that the result was unfair to Ingle? What do you imagine is the story behind the termination of Ingle?

4. If Ingle had convinced the court of the correctness of his claim of unfair treatment, what would the appropriate remedy have been? Would Ingle have a job for life? What if the Glamores wanted to sell their interest in the corporation?

Brodie v. Jordan

447 Mass. 866, 857 N.E.2d 1076 (2006).

. . .

1. *Background.* Malden is a Massachusetts corporation that operates a small machine shop and produces metal objects such as ball bearings. The plaintiff's now deceased husband, Walter S. Brodie (Walter), was one of the founding members of the company and served as its president from 1979 to 1992. Barbuto has been a shareholder, a director, and the treasurer of the company since its formation. Jordan has been an employee of the company since 1975 and a shareholder, director, and officer since 1984; he is the one responsible for the day-to-day operation of the business. Beginning in 1984, Walter, Barbuto, and Jordan each held one-third of the shares of the corporation and all three served as directors. By 1988, however, Walter was no longer involved in the company's day-to-day operation and only met with Barbuto and Jordan two to three times each year. After Walter and the defendants began to disagree over various management issues, Walter made a number of requests that the company purchase his shares, but those requests were rejected. Neither the articles of organization nor any corporate bylaw obligated Malden or the defendants to purchase the stock of a shareholder.

The corporation has not paid any dividends to shareholders since 1989. As an employee, Jordan receives a salary at a rate set by the board of directors (Barbuto and himself). Jordan participates in a profit-sharing plan made available by the corporation and has the use of a company vehicle. Barbuto received director's fees from the corporation until 1998. He owns the building that houses Malden's corporate offices and receives rent from the corporation. Barbuto also owns a separate corporation, Barco Engineering, Inc., which is a customer of Malden and for which Malden regularly performs services on an open credit account. Walter received compensation from the company prior to 1992, and was paid a consultant's fee in 1994 and 1995. However, neither Walter nor the plaintiff [Mary Brodie, Walter's wife] appears to have received any compensation or other money from the corporation since 1995.

In 1992, Walter was voted out as president and director of Malden, and Jordan was elected president. Walter died in 1997. The plaintiff was appointed Walter's executrix and inherited his one-third interest in Malden. She attended a Malden shareholders' meeting in July, 1997, at which she nominated herself, through counsel, as a director, but Barbuto and Jordan voted against her election. At this same meeting, the plaintiff asked Jordan and Barbuto to perform a valuation of the company so that she could ascertain the value of her shares, but such a valuation was never performed.

In 1998, the plaintiff filed the instant suit. Prior to and since that time, the defendants failed to provide her with various financial and operational company information that she requested. At the time of trial, the defendants had failed to hold an annual shareholder's meeting for the previous five years, and the plaintiff had not participated in any company decision-making.

2. *Discussion*. The parties do not dispute that Malden is a close corporation . . . "[S]tockholders in [a] close corporation owe one another substantially the same fiduciary duty in the operation of the enterprise that partners owe to one another" (footnotes omitted), [Donahue v. Rodd Electrotype Co. of New England, Inc., 328 N.E.2d 505 (1975)] . . .,, that is, a duty of "utmost good faith and loyalty," id., quoting Cardullo v. Landau, 329 Mass. 5, 8, 105 N.E.2d 843 (1952).

Majority shareholders in a close corporation violate this duty when they act to "freeze out" the minority. We have defined freeze-outs by way of example:

> The squeezers [those who employ the freeze-out techniques] may refuse to declare dividends; they may drain off the corporation's earnings in the form of exorbitant salaries and bonuses to the majority shareholder-officers and perhaps to their relatives, or in the form of high rent by the corporation for property leased from majority shareholders . . . ; they may deprive minority shareholders of corporate offices and of employment by the company; they may cause the corporation to sell its assets at an inadequate price to the majority shareholders. . . .

Donahue v. Rodd Electrotype Co. of New England, Inc., supra at 588–589, 328 N.E.2d 505, quoting F.H. O'Neal & J. Derwin, Expulsion or Oppression of Business Associates 42 (1961). What these examples have in common is that, in each, the majority frustrates the minority's reasonable expectations of benefit from their ownership of shares.

We have previously analyzed freeze-outs in terms of shareholders' "reasonable expectations" both explicitly and implicitly. . . . A number of other jurisdictions, either by judicial decision or by statute, also look to shareholders' "reasonable expectations" in determining whether to grant relief to an aggrieved minority shareholder in a close corporation.

In the present case, the Superior Court judge properly analyzed the defendants' liability in terms of the plaintiff's reasonable expectations of benefit. The judge found that the defendants had interfered with the plaintiff's reasonable expectations by excluding her from corporate decision-making, denying her access to company information, and hindering her ability to sell her shares in the open market. In addition, the judge's findings reflect a state of affairs in which the defendants were the only ones receiving any financial benefit from the corporation. The Appeals Court determined that the findings were warranted, and the defendants have not sought further appellate review with respect to liability. Thus, the only question before us is whether, on this record, the plaintiff was entitled to the remedy of a forced buyout of her shares by the majority. We conclude that she was not so entitled.

a. *Remedies for freeze-out of minority shareholder*. The proper remedy for a freeze-out is "to restore [the minority shareholder] as nearly as possible to the position [s]he would have been in had there been no wrongdoing." Zimmerman v. Bogoff, 402 Mass. 650, 661, 524 N.E.2d 849 (1988). Because the wrongdoing in a freeze-out is the denial by the majority of the minority's reasonable expectations of benefit, it follows that the remedy should, to the extent possible, restore to the minority shareholder those benefits which she reasonably expected, but has not received because of the fiduciary breach.

If, for example, a minority shareholder had a reasonable expectation of employment by the corporation and was terminated wrongfully, the remedy may be reinstatement, back pay, or both. See Wilkes v. Springside Nursing Home, Inc., . . . 353 N.E.2d 657. . . . Similarly, if a minority shareholder has a reasonable expectation of sharing in company profits and has been denied this opportunity, she may be "entitled to participate in the favorable results of operations to the extent that those results have been wrongly appropriated by the majority." Crowley v. Communications for Hosps., Inc., 30 Mass. App. Ct. 751, 768, 573 N.E.2d 996 (1991). . . .

b. *The Superior Court judge's remedy*. Courts have broad equitable powers to fashion remedies for breaches of fiduciary duty in a close corporation, . . . and their choice of a particular remedy is reviewed for abuse of discretion. . . . Here, the Superior Court judge ordered the defendants to buy out the plaintiff at the price of an expert's estimate of her share of the corporation, a remedy that no Massachusetts appellate court has previously authorized. The problem with this remedy is that it placed the plaintiff in a significantly better position than she would have enjoyed absent the wrongdoing, and well exceeded her reasonable expectations of benefit from her shares.

. . . In this case, it is undisputed that neither the articles of organization nor any corporate bylaw obligates Malden or the defendants to purchase the plaintiff's shares. Thus, there is nothing in the background law, the governing rules of this particular close corporation, or any other circumstance that could have given the plaintiff a reasonable expectation of having her shares bought out.

In ordering the defendants to purchase the plaintiff's stock at the price of her share of the company, the judge created an artificial market for the plaintiff's minority share of a close corporation-an asset that, by definition, has little or no market value. . . . Thus, the remedy had the perverse effect of placing the plaintiff in a position superior to that which she would have enjoyed had there been no wrongdoing. . . .

c. *Considerations on remand*. As we have indicated, the remedy for the defendants' breach of fiduciary duty is one that protects the plaintiff's reasonable expectations of benefit from the corporation and that compensates her for their denial in the past. An evidentiary hearing is appropriate to determine her reasonable expectations of ownership; whether such expectations have been frustrated; and, if so, the means by which to vindicate the plaintiff's interests. For breaches visited upon the plaintiff resulting in deprivations that can be quantified, money damages will be the appropriate remedy. Prospective injunctive relief may be granted to ensure that the plaintiff is allowed to participate in company governance, and to enjoy financial or other benefits from the business, to the extent that her ownership interest justifies.

In devising a remedy that grants the plaintiff her reasonable expectations of benefit from stock ownership in Malden, the judge may consider the fact that the plaintiff has received no economic benefit from her shares. If the defendants have denied the plaintiff any return on her investment while "drain[ing] off the corporation's earnings" for themselves, Donahue v. Rodd Electrotype Co. of New England, Inc., . . . 328 N.E.2d 505, the judge may consider, among other possibilities the propriety, of compelling the declaration of dividends.

So ordered.

ANALYSIS

1. What might the defendants have done, beginning around 1990, to deprive Ms. Brodie of basis for a suit against them or the corporation—without giving up much of substance? In other words, what was the minimum "fiduciary obligation" of the defendants toward Ms. Brodie?

2. On remand, whose "reasonable expectations" are to be determined? What evidence might each of the parties offer as to their expectations?

3. Does the *Brodie* reasonable expectations standard replace the *Wilkes* three-step test? If not, what does the relationship between the two appear to be?

4. Who won, Ms. Brodie or the defendants? What is the likely effect of the decision on settlement negotiations?

Smith v. Atlantic Properties, Inc.

12 Mass.App.Ct. 201, 422 N.E.2d 798 (1981).

In December, 1951, Dr. Louis E. Wolfson agreed to purchase land in Norwood for $350,000, with an initial cash payment of $50,000 and a mortgage note of $300,000 payable in thirty-three months. Dr. Wolfson offered a quarter interest each in the land to Mr. Paul T. Smith, Mr. Abraham Zimble, and William H. Burke. Each paid to Dr. Wolfson $12,500, one quarter of the initial payment. Mr. Smith, an attorney, organized the defendant corporation (Atlantic) in 1951 to operate the real estate. Each of the four subscribers received twenty-five shares of stock. Mr. Smith included, both in the corporation's articles of organization and in its by-laws, a provision reading, "No election, appointment or resolution by the Stockholders and no election, appointment, resolution, purchase, sale, lease, contract, contribution, compensation, proceeding or act by the Board of Directors or by any officer or officers shall be valid or binding upon the corporation until effected, passed, approved or ratified by an affirmative vote of eighty (80%) per cent of the capital stock issued outstanding and entitled to vote." This provision (hereafter referred to as the 80% provision) was included at Dr. Wolfson's request and had the effect of giving to any one of the four original shareholders a veto in corporate decisions.

Atlantic purchased the Norwood land. Some of the land and other assets were sold for about $220,000. Atlantic retained twenty-eight acres on which stood about twenty old brick or wood mill-type structures, which required expensive and constant repairs. After the first year, Atlantic became profitable and showed a profit every year prior to 1969, ranging from a low of $7,683 in 1953 to a high of $44,358 in 1954. The mortgage was paid by 1958 and Atlantic has incurred no long-term debt thereafter. Salaries of about $25,000 were paid only in 1959 and 1960. Dividends in the total amount of $10,000 each were paid in 1964 and 1970. By 1961, Atlantic had about $172,000 in retained earnings, more than half in cash.

For various reasons, which need not be stated in detail, disagreements and ill will soon arose between Dr. Wolfson, on the one hand, and the other stockholders as a group.[3] Dr. Wolfson wished to see Atlantic's earnings devoted to repairs and possibly some improvements in its existing buildings and adjacent facilities. The other stockholders desired the declaration of dividends. Dr. Wolfson fairly steadily refused to vote for any dividends. Although it was pointed out to him that failure to declare dividends might result in the imposition by the Internal Revenue Service of a penalty under the Internal Revenue Code, I.R.C. § 531 et seq. (relating to unreasonable accumulation of corporate earnings and profits), Dr. Wolfson persisted in his refusal to declare dividends. The other shareholders did agree over the years to making at least the most urgent repairs to Atlantic's buildings, but did not agree to make all repairs and improvements which were recommended in a 1962 report by an engineering firm retained by Atlantic to make a complete estimate of all repairs and improvements which might be beneficial.

The fears of an Internal Revenue Service assessment of a penalty tax were soon realized. Penalty assessments were made in 1962, 1963, and 1964. These were settled by Dr. Wolfson for $11,767.71 in taxes and interest. Despite this settlement, Dr. Wolfson continued his opposition to declaring dividends. The record does not indicate that he developed any specific and definitive schedule or plan for a series of necessary or desirable repairs and improvements to Atlantic's properties. At least none was proposed which would have had a reasonable chance of satisfying the Internal Revenue Service that expenditures for such repairs and improvements constituted "reasonable needs of the business," I.R.C. § 534(c), a term which includes (see I.R.C. § 537) "the reasonably anticipated needs of the business." Predictably, despite further warnings by Dr. Wolfson's shareholder colleagues, the Internal Revenue Service assessed further penalty taxes for the years 1965, 1966, 1967, and 1968. These taxes were upheld by the United States Tax Court in Atlantic Properties, Inc. v. Commissioner of Int. Rev., 62 T.C. 644 (1974), and on appeal in 519 F.2d 1233 (1st Cir.1975). . . .

---

[3] At least one cause of ill will on Dr. Wolfson's part may have been the refusal of the other shareholders to consent to his transferring his shares in Atlantic to the Louis E. Wolfson Foundation, a charitable foundation created by Dr. Wolfson.

An examination of these decisions makes it apparent that Atlantic has incurred substantial penalty taxes and legal expense largely because of Dr. Wolfson's refusal to vote for the declaration of sufficient dividends to avoid the penalty, a refusal which was (in the Tax Court and upon appeal) attributed in some measure to a tax avoidance purpose on Dr. Wolfson's part.

On January 30, 1967, the shareholders, other than Dr. Wolfson, initiated this proceeding in the Superior Court, later supplemented to reflect developments after the original complaint. The plaintiffs sought a court determination of the dividends to be paid by Atlantic, the removal of Dr. Wolfson as a director, and an order that Atlantic be reimbursed by him for the penalty taxes assessed against it and related expenses. . . .

The trial judge made findings (but in more detail) of essentially the facts outlined above and concluded that Dr. "Wolfson's obstinate refusal to vote in favor of . . . dividends was . . . caused more by his dislike for other stockholders and his desire to avoid additional tax payments than . . . by any genuine desire to undertake a program for improving . . . [Atlantic] property." She also determined that Dr. Wolfson was liable to Atlantic for taxes and interest amounting to "$11,767.11 plus interest from the commencement of this action, plus $35,646.14 plus interest from August 11, 1975," the date of the First Circuit decision affirming the second penalty tax assessment. The latter amount includes an attorney's fee of $7,500 in the Federal tax cases. She also ordered the directors of Atlantic to declare "a reasonable dividend at the earliest practical date and reasonable dividends annually thereafter consistent with good business practice." In addition, the trial judge directed that jurisdiction of the case be retained in the Superior Court "for a period of five years to [e]nsure compliance." Judgment was entered pursuant to the trial judge's order. . . .

After the entry of judgment, Dr. Wolfson and Atlantic filed a motion for a new trial and to amend the judge's findings. This motion, after hearing, was denied, and Dr. Wolfson and Atlantic claimed an appeal from the judgment and the former from the denial of the motion. The plaintiffs . . . requested payment of their attorneys' fees in this proceeding and filed supporting affidavits. The motion was denied, and the plaintiffs appealed.

1. The trial judge, in deciding that Dr. Wolfson had committed a breach of his fiduciary duty to other stockholders, relied greatly on broad language in Donahue v. Rodd Electrotype Co., 367 Mass. 578, 586–597 (1975), in which the Supreme Judicial Court afforded to a minority stockholder in a close corporation equality of treatment (with members of a controlling group of shareholders) in the matter of the redemption of shares. The court (at 592–593) relied on the resemblance of a close corporation to a partnership and held that "stockholders in the close corporation owe one another substantially the same fiduciary duty in the operation of the enterprise that partners owe to one another" (footnotes omitted). That standard of duty, the court said, was the "utmost good faith and loyalty." The court went on to say that such stockholders "may not act out of avarice, expediency or self-interest in derogation of their duty of loyalty to the other stockholders and to the corporation." Similar principles were stated in Wilkes v. Springside Nursing Home, Inc., 370

Mass. 842, 848–852, (1976), but with some modifications . . . of the sweeping language of the *Donahue* case. . . .

In the *Donahue* case, 367 Mass. at 593 n. 17, the court recognized that cases may arise in which, in a close corporation, majority stockholders may ask protection from a minority stockholder. Such an instance arises in the present case because Dr. Wolfson has been able to exercise a veto concerning corporate action on dividends by the 80% provision (in Atlantic's articles or organization and by-laws) already quoted. The 80% provision may have substantially the effect of reversing the usual roles of the majority and the minority shareholders. The minority, under that provision, becomes an ad hoc controlling interest.[6]

. . . In the present case, Dr. Wolfson testified that he requested the inclusion of the 80% provision "in case the people [the other shareholders] whom I knew, but not very well, ganged up on me." The possibilities of shareholder disagreement on policy made the provision seem a sensible precaution.[8] A question is presented, however, concerning the extent to which such a veto power possessed by a minority stockholder may be exercised as its holder may wish, without a violation of the "fiduciary duty" referred to in the *Donahue* case, 367 Mass. at 593, 328 N.E.2d 505, as modified in the *Wilkes* case. . . .

2. With respect to the past damage to Atlantic caused by Dr. Wolfson's refusal to vote in favor of any dividends, the trial judge was justified in finding that his conduct went beyond what was reasonable. The other stockholders shared to some extent responsibility for what occurred by failing to accept Dr. Wolfson's proposals with much sympathy, but the inaction on dividends seems the principal cause of the tax penalties. Dr. Wolfson had been warned of the dangers of an assessment under the Internal Revenue Code, I.R.C. § 531 et seq. He had refused to vote dividends in any amount adequate to minimize that danger and had failed to bring forward, within the relevant taxable years, a convincing, definitive program of appropriate improvements which could withstand scrutiny by the Internal Revenue Service. Whatever may have been the reason for Dr. Wolfson's refusal to declare dividends (and even if in any particular year he may have gained slight, if any, tax advantage from withholding dividends) we think that he recklessly ran serious and unjustified risks of precisely the penalty taxes eventually assessed, risks which were inconsistent with any reasonable interpretation of a duty of "utmost good faith and loyalty." The trial judge (despite the fact that the other shareholders helped to create the voting deadlock and despite the novelty of the situation) was justified in

---

[6] The majority shareholders, in the event of a deadlock, at least may seek dissolution of the corporation if forty percent of the voting power can be mustered, whereas a single stockholder with only twenty-five percent of the stock may not do so. See G.L. c. 156B, § 99(*b*), as amended by St.1969, c. 392, § 23.

[8] . . . It was reasonably foreseeable that there might be differences of opinion between Dr. Wolfson, a man with substantial income likely to be in a high income tax bracket, and less affluent shareholders on such matters of policy as dividend declarations, salaries, and investment in improvements in the property. The other shareholders, two of whom were attorneys, should have known that it was as open to Dr. Wolfson reasonably to exercise the veto provided to him by the 80% provision in favor of a policy of reinvestment of earnings in Atlantic's properties, which would probably avoid taxes and increase the value of the corporate assets, as it was for them (possessed of the same veto) to use reasonably their voting power in favor of a more generous dividend and salary policy.

charging Dr. Wolfson with the out-of-pocket expenditure incurred by Atlantic for the penalty taxes and related counsel fees of the tax cases.[10]

ANALYSIS

1. What is the logic of the case? Why is the problem Wolfson's fault?

2. If you had been Wolfson's lawyer and he had told you he was adamant in his intention to use earnings for rehabilitation, what would you have advised him to do? What does your answer tell you about the legal doctrine of the decision and about the effect of that doctrine on behavior and on economic entitlements?

PLANNING

How could the problems encountered by the investors in this case have been avoided by adoption of appropriate provisions at the time of formation of the enterprise?

NOTE AND QUESTIONS

In Nixon v. Blackwell, 626 A.2d 1366, 1379–81 (Del.1993) (en banc), the Delaware Supreme Court offered the following comments (which were not necessary to analysis of the legal issues raised by the case):

> The case at bar points up the basic dilemma of minority stockholders in receiving fair value for their stock as to which there is no market and no market valuation. It is not difficult to be sympathetic, in the abstract, to a stockholder who finds himself or herself in that position. A stockholder who bargains for stock in a closely held corporation . . . can make a business judgment whether to buy into such a minority position, and if so on what terms. One could bargain for definitive provisions of self-ordering permitted to a Delaware corporation through the certificate of incorporation or by-laws by reason of the provisions in 8 Del.C. §§ 102, 109, and 141(a). Moreover, in addition to such mechanisms, a stockholder intending to buy into a minority position in a Delaware corporation may enter into definitive stockholder agreements, and such agreements may provide for elaborate earnings tests, buy-out provisions, voting trusts, or other voting agreements. . . .
>
> The tools of good corporate practice are designed to give a purchasing minority stockholder the opportunity to bargain for protection before parting with consideration. It would do violence to normal corporate practice and our corporation law to fashion an ad hoc ruling which would result in a court-imposed stockholder buy-out for which the parties had not contracted. . . .
>
> It would . . . be inappropriate judicial legislation for this Court to fashion a special judicially created rule for minority

[10] We do not now suggest that the standard of "utmost good faith and loyalty" may require some relaxation when applied to a minority ad hoc controlling interest, created by some device, similar to the 80% provision, designed in part to protect the selfish interests of a minority shareholder. This seems to us a difficult area of the law best developed on a case by case basis.

> investors when . . . there are no negotiated special provisions in the certificate of incorporation, by-laws, or stockholder agreements.

1. How would *Wilkes* have been decided under Delaware law?

2. Which approach do you prefer—Delaware's (you made your bed and you must lie in it) or Massachusetts's (the Golden Rule)? Why? What are the likely consequences of each approach?

Jordan v. Duff and Phelps, Inc.

815 F.2d 429 (7th Cir.1987), cert. dismissed, 485 U.S. 901 (1988).

■ BEFORE CUDAHY, POSNER, and EASTERBROOK, CIRCUIT JUDGES.

■ EASTERBROOK, CIRCUIT JUDGE.

. . .

I

The case is here following a grant of summary judgment for the defendants [in an action founded on § 10(b) and Rule 10b–5, common law fraud, and breach of fiduciary duty].

Duff and Phelps, Inc., evaluates the risk and worth of firms and their securities. It sells credit ratings, investment research, and financial consulting services to both the firms under scrutiny and potential investors in them. Jordan started work at Duff & Phelps in May 1977 and was viewed as a successful securities analyst. In 1981 the firm offered Jordan the opportunity to buy some stock. By November 1983 Jordan had purchased 188 of the 20,100 shares outstanding. He was making installment payments on another 62 shares. Forty people other than Jordan held stock in Duff & Phelps.

Jordan purchased his stock at its "book value" (the accounting net worth of Duff & Phelps, divided by the number of shares outstanding). Before selling him any stock, Duff & Phelps required Jordan to sign a "Stock Restriction and Purchase Agreement" (the Agreement). This provided in part:

> Upon the termination of any employment with the Corporation . . . for any reason, including resignation, discharge, death, disability or retirement, the individual whose employment is terminated or his estate shall sell to the Corporation, and the Corporation shall buy, all Shares of the Corporation then owned by such individual or his estate. The price to be paid for such Shares shall be equal to the adjusted book value (as hereinafter defined) of the Shares on the December 31 which coincides with, or immediately precedes, the date of termination of such individual's employment.

Duff & Phelps enforced this restriction with but a single exception. During 1983 the board of directors of Duff & Phelps adopted a resolution—of which Jordan did not learn until 1984—allowing employees fired by the firm to keep their stock for five years. The resolution followed the discharge of Carol Franchik, with whom Claire Hansen, the (married) chairman of the board, had been having an affair. When Franchik threatened suit, the board allowed her to keep her stock.

While Jordan was accumulating stock, Hansen, the chairman of the board, was exploring the possibility of selling the firm. Between May and August 1983 Hansen and Francis Jeffries, another officer of Duff & Phelps, negotiated with Security Pacific Corp., a bank holding company. The negotiators reached agreement on a merger, in which Duff & Phelps would be valued at $50 million, but a higher official within Security Pacific vetoed the deal on August 11, 1983. As of that date, Duff & Phelps had no irons in the fire.

Jordan, however, was conducting a search of his own—for a new job. Jordan's family lived near Chicago, the headquarters of Duff & Phelps, and Jordan's wife did not get along with Jordan's mother. The strain between the two occasionally left his wife in tears. He asked Duff & Phelps about the possibility of a transfer to the firm's only branch office, in Cleveland, but the firm did not need Jordan's services there. Concluding that it was time to choose between his job and his wife, Jordan chose his wife and started looking for employment far away from Chicago. His search took him to Houston, where Underwood Neuhaus & Co., a broker-dealer in securities, offered him a job at a salary ($110,000 per year) substantially greater than his compensation ($67,000) at Duff & Phelps. Jordan took the offer on the spot during an interview in Houston, but Underwood would have allowed Jordan to withdraw this oral acceptance.

On November 16, 1983, Jordan told Hansen that he was going to resign and accept employment with Underwood. Jordan did not ask Hansen about potential mergers; Hansen did not volunteer anything. Jordan delivered a letter of resignation, which Duff & Phelps accepted the same day. By mutual agreement, Jordan worked the rest of the year for Duff & Phelps even though his loyalties had shifted. He did this so that he could receive the book value of the stock as of December 31, 1983—for under the Agreement a departure in November would have meant valuation as of December 31, 1982. Jordan delivered his certificates on December 30, 1983, and the firm mailed him a check for $23,225, the book value (at $123.54 per share) of the 188 shares of stock. Jordan surrendered, as worthless under the circumstances, the right to buy the remaining 62 shares.

Before Jordan cashed the check, however, he was startled by the announcement on January 10, 1984, of a merger between Duff & Phelps and a subsidiary of Security Pacific. Under the terms of the merger Duff & Phelps would be valued at $50 million. If Jordan had been an employee on January 10, had quickly paid for the other 62 shares, and the merger had closed that day, he would have received $452,000 in cash and the opportunity to obtain as much as $194,000 more in "earn out" (a percentage of Duff & Phelps's profits to be paid to the former investors—an arrangement that keeps the employees' interest in the firm keen and reduces the buyer's risk if profits fall short). Jordan refused to cash the check and demanded his stock back; Duff & Phelps told him to get lost. He filed this suit in March 1984, asking for damages measured by the value his stock would have had under the terms of the acquisition.

The public announcement on January 10 explained that the boards of the two firms had reached an agreement in principle on January 6. The definitive agreement was signed on March 23. Because Security Pacific is a bank holding company, the acquisition required the approval of the Board of Governors of the Federal Reserve. The Fed granted approval, but with a condition so onerous that the firms abandoned the transaction. The Fed objected to Security Pacific's acquisition of Duff & Phelps's credit rating business. 71 Fed. Res. Bull. 118 (1985). The agreement was formally cancelled on January 9, 1985. Duff & Phelps quickly asked the district court to dismiss Jordan's suit, on the ground that he could not establish damages. Jordan responded by amending his complaint, with Judge Hart's permission, to ask for rescission rather than damages.

Throughout 1985 Duff & Phelps continued looking for a partner; finding none, it decided to dance with itself. The firm's management formed an "Employee Stock Ownership Trust", which was able to borrow $40 million against the security of the firm's assets and business. The Trust acquired Duff & Phelps through a new firm, Duff Research, Inc. This transaction occurred in December 1985. The employees at the time, together with Carol Franchik, received cash, notes, and beneficial interests in the Trust. Jordan asserts that the package was worth almost $2000 per share, or $497,000 if he had held 250 shares in December 1985.

. . .

II

Michaels [v. Michaels, 767 F.2d 1185, 1194–97 (7th Cir.1985)] holds that close corporations that purchase their own stock must disclose to the sellers all information that meets the standard of "materiality" set out in TSC Industries, Inc. v. Northway, Inc., 426 U.S. 438, 449, 48 L.Ed. 2d 757, 96 S.Ct. 2126 (1976). . . . A jury would be free under *Michaels* to conclude that the board's decision of November 14 to seek a buyer for Duff & Phelps—coupled with the fact that at least one putative buyer thought Duff & Phelps worth $50 million, which casts an important light on the prospect of a profitable conclusion to the search—was "material" under the standard of TSC Industries. That is, there is a "substantial likelihood that, under all the circumstances, the omitted fact would have assumed actual significance in the deliberations of the reasonable shareholder" and "would have been viewed by the reasonable investor as having significantly altered the 'total mix' of information made available." 426 U.S. at 449 (footnote omitted.)

. . .

[T]his supposes that Duff & Phelps had a duty to disclose anything to Jordan. Most people are free to buy and sell stock on the basis of valuable private knowledge without informing their trading partners. Strangers transact in markets all the time using private information that might be called "material" and, unless one has a duty to disclose, both may keep their counsel. Dirks v. SEC, 463 U.S. 646, 653–64, 77 L.Ed. 2d 911, 103 S.Ct. 3255 (1983); Chiarella v. United States, 445 U.S. 222, 227–35, 63 L.Ed. 2d 348, 100 S.Ct. 1108 (1980);. . . . The ability to make profits from the possession of information is the principal spur to create the information, which the parties and the market as a whole may find valuable. The absence of a duty to disclose may not justify a lie about a material fact, but Duff & Phelps did not lie to Jordan. It simply remained silent when Jordan quit and tendered the stock, and it offered the payment required by the Agreement.

This argument is unavailing on the facts as we know them. The "duty" in question is the fiduciary duty of corporate law. Close corporations buying their own stock, like knowledgeable insiders of closely held firms buying from outsiders, have a fiduciary duty to disclose material facts. . . . The "special facts" doctrine developed by several courts at the turn of the century is based on the principle that insiders in closely held firms may not buy stock from outsiders in person-to-person transactions without informing them of new events that substantially affect the value of the stock. . . .

Because the fiduciary duty is a standby or off-the-rack guess about what parties would agree to if they dickered about the subject explicitly, parties may contract with greater specificity for other arrangements. It is a violation of duty to steal from the corporate treasury; it is not a violation to write oneself a check that the board has approved as a bonus. . . . The obligation to break silence is itself based on state law, . . . and so may be redefined to the extent state law permits. . . . But we need not decide how far contracts can redefine obligations to disclose. Jordan was an employee at will; he signed no contract.

The stock was designed to bind Duff & Phelps's employees loyally to the firm. The buy-sell agreement tied ownership to employment. Understandably Duff & Phelps did not want a viper in its nest, a disgruntled employee remaining only in the hope of appreciation of his stock. So there could have been reason to divorce the employment decision from the value of the stock. Perhaps it would have been rational for each employee to agree with Duff & Phelps to look to salary alone in deciding whether to stay. A contractual agreement that the firm had no duty to disclose would have uncoupled the investment decision from the employment decision, leaving whoever was in the firm on the day of a merger to receive a surprise appreciation. . . .

Yet an explicit agreement to make all employment decisions in ignorance of the value of the stock might not have been in the interests of the firm or its employees. Duff & Phelps was trying to purchase loyalty by offering stock to its principal employees. The package of compensation contained salary and the prospect of appreciation of the stock. Perhaps it paid a lower salary than, say, Underwood Neuhaus & Co., because its package contained a higher component of gain from anticipated appreciation in the stock. It is therefore unwarranted to say that the implicit understanding between Jordan and Duff & Phelps should be treated as if it had such a no-duty clause; we are not confident that this is the clause firms and their employees regularly would prefer. . . .

The course of dealing between Jordan and Duff & Phelps suggests that the firm did not demand that employees decide whether to stay or go without regard to the value of the stock. It apparently informed Jordan what the book value was expected to be on December 31, 1983, so that Jordan could decide whether to leave in November (receiving the value as of December 31, 1982) or stay for another six weeks. The firm did not demand that Jordan depart as soon as it learned he had switched loyalties; it allowed employees to time their departures to obtain the maximum advantage from their stock. The Agreement did not ensure that employees disregard the value of the stock when deciding what to do, and neither did the usual practice at Duff & Phelps. So the possibility that a firm could negotiate around the fiduciary duty does not assist Duff & Phelps; it did not obtain such an agreement, express or implied.

The closest Duff & Phelps came is the provision in the Agreement fixing the price of the stock at book value. Yet although the Agreement fixed the price to be paid those who quit, it did not establish the terms on which anyone would leave. Thus cases such as Toledo Trust [Co. v. Nye, 588 F.2d 202, 206 (6th Cir.1978)] and St. Louis Union Trust Co. v. Merrill Lynch, Pierce, Fenner & Smith, Inc., 562 F.2d 1040 (8th Cir.1977), do not assist Duff & Phelps. These cases dealt with agreements calling for valuation at a formula price on a fixed date. In *St. Louis Union Trust* the date was the death of the employee, the formula was book value. The court of appeals held that there was no need to pay the employee's estate a different price, just because a few weeks later Merrill Lynch went public at a higher price. The employee presumably did not take the possibility of a merger into account in deciding whether to die, and the formula price made "disclosure" irrelevant. *Toledo Trust*, too, discussed a buy back triggered by death. . . . Jordan, though, exercised choice about the date on which the formula would be triggered. He could have remained at Duff & Phelps; his decision to depart was affected by his wife's distress, his salary, his working conditions, the enjoyment he received from the job, and the value of his stock. The departure of such an employee is an investment decision as much as it is an employment decision. It is not fanciful to suppose that Mrs. Jordan would have found her mother in law a whole lot more tolerable if she had known that Jordan's stock might shortly be worth 20 times book value.

. . .

Our dissenting colleague concludes that all of this is beside the point because Hansen could have said, on receiving Jordan's letter on November 16: "In a few weeks we will pull off a merger that would have made your stock 20 times more valuable. It's a shame you so foolishly resigned. But even if you hadn't resigned, we would have fired you, the better to engross the profits of the merger for ourselves. So long, sucker." This would have been permissible, under our colleague's interpretation, because Jordan was an employee at will and therefore could have been fired at any time, even the day before the merger, for any reason—including the desire to deprive Jordan of a share of the profits. The ability to fire Jordan enabled the firm to "call" his shares, at book value, on whim. On this view, it is foolish to say that Duff & Phelps had a duty to disclose, because disclosure would have been no use to Jordan. (Perhaps this is really an argument about "causation" rather than "duty," but the terminology is unimportant.) But Duff & Phelps itself does not press this argument, and in civil litigation an appellate court ought not put words in a party's mouth and use them as the grounds on which to decide. . . . Perhaps Duff & Phelps does not want to establish a reputation for shoddy dealing; as our dissenting brother observes, a firm's desire to preserve its reputation is a powerful inducement to treat its contractual partners well. To attribute to a litigant an argument that it will take every possible advantage is to assume that the party wishes to dissipate its reputation, and the assumption is unwarranted.

More than that, a person's status as an employee "at will" does not imply that the employer may discharge him for every reason. Illinois, where Jordan was employed, has placed some limits on the discharge of at-will employees. . . . But employment at will is still a contractual relation, one in which a particular duration ("at will") is implied in the absence of a contrary expression. . . . One term implied in every unwritten contract and therefore, we suppose, every written one, is that neither party will try to take opportunistic advantage of the other. "[T]he fundamental function of contract law (and recognized as such at least since Hobbes's day) is to deter people from behaving opportunistically toward their contracting parties, in order to encourage the optimal timing of economic activity and to make costly self-protective measures unnecessary." Richard A. Posner, Economic Analysis of Law 81 (3d ed. 1986). . . .

Employment creates occasions for opportunism. . . . The difficulties of separating opportunistic conduct from honest differences of opinion about an employee's performance on the job may lead firms and their employees to transact on terms that keep such disputes out of court—which employment at will usually does. But no one . . . doubts that an avowedly opportunistic discharge is a breach of contract, although the employment is at-will. . . .

. . . We do not suppose for a second that if Jordan had not resigned on November 16, the firm could have fired him on January 9 with a little note saying: "Dear Mr. Jordan: There will be a lucrative merger tomorrow. You have been a wonderful employee, but in order to keep the proceeds of the merger for ourselves, we are letting you go, effective this instant. Here is the $23,000 for your shares." Had the firm fired Jordan for this stated reason, it would have broken an implied pledge to avoid opportunistic conduct. . . .

The timing of the sale and the materiality of the information Duff & Phelps withheld on November 16 are for the jury to determine. Our dissenting colleague stresses that businesses would be shocked to learn that they must disclose valuable corporate information to fickle employees. If disclosure is unthinkable, however, Jordan may have trouble establishing that Duff & Phelps acted with intent to defraud, a necessary element of a case under Rule 10b–5. . . .

III

. . . Jordan is entitled only to damages, as his initial complaint requested. . . . But what might the damages be? Judge Leinenweber held that there are none, as a matter of law, because the merger with Security Pacific fell through. Doubtless the news of the deal with Security Pacific was the reason Jordan filed this suit. Yet the rationale of finding a securities violation—if there was one, a qualification we will not repeat—is that Jordan sold his stock in ignorance of facts that would have established a higher value. The relevance of the fact does not depend on how things turn out. Just as a lie that overstates a firm's prospects is a violation even if, against all odds, every fantasy comes true, . . . so a failure to disclose an important beneficent event is a violation even if things later go sour. The news, here that some firm was willing to pay $50 million for Duff & Phelps in an arms' length transaction, allows investors to assess the worth of the stock. If one deal for $50 million falls through, another may be possible at a similar price. Investors will either hold the stock or demand a price that reflects the value of that information. The conclusion that because the first deal collapsed there are no damages must reflect a belief that if the firm was not worth $50 million, then it was worth only $2.5 million (its book value). That is implausible. Security Pacific was willing to pay $50 million because, it concluded, Duff & Phelps was worth that much. If it was worth that much to Security Pacific, it was worth that much to someone else. Some value may be produced by interactions unique to Security Pacific, but there is no reason to think that Security Pacific would pay the investors of Duff & Phelps for the elements of value Security Pacific brought to the deal. The price of an asset usually is what the second-highest bidder will pay. So if Security Pacific bid $50 million, it believed that someone else would pay that much too (or that Duff & Phelps would hold out as part of a risky gaming strategy); otherwise Security Pacific would have bid less. The end of Security Pacific's bid—for reasons unrelated to a reassessment of the value of Duff & Phelps—therefore does not show that Jordan was uninjured. And less than a year later Duff & Phelps sold the firm to a trust (which is to say, to the syndicate of banks that loaned the money to the trust) for about $40 million.

The sticky problem is not whether Jordan can show some damages in principle but whether he can establish causation. . . . Because of the Agreement, employment and ownership of the shares were tied. Jordan could sell his stock in two ways: by leaving the firm and receiving book value, or by holding the stock until a merger or LBO [that is, leveraged buyout, which is the type of transaction that was ultimately concluded] and receiving the offered price. Even if the stock was worth more than book value, Jordan could not receive that price without holding on. So it seems that to recover, Jordan must establish that on learning of the negotiations with Security Pacific he would have dropped plans to go to Houston, and that even after the disappointment of the Fed's action that scuttled the deal with Security Pacific Jordan would have stuck around until the end of 1985, finally receiving the payment from the LBO. Judge Hart denied defendants' motion for summary judgment, holding that causation is a question for the jury. We think that right. Because a reasonable investor would not conclude that the withdrawal of one bid implies that there will be no others—and because Jordan would have known of the board's decision to sell the firm—a jury would be entitled to conclude that Jordan would have stuck around. Difficulties with a mother-in-law are a strain, but families bear strains greater than that for the prospect of financial gain.

. . .

REVERSED AND REMANDED

[The short concurring opinion of Judge Cudahy is omitted.]

■ POSNER, CIRCUIT JUDGE, dissenting. A corporate employee at will quit, owning shares that he had agreed to sell back to the corporation at book value. The agreement was explicit that his status as a shareholder conferred no job rights on him. Nevertheless the court holds that the corporation had, as a matter of law, a duty, enforceable by proceedings under Rule 10b–5 of the Securities Exchange Act, to volunteer to the employee information about the corporation's prospects that might have led him to change his mind about quitting, although as an employee at will he had no right to change his mind. I disagree with this holding. The terms of the stockholder agreement show that there was no duty of disclosure, and since there was no duty there was no violation of Rule 10b–5.

. . .

We should ask why liability for failing to disclose, as distinct from liability for outright misrepresentation, depends on proof of duty. The reason is that information is a valuable commodity, and its production is discouraged if the producer must share it with the whole world. Hence an investor is not required to blurt out his secrets, and a skilled investor is not required to disclose the results of his research and insights before he is able to profit from them. . . . But one who makes a contract, express or implied, to disclose information to another acts wrongfully if he then withholds the information. The question is whether Duff and Phelps made an undertaking, and therefore assumed a duty, to disclose to any stockholding employee who announced his resignation information regarding the prospects for a profitable sale of the company.

My brethren find such a duty implicit in the fiduciary relationship between a closely held corporation and its shareholders. By this approach, what should be the beginning of analysis becomes its end. . . . [T]he mere existence of a fiduciary relationship between a corporation and its shareholders does not require disclosure of material information to the shareholders. A further inquiry is necessary, and here must focus on the particulars of Jordan's relationship with Duff and Phelps.

. . . The contingent nature of Jordan's status as a shareholder [that is, he could remain a shareholder only if he also remained an employee] has a twofold significance. First, it raises a question about the applicability of the majority's rule requiring disclosure "in the course of negotiating to purchase stock." One may doubt whether there was any real negotiation in this case, for once Jordan resigned he was contractually obligated to sell back his stock at a predetermined price. Second, and more important, the contingent nature of Jordan's status as a shareholder negates the existence of a right to be informed and hence a duty to disclose. This point is central to my dissent and has now to be explained.

Jordan's deal with Duff and Phelps required him to surrender his stock at book value if he left the company. It didn't matter whether he quit or was fired, retired or died; the agreement is explicit on these matters. My brethren hypothesize "implicit parts of the relations between Duff & Phelps and its employees." But those relations are totally defined by (1) the absence of an employment contract, which made Jordan an employee at will; (2) the shareholder agreement, which has no "implicit parts" that bear on Duff and Phelps' duty to Jordan, and explicitly ties his rights as a shareholder to his status as an employee at will; (3) a provision in the stock purchase agreement between Jordan and Duff and Phelps (signed at the same time as the shareholder agreement) that "nothing herein contained shall confer on the Employee any right to be continued in the employment of the Corporation." There is no occasion to speculate about "the implicit understanding" between Jordan and Duff and Phelps. The parties left nothing to the judicial imagination. The effect of the shareholder and stock purchase agreements (which for simplicity I shall treat as a single "stockholder agreement"), against a background of employment at will, was to strip Jordan of any contractual protection against what happened to him, and indeed against worse that might have happened to him. Duff and Phelps points out that it would not have had to let Jordan withdraw his resignation had he gotten wind of the negotiations with Security Pacific and wanted to withdraw it. On November 14 Hansen could have said to Jordan, "I accept your resignation effective today; we hope to sell Duff and Phelps for $50 million but have no desire to see you participate in the resulting bonanza. You will receive the paltry book value of your shares as of December 31, 1982." The "nothing herein contained" provision in the stockholder agreement shows that this tactic is permitted. Equally, on November 14, at the board meeting before Hansen knew that Jordan wanted to quit, the board could have decided to fire Jordan in order to increase the value of the deal with Security Pacific to the remaining shareholders.

. . .

My brethren correctly observe that, "Because the fiduciary duty is a standby or off-the-rack guess about what parties would agree to if they dickered about the subject explicitly, parties may contract with greater specificity for other arrangements." But, they add, "we need not decide how far contracts can redefine obligations to disclose. Jordan was an employee at will; he signed no contract." It is true that he signed no contract of employment, but he signed a stockholder agreement that defined his rights as a shareholder "with greater specificity." The agreement entitled Duff and Phelps to terminate Jordan as shareholder, subject only to a duty to buy back his shares at book value. The arrangement that resulted (call it "shareholder at will") is incompatible with an inference that Duff and Phelps undertook to keep him abreast of developments affecting the value of the firm.

. . .

Since receipt of the information would have conferred no right on Jordan to benefit from the information, how can the parties be thought to have intended Duff and Phelps to have an enforceable duty to disclose the information to him? There is no duty to give shareholders information that they have no right to benefit from. . . . By signing the stockholder agreement Jordan gave Duff and Phelps in effect an option . . . to buy back his stock at any time at a fixed price. The grant of the option denied Jordan the right to profit from any information that the company might have about its prospects but prefer not to give him. If Hansen had known of the rule of law that my brethren adopt today, he could have avoided liability simply by telling Jordan that, come what may, December 30 would be Jordan's last day working for Duff and Phelps. Failure to disclose would be immaterial because Jordan could not act on the disclosure. Only because Hansen failed to make Jordan's resignation effective immediately (a generous gesture, which we have given Hansen cause to regret), as he could have done without violating any contractual obligation, is he held to have violated a duty of disclosure.

. . .

Was Jordan a fool to have become a shareholder of Duff and Phelps on such disadvantageous terms as I believe he agreed to? (If so, that might be a reason for doubting whether those were the real terms.) He was not. Few business executives in this country have contractual entitlements to earnings, bonuses, or even retention of their jobs. They would rather take their chances on their employer's good will and interest in reputation, and on their own bargaining power and value to the firm, than pay for contract rights that are difficult and costly to enforce. . . . If Jordan had had greater rights as a shareholder he would have had a lower salary; when he went to work for a new employer in Houston and received no stock rights he got a higher salary.

I go further: Jordan was protected by Duff and Phelps' own self-interest from being exploited. The principal asset of a service company such as Duff and Phelps is good will. It is a product largely of its employees' efforts and skills. If Jordan were a particularly valuable employee, so that the firm would be worth less without him, Hansen, desiring as he did to sell the firm for the highest possible price, would have told him about the prospects for selling the company. If Jordan was not a particularly valuable employee—if his departure would not reduce the value of the firm—there was no reason why he should participate in the profits from the sale of the firm, unless perhaps he had once been a particularly valuable employee but had ceased to be so. That possibility might, but did not, lead him to negotiate for an employment contract, or for stock rights that would outlast his employment. By the type of agreement that he made with Duff and Phelps, Jordan gambled that he was and would continue to be such a good employee that he would be encouraged to stay long enough to profit from the firm's growth. The relationship that the parties created aligned their respective self-interests better than the legal protections that the court devises today.

My brethren are well aware that Duff and Phelps faced market constraints against exploiting its employee shareholders, but seem to believe that this implies that the company also assumed contractual duties. Businessmen, however, are less enthusiastic about contractual duties than lawyers are, . . . so it is incorrect to infer from the existence of market constraints against exploitation that the parties also imposed a contractual duty against exploitation. Contractual obligation is a source of uncertainty and cost, and is therefore an expensive way of backstopping market forces. That is why employment at will is such a common form of employment relationship. It is strange to infer that firms invariably assume a legal obligation not to do what is not in their self-interest to do, and stranger to suppose—in the face of an explicit disclaimer—that by "allowing employees to time their departures to obtain the maximum advantage from their stock," Duff and Phelps obligated itself to allow them to do this.

Having earlier in its opinion tried to get mileage out of the fact that Jordan "signed no [employment] contract," the majority later tries to get additional mileage from the observation that employment at will is a "contractual relation." This is the kind of legal half-truth that should make us thankful that our opinions are not subject to Rule 10b–5. Employment at will is a voluntary relationship, and thus contractual in the sense in which the word contract is used in the expression "freedom of contract." And the relationship can provide a framework for contracting: if Duff and Phelps had not paid Jordan his agreed-on wage after he had earned it, he could have sued the company for breach of contract. But the only element of employment at will that is relevant to this case is that employment at will is terminable at will, meaning that the employer can fire the employee without worrying about legal sanctions and likewise the employee can quit without worrying about them. Freedom of contract includes freedom not to contract.

. . .

The inroads that the majority opinion makes on freedom of contract are not justified by its quotation from my academic writings concerning the purpose of contract law (which presupposes an agreement that the parties regard as legally enforceable) or by the possibility that corporations will exploit their junior executives, which may well be the least urgent problem facing our nation. The majority's statement that "one term implied in every written contract and therefore, we suppose, every unwritten one, is that neither party will try to take opportunistic advantage of the other" confuses the underlying rationale of contract law with the actual requirements of that law, and is anyway irrelevant since the parties decided not to subject the relevant parts of their relationship to the law of contracts and not to give Jordan any contractual protections against being fired. There was no "implied pledge to avoid opportunistic conduct" any more than there were "implicit parts of the relations" giving rise to contractual obligations. . . .

. . .

ANALYSIS

1. What relationship should be the focus of attention in this case: employer and employee, corporation and shareholder, or majority shareholder and minority shareholder? In other words, is this an employee-compensation case or a shareholder-oppression case? Or is it just an old-fashioned contract case, with the terms incompletely specified?

2. What is the relevance, if any, of fraud or fiduciary obligation? How do these questions bear on the question whether the plaintiff is entitled to relief under § 10(b) and Rule 10b–5? Is it possible to ignore all the linguistic frameworks, the legal "cubbyholes," and examine the case in some other, more fundamental way? One possibility is to describe the facts as objectively as possible and then to examine various possible outcomes in light of the goals or criteria of a good system of rules of law for such situations. What are those goals or criteria? What are the implicit criteria applied by Judge Easterbrook? By Judge Posner?

3. Judge Easterbrook asserts, "Duff & Phelps was trying to purchase loyalty by offering stock to its principal employees." Is that statement accurate? Helpful?

4. Suppose Jordan's contract with Duff & Phelps made clear that his employment could be terminated at any time, even if termination meant that he would lose out on an expected appreciation in the value of his shares, and that Duff & Phelps had no obligation to provide him with any information regarding the value of his shares. Or suppose that the contract had provided clearly that all that Jordan could ever expect was the book value of his shares; that he would never be entitled to the benefit of a sale of the entire corporation. Would Jordan have been foolish to accept employment on those terms? Would enforcement of such a term in the contract be "opportunistic"? A violation of Rule 10b–5?

5. How would Jordan have fared (without benefit of litigation) if his contract with Duff & Phelps had provided for a buyout at "fair market value" rather than book value? Why did the parties use book value?

5. CONTROL, DURATION, AND STATUTORY DISSOLUTION

In this section, as in the preceding section, we examine situations in which minority shareholders of closely held corporations claim that they have been treated unfairly by the majority. In the cases in this section, however, the minority shareholders have invoked special statutory provisions allowing the courts to order dissolution in certain circumstances and the general equitable powers of the courts. We will now focus our attention on those statutory provisions and equitable powers, on the remedies available under them, and on the strategies both majority and minority shareholders should consider.

Alaska Plastics, Inc. v. Coppock

621 P.2d 270 (Alaska 1980).

The issue in this case involves the rights of a minority shareholder in a close corporation who allegedly has been deprived of benefits accorded other shareholders. The trial judge concluded that the corporation was obligated to buy the minority shareholder's stock at its fair value. We have concluded that this remedy is not available on the present record as a matter of law. Accordingly, we remand to the superior court to determine whether, based upon adequate findings of fact and conclusions of law, a remedy more appropriate to the alleged facts is available.

Those facts which the parties have stipulated to or which appear to be undisputed in the record are summarized below.

In 1961 the three individual appellants, Ralph Stefano, C. Harold Gillam, and Robert Crow formed a corporation known as Alaska Plastics and began to produce foam insulation at a building they bought in Fairbanks. Each of the three incorporators held 300 shares of stock. In 1970 Crow was divorced and, as part of a property settlement, gave his former wife, Patricia Muir, 150 shares or a one-sixth interest in the corporation.[1] From the time of incorporation until this lawsuit, Stefano, Gillam and Crow have been the only directors and officers of Alaska Plastics.

Stefano conceded at trial that the corporation forgot to notify Muir of annual shareholders meetings in 1971 and 1974. It was also undisputed that Muir was not notified of a shareholders meeting in 1972. According to Muir's testimony she was told of the 1973 shareholders meeting about three hours before the meeting was held.

In 1971 and 1972, Stefano, Gillam and Crow held the shareholders meetings in Seattle. It appears from Stefano's testimony that he and Gillam also brought their wives to these meetings at company expense, but he conceded that there was no business purpose for doing so.

In 1971, Stefano, Gillam and Crow voted themselves each a $3,000 annual director's fee. Although director's fees were apparently paid from 1971 through 1974, the three directors have never authorized Alaska Plastics to pay dividends. In 1974 the three board members also authorized an annual salary of $30,000 a year for Gillam, who was then

1 At the time this action was filed Muir had remarried and assumed the name of Patricia Coppock. She has since that time resumed using her maiden name.

employed as general manager of Alaska Plastics. Muir testified that she has never received any money from the corporation.

At the 1974 board meeting Stefano, Gillam and Crow also decided to offer Muir $15,000 for her shares and on May 1, 1974, Stefano wrote Muir informing her of the corporation's offer. Thinking the firm's offer was too low, Muir retained a lawyer who wrote the corporation expressing her concern both regarding the offered price and regarding the corporation's failure to inform Muir of shareholders meetings. In July, 1974, Muir's lawyer made a further demand on the corporation to inspect the books and records of the corporation. Gillam apparently advised Muir where the firm kept its books and told her they could be made available. An accountant employed by Muir did investigate the company's books and estimated that the shares might have a value somewhere between $23,000 and $40,000. Muir also ordered an appraisal of Alaska Plastics' Fairbanks property.

Later that same year, at a special director's meeting in October, 1974, the three board members agreed to make a $50,000 offer for Broadwater Industries, a firm located near Palmer that made a type of plastic foam insulation similar to that produced by Alaska Plastics at their Fairbanks plant. The purchase was apparently accomplished at some time between October and the next shareholders meeting, which was held on April 25, 1975. Muir testified that she was never consulted about the purchase and first learned about it at the 1975 meeting. At that meeting, however, she did not dissent from a shareholder vote ratifying all the acts of the directors and officers for the previous year.

Broadwater Industries was subsequently renamed Valley Plastics and is now a wholly-owned subsidiary of Alaska Plastics. The directors and officers of Valley Plastics are Stefano, Gillam and Crow.

At the 1975 shareholders meeting, Muir offered her stock to the corporation for $40,000. In June, 1975, the board raised its offer to $20,000, which Muir again rejected.

Shortly after these negotiations failed, Alaska Plastics' Fairbanks plant, which was not insured, burned to the ground. The fire caused a total loss. Since the fire, Alaska Plastics has ceased production from Fairbanks and the corporation has not made an attempt to resume production in Fairbanks. All the remaining manufacturing and sales of Alaska Plastics are accomplished through its subsidiary, Valley Plastics. The fire, in effect, turned Alaska Plastics into a holding company for its affiliate.

About a year after the fire, in 1976, Stefano, acting as an individual, made a further offer of $20,000 to Muir, but the purchase never took place. Further attempts by the parties to negotiate a purchase or settlement failed and a lawsuit was filed in October 1976.

An amended complaint alleges ten separate causes of action, and prays for relief both in the name of the corporation and individually for Muir. After trial, . . . the trial judge issued a judgment which states in part:

> "[T]he continued retention by Plaintiff of one-sixth of the shares in Alaska Plastics, Inc. following the offer on April 1974 was oppressive to Plaintiff and . . . an appropriate remedy would be

to direct the transfer of Plaintiff's shares to Alaska Plastics, Inc. in exchange for a fair and equitable value. . . ."

A total judgment was entered against the three individual appellants and Alaska Plastics for $52,314, which represented $32,000 for the value of the shares, $5,200 for attorney's fees, and $15,144 in interest and costs. Muir was in turn required to convey her shares to Alaska Plastics. Both sides subsequently filed appeals.

I. SHAREHOLDER REMEDIES

In a corporation with publicly traded stock, dissatisfied shareholders can sell their stock on the market, recover their assets, and invest elsewhere. In a close corporation there is not likely to be a ready market for the corporation's shares. The corporation itself, or one of the other individual shareholders of the corporation, who are likely to provide the only market, may not be interested in buying out another shareholder. If they are interested, majority shareholders who control operating policy are in a unique position to "squeeze out" a minority shareholder at an unreasonably low price.

From a dissatisfied shareholder's point of view, the most successful remedy is likely to be a requirement that the corporation buy his or her shares at their fair value. Ordinarily, there are four ways in which this can occur. First, there may be a provision in the articles of incorporation or by-laws that provides for the purchase of shares by the corporation, contingent upon the occurrence of some event, such as the death of a shareholder or transfer of shares. Second, the shareholder may petition the court for involuntary dissolution of the corporation. Third, upon some significant change in corporate structure, such as a merger, the shareholder may demand a statutory right of appraisal. Finally, in some circumstances, a purchase may be justified as an equitable remedy upon a finding of a breach of a fiduciary duty between directors and shareholders and the corporation or other shareholders.

It does not appear from the record that there is any provision in the articles of incorporation or by-laws which would allow Muir to force Alaska Plastics to purchase her shares. Muir has not suggested that there is such provision, and we, therefore, do not consider the availability of this first method.

As to the second method, Alaska's corporation code provides in AS 10.05.540(2) that a shareholder may bring an action to liquidate the assets of a corporation upon a showing that "the acts of the directors or those in control of the corporation are illegal, oppressive or fraudulent. . . ." A shareholder may also seek liquidation when "corporate assets are being misapplied or wasted." AS 10.05.540(4). Upon a liquidation of assets all creditors and the cost of liquidation must be paid and the remainder distributed among all the shareholders "according to their respective rights and interests." AS 10.05.561. There is no indication whether Muir would have received more or less than the $32,000 price for her shares ordered by the court if Alaska Plastics had been liquidated.

Liquidation is an extreme remedy. In a sense, forced dissolution allows minority shareholders to exercise retaliatory oppression against the majority. Absent compelling circumstances, courts often are reluctant to order involuntary dissolution. . . . As a result, courts have recognized alternative remedies based upon their inherent equitable powers. Thus in Baker [v. Commercial Body Builders, Inc., 264 Or. 614, 507 P.2d 387, 395–97 (1973)], interpreting a statute substantially similar to AS 10.05.540, the court authorized numerous alternative remedies for oppressive or fraudulent conduct by the majority. Among those would be:

> "an order requiring the corporation or a majority of its stockholders to purchase the stock of the minority shareholders at a price to be determined according to a specified formula or at a price determined by the court to be a fair and reasonable price." (footnote omitted).

Baker, 507 P.2d at 396. . . .

We are persuaded by *Baker* and conclude that Muir's request in her amended complaint for liquidation, although not actively pursued, could justify the trial court's order as an equitable remedy less drastic than liquidation. To prevail on this basis, Muir must establish on remand that the acts of Stefano, Gillam and Crow were "illegal, oppressive or fraudulent," AS 10.05.540(2), or alternatively, constituted a waste or misapplication of corporate assets. AS 10.05.540(4). Because the trial court did not reach the issue, we express no opinion here on whether Muir has satisfied the statutory standards of AS 10.05.540.

The third method of forcing a corporation to purchase a minority shareholder's shares is a statutory appraisal remedy, which may be available under the Alaska Business Corporation Act in two circumstances where there is some fundamental corporate change. The remedy is available upon the merger or consolidation with another corporation, AS 10.05.417, or upon a sale of substantially all of the corporation's assets. AS 10.05.447. There is no suggestion that either statute is applicable in this case. In some circumstances, however, courts have found that a corporate transaction so fundamentally changes the nature of the business that there is a "de facto" merger which triggers the same statutory appraisal remedy.

[The court concludes that the "de facto" merger doctrine is not applicable in this case. That doctrine is examined later in this casebook. Chapter 6, Sec. 1.]

We turn, then, to the fourth possibility by which a minority shareholder may force a corporation to purchase his or her shares. Two leading cases have concluded that transactions by one group of shareholders that enable it to derive some special benefit not shared in common by all shareholders should be subject to close judicial scrutiny. The Massachusetts Supreme Judicial Court concluded that shareholders in closely held corporations owe one another a fiduciary duty:

> "Because of the fundamental resemblance of the close corporation to the partnership, the trust and confidence which are essential to this scale and manner of enterprise, and the inherent danger to minority interests in the close corporation, we hold that stockholders in the close corporation owe one another substantially the same fiduciary duty in the operation of the enterprise that partners owe to one another. In our previous decisions, we have defined the standard of duty owed by partners to one another as the 'utmost good faith and loyalty.' " (footnotes and citations omitted).

Donahue v. Rodd Electrotype Co., 367 Mass. 578, 328 N.E.2d 505, 515 (1975). The California Supreme Court concluded that a controlling group of shareholders owes a similar duty to minority shareholders. In Jones v. H.F. Ahmanson & Co., 1 Cal.3d 93, 81 Cal.Rptr. 592, 460 P.2d 464 (1969), the court held that a control block of stock could not be used to give the majority benefits that were not shared with the minority.

We believe that *Donahue* and *Ahmanson* correctly state the law applicable to the relationship between shareholders in closely held corporations, or between those holding a controlling block of stock, and minority shareholders. We do not believe, though, that the existence and breach of a fiduciary duty among corporate shareholders supports the appraisal remedy ordered by the trial court in this case.

The trial judge made no findings of fact or conclusions of law, but the basis for his decision is clear from extensive discussions that took place prior to instructing the jury and the form of the judge's final order. The court concluded that once the corporation made an offer to Muir it was under an obligation to purchase her stock at a "fair" price, regardless of what price the corporation had initially offered. Had Muir actually sold the stock at an unfairly low price, she might have brought an action to set the transaction aside. The existence of a fiduciary duty between shareholders would justify careful scrutiny and shifting the burden onto the defendants to show that the transaction was fail. . . . In this case, however, Muir rejected both of the corporation's offers. We are not aware of any authority which would allow a court to order specific performance on the basis of an unaccepted offer, particularly on terms totally different from those offered. Such a rule would place a court in the impossible position of making and enforcing contracts between unwilling parties.

Donahue and *Ahmanson* do suggest the appropriate form of a remedy in this case, however. In *Donahue,* one of the controlling shareholders caused the corporation to purchase forty-five of his shares, but then refused to buy an equal number of shares held by a minority shareholder. The court first noted the benefit that a shareholder in a close corporation gained by forcing the corporation to buy his shares.

> "The benefits conferred by the purchase are twofold: (1) provision of a market for shares; (2) access to corporate assets for personal use. By definition, there is no ready market for shares of a close corporation. The purchase creates a market for shares which previously had been unmarketable. It transforms a previously illiquid investment into a liquid one."

328 N.E.2d at 518. The court then went on to conclude that where a controlling shareholder took advantage of such a special benefit, the fiduciary duty owed to other shareholders required that the corporation offer such a benefit equally:

> "The rule of equal opportunity in stock purchases by close corporations provides equal access to these benefits for all stockholders."

Id. at 519.

In *Ahmanson,* the controlling group of shareholders transferred its control block of stock to a holding company which in turn offered its stock to the public. There were relatively few shares of stock in the active company in which the plaintiffs owned shares, and the price of each share was so high that they had little market appeal. The holding company, on the other hand, offered numerous shares at far lower prices. Because of the ready market for holding company shares, the controlling shareholders were able to sell part of their investment in the active company through the holding company at a huge profit. The court held that the majority shareholders had to offer this same opportunity to minority shareholders.

As we read Muir's complaint, the essence of her action is that Stefano, Gillam and Crow enjoyed benefits from the corporation which should have been shared equally with her. None of the other shareholders of Alaska Plastics have sold their stock to the corporation so it would not be appropriate to order the corporation to purchase Muir's stock. Unlike *Donahue,* this was not one of the benefits which the majority received and which they did not share with Muir. There was evidence, however, that the corporation paid Stefano, Gillam and Crow "director's fees." Gillam received a substantial salary. The corporation apparently paid some of the personal expenses of the directors' wives. Regardless of how the corporation labels these expenditures, if they were not made for the reasonable value of services rendered to the corporation, some portion of these payments might be characterized as constructive dividends.

We express no opinion as to whether Muir has shown that these payments were a distribution of dividends, whether she was deprived of other corporate benefits which she should have shared in equally with the other three shareholders, or whether the majority shareholders violated AS 10.05.540. The case must be remanded to the trial court to make appropriate findings of fact and conclusions of law based upon the present record.

II. THE DERIVATIVE CLAIM

At the conclusion of trial, the judge dismissed Muir's derivative suit. In her brief, Muir suggests that a number of acts taken by the corporation amounted to a breach of the director's duty of care toward the corporation. For example, the directors failed to insure the Fairbanks plant, they kept large reserves of cash in noninterest-bearing checking accounts, and they loaned an employee money at a rate below prevailing rates of interest. Viewing the plaintiff's evidence alone, which amounted to little more than the fact that these acts had taken place, we conclude that the evidence was insufficient to establish a breach of duty towards the corporation.

Judges are not business experts, Dodge v. Ford Motor Co., 204 Mich. 459, 170 N.W. 668, 684 (1919), a fact which has become expressed in the so-called "business judgment rule." The essence of that doctrine is that courts are reluctant to substitute their judgment for that of the board of directors unless the board's decisions are unreasonable. No *proof* was presented that the alleged acts were unreasonable in the sense that they would not have been taken by "an ordinarily prudent man . . . in the management of his own affairs of like magnitude and importance." Nanfito v. Tekseed Hybrid Co., 341 F.Supp. 240, 244 (D.Neb.1972). The proof offered was therefore insufficient to present a question for the trier of fact.

In Santarelli v. Katz, 270 F.2d 762 (7th Cir.1959), the evidence showed that one of the director's wives in a closely held corporation had been receiving thousands of dollars a year to attend three or four conventions. In a stockholders derivative suit, the court noted:

> "[I]f a stockholder is being unjustly deprived of dividends that should be his, a court of equity will not permit management to cloak itself in the immunity of the business judgment rule."

Id. at 768.

There is thus authority for concluding that an unfair distribution of corporate funds would be a proper subject for a derivative suit. Nevertheless, as we read the gravamen of Muir's complaint, it is that she was harmed as an individual by not receiving the same benefits as the other shareholders received, not that the corporation itself was harmed. Therefore, we believe that a derivative action would not be the appropriate form of action in this case, . . . Furthermore, Muir's rights are adequately protected by an individual action. The trial court thus properly dismissed this claim.

The case is REMANDED to the superior court for further proceedings in accordance with this opinion.

AFTERMATH

On remand, the trial court entered a judgment for Muir for $32,000 as the fair and reasonable value of her shares. On appeal, the Supreme Court upheld the trial court's "findings of oppressive or fraudulent conduct sufficient to warrant a remedy as 'drastic' as involuntary dissolution of the corporation or a forced buy-out of Muir's shares." Stefano v. Coppock, 705 P.2d 443 (Alaska 1985). The Supreme Court stated:

> It is clear that AS § 10.05.540(2) allows the superior court to liquidate a corporation when it is shown that the acts of those in control are oppressive or fraudulent. However, courts retain equitable authority to fashion a less drastic remedy to fit the parties' situation.

NOTE ON MEISELMAN V. MEISELMAN

In a leading case, Meiselman v. Meiselman, 309 N.C. 279, 307 S.E.2d 551 (1983), the corporation owned movie theaters and real estate, with a book value of over $11 million. The shareholders were brothers, Ira and Michael Meiselman, whose father had founded the business. Ira, the younger of the brothers, was the majority shareholder (by virtue of disproportionate gifts from the father) and ran the business. Michael had been excluded from management decision-making but had been employed in the business and had drawn a salary for many years. Over the years there had been personal antagonism between Ira and Michael. In 1979, Michael filed suit against Ira, complaining of the fact that Ira owned 100 percent of the shares of a company that provided management services to the jointly owned corporation. Shortly thereafter, Michael was fired and thereby lost his salary and fringe benefits. He did, however, receive dividends ($54,591 in 1979 and $61,845 in 1980). Michael then filed the suit that gave rise to the cited decision. Initially he sought dissolution but subsequently changed the claim for relief and sought to compel the corporation to buy his shares for a fair price.

Michael invoked N.C.G.S. § 55–125(a), which allows a court to order dissolution where such relief is "reasonably necessary for the protection of the rights and interests of the complaining shareholder." Under § 55–125.1, the court may, as an alternative to dissolution, order a buy-out of the complaining shareholder's shares. The trial court denied relief. The Supreme Court returned the case to the trial court, holding that, at least in cases involving close corporations, the complaining shareholder need not establish oppressive or fraudulent conduct by the controlling shareholder or shareholders. Instead, it said, "rights and interests," under the statute include "reasonable expectations," which include expectations that the minority shareholder "will participate in the management of the business or be employed by the company," but limited to "expectations embodied in understandings, express or implied, among the participants." In its lengthy opinion, the court referred to the statutes of seven states (Illinois, Maryland, Michigan, New Jersey, New York, South Carolina, and Virginia) in which dissolution may be granted for oppressive conduct, with some decisions under these statutes interpreting "oppressive" broadly; and statutes in three states (California, Michigan, and New Jersey) in which dissolution (or other relief) may be granted for "unfair" conduct. The court also relied on the writings of Professors O'Neal and Hetherington in support of the idea that it is often unrealistic to expect minority shareholders in close corporations to bargain for protection of their expectations and that, consequently, judicial intervention on their behalf is appropriate.

ANALYSIS AND PLANNING

1. In Alaska Plastics, Inc. v. Coppock, did the trial court have authority to order dissolution? If it had ordered dissolution, what do you suppose would have happened?

2. What was the legal theory for the remedy that the court ordered on remand? What was the virtue of that remedy? What other remedies might the court have ordered and what are the virtues and defects of each?

3. Why was Muir not required to pursue her derivative action? Would a judgment on the derivative claim have given Muir all that to which she was entitled?

4. Suppose that the individual defendants had caused the corporation to offer either to buy Muir's one-sixth interest in the corporation for $25,000 or to sell the other five-sixths of the corporation to her for the same pro rata price, $125,000, and she had refused either to sell or to buy. Would the trial court still have had authority to order that her shares be purchased for $32,000?

5. Suppose the defendants had never offered to buy Muir's shares. Would Muir's case have been weaker or stronger?

6. Suppose that before the case came to trial the individual defendants had each repaid to the corporation $2,500 of their annual directors' fees, plus the expenses for which they had been reimbursed for attending meetings of the board, plus interest. Could the trial court still have ordered the defendants to buy Muir's shares?

7. Suppose you had represented Patricia Muir at the time of her divorce from Robert Crow and that Crow had no cash to buy out Muir's

interest in the shares of stock of the corporation. What kind of deal would you have sought with respect to the shares?

8. Suppose you had represented all three of the original investors at the time of the formation of the corporation and you had been aware that Crow's marriage was in difficulty. What would you have advised in anticipation of the possibility that Muir might claim a right to half of the shares of stock of the corporation that were to be issued to Crow?

NOTE AND QUESTION ON LIMITED LIABILITY COMPANIES

Under the Delaware Limited Liability Co. Act, § 18–604:

> [U]pon resignation, any resigning member is entitled to receive any distribution to which he is entitled under a limited liability company agreement and, if not otherwise provided in a limited liability company agreement, he is entitled to receive, within a reasonable time after resignation, the fair value of his limited liability company interest as of the date of resignation based upon his right to share in distributions from the limited liability company.

This provision roughly parallels the partnership rules outlined in Chapter 2, Sections 1 and 8.

Consider the implications. If investors form a corporation, the default rule generally will be one of no right to dissolution or buyout. If investors want the right to "put" their stock to the firm, they must so provide in their charter or a shareholders' agreement. If they instead form an LLC, the default rule will grant them that right. Granted, LLC members can modify the default rule through their organizational documents. What modifications are likely to be desirable?

Haley v. Talcott

864 A.2d 86 (Del. Ch. 2004).

Plaintiff Matthew James Haley has moved for summary judgment of his claim seeking dissolution of Matt and Greg Real Estate, LLC ("the LLC"). Haley and defendant Gregory L. Talcott are the only members of the LLC, each owning a 50% interest in the LLC. Haley brings this action in reliance upon § 18–802 of the Delaware Limited Liability Company Act which permits this court to "decree dissolution of a limited liability company whenever it is not reasonably practicable to carry on the business in conformity with a limited liability company agreement." The question before the court is whether dissolution of the LLC should be granted, as Haley requests, or whether, as Talcott contends, Haley is limited to the contractually-provided exit mechanism in the LLC Agreement.

Haley and Talcott have suffered, to put it mildly, a falling out. There is no rational doubt that they cannot continue to do business as 50% members of an LLC. But the path to separating their interests is complicated by a second company, Delaware Seafood, also known as the Redfin Seafood Grill ("Redfin Grill"), a restaurant that, at the risk of slightly oversimplifying, was owned by Talcott and, before the falling out, operated by Haley under an employment contract that gave him a 50%

share in the profits. The LLC owns the land that the Redfin Grill occupies under an expired lease. The resolution of the current case and the ultimate fate of the LLC therefore critically affect the continued existence of a second business that one party owns and that the other bitterly contends, in other litigation pending before this court, wrongly terminated him.

The question before the court is essentially how the interests of the members of the LLC are to be separated. . . .

I. *Factual Background*

. . . Haley and Talcott have known each other since the 1980s. . . . In 2001, Haley found the location for what would become the Redfin Grill. Talcott contributed substantial start-up money and Haley managed the Redfin Grill without drawing a salary for the first year.

The structure of the agreements between the parties forming the Redfin Grill is complex and the subject of additional litigation before this court. For reasons that are not relevant, Haley and Talcott chose to create and operate the Redfin Grill as an entity solely owned by Talcott, with Haley's rights and obligations being defined by a series of contracts. . . .

The Employment Contract, although structured as an agreement between an employer and an employee, makes clear that the parties were operating the business as a joint venture. The Employment Contract specified that Haley reported to Talcott and that Talcott had the right to reevaluate and revise Haley's decisions, but indicated that "such action is not anticipated." It also provided that Haley's "bonus" would be one half of the net profits of the Redfin Grill, after the initial loan from Talcott was repaid. Moreover, Talcott would materially breach the Employment Contract, and Haley could end his employment for cause, if Talcott amended Haley's duties such that his position as "Operations Director" became one of "less dignity, responsibility, importance or scope." The Employment Contract further clarified Haley's importance to the enterprise by awarding him one half of any proceeds from any sale of the Redfin Grill. Finally, the Employment Contract limited Talcott's ability to remove Haley from his active role:

> [N]otwithstanding the language in the Employment Agreement relating to termination, individually, I [Talcott] will assure you that the Employment Agreement will not be terminable under any circumstances unless an event occurs that would entitle you payment of a Retention Bonus as set forth in the Retention Bonus Agreement that is part of this transaction. Such an event would be a "Business Sale". . . .

The Employment Contract therefore establishes a relationship more similar to a partnership than a typical employer/employee relationship.

The equivalent nature of the parties' contributions is further confirmed by the Real Estate Agreement. In that agreement, Talcott granted Haley the right to participate in an option to purchase the property where the Redfin Grill was situated which is located at 1111 Highway One in Bethany Beach, Delaware (the "Property"). Talcott had obtained the option personally when the Redfin Grill first leased the Property from the then-owner in February of 2001. Talcott provided this valuable right to participate for the nominal price of $10.00. The agreement provided that if the option were exercised, Haley would shoulder 50% of the burden of the purchase, and would be either a 50% owner of the land or a 50% owner of the entity formed to hold the land. FN11. See Pl. Ex. 1D.

From late 2001 into 2003, under Haley's supervision, the Redfin Grill grew into a successful business. By the second year of its existence, the start-up money had been repaid to Talcott with interest, both parties were drawing salaries (Talcott's substantially smaller since he was not participating in day-to-day management), and the parties each received approximately $150,000 in profit sharing. In 2003, the parties formed Matt & Greg Real Estate, LLC to take advantage of the option to purchase the Property that was the subject of the Real Estate Agreement. The option price was $720,000 and the new LLC took out a mortgage from County Bank in Rehoboth Beach, Delaware, for that amount, exercised the option, and obtained the deed to the Property on or about May 23, 2003. Importantly, both Haley and Talcott, individually, signed personal guaranties for the entire amount of the mortgage in order to secure the loan. The Redfin Grill continued to operate at the site, paying the LLC $6,000 per month in rent, a payment sufficient to cover the LLC's monthly obligation under the mortgage. Thus by mid-2003, the parties appeared poised to reap the fruits of their labors; unfortunately, at that point their personal relationship began to deteriorate.

Haley, having managed the restaurant from the time it opened in May 2001, and having formalized his management position in the Employment Contract, apparently believed that the relationship would be reformulated to provide him a direct stock ownership interest in the Redfin Grill at some point. The reasons underlying that belief are not important here, but in late October they caused a rift to develop between the parties. On or about October 27, 2003, the conflict that had been brewing between the parties led to some kind of confrontation. As a result, Talcott sent a letter of understanding to Haley dated October 27, 2003, purporting to accept his resignation and forbidding him to enter the premises of the Redfin Grill.

Haley responded on November 3, 2003 with two separate letters from his counsel to Talcott. In the first, Haley asserts that he did not resign, and that he regarded Talcott's October 27, 2003 letter of understanding as terminating him without cause in breach of the Employment Contract. Haley goes on to express his intent to pursue legal remedies, an intent that he acted upon in the related case in this court. In his second November 3, 2003 letter, Haley purported to take several positions expressly as a 50% member in the LLC including: 1) rejecting the new lease proposed by Talcott for the Redfin Grill; 2) voting to revoke any consent to possession by the Redfin Grill and terminating any lease by which the Redfin Grill asserts the right to possession; and 3) voting that the Property be put up for sale on the open market.

Of course, as a 50% member, Haley could not force the LLC to take action on these proposals because Talcott opposed them. As a result, the pre-existing status quo continued by virtue of the stalemate—a result that Talcott favored. The Redfin Grill's lease has expired and, as a consequence, the Redfin Grill continues to pay $6,000 per month to the LLC in a month-to-month arrangement. The $6,000 rent exceeds the LLC's required mortgage payment by $800 per month, so the situation remains stable. With only a 50% ownership interest, Haley cannot force the termination of the Redfin Grill's lease and evict the Redfin Grill as a tenant; neither can he force the sale of the Property, land that was appraised as of June 14, 2004 at $1.8 million. In short, absent intervention by this court, Haley is stuck, unless he chooses to avail himself of the exit mechanism provided in the LLC Agreement.

That exit mechanism, like judicial dissolution, would provide Haley with his share of the fair market value of the LLC, including the Property. Section 18 of the LLC Agreement provides that upon written notice of election to "quit" the company, the remaining member may elect, in writing, to purchase the departing member's interest for fair market value. If the remaining member elects to purchase the departing member's interest, the parties may agree on fair value, or have the fair value determined by three arbitrators, one chosen by each member and a third chosen by the first two arbitrators. The departing member pays the reasonable expenses of the three arbitrators. Once a fair price is determined, it may be paid in cash, or over a term if secured by: 1) a note signed by the company and personally by the remaining member; 2) a security agreement; and 3) a recorded UCC lien. Only if the remaining member fails to elect to purchase the departing member's interest is the company to be liquidated.

The LLC agreement describes additional details regarding the term and interest rate of any installment payments and defines penalty, default, and acceleration terms to be contained in the securing note. Although these details are not critical to a comparison between a contractual separation under the LLC Agreement and a judicial dissolution, they demonstrate the level of detail that the parties considered in crafting the exit mechanism. But despite this level of detail, the exit provision does not expressly provide a release from the personal guaranties that both Haley and Talcott signed to secure the mortgage on the Property. Nor does the exit provision state that any member dissatisfied with the status quo must break an impasse by exit rather than a suit for dissolution.

Rather than use the exit mechanism, Haley has simultaneously sought: 1) dissolution of the LLC; and 2) relief in an employment litigation filed against Talcott and Redfin Grill, a case also pending in this court. Haley does not view himself as being obligated by the LLC Agreement to be the one who exits; moreover, he would bear the cost of the exit mechanism and that mechanism, as will be discussed, would not release him from the guaranty.

. . .

III. *Legal Analysis*

A. *Procedural Framework*

. . . Section 18–802 provides in its entirety:

> On application by or for a member or manager the Court of Chancery may decree dissolution of a limited liability company whenever it is not reasonably practicable to carry on the business in conformity with a limited liability company agreement. . . .

B. *Case Law Under § 273 Of The Delaware General Corporate Law ("DGCL") Provides An Appropriate Framework For Analysis*

Section 18–802 of the Delaware LLC Act . . . plays a role for LLCs similar to the role that § 273 of the DGCL plays for joint venture corporations with only two stockholders. When a limited liability agreement provides for the company to be governed by its members, when there are only two members, and when those members are at permanent odds, § 273 provides relevant insight into what should happen. To wit, § 273(a) provides, in relevant part, that:

> If the stockholders of a corporation of this state, having only 2 stockholders each of whom own 50% of the stock therein, shall be engaged in a joint venture and if such stockholders shall be unable to agree upon the desirability of discontinuing such joint venture and disposing of the assets used in such venture, either stockholder may, unless otherwise provided in the certificate of incorporation of the corporation or in a written agreement between stockholders, file with the Court of Chancery a petition stating that it desires to discontinue such joint venture and to dispose of the assets used in such venture in accordance with a plan to be agreed on by both stockholders or that, if no such plan shall be agreed upon by both stockholders, the corporation be dissolved.

Section 273 essentially sets forth three pre-requisites for a judicial order of dissolution: 1) the corporation must have two 50% stockholders, 2) those stockholders must be engaged in a joint venture, and 3) they must be unable to agree upon whether to discontinue the business or how to dispose of its assets. Here, by analogy, each of the three provisions is indisputably met.

First, there is no dispute that the parties are 50% members of the LLC. . . .

Second, there is no rational doubt that the parties intended to be and are engaged in a joint venture. . . . The relationship between Haley and Talcott indicates active involvement by both parties in creating a restaurant for their mutual benefit and profit, and the Employment Contract shows that Haley was to be the "Operations Director" of the Redfin Grill, a position that, according to the Side Letter Agreement, would only be terminated if the restaurant was sold. Haley was also entitled to a 50% share of the Redfin Grill's profits. In short, Haley and Talcott were in it together for as long as they owned the restaurant, equally sharing the profits as provided in the Employment Contract.

Most importantly, Haley never agreed to be a passive investor in the LLC who would be subject to Talcott's unilateral dominion. Instead, the LLC agreement provided that: "no member/managers may, *without the agreement of a majority vote of the managers' interest,* act on behalf of the company." [Ed.: Emphasis added by the court.] Acts of the company expressly include: borrowing money in the company name; using company property as collateral; binding the company to any obligation such as a guarantor or surety; selling, mortgaging or encumbering any personal or real property of the company except for business purposes for proper consideration; lending company funds; contracting for any debt except for a proper company purpose; and drawing checks on the company account in excess of $5,000. Under these terms, as a 50% member/manager, no major action of the LLC could be taken without Haley's approval. Thus, Haley is entitled to a continuing say in the operation of the LLC.

Finally, the evidence clearly supports a finding of deadlock between the parties about the business strategy and future of the LLC. . . .

. . . The parties have not interacted since their falling out in October, 2003. Clearly, Talcott understands that the end of Haley's managerial role from the Redfin Grill profoundly altered their relationship as co-members of the LLC. After all, it has left Haley on the outside, looking in, with no power. Of course, Talcott insists that the LLC can and does continue to function for its intended purpose and in conformity with the agreement, receiving payments from the Redfin Grill and writing checks to meet its obligations under the mortgage on Talcott's authority. But that reality does not mean that the LLC is operating in accordance with the LLC Agreement. Although the LLC is technically functioning at this point, this operation is purely a residual, inertial status quo that just happens to exclusively benefit one of the 50% members, Talcott, as illustrated by the hands-tied continuation of the expired lease with the Redfin Grill. With strident disagreement between the parties regarding the appropriate deployment of the asset of the LLC, and open hostility as evidenced by the related suit in this matter, it is not credible that the LLC could, if necessary, take any important action that required a vote of the members. Abundant, uncontradicted documents in the record demonstrate the inability of the parties to function together.

For all these reasons, if the LLC were a corporation, there would be no question that Haley's request to dissolve the entity would be granted. But this case regards an LLC, not a corporation, and more importantly, an LLC with a detailed exit provision. That distinguishing factor must and is considered next.

C. *Even Given The Contractual Emphasis Of The Delaware LLC Act, The Exit Remedy Provided In The LLC Agreement Is An Insufficient Alternative To Dissolution*

The Delaware LLC Act is grounded on principles of freedom of contract. For that reason, the presence of a reasonable exit mechanism bears on the propriety of ordering dissolution under § 18–802. When the agreement itself provides a fair opportunity for the dissenting member who disfavors the inertial status quo to exit and receive the fair market value of her interest, it is at least arguable that the limited liability company may still proceed to operate practicably under its contractual charter because the charter itself provides an equitable way to break the impasse.

Here, that reasoning might be thought apt because Haley has already "voted" as an LLC member to sell the LLC's only asset, the Property, presumably because he knew he could not secure sole control of both the LLC and the Redfin Grill. Given that reality, so long as Haley can actually extract himself fairly, it arguably makes sense for this court to stay its hand in an LLC case and allow the contract itself to solve the problem.

Notably, reasoning of this nature has been applied in the § 273 context. Even under § 273, this court's authority to order dissolution remains discretionary and may be influenced by the particular circumstances. Talcott rightly argues that the situation here is somewhat analogous to that in *In re Delaware Bay Surgical Services* where this court declined to dissolve a corporation under § 273 in part because a mechanism existed for the repurchase of the complaining member's 50% interest.[32]

But, this matter differs from *Surgical Services* in two important respects. First, in *Surgical Services*, the respondent doctor had owned the company before admitting the petitioner to his practice as a 50% stakeholder. The court found that both parties clearly intended, upon entering the contract, that if the parties ended their contractual relationship, the respondent would be the one permitted to keep the company. By contrast, no such obvious priority of interest exists here. Haley and Talcott created the LLC together and while the detailed exit provision provided in the formative LLC Agreement allows either party to leave voluntarily, it provides no insight on who should retain the LLC if both parties would prefer to buy the other out, and neither party desires to leave. . . . [In this case,] forcing Haley to exercise the contractual exit mechanism would not permit the LLC to proceed in a practicable way that accords with the LLC Agreement, but would instead permit Talcott to penalize Haley without express contractual authorization.[35]

Why? Because the parties agree that exit mechanism in the LLC Agreement would not relieve Haley of his obligation under the personal guaranty that he signed to secure the mortgage from County Bank. If Haley is forced to use the exit mechanism, Talcott and he both believe that Haley would still be left holding the bag on the guaranty. It is therefore not equitable to force Haley to use the exit mechanism in this circumstance. While the exit mechanism may be workable in a friendly departure when both parties cooperate to reach an adequate alternative agreement with the bank, the bank cannot be compelled to accept the removal of Haley as a personal guarantor. Thus, the exit mechanism fails as an adequate remedy for Haley because it does not equitably effect the separation of the parties. Rather, it would leave Haley with no upside potential, and no protection over the considerable downside risk that he would have to make good on any future default by the LLC (over whose operations he would have no control) to its mortgage lender. Thus here, unlike in Surgical Services, the parties do not, in fact, "have at their

---

[32] In re Delaware Bay Surgical Services, C.A. No. 2121–S (Del.Ch. Jan. 28, 2002) (resolving cross summary judgment motions).

[35] Stated plainly and putting aside Haley's proposal to sell the Property, it is an interesting question whether the 50% member of an LLC that operates an on-going business, and who does not favor inertial policy, must exit rather than force dissolution, particularly when the cost of the exit procedure would, as here, be borne solely by him. Arguably, it is economically more efficient—absent an explicit requirement that the party disfavoring inertia exit if he is dissatisfied—to order dissolution, and allow both parties to bid as purchasers, with the assets going to the highest bidder (inside or outside) who presumably will deploy the asset to its most valuable use. It is also concomitantly arguable that if parties wish to force the co-equal member disfavoring inertia to exit rather than seek dissolution, then they should explicitly contract upfront in the LLC agreement that exit (or the triggering of a buy-sell procedure, giving incentives for the business to be retained by the member willing to pay the highest value) is the required method of breaking any later-arising stalemate.

disposal a far less drastic means to resolve their personal disagreement."[37]

IV. *Conclusion*

For the reasons discussed above, I find that it is not reasonably practicable for the LLC to continue to carry on business in conformity with the LLC Agreement. The parties shall confer and, within four weeks, submit a plan for the dissolution of the LLC. The plan shall include a procedure to sell the Property owned by the LLC within a commercially reasonable time frame. Either party may, of course, bid on the Property.

ANALYSIS

1. What is the "business" of the LLC? Why is it "not reasonably practicable to carry on [that] business"?

2. Is the Redfin Grill business legally a partnership, with Haley and Talcott as partners?

3. Why didn't Haley simply resign and exercise his rights under Section 604 of the Delaware LLC Code, as described in the Note preceding the case?

4. The court states that the "key facts about the parties' ability to work together are not rationally disputable." With respect to the LLC, what is the "work" that they must do together? Might there in fact be key facts that could be relevant but that neither of the parties' lawyers wanted the court to consider?

5. What happens next? The court refers to the possibility of an auction at which both parties can bid. If such an auction is held, what happens to the bank loan? How does the decision of the court affect the bargaining position of each party?

6. Do you agree that there was, as the court put it, "no reasonable alternative to dissolution"?

7. The exit provision of the LLC agreement did not work. Whose fault is that? If you had represented Talcott, how would you have drafted it? What if you had represented Haley?

PLANNING

Suppose the parties had explicitly bargained over the following questions: (1) Should the exiting LLC member be released from the personal guarantee of the mortgage? (2) Is the contractual exit provision the sole ground on which a member may depart the LLC or may such a member invoke the statutory provisions for dissolution. Is there a clear answer to these questions that most parties would give? If not, how could the law facilitate their efforts at private ordering of the problem?

---

[37] In re Delaware Bay Surgical Services, C.A. No. 2121–S, at 5 (Del.Ch. Jan. 28, 2002).

Pedro v. Pedro

489 N.W.2d 798 (Minn.App.1992).

After a request for dissolution of The Pedro Companies by respondent, Alfred Pedro, appellants, Carl and Eugene Pedro and The Pedro Companies, moved that the action proceed as a buyout pursuant to Minn. Stat. § 302A.751 (1990).*

After a jury awarded damages, this court determined the jury's verdict was merely advisory and remanded the case to the trial court to make findings. Pedro v. Pedro, 463 N.W.2d 285 (Minn.App.1990) (Pedro 1), pet. for rev. denied (Minn. Jan. 24, 1991). On remand, the trial court awarded damages for breach of fiduciary duty and for wrongful termination of lifetime employment. In addition to other issues, appellants challenge the propriety of the trial court's rulings on these matters.

Facts

Alfred, Carl, and Eugene Pedro are brothers who each owned a one-third interest in The Pedro Companies ("TPC"), a closely held Minnesota corporation, which manufactures and sells luggage and leather products. All three brothers worked in the business for all or most of their adult lives. TPC has annual sales of approximately $6 million. Carl has worked for TPC since 1940 and he is currently employed by the company. Eugene has worked for TPC since 1939 and is also currently employed by the company. Alfred worked for TPC for 45 years and was fired in 1987 at the age of 62. Each brother, as an equal shareholder, received the same benefit and compensation as the others. Each shareholder had an equal vote in the management of the company.

In 1968, all of the company's shareholders (the three brothers and their father) entered into a stock retirement agreement ("SRA") which was designed to facilitate the purchase of the shareholder's stock upon death, or when a living shareholder wished to sell his stock. In 1975, the father died and the company purchased his stock from his estate, pursuant to the terms of the SRA.

In 1979, the remaining shareholders (the three brothers) modified and re-executed the SRA, reducing the purchase price of the shares. The agreement provided in part:

> Until and unless changed the value of each share of stock shall be as follows: 75% of net book value at the end of the preceding

---

* [Eds.—This section of the Minnesota Business Corporations law provides for judicial dissolution at the request of a shareholder on a finding of deadlock among directors or shareholders, or waste of assets, or if "those in control have acted fraudulently, illegally, or in a manner unfairly prejudicial toward one or more shareholders," etc. As a remedy, in the case of a "closely held corporation," the court may order a buy-out of the shares of either party, at "fair value," with the purchase price payable in installments, but with the purchaser required to post a bond for the purchase price. A "closely held corporation" is one with not more than 35 shareholders. Minn. Stat. § 302A.011, subd. 6a.

In its earlier opinion in this case, the court described this provision as follows:

> [I]t provides the courts with equitable authority to protect the rights and *reasonable expectations* of minority shareholders. . . . [T]he primary expectations of minority shareholders include *an active voice in management* of the corporation and *input as an employee*.

463 N.W.2d at 289 (emphasis supplied.)]

calendar year. It is the intent of the parties that the value of a Stockholder's interest as herein determined does include good will.

The relationship between respondent and the other two shareholders deteriorated through 1987 and 1988, after Alfred discovered an apparent discrepancy of almost $330,000 between the internal accounting records and the TPC checking account. Approximately $40,000 was discovered in an emergency investigation, yet about $270,000 of the discrepancy remained unexplained.

Alfred was very concerned and insisted that an independent accountant be retained to locate the source of the discrepancy. In May 1987, Carl and Eugene agreed to retain an accountant to investigate the cash shortage. After a month with no results, TPC dismissed the accountant. Alfred testified that soon afterwards, the corporate accountant admitted in a meeting with all three brothers that there was a $140,000 to $147,000 discrepancy which was unexplainable.

Alfred testified that during this time, Eugene would interfere with his area of responsibility in the TPC plant and undermine his management authority. Alfred testified that he was told to cooperate, resign or be fired. He was told if he did not forget about the apparent discrepancy, his brothers would fire him. Alfred again repeated his demand that the corporation hire an independent accountant to investigate the situation.

In October 1987, a second independent accountant was hired to investigate the shortage. After concluding his investigation, the accountant issued a report identifying a $140,000 discrepancy which could not be reconciled. He testified that throughout his investigation, he was refused access to numerous documents. He also stated there were over 20 leads never followed up before he ended his investigation.

Alfred was placed on a mandatory leave of absence from TPC on October 27, 1987. In December 1987, Alfred received a written notice that he was fired and all of his pay and benefits were discontinued. Employees were informed that Alfred had a nervous breakdown.

Alfred commenced this action in February 1988. Upon remand from this court on the earlier appeal, the trial court made the following findings of fact and conclusions of law. The court awarded Alfred $766,582.33 as damages for his one-third ownership in TPC which was determined by the terms of the SRA.* Alfred was awarded $58,260.69 for prejudgment interest on this award.

The trial court also awarded Alfred $563,417.67 based on its finding that the individual defendants had breached their fiduciary duties to Alfred. The award represented the difference between the fair market value of Alfred Pedro's stock as determined by the trial court and the value provided by the SRA. In addition, the trial court awarded $68,690.05 for prejudgment interest on this award.

The trial court further found that Alfred had a contract of lifetime employment with TPC. The court found wrongful termination and

* [Eds.—In its earlier (1990) opinion in the case, the court had held, "Inasmuch as appellants' breaches of fiduciary duty forced the buyout, they cannot benefit from wrongful treatment of their fellow shareholder and must disgorge any such gain." 463 N.W.2d at 288.]

awarded him $256,740 as compensation for lost wages. Because the contract was for lifetime employment, the award represented lost wages until he reached the age of 72. The court reduced this award by payments made to Alfred since December 1989. Moreover, the court awarded prejudgment interest in the sum of $31,750.37 on this award.

The trial court also awarded Alfred $200,000 for attorney fees and expenses incurred by him. This award was based on the trial court's finding that appellants had acted in a manner which was "arbitrary, vexatious and otherwise not in good faith . . . prior to and during this action." The court awarded Alfred an additional $6,063 for attorney fees for having to respond to appellants' motion to recuse the trial judge and for the preparation of Findings of Fact, Conclusions of Law and Order for Judgment.

Issues

1. Was the evidence sufficient to support the trial court's finding of breach of fiduciary duty?

2. Did the trial court properly determine Alfred Pedro had a reasonable expectation of lifetime employment, thereby awarding him damages for lost wages following the buyout until he reached age 72?

3. Did the trial court make proper determinations regarding joint and several liability, prejudgment interest, recusal of the trial judge, and attorney fees?

Analysis

I.

. . .

The relationship among shareholders in closely held corporations is analogous to that of partners. . . . Shareholders in closely held corporations owe one another a fiduciary duty. . . . Owing a fiduciary duty includes dealing "openly, honestly and fairly with other shareholders." Evans [v. Blesi, 345 N.W.2d 775, 779 (Minn.App.1984)].

The court's findings of fact contain many examples where appellants did not act openly, honestly, and fairly with respondent Alfred Pedro. The trial court found that at no time since the action was commenced, did appellants ever implement payments admittedly due under the SRA. Appellants interfered with respondent's responsibilities in TPC and hired a private investigator to follow him when he was not in the office. The court found appellants fabricated accusations of neglect and malfeasance which were not substantiated during the trial.

Moreover, an employee testified that after respondent was terminated, employees were informed that he had a nervous breakdown. Also, respondent testified he was told if he did not forget about the discrepancies in the financial records, his brothers would fire him. Finally, appellants admitted in their motion requesting a buyout, that they were acting "in a manner unfairly prejudicial" toward respondent pursuant to Minn. Stat. § 302A.751, subd. 1(b)(2) (1990). This admission supports a finding of breach of fiduciary duty.

Appellants claim no breach of fiduciary duty can exist because there has been no diminution in the value of the corporation or the stock value of respondent's shares. In support of this assertion, appellants cite several cases where actions by an officer or director did reduce the value of the corporation, constituting a breach of fiduciary duty. . . .

However, an action depleting a corporation's value is not the exclusive method of breaching one's fiduciary duties. See *Evans*, 345 N.W.2d at 779–80 (majority shareholders breached fiduciary duty to minority shareholder by forcing his resignation). Moreover, loss in value of a shareholder's stock is not the only measure of damages. See Pavlidis v. New England Patriots Football Club, Inc., 675 F.Supp. 701, 703 (D.Mass.1987) (damages for corporate director's breach of fiduciary duty was either profits made by director or value of property at time of breach plus interest).

Moreover, the measure of damages for the buyout was proper. In *Pedro 1* [Pedro v. Pedro, 463 N.W.2d 285 (Minn.App.1990) (an earlier decision in this case)], this court stated:

> If the fair value of the shares is greater than the purchase price for the buyout as calculated from the formula in the SRA, the difference is the measure of respondent's damage resulting from having been forced to sell his shares in the company.

Pedro, 463 N.W.2d at 288. Here there was evidence in the record that the fair market value of respondent's shares equalled $1,330,000. After subtracting the undisputed purchase price set forth under the SRA of $766,582.33, the trial court properly awarded damages for breach of fiduciary duty of $563,417.67.

II.

Appellants claim the evidence was insufficient for the court to find a contract for lifetime employment. They also assert damages for lost wages following the buyout were improper. Again, we are unable to set aside findings of fact unless they are clearly erroneous. . . . Based upon the unique facts in this case, we affirm the trial court's award of damages for lost wages.

Trial courts have broad equitable powers in fashioning relief for the buyout of shareholders in a closely held corporation. Minn. Stat. § 302A.751, subd. 3a provides:

> In determining whether to order equitable relief, dissolution, or a buy-out, the court shall take into consideration the duty which all shareholders in a closely held corporation owe one another to act in an honest, fair and reasonable manner in the operation of the corporation and the reasonable expectations of the shareholders as they exist at the inception and develop during the course of the shareholders' relationship with the corporation and with each other.

This section allows courts to look to respondent's reasonable expectations when awarding damages. In addition to an ownership interest,

> the reasonable expectations of such a shareholder are a job, salary, a significant place in management, and economic security for his family.

Joseph E. Olson, A Statutory Elixir for the Oppression Malady, 36 Mercer L. Rev. 627, 629 (1985) (footnote omitted).

In Pine River State Bank v. Mettille, 333 N.W.2d 622 (Minn.1983), the supreme court explained that the court must ascertain the intent of the parties to the employment contract. Id. at 628. When ascertaining the intent, trial courts must consider the written and oral negotiations of the parties as well as the parties' situation, the type of employment and the particular circumstances of the case. Eklund v. Vincent Brass and Aluminum Co., 351 N.W.2d 371, 376 (Minn.App.1984), pet. for rev. denied (Minn. Nov. 1, 1984).

> In a closely held corporation the nature of the employment of a shareholder may create a reasonable expectation by the employee-owner that his employment is not terminable at will.

Pedro, 463 N.W.2d at 289.

The unique facts in the record support the trial court's finding of an agreement to provide lifetime employment to respondent. Carl Pedro, Sr. worked at the corporation until his death. Eugene Pedro, who worked for over 50 years at TPC, testified that he intended to always work for the company. Carl Pedro, Jr. worked at TPC for over 34 years. Alfred Pedro testified of his expectation of a lifetime job like his father. He had already been employed by TPC for 45 years. Even the corporate accountant testified regarding Carl's and Eugene's expectations that they would work for the corporation as long as they wanted. Based upon this evidence it was reasonable for the trial court to determine that the parties did in fact have a contract that was not terminable at will.

Appellants claim a grant of damages for both lost wages and breach of fiduciary duty under § 302A.751, subd. 3a allows respondent a double recovery. . . . Even appellants concede respondent has two separate interests, as owner and employee. Thus, allowing recovery for each interest is appropriate and will not be considered a double recovery.

Finally, appellants dispute the trial court's award of damages for lost wages following the buyout. They claim once respondent's ownership interest is severed, he has no right to damages for lost wages. We believe the trial court's award of future damages for lost wages is wholly consistent with the court's broad equitable powers found in § 302A.751, subd. 3a and is warranted based upon its finding of a contract for lifetime employment.

III.

. . .

[A]ppellants challenge the trial court's award of attorney fees. Under section 302A.751, subd. 4, if the court finds a party to a proceeding brought under this section has acted arbitrarily, vexatiously or otherwise not in good faith, it may, in its discretion, award reasonable expenses, including attorneys fees and disbursements to any of the other parties. Here, the trial court made specific findings that appellants both breached fiduciary duties and acted arbitrarily, vexatiously or otherwise not in good faith. Once this has been done, the trial court has discretion to award attorney fees. . . .

Decision

The facts of this case support the trial court's findings that appellants breached their fiduciary duties to respondent and wrongfully terminated his contract for lifetime employment.

Affirmed.

ANALYSIS

1. How would you have drafted the SRA?

2. Could the parties have avoided the court's result by drafting the contract differently? Would they have wanted to do so? Does the court interpret the SRA or does it impose mandatory contractual terms?

3. Does the Minnesota statute, with its interpretation in *Pedro,* reduce the need for buy/sell agreements in closely held corporations? Eliminate them? Suppose you are about to invest in such a corporation. If you tell the other investors that you do not like the state's "default" rule and want to hammer out a control agreement, employment agreements, and a buy/sell agreement, what adverse message might you be conveying?

PLANNING ISSUE

How do the rules encountered in this section affect your judgment about the need for a buy-sell agreement in closely held corporations?

Stuparich v. Harbor Furniture Mfg., Inc.

83 Cal.App.4th 1268, 100 Cal.Rptr.2d 313 (2000).

This is a dispute concerning a closely held family corporation. Plaintiffs and appellants, Ann Stuparich and Candi Tuttleton, appeal from judgment entered in favor of the corporation after the trial court granted summary judgment against them. The sole issue on appeal is whether plaintiffs raised a triable issue of material fact regarding their claim that dissolution was appropriate under Corporations Code § 1800(b)(5). . . . That statute provides for the involuntary dissolution of a corporation where "In the case of any corporation with 35 or fewer shareholders . . . liquidation is reasonably necessary for the protection of the rights or interests of the complaining shareholder or shareholders."

We conclude that plaintiffs did not raise a triable issue of material fact that dissolution of the corporation was reasonably necessary to protect their rights, and interests, and affirm the judgment.

FACTUAL AND PROCEDURAL SUMMARY

Plaintiffs are sisters. Harbor Furniture was founded by their grandfather in 1929 as a furniture manufacturing business. A short time later, ownership of the company was divided between the grandfather and his wife (50 percent) and their son, Malcolm Tuttleton, Sr. and his wife, Ilo Tuttleton (50 percent). In 1946, Harbor Furniture purchased land in Los Angeles County as an investment. Harbor Furniture was incorporated in 1957. In 1965, the Los Angeles County land was developed into a mobile home park named "The Californian," which continues to be owned and operated by Harbor Furniture. The corporation also continues to manufacture furniture.

It is undisputed that Malcolm, Jr. worked with his father, Malcolm, Sr., in the day-to-day operation of Harbor Furniture beginning in 1961. Malcolm, Jr. is the plaintiffs' brother. In 1982, Malcolm, Sr. turned over the position of Chief Executive Officer to Malcolm, Jr. Malcolm, Jr. received an annual salary of $153,000 plus bonuses. His wife, Jocelle, is employed by Harbor Furniture as an office manager and she also oversees production. Her annual salary is $49,000. Malcolm, Jr.'s son, Brent, is employed by Harbor Furniture as a salesman. He receives a guaranteed annual salary of $27,000 plus commissions. Other than by attendance at board meetings, neither plaintiff has been involved in the operation of the company.

Plaintiffs obtained shares in Harbor Furniture through gifts and inheritance. When they filed the dissolution proceeding on December 17, 1996, they each held 19.05 percent of voting shares and 33.33 percent of non-voting shares in the corporation. In March 1996, their father, Malcolm, Sr., sold his voting stock to his son, Malcolm, Jr. This transaction gave Malcolm, Jr. 51.56 percent of the voting shares and 33.33 percent of the non-voting shares. (Plaintiffs characterize this transaction as "clandestine" and assert that they first learned of it through discovery conducted in this action.) The remaining 10.34 percent of shares are held by unidentified others. It is undisputed that the total number of shareholders is less than 35.

Plaintiffs became dissatisfied with the failure of the company to observe various formalities. At Ann Stuparich's insistence, the corporation began holding annual meetings in 1990. She served as chairman of the board of directors between 1990 and 1996. Both plaintiffs were on the board of directors for that period. The other members of the board included Malcolm Jr., Malcolm Sr., and his wife, Ilo. Candi Tuttleton became secretary of the board of directors in 1993. Malcolm, Sr. was president and Malcolm, Jr. was vice-president.

Confusion and a dispute arose in late 1995 when the company's certified public accountant, John Rohm, circulated a proposal regarding disposition of Ilo Tuttleton's stock following her death. Plaintiffs believed that they had acquired a controlling share of the stock in the corporation. They proposed formally separating the mobile home park operation from the furniture manufacturing operation by creating separate divisions. This was because the furniture business was incurring financial losses each year while the mobile home park was very profitable. Ann Stuparich intended to insulate the profits of the mobile home park from the furniture losses through this reorganization. Candi Tuttleton concurred in her sister's proposal.

According to Ann Stuparich's declaration, "Shortly thereafter, I was notified by John Rohm that his initial communication had been in error. The stock [distribution] had not given voting control to my sister and I. At approximately the same time I was notified by my brother [Malcolm, Jr.] that my meeting notice was defective and that no meeting would be held to discuss my restructuring proposal. When I was unable to obtain a satisfactory explanation as to how the voting/non-voting . . . discrepancy had arisen, I threw up my hands in frustration."

Plaintiffs' separate statement of disputed facts, which is supported by their declarations, states: "Although given titles of authority, Plaintiffs never had any real power or role in the corporation. Plaintiffs in 1996 realized that their efforts were futile, and that there never would be meaningful discussion of subjects of concern to them. Rather than continue efforts in frustration and futility, Plaintiffs stopped attending annual meetings." Malcolm, Jr. refused plaintiffs' request to buy out their shares.

It is undisputed that plaintiffs received monthly dividends from corporate profits from 1984 to 1996. The dividend payments tripled during this period from $1,000 per month to $3,000 per month. With additional quarterly payments, each plaintiff has received more than $800,000 in dividends since 1984. Harbor Furniture has distributed in excess of $2,700,000 in dividends to its shareholders since 1984, although the furniture portion of the business suffered losses of $2,577,682 in the fiscal years from 1990 through 1998.

Plaintiffs filed a verified complaint against Harbor Furniture Manufacturing, Inc., Malcolm, Jr., Malcolm, Sr., Malcolm, Jr.'s wife, Jocelle and son, Brent. They sought involuntary dissolution of the corporation under § 1800(b)(4) and (5); declaratory relief; and damages for fraud, conspiracy and negligence. The individual defendants and all causes of action other than that for dissolution under § 1800(b)(5) subsequently were dismissed by stipulation of the parties. After the action was filed, there was a serious argument between Candi Tuttleton and Malcolm, Jr. which resulted in physical injuries to Ms. Tuttleton.

Harbor Manufacturing moved for summary judgment. . . . The trial court granted the motion for summary judgment. In its minute order, the court found, "Plaintiff [sic] seek involuntary dissolution on the ground that the animosity between them and their brother makes it impossible to participate in corporate activities. However, as the moving papers indicate, plaintiffs could pursue a representative on the board of directors to represent their interests in the corporation. Further, plaintiff's [sic] rights are not in need of protection as they have consistently received the dividends owed them as shareholders."

DISCUSSION

. . .

The sole issue in this appeal is whether plaintiffs raised a triable issue of material fact as to their right to involuntary dissolution of the corporation under § 1800(b)(5) which applies where "liquidation is reasonably necessary for the protection of the rights or interests of the complaining shareholder or shareholders." The Legislative Committee Comment to § 1800 notes that the enacting legislation was intended to expand the authority to initiate an involuntary dissolution in specified situations. (Assem. Legis. Com. com., reprinted at 23E West's Ann. Corp.Code (1990 ed.) foll. § 1800, p. 481 (Legislative Committee comment)). The Legislative Committee comment specifically addresses involuntary dissolution in a close corporation. "The new law specifically authorizes the formation of 'close corporations' and the agreements necessary to 'close' the corporation. To provide close corporation shareholders with a remedy, this section permits any shareholder of a close corporation to initiate involuntary dissolution. . . . Since this section permits a going concern to be involuntarily terminated, the application of such a drastic remedy should be appropriately limited. Subdivision (b)(5) of this section states a relatively broad ground for involuntary dissolution proceedings and, in light of the expansion of authority to bring such an action, this provision is limited to corporations with 35 or fewer shareholders."

There are two cases addressing the right of minority shareholders to force dissolution of a corporation because their interests and rights cannot be protected. The first, Stumpf v. C.E. Stumpf & Sons, Inc. (1975) 47 Cal.App.3d 230, 120 Cal.Rptr. 671, was decided under former § 4651, the predecessor to § 1800. Former § 4651(f) allowed involuntary dissolution where "The liquidation is reasonably necessary for the protection of the rights or interests of any substantial number of the shareholders, or of the complaining shareholders. (Id. at p. 233, fn. 2, 120 Cal.Rptr. 671.) The corporation in *Stumpf* was wholly owned in equal shares by C.G. Stumpf, Sr. and his two sons. One of the sons, Donald Stumpf, left employment with the corporation after a managerial dispute. He was removed as an officer of the corporation. He did not seek to participate in the family business after that, and was not asked to do so. The trial court granted his request for involuntary dissolution of the corporation. On appeal, the corporation argued that dissolution was inappropriate absent some finding of deadlock, mismanagement, or unfairness toward Donald. Deadlock and mismanagement were other grounds for dissolution set out in former § 4651. The trial court specifically found there had been no mismanagement or unfairness and there was no evidence of a corporate deadlock.

The *Stumpf* court affirmed the order of dissolution. It concluded that subdivision (f) of section 4651 was not limited to situations of the kind specified in the other subdivisions of the section. . . . It read former § 4658, which allowed a majority to preserve the corporation by buying out the minority, with former § 4651, as demonstrating a legislative intent "to empower the courts to order dissolution when required to assure fairness to minority shareholders and at the same time to lessen the danger of minority abuse." . . .

Based on evidence of the extreme hostility between the two brothers—which had forced Donald Stumpf to sever contact with the family and had shown that Donald had no say in the operation of the business and that he received no salary, dividends, or other revenue from his investment in the corporation after he withdrew from the business—the court concluded that the trial court's judgment granting dissolution was supported by substantial evidence. It found no abuse of discretion.

The second case is Bauer v. Bauer, [1996] 46 Cal.App.4th 1106, 54 Cal.Rptr.2d 377. In that case, minority shareholders of West Coast, a closely held corporation, sought involuntary dissolution. The minority shareholders went into business in direct competition with West Coast and had been ousted as employees of West Coast. Following trial, the court refused to grant dissolution. On appeal, the minority shareholders argued that dissolution was appropriate both under § 1800(b)(4) (persistent fraud, mismanagement, abuse of authority or persistent unfairness toward shareholders) and (b)(5) (dissolution necessary to protect rights or interests of complaining shareholders). The Court of Appeal held that in enacting subdivisions (b)(4) and (b)(5) of § 1800, "the Legislature clearly distinguished between a cause of action for involuntary dissolution based on the controlling shareholders' misconduct, and one based specifically on protection of the rights, interests and expectations of complaining minority shareholders. . . . The Bauer court concluded that the grounds for dissolution under subdivision (b)(5) are considerably broader than those in subdivision (b)(4). . . .

The *Bauer* court applied an abuse of discretion standard. . . . It concluded that in light of the bad faith conduct of the minority shareholders in setting up a competing business and soliciting West Coast's customers, the trial court did not abuse its discretion in concluding that the "drastic relief of involuntary liquidation" was not " 'reasonably necessary' " to protect the minority shareholders' interests. The appellate court also found that nonpayment of corporate dividends was not a basis for granting dissolution because of evidence that there were no profits from which dividends could be paid. Finally, it found that under the circumstances, the minority shareholders did not have a reasonable expectation of receiving either dividends or salaries from West Coast. It affirmed the trial court's judgment denying involuntary dissolution because involuntary dissolution was not " 'reasonably necessary' " to protect the minority shareholders' rights and interests. . . . With these decisions in mind, we turn to plaintiffs' arguments on appeal.

The issue is whether plaintiffs raised a triable issue of material fact as to whether dissolution is "reasonably necessary" to protect their rights or interests. Plaintiffs point to the following evidence, presented in opposition to the motion for summary judgment: (1) their brother, Malcolm, Jr., has voting control of the corporation; (2) plaintiffs are not allowed meaningful participation in the corporation; (3) the dispute with their brother gave rise to a violent confrontation between Malcolm, Jr. and Candi Tuttleton; and (4) plaintiffs have an economic interest in reducing or ending the significant losses the furniture manufacturing business has suffered over the last 10 years, but Malcolm, Jr. and his family draw benefits from the furniture operation in the form of salaries and bonuses.

First, it is undisputed that Malcolm, Jr., with 51.56 percent of the voting shares, can outvote plaintiffs on any issue. California law allows corporations to issue both voting and nonvoting stock. (§ 400, subd. (a).) . . .

It is also undisputed that Malcolm, Sr. turned over the operation of Harbor Furniture to Malcolm, Jr. and that plaintiffs have played no part in the daily operation of either the furniture manufacturing or mobile home park operations of the corporation. In addition, while characterizing Malcolm, Sr.'s sale of his voting stock to his son as "clandestine," plaintiffs do not dispute his right to make the sale.

Thus, the distribution of voting shares in the corporation is consistent with California law, and does not, in itself, present a "reasonable" necessity for dissolution. The other issues briefed by plaintiffs are related. They cite their inability to play a meaningful role in the operation of the corporation, the complete breakdown of their relationship with their brother, and the continuing losses incurred by the furniture manufacturing operation, which reduced profits. Plaintiffs rely on their declarations, in which they describe their efforts to participate in corporate operations or policy as frustrating and futile. As evidence of their treatment as "second class" shareholders, plaintiffs cite Malcolm, Jr.'s concealment of his acquisition of a controlling share of voting stock. As we have discussed, plaintiffs do not challenge Malcolm, Sr.'s right to sell these shares to his son. Plaintiffs contend that the sale was made at steeply discounted values, arguing "the entire secretive transaction is merely one more example of actions that disadvantage and disregard the sisters, who after all do in fact own the majority of all shares in the corporation. But Malcolm, Sr. was privileged to sell his shares to his son at whatever price he chose.

In essence, the corporation argues that as minority shareholders, plaintiffs' only right and interest is in continuing to receive dividends. It points to undisputed evidence that plaintiffs, as well as the other shareholders, were paid significant dividends in the period preceding the filing of the dissolution action. It invokes the business judgment rule of deference to corporate directors in making decisions regarding the operation of the company,. . . . In response to plaintiffs' argument that the corporation would make more money if the furniture manufacturing operation were eliminated, Harbor Furniture argues that this does not raise a triable issue of material fact because it can always be argued that more profits could be made. It contends that courts should not be involved "in the tweaking of corporate performance. Such is the reason for the 'business judgment' rule." The corporation also suggests that plaintiffs elect someone other than themselves to represent their interests on the board of directors. It argues "An opportunity to participate and speak is all a minority shareholder is entitled to and may expect." . . .

On this undisputed record, we cannot say that the trial court erred in finding as a matter of law that the drastic remedy of liquidation is not reasonably necessary for the protection of the rights or interests of the complaining shareholder or shareholders. . . . As holders of a minority of the voting shares, plaintiffs are not entitled to substitute their business judgment for their brother's with respect to viability of the furniture operations. . . .

The judgment is affirmed.

ANALYSIS

1. What is the relevance of the altercation between Candi Tuttleton and Malcolm Tuttleton, Jr., that led to "physical injuries" to Candi?

2. What is the relevance of the fact that Malcolm, Jr., and his wife and son received salaries and the sisters did not?

3. How can the outcome in this case be reconciled with the outcomes in *Alaska Plastics* and Pedro v. Pedro?

4. What happens next? The dueling family factions seem to be stuck with one another. Suppose Malcolm, Jr. asks for your advice. He suggests that he might want to reduce dividends, using the money to modernize the furniture factory, and that he might offer to buy out his sisters if they are willing to sell at a low enough price. What advice do you offer?

6. TRANSFER OF CONTROL

Frandsen v. Jensen-Sundquist Agency, Inc.

802 F.2d 941 (7th Cir.1986).

■ POSNER, CIRCUIT JUDGE.

The appeals in this diversity suit require us to consider issues of Wisconsin contract and tort law in the settling of a dispute over the rights of a minority shareholder in a closely held corporation. The facts are as follows. In 1975 Walter Jensen owned all the stock of Jensen-Sundquist Agency, Inc., a holding company whose principal asset was a majority of the stock of the First Bank of Grantsburg; Jensen-Sundquist also owned a small insurance company. That year Jensen sold 52 percent of his stock in the holding company to members of his family—the "majority bloc," as we shall call them and the interest they acquired; 8 percent to Dennis Frandsen, a substantial businessman who was not a member of Jensen's family and who paid Jensen $97,000 for the stock; and the rest, in smaller chunks, to other non-family members. By a stockholder agreement drafted by Jensen and a lawyer representing the bank and Jensen's family, the majority bloc agreed "that should they at any time offer to sell their stock in Jensen-Sundquist, Inc., . . . they will first offer their stock to [Frandsen and six other minority shareholders who had negotiated for this provision] at the same price as may be offered to [the majority bloc] . . . and . . . they will not sell their stock to any other person, firm, or organization without first offering said stock" to these minority shareholders "at the same price and upon the same terms." The majority bloc also agreed not to "sell any of their shares to anyone without at the same time offering to purchase all the shares of" these minority shareholders "at the same price." Thus if the majority bloc offered to sell its shares it had to give Frandsen a right to buy the shares at the offer price. If Frandsen declined, the second protective provision came into play: the majority bloc had to offer to buy his shares at the same price at which it sold its own shares.

In 1984 the president of Jensen-Sundquist began discussions with First Wisconsin Corporation, Wisconsin's largest bank holding company, looking to the acquisition by First Wisconsin of First Bank of Grantsburg, Jensen-Sundquist's principal property. A price of $88 per share of stock in the First Bank of Grantsburg was agreed to in principle. The acquisition was to be effected (we simplify slightly) by First Wisconsin's buying Jensen-Sundquist for cash, followed by a merger of First Bank of Grantsburg into a bank subsidiary of First Wisconsin. Each stockholder of Jensen-Sundquist would receive $62 per share, which would translate into $88 per share of the bank. (The reasons that the share values were not the same were that there were more holding company shares than bank shares and that the holding company had another asset besides the bank—the insurance company.) Jensen-Sundquist asked each of the minority shareholders to sign a waiver of any rights he "may have" in the transaction, rights arising from the stockholder agreement, but advised each shareholder that in counsel's opinion the shareholder had no rights other than to receive $62 per share.

Each of the minority shareholders except Frandsen signed or was expected to sign the waiver. Frandsen not only refused to sign but announced that he was exercising his right of first refusal and would buy the majority bloc's shares at $62 a share. (He also offered to buy out the other minority shareholders.) The majority did not want to sell its shares to him—Frandsen says because the president of Jensen-Sundquist, who was also the chairman of the board of First Bank of Grantsburg and a member of the majority bloc, was afraid he would lose his job if Frandsen took over. The deal was restructured. Jensen-Sundquist agreed to sell its shares in First Bank of Grantsburg to First Wisconsin at $88 a share and then liquidate, so that in the end all the stockholders would end up with cash plus the insurance company and First Wisconsin would end up with the bank, which was all it had ever wanted out of the deal. All this was done over Frandsen's protest. He then brought this suit against the majority bloc, charging breach of the stockholder agreement. . .. The district judge granted summary judgment for the defendants and Frandsen appeals. . . .

The case would be easy if the transaction had been structured from the start as a simple acquisition by First Wisconsin of First Bank of Grantsburg from Jensen-Sundquist. Nothing in the stockholder agreement suggests that any minority shareholder has the right to block the sale by Jensen-Sundquist of any of its assets, including its principal asset, a controlling interest in First Bank of Grantsburg. The right of first refusal is a right to buy the shares of the majority bloc in Jensen-Sundquist if they are offered for sale, and there would be no offer of sale if Jensen-Sundquist simply sold some or for that matter all of its assets and became an investment company instead of a bank holding company. Nor did the contract entitle Frandsen to insist that the deal be configured so as to trigger his right of first refusal. . . .

The case is a little harder because the transaction was originally configured as a purchase of the holding company rather than just of the bank, an asset of the holding company. . . . And Frandsen points out that under the stockholder agreement his right of first refusal was triggered by an *offer,* so that the fact the offer was later withdrawn would not affect his right of first refusal if he had already tried to exercise it—and he had tried, before the defendants reconfigured the transaction. But the point is academic, because we agree with the district judge that there never was an offer within the scope of the agreement. The part of the agreement that grants a right of first refusal refers to an offer to sell "their stock," and to a sale of "their stock," and the "their" refers to the majority shareholders. They never offered to sell their stock to First Wisconsin. First Wisconsin was not interested in becoming a majority shareholder of Jensen-Sundquist, in owning an insurance company, and in dealing with Frandsen and the other minority shareholders. It just wanted the bank.

What is more, a sale of stock was never contemplated, again for the reason that First Wisconsin was not interested in becoming a shareholder of Jensen-Sundquist. The transaction originally contemplated was a merger of Jensen-Sundquist into First Wisconsin. In a merger, as the word implies, the acquired firm disappears as a distinct legal entity. . . . In effect, the shareholders of the merged firm yield up all of the assets of the firm, receiving either cash or securities in exchange, and the firm dissolves. . . . In this case the shareholders would have received cash. Their shares would have disappeared but not by sale, for in a merger the shares of the acquired firm are not bought, they are extinguished. There would have been no Jensen-Sundquist after the merger, and no shareholders in Jensen-Sundquist.

The distinction between a sale of shares and a merger is such a familiar one in the business world that it is unbelievable that so experienced a businessman as Frandsen would have overlooked it. It is true that he was not represented by a lawyer in connection with the stockholder agreement, but when an experienced businessman deliberately eschews legal assistance in making a contract he cannot by doing so obtain a legal advantage over a represented party should a dispute arise.

Nor are we persuaded by Frandsen's argument that if interpreted literally the stockholder agreement gave him no right of first refusal worthy of the name. It is true that under that interpretation if as happened the majority bloc did not want to sell out to him, all it had to do was find a merger partner. But these alternatives are not identical in all but form, as he argues. The majority bloc was only 52 percent. If the majority wanted to sell its stock to someone who wanted a controlling interest in the company rather than the company itself or an asset of the company such as the First Bank of Grantsburg, it had to offer its shares to Frandsen first (and to the other six minority shareholders who had a right of first refusal—what would have happened if all had exercised their right we need not speculate about). If it wanted to bypass Frandsen it had to find someone willing to buy not just its shares, but the company.

Most important, Frandsen may have been concerned not with a sale of the company itself at a price agreeable to a majority and therefore likely to be attractive to him as well, but with a sale of the majority bloc that would leave him a minority shareholder in a company owned by strangers. The lot of a minority shareholder in a closely held company is not an enviable one, even in the best of circumstances. A majority coalition may gang up on him. And he may not have the usual recourse of a victimized minority shareholder—to sell out. For there may be no market for his shares, except the very people who have ganged up on him. . . . Frandsen may just have wanted to protect himself against being put at the mercy of a new and perhaps hostile majority bloc. The right of first refusal was one protection against this danger.

Against this Frandsen argues that the right of first refusal must have had an additional purpose, for otherwise it would merely have duplicated the second protective provision in the stockholder agreement, which guaranteed that the majority bloc if it sold its shares would offer to buy his shares at the same price. It is true that this provision protected Frandsen against finding himself a minority shareholder in a company controlled by persons other than the members of the original majority bloc, but it did so at the price of forcing him to leave the company. The right of first refusal enabled him to remain in the company by buying out the majority bloc at the same price that the bloc was willing to sell its shares to others. It thus gave him additional protection. It did not give him protection against a sale of the company itself but this does not make the agreement incoherent or unclear, for his only concern may have been with the possibility of finding himself confronted with a new majority bloc, and that is the only possibility he may have thought it important to negotiate with reference to.

We note in this connection that Frandsen himself had once taken over a bank by paying a premium to a majority of shareholders and then, after he acquired control in this way, buying out the minority shareholders at a lower price. Evidently he wanted to make sure that no one did this to him in Jensen-Sundquist by buying the majority bloc and then making life uncomfortable for him and the other minority shareholders so that they would sell their shares on the cheap. The stockholder agreement that he negotiated with Jensen was well designed to protect him against a maneuver that he had practiced himself. The defendants' efforts to get Frandsen to sign a waiver do not as he argues establish a practical construction of the stockholder agreement as entitling him to exercise his right of first refusal in the event of a proposed merger. A waiver is like a quitclaim deed: the signer waives whatever rights he may have, but does not warrant that he has any rights to waive.

Frandsen's principal argument is that the word "sell" is sufficiently ambiguous to embrace a disposition that has the same practical effect as a sale of the majority bloc's shares. This may be; Wilson v. Whinery, 37 Wash.App. 24, 28–29, 678 P.2d 354, 357 (1984), held that a transfer of all beneficial use of parcel B, "thereby granting [the transferee] substantial control over parcel B," was a sale of B for purposes of a right of first refusal triggered by such a sale. But our main point has been that a sale of the majority bloc's shares is not the same thing as a sale of either all or some of the holding company's assets. The sale of assets does not result in substituting a new majority bloc, and that is the possibility at which the protective provisions are aimed. This appears with sufficient clarity, moreover, to justify the district judge's refusal to go outside the text of the contract to find its meaning.

Any lingering doubts of the propriety of this course are dispelled by the rule that rights of first refusal are to be interpreted narrowly. . . . This may seem to be one of those fusty "canons of construction" that invite ridicule because they have no basis and contradict each other and are advanced simply as rhetorical flourishes to embellish decisions reached on other, more practical grounds. . . . But actually it makes some sense. The effect of a right of first refusal is to add a party to a transaction, for the right is triggered by an offer of sale, and the effect is therefore to inject the holder of the right into the sale transaction. Adding a party to a transaction increases the costs of transacting exponentially; the formula for the number of links required to connect up all the members of an n-member set is n(n–1)/2, meaning that, for example, increasing the number of parties to a transaction from three to four increases the number of required linkages from three to six. Certainly the claim of a right of first refusal complicated the transaction here! If all the costs of the more complicated transaction were borne by the parties, it would hardly be a matter of social concern. But some of the costs are borne by the taxpayers who support the court system, and the courts are not enthusiastic about this, and have decided not to be hospitable to such rights. The right is enforceable but only if the contract clearly confers it. . . .

The district judge correctly dismissed all of Frandsen's claims.

AFFIRMED.

Zetlin v. Hanson Holdings, Inc.

48 N.Y.2d 684, 421 N.Y.S.2d 877, 397 N.E.2d 387 (1979).

Plaintiff Zetlin owned approximately 2% of the outstanding shares of Gable Industries, Inc., with defendants Hanson Holdings, Inc., and Sylvestri together with members of the Sylvestri family, owning 44.4% of Gable's shares. The defendants sold their interests to Flintkote Co. for a premium price of $15 per share, at a time when Gable was selling on the open market for $7.38 per share. It is undisputed that the 44.4% acquired by Flintkote represented effective control of Gable.

Recognizing that those who invest the capital necessary to acquire a dominant position in the ownership of a corporation have the right of controlling that corporation, it has long been settled law that, absent looting of corporate assets, conversion of a corporate opportunity, fraud or other acts of bad faith, a controlling stockholder is free to sell, and a purchaser is free to buy, that controlling interest at a premium price. . . .

Certainly, minority shareholders are entitled to protection against such abuse by controlling shareholders. They are not entitled, however, to inhibit the legitimate interests of the other stockholders. It is for this reason that control shares usually command a premium price. The premium is the added amount an investor is willing to pay for the privilege of directly influencing the corporation's affairs.

In this action plaintiff Zetlin contends that minority stockholders are entitled to an opportunity to share equally in any premium paid for a controlling interest in the corporation. This rule would profoundly affect the manner in which controlling stock interests are now transferred. It would require, essentially, that a controlling interest be transferred only by means of an offer to all stockholders, i.e., a tender offer. This would be contrary to existing law and if so radical a change is to be effected it would best be done by the Legislature.

Order affirmed.

NOTE AND QUESTIONS ON CONTROL PREMIUMS

The underlying issue in sale-of-control cases can be reflected by two paradigms. For the *first paradigm,* suppose there is a business firm that produces earnings of $200,000 per year before any payment of salary to its manager and suppose that a reasonable salary for the manager is $50,000 per year, so the net earnings are $150,000 per year. Suppose further that the market value of the firm is a multiple of five times the net earnings, or $750,000; that the firm is incorporated, with 1,500 common shares outstanding; that 1,000 (or 2/3) of these shares are owned by C (the controlling shareholder) and 500 by M (the minority shareholder); and that C has been acting as manager and taking a salary of $50,000 per year. Thus, the financial picture looks like this:

Gross earnings	$200,000
Reasonable salary	$ 50,000
Net earnings	$150,000
Market value of firm (5 times net earnings)	$750,000
C's shares	1,000
M's shares	500
Earnings allocable to C	$100,000
Earnings allocable to M	$ 50,000
Market value of C's shares	$500,000
Market value of M's shares	$250,000

Now suppose C's shares are bought by B, who elects his representatives to the board of directors, and that the board installs B's son, S, as manager; that S, as a manager, is competent but has no special qualities that add value to the business; that the board sets S's salary at $110,000 per year; and that, given the traditional judicial deference to decisions of boards of directors, there is no realistic prospect that a legal attack on this salary would be successful. The financial picture now looks like this:

Gross earnings	$200,000
S's salary	$110,000
Net earnings	$ 90,000
B's shares	1,000
M's shares	500
Earnings allocable to B	$ 60,000
Additional value to B from S's excess salary (yearly)	$ 60,000
Total annual return to B	$120,000
Market value of B's shares	$600,000
Earnings allocable to M	$ 30,000
Market value of M's shares	$150,000

On these assumed facts, which are extreme but may fairly depict reality in some situations, B has been able to shift $100,000 of the value of the firm from M to himself.* Thus, B might have been willing to pay C a premium (that is, an amount in excess of C's allocable share of the total fair market value of the firm) for his shares. If, for example, B had paid $550,000 for C's 1,000 shares, C and B each would profit by $50,000—at the expense of M. On this view of control premiums, the premium is paid for control because the buyer intends to milk, or (a more extreme version) loot, the corporation. In thinking about this view of reality, however, one must wonder why (returning to our hypothetical facts) C had been paying himself a salary of only $50,000. If C had been paying himself $110,000,

* A thoughtful reader may detect a problem with the assumed facts. If it is so easy to increase the salary of the controlling shareholder or his son, why would M's shares initially be worth $250,000? Why would there not be at least some discount to reflect the prospect that the controlling shareholder would extract benefits not shared with the minority shareholder? The answer is that the initially assumed facts may in fact be unrealistic to some degree, but the observations generated by the facts assumed are nonetheless interesting and useful. The implications of the thoughtful reader's concern with the realism of the assumed facts might be explored by starting with the firm under B's ownership, with B's shares worth $600,000 and M's shares worth $150,000, and asking how one's reactions to sale of control shares for a premium price change if it is now B, rather than C, who is selling the shares.

then C's shares would have been worth more than M's, but the sale of those shares to B, at a price in excess of the value of M's shares, would not have harmed M. The question left by this paradigm is, why not, by some legal rule or device, provide that a buyer such as B, who is willing to pay a premium for a controlling number of shares, must buy pro rata from all shareholders?

For the *second paradigm,* assume that we begin with the same facts as in the first paradigm, with the firm earning net revenues of $150,000 (after the $50,000 salary to C), and with C owning 1,000 shares worth $500,000 and M owning 500 shares worth $250,000. Along comes E, a successful entrepreneur, who examines the firm's methods of operations and concludes that by making some changes and by replacing C, as manager, with her own person (who will be willing to accept the same $50,000 salary), she can increase the net earnings to $200,000.** If E is right, she can increase the value of the firm from $750,000 to $1,000,000. Suppose E buys C's shares for $600,000. Everyone has an increase in wealth. C has sold shares worth $500,000 for $600,000, for a gain of $100,000. E has paid $600,000 for shares that should now be worth $666,667 (2/3 of the $1,000,000 total value). And M's shares should increase in value from $250,000 to $333,333 (1/3 of $1,000,000), a gain of $83,333. The total gain is $250,000, which, of course, is the total increase in the value of the firm. It is difficult to see any basis for objection to the sale from C to E. But is this a realistic paradigm? In challenging the realism, a person might ask why, since E expected to make a profit from the purchase of C's shares at a 20 percent premium,* was she not also willing to offer the same premium for M's shares? Does the failure to do so necessarily establish that E does not genuinely expect to increase the firm's earnings, but rather intends to exploit the firm for her own personal advantage, as in the first paradigm?

PLANNING PROBLEM

Recall that in the *Frandsen* case, a minority shareholder bargained for a "take-me-along" or "equal-opportunity" provision. It was described by the court as follows:

> [I]f the majority bloc offered to sell its shares it had to give Frandsen a right to buy the shares at the offer price. If Frandsen declined, the second protective provision came into play: the majority bloc had to offer to buy his shares at the same price at which it sold its own shares.

Suppose that you are practicing law and that three people come to you and ask you to advise and assist them in forming a business organization to manufacture and sell computer components. The three individuals are Ida, Sally, and Maria. Ida has the product ideas and technical competence and will supervise production. Sally will be in

---

** Again the thoughtful reader might wonder why the initial value of the shares was not at least slightly greater than $750,000, to reflect the prospect that the earnings might be increased through better strategies and management, or to reflect the probability that C was gaining intangible benefits from managing the firm in his own relatively inefficient way. Changing the facts to reflect this possibility would add complexity without altering the important implications.

* It was assumed that C's shares were initially worth $500,000. E paid $600,000, which includes a premium of $100,000 over the initial worth. $100,000 is 20 percent of $500,000.

charge of sales and promotion. Maria will supply the money for the start-up phase; she will play no active role in the business. The three principals tell you that if all goes well they expect to become rich from this venture (or, in Maria's case, richer). What advice would you give them about adopting an equal-opportunity provision? Would your advice change if you knew that Ida and Sally were sisters and always acted together, as if they were one person? (By the way, do you have a problem with advising all three?)

Perlman v. Feldmann

219 F.2d 173 (2d Cir.), cert. denied, 349 U.S. 952 (1955).

■ CLARK, CHIEF JUDGE.

This is a derivative action brought by minority stockholders of Newport Steel Corporation to compel accounting for, and restitution of, allegedly illegal gains which accrued to defendants as a result of the sale in August, 1950, of their controlling interest in the corporation. The principal defendant, C. Russell Feldmann, who represented and acted for the others, members of his family,[1] was at that time not only the dominant stockholder, but also the chairman of the board of directors and the president of the corporation. Newport, an Indiana corporation, operated mills for the production of steel sheets for sale to manufacturers of steel products, first at Newport, Kentucky, and later also at other places in Kentucky and Ohio. The buyers, a syndicate organized as Wilport Company, a Delaware corporation, consisted of end-users of steel who were interested in securing a source of supply in a market becoming ever tighter in the Korean War. Plaintiffs contend that the consideration paid for the stock included compensation for the sale of a corporate asset, a power held in trust for the corporation by Feldmann as its fiduciary. This power was the ability to control the allocation of the corporate product in a time of short supply, through control of the board of directors; and it was effectively transferred in this sale by having Feldmann procure the resignation of his own board and the election of Wilport's nominees immediately upon consummation of the sale.

. . .

Newport was a relative newcomer in the steel industry with predominantly old installations which were in the process of being supplemented by more modern facilities. Except in times of extreme shortage Newport was not in a position to compete profitably with other steel mills for customers not in its immediate geographical area. Wilport, the purchasing syndicate, consisted of geographically remote end-users of steel who were interested in buying more steel from Newport than they had been able to obtain during recent periods of tight supply. The price of $20 per share was found by Judge Hincks to be a fair one for a control block of stock, although the over-the-counter market price had not exceeded $12 and the book value per share was $17.03. . . .

[1] The stock was not held personally by Feldmann in his own name, but was held by the members of his family and by personal corporations. The aggregate of stock thus had amounted to 33% of the outstanding Newport stock and gave working control to the holder. The actual sale included 55,552 additional shares held by friends and associates of Feldmann, so that a total of 37% of the Newport stock was transferred.

Both as director and as dominant stockholder, Feldmann stood in a fiduciary relationship to the corporation and to the minority stockholders as beneficiaries thereof. . . .

It is true, as defendants have been at pains to point out, that this is not the ordinary case of breach of fiduciary duty. We have here no fraud, no misuse of confidential information, no outright looting of a helpless corporation. But on the other hand, we do not find compliance with that high standard which we have just stated and which we and other courts have come to expect and demand of corporate fiduciaries. . . . The actions of defendants in siphoning off for personal gain corporate advantages to be derived from a favorable market situation do not betoken the necessary undivided loyalty owed by the fiduciary to his principal.

The corporate opportunities of whose misappropriation the minority stockholders complain need not have been an absolute certainty in order to support this action against Feldmann. . . . [I]n Irving Trust Co. v. Deutsch, 2 Cir., 73 F.2d 121, 124, an accounting was required of corporate directors who bought stock for themselves for corporate use, even though there was an affirmative showing that the corporation did not have the finances itself to acquire the stock. Judge Swan speaking for the court pointed out that "The defendants' argument, contrary to Wing v. Dillingham [5 Cir., 239 F. 54], that the equitable rule that fiduciaries should not be permitted to assume a position in which their individual interests might be in conflict with those of the corporation can have no application where the corporation is unable to undertake the venture, is not convincing. If directors are permitted to justify their conduct on such a theory, there will be a temptation to refrain from exerting their strongest efforts on behalf of the corporation since, if it does not meet the obligations, an opportunity of profit will be open to them personally."

This rationale is equally appropriate to a consideration of the benefits which Newport might have derived from the steel shortage. In the past Newport had used and profited by its market leverage by operation of what the industry had come to call the "Feldmann Plan." This consisted of securing interest-free advances from prospective purchasers of steel in return for firm commitments to them from future production. The funds thus acquired were used to finance improvements in existing plants and to acquire new installations. In the summer of 1950 Newport had been negotiating for cold-rolling facilities which it needed for a more fully integrated operation and a more marketable product, and Feldmann plan funds might well have been used toward this end.

Further, as plaintiffs alternatively suggest, Newport might have used the period of short supply to build up patronage in the geographical area in which it could compete profitably even when steel was more abundant. Either of these opportunities was Newport's, to be used to its advantage only. Only if defendants had been able to negate completely any possibility of gain by Newport could they have prevailed. . . .

Defendants seek to categorize the corporate opportunities which might have accrued to Newport as too unethical to warrant further consideration. It is true that reputable steel producers were not participating in the gray market brought about by the Korean War and were refraining from advancing their prices, although to do so would not have been illegal. But Feldmann plan transactions were not considered within this self-imposed interdiction; the trial court found that around the time of the Feldmann sale Jones & Laughlin Steel Corporation, Republic Steel Company, and Pittsburgh Steel Corporation were all participating in such arrangements. In any event, it ill becomes the defendants to disparage as unethical the market advantages from which they themselves reaped rich benefits.

We do not mean to suggest that a majority stockholder cannot dispose of his controlling block of stock to outsiders without having to account to his corporation for profits or even never do this with impunity when the buyer is an interested customer, actual or potential, for the corporation's product. But when the sale necessarily results in a sacrifice of this element of corporate good will and consequent unusual profit to the fiduciary who has caused the sacrifice, he should account for his gains. So in a time of market shortage, where a call on a corporation's product commands an unusually large premium, in one form or another, we think it sound law that a fiduciary may not appropriate to himself the value of this premium. . . .

Hence to the extent that the price received by Feldmann and his co-defendants included such a bonus, he is accountable to the minority stockholders who sue here. . . . And plaintiffs, as they contend, are entitled to a recovery in their own right, instead of in right of the corporation (as in the usual derivative actions), since neither Wilport nor their successors in interest should share in any judgment which may be rendered. . . .

■ SWAN, CIRCUIT JUDGE (dissenting).

With the general principles enunciated in the majority opinion as to the duties of fiduciaries I am, of course, in thorough accord. But, as Mr. Justice Frankfurter stated in Securities and Exchange Comm. v. Chenery Corp., 318 U.S. 80, 85, "to say that a man is a fiduciary only begins analysis; it gives direction to further inquiry. To whom is he a fiduciary? What obligations does he owe as a fiduciary? In what respect has he failed to discharge these obligations?" My brothers' opinion does not specify precisely what fiduciary duty Feldmann is held to have violated or whether it was a duty imposed upon him as the dominant stockholder or as a director of Newport. . . .

The power to control the management of a corporation, that is, to elect directors to manage its affairs, is an inseparable incident to the ownership of a majority of its stock, or sometimes, as in the present instance, to the ownership of enough shares, less than a majority, to control an election. Concededly a majority or dominant shareholder is ordinarily privileged to sell his stock at the best price obtainable from the purchaser. In so doing he acts on his own behalf, not as an agent of the corporation. If he knows or has reason to believe that the purchaser intends to exercise to the detriment of the corporation the power of management acquired by the purchase, such knowledge or reasonable suspicion will terminate the dominant shareholder's privilege to sell and will create a duty not to transfer the power of management to such purchaser. The duty seems to me to resemble the obligation which everyone is under not to assist another to commit a tort rather than the obligation of a fiduciary. But whatever the nature of the duty, a violation of it will subject the violator to liability for damages sustained by the corporation. Judge Hincks found that Feldmann had no reason to think that Wilport would use the power of management it would acquire by the purchase to injure Newport, and that there was no proof that it ever was so used. Feldmann did know, it is true, that the reason Wilport wanted the stock was to put in a board of directors who would be likely to permit Wilport's members to purchase more of Newport's steel than they might otherwise be able to get. But there is nothing illegal in a dominant shareholder purchasing from his own corporation at the same prices it offers to other customers. That is what the members of Wilport did, and there is no proof that Newport suffered any detriment therefrom.

My brothers say that "the consideration paid for the stock included compensation for the sale of a corporate asset," which they describe as "the ability to control the allocation of the corporate product in a time of short supply, through control of the board of directors; and it was effectively transferred in this sale by having Feldmann procure the resignation of his own board and the election of Wilport's nominees immediately upon consummation of the sale." The implications of this are not clear to me. If it means that when market conditions are such as to induce users of a corporation's product to wish to buy a controlling block of stock in order to be able to purchase part of the corporation's output at the same mill list prices as are offered to other customers, the dominant stockholder is under a fiduciary duty not to sell his stock, I cannot agree. For reasons already stated, in my opinion Feldmann was not proved to be under any fiduciary duty as a stockholder not to sell the stock he controlled.

Feldmann was also a director of Newport. Perhaps the quoted statement means that as a director he violated his fiduciary duty in voting to elect Wilport's nominees to fill the vacancies created by the resignations of the former directors of Newport. As a director Feldmann was under a fiduciary duty to use an honest judgment in acting on the corporation's behalf. A director is privileged to resign, but so long as he remains a director he must be faithful to his fiduciary duties and must not make a personal gain from performing them. Consequently, if the price paid for Feldmann's stock included a payment for voting to elect the new directors, he must account to the corporation for such payment, even though he honestly believed that the men he voted to elect were well qualified to serve as directors. He can not take pay for performing his fiduciary duty. . . .

The final conclusion of my brothers is that the plaintiffs are entitled to recover in their own right instead of in the right of the corporation. This appears to be completely inconsistent with the theory advanced at the outset of the opinion, namely, that the price of the stock "included compensation for the sale of a corporate asset." If a corporate asset was sold, surely the corporation should recover the compensation received for it by the defendants. . . .

ANALYSIS

1. What did Feldmann do wrong? In what capacity?

2. How were plaintiffs harmed by the defendants' sale of their shares?

3. Why is this a derivative action?

Essex Universal Corporation v. Yates

305 F.2d 572 (2d Cir.1962).

■ BEFORE LUMBARD, CHIEF JUDGE, and CLARK and FRIENDLY, CIRCUIT JUDGES.

■ LUMBARD, CHIEF JUDGE.

. . .

The defendant Herbert J. Yates, a resident of California, was president and chairman of the board of directors of Republic Pictures Corporation, a New York corporation which at the time relevant to this suit had 2,004,190 shares of common stock outstanding. Republic's stock was listed and traded on the New York Stock Exchange. In August 1957, Essex Universal Corporation, a Delaware corporation owning stock in various diversified businesses, learned of the possibility of purchasing from Yates an interest in Republic. Negotiations proceeded rapidly, and on August 28 Yates and Joseph Harris, the president of Essex, signed a contract in which Essex agreed to buy, and Yates agreed "to sell or cause to be sold" at least 500,000 and not more than 600,000 shares of Republic stock. The price was set at eight dollars a share, roughly two dollars above the then market price on the Exchange. . . . In addition to other provisions not relevant to the present motion, the contract contained the following paragraph:

> "6. Resignations.
>
> Upon and as a condition to the closing of this transaction if requested by Buyer at least ten (10) days prior to the date of the closing:
>
> (a) Seller will deliver to Buyer the resignations of the majority of the directors of Republic.
>
> (b) Seller will cause a special meeting of the board of directors of Republic to be held, legally convened pursuant to law and the by-laws of Republic, and simultaneously with the acceptance of the directors' resignations set forth in paragraph 6(a) immediately preceding will cause nominees of Buyer to be elected directors of Republic in place of the resigned directors."

Before the date of the closing, as provided in the contract, Yates notified Essex that he would deliver 566,223 shares, or 28.3 per cent of the Republic stock then outstanding, and Essex formally requested Yates to arrange for the replacement of a majority of Republic's directors with Essex nominees pursuant to paragraph 6 of the contract. This was to be accomplished by having eight of the fourteen directors resign seriatim, each in turn being replaced by an Essex nominee elected by the others; such a procedure was in form permissible under the charter and by-laws of Republic, which empowered the board to choose the successor of any of its members who might resign.

On September 18, the parties met as arranged for the closing at Republic's office in New York City. Essex tendered bank drafts and cashier's checks totalling $1,698,690, which was the 37½ per cent of the total price of $4,529,784 due at this time. The drafts and checks were payable to one Benjamin C. Cohen, who was Essex' banker and had arranged for the borrowing of the necessary funds. Although Cohen was prepared to endorse these to Yates, Yates upon advice of his lawyer rejected the tender as "unsatisfactory" and said, according to his deposition testimony, "Well, there can be no deal. We can't close it."

Essex began this action in the New York Supreme Court, and it was removed to the district court on account of diversity of citizenship. Essex seeks damages of $2,700,000, claiming that at the time of the aborted closing the stock was in actuality worth more than $12.75 a share. Yates' answer raised a number of defenses, but the motion for summary judgment now before us was made and decided only on the theory that the provision in the contract for immediate transfer of control of the board of directors was illegal *per se* and tainted the entire contract. We have no doubt, and the parties agree, that New York law governs. . . .

Up to this point my brethren and I are in agreement. The following analysis is my own, except insofar as the separate opinions of Judges Clark and Friendly may indicate agreement.

It is established beyond question under New York law that it is illegal to sell corporate office or management control by itself (that is, accompanied by no stock or insufficient stock to carry voting control). . . . The same rule apparently applies in all jurisdictions where the question has arisen. . . . The rationale of the rule is undisputable: persons enjoying management control hold it on behalf of the corporation's stockholders, and therefore may not regard it as their own personal property to dispose of as they wish. . . .

Essex was, however, contracting with Yates for the purchase of a very substantial percentage of Republic stock. If, by virtue of the voting power carried by this stock, it could have elected a majority of the board of directors, then the contract was not a simple agreement for the sale of office to one having no ownership interest in the corporation, and the question of its legality would require further analysis. Such stock voting control would incontestably belong to the owner of a majority of the voting stock, and it is commonly known that equivalent power usually accrues to the owner of 28.3% of the stock. For the purpose of this analysis, I shall assume that Essex was contracting to acquire a majority of the Republic stock, deferring consideration of the situation where, as here, only 28.3% is to be acquired.

Republic's board of directors at the time of the aborted closing had fourteen members divided into three classes, each class being "as nearly as may be" of the same size. Directors were elected for terms of three years, one class being elected at each annual shareholder meeting on the first Tuesday in April. Thus, absent the immediate replacement of directors provided for in this contract, Essex as the hypothetical new majority shareholder of the corporation could not have obtained managing control in the form of a majority of the board in the normal course of events until April 1959, some eighteen months after the sale of the stock. . . .

There is no question of the right of a controlling shareholder under New York law normally to derive a premium from the sale of a controlling block of stock. In other words, there was no impropriety *per se* in the fact that Yates was to receive more per share than the generally prevailing market price for Republic stock . . . .

The next question is whether it is legal to give and receive payment for the immediate transfer of management control to one who has achieved majority share control but would not otherwise be able to convert that share control into operating control for some time. I think that it is.

. . .

The easy and immediate transfer of corporate control to new interests is ordinarily beneficial to the economy and it seems inevitable that such transactions would be discouraged if the purchaser of a majority stock interest were required to wait some period before his purchase of control could become effective. Conversely it would greatly hamper the efforts of any existing majority group to dispose of its interest if it could not assure the purchaser of immediate control over corporation operations. I can see no reason why a purchaser of majority control should not ordinarily be permitted to make his control effective from the moment of the transfer of stock.

Thus if Essex had been contracting to purchase a majority of the stock of Republic, it would have been entirely proper for the contract to contain the provision for immediate replacement of directors. Although in the case at bar only 28.3 per cent of the stock was involved, it is commonly known that a person or group owning so large a percentage of the voting stock of a corporation which, like Republic, has at least the 1,500 shareholders normally requisite to listing on the New York Stock Exchange, is almost certain to have share control as a practical matter. If Essex was contracting to acquire what in reality would be equivalent to ownership of a majority of stock, i.e., if it would as a practical certainty have been guaranteed of the stock voting power to choose a majority of the directors of Republic in due course, there is no reason why the contract should not similarly be legal. Whether Essex was thus to acquire the equivalent of majority stock control would, if the issue is properly raised by the defendants, be a factual issue to be determined by the district court on remand.

Because 28.3 per cent of the voting stock of a publicly owned corporation is usually tantamount to majority control, I would place the burden of proof on this issue on Yates as the party attacking the legality of the transaction. Thus, unless on remand Yates chooses to raise the question whether the block of stock in question carried the equivalent of majority control, it is my view that the trial court should regard the contract as legal and proceed to consider the other issues raised by the pleadings. If Yates chooses to raise the issue, it will, on my view, be necessary for him to prove the existence of circumstances which would have prevented Essex from electing a majority of the Republic board of directors in due course. . . .

■ CLARK, CIRCUIT JUDGE (concurring in the result).

Since Barnes v. Brown, 80 N.Y. 527, teaches us that not all contracts like the one before us are necessarily illegal, summary judgment seems definitely improper and the action should be remanded for trial. But particularly in view of our lack of knowledge of corporate realities and the current standards of business morality, I should prefer to avoid too precise instructions to the district court in the hope that if the action again comes before us the record will be generally more instructive on this important issue than it now is. . . .

. . .

■ FRIENDLY, CIRCUIT JUDGE (concurring).

I have no doubt that many contracts, drawn by competent and responsible counsel, for the purchase of blocks of stock from interests thought to "control" a corporation although owning less than a majority, have contained provisions like paragraph 6 of the contract *sub judice*. However, developments over the past decades seem to me to show that such a clause violates basic principles of corporate democracy. To be sure, stockholders who have allowed a set of directors to be placed in office, whether by their vote or their failure to vote, must recognize that death, incapacity or other hazard may prevent a director from serving a full term, and that they will have no voice as to his immediate successor. But the stockholders are entitled to expect that, in that event, the remaining directors will fill the vacancy in the exercise of their fiduciary responsibility. A mass seriatim resignation directed by a selling stockholder, and the filling of vacancies by his henchmen at the dictation of a purchaser and without any consideration of the character of the latter's nominees, are beyond what the stockholders contemplated or should have been expected to contemplate. . . .

Hence, I am inclined to think that if I were sitting on the New York Court of Appeals, I would hold a provision like paragraph 6 violative of public policy save when it was entirely plain that a new election would be a mere formality—i.e., when the seller owned more than 50% of the stock. . . . Moreover, in view of the perhaps unexpected character of such a holding, I doubt that I would give it retrospective effect.

NOTE ON WHAT IS A CONTROL BLOCK OF SHARES

In Essex Universal Corporation v. Yates the selling shareholder, Yates, was the incumbent—that is, Yates had control of the board of directors and of the management of the corporation. Control gave him, among other things, access to the corporation's list of shareholders and its funds (for waging a campaign to line up the votes of other shareholders in a proxy fight), and the advantage of inertia. Since he already held 28.3 percent of the voting shares, a challenger to his control would have been required to buy shares from the holders of the remaining 71.7 percent. The incumbent had a sufficiently large stake in the corporation to have a strong incentive to resist challenge. Given the likelihood of resistance, a battle for control might leave little gain for the challenger, even if the challenger did gain control. In this setting, the 28.3 percent voting block provides effective control.

Where there is an incumbent management team and board of directors that does not have a significant percentage of the voting shares, an outsider who acquires a large, but less-than-majority block of voting shares may well be unable to exert any control over the corporation. Indeed, it is not uncommon that outsiders who acquire substantial minority positions are denied any representation whatever on the board of directors, even though the incumbent directors collectively own far fewer shares than the outsider.

ANALYSIS

1. Suppose all the facts of the *Yates* case are as stated by the court except that Mr. Yates held, and sold, only 3 percent of the voting shares. What would the result have been?

2. Suppose a shareholder other than Yates had objected to the contract between Yates and Essex Universal Corporation. How might such a shareholder have challenged the contract, or its consequences, and what would have been the likelihood of success?

3. In *Yates,* the board was said to have been "classified." (Often the word used to describe the type of board encountered in the case is "staggered." A "classified" board, by contrast, is one for which different classes of stock elect different sets of directors.) How did the constitution of the board affect the strategy for the sale of the controlling block? How would the strategy have changed if the board had not been classified (that is, staggered)? In answering this question, assume that the time is now and that the applicable law is that of New York. Here are the relevant provisions:

§ 602. Meetings of shareholders

. . .

(b) A meeting of shareholders shall be held annually for the election of directors and the transaction of other business on a date fixed by or under the by-laws.

(c) Special meetings of the shareholders may be called by the board and by such person or persons as may be so authorized by the certificate of incorporation or the by-laws. . . .

§ 702. Number of directors

. . .

(b) The number of directors may be increased or decreased by amendment of the by-laws, or by action of the shareholders or of the board under specific provisions of a by-law adopted by the shareholders. . . .

§ 703. Election and term of directors

(a) At each annual meeting of shareholders, directors shall be elected to hold office until the next annual meeting except as authorized by § 704 (classification of directors). The certificate of incorporation may provide for the election of one or more directors by the holders of the shares of any class or series, . . . voting as a class.

(b) Each director shall hold office until the expiration of the term for which he is elected, and until his successor has been elected and qualified.

§ 704. Classification of directors

(a) The certificate of incorporation or the specific provisions of a by-law adopted by the shareholders may provide that the directors be divided into two, three, or four classes. All classes shall be as nearly equal in number as possible, and no class shall include less than three directors. The terms of office of the directors initially classified shall be as follows: that of the first class shall expire at the next annual meeting of shareholders, the second class at the succeeding annual meeting, the third class, if any, at the third succeeding annual meeting, and the fourth class, if any, at the fourth succeeding annual meeting.

(b) At each annual meeting after such initial classification, directors to replace those whose terms expire at such annual meeting shall be elected to hold office until the second succeeding annual meeting if there are two classes, the third succeeding annual meeting if there are three classes, or the fourth succeeding annual meeting if there are four classes.

(c) If directors are classified and the number of directors is thereafter changed:

(1) Any newly created directorships or any decrease in directorships shall be so apportioned among the classes as to make all classes as nearly equal in number as possible.

(2) When the number of directors is increased by the board and any newly created directorships are filled by the board, there shall be no classification of the additional directors until the next annual meeting of shareholders.

§ 705. Newly created directorships and vacancies

(a) Newly created directorships resulting from an increase in the number of directors and vacancies occurring in the board for any reason except the removal of directors without cause may be filled by vote of the board. . . .Nothing in this paragraph shall affect any provision of the certificate of incorporation or the by-laws which provides that such newly created directorships or vacancies shall be filled by vote of the shareholders. . . .

(b) Unless the certificate of incorporation or the specific provisions of a by-law adopted by the shareholders provides that the board may fill vacancies occurring by reason of the removal of directors without cause, such vacancies may be filled only by vote of the shareholders.

. . .

§ 706. Removal of directors

(a) Any or all of the directors may be removed for cause by vote of the shareholders. The certificate of incorporation or the specific provisions of a by-law adopted by the shareholders may provide for such removal by action of the board. . . .

(b) If the certificate of incorporation or the by-laws so provide, any or all of the directors may be removed without cause by vote of the shareholders.

(c) The removal of directors, with or without cause, as provided in paragraphs (a) and (b) is subject to the following:

(1) In the case of a corporation having cumulative voting, no director may be removed when the votes cast against his removal would be sufficient to elect him. . . .

(2) When by the provisions of the certificate of incorporation the holders of the shares of any class or series . . . voting as a

class, are entitled to elect one or more directors, any director so elected may be removed only by the applicable vote of the holders of that class or series, . . . voting as a class.

4. The Delaware General Corporation Law, § 141(k), provides that "any director or the entire board of directors may be removed, with or without cause, by the holders of a majority of the shares then entitled to vote at an election of directors," with exceptions protecting cumulative voting, and with an exception that: "Unless the certificate of incorporation otherwise provides, in the case of a corporation whose board is classified as provided in subsection (d) of this section, shareholders may effect such removal only for cause." Subsection (d) of § 141 permits the certificate or the by-laws to provide that the board may be "divided into one, two, or three classes" to achieve staggered terms and for classification of shares for the purpose of electing directors. How, if at all, does the Delaware law differ from the New York law?

Amendment of the articles of incorporation of a corporation requires, first, the adoption by the board of a resolution incorporating the amendment and, second, approval by a vote of the shareholders. See Del.Gen.Corp.Law § 242(b); N.Y.Bus.Corp.Law § 803 (following the basic two-step pattern but allowing certain minor amendments by action of the board alone).

PROBLEMS

1. Suppose Basic Press, Inc. has 100,000 shares outstanding, and is publicly held. You own 30,000 shares. The shares trade at $5.00 per share, but you have negotiated to sell your shares to the giant East Publishing Co. at $8.00 per share. Is there any legal impediment to the sale?

2. Suppose, instead, that Basic Press, Inc. has only four shareholders. Three of the shareholders own 30,000 shares each, and the fourth owns 10,000 shares. There is no market for the stock, and the company has issued no dividends for ten years. Suppose that the three major shareholders negotiate a sale of their stock to the East Publishing Co. Is there any legal impediment to the sale? Any ethical impediment?

3. Suppose, once again, that Basic Press is publicly held, and that you own 30,000 shares. You have negotiated a sale of your stock to the East Publishing Co.

(a) As a condition for closing the sale, East insists that Basic first replace its directors with East nominees. Is the agreement legally permissible?

(b) As a condition for closing the sale, East insists that Basic replace *one* of its directors with an East nominee. Is the agreement legally permissible?

(c) As a condition for closing the sale, East insists that the Basic directors appoint Mr. Greensmith, the CEO of East, to be the CEO of Basic. Is the agreement legally enforceable?

(d) Suppose that Basic is a closely held corporation. Would East be able to insist that Basic appoint Greensmith to be CEO of Basic?

CHAPTER 7

MERGERS, ACQUISITIONS, AND TAKEOVERS

1. MERGERS AND ACQUISITIONS

A. THE DE FACTO MERGER DOCTRINE

INTRODUCTION

In the first case that follows, Farris v. Glen Alden Corporation, two corporations, List Industries Corporation and Glen Alden Corporation, sought to combine. List was worth about three times as much as Glen Alden, so the List shareholders would wind up with about three quarters, and the Glen Alden shareholders one quarter, of the shares of the surviving corporation. Normally one would describe the combination as an acquisition of Glen Alden by List. One simple and obvious way to accomplish the combination would have been by a statutory merger.

A statutory merger is a combination accomplished by using a procedure prescribed in the state corporation laws (most of which are essentially the same in this respect). Under a statutory merger the terms of merger are spelled out in a document called a merger agreement, drafted by the parties, which prescribes, among other things, the treatment of the shareholders of each corporation. Considerable flexibility is available. In Farris v. Glen Alden, it was contemplated that the shareholders of each corporation would wind up owning stock in the surviving corporation. Thus, if the statutory merger procedure had been used, the merger agreement would have specified how many shares would go to the shareholders of each of the two corporations. It would have been natural to use List as the surviving corporation. Upon the filing of the merger agreement with the appropriate state official, Glen Alden would have disappeared and all the property interests, rights, and obligations of Glen Alden would have passed by law (under the merger provision of the corporation law) to List.

If the statutory merger procedure had been used, approval by votes of the boards of directors and the shareholders of each of the two corporations would have been required.* In addition, shareholders of each corporation who voted against the merger would have been entitled to demand that they be paid in cash the fair value of their shares (determined by agreement or, failing agreement, by a judicial proceeding). This right to be paid off is called the "appraisal right."

There are other ways in which combinations or, if you will, acquisitions, can be accomplished. These alternative methods are sometimes called "practical" mergers because they do not use the

* Under the current laws of some states, no vote of a corporation's shareholders is required if the acquisition does not substantially diminish their control. See, e.g., Del.Gen.Corp.L. § 251(f) (no vote necessary if new voting rights are less than 20 percent of total).

statutory procedure. One such alternative method would be that List would offer its shares to the shareholders of Glen Alden in return for their Glen Alden shares. By this method, List would seek to acquire enough Glen Alden shares to gain control of Glen Alden (and the offer could be made contingent on that outcome). Since the transaction would be between List and the individual shareholders of Glen Alden, no votes of the Glen Alden directors or shareholders would be required. Neither would there be any appraisal rights. Once it gained sufficient control of Glen Alden (typically, 90 percent), List could use a special procedure called a "short-form merger" to merge Glen Alden into List. List might also acquire Glen Alden shares for cash. And it might use a subsidiary to accomplish the acquisition. The common element would be a sale by the individual Glen Alden shareholders of their shares, for shares of List or for cash.

Another method of combination or acquisition would have List buy all the assets of Glen Alden for List stock (or for cash). Here List would deal with Glen Alden rather than with its shareholders. One supposed advantage of an assets acquisition is that the acquiring corporation does not succeed to unforeseen liabilities of the acquired corporation as it would under a statutory merger. (Known liabilities will be satisfied by the seller or assumed by the buyer and taken into account in the purchase price.) There is authority, however, for holding an acquiring corporation in an assets acquisition liable for product liabilities of the acquired corporation that did not arise until years after the asset transfer. See, e.g., Knapp v. North American Rockwell Corp., 506 F.2d 361 (3d Cir.1974), cert. denied, 421 U.S. 965 (1975).

If the assets-acquisition method had been used, Glen Alden would have been left with nothing but shares of List. Ordinarily, it would then have liquidated and distributed these shares to its shareholders. Glen Alden would have ceased to exist.

State laws vary on the requirement of a shareholder vote and on the availability of an appraisal right where a combination is accomplished by an asset acquisition.

In Farris v. Glen Alden the combination was accomplished by having Glen Alden, the smaller corporation, acquire the assets of List (the minnow swallows the whale). To pay for the List assets, Glen Alden issued new shares to List, which in turn distributed them to its shareholders. The number of these shares was such that the List shareholders wound up owning 76.5 percent of the total number of outstanding shares of the surviving corporation, Glen Alden, which changed its name to List Alden.

Glen Alden was incorporated in Pennsylvania and List in Delaware. Under Delaware law, the sale of substantially all of the assets of List required the approval of a majority of the List shareholders, but the List shareholders did not have appraisal rights. Under Pennsylvania law, if Glen Alden had sold its assets to List, approval by a majority of the Glen Alden shareholders would have been required and dissenting shareholders would have had appraisal rights. Since, formally, Glen Alden acquired the assets of List, its position was that its shareholders were not entitled to appraisal rights (though a vote was required to authorize the issuance of the additional Glen Alden shares needed as consideration for the List assets).

It seems that the objective of casting the merger in the form that it took was to avoid appraisal rights. According to footnote 5 in the opinion, appraisal rights might have resulted in a cash drain that List considered unacceptable. It is not entirely clear why this should be a problem. If List were required to acquire shares for cash, it could sell new shares to the public to replace that cash. The result would be simply a new set of shareholders (as if the dissenting shareholders had sold their shares in the stock market). But that is easier said than done. Because of state and federal securities laws, selling shares to the public is sometimes costly and time consuming. Moreover, if appraisal rights had been available List could not have been certain of the total price that it would ultimately pay for Glen Alden.

It is also unclear why any Glen Alden shareholders would want appraisal rights. A majority of the Glen Alden shareholders did approve the transaction (in connection with approval of the issuance of new shares). Apparently, those shareholders found the deal attractive, which means that they thought their shares would not decline in value. Shareholders who did not like the idea of the combination with List could have sold their shares. It is difficult to see why they should be entitled to anything more in an appraisal proceeding than what they could have realized by a sale in the public market. This line of thought may explain why Delaware did not provide for appraisal rights in the case of a sale of substantially all the assets of a corporation and why, under present Delaware law, appraisal is not available in a merger if the shares relinquished are "(i) listed in a national securities exchange or (ii) held of record by more than 2,000 stockholders," and if the shares received have similar characteristics (e.g., voting and dividend rights). Del.Gen.Corp. Law § 262(b)(1).

Farris v. Glen Alden Corporation

393 Pa. 427, 143 A.2d 25 (1958).

Glen Alden is a Pennsylvania corporation engaged principally in the mining of anthracite coal and lately in the manufacture of air conditioning units and fire-fighting equipment. In recent years the company's operating revenue has declined substantially, and in fact, its coal operations have resulted in tax loss carryovers of approximately $14,000,000. In October 1957, List [Industries Corporation], a Delaware holding company owning interests in motion picture theaters, textile companies and real estate, and to a lesser extent, in oil and gas operations, warehouses and aluminum piston manufacturing, purchased through a wholly owned subsidiary 38.5% of Glen Alden's outstanding stock. This acquisition enabled List to place three of its directors on the Glen Alden board.

On March 20, 1958, the two corporations entered into a "reorganization agreement," subject to stockholder approval, which contemplated the following actions:

1. Glen Alden is to acquire all of the assets of List, excepting a small amount of cash reserved for the payment of List's expenses in connection with the transaction. These assets include over $8,000,000 in cash held chiefly in the treasuries of List's wholly owned subsidiaries.

2. In consideration of the transfer, Glen Alden is to issue 3,621,703 shares of stock to List. List in turn is to distribute the stock to its shareholders. . . .

3. Further, Glen Alden is to assume all of List's liabilities including a $5,000,000 note incurred by List in order to purchase Glen Alden stock in 1957, outstanding stock options, incentive stock options plans, and pension obligations.

4. Glen Alden is to change its corporate name from Glen Alden Corporation to List Alden Corporation.

5. The present directors of both corporations are to become directors of List Alden.

6. List is to be dissolved and List Alden is to then carry on the operations of both former corporations.

Two days after the agreement was executed notice of the annual meeting of Glen Alden to be held on April 11, 1958, was mailed to the shareholders together with a proxy statement analyzing the reorganization agreement and recommending its approval as well as approval of certain amendments to Glen Alden's articles of incorporation and bylaws necessary to implement the agreement. At this meeting the holders of a majority of the outstanding shares, (not including those owned by List), voted in favor of a resolution approving the reorganization agreement.

On the day of the shareholders' meeting, plaintiff, a shareholder of Glen Alden, filed a complaint in equity against the corporation and its officers seeking to enjoin them temporarily until final hearing, and perpetually thereafter, from executing and carrying out the agreement.

The gravamen of the complaint was that the notice of the annual shareholders' meeting did not conform to the requirements of the Business Corporation Law, 15 P.S. § 2852–1 et seq., in three respects: (1) It did not give notice to the shareholders that the true intent and purpose of the meeting was to effect a merger or consolidation of Glen Alden and List; (2) It failed to give notice to the shareholders of their right to dissent to the plan of merger or consolidation and claim fair value for their shares, and (3) It did not contain copies of the text of certain sections of the Business Corporation Law as required.[3]

By reason of these omissions, plaintiff contended that the approval of the reorganization agreement by the shareholders at the annual meeting was invalid and unless the carrying out of the plan were enjoined, he would suffer irreparable loss by being deprived of substantial property rights.

The defendants answered admitting the material allegations of fact in the complaint but denying that they gave rise to a cause of action because the transaction complained of was a purchase of corporate assets

---

[3] The proxy statement included the following declaration: "Appraisal Rights. In the opinion of counsel, the shareholders of neither Glen Alden nor List Industries will have any rights of appraisal or similar rights of dissenters with respect to any matter to be acted upon at their respective meetings."

as to which shareholders had no rights of dissent or appraisal. For these reasons the defendants then moved for judgment on the pleadings.[5]

The court below concluded that the reorganization agreement entered into between the two corporations was a plan for a *de facto* merger, and that therefore the failure of the notice of the annual meeting to conform to the pertinent requirements of the merger provisions of the Business Corporation Law rendered the notice defective and all proceedings in furtherance of the agreement void. Wherefore, the court entered a final decree denying defendants' motion for judgment on the pleadings, entering judgment upon plaintiff's complaint and granting the injunctive relief therein sought. This appeal followed.

When use of the corporate form of business organization first became widespread, it was relatively easy for courts to define a "merger" or a "sale of assets" and to label a particular transaction as one or the other. . . . But prompted by the desire to avoid the impact of adverse, and to obtain the benefits of favorable, government regulations, particularly federal tax laws, new accounting and legal techniques were developed by lawyers and accountants which interwove the elements characteristic of each, thereby creating hybrid forms of corporate amalgamation. Thus, it is no longer helpful to consider an individual transaction in the abstract and solely by reference to the various elements therein determine whether it is a "merger" or a "sale." Instead, to determine properly the nature of a corporate transaction, we must refer not only to all the provisions of the agreement, but also to the consequences of the transaction and to the purposes of the provisions of the corporation law said to be applicable. We shall apply this principle to the instant case.

Section 908, subd. A of the Pennsylvania Business Corporation Law provides: "If any shareholder of a domestic corporation which becomes a party to a plan of merger or consolidation shall object to such plan of merger or consolidation, such shareholder shall be entitled to . . . [the fair value of his shares upon surrender of the share certificate or certificates representing his shares]." Act of May 5, 1933, P.L. 364, as amended, 15 P.S. § 2852–908, subd. A.

This provision had its origin in the early decision of this Court in Lauman v. Lebanon Valley R.R. Co., 1858, 30 Pa. 42. There a shareholder who objected to the consolidation of his company with another was held to have a right in the absence of statute to treat the consolidation as a dissolution of his company and to receive the value of his shares upon their surrender.

The rationale of the *Lauman* case, and of the present section of the Business Corporation Law based thereon, is that when a corporation combines with another so as to lose its essential nature and alter the original fundamental relationships of the shareholders among themselves and to the corporation, a shareholder who does not wish to continue his membership therein may treat his membership in the

[5] Counsel for the defendants concedes that if the corporation is required to pay the dissenting shareholders the appraised fair value of their shares, the resultant drain of cash would prevent Glen Alden from carrying out the agreement. On the other hand, plaintiff contends that if the shareholders had been told of their rights as dissenters, rather than specifically advised that they had no such rights, the resolution approving the reorganization agreement would have been defeated.

original corporation as terminated and have the value of his shares paid to him. . . .

Does the combination outlined in the present "reorganization" agreement so fundamentally change the corporate character of Glen Alden and the interest of the plaintiff as a shareholder therein, that to refuse him the rights and remedies of a dissenting shareholder would in reality force him to give up his stock in one corporation and against his will accept shares in another? If so, the combination is a merger within the meaning of section 908, subd. A of the corporation law. . . .

If the reorganization agreement were consummated plaintiff would find that the "List Alden" resulting from the amalgamation would be quite a different corporation than the "Glen Alden" in which he is now a shareholder. Instead of continuing primarily as a coal mining company, Glen Alden would be transformed, after amendment of its articles of incorporation, into a diversified holding company whose interests would range from motion picture theaters to textile companies. Plaintiff would find himself a member of a company with assets of $169,000,000 and a long-term debt of $38,000,000 in lieu of a company one-half that size and with but one-seventh the long-term debt.

While the administration of the operations and properties of Glen Alden as well as List would be in the hands of management common to both companies, since all executives of List would be retained in List Alden, the control of Glen Alden would pass to the directors of List; for List would hold eleven of the seventeen directorships on the new board of directors.

As an aftermath of the transaction plaintiff's proportionate interest in Glen Alden would have been reduced to only two-fifths of what it presently is because of the issuance of an additional 3,621,703 shares to List which would not be subject to preemptive rights. In fact, ownership of Glen Alden would pass to the stockholders of List who would hold 76.5% of the outstanding shares as compared with but 23.5% retained by the present Glen Alden shareholders.

Perhaps the most important consequence to the plaintiff, if he were denied the right to have his shares redeemed at their fair value, would be the serious financial loss suffered upon consummation of the agreement. While the present book value of his stock is $38 a share after combination it would be worth only $21 a share. In contrast, the shareholders of List who presently hold stock with a total book value of $33,000,000 or $7.50 a share, would receive stock with a book value of $76,000,000 or $21 a share.

Under these circumstances it may well be said that if the proposed combination is allowed to take place without right of dissent, plaintiff would have his stock in Glen Alden taken away from him and the stock of a new company thrust upon him in its place. He would be projected against his will into a new enterprise under terms not of his own choosing. It was to protect dissident shareholders against just such a result that this Court one hundred years ago in the Lauman case, and the legislature thereafter in section 908, subd. A, granted the right of dissent. And it is to accord that protection to the plaintiff that we conclude that the combination proposed in the case at hand is a merger within the intendment of section 908, subd. A.

Nevertheless, defendants contend that the 1957 amendments to sections 311 and 908 of the corporation law preclude us from reaching this result and require the entry of judgment in their favor. Subsection F of section 311 dealing with the voluntary transfer of corporate assets provides: "The shareholders of a business corporation which acquires by sale, lease or exchange all or substantially all of the property of another corporation by the issuance of stock, securities or otherwise shall not be entitled to the rights and remedies of dissenting shareholders. . . ." Act of July 11, 1957, P.L. 711, § 1, 15 P.S. § 2852–311, subd. F.

And the amendment to section 908 reads as follows: "The right of dissenting shareholders . . . shall not apply to the purchase by a corporation of assets whether or not the consideration therefor be money or property, real or personal, including shares or bonds or other evidences of indebtedness of such corporation. The shareholders of such corporation shall have no right to dissent from any such purchase." Act of July 11, 1957, P.L. 711, § 1, 15 P.S. § 2852–908, subd. C.

Defendants view these amendments as abridging the right of shareholders to dissent to a transaction between two corporations which involves a transfer of assets for a consideration even though the transfer has all the legal incidents of a merger. They claim that only if the merger is accomplished in accordance with the prescribed statutory procedure does the right of dissent accrue. In support of this position they cite to us the comment on the amendments by the Committee on Corporation Law of the Pennsylvania Bar Association, the committee which originally drafted these provisions. The comment states that the provisions were intended to overrule cases which granted shareholders the right to dissent to a sale of assets when accompanied by the legal incidents of a merger. See 61 Ann.Rep.Pa.Bar Ass'n 277, 284 (1957).[7] Whatever may have been the intent of the *committee,* there is no evidence to indicate that the *legislature* intended the 1957 amendments to have the effect contended for. But furthermore, the language of these two provisions does not support the opinion of the committee and is inapt to achieve any such purpose. The amendments of 1957 do not provide that a transaction between two corporations which has the effect of a merger but which includes a transfer of assets for consideration is to be exempt from the protective provisions of sections 908, subd. A and 515. They provide only that the shareholders of a corporation which acquires the property or purchases the assets of another corporation, *without more,* are not entitled to the right to dissent from the transaction. So, as in the present

[7] "The amendment to Section 311 expressly provides that a sale, lease or exchange of substantially all corporate assets in connection with its liquidation or dissolution is subject to the provisions of Article XI of the Act, and that no consent or authorization of shareholders other than what is required by Article XI is necessary. The recent decision in Marks v. Autocar Co., D.C.E.D.Pa., Civil Action No. 16075 [153 F.Supp. 768] is to the contrary. This amendment, together with the proposed amendment to Section 1104 expressly permitting the directors in liquidating the corporation to sell only such assets as may be required to pay its debts and distribute any assets remaining among shareholders (Section 1108, [subd.] B now so provides in the case of receivers) have the effect of overruling Marks v. Autocar Co.,. . . . which permits a shareholder dissenting from such a sale to obtain the fair value of his shares. The Marks case relies substantially on Bloch v. Baldwin Locomotive Works, 75 [Pa.] Dist. & Co. R. 24, also believed to be an undesirable decision. That case permitted a holder of stock in a corporation which *purchased* for stock all the assets of another corporation to obtain the fair value of his shares. That case is also in effect overruled by the new Sections 311 [subd.] F and 908 [subd.] C." 61 Ann.Rep.Pa.Bar Ass'n, 277, 284 (1957).

case, when as part of a transaction between two corporations, one corporation dissolves, its liabilities are assumed by the survivor, its executives and directors take over the management and control of the survivor, and, as consideration for the transfer, its stockholders acquire a majority of the shares of stock of the survivor, then the transaction is no longer simply a purchase of assets or acquisition of property to which sections 311, subd. F and 908, subd. C apply, but a merger governed by section 908, subd. A of the corporation law. To divest shareholders of their right of dissent under such circumstances would require express language which is absent from the 1957 amendments.

Even were we to assume that the combination provided for in the reorganization agreement is a "sale of assets" to which section 908, subd. A does not apply, it would avail the defendants nothing; we will not blind our eyes to the realities of the transaction. Despite the designation of the parties and the form employed, Glen Alden does not in fact acquire List, rather, List acquires Glen Alden, . . . and under section 311, subd. D[8] the right of dissent would remain with the shareholders of Glen Alden.

We hold that the combination contemplated by the reorganization agreement, although consummated by contract rather than in accordance with the statutory procedure, is a merger within the protective purview of sections 908, subd. A and 515 of the corporation law. The shareholders of Glen Alden should have been notified accordingly and advised of their statutory rights of dissent and appraisal. The failure of the corporate officers to take these steps renders the stockholder approval of the agreement at the 1958 shareholders' meeting invalid. The lower court did not err in enjoining the officers and directors of Glen Alden from carrying out this agreement.

Decree affirmed at appellants' cost.

AFTERMATH

After the decision in Farris v. Glen Alden, the Pennsylvania legislature again modified its corporation law in an effort to defeat the de facto merger doctrine. The new law was tested in Terry v. Penn Central Corporation, 668 F.2d 188 (3d Cir.1981). Penn Central had embarked on a program of acquisitions. To accomplish these acquisitions it formed a wholly owned subsidiary. The subsidiary, rather than Penn Central, acquired the target corporations, through mergers. One of the questions presented in *Terry* was whether an acquisition by merger with a subsidiary should be treated as a de facto merger with the parent, Penn Central, thereby giving the parent shareholders voting and appraisal rights. The court held that it should not, relying on the modifications in the Pennsylvania law and on a statement in a preamble to the new law stating that the objective was to "abolish the doctrine of de facto mergers."*

---

[8] "If any shareholder of a business corporation which sells, leases or exchanges all or substantially all of its property and assets otherwise than (1) in the usual and regular course of its business, (2) for the purpose of relocating its business, or (3) in connection with its dissolution and liquidation, shall object to such sale, lease or exchange and comply with the provisions of section 515 of this act, such shareholder shall be entitled to the rights and remedies of dissenting shareholders as therein provided." Act of July 11, 1957, P.L. 711, 15 P.S. § 2852–311, subd. D.

* To confuse matters, however, the court in *Terry* added, "A different result might be reached if here, as in *Farris,* the acquiring corporation were significantly smaller than the

ANALYSIS

1. How should the language of the Pennsylvania corporate law applicable in Farris v. Glen Alden have been drafted to accomplish the apparent objective of the members of the Committee on Corporation Law of the Pennsylvania Bar Association? What arguments would you offer in support of that objective?

2. Why does the court hold that the transaction was de facto a merger rather than an asset acquisition by List? Would it make any difference?

3. Suppose Glen Alden had had a market value of $10,000,000 and 1 million shares outstanding and that it had sold 3 million new shares for $30,000,000 cash and used the cash to buy all the assets of List. If the de facto merger doctrine were still the law (as it is in some other states*), would it apply to these facts?

Hariton v. Arco Electronics, Inc.

188 A.2d 123 (Del.1963).

This case involves a sale of assets under § 271 of the corporation law, 8 Del.C. [The issue] may be stated as follows: A sale of assets is effected under § 271 in consideration of shares of stock of the purchasing corporation. The agreement of sale embodies also a plan to dissolve the selling corporation and distribute the shares so received to the stockholders of the seller, so as to accomplish the same result as would be accomplished by a merger of the seller into the purchaser. Is the sale legal? . . .

The defendant Arco and Loral Electronics Corporation, a New York corporation, are both engaged, in somewhat different forms, in the electronic equipment business. In the summer of 1961 they negotiated for an amalgamation of the companies. As of October 27, 1961, they entered into a "Reorganization Agreement and Plan." The provisions of this Plan pertinent here are in substance as follows:

> 1. Arco agrees to sell all its assets to Loral in consideration (inter alia) of the issuance to it of 283,000 shares of Loral.
>
> 2. Arco agrees to call a stockholders meeting for the purpose of approving the Plan and the voluntary dissolution.
>
> 3. Arco agrees to distribute to its stockholders all the Loral shares received by it as a part of the complete liquidation of Arco.

At the Arco meeting all the stockholders voting (about 80%) approved the Plan. It was thereafter consummated.

Plaintiff, a stockholder who did not vote at the meeting, sued to enjoin the consummation of the Plan on the grounds (1) that it was

---

acquired corporation such that the acquisition greatly transformed the nature of the successor corporation." in Terry v. Penn Central Corporation, 668 F.2d 188, 194 n.7 (3d Cir.1981).

* See Rath v. Rath Packing Co., 257 Iowa 1277, 136 N.W.2d 410 (1965); Applestein v. United Board & Carton Corp., 60 N.J.Super. 333, 159 A.2d 146, aff'd, 33 N.J. 72, 161 A.2d 474 (1960).

illegal, and (2) that it was unfair. The second ground was abandoned. Affidavits and documentary evidence were filed, and defendant moved for summary judgment and dismissal of the complaint. The Vice Chancellor granted the motion and plaintiff appeals.

. . . Plaintiff's argument that the sale is illegal runs as follows: The several steps taken here accomplish the same result as a merger of Arco into Loral. In a "true" sale of assets, the stockholder of the seller retains the right to elect whether the selling company shall continue as a holding company. Moreover, the stockholder of the selling company is forced to accept an investment in a new enterprise without the right of appraisal granted under the merger statute. § 271 cannot therefore be legally combined with a dissolution proceeding under § 275 and a consequent distribution of the purchaser's stock. Such a proceeding is a misuse of the power granted under § 271, and a *de facto* merger results.

Plaintiff's contention that this sale has achieved the same result as a merger is plainly correct. . . . Accepting it as correct, we noted that this result is made possible by the overlapping scope of the merger statute and section 271. . . .

We . . . hold that the reorganization here accomplished through § 271 and a mandatory plan of dissolution and distribution is legal. This is so because the sale-of-assets statute and the merger statute are independent of each other. They are, so to speak, of equal dignity, and the framers of a reorganization plan may resort to either type of corporate mechanics to achieve the desired end. This is not an anomalous result in our corporation law. As the Vice Chancellor pointed out, the elimination of accrued dividends, though forbidden under a charter amendment . . . may be accomplished by a merger. . . .

Plaintiff concedes, as we read his brief, that if the several steps taken in this case had been taken separately they would have been legal. That is, he concedes that a sale of assets, followed by a separate proceeding to dissolve and distribute, would be legal, even though the same result would follow. This concession exposes the weakness of his contention. To attempt to make any such distinction between sales under § 271 would be to create uncertainty in the law and invite litigation.

ANALYSIS

Is there any good reason why the Delaware legislature would allow shareholders to choose appraisal rights in a statutory merger but not in an asset sale that accomplishes the same result as a statutory merger?

PROBLEM

Suppose you represent Donna, who has just agreed with Eve and Fred to form a Delaware corporation to own and operate a furniture manufacturing business. They have hired a lawyer, who is in the process of creating a simple form-book corporation with no ancillary agreements. They contemplate that Donna will be responsible for marketing and sales, Eve for manufacturing and operations, and Fred for research, design, and development. Each will own one-third of the shares of common stock of the corporation. Donna tells you that in the furniture manufacturing business, mergers and acquisitions are commonplace. In fact, she and Eve and Fred all expect that once their company has established itself, their best prospects for further growth will probably require some sort of combination with one or more other firms. Donna also tells you that Eve and Fred have been friends for a few years and she is concerned that they might act together in ways that might be to her detriment (for example, by approving a merger that would result in a firm in which they would have lucrative jobs but she would not). On the other hand, Donna thinks that both Eve and Fred tend at times to be petulant and petty. Donna can easily imagine a falling out between Eve and Fred and an alliance of herself with one of them. She asks for your advice on what she might do to protect herself in the event of a merger. What is your response?

B. FREEZE-OUT MERGERS

Weinberger v. UOP, Inc.

457 A.2d 701 (Del.Sup.1983) (en banc).

This post-trial appeal was reheard en banc from a decision of the Court of Chancery. It was brought by the class action plaintiff below, a former shareholder of UOP, Inc., who challenged the elimination of UOP's minority shareholders by a cash-out merger between UOP and its majority owner, The Signal Companies, Inc. Originally, the defendants in this action were Signal, UOP, certain officers and directors of those companies, and UOP's investment banker, Lehman Brothers Kuhn Loeb, Inc. The present Chancellor held that the terms of the merger were fair to the plaintiff and the other minority shareholders of UOP. Accordingly, he entered judgment in favor of the defendants.

Numerous points were raised by the parties, but we address only the following questions presented by the trial court's opinion:

1) The plaintiff's duty to plead sufficient facts demonstrating the unfairness of the challenged merger;

2) The burden of proof upon the parties where the merger has been approved by the purportedly informed vote of a majority of the minority shareholders;

3) The fairness of the merger in terms of adequacy of the defendants' disclosures to the minority shareholders;

4) The fairness of the merger in terms of adequacy of the price paid for the minority shares and the remedy appropriate to that issue; and

5) The continued force and effect of Singer v. Magnavox Co., Del.Supr., 380 A.2d 969, 980 (1977), and its progeny.

In ruling for the defendants, the Chancellor re-stated his earlier conclusion that the plaintiff in a suit challenging a cash-out merger must allege specific acts of fraud, misrepresentation, or other items of misconduct to demonstrate the unfairness of the merger terms to the minority. We approve this rule and affirm it.

The Chancellor also held that even though the ultimate burden of proof is on the majority shareholder to show by a preponderance of the evidence that the transaction is fair, it is first the burden of the plaintiff attacking the merger to demonstrate some basis for invoking the fairness obligation. We agree with that principle. However, where corporate action has been approved by an informed vote of a majority of the minority shareholders, we conclude that the burden entirely shifts to the plaintiff to show that the transaction was unfair to the minority. . . . But in all this, the burden clearly remains on those relying on the vote to show that they completely disclosed all material facts relevant to the transaction.

Here, the record does not support a conclusion that the minority stockholder vote was an informed one. Material information, necessary to acquaint those shareholders with the bargaining positions of Signal and UOP, was withheld under circumstances amounting to a breach of fiduciary duty. We therefore conclude that this merger does not meet the test of fairness, at least as we address that concept, and no burden thus shifted to the plaintiff by reason of the minority shareholder vote. Accordingly, we reverse and remand for further proceedings consistent herewith.

In considering the nature of the remedy available under our law to minority shareholders in a cash-out merger, we believe that it is, and hereafter should be, an appraisal under 8 Del.C. § 262 as hereinafter construed. . . . But to give full effect to section 262 within the framework of the General Corporation Law we adopt a more liberal, less rigid and stylized, approach to the valuation process than has heretofore been permitted by our courts. While the present state of these proceedings does not admit the plaintiff to the appraisal remedy per se, the practical effect of the remedy we do grant him will be co-extensive with the liberalized valuation and appraisal methods we herein approve for cases coming after this decision.

Our treatment of these matters has necessarily led us to a reconsideration of the business purpose rule announced in the trilogy of *Singer v. Magnavox Co.,* supra; Tanzer v. International General Industries, Inc., Del.Supr., 379 A.2d 1121 (1977); and Roland International Corp. v. Najjar, Del.Supr., 407 A.2d 1032 (1979). For the reasons hereafter set forth we consider that the business purpose requirement of these cases is no longer the law of Delaware.

I.

. . .

Signal is a diversified, technically based company operating through various subsidiaries. Its stock is publicly traded on the New York, Philadelphia and Pacific Stock Exchanges. UOP, formerly known as Universal Oil Products Company, was a diversified industrial company engaged in various lines of business, including petroleum and petrochemical services and related products, construction, fabricated metal products, transportation equipment products, chemicals and plastics, and other products and services including land development, lumber products and waste disposal. Its stock was publicly held and listed on the New York Stock Exchange.

In 1974 Signal sold one of its wholly-owned subsidiaries for $420,000,000 in cash. . . . While looking to invest this cash surplus, Signal became interested in UOP as a possible acquisition. Friendly negotiations ensued, and Signal proposed to acquire a controlling interest in UOP at a price of $19 per share. UOP's representatives sought $25 per share. In the arm's length bargaining that followed, an understanding was reached whereby Signal agreed to purchase from UOP 1,500,000 shares of UOP's authorized but unissued stock at $21 per share.

This purchase was contingent upon Signal making a successful cash tender offer for 4,300,000 publicly held shares of UOP, also at a price of $21 per share. This combined method of acquisition permitted Signal to acquire 5,800,000 shares of stock, representing 50.5% of UOP's outstanding shares. The UOP board of directors advised the company's shareholders that it had no objection to Signal's tender offer at that price. Immediately before the announcement of the tender offer, UOP's common stock had been trading on the New York Stock Exchange at a fraction under $14 per share.

The negotiations between Signal and UOP occurred during April 1975, and the resulting tender offer was greatly oversubscribed. However, Signal limited its total purchase of the tendered shares so that, when coupled with the stock bought from UOP, it had achieved its goal of becoming a 50.5% shareholder of UOP.

Although UOP's board consisted of thirteen directors, Signal nominated and elected only six. Of these, five were either directors or employees of Signal. The sixth, a partner in the banking firm of Lazard Freres & Co., had been one of Signal's representatives in the negotiations and bargaining with UOP concerning the tender offer and purchase price of the UOP shares.

However, the president and chief executive officer of UOP retired during 1975, and Signal caused him to be replaced by James V. Crawford, a long-time employee and senior executive vice president of one of Signal's wholly-owned subsidiaries. Crawford succeeded his predecessor on UOP's board of directors and also was made a director of Signal.

By the end of 1977 Signal basically was unsuccessful in finding other suitable investment candidates for its excess cash, and by February 1978 considered that it had no other realistic acquisitions available to it on a friendly basis. Once again its attention turned to UOP.

The trial court found that at the instigation of certain Signal management personnel, including William W. Walkup, its board chairman, and Forrest N. Shumway, its president, a feasibility study was made concerning the possible acquisition of the balance of UOP's outstanding shares. This study was performed by two Signal officers, Charles S. Arledge, vice president (director of planning), and Andrew J. Chitiea, senior vice president (chief financial officer). Messrs. Walkup, Shumway, Arledge and Chitiea were all directors of UOP in addition to their membership on the Signal board.

Arledge and Chitiea concluded that it would be a good investment for Signal to acquire the remaining 49.5% of UOP shares at any price up to $24 each. Their report was discussed between Walkup and Shumway who, along with Arledge, Chitiea and Brewster L. Arms, internal counsel for Signal, constituted Signal's senior management. In particular, they talked about the proper price to be paid if the acquisition was pursued, purportedly keeping in mind that as UOP's majority shareholder, Signal owed a fiduciary responsibility to both its own stockholders as well as to UOP's minority. It was ultimately agreed that a meeting of Signal's executive committee would be called to propose that Signal acquire the remaining outstanding stock of UOP through a cash-out merger in the range of $20 to $21 per share.

The executive committee meeting was set for February 28, 1978. As a courtesy, UOP's president, Crawford, was invited to attend, although he was not a member of Signal's executive committee. On his arrival, and prior to the meeting, Crawford was asked to meet privately with Walkup and Shumway. He was then told of Signal's plan to acquire full ownership of UOP and was asked for his reaction to the proposed price range of $20 to $21 per share. Crawford said he thought such a price would be "generous," and that it was certainly one which should be submitted to UOP's minority shareholders for their ultimate consideration.

Thus, Crawford voiced no objection to the $20 to $21 price range, nor did he suggest that Signal should consider paying more than $21 per share for the minority interests. Later, at the executive committee meeting the same factors were discussed, with Crawford repeating the position he earlier took with Walkup and Shumway. Also considered was the 1975 tender offer and the fact that it had been greatly oversubscribed at $21 per share.

Thus, it was the consensus that a price of $20 to $21 per share would be fair to both Signal and the minority shareholders of UOP. Signal's executive committee authorized its management "to negotiate" with UOP "for a cash acquisition of the minority ownership in UOP, Inc., with the intention of presenting a proposal to [Signal's] board of directors . . . on March 6, 1978." . . .

Between Tuesday, February 28, 1978 and Monday, March 6, 1978, a total of four business days, Crawford spoke by telephone with all of UOP's non-Signal, i.e., outside, directors. Also during that period, Crawford retained Lehman Brothers to render a fairness opinion as to the price offered the minority for its stock. He gave two reasons for this choice. First, the time schedule between the announcement and the board meetings was short (by then only three business days) and since Lehman Brothers had been acting as UOP's investment banker for many years, Crawford felt that it would be in the best position to respond on such brief notice. Second, James W. Glanville, a long-time director of UOP and a partner in Lehman Brothers, had acted as a financial advisor to UOP for many years. Crawford believed that Glanville's familiarity with UOP, as a member of its board, would also be of assistance in enabling Lehman Brothers to render a fairness opinion within the existing time constraints.

Crawford telephoned Glanville, who gave his assurance that Lehman Brothers had no conflicts that would prevent it from accepting the task. Glanville's immediate personal reaction was that a price of $20 to $21 would certainly be fair, since it represented almost a 50% premium over UOP's market price. . . .

Glanville assembled a three-man Lehman Brothers team to do the work on the fairness opinion. These persons examined relevant documents and information concerning UOP, including its annual reports and its Securities and Exchange Commission filings from 1973 through 1976, as well as its audited financial statements for 1977, its interim reports to shareholders, and its recent and historical market prices and trading volumes. In addition, on Friday, March 3, 1978, two members of the Lehman Brothers team flew to UOP's headquarters in Des Plaines, Illinois, to perform a "due diligence" visit, during the course of which they interviewed Crawford as well as UOP's general counsel, its chief financial officer, and other key executives and personnel.

As a result, the Lehman Brothers team concluded that "the price of either $20 or $21 would be a fair price for the remaining shares of UOP." They telephoned this impression to Glanville, who was spending the weekend in Vermont.

. . .

On March 6, 1978, both the Signal and UOP boards were convened to consider the proposed merger. . . .

First, Signal's board unanimously adopted a resolution authorizing Signal to propose to UOP a cash merger of $21 per share as outlined in a certain merger agreement and other supporting documents. This proposal required that the merger be approved by a majority of UOP's outstanding minority shares voting at the stockholders meeting at which the merger would be considered, and that the minority shares voting in favor of the merger, when coupled with Signal's 50.5% interest would have to comprise at least two-thirds of all UOP shares. Otherwise the proposed merger would be deemed disapproved.

UOP's board then considered the proposal. Copies of the agreement were delivered to the directors in attendance, and other copies had been forwarded earlier to the directors participating by telephone. They also had before them UOP financial data for 1974–1977, UOP's most recent financial statements, market price information, and budget projections for 1978. In addition they had Lehman Brothers' hurriedly prepared fairness opinion letter finding the price of $21 to be fair. Glanville, the Lehman Brothers partner, and UOP director, commented on the information that had gone into preparation of the letter.

. . .

. . . While Signal's men on UOP's board participated in various aspects of the meeting, they abstained from voting. However, the minutes show that each of them "if voting would have voted yes."

. . .

Despite the swift board action of the two companies, the merger was not submitted to UOP's shareholders until their annual meeting on May 26, 1978. . . .

As of the record date of UOP's annual meeting, there were 11,488,302 shares of UOP common stock outstanding, 5,688,302 of which were owned by the minority. At the meeting only 56%, or 3,208,652, of the minority shares were voted. Of these, 2,953,812, or 51.9% of the total minority, voted for the merger, and 254,840 voted against it. When Signal's stock was added to the minority shares voting in favor, a total of 76.2% of UOP's outstanding shares approved the merger while only 2.2% opposed it.

By its terms the merger became effective on May 26, 1978, and each share of UOP's stock held by the minority was automatically converted into a right to receive $21 cash.

II.

A.

A primary issue mandating reversal is the preparation by two UOP directors, Arledge and Chitiea, of their feasibility study for the exclusive use and benefit of Signal. This document was of obvious significance to both Signal and UOP. Using UOP data, it described the advantages to Signal of ousting the minority at a price range of $21–$24 per share. . . .

Having written [their report] solely for the use of Signal, it is clear from the record that neither Arledge nor Chitiea shared this report with their fellow directors of UOP. We are satisfied that no one else did either. This conduct hardly meets the fiduciary standards applicable to such a transaction. . . .

The Arledge-Chitiea report speaks for itself in supporting the Chancellor's finding that a price of up to $24 was a "good investment" for Signal. It shows that a return on the investment at $21 would be 15.7% versus 15.5% at $24 per share. This was a difference of only two-tenths of one percent, while it meant over $17,000,000 to the minority. Under such circumstances, paying UOP's minority shareholders $24 would have had relatively little long-term effect on Signal, and the Chancellor's findings concerning the benefit to Signal, even at a price of $24, were obviously correct. . . .

Certainly, this was a matter of material significance to UOP and its shareholders. Since the study was prepared by two UOP directors, using UOP information for the exclusive benefit of Signal, and nothing whatever was done to disclose it to the outside UOP directors or the minority shareholders, a question of breach of fiduciary duty arises. This problem occurs because there were common Signal-UOP directors participating, at least to some extent, in the UOP board's decision-making processes without full disclosure of the conflicts they faced.[7]

B.

In assessing this situation, the Court of Chancery was required to:

> [E]xamine what information defendants had and to measure it against what they gave to the minority stockholders, in a context in which "complete candor" is required. In other words, the limited function of the Court was to determine whether defendants had disclosed all information in their possession germane to the transaction in issue. And by "germane" we mean, for present purposes, information such as a reasonable shareholder would consider important in deciding whether to sell or retain stock. . . .
>
> . . . Completeness, not adequacy, is both the norm and the mandate under present circumstances.

[7] Although perfection is not possible, or expected, the result here could have been entirely different if UOP had appointed an independent negotiating committee of its outside directors to deal with Signal at arm's length. . . . Since fairness in this context can be equated to conduct by a theoretical, wholly independent, board of directors acting upon the matter before them, it is unfortunate that this course apparently was neither considered nor pursued. . . . Particularly in a parent-subsidiary context, a showing that the action taken was as though each of the contending parties had in fact exerted its bargaining power against the other at arm's length is strong evidence that the transaction meets the test of fairness. . . .

Lynch v. Vickers Energy Corp., Del.Supr., 383 A.2d 278, 281 (1977) (*Lynch I*). This is merely stating in another way the long-existing principle of Delaware law that these Signal designated directors on UOP's board still owed UOP and its shareholders an uncompromising duty of loyalty. . . .

Given the absence of any attempt to structure this transaction on an arm's length basis, Signal cannot escape the effects of the conflicts it faced, particularly when its designees on UOP's board did not totally abstain from participation in the matter. There is no "safe harbor" for such divided loyalties in Delaware. When directors of a Delaware corporation are on both sides of a transaction, they are required to demonstrate their utmost good faith and the most scrupulous inherent fairness of the bargain. . . .

C.

The concept of fairness has two basic aspects: fair dealing and fair price. The former embraces questions of when the transaction was timed, how it was initiated, structured, negotiated, disclosed to the directors, and how the approvals of the directors and the stockholders were obtained. The latter aspect of fairness relates to the economic and financial considerations of the proposed merger, including all relevant factors: assets, market value, earnings, future prospects, and any other elements that affect the intrinsic or inherent value of a company's stock. . . . However, the test for fairness is not a bifurcated one as between fair dealing and price. All aspects of the issue must be examined as a whole since the question is one of entire fairness. However, in a non-fraudulent transaction we recognize that price may be the preponderant consideration outweighing other features of the merger. Here, we address the two basic aspects of fairness separately because we find reversible error as to both.

D.

Part of fair dealing is the obvious duty of candor required by *Lynch I, supra*. Moreover, one possessing superior knowledge may not mislead any stockholder by use of corporate information to which the latter is not privy. . . . Delaware has long imposed this duty even upon persons who are not corporate officers or directors, but who nonetheless are privy to matters of interest or significance to their company. . . . With the well-established Delaware law on the subject, and the Court of Chancery's findings of fact here, it is inevitable that the obvious conflicts posed by Arledge and Chitiea's preparation of their "feasibility study," derived from UOP information, for the sole use and benefit of Signal, cannot pass muster.

The Arledge-Chitiea report is but one aspect of the element of fair dealing. How did this merger evolve? It is clear that it was entirely initiated by Signal. The serious time constraints under which the principals acted were all set by Signal. It had not found a suitable outlet for its excess cash and considered UOP a desirable investment, particularly since it was now in a position to acquire the whole company for itself. For whatever reasons, and they were only Signal's, the entire transaction was presented to and approved by UOP's board within four business days. Standing alone, this is not necessarily indicative of any lack of fairness by a majority shareholder. It was what occurred, or more properly, what did not occur, during this brief period that makes the time constraints imposed by Signal relevant to the issue of fairness.

The structure of the transaction, again, was Signal's doing. So far as negotiations were concerned, it is clear that they were modest at best. Crawford, Signal's man at UOP, never really talked price with Signal, except to accede to its management's statements on the subject, and to convey to Signal the UOP outside directors' view that as between the $20–$21 range under consideration, it would have to be $21. The latter is not a surprising outcome, but hardly arm's length negotiations. Only the protection of benefits for UOP's key employees and the issue of Lehman Brothers' fee approached any concept of bargaining.

As we have noted, the matter of disclosure to the UOP directors was wholly flawed by the conflicts of interest raised by the Arledge-Chitiea report. All of those conflicts were resolved by Signal in its own favor without divulging any aspect of them to UOP.

This cannot but undermine a conclusion that this merger meets any reasonable test of fairness. The outside UOP directors lacked one material piece of information generated by two of their colleagues, but shared only with Signal. True, the UOP board had the Lehman Brothers' fairness opinion, but that firm has been blamed by the plaintiff for the hurried task it performed, when more properly the responsibility for this lies with Signal. There was no disclosure of the circumstances surrounding the rather cursory preparation of the Lehman Brothers' fairness opinion. Instead, the impression was given UOP's minority that a careful study had been made, when in fact speed was the hallmark, and Mr. Glanville, Lehman's partner in charge of the matter, and also a UOP director, having spent the weekend in Vermont, brought a draft of the "fairness opinion letter" to the UOP directors' meeting on March 6, 1978 with the price left blank. We can only conclude from the record that the rush imposed on Lehman Brothers by Signal's timetable contributed to the difficulties under which this investment banking firm attempted to perform its responsibilities. Yet, none of this was disclosed to UOP's minority.

Finally, the minority stockholders were denied the critical information that Signal considered a price of $24 to be a good investment. Since this would have meant over $17,000,000 more to the minority, we cannot conclude that the shareholder vote was an informed one. Under the circumstances, an approval by a majority of the minority was meaningless. . . .

Given these particulars and the Delaware law on the subject, the record does not establish that this transaction satisfies any reasonable concept of fair dealing, and the Chancellor's findings in that regard must be reversed.

E.

Turning to the matter of price, plaintiff also challenges its fairness. His evidence was that on the date the merger was approved the stock was worth at least $26 per share. In support, he offered the testimony of a chartered investment analyst who used two basic approaches to valuation: a comparative analysis of the premium paid over market in ten other tender offer-merger combinations, and a discounted cash flow analysis.

In this breach of fiduciary duty case, the Chancellor perceived that the approach to valuation was the same as that in an appraisal proceeding. Consistent with precedent, he rejected plaintiff's method of proof and accepted defendants' evidence of value as being in accord with practice under prior case law. This means that the so-called "Delaware block" or weighted average method was employed wherein the elements of value, i.e., assets, market price, earnings, etc., were assigned a particular weight and the resulting amounts added to determine the value per share. . . . This procedure has been in use for decades. However, to the extent it excludes other generally accepted techniques used in the financial community and the courts, it is now clearly outmoded. It is time we recognize this in appraisal and other stock valuation proceedings and bring our law current on the subject.

While the Chancellor rejected plaintiff's discounted cash flow method of valuing UOP's stock, as not corresponding with "either logic or the existing law" (426 A.2d at 1360), it is significant that this was essentially the focus, i.e., earnings potential of UOP, of Messrs. Arledge and Chitiea in their evaluation of the merger. Accordingly, the standard "Delaware block" or weighted average method of valuation, formerly employed in appraisal and other stock valuation cases, shall no longer exclusively control such proceedings. We believe that a more liberal approach must include proof of value by any techniques or methods which are generally considered acceptable in the financial community and otherwise admissible in court, subject only to our interpretation of 8 Del.C. § 262(h), *infra*. . . .

Fair price obviously requires consideration of all relevant factors involving the value of a company. . . .

This is not only in accord with the realities of present day affairs, but it is thoroughly consonant with the purpose and intent of our statutory law. Under 8 Del.C. § 262(h), the Court of Chancery:

> shall appraise the shares, determining their *fair* value exclusive of any element of value arising from the accomplishment or expectation of the merger, together with a fair rate of interest, if any, to be paid upon the amount determined to be the *fair* value. In determining such *fair* value, the Court shall take into account *all relevant factors* . . . (Emphasis added) . . .

It is significant that section 262 now mandates the determination of "fair" value based upon "all relevant factors." Only the speculative elements of value that may arise from the "accomplishment or expectation" of the merger are excluded. We take this to be a very narrow exception to the appraisal process, designed to eliminate use of *pro forma* data and projections of a speculative variety relating to the completion of a merger. But elements of future value, including the nature of the enterprise, which are known or susceptible of proof as of the date of the merger and not the product of speculation, may be considered. When the trial court deems it appropriate, fair value also includes any damages, resulting from the taking, which the stockholders sustain as a class. . . .

Although the Chancellor received the plaintiff's evidence, his opinion indicates that the use of it was precluded because of past Delaware practice. While we do not suggest a monetary result one way or the other, we do think the plaintiff's evidence should be part of the factual mix and weighed as such. Until the $21 price is measured on remand by the valuation standards mandated by Delaware law, there can be no finding at the present stage of these proceedings that the price is fair. Given the lack of any candid disclosure of the material facts surrounding establishment of the $21 price, the majority of the minority vote, approving the merger, is meaningless.

. . .

While a plaintiff's monetary remedy ordinarily should be confined to the more liberalized appraisal proceeding herein established, we do not intend any limitation on the historic powers of the Chancellor to grant such other relief as the facts of a particular case may dictate. The appraisal remedy we approve may not be adequate in certain cases, particularly where fraud, misrepresentation, self-dealing, deliberate waste of corporate assets, or gross and palpable overreaching are involved. . . . Under such circumstances, the Chancellor's powers are complete to fashion any form of equitable and monetary relief as may be appropriate, including rescissory damages. Since it is apparent that this long completed transaction is too involved to undo, and in view of the Chancellor's discretion, the award, if any, should be in the form of monetary damages based upon entire fairness standards, i.e., fair dealing and fair price.

. . .

III.

Finally, we address the matter of business purpose. The defendants contend that the purpose of this merger was not a proper subject of inquiry by the trial court. The plaintiff says that no valid purpose existed—the entire transaction was a mere subterfuge designed to eliminate the minority. The Chancellor ruled otherwise, but in so doing he clearly circumscribed the thrust and effect of *Singer*. . . . This has led to the thoroughly sound observation that the business purpose test "may be . . . virtually interpreted out of existence, as it was in *Weinberger*."[9]

The requirement of a business purpose is new to our law of mergers and was a departure from prior case law. . . .

In view of the fairness test which has long been applicable to parent-subsidiary mergers, . . . the expanded appraisal remedy now available to shareholders, and the broad discretion of the Chancellor to fashion such relief as the facts of a given case may dictate, we do not believe that any additional meaningful protection is afforded minority shareholders by the business purpose requirement. . . . Accordingly, such requirement shall no longer be of any force or effect.

The judgment of the Court of Chancery, finding both the circumstances of the merger and the price paid the minority shareholders to be fair, is reversed. The matter is remanded for further proceedings consistent herewith. Upon remand the plaintiff's post-trial motion to enlarge the class should be granted.

---

[9] Weiss, *The Law of Take Out Mergers: A Historical Perspective,* 56 N.Y.U.L.Rev. 624, 671, n. 300 (1981).

ANALYSIS

1. If the Signal directors on the UOP board had fought for a price of $24 for the minority UOP shareholders, and in doing so had revealed the contents of the Arledge-Chitiea report, might they have subjected themselves to liability to the Signal shareholders?

2. If you had been counsel to the Signal board before any steps had been taken, how would you have advised them (with the benefit of hindsight) on how to proceed in the acquisition of the UOP minority shares?

3. In Weinberger, the Delaware Supreme Court held that "a plaintiff's monetary remedy ordinarily should be confined to the more liberalized appraisal proceeding herein established." The court acknowledged that appraisal might not be "adequate in certain cases, particularly where fraud, misrepresentation, self-dealing, deliberate waste of corporate assets, or gross and palpable overreaching are involved." In the absence of such abuses, however, plaintiffs would not be permitted to bring a class action on behalf of all shareholders but rather would be limited to pursuing their own rights in an appraisal proceeding.

If that was what the Court intended, it would have left minority shareholders subjected to a freeze-out merger by a controlling shareholder with minimal protections. The Delaware appraisal statute contains several traps for the unwary, especially the requirement that a shareholder perfect his appraisal rights by giving the corporation written notice of his intent to demand appraisal before the shareholder vote on the merger. Facts tending to show that the price was unfair may not be discovered until after the shareholder vote. As a result, shareholders often fail to perfect their appraisal rights and would therefore be left without a remedy under a literal reading of Weinberger's statement that appraisal is normally to be their exclusive remedy.

In Rabkin v. Philip A. Hunt Chemical Corp., 498 A.2d 1099 (Del. 1985), however, the Court held that appraisal is the exclusive remedy only if the stockholders' complaints are limited to "judgmental factors of valuation." Id. at 1108. Accordingly, "Rabkin . . . effectively eliminated appraisal as the exclusive remedy for any claim alleging breach of the duty of entire fairness." Glassman v. Unocal Exploration Corp., 777 A.2d 242, 247 (Del. 2001).

As a policy matter, should the court have retained appraisal as the exclusive remedy?

Kahn v. M & F Worldwide Corp.

88 A.3d 635 (Del 2014).

This is an appeal from a final judgment entered by the Court of Chancery in a proceeding that arises from a 2011 acquisition by MacAndrews & Forbes Holdings, Inc. ("M & F" or "MacAndrews & Forbes")—a 43% stockholder in M & F Worldwide Corp. ("MFW")—of the remaining common stock of MFW (the "Merger"). From the outset, M & F's proposal to take MFW private was made contingent upon two stockholder-protective procedural conditions. First, M & F required the Merger to be negotiated and approved by a special committee of independent MFW directors (the "Special Committee"). Second, M & F required that the Merger be approved by a majority of stockholders unaffiliated with M & F. The Merger closed in December 2011, after it was approved by a vote of 65.4% of MFW's minority stockholders.

FACTS

MFW and M & F

MFW is a holding company incorporated in Delaware. . . .

The MFW board had thirteen members. They were: Ronald Perelman, Barry Schwartz, William Bevins, Bruce Slovin, Charles Dawson, Stephen Taub, John Keane, Theo Folz, Philip Beekman, Martha Byorum, Viet Dinh, Paul Meister, and Carl Webb. Perelman, Schwartz, and Bevins were officers of both MFW and MacAndrews & Forbes. Perelman was the Chairman of MFW and the Chairman and CEO of MacAndrews & Forbes; Schwartz was the President and CEO of MFW and the Vice Chairman and Chief Administrative Officer of MacAndrews & Forbes; and Bevins was a Vice President at MacAndrews & Forbes.

The Taking MFW Private Proposal

In May 2011, Perelman began to explore the possibility of taking MFW private. At that time, MFW's stock price traded in the $20 to $24 per share range. MacAndrews & Forbes engaged a bank, Moelis & Company, to advise it. After preparing valuations based on projections that had been supplied to lenders by MFW in April and May 2011, Moelis valued MFW at between $10 and $32 a share.

On June 10, 2011, MFW's shares closed on the New York Stock Exchange at $16.96. The next business day, June 13, 2011, Schwartz sent a letter proposal ("Proposal") to the MFW board to buy the remaining MFW shares for $24 in cash. The Proposal stated, in relevant part:

> The proposed transaction would be subject to the approval of the Board of Directors of the Company [*i.e.*, MFW] and the negotiation and execution of mutually acceptable definitive transaction documents. It is our expectation that the Board of Directors will appoint a special committee of independent directors to consider our proposal and make a recommendation to the Board of Directors. *We will not move forward with the transaction unless it is approved by such a special committee. In addition, the transaction will be subject to a non-waivable condition requiring the approval of a majority of the shares of the Company not owned by M & F or its affiliates. . . .*
>
> . . . In considering this proposal, you should know that in our capacity as a stockholder of the Company we are interested only in acquiring the shares of the Company not already owned by us and that in such capacity we have no interest in selling any of the shares owned by us in the Company nor would we expect, in our capacity as a stockholder, to vote in favor of any alternative sale, merger or similar transaction involving the Company. If the special committee does not recommend or the public stockholders of the Company do not approve the proposed transaction, such determination would not adversely affect our future relationship with the Company and we would intend to remain as a long-term stockholder.

. . .

The Special Committee Is Formed

The MFW board met the following day to consider the Proposal. . . . Schwartz and Bevins, as the two directors present who were also directors of MacAndrews & Forbes, recused themselves from the meeting, as did Dawson . . . who had previously expressed support for the proposed offer.

. . . The independent directors decided to form the Special Committee, and resolved further that:

> [T]he Special Committee is empowered to: (i) make such investigation of the Proposal as the Special Committee deems appropriate; (ii) evaluate the terms of the Proposal; (iii) negotiate with Holdings [*i.e.,* MacAndrews & Forbes] and its representatives any element of the Proposal; (iv) negotiate the terms of any definitive agreement with respect to the Proposal (it being understood that the execution thereof shall be subject to the approval of the Board); (v) report to the Board its recommendations and conclusions with respect to the Proposal, including a determination and *recommendation as to whether the Proposal is fair and in the best interests of the stockholders of the Company other than Holdings* and its affiliates and should be approved by the Board; and (vi) determine to elect not to pursue the Proposal. . . .
>
> . . . .
>
> . . . [T]he Board shall not approve the Proposal without a prior favorable recommendation of the Special Committee. . . .
>
> . . . [T]he Special Committee [is] empowered to retain and employ legal counsel, a financial advisor, and such other agents as the Special Committee shall deem necessary or desirable in connection with these matters. . . .

The Special Committee consisted of Byorum, Dinh, Meister (the chair), Slovin, and Webb. The following day, Slovin recused himself because, although the MFW board had determined that he qualified as an independent director under the rules of the New York Stock Exchange, he had "some current relationships that could raise questions about his independence for purposes of serving on the Special Committee."

ANALYSIS

What Should Be The Review Standard?

Where a transaction involving self-dealing by a controlling stockholder is challenged, the applicable standard of judicial review is "entire fairness," with the defendants having the burden of persuasion.[5]

---

[5] Kahn v. Tremont Corp., 694 A.2d 422, 428 (Del.1997); Weinberger v. UOP, Inc., 457 A.2d 701, 710 (Del.1983); . . . . [Eds.: See generally Weinberger v. UOP, Inc., 457 A.2d 701, 711 (Del. 1983). ("The concept of fairness has two basic aspects: fair dealing and fair price. The former embraces questions of when the transaction was timed, how it was initiated, structured, negotiated, disclosed to the directors, and how the approvals of the directors and the stockholders were obtained. The latter aspect of fairness relates to the economic and financial considerations of the proposed merger, including all relevant factors: assets, market value, earnings, future prospects, and any other elements that affect the intrinsic or inherent value of a company's stock. . . . However, the test for fairness is not a bifurcated one as between fair

In *Kahn v. Lynch Communication Systems, Inc.*,[6] however, this Court held that in "entire fairness" cases, the defendants may shift the burden of persuasion to the plaintiff if either (1) they show that the transaction was approved by a well-functioning committee of independent directors; **or** (2) they show that the transaction was approved by an informed vote of a majority of the minority stockholders.

This appeal presents a question of first impression: what should be the standard of review for a merger between a controlling stockholder and its subsidiary, where the merger is conditioned *ab initio* upon the approval of **both** an independent, adequately-empowered Special Committee that fulfills its duty of care, and the uncoerced, informed vote of a majority of the minority stockholders. . . .

The Court of Chancery held that the consequence should be that the business judgment standard of review* will govern going private mergers with a controlling stockholder that are conditioned *ab initio* upon (1) the approval of an independent and fully-empowered Special Committee that fulfills its duty of care and (2) the uncoerced, informed vote of the majority of the minority stockholders.

The Court of Chancery rested its holding upon the premise that the common law equitable rule that best protects minority investors is one that encourages controlling stockholders to accord the minority both procedural protections. A transactional structure subject to both conditions differs fundamentally from a merger having only one of those protections, in that:

> By giving controlling stockholders the opportunity to have a going private transaction reviewed under the business judgment rule, a strong incentive is created to give minority stockholders much broader access to the transactional structure that is most likely to effectively protect their interests. . . . That structure, it is important to note, is critically different than a structure that uses only *one* of the procedural protections. The "or" structure does not replicate the protections of a third-party merger under the DGCL approval process, because it only requires that one, and not both, of the statutory requirements of director and stockholder approval be accomplished by impartial decisionmakers. The "both" structure, by contrast, replicates the arm's-length merger steps of the DGCL by "requir[ing] two independent approvals, which it is fair to say serve independent integrity-enforcing functions."[10]

. . . [The] Appellants . . . argue that neither procedural protection is adequate to protect minority stockholders, because "possible ineptitude and timidity of directors" may undermine the special committee

---

dealing and price. All aspects of the issue must be examined as a whole since the question is one of entire fairness.").

[6] Kahn v. Lynch Comc'n Sys., Inc., 638 A.2d 1110 (Del.1994).

* [Eds.: As the Delaware Chancery Court has observed, review under the business judgment rule is much more favorable to the defendants than would be review under the entire fairness standard. See, e.g., In re Citigroup Inc. Shareh'r Derivative Litig., 964 A.2d 106, 125 (Del. Ch. 2009) (stating that "the burden required for a plaintiff to rebut the presumption of the business judgment rule . . . is a difficult one").

[10] In re MFW Shareholders Litigation, 67 A.3d 496, 528 (Del.Ch.2013) (citing In re Cox Commc'ns, Inc. S'holders Litig., 879 A.2d 604, 618 (Del.Ch.2005)).

protection, and because majority-of-the-minority votes may be unduly influenced by arbitrageurs that have an institutional bias to approve virtually any transaction that offers a market premium, however insubstantial it may be. Therefore, the Appellants claim, these protections, even when combined, are not sufficient to justify "abandon[ing]" the entire fairness standard of review.

With regard to the Special Committee procedural protection, the Appellants' assertions regarding the MFW directors' inability to discharge their duties are not supported either by the record or by well-established principles of Delaware law. As the Court of Chancery correctly observed:

> Although it is possible that there are independent directors who have little regard for their duties or for being perceived by their company's stockholders (and the larger network of institutional investors) as being effective at protecting public stockholders, the court thinks they are likely to be exceptional, and certainly our Supreme Court's jurisprudence does not embrace such a skeptical view.

Regarding the majority-of-the-minority vote procedural protection, as the Court of Chancery noted, "plaintiffs themselves do not argue that minority stockholders will vote against a going private transaction because of fear of retribution." Instead, as the Court of Chancery summarized, the Appellants' argued as follows:

> [Plaintiffs] just believe that most investors like a premium and will tend to vote for a deal that delivers one and that many longterm investors will sell out when they can obtain most of the premium without waiting for the ultimate vote. But that argument is not one that suggests that the voting decision is not voluntary, it is simply an editorial about the motives of investors and does not contradict the premise that a majority-of-the-minority condition gives minority investors a free and voluntary opportunity to decide what is fair for themselves.

Business Judgment Review Standard Adopted

We hold that business judgment is the standard of review that should govern mergers between a controlling stockholder and its corporate subsidiary, where the merger is conditioned *ab initio* upon both the approval of an independent, adequately-empowered Special Committee that fulfills its duty of care; and the uncoerced, informed vote of a majority of the minority stockholders. We so conclude for several reasons.

First, entire fairness is the highest standard of review in corporate law. It is applied in the controller merger context as a substitute for the dual statutory protections of disinterested board and stockholder approval, because both protections are potentially undermined by the influence of the controller. However, as this case establishes, that undermining influence does not exist in every controlled merger setting, regardless of the circumstances. The simultaneous deployment of the procedural protections employed here create a countervailing, offsetting influence of equal—if not greater—force. That is, where the controller irrevocably and publicly disables itself from using its control to dictate the outcome of the negotiations and the shareholder vote, the controlled merger then acquires the shareholder-protective characteristics of third-party, arm's-length mergers, which are reviewed under the business judgment standard.

Second, the dual procedural protection merger structure optimally protects the minority stockholders in controller buyouts. As the Court of Chancery explained:

> [W]hen these two protections are established up-front, a potent tool to extract good value for the minority is established. From inception, the controlling stockholder knows that it cannot bypass the special committee's ability to say no. And, the controlling stockholder knows it cannot dangle a majority-of-the-minority vote before the special committee late in the process as a deal-closer rather than having to make a price move.

Third, and as the Court of Chancery reasoned, applying the business judgment standard to the dual protection merger structure:

> . . . is consistent with the central tradition of Delaware law, which defers to the informed decisions of impartial directors, especially when those decisions have been approved by the disinterested stockholders on full information and without coercion. Not only that, the adoption of this rule will be of benefit to minority stockholders because it will provide a strong incentive for controlling stockholders to accord minority investors the transactional structure that respected scholars believe will provide them the best protection, a structure where stockholders get the benefits of independent, empowered negotiating agents to **bargain for the best price and say no** if the agents believe the deal is not advisable for any proper reason, plus the critical ability to determine for themselves whether to accept any deal that their negotiating agents recommend to them. A transactional structure with both these protections is fundamentally different from one with only one protection.

Fourth, the underlying purposes of the dual protection merger structure utilized here and the entire fairness standard of review both converge and are fulfilled at the same critical point: **price.** Following *Weinberger v. UOP, Inc.,* this Court has consistently held that, although entire fairness review comprises the dual components of fair dealing and fair price, in a non-fraudulent transaction "price may be the preponderant consideration outweighing other features of the merger."[12] The dual protection merger structure requires two price-related pretrial determinations: first, that a fair price was achieved by an empowered, independent committee that acted with care; and, second, that a fully informed, uncoerced majority of the minority stockholders voted in favor of the price that was recommended by the independent committee.

The New Standard Summarized

To summarize our holding, in controller buyouts, the business judgment standard of review will be applied *if and only if:* (i) the controller conditions the procession of the transaction on the approval of

---

[12] Weinberger v. UOP, Inc., 457 A.2d 701, 711 (Del.1983).

both a Special Committee and a majority of the minority stockholders; (ii) the Special Committee is independent; (iii) the Special Committee is empowered to freely select its own advisors and to say no definitively; (iv) the Special Committee meets its duty of care in negotiating a fair price; (v) the vote of the minority is informed; and (vi) there is no coercion of the minority.[14]

If a plaintiff that can plead a reasonably conceivable set of facts showing that any or all of those enumerated conditions did not exist, that complaint would state a claim for relief that would entitle the plaintiff to proceed and conduct discovery. If, after discovery, triable issues of fact remain about whether either or both of the dual procedural protections were established, or if established were effective, the case will proceed to a trial in which the court will conduct an entire fairness review.

. . . A controller that employs and/or establishes only one of these dual procedural protections would continue to receive burden-shifting within the entire fairness standard of review framework. . . .

Having articulated the circumstances that will enable a controlled merger to be reviewed under the business judgment standard, we next address whether those circumstances have been established as a matter of undisputed fact and law in this case.

Dual Protection Inquiry

. . .

We begin by reviewing the record relating to the independence, mandate, and process of the Special Committee. . . . ". . . [T]he controlling stockholder must do more than establish a perfunctory special committee of outside directors."[18]

Rather, the special committee must "function in a manner which indicates that the controlling stockholder did not dictate the terms of the transaction and that the committee exercised real bargaining power 'at an arms-length.' "[19] . . .

The Special Committee Was Independent

The Appellants do not challenge the independence of the Special Committee's Chairman, Meister. They claim, however, that the three other Special Committee members—Webb, Dinh, and Byorum—were

---

[14] The Verified Consolidated Class Action Complaint would have survived a motion to dismiss under this new standard. First, the complaint alleged that Perelman's offer "value[d] the company at just four times" MFW's profits per share and "five times 2010 pre-tax cash flow," and that these ratios were "well below" those calculated for recent similar transactions. Second, the complaint alleged that the final Merger price was two dollars per share lower than the trading price only about two months earlier. Third, the complaint alleged particularized facts indicating that MWF's share price was depressed at the times of Perelman's offer and the Merger announcement due to short-term factors such as MFW's acquisition of other entities and Standard & Poor's downgrading of the United States' creditworthiness. Fourth, the complaint alleged that commentators viewed both Perelman's initial $24 per share offer and the final $25 per share Merger price as being surprisingly low. These allegations about the sufficiency of the price call into question the adequacy of the Special Committee's negotiations, thereby necessitating discovery on all of the new prerequisites to the application of the business judgment rule.

[18] Kahn v. Tremont Corp., 694 A.2d 422, 429 (Del.1997) (citation omitted). . . .

[19] Kahn v. Tremont Corp., 694 A.2d at 429 (citation omitted).

beholden to Perelman because of their prior business and/or social dealings with Perelman or Perelman-related entities.

The Appellants . . . urged that Webb and Perelman shared a "longstanding and lucrative business partnership" between 1983 and 2002 which included acquisitions of thrifts and financial institutions, and which led to a 2002 asset sale to Citibank in which Webb made "a significant amount of money." The Court of Chancery concluded, however, that the fact of Webb having engaged in business dealings with Perelman nine years earlier did not raise a triable fact issue regarding his ability to evaluate the Merger impartially. We agree.[21]

Second, the Appellants argued that there were triable issues of fact regarding Dinh's independence. The Appellants demonstrated that between 2009 and 2011, Dinh's law firm, Bancroft PLLC, advised M & F and Scientific Games (in which M & F owned a 37.6% stake), during which time the Bancroft firm earned $200,000 in fees. The record reflects that Bancroft's limited prior engagements, which were inactive by the time the Merger proposal was announced, were fully disclosed to the Special Committee soon after it was formed. The Court of Chancery found that the Appellants failed to proffer any evidence to show that compensation received by Dinh's law firm was material to Dinh, in the sense that it would have influenced his decisionmaking with respect to the M & F proposal. The only evidence of record, the Court of Chancery concluded, was that these fees were "*de minimis*" and that the Appellants had offered no contrary evidence that would create a genuine issue of material fact.

The Court of Chancery also found that the relationship between Dinh, a Georgetown University Law Center professor, and M & F's Barry Schwartz, who sits on the Georgetown Board of Visitors, did not create a triable issue of fact as to Dinh's independence. No record evidence suggested that Schwartz could exert influence on Dinh's position at Georgetown based on his recommendation regarding the Merger. Indeed, Dinh had earned tenure as a professor at Georgetown before he ever knew Schwartz.

The Appellants also argue that Schwartz's later invitation to Dinh to join the board of directors of Revlon, Inc. "illustrates the ongoing personal relationship between Schwartz and Dinh." There is no record evidence that Dinh expected to be asked to join Revlon's board at the time he served on the Special Committee. Moreover, the Court of Chancery noted, Schwartz's invitation for Dinh to join the Revlon board of directors occurred months after the Merger was approved and did not raise a triable fact issue concerning Dinh's independence from Perelman. We uphold the Court of Chancery's findings relating to Dinh.

Third, the Appellants urge that issues of material fact permeate Byorum's independence and, specifically, that Byorum "had a business relationship with Perelman from 1991 to 1996 through her executive position at Citibank." The Court of Chancery concluded, however, the Appellants presented no evidence of the nature of Byorum's interactions

---

[21] Beam ex rel. Martha Stewart Living Omnimedia, Inc. v. Stewart, 845 A.2d 1040, 1051 (Del.2004) ("Allegations that [the controller] and the other directors . . . developed business relationships before joining the board . . . are insufficient, without more, to rebut the presumption of independence.").

with Perelman while she was at Citibank. Nor was there evidence that after 1996 Byorum had an ongoing economic relationship with Perelman that was material to her in any way. Byorum testified that any interactions she had with Perelman while she was at Citibank resulted from her role as a senior executive, because Perelman was a client of the bank at the time. Byorum also testified that she had no business relationship with Perelman between 1996 and 2007, when she joined the MFW Board.

The Appellants also contend that Byorum performed advisory work for Scientific Games in 2007 and 2008 as a senior managing director of Stephens Cori Capital Advisors ("Stephens Cori"). The Court of Chancery found, however, that the Appellants had adduced no evidence tending to establish that the $100,000 fee Stephens Cori received for that work was material to either Stephens Cori or to Byorum personally.[24] Stephens Cori's engagement for Scientific Games, which occurred years before the Merger was announced and the Special Committee was convened, was fully disclosed to the Special Committee, which concluded that "it was not material, and it would not represent a conflict." We uphold the Court of Chancery's findings relating to Byorum as well.

To evaluate the parties' competing positions on the issue of director independence, the Court of Chancery applied well-established Delaware legal principles. To show that a director is not independent, a plaintiff must demonstrate that the director is "beholden" to the controlling party "or so under [the controller's] influence that [the director's] discretion would be sterilized."[27] Bare allegations that directors are friendly with, travel in the same social circles as, or have past business relationships with the proponent of a transaction or the person they are investigating are not enough to rebut the presumption of independence.

A plaintiff seeking to show that a director was not independent must satisfy a materiality standard. The court must conclude that the director in question had ties to the person whose proposal or actions he or she is evaluating that are sufficiently substantial that he or she could not objectively discharge his or her fiduciary duties. Consistent with that predicate materiality requirement, the existence of some financial ties between the interested party and the director, without more, is not disqualifying. The inquiry must be whether, applying a subjective standard, those ties were *material,* in the sense that the alleged ties could have affected the impartiality of the individual director.

. . .

The record supports the Court of Chancery's holding that none of the Appellants' claims relating to Webb, Dinh or Byorum raised a triable issue of material fact concerning their individual independence or the Special Committee's collective independence.

The Special Committee Was Empowered

It is undisputed that the Special Committee was empowered to hire its own legal and financial advisors, and it retained Willkie Farr &

---

[24] The Court of Chancery observed that Stephens Cori's fee from the Scientific Games engagement was "only one tenth of the $1 million that Stephens Cori would have had to have received for Byroum not to be considered independent under NYSE rules."

[27] Rales v. Blasband, 634 A.2d 927, 936 (Del.1993) (citing Aronson v. Lewis, 473 A.2d 805, 815 (Del.1984)).

Gallagher LLP as its legal advisor. After interviewing four potential financial advisors, the Special Committee engaged Evercore Partners ("Evercore"). The qualifications and independence of Evercore and Willkie Farr & Gallagher LLP are not contested.

Among the powers given the Special Committee in the board resolution was the authority to "report to the Board its recommendations and conclusions with respect to the [Merger], including a determination and recommendation as to whether the Proposal is fair and in the best interests of the stockholders. . . ." The Court of Chancery also found that it was "undisputed that the [S]pecial [C]ommittee was empowered not simply to 'evaluate' the offer, like some special committees with weak mandates, but to negotiate with [M & F] over the terms of its offer to buy out the noncontrolling stockholders. This negotiating power was accompanied by the clear authority to say no definitively to [M & F]" and to "make that decision stick." . . . Therefore, the Court of Chancery concluded, "the MFW committee did not have to fear that if it bargained too hard, MacAndrews & Forbes could bypass the committee and make a tender offer directly to the minority stockholders." The Court of Chancery acknowledged that even though the Special Committee had the authority to negotiate and "say no," it did not have the authority, as a practical matter, to sell MFW to other buyers. MacAndrews & Forbes stated in its announcement that it was not interested in selling its 43% stake. Moreover, under Delaware law, MacAndrews & Forbes had no duty to sell its block, which was large enough, again as a practical matter, to preclude any other buyer from succeeding unless MacAndrews & Forbes decided to become a seller. Absent such a decision, it was unlikely that any potentially interested party would incur the costs and risks of exploring a purchase of MFW.

Nevertheless, the . . . undisputed record shows that the Special Committee, with the help of its financial advisor, did consider whether there were other buyers who might be interested in purchasing MFW, and whether there were other strategic options, such as asset divestitures, that might generate more value for minority stockholders than a sale of their stock to MacAndrews & Forbes.

The Special Committee Exercised Due Care

. . .

In scrutinizing the Special Committee's execution of its broad mandate, the Court of Chancery determined there was no "evidence indicating that the independent members of the special committee did not meet their duty of care. . . ." To the contrary, the Court of Chancery found, the Special Committee "met frequently and was presented with a rich body of financial information relevant to whether and at what *price* a going private transaction was advisable." The Court of Chancery ruled that "the plaintiffs d[id] not make any attempt to show that the MFW Special Committee failed to meet its duty of care. . . ." Based on the undisputed record, the Court of Chancery held that, "there is no triable issue of fact regarding whether the [S]pecial [C]ommittee fulfilled its duty of care." . . .

Majority of Minority Stockholder Vote

We now consider the second procedural protection invoked by M & F—the majority-of-the-minority stockholder vote. Consistent with the second condition imposed by M & F at the outset, the Merger was then put before MFW's stockholders for a vote. On November 18, 2011, the stockholders were provided with a proxy statement, which contained the history of the Special Committee's work and recommended that they vote in favor of the transaction at a price of $25 per share.

. . . MFW's stockholders—representing more than 65% of the minority shares—approved the Merger. . . . The Court of Chancery found that "the plaintiffs themselves do not dispute that the majority-of-the-minority vote was fully informed and uncoerced, because they fail to allege any failure of disclosure or any act of coercion."

. . .

Conclusion

For the above-stated reasons, the judgment of the Court of Chancery is affirmed.

ANALYSIS

1. The Delaware Supreme Court advanced four justifications for its ruling. In the lower court decision affirmed here, the Chancery Court offered a fifth reason: "Under Delaware law, it has long been thought beneficial to investors for courts, which are not experts in business, to defer to the disinterested decisions of directors, who are expert, and stockholders, whose money is at stake." In re MFW S'holders Litig., 67 A.3d 496, 526 (Del. Ch. 2013), aff'd sub nom., Kahn v. M & F Worldwide Corp., ___ A.3d ___, 2014 WL 996270 (Del. 2014). What benefits does such deference provide? What costs does such deference create, if any?

2. If the Special Committee had rejected the offer, would Perelman have been precluded from making a tender offer? Forever? Why was it important to the court that Perelman had indicated that he would not follow a rejection of his offer with a tender offer? How would such a strategy coerce shareholders?

3. How meaningful is the shareholder right to vote on the offer? What is the role of institutional holders and arbitrageurs?

4. Just how independent was Byorum? The court dismisses as trivial the fact that she was friends with Perelman. Do you agree?

5. Why might a controlling shareholder decide not to structure the acquisition so as to gain the benefit of the business judgment rule?

6. How easy is it likely to be for defendants to prevail on a motion to dismiss on the pleadings for failure to state a claim as opposed to a motion for summary judgment following discovery? Would it have been easier for them to do so under the Chancery Court two-protection approach?

Coggins v. New England Patriots Football Club, Inc.

397 Mass. 525, 492 N.E.2d 1112 (1986).

On November 18, 1959, William H. Sullivan, Jr. (Sullivan), purchased an American Football League (AFL) franchise for a professional football team. The team was to be the last of the eight original teams set up to form the AFL (now the American Football Conference of the National Football League). For the franchise, Sullivan paid $25,000. Four months later, Sullivan organized a corporation, the American League Professional Football Team of Boston, Inc. Sullivan contributed his AFL franchise; nine other persons each contributed $25,000. In return, each of the ten investors received 10,000 shares of voting common stock in the corporation. Another four months later, in July, 1960, the corporation sold 120,000 shares of nonvoting common stock to the public at $5 a share.

Sullivan had effective control of the corporation from its inception until 1974. By April 1974, Sullivan had increased his ownership of shares from 10,000 shares of voting stock to 23,718 shares, and also had acquired 5,499 shares of nonvoting stock. Nevertheless, in 1974 the other voting stockholders ousted him from the presidency and from operating control of the corporation. He then began the effort to regain control of the corporation—an effort which culminated in this and other law suits.

In November, 1975, Sullivan succeeded in obtaining ownership or control of all 100,000 of the voting shares, at a price of approximately $102 a share (adjusted cash value), of the corporation, by that time renamed the New England Patriots Football Club, Inc. (Old Patriots). Upon completion of the purchase, he immediately used his 100% control to vote out the hostile directors, elect a friendly board and arrange his resumption of the presidency and the complete control of the Patriots. In order to finance this coup, Sullivan borrowed approximately $5,348,000 from the Rhode Island Hospital National Bank and the LaSalle National Bank of Chicago. As a condition of these loans, Sullivan was to use his best efforts to reorganize the Patriots so that the income of the corporation could be devoted to the payment of these personal loans and the assets of the corporation pledged to secure them. At this point they were secured by all of the voting shares held by Sullivan. In order to accomplish in effect the assumption by the corporation of Sullivan's personal obligations, it was necessary, as a matter of corporate law, to eliminate the interest of the nonvoting shares.

On October 20, 1976, Sullivan organized a new corporation called the New Patriots Football Club, Inc. (New Patriots). The board of directors of the Old Patriots and the board of directors of the New Patriots[5] executed an agreement of merger of the two corporations providing that, after the merger, the voting stock of the Old Patriots would be extinguished, the nonvoting stock would be exchanged for cash at the rate of $15 a share, and the name of the New Patriots would be changed to the name formerly used by the Old Patriots.[6] As part of this

5 The two boards were identical.

6 Additional findings as to the purpose of this merger made by the Federal judge, as adopted by the trial judge, are: "Purported reasons for the merger [were] stated in the [proxy materials]. Three reasons are given: (1) the policy of the [National Football League] to discourage public ownership of member football teams, (2) the difficulty in reconciling management's obligations to the NFL with its obligations to public stockholders, and (3) the cost and possible revelation of confidential information resulting from the obligations of publicly owned corporations to file reports with various public bodies. . . . I find, however, that while some of the stated reasons may have been useful by-products of the merger, the true reason for the merger was to enable Sullivan to satisfy his $5,348,000 personal obligation to the banks. The merger would not have occurred for the considerations stated as reasons in the Proxy Statement. . . . The Proxy Statement is an artful attempt to minimize the future profitability of

plan, Sullivan gave the New Patriots his 100,000 voting shares of the Old Patriots in return for 100% of the New Patriots stock.

General Laws c. 156B, § 78(c)(1)(iii), as amended through St.1976, c. 327, required approval of the merger agreement by a majority vote of each class of affected stock. Approval by the voting class, entirely controlled by Sullivan, was assured. The merger was approved by the class of nonvoting stockholders at a special meeting on December 8, 1976. On January 31, 1977, the merger of the New Patriots and the Old Patriots was consummated.

David A. Coggins (Coggins) was the owner of ten shares of nonvoting stock in the Old Patriots. Coggins, a fan of the Patriots from the time of their formation, was serving in Vietnam in 1967 when he purchased the shares through his brother. Over the years, he followed the fortunes of the team, taking special pride in his status as an owner.[8] When he heard of the proposed merger, Coggins was upset that he could be forced to sell. Coggins voted against the merger and commenced this suit on behalf of those stockholders, who, like himself, believed the transaction to be unfair and illegal. A judge of the Superior Court certified the class as "stockholders of New England Patriots Football Club, Inc. who have voted against the merger . . . but who have neither turned in their shares nor perfected their appraisal rights . . . [and who] desire only to void the merger."

The trial judge found in favor of the Coggins class but determined that the merger should not be undone. Instead, he ruled that the plaintiffs are entitled to rescissory damages, and he ordered that further hearings be held to determine the amount of damages. . . .

We conclude that the trial judge was correct in ruling that the merger was illegal and that the plaintiffs have been wronged. Ordinarily, rescission of the merger would be the appropriate remedy. This merger, however, is now nearly ten years old, and, because an effective and orderly rescission of the merger now is not feasible, we remand the case for proceedings to determine the appropriate monetary damages to compensate the plaintiffs. . . .

Scope of Judicial Review. In deciding this case, we address an important corporate law question: What approach will a Massachusetts court reviewing a cash freeze-out merger employ? This question has been considered by courts in a number of other States. . . .

The parties have urged us to consider the views of a court with great experience in such matters, the Supreme Court of Delaware. We note that the Delaware court announced one test in 1977, but recently has changed to another. In Singer v. Magnavox Co., 380 A.2d 969, 980 (Del.1977), the Delaware court established the so-called "business-purpose" test, holding that controlling stockholders violate their fiduciary duties when they "cause a merger to be made for the sole purpose of eliminating a minority on a cash-out basis." Id. at 978. In 1983, Delaware jettisoned the business-purpose test, satisfied that the "fairness" test "long . . . applicable to parent-subsidiary mergers, . . . the

---

the Patriots and to put a wash of corporate respectability over Sullivan's diversion of the corporation's income for his own purposes."

[8] It was, in part, the goal of the Old Patriots, in offering stock to the public, to generate loyal fans.

expanded appraisal remedy now available to stockholders, and the broad discretion of the Chancellor to fashion such relief as the facts of a given case may dictate" provided sufficient protection to the frozen-out minority. Weinberger v. UOP, Inc., 457 A.2d 701, 715 (Del.1983).[11] "The requirement of fairness is unflinching in its demand that where one stands on both sides of a transaction, he has the burden of establishing its entire fairness, sufficient to pass the test of careful scrutiny by the courts." Id. at 710. "The concept of fairness has two basic aspects: fair dealing and fair price." Id. at 711. We note that the "fairness" test to which the Delaware court now has adhered is, as we later show, closely related to the views expressed in our decisions. Unlike the Delaware court, however, we believe that the "business-purpose" test is an additional useful means under our statutes and case law for examining a transaction in which a controlling stockholder eliminates the minority interest in a corporation. Cf. Wilkes v. Springside Nursing Home, Inc., 370 Mass. 842, 851, 353 N.E.2d 657 (1976). This concept of fair dealing is not limited to close corporations but applies to judicial review of cash freeze-out mergers. . . .

The dangers of self-dealing and abuse of fiduciary duty are greatest in freeze-out situations like the Patriots merger, where a controlling stockholder and corporate director chooses to eliminate public ownership. It is in these cases that a judge should examine with closest scrutiny the motives and the behavior of the controlling stockholder. A showing of compliance with statutory procedures is an insufficient substitute for the inquiry of the courts when a minority stockholder claims that the corporate action "will be or is illegal or fraudulent as to him." G.L. c. 156B, § 98.

A controlling stockholder who is also a director standing on both sides of the transaction bears the burden of showing that the transaction does not violate fiduciary obligations. . . . Judicial inquiry into a freeze-out merger in technical compliance with the statute may be appropriate, and the dissenting stockholders are not limited to the statutory remedy of judicial appraisal where violations of fiduciary duties are found.

Factors in judicial review. The defendants concentrate their arguments on the finding of the Superior Court judge that the offered price for nonvoting shares was inadequate. They claim that his conclusion that rescissory damages are due these plaintiffs is based wholly on a finding of price inadequacy. The trial judge, however, considered the totality of circumstances, including the purpose of the merger, the accuracy and adequacy of disclosure in connection with the merger, and the fairness of the price. The trial judge correctly considered the totality of circumstances, even though he failed to attach adequate significance to each of these factors and to structure them correctly in his analysis.

Judicial scrutiny should begin with recognition of the basic principle that the duty of a corporate director must be to further the legitimate goals of the corporation. The result of a freeze-out merger is the elimination of public ownership in the corporation. The controlling faction increases its equity from a majority to 100%, using corporate

[11] . . . . That the new Delaware approach is not without its difficulties is illustrated by the opinion in Rabkin v. Philip A. Hunt Chem. Corp., 498 A.2d 1099 (Del.1985).

processes and corporate assets. The corporate directors who benefit from this transfer of ownership must demonstrate how the legitimate goals of the corporation are furthered. A director of a corporation violates his fiduciary duty when he uses the corporation for his or his family's personal benefit in a manner detrimental to the corporation. . . . Because the danger of abuse of fiduciary duty is especially great in a freeze-out merger, the court must be satisfied that the freeze-out was for the advancement of a legitimate corporate purpose. If satisfied that elimination of public ownership is in furtherance of a business purpose, the court should then proceed to determine if the transaction was fair by examining the totality of the circumstances.

The plaintiffs here adequately alleged that the merger of the Old Patriots and New Patriots was a freeze-out merger undertaken for no legitimate business purpose, but merely for the personal benefit of Sullivan. While we have recognized the right to "selfish ownership" in a corporation, such a right must be balanced against the concept of the majority stockholder's fiduciary obligation to the minority stockholders. Wilkes v. Springside Nursing Home, Inc., 370 Mass. 842, 851, 353 N.E.2d 657 (1976). Consequently, the defendants bear the burden of proving, first, that the merger was for a legitimate business purpose, and, second, that, considering totality of circumstances, it was fair to the minority.

The decision of the Superior Court judge includes a finding that "the defendants have failed to demonstrate that the merger served any valid corporate objective unrelated to the personal interests of the majority shareholders. It thus appears that the sole reason for the merger was to effectuate a restructuring of the Patriots that would enable the repayment of the [personal] indebtedness incurred by Sullivan. . . ." The trial judge considered the defendants' claims that the policy of the National Football League (NFL) requiring majority ownership by a single individual or family made it necessary to eliminate public ownership. He found that "the stock ownership of the Patriots as it existed just prior to the merger fully satisfied the rationale underlying the policy as expressed by NFL Commissioner Pete Rozelle. Having acquired 100% control of the voting common stock of the Patriots, Sullivan possessed unquestionable authority to act on behalf of the franchise at League meetings and effectively foreclosed the possible recurrence of the internal management disputes that had existed in 1974. Moreover, as the proxy statement itself notes, the Old Patriots were under no legal compulsion to eliminate public ownership." Likewise, the defendants did not succeed in showing a conflict between the interests of the league owners and the Old Patriots' stockholders. We perceive no error in these findings. They are fully supported by the evidence. Under the approach we set forth above, there is no need to consider further the elements of fairness of a transaction that is not related to a valid corporate purpose.

Remedy. The plaintiffs are entitled to relief. They argue that the appropriate relief is rescission of the merger and restoration of the parties to their positions of 1976. We agree that the normally appropriate remedy for an impermissible freeze-out merger is rescission. Because Massachusetts statutes do not bar a cash freeze-out, however, numerous third parties relied in good faith on the outcome of the merger. The trial judge concluded that the expectations of those parties should not be upset, and so chose to award damages rather than rescission.

. . . The passage of time has made the 1976 position of the parties difficult, if not impossible, to restore. A substantial number of former stockholders have chosen other courses and should not be forced back into the Patriots corporation. In these circumstances the interests of the corporation and of the plaintiffs will be furthered best by limiting the plaintiffs' remedy to an assessment of damages. . . . On remand, the judge is to take further evidence on the present value of the Old Patriots on the theory that the merger had not taken place. Each share of the Coggins class is to receive, as rescissory damages, its aliquot share of the present assets.

The trial judge dismissed the plaintiffs' claims against the individual defendants based on waste of corporate assets. The remedy we order is intended to give the plaintiffs what they would have if the merger were undone and the corporation were put back together again. The trial judge's finding that the sole purpose of the merger was the personal financial benefit of William H. Sullivan, Jr., and the use of corporate assets to accomplish this impermissible purpose, leads inescapably to the conclusion that part of what the plaintiffs otherwise would have benefitted by, was removed from the corporation by the individual defendants. We reverse the dismissal of the claim for waste of corporate assets and remand this question to the trial court. The present value of the Patriots, as determined on remand, should include the amount wrongfully removed or diverted from the corporate coffers by the individual defendants.

We do not think it appropriate, however, to award damages based on a 1976 appraisal value. To do so would make this suit a nullity, leaving the plaintiffs with no effective remedy except appraisal, a position we have already rejected. Rescissory damages must be determined based on the present value of the Patriots, that is, what the stockholders would have if the merger were rescinded. . . .

NOTE

Sarrouf v. New England Patriots Football Club, Inc., 397 Mass. 542, 492 N.E.2d 1122 (1986), was the appeal from the appraisal proceeding for those shareholders who had rejected the offered price of $15 per share and had perfected their appraisal rights. The Supreme Judicial Court upheld the trial court finding that the value was $80 per share.

ANALYSIS

1. What is a legitimate business purpose? Suppose Sullivan wanted a winning team and was not much concerned about profit, while most of the nonvoting shareholders wanted to maximize profits. Would that difference in goals have provided a legitimate business purpose to justify the cash-out merger of the nonvoting shares? What if the objectives of Sullivan and the nonvoting shareholders as to profit maximization had been reversed and for years nonvoting shareholders had been confronting Sullivan, demanding that he spend money to create a better team?

2. One benefit of going private is that the corporation saves various expenses of being a public corporation (annual reports to the SEC and the shareholders, legal fees, accounting fees, etc.). Is the elimination of

these expenses a legitimate business purpose? If so, will it always be possible for a public corporation seeking to go private to satisfy the business purpose test?

3. What was wrong about Sullivan's actual purpose? Suppose he needed money for another business venture and had caused the Patriots corporation to borrow money and declare a large dividend payable to all shareholders. Assume that this action did not threaten the corporation with insolvency or require any significant change in its operations. Would a shareholder such as Coggins have been entitled to an injunction to prevent the payment of the dividend?

4. What if Sullivan had had "good" motives as well as the "bad" one on which the court focused? Suppose, for example, that Sullivan had been concerned about the expenses and the staff time associated with the fact that the Patriots corporation was public, that he had been vexed and distracted by confrontations with nonvoting shareholders over policies and strategies, and that he found it disadvantageous to be required, as a public company, to disclose financial data. Suppose that because of these considerations he had been considering a cash-out merger of the nonvoting shareholders and that while the cash-out merger was under consideration his personal bankers had, in effect, insisted that he do it. Would Coggins have been entitled to block the merger, or would appraisal have been his sole remedy?

5. Apart from the unique facts of *Coggins,* can you think of any reason why a majority would want to buy out a minority at a fair price (presumably assured by the appraisal right) except for some business purpose?

6. On the question of damages, the court states, "each share of the Coggins class is to receive . . . its aliquot share of the present assets." In the next paragraph the court says that the "present value . . . should include the amount wrongfully removed or diverted from the corporate coffers by the individual defendants." What if the corporation had paid normal, legally permissible dividends?

C. DE FACTO NON-MERGER

Rauch v. RCA Corporation

861 F.2d 29 (2d Cir.1988).

Background

This case arises from the acquisition of RCA Corporation ("RCA") by General Electric Company ("GE"). On or about December 11, 1985, RCA, GE and Gesub, Inc. ("Gesub"), a wholly owned Delaware subsidiary of GE, entered into an agreement of merger. Pursuant to the terms of the agreement, all common and preferred shares of RCA stock (with one exception) were converted to cash. . . . Specifically, the merger agreement provided (subject in each case to the exercise of appraisal rights) that each share of RCA common stock would be converted into $66.50 . . . and each share of $3.50 cumulative first preferred stock (the stock held by plaintiff and in issue here, hereinafter the "Preferred Stock") would be converted into $40.00. . . .

On February 27, 1986, plaintiff, a holder of 250 shares of Preferred Stock, commenced this diversity class action on behalf of a class consisting of the holders of Preferred Stock. It is undisputed that this action is governed by the law of Delaware, the state of incorporation of both RCA and Gesub. Plaintiff claimed that the merger constituted a "liquidation or dissolution or winding up of RCA and a redemption of the [Preferred Stock]," as a result of which holders of the Preferred Stock were entitled to $100 per share in accordance with the redemption provisions of RCA's certificate of incorporation,[2] that defendants were in violation of the rights of the holders of Preferred Stock as thus stated; and that defendants thereby wrongfully converted substantial sums of money to their own use. Plaintiff sought damages and injunctive relief.

Defendants moved to dismiss the complaint pursuant to Fed.R.Civ.P. 12(b)(6), and plaintiff cross-moved for summary judgment. The district court concluded that the transaction at issue was a bona fide merger carried out in accordance with the relevant provisions of the Delaware General Corporation Law. Accordingly, the district court held that plaintiff's action was precluded by Delaware's doctrine of independent legal significance, and dismissed the complaint.

Discussion

. . .

According to RCA's Restated Certificate of Incorporation, the owners of the Preferred Stock were entitled to $100 per share, plus accrued dividends, upon the redemption of such stock at the election of the corporation. Plaintiff contends that the merger agreement, which compelled the holders of Preferred Stock to sell their shares to RCA for $40.00, effected a redemption whose nature is not changed by referring to it as a conversion of stock to cash pursuant to a merger. Plaintiff's argument, however, is not in accord with Delaware law.

It is clear that under the Delaware General Corporation Law, a conversion of shares to cash that is carried out in order to accomplish a merger is legally distinct from a redemption of shares by a corporation. Section 251 of the Delaware General Corporation Law allows two corporations to merge into a single corporation by adoption of an agreement that complies with that section. Del.Code Ann. tit. viii, § 251(c) (1983). The merger agreement in issue called for the conversion of the shares of the constituent corporations into cash. The statute specifically authorizes such a transaction:

> The agreement shall state . . . the manner of converting the shares of each of the constituent corporations into shares or other securities of the corporation surviving or resulting from the merger or consolidation and, if any shares of any of the constituent corporations are not to be converted solely into

[2] RCA's Restated Certificate of Incorporation, paragraph Fourth, Part I, provides in relevant part:

> (c) The First Preferred Stock at any time outstanding *may be redeemed by the Corporation,* in whole or in part, *at its election,* expressed by resolution of the Board of Directors, at any time or times upon not less than sixty (60) days' previous notice to the holders of record of the First Preferred Stock to be redeemed, given as hereinafter provided, at the price of one hundred dollars ($100) per share and all dividends accrued or in arrears. . . . (emphasis added).

> shares or other securities of the surviving or resulting corporations, *the cash . . . which the holders of such shares are to receive* in exchange for, or upon conversion of such shares . . ., *which cash . . . may be* in addition to or *in lieu of shares* or other securities of the surviving or resulting corporation. . . .

Id. § 251(b) (emphasis added). Thus, the RCA-GE merger agreement complied fully with the merger provision in question, and plaintiff does not argue to the contrary.

Redemption, on the other hand, is governed by sections 151(b) and 160(a) of the Delaware General Corporation Law. Section 151(b) provides that a corporation may subject its preferred stock to redemption "by the corporation at its option or at the option of the holders of such stock or upon the happening of a specified event." Del.Code Ann. tit. viii, § 151(b) (1983). In this instance, the Preferred Stock was subject to redemption by RCA *at its election.* See supra note 2. Nothing in RCA's certificate of incorporation indicated that the holders of Preferred Stock could initiate a redemption, nor was there provision for any specified event, such as the Gesub-RCA merger, to trigger a redemption.[3]

Plaintiff's contention that the transaction was essentially a redemption rather than a merger must therefore fail. RCA chose to convert its stock to cash to accomplish the desired merger, and in the process chose not to redeem the Preferred Stock. It had every right to do so in accordance with Delaware law. As the district court aptly noted, to accept plaintiff's argument "would render nugatory the conversion provisions within Section 251 of the Delaware Code."

Delaware courts have long held that such a result is unacceptable. Indeed, it is well settled under Delaware law that "action taken under one section of [the Delaware General Corporation Law] is legally independent, and its validity is not dependent upon, nor to be tested by the requirements of other unrelated sections under which the same final result might be attained by different means." Rothschild Int'l Corp. v. Liggett Group, 474 A.2d 133, 136 (Del.1984) (quoting Orzeck v. Englehart, 41 Del.Ch. 361, 365, 195 A.2d 375, 378 (Del.1963)). The rationale of the doctrine is that the various provisions of the Delaware General Corporation Law are of equal dignity, and a corporation may resort to one section thereof without having to answer for the consequences that would have arisen from invocation of a different section. See Hariton v. Arco Electronics, Inc., 41 Del.Ch. 74, 77, 188 A.2d 123, 125 (Del.1963). . . .

We note in this regard that plaintiff's complaint nowhere alleges that the $40.00 per share conversion rate for the Preferred Stock was unfair. Rather, "[p]laintiff is complaining of a breach of *contractual* rights, entirely divorced from the purported 'fairness' of the transaction."

---

[3] Plaintiff points, however, to Del.Code Ann. tit. viii, § 251(e) (1983), which provides that "[i]n the case of a merger, the certificate of incorporation of the surviving corporation shall automatically be amended to the extent, if any, that changes in the certificate of incorporation are set forth in the agreement of merger." Plaintiff contends that the agreement of merger "purports to alter or impair existing preferential rights," Brief for Plaintiff-Appellant at 14, thus requiring a class vote under other provisions of Delaware law. There are a number of problems with this contention, but the decisive threshold difficulty is that no "existing preferential rights" are altered or impaired in any way, since the holders of Preferred Stock never had any right to initiate a redemption.

Brief for Plaintiff-Appellant at 23. Moreover, as the district court stated: "Delaware provides specific protection to shareholders who believe that they have received insufficient value for their stock as the result of a merger: they may obtain an appraisal under § 262 of the General Corporation Law." Plaintiff, however, explicitly disavows any appraisal theory or remedy, consistent with her position that fairness is not the issue.

. . .

ANALYSIS

In *Rauch,* the plaintiff urged adoption of, and the court rejected, what might be called a "de facto non-merger" doctrine. The transaction took the form of a merger but the plaintiff argued that it was in substance, or de facto, a sale of assets followed by a redemption. If the sale-of-assets route had been followed, then, in the absence of any change in the redemption price of the preferred shares, those shares would have been entitled to $100 per share, plus any previously unpaid dividends, before the common shares received anything. Under Delaware General Corporation Law § 242(b)(2), however, the redemption price could have been altered by a majority vote of the preferred shares. A sale-of-assets transaction might have been made contingent on a prior vote of the preferred shares, approving amendment of the certificate of incorporation to lower the liquidation preference to $40 per share.*

Why might a majority of the preferred shareholders have voted to approve the reduction of their liquidation preference? What does your answer tell you about why the plaintiff in *Rauch* did not challenge the fairness of the transaction and did not pursue her appraisal remedy? What does your answer to both of these questions tell you about the possible limitations on the legal rule applied in *Rauch?*

PROBLEM

Buyer Corp. has proposed to buy all the assets of Seller Corp. for $150 million. Seller has 10 million shares of common stock outstanding. The most recent market price of the common is $10 per share, making the total market value of all the common $100 million. Seller also has 1 million shares of preferred stock outstanding. The preferred shares are entitled to an annual dividend of $3 per share, which has always been paid as due. The preferred shares are entitled on liquidation to receive

* See Goldman v. Postal Telegraph, Inc., 52 F.Supp. 763 (D.Del.1943). In *Goldman*, which arose under Delaware law, no dividends had been paid on Postal Telegraph's preferred shares for many years. The corporation was on the verge of insolvency and going downhill. If the corporation had been liquidated, the common shareholders would have received nothing; the liquidation preference of the preferred far exceeded the value of the corporate assets. But the preferred shareholders did not have the legal right to force liquidation. Western Union offered to acquire the Postal Telegraph assets for Western Union shares. About one-sixth of those shares were to go to the Postal Telegraph common shareholders and the rest to its preferred shareholders. This plan required, and was made contingent upon, voting approval of both the classes of Postal Telegraph shareholders. After such voting approval was obtained, a preferred shareholder objected and brought suit. The court upheld the plan, stating, "I can see no reason why a Delaware corporation cannot agree to sell its assets conditioned upon the seller amending its certificate of incorporation as a part of the transaction. . . . The reality of the situation called for some inducement to be offered to the common stockholders to secure their favorable vote for the plan."

$100 per share before the common shares receive anything. The recent price of the preferred shares is $30 per share, making the total market value of all the preferred shares $30 million. Seller has no debt. Thus, its capital is:

	Common	Preferred
Per share market price	$10	$30
Number of shares	10 million	1 million
Liquidation Preference	–	$100 million
Market Value	$100 million	$ 30 million

You are outside general counsel for Seller. Both Buyer and Seller are Delaware corporations. Buyer's representatives have said that they are indifferent about how the total $150 million consideration is divided between the common and the preferred so long as whatever division is adopted will sustain legal challenge. The board of directors of Seller has asked for your legal advice on how the total consideration should be divided. What is your response? What if the market value of the common is $10 million, the market value of the preferred is $40 million and the consideration to be paid is $60 million?

D. LLC MERGERS

VGS, Inc. v. Castiel

2000 WL 1277372 (Del.Ch.), aff'd mem., 781 A.2d 696 (Del.Supr. 2001).

One entity controlled by a single individual forms a one "member" limited liability company. Shortly thereafter, two other entities, one of which is controlled by the owner of the original member, become members of the LLC. The LLC Agreement creates a three-member Board of Managers with sweeping authority to govern the LLC. The individual owning the original member has the authority to name and remove two of the three managers. He also acts as CEO. The unaffiliated third member becomes disenchanted with the original member's leadership. Ultimately the third member's owner, also the third manager, convinces the original member's owner's appointed manager to join him in a clandestine strategic move to merge the LLC into a Delaware corporation. The appointed manager and the disaffected third member do not give the original member's owner, still a member of the LLC's board of managers, notice of their strategic move. After the merger, the original member finds himself relegated to a minority position in the surviving corporation. While a majority of the board acted by written consent, as all involved surely knew, had the original member's manager received notice beforehand that his appointed manager contemplated action against his interests he would have promptly attempted to remove him. Because the two managers acted without notice to the third manager under circumstances where they knew that with notice that he could have acted to protect his majority interest, they breached their duty of loyalty to the original member and their fellow manager by failing to act in good faith. The purported merger must therefore be declared invalid.

. . .

I. Facts

David Castiel formed Virtual Geosatellite LLC (the "LLC") on January 6, 1999 in order to pursue a Federal Communications Commission ("FCC") license to build and operate a satellite system which its proponents claim could dramatically increase the "real estate" in outer space capable of transmitting high speed internet traffic and other communications. When originally formed, it had only one Member—Virtual Geosatellite Holdings, Inc. ("Holdings"). On January 8, 1999, Ellipso, Inc. ("Ellipso") joined the LLC as its second Member. Several weeks later, on January 29, 1999, Sahagen Satellite Technology Group LLC ("Sahagen Satellite") became the third Member of the LLC. David Castiel controls both Holdings and Ellipso. Peter Sahagen, an aggressive and apparently successful venture capitalist, controls Sahagen Satellite.

Pursuant to the LLC Agreement, Holdings received 660 units (representing 63.46% of the total equity in the LLC), Sahagen Satellite received 260 units (representing 25%), and Ellipso received 120 units (representing 11.54%). The founders vested management of the LLC in a Board of Managers. As the majority unitholder, Castiel had the power to appoint, remove, and replace two of the three members of the Board of Managers. Castiel, therefore, had the power to prevent any Board decision with which he disagreed. Castiel named himself and Tom Quinn to the Board of Managers. Sahagen named himself as the third member of the Board.

Not long after the formation of the LLC, Castiel and Sahagen were at odds. Castiel contends that Sahagen wanted to control the LLC ever since he became involved, and that Sahagen repeatedly offered, unsuccessfully, to buy control of the LLC. Sahagen maintains that Castiel ran the LLC so poorly that its mission had become untracked, additional necessary capital could not be raised, and competent managers could not be attracted to join the enterprise. Further, Sahagen claims that Castiel directed LLC assets to Ellipso in order to prop up a failing, cash-strapped Ellipso. At trial, these issues and other similar accusations from both sides were explored in great detail. For our purposes here, all that need be concluded is the unarguable fact that Castiel and Sahagen had very different ideas about how the LLC should be managed and operated.

Sahagen ultimately convinced Quinn that Castiel must be ousted from leadership in order for the LLC to prosper. As a result, Quinn (Castiel's nominee) covertly "defected" to Sahagen's camp, and he and Sahagen decided to wrest control of the LLC from Castiel. Many LLC employees and even some of Castiel's lieutenants testified that they believed it to be in the LLC's best interest to take control from Castiel.

On April 14, 2000, without notice to Castiel, Quinn and Sahagen acted by written consent to merge the LLC under Delaware law into VGS, Inc. ("VGS"), a Delaware corporation. Accordingly, the LLC ceased to exist, its assets and liabilities passed to VGS, and VGS became the LLC's legal successor-in-interest. VGS's Board of Directors is comprised of Sahagen, Quinn, and Neel Howard. Of course, the incorporators did not name Castiel to VGS's Board.

On the day of the merger, Sahagen executed a promissory note to VGS in the amount of $10 million plus interest. In return, he received two million shares of VGS Series A Preferred Stock. VGS also issued 1,269,200 shares of common stock to Holdings, 230,800 shares of common stock to Ellipso, and 500,000 shares of common stock to Sahagen Satellite. Once one does the math, it is apparent that Holdings and Ellipso went from having a 75% controlling combined ownership interest in the LLC to having only a 37.5% interest in VGS. On the other hand, Sahagen and Sahagen Satellite went from owning 25% of the LLC to owning 62.5% of VGS.

There can be no doubt why Sahagen and Quinn, acting as a majority of the LLC's board of managers did not notify Castiel of the merger plan. Notice to Castiel would have immediately resulted in Quinn's removal from the board and a newly constituted majority which would thwart the effort to strip Castiel of control. Had he known in advance, Castiel surely would have attempted to replace Quinn with someone loyal to Castiel who would agree with his views. Clandestine machinations were, therefore, essential to the success of Quinn and Sahagen's plan.

II. Analysis

A. The Board of Managers did have authority to act by majority vote.

The LLC Agreement does not expressly state whether the Board of Managers must act unanimously or by majority vote. Sahagen and Quinn contend that because a number of provisions would be rendered meaningless if a unanimous vote was required, a majority vote is implied. Castiel, however, maintains that a unanimous vote must be implied when the majority owner has blocking power.

Section 8.01(b)(i) of the LLC Agreement states that, "[t]he Board of Managers shall initially be composed of three (3) Managers." Sahagen Satellite has the right to designate one member of the initial board, and if the Board of Managers increased in number, Sahagen Satellite could "designate a number of representatives on the Board of Managers that is less than Sahagen's then current Percentage Interest." If unanimity were required, the number of managers would be irrelevant—Sahagen, and his minority interest, would have veto power in any event. The existence of language in the LLC Agreement discussing expansion of the Board is therefore quite telling.

Also persuasive is the fact that Section 8.01(c) of the LLC Agreement, entitled "Matters Requiring Consent of Sahagen," provides that Sahagen's approval is needed for a merger, consolidation, or reorganization of the LLC. If a unanimity requirement indeed existed, there would have been no need to expressly list matters on which Sahagen's minority interest had veto power.

Section 12.01(a)(i) of the LLC Agreement also supports Sahagen's argument. This section provides that the LLC may be dissolved by written consent by either the Board of Managers or by Members holding two-thirds of the Common Units. The effect of this Section is to allow any combination of Holdings and Sahagen Satellite, or Holdings and Ellipso, as Members, to dissolve the LLC. It seems unlikely that the Members designed the LLC Agreement to permit Members holding two-thirds of the Common Units to dissolve the LLC but denied their appointed Managers the power to reach the same result unless the minority manager agreed.

Castiel takes the position that while the Members can act by majority vote, the Board of Managers can act only by unanimous vote. He maintains that if the Board fails to agree unanimously on an issue the issue should be put to an LLC Members' vote with the majority controlling. The practical effect of Castiel's interpretation would be that whenever Castiel and Sahagen disagreed, Castiel would prevail because the issue would be submitted to the Members where Castiel's controlling interest would carry the vote. If that were the case, both Sahagen's Board position and Quinn's Board position would be superfluous. I am confident that the parties never intended that result, or if they had so intended, that they would have included plain and simple language in the agreement spelling it out clearly.

B. By failing to give notice of their proposed action, Sahagen and Quinn failed to discharge their duty of loyalty to Castiel in good faith

Section 18–404(d) of the LLC Act states in pertinent part:

> Unless otherwise provided in a limited liability company agreement, on any matter that is to be voted on by managers, the managers may take such action without a meeting, without prior notice and without a vote if a consent or consents in writing, setting forth the action so taken, shall be signed by the managers having not less than the minimum number of votes that would be necessary to authorize such action at a meeting.

Therefore, the LLC Act, read literally, does not require notice to Castiel before Sahagen and Quinn could act by written consent. The LLC Agreement does not purport to modify the statute in this regard.

Those observations cannot complete the analysis of Sahagen and Quinn's actions, however. Sahagen and Quinn knew what would happen if they notified Castiel of their intention to act by written consent to merge the LLC into VGS, Inc. Castiel would have attempted to remove Quinn, and block the planned action. Regardless of his motivation in doing so, removal of Quinn in that circumstance would have been within Castiel's rights as the LLC's controlling owner under the Agreement. Section 18–404(d) has yet to be interpreted by this Court or the Supreme Court. Nonetheless, it seems clear that the purpose of permitting action by written consent without notice is to enable LLC managers to take quick, efficient action in situations where a minority of managers could not block or adversely affect the course set by the majority even if they were notified of the proposed action and objected to it. The General Assembly never intended, I am quite confident, to enable two managers to deprive, clandestinely and surreptitiously, a third manager representing the majority interest in the LLC of an opportunity to protect that interest by taking an action that the third manager's member would surely have opposed if he had knowledge of it. My reading of Section 18–404(d) is grounded in a classic maxim of equity—"Equity looks to the intent rather than to the form."[3] In this hopefully unique situation, this application of the maxim requires construction of the statute to allow action without notice only by a constant or fixed majority. It cannot apply

---

[3] DONALD J. WOLFE, JR. & MICHAEL A. PITTENGER, CORPORATE AND COMMERCIAL PRACTICE IN THE DELAWARE COURT OF CHANCERY, at vii (1998) (listing the maxims of equity). . . .

to an illusory, will-of-the wisp majority which would implode should notice be given. Nothing in the statute suggests that this court of equity should blind its eyes to a shallow, too clever by half, manipulative attempt to restructure an enterprise through an action taken by a "majority" that existed only so long as it could act in secrecy.

Sahagen and Quinn each owed a duty of loyalty to the LLC, its investors and Castiel, their fellow manager. Castiel or his entities owned a majority interest in the LLC and he sat as a member of the board representing entities and interests empowered by the Agreement to control the majority membership of the board. The majority investor protected his equity interest in the LLC through the mechanism of appointment to the board rather than by the statutorily sanctioned mechanism of approval by members owning a majority of the LLC's equity interests. It may seem somewhat incongruous, but this Agreement allows the action to merge, dissolve or change to corporate status to be taken by a simple majority vote of the board of managers rather than rely upon the default position of the statute which requires a majority vote of the equity interest. Instead the drafters made the critical assumption, known to all the players here, that the holder of the majority equity interest has the right to appoint and remove two managers, ostensibly guaranteeing control over a three member board. When Sahagen and Quinn, fully recognizing that this was Castiel's protection against actions adverse to his majority interest, acted in secret, without notice, they failed to discharge their duty of loyalty to him in good faith. They owed Castiel a duty to give him prior notice even if he would have interfered with a plan that they conscientiously believed to be in the best interest of the LLC.[4] Instead, they launched a preemptive strike that furtively converted Castiel's controlling interest in the LLC to a minority interest in VGS without affording Castiel a level playing field on which to defend his interest. "[Another] traditional maxim of equity holds that equity regards and treats that as done which in good conscience ought to be done."[5] In good conscience, under these circumstances, Sahagen and Quinn should have given Castiel prior notice.

Many hours were spent at trial focusing on contentions that Castiel has proved to be an ineffective leader in whom employees and investors have lost confidence. I listened to testimony regarding delayed FCC licensing, a suggested new management team for the LLC, and the alleged unlocked value of the LLC. A substantial record exists fully flushing out the rancorous relationships of the members and their wildly disparate views on the existing state of affairs as well as the LLC's prospects for the future. But the issue of who is best suited to run the LLC should not be resolved here but in board meetings where all managers are present and all members appropriately represented, and/or in future litigation, if it unfortunately becomes necessary.

Likewise, the parties spent much time and effort arguing over the standard to be applied to the actions taken by Sahagen and Quinn. Specifically, the parties debated whether the standard should be entire

---

[4] I make no ruling here as to whether I believe the merger and the resulting recapitalization of the LLC was in the LLC's best interests, nor do I rule here regarding the wisdom of Castiel's actions had he in fact been able to remove Quinn before the merger.

[5] WOLFE & PITTENGER, supra, at § 2–3(b)(1)(i), citing 2 JOHN NORTON POMEROY, A TREATISE ON EQUITY JURISPRUDENCE § 363 et seq. (5th ed. (1941)).

fairness or the business judgment rule. It should be clear that the actions of Sahagen and Quinn, in their capacity as managers constituted a breach of their duty of loyalty and that those actions do not, therefore, entitle them to the benefit or protection of the business judgment rule. They intentionally used a flawed process to merge the LLC into VGS, Inc., in an attempt to prevent the member with majority equity interest in the LLC from protecting his interests in the manner contemplated by the very LLC Agreement under which they purported to act. Analysis beyond a look at the process is clearly unnecessary. Perhaps, had notice been given and an attempt then made to block Castiel's anticipated action to replace Quinn, the allegedly disinterested and independent member that Castiel himself had appointed, the analysis might be different. However, this, as all cases must be reviewed as it is presented, not as it might have been.

III. Conclusion

For the reasons stated above, I find that a majority vote of the LLC's Board of Managers could properly effect a merger. But, I also find that Sahagen and Quinn failed to discharge their duty of loyalty to Castiel in good faith by failing to give him advance notice of their merger plans under the unique circumstances of this case and the structure of this LLC Agreement. Accordingly, I declare that the acts taken to merge the LLC into VGS, Inc. to be invalid and the merger is ordered rescinded.

ANALYSIS

1. The court states that "Section 8.01(c) of the LLC Agreement, entitled 'Matters Requiring Consent of Sahagen,' provides that Sahagen's approval is needed for a merger, consolidation, or reorganization of the LLC." Castiel did not have a similar veto power. Why not?

2. Is this decision consistent with that of the Delaware Supreme Court in Hariton v. Arco Electronics, Inc. (Chap. 7 Sec. I.A.)?

3. On the court's view of how the Board of Managers should operate, what is Quinn, a potted plant?

4. The court states that "Sahagen and Quinn each owed a duty of loyalty to the LLC, its investors and Castiel, their fellow manager." Suppose that Sahagen and Quinn firmly and sincerely believed that ousting Castiel from control was essential for the financial well-being of the LLC and that the plan for taking control from Castiel that they adopted was the only feasible one. If they failed to adopt that plan would they have failed in their duty of loyalty?

2. TAKEOVERS

A. INTRODUCTION

Cheff v. Mathes

41 Del.Ch. 494, 199 A.2d 548 (1964).

This is an appeal from the decision of the Vice-Chancellor in a derivative suit holding certain directors of Holland Furnace Company liable for loss allegedly resulting from improper use of corporate funds to purchase shares of the company. . . .

Holland Furnace Company, a corporation of the State of Delaware, manufactures warm air furnaces, air conditioning equipment, and other home heating equipment. At the time of the relevant transactions, the board of directors was composed of the seven individual defendants. Mr. Cheff had been Holland's Chief Executive Officer since 1933, received an annual salary of $77,400, and personally owned 6,000 shares of the company. He was also a director. Mrs. Cheff, the wife of Mr. Cheff, was a daughter of the founder of Holland and had served as a director since 1922. She personally owned 5,804 shares of Holland and owned 47.9 percent of Hazelbank United Interest, Inc. Hazelbank is an investment vehicle for Mrs. Cheff and members of the Cheff-Landwehr family group, which owned 164,950 shares of the 883,585 outstanding shares of Holland. As a director, Mrs. Cheff received a compensation of $200.00 for each monthly board meeting, whether or not she attended the meeting.

The third director, Edgar P. Landwehr, is the nephew of Mrs. Cheff and personally owned 24,010 shares of Holland and 8.6 percent of the outstanding shares of Hazelbank. He received no compensation from Holland other than the monthly director's fee.

Robert H. Trenkamp is an attorney who first represented Holland in 1946. In May 1953, he became a director of Holland and acted as general counsel for the company. During the period in question, he received no retainer from the company, but did receive substantial sums for legal services rendered the company. Apart from the above-described payments, he received no compensation from Holland other than the monthly director's fee. He owned 200 shares of Holland Furnace stock. Although he owned no shares of Hazelbank, at the time relevant to this controversy, he was serving as a director and counsel of Hazelbank.

John D. Ames was then a partner in the Chicago investment firm of Bacon, Whipple & Co. and joined the board at the request of Mr. Cheff. During the periods in question, his stock ownership varied between ownership of no shares to ownership of 300 shares. He was considered by the other members of the Holland board to be the financial advisor to the board. He received no compensation from Holland other than the normal director's fee.

[There were two other directors, Boalt and Spatta, who were not substantial shareholders and were not employees of the firm. Both were businessmen who had become directors at the request of Mr. Cheff.]

The board of directors of Hazelbank included the five principal shareholders: Mrs. Cheff; Leona Kolb, who was Mrs. Cheff's daughter; Mr. Landwehr; Mrs. Bowles, who was Mr. Landwehr's sister; Mrs. Putnam, who was also Mr. Landwehr's sister; Mr. Trenkamp; and Mr. William DeLong, an accountant.

Prior to the events in question, Holland employed approximately 8500 persons and maintained 400 branch sales offices located in 43 states. The volume of sales had declined from over $41,000,000 in 1948 to less than $32,000,000 in 1956. Defendants contend that the decline in earnings is attributable to the artificial post-war demand generated in the 1946–1948 period. In order to stabilize the condition of the company, the sales department apparently was reorganized and certain unprofitable branch offices were closed. By 1957 this reorganization had been completed and the management was convinced that the changes were manifesting beneficial results. The practice of the company was to directly employ the retail salesman, and the management considered that practice—unique in the furnace business—to be a vital factor in the company's success.

During the first five months of 1957, the monthly trading volume of Holland's stock on the New York Stock Exchange ranged between 10,300 shares to 24,200 shares. In the last week of June 1957, however, the trading increased to 37,800 shares, with a corresponding increase in the market price. In June of 1957, Mr. Cheff met with Mr. Arnold H. Maremont, who was President of Maremont Automotive Products, Inc. and Chairman of the boards of Motor Products Corporation and Allied Paper Corporation. Mr. Cheff testified, on deposition, that Maremont generally inquired about the feasibility of merger between Motor Products and Holland. Mr. Cheff testified that, in view of the difference in sales practices between the two companies, he informed Mr. Maremont that a merger did not seem feasible. In reply, Mr. Maremont stated that, in the light of Mr. Cheff's decision, he had no further interest in Holland nor did he wish to buy any of the stock of Holland.

None of the members of the board apparently connected the interest of Mr. Maremont with the increased activity of Holland stock. However, Mr. Trenkamp and Mr. Staal, the Treasurer of Holland, unsuccessfully made an informal investigation in order to ascertain the identity of the purchaser or purchasers. The mystery was resolved, however, when Maremont called Ames in July of 1957 to inform the latter that Maremont then owned 55,000 shares of Holland stock. At this juncture, no requests for change in corporate policy were made, and Maremont made no demand to be made a member of the board of Holland.

Ames reported the above information to the board at its July 30, 1957 meeting. Because of the position now occupied by Maremont, the board elected to investigate the financial and business history of Maremont and corporations controlled by him. Apart from the documentary evidence produced by this investigation, which will be considered infra, Staal testified, on deposition, that "leading bank officials" had indicated that Maremont "had been a participant, or had attempted to be, in the liquidation of a number of companies." Staal specifically mentioned only one individual giving such advice, the Vice President of the First National Bank of Chicago. Mr. Cheff testified, at trial, of Maremont's alleged participation in liquidation activities. Mr. Cheff testified that: "Throughout the whole of the Kalamazoo-Battle Creek area, and Detroit too, where I spent considerable time, he is well known and not highly regarded by any stretch." This information was communicated to the board.

On August 23, 1957, at the request of Maremont, a meeting was held between Mr. Maremont and Cheff. At this meeting, Cheff was informed that Motor Products then owned approximately 100,000 shares of Holland stock. Maremont then made a demand that he be named to the board of directors, but Cheff refused to consider it. Since considerable controversy has been generated by Maremont's alleged threat to liquidate the company or substantially alter the sales force of Holland, we believe it desirable to set forth the testimony of Cheff on this point:

"Now we have 8500 men, direct employees, so the problem is entirely different. He indicated immediately that he had no interest in that type of distribution, that he didn't think it was modern, that he felt furnaces could be sold as he sold mufflers, through half a dozen salesmen in a wholesale way."

Testimony was introduced by the defendants tending to show that substantial unrest was present among the employees of Holland as a result of the threat of Maremont to seek control of Holland. Thus, Mr. Cheff testified that the field organization was considering leaving in large numbers because of a fear of the consequences of a Maremont acquisition; he further testified that approximately "25 of our key men" were lost as the result of the unrest engendered by the Maremont proposal. Staal, corroborating Cheff's version, stated that a number of branch managers approached him for reassurances that Maremont was not going to be allowed to successfully gain control. Moreover, at approximately this time, the company was furnished with a Dun and Bradstreet report, which indicated the practice of Maremont to achieve quick profits by sales or liquidations of companies acquired by him. The defendants were also supplied with an income statement of Motor Products, Inc., showing a loss of $336,121.00 for the period in 1957.

On August 30, 1957, the board was informed by Cheff of Maremont's demand to be placed upon the board and of Maremont's belief that the retail sales organization of Holland was obsolete. The board was also informed of the results of the investigation by Cheff and Staal. Predicated upon this information, the board authorized the purchase of company stock on the market with corporate funds, ostensibly for use in a stock option plan.

Subsequent to this meeting, substantial numbers of shares were purchased and, in addition, Mrs. Cheff made alternate personal purchases of Holland stock. As a result of purchases by Maremont, Holland and Mrs. Cheff, the market price rose. On September 13, 1957, Maremont wrote to each of the directors of Holland and requested a broad engineering survey to be made for the benefit of all stockholders. During September, Motor Products released its annual report, which indicated that the investment in Holland was a "special situation" as opposed to the normal policy of placing the funds of Motor Products into "an active company." On September 4th, Maremont proposed to sell his current holdings of Holland to the corporation for $14.00 a share. However, because of delay in responding to this offer, Maremont withdrew the offer. At this time, Mrs. Cheff was obviously quite concerned over the prospect of a Maremont acquisition, and had stated her willingness to expend her personal resources to prevent it.

On September 30, 1957, Motor Products Corporation, by letter to Mrs. Bowles, made a buy-sell offer to Hazelbank. At the Hazelbank meeting of October 3, 1957, Mrs. Bowles presented the letter to the board. The board took no action, but referred the proposal to its finance committee. Although Mrs. Bowles and Mrs. Putnam were opposed to any acquisition of Holland stock by Hazelbank, Mr. Landwehr conceded that a majority of the board were in favor of the purchase. Despite this fact, the finance committee elected to refer the offer to the Holland board on the grounds that it was the primary concern of Holland.

Thereafter, Mr. Trenkamp arranged for a meeting with Maremont, which occurred on October 14–15, 1957, in Chicago. Prior to this meeting, Trenkamp was aware of the intentions of Hazelbank and Mrs. Cheff to purchase all or portions of the stock then owned by Motor Products if Holland did not so act. As a result of the meeting, there was a tentative agreement on the part of Motor Products to sell its 155,000 shares at $14.40 per share. On October 23, 1957, at a special meeting of the Holland board, the purchase was considered. All directors, except Spatta, were present. The dangers allegedly posed by Maremont were again reviewed by the board. Trenkamp and Mrs. Cheff agree that the latter informed the board that either she or Hazelbank would purchase part or all of the block of Holland stock owned by Motor Products if the Holland board did not so act. The board was also informed that in order for the corporation to finance the purchase, substantial sums would have to be borrowed from commercial lending institutions. A resolution authorizing the purchase of 155,000 shares from Motor Products was adopted by the board. The price paid was in excess of the market price prevailing at the time, and the book value of the stock was approximately $20.00 as compared to approximately $14.00 for the net quick asset value. The transaction was subsequently consummated. The stock option plan mentioned in the minutes has never been implemented. In 1959, Holland stock reached a high of $15.25 a share.*

On February 6, 1958, plaintiffs, owners of 60 shares of Holland stock, filed a derivative suit in the court below naming all of the individual directors of Holland, Holland itself and Motor Products Corporation as defendants. The complaint alleged that all of the purchases of stock by Holland in 1957 were for the purpose of insuring the perpetuation of control by the incumbent directors. . . .

After trial, the Vice Chancellor found the following facts: (a) Holland directly sells to retail consumers by means of numerous branch offices. There were no intermediate dealers. (b) Immediately prior to the complained-of transactions, the sales and earnings of Holland had declined and its marketing practices were under investigation by the Federal Trade Commission. (c) Mr. Cheff and Trenkamp had received substantial sums as Chief Executive and attorney of the company, respectively. (d) Maremont, on August 23rd, 1957, demanded a place on the board. (e) At the October 14th meeting between Trenkamp, Staal and Maremont, Trenkamp and Staal were authorized to speak for Hazelbank and Mrs. Cheff as well as Holland. (f) Only Mr. Cheff, Mrs. Cheff, Mr. Landwehr, and Mr. Trenkamp clearly understood, prior to the October 23rd meeting, that either Hazelbank or Mrs. Cheff would have utilized their funds to purchase the Holland stock if Holland had not acted. (g) There was no real threat posed by Maremont and no substantial evidence of intention by Maremont to liquidate Holland. (h) Any employee unrest could have been caused by factors other than Maremont's intrusion and

* [Eds.—The following data reveals Maremont's profit and his advantage over other shareholders. The closing price of Holland shares on October 23 (when the Holland board resolved to buy out Maremont at $14 per share) was $11–1/8. Wall St. J., Oct. 24, 1957, p. 26, col. 3. The range of prices in the first five months of 1957, when Maremont (or his corporation) acquired his shares, was $9–1/4 to $11–3/8. Wall St. J., June 3, 1957, p. 22, col. 3. The closing price on May 31 was $9–1/4. Id. If Maremont paid an average of $10.40 for his 155,000 shares, he made a profit of $4 per share or $620,000, on an investment of $1,612,000—in less than six months. Note, however, the court's statement that the share price rose to $15.25 in 1959.]

"only one important employee was shown to have left, and his motive for leaving is not clear." (i) The Court rejected the stock option plan as a meaningful rationale for the purchase from Maremont or the prior open market purchases.

The Court then found that the actual purpose behind the purchase was the desire to perpetuate control, but because of its finding that only the four above-named directors knew of the "alternative," the remaining directors were exonerated. No appeal was taken by plaintiffs from that decision.

. . .

Under the provisions of 8 Del.C. § 160, a corporation is granted statutory power to purchase and sell shares of its own stock. Such a right, as embodied in the statute, has long been recognized in this State. . . . The charge here is not one of violation of statute, but the allegation is that the true motives behind such purchases were improperly centered upon perpetuation of control. In an analogous field, courts have sustained the use of proxy funds to inform stockholders of management's views upon the policy questions inherent in an election to a board of directors, but have not sanctioned the use of corporate funds to advance the selfish desires of directors to perpetuate themselves in office. . . . Similarly, if the actions of the board were motivated by a sincere belief that the buying out of the dissident stockholder was necessary to maintain what the board believed to be proper business practices, the board will not be held liable for such decision, even though hindsight indicates the decision was not the wisest course. See Kors v. Carey, Del.Ch., 158 A.2d 136. On the other hand, if the board has acted solely or primarily because of the desire to perpetuate themselves in office, the use of corporate funds for such purposes is improper. See Bennett v. Propp, Del., 187 A.2d 405. . . .

Our first problem is the allocation of the burden of proof to show the presence or lack of good faith on the part of the board in authorizing the purchase of shares. Initially, the decision of the board of directors in authorizing a purchase was presumed to be in good faith and could be overturned only by a conclusive showing by plaintiffs of fraud or other misconduct. . . . In *Kors,* cited supra, the court merely indicated that the directors are presumed to act in good faith and the burden of proof to show to the contrary falls upon the plaintiff. However, in Bennett v. Propp, supra, we stated:

> "We must bear in mind the inherent danger in the purchase of shares with corporate funds to remove a threat to corporate policy when a threat to control is involved. The directors are of necessity confronted with a conflict of interest, and an objective decision is difficult. . . . Hence, in our opinion, the burden should be on the directors to justify such a purchase as one primarily in the corporate interest." (187 A.2d 409, at page 409).

. . .

To say that the burden of proof is upon the defendants is not to indicate, however, that the directors have the same "self-dealing interest" as is present, for example, when a director sells property to the corporation. The only clear pecuniary interest shown on the record was held by Mr. Cheff, as an executive of the corporation, and Trenkamp, as its attorney. The mere fact that some of the other directors were substantial shareholders does not create a personal pecuniary interest in the decisions made by the board of directors, since all shareholders would presumably share the benefit flowing to the substantial shareholder. . . . Accordingly, these directors other than Trenkamp and Cheff, while called upon to justify their actions, will not be held to the same standard of proof required of those directors having personal and pecuniary interest in the transaction.

As noted above, the Vice Chancellor found that the stock option plan, mentioned in the minutes as a justification for the purchases, was not a motivating reason for the purchases. This finding we accept, since there is evidence to support it; in fact, Trenkamp admitted that the stock option plan was not the motivating reason.

. . .

Plaintiffs urge that the sale price was unfair in view of the fact that the price was in excess of that prevailing on the open market. However, as conceded by all parties, a substantial block of stock will normally sell at a higher price than that prevailing on the open market, the increment being attributable to a "control premium." Plaintiffs argue that it is inappropriate to require the defendant corporation to pay a control premium, since control is meaningless to an acquisition by a corporation of its own shares. However, it is elementary that a holder of a substantial number of shares would expect to receive the control premium as part of his selling price, and if the corporation desired to obtain the stock, it is unreasonable to expect that the corporation could avoid paying what any other purchaser would be required to pay for the stock. In any event, the financial expert produced by defendant at trial indicated that the price paid was fair and there was no rebuttal. Ames, the financial man on the board, was strongly of the opinion that the purchase was a good deal for the corporation. The Vice Chancellor made no finding as to the fairness of the price other than to indicate the obvious fact that the market price was increasing as a result of open market purchases by Maremont, Mrs. Cheff and Holland.

The question then presented is whether or not defendants satisfied the burden of proof of showing reasonable grounds to believe a danger to corporate policy and effectiveness existed by the presence of the Maremont stock ownership. It is important to remember that the directors satisfy their burden by showing good faith and reasonable investigation; the directors will not be penalized for an honest mistake of judgment, if the judgment appeared reasonable at the time the decision was made. . . .

In holding that employee unrest could as well be attributed to a condition of Holland's business affairs as to the possibility of Maremont's intrusion, the Vice Chancellor must have had in mind one or both of two matters: (1) the pending proceedings before the Federal Trade Commission concerning certain sales practices of Holland; (2) the decrease in sales and profits during the preceding several years. Any other possible reason would be pure speculation. In the first place, the adverse decision of the F.T.C. was not announced until *after* the complained-of transaction. Secondly, the evidence clearly shows that the downward trend of sales and profits had reversed itself, presumably because of the reorganization which had then been completed. Thirdly, everyone who testified on the point said that the unrest was due to the possible threat presented by Maremont's purchases of stock. There was, in fact, no *testimony* whatever of any connection between the unrest and either the F.T.C. proceedings or the business picture.

The Vice Chancellor found that there was no substantial evidence of a liquidation posed by Maremont. This holding overlooks an important contention. The fear of the defendants, according to their testimony, was not limited to the possibility of liquidation; it included the alternate possibility of a material change in Holland's sales policies, which the board considered vital to its future success. The *unrebutted* testimony before the court indicated: (1) Maremont had deceived Cheff as to his original intentions, since his open market purchases were contemporaneous with his disclaimer of interest in Holland; (2) Maremont had given Cheff some reason to believe that he intended to eliminate the retail sales force of Holland; (3) Maremont demanded a place on the board; (4) Maremont substantially increased his purchases after having been refused a place on the board; (5) the directors had good reason to believe that unrest among key employees had been engendered by the Maremont threat; (6) the board had received advice from Dun and Bradstreet indicating the past liquidation or quick sale activities of Motor Products; (7) the board had received professional advice from the firm of Merrill Lynch, Fenner & Beane, who recommended that the purchase from Motor Products be carried out; (8) the board had received competent advice that the corporation was over-capitalized; (9) Staal and Cheff had made informal personal investigations from contacts in the business and financial community and had reported to the board of the alleged poor reputation of Maremont. The board was within its rights in relying upon that investigation, since 8 Del.C. § 141(f) allows the directors to reasonably rely upon a report provided by corporate officers. . . .

Accordingly, we are of the opinion that the evidence presented in the court below leads inevitably to the conclusion that the board of directors, based upon direct investigation, receipt of professional advice, and personal observations of the contradictory action of Maremont and his explanation of corporate purpose, believed, with justification, that there was a reasonable threat to the continued existence of Holland, or at least existence in its present form, by the plan of Maremont to continue building up his stock holdings. We find no evidence in the record sufficient to justify a contrary conclusion. The opinion of the Vice Chancellor that employee unrest may have been engendered by other factors or that the board had no grounds to suspect Maremont is not supported in any manner by the evidence.

As noted above, the Vice-Chancellor found that the purpose of the acquisition was the improper desire to maintain control, but, at the same time, he exonerated those individual directors whom he believed to be unaware of the possibility of using non-corporate funds to accomplish this purpose. Such a decision is inconsistent with his finding that the motive was improper. . . . If the actions were in fact improper because of a desire to maintain control, then the presence or absence of a non-corporate alternative is irrelevant, as corporate funds may not be used to advance an improper purpose even if there is no non-corporate alternative available. Conversely, if the actions were proper because of a decision by the board made in good faith that the corporate interest was served thereby, they are not rendered improper by the fact that some individual directors were willing to advance personal funds if the corporation did not. It is conceivable that the Vice Chancellor considered this feature of the case to be of significance because of his apparent belief that any excess corporate funds should have been used to finance a subsidiary corporation. That action would not have solved the problem of Holland's over-capitalization. In any event, this question was a matter of business judgment, which furnishes no justification for holding the directors personally responsible in this case.

Accordingly, the judgment of the court below is reversed and remanded with instruction to enter judgment for the defendants.

OTHER FACTS

As the court in Cheff v. Mathes suggests, at the time of the events giving rise to the case, the Federal Trade Commission had been investigating the sales practices of the Holland Furnace Company for more than a year. As a result of the investigation, it eventually ordered Holland to cease and desist from "unfair and deceptive" practices. The Court of Appeals for the Seventh Circuit, on appeal, upheld the order in 1961, in Holland Furnace Company v. Federal Trade Commission, 295 F.2d 302. Most of Holland's business was in replacement furnaces. The evidence showed that Holland salesmen had gone door to door posing as inspectors from the government or a utility company. They would then dismantle a furnace and refuse to reassemble it, claiming that the furnace was unsafe and that parts necessary to make it safe were unavailable.

In 1965, the court of appeals found that Holland and Mr. Cheff had violated its order and held both in contempt. It found that Cheff had "knowingly, willfully and intentionally violated" the order by continuing Holland's deceptive practices, while disguising them through various schemes. It fined Holland and sent Cheff to prison for six months. See In re Holland Furnace Company, 341 F.2d 548 (7th Cir.1965), affirmed sub nom. Cheff v. Schnackenberg, 384 U.S. 373 (1966).

The Delaware Supreme Court in *Cheff* states that at the time Maremont was bought out, in 1957, the "downward trend of sales and profits had reversed itself." The court fails to note that soon the downward trend resumed. In 1958, net income was $795,352 on sales of $31.3 million. In 1960, sales were $29.6 million and net income $76,745, and in 1961 sales were $24.2 million and there was a net loss of $1.2 million. From then on the company went rapidly downhill, with total losses over the next four years of $13.8 million. Sales in 1965 were $1.1 million, and the stock traded at a high of $1.63 and a low of 38 cents. See Moody's Industrial Manual, 1958–1965. By 1966 Holland apparently was out of business; it was not listed in Moody's in that year.

Arnold Maremont died in 1978 at the age of 74. According to his obituary in the New York Times (Nov. 9, 1978, at D19), he had been a "well-known art collector and civic leader," and "a governing life member of the Art Institute of Chicago and a former trustee of the Lyric Opera and the Ballet Theater." The obituary also states that "Mr. Maremont was the first Illinois industrialist to back a law ending discrimination against hiring Negroes and, as chairman of the Illinois Public Aid

Commission in the early 60's, he campaigned for publicly supported birth control for welfare families."

NOTE ON "GREENMAIL"

During the 1980's, the purchase by a corporation of a potential acquirer's stock, at a premium over the market price, came to be called "greenmail." Buying off one person, however, provides no protection against later pursuers, except possibly to the extent that the premium paid to the first pursuer depletes the corporate resources and makes it a less attractive target. Such reduction in corporate resources could, of course, be achieved by managers simply by paying a dividend to all shareholders or by buying the corporation's shares from all shareholders wanting to sell.

Section 5881 of the Internal Revenue Code, enacted in 1987, imposes a penalty tax of 50 percent on the gain from greenmail, which is defined as gain from the sale of stock that was held for less than two years and sold to the corporation pursuant to an offer that "was not made on the same terms to all shareholders."

ANALYSIS

1. The court in *Cheff* seems to view the case as one involving a difference in business strategy, with the board concluding that the value of the corporation would be maximized by continuing the existing strategy and Maremont concluding that a different strategy was required. Should the choice of strategies have been put to the shareholders? How?

2. According to the defendants, what was the threat posed by Maremont that justified their purchase of his shares? How else might they have responded to this threat?

3. The court in *Cheff* observes that corporate control struggles pose a potential conflict of interest between the shareholders and members of the board. The potential acquirer generally challenges the board's judgment and sometimes poses a threat to the incumbents' salaries or other substantial benefits (e.g., legal fees). In response to this conflict, the court shifts the burden of proof to the board members (to different degrees, depending on what they have at stake), but still applies the business judgment rule (requiring only good faith and reasonable investigation). Does this go far enough? What do you think is the proper test for determining whether a corporation should be permitted to buy out a dissident shareholder? Should the test be the same where the plaintiff seeks an injunction as where the plaintiff seeks money damages?

4. Should any of the events after 1957 have been treated as relevant to the decision?

5. What more might the board members have done to protect themselves against attack on their decision to buy Maremont's shares?

6. Suppose it was clear that Maremont intended to liquidate; that upon liquidation the shareholders would receive $20 per share; and that the present market price was $13 per share. What possible grounds would the directors have had for the purchase of Maremont's shares? Suppose you are a shareholder and support Maremont's plan to liquidate

and one of the directors says to you, "A year from now the shares will be worth $25, so it would be foolish to take $20 now." What is your response? Think of yourself as a litigator preparing to cross-examine the director on that statement. What questions might you pose?

PROBLEM

Five individuals form a corporation to manufacture maternity dresses. They have all had experience in the business and expect to be involved in various roles in its operation. They pooled their own resources and borrowed money to buy the plant and various other assets of a corporation that recently became bankrupt. They intend to sell shares to the public to raise operating funds. You represent one of the founders, who asks you for a list of the pros and cons on a provision in the articles of incorporation that would prohibit the corporation from buying its own shares except in stock market transactions or pursuant to an offer to all shareholders. What is your response?

B. DEVELOPMENT

INTRODUCTION

In the next case, Unocal Corporation v. Mesa Petroleum Co., the court discusses, and criticizes, the "two-tier 'front loaded' cash tender offer." Such offers were widely discussed and criticized in the 1980s, although in fact they were relatively uncommon. It soon became clear, moreover, at least after the decision in *Unocal*, that they were not difficult for a determined board of directors to resist and by the 1990s they had virtually disappeared. In any event, *Unocal* is an important case for its broader doctrine and it cannot be understood without an understanding of how such offers work and why the court thought them to be "coercive." So here is a simplified version: Suppose you own shares in Sloth Co. Sloth trades at $50 per share, and T. Boone Pickens has announced a standard one-tiered tender offer for Sloth Co. at $60 per share with no limit on the number of shares he is willing to take, but conditioned on his acquiring at least 51 percent of the shares. Shareholders who think this is the best offer they are likely to receive can tender; those who think another raider will raise the stakes further can refuse.

Suppose, however, that Pickens instead uses a "two-tiered front-end-loaded" tender offer. For example, he could offer to buy 51 percent of the stock at $65 (the front end), and announce that he will thereafter merge Sloth into his own firm in a transaction that pays $55 cash per share for the remaining 49 percent of the stock (the back end).* Suppose further that you believe that, if the Pickens bid fails, rival raiders will bid the price of Sloth stock up to $70.

* Hence the term "cash-out merger." See generally Section 1 of this chapter. The tender offer is "front-end loaded" because the front end offers a higher price ($65) than the back end ($55). A two-tiered offer can be "coercive" even if the front end is an any-and-all offer rather than an offer for 51 percent of the stock.

Consider your options:

(a) You tender your stock and the deal goes through. You will receive $65 for at least 51 percent of your stock (a larger percentage if some shareholders fail to tender) and $55 for the rest.

(b) You do not tender and the deal goes through. You will receive $55 (the back-end price) for all your stock.

(c) The deal does not go through. You will sell your stock for $70 regardless of whether you tender.

Of these options, (a) is a better deal than (b), and (c) is better than (a). If you owned enough stock to affect the chance that Pickens's bid would succeed, you might refuse to tender. But if Sloth Co. is a large company and you own only a few shares, your decision to tender will not noticeably affect the probability of success of the offer. As a result, you will calculate that (i) if you tender, you will receive up to $65 if Pickens succeeds and $70 if he fails, and (ii) if you do not tender, you will receive $55 if Pickens succeeds and $70 if he fails. Notwithstanding that you hope Pickens fails, you probably will tender your shares, as will your fellow shareholders, and the bid is likely to succeed. Even though all shareholders would prefer to see the bid fail, most are likely to tender (because of the fear of being left with the back-end price ($55)) and the bid is likely to succeed. Each will think as follows: If the bid fails, I will wind up with $70 per share. If it succeeds, I will receive either $55 or $65 per share, depending on what I do. Since I own so few shares, my decision is not likely to affect the outcome. So I had better tender and pin down my right to $65 per share for at least 51 percent of my shares if the offer succeeds. Thus, the two-tiered front-end-loaded offer "coerces" each shareholder into tendering, and forecloses a more advantageous auction for the stock.

This may not be the whole story. Suppose again that Sloth stock trades at $50 and Pickens makes a one-tiered tender offer at $60. Why is Pickens offering so much? Pickens is no fool, and does not run a charity. Hence, you may well conclude that he is willing to offer $60 because he thinks he can (by revamping Sloth Co. management) increase the value of Sloth stock to more than $60. After all, if he cannot raise the price of the stock above $60, he will make no money from the deal—and Pickens always tries to make money. Suppose, therefore, that you conclude that Pickens will increase the value of Sloth stock to $70 per share.

Consider again your options:

(a) You *do* tender and the tender offer at $60 goes through. You will get $60.

(b) You do *not* tender and the tender offer goes through. You will get $70. In effect, you will "free-ride" on Pickens's efforts to turn the company around.

(c) The tender offer does not go through. You will be left with stock worth the same amount regardless of what you do.

Given these choices, you have a strong incentive not to tender, hoping the offer will succeed and your stock will be worth $70 per share. If many other shareholders make the same calculation, relatively few people will tender. As a result, shareholders may tender less than 51 percent of the stock, and the tender offer will fail. Even though Pickens could turn Sloth

Co. into a more profitable company, shareholders will try to free-ride on his efforts, and his tender offer probably will fail. According to this scenario, the "two-tiered offer" is simply an ingenious and efficient solution to this free-riding problem.

At the time the *Unocal* case arose many major oil companies such as Unocal had vast oil reserves (that is, they owned oil in the ground). For some of these companies, the value of the reserves substantially exceeded the aggregate market price of the company's securities. Thus, as the saying went, it was cheaper to buy oil on Wall Street than to drill for it in the field. How could it be that the total value of the securities of a corporation could be substantially less than the readily determinable value of its assets? One plausible explanation was that incumbent managers were committed, for reasons having to do with their own egos and self-interest, to maintaining exploration and development programs that had subnormal rates of return—basically, wasting the valuable assets of the corporation.*

Unocal Corporation v. Mesa Petroleum Co.

493 A.2d 946 (Del.1985).

We confront an issue of first impression in Delaware—the validity of a corporation's self-tender for its own shares which excludes from participation a stockholder making a hostile tender offer for the company's stock.

The Court of Chancery granted a preliminary injunction to the plaintiffs, Mesa Petroleum Co., Mesa Asset Co., Mesa Partners II, and Mesa Eastern, Inc. (collectively "Mesa"),[1] enjoining an exchange offer of the defendant, Unocal Corporation (Unocal) for its own stock. The trial court concluded that a selective exchange offer, excluding Mesa, was legally impermissible. We cannot agree with such a blanket rule. The factual findings of the Vice Chancellor, fully supported by the record, establish that Unocal's board, consisting of a majority of independent directors, acted in good faith, and after reasonable investigation found that Mesa's tender offer was both inadequate and coercive. Under the circumstances the board had both the power and duty to oppose a bid it perceived to be harmful to the corporate enterprise. On this record we are satisfied that the device Unocal adopted is reasonable in relation to the threat posed, and that the board acted in the proper exercise of sound business judgment. We will not substitute our views for those of the board if the latter's decision can be "attributed to any rational business purpose." Sinclair Oil Corp. v. Levien, Del.Supr., 280 A.2d 717, 720

---

* For empirical support of this theory, see Michael C. Jensen, The Takeover Controversy: Analysis and Evidence, in Knights, Raiders, and Targets 320 (John C. Coffee, Jr., et al., eds. 1988). Jensen claims that the defeat of the Pickens offer resulted in a loss to the Unocal shareholders of $1.1 billion (the difference between the value of the Pickens offer and the value of what the shareholders were left with when it was defeated), even though the financial restructuring that Unocal was forced to adopt in response to Pickens's tender offer increased the value of the firm by $2.1 billion. Despite his "service" to the shareholders, says Jensen, Pickens was "vilified in the press . . . .—obviously a perversion of incentives." Id. at 345.

[1] T. Boone Pickens, Jr., is President and Chairman of the Board of Mesa Petroleum and President of Mesa Asset and controls the related Mesa entities.

(1971). Accordingly, we reverse the decision of the Court of Chancery and order the preliminary injunction vacated.

I.

The factual background of this matter bears a significant relationship to its ultimate outcome.

On April 8, 1985, Mesa, the owner of approximately 13% of Unocal's stock, commenced a two-tier "front loaded" cash tender offer for 64 million shares, or approximately 37%, of Unocal's outstanding stock at a price of $54 per share. The "back-end" was designed to eliminate the remaining publicly held shares by an exchange of securities purportedly worth $54 per share. However, pursuant to an order entered by the United States District Court for the Central District of California on April 26, 1985, Mesa issued a supplemental proxy statement to Unocal's stockholders disclosing that the securities offered in the second-step merger would be highly subordinated, and that Unocal's capitalization would differ significantly from its present structure. Unocal has rather aptly termed such securities "junk bonds."

Unocal's board consists of eight independent outside directors and six insiders. It met on April 13, 1985, to consider the Mesa tender offer. Thirteen directors were present, and the meeting lasted nine and one-half hours. The directors were given no agenda or written materials prior to the session. However, detailed presentations were made by legal counsel regarding the board's obligations under both Delaware corporate law and the federal securities laws. The board then received a presentation from Peter Sachs on behalf of Goldman Sachs & Co. (Goldman Sachs) and Dillon, Read & Co. (Dillon Read) discussing the bases for their opinions that the Mesa proposal was wholly inadequate. Mr. Sachs opined that the minimum cash value that could be expected from a sale or orderly liquidation for 100% of Unocal's stock was in excess of $60 per share. In making his presentation, Mr. Sachs showed slides outlining the valuation techniques used by the financial advisors, and others, depicting recent business combinations in the oil and gas industry. The Court of Chancery found that the Sachs presentation was designed to apprise the directors of the scope of the analyses performed rather than the facts and numbers used in reaching the conclusion that Mesa's tender offer price was inadequate.

Mr. Sachs also presented various defensive strategies available to the board if it concluded that Mesa's two-step tender offer was inadequate and should be opposed. One of the devices outlined was a self-tender by Unocal for its own stock with a reasonable price range of $70 to $75 per share. The cost of such a proposal would cause the company to incur $6.1—6.5 billion of additional debt, and a presentation was made informing the board of Unocal's ability to handle it. The directors were told that the primary effect of this obligation would be to reduce exploratory drilling, but that the company would nonetheless remain a viable entity.

The eight outside directors, comprising a clear majority of the thirteen members present, then met separately with Unocal's financial advisors and attorneys. Thereafter, they unanimously agreed to advise the board that it should reject Mesa's tender offer as inadequate, and that Unocal should pursue a self-tender to provide the stockholders with a fairly priced alternative to the Mesa proposal. The board then reconvened and unanimously adopted a resolution rejecting as grossly inadequate Mesa's tender offer. Despite the nine and one-half hour length of the meeting, no formal decision was made on the proposed defensive self-tender.

On April 15, the board met again with four of the directors present by telephone and one member still absent. This session lasted two hours. Unocal's Vice President of Finance and its Assistant General Counsel made a detailed presentation of the proposed terms of the exchange offer. A price range between $70 and $80 per share was considered, and ultimately the directors agreed upon $72. The board was also advised about the debt securities that would be issued, and the necessity of placing restrictive covenants upon certain corporate activities until the obligations were paid. The board's decisions were made in reliance on the advice of its investment bankers, including the terms and conditions upon which the securities were to be issued. Based upon this advice, and the board's own deliberations, the directors unanimously approved the exchange offer. Their resolution provided that if Mesa acquired 64 million shares of Unocal stock through its own offer (the Mesa Purchase Condition), Unocal would buy the remaining 49% outstanding for an exchange of debt securities having an aggregate par value of $72 per share. The board resolution also stated that the offer would be subject to other conditions that had been described to the board at the meeting, or which were deemed necessary by Unocal's officers, including the exclusion of Mesa from the proposal (the Mesa exclusion). Any such conditions were required to be in accordance with the "purport and intent" of the offer.

Unocal's exchange offer was commenced on April 17, 1985, and Mesa promptly challenged it by filing this suit in the Court of Chancery. On April 22, the Unocal board met again and was advised by Goldman Sachs and Dillon Read to waive the Mesa Purchase Condition as to 50 million shares. This recommendation was in response to a perceived concern of the shareholders that, if shares were tendered to Unocal, no shares would be purchased by either offeror. The directors were also advised that they should tender their own Unocal stock into the exchange offer as a mark of their confidence in it.

Another focus of the board was the Mesa exclusion. Legal counsel advised that under Delaware law Mesa could only be excluded for what the directors reasonably believed to be a valid corporate purpose. The directors' discussion centered on the objective of adequately compensating shareholders at the "back-end" of Mesa's proposal, which the latter would finance with "junk bonds." To include Mesa would defeat that goal, because under the proration aspect of the exchange offer (49%) every Mesa share accepted by Unocal would displace one held by another stockholder. Further, if Mesa were permitted to tender to Unocal, the latter would in effect be financing Mesa's own inadequate proposal.

On April 24, 1985 Unocal issued a supplement to the exchange offer describing the partial waiver of the Mesa Purchase Condition. On May 1, 1985, in another supplement, Unocal extended the withdrawal, proration and expiration dates of its exchange offer to May 17, 1985.

Meanwhile, on April 22, 1985, Mesa amended its complaint in this action to challenge the Mesa exclusion. A preliminary injunction hearing was scheduled for May 8, 1985. However, on April 23, 1985, Mesa moved for a temporary restraining order in response to Unocal's announcement that it was partially waiving the Mesa Purchase Condition. After expedited briefing, the Court of Chancery heard Mesa's motion on April 26.

On April 29, 1985, the Vice Chancellor temporarily restrained Unocal from proceeding with the exchange offer unless it included Mesa. The trial court recognized that directors could oppose, and attempt to defeat, a hostile takeover which they considered adverse to the best interests of the corporation. However, the Vice Chancellor decided that in a selective purchase of the company's stock, the corporation bears the burden of showing: (1) a valid corporate purpose, and (2) that the transaction was fair to all of the stockholders, including those excluded.

. . .

II.

The issues we address involve these fundamental questions: Did the Unocal board have the power and duty to oppose a takeover threat it reasonably perceived to be harmful to the corporate enterprise, and if so, is its action here entitled to the protection of the business judgment rule?

Mesa contends that the discriminatory exchange offer violates the fiduciary duties Unocal owes it. Mesa argues that because of the Mesa exclusion the business judgment rule is inapplicable, because the directors by tendering their own shares will derive a financial benefit that is not available to *all* Unocal stockholders. Thus, it is Mesa's ultimate contention that Unocal cannot establish that the exchange offer is fair to *all* shareholders, and argues that the Court of Chancery was correct in concluding that Unocal was unable to meet this burden.

Unocal answers that it does not owe a duty of "fairness" to Mesa, given the facts here. Specifically, Unocal contends that its board of directors reasonably and in good faith concluded that Mesa's $54 two-tier tender offer was coercive and inadequate, and that Mesa sought selective treatment for itself. Furthermore, Unocal argues that the board's approval of the exchange offer was made in good faith, on an informed basis, and in the exercise of due care. Under these circumstances, Unocal contends that its directors properly employed this device to protect the company and its stockholders from Mesa's harmful tactics.

III.

We begin with the basic issue of the power of a board of directors of a Delaware corporation to adopt a defensive measure of this type. Absent such authority, all other questions are moot. Neither issues of fairness nor business judgment are pertinent without the basic underpinning of a board's legal power to act.

The board has a large reservoir of authority upon which to draw. Its duties and responsibilities proceed from the inherent powers conferred by 8 Del.C. § 141(a), respecting management of the corporation's "business and affairs."[6] Additionally, the powers here being exercised

---

[6] The general grant of power to a board of directors is conferred by 8 Del.C. § 141(a), which provides:

derive from 8 Del.C. § 160(a), conferring broad authority upon a corporation to deal in its own stock.[7] From this it is now well established that in the acquisition of its shares a Delaware corporation may deal selectively with its stockholders, provided the directors have not acted out of a sole or primary purpose to entrench themselves in office. Cheff v. Mathes, Del.Supr., 199 A.2d 548, 554 (1964); Bennett v. Propp, Del.Supr., 187 A.2d 405, 408 (1962);. . . .

Finally, the board's power to act derives from its fundamental duty and obligation to protect the corporate enterprise, which includes stockholders, from harm reasonably perceived, irrespective of its source. . . .

Thus, we are satisfied that in the broad context of corporate governance, including issues of fundamental corporate change, a board of directors is not a passive instrumentality.

Given the foregoing principles, we turn to the standards by which director action is to be measured. In Pogostin v. Rice, Del.Supr., 480 A.2d 619 (1984), we held that the business judgment rule, including the standards by which director conduct is judged, is applicable in the context of a takeover. Id. at 627. The business judgment rule is a "presumption that in making a business decision the directors of a corporation acted on an informed basis, in good faith and in the honest belief that the action taken was in the best interests of the company." Aronson v. Lewis, Del.Supr., 473 A.2d 805, 812 (1984) (citations omitted). . . .

When a board addresses a pending takeover bid it has an obligation to determine whether the offer is in the best interests of the corporation and its shareholders. In that respect a board's duty is no different from any other responsibility it shoulders, and its decisions should be no less entitled to the respect they otherwise would be accorded in the realm of business judgment. . . . There are, however, certain caveats to a proper exercise of this function. Because of the omnipresent specter that a board may be acting primarily in its own interests, rather than those of the corporation and its shareholders, there is an enhanced duty which calls for judicial examination at the threshold before the protections of the business judgment rule may be conferred.

This Court has long recognized that:

> We must bear in mind the inherent danger in the purchase of shares with corporate funds to remove a threat to corporate policy when a threat to control is involved. The directors are of necessity confronted with a conflict of interest, and an objective decision is difficult.

Bennett v. Propp, Del.Supr., 187 A.2d 405, 409 (1962). In the face of this inherent conflict directors must show that they had reasonable grounds for believing that a danger to corporate policy and effectiveness existed

---

> (a) The business *and affairs* of every corporation organized under this chapter shall be managed by or under the direction of a board of directors, except as may be otherwise provided in this chapter or in its certificate of incorporation. . . .

[7] This power under 8 Del.C. § 160(a), with certain exceptions not pertinent here, is as follows:

> (a) Every corporation may purchase, redeem, receive, take or otherwise acquire, own and hold, sell, lend, exchange, transfer or otherwise dispose of, pledge, use and otherwise deal in and with its own shares. . . .

because of another person's stock ownership. Cheff v. Mathes, 199 A.2d at 554–55. However, they satisfy that burden "by showing good faith and reasonable investigation. . . ." Id. at 555. Furthermore, such proof is materially enhanced, as here, by the approval of a board comprised of a majority of outside independent directors who have acted in accordance with the foregoing standards. . . .

IV.

A.

In the board's exercise of corporate power to forestall a takeover bid our analysis begins with the basic principle that corporate directors have a fiduciary duty to act in the best interests of the corporation's stockholders. . . . As we have noted, their duty of care extends to protecting the corporation and its owners from perceived harm whether a threat originates from third parties or other shareholders.[10] But such powers are not absolute. A corporation does not have unbridled discretion to defeat any perceived threat by any Draconian means available.

The restriction placed upon a selective stock repurchase is that the directors may not have acted solely or primarily out of a desire to perpetuate themselves in office. See Cheff v. Mathes, 199 A.2d at 556. . . . Of course, to this is added the further caveat that inequitable action may not be taken under the guise of law. . . . The standard of proof established in *Cheff v. Mathes* and discussed supra, is designed to ensure that a defensive measure to thwart or impede a takeover is indeed motivated by a good faith concern for the welfare of the corporation and its stockholders, which in all circumstances must be free of any fraud or other misconduct. . . . However, this does not end the inquiry.

B.

A further aspect is the element of balance. If a defensive measure is to come within the ambit of the business judgment rule, it must be reasonable in relation to the threat posed. This entails an analysis by the directors of the nature of the takeover bid and its effect on the corporate enterprise. Examples of such concerns may include: inadequacy of the price offered, nature and timing of the offer, questions of illegality, the impact on "constituencies" other than shareholders (i.e., creditors, customers, employees, and perhaps even the community generally), the risk of nonconsummation, and the quality of securities being offered in the exchange. . . . While not a controlling factor, it also seems to us that a board may reasonably consider the basic stockholder interests at stake, including those of short term speculators, whose actions may have fueled the coercive aspect of the offer at the expense of the long term investor. Here, the threat posed was viewed by the Unocal board as a grossly inadequate two-tier coercive tender offer coupled with the threat of greenmail.

Specifically, the Unocal directors had concluded that the value of Unocal was substantially above the $54 per share offered in cash at the front end. Furthermore, they determined that the subordinated securities to be exchanged in Mesa's announced squeeze out of the remaining shareholders in the "back-end" merger were "junk bonds"

[10] It has been suggested that a board's response to a takeover threat should be a passive one. . . . However, that clearly is not the law of Delaware, and as the proponents of this rule of passivity readily concede, it has not been adopted either by courts or state legislatures. . . .

worth far less than $54. It is now well recognized that such offers are a classic coercive measure designed to stampede shareholders into tendering at the first tier, even if the price is inadequate, out of fear of what they will receive at the back end of the transaction. Wholly beyond the coercive aspect of an inadequate two-tier tender offer, the threat was posed by a corporate raider with a national reputation as a "greenmailer."[13]

In adopting the selective exchange offer, the board stated that its objective was either to defeat the inadequate Mesa offer or, should the offer still succeed, provide the 49% of its stockholders, who would otherwise be forced to accept "junk bonds," with $72 worth of senior debt. We find that both purposes are valid.

However, such efforts would have been thwarted by Mesa's participation in the exchange offer. First, if Mesa could tender its shares, Unocal would effectively be subsidizing the former's continuing effort to buy Unocal stock at $54 per share. Second, Mesa could not, by definition, fit within the class of shareholders being protected from its own coercive and inadequate tender offer.

Thus, we are satisfied that the selective exchange offer is reasonably related to the threats posed. It is consistent with the principle that "the minority stockholder shall receive the substantial equivalent in value of what he had before." Sterling v. Mayflower Hotel Corp., Del.Supr., 93 A.2d 107, 114 (1952). . . .

This concept of fairness, while stated in the merger context, is also relevant in the area of tender offer law. Thus, the board's decision to offer what it determined to be the fair value of the corporation to the 49% of its shareholders, who would otherwise be forced to accept highly subordinated "junk bonds," is reasonable and consistent with the directors' duty to ensure that the minority stockholders receive equal value for their shares.

V.

Mesa contends that it is unlawful, and the trial court agreed, for a corporation to discriminate in this fashion against one shareholder. It argues correctly that no case has ever sanctioned a device that precludes a raider from sharing in a benefit available to all other stockholders. However, as we have noted earlier, the principle of selective stock repurchases by a Delaware corporation is neither unknown nor unauthorized. . . . The only difference is that heretofore the approved transaction was the payment of "greenmail" to a raider or dissident posing a threat to the corporate enterprise. All other stockholders were denied such favored treatment, and given Mesa's past history of greenmail, its claims here are rather ironic.

. . .

[13] The term "greenmail" refers to the practice of buying out a takeover bidder's stock at a premium that is not available to other shareholders in order to prevent the takeover. The Chancery Court noted that "Mesa has made tremendous profits from its takeover activities although in the past few years it has not been successful in acquiring any of the target companies on an unfriendly basis." Moreover, the trial court specifically found that the actions of the Unocal board were taken in good faith to eliminate both the inadequacies of the tender offer and to forestall the payment of "greenmail."

Thus, while the exchange offer is a form of selective treatment, given the nature of the threat posed here the response is neither unlawful nor unreasonable. If the board of directors is disinterested, has acted in good faith and with due care, its decision in the absence of an abuse of discretion will be upheld as a proper exercise of business judgment.

To this Mesa responds that the board is not disinterested, because the directors are receiving a benefit from the tender of their own shares, which because of the Mesa exclusion, does not devolve upon *all* stockholders equally. . . . However, Mesa concedes that if the exclusion is valid, then the directors and all other stockholders share the same benefit. The answer of course is that the exclusion is valid, and the directors' participation in the exchange offer does not rise to the level of a disqualifying interest. . . .

VI.

In conclusion, there was directorial power to oppose the Mesa tender offer, and to undertake a selective stock exchange made in good faith and upon a reasonable investigation pursuant to a clear duty to protect the corporate enterprise. Further, the selective stock repurchase plan chosen by Unocal is reasonable in relation to the threat that the board rationally and reasonably believed was posed by Mesa's inadequate and coercive two-tier tender offer. Under those circumstances the board's action is entitled to be measured by the standards of the business judgment rule. Thus, unless it is shown by a preponderance of the evidence that the directors' decisions were primarily based on perpetuating themselves in office, or some other breach of fiduciary duty such as fraud, overreaching, lack of good faith, or being uninformed, a Court will not substitute its judgment for that of the board.

. . .

NOTE ON SEC REACTION AND POISON PILLS

After the *Unocal* decision, the SEC demonstrated its disapproval of discriminatory self-tenders by amending its rules to prohibit issuer tender offers other than those made to all shareholders. Rule 13e–4(f)(8). The SEC rule does not, however, prohibit "poison pills," which can have much the same effect. Poison pills are widely used, highly complex plans designed to provide varying degrees of protection against takeovers.

Pills take a wide variety of forms, but most are based on a form of security known as a "right." (Hence, the pill's official name, the Shareholder Rights Plan.) A traditional right, typically known as a warrant, grants the holder the option to purchase new shares of stock of the issuing corporation. Warrants are traded as separate securities, having value because they typically confer on the holder the right to buy issuer common stock at a discount from the prevailing market price. The poison pill variant of the right adds three additional elements not found in traditional rights: a "flip-in" element, a "flip-over" element, and a redemption provision.

The pill is typically adopted by the board of directors without any shareholder action. When adopted, the rights attach to the corporation's outstanding common stock, cannot be traded separately from the common stock, and are priced so that exercise of the option would be economically irrational. The rights become exercisable, and can be traded separately from the common stock, upon a so-called distribution event, which is typically defined as the acquisition of, or announcement of an intent to acquire, some specified percentage of the issuer's stock by a prospective acquirer. (Twenty percent is a commonly used trigger level.) Although the rights are now exercisable, and will remain so for the remainder of their specified life (typically ten years), they remain "out of the money."

The pill's flip-in element is triggered, typically, by the actual acquisition of some specified percentage of the issuer's common stock. (Again, 20 percent is a commonly used trigger.) If triggered, the flip-in pill entitles the holder of each right—except, and this is key, the acquirer and its affiliates or associates—to buy two shares of the target issuer's common stock or other securities at half price. In other words, the value of the stock received when the right is exercised is equal to two times the exercise price of the right. The deterrent effect of such a flip-in pill arises out of the massive dilution the pill causes to the value of the target stock owned by unwanted acquirer.

The pill's "flip-over" feature typically is triggered if, following the acquisition of a specified percentage of the target's common stock, the target is subsequently merged into the acquirer or one of its affiliates. In such an event, the holder of each right becomes entitled to purchase common stock of the acquiring company, again at half-price, thereby impairing the acquirer's capital structure and drastically diluting the interest of the acquirer's other stockholders.

Because the rights trade separately from the issuer's common stock, an acquirer remains subject to the pill's poisonous effects even if an overwhelming majority of the target's shareholders accept the bidder's tender offer. In the face of a pill, a prospective acquirer thus has a strong incentive to negotiate with the target's board. Most pills include a redemption provision pursuant to which the board may redeem the rights at a nominal price at any time prior to the right being exercised. (Some pills become non-redeemable after the triggering event.) Proponents of pills contend that these plans thus do not deter takeover bids, but rather simply give the target board leverage to negotiate the best possible deal for their shareholders.

In Moran v. Household International, Inc., 500 A.2d 1346 (Del.1985), the Delaware Supreme Court upheld a flip-over pill against a *Unocal*-based. The court claimed that the pill allowed the Household board to prevent coercive offers and to ensure that, if the company were to be sold, an auction or bidding process could be initiated so that the shareholders would obtain the highest possible price for their shares.

NOTE ON "JUNK" BONDS AS THE BACK-END CONSIDERATION

The court in *Unocal* wrote that one of the factors a board may consider in determining how to react to a takeover threat is "the quality of the securities being offered." Later it stated that but for the board's action the shareholders would have been "forced to accept highly subordinated 'junk bonds.' " Junk bonds are debt obligations of a corporation that are usually subordinate to other debt (they are comparable to a second or third mortgage on a personal residence) and bear a relatively high level of risk and high interest rate. It is by no means clear that shareholders should be concerned about the riskiness of such obligations, for at least two reasons. First, while a corporation's junk bonds are riskier than its investment-grade bonds, they are less risky than the common stock that the shareholder already owns. Second, a person who is reluctant to hold junk bonds received in an exchange can sell them. That being so, the only rational concern should be the value of such bonds. On the other hand, the value of junk bonds offered in an exchange such as the one proposed by Pickens in *Unocal* may be difficult to determine. One might well ask Pickens, "If the bonds you offer are worth what you say they are worth, why don't you just sell them to the public, or to institutions such as insurance companies or mutual funds or pension funds, and pay us in cash?" Nevertheless, what is important (assuming marketability) is value, not "quality." Asking which is more valuable, $100 worth of junk bonds or $100 worth of investment-grade bonds, assuming both are readily salable, is like asking which is heavier, a pound of lead or a pound of feathers.

ANALYSIS

1. If the trial court in a case involving a defense against a hostile takeover bid finds that independent members of the board acted in good faith and with reasonable investigation (as required by the business judgment rule), is the board's defensive action immune from judicial review?

2. What is the relevance, if any, of the fact that Pickens had a reputation as a "greenmailer"? As a greenmailer, what threat did he pose?

3. Suppose Pickens had had a reputation not as a greenmailer but as a liquidator. Suppose, for example, that it had been clear that it was Pickens's intent, if he was successful in his takeover attempt, to reduce substantially Unocal's exploration and drilling program and fire a substantial number of employees involved in that program. What relevance would that have had?

4. Suppose Pickens had offered $54 cash for any and all shares, with a commitment, if successful in acquiring control, to effect a cash-out merger of the remaining shares at the same price. Suppose, further, that there was no reason to believe that Pickens would liquidate assets or fire employees, other than a few of the top executives, who would receive generous severance compensation. Would the board still have been justified in resisting the takeover? In using a discriminatory self-tender?

Revlon, Inc. v. MacAndrews & Forbes Holdings, Inc.

506 A.2d 173 (Del.1985).

In this battle for corporate control of Revlon, Inc. (Revlon), the Court of Chancery enjoined certain transactions designed to thwart the efforts of Pantry Pride, Inc. (Pantry Pride) to acquire Revlon. The defendants are Revlon, its board of directors, and Forstmann Little & Co. and the latter's affiliated limited partnership (collectively, Forstmann). The injunction barred consummation of an option granted Forstmann to purchase certain Revlon assets (the lock-up option), a promise by Revlon to deal exclusively with Forstmann in the face of a takeover (the no-shop provision), and the payment of a $25 million cancellation fee to Forstmann if the transaction was aborted. The Court of Chancery found that the Revlon directors had breached their duty of care by entering into the foregoing transactions and effectively ending an active auction for the company. The trial court ruled that such arrangements are not illegal *per se* under Delaware law, but that their use under the circumstances here was impermissible. We agree. . . .

Additionally, we address for the first time the extent to which a corporation may consider the impact of a takeover threat on constituencies other than shareholders. See Unocal Corp. v. Mesa Petroleum Co., Del.Supr., 493 A.2d 946, 955 (1985).

In our view, lock-ups and related agreements are permitted under Delaware law where their adoption is untainted by director interest or other breaches of fiduciary duty. The actions taken by the Revlon directors, however, did not meet this standard. Moreover, while concern for various corporate constituencies is proper when addressing a takeover threat, that principle is limited by the requirement that there be some rationally related benefit accruing to the stockholders. We find no such benefit here.

Thus, under all the circumstances we must agree with the Court of Chancery that the enjoined Revlon defensive measures were inconsistent with the directors' duties to the stockholders. Accordingly, we affirm.

I.

The somewhat complex maneuvers of the parties necessitate a rather detailed examination of the facts. The prelude to this controversy began in June 1985, when Ronald O. Perelman, chairman of the board and chief executive officer of Pantry Pride, met with his counterpart at Revlon, Michel C. Bergerac, to discuss a friendly acquisition of Revlon by Pantry Pride. Perelman suggested a price in the range of $40–50 per share, but the meeting ended with Bergerac dismissing those figures as considerably below Revlon's intrinsic value. All subsequent Pantry Pride overtures were rebuffed, perhaps in part based on Mr. Bergerac's strong personal antipathy to Mr. Perelman.

Thus, on August 14, Pantry Pride's board authorized Perelman to acquire Revlon, either through negotiation in the $42–$43 per share range, or by making a hostile tender offer at $45. Perelman then met with Bergerac and outlined Pantry Pride's alternate approaches. Bergerac remained adamantly opposed to such schemes and conditioned any further discussions of the matter on Pantry Pride executing a standstill agreement prohibiting it from acquiring Revlon without the latter's prior approval.

On August 19, the Revlon board met specially to consider the impending threat of a hostile bid by Pantry Pride.[3] At the meeting, Lazard Freres, Revlon's investment banker, advised the directors that

[3] There were 14 directors on the Revlon board. Six of them held senior management positions with the company, and two others held significant blocks of its stock. Four of the remaining six directors were associated at some point with entities that had various business relationships with Revlon. On the basis of this limited record, however, we cannot conclude that this board is entitled to certain presumptions that generally attach to the decisions of a board whose majority consists of truly outside independent directors.

$45 per share was a grossly inadequate price for the company. Felix Rohatyn and William Loomis of Lazard Freres explained to the board that Pantry Pride's financial strategy for acquiring Revlon would be through "junk bond" financing followed by a break-up of Revlon and the disposition of its assets. With proper timing, according to the experts, such transactions could produce a return to Pantry Pride of $60 to $70 per share, while a sale of the company as a whole would be in the "mid 50" dollar range. Martin Lipton, special counsel for Revlon, recommended two defensive measures: first, that the company repurchase up to 5 million of its nearly 30 million outstanding shares; and second, that it adopt a Note Purchase Rights Plan. Under this plan, each Revlon shareholder would receive as a dividend one Note Purchase Right (the Rights) for each share of common stock, with the Rights entitling the holder to exchange one common share for a $65 principal Revlon note at 12% interest with a one-year maturity. The Rights would become effective whenever anyone acquired beneficial ownership of 20% or more of Revlon's shares, unless the purchaser acquired all the company's stock for cash at $65 or more per share. In addition, the Rights would not be available to the acquiror, and prior to the 20% triggering event the Revlon board could redeem the rights for 10 cents each. Both proposals were unanimously adopted.

Pantry Pride made its first hostile move on August 23 with a cash tender offer for any and all shares of Revlon at $47.50 per common share and $26.67 per preferred share, subject to (1) Pantry Pride's obtaining financing for the purchase, and (2) the Rights being redeemed, rescinded or voided.

The Revlon board met again on August 26. The directors advised the stockholders to reject the offer. Further defensive measures also were planned. On August 29, Revlon commenced its own offer for up to 10 million shares, exchanging for each share of common stock tendered one Senior Subordinated Note (the Notes) of $47.50 principal at 11.75% interest, due 1995, and one-tenth of a share of $9.00 Cumulative Convertible Exchangeable Preferred Stock valued at $100 per share. Lazard Freres opined that the notes would trade at their face value on a fully distributed basis.[4] Revlon stockholders tendered 87 percent of the outstanding shares (approximately 33 million), and the company accepted the full 10 million shares on a pro rata basis. The new Notes contained covenants which limited Revlon's ability to incur additional debt, sell assets, or pay dividends unless otherwise approved by the "independent" (non-management) members of the board.

At this point, both the Rights and the Note covenants stymied Pantry Pride's attempted takeover. The next move came on September 16, when Pantry Pride announced a new tender offer at $42 per share, conditioned upon receiving at least 90% of the outstanding stock. Pantry Pride also indicated that it would consider buying less than 90%, and at an increased price, if Revlon removed the impeding Rights. While this offer was lower on its face than the earlier $47.50 proposal, Revlon's

[4] Like bonds, the Notes actually were issued in denominations of $1,000 and integral multiples thereof. A separate certificate was issued in a total principal amount equal to the remaining sum to which a stockholder was entitled. Likewise, in the esoteric parlance of bond dealers, a Note trading at par ($1,000) would be quoted on the market at 100.

investment banker, Lazard Freres, described the two bids as essentially equal in view of the completed exchange offer.

The Revlon board held a regularly scheduled meeting on September 24. The directors rejected the latest Pantry Pride offer and authorized management to negotiate with other parties interested in acquiring Revlon. Pantry Pride remained determined in its efforts and continued to make cash bids for the company, offering $50 per share on September 27, and raising its bid to $53 on October 1, and then to $56.25 on October 7.

In the meantime, Revlon's negotiations with Forstmann and the investment group Adler & Shaykin had produced results. The Revlon directors met on October 3 to consider Pantry Pride's $53 bid and to examine possible alternatives to the offer. Both Forstmann and Adler & Shaykin made certain proposals to the board. As a result, the directors unanimously agreed to a leveraged buyout by Forstmann. The terms of this accord were as follows: each stockholder would get $56 cash per share; management would purchase stock in the new company by the exercise of their Revlon "golden parachutes";[5] Forstmann would assume Revlon's $475 million debt incurred by the issuance of the Notes; and Revlon would redeem the Rights and waive the Notes covenants for Forstmann or in connection with any other offer superior to Forstmann's. The board did not actually remove the covenants at the October 3 meeting, because Forstmann then lacked a firm commitment on its financing, but accepted the Forstmann capital structure, and indicated that the outside directors would waive the covenants in due course. Part of Forstmann's plan was to sell Revlon's Norcliff Thayer and Reheis divisions to American Home Products for $335 million. Before the merger, Revlon was to sell its cosmetics and fragrance division to Adler & Shaykin for $905 million. These transactions would facilitate the purchase by Forstmann or any other acquiror of Revlon.

When the merger, and thus the waiver of the Notes covenants, was announced, the market value of these securities began to fall. The Notes, which originally traded near par, around 100, dropped to 87.50 by October 8. One director later reported (at the October 12 meeting) a "deluge" of telephone calls from irate noteholders, and on October 10 the Wall Street Journal reported threats of litigation by these creditors.

Pantry Pride countered with a new proposal on October 7, raising its $53 offer to $56.25, subject to nullification of the Rights, a waiver of the Notes covenants, and the election of three Pantry Pride directors to the Revlon board. On October 9, representatives of Pantry Pride, Forstmann and Revlon conferred in an attempt to negotiate the fate of Revlon, but could not reach agreement. At this meeting Pantry Pride announced that it would engage in fractional bidding and top any Forstmann offer by a slightly higher one. It is also significant that Forstmann, to Pantry Pride's exclusion, had been made privy to certain Revlon financial data. Thus, the parties were not negotiating on equal terms.

Again privately armed with Revlon data, Forstmann met on October 11 with Revlon's special counsel and investment banker. On October 12,

[5] In the takeover context "golden parachutes" generally are understood to be termination agreements providing substantial bonuses and other benefits for managers and certain directors upon a change in control of a company.

Forstmann made a new $57.25 per share offer, based on several conditions.[6] The principal demand was a lock-up option to purchase Revlon's Vision Care and National Health Laboratories divisions for $525 million, some $100–$175 million below the value ascribed to them by Lazard Freres, if another acquiror got 40% of Revlon's shares. Revlon also was required to accept a no-shop provision. The Rights and Notes covenants had to be removed as in the October 3 agreement. There would be a $25 million cancellation fee to be placed in escrow, and released to Forstmann if the new agreement terminated or if another acquiror got more than 19.9% of Revlon's stock. Finally, there would be no participation by Revlon management in the merger. In return, Forstmann agreed to support the par value of the Notes, which had faltered in the market, by an exchange of new notes. Forstmann also demanded immediate acceptance of its offer, or it would be withdrawn. The board unanimously approved Forstmann's proposal because: (1) it was for a higher price than the Pantry Pride bid, (2) it protected the noteholders, and (3) Forstmann's financing was firmly in place.[7] The board further agreed to redeem the rights and waive the covenants on the preferred stock in response to any offer above $57 cash per share. The covenants were waived, contingent upon receipt of an investment banking opinion that the Notes would trade near par value once the offer was consummated.

Pantry Pride, which had initially sought injunctive relief from the Rights plan on August 22, filed an amended complaint on October 14 challenging the lock-up, the cancellation fee, and the exercise of the Rights and the Notes covenants. Pantry Pride also sought a temporary restraining order to prevent Revlon from placing any assets in escrow or transferring them to Forstmann. Moreover, on October 22, Pantry Pride again raised its bid, with a cash offer of $58 per share conditioned upon nullification of the Rights, waiver of the covenants, and an injunction of the Forstmann lock-up.

On October 15, the Court of Chancery prohibited the further transfer of assets, and eight days later enjoined the lock-up, no-shop, and cancellation fee provisions of the agreement. The trial court concluded that the Revlon directors had breached their duty of loyalty by making concessions to Forstmann, out of concern for their liability to the noteholders, rather than maximizing the sale price of the company for the stockholders' benefit. . . .

[6] Forstmann's $57.25 offer ostensibly is worth $1 more than Pantry Pride's $56.25 bid. However, the Pantry Pride offer was immediate, while the Forstmann proposal must be discounted for the time value of money because of the delay in approving the merger and consummating the transaction. The exact difference between the two bids was an unsettled point of contention even at oral argument.

[7] Actually, at this time about $400 million of Forstmann's funding was still subject to two investment banks using their "best efforts" to organize a syndicate to provide the balance. Pantry Pride's entire financing was not firmly committed at this point either, although Pantry Pride represented in an October 11 letter to Lazard Freres that its investment banker, Drexel Burnham Lambert, was highly confident of its ability to raise the balance of $350 million. Drexel Burnham had a firm commitment for this sum by October 18.

II.

. . .

A.

. . .

If the business judgment rule applies, there is a "presumption that in making a business decision the directors of a corporation acted on an informed basis, in good faith and in the honest belief that the action taken was in the best interests of the company." Aronson v. Lewis, 473 A.2d [805, 812 (Del.1984)]. However, when a board implements anti-takeover measures there arises "the omnipresent specter that a board may be acting primarily in its own interests, rather than those of the corporation and its shareholders . . ." Unocal Corp. v. Mesa Petroleum Co., 493 A.2d at 954. This potential for conflict places upon the directors the burden of proving that they had reasonable grounds for believing there was a danger to corporate policy and effectiveness, a burden satisfied by a showing of good faith and reasonable investigation. Id. at 955. In addition, the directors must analyze the nature of the takeover and its effect on the corporation in order to ensure balance—that the responsive action taken is reasonable in relation to the threat posed. Id.

B.

The first relevant defensive measure adopted by the Revlon board was the Rights Plan, which would be considered a "poison pill" in the current language of corporate takeovers—a plan by which shareholders receive the right to be bought out by the corporation at a substantial premium on the occurrence of a stated triggering event. . . . [T]he board clearly had the power to adopt the measure. . . . Thus, the focus becomes one of reasonableness and purpose.

The Revlon board approved the Rights Plan in the face of an impending hostile takeover bid by Pantry Pride at $45 per share, a price which Revlon reasonably concluded was grossly inadequate. Lazard Freres had so advised the directors, and had also informed them that Pantry Pride was a small, highly leveraged company bent on a "bust-up" takeover by using "junk bond" financing to buy Revlon cheaply, sell the acquired assets to pay the debts incurred, and retain the profit for itself.[12] In adopting the Plan, the board protected the shareholders from a hostile takeover at a price below the company's intrinsic value, while retaining sufficient flexibility to address any proposal deemed to be in the stockholders' best interests.

To that extent the board acted in good faith and upon reasonable investigation. Under the circumstances it cannot be said that the Rights Plan as employed was unreasonable, considering the threat posed. Indeed, the Plan was a factor in causing Pantry Pride to raise its bids from a low of $42 to an eventual high of $58. At the time of its adoption the Rights Plan afforded a measure of protection consistent with the directors' fiduciary duty in facing a takeover threat perceived as detrimental to corporate interests. . . .

---

[12] . . . . [A] "bust-up" takeover generally refers to a situation in which one seeks to finance an acquisition by selling off pieces of the acquired company, presumably at a substantial profit.

Far from being a "show-stopper," . . . the measure spurred the bidding to new heights, a proper result of its implementation. . . .

Although we consider adoption of the Plan to have been valid under the circumstances, its continued usefulness was rendered moot by the directors' actions on October 3 and October 12. At the October 3 meeting the board redeemed the Rights conditioned upon consummation of a merger with Forstmann, but further acknowledged that they would also be redeemed to facilitate any more favorable offer. On October 12, the board unanimously passed a resolution redeeming the Rights in connection with any cash proposal of $57.25 or more per share. Because all the pertinent offers eventually equalled or surpassed that amount, the Rights clearly were no longer any impediment in the contest for Revlon. This mooted any question of their propriety under *Moran* or *Unocal.*

C.

The second defensive measure adopted by Revlon to thwart a Pantry Pride takeover was the company's own exchange offer for 10 million of its shares. The directors' general broad powers to manage the business and affairs of the corporation are augmented by the specific authority conferred under 8 Del.C. § 160(a), permitting the company to deal in its own stock. . . . However, when exercising that power in an effort to forestall a hostile takeover, the board's actions are strictly held to the fiduciary standards outlined in *Unocal.* These standards require the directors to determine the best interests of the corporation and its stockholders, and impose an enhanced duty to abjure any action that is motivated by considerations other than a good faith concern for such interests. . . .

The Revlon directors concluded that Pantry Pride's $47.50 offer was grossly inadequate. In that regard the board acted in good faith, and on an informed basis, with reasonable grounds to believe that there existed a harmful threat to the corporate enterprise. The adoption of a defensive measure, reasonable in relation to the threat posed, was proper and fully accorded with the powers, duties, and responsibilities conferred upon directors under our law. . . .

D.

However, when Pantry Pride increased its offer to $50 per share, and then to $53, it became apparent to all that the break-up of the company was inevitable. The Revlon board's authorization permitting management to negotiate a merger or buyout with a third party was a recognition that the company was for sale. The duty of the board had thus changed from the preservation of Revlon as a corporate entity to the maximization of the company's value at a sale for the stockholders' benefit. This significantly altered the board's responsibilities under the *Unocal* standards. It no longer faced threats to corporate policy and effectiveness, or to the stockholders' interests, from a grossly inadequate bid. The whole question of defensive measures became moot. The directors' role changed from defenders of the corporate bastion to auctioneers charged with getting the best price for the stockholders at a sale of the company.

III.

This brings us to the lock-up with Forstmann and its emphasis on shoring up the sagging market value of the Notes in the face of threatened litigation by their holders. Such a focus was inconsistent with the changed concept of the directors' responsibilities at this stage of the developments. The impending waiver of the Notes covenants had caused the value of the Notes to fall, and the board was aware of the noteholders' ire as well as their subsequent threats of suit. The directors thus made support of the Notes an integral part of the company's dealings with Forstmann, even though their primary responsibility at this stage was to the equity owners.

The original threat posed by Pantry Pride—the break-up of the company—had become a reality which even the directors embraced. Selective dealing to fend off a hostile but determined bidder was no longer a proper objective. Instead, obtaining the highest price for the benefit of the stockholders should have been the central theme guiding director action. Thus, the Revlon board could not make the requisite showing of good faith by preferring the noteholders and ignoring its duty of loyalty to the shareholders. The rights of the former already were fixed by contract. . . . The noteholders required no further protection, and when the Revlon board entered into an auction-ending lock-up agreement with Forstmann on the basis of impermissible considerations at the expense of the shareholders, the directors breached their primary duty of loyalty.

The Revlon board argued that it acted in good faith in protecting the noteholders because *Unocal* permits consideration of other corporate constituencies. Although such considerations may be permissible, there are fundamental limitations upon that prerogative. A board may have regard for various constituencies in discharging its responsibilities, provided there are rationally related benefits accruing to the stockholders. However, such concern for non-stockholder interests is inappropriate when an auction among active bidders is in progress, and the object no longer is to protect or maintain the corporate enterprise but to sell it to the highest bidder.

Revlon also contended that it had contractual and good faith obligations to consider the noteholders. However, any such duties are limited to the principle that one may not interfere with contractual relationships by improper actions. Here, the rights of the noteholders were fixed by agreement, and there is nothing of substance to suggest that any of those terms were violated. The Notes covenants specifically contemplated a waiver to permit sale of the company at a fair price. The Notes were accepted by the holders on that basis, including the risk of an adverse market effect stemming from a waiver. Thus, nothing remained for Revlon to legitimately protect, and no rationally related benefit thereby accrued to the stockholders. Under such circumstances we must conclude that the merger agreement with Forstmann was unreasonable in relation to the threat posed.

A lock-up is not *per se* illegal under Delaware law. . . . Such options can entice other bidders to enter a contest for control of the corporation, creating an auction for the company and maximizing shareholder profit. Current economic conditions in the takeover market are such that a "white knight" like Forstmann might only enter the bidding for the target company if it receives some form of compensation to cover the risks and costs involved. . . .

However, while those lock-ups which draw bidders into the battle benefit shareholders, similar measures which end an active auction and foreclose further bidding operate to the shareholders' detriment. . . .

The Forstmann option had a . . . destructive effect on the auction process. Forstmann had already been drawn into the contest on a preferred basis, so the result of the lock-up was not to foster bidding, but to destroy it. The board's stated reasons for approving the transactions were: (1) better financing, (2) noteholder protection, and (3) higher price. As the Court of Chancery found, and we agree, any distinctions between the rival bidders' methods of financing the proposal were nominal at best, and such a consideration has little or no significance in a cash offer for any and all shares. The principal object, contrary to the board's duty of care, appears to have been protection of the noteholders over the shareholders' interests.

While Forstmann's $57.25 offer was objectively higher than Pantry Pride's $56.25 bid, the margin of superiority is less when the Forstmann price is adjusted for the time value of money. In reality, the Revlon board ended the auction in return for very little actual improvement in the final bid. The principal benefit went to the directors, who avoided personal liability to a class of creditors to whom the board owed no further duty under the circumstances. . . .

In addition to the lock-up option, the Court of Chancery enjoined the no-shop provision as part of the attempt to foreclose further bidding by Pantry Pride. . . . The no-shop provision, like the lock-up option, while not *per se* illegal, is impermissible under the *Unocal* standards when a board's primary duty becomes that of an auctioneer responsible for selling the company to the highest bidder. The agreement to negotiate only with Forstmann ended rather than intensified the board's involvement in the bidding contest.

It is ironic that the parties even considered a no-shop agreement when Revlon had dealt preferentially, and almost exclusively, with Forstmann throughout the contest. After the directors authorized management to negotiate with other parties, Forstmann was given every negotiating advantage that Pantry Pride had been denied: cooperation from management, access to financial data, and the exclusive opportunity to present merger proposals directly to the board of directors. Favoritism for a white knight to the total exclusion of a hostile bidder might be justifiable when the latter's offer adversely affects shareholder interests, but when bidders make relatively similar offers, or dissolution of the company becomes inevitable, the directors cannot fulfill their enhanced *Unocal* duties by playing favorites with the contending factions. Market forces must be allowed to operate freely to bring the target's shareholders the best price available for their equity. Thus, as the trial court ruled, the shareholders' interests necessitated that the board remain free to negotiate in the fulfillment of that duty.

The court below similarly enjoined the payment of the cancellation fee, pending a resolution of the merits, because the fee was part of the overall plan to thwart Pantry Pride's efforts. We find no abuse of discretion in that ruling.

. . .

V.

In conclusion, the Revlon board was confronted with a situation not uncommon in the current wave of corporate takeovers. A hostile and determined bidder sought the company at a price the board was convinced was inadequate. The initial defensive tactics worked to the benefit of the shareholders, and thus the board was able to sustain its *Unocal* burdens in justifying those measures. However, in granting an asset option lock-up to Forstmann, we must conclude that under all the circumstances the directors allowed considerations other than the maximization of shareholder profit to affect their judgment, and followed a course that ended the auction for Revlon, absent court intervention, to the ultimate detriment of its shareholders. No such defensive measure can be sustained when it represents a breach of the directors' fundamental duty of care. See Smith v. Van Gorkom, Del.Supr., 488 A.2d 858, 874 (1985). In that context the board's action is not entitled to the deference accorded it by the business judgment rule. The measures were properly enjoined. The decision of the Court of Chancery, therefore, is

AFFIRMED.

SIDELIGHTS

The clash between Perelman of Pantry Pride and Bergerac of Revlon involved personalities as well as money and power. In a fascinating account of Perelman's eventually successful takeover (which ultimately resulted in Perelman becoming one of the richest people in America), Bergerac is described as "a courtly, somewhat imperious, urbane, witty Frenchman," while Perelman is "crude, brusque, humorless, speaks in a staccato manner and perpetually puffs on a cigar." C. Bruck, The Predators' Ball 194 (1988) (the story of Michael Milken of Drexel Burnham Lambert, who provided the financing for Perelman). Thus, the Revlon takeover was "a class war, between the corporate America and Wall Street elite, and the Drexel arrivistes." Id. at 197. Perelman won that war, but Bergerac's defeat was softened with $35 million in severance pay (id. at 232)—the corporate world's version of the Marshall plan.

ANALYSIS

1. The court states that Revlon had about 30 million shares outstanding. Thus, Perelman's offer of $56 (roughly) per share implied that he was willing to pay $1,680 million for the entire firm. Suppose that in fact he had decided that he would bid as high as $1,800 million and that raising his offer to this amount would not impose any additional legal, accounting, or other such costs on him. Suppose further that Forstmann had decided that he would be willing to bid as high as $1,700 million, after taking account of legal and accounting costs of $10 million. In the absence of a termination fee or other lockup, who prevails and at what price in a fair auction? Forstmann will be unwilling to bid, because he will be reasonably certain that Perelman will outbid him and that he will therefore waste his $10 million. Suppose that the Revlon board offers Forstmann a termination fee of $12 million in return for a bid of $1,700 million. Forstmann will be happy to accept the offer. Perelman will then

bid, say, $1,701 million. If the Revlon board accepts the $1,701 million Perelman bid, Revlon's shareholders will net $1,701 million. The $12 million payable to Forstmann will come from the Revlon assets and will therefore be paid, in effect, by Perelman. The Revlon shareholders will have increased their total proceeds by $21 million (the $1,701 million final bid less the $1,680 million prior bid). Forstmann will be ahead $2 million for his efforts. Perelman will have bought the company for $1,713 million (his bid of $1,701 million plus the termination fee of $12 million).

What if the Revlon board offers Forstmann a termination fee of $20 million in return for a bid of $1,750 million? This would be a tough one for Forstmann—unless he is certain that Perelman will outbid him. If Perelman does not do so, Forstmann winds up buying the company for $50 million more than it is worth to him, and, of course, there is no termination fee. In fact, if Perelman values the company at $1,800 million, he will bid up to $1,780 million when the termination fee is $20 million, but Forstmann may not be sure of that. Note that the termination fee does not fall from heaven. It comes from Revlon and reduces the amount the Perelman is willing to pay and that the Revlon shareholders will receive.

Finally, suppose the board offers a termination fee of $150 million in return for a bid of $1,700 million. The termination fee reduces the value to Perelman to $1,650 million, so he will not outbid Forstmann. Thus, the company goes to Forstmann for $1,700 million even though Perelman values it at $1,800 million. (Although, once Forstmann owns Revlon, which he values at $1,700 million, if he is a rational maximizer, he would sell it to Perlman. Consequently, once again, Revlon should wind up in the hands of the holder who values it most highly.)

Return to the facts as originally stated, with a termination fee of $12 million. In the end, everyone is better off, but there has been a waste of $10 million in expenses incurred by Forstmann. Is there a better way to induce Perelman to increase his bid—a way that avoids the waste?

2. In *Revlon,* precisely when was it that the duty of the board to step back and act as auctioneers arose?

3. Does the board of directors of a Delaware corporation have "fiduciary" obligations to its creditors? Should it have?

4. How much of an advantage will white knights generally have? What was Forstmann's informational advantage? Consider the following recollection from Steve Fraidin of Fried, Frank, Shriver & Jacobson:

> I represented Forstmann Little. At one point there was a negotiation between the parties to try to settle the situation, and my client tells Perelman, "We have a big advantage: we have confidential information, you don't have any. We know what to bid and you do not." Perelman, who was a smart man, said, "Actually, I have even better information than you because I know what you're bidding. And once I know what you're bidding and I know how smart you are and I know that you have all the confidential information, I know I can bid a nickel more and still have a good deal." And he was absolutely right.

Quoted in Guhan Subramanian, The Drivers of Market Efficiency in Revlon Transactions, 28 J. Corp. L. 691 (2003).

Paramount Communications, Inc. v. Time Incorporated

571 A.2d 1140 (Del.1989).

. . .

Time is a Delaware corporation with its principal offices in New York City. Time's traditional business is publication of magazines and books; however, Time also provides pay television programming through its Home Box Office, Inc. and Cinemax subsidiaries. In addition, Time owns and operates cable television franchises through its subsidiary, American Television and Communication Corporation. During the relevant time period, Time's board consisted of sixteen directors. Twelve of the directors were "outside," nonemployee directors. Four of the directors were also officers of the company. . . .

As early as 1983 and 1984, Time's executive board began considering expanding Time's operations into the entertainment industry. . . .

In late spring of 1987, a meeting took place between Steve Ross, CEO of Warner Brothers, and N.J. Nicholas [President and a director] of Time. Ross and Nicholas discussed the possibility of a joint venture between the two companies through the creation of a jointly-owned cable company. Time would contribute its cable system and HBO. Warner would contribute its cable system and provide access to Warner Brothers Studio. The resulting venture would be a larger, more efficient cable network, able to produce and distribute its own movies on a world-wide basis. Ultimately the parties abandoned this plan, determining that it was impractical for several reasons, chief among them being tax considerations.

On August 11, 1987, Gerald M. Levin, Time's vice chairman and chief strategist, wrote J. Richard Munro [Time Chairman] a confidential memorandum in which he strongly recommended a strategic consolidation with Warner. In June 1988, Nicholas and Munro sent to each outside director a copy of the "comprehensive long-term planning document" prepared by the committee of Time executives that had been examining strategies for the 1990s. The memo included reference to and a description of Warner as a potential acquisition candidate.

. . . On July 21, 1988, Time's board met, with all outside directors present. The meeting's purpose was to consider Time's expansion into the entertainment industry on a global scale. . . .

Without any definitive decision on choice of a company, the board approved in principle a strategic plan for Time's expansion. . . .

The board's consensus was that a merger of Time and Warner was feasible, but only if Time controlled the board of the resulting corporation and thereby preserved a management committed to Time's journalistic integrity. . . .

Of a wide range of companies considered by Time's board as possible merger candidates, Warner Brothers, Paramount, Columbia, M.C.A., Fox, MGM, Disney, and Orion, the board, in July 1988, concluded that Warner was the superior candidate for a consolidation. . . .

From the outset, Time's board favored an all-cash or cash and securities acquisition of Warner as the basis for consolidation. Bruce

Wasserstein, Time's financial advisor, also favored an outright purchase of Warner. However, Steve Ross, Warner's CEO, was adamant that a business combination was only practicable on a stock-for-stock basis. . . .

Eventually Time acquiesced in Warner's insistence on a stock-for-stock deal, but talks broke down over corporate governance issues. Time wanted Ross' position as a co-CEO to be temporary and wanted Ross to retire in five years. Ross, however, refused to set a time for his retirement and viewed Time's proposal as indicating a lack of confidence in his leadership. . . .

Warner and Time resumed negotiations in January 1989. The catalyst for the resumption of talks was a private dinner between Steve Ross and Time outside director, Michael Dingman. Dingman was able to convince Ross that the transitional nature of the proposed co-CEO arrangement did not reflect a lack of confidence in Ross. Ross agreed that this course was best for the company and a meeting between Ross and Munro resulted. Ross agreed to retire in five years and let Nicholas succeed him. . . .

Time insider directors Levin and Nicholas met with Warner's financial advisors to decide upon a stock exchange ratio. Time's board had recognized the potential need to pay a premium in the stock ratio in exchange for dictating the governing arrangement of the new Time-Warner. . . . Warner's financial advisors informed its board that any exchange rate over .400 was a fair deal and any exchange rate over .450 was "one hell of a deal." The parties ultimately agreed upon an exchange rate favoring Warner of .465. On that basis, Warner stockholders would have owned approximately 62% of the common stock of Time-Warner.

On March 3, 1989, Time's board, with all but one director in attendance, met and unanimously approved the stock-for-stock merger with Warner. Warner's board likewise approved the merger. . . .

At its March 3, 1989 meeting, Time's board adopted several defensive tactics. Time entered an automatic share exchange agreement with Warner. Time would receive 17,292,747 shares of Warner's outstanding common stock (9.4%) and Warner would receive 7,080,016 shares of Time's outstanding common stock (11.1%). Either party could trigger the exchange. Time sought out and paid for "confidence" letters from various banks with which it did business. In these letters, the banks promised not to finance any third-party attempt to acquire Time. Time argues these agreements served only to preserve the confidential relationship between itself and the banks. The Chancellor found these agreements to be inconsequential and futile attempts to "dry up" money for a hostile takeover. Time also agreed to a "no-shop" clause, preventing Time from considering any other consolidation proposal, thus relinquishing its power to consider other proposals, regardless of their merits. Time did so at Warner's insistence. Warner did not want to be left "on the auction block" for an unfriendly suitor, if Time were to withdraw from the deal. . . .

Time representatives lauded the lack of debt to the United States Senate and to the President of the United States. Public reaction to the announcement of the merger was positive. Time-Warner would be a media colossus with international scope. The board scheduled the stockholder vote for June 23; and a May 1 record date was set. On May

24, 1989, Time sent out extensive proxy statements to the stockholders regarding the approval vote on the merger. In the meantime, with the merger proceeding without impediment, the special committee had concluded, shortly after its creation, that it was not necessary either to retain independent consultants, legal or financial, or even to meet. Time's board was unanimously in favor of the proposed merger with Warner; and, by the end of May, the Time-Warner merger appeared to be an accomplished fact.

On June 7, 1989, these wishful assumptions were shattered by Paramount's surprising announcement of its all-cash offer to purchase all outstanding shares of Time for $175 per share. The following day, June 8, the trading price of Time's stock rose from $126 to $170 per share. Paramount's offer was said to be "fully negotiable."

Time found Paramount's "fully negotiable" offer to be in fact subject to at least three conditions. First, Time had to terminate its merger agreement and stock exchange agreement with Warner, and remove certain other of its defensive devices, including the redemption of Time's shareholder rights. Second, Paramount had to obtain the required cable franchise transfers from Time in a fashion acceptable to Paramount in its sole discretion. Finally, the offer depended upon a judicial determination that section 203 of the General Corporate Law of Delaware (The Delaware Anti-Takeover Statute [discussed after the *CTS* case, below]) was inapplicable to any Time-Paramount merger. . . .

On June 8, 1989, Time formally responded to Paramount's offer. Time's chairman and CEO, J. Richard Munro, sent an aggressively worded letter to Paramount's CEO, Martin Davis. Munro's letter attacked Davis' personal integrity and called Paramount's offer "smoke and mirrors."

. . .

Over the following eight days, Time's board met three times to discuss Paramount's $175 offer. The board viewed Paramount's offer as inadequate and concluded that its proposed merger with Warner was the better course of action. Therefore, the board declined to open any negotiations with Paramount and held steady its course toward a merger with Warner.

[On] June 16, Time's board met to take up Paramount's offer. The board's prevailing belief was that Paramount's bid posed a threat to Time's control of its own destiny and retention of the "Time Culture." Even after Time's financial advisors made another presentation of Paramount and its business attributes, Time's board maintained its position that a combination with Warner offered greater potential for Time. . . .

At the same meeting, Time's board decided to recast its consolidation with Warner into an outright cash and securities acquisition of Warner by Time; and Time so informed Warner. Time accordingly restructured its proposal to acquire Warner as follows: Time would make an immediate all-cash offer for 51% of Warner's outstanding stock at $70 per share. The remaining 49% would be purchased at some later date for a mixture of cash and securities worth $70 per share. To provide the funds required for its outright acquisition of Warner, Time would assume 7–10 billion dollars worth of debt, thus eliminating one of the principal transaction-related benefits of the original merger agreement. Nine billion dollars of the total purchase price would be allocated to the purchase of Warner's goodwill.

. . .

On June 23, 1989, Paramount raised its all-cash offer to buy Time's outstanding stock to $200 per share. Paramount still professed that all aspects of the offer were negotiable. Time's board met on June 26, 1989 and formally rejected Paramount's $200 per share second offer. The board reiterated its belief that, despite the $25 increase, the offer was still inadequate. The Time board maintained that the Warner transaction offered a greater long-term value for the stockholders and, unlike Paramount's offer, did not pose a threat to Time's survival and its "culture." Paramount then filed this action in the Court of Chancery.*

II

The Shareholder Plaintiffs first assert a *Revlon* claim. They contend that the March 4 Time-Warner agreement effectively put Time up for sale, triggering *Revlon* duties, requiring Time's board to enhance short-term shareholder value and to treat all other interested acquirors on an equal basis. The Shareholder Plaintiffs base this argument on two facts: (i) the ultimate Time-Warner exchange ratio of .465 favoring Warner, resulting in Warner shareholders' receipt of 62% of the combined company; and (ii) the subjective intent of Time's directors as evidenced in their statements that the market might perceive the Time-Warner merger as putting Time up "for sale" and their adoption of various defensive measures.

The Shareholder Plaintiffs further contend that Time's directors, in structuring the original merger transaction to be "takeover-proof," triggered *Revlon* duties by foreclosing their shareholders from any prospect of obtaining a control premium. In short, plaintiffs argue that Time's board's decision to merge with Warner imposed a fiduciary duty to maximize immediate share value and not erect unreasonable barriers to further bids. Therefore, they argue, the Chancellor erred in finding: that Paramount's bid for Time did not place Time "for sale"; that Time's transaction with Warner did not result in any transfer of control; and that the combined Time-Warner was not so large as to preclude the possibility of the stockholders of Time-Warner receiving a future control premium.

Paramount asserts only a *Unocal* claim in which the shareholder plaintiffs join. Paramount contends that the Chancellor, in applying the first part of the *Unocal* test, erred in finding that Time's board had reasonable grounds to believe that Paramount posed both a legally cognizable threat to Time shareholders and a danger to Time's corporate policy and effectiveness. Paramount also contests the court's finding that Time's board made a reasonable and objective investigation of Paramount's offer so as to be informed before rejecting it. Paramount further claims that the court erred in applying *Unocal's* second part in finding Time's response to be "reasonable." Paramount points primarily to the preclusive effect of the revised agreement which denied Time shareholders the opportunity both to vote on the agreement and to

---

* [Eds.—Suits filed subsequently on behalf of Time shareholders were ultimately consolidated with the Paramount action.]

respond to Paramount's tender offer. Paramount argues that the underlying motivation of Time's board in adopting these defensive measures was management's desire to perpetuate itself in office.

. . .

A.

We first take up plaintiffs' principal *Revlon* argument, summarized above. In rejecting this argument, the Chancellor found the original Time-Warner merger agreement not to constitute a "change of control" and concluded that the transaction did not trigger *Revlon* duties. The Chancellor's conclusion is premised on a finding that "[b]efore the merger agreement was signed, control of the corporation existed in a fluid aggregation of unaffiliated shareholders representing a voting majority—in other words, in the market." The Chancellor's findings of fact are supported by the record and his conclusion is correct as a matter of law. However, we premise our rejection of plaintiffs' *Revlon* claim on different grounds, namely, the absence of any substantial evidence to conclude that Time's board, in negotiating with Warner, made the dissolution or break-up of the corporate entity inevitable, as was the case in *Revlon*.

Under Delaware law there are, generally speaking and without excluding other possibilities, two circumstances which may implicate *Revlon* duties. The first, and clearer one, is when a corporation initiates an active bidding process seeking to sell itself or to effect a business reorganization involving a clear break-up of the company. . . . However, *Revlon* duties may also be triggered where, in response to a bidder's offer, a target abandons its long-term strategy and seeks an alternative transaction involving the breakup of the company. Thus, in *Revlon,* when the board responded to Pantry Pride's offer by contemplating a "bust-up" sale of assets in a leveraged acquisition, we imposed upon the board a duty to maximize immediate shareholder value and an obligation to auction the company fairly. If, however, the board's reaction to a hostile tender offer is found to constitute only a defensive response and not an abandonment of the corporation's continued existence, *Revlon* duties are not triggered, though *Unocal* duties attach. . . .

The plaintiffs insist that even though the original Time-Warner agreement may not have worked "an objective change of control," the transaction made a "sale" of Time inevitable. Plaintiffs rely on the subjective intent of Time's board of directors and principally upon certain board members' expressions of concern that the Warner transaction *might* be viewed as effectively putting Time up for sale. Plaintiffs argue that the use of a lock-up agreement, a no-shop clause, and so-called "dry-up" agreements prevented shareholders from obtaining a control premium in the immediate future and thus violated *Revlon.*

We agree with the Chancellor that such evidence is entirely insufficient to invoke *Revlon* duties; and we decline to extend *Revlon's* application to corporate transactions simply because they might be construed as putting a corporation either "in play" or "up for sale." . . . The adoption of structural safety devices alone does not trigger *Revlon.* Rather, as the Chancellor stated, such devices are properly subject to a *Unocal* analysis.

. . .

B.

We turn now to plaintiffs' *Unocal* claim. We begin by noting, as did the Chancellor, that our decision does not require us to pass on the wisdom of the board's decision to enter into the original Time-Warner agreement. That is not a court's task. Our task is simply to review the record to determine whether there is sufficient evidence to support the Chancellor's conclusion that the initial Time-Warner agreement was the product of a proper exercise of business judgment. . . .

Time's decision in 1988 to combine with Warner was made only after what could be fairly characterized as an exhaustive appraisal of Time's future as a corporation. . . .

We find ample evidence in the record to support the Chancellor's conclusion that the Time board's decision to expand the business of the company through its March 3 merger with Warner was entitled to the protection of the business judgment rule. . . .

The Chancellor reached a different conclusion in addressing the Time-Warner transaction as revised three months later. He found that the revised agreement was defense-motivated and designed to avoid the potentially disruptive effect that Paramount's offer would have had on consummation of the proposed merger were it put to a shareholder vote. Thus, the court declined to apply the traditional business judgment rule to the revised transaction and instead analyzed the Time board's June 16 decision under *Unocal.* The court ruled that *Unocal* applied to all director actions taken, following receipt of Paramount's hostile tender offer, that were reasonably determined to be defensive. Clearly that was a correct ruling and no party disputes that ruling.

. . .

Unocal involved a two-tier, highly coercive tender offer. In such a case, the threat is obvious: shareholders may be compelled to tender to avoid being treated adversely in the second stage of the transaction. . . . In subsequent cases, the Court of Chancery has suggested that an all-cash, all-shares offer, falling within a range of values that a shareholder might reasonably prefer, cannot constitute a legally recognized "threat" to shareholder interests sufficient to withstand a *Unocal* analysis. . . . In those cases, the Court of Chancery determined that whatever threat existed related only to the shareholders and only to price and not to the corporation.

From those decisions by our Court of Chancery, Paramount and the individual plaintiffs extrapolate a rule of law that an all-cash, all-shares offer with values reasonably in the range of acceptable price cannot pose any objective threat to a corporation or its shareholders. Thus, Paramount would have us hold that only if the value of Paramount's offer were determined to be clearly inferior to the value created by management's plan to merge with Warner could the offer be viewed—objectively—as a threat.

Implicit in the plaintiffs' argument is the view that a hostile tender offer can pose only two types of threats: the threat of coercion that results from a two-tier offer promising unequal treatment for nontendering shareholders; and the threat of inadequate value from an all-shares, all-cash offer at a price below what a target board in good faith deems to be the present value of its shares. . . . Since Paramount's offer was all-cash, the only conceivable "threat" plaintiffs argue, was inadequate value. We disapprove of such a narrow and rigid construction of *Unocal,* for the reasons which follow.

Plaintiffs' position represents a fundamental misconception of our standard of review under *Unocal* principally because it would involve the court in substituting its judgment as to what is a "better" deal for that of a corporation's board of directors. . . .

In this case, the Time board reasonably determined that inadequate value was not the only legally cognizable threat that Paramount's all-cash, all-shares offer could present. Time's board concluded that Paramount's eleventh hour offer posed other threats. One concern was that Time shareholders might elect to tender into Paramount's cash offer in ignorance or a mistaken belief of the strategic benefit which a business combination with Warner might produce. . . . Further, the timing of Paramount's offer to follow issuance of Time's proxy notice was viewed as arguably designed to upset, if not confuse, the Time stockholders' vote. . . .

Paramount also contends that the Time board had not duly investigated Paramount's offer. Therefore, Paramount argues, Time was unable to make an informed decision that the offer posed a threat to Time's corporate policy. Although the Chancellor did not address this issue directly, his findings of fact do detail Time's exploration of the available entertainment companies, including Paramount, before determining that Warner provided the best strategic "fit." . . . Thus, the record does, in our judgment, demonstrate that Time's board was adequately informed of the potential benefits of a transaction with Paramount. . . .

We turn to the second part of the *Unocal* analysis. The obvious requisite to determining the reasonableness of a defensive action is a clear identification of the nature of the threat. . . . Paramount argues that, assuming its tender offer posed a threat, Time's response was unreasonable in precluding Time's shareholders from accepting the tender offer or receiving a control premium in the immediately foreseeable future. Once again, the contention stems, we believe, from a fundamental misunderstanding of where the power of corporate governance lies. Delaware law confers the management of the corporate enterprise to the stockholders' duly elected board representatives. . . . The fiduciary duty to manage a corporate enterprise includes the selection of a time frame for achievement of corporate goals. That duty may not be delegated to the stockholders. . . . Directors are not obliged to abandon a deliberately conceived corporate plan for a short-term shareholder profit unless there is clearly no basis to sustain the corporate strategy. . . .

. . .

Here, on the record facts, the Chancellor found that Time's responsive action to Paramount's tender offer was not aimed at "cramming down" on its shareholders a management-sponsored alternative, but rather had as its goal the carrying forward of a pre-existing transaction in an altered form.[19] Thus, the response was reasonably related to the threat. . . .

Conclusion

Applying the test for grant or denial of preliminary injunctive relief, we find plaintiffs failed to establish a reasonable likelihood of ultimate success on the merits. Therefore, we affirm.

NOTE

As the opinion in this case indicates, Paramount, on June 23, 1989, offered the Time, Inc. shareholders $200 per share for their shares and shortly thereafter the Time board rejected this offer as "inadequate." The decision of the Delaware Supreme Court was announced on July 24, 1989. The closing price of Time, Inc. shares on the New York Stock Exchange on July 25, 1989 was $137.50. The closing price on July 25, 1990, was $93.00 (with about 64.1 million shares outstanding).

ANALYSIS

1. The decision in this case allowed the board of directors to deny the shareholders an opportunity to choose between the Paramount offer of $200 per share and the alternative involving the combination with Warner. Given that most of the shares were held by institutions (e.g., mutual funds and pension funds), run by savvy people, what is the justification for that?

2. Did the merger of Time and Warner deprive the Time shareholders of the opportunity in the future to realize a premium for sale of control? After the merger, could Paramount, or some other corporation, have mounted a new takeover bid for the combined corporations? Is that relevant?

3. Recall the facts in *Revlon*, supra. Suppose that before Perelman had shown an interest in Revlon, a group of Revlon managers, together with Forstmann Little & Co., had been in negotiations to buy the company for $53 per share, a price that a reputable investment banker had advised, after thorough investigation, was a good one. Assume that it was contemplated that none of the Revlon divisions would be sold off; the company would be kept intact. Suppose that then Perelman had made an offer of $56 per share, all cash, no strings. Suppose all the members of the board strongly favored the sale to the management/Forstmann group and sought your advice on how to proceed. What would your response have been?

---

[19] The Chancellor cited Shamrock Holdings, Inc. v. Polaroid Corp., Del.Ch., 559 A.2d 257 (1989), as a closely analogous case. In that case, the Court of Chancery upheld, in the face of a takeover bid, the establishment of an employee stock ownership plan that had a significant anti-takeover effect. The Court of Chancery upheld the board's action largely because the ESOP had been adopted *prior* to any contest for control and was reasonably determined to increase productivity and enhance profits. The ESOP did not appear to be primarily a device to affect or secure corporate control.

Paramount Communications Inc. v. QVC Network Inc.

637 A.2d 34 (Del.1994).

In this appeal we review an order of the Court of Chancery dated November 24, 1993 . . ., preliminarily enjoining certain defensive measures designed to facilitate a so-called strategic alliance between Viacom Inc. ("Viacom") and Paramount Communications Inc. ("Paramount") approved by the board of directors of Paramount (the "Paramount Board" or the "Paramount directors") and to thwart an unsolicited, more valuable, tender offer by QVC Network Inc. ("QVC"). In affirming, we hold that the sale of control in this case, which is at the heart of the proposed strategic alliance, implicates enhanced judicial scrutiny of the conduct of the Paramount Board under Unocal Corp. v. Mesa Petroleum Co., Del.Supr. 493 A.2d 946 (1985), and Revlon, Inc. v. MacAndrews & Forbes Holdings, Inc., Del.Supr., 506 A.2d 173 (1985).

. . .

I. FACTS

. . .

Paramount is a Delaware corporation with its principal offices in New York City. Approximately 118 million shares of Paramount's common stock are outstanding and traded on the New York Stock Exchange. The majority of Paramount's stock is publicly held by numerous unaffiliated investors. Paramount owns and operates a diverse group of entertainment businesses, including motion picture and television studios, book publishers, professional sports teams and amusement parks.

There are 15 persons serving on the Paramount Board. Four directors are officer-employees of Paramount: Martin S. Davis ("Davis"), Paramount's Chairman and Chief Executive Officer since 1983; Donald Oresman ("Oresman"), Executive Vice-President, Chief Administrative Officer, and General Counsel; Stanley R. Jaffe, President and Chief Operating Officer; and Ronald L. Nelson, Executive Vice President and Chief Financial Officer. . . .

Viacom is a Delaware corporation with its headquarters in Massachusetts. Viacom is controlled by Sumner M. Redstone ("Redstone"), its Chairman and Chief Executive Officer, who owns indirectly approximately 85.2 percent of Viacom's voting Class A stock and approximately 69.2 percent of Viacom's nonvoting Class B stock through National Amusements, Inc. ("NAI"), an entity 91.7 percent owned by Redstone. Viacom has a wide range of entertainment operations, including a number of well-known cable television channels such as MTV, Nickelodeon, Showtime, and The Movie Channel. . . .

QVC is a Delaware corporation with its headquarters in West Chester, Pennsylvania. QVC has several large stockholders, including Liberty Media Corporation, Comcast Corporation, Advance Publications, Inc., and Cox Enterprises Inc. Barry Diller ("Diller"), the Chairman and Chief Executive Officer of QVC, is also a substantial stockholder. QVC sells a variety of merchandise through a televised shopping channel. . . .

Beginning in the late 1980s, Paramount investigated the possibility of acquiring or merging with other companies in the entertainment, media, or communications industry. . . . Consistent with its goal of strategic expansion, Paramount made a tender offer for Time Inc. in 1989, but was ultimately unsuccessful. . . .

Although Paramount had considered a possible combination of Paramount and Viacom as early as 1990, recent efforts to explore such a transaction began at a dinner meeting between Redstone and Davis on April 20, 1993. . . . After several more meetings between Redstone and Davis, serious negotiations began taking place in early July.

It was tentatively agreed that Davis would be the chief executive officer and Redstone would be the controlling stockholder of the combined company, but the parties could not reach agreement on the merger price and the terms of a stock option to be granted to Viacom. With respect to price, Viacom offered a package of cash and stock (primarily Viacom Class B nonvoting stock) with a market value of approximately $61 per share, but Paramount wanted at least $70 per share.

Shortly after negotiations broke down in July 1993, two notable events occurred. First, Davis apparently learned of QVC's potential interest in Paramount, and told Diller over lunch on July 21, 1993, that Paramount was not for sale. Second, the market value of Viacom's Class B nonvoting stock increased from $46.875 on July 6 to $57.25 on August 20. QVC claims (and Viacom disputes) that this price increase was caused by open market purchases of such stock by Redstone or entities controlled by him.

On August 20, 1993, discussions between Paramount and Viacom resumed. . . . On September 9, 1993, the Paramount Board was informed about the status of the negotiations and was provided information by [financial advisers] Lazard [Freres & Co.], including an analysis of the proposed transaction.

On September 12, 1993, the Paramount Board met again and unanimously approved the Original Merger Agreement whereby Paramount would merge with and into Viacom. The terms of the merger provided that each share of Paramount common stock would be converted into 0.10 shares of Viacom Class A voting stock, 0.90 shares of Viacom Class B nonvoting stock, and $9.10 in cash. In addition, the Paramount Board agreed to amend its "poison pill" Rights Agreement to exempt the proposed merger with Viacom. The Original Merger Agreement also contained several provisions designed to make it more difficult for a potential competing bid to succeed. We focus, as did the Court of Chancery, on three of these defensive provisions: a "no-shop" provision (the "No-Shop Provision"), the Termination Fee, and the Stock Option Agreement.

First, under the No-Shop Provision, the Paramount Board agreed that Paramount would not solicit, encourage, discuss, negotiate, or endorse any competing transaction unless: (a) a third party "makes an unsolicited written, bona fide proposal, which is not subject to any material contingencies relating to financing"; and (b) the Paramount Board determines that discussions or negotiations with the third party are necessary for the Paramount Board to comply with its fiduciary duties.

Second, under the Termination Fee provision, Viacom would receive a $100 million termination fee if: (a) Paramount terminated the Original Merger Agreement because of a competing transaction; (b) Paramount's stockholders did not approve the merger; or (c) the Paramount Board recommended a competing transaction.

The third and most significant deterrent device was the Stock Option Agreement, which granted to Viacom an option to purchase approximately 19.9 percent (23,699,000 shares) of Paramount's outstanding common stock at $69.14 per share if any of the triggering events for the Termination Fee occurred. In addition to the customary terms that are normally associated with a stock option, the Stock Option Agreement contained two provisions that were both unusual and highly beneficial to Viacom: (a) Viacom was permitted to pay for the shares with a senior subordinated note of questionable marketability instead of cash, thereby avoiding the need to raise the $1.6 billion purchase price (the "Note Feature"); and (b) Viacom could elect to require Paramount to pay Viacom in cash a sum equal to the difference between the purchase price and the market price of Paramount's stock (the "Put Feature"). Because the Stock Option Agreement was not "capped" to limit its maximum dollar value, it had the potential to reach (and in this case did reach) unreasonable levels.

After the execution of the Original Merger Agreement and the Stock Option Agreement on September 12, 1993, Paramount and Viacom announced their proposed merger. In a number of public statements, the parties indicated that the pending transaction was a virtual certainty. . . .

Despite these attempts to discourage a competing bid, Diller sent a letter to Davis on September 20, 1993, proposing a merger in which QVC would acquire Paramount for approximately $80 per share, consisting of 0.893 shares of QVC common stock and $30 in cash. QVC also expressed its eagerness to meet with Paramount to negotiate the details of a transaction. When the Paramount Board met on September 27, it was advised by Davis that the Original Merger Agreement prohibited Paramount from having discussions with QVC (or anyone else) unless certain conditions were satisfied. In particular, QVC had to supply evidence that its proposal was not subject to financing contingencies. . . .

On October 5, 1993, QVC provided Paramount with evidence of QVC's financing. The Paramount Board then held another meeting on October 11, and decided to authorize management to meet with QVC. Davis also informed the Paramount Board that Booz-Allen & Hamilton ("Booz-Allen"), a management consulting firm, had been retained to assess, inter alia, the incremental earnings potential from a Paramount-Viacom merger and a Paramount-QVC merger. . . .

On October 21, 1993, QVC filed this action and publicly announced an $80 cash tender offer for 51 percent of Paramount's outstanding shares (the "QVC tender offer"). Each remaining share of Paramount common stock would be converted into 1.42857 shares of QVC common stock in a second-step merger. The tender offer was conditioned on, among other things, the invalidation of the Stock Option Agreement, which was worth over $200 million by that point.[5] . . .

---

[5] By November 15, 1993, the value of the Stock Option Agreement had increased to nearly $500 million based on the $90 QVC bid. . . .

Confronted by QVC's hostile bid, which on its face offered over $10 per share more than the consideration provided by the Original Merger Agreement, Viacom realized that it would need to raise its bid in order to remain competitive. Within hours after QVC's tender offer was announced, Viacom entered into discussions with Paramount concerning a revised transaction. These discussions led to serious negotiations concerning a comprehensive amendment to the original Paramount-Viacom transaction. In effect, the opportunity for a "new deal" with Viacom was at hand for the Paramount Board. With the QVC hostile bid offering greater value to the Paramount stockholders, the Paramount Board had considerable leverage with Viacom.

At a special meeting on October 24, 1993, the Paramount Board approved the Amended Merger Agreement and an amendment to the Stock Option Agreement. The Amended Merger Agreement was, however, essentially the same as the Original Merger Agreement, except that it included a few new provisions. One provision related to an $80 per share cash tender offer by Viacom for 51 percent of Paramount's stock, and another changed the merger consideration so that each share of Paramount would be converted into 0.20408 shares of Viacom Class A voting stock, 1.08317 shares of Viacom Class B nonvoting stock, and 0.20408 shares of a new series of Viacom convertible preferred stock. The Amended Merger Agreement also added a provision giving Paramount the right not to amend its Rights Agreement to exempt Viacom if the Paramount Board determined that such an amendment would be inconsistent with its fiduciary duties because another offer constituted a "better alternative." Finally, the Paramount Board was given the power to terminate the Amended Merger Agreement if it withdrew its recommendation of the Viacom transaction or recommended a competing transaction. . . .

Viacom's tender offer commenced on October 25, 1993, and QVC's tender offer was formally launched on October 27, 1993. . . . On November 6, 1993, Viacom unilaterally raised its tender offer price to $85 per share in cash and offered a comparable increase in the value of the securities being proposed in the second-step merger. At a telephonic meeting held later that day, the Paramount Board agreed to recommend Viacom's higher bid to Paramount's stockholders.

QVC responded to Viacom's higher bid on November 12 by increasing its tender offer to $90 per share and by increasing the securities for its second-step merger by a similar amount. In response to QVC's latest offer, the Paramount Board scheduled a meeting for November 15, 1993. . . . At its meeting on November 15, 1993, the Paramount Board determined that the new QVC offer was not in the best interests of the stockholders. The purported basis for this conclusion was that QVC's bid was excessively conditional. . . .

II. APPLICABLE PRINCIPLES OF ESTABLISHED DELAWARE LAW

. . . . Under normal circumstances, neither the courts nor the stockholders should interfere with the managerial decisions of the directors. The business judgment rule embodies the deference to which such decisions are entitled.

Nevertheless, there are rare situations which mandate that a court take a more direct and active role in overseeing the decisions made and actions taken by directors. In these situations, a court subjects the directors' conduct to enhanced scrutiny to ensure that it is reasonable.[9] . . . The case at bar implicates two such circumstances: (1) the approval of a transaction resulting in a sale of control, and (2) the adoption of defensive measures in response to a threat to corporate control.

A. The Significance of a Sale or Change of Control

When a majority of a corporation's voting shares are acquired by a single person or entity, or by a cohesive group acting together, there is a significant diminution in the voting power of those who thereby become minority stockholders . . . Because of the overriding importance of voting rights, this Court and the Court of Chancery have consistently acted to protect stockholders from unwarranted interference with such rights.

In the absence of devices protecting the minority stockholders, stockholder votes are likely to become mere formalities where there is a majority stockholder. . . . Absent effective protective provisions, minority stockholders must rely for protection solely on the fiduciary duties owed to them by the directors and the majority stockholder, since the minority stockholders have lost the power to influence corporate direction through the ballot. . . .

In the case before us, the public stockholders (in the aggregate) currently own a majority of Paramount's voting stock. . . . In the event the Paramount-Viacom transaction is consummated, the public stockholders will receive cash and a minority equity voting position in the surviving corporation. Following such consummation, there will be a controlling stockholder who will have the voting power to: (a) elect directors; (b) cause a break-up of the corporation; (c) merge it with another company; (d) cash-out the public stockholders; (e) amend the certificate of incorporation; (f) sell all or substantially all of the corporate assets; or (g) otherwise alter materially the nature of the corporation and the public stockholders' interests. . . .

Because of the intended sale of control, the Paramount-Viacom transaction has economic consequences of considerable significance to the Paramount stockholders. Once control has shifted, the current Paramount stockholders will have no leverage in the future to demand another control premium. As a result, the Paramount stockholders are entitled to receive, and should receive, a control premium and/or protective devices of significant value. There being no such protective provisions in the Viacom-Paramount transaction, the Paramount directors had an obligation to take the maximum advantage of the current opportunity to realize for the stockholders the best value reasonably available.

B. The Obligations of Directors in a Sale or Change of Control Transaction

The consequences of a sale of control impose special obligations on the directors of a corporation. In particular, they have the obligation of acting reasonably to seek the transaction offering the best value

---

[9] Where actual self-interest is present and affects a majority of the directors approving a transaction, a court will apply even more exacting scrutiny to determine whether the transaction is entirely fair to the stockholders.

reasonably available to the stockholders. The courts will apply enhanced scrutiny to ensure that the directors have acted reasonably.

In the sale of control context, the directors must focus on one primary objective—to secure the transaction offering the best value reasonably available for the stockholders—and they must exercise their fiduciary duties to further that end. . . .

[S]ome of the methods by which a board can fulfill its obligation . . . include conducting an auction, canvassing the market, etc. Delaware law recognizes that there is "no single blueprint" that directors must follow. . . .

In determining which alternative provides the best value for the stockholders, a board of directors is not limited to considering only the amount of cash involved, and is not required to ignore totally its view of the future value of a strategic alliance. . . . Instead, the directors should analyze the entire situation and evaluate in a disciplined manner the consideration being offered. . . . Having informed themselves of all material information reasonably available, the directors must decide which alternative is most likely to offer the best value reasonably available to the stockholders.

C. Enhanced Judicial Scrutiny of a Sale or Change of Control Transaction

Board action in the circumstances presented here is subject to enhanced scrutiny. Such scrutiny is mandated by: (a) the threatened diminution of the current stockholders' voting power; (b) the fact that an asset belonging to public stockholders (a control premium) is being sold and may never be available again: and (c) the traditional concern of Delaware courts for actions which impair or impede stockholder voting rights. . . .

The key features of an enhanced scrutiny test are: (a) a judicial determination regarding the adequacy of the decisionmaking process employed by the directors, including the information on which the directors based their decision; and (b) a judicial examination of the reasonableness of the directors' action in light of the circumstances then existing. The directors have the burden of proving that they were adequately informed and acted reasonably. . . .

D. *Revlon* and *Time-Warner* Distinguished

The Paramount defendants and Viacom assert that the fiduciary obligations and the enhanced judicial scrutiny discussed above are not implicated in this case in the absence of a "break-up" of the corporation, and that the order granting the preliminary injunction should be reversed. This argument is based on their erroneous interpretation of our decisions in *Revlon* and *Time-Warner*.

In *Revlon*, we reviewed the actions of the board of directors of Revlon, Inc. ("Revlon"), which had rebuffed the overtures of Pantry Pride, Inc. and had instead entered into an agreement with Forstmann Little & Co. ("Forstmann") providing for the acquisition of 100 percent of Revlon's outstanding stock by Forstmann and the subsequent break-up of Revlon. Based on the facts and circumstances present in *Revlon*, we held that "the directors' role changed from defenders of the corporate bastion to auctioneers charged with getting the best price for the stockholders at a sale of the company." 506 A.2d at 182. We further held that "when a board ends an intense bidding contest on an insubstantial basis, . . . [that] action cannot withstand the enhanced scrutiny which Unocal requires of director conduct." Id. at 184.

It is true that one of the circumstances bearing on these holdings was the fact that "the break-up of the company . . . had become a reality which even the directors embraced." Id. at 182. It does not follow, however, that a "break-up" must be present and "inevitable" before directors are subject to enhanced judicial scrutiny and are required to pursue a transaction that is calculated to produce the best value reasonably available to the stockholders. In fact, we stated in *Revlon* that "when bidders make relatively similar offers, or dissolution of the company becomes inevitable, the directors cannot fulfill their enhanced *Unocal* duties by playing favorites with the contending factions." Id. at 184 (emphasis added). *Revlon* thus does not hold that an inevitable dissolution or "break-up" is necessary.

The decisions of this Court following *Revlon* reinforced the applicability of enhanced scrutiny and the directors' obligation to seek the best value reasonably available for the stockholders where there is a pending sale of control, regardless of whether or not there is to be a break-up of the corporation. . . .

[W]hen a corporation undertakes a transaction which will cause: (a) a change in corporate control; or (b) a break-up of the corporate entity, the directors' obligation is to seek the best value reasonably available to the stockholders. This obligation arises because the effect of the Viacom-Paramount transaction, if consummated, is to shift control of Paramount from the public stockholders to a controlling stockholder, Viacom. Neither *Time-Warner* nor any other decision of this Court holds that a "break-up" of the company is essential to give rise to this obligation where there is a sale of control.

III. BREACH OF FIDUCIARY DUTIES BY PARAMOUNT BOARD

. . .

A. The Specific Obligations of the Paramount Board

Under the facts of this case, the Paramount directors had the obligation: (a) to be diligent and vigilant in examining critically the Paramount-Viacom transaction and the QVC tender offers; (b) to act in good faith; (c) to obtain, and act with due care on, all material information reasonably available, including information necessary to compare the two offers to determine which of these transactions, or an alternative course of action, would provide the best value reasonably available to the stockholders; and (d) to negotiate actively and in good faith with both Viacom and QVC to that end.

Having decided to sell control of the corporation, the Paramount directors were required to evaluate critically whether or not all material aspects of the Paramount-Viacom transaction (separately and in the aggregate) were reasonable and in the best interests of the Paramount stockholders in light of current circumstances, including: the change of control premium, the Stock Option Agreement, the Termination Fee, the coercive nature of both the Viacom and QVC tender offers,[18] the No-Shop Provision, and the proposed disparate use of the Rights Agreement as to the Viacom and QVC tender offers, respectively.

These obligations necessarily implicated various issues, including the questions of whether or not those provisions and other aspects of the Paramount-Viacom transaction (separately and in the aggregate): (a) adversely affected the value provided to the Paramount stockholders; (b) inhibited or encouraged alternative bids; (c) were enforceable contractual obligations in light of the directors' fiduciary duties; and (d) in the end would advance or retard the Paramount directors' obligation to secure for the Paramount stockholders the best value reasonably available under the circumstances.

The Paramount defendants contend that they were precluded by certain contractual provisions, including the No-Shop Provision, from negotiating with QVC or seeking alternatives. Such provisions, whether or not they are presumptively valid in the abstract, may not validly define or limit the directors' fiduciary duties under Delaware law or prevent the Paramount directors from carrying out their fiduciary duties under Delaware law. To the extent such provisions are inconsistent with those duties, they are invalid and unenforceable. . . .

Since the Paramount directors had already decided to sell control, they had an obligation to continue their search for the best value reasonably available to the stockholders. This continuing obligation included the responsibility, at the October 24 board meeting and thereafter, to evaluate critically both the QVC tender offers and the Paramount-Viacom transaction to determine if: (a) the QVC tender offer was, or would continue to be, conditional; (b) the QVC tender offer could be improved; (c) the Viacom tender offer or other aspects of the Paramount-Viacom transaction could be improved; (d) each of the respective offers would be reasonably likely to come to closure, and under what circumstances; (e) other material information was reasonably available for consideration by the Paramount directors; (f) there were viable and realistic alternative courses of action; and (g) the timing constraints could be managed so the directors could consider these matters carefully and deliberately.

B. The Breaches of Fiduciary Duty by the Paramount Board

The Paramount directors made the decision on September 12, 1993, that, in their judgment, a strategic merger with Viacom on the economic terms of the Original Merger Agreement was in the best interests of Paramount and its stockholders. Those terms provided a modest change of control premium to the stockholders. The directors also decided at that time that it was appropriate to agree to certain defensive measures (the Stock Option Agreement, the Termination Fee, and the No-Shop Provision) insisted upon by Viacom as part of that economic transaction. . . . We conclude that the Paramount directors' process was

---

[18] Both the Viacom and the QVC tender offers were for 51 percent cash and a "back-end" of various securities, the value of each of which depended on the fluctuating value of Viacom and QVC stock at any given time. Thus, both tender offers were two-tiered, front-end loaded, and coercive. Such coercive offers are inherently problematic and should be expected to receive particularly careful analysis by a target board. See *Unocal,* 493 A.2d at 956.

not reasonable, and the result achieved for the stockholders was not reasonable under the circumstances.

. . . The Stock Option Agreement had a number of unusual and potentially "draconian" provisions, including the Note Feature and the Put Feature. Furthermore, the Termination Fee, whether or not unreasonable by itself, clearly made Paramount less attractive to other bidders, when coupled with the Stock Option Agreement. Finally, the No-Shop Provision inhibited the Paramount Board's ability to negotiate with other potential bidders, particularly QVC which had already expressed an interest in Paramount.

Throughout the applicable time period, and especially from the first QVC merger proposal on September 20 through the Paramount Board meeting on November 15, QVC's interest in Paramount provided the opportunity for the Paramount Board to seek significantly higher value for the Paramount stockholders than that being offered by Viacom. . . .

The Paramount directors had the opportunity in the October 23–24 time frame, when the Original Merger Agreement was renegotiated, to take appropriate action to modify the improper defensive measures as well as to improve the economic terms of the Paramount-Viacom transaction. Under the circumstances existing at that time, it should have been clear to the Paramount Board that the Stock Option Agreement, coupled with the Termination Fee and the No-Shop Clause, were impeding the realization of the best value reasonably available to the Paramount stockholders. Nevertheless, the Paramount Board made no effort to eliminate or modify these counterproductive devices, and instead continued to cling to its vision of a strategic alliance with Viacom.

. . .

IV. VIACOM'S CLAIM OF VESTED CONTRACT RIGHTS

Viacom argues that it had certain "vested" contract rights with respect to the No-Shop Provision and the Stock Option Agreement. In effect, Viacom's argument is that the Paramount directors could enter into an agreement in violation of their fiduciary duties and then render Paramount, and ultimately its stockholders, liable for failing to carry out an agreement in violation of those duties. Viacom's protestations about vested rights are without merit. . . .

AFTERMATH

After the Delaware Supreme Court issued its order, the Paramount board adopted procedures to encourage Viacom and QVC to bid against one another so as to maximize the consideration to be paid to Paramount's shareholders. Ultimately, Viacom prevailed, with a combination of cash and securities worth a total of about $10 billion, compared with a value of about $8 billion for the cash and securities that had been approved by the Paramount board for the friendly acquisition, before the offer by QVC.

ANALYSIS

1. What would the result have been if the Viacom bid had been such that Viacom would have wound up with only 49 percent of the voting shares of the surviving corporation?

2. If there is no conflict of interest on the part of the independent directors of Paramount, why should there be "enhanced scrutiny." Why not simply apply the business judgment rule?

3. Suppose a potential buyer of a public corporation suggests that it might make an offer at a significant premium but that it is not willing to be a "stalking horse," and therefore will make the offer only if it receives a no-shop clause and a termination fee. How should the board proceed?

4. The American Law Institute (ALI) took the following approach in its Principles of Corporate Governance: Analysis and Recommendations (1994):*

> § 6.02. Action of Directors That Has the Foreseeable Effect of Blocking Unsolicited Tender Offers.
>
> (a) The board of directors may take an action that has the foreseeable effect of blocking an unsolicited tender offer, if the action is a reasonable response to the offer.
>
> (b) In considering whether its action is a reasonable response to the offer:
>
> (1) The board may take into account all factors relevant to the best interests of the corporation and shareholders, including, among other things, questions of legality and whether the offer, if successful, would threaten the corporation's essential economic prospects; and
>
> (2) The board may, in addition to the analysis under § 6.02(b)(1), have regard for interests or groups (other than shareholders) with respect to which the corporation has a legitimate concern if to do so would not significantly disfavor the long-term interests of shareholders.
>
> (c) A person who challenges an action of the board on the ground that it fails to satisfy the standards of Subsection (a) has the burden of proof that the board's action is an unreasonable response to the offer.
>
> (d) An action that does not meet the standards of Subsection (a) may be enjoined or set aside, but directors who authorize such an action are not subject to liability for damages if their conduct meets the standard of the business judgment rule.

Would any of the cases in this section have come out differently under the ALI proposal than as they were decided under Delaware law? Is the ALI proposal preferable as a policy matter?

NOTE ON SUBSEQUENT DELAWARE DEVELOPMENTS

In Unitrin v. American General Corp., 651 A.2d 1361 (Del.1995), the court approved a defensive repurchase of shares and in the process generated a couple of new phrases. A defensive measure approved by an independent board is permissible if it is not "draconian," which means that it is not "coercive or preclusive." In the case itself, the shareholders, according to the court, were not foreclosed from receiving a control premium in the future and a change of control by proxy battle was still possible. The court emphasized the discretion of the board to choose a defensive measure from among alternatives that are within the "range of reasonableness" (from *QVC*). If the measure adopted is within this range, the plaintiff will not be heard to argue that another measure might have been better.

In Carmody v. Toll Brothers, Inc., 723 A.2d 1180 (Del.Ch.1998), the Delaware Chancery Court addressed the validity of a so-called "dead hand poison pill." In addition to fairly standard flip-in and flip-over features, the Toll Brothers pill provided that the pill could be redeemed only by those directors who had been in office when the shareholder rights constituting the pill had become exercisable (or their approved successors). This provision was intended to foreclose a loophole in standard poison pills. Most pills are subject to redemption at nominal cost by the target's board of directors. Such redemption provisions purportedly allow the target's board to use the pill as a negotiating device: The poison pill makes an acquisition of the target prohibitively expensive. If the prospective acquirer makes a sufficiently attractive offer, however, the board may redeem the pill and allow the offer to go forward unimpaired by the pill's dilutive effects. Although such redemption provisions gave the target's board considerable negotiating leverage, and were one of the justifications used to defend the whole idea of the poison pill, they also made the target vulnerable to a combined tender offer and proxy contest. The prospective acquirer could trigger the pill, conduct a proxy contest to elect a new board, which, if elected, would then redeem the pill to permit the tender offer to go forward. The dead hand pill was intended to close this loophole by depriving any such newly elected directors of the right to redeem the pill.

In denying Toll Brothers' motion to dismiss for failure to state a claim a shareholder suit challenging the validity of the dead hand pill, Vice Chancellor Jacobs indicated that the pill likely ran afoul of several aspects of Delaware law. First, it implicated the Delaware statutes governing the powers of directors: "Absent express language in the charter, nothing in Delaware law suggests that some directors of a public corporation may be created less equal than other directors, and certainly not by unilateral board action." Id. at 1191. Second, the dead hand pill effectively disenfranchised shareholders who wished to elect a board committed to redeeming the pill by deterring proxy contests by prospective acquirers. Accordingly, the challenge to the pill stated a claim under the Delaware Supreme Court's holding in Stroud v. Grace, 606 A.2d 75, 92 n. 3 (Del.1992), that defensive measures that disenfranchise shareholders are strongly suspect and cannot be sustained absent a compelling justification. *Toll Brothers*, 723 A.2d at 1193–94. Finally, the shareholder had also stated a "far from conclusory" claim under Unocal Corp. v. Mesa Petroleum Co., 493 A.2d 946 (Del.1985). Although standard pills had been upheld under the *Unocal* standard, the dead hand pill was both preclusive and coercive. It was coercive because the pill effectively forced shareholders to re-elect the incumbent directors if they wished to be represented by a board entitled to exercise its full statutory powers. The pill was preclusive because the added deterrent effect of the dead hand provision made a takeover prohibitively expensive and effectively impossible. *Toll Brothers*, 723 A.2d at 1195.

In Mentor Graphics Corp. v. Quickturn Design Systems, Inc., 728 A.2d 25 (Del.Ch.1998), Vice Chancellor Jacobs invalidated (after trial) a so-called "no hand" pill, which he distinguished from the Toll Brothers pill as follows:

> The "no hand" poison pill being challenged here is a variation of, and operates in a different manner from, the "dead hand" pill addressed in *Toll Brothers*. The pill in *Toll Brothers* created two classes of directors. One would have the power to redeem and the other would not. That limitation would last the entire lifetime of the pill. In contrast, the "no hand" pill in this case would create no classes. It would evenhandedly prevent all members of a newly elected target board, whose majority is nominated or supported by the hostile bidder, from redeeming the rights to facilitate an acquisition by the bidder. The duration of this "no hand" pill would be for six months after the new directors take office.

728 A.2d at 28. The target "board's stated rationale for adopting the [no hand pill] was to afford any newly elected board sufficient time to adequately inform itself about Quickturn, its business, and its true value, and also to allow stockholders sufficient time to consider alternatives, before the board decided to sell the company to any acquiror." 728 A.2d at 36. Jacobs concluded that the no hand pill violated the target board's *Unocal* duties and, accordingly, declined to address plaintiff's statutory and *Stroud*-based claims. As to the former, his analysis began with the Delaware Supreme Court's statement in Unitrin v. American General Corp., 651 A.2d 1361 (Del.1995), that Delaware law recognized three basic categories of threats to corporate policy and effectiveness for purposes of *Unocal*'s first prong:

> (i) opportunity loss . . . [where] a hostile offer might deprive target shareholders of the opportunity to select a superior alternative offered by target management [or, we would add, offered by another bidder]; (ii) structural coercion, . . . the risk that disparate treatment of non-tendering shareholders might distort shareholders' tender decisions; and . . . (iii) substantive coercion, . . . the risk that shareholders will mistakenly accept an underpriced offer because they disbelieve management's representations of intrinsic value.

Mentor Graphics, 728 A.2d at 45. Jacobs found that the board reasonably and in good faith believed that the prospective acquirer's offer was inadequate, hence invoking the substantive coercion threat. Id. at 47. Jacobs concluded, however, that the pill ran afoul of *Unocal*'s second prong. Although the board claimed the no hand provision was intended to give a new board time to learn about the target before deciding whether to sell the company, the pill in fact precluded only a sale to the initial bidder. Sales to other potential buyers were not foreclosed. In addition, the board failed to explain why the six-month delay on such a sale imposed by the no hand provision was reasonable. Accordingly, Jacobs held that the pill was disproportionate to the claimed substantive coercion threat. Id. at 47–51.

The Delaware Supreme Court affirmed, but on different grounds. Quickturn Design Systems, Inc. v. Mentor Graphics Corporation, 721 A.2d 1281 (Del.1998). The court explained:

> One of the most basic tenets of Delaware corporate law is that the board of directors has the ultimate responsibility for managing the business and affairs of a corporation. Section 141(a) requires that any limitation on the board's authority be set out in the certificate of incorporation. The Quickturn certificate of incorporation contains no provision purporting to limit the authority of the board in any way. The Delayed Redemption Provision, however, would prevent a newly elected board of directors from completely discharging its fundamental management duties to the corporation and its stockholders for six months. While the Delayed Redemption Provision limits the board of directors' authority in only one respect, the suspension of the Rights Plan, it nonetheless restricts the board's power in an area of fundamental importance to the shareholders—negotiating a possible sale of the corporation. Therefore, we hold that the Delayed Redemption Provision is invalid under Section 141(a), which confers upon any newly elected board of directors full power to manage and direct the business and affairs of a Delaware corporation.
>
> In discharging the statutory mandate of Section 141(a), the directors have a fiduciary duty to the corporation and its shareholders. . . .
>
> This Court has recently observed that "although the fiduciary duty of a Delaware director is unremitting, the exact course of conduct that must be charted to properly discharge that responsibility will change in the specific context of the action the director is taking with regard to either the corporation or its shareholders." This Court has held "to the extent that a contract, or a provision thereof, purports to require a board to act or not act in such a fashion as to limit the exercise of fiduciary duties, it is invalid and unenforceable." The Delayed Redemption Provision "tends to limit in a substantial way the freedom of [newly elected] directors' decisions on matters of management policy." Therefore, "it violates the duty of each [newly elected] director to exercise his own best judgment on matters coming before the board."

Id. at 1291–92.

Lyondell Chemical Company v. Ryan

970 A.2d 235 (Del. 2009).

. . .

FACTUAL AND PROCEDURAL BACKGROUND

Before the merger at issue, Lyondell Chemical Company ("Lyondell") was the third largest independent, publicly traded chemical company in North America. Dan Smith ("Smith") was Lyondell's Chairman and CEO. Lyondell's other ten directors were independent and many were, or had been, CEOs of other large, publicly traded companies. Basell AF

("Basell") is a privately held Luxembourg company owned by Leonard Blavatnik ("Blavatnik") through his ownership of Access Industries. Basell is in the business of polyolefin technology, production and marketing.

In April 2006, Blavatnik told Smith that Basell was interested in acquiring Lyondell. A few months later, Basell sent a letter to Lyondell's board offering \$26.50–\$28.50 per share. Lyondell determined that the price was inadequate and that it was not interested in selling. During the next year, Lyondell prospered and no potential acquirors expressed interest in the company. In May 2007, an Access affiliate filed a Schedule 13D with the Securities and Exchange Commission disclosing its right to acquire an 8.3% block of Lyondell stock owned by Occidental Petroleum Corporation. The Schedule 13D also disclosed Blavatnik's interest in possible transactions with Lyondell.

In response to the Schedule 13D, the Lyondell board immediately convened a special meeting. The board recognized that the 13D signaled to the market that the company was "in play," but the directors decided to take a "wait and see" approach. . . . In late June 2007, Basell announced that it had entered into a \$9.6 billion merger agreement with Huntsman Corporation ("Huntsman"), a specialty chemical company. Basell apparently reconsidered, however, after Hexion Specialty Chemicals, Inc. made a topping bid for Huntsman. Faced with competition for Huntsman, Blavatnik returned his attention to Lyondell.

On July 9, 2007, Blavatnik met with Smith to discuss an all-cash deal at \$40 per share. Smith responded that \$40 was too low, and Blavatnik raised his offer to \$44–\$45 per share. Smith told Blavatnik that he would present the proposal to the board, but that he thought the board would reject it. Smith advised Blavatnik to give Lyondell his best offer, since Lyondell really was not on the market. The meeting ended at that point, but Blavatnik asked Smith to call him later in the day. When Smith called, Blavatnik offered to pay \$48 per share. Under Blavatnik's proposal, Basell would require no financing contingency, but Lyondell would have to agree to a \$400 million break-up fee and sign a merger agreement by July 16, 2007.

Smith called a special meeting of the Lyondell board on July 10, 2007 to review and consider Basell's offer. The meeting lasted slightly less than one hour, during which time the board reviewed valuation material that had been prepared by Lyondell management for presentation at the regular board meeting, which was scheduled for the following day. The board also discussed the Basell offer, the status of the Huntsman merger, and the likelihood that another party might be interested in Lyondell. The board instructed Smith to obtain a written offer from Basell and more details about Basell's financing.

Blavatnik agreed to the board's request, but also made an additional demand. Basell had until July 11 to make a higher bid for Huntsman, so Blavatnik asked Smith to find out whether the Lyondell board would provide a firm indication of interest in his proposal by the end of that day. The Lyondell board met on July 11, again for less than one hour, to consider the Basell proposal and how it compared to the benefits of remaining independent. The board decided that it was interested, authorized the retention of Deutsche Bank Securities, Inc. ("Deutsche

Bank") as its financial advisor, and instructed Smith to negotiate with Blavatnik.

Basell then announced that it would not raise its offer for Huntsman, and Huntsman terminated the Basell merger agreement. From July 12–July 15 the parties negotiated the terms of a Lyondell merger agreement; Basell conducted due diligence; Deutsche Bank prepared a "fairness" opinion; and Lyondell conducted its regularly scheduled board meeting. The Lyondell board discussed the Basell proposal again on July 12, and later instructed Smith to try to negotiate better terms. Specifically, the board wanted a higher price, a go-shop provision,[2] and a reduced break-up fee. As the trial court noted, Blavatnik was "incredulous." He had offered his best price, which was a substantial premium, and the deal had to be concluded on his schedule. As a sign of good faith, however, Blavatnik agreed to reduce the break-up fee from $400 million to $385 million.

On July 16, 2007, the board met to consider the Basell merger agreement. Lyondell's management, as well as its financial and legal advisers, presented reports analyzing the merits of the deal. The advisors explained that, notwithstanding the no-shop provision in the merger agreement, Lyondell would be able to consider any superior proposals that might be made because of the "fiduciary out" provision. In addition, Deutsche Bank reviewed valuation models derived from "bullish" and more conservative financial projections. Several of those valuations yielded a range that did not even reach $48 per share, and Deutsche Bank opined that the proposed merger price was fair. Indeed, the bank's managing director described the merger price as "an absolute home run." Deutsche Bank also identified other possible acquirors and explained why it believed no other entity would top Basell's offer. After considering the presentations, the Lyondell board voted to approve the merger and recommend it to the stockholders. At a special stockholders' meeting held on November 20, 2007, the merger was approved by more than 99% of the voted shares. . . .

DISCUSSION

The class action complaint challenging this $13 billion cash merger alleges that the Lyondell directors breached their "fiduciary duties of care, loyalty and candor . . . and . . . put their personal interests ahead of the interests of the Lyondell shareholders." . . . The trial court rejected all claims except those directed at the process by which the directors sold the company and the deal protection provisions in the merger agreement.

The remaining claims are but two aspects of a single claim, under *Revlon v. MacAndrews & Forbes Holdings, Inc.*,[6] that the directors failed to obtain the best available price in selling the company. . . . The trial court reviewed the record, and found that Ryan might be able to prevail at trial on a claim that the Lyondell directors breached their duty of care. But Lyondell's charter includes an exculpatory provision, pursuant to 8 Del. C. § 102(b)(7), protecting the directors from personal liability for breaches of the duty of care. Thus, this case turns on whether any arguable shortcomings on the part of the Lyondell directors also

[2] A "go-shop" provision allows the seller to seek other buyers for a specified period after the agreement is signed.

[6] 506 A.2d 173, 182 (Del.1986).

implicate their duty of loyalty, a breach of which is not exculpated. Because the trial court determined that the board was independent and was not motivated by self-interest or ill will, the sole issue is whether the directors are entitled to summary judgment on the claim that they breached their duty of loyalty by failing to act in good faith.

This Court examined "good faith"[8] in two recent decisions. In *In re Walt Disney Co. Deriv. Litig.*,[9] the Court [held that]:

> [A]t least three different categories of fiduciary behavior are candidates for the "bad faith" pejorative label. The first category involves so-called "subjective bad faith," that is, fiduciary conduct motivated by an actual intent to do harm. . . . [S]uch conduct constitutes classic, quintessential bad faith. . . .
>
> The second category of conduct, which is at the opposite end of the spectrum, involves lack of due care-that is, fiduciary action taken solely by reason of gross negligence and without any malevolent intent. . . . [W]e address the issue of whether gross negligence (including failure to inform one's self of available material facts), without more, can also constitute bad faith. The answer is clearly no.
>
> That leaves the third category of fiduciary conduct, which falls in between the first two categories. . . . This third category is what the Chancellor's definition of bad faith-intentional dereliction of duty, a conscious disregard for one's responsibilities-is intended to capture. The question is whether such misconduct is properly treated as a non-exculpable, nonindemnifiable violation of the fiduciary duty to act in good faith. In our view, it must be. . . .[10]

A few months later, in *Stone v. Ritter*,[11] this Court . . . clarified any possible ambiguity about the directors' mental state, holding that "imposition of liability requires a showing that the directors knew that they were not discharging their fiduciary obligations."[13]

The Court of Chancery recognized these legal principles, but it denied summary judgment in order to obtain a more complete record before deciding whether the directors had acted in bad faith. . . . [H]owever, the trial court reviewed the existing record under a mistaken view of the applicable law. Three factors contributed to that mistake. First, the trial court imposed *Revlon* duties on the Lyondell directors before they either had decided to sell, or before the sale had become inevitable. Second, the court read *Revlon* and its progeny as creating a set of requirements that must be satisfied during the sale process. Third, the trial court equated an arguably imperfect attempt to carry out *Revlon* duties with a knowing disregard of one's duties that constitutes bad faith.

---

[8] Our corporate decisions tend to use the terms "bad faith" and "failure to act in good faith" interchangeably, although in a different context we noted that, "[t]he two concepts-bad faith and conduct not in good faith are not necessarily identical." 25 Massachusetts Avenue Property LLC v. Liberty Property Limited Partnership, Del.Supr., No. 188, 2008, Order at p. 5, (November 25, 2008). For purposes of this appeal, we draw no distinction between the terms.

[9] 906 A.2d 27 (Del.2006).

[10] Id. at 64–66.

[11] 911 A.2d 362 (Del.2006).

[13] *Stone*, 911 A.2d at 370.

. . . The Court of Chancery identified several undisputed facts that would support the entry of judgment in favor of the Lyondell directors: the directors were "active, sophisticated, and generally aware of the value of the Company and the conditions of the markets in which the Company operated." They had reason to believe that no other bidders would emerge, given the price Basell had offered and the limited universe of companies that might be interested in acquiring Lyondell's unique assets. Smith negotiated the price up from $40 to $48 per share—a price that Deutsche Bank opined was fair. Finally, no other acquiror expressed interest during the four months between the merger announcement and the stockholder vote.

Other facts, however, led the trial court to "question the adequacy of the Board's knowledge and efforts. . . ." After the Schedule 13D was filed in May, the directors apparently took no action to prepare for a possible acquisition proposal. The merger was negotiated and finalized in less than one week, during which time the directors met for a total of only seven hours to consider the matter. The directors did not seriously press Blavatnik for a better price, nor did they conduct even a limited market check. Moreover, although the deal protections were not unusual or preclusive, the trial court was troubled by "the Board's decision to grant considerable protection to a deal that may not have been adequately vetted under Revlon."

The trial court found the directors' failure to act during the two months after the filing of the Basell Schedule 13D critical to its analysis of their good faith. The court pointedly referred to the directors' "two months of slothful indifference despite knowing that the Company was in play," and the fact that they "languidly awaited overtures from potential suitors. . . ." In the end, the trial court found that it was this "failing" that warranted denial of their motion for summary judgment. . . .

The problem with the trial court's analysis is that *Revlon* duties do not arise simply because a company is "in play." The duty to seek the best available price applies only when a company embarks on a transaction—on its own initiative or in response to an unsolicited offer—that will result in a change of control. Basell's Schedule 13D did put the Lyondell directors, and the market in general, on notice that Basell was interested in acquiring Lyondell. The directors responded by promptly holding a special meeting to consider whether Lyondell should take any action. The directors decided that they would neither put the company up for sale nor institute defensive measures to fend off a possible hostile offer. Instead, they decided to take a "wait and see" approach. That decision was an entirely appropriate exercise of the directors' business judgment. The time for action under *Revlon* did not begin until July 10, 2007, when the directors began negotiating the sale of Lyondell.

The Court of Chancery focused on the directors' two months of inaction, when it should have focused on the one week during which they considered Basell's offer. During that one week, the directors met several times; their CEO tried to negotiate better terms; they evaluated Lyondell's value, the price offered and the likelihood of obtaining a better price; and then the directors approved the merger. The trial court acknowledged that the directors' conduct during those seven days might not demonstrate anything more than lack of due care. But the court remained skeptical about the directors' good faith—at least on the present record. That lingering concern was based on the trial court's synthesis of the *Revlon* line of cases, which led it to the erroneous conclusion that directors must follow one of several courses of action to satisfy their *Revlon* duties.

There is only one Revlon duty—to "[get] the best price for the stockholders at a sale of the company."[26] No court can tell directors exactly how to accomplish that goal, because they will be facing a unique combination of circumstances, many of which will be outside their control. [The trial court, however, held that] directors must "engage actively in the sale process," and they must confirm that they have obtained the best available price either by conducting an auction, by conducting a market check, or by demonstrating "an impeccable knowledge of the market."

The Lyondell directors did not conduct an auction or a market check, and they did not satisfy the trial court that they had the "impeccable" market knowledge that the court believed was necessary to excuse their failure to pursue one of the first two alternatives. As a result, the Court of Chancery was unable to conclude that the directors had met their burden under *Revlon*. . . . Where, as here, the issue is whether the directors failed to act in good faith, [however,] the existing record mandates the entry of judgment in favor of the directors.

As discussed above, bad faith will be found if a "fiduciary intentionally fails to act in the face of a known duty to act, demonstrating a conscious disregard for his duties." The trial court decided that the *Revlon* sale process must follow one of three courses, and that the Lyondell directors did not discharge that "known set of [*Revlon*] 'duties'." But, as noted, there are no legally prescribed steps that directors must follow to satisfy their *Revlon* duties. Thus, the directors' failure to take any specific steps during the sale process could not have demonstrated a conscious disregard of their duties. More importantly, there is a vast difference between an inadequate or flawed effort to carry out fiduciary duties and a conscious disregard for those duties.

. . . "In the transactional context, [an] extreme set of facts [is] required to sustain a disloyalty claim premised on the notion that disinterested directors were intentionally disregarding their duties."[34] . . . [I]f the directors failed to do all that they should have under the circumstances, they breached their duty of care. Only if they knowingly and completely failed to undertake their responsibilities would they breach their duty of loyalty. The trial court approached the record from the wrong perspective. Instead of questioning whether disinterested, independent directors did everything that they (arguably) should have done to obtain the best sale price, the inquiry should have been whether those directors utterly failed to attempt to obtain the best sale price.

Viewing the record in this manner leads to only one possible conclusion. The Lyondell directors met several times to consider Basell's premium offer. They were generally aware of the value of their company and they knew the chemical company market. The directors solicited and followed the advice of their financial and legal advisors. They attempted

[26] *Revlon*, 506 A.2d at 182.

[34] In re Lear Corp. S'holder Litig., 2008 WL 4053221 at *11 (Del.Ch.).

to negotiate a higher offer even though all the evidence indicates that Basell had offered a "blowout" price. Finally, they approved the merger agreement, because "it was simply too good not to pass along [to the stockholders] for their consideration." [T]his record clearly establishes that the Lyondell directors did not breach their duty of loyalty by failing to act in good faith. In concluding otherwise, the Court of Chancery reversibly erred. . . .

ANALYSIS

1. Just how incompetent would Lyondell's board of directors have had to have been in order to have "knowingly and completely failed to undertake their responsibilities"?

2. Does *Lyondell* stand for the proposition that *Revlon* duties are violated only when the target's directors act in bad faith? If so, should the results in *Revlon* or *QVC* have been different? Or did those cases differ from this one in important respects?

3. What would trigger *Revlon* duties after *Lyondell*?

4. What does *Lyondell* imply about the relationship between the *Revlon* and *Unocal* standards of review?

PROBLEMS

1. Smith, the CEO of Lyondell, reports to the board, at a regular quarterly meeting, that Blavatnik has made an offer to buy the corporation for cash at a price per share that represents about a 40 percent premium over the current market price. For purposes of this question only, suppose that Peter Bumbler, one of the directors, realizing that a majority of the directors dislike Blavatnik and are content with things as they are, states, "Let's not waste our time on this; let's just ignore the guy and hope he goes away. But I suppose we have to jump through some hoops so we don't get sued. So what should we do, Joe?" You are Joe, the general counsel of the corporation. What do you say?

2. Smith, the CEO of Lyondell, reports to the board, at a regular quarterly meeting, that Blavatnik has made an offer to buy the corporation for cash at a price per share that represents about a 40 percent premium over the current market price. For purposes of this question only, suppose a member of the board, after hearing the offer, says, "Sounds good, but I'm just too busy now to spend time on it." A majority of the members of the board say, in effect, "me too." So they take no action on the offer and Blavatnik, after a couple of weeks with no response, becomes exasperated and gives up. A shareholder brings suit for damages against the directors. Assume that the corporation has in place an exculpatory provision consistent with DGCL § 107(b)(2). Will the exculpatory clause preclude liability here?

3. C Corporation, Inc., a public corporation incorporated in Delaware, is in dire financial condition, operating at a loss and about to run out of cash. P Corporation, Inc., a privately held corporation in the same line of business as C Corp., presents an unsolicited offer to invest enough money to give C Corp. a reasonable chance of recovery. In return for the investment, P Corp. would receive 35 percent of the equity in C Corp., the right to fill three seats on the nine-member board, and the

right to demand the replacement of the current CEO plus a veto power in the selection of her successor. (a) Does this offer trigger *Revlon* duties? (b) What if P Corp.'s offer had been, again, for 35 percent of the equity but in the form of a new class of common shares with the right to elect five members of the nine-member board? (c) Would your answer to (a) or (b) change if P were publicly held? (d) What if, before receiving the offer from F Corp., C Corp. had sought equity investments from a couple of private-equity funds (that is, funds that invest on behalf of their wealthy clients)?

C. EXTENSION OF THE *UNOCAL/REVLON* FRAMEWORK TO NEGOTIATED ACQUISITIONS

Omnicare, Inc. v. NCS Healthcare, Inc.

818 A.2d 914 (Del. 2003).

■ HOLLAND, JUSTICE, for the majority:

NCS Healthcare, Inc. ("NCS"), a Delaware corporation, was the object of competing acquisition bids, one by Genesis Health Ventures, Inc. ("Genesis"), a Pennsylvania corporation, and the other by Omnicare, Inc. ("Omnicare"), a Delaware corporation. . . .

The Parties

. . . NCS is a leading independent provider of pharmacy services to long-term care institutions. . . . NCS common stock consists of Class A shares and Class B shares. The Class B shares are entitled to ten votes per share and the Class A shares are entitled to one vote per share. The shares are virtually identical in every other respect.

The defendant Jon H. Outcalt is Chairman of the NCS board of directors. Outcalt owns 202,063 shares of NCS Class A common stock and 3,476,086 shares of Class B common stock. The defendant Kevin B. Shaw is President, CEO and a director of NCS. At the time the merger agreement at issue in this dispute was executed with Genesis, Shaw owned 28,905 shares of NCS Class A common stock and 1,141,134 shares of Class B common stock.

The NCS board has two other members, defendants Boake A. Sells and Richard L. Osborne. Sells is a graduate of the Harvard Business School. He was Chairman and CEO at Revco Drugstores in Cleveland, Ohio from 1987 to 1992. . . . Osborne is a full-time professor at the Weatherhead School of Management at Case Western Reserve University. . . .

The defendant Genesis is a Pennsylvania corporation with its principal place of business in Kennett Square, Pennsylvania. It is a leading provider of healthcare and support services to the elderly. The defendant Geneva Sub, Inc., a wholly owned subsidiary of Genesis, is a Delaware corporation formed by Genesis to acquire NCS. . . .

Omnicare is a Delaware corporation with its principal place of business in Covington, Kentucky. . . .

FACTUAL BACKGROUND

. . .

NCS Seeks Restructuring Alternatives

Beginning in late 1999, changes in the timing and level of reimbursements by government and third-party providers adversely affected market conditions in the health care industry. As a result, NCS began to experience greater difficulty in collecting accounts receivables, which led to a precipitous decline in the market value of its stock. NCS common shares that traded above $20 in January 1999 were worth as little as $5 at the end of that year. By early 2001, NCS was in default on approximately $350 million in debt, including $206 million in senior bank debt and $102 million of its 5 3/4 %Convertible Subordinated Debentures (the "Notes"). After these defaults, NCS common stock traded in a range of $0.09 to $0.50 per share until days before the announcement of the transaction at issue in this case.

NCS began to explore strategic alternatives that might address the problems it was confronting. As part of this effort, in February 2000, NCS retained UBS Warburg, L.L.C. to identify potential acquirers and possible equity investors. UBS Warburg contacted over fifty different entities to solicit their interest in a variety of transactions with NCS. UBS Warburg had marginal success in its efforts. By October 2000, NCS had only received one non-binding indication of interest valued at $190 million, substantially less than the face value of NCS's senior debt. This proposal was reduced by 20% after the offeror conducted its due diligence review.

NCS Financial Deterioration

In December 2000, NCS terminated its relationship with UBS Warburg and retained Brown, Gibbons, Lang & Company as its exclusive financial advisor. During this period, NCS's financial condition continued to deteriorate. In April 2001, NCS received a formal notice of default and acceleration from the trustee for holders of the Notes. As NCS's financial condition worsened, the Noteholders formed a committee to represent their financial interests (the "Ad Hoc Committee"). At about that time, NCS began discussions with various investor groups regarding a restructuring in a "pre-packaged" bankruptcy. NCS did not receive any proposal that it believed provided adequate consideration for its stakeholders. At that time, full recovery for NCS's creditors was a remote prospect, and any recovery for NCS stockholders seemed impossible.

Omnicare's Initial Negotiations

In the summer of 2001, NCS invited Omnicare, Inc. to begin discussions with Brown Gibbons regarding a possible transaction. On July 20, Joel Gemunder, Omnicare's President and CEO, sent Shaw a written proposal to acquire NCS in a bankruptcy sale under Section 363 of the Bankruptcy Code. This proposal was for $225 million subject to satisfactory completion of due diligence. . . .

In August 2001, Omnicare increased its bid to $270 million, but still proposed to structure the deal as an asset sale in bankruptcy. Even at $270 million, Omnicare's proposal was substantially lower than the face value of NCS's outstanding debt. It would have provided only a small recovery for Omnicare's Noteholders and no recovery for its stockholders. . . .

There was no further contact between Omnicare and NCS between November 2001 and January 2002. Instead, Omnicare began secret discussions with Judy K. Mencher, a representative of the Ad Hoc Committee. In these discussions, Omnicare continued to pursue a transaction structured as a sale of assets in bankruptcy. In February 2002, the Ad Hoc Committee notified the NCS board that Omnicare had proposed an asset sale in bankruptcy for $313,750,000.

NCS Independent Board Committee

In January 2002, Genesis was contacted by members of the Ad Hoc Committee concerning a possible transaction with NCS. Genesis executed NCS's standard confidentiality agreement and began a due diligence review. Genesis had recently emerged from bankruptcy because, like NCS, it was suffering from dwindling government reimbursements.

Genesis previously lost a bidding war to Omnicare in a different transaction. This led to bitter feelings between the principals of both companies. More importantly, this bitter experience for Genesis led to its insistence on exclusivity agreements and lock-ups in any potential transaction with NCS.

NCS Financial Improvement

NCS's operating performance was improving by early 2002. As NCS's performance improved, the NCS directors began to believe that it might be possible for NCS to enter into a transaction that would provide some recovery for NCS stockholders' equity. In March 2002, NCS decided to form an independent committee of board members who were neither NCS employees nor major NCS stockholders (the "Independent Committee"). The NCS board thought this was necessary because, due to NCS's precarious financial condition, it felt that fiduciary duties were owed to the enterprise as a whole rather than solely to NCS stockholders.

Sells and Osborne were selected as the members of the committee, and given authority to consider and negotiate possible transactions for NCS. The entire four member NCS board, however, retained authority to approve any transaction. The Independent Committee retained the same legal and financial counsel as the NCS board. . . .

Genesis Initial Proposal

Two days later, on May 16, 2002, Scott Berlin of Brown Gibbons, Glen Pollack and Boake Sells met with George Hager, CFO of Genesis, and Michael Walker, who was Genesis's CEO. At that meeting, Genesis made it clear that if it were going to engage in any negotiations with NCS, it would not do so as a "stalking horse." . . .

In June 2002, Genesis proposed a transaction that would take place outside the bankruptcy context. Although it did not provide full recovery for NCS's Noteholders, it provided the possibility that NCS stockholders would be able to recover something for their investment. As discussions continued, the terms proposed by Genesis continued to improve. On June 25, the economic terms of the Genesis proposal included repayment of the NCS senior debt in full, full assumption of trade credit obligations, an exchange offer or direct purchase of the NCS Notes providing NCS

Noteholders with a combination of cash and Genesis common stock equal to the par value of the NCS Notes (not including accrued interest), and $20 million in value for the NCS common stock. Structurally, the Genesis proposal continued to include consents from a significant majority of the Noteholders as well as support agreements from stockholders owning a majority of the NCS voting power.

Genesis Exclusivity Agreement

. . . Genesis agreed to offer a total of $24 million in consideration for the NCS common stock, or an additional $4 million, in the form of Genesis common stock. [But] Genesis's representatives demanded that, before any further negotiations take place, NCS agree to enter into an exclusivity agreement with it. . . . On June 27, 2002, Genesis's legal counsel delivered a draft form of exclusivity agreement for review and consideration by NCS's legal counsel.

The Independent Committee met on July 3, 2002, to consider the proposed exclusivity agreement. Pollack presented a summary of the terms of a possible Genesis merger, which had continued to improve. . . .

After NCS executed the exclusivity agreement, Genesis provided NCS with a draft merger agreement, a draft Noteholders' support agreement, and draft voting agreements for Outcalt and Shaw, who together held a majority of the voting power of the NCS common stock. Genesis and NCS negotiated the terms of the merger agreement over the next three weeks. During those negotiations, the Independent Committee and the Ad Hoc Committee persuaded Genesis to improve the terms of its merger. . . .

Omnicare Proposes Negotiations

By late July 2002, Omnicare came to believe that NCS was negotiating a transaction, possibly with Genesis or another of Omnicare's competitors, that would potentially present a competitive threat to Omnicare. Omnicare also came to believe, in light of a run-up in the price of NCS common stock, that whatever transaction NCS was negotiating probably included a payment for its stock. . . .

On the afternoon of July 26, 2002, Omnicare faxed to NCS a letter outlining a proposed acquisition. The letter suggested a transaction in which Omnicare would retire NCS's senior and subordinated debt at par plus accrued interest, and pay the NCS stockholders $3 cash for their shares. Omnicare's proposal, however, was expressly conditioned on negotiating a merger agreement, obtaining certain third party consents, and completing its due diligence. . . .

Late in the afternoon of July 26, 2002, NCS representatives received voicemail messages from Omnicare asking to discuss the letter. The exclusivity agreement prevented NCS from returning those calls. In relevant part, that agreement precluded NCS from "engag[ing] or participat[ing] in any discussions or negotiations with respect to a Competing Transaction or a proposal for one." The July 26 letter from Omnicare met the definition of a "Competing Transaction."

Despite the exclusivity agreement, the Independent Committee met to consider a response to Omnicare. It concluded that discussions with Omnicare about its July 26 letter presented an unacceptable risk that Genesis would abandon merger discussions. The Independent Committee believed that, given Omnicare's past bankruptcy proposals and unwillingness to consider a merger, as well as its decision to negotiate exclusively with the Ad Hoc Committee, the risk of losing the Genesis proposal was too substantial. Nevertheless, the Independent Committee instructed Pollack to use Omnicare's letter to negotiate for improved terms with Genesis.

Genesis Merger Agreement And Voting Agreements

Genesis responded to the NCS request to improve its offer as a result of the Omnicare fax the next day. On July 27, Genesis proposed substantially improved terms. First, it proposed to retire the Notes in accordance with the terms of the indenture, thus eliminating the need for Noteholders to consent to the transaction. This change involved paying all accrued interest plus a small redemption premium. Second, Genesis increased the exchange ratio for NCS common stock to one-tenth of a Genesis common share for each NCS common share, an 80% increase. Third, it agreed to lower the proposed termination fee in the merger agreement from $10 million to $6 million. In return for these concessions, Genesis stipulated that the transaction had to be approved by midnight the next day, July 28, or else Genesis would terminate discussions and withdraw its offer.

The Independent Committee and the NCS board both scheduled meetings for July 28. The committee met first. Although that meeting lasted less than an hour, the Court of Chancery determined the minutes reflect that the directors were fully informed of all material facts relating to the proposed transaction. After concluding that Genesis was sincere in establishing the midnight deadline, the committee voted unanimously to recommend the transaction to the full board.

The full board met thereafter. After receiving similar reports and advice from its legal and financial advisors, the board concluded that "balancing the potential loss of the Genesis deal against the uncertainty of Omnicare's letter, results in the conclusion that the only reasonable alternative for the Board of Directors is to approve the Genesis transaction." The board first voted to authorize the voting agreements with Outcalt and Shaw. . . . The board was advised by its legal counsel that "under the terms of the merger agreement and because NCS shareholders representing in excess of 50% of the outstanding voting power would be *required* by Genesis to enter into stockholder voting agreements contemporaneously with the signing of the merger agreement, and would agree to vote their shares in favor of the merger agreement, shareholder approval of the merger would be assured even if the NCS Board were to withdraw or change its recommendation. *These facts would prevent NCS from engaging in any alternative or superior transaction in the future.*" (emphasis added).

After listening to a *summary* of the merger terms, the board then resolved that the merger agreement and the transactions contemplated thereby were advisable and fair and in the best interests of all the NCS stakeholders. The NCS board further resolved to recommend the transactions to the stockholders for their approval and adoption. A definitive merger agreement between NCS and Genesis and the stockholder voting agreements were executed later that day. . . .

NCS / Genesis Merger Agreement

Among other things, the NCS/Genesis merger agreement provided the following:

NCS stockholders would receive 1 share of Genesis common stock in exchange for every 10 shares of NCS common stock held;

NCS stockholders could exercise appraisal rights under 8 Del. C. § 262;

NCS would redeem NCS's Notes in accordance with their terms;

NCS would submit the merger agreement to NCS stockholders regardless of whether the NCS board continued to recommend the merger;

NCS would not enter into discussions with third parties concerning an alternative acquisition of NCS, or provide non-public information to such parties, unless (1) the third party provided an unsolicited, *bona fide* written proposal documenting the terms of the acquisition; (2) the NCS board believed in good faith that the proposal was or was likely to result in an acquisition on terms superior to those contemplated by the NCS/Genesis merger agreement; and (3) before providing non-public information to that third party, the third party would execute a confidentiality agreement at least as restrictive as the one in place between NCS and Genesis; and

If the merger agreement were to be terminated, under certain circumstances NCS would be required to pay Genesis a $6 million termination fee and/or Genesis's documented expenses, up to $5 million.

Voting Agreements

Outcalt and Shaw, in their capacity as NCS stockholders, entered into voting agreements with Genesis.* NCS was also required to be a party to the voting agreements by Genesis. Those agreements provided, among other things, that:

Outcalt and Shaw were acting in their capacity as NCS stockholders in executing the agreements, not in their capacity as NCS directors or officers;

Neither Outcalt nor Shaw would transfer their shares prior to the stockholder vote on the merger agreement;

Outcalt and Shaw agreed to vote all of their shares in favor of the merger agreement; and Outcalt and Shaw granted to Genesis an irrevocable proxy to vote their shares in favor of the merger agreement.

The voting agreement was specifically enforceable by Genesis.

---

* [Eds.: By virtue of the super-voting rights of their Class B stock, Outcalt and Shaw had effective voting control of NCS. If Outcalt and Shaw sold those shares, the shares automatically converted to Class A stock, having only one vote per share, which is why they did not simply sell their shares to Omnicare. Indeed, in a separate part of the litigation, Genesis unsuccessfully argued that the voting agreement itself constituted an automatic conversion of the Class B stock into Class A.]

The merger agreement further provided that if either Outcalt or Shaw breached the terms of the voting agreements, Genesis would be entitled to terminate the merger agreement and potentially receive a $6 million termination fee from NCS. Such a breach was impossible since Section 6 provided that the voting agreements were specifically enforceable by Genesis.

Omnicare's Superior Proposal

On July 29, 2002, hours after the NCS/Genesis transaction was executed, Omnicare faxed a letter to NCS restating its conditional proposal and attaching a draft merger agreement. Later that morning, Omnicare issued a press release publicly disclosing the proposal.

On August 1, 2002, Omnicare filed a lawsuit attempting to enjoin the NCS/Genesis merger, and announced that it intended to launch a tender offer for NCS's shares at a price of $3.50 per share. On August 8, 2002, Omnicare began its tender offer. By letter dated that same day, Omnicare expressed a desire to discuss the terms of the offer with NCS. Omnicare's letter continued to condition its proposal on satisfactory completion of a due diligence investigation of NCS.

On August 8, 2002, and again on August 19, 2002, the NCS Independent Committee and full board of directors met separately to consider the Omnicare tender offer in light of the Genesis merger agreement. NCS's outside legal counsel and NCS's financial advisor attended both meetings. The board was unable to determine that Omnicare's expressions of interest were likely to lead to a "Superior Proposal," as the term was defined in the NCS/Genesis merger agreement. On September 10, 2002, NCS requested and received a waiver from Genesis allowing NCS to enter into discussions with Omnicare without first having to determine that Omnicare's proposal was a "Superior Proposal."

On October 6, 2002, Omnicare irrevocably committed itself to a transaction with NCS. Pursuant to the terms of its proposal, Omnicare agreed to acquire all the outstanding NCS Class A and Class B shares at a price of $3.50 per share in cash. As a result of this irrevocable offer, on October 21, 2002, the NCS board withdrew its recommendation that the stockholders vote in favor of the NCS/Genesis merger agreement. NCS's financial advisor withdrew its fairness opinion of the NCS/Genesis merger agreement as well.

Genesis Rejection Impossible

The Genesis merger agreement [provides that even] if the NCS board "changes, withdraws or modifies" its recommendation, as it did, it must still submit the merger to a stockholder vote.

A subsequent filing with the Securities and Exchange Commission ("SEC") states: "the NCS independent committee and the NCS board of directors have determined to withdraw their recommendations of the Genesis merger agreement and recommend that the NCS stockholders vote against the approval and adoption of the Genesis merger." In that same SEC filing, however, the NCS board explained why the success of the Genesis merger had already been predetermined [by the voting agreements]. . . . This litigation was commenced to prevent the consummation of the inferior Genesis transaction.

LEGAL ANALYSIS

Business Judgment or Enhanced Scrutiny

. . . The prior decisions of this Court have identified the circumstances where board action must be subjected to enhanced judicial scrutiny before the presumptive protection of the business judgment rule can be invoked. One of those circumstances was described in *Unocal*: when a board adopts defensive measures in response to a hostile takeover proposal that the board reasonably determines is a threat to corporate policy and effectiveness. . . . Other circumstances requiring enhanced judicial scrutiny give rise to what are known as *Revlon* duties, such as when the board enters into a merger transaction that will cause a change in corporate control, initiates an active bidding process seeking to sell the corporation, or makes a break up of the corporate entity inevitable. . . .

Deal Protection Devices Require Enhanced Scrutiny

The dispositive issues in this appeal involve the defensive devices that protected the Genesis merger agreement. . . .

It is well established that conflicts of interest arise when a board of directors acts to prevent stockholders from effectively exercising their right to vote contrary to the will of the board. The "omnipresent specter" of such conflict may be present whenever a board adopts defensive devices to protect a merger agreement.[27] The stockholders' ability to effectively reject a merger agreement is likely to bear an inversely proportionate relationship to the structural and economic devices that the board has approved to protect the transaction. . . .

. . . Accordingly, . . . defensive devices adopted by the board to protect the original merger transaction must withstand enhanced judicial scrutiny under the *Unocal* standard of review, even when that merger transaction does not result in a change of control.

Enhanced Scrutiny Generally

In *Paramount v. QVC*, this Court identified the key features of an enhanced judicial scrutiny test. The first feature is a "judicial determination regarding the adequacy of the decisionmaking process employed by the directors, including the information on which the directors based their decision."[35] The second feature is "a judicial examination of the reasonableness of the directors' action in light of the circumstances then existing."[36] We also held that "the directors have the burden of proving that they were adequately informed and acted reasonably."[37]

In *QVC*, we explained that the application of an enhanced judicial scrutiny test involves a judicial "review of the reasonableness of the substantive merits of the board's actions."[38] In applying that standard, we held that "a court should not ignore the complexity of the directors' task" in the context in which action was taken.[39] Accordingly, we

---

[27] See Unocal Corp. v. Mesa Petroleum Co., 493 A.2d 946, 954 (Del.1985).

[35] Paramount Communications Inc. v. QVC Network Inc., 637 A.2d 34, 45 (Del.1993).

[36] Id.

[37] Id.

[38] Id. (footnote omitted).

[39] Id.

concluded that a court applying enhanced judicial scrutiny should not decide whether the directors made a perfect decision but instead should decide whether "the directors' decision was, on balance, within a range of reasonableness."[40] . . .

Deal Protection Devices

Deal protection devices need not all be in the merger agreement itself. In this case, for example, the Section 251(c) provision in the merger agreement was combined with the separate voting agreements to provide a structural defense for the Genesis merger agreement against any subsequent superior transaction.* Genesis made the NCS board's defense of its transaction absolute by insisting on the omission of any effective fiduciary out clause in the NCS merger agreement.

Genesis argues that stockholder voting agreements cannot be construed as deal protection devices taken by a board of directors because stockholders are entitled to vote in their own interest. . . .

In this case, the stockholder voting agreements were inextricably intertwined with the defensive aspects of the Genesis merger agreement. In fact, the voting agreements with Shaw and Outcalt were the linchpin of Genesis' proposed tripartite defense. Therefore, Genesis made the execution of those voting agreements a non-negotiable condition precedent to its execution of the merger agreement. . . .

With the assurance that Outcalt and Shaw would irrevocably agree to exercise their majority voting power in favor of its transaction, Genesis insisted that the merger agreement reflect the other two aspects of its concerted defense, i.e., the inclusion of a Section 251(c) provision and the omission of any effective fiduciary out clause. Those dual aspects of the merger agreement would not have provided Genesis with a complete defense in the absence of the voting agreements with Shaw and Outcalt.

---

[40] Id. (citations omitted).

* [Eds.: DGCL § 251(c) provides, in pertinent part: "The terms of the agreement may require that the agreement be submitted to the stockholders whether or not the board of directors determines at any time subsequent to declaring its advisability that the agreement is no longer advisable and recommends that the stockholders reject it." Elsewhere in the opinion, the majority further explained:

> . . . Section 251(c) of the Delaware General Corporation Law now permits boards to agree to submit a merger agreement for a stockholder vote, even if the Board later withdraws its support for that agreement and recommends that the stockholders reject it. [Section 251(c) was amended in 1998 to allow for the inclusion in a merger agreement of a term requiring that the agreement be put to a vote of stockholders whether or not their directors continue to recommend the transaction. Before this amendment, Section 251 was interpreted as precluding a stockholder vote if the board of directors, after approving the merger agreement but before the stockholder vote, decided no longer to recommend it. See Smith v. Van Gorkom, 488 A.2d 858, 887–88 (Del.1985).] The Court of Chancery also noted that stockholder voting agreements are permitted by Delaware law. . . .
>
> Taking action that is otherwise legally possible, however, does not ipso facto comport with the fiduciary responsibilities of directors in all circumstances. The synopsis to the amendments that resulted in the enactment of Section 251(c) in the Delaware corporation law statute specifically provides: "the amendments are not intended to address the question of whether such a submission requirement is appropriate in any particular set of factual circumstances." Section 251 provisions . . . are "presumptively valid in the abstract." Such provisions in a merger agreement may not, however, "validly define or limit the directors' fiduciary duties under Delaware law or prevent the [NCS] directors from carrying out their fiduciary duties under Delaware law." [Paramount Communications Inc. v. QVC Network Inc., 637 A.2d at 48.]]

These Deal Protection Devices Unenforceable

. . . Pursuant to the judicial scrutiny required under *Unocal*'s two-stage analysis, the NCS directors must first demonstrate "that they had reasonable grounds for believing that a danger to corporate policy and effectiveness existed. . . ."[61] To satisfy that burden, the NCS directors are required to show they acted in good faith after conducting a reasonable investigation. The threat identified by the NCS board was the possibility of losing the Genesis offer and being left with no comparable alternative transaction.

The second stage of the *Unocal* test requires the NCS directors to demonstrate that their defensive response was "reasonable in relation to the threat posed."[63] This inquiry involves a two-step analysis. The NCS directors must first establish that the merger deal protection devices adopted in response to the threat were not "coercive" or "preclusive," and then demonstrate that their response was within a "range of reasonable responses" to the threat perceived.[64] In *Unitrin*, we stated:

> A response is "coercive" if it is aimed at forcing upon stockholders a management-sponsored alternative to a hostile offer.[65]
>
> A response is "preclusive" if it deprives stockholders of the right to receive all tender offers or precludes a bidder from seeking control by fundamentally restricting proxy contests or otherwise.[66]

This aspect of the *Unocal* standard provides for a disjunctive analysis. If defensive measures are either preclusive or coercive they are draconian and impermissible. In this case, the deal protection devices of the NCS board were both preclusive and coercive.

. . . A stockholder vote may be nullified by wrongful coercion "where the board or some other party takes actions which have the effect of causing the stockholders to vote in favor of the proposed transaction for some reason other than the merits of that transaction."[68] . . .

Although the minority stockholders were not forced to vote for the Genesis merger, they were required to accept it because it was a fait accompli. The record reflects that the defensive devices employed by the NCS board are preclusive and coercive in the sense that they accomplished a fait accompli. In this case, despite the fact that the NCS board has withdrawn its recommendation for the Genesis transaction and recommended its rejection by the stockholders, the deal protection devices approved by the NCS board operated in concert to have a preclusive and coercive effect. Those tripartite defensive measures—the Section 251(c) provision, the voting agreements, and the absence of an effective fiduciary out clause—made it "mathematically impossible" and

---

61 Unocal Corp. v. Mesa Petroleum Co., 493 A.2d 946, 955 (Del.1985) (citation omitted).

63 Id.

64 Unitrin, Inc. v. Am. Gen. Corp., 651 A.2d 1361, 1387–88 (Del.1995).

65 Id. at 1387. . . .

66 Id.

68 [Williams v. Geier, 671 A.2d 1368, 1382–83 (Del.1996) (citations omitted).]

"realistically unattainable" for the Omnicare transaction or any other proposal to succeed, no matter how superior the proposal.[72]

. . . Accordingly, we hold that those deal protection devices are unenforceable.

Effective Fiduciary Out Required

The defensive measures that protected the merger transaction are unenforceable not only because they are preclusive and coercive but, alternatively, they are unenforceable because they are invalid as they operate in this case. Given the specifically enforceable irrevocable voting agreements, the provision in the merger agreement requiring the board to submit the transaction for a stockholder vote and the omission of a fiduciary out clause in the merger agreement completely prevented the board from discharging its fiduciary responsibilities to the minority stockholders when Omnicare presented its superior transaction. . . .

. . . We hold that the NCS board did not have authority to accede to the Genesis demand for an absolute "lock-up."

. . . Instead of agreeing to the absolute defense of the Genesis merger from a superior offer, however, the NCS board was required to negotiate a fiduciary out clause to protect the NCS stockholders if the Genesis transaction became an inferior offer. By acceding to Genesis' ultimatum for complete protection in futuro, the NCS board disabled itself from exercising its own fiduciary obligations at a time when the board's own judgment is most important, i.e. receipt of a subsequent superior offer.

Any board has authority to give the proponent of a recommended merger agreement reasonable structural and economic defenses, incentives, and fair compensation if the transaction is not completed. To the extent that defensive measures are economic and reasonable, they may become an increased cost to the proponent of any subsequent transaction. Just as defensive measures cannot be draconian, however, they cannot limit or circumscribe the directors' fiduciary duties. Notwithstanding the corporation's insolvent condition, the NCS board had no authority to execute a merger agreement that subsequently prevented it from effectively discharging its ongoing fiduciary responsibilities.

. . . The issues in this appeal do not involve the general validity of either stockholder voting agreements or the authority of directors to insert a Section 251(c) provision in a merger agreement. In this case, the NCS board combined those two otherwise valid actions and caused them to operate in concert as an absolute lock up, in the absence of an effective fiduciary out clause in the Genesis merger agreement.

In the context of this preclusive and coercive lock up case, the protection of Genesis' contractual expectations must yield to the supervening responsibility of the directors to discharge their fiduciary duties on a continuing basis. The merger agreement and voting agreements, as they were combined to operate in concert in this case, are inconsistent with the NCS directors' fiduciary duties. To that extent, we hold that they are invalid and unenforceable. . . .

---

[72] See Unitrin, Inc. v. Am. Gen. Corp., 651 A.2d at 1388–89; see also Carmody v. Toll Bros., Inc., 723 A.2d 1180, 1195 (Del.Ch.1998) (citations omitted).

■ VEASEY, CHIEF JUSTICE, with whom STEELE, JUSTICE, joins dissenting.

. . . The Majority adopts a new rule of law that imposes a prohibition on the NCS board's ability to act in concert with controlling stockholders to lock up this merger. The Majority reaches this conclusion by analyzing the challenged deal protection measures as isolated board actions. The Majority concludes that the board owed a duty to the NCS minority stockholders to refrain from acceding to the Genesis demand for an irrevocable lock-up notwithstanding the compelling circumstances confronting the board and the board's disinterested, informed, good faith exercise of its business judgment.

Because we believe this Court must respect the reasoned judgment of the board of directors and give effect to the wishes of the controlling stockholders, we respectfully disagree with the Majority's reasoning that results in a holding that the confluence of board and stockholder action constitutes a breach of fiduciary duty. The essential fact that must always be remembered is that this agreement and the voting commitments of Outcalt and Shaw concluded a lengthy search and intense negotiation process in the context of insolvency and creditor pressure where no other viable bid had emerged. . . .

. . . It is now known, of course, after the case is over, that the stockholders of NCS will receive substantially more by tendering their shares into the topping bid of Omnicare than they would have received in the Genesis merger, as a result of the post-agreement Omnicare bid and the injunctive relief ordered by the Majority of this Court. Our jurisprudence cannot, however, be seen as turning on such ex post felicitous results. Rather, the NCS board's good faith decision must be subject to a real-time review of the board action before the NCS-Genesis merger agreement was entered into.

An Analysis of the Process Leading to the Lock-up Reflects a Quintessential, Disinterested and Informed Board Decision Reached in Good Faith

The Majority has adopted the Vice Chancellor's findings and has assumed arguendo that the NCS board fulfilled its duties of care, loyalty, and good faith by entering into the Genesis merger agreement. . . . The problem is that the Majority has removed from their proper context the contractual merger protection provisions. The lock-ups here cannot be reviewed in a vacuum. A court should review the entire bidding process to determine whether the independent board's actions permitted the directors to inform themselves of their available options and whether they acted in good faith.

Going into negotiations with Genesis, the NCS directors knew that, up until that time, NCS had found only one potential bidder, Omnicare. Omnicare had refused to buy NCS except at a fire sale price through an asset sale in bankruptcy. Omnicare's best proposal at that stage would not have paid off all creditors and would have provided nothing for stockholders. The Noteholders, represented by the Ad Hoc Committee, were willing to oblige Omnicare and force NCS into bankruptcy if Omnicare would pay in full the NCS debt. Through the NCS board's efforts, Genesis expressed interest that became increasingly attractive. Negotiations with Genesis led to an offer paying creditors off and conferring on NCS stockholders $24 million—an amount infinitely superior to the prior Omnicare proposals.

But there was, understandably, a *sine qua non*. In exchange for offering the NCS stockholders a return on their equity and creditor payment, Genesis demanded certainty that the merger would close. If the NCS board would not have acceded to the Section 251(c) provision, if Outcalt and Shaw had not agreed to the voting agreements and if NCS had insisted on a fiduciary out, there would have been no Genesis deal! Thus, the only value-enhancing transaction available would have disappeared. NCS knew that Omnicare had spoiled a Genesis acquisition in the past, and it is not disputed by the Majority that the NCS directors made a reasoned decision to accept as real the Genesis threat to walk away.

When Omnicare submitted its conditional eleventh-hour bid, the NCS board had to weigh the economic terms of the proposal against the uncertainty of completing a deal with Omnicare. Importantly, because Omnicare's bid was conditioned on its satisfactorily completing its due diligence review of NCS, the NCS board saw this as a crippling condition, as did the Ad Hoc Committee. As a matter of business judgment, the risk of negotiating with Omnicare and losing Genesis at that point outweighed the possible benefits. . . .

A lock-up permits a target board and a bidder to "exchange certainties."[97] Certainty itself has value. The acquirer may pay a higher price for the target if the acquirer is assured consummation of the transaction. The target company also benefits from the certainty of completing a transaction with a bidder because losing an acquirer creates the perception that a target is damaged goods, thus reducing its value. . . .

. . . If the creditors decided to force NCS into bankruptcy, which could have happened at any time as NCS was unable to service its obligations, the stockholders would have received nothing. The NCS board also did not know if the NCS business prospects would have declined again, leaving NCS less attractive to other bidders, including Omnicare, which could have changed its mind and again insisted on an asset sale in bankruptcy.

Situations will arise where business realities demand a lock-up so that wealth-enhancing transactions may go forward. Accordingly, any bright-line rule prohibiting lock-ups could, in circumstances such as these, chill otherwise permissible conduct. . . .

An Absolute Lock-up is Not a Per Se Violation of Fiduciary Duty

We respectfully disagree with the Majority's conclusion that the NCS board breached its fiduciary duties to the Class A stockholders by failing to negotiate a "fiduciary out" in the Genesis merger agreement. What is the practical import of a "fiduciary out?" It is a contractual provision, articulated in a manner to be negotiated, that would permit the board of the corporation being acquired to exit without breaching the merger agreement in the event of a superior offer.

In this case, Genesis made it abundantly clear early on that it was willing to negotiate a deal with NCS but only on the condition that it

[97] See Rand v. Western Air Lines, 1994 WL 89006 at *6 (Del.Ch.).

would not be a "stalking horse." Thus, it wanted to be certain that a third party could not use its deal with NCS as a floor against which to begin a bidding war. As a result of this negotiating position, a "fiduciary out" was not acceptable to Genesis. The Majority Opinion holds that such a negotiating position, if implemented in the agreement, is invalid per se where there is an absolute lock-up. We know of no authority in our jurisprudence supporting this new rule, and we believe it is unwise and unwarranted. . . .

ANALYSIS

1. The majority emphasized "the board's continuing responsibility to effectively exercise its fiduciary duties at all times after the merger agreement is executed." Does this statement suggest that any attempt by a board of directors to precommit the corporation to a particular course of conduct is inherently invalid?

2. Does "shaming," as Justice Steele observed in dissent, seem a plausible goal of corporate law jurisprudence?

3. In a portion of the majority opinion omitted from the excerpt above, the majority stated:

> Under the circumstances presented in this case, where a cohesive group of stockholders with majority voting power was irrevocably committed to the merger transaction, "[e]ffective representation of the financial interests of the minority shareholders imposed upon the [NCS board] an affirmative responsibility to protect those minority shareholders' interests." The NCS board could not abdicate its fiduciary duties to the minority by leaving it to the stockholders alone to approve or disapprove the merger agreement because two stockholders had already combined to establish a majority of the voting power that made the outcome of the stockholder vote a foregone conclusion.

What could the NCS board have done, however, if Outcalt and Shaw insisted on supporting Omnicare?

D. EXTENSION OF THE *UNOCAL/REVLON* FRAMEWORK TO SHAREHOLDER DISENFRANCHISEMENT

Hilton Hotels Corp. v. ITT Corp.

978 F.Supp. 1342 (D.Nev.1997).

. . .

I. FACTS

On January 27, 1997, Hilton announced a $55.00 per share tender offer for the stock of ITT, and announced plans for a proxy contest at ITT's 1997 annual meeting. This litigation commenced on the same date with the filing of Hilton's Complaint for Injunctive and Declaratory Relief. . . .

On February 11, 1997, ITT formally rejected Hilton's tender offer. ITT proceeded to sell several of its non-core assets and opposed Hilton's takeover attempt before gaming regulatory bodies in Nevada, New Jersey and Mississippi.

When it became apparent that ITT would not conduct its annual meeting in May 1997, as it had customarily done in preceding years, Hilton filed a motion for a mandatory injunction to compel ITT to conduct the annual meeting in May. On April 21, 1997, this Court denied Hilton's Motion finding that Nevada law and ITT's by-laws did not require that ITT conduct its annual meeting within twelve months of the prior meeting, but rather that ITT had eighteen months within which to do so. . . .

On July 15, 1997, ITT announced a Comprehensive Plan which, among other things, proposed to split ITT into three new entities, the largest of which would become ITT Destinations. ITT Destinations would be comprised of the current ITT's hotel and gaming business[es] which account for approximately 93% of ITT's current assets. A second entity, ITT Educational Services, would consist of the current ITT's technical schools, and ITT's European Yellow Pages Division would remain with the current ITT as ITT World Directories.

Most significantly, under the Comprehensive Plan, the board of directors of the new ITT Destinations would be comprised of the members of ITT's current board with one important distinction. The new board would be a "classified" or "staggered" board divided into three classes with each class of directors serving for a term of three years, and with one class to be elected each year. Moreover, a shareholder vote of 80% would be required to remove directors without cause, and [an] 80% shareholder vote would also be required to repeal the classified board provision or the 80% requirement to remove directors without cause.*

Additionally, the record fairly supports Hilton's contention that the Comprehensive Plan contains a "poison pill" resulting in a $1.4 billion tax liability which would be triggered if Hilton successfully acquired

---

* [Eds.—Nevada corporation code section 330 (Nev. Rev. Stat. § 78.330) provides, in pertinent part:

> 1. . . . [D]irectors of every corporation must be elected at the annual meeting of the stockholders by a plurality of the votes cast at the election. Unless otherwise provided in the bylaws, the board of directors have the authority to set the date, time and place for the annual meeting of the stockholders. If for any reason directors are not elected . . . at the annual meeting of the stockholders, they may be elected at any special meeting of the stockholders which is called and held for that purpose.
>
> 2. The articles of incorporation or the bylaws may provide for the classification of directors as to the duration of their respective terms of office or as to their election by one or more authorized classes or series of shares, but at least one-fourth in number of the directors of every corporation must be elected annually.
>
> 3. The articles of incorporation may provide that the voting power of individual directors or classes of directors may be greater than or less than that of any other individual directors or classes of directors, and the different voting powers may be stated in the articles of incorporation or may be dependent upon any fact or event that may be ascertained outside the articles of incorporation if the manner in which the fact or event may operate on those voting powers is stated in the articles of incorporation. If the articles of incorporation provide that any directors may have voting power greater than or less than other directors, every reference in this chapter to a majority or other proportion of directors shall be deemed to refer to a majority or other proportion of the voting power of all of the directors or classes of directors, as may be required by the articles of incorporation.]

more than 50% of ITT Destinations and that Hilton would be liable for 90% of the tax bill.

Finally, and critical to this Court's analysis, ITT seeks to implement the Comprehensive Plan prior to ITT's 1997 annual meeting and without obtaining shareholder approval.

II. THE PARTIES' CONTENTIONS AND APPLICABLE LEGAL STANDARDS

. . .

Shortly after ITT's announcement of its Comprehensive Plan, Hilton announced an amended tender offer of $70.00 per share, which was rejected by ITT. On August 26, 1997, Hilton filed its Motion for Injunctive and Declaratory Relief (#29) seeking:

1. A preliminary and permanent injunction enjoining ITT from proceeding with its Comprehensive Plan;

2. Declaring that by adopting the Comprehensive Plan, ITT's directors had breached their fiduciary duties to ITT and its shareholders;

3. Declaring that ITT may not implement its Comprehensive Plan without obtaining a shareholder vote; and

4. Requiring ITT to conduct its 1997 annual meeting for the election of directors not later than November 14, 1997.

. . .

Where, as here, Hilton's Motion seeks mandatory injunctive relief in the sense that a trial on the merits could not practically reverse a preliminary decision enjoining implementation of ITT's Comprehensive Plan until after the 1997 annual meeting, the Motion is subject to heightened scrutiny and the injunction requested should not issue unless the facts and the law clearly favor the party requesting such relief. . . . Therefore, this Court will apply the standard for permanent injunctive relief with regard to Hilton's Motion.

[Hilton must show irreparable injury and] "must actually succeed on the merits of their claims." Coleman v. Wilson, 912 F.Supp. 1282, 1311 (E.D.Ca.1995) (citing Sierra Club v. Penfold, 857 F.2d 1307, 1318 (9th Cir.1988)).

. . .

III. DISCUSSION

This case involves consideration of the powers and duties of the board of directors of a Nevada corporation in responding to a hostile takeover attempt, and the importance of protecting the franchise of the shareholders of the corporation in the process. Many courts have grappled with legal issues presented by the strategies employed by hostile bidders, such as Hilton, and the concomitant anti-takeover defensive measures utilized by target companies, such as ITT. Coupling an unsolicited tender offer with a proxy contest to replace the incumbent board is a favored strategy of would-be acquirors. A variety of sophisticated defensive measures, including "poison pill" plans have also evolved to frustrate a host of takeover attempts. As a result, "replacing the incumbent directors of the target corporation is viewed as an efficient way to eliminate the target company's ability to utilize these anti-takeover defenses." Kidsco v. Dinsmore III, 674 A.2d 483, 490 (Del.Ch.1995). . . .

Nevada state case law is virtually silent on the subject. However, provisions of Chapter 78 of the Nevada Revised Statutes ("N.R.S.") speak to the respective rights and duties of directors and officers of corporations, and the rights of corporate stockholders. Nevada's statutory scheme does not, however, provide clear guidance in this case. While N.R.S. § 78.138 addresses several powers of a corporate board in undertaking defensive measures to resist a hostile takeover,* nothing in the Nevada statutes, or elsewhere in the law of Nevada, authorizes the incumbent board of a corporation to entrench itself by effectively removing the right of the corporation's shareholders to vote on who may serve on the board of the corporation in which they own a share. Whether a target corporation such as ITT can do so in the face of a hostile takeover attempt by Hilton is the dispositive issue presented in this case.

Where, as here, there is no Nevada statutory or case law on point for an issue of corporate law, this Court finds persuasive authority in Delaware case law,. . .

---

* [Eds.—Nevada corporation code § 138 (Nev. Rev. Stat. § 78.138) provides, in pertinent part:

1. Directors and officers shall exercise their powers in good faith and with a view to the interests of the corporation. . . .

3. Directors and officers, in exercising their respective powers with a view to the interests of the corporation, may consider:

(a) The interests of the corporation's employees, suppliers, creditors and customers;

(b) The economy of the state and nation;

(c) The interests of the community and of society; and

(d) The long-term as well as short-term interests of the corporation and its stockholders, including the possibility that these interests may be best served by the continued independence of the corporation.

This subsection does not create or authorize any causes of action against the corporation or its directors or officers.

4. Directors may resist a change or potential change in control of the corporation if the directors by a majority vote of a quorum determine that the change or potential change is opposed to or not in the best interest of the corporation:

(a) Upon consideration of the interests of the corporation's stockholders and any of the matters set forth in subsection 3; or

(b) Because the amount or nature of the indebtedness and other obligations to which the corporation or any successor to the property of either may become subject in connection with the change or potential change in control provides reasonable grounds to believe that, within a reasonable time:

(1) The assets of the corporation or any successor would be or become less than its liabilities;

(2) The corporation or any successor would be or become insolvent; or

(3) Any voluntary or involuntary proceeding under the federal bankruptcy laws concerning the corporation or any successor would be commenced by any person.

Consider also Nevada Corporate Code § 120 (Nev. Rev. Stat. § 78.120), which provides in pertinent part:

1. Subject only to such limitations as may be provided by this chapter, or the articles of incorporation of the corporation, the board of directors has full control over the affairs of the corporation.

3. The selection of a period for the achievement of corporate goals is the responsibility of the directors.]

A. Legal Framework for Board Action in Response to a Proxy Contest and Tender Offer.

As this case involves both a tender offer and a proxy contest by Hilton, the proper legal standard is a *Unocal/Blasius** analysis as articulated in Stroud v. Grace, 606 A.2d 75, 92 n. 3 (Del.1992), and Unitrin, [Inc. v. American Gen. Corp., 651 A.2d 1361], 1379 [(Del.1995)].

> In assessing a challenge to defensive actions by a target corporation's board of directors in a takeover context, this Court has held that the Court of Chancery should evaluate the board's overall response, including the justification for each contested defensive measure, and the results achieved thereby. Where all of the target board's defensive actions are *inextricably related*, the principles of *Unocal* require that such actions be scrutinized collectively as a unitary response to the perceived threat.

Unitrin, 651 A.2d at 1386–87 (emphasis supplied).

Where an acquiror launches both a proxy fight and a tender offer, it

> "necessarily invoke[s] both *Unocal* and *Blasius*" because "both [tests] recognize the inherent conflicts of interest that arise when shareholders are not permitted free exercise of their franchise. . . . [I]n certain circumstances, [the judiciary] must recognize the special import of protecting the shareholders' franchise within *Unocal*'s requirement that any defensive measure be proportionate and 'reasonable in relation to the threat posed.' "

Unitrin, 651 A.2d at 1379 (quoting *Stroud*, 606 A.2d at 92 n. 3).

> A board's unilateral decision to adopt a defensive measure touching "upon issues of control" that purposefully disenfranchises its shareholders is strongly suspect under *Unocal*, and cannot be sustained without a "compelling justification."

Stroud, 606 A.2d at 92 n. 3.

These cases have drawn a distinction between the exercise of two types of corporate power: 1) power over the assets of the corporation and 2) the power relationship between the board (management) and the shareholders. Actions involving the first type of power invoke the business judgment rule, or *Unocal* if an action is in response to a reasonably perceived threat to the corporation. Actions involving the second power invoke a *Blasius* analysis. The issues raised in this case require the Court to focus on the power relationship between ITT's board and ITT shareholders, not on the ITT board's actions relating to corporate assets.

Several amicus briefs have been filed on behalf of ITT shareholders, urging that they be allowed to vote on the Comprehensive Plan and the

* [Eds.—In Stroud v. Grace, 606 A.2d 75 (Del.1992), and Blasius Indus. v. Atlas Corp., 564 A.2d 651 (Del. Ch. 1988), the Delaware courts held that board action intended to thwart the free exercise of the shareholder franchise must satisfy the "heavy burden" of demonstrating a "compelling justification" for their action. In cases, such as *Hilton*, in which the board's action takes place in the context of an unsolicited tender offer, *Unocal* provides the basic standard of review for the board's actions, but in applying *Unocal*'s proportionality prong the courts will treat board action that purposefully disenfranchises the shareholders as "strongly suspect."]

board of directors at the 1997 annual meeting. This Court has found no legal basis mandating a shareholder vote on the adoption of ITT's Comprehensive Plan in its entirety. However, as the Court finds that the Comprehensive Plan would violate the power relationship between ITT's board and ITT's shareholders by impermissibly infringing on the shareholders' right to vote on members of the board of directors, it must be enjoined.

ITT argues that Nevada does not follow Delaware case law since N.R.S. § 78.138 provides that a board, exercising its powers in good faith and with an view to the interests of the corporation can resist potential changes in control of a corporation based on the effect [on] constituencies other than the shareholders. However, the corporate rights provided under N.R.S. § 78.138 are not incompatible with the duties articulated in [the Delaware cases].

Delaware case law merely clarifies the basic duties established by the Nevada statutes. . . .

Thus, Delaware precedent establishes that a board has power over the management and assets of a corporation, but that power is not unbridled. That power is limited by the right of shareholders to vote for the members of the board. . . .

Unocal requires the Court to consider the following two questions: 1) Does ITT have reasonable grounds for believing a danger to corporate policy and effectiveness exists? 2) Is the response reasonable in relation to the threat? If it is a defensive measure touching on issues of control, the court must examine whether the board purposefully disenfranchised its shareholders, an action that cannot be sustained without a compelling justification. *Stroud*, 606 A.2d at 92 n. 3.

1. The Classified Board for ITT Destinations

The first defensive action this Court will analyze under the *Unocal* standard is the provision in the Comprehensive Plan for a classified board for ITT Destinations.

a. Reasonable Grounds for Believing a Threat to Corporate Policy and Effectiveness Exists.

Nine of ITT's eleven directors are outside directors. Under *Unocal*, such a majority materially enhances evidence that a hostile offer presents a threat warranting a defensive response. *Unitrin*, 651 A.2d at 1375.

ITT argues strenuously that the Comprehensive Plan is better than Hilton's offer. This is not for the Court to decide, and it is not determinative under its analysis. Under *Unocal*, a court must first determine if there is a threat to corporate policy and effectiveness. ITT has failed to demonstrate such a threat.

ITT has made no showing that Hilton will pursue a different corporate policy than ITT seeks to implement through its Comprehensive Plan. In fact, over the past few months, ITT has to a large extent adopted Hilton's proposed strategy of how it says it will govern ITT if its slate of directors is elected. There has also been no showing of Hilton's inability or ineffectiveness to run ITT if it does succeed in its takeover attempt. . . .

The ITT board has also failed to meet its burden of showing "good faith and reasonable investigation" of a threat to corporate policy or effectiveness which would meet the burden placed on the board under the first prong of the *Unocal* test. Since Hilton's tender offer was announced, the ITT board has not met with Hilton to discuss the offer. Moreover the overwhelming majority of ITT's evidence of good faith relates to its approval of the Comprehensive Plan, not to the inadequacy of Hilton's offer.

The sole "threat" ITT points to is that Hilton's offer of $70 a share is inadequate, primarily because this price does not contain a control premium. However, at the August 14, 1997, ITT board meeting, Goldman Sachs told the ITT board that the market valued ITT's plan at $62 to $64 dollars a share. This contradicts ITT's argument that there is no control premium over market price contained in Hilton's offer. That ITT itself was offering to buy back roughly 26% of its stock at $70 a share does not nullify this fact.

The only attempt ITT has made to satisfy the first prong of the *Unocal* analysis is to argue that Hilton's price is inadequate. However, while inadequacy of an offer is a legally cognizable threat, Paramount Communications, Inc. v. Time, Inc., 571 A.2d 1140, 1153 (Del.1989), ITT has shown no real harm to corporate policy or effectiveness. The facts in *Unocal* illustrate this point well. *Unocal* involved a tender offer with a back-end offer of junk bonds. Junk bond financing could reasonably harm the future policy and effectiveness of a company. As ITT itself is offering only $70 a share, and the Comprehensive Plan involves greatly increasing the leveraging of ITT, its claim that Hilton's offer of $70 a share is a threat to policy or effectiveness is unpersuasive. In light of these facts, the alleged inadequacy of Hilton's offer is not a severe threat to ITT. Under the proportionality requirement, the nature of Hilton's threat will set the parameters for the range of permissible defensive tactics under the second prong of the *Unocal* test.

b. ITT's Response was Preclusive

Assuming Hilton's offer constitutes a cognizable threat under *Unocal*, ITT's response cannot be preclusive or coercive, and it must be within the range of reasonableness. As articulated in *Unitrin*, a board cannot "cram down" on shareholders a management sponsored alternative. The installation of a classified board for ITT Destinations, a company which will encompass 93% of the current ITT's assets and 87% of its revenues, is clearly preclusive and coercive under *Unitrin*. The classified board provision for ITT Destinations will preclude current ITT shareholders from exercising a right they currently possess—to determine the membership of the board of ITT. At the very minimum, ITT shareholders will have no choice but to accept the Comprehensive Plan and a majority of ITT's incumbent board members for another year. Therefore, the Comprehensive Plan is preclusive.

c. The Primary Purpose of the Comprehensive Plan is to Interfere with Shareholder Franchise

ITT's response to Hilton's tender offer touches upon issues of control, and this Court must determine whether the response purposefully disenfranchises ITT's shareholders. If so, under the analysis of *Stroud* and *Unitrin*, it is not a reasonable response unless a "compelling justification" exists. It is important to note that in *Blasius*, the board did something that normally would be entirely permissible under Delaware law and its own by-laws: it expanded the board from seven to nine individuals. It did this in the face of a hostile takeover by a company financed through "junk bonds" and two individuals who sought to substantially "cash out" many of the target corporation's assets. Still, while the board in *Blasius* had a good faith reason to act as it did, and it acted with appropriate care, the board could not lawfully prevent the shareholders from electing a majority of new directors.

Blasius' factual scenario is strikingly similar to the circumstances surrounding ITT's actions. Normally, a corporation is free to adopt a classified board structure. In fact many companies, including Hilton, have classified boards. As long as the classified board is adopted in the proper manner, whether through charter amendment, changes in the by-laws of a company or through shareholder vote, it is permissible. However, *Blasius* illustrates that even if an action is normally permissible, and the board adopts it in good faith and with proper care, a board cannot undertake such action if the primary purpose is to disenfranchise the shareholders in light of a proxy contest. Thus, while ITT could normally adopt a classified board or issue a dividend of shares creating ITT Destinations, it cannot undertake these actions if the primary purpose is to disenfranchise ITT shareholders in light of Hilton's tender offer and proxy contest.

As a board would likely never concede that its primary purpose was to entrench itself, this Court must look to circumstantial evidence to determine the primary purpose of ITT's action touching upon issues of control. While none of the following factors are dispositive, collectively they eliminate all questions of material fact, and demonstrate that the primary purpose of ITT's Comprehensive Plan was to disenfranchise its shareholders.

i. Timing

The intent evidenced by the timing of the Comprehensive Plan is transparent. Although ITT claims that a spin-off or sale was contemplated before Hilton's tender offer, it makes no mention of when the board determined to move from an annually elected board to a classified board. Moreover, all aspects of ITT's Comprehensive Plan were formulated against the backdrop of Hilton's tender offer and proxy contest, and the Plan was not announced until well after Hilton's initial tender offer. Finally, this major restructuring of ITT was announced and to be implemented in a little over two months, and designed to take effect less than two months before the annual meeting was to be held at which shareholders would have the opportunity to vote on an annually elected rather than a classified board.

ii. Entrenchment

The ITT directors who are approving the Comprehensive Plan are the same directors who will fill the classified board positions of ITT Destinations. ITT and its advisors recognized from the outset that they were vulnerable because they did not have a staggered board of directors. The members of ITT's board are appointing themselves to new, more insulated positions, and at least seven of the eleven directors are avoiding the shareholder vote that would otherwise occur at ITT's 1997 annual meeting. While companies may convert from annual to classified boards, as *Blasius* illustrates, the rub is in the details. It is the manner of adopting the Comprehensive Plan with its provision for a new certified board comprised of incumbent ITT directors which supports the conclusion that ITT's Plan is primarily designed to entrench the incumbent board.

iii. ITT's Stated Purpose

ITT has offered no credible justification for not seeking shareholder approval of the Comprehensive Plan. ITT simply claims that it wants to "avoid market risks and other business problems." . . . Such vague generalizations do not approach the required showing of a reasonable justification other than entrenchment for the board's action. Simply stating that its "advisors" suggested a rapid implementation of the Comprehensive Plan, without pointing to a specific risk or problem, is insufficient to meet ITT's burden.

iv. Benefits of Comprehensive Plan

ITT argues that there are economic benefits to the Comprehensive Plan, and general benefits of the classified board provision for ITT Destinations, That may be true, but the additional benefits of a plan infringing on shareholder voting rights do not remedy the fundamental flaw of board entrenchment.

v. Effect of Classified Board

The classified board provision for ITT Destinations under ITT's Comprehensive Plan ensures that ITT shareholders will be absolutely precluded from electing a majority of the directors nominated under Hilton's proxy contest at the 1997 annual meeting. Such a Plan, coupled with ITT's vehement opposition to Hilton's tender offer, is inconsistent with ITT's earlier argument that a delay of the 1997 annual meeting from May to November would afford shareholders additional time to inform themselves and more fully consider the implications of their vote for directors at the 1997 annual meeting.

ITT's position is particularly anomalous given the fact that when ITT previously split the company in 1995, it sought shareholder approval. While shareholder approval may not be absolutely required to split ITT now any more than it was in 1995, the fact that the ITT board decided to subject the 1995 split of the company to a shareholder vote is strong evidence that the primary purpose of its attempts to implement the Comprehensive Plan prior to the 1997 annual meeting is to entrench the incumbent ITT board.

vi. Failure to Obtain an IRS Opinion as to Effects of the Comprehensive Plan

ITT is not seeking an Internal Revenue Service opinion regarding the tax consequences of the three-way split of ITT under the Comprehensive Plan. It is doubtful that an Internal Revenue Service opinion on the matter could be obtained before ITT's 1997 annual meeting. Furthermore, there are serious questions as to the extent to which implementation of the Comprehensive Plan will constitute a taxable event to ITT and its shareholders, or the extent to which Hilton would incur adverse tax consequences if it attempted to take over ITT Destinations once the Comprehensive Plan is implemented. . . . While obtaining a tax opinion from the Internal Revenue Service may not be mandatory, ITT's failure to seriously consider obtaining such an opinion provides additional evidence that ITT's primary intention in implementing the Comprehensive Plan at this time was to impede the shareholder franchise.

2. Other Provisions of the Comprehensive Plan

This Court's analysis regarding the threat to ITT under the first prong of *Unocal* is equally applicable to the remaining elements of the Comprehensive Plan. Whether the other aspects of ITT's Comprehensive Plan violate the second step of the *Unocal* analysis, that is, whether they are preclusive or coercive, is problematic. Certainly the record before the Court supports Hilton's contention that the "tax poison pill" relating to its potential purchase of ITT Destinations is preclusive and coercive. . . .

. . . This Court finds it unnecessary . . . to undertake an exhaustive analysis of the laundry list of issues presented by both parties. The different provisions of the Comprehensive Plan are inextricably related, and this Court has already concluded that the staggered board provision is preclusive and was enacted for the primary purpose of entrenching the current board. Therefore, the entire Comprehensive Plan must be enjoined.

3. Duty to Maximize Value to Shareholders Under *Revlon*

Hilton further argues that injunctive relief is warranted based on an analysis of the Comprehensive Plan under the *Revlon* standard. The Court finds that Hilton has not extinguished all material facts as to whether the Comprehensive Plan involves: 1) an abandonment of the long-term strategy of ITT involving a breakup of the company or 2) a sale of control is contemplated in *Revlon* and Paramount v. QVC, 637 A.2d 34 (Del.1994). Therefore, permanent injunctive relief on this basis is not warranted.

IV. CONCLUSION

. . .

Shareholders do not exercise day-to-day business judgments regarding the operation of a corporation—those are matters left to the reasonable discretion of directors, officers and the corporation's management team. Corporate boards have great latitude in exercising their business judgments as they should. As a result, shareholders generally have only two protections against perceived inadequate business performance. They may sell their stock or vote to replace incumbent board members. For this reason, interference with the shareholder franchise is especially serious. It is not to be left to the board's business judgment, precisely because it undercuts a primary justification for allowing directors to rely on their business judgment in almost every other context. . . .

ITT strongly argues that its Comprehensive Plan is superior to Hilton's alternative tender offer. This argument should be directed to ITT's shareholders, not this Court.

. . .

This Court concludes that the structure and timing of ITT's Comprehensive Plan with its classified board provision for ITT Destinations, is preclusive and leaves no doubt that the primary purpose for ITT's proposed implementation of the Comprehensive Plan before the 1997 annual meeting is to impermissibly impede the exercise of the shareholder franchise by depriving shareholders of the opportunity to vote to re-elect or to oust all or as many of the incumbent ITT directors as they may choose at the upcoming annual meeting. It has as its primary purpose the entrenchment of the incumbent ITT board. As a result, the Court concludes that Hilton has prevailed on the merits of its claim for permanent injunctive relief.

IT IS THEREFORE ORDERED that Hilton's Motion for Permanent Injunctive Relief is granted to the extent that ITT is hereby enjoined from implementing its Comprehensive Plan announced July 15, 1997.

IT IS FURTHER ORDERED that ITT's annual meeting shall be held no later than November 14, 1997.

. . .

AFTERMATH

In September 1997, Starwood Lodging, Inc. launched a competing bid for ITT. ITT's board announced its support for the Starwood offer. Hilton started a proxy fight to install its slate of directors for ITT, but at the November shareholder meeting the directors supported by ITT and Starwood were elected, whereupon Hilton withdrew its offer (which caused the market price of its shares to rise, a sign that people who followed the stock thought that Hilton had offered more for ITT than it was worth).

ANALYSIS

1. How persuasive is the court's finding that the classified board scheme was "preclusive"? Suppose ITT had been allowed to set up ITT Destinations, with a classified board. If Hilton had thereupon acquired a majority of ITT Destination's stock, would Hilton's efforts to obtain control of ITT in fact have been significantly impeded?

2. Why didn't ITT's board of directors simply adopt a by-law creating a classified board without going through the rigmarole of establishing three new corporations? Would your answer change under Delaware law?

3. The court appears to assume that Nevada courts would follow *Revlon*, as interpreted by *Time* and *QVC*. In light of Nev. Rev. Stat. §§ 78.120(3) and 78.138, does that conclusion appear plausible?

4. The court dismisses Hilton's *Revlon* claims on procedural grounds relating to the standard for granting injunctions. If the court had reached the merits of those claims, how should it have ruled?

5. Would the result in this case have changed if Hilton had not launched a proxy contest concurrently with its tender offer? Why did Hilton do so?

6. In view of the Delaware Supreme Court's holdings in Paramount Communications, Inc. v. Time Inc., was the *Hilton* court correct in holding that the only legally cognizable threat for purposes of *Unocal*'s first prong was price inadequacy? Did Hilton's bid raise any of the other threats validated by the Delaware Supreme Court in *Time*?

7. The court states, in connection with its discussion of *Unocal*, "Junk bond financing could . . . harm the future policy and effectiveness

of the company." So what? Should the shareholders care? Suppose a corporation's board decides on a policy of expansion that is to be financed by junk bonds and a shareholder challenges that policy in a derivative action. What would the shareholder be required to prove in order to prevail?

E. STATE AND FEDERAL LEGISLATION

CTS Corporation v. Dynamics Corporation of America

481 U.S. 69, 107 S.Ct. 1637, 95 L.Ed.2d 67 (1987).

■ JUSTICE POWELL delivered the opinion of the Court.

This case presents the questions whether the Control Share Acquisitions Chapter of the Indiana Business Corporation Law . . . is preempted by the Williams Act . . . or violates the Commerce Clause of the Federal Constitution, Art. I, § 8, cl. 3.

I

A

On March 4, 1986, the Governor of Indiana signed a revised Indiana Business Corporation Law, Ind.Code § 23–1–17–1 et seq. (Supp.1986). That law included the Control Share Acquisitions Chapter (Indiana Act or Act). Beginning on August 1, 1987, the Act will apply to any corporation incorporated in Indiana, § 23–1–17–3(a), unless the corporation amends its articles of incorporation or bylaws to opt out of the Act, § 23–1–42–5. Before that date, any Indiana corporation can opt into the Act by resolution of its board of directors. § 23–1–17–3(b). The Act applies only to "issuing public corporations." The term "corporation" includes only businesses incorporated in Indiana. See § 23–1–20–5. An "issuing public corporation" is defined as:

"a corporation that has:

"(1) one hundred (100) or more shareholders;

"(2) its principal place of business, its principal office, or substantial assets within Indiana; and

"(3) either:

"(A) more than ten percent (10%) of its shareholders resident in Indiana;

"(B) more than ten percent (10%) of its shares owned by Indiana residents; or

"(C) ten thousand (10,000) shareholders resident in Indiana." § 23–1–42–4(a).

The Act focuses on the acquisition of "control shares" in an issuing public corporation. Under the Act, an entity acquires "control shares" whenever it acquires shares that, but for the operation of the Act, would bring its voting power in the corporation to or above any of three thresholds: 20%, 33⅓%, or 50%. § 23–1–42–1. An entity that acquires control shares does not necessarily acquire voting rights. Rather, it gains those rights only "to the extent granted by resolution approved by the shareholders of the issuing public corporation." § 23–1–42–9(a). Section 9 requires a majority vote of all disinterested[2] shareholders holding each class of stock for passage of such a resolution. § 23–1–42–9(b). The practical effect of this requirement is to condition acquisition of control of a corporation on approval of a majority of the pre-existing disinterested shareholders.

The shareholders decide whether to confer rights on the control shares at the next regularly scheduled meeting of the shareholders, or at a specially scheduled meeting. The acquiror can require management of the corporation to hold such a special meeting within 50 days if it files an "acquiring person statement,"[4] requests the meeting, and agrees to pay the expenses of the meeting. See § 23–1–42–7. If the shareholders do not vote to restore voting rights to the shares, the corporation may redeem the control shares from the acquiror at fair market value, but it is not required to do so. § 23–1–42–10(b). Similarly, if the acquiror does not file an acquiring person statement with the corporation, the corporation may, if its bylaws or articles of incorporation so provide, redeem the shares at any time after 60 days after the acquiror's last acquisition. § 23–1–42–10(a).

B

On March 10, 1986, appellee Dynamics Corporation of America (Dynamics) owned 9.6% of the common stock of appellant CTS Corporation, an Indiana corporation. On that day, six days after the Act went into effect, Dynamics announced a tender offer for another million shares in CTS; purchase of those shares would have brought Dynamics' ownership interest in CTS to 27.5%. Also on March 10, Dynamics filed suit in the United States District Court for the Northern District of Illinois, alleging that CTS had violated the federal securities laws in a number of respects no longer relevant to these proceedings. On March 27, the Board of Directors of CTS, an Indiana corporation, elected to be governed by the provisions of the Act, see § 23–1–17–3.

Four days later, on March 31, Dynamics moved for leave to amend its complaint to allege that the Act is pre-empted by the Williams Act, 15 U.S.C. §§ 78m(d)–(e) and 78n(d)–(f) (1982 ed. and Supp. III), and violates the Commerce Clause, Art. I, § 8, cl. 3. Dynamics sought a temporary restraining order, a preliminary injunction, and declaratory relief against CTS's use of the Act. On April 9, the District Court ruled that the Williams Act pre-empts the Indiana Act and granted Dynamics' motion for declaratory relief. 637 F.Supp. 389 (N.D.Ill.1986). Relying on Justice WHITE's plurality opinion in Edgar v. MITE Corp., 457 U.S. 624 (1982), the court concluded that the Act "wholly frustrates the purpose and objective of Congress in striking a balance between the investor, management, and the takeover bidder in takeover contests." 637 F.Supp., at 399. A week later, on April 17, the District Court issued an opinion accepting Dynamics' claim that the Act violates the Commerce Clause. This holding rested on the court's conclusion that "the substantial

[2] "Interested shares" are shares with respect to which the acquiror, an officer or an inside director of the corporation "may exercise or direct the exercise of the voting power of the corporation in the election of directors." § 23–1–42–3. . . .

[4] An "acquiring person statement" is an information statement describing, *inter alia,* the identity of the acquiring person and the terms and extent of the proposed acquisition. See § 23–1–42–6.

interference with interstate commerce created by the [Act] outweighs the articulated local benefits so as to create an impermissible indirect burden on interstate commerce." Id., at 406. The District Court certified its decisions on the Williams Act and Commerce Clause claims as final under Fed.Rule Civ.Proc. 54(b). Ibid.

[The Court of Appeals, in an opinion by Judge Richard Posner, affirmed.]

After disposing of a variety of questions not relevant to this appeal, the Court of Appeals examined Dynamics' claim that the Williams Act pre-empts the Indiana Act. The court looked first to the plurality opinion in Edgar v. MITE Corp., supra, in which three Justices found that the Williams Act pre-empts state statutes that upset the balance between target management and a tender offeror. The court noted that some commentators had disputed this view of the Williams Act, concluding instead that the Williams Act was "an anti-takeover statute, expressing a view, however benighted, that hostile takeovers are bad." Id., at 262. It also noted:

> "[I]t is a big leap from saying that the Williams Act does not itself exhibit much hostility to tender offers to saying that it implicitly forbids states to adopt more hostile regulations. . . . But whatever doubts of the Williams' Act preemptive intent we might entertain as an original matter are stilled by the weight of precedent." Ibid.

Once the court had decided to apply the analysis of the *MITE* plurality, it found the case straightforward:

> "Very few tender offers could run the gauntlet that Indiana has set up. In any event, if the Williams Act is to be taken as a congressional determination that a month (roughly) is enough time to force a tender offer to be kept open, 50 days is too much; and 50 days is the minimum under the Indiana act if the target corporation so chooses." Id., at 263.

The court next addressed Dynamic's Commerce Clause challenge to the Act. Applying the balancing test articulated in Pike v. Bruce Church, Inc., 397 U.S. 137 (1970), the court found the Act unconstitutional:

> "Unlike a state's blue sky law the Indiana statute is calculated to impede transactions between residents of other states. For the sake of trivial or even negative benefits to its residents Indiana is depriving nonresidents of the valued opportunity to accept tender offers from other nonresidents.
>
> ". . . Even if a corporation's tangible assets are immovable, the efficiency with which they are employed and the proportions in which the earnings they generate are divided between management and shareholders depends on the market for corporate control—an interstate, indeed international, market that the State of Indiana is not authorized to opt out of, as in effect it has done in this statute." 794 F.2d, at 264.

Finally, the court addressed the "internal affairs" doctrine, a "principle of conflict of laws . . . designed to make sure that the law of only one state shall govern the internal affairs of a corporation or other association." Ibid. It stated:

> "We may assume without having to decide that Indiana has a broad latitude in regulating those affairs, even when the consequence may be to make it harder to take over an Indiana corporation. . . . But in this case the effect on the interstate market in securities and corporate control is direct, intended, and substantial. . . . [T]hat the mode of regulation involves jiggering with voting rights cannot take it outside the scope of judicial review under the commerce clause." Ibid.

Accordingly, the court affirmed the judgment of the District Court.

. . .

II

The first question in this case is whether the Williams Act pre-empts the Indiana Act. As we have stated frequently, absent an explicit indication by Congress of an intent to pre-empt state law, a state statute is pre-empted only

> " 'where compliance with both federal and state regulations is a physical impossibility . . .,' *Florida Lime & Avocado Growers, Inc. v. Paul,* 373 U.S. 132, 142–143 (1963), or where the state 'law stands as an obstacle to the accomplishment and execution of the full purposes and objectives of Congress.' *Hines v. Davidowitz,* 312 U.S. 52, 67 [61 S.Ct. 399, 404, 85 L.Ed. 581] (1941). . . ." *Ray v. Atlantic Richfield Co.,* 435 U.S. 151 (1978).

Because it is entirely possible for entities to comply with both the Williams Act and the Indiana Act, the state statute can be pre-empted only if it frustrates the purposes of the federal law.

A

Our discussion begins with a brief summary of the structure and purposes of the Williams Act. Congress passed the Williams Act in 1968 in response to the increasing number of hostile tender offers. Before its passage, these transactions were not covered by the disclosure requirements of the federal securities laws. . . .

The Williams Act, backed by regulations of the Securities and Exchange Commission (SEC), imposes requirements in two basic areas. First, it requires the offeror to file a statement disclosing information about the offer, including: the offeror's background and identity; the source and amount of the funds to be used in making the purchase; the purpose of the purchase, including any plans to liquidate the company or make major changes in its corporate structure; and the extent of the offeror's holdings in the target company.

Second, the Williams Act, and the regulations that accompany it, establish procedural rules to govern tender offers. For example, stockholders who tender their shares may withdraw them during the first 15 business days of the tender offer and, if the offeror has not purchased their shares, any time after 60 days from commencement of the offer. . . . The offer must remain open for at least 20 business days. . . . If more shares are tendered than the offeror sought to purchase, purchases must be made on a pro rata basis from each tendering shareholder. . . . Finally, the offeror must pay the same price for all purchases; if the offering price is increased before the end of the offer, those who already have tendered must receive the benefit of the increased price. . . .

B

The Indiana Act differs in major respects from the Illinois statute that the Court considered in Edgar v. MITE Corp., 457 U.S. 624 (1982). After reviewing the legislative history of the Williams Act, Justice WHITE, joined by Chief Justice Burger and Justice BLACKMUN (the plurality), concluded that the Williams Act struck a careful balance between the interests of offerors and target companies, and that any state statute that "upset" this balance was pre-empted. Id., at 632–634.

The plurality then identified three offending features of the Illinois statute. Justice WHITE's opinion first noted that the Illinois statute provided for a 20-day precommencement period. During this time, management could disseminate its views on the upcoming offer to shareholders, but offerors could not publish their offers. The plurality found that this provision gave management "a powerful tool to combat tender offers." Id., at 635. This contrasted dramatically with the Williams Act; Congress had deleted express precommencement notice provisions from the Williams Act. According to the plurality, Congress had determined that the potentially adverse consequences of such a provision on shareholders should be avoided. Thus, the plurality concluded that the Illinois provision "frustrate[d] the objectives of the Williams Act." Ibid. The second criticized feature of the Illinois statute was a provision for a hearing on a tender offer that, because it set no deadline, allowed management " 'to stymie indefinitely a takeover,' " id., at 637 (quoting MITE Corp. v. Dixon, 633 F.2d 486, 494 (C.A.7 1980)). The plurality noted that " 'delay can seriously impede a tender offer,' " 457 U.S., at 637, (quoting Great Western United Corp. v. Kidwell, 577 F.2d 1256, 1277 (C.A.5 1978) (per Wisdom, J.)), and that "Congress anticipated that investors and the takeover offeror would be free to go forward without unreasonable delay," 457 U.S., at 639. Accordingly, the plurality concluded that this provision conflicted with the Williams Act. The third troublesome feature of the Illinois statute was its requirement that the fairness of tender offers would be reviewed by the Illinois Secretary of State. Noting that "Congress intended for investors to be free to make their own decisions," the plurality concluded that " '[t]he state thus offers investor protection at the expense of investor autonomy—an approach quite in conflict with that adopted by Congress.' " Id., at 639–640 (quoting MITE Corp. v. Dixon, supra, at 494).

C

As the plurality opinion in *MITE* did not represent the views of a majority of the Court, we are not bound by its reasoning. We need not question that reasoning, however, because we believe the Indiana Act passes muster even under the broad interpretation of the Williams Act articulated by Justice WHITE in *MITE*. As is apparent from our summary of its reasoning, the overriding concern of the *MITE* plurality was that the Illinois statute considered in that case operated to favor management against offerors, to the detriment of shareholders. By contrast, the statute now before the Court protects the independent shareholder against both of the contending parties. Thus, the Act furthers a basic purpose of the Williams Act, " 'plac[ing] investors on an equal footing with the takeover bidder,' " Piper v. Chris-Craft Industries,

[430 U.S. 1, 30 (1977)] (quoting the Senate Report accompanying the Williams Act, S.Rep. No. 550, 90th Cong., 1st Sess., 4 (1967)).

The Indiana Act operates on the assumption, implicit in the Williams Act, that independent shareholders faced with tender offers often are at a disadvantage. By allowing such shareholders to vote as a group, the Act protects them from the coercive aspects of some tender offers. If, for example, shareholders believe that a successful tender offer will be followed by a purchase of nontendering shares at a depressed price, individual shareholders may tender their shares—even if they doubt the tender offer is in the corporation's best interest—to protect themselves from being forced to sell their shares at a depressed price.... In such a situation under the Indiana Act, the shareholders as a group, acting in the corporation's best interest, could reject the offer, although individual shareholders might be inclined to accept it....

In implementing its goal, the Indiana Act avoids the problems the plurality discussed in *MITE*. Unlike the *MITE* statute, the Indiana Act does not give either management or the offeror an advantage in communicating with the shareholders about the impending offer. The Act also does not impose an indefinite delay on tender offers. Nothing in the Act prohibits an offeror from consummating an offer on the 20th business day, the earliest day permitted under applicable federal regulations, see 17 CFR § 240.14e–1(a) (1986). Nor does the Act allow the state government to interpose its views of fairness between willing buyers and sellers of shares of the target company. Rather, the Act allows *shareholders* to evaluate the fairness of the offer collectively.

D

The Court of Appeals based its finding of pre-emption on its view that the practical effect of the Indiana Act is to delay consummation of tender offers until 50 days after the commencement of the offer. 794 F.2d, at 263. As did the Court of Appeals, Dynamics reasons that no rational offeror will purchase shares until it gains assurance that those shares will carry voting rights. Because it is possible that voting rights will not be conferred until a shareholder meeting 50 days after commencement of the offer, Dynamics concludes that the Act imposes a 50-day delay. This, it argues, conflicts with the shorter 20-business-day period established by the SEC as the minimum period for which a tender offer may be held open.... We find the alleged conflict illusory.

The Act does not impose an absolute 50-day delay on tender offers, nor does it preclude an offeror from purchasing shares as soon as federal law permits. If the offeror fears an adverse shareholder vote under the Act, it can make a conditional tender offer, offering to accept shares on the condition that the shares receive voting rights within a certain period of time. The Williams Act permits tender offers to be conditioned on the offeror's subsequently obtaining regulatory approval. . . . There is no reason to doubt that this type of conditional tender offer would be legitimate as well.

Even assuming that the Indiana Act imposes some additional delay, nothing in *MITE* suggested that *any* delay imposed by state regulation, however short, would create a conflict with the Williams Act. The plurality argued only that the offeror should "be free to go forward without *unreasonable* delay." 457 U.S., at 639, 102 S.Ct., at 2639 (emphasis added). In that case, the Court was confronted with the potential for indefinite delay and presented with no persuasive reason why some deadline could not be established. By contrast, the Indiana Act provides that full voting rights will be vested—if this eventually is to occur—within 50 days after commencement of the offer. . . .

Finally, we note that the Williams Act would pre-empt a variety of state corporate laws of hitherto unquestioned validity if it were construed to pre-empt any state statute that may limit or delay the free exercise of power after a successful tender offer. State corporate laws commonly permit corporations to stagger the terms of their directors. . . .

By staggering the terms of directors, and thus having annual elections for only one class of directors each year, corporations may delay the time when a successful offeror gains control of the board of directors. Similarly, state corporation laws commonly provide for cumulative voting. . . . By enabling minority shareholders to assure themselves of representation in each class of directors, cumulative voting provisions can delay further the ability of offerors to gain untrammeled authority over the affairs of the target corporation. . . .

In our view, the possibility that the Indiana Act will delay some tender offers is insufficient to require a conclusion that the Williams Act pre-empts the Act. . . .

III

As an alternative basis for its decision, the Court of Appeals held that the Act violates the Commerce Clause of the Federal Constitution. We now address this holding. On its face, the Commerce Clause is nothing more than a grant to Congress of the power "[t]o regulate Commerce . . . among the several States . . .," Art. I, § 8, cl. 3. But it has been settled for more than a century that the Clause prohibits States from taking certain actions respecting interstate commerce even absent congressional action. . . .

A

The principal objects of dormant Commerce Clause scrutiny are statutes that discriminate against interstate commerce. . . . The Indiana Act is not such a statute. It has the same effects on tender offers whether or not the offeror is a domiciliary or resident of Indiana. . . .

Dynamics nevertheless contends that the statute is discriminatory because it will apply most often to out-of-state entities. This argument rests on the contention that, as a practical matter, most hostile tender offers are launched by offerors outside Indiana. But this argument avails Dynamics little. "The fact that the burden of a state regulation falls on some interstate companies does not, by itself, establish a claim of discrimination against interstate commerce." Exxon Corp. v. Governor of Maryland, 437 U.S. 117, 126, 98 S.Ct. 2207, 2214, 57 L.Ed.2d 91 (1978). . . .

B

This Court's recent Commerce Clause cases also have invalidated statutes that adversely may affect interstate commerce by subjecting activities to inconsistent regulations. . . . The Indiana Act poses no such problem. So long as each State regulates voting rights only in the corporations it has created, each corporation will be subject to the law of only one State. No principle of corporation law and practice is more firmly established than a State's authority to regulate domestic corporations, including the authority to define the voting rights of shareholders. . . .

C

The Court of Appeals did not find the Act unconstitutional for either of these threshold reasons. Rather, its decision rested on its view of the Act's potential to hinder tender offers. We think the Court of Appeals failed to appreciate the significance for Commerce Clause analysis of the fact that state regulation of corporate governance is regulation of entities whose very existence and attributes are a product of state law. . . .

Every State in this country has enacted laws regulating corporate governance. By prohibiting certain transactions, and regulating others, such laws necessarily affect certain aspects of interstate commerce. This necessarily is true with respect to corporations with shareholders in States other than the State of incorporation. . . .

These regulatory laws may affect directly a variety of corporate transactions. Mergers are a typical example. In view of the substantial effect that a merger may have on the shareholders' interests in a corporation, many States require supermajority votes to approve mergers. . . .

By requiring a greater vote for mergers than is required for other transactions, these laws make it more difficult for corporations to merge. State laws also may provide for "dissenters' rights" under which minority shareholders who disagree with corporate decisions to take particular actions are entitled to sell their shares to the corporation at fair market value. . . . By requiring the corporation to purchase the shares of dissenting shareholders, these laws may inhibit a corporation from engaging in the specified transactions.

It thus is an accepted part of the business landscape in this country for States to create corporations, to prescribe their powers, and to define the rights that are acquired by purchasing their shares. A State has an interest in promoting stable relationships among parties involved in the corporations it charters, as well as in ensuring that investors in such corporations have an effective voice in corporate affairs.

There can be no doubt that the Act reflects these concerns. The primary purpose of the Act is to protect the shareholders of Indiana corporations. It does this by affording shareholders, when a takeover offer is made, an opportunity to decide collectively whether the resulting change in voting control of the corporation, as they perceive it, would be desirable. A change of management may have important effects on the shareholders' interests; it is well within the State's role as overseer of corporate governance to offer this opportunity. The autonomy provided by allowing shareholders collectively to determine whether the takeover is advantageous to their interests may be especially beneficial where a hostile tender offer may coerce shareholders into tendering their shares.

Appellee Dynamics responds to this concern by arguing that the prospect of coercive tender offers is illusory, and that tender offers generally should be favored because they reallocate corporate assets into the hands of management who can use them most effectively. . . . Indiana's concern with tender offers is not groundless. Indeed, the potentially coercive aspects of tender offers have been recognized by the

Securities and Exchange Commission, . . . and by a number of scholarly commentators. . . . The Constitution does not require the States to subscribe to any particular economic theory. We are not inclined "to second-guess the empirical judgments of lawmakers concerning the utility of legislation," Kassel v. Consolidated Freightways Corp., [450 U.S., 662, 679 (1981)] (Brennan, J., concurring in judgment). In our view, the possibility of coercion in some takeover bids offers additional justification for Indiana's decision to promote the autonomy of independent shareholders.

Dynamics argues in any event that the State has " 'no legitimate interest in protecting the nonresident shareholders.' " Brief for Appellee Dynamics Corp. of America 21 (quoting Edgar v. MITE Corp., 457 U.S., at 644). Dynamics relies heavily on the statement by the *MITE* Court that "[i]nsofar as the . . . law burdens out-of-state transactions, there is nothing to be weighed in the balance to sustain the law." 457 U.S., at 644. But that comment was made in reference to an Illinois law that applied as well to out-of-state corporations as to in-state corporations. We agree that Indiana has no interest in protecting non-resident shareholders *of nonresident corporations.* But this Act applies only to corporations incorporated in Indiana. We reject the contention that Indiana has no interest in providing for the shareholders of its corporations the voting autonomy granted by the Act. . . .

IV

On its face, the Indiana Control Share Acquisitions Chapter evenhandedly determines the voting rights of shares of Indiana corporations. The Act does not conflict with the provisions or purposes of the Williams Act. To the limited extent that the Act affects interstate commerce, this is justified by the State's interests in defining the attributes of shares in its corporations and in protecting shareholders. . . . Accordingly, we reverse the judgment of the Court of Appeals.

It is so ordered.

■ JUSTICE SCALIA, concurring in part and concurring in the judgment.

. . .

One commentator has suggested that, at least much of the time, we do not in fact mean what we say when we declare that statutes which neither discriminate against commerce nor present a threat of multiple and inconsistent burdens might nonetheless be unconstitutional under a "balancing" test. See Regan, The Supreme Court and State Protectionism: Making Sense of the Dormant Commerce Clause, 84 Mich.L.Rev. 1091 (1986). If he is not correct, he ought to be. As long as a State's corporation law governs only its own corporations and does not discriminate against out-of-state interests, it should survive this Court's scrutiny under the Commerce Clause, whether it promotes shareholder welfare or industrial stagnation. Beyond that, it is for Congress to prescribe its invalidity.

. . .

I do not share the Court's apparent high estimation of the beneficence of the state statute at issue here. But a law can be both economic folly and constitutional. The Indiana Control Shares

Acquisition Chapter is at least the latter. I therefore concur in the judgment of the Court.

■ JUSTICE WHITE, with whom JUSTICE BLACKMUN and JUSTICE STEVENS join as to Part II, dissenting.

The majority today upholds Indiana's Control Share Acquisitions Chapter, a statute which will predictably foreclose completely some tender offers for stock in Indiana corporations. I disagree with the conclusion that the Chapter is neither preempted by the Williams Act nor in conflict with the Commerce Clause. The Chapter undermines the policy of the Williams Act by effectively preventing minority shareholders, in some circumstances, from acting in their own best interests by selling their stock. In addition, the Chapter will substantially burden the interstate market in corporate ownership, particularly if other States follow Indiana's lead as many already have done. The Chapter, therefore, directly inhibits interstate commerce, the very economic consequences the Commerce Clause was intended to prevent. The opinion of the Court of Appeals is far more persuasive than that of the majority today, and the judgment of that court should be affirmed.

. . .

ANALYSIS

1. Underlying the decision in *CTS* is a nearly universal choice-of-law rule under which the law of the state of incorporation governs a corporation's "internal affairs" (which includes voting rights and other matters relating to the structure of ownership). Is this a sound rule? Why should it be, for example, that the law of Delaware governs the structure of about half of all major corporations in the United States? Does Congress have the power to impose a uniform federal law for the internal affairs of corporations?

2. Does the Indiana statute seem to you to be a justifiable response, as the Court suggests, to the need "to protect shareholders of Indiana corporations from [two-tier] coercive offer[s]"? If the objective was to protect shareholders from coercive bids, what aspect of the Indiana statute might seem incongruous? If the Supreme Court had found that the purpose of the Indiana statute was to protect local employees and business rather than shareholders, what relevance would, and should, that finding have had?

3. Think about how the Indiana law works. Suppose that on Day 1 a bidder announces a tender offer. At the same time it requests a special shareholder meeting to confer voting rights. Its offer is made contingent on a favorable vote on its voting rights. What is the timetable thereafter? How much disadvantage does the bidder suffer by virtue of the control share acquisition law?

4. Although the Court in *CTS* ducks the issue, many states adopted their anti-takeover statutes straightforwardly to protect specific local managerial interests. Indiana adopted the statute in *CTS,* for example, to protect Arvin Industries. Headquartered in Columbus, Indiana (population 30,000), Arvin had made auto parts and employed about 2000 workers. It supported the local public schools and maintained good relations with the town. In December 1985, the Belzberg family

(noted for greenmail attempts) threatened a takeover. Arvin responded by enlisting the aid of a friendly state legislator and had its lawyer write the first draft of what would become the Control Share Acquisition Chapter. The legislature adopted the bill and Arvin escaped the takeover. Similarly, the Wisconsin legislature adopted its statute in 1987 to protect the G. Heileman Brewing Company. An Australian firm threatened to take over the firm, and Heileman's lawyers responded by drafting protective legislation.* Should such evidence matter?

NOTES AND QUESTIONS ON OTHER STATE ANTI-TAKEOVER LEGISLATION

Several states had adopted anti-takeover statutes by the time of the Supreme Court's decision in *MITE* (discussed in *CTS*). After *MITE,* states adopted a second wave of statutes designed to block takeovers, but now designed them to fit within the strictures of *MITE.* After *CTS,* a third wave followed.

Particularly important is the 1988 Delaware anti-takeover statute. Del.Gen.Corp.Law § 203. Sometimes called a moratorium statute, the law kicks in if a bidder acquires at least 15 percent of a target's stock. Thereafter, the bidder may not engage in a "business combination" with the target for three years. The statute defines "business combination" broadly to include a merger between the bidder and the target, and a host of other transactions that accomplish much the same effect. Often, this inability to engage in a merger (particularly cash-out mergers to eliminate the minority shareholders) will chill any potential bidder's interest.

The Delaware statute has three important exceptions to the general ban. First, should a bidder acquire 85 percent or more of a target's stock, the ban will not apply. If the bidder buys a large enough stake, in other words, it may merge the target into itself.

Second, should a target board approve a tender offer or business combination *before* a bidder acquires 15 percent, the ban will not apply. If a bidder starts by cutting a deal with the target board, in short, the statute will let it later do a cash-out merger.

Last, the ban will not apply if a target board approves a merger after the bidder acquires its 15 percent threshold stake and ⅔ of the shares (other than shares held by the bidder) also approve the merger. Suppose, in other words, that the bidder acquires its stock and then replaces the board through a proxy fight. If it wants to cash-out the remaining target shareholders, it will need the approval of ⅔ of the other shares as well as the approval of the new board.

The Delaware statute allows corporations to opt out of the anti-takeover statute by so stating in their charter or by-laws. Note, however, that such an opt-out will not take effect for twelve months. Neither will it apply to any bidder who bought 15 percent before the amendment.

---

* Respectively, see Miller, Safe at Home: How Indiana Shielded a Firm and Changed the Takeover Business, Wall Street Journal, July 1, 1987, at 1, col. 6; Kenneth Davis, Epilogue: The Role of the Hostile Takeover and the Role of the States, 1988 Wis.L.Rev. 491, 493–97.

In contrast, Pennsylvania enacted a far more draconian set of anti-takeover rules. As later amended, Pennsylvania law contains the following provisions:

First, directors are allowed to take account of the interests not only of shareholders but also of "employees, suppliers, customers and creditors of the corporation, and . . . communities in which offices or other establishments of the corporation are located." Penn.Consol.Stat. Title 15, §§ 515(a)(1), 1715(a)(1). Even more important, the directors are expressly relieved of any obligation to treat the interests of shareholders as "dominant or controlling." §§ 515(b), 1715(b). These rules expressly apply to decisions about redeeming rights under a poison pill plan and to other decisions relating to takeovers. § 1715(c)(1). Thus, even if a change in control is inevitable and even if the result of refusing to redeem a poison pill right will be that the price paid for shares will be less than what the shareholders might have received from a hostile bidder, the board is not obligated to redeem. These rules were initially subject to a limited opt-out provision: the board (not the shareholders) could elect to opt out within 90 days of the effective date of the new law (one year in case of non-publicly traded corporations). Corporations formed after the effective date must opt out at the time of formation or soon thereafter. § 1711(b). There is still a requirement that directors must act in "good faith," which provides the authority for a court to intervene in extreme cases, but lack of good faith must be proved by "clear and convincing evidence." § 1715(d).

Second, there are provisions on control-share acquisitions (again, subject to the limited opt-out). §§ 2561–2658. In part, they follow the pattern of the Indiana law described in *CTS*. If a bidder acquires a controlling interest (20, 33⅓, or 50 percent of the voting power), the bidder loses voting rights unless it gains approval of a majority of the "disinterested" shares and a majority of all shares (other than its own). Disinterested shares are those that have been held the later of (i) twelve months before the record date for voting or (ii) five days before the first disclosure of the takeover bid. The vote-stripping rule does not apply to a person who acquires less than a controlling interest and then acquires additional voting power by obtaining revocable proxies obtained without consideration. A bidder is entitled to a special meeting on restoration of voting rights within 50 days of a request for such a meeting.

Third, and perhaps most innovative, is a provision calling for disgorgement (that is, payment to the corporation) of any gain from the sale of a corporation's shares by a person within 18 months after that person has sought or expressed an intent to seek control (20 percent of the voting power). §§ 2571–2576. The expressed intention of this provision is to remove the profit from greenmail or from putting a corporation "in play." Exemptions may be granted with the approval of both the board and the shareholders. Proxy contests are not covered if the objective was not to put the corporation "in play." Jurisdiction is asserted over persons and transactions having no connection with Pennsylvania other than purchase and sale of shares of a Pennsylvania corporation. Actions to enforce the corporation's right of recovery may be brought by a shareholder if the corporation fails to act; the shareholder is entitled to costs and attorney fees.

Fourth, there is a "tin parachute"—a provision for severance pay for all employees. An employee who is fired as a result of a takeover is entitled to a week's pay for each year of prior employment (with a maximum of 26 weeks' pay). §§ 2581–2583. This right applies only to employment in Pennsylvania. A similar tin parachute provision in the Massachusetts law has been held preempted by the federal Employee Retirement Income Security Act (ERISA), which explicitly preempts "any and all State laws" that "relate to any employee benefit plan." Simas v. Quaker Fabric Corp. of Fall River, 6 F.3d 849 (1st Cir.1993).

Finally, the new law provides that after a takeover all labor contracts are to remain in force. §§ 2585–2588.

1. The Delaware takeover statute has passed constitutional muster on several occasions. See, e.g., BNS Inc. v. Koppers Co., Inc., 683 F. Supp. 458 (D. Del. 1988) (holding that states must preserve a "meaningful opportunity" for hostile offers that are beneficial to target shareholders to succeed and finding that Delaware had done so). But what about the more draconian Pennsylvania law. Are any parts of the Pennsylvania law preempted by the Williams Act? Do any parts of the Pennsylvania law violate the Commerce Clause?

2. What, if anything, should Congress do in response to the Pennsylvania law? Is there reason to suppose that Congress would be more likely than the states to favor shareholder interests over the interests of others?

3. How would the adoption of the Pennsylvania law affect your decision to invest in a corporation incorporated in Pennsylvania that did not opt out of the provisions that are optional?

4. Are there better ways than the Pennsylvania legislation to protect nonshareholder interests? Is corporate law ever a good device for protecting nonshareholder interests?

CHAPTER 8

CORPORATE DEBT

1. INTRODUCTION

In this chapter we examine some aspects of corporate bonds and debentures. Debentures are long-term unsecured debt obligations, while bonds are long-term debt obligations secured by property of the debtor, but the word "bonds" is often used (and will be used here) in referring to debentures as well as bonds. Bonds and debentures are forms of debt owed by corporations, typically to individuals and to institutions such as pension funds, insurance companies, and mutual funds. The legal and economic issues presented in these debt instruments are much the same as those arising with bank debt (generally memorialized in a "loan agreement") and other financing. In financial parlance, corporations are said to "issue" bonds and debentures, but they "borrow" from banks; the financial relationship is essentially the same regardless of the lingo. Currently, most debt obligations to banks are secured but most other debt obligations are not. The aversion to secured debt in nonbank borrowing reflects the fact that a security interest in a corporation's property disadvantageously constrains business decisions; with a single lender, like a bank, it may be feasible to waive the constraint, while with debt held by many persons that may not be so. Moreover, the main function of a security interest is to give some creditors priority over others and there is an alternative method of doing that. The alternative is the subordination agreement, which allows debt to be issued in layers of priority. Thus, for example, a corporation might issue senior debentures and subordinated debentures, with the latter being entitled to payment only after the claims of the former have been fully satisfied.

The rights of bondholders are largely governed by private contract. Most of the contractual terms are contained in a document called an indenture, which includes, among other things, various covenants (promises). Bond indenture forms have evolved over the years and are often long and complex. Yet in the case of publicly issued bonds, the evolution is a slow process and the contractual language is highly standardized. Lenders are most concerned about the financial soundness of the borrower and the interest rate to be paid. Covenants and other terms are relatively less important and it is not practical to negotiate over these terms every time a new bond is issued. In addition to the cost of negotiation is the problem of explaining new terms to a large number of potential buyers of the bonds. This is true even though most bonds these days are sold to sophisticated institutional buyers. With sizable bank loans, however, the terms of the loan agreement may be the subject of considerable negotiation and sometimes even some innovation—not to mention hair-splitting.

Generally a corporate trustee is appointed to enforce the terms of the indenture. Corporate indenture trustees are subject to certain conflicts of interest. For one thing, the corporate trustee is likely to be part of a bank, which may have loaned money to the corporation that issued the debenture, and occasions can arise when there will be a conflict between the interests of the bank, as lender, and the interests of the debenture holders. When this happens suspicions are aroused about the loyalties of the trustee to the debenture holders. A more subtle, but perhaps more important, influence arises from the trustee's need to attract new business and from the fact that trustees are selected by issuers (who are in turn advised by people called investment bankers). The effect of this reality was illustrated in Broad v. Rockwell International Corporation, 642 F.2d 929 (5th Cir.), cert. denied, 454 U.S. 965 (1981). The issuer of the debentures in that case was merged into another firm and a question arose as to the effect on a conversion privilege (that is, a right to convert the debentures into common stock). The trustee consulted its own lawyers, who took a position contrary to that of the issuer and unfavorable to it. This gave rise to "heated disagreement" between the lawyers for the issuer and the lawyers for the trustee. There was "evidence in the record indicating that [the issuer] exerted considerable pressure on the [trustee] to change its position, threatening the withdrawal of certain other business from the [trustee] and possible litigation if the [trustee] blocked the merger by refusing to execute a supplemental indenture." 642 F.2d at 936. The upshot was that the trustee decided to "refuse to take a position as to the rights of the holders of the Debentures after the merger, relying on the provisions in the Indenture and in the supplemental indenture by which [the issuer] would indemnify the [trustee] in any lawsuits that might later be brought." Id.

2. DEBTOR'S SALE OF SUBSTANTIALLY ALL ITS ASSETS

Sharon Steel Corporation v. Chase Manhattan Bank, N.A.

691 F.2d 1039 (2d Cir.1982), cert. denied, 460 U.S. 1012 (1983).

[Several years before the events giving rise to this case, UV Industries (UV) had issued certain debentures. These debentures bore interest at rates lower than the prevailing market rates for newly issued obligations with similar characteristics. Because of the low interest rates, the debentures' market value was less than their face amount (that is, the amount payable on maturity).

Early in 1979, UV adopted a plan to liquidate by selling all its assets and distributing the proceeds to its shareholders. Under tax rules in effect at the time (but not now), it was important that the liquidation be accomplished within twelve months.

UV had three lines of business. One was carried on by a subsidiary called Federal Pacific Electric Company (Federal), which generated 60 percent of UV's operating revenue and 81 percent of its operating profits. The second line of business consisted of oil and gas properties that generated 2 percent of operating revenues and 6 percent of operating profits. The third line of business, involving metal mining and manufacturing, was carried on largely by a subsidiary called Mueller Brass Company, and accounted for 38 percent of operating revenues and 13 percent of operating profits. UV also held substantial cash and other liquid assets.

On March 29, 1979, UV sold Federal to Reliance Electric Company for $345 million in cash, part of which was distributed to the UV shareholders.

On October 2, UV sold the oil and gas properties to Tenneco Oil Company for $135 million in cash.

These transactions left UV with Mueller Brass and some mining properties, plus cash of $322 million, subject to the claim of the debenture holders in a total face amount of about $123 million. On November 26, Sharon Steel Corporation (Sharon) bought all of UV's remaining assets (including the cash). Sharon paid with cash of $107 million plus its subordinated debentures that had a market value of about $353 million. As previously mentioned the market value of the $123 million of UV debentures was less than their face amount because they had been issued at a time when interest rates were lower. Apparently it was not feasible for UV or Sharon to buy back the debentures in market transactions (presumably because, as bondholders became aware of efforts by UV or Sharon to purchase, they would hold out for a higher-than-market price). The question then arose whether, by virtue of the liquidation of UV, the debentures became due and payable. If they did, then the debenture holders would be better off. They would receive the face amount of the debentures and could reinvest at current interest rates. Correspondingly, Sharon would need to borrow at a higher interest cost.[1]

The following provision, from one of the indentures at issue in the case, uses typical language relating to assumption of indebtedness in the event of merger, consolidation, or sale of all or substantially all of the assets of the debtor:

> *Company May Consolidate, etc., on Certain Terms.* Nothing contained in this Indenture or in any of the Notes shall prevent any consolidation or merger of the Company with or into any other corporation or corporations (whether or not affiliated with the Company), . . . or shall prevent any sale, conveyance or lease of all or substantially all of the property of the Company to any other corporation (whether or not affiliated with the Company) authorized to acquire and operate the same; *provided, however,* and the Company hereby covenants and agrees, that any such consolidation, merger, sale, conveyance or lease shall be upon the condition that (a) immediately after such consolidation, merger, sale, conveyance or lease the corporation (whether the Company or such other corporation) formed by or surviving any such consolidation or merger, or to which such sale, conveyance or lease shall have been made, shall not be in default in the performance or observance of any of the terms, covenants and conditions of this Indenture to be kept or performed by the Company; (b) the corporation (if other than the Company)

---

1 Suppose, for example, that the interest rate on the debentures was 7 percent. The total interest payments would be 7 percent of $123 million, or $8.61 million. Suppose the current interest rate was 10 percent. If Sharon were required to redeem the debentures for the face amount of $123 million, the holders could reinvest that amount and earn 10 percent, or $12.3 million, annually, and Sharon's interest cost for replacing the funds would be the same amount (or perhaps more since Sharon was already apparently heavily laden with debt). The total value to the debenture holders, and the total cost to Sharon, over time would depend on the number of years until the debentures would be paid off in any event—that is, the number of years to maturity.

> formed by or surviving any such consolidation or merger, or to which such sale, conveyance or lease shall have been made, shall be a corporation organized under the laws of the United States of America or any State thereof; and (c) the due and punctual payment of the principal of and interest on all of the Notes, according to their tenor, and the due and punctual performance and observance of all of the covenants and conditions of this Indenture to be performed or observed by the Company, shall be expressly assumed, by supplemental indenture satisfactory in form to the Trustee, executed and delivered to the Trustee, by the corporation (if other than the Company) formed by such consolidation . . ., or by the corporation which shall have acquired or leased such property.
>
> The opinion of the court, by Ralph K. Winter, Circuit Judge, follows.]

Sharon Steel argues that [the trial judge] erred in not submitting to the jury issues going to the meaning of the successor obligor clauses. We disagree.

Successor obligor clauses are "boilerplate" or contractual provisions which are standard in a certain genre of contracts. Successor obligor clauses are thus found in virtually all indentures. Such boilerplate must be distinguished from contractual provisions which are peculiar to a particular indenture and [thus such boilerplate] must be given a consistent, uniform interpretation. As the American Bar Foundation *Commentaries on Indentures* (1971) ("*Commentaries*") state:

> Since there is seldom any difference in the intended meaning, [boilerplate] provisions are susceptible of standardized expression. The use of standardized language can result in a better and quicker understanding of those provisions and a substantial saving of time not only for the draftsman but also for the parties and all others who must comply with or refer to the indenture, including governmental bodies whose approval or authorization of the issuance of the securities is required by law.

Id.

Boilerplate provisions are thus not the consequence of the relationship of particular borrowers and lenders and do not depend upon particularized intentions of the parties to an indenture. There are no adjudicative facts relating to the parties to the litigation for a jury to find and the meaning of boilerplate provisions is, therefore, a matter of law rather than fact.

Moreover, uniformity in interpretation is important to the efficiency of capital markets. . . . Whereas participants in the capital market can adjust their affairs according to a uniform interpretation, whether it be correct or not as an initial proposition, the creation of enduring uncertainties as to the meaning of boilerplate provisions would decrease the value of all debenture issues and greatly impair the efficient working of capital markets. . . .

We turn now to the meaning of the successor obligor clauses. Interpretation of indenture provisions is a matter of basic contract law. As the *Commentaries* at 2 state:

> The second fundamental characteristic of long term debt financing is that the rights of holders of the debt securities are largely a matter of contract. There is no governing body of statutory or common law that protects the holder of unsecured debt securities against harmful acts by the debtor except in the most extreme situations . . . [T]he debt securityholder can do nothing to protect himself against actions of the borrower which jeopardize its ability to pay the debt unless he . . . establishes his rights through contractual provisions set forth in the . . . indenture.

Contract language is thus the starting point in the search for meaning and Sharon argues strenuously that the language of the successor obligor clauses clearly permits its assumption of UV's public debt. Sharon's argument is a masterpiece of simplicity: on November 26, 1979, it bought everything UV owned; therefore, the transaction was a "sale" of "all" UV's "assets." In Sharon's view, the contention of the Indenture Trustees and Debentureholders that proceeds from earlier sales in a predetermined plan of piecemeal liquidation may not be counted in determining whether a later sale involves "all assets" must be rejected because it imports a meaning not evident in the language.

Sharon's literalist approach simply proves too much. If proceeds from earlier piecemeal sales are "assets," then UV continued to own "all" its "assets" even after the Sharon transaction since the proceeds of that transaction, including the $107 million cash for cash "sale," went into the UV treasury. If the language is to be given the "literal" meaning attributed to it by Sharon, therefore, UV's "assets" were not "sold" on November 26 and the ensuing liquidation requires the redemption of the debentures by UV. Sharon's literal approach is thus self-defeating.

The words "all or substantially all" are used in a variety of statutory and contractual provisions relating to transfers of assets and have been given meaning in light of the particular context and evident purpose. . . . [A] literal reading of the words "all or substantially all" is not helpful apart from reference to the underlying purpose to be served. We turn, therefore, to that purpose.

Sharon argues that the sole purpose of successor obligor clauses is to leave the borrower free to merge, liquidate or to sell its assets in order to enter a wholly new business free of public debt and that they are not intended to offer any protection to lenders. On their face, however, they seem designed to protect lenders as well by assuring a degree of continuity of assets. Thus, a borrower which sells all its assets does not have an option to continue holding the debt. It must either assign the debt or pay it off.

Where contractual language seems designed to protect the interests of both parties and where conflicting interpretations are argued, the contract should be construed to sacrifice the principal interests of each party as little as possible. An interpretation which sacrifices a major interest of one of the parties while furthering only a marginal interest of the other should be rejected in favor of an interpretation which sacrifices marginal interests of both parties in order to protect their major concerns.

Of the contending positions, we believe that of the Indenture Trustees and Debentureholders best accommodates the principal interests of corporate borrowers and their lenders. Even if the UV/Sharon transaction is held not to be covered by the successor obligor clauses, borrowers are free to merge, consolidate or dispose of the operating assets of the business. Accepting Sharon's position, however, would severely impair the interests of lenders. Sharon's view would allow a borrowing corporation to engage in a piecemeal sale of assets, with concurrent liquidating dividends to that point at which the asset restrictions of an indenture prohibited further distribution. A sale of "all or substantially all" of the remaining assets could then be consummated, a new debtor substituted, and the liquidation of the borrower completed. The assignment of the public debt might thus be accomplished, even though the last sale might be nothing more than a cash for cash transaction in which the buyer purchases the public indebtedness. The UV/Sharon transaction is not so extreme, but the sale price paid by Sharon did include a cash for cash exchange of $107 million. Twenty-three percent of the sale price was, in fact, an exchange of dollars for dollars. Such a transaction diminishes the protection for lenders in order to facilitate deals with little functional significance other than substituting a new debtor in order to profit on a debenture's low interest rate. We hold, therefore, that boilerplate successor obligor clauses do not permit assignment of the public debt to another party in the course of a liquidation unless "all or substantially all" of the assets of the company at the time the plan of liquidation is determined upon are transferred to a single purchaser.

The application of this rule to the present case is not difficult. The plan of liquidation was approved by UV's shareholders on March 26, 1978. Since the Indenture Trustees make no claim as to an earlier time, e.g., the date of the Board recommendation, we accept March 26 as the appropriate reference date. The question then is whether "all or substantially all" of the assets held by UV on that date were transferred to Sharon. That is easily answered. The assets owned by UV on March 26 and later transferred to Sharon were Mueller Brass, certain metals mining property, and substantial amounts of cash and other liquid assets. . . . Mueller Brass and the metals mining properties were responsible for only 38% of UV's 1978 operating revenues and 13% of its operating profits. They constitute 41% of the book value of UV's operating properties. When the cash and other liquid assets are added, the transaction still involved only 51% of the book value of UV's total assets.

Since we do not regard the question in this case as even close, we need not determine how the substantiality of corporate assets is to be measured, what percentage meets the "all or substantially all" test or what role a jury might play in determining those issues. Even when the liquid assets (other than proceeds from the sale of Federal and the oil and gas properties) are aggregated with the operating properties, the transfer to Sharon accounted for only 51% of the total book value of UV's assets. In no sense, therefore, are they "all or substantially all" of those assets. The successor obligor clauses are, therefore, not applicable. UV is thus in default on the indentures and the debentures are due and payable.

. . .

CONCLUSION

We affirm [the trial judge's] dismissal of Sharon's amended complaint and award of judgment to the Indenture Trustees and Debentureholders on their claim that the debentures are due and payable. . . .

ANALYSIS

1. If the decision had been in favor of Sharon, what, if any, meaning and effect would the "substantially all" language have had?

2. UV was constrained by federal tax rules in effect at the time the case arose. Under those rules, in order to avoid corporate tax on the sale of its assets, UV needed to sell all its assets and distribute the proceeds within a twelve-month period following the adoption of the liquidation plan. Had it not been for this tax constraint, how would you have advised UV to proceed with its liquidation, given its goal of preserving the favorable loans.

3. The court also says, "Accepting Sharon's position . . . would severely impair the interests of lenders." Do you agree? By comparison, suppose Jack buys a house, for use as a personal residence, for $100,000, using $20,000 of his own money and $80,000 from a nonrecourse 30-year loan. Two years later the amount that remains due on the loan is $79,000; the market value of the house has declined to $78,000, but interest rates have risen and the value of the loan has declined to $70,000. Jack then sells the house to Jill, who pays Jack $8,000 and assumes the mortgage, which is assignable and does not include a due-on-sale clause. Does the transfer harm the lender? Is this situation different from that in *Sharon Steel*?

PLANNING

Suppose you had represented UV at the time it prepared to issue the debentures and that you had anticipated the problem that gave rise to the *Sharon Steel* decision. Suppose further that the debentures were to be sold to a small number of large insurance companies represented by shrewd, tough-minded, but reasonable, lawyers. What language might you have sought to include in the indenture to allow UV to take full advantage of a favorable loan in the event of a liquidation subject to the tax constraint?

3. INCURRENCE OF ADDITIONAL DEBT

Metropolitan Life Insurance Company v. RJR Nabisco, Inc.

716 F.Supp. 1504 (S.D.N.Y.1989).

I. Introduction

The corporate parties to this action are among the country's most sophisticated financial institutions, as familiar with the Wall Street investment community and the securities market as American consumers are with the Oreo cookies and Winston cigarettes made by defendant RJR Nabisco, Inc. (sometimes "the company" or "RJR Nabisco"). The present action traces its origins to October 20, 1988, when F. Ross Johnson, then the Chief Executive Officer of RJR Nabisco, proposed a $17 billion leveraged buy-out ("LBO") of the company's shareholders, at $75 per share. Within a few days, a bidding war developed among the investment group led by Johnson and the investment firm of Kohlberg Kravis Roberts & Co. ("KKR"), and others. On December 1, 1988, a special committee of RJR Nabisco directors, established by the company specifically to consider the competing proposals, recommended that the company accept the KKR proposal, a $24 billion LBO that called for the purchase of the company's outstanding stock at roughly $109 per share.

. . .

Plaintiffs . . . allege, in short, that RJR Nabisco's actions have drastically impaired the value of bonds previously issued to plaintiffs by, in effect, misappropriating the value of those bonds to help finance the LBO and to distribute an enormous windfall to the company's shareholders. As a result, plaintiffs argue, they have unfairly suffered a multimillion dollar loss in the value of their bonds.

. . .

Plaintiffs move for summary judgment pursuant to Fed.R.Civ.P. 56 against the company on Count I, which alleges a "Breach of Implied Covenant of Good Faith and Fair Dealing," and against both defendants on Count V, which is labeled simply "In Equity."

Although the numbers involved in this case are large, and the financing necessary to complete the LBO unprecedented, the legal principles nonetheless remain discrete and familiar. Yet while the instant motions thus primarily require the Court to evaluate and apply traditional rules of equity and contract interpretation, plaintiffs do raise issues of first impression in the context of an LBO. At the heart of the present motions lies plaintiffs' claim that RJR Nabisco violated a restrictive covenant—not an explicit covenant found within the four corners of the relevant bond indentures, but rather an *implied* covenant of good faith and fair dealing—not to incur the debt necessary to facilitate the LBO and thereby betray what plaintiffs claim was the fundamental basis of their bargain with the company. The company, plaintiffs assert, consistently reassured its bondholders that it had a "mandate" from its Board of Directors to maintain RJR Nabisco's preferred credit rating. Plaintiffs ask this Court first to imply a covenant of good faith and fair dealing that would prevent the recent transaction, then to hold that this covenant has been breached, and finally to require RJR Nabisco to redeem their bonds.

RJR Nabisco defends the LBO by pointing to express provisions in the bond indentures that, *inter alia,* permit mergers and the assumption of additional debt. These provisions, as well as others that could have been included but were not, were known to the market and to plaintiffs, sophisticated investors who freely bought the bonds and were equally free to sell them at any time. Any attempt by this Court to create contractual terms *post hoc,* defendants contend, not only finds no basis in the controlling law and undisputed facts of this case, but also would constitute an impermissible invasion into the free and open operation of the marketplace.

For the reasons set forth below, this Court agrees with defendants. There being no express covenant between the parties that would restrict the incurrence of new debt, and no perceived direction to that end from covenants that are express, this Court will not imply a covenant to prevent the recent LBO and thereby create an indenture term that, while bargained for in other contexts, was not bargained for here and was not even within the mutual contemplation of the parties.

II. Background

. . .

A. The Parties:

Metropolitan Life Insurance Co. ("MetLife"), incorporated in New York, is a life insurance company that provides pension benefits for 42 million individuals. According to its most recent annual report, MetLife's assets exceed $88 billion and its debt securities holdings exceed $49 billion. . . . MetLife alleges that it owns $340,542,000 in principal amount of six separate RJR Nabisco debt issues, bonds allegedly purchased between July 1975 and July 1988. Some bonds become due as early as this year; others will not become due until 2017. The bonds bear interest rates of anywhere from 8 to 10.25 percent. MetLife also owned 186,000 shares of RJR Nabisco common stock at the time this suit was filed.

Jefferson-Pilot Life Insurance Co. ("Jefferson-Pilot") is a North Carolina company that has more than $3 billion in total assets, $1.5 billion of which are invested in debt securities. Jefferson-Pilot alleges that it owns $9.34 million in principal amount of three separate RJR Nabisco debt issues, allegedly purchased between June 1978 and June 1988. Those bonds, bearing interest rates of anywhere from 8.45 to 10.75 percent, become due in 1993 and 1998.

RJR Nabisco, a Delaware corporation, is a consumer products holding company that owns some of the country's best known product lines, including LifeSavers candy, Oreo cookies, and Winston cigarettes. The company was formed in 1985, when R.J. Reynolds Industries, Inc. ("R.J. Reynolds") merged with Nabisco Brands, Inc. ("Nabisco Brands"). In 1979, and thus before the R.J. Reynolds-Nabisco Brands merger, R.J. Reynolds acquired the Del Monte Corporation ("Del Monte"), which distributes canned fruits and vegetables. From January 1987 until February 1989, co-defendant Johnson served as the company's CEO. KKR, a private investment firm, organizes funds through which investors provide pools of equity to finance LBOs.

B. The Indentures:

The bonds[9] implicated by this suit are governed by long, detailed indentures, which in turn are governed by New York contract law.[10] No one disputes that the holders of public bond issues, like plaintiffs here, often enter the market after the indentures have been negotiated and

[9] For the purposes of this Opinion, the terms "bonds," "debentures," and "notes" will be used interchangeably. Any distinctions among these terms are not relevant to the present motions.

[10] Both sides agree that New York law controls this Court's interpretation of the indentures, which contain explicit designations to that effect. . . .

memorialized. Thus, those indentures are often not the product of face-to-face negotiations between the ultimate holders and the issuing company. What remains equally true, however, is that underwriters ordinarily negotiate the terms of the indentures with the issuers. Since the underwriters must then sell or place the bonds, they necessarily negotiate in part with the interests of the buyers in mind. Moreover, these indentures were not secret agreements foisted upon unwitting participants in the bond market. No successive holder is required to accept or to continue to hold the bonds, governed by their accompanying indentures; indeed, plaintiffs readily admit that they could have sold their bonds right up until the announcement of the LBO. Instead, sophisticated investors like plaintiffs are well aware of the indenture terms and, presumably, review them carefully before lending hundreds of millions of dollars to any company.

Indeed, the prospectuses for the indentures contain a statement relevant to this action:

> The Indenture contains no restrictions on the creation of unsecured short-term debt by [RJR Nabisco] or its subsidiaries, no restriction on the creation of unsecured Funded Debt by [RJR Nabisco] or its subsidiaries which are not Restricted Subsidiaries, and no restriction on the payment of dividends by [RJR Nabisco].

Further, as plaintiffs themselves note, the contracts at issue "[do] not impose debt limits, since debt is assumed to be used for productive purposes."

1. The relevant Articles:

A typical RJR Nabisco indenture contains thirteen Articles. At least four of them are relevant to the present motions and thus merit a brief review.

Article Three delineates the covenants of the issuer. Most important, it first provides for payment of principal and interest. It then addresses various mechanical provisions regarding such matters as payment terms and trustee vacancies. The Article also contains "negative pledge" and related provisions, which restrict mortgages or other liens on the assets of RJR Nabisco or its subsidiaries and seek to protect the bondholders from being subordinated to other debt.

Article Five describes various procedures to remedy defaults and the responsibilities of the Trustee. This Article includes the distinction in the indentures noted above. . . . In seven of the nine securities at issue, a provision in Article Five prohibits bondholders from suing for any remedy based on rights in the indentures unless 25 percent of the holders have requested in writing that the indenture trustee seek such relief, and, after 60 days, the trustee has not sued. Defendants argue that this provision precludes plaintiffs from suing on these seven securities. Given its holdings today, see infra, the Court need not address this issue.

. . .

Article Ten addresses a potential "Consolidation, Merger, Sale or Conveyance," and explicitly sets forth the conditions under which the company can consolidate or merge into or with any other corporation. It provides explicitly that RJR Nabisco "may consolidate with, or sell or convey, all or substantially all of its assets to, or merge into or with any other corporation," so long as the new entity is a United States corporation, and so long as it assumes RJR Nabisco's debt. The Article also requires that any such transaction not result in the company's default under any indenture provision.

2. The elimination of restrictive covenants:

In its Amended Complaint, MetLife lists the six debt issues on which it bases its claims. Indentures for two of those issues . . . once contained express covenants that, among other things, restricted the company's ability to incur precisely the sort of debt involved in the recent LBO. In order to eliminate those restrictions, the parties to this action renegotiated the terms of those indentures, first in 1983 and then again in 1985.

. . .

3. The recognition and effect of the LBO trend:

Other internal MetLife documents help frame the background to this action, for they accurately describe the changing securities markets and the responses those changes engendered from sophisticated market participants, such as MetLife and Jefferson-Pilot. At least as early as 1982, MetLife recognized an LBO's effect on bond values. In the spring of that year, MetLife participated in the financing of an LBO of a company called Reeves Brothers ("Reeves"). At the time of that LBO, MetLife also held bonds in that company. Subsequent to the LBO, as a MetLife memorandum explained, the "Debentures of Reeves were downgraded by Standard & Poor's from BBB to B and by Moody's from Baal to Ba3, thereby lowering the value of the Notes and Debentures held by [MetLife]." MetLife Memorandum, dated August 20, 1982.

MetLife further recognized its "inability to force any type of payout of the [Reeves'] Notes or the Debentures as a result of the buy-out [which] was somewhat disturbing at the time we considered a participation in the new financing. However," the memorandum continued,

> our concern was tempered since, as a stockholder in [the holding company used to facilitate the transaction], we would benefit from the increased net income attributable to the continued presence of the low coupon indebtedness. The recent downgrading of the Reeves Debentures and the consequent "loss" in value has again raised questions regarding our ability to have forced a payout. *Questions have also been raised about our ability to force payouts in similar future situations, particularly when we would not be participating in the buyout financing.*

Id. (emphasis added). In the memorandum, MetLife sought to answer those very "questions" about how it might force payouts in "similar future situations."

> *A method of closing this apparent "loophole," thereby forcing a payout of [MetLife's] holdings, would be through a covenant dealing with a change in ownership.* Such a covenant is fairly standard in financings with privately-held companies . . . It provides the lender with an option to end a particular borrowing relationship via some type of special redemption . . .

Id., at 2 (emphasis added).

A more comprehensive memorandum, prepared in late 1985, evaluated and explained several aspects of the corporate world's increasing use of mergers, takeovers and other debt-financed transactions. That memorandum first reviewed the available protection for lenders such as MetLife:

> Covenants are incorporated into loan documents to ensure that after a lender makes a loan, the creditworthiness of the borrower and the lender's ability to reach the borrower's assets do not deteriorate substantially. *Restrictions on the incurrence of debt,* sale of assets, mergers, dividends, restricted payments and loans and advances to affiliates *are some of the traditional negative covenants that can help protect lenders in the event their obligors become involved in undesirable merger/takeover situations.*

MetLife Northeastern Office Memorandum, dated November 27, 1985, (emphasis added). The memorandum then surveyed market realities:

> Because almost any industrial company is apt to engineer a takeover or be taken over itself, *Business Week* says that investors are beginning to view debt securities of high grade industrial corporations as Wall Street's riskiest investments. In addition, *because public bondholders do not enjoy the protection of any restrictive covenants,* owners of high grade corporates face substantial losses from takeover situations, if not immediately, then when the bond market finally adjusts. . . . [T]here have been 10–15 merger/takeover/LBO situations where, *due to the lack of covenant protection, [MetLife] has had no choice but to remain a lender to a less creditworthy obligor. . . . The fact that the quality of our investment portfolio is greater than the other large insurance companies . . . may indicate that we have negotiated better covenant protection than other institutions, thus generally being able to require prepayment when situations become too risky . . . [However,] a problem exists. And* because the current merger craze is not likely to decelerate *and because there exist vehicles to circumvent traditional covenants, the problem will probably continue. Therefore,* perhaps it is time to institute appropriate language designed to protect Metropolitan from the negative implications of mergers and takeovers.

Id. at 2–4 (emphasis added).

Indeed, MetLife does not dispute that, as a member of a bondholders' association, it received and discussed a proposed model indenture, which included a "comprehensive covenant" entitled "Limitations on Shareholders' Payments."[16] As becomes clear from reading the proposed—but never adopted—provision, it was "intend[ed] to provide protection against all of the types of situations in which shareholders profit at the expense of bondholders." Id. The provision dictated that the

[16] See Bradley Resp.Aff.Exh.F. That exhibit is an August 5, 1988 letter from the New York law firm of Kaye, Scholer, Fierman, Hays & Handler. A partner at that firm sent the letter to "Indenture Group Members," including MetLife, who participated in the Institutional Bondholders' Rights Association ("the IBRA"). The "Limitations on Shareholders' Payments" provision appears in a draft IBRA model indenture.

"[c]orporation will not, and will not permit any [s]ubsidiary to, directly or indirectly, make any [s]hareholder [p]ayment unless . . . (1) the aggregate amount of all [s]hareholder payments during the period [at issue] . . . shall not exceed [figure left blank]." The term "shareholder payments" is defined to include "restructuring distributions, stock repurchases, debt incurred or guaranteed to finance merger payments to shareholders, etc."

Apparently, that provision—or provisions with similar intentions—never went beyond the discussion stage at MetLife. That fact is easily understood; indeed, MetLife's own documents articulate several reasonable, undisputed explanations:

> While it would be possible to broaden the change in ownership covenant to cover any acquisition-oriented transaction, *we might well encounter significant resistance in implementation with larger public companies*. . . . With respect to implementation, we would be faced with the task of imposing a non-standard limitation on potential borrowers, *which could be a difficult task in today's highly competitive marketplace. Competitive pressures notwithstanding, it would seem that management of larger public companies would be particularly opposed to such a covenant since its effect would be to increase the cost of an acquisition* (due to an assumed debt repayment), a factor that could well lower the price of any tender offer (thereby impacting shareholders).

Bradley Reply Aff.Exh.D, at 3 (emphasis added). The November 1985 memorandum explained that

> [o]bviously, our ability to implement methods of takeover protection will vary between the public and private market. In that public securities do not contain any meaningful covenants, it would be very difficult for [MetLife] to demand takeover protection in public bonds. Such a requirement would effectively take us out of the public industrial market. A recent *Business Week* article does suggest, however, that there is increasing talk among lending institutions about requiring blue chip companies to compensate them for the growing risk of downgradings. *This talk, regarding such protection as restrictions on future debt financings, is met with skepticism by the investment banking community which feels that CFO's [chief financial officers] are not about to give up the option of adding debt and do not really care if their companies' credit ratings drop a notch or two.*

The Court quotes these documents at such length not because they represent an "admission" or "waiver" from MetLife, or an "assumption of risk" in any tort sense, or its "consent" to any particular course of conduct—all terms discussed at even greater length in the parties' submissions. Rather, the documents set forth the background to the present action, and highlight the risks inherent in the market itself, for any investor. Investors as sophisticated as MetLife and Jefferson-Pilot would be hard-pressed to plead ignorance of these market risks. Indeed, MetLife has not disputed the facts asserted in its own internal documents. Nor has Jefferson-Pilot—presumably an institution no less sophisticated than MetLife—offered any reason to believe that its understanding of the securities market differed in any material respect from the description and analysis set forth in the MetLife documents.

Those documents, after all, were not born in a vacuum. They are descriptions of, and responses to, the market in which investors like MetLife and Jefferson-Pilot knowingly participated.

These documents must be read in conjunction with plaintiffs' Amended Complaint. That document asserts that the LBO "undermines the foundation of the investment grade debt market . . .,"; that, although "the indentures do not purport to limit dividends or debt . . . [s]uch covenants were believed unnecessary with blue chip companies . . ."; that "the transaction contradicts the premise of the investment grade market . . ."; and, finally, that "[t]his buy-out was not contemplated at the time the debt was issued, contradicts the premise of the investment grade ratings that RJR Nabisco actively solicited and received, and is inconsistent with the understandings of the market . . . which [p]laintiffs relied upon."

Solely for the purposes of these motions, the Court accepts various factual assertions advanced by plaintiffs: first, that RJR Nabisco actively solicited "investment grade" ratings for its debt; second, that it relied on descriptions of its strong capital structure and earnings record which included prominent display of its ability to pay the interest obligations on its long-term debt several times over, Am.Comp. & 14; and third, that the company made express or implied representations not contained in the relevant indentures concerning its future creditworthiness. Id. & 15. In support of those allegations, plaintiffs have marshaled a number of speeches made by co-defendant Johnson and other executives of RJR Nabisco.[18]

. . .

III. Discussion

At the outset, the Court notes that nothing in its evaluation is substantively altered by the speeches given or remarks made by RJR Nabisco executives, or the opinions of various individuals—what, for instance, former RJR Nabisco Treasurer Dowdle personally did or did not "firmly believe" the indentures meant. The parol evidence rule bars plaintiffs from arguing that the speeches made by company executives prove defendants agreed or acquiesced to a term that does not appear in the indenture. . . .

The indentures at issue clearly address the eventuality of a merger. They impose certain related restrictions not at issue in this suit, but no restriction that would prevent the recent RJR Nabisco merger transaction. . . .

Under certain circumstances, however, courts will, as plaintiffs note, consider extrinsic evidence to evaluate the scope of an implied covenant of good faith. See Valley National Bank v. Babylon Chrysler-Plymouth, Inc., 53 Misc.2d 1029, 1031–32, 280 N.Y.S.2d 786, 788–89

[18] See, e.g., Address by F. Ross Johnson, November 12, 1987, P.Exh. 8, at 5 ("Our strong balance sheet is a cornerstone of our strategies. It gives us the resources to modernize facilities, develop new technologies, bring on new products, and support our leading brands around the world."); Remarks of Edward J. Robinson, Executive Vice President and Chief Financial Officer, February 15, 1988, P.Exh. 6, at 1 ("RJR Nabisco's financial strategy is . . . to enhance the strength of the balance sheet by reducing the level of debt as well as lowering the cost of existing debt."); Remarks by Dr. Robert J. Carbonell, Vice Chairman of RJR Nabisco, June 3, 1987, P.Exh. 10, at 5 ("We will not sacrifice our longer-term health for the sake of short term heroics.").

(Sup.Ct.Nassau), aff'd, 28 A.D.2d 1092, 284 N.Y.S.2d 849 (2d Dep't 1967) (Relying on custom and usage because "[w]hen a contract fails to establish the time for performance, the law implies that the act shall be done within a reasonable time . . ."). However, the Second Circuit has established a different rule for customary, or boilerplate, provisions of detailed indentures used and relied upon throughout the securities market, such as those at issue. Ignoring these principles, plaintiffs would have this Court vary what they themselves have admitted is "indenture boilerplate" of "standard" agreements to comport with collateral representations and their subjective understandings.[20]

A. *Plaintiffs' Case Against the RJR Nabisco LBO:*

1. Count One: The implied covenant:

> In their first count, plaintiffs assert that [d]efendant RJR Nabisco owes a continuing duty of good faith and fair dealing in connection with the contract [i.e., the indentures] through which it borrowed money from MetLife, Jefferson-Pilot and other holders of its debt, including a duty not to frustrate the purpose of the contracts to the debtholders or to deprive the debtholders of the intended object of the contracts—purchase of investment-grade securities.
>
> In the "buy-out," the [c]ompany breaches the duty [or implied covenant] of good faith and fair dealing by, *inter alia,* destroying the investment grade quality of the debt and transferring that value to the "buy-out" proponents and to the shareholders.

In effect, plaintiffs contend that express covenants were not necessary because an *implied* covenant would prevent what defendants have now done.

A plaintiff always can allege a violation of an express covenant. If there has been such a violation, of course, the court need not reach the question of whether or not an *implied* covenant has been violated.

In contracts like bond indentures, "an implied covenant . . . derives its substance directly from the language of the Indenture, and 'cannot give the holders of Debentures any rights inconsistent with those set out in the Indenture.' *[Where] plaintiffs' contractual rights [have not been] violated, there can have been no breach of an implied covenant.*" Gardner & Florence Call Cowles Foundation v. Empire Inc., 589 F.Supp. 669, 673 (S.D.N.Y.1984), vacated on procedural grounds, 754 F.2d 478 (2d Cir.1985) (quoting Broad v. Rockwell, 642 F.2d 929, 957 (5th Cir.) (en banc), cert. denied, 454 U.S. 965, 102 S.Ct. 506, 70 L.Ed.2d 380 (1981)) (emphasis added).

---

20 To a certain extent, this discussion is academic. Even if the Court did consider the extrinsic evidence offered by plaintiffs, its ultimate decision would be no different. Based on that extrinsic evidence, plaintiffs attempt to establish that an implied covenant of good faith is necessary to protect the benefits of their agreements. That inquiry necessarily asks the Court to determine whether the existing contractual terms should be construed to preclude defendants from engaging in an LBO along the lines of the recently completed transaction. However, even evaluating *all* facts—such as the public statements made by company executives—in the light most favorable to plaintiffs, these plaintiffs fail as a matter of law to establish that the purported "fundamental basis" of their bargain with defendants created a contractual obligation on the part of the defendants not to engage in an LBO. . . .

. . .

The appropriate analysis, then, is first to examine the indentures to determine "the fruits of the agreement" between the parties, and then to decide whether those "fruits" have been spoiled—which is to say, whether plaintiffs' contractual rights have been violated by defendants.

The American Bar Foundation's *Commentaries on Indentures* ("the *Commentaries*"), relied upon and respected by both plaintiffs and defendants, describes the rights and risks generally found in bond indentures like those at issue:

> The most obvious and important characteristic of long-term debt financing is that the holder ordinarily has not bargained for and does not expect any substantial gain in the value of the security to compensate for the risk of loss . . . [T]he significant fact, *which accounts in part for the detailed protective provisions of the typical long-term debt financing instrument,* is that *the lender (the purchaser of the debt security) can expect only interest at the prescribed rate plus the eventual return of the principal.* Except for possible increases in the market value of the debt security because of changes in interest rates, the debt security will seldom be worth more than the lender paid for it . . . It may, of course, become worth much less. Accordingly, the typical investor in a long-term debt security is primarily interested in every reasonable assurance that the principal and interest will be paid when due. . . . Short of bankruptcy, *the debt security holder can do nothing to protect himself against actions of the borrower which jeopardize its ability to pay the debt unless he . . . establishes his rights through contractual provisions set forth in the debt agreement or indenture.*

Id. at 1–2 (1971) (emphasis added).

A review of the parties' submissions and the indentures themselves satisfies the Court that the substantive "fruits" guaranteed by those contracts and relevant to the present motions include the periodic and regular payment of interest and the eventual repayment of principal. . . .

It is not necessary to decide that indentures like those at issue could never support a finding of additional benefits, under different circumstances with different parties. Rather, for present purposes, it is sufficient to conclude what obligation is *not* covered, either explicitly or implicitly, by these contracts held by these plaintiffs. Accordingly, this Court holds that the "fruits" of these indentures do not include an implied restrictive covenant that would prevent the incurrence of new debt to facilitate the recent LBO. To hold otherwise would permit these plaintiffs to straightjacket the company in order to guarantee their investment. These plaintiffs do not invoke an implied covenant of good faith to protect a legitimate, mutually contemplated benefit of the indentures; rather, they seek to have this Court create an additional benefit for which they did not bargain.

. . .

The sort of unbounded and one-sided elasticity urged by plaintiffs would interfere with and destabilize the market. And this Court, like the parties to these contracts, cannot ignore or disavow the marketplace in which the contract is performed. Nor can it ignore the expectations of that market—expectations, for instance, that the terms of an indenture will be upheld, and that a court will not, *sua sponte,* add new substantive terms to that indenture as it sees fit. The Court has no reason to believe that the market, in evaluating bonds such as those at issue here, did not discount for the possibility that any company, even one the size of RJR Nabisco, might engage in an LBO heavily financed by debt. That the bonds did not lose any of their value until the October 20, 1988 announcement of a possible RJR Nabisco LBO only suggests that the market had theretofore evaluated the risks of such a transaction as slight.

. . .

Ultimately, plaintiffs cannot escape the inherent illogic of their argument. On the one hand, it is undisputed that investors like plaintiffs recognized that companies like RJR Nabisco strenuously opposed additional restrictive covenants that might limit the incurrence of new debt or the company's ability to engage in a merger. Furthermore, plaintiffs argue that they had no choice other than to accept the indentures as written, without additional restrictive covenants, or to "abandon" the market.

Yet on the other hand, plaintiffs ask this Court to imply a covenant that would have just that restrictive effect because, they contend, it reflects precisely the fundamental assumption of the market and the fundamental basis of their bargain with defendants. If that truly were the case here, it is difficult to imagine why an insistence on that term would have forced the plaintiffs to abandon the market. The Second Circuit has offered a better explanation: "[a] promise by the defendant should be implied only if the court may rightfully assume that the parties would have included it in their written agreement had their attention been called to it . . . *Any such assumption in this case would be completely unwarranted.*" Neuman v. Pike, 591 F.2d 191, 195 (2d Cir.1979) (emphasis added, citations omitted).

In the final analysis, plaintiffs offer no objective or reasonable standard for a court to use in its effort to define the sort of actions their "implied covenant" would permit a corporation to take, and those it would not.[28] . . .

2. Count Five: In Equity:

Count Five substantially restates and realleges the contract claims advanced in Count I. . . . For present purposes, it makes no difference how plaintiffs characterize their arguments. Their equity claims cannot survive defendants' motion for summary judgment.

In their papers, plaintiffs variously attempt to justify Count V as being based on unjust enrichment, frustration of purpose, an alleged breach of something approaching a fiduciary duty, or a general claim of unconscionability. Each claim fails.

---

[28] Under plaintiffs' theory, bondholders might ask a court to prohibit a company like RJR Nabisco not only from engaging in an LBO, but also from entering a new line of business—with the attendant costs of building new physical plants and hiring new workers—or from acquiring new businesses such as RJR Nabisco did when it acquired Del Monte.

B. Defendant's Remaining Motions:

. . .

1. Rule 10b–5:

Defendants move to dismiss pursuant to Fed.R.Civ.P. 12(c) Count III, the Rule 10b–5 counts, as to those six debt issues purchased by plaintiffs prior to September 1987, which is when plaintiffs allege in their complaint that defendants first began to develop an LBO plan. Plaintiffs admit that Rule 10b–5 is limited to purchases or sales during the period of non-disclosure or misrepresentation. . . . The rule does not afford relief to those who forgo a purchase or sale and instead merely hold in reliance of a nondisclosure or misrepresentation. . . .

The first, second, third, fifth, seventh and eighth securities listed in the Amended Complaint fail to satisfy this requirement, at least on the facts as presently pleaded. Accordingly, the Court grants defendants' motion on Count III as to those issues. Plaintiffs correctly note, however, that the disclosure-related common law fraud claims are not restricted to purchases and sales. . . . Thus, the Court denies defendants' motion to dismiss Count II on this basis.

AFTERMATH

The decision of the district court in *MetLife* left various claims pending, including claims of fraud and fraudulent conveyance. In January 1991, the case was settled. A Wall Street Journal article stated that the settlement "restore[d] much of the value of the RJR bonds that was lost when RJR was taken private in 1989." Hylton, Metropolitan Life Settles Bond Rift With RJR Nabisco, Wall St.J., Jan. 25, 1991, at C1, col. 1. The settlement was only for the benefit of MetLife and Jefferson-Pilot, but MetLife said that it would be willing to buy the bonds of other investors "at par or near par." A MetLife representative was quoted as saying, " 'Our claim was to be paid in full right away, and we're not getting that but we're very satisfied.' " In the settlement, MetLife and Jefferson-Pilot became entitled to receive a combination of cash, new debt securities, common stock, and a shorter duration for some of the existing debt. In addition, RJR agreed to pay MetLife's and Jefferson-Pilot's legal fees and other expenses of about $15 million.

ANALYSIS

1. Given MetLife's awareness of the risks associated with the RJR Nabisco bonds that it held, why did it not simply sell those bonds and invest in U.S. Treasury obligations?

2. In discussing the plaintiffs' argument based on a theory of implied covenant of good faith and fair dealing, the court says that it must "decide whether [the] 'fruits' of the agreement have been spoiled." It later says that the fruits "include the periodic and regular payment of interest and the eventual repayment of principal," and concludes that these fruits were not spoiled. Is this mode of analysis helpful? Why did the value of the RJR Nabisco debentures held by MetLife decline?

3. When a bank lends money to an individual to finance the purchase of a personal residence or an automobile, what type of provision is included in the loan that protects against the dilution of the value of

the bank's claim by the borrower incurring additional debt? Do you suppose that similar protection is found in some corporate debt obligations? What other type of protective provision might a lender demand to protect itself from such dilution?*

4. Suppose that you are outside counsel to a major institutional investor such as an insurance company, a pension fund, or a mutual fund, and have been asked to devise new provisions to protect against the type of loss experienced by the plaintiffs in *MetLife*. A lawyer from another firm has proposed a covenant stating that the debtor "will take no action that will materially reduce the probability that it will pay interest and principal when it is due." What is your reaction?

5. The court in *MetLife* quotes the American Bar Foundation's Commentaries on Indentures, which asserts, "Except for possible increases in the market value of the debt security because of changes in interest rates, the debt security will seldom be worth more than the lender paid for it." Consider the new debentures issued by RJR Nabisco to finance the LBO. These debentures paid a high rate of interest because of a significant risk of default on the obligation to pay interest and to repay principal. They were known as "high-yield" or "junk" bonds. Suppose that two years after the LBO, RJR Nabisco has been extremely successful and the value of its equity has risen substantially. What would be the effect of such success on the value of the debentures? How, if at all, is your answer to that question relevant to the legal doctrine on responsibilities of directors toward debenture holders?

6. Do you agree with the outcome in the case? Compare Wilkes v. Springside Nursing Home, Inc., supra Chapter 6. There the plaintiff was a shareholder in a closely held corporation who complained about being ousted from his job with the corporation. Despite the fact that he had no employment contract, the court granted relief, relying on the conclusory statement that the majority owed the plaintiff a fiduciary duty. How can *Wilkes* and *MetLife* be reconciled?

7. Generally mergers must be approved by a vote of the shareholders. Why is a vote of the debenture holders not also required? Approval by debenture holders could be required by contract by including in the indenture a prohibition on mergers, together with a general provision (common in indentures) allowing waiver of indenture obligations by vote of the debenture holders. Another possibility would be a federal law,** comparable to the rule found in typical state

---

* One possibility (there are others) is, ironically, found in one of the indentures issued by the newly formed corporation, RJR Holdings Capital Corp., that was used as the vehicle for effectuating the RJR Nabisco LBO. The indenture provides that if a "Change of Control" occurs, each debenture holder may require that the issuer redeem its debenture for 101 percent of the principal amount plus accrued interest. "Change of Control" is defined, in part, as "the ownership of KKR and its affiliates, directly or indirectly, of less than 40% of the total voting power . . . of the Company. . . ." The debentures were also protected by a covenant severely limiting the amount of additional debt that the company might incur. See Prospectus dated April 4, 1989, for $750,000,000 **% Subordinated Debentures due 2001 and $750,000,000 Subordinated Extendible Reset Debentures.

** The state law applicable to relationships among shareholders (or, if you will, between the shareholders and the abstraction called the corporation) is, as we have seen in earlier chapters, that of the state of incorporation. The rule for choice of state law for debt instruments is essentially the common-law conflicts-of-law rule relating to contracts, which allows the parties to specify the state whose law they wish to apply. This choice-of-law rule could, however, be overridden by a state regulatory provision intended to affect transactions within the state. It

corporations codes for shareholders, requiring creditor approval of any merger. Assuming you think creditor approval is a good idea, which would be the better approach? If the federal-law approach were adopted, should the rule be one that the parties to a loan can reject?

NEGATIVE PLEDGE COVENANT AND CURE PERIOD

Another aspect of the litigation between MetLife and RJR Nabisco arose from a negative pledge covenant. A negative pledge covenant prohibits a debtor from mortgaging specified assets to any lender without providing "equal and ratable" mortgage protection to the obligations covered by the covenant. Violation of this covenant would be an act of default, which would, among other things, accelerate the repayment obligation. Some of the RJR Nabisco obligations included negative pledge clauses but provided a "cure period"—a period of 90 days following a notice of default, during which time RJR Nabisco could cure the default.

To finance the LBO, the new owners had agreed to a requirement that RJR Nabisco would sell $5.5 billion of its assets and use the proceeds to repay certain debts incurred in connection with the LBO. MetLife (and other debenture holders) claimed that this violated the negative pledge covenant. RJR Nabisco went to the federal district court in New York for a declaratory judgment that its agreement did not constitute a violation of the covenant. Since this litigation would take more than 90 days (the debenture holders claimed they needed at least four months for discovery), it sought an order tolling the cure period. The district court granted the request for that order (Metropolitan Life Insurance Company v. RJR Nabisco, Inc., 716 F.Supp. 1526 (S.D.N.Y.1989), but was reversed on appeal. 906 F.2d 884 (2d Cir.1990). The Second Circuit, in a 2–1 decision, adopted a strong strict constructionist position, stating that the "cure provisions at issue here are unambiguous" and include "no mention . . . of a period for adjudication of any notice of default . . . [or] of an automatic extension of the cure period in the event of litigation over the merits of the default notice." Having thus demonstrated its support for the principle "you made your bed, now you must lie in it," the majority went on, however, to hold that in order to expedite the proceeding, the trial court could limit discovery and could "in order to protect both the right of the lender to obtain admissible evidence of default and the right of the borrower to use the full cure period to secure an adjudication, stay the running of the cure period for such time as the lender needs for discovery."

---

turns out that most publicly traded debt obligations are governed by New York law, because such obligations are issued through Wall Street investment bankers and it is customary to specify that New York law applies. The New York legislature might be reluctant to impose a rule that issuers of debt found onerous, for fear of driving business away from Wall Street, and doubts might arise about the scope of any state's authority to control the terms of transactions with strong connections with other states. There is no doubt, however, about the authority of Congress to control the terms of any transaction that has an adequate impact, which generally need be only minimal, on interstate commerce.

Bank of New York Mellon v. Realogy Corporation

979 A.2d 1113 (Del. Ch. 2008).

I

. . .

Defendant Realogy Corporation is a Delaware Corporation [that provides] real estate and relocation services, and includes such well-known brands as Century 21, Coldwell Banker, and Sotheby's International Realty.

. . . Realogy was a publicly traded corporation . . . until it was taken private by an affiliate of Apollo Management, L.P. (collectively with its affiliates, "Apollo") in April 2007, during the height of the private equity boom.

In order to provide the large amount of debt financing necessary to complete Apollo's acquisition of Realogy, Realogy issued a number of debt instruments.

[Editors: Here is a simplified description of the outstanding debt that Realogy had issued.

Level I is the most senior debt, with a total in principal amount of $3.92 billion. It is "secured by a first lien on substantially all of the assets of Realogy." The terms of this debt include a provision referred to as an "accordion" feature, allowing Realogy to issue additional debt obligations (called "Other Term Loans"), up $650 million, to new lenders, on the same terms as the other Level I debt or on "such other alternative terms as [the lenders' agent] should deem satisfactory."

Level II debt is unsecured and includes two sets of obligations that differ only in the terms for payment of interest. The "Cash Notes," in a principal amount of $1.7 billion, with interest at 10.50 percent, require the normal semi-annual cash payment of interest. The "Toggle Notes," in a principal amount of $582 million, with interest at 11.375 percent, allow the issuer (Realogy) to pay in cash or to pay in kind (PIK). The payment in kind is accomplished by issuing new notes, for the interest due on the old notes, on the same terms as the original notes. The Level II notes are "pari passu" with the Level I obligations, which means that in liquidation the two sets of obligations share pro rata, by the face value of their claims, in the available proceeds. However, since the Level I obligations are secured by "substantially all of" Realogy's assets and the Level II obligations are not, there might be little, if anything, left to share after the Level I notes have exercised their lien on the assets.

Level III debt, in a principal amount of $875 million, with interest at 12.375 percent, is unsecured and is subordinated to the Level I and the Level II debt. That is, in the event of insolvency, the Level III claim is entitled to a payout only after the Level I and II claims have been fully satisfied.]

Like the rest of the residential real estate industry, Realogy has fallen on hard times since the closing of its [debt-financed purchase by Apollo]. As evidence of the market's evaluation of Realogy's diminished prospects to pay back its debt, the [Level II] Cash Notes presently trade at just below 18 cents on the dollar, the [Level II] Toggle Notes at approximately 13 cents on the dollar, and the [Level III] Notes at just below 12 cents on the dollar. . . .

On November 13, 2008, Realogy issued a press release announcing the terms and conditions of a proposed debt refinancing. According to the terms of the offer (as finally amended), eligible noteholders are invited to participate as lenders under a new $500 million term lending facility. The term lending facility would consist of Term C and Term D Loans under the Other Term Loans accordion feature of the Credit Agreement, and would be secured by a second lien on substantially all of the assets of Realogy. Instead of funding these term loans with cash, the participating noteholders would fund their obligations under the new term loans with the delivery of existing notes. . . . [F]or each $100,000 in term loan commitment, holders of:

(1) [the Level III debt] would be required to deliver $277,477.48 in principal value of [this debt]. . . .[4]

(2) [the Level II] Cash Notes would be required to deliver $198,709.68 in principal value of [these] Cash Notes. . . .[5]

(3) [the Level II] Toggle Notes would be required to deliver $212,030.08 in principal value of [these] Toggle Notes. . . .[6]

[The proposal included a provision for priority among the three classes of debtholders in the opportunity to exchange their current obligations for the new secured term notes, with the Level III holders coming first with an entitlement to take up to $125 million of the new term loan notes, the Level II Cash Notes holders coming next for the difference between $500 million and the amount taken by the Level III holders, then, finally, the Level II Toggle Notes holders for whatever was left.]

[T]he new term loans would be pari passu to the existing indebtedness under the [Level I] Credit Agreement as well as the [Level II] Notes. Unlike the [Level II] Notes, however, the new term loans would be secured debt. This security would give the holders of the new term loans an effectively higher priority in any potential bankruptcy proceeding than any of the [Level II] Notes or the [Level III] Notes. . . .

On November 24, 2008, counsel for the majority of the [Level II] Toggle Noteholders demanded in writing that Realogy confirm that it would terminate the proposed exchange transaction, citing, inter alia, allegations of certain covenant breaches of the indenture governing the [Level II] Toggle Notes (the "Indenture"). Realogy replied on November 25, 2008 that it intended to proceed with the transaction. . . .

On November 26, 2008, the Trustee [for the Level II Toggle Notes]* similarly demanded that Realogy . . . immediately terminate the proposed exchange transaction. Included in the Trustee's grounds for this demand was the claim that the exchange transaction would constitute a breach of Section 4.12 of the Indenture.

---

4 Implying a principal value exchange rate of approximately 36 cents on the dollar.

5 Implying a principal value exchange rate of approximately 50 cents on the dollar.

6 Implying a principal value exchange rate of approximately 47 cents on the dollar.

* [Eds.—A trustee is an institution, in this case The Bank of New York Mellon, appointed in the indenture (or other loan agreement), with the obligation to enforce the terms of the indenture.]

C. Procedural History

[The case proceeded, on an expedited schedule, on cross motions for summary judgment.]

. . .

III.

The Trustee makes a number of arguments as to why the proposed exchange transaction violates the [Level II] Indenture. All of the Trustee's arguments, however, boil down to variants of the same proposition: the proposed transaction violates the [Level I] Credit Agreement.* [Section 4.12, filled with lawyerly cover-all-bases language, provides in essence that Realogy is not permitted to grant any liens to secure new loans other than those permitted under the Level I Credit Agreement's accordion provision. Thus, the question became whether the new "loan," funded by cancellation of existing unsecured debt, is permitted under that accordion provision. The court treats this as a question of law, applying the rules for contract interpretation to the language of the Credit Agreement, which the court describes as unambiguous. The court states that " '[c]ontractual language whose meaning is otherwise plain is not ambiguous merely because the parties urge different interpretations in the litigation,' " citing First Lincoln Holdings, Inc. v. Equitable Life Assurance Society, 164 F.Supp.2d 383, 393 (S.D.N.Y.2001), which in turn quotes U.S. Trust Co. of New York v. Jenner, 168 F.3d 630, 632 (2d Cir.1999)).]

IV

The Trustee urges that the [new] Second Lien Term Loans [that Realogy proposes to issue] cannot be Loans under the Credit Agreement because they are not funded in cash. In support of its position, the Trustee makes two basic arguments: (1) the plain meaning of "loan" does not encompass non-cash funded transactions; (2) non-cash funded loans are in any event not permitted by the terms of the Credit Agreement.

A. Does "Loan" Necessarily Imply Cash Funding?

Realogy purports that the new Second Lien Term Loans will be created as Other Term Loans pursuant to Section 2.20 of the Credit Agreement. "Other Term Loans" is defined in Section 2.20 as "term loans with pricing and/or amortization terms different from the Term B Loans." The Trustee argues that the plain meaning of the word "loans" does not permit the funding of borrowings other than in cash. Thus, because the borrowings will not be funded with cash, they cannot be Other Term Loans, and therefore cannot be authorized under Section 2.20.

---

* [Eds.—It seems odd that the Trustee relies on a Level I agreement in support of a Level II claim. At the end of the opinion, in footnote 59, the court observes:

> The court notes the irony contained in the present situation. The Trustee [for the Level II Toggle Notes], a non-party to the [Level I] Credit Agreement, is suing to enforce a document whose terms are not for the Trustee's benefit. Moreover, those terms can be amended to remedy the prohibitions the Trustee relies on at any time, without the consent of the Trustee or the Toggle Noteholders. Thus, as to the Trustee and the Toggle Noteholders, it is little more than fortunate happenstance that they are able to find a provision in the Credit Agreement on which to rely to block the proposed transaction. Nevertheless, the court must construe the agreements as they stand, not as they might be.]

The court finds this argument uncompelling. The fundamental feature of a loan is the advancement of some valuable property in exchange for a promise to repay that advancement. Generally the repayment is required to be in cash, even if the initial value given is not. There are many commercial examples of loans which are not funded in cash but which are repaid in cash, such as traditional vendor and seller financing agreements.[39] The fact that loans under credit agreements are typically funded in cash does not mean that the word "loan" cannot even in that context encompass borrowings funded otherwise. Moreover, such hyper-technical arguments seem out of place when made by a non-party to the contract being interpreted.

B. Does The Credit Agreement Require Loans To Be Funded With Cash?

The Trustee relies on a number of provisions, taken in the aggregate, in an attempt to prove that the Credit Agreement does not permit the creation of loans funded other than with cash. These arguments fundamentally fall into two categories: (1) arguments based on the use of loan denominations in terms of amounts of currency; and (2) arguments based on various procedural and ministerial provisions.

1. Arguments Based On Currency Terms

The Trustee points out that the Credit Agreement frequently speaks about loans in terms of quantities of currency, and cites to these provisions as evidence that only cash loans are permitted. . . . The court is unconvinced. The use of the term "principal," denominated in dollars, still has an obvious meaning with respect to the [proposed] Second Lien Term Loans. It is the amount that Realogy will be required to repay to the Incremental Term Lenders upon maturation of the Second Lien Term Loans. This is no different than any other term loan, whether originally funded in cash or other valuable consideration. . . .

2. Arguments Based On Procedural And Ministerial Terms

The Trustee points to certain procedural and administrative provisions of the Credit Agreement as evidence that only cash-funded loans are permitted. Section 2.03, entitled "Requests for Borrowings," requires that as part of the required notice of a borrowing request, Realogy "shall specify . . . the location and number of the Borrower's account to which funds are to be disbursed." Because, the Trustee argues, Section 2.03 states that Realogy "shall specify" bank account information in borrowing requests, it must be that all loans are required to be funded in cash. "Otherwise," the Trustee seemingly asks, "why require the bank account?" The purpose of Section 2.03 is to specify the process for initiating a loan. In a typical borrowing under the Credit Agreement, the new loan will be funded in cash. . . . In order to facilitate this process, the borrowing request procedure thus "requires" an account into which funds are to be disbursed. It proves too much, however, to read this as permitting only transactions in which a disbursal account would be

---

[39] The court also notes the existence of "consolidation loans" for student loan indebtedness. These consolidation loans are often offered by the same lender that made the original loans to the student borrower. Thus a lender funds the new consolidation loan by tendering all of the borrower's earlier incurred promissory notes. The lender then takes back from the borrower a new promissory note evidencing the aggregate indebtedness. This new promissory note often contains materially different terms than the original notes.

necessary. Such a requirement would prohibit transactions explicitly anticipated and authorized by the very same section of the Credit Agreement. . . . [The court proceeds to serve up a lengthy and complex analysis of certain provisions of the Credit Agreement.]

The court finds the Trustee's argument that the Credit Agreement forbids the proposed transaction because it is not funded in cash unconvincing for another reason as well. The Trustee does not appear to dispute that (at least in the absence of the restriction in Section 6.09 discussed below) the proposed refinancing would be permissible if the [proposed] Second Lien Term Loans were funded in cash. Thus, for example, [the transaction could be restructured by having the Noteholders commit to paying cash for the new term loans while at the same time having Realogy agree to buy the existing notes, from the Noteholders, for cash, at the proposed reduced price. The result would be that the Noteholders would pay cash to Realogy for new term loans and Realogy in turn would pay cash to the Noteholders to redeem the existing notes, with these transaction carried out through a financial institution acting as intermediary.] [E]ach lender would receive the exact amount of cash they had [paid to Realogy in] this Rube Goldbergesque hypothetical transaction. The entire transfer of money from the lenders . . . to Realogy, . . ., and back to the lenders, would have, taken as a whole, no economic reality whatsoever. The final state of affairs, meanwhile, would be identical to that of the actual proposed transaction. . . . Thus, in the Trustee's view, the actual proposed transaction, while far simpler and more efficient, would be prohibited. Meanwhile, the economically equivalent hypothetical transaction, with all its unnecessary complication, would be permitted. It strikes the court as less than commercially reasonable that the parties to the Credit Agreement would have intended such a result, at least in the absence of more explicit language requiring it. It only tends to fuel the court's skepticism that it is a non-party to the Credit Agreement that urges this absurdist conclusion, purely for its own benefit.

V.

The Trustee also urges that the proposed transaction is prohibited by [a covenant in] the Credit Agreement [under which, after a somewhat complex journey through the terms of the indenture, Realogy is prohibited from engaging in the proposed transaction unless the new term loans fit the definition of "Permitted Refinancing Indebtedness." That definition includes the language, "no Permitted Refinancing Indebtedness shall have different obligors, or greater guarantees or security, than the Indebtedness being Refinanced." Realogy relied on a somewhat ambiguous exception to this provision. The court notes the "admittedly strange structure" of the relevant portions of the indenture; reasons that the Realogy interpretation would "allow a mere proviso clause to entirely sap the vitality of what would otherwise be a significant proviso"; concludes that "[t]he Trustee's interpretation is the better one"; and, on this basis, grants judgment for the Trustee.]

ANALYSIS

1. Why did Realogy wind up with such a complex set of debt obligations? Why not, for example, just issue two types of debt—senior and subordinated? Or maybe even just one type—senior secured?

2. Why would a person buy the Level II or Level III debt rather than the Level I debt?

3. What is the function of the "Toggle" feature? Why did Realogy want it? Why were investors willing to accept it?

4. What is the purpose or function of the "accordion" feature of the Level I debt?

5. Why did the holders of the Toggle Notes challenge the proposed refinancing?

6. At the end of Section IV(A) of the opinion the court states that the Trustee's "hyper-technical arguments seem out of place when made by a non-party to the contract being interpreted." What does the court have in mind in describing the argument as "hyper-technical"? Why should it matter that the Trustee is not a party to the contract on whose language it relies?

7. Near the end of part IV(B)(2) of the opinion the court poses an alternative transaction that, it states, "would have, taken as a whole, no economic reality whatsoever." Despite this description, the court implies that it would have respected the form of the transaction. Do you agree that it would have been required to do so?

8. Why are the loan documents so complex and difficult to follow and interpret (take our word for it)?

4. EXCHANGE OFFERS

BACKGROUND NOTE

Most indentures include a provision permitting amendment by a vote of the bondholders, but for publicly issued debt, the federal Trust Indenture Act of 1939 prohibits the alteration of "core" terms—including interest payment, principal amount, and duration—without unanimous consent of the holders. This prohibition does not apply, however, to important protective covenants such as those limiting the payment of dividends and those requiring the maintenance of a specified ratio of equity to debt. The procedure for altering or eliminating such covenants is specified in the indenture; it is a matter of private law. Many indentures allow alteration or elimination of non-core covenants with the approval of a majority or, often, some higher percentage (e.g., two-thirds) of the debenture holders, with voting power based on face amounts of the debentures. Where such voting is permitted, however, the typical indenture will prohibit the voting of debentures "owned" (other terms of similar effect are also sometimes used) by the debtor.

Review the material on two-tier tender offers in Chapter 6, Section 2(B).

Katz v. Oak Industries, Inc.

508 A.2d 873 (Del.Ch.1986).

. . .

Plaintiff is the owner of long-term debt securities issued by Oak Industries, Inc. ("Oak"), a Delaware corporation; in this class action he seeks to enjoin the consummation of an exchange offer and consent solicitation made by Oak to holders of various classes of its long-term debt. As detailed below that offer is an integral part of a series of transactions that together would effect a major reorganization and recapitalization of Oak. The claim asserted is in essence, that the exchange offer is a coercive device and, in the circumstances, constitutes a breach of contract. This is the Court's opinion on plaintiff's pending application for a preliminary injunction.

I.

The background facts are involved even when set forth in the abbreviated form the decision within the time period currently available requires.

Through its domestic and foreign subsidiaries and affiliated entities, Oak manufactures and markets component equipment used in consumer, industrial and military products (the "Components Segment"); produces communications equipment for use in cable television systems and satellite television systems (the "Communications Segment"); and manufactures and markets laminates and other materials used in printed circuit board applications (the "Materials Segment"). During 1985, the Company has terminated certain other unrelated businesses. As detailed below, it has now entered into an agreement with Allied-Signal, Inc. for the sale of the Materials Segment of its business and is currently seeking a buyer for its Communications Segment.

Even a casual review of Oak's financial results over the last several years shows it unmistakably to be a company in deep trouble. During the period from January 1, 1982 through September 30, 1985, the Company has experienced unremitting losses from operations. . . . Financial markets, of course, reflected this gloomy history.[2]

Unless Oak can be made profitable within some reasonably short time it will not continue as an operating company. Oak's board of directors, comprised almost entirely of outside directors, has authorized steps to buy the company time. In February, 1985, in order to reduce a burdensome annual cash interest obligation on its $230 million of then outstanding debentures, the Company offered to exchange such debentures for a combination of notes, common stock and warrants. As a result, approximately $180 million principal amount of the then outstanding debentures were exchanged. Since interest on certain of the notes issued in that exchange offer is payable in common stock, the effect of the 1985 exchange offer was to reduce to some extent the cash drain on the Company caused by its significant debt.

About the same time that the 1985 exchange offer was made, the Company announced its intention to discontinue certain of its operations and sell certain of its properties. Taking these steps, while effective to stave off a default and to reduce to some extent the immediate cash drain, did not address Oak's longer-range problems. Therefore, also during 1985 representatives of the Company held informal discussions with several interested parties exploring the possibility of an investment from, combination with or acquisition by another company. As a result of these

[2] The price of the company's common stock has fallen from over $30 per share on December 31, 1981 to approximately $2 per share recently. The debt securities that are the subject of the exchange offer here involved have traded at substantial discounts.

discussions, the Company and Allied-Signal, Inc. entered into two agreements. The first, the Acquisition Agreement, contemplates the sale to Allied-Signal of the Materials Segment for $160 million in cash. The second agreement, the Stock Purchase Agreement, provides for the purchase by Allied-Signal for $15 million cash of 10 million shares of the Company's common stock together with warrants to purchase additional common stock.

The Stock Purchase Agreement provides as a condition to Allied-Signal's obligation that at least 85% of the aggregate principal amount of all of the Company's debt securities shall have tendered and accepted the exchange offers that are the subject of this lawsuit. Oak has six classes of such long term debt. If less than 85% of the aggregate principal amount of such debt accepts the offer, Allied-Signal has an option, but no obligation, to purchase the common stock and warrants contemplated by the Stock Purchase Agreement. . . .

Thus, as part of the restructuring and recapitalization contemplated by the Acquisition Agreement and the Stock Purchase Agreement, the Company has extended an exchange offer to each of the holders of the six classes of its long-term debt securities. These pending exchange offers include a Common Stock Exchange Offer (available only to holders of the 9⅝% convertible notes) and the Payment Certificate Exchange Offers (available to holders of all six classes of Oak's long-term debt securities). The Common Stock Exchange Offer currently provides for the payment to each tendering noteholder of 407 shares of the Company's common stock in exchange for each $1,000 9⅝% note accepted. The offer is limited to $38.6 million principal amount of notes (out of approximately $83.9 million outstanding).

The Payment Certificate Exchange Offer is an any and all offer. Under its terms, a payment certificate, payable in cash five days after the closing of the sale of the Materials Segment to Allied-Signal, is offered in exchange for debt securities. The cash value of the Payment Certificate will vary depending upon the particular security tendered. In each instance, however, that payment will be less than the face amount of the obligation. The cash payments range in amount, per $1,000 of principal, from $918 to $655. These cash values however appear to represent a premium over the market prices for the Company's debentures as of the time the terms of the transaction were set.

The Payment Certificate Exchange Offer is subject to certain important conditions before Oak has an obligation to accept tenders under it. First, it is necessary that a minimum amount ($38.6 million principal amount out of $83.9 total outstanding principal amount) of the 9⅝% notes be tendered pursuant to the Common Stock Exchange Offer. Secondly, it is necessary that certain minimum amounts of each class of debt securities be tendered, together with consents to amendments to the underlying indentures. Indeed, under the offer one may not tender securities unless at the same time one consents to the proposed amendments to the relevant indentures.

The condition of the offer that tendering security holders must consent to amendments in the indentures governing the securities gives rise to plaintiff's claim of breach of contract in this case. Those amendments would, if implemented, have the effect of removing significant negotiated protections to holders of the Company's long-term debt including the deletion of all financial covenants. Such modification may have adverse consequences to debt holders who elect not to tender pursuant to either exchange offer.

Allied-Signal apparently was unwilling to commit to the $15 million cash infusion contemplated by the Stock Purchase Agreement, unless Oak's long-term debt is reduced by 85% (at least that is a condition of their obligation to close on that contract). . . . But existing indenture covenants prohibit the Company, so long as any of its long-term notes are outstanding, from issuing any obligation (including the Payment Certificates) in exchange for any of the debentures. Thus, in this respect, amendment to the indentures is required in order to close the Stock Purchase Agreement as presently structured.

. . .

II.

. . .

As amplified in briefing on the pending motion, plaintiff's claim is that no free choice is provided to bondholders by the exchange offer and consent solicitation. Under its terms, a rational bondholder is "forced" to tender and consent. Failure to do so would face a bondholder with the risk of owning a security stripped of all financial covenant protections and for which it is likely that there would be no ready market. A reasonable bondholder, it is suggested, cannot possibly accept those risks and thus such a bondholder is coerced to tender and thus to consent to the proposed indenture amendments.[6]

. . .

III.

. . .

I turn first to an evaluation of the probability of plaintiff's ultimate success on the merits of his claim. I begin that analysis with two preliminary points. The first concerns what is not involved in this case. To focus briefly on this clears away much of the corporation law case law of this jurisdiction upon which plaintiff in part relies. This case does not involve the measurement of corporate or directorial conduct against that high standard of fidelity required of fiduciaries when they act with respect to the interests of the beneficiaries of their trust. Under our law—and the law generally—the relationship between a corporation and the holders of its debt securities, even convertible debt securities, is contractual in nature. . . . Arrangements among a corporation, the underwriters of its debt, trustees under its indentures and sometimes ultimate investors are typically thoroughly negotiated and massively documented. The rights and obligations of the various parties are or should be spelled out in that documentation. The terms of the contractual

---

[6] It is worthy of note that a very high percentage of the principal value of Oak's debt securities are owned in substantial amounts by a handful of large financial institutions. Almost 85% of the value of the 13.50% Notes is owned by four such institutions (one investment banker owns 55% of that issue); 69.1% of the 9⅝% Notes are owned by four financial institutions (the same investment banker owning 25% of that issue) and 85% of the 11⅝% Notes are owned by five such institutions. Of the debentures, 89% of the 13.65% debentures are owned by four large banks; and approximately 45% of the two remaining issues is owned by two banks.

relationship agreed to and not broad concepts such as fairness define the corporation's obligation to its bondholders.[7]

Thus, the first aspect of the pending Exchange Offers about which plaintiff complains—that "the purpose and effect of the Exchange Offers is to benefit Oak's common stockholders at the expense of the Holders of its debt"—does not itself appear to allege a cognizable legal wrong. It is the obligation of directors to attempt, within the law, to maximize the long-run interests of the corporation's stockholders; that they may sometimes do so "at the expense" of others (even assuming that a transaction which one may refuse to enter into can meaningfully be said to be at his expense) does not for that reason constitute a breach of duty. It seems likely that corporate restructurings designed to maximize shareholder values may in some instances have the effect of requiring bondholders to bear greater risk of loss and thus in effect transfer economic value from bondholders to stockholders. . . . But if courts are to provide protection against such enhanced risk, they will require either legislative direction to do so or the negotiation of indenture provisions designed to afford such protection.

The second preliminary point concerns the limited analytical utility, at least in this context, of the word "coercive" which is central to plaintiff's own articulation of his theory of recovery. . . . Clearly some "coercion" is legally unproblematic. Parents may "coerce" a child to study with the threat of withholding an allowance; employers may "coerce" regular attendance at work by either docking wages for time absent or by rewarding with a bonus such regular attendance. Other "coercion" so defined clearly would be legally relevant (to encourage regular attendance by corporal punishment, for example). Thus, for purposes of legal analysis, the term "coercion" itself—covering a multitude of situations—is not very meaningful. For the word to have much meaning for purposes of legal analysis, it is necessary in each case that a normative judgment be attached to the concept ("inappropriately coercive" or "wrongfully coercive", etc.). But, it is then readily seen that what is legally relevant is not the conclusory term "coercion" itself but rather the norm that leads to the adverb modifying it.

In this instance, assuming that the Exchange Offers and Consent Solicitation can meaningfully be regarded as "coercive" (in the sense that Oak has structured it in a way designed—and I assume effectively so—to "force" rational bondholders to tender), the relevant legal norm that will support the judgment whether such "coercion" is wrongful or not will, for the reasons mentioned above, be derived from the law of contracts. I turn then to that subject to determine the appropriate legal test or rule.

Modern contract law has generally recognized an implied covenant to the effect that each party to a contract will act with good faith towards the other with respect to the subject matter of the contract. . . .

It is this obligation to act in good faith and to deal fairly that plaintiff claims is breached by the structure of Oak's coercive exchange offer. Because it is an implied *contractual* obligation that is asserted as the

---

[7] To say that the broad duty of loyalty that a director owes to his corporation and ultimately its shareholders is not implicated in this case is not to say, as the discussion below reflects, that as a matter of contract law a corporation owes no duty to bondholders of good faith and fair dealing. *See, Restatement of Law, Contracts 2d,* § 205 (1979). Such a duty, however, is quite different from the congeries of duties that are assumed by a fiduciary. . . .

basis for the relief sought, the appropriate legal test is not difficult to deduce. It is this: is it clear from what was expressly agreed upon that the parties who negotiated the express terms of the contract would have agreed to proscribe the act later complained of as a breach of the implied covenant of good faith—had they thought to negotiate with respect to that matter. If the answer to this question is yes, then, in my opinion, a court is justified in concluding that such act constitutes a breach of the implied covenant of good faith. . . .

With this test in mind, I turn now to a review of the specific provisions of the various indentures from which one may be best able to infer whether it is apparent that the contracting parties—had they negotiated with the exchange offer and consent solicitation in mind—would have expressly agreed to prohibit contractually the linking of the giving of consent with the purchase and sale of the security.

IV.

Applying the foregoing standard to the exchange offer and consent solicitation, I find first that there is nothing in the indenture provisions granting bondholders power to veto proposed modifications in the relevant indenture that implies that Oak may not offer an inducement to bondholders to consent to such amendments. Such an implication, at least where, as here, the inducement is offered on the same terms to each holder of an affected security, would be wholly inconsistent with the strictly commercial nature of the relationship.

Nor does the second pertinent contractual provision supply a ground to conclude that defendant's conduct violates the reasonable expectations of those who negotiated the indentures on behalf of the bondholders. Under that provision Oak may not vote debt securities held in its treasury. Plaintiff urges that Oak's conditioning of its offer to purchase debt on the giving of consents has the effect of subverting the purpose of that provision; it permits Oak to "dictate" the vote on securities which it could not itself vote.

The evident purpose of the restriction on the voting of treasury securities is to afford protection against the issuer voting as a bondholder in favor of modifications that would benefit it as issuer, even though such changes would be detrimental to bondholders. But the linking of the exchange offer and the consent solicitation does not involve the risk that bondholder interests will be affected by a vote involving anyone with a financial interest in the subject of the vote other than a bondholder's interest. That the consent is to be given concurrently with the transfer of the bond to the issuer does not in any sense create the kind of conflict of interest that the indenture's prohibition on voting treasury securities contemplates. Not only will the proposed consents be granted or withheld only by those with a financial interest to maximize the return on their investment in Oak's bonds, but the incentive to consent is equally available to all members of each class of bondholders. Thus the "vote" implied by the consent solicitation is not affected in any sense by those with a financial conflict of interest.

In these circumstances, while it is clear that Oak has fashioned the exchange offer and consent solicitation in a way designed to encourage consents, I cannot conclude that the offer violates the intendment of any of the express contractual provisions considered or, applying the test set out above, that its structure and timing breaches an implied obligation of good faith and fair dealing.

One further set of contractual provisions should be touched upon: Those granting to Oak a power to redeem the securities here treated at a price set by the relevant indentures. Plaintiff asserts that the attempt to force all bondholders to tender their securities at less than the redemption price constitutes, if not a breach of the redemption provision itself, at least a breach of an implied covenant of good faith and fair dealing associated with it. The flaw, or at least one fatal flaw, in this argument is that the present offer is not the functional equivalent of a redemption which is, of course, an act that the issuer may take unilaterally. In this instance it may happen that Oak will get tenders of a large percentage of its outstanding long-term debt securities. If it does, that fact will, in my judgment, be in major part a function of the merits of the offer (i.e., the price offered in light of the Company's financial position and the market value of its debt). To answer plaintiff's contention that the *structure* of the offer "forces" debt holders to tender, one only has to imagine what response this offer would receive if the price offered did not reflect a premium over market but rather was, for example, ten percent of market value. The exchange offer's success ultimately depends upon the ability and willingness of the issuer to extend an offer that will be a financially attractive alternative to holders. This process is hardly the functional equivalent of the unilateral election of redemption and thus cannot be said in any sense to constitute a subversion by Oak of the negotiated provisions dealing with redemption of its debt.

Accordingly, I conclude that plaintiff has failed to demonstrate a probability of ultimate success on the theory of liability asserted.

PROBLEM

Suppose that Sleeze Corp. has outstanding $10 million worth of debentures, in denominations of $1,000 each. These debentures are held by 500 separate individuals, no one of whom holds more than 50 of them. The debentures are infrequently traded so it is difficult to establish a market price. The most recent reported sale was at a price of $850. Sleeze Corp. has the right to call the debentures for redemption at any time at a price of $1,050.

Sleeze Corp. has recently sold one of its divisions and wants to distribute the proceeds of that sale to its shareholders as a dividend. The payment of this extraordinary dividend is prohibited, however, by a covenant in the indenture for the debentures. Were it not for this covenant, there would be no legal objection to the payment of the dividend. The covenant may be eliminated by a vote of a majority of the debentures.

Sleeze Corp. makes a tender offer of $860 per debenture. It is conditioned on a tender of at least 51 percent of the debentures and on submission of an "exit consent," which would vote the tendered debentures in favor of an indenture amendment eliminating the covenant that restricts the payment of dividends. In the written materials accompanying the tender offer, Sleeze Corp. states that if the tender is successful it intends to pay the extraordinary dividend. It is reasonable to expect that if the dividend is paid, the value of the debentures will be $800.

(a) Suppose you hold 10 of the debentures and do not wish to file a lawsuit. You think the debentures are worth $900 or more but your broker tells you that he cannot find a buyer at any price above $850. Do you tender?

(b) Suppose you are retained by a group of debenture holders to seek an injunction against the Sleeze Corp. tender offer and that the relevant law is that of Delaware, as set forth in Katz v. Oak Industries, Inc. On what theory, or theories, would you rely and how would you distinguish that case?

ANALYSIS

In Katz v. Oak Industries, Inc., a procedure was adopted to bring about a redemption, at less than face value (or, in Wall Street lingo, with a "haircut"), of substantially all of the debt obligations. That procedure consisted of a tender offer conditioned on the holder of each obligation submitting an exit consent voting that obligation in favor of the elimination of certain restrictive covenants. Under an alternative approach, the debtor corporation could have made a tender offer conditioned on a tender of, say, eighty-five percent of the obligations and on a *prior* vote eliminating the restrictive covenants. In a situation like that in Katz v. Oak Industries, Inc., is it likely that the outcome of the tender would have been different under the alternative approach from what it was under the approach in fact adopted? Might the outcome be different under the two approaches in other situations? What do your answers to these questions suggest about drafting provisions relating to the indenture amendments?

5. REDEMPTION AND CALL PROTECTION

Morgan Stanley & Co. v. Archer Daniels Midland Company

570 F.Supp. 1529 (S.D.N.Y.1983).

[This suit arose from the redemption by Archer Daniels Midland Company (ADM) of $125 million of debentures bearing an interest rate of 16 percent. The plaintiff, Morgan Stanley & Company, Inc. (Morgan Stanley), claimed that the redemption violated a contractual prohibition and that it violated certain securities laws, including § 10(b) of the '34 Act. The reported decision in this case includes an opinion in support of the court's denial of the plaintiff's request for a preliminary injunction, followed by an opinion on the parties' cross motions for summary judgment. The former opinion, which contains a substantial discussion of the plaintiff's claims under the securities laws, as well as a discussion of its contract-law claims, is omitted.]

. . .

FACTS

In May, 1981, Archer Daniels issued $125,000,000 of 16% Sinking Fund Debentures due May 15, 2011. . . . The Debentures state in relevant part:

> The Debentures are subject to redemption upon not less than 30 nor more than 60 days' notice by mail, at any time, in whole or in part, at the election of the Company, at the following optional Redemption Price (expressed in percentages of the principal amount), together with accrued interest to the Redemption Date . . ., all as provided in the Indenture: If redeemed during the twelve-month period beginning May 15 of the years indicated:
>
> | Year | Percentage | Year | Percentage |
> |---|---|---|---|
> | 1981 | 115.500 % | 1991 | 107.750 % |
> | 1982 | 114.725 | 1992 | 106.975 |
> | 1983 | 113.950 | 1993 | 106.200 |
> | 1984 | 113.175 | 1994 | 105.425 |
> | 1985 | 112.400 | 1995 | 104.650 |
> | 1986 | 111.625 | 1996 | 103.875 |
> | 1987 | 110.850 | 1997 | 103.100 |
> | 1988 | 110.075 | 1998 | 102.325 |
> | 1989 | 109.300 | 1999 | 101.550 |
> | 1990 | 108.525 | 2000 | 100.775 |
>
> and thereafter at 100%; provided, however, that prior to May 15, 1991, the Company may not redeem any of the Debentures pursuant to such option from the proceeds, or in anticipation, of the issuance of any indebtedness for money borrowed by or for the account of the Company or any Subsidiary (as defined in the Indenture) or from the proceeds, or in anticipation of a sale and leaseback transaction (as defined in Section 1008 of the Indenture), if, in either case, the interest cost or interest factor applicable thereto (calculated in accordance with generally accepted financial practice) shall be less than 16.08% per annum.

The May 12, 1981 Prospectus and the Indenture pursuant to which the Debentures were issued contain substantially similar language.[1] The

---

[1] The May 12, 1981 Prospectus announcing the issuance of the Debentures provides, in relevant part:

> The Sinking Fund Debentures will be subject to redemption, . . . provided, however, that the Company will not be entitled to redeem any of the Sinking Fund Debentures prior to May 15, 1991 *as part of a refunding or anticipated refunding operation by the application, directly or indirectly,* of the proceeds of indebtedness for money borrowed which shall have an interest cost of less than 16.03% per annum.

The Indenture provides, in relevant part:

> The Debentures may be redeemed, . . . provided, however, that prior to May 15, 1991, the Company may not redeem any of the Debentures pursuant to such option *from the proceeds, or in anticipation, of the issuance of any indebtedness* for money borrowed by or for the account of the Company or any Subsidiary or from the proceeds, or in anticipation, of a sale and leaseback transaction (as defined in Section 1008), if, in either case, the interest cost or interest factor applicable thereto (calculated in accordance with generally accepted financial practice) shall be less than 16.08% per annum.

[Eds.—Emphasis supplied.]

Moody's Bond Survey of April 27, 1981, in reviewing its rating of the Debentures, described the redemption provision in the following manner:

> "The 16% sinking fund debentures are nonrefundable with lower cost interest debt before April 15, 1991. Otherwise, they are callable in whole or in part at prices to be determined.

The proceeds of the Debenture offering were applied to the purchase of long-term government securities bearing rates of interest below 16.089%.

ADM raised money through public borrowing at interest rates less than 16.08% on at least two occasions subsequent to the issuance of the Debentures. On May 7, 1982, over a year before the announcement of the planned redemption, ADM borrowed $50,555,500 [at] an effective interest rate of less than 16.08%. On March 10, 1983, ADM raised an additional $86,400,000 [at] an effective interest rate of less than 16.08%. . . .

In the period since the issuance of the Debentures, ADM also raised money through two common stock offerings. Six million shares of common stock were issued by prospectus dated January 28, 1983, resulting in proceeds of $131,370,000. And by a prospectus supplement dated June 1, 1983, ADM raised an additional $15,450,000 by issuing 600,000 shares of common stock.

Morgan Stanley, the plaintiff in this action, bought $15,518,000 principal amount of the Debentures at $1,252.50 per $1,000 face amount on May 5, 1983, and $500,000 principal amount at $1,200 per $1,000 face amount on May 31, 1983. The next day, June 1, ADM announced that it was calling for the redemption of the 16% Sinking Fund Debentures, effective August 1, 1983. The direct source of funds was . . . the two ADM common stock offerings of January and June, 1983. . . .

Prior to the announcement of the call for redemption, the Debentures were trading at a price in excess of the $1,139.50 call price. At no time prior to the June 1 announcement did ADM indicate in any of its materials filed with the Securities and Exchange Commission or otherwise that it intended to exercise its redemption rights if it felt it was in its self-interest to do so. Nor did it express any contemporaneous opinion as to whether it was entitled under the terms of the Indenture to call the Debentures when it was borrowing funds at an interest rate less than 16.08% if the source of such redemption was other than the issuance of debt.

Plaintiff . . . contends that the proposed redemption is barred by the express terms of the call provisions of the Debenture and the Indenture Agreement, and that consummation of the plan would violate the Trust Indenture Act of 1939, 15 U.S.C. § 77aaa *et seq.* and common law principles of contract law. The plaintiff's claim is founded on the language contained in the Debenture and Trust Indenture that states that the company may not redeem the Debentures "from the proceeds, or in anticipation, of the issuance of any indebtedness . . . if . . . the interest cost or interest factor . . . [is] less than 16.08% per annum." Plaintiff points to the $86,400,000 raised by the . . . transaction within 90 days of the June 1 redemption announcement, and the $50,555,500 raised by the . . . transaction in May, 1982—both at interest rates below 16.08%—as proof that the redemption is being funded, at least indirectly, from the proceeds of borrowing in violation of the Debentures and Indenture agreement. The fact that ADM raised sufficient funds to redeem the Debentures entirely through the issuance of common stock is, according to the plaintiffs, an irrelevant "juggling of funds" used to circumvent the protections afforded investors by the redemption provisions of the Debenture. Plaintiff would have the Court interpret the provision as barring redemption during any period when the issuer has borrowing at a rate lower than that prescribed by the Debentures, regardless of whether the direct source of the funds is the issuance of equity, the sale of assets, or merely cash on hand.

The defendant would have the Court construe the language more narrowly as barring redemption only where the direct or indirect source of the funds is a debt instrument issued at a rate lower than that it is paying on the outstanding Debentures. Where, as here, the defendant can point directly to a non-debt source of funds (the issuance of common stock), the defendant is of the view that the general redemption schedule applies.

. . .

According to Morgan Stanley, the fact that the Debentures were trading at levels above the call price prior to the redemption announcement bolsters the argument that the investing public thought it was protected against early redemption. The plaintiff asserts that it would not have bought the Debentures without what it perceived to be protection against premature redemption.

ADM contends that plaintiff's allegations of securities fraud stem in the first instance from its strained and erroneous interpretation of the redemption language. Defendant argues that the redemption language itself—a boilerplate provision found in numerous Indenture Agreements—was sufficient disclosure. Moreover, defendant asserts that it had no plan or scheme at the time the Debentures were issued to exercise its call rights in conjunction with speculation in government securities or otherwise and that the provision existed solely to offer the issuer "financial flexibility." More important, defendant contends that its view of the Debenture language was the one commonly accepted by both bondholders and the investing public. . . .

ON MOTION FOR SUMMARY JUDGMENT

Contract Claims

The plaintiff's contract claims arise out of alleged violations of state contract law. Section 113 of the Indenture provides that the Indenture and the Debentures shall be governed by New York law. Under New York law, the terms of the Debentures constitute a contract between ADM and the holders of the Debentures, including Morgan Stanley. . . .

We note as an initial matter that where, as here, the contract language in dispute is a "boilerplate" provision found in numerous debentures and indenture agreements, the desire to give such language a consistent, uniform interpretation requires that the Court construe the language as a matter of law.

In Franklin Life Insurance Co. v. Commonwealth Edison Co., 451 F.Supp. 602 (S.D.Ill.1978), aff'd per curiam on the opinion below, 598 F.2d 1109 (7th Cir.), rehearing and rehearing en banc denied, id., cert.

denied, 444 U.S. 900, 100 S.Ct. 210, 62 L.Ed.2d 136 (1979), the district court found, with respect to language nearly identical to that now before us, that an early redemption of preferred stock was lawful where funded directly from the proceeds of a common stock offering.

Morgan Stanley argues, however, that *Franklin* was incorrectly decided and should therefore be limited to its facts. We find any attempt to distinguish *Franklin* on its facts to be wholly unpersuasive. Commonwealth Edison, the defendant in *Franklin,* issued 9.44% Cumulative Preferred Stock in 1970. The stock agreement contained a redemption provision virtually identical to that at issue in this litigation. The prospectus announcing the preferred stock would be used primarily for interim financing of a long-term construction program. The construction program required an estimated expenditure of approximately $2,250,000,000, of which $1,150,000,000 would have to be raised through the sale of additional securities of the company. *Franklin, supra,* 451 F.Supp. at 605. In accord with this estimate, Commonwealth Edison's long-term debt increased from $1.849 billion at the end of 1971 to an amount in excess of $3 billion by the time of trial in 1978. All of this debt was issued at interest rates below 9.44%. In January of 1972, Commonwealth Edison announced its intention to redeem the preferred stock with the proceeds of a common stock issue.

The Franklin Life Insurance Company brought suit, contending that the language of the redemption provision barred redemption where Commonwealth Edison had been borrowing at interest rates below 9.44%, and expected to continue borrowing at such rates in the near future. The district court rejected plaintiff's claims, and held that the redemption was lawful because the refunding was accomplished solely from the proceeds of the common stock issue. In adopting a rule that looked to the source of the proceeds for redemption, the court rejected a "net borrower" theory that would have examined the issuer's general corporate borrowing history. Thus, Edison's borrowing projections and the sizable anticipated increase in its long-term, lower-cost debt was irrelevant, given that the undisputed source of the redemption was the common stock issue.

. . .

Morgan Stanley contends . . . that *Franklin* was wrongly decided, as a matter of law, and that a fresh examination of the redemption language in light of the applicable New York cases would lead us to reject the "source" rule. In this regard, Morgan Stanley suggests a number of universal axioms of contract construction intended to guide us in construing the redemption language as a matter of first impression. For example, Morgan counsels that we should construe the contract terms in light of their "plain meaning," and should adopt the interpretation that best accords with all the terms of the contract. . . . Words are not to be construed as meaningless if they can be made significant by a reasonable construction of the contract. . . . Where several constructions are possible, the court may look to the surrounding facts and circumstances to determine the intent of the parties. Finally, Morgan Stanley urges that all ambiguities should be resolved against the party that drafted the agreement. . . .

We find these well-accepted and universal principles of contract construction singularly unhelpful in construing the contract language before us. Several factors lead us to this conclusion. First, there is simply no "plain meaning" suggested by the redemption language that would imbue all the contract terms with a significant meaning. Either party's interpretation of the redemption language would dilute the meaning of at least some of the words—either the "indirectly or directly," "in anticipation of" language, were we to adopt defendant's "source" rule, or the "from the proceeds," "as part of a refunding operation" language, were we to adopt the plaintiff's interpretation. Any attempt to divine the "plain meaning" of the redemption language would be disingenuous at best.

Equally fruitless would be an effort to discern the "intent of the parties" under the facts of this case. It may very well be that ADM rejected an absolute no-call provision in its negotiations with the underwriters in favor of language it viewed as providing "greater flexibility." It is also clear, however, that neither the underwriters nor ADM knew whether such "flexibility" encompassed redemption under the facts of this case. The deposition testimony of ADM officials suggesting that they believed at the time they negotiated the Indenture that they could redeem the Debentures at any time except through lower-cost debt merely begs the question. Had ADM management so clearly intended the Indenture to allow refunding under the circumstances of this case, it surely would have considered that option prior to the suggestions of Merrill Lynch, which appears to represent the first time the idea of early redemption funded directly by the proceeds of a stock issue was presented by any of ADM's investment advisors.

Finally, we view this as a most inappropriate case to construe ambiguous contract language against the drafter. The Indenture was negotiated by sophisticated bond counsel on both sides of the bargaining table. There is no suggestion of disparate bargaining power in the drafting of the Indenture, nor could there be. Moreover, even if we were to adopt this rule, it is not at all clear that ADM would be considered the drafter of the Indenture, given the active participation of the managing underwriter. Indeed, it is arguable that the ambiguous language should be construed in favor of ADM. See Broad v. Rockwell International Corp., [642 F.2d 929, 947 n. 20 (5th Cir.), cert. denied, 454 U.S. 965 (1981)] (purchaser of Debentures may stand in the shoes of the underwriters that originally negotiated and drafted the Debentures).

Not only do the rules of contract construction provide little aid on the facts before us, but we find the equities in this action to be more or less in equilibrium. Morgan Stanley now argues, no doubt in good faith, that the redemption is unlawful under the Indenture. Nevertheless, . . . Morgan Stanley employees were fully aware of the uncertain legal status of an early call at the time they purchased the ADM Debentures. To speak of upsetting Morgan's "settled expectations" would thus be rather misleading under the circumstances. By the same token, however, it is also clear that ADM had no expectations with respect to the availability of an early redemption call until the idea was first suggested by Merrill Lynch.

Because we find equitable rules of contract construction so unhelpful on the facts of this case, the decision in *Franklin* takes on added importance. While it is no doubt true that the decision in that case was a difficult one and in no sense compelled under existing law, we find the reasoning of the court thoroughly convincing given the obvious ambiguity of the language it was asked to construe. We also find the result to be a fair one. . . . Moreover, we note that the decision in *Franklin* preceded the drafting of the ADM Indenture by several years. We must assume, therefore, that the decision was readily available to bond counsel for all parties. That the parties may not in fact have been aware of the decision at the time the Indenture was negotiated is not dispositive, for the law in force at the time a contract is entered into becomes a part of the contract. . . . While *Franklin* was decided under Illinois law and is therefore not binding on the New York courts, we cannot ignore the fact that it was the single existing authority on this issue, and was decided on the basis of universal contract principles. Under these circumstances, it was predictable that *Franklin* would affect any subsequent decision under New York law. *Franklin* thus adds an unavoidable gloss to any interpretation of the redemption language.

Finally, we note that to cast aside the holding in *Franklin* would, in effect, result in the very situation the Second Circuit sought to avoid in *Sharon Steel,* supra. In that case, the Court warned that allowing juries to construe boilerplate language as they saw fit would likely result in intolerable uncertainty in the capital markets. To avoid such an outcome, the Court found that the interpretation of boilerplate should be left to the Court as a matter of law. *Sharon Steel,* supra, 691 F.2d at 1048. While the Court in *Sharon Steel* was addressing the issue of varying interpretations by juries rather than by the courts, this distinction does not diminish the uncertainty that would result were we to reject the holding in *Franklin.* Given the paramount interest in uniformly construing boilerplate provisions, and for all the other reasons stated above and in our prior Opinion, we chose to follow the holding in *Franklin.*[4]

Accordingly, we find that the ADM redemption was lawful under the terms of the Debentures and the Indenture, and that therefore defendant's motion for summary judgment on Counts VI and X through XII is hereby granted.

---

[4] We note in this regard that the "source" rule adopted in *Franklin* in no sense constitutes a license to violate the refunding provision. The court is still required to make a finding of the true source of the proceeds for redemption. Where the facts indicate that the proposed redemption was indirectly funded by the proceeds of anticipated debt borrowed at a prohibited interest rate, such redemption would be barred regardless of the name of the account from which the funds were withdrawn. Thus, a different case would be before us if ADM, contemporaneously with the redemption, issued new, lower-cost debt and used the proceeds of such debt to repurchase the stock issued in the first instance to finance the original redemption. On those facts, the redemption could arguably be said to have been indirectly funded through the proceeds of anticipated lower-cost debt, since ADM would be in virtually the same financial posture after the transaction as it was before the redemption—except that the new debt would be carried at a lower interest rate. Here, by contrast, there is no allegation that ADM intends to repurchase the common stock it issued to fund the redemption. The issuance of stock, with its concomitant effect on the company's debt/equity ratio, is exactly the type of substantive financial transaction the proceeds of which may be used for early redemption.

Moreover, we fail to see how, on the facts of this case, the redemption could be argued to be a refunding from the proceeds of lower-cost debt. The [$50.5 million] transaction occurred over a year before the redemption and appears completely unrelated to it. The proceeds of that transaction were used to purchase government securities that remain in ADM's portfolio. The [$86.4 million] transaction, while closer in time, similarly is not fairly viewed as the source of the redemption, given that the proceeds of that transaction were applied directly to reducing ADM's short-term debt. To view the redemption as having been funded *indirectly* "from the proceeds" of the [$86.4 million] transaction would require us to ignore the *direct* source of the refunding, the two ADM common stock issues.

. . .

AFTERMATH

A leading treatise on bonds, in discussing the ADM redemption, states, "Investors don't readily forget the times that they lost money, especially if they felt that they might have been 'bamboozled.' " ADM's next bond issue, in 1984, containing the same, standard refunding provision that gave rise to the litigation with Morgan Stanley, "was not well received." Over a year later, when ADM again sold debentures, the obligations were noncallable for life (20 years).* And in 1986, when ADM sought to redeem high-interest bonds, it did so by a tender offer, at an above-market price. R. Wilson and F. Fabozzi, The New Corporate Bond Market 188 (1990).

PROBLEM

In 1986, X Corp. issued $10 million of 15 percent subordinated debentures due January 15, 2006, which contained a prohibition on lower-rate refunding, using language identical to that in the *Archer Daniels Midland* case. In 1988, X Corp. built a new manufacturing plant to replace one that it had used for many years and was no longer large enough for its operations. The cost of the new plant was $20 million. It borrowed $18 million short term from a bank to finance the construction. On January 10, 1989, X Corp. moved its manufacturing operations to the new plant. On January 20, it raised $18 million by a public sale of $18 million of 12 percent subordinated debentures due January 20, 2009. It deposited the proceeds of the loan in a special account and on January 21, 1989, used those proceeds to pay off the bank loan. On January 25, X Corp. sold its old plant for $10 million, deposited the proceeds in its general account, and used those proceeds to redeem the 15 percent debentures. Did X Corp. violate the refunding prohibition? What if it had sold the old plant two days before it issued the 12 percent debentures, deposited the proceeds of both transactions in its general account, then paid off the 12 percent debentures and, an hour later, paid off the bank loan?

PLANNING

1. What language could have been included in the ADM debenture to give Morgan Stanley the protection that it claimed it had?

2. How might the redemption price on debentures be set so as to eliminate the problem that arose in the *Archer Daniels Midland* case? In answering this question, bear in mind that the value of a debenture can rise because (a) the market rate of interest has fallen or because (b) the issuer's creditworthiness has improved.

* Redemption provisions making a bond "noncallable," as opposed to "nonrefundable," had been familiar to issuers and lenders at the time ADM issued the bonds that gave rise to the litigation with Morgan Stanley.

INDEX

References are to Pages

DIRECTORS

PERSONAL HOLDING COMPANIES

PIERCING THE CORPORATE VEIL

POISON PILLS

POLICY CONSIDERATIONS

POWERS

PRIVATE RIGHTS OF ACTION

PROFIT AND LOSS SHARING

PROMOTERS

PROPERTY

PROXY FIGHTS

PUBLIC CORPORATIONS

PUBLIC POLICY

RATIFICATION